Japan

WORLD BIBLIOGRAPHICAL SERIES

General Editors:
Robert G. Neville (Executive Editor)
John J. Horton   Ian Wallace
Hans H. Wellisch   Ralph Lee Woodward, Jr.

John J. Horton is Deputy Librarian of the University of Bradford and currently Chairman of its Academic Board of Studies in Social Sciences. He has maintained a longstanding interest in the discipline of area studies and its associated bibliographical problems, with special reference to European Studies. In particular he has published in the field of Icelandic and of Yugoslav studies, including the two relevant volumes in the World Bibliographical Series.

Ian Wallace is Professor of Modern Languages at Loughborough University of Technology. A graduate of Oxford in French and German, he also studied in Tübingen, Heidelberg and Lausanne before taking teaching posts at universities in the USA, Scotland and England. He specializes in East German affairs, especially literature and culture, on which he has published numerous articles and books. In 1979 he founded the journal *GDR Monitor*, which he continues to edit.

Hans H. Wellisch is Professor emeritus at the College of Library and Information Services, University of Maryland. He was President of the American Society of Indexers and was a member of the International Federation for Documentation. He is the author of numerous articles and several books on indexing and abstracting, and has published *The Conversion of Scripts* and *Indexing and Abstracting: an International Bibliography*. He also contributes frequently to *Journal of the American Society for Information Science, The Indexer* and other professional journals.

Ralph Lee Woodward, Jr. is Chairman of the Department of History at Tulane University, New Orleans, where he has been Professor of History since 1970. He is the author of *Central America, a Nation Divided*, 2nd ed. (1985), as well as several monographs and more than sixty scholarly articles on modern Latin America. He has also compiled volumes in the World Bibliographical Series on *Belize* (1980), *Nicaragua* (1983), and *El Salvador* (1988). Dr. Woodward edited the Central American section of the *Research Guide to Central America and the Caribbean* (1985) and is currently editor of the Central American history section of the *Handbook of Latin American Studies*.

VOLUME 103

Japan

Frank Joseph Shulman

CLIO PRESS

**OXFORD, ENGLAND · SANTA BARBARA, CALIFORNIA
DENVER, COLORADO**

Kenneth Berger   11-12-90

This volume has been published with the generous financial assistance of the Japan Foundation (Tokyo), the Suntory Foundation (Osaka) and the Great Britain–Sasakawa Foundation (London).

British Library Cataloguing-in-Publication Data

Shulman, Frank Joseph, 1943–
Japan.— (World bibliographical series, 103).
1. Japan – Bibliographies
I. Title   II. Series
016.952

Library of Congress Cataloging-in-Publication Data
Shulman, Frank Joseph, 1943–
Japan / Frank Joseph Shulman.
(World bibliographical series; v. 103)
Includes bibliographical references.
ISBN 1–85109–074–6
1. Japan – Bibliography.   I. Title.   II. Series.
Z3301.S475   1989
[DS806]
016.952–dc20

ISBN 1–85109–074–6 (alk. paper)

The paper used in this publication meets the requirements of the ANSI Standard Z39.48–1984 (Permanence of Paper).

Clio Press Ltd.,
55 St. Thomas' Street, Oxford OX1 1JG, England.

ABC-CLIO,
130 Cremona Drive, Santa Barbara, CA 93117, USA.

Distributed in Japan by Publishers International Corporation
2nd Newfield Building, 42-3 Ohtsuka 3-chome,
Bunkyo-ku, Tokyo 112, Japan.

Designed by Bernard Crossland.
Typeset by Columns Design and Production Services, Reading, England.
Printed and bound in Great Britain by
Billing and Sons Ltd., Worcester.

THE WORLD BIBLIOGRAPHICAL SERIES

This series, which is principally designed for the English speaker, will eventually cover every country in the world, each in a separate volume comprising annotated entries on works dealing with its history, geography, economy and politics; and with its people, their culture, customs, religion and social organization. Attention will also be paid to current living conditions – housing, education, newspapers, clothing, etc.– that are all too often ignored in standard bibliographies; and to those particular aspects relevant to individual countries. Each volume seeks to achieve, by use of careful selectivity and critical assessment of the literature, an expression of the country and an appreciation of its nature and national aspirations, to guide the reader towards an understanding of its importance. The keynote of the series is to provide, in a uniform format, an interpretation of each country that will express its culture, its place in the world, and the qualities and background that make it unique. The views expressed in individual volumes, however, are not necessarily those of the publisher.

VOLUMES IN THE SERIES

1 *Yugoslavia*, John J. Horton
2 *Lebanon*, Shereen Khairallah
3 *Lesotho*, Shelagh M. Willet and David Ambrose
4 *Rhodesia/Zimbabwe*, Oliver B. Pollack and Karen Pollack
5 *Saudi Arabia*, Frank A. Clements
6 *USSR*, Anthony Thompson
7 *South Africa*, Reuben Musiker
8 *Malawi*, Robert B. Boeder
9 *Guatemala*, Woodman B. Franklin
10 *Pakistan*, David Taylor
11 *Uganda*, Robert L. Collison
12 *Malaysia*, Ian Brown and Rajeswary Ampalavanar
13 *France*, Frances Chambers
14 *Panama*, Eleanor DeSelms Langstaff
15 *Hungary*, Thomas Kabdebo
16 *USA*, Sheila R. Herstein and Naomi Robbins
17 *Greece*, Richard Clogg and Mary Jo Clogg
18 *New Zealand*, R. F. Grover
19 *Algeria*, Richard I. Lawless
20 *Sri Lanka*, Vijaya Samaraweera
21 *Belize*, Ralph Lee Woodward, Jr.
23 *Luxembourg*, Carlo Hury and Jul Christophory
24 *Swaziland*, Balam Nyeko
25 *Kenya*, Robert L. Collison
26 *India*, Brijen K. Gupta and Datta S. Kharbas
27 *Turkey*, Merel Güçlü
28 *Cyprus*, P. M. Kitromilides and M. L. Evriviades
29 *Oman*, Frank A. Clements
31 *Finland*, J. E. O. Screen
32 *Poland*, Richard C. Lewański
33 *Tunisia*, Allan M. Findlay, Anne M. Findlay and Richard I. Lawless
34 *Scotland*, Eric G. Grant
35 *China*, Peter Cheng
36 *Qatar*, P. T. H. Unwin
37 *Iceland*, John J. Horton
38 *Nepal*, John Whelpton
39 *Haiti*, Frances Chambers
40 *Sudan*, M. W. Daly
41 *Vatican City State*, Michael J. Walsh
42 *Iraq*, A. J. Abdulrahman
43 *United Arab Emirates*, Frank A. Clements
44 *Nicaragua*, Ralph Lee Woodward, Jr.
45 *Jamaica*, K. E. Ingram
46 *Australia*, I. Kepars

47 *Morocco*, Anne M. Findlay, Allan M. Findlay and Richard I. Lawless
48 *Mexico*, Naomi Robbins
49 *Bahrain*, P. T. H. Unwin
50 *The Yemens*, G. Rex Smith
51 *Zambia*, Anne M. Bliss and J. A. Rigg
52 *Puerto Rico*, Elena E. Cevallos
53 *Namibia*, Stanley Schoeman and Elna Schoeman
54 *Tanzania*, Colin Darch
55 *Jordan*, Ian J. Seccombe
56 *Kuwait*, Frank A. Clements
57 *Brazil*, Solena V. Bryant
58 *Israel*, Esther M. Snyder (preliminary compilation E. Kreiner)
59 *Romania*, Andrea Deletant and Dennis Deletant
60 *Spain*, Graham J. Shields
61 *Atlantic Ocean*, H. G. R. King
63 *Cameroon*, Mark W. DeLancey and Peter J. Schraeder
64 *Malta*, John Richard Thackrah
65 *Thailand*, Michael Watts
66 *Austria*, Denys Salt with the assistance of Arthur Farrand Radley
67 *Norway*, Leland B. Sather
68 *Czechoslovakia*, David Short
69 *Irish Republic*, Michael Owen Shannon
70 *Pacific Basin and Oceania*, Gerald W. Fry and Rufino Mauricio
71 *Portugal*, P. T. H. Unwin
72 *West Germany*, Donald S. Detwiler and Ilse E. Detwiler
73 *Syria*, Ian J. Seccombe
74 *Trinidad and Tobago*, Frances Chambers
76 *Barbados*, Robert B. Potter and Graham M. S. Dann
77 *East Germany*, Ian Wallace
78 *Mozambique*, Colin Darch
79 *Libya*, Richard I. Lawless
80 *Sweden*, Leland B. Sather and Alan Swanson

81 *Iran*, Reza Navabpour
82 *Dominica*, Robert A. Myers
83 *Denmark*, Kenneth E. Miller
84 *Paraguay*, R. Andrew Nickson
85 *Indian Ocean*, Julia J. Gotthold with the assistance of Donald W. Gotthold
86 *Egypt*, Ragai N. Makar
87 *Gibraltar*, Graham J. Shields
88 *The Netherlands*, Peter King and Michael Wintle
89 *Bolivia*, Gertrude M. Yeager
90 *Papua New Guinea*, Fraiser McConnell
91 *The Gambia*, David P. Gamble
92 *Somalia*, Mark W. DeLancey, Sheila L. Elliott, December Green, Kenneth J. Menkhaus, Mohammad Haji Moqtar, Peter J. Schraeder
93 *Brunei*, Sylvia C. Engelen Krausse, Gerald H. Krausse
94 *Albania*, William B. Bland
95 *Singapore*, Stella R. Quah, Jon S. T. Quah
96 *Guyana*, Frances Chambers
97 *Chile*, Harold Blakemore
98 *El Salvador*, Ralph Lee Woodward, Jr.
99 *The Arctic*, H.G.R. King
100 *Nigeria*, Robert A. Myers
101 *Ecuador*, David Corkill
102 *Uruguay*, Henry Finch with the assistance of Alicia Casas de Barrán
103 *Japan*, Frank Joseph Shulman
104 *Belgium*, R.C. Riley
105 *Macau*, Richard Louis Edmonds
106 *Philippines*, Jim Richardson
107 *Bulgaria*, Richard J. Crampton
108 *The Bahamas*, Paul G. Boultbee
109 *Peru*, John R. Fisher
110 *Venezuela*, D. A. G. Waddell
111 *Dominican Republic*, Kai Schoenhals

For Ron and Jackie Morse

Contents

INTRODUCTION xiii

CHRONOLOGY: HISTORICAL PERIODS AND HISTORICAL
           EVENTS REFERRED TO WITHIN THE
           BIBLIOGRAPHY xix

THE COUNTRY AND ITS PEOPLE 1

GEOGRAPHY AND GEOLOGY 17
    General 17
    Maps and Atlases 21

FLORA AND FAUNA 24

TRAVELLERS' ACCOUNTS 28

TOURISM AND TRAVEL GUIDES 32

PREHISTORY AND ARCHAEOLOGY 42

HISTORY 46
    General Histories 46
    AD 550–1600 53
    1600–1868 (Tokugawa Period) 66
    1868–1945 (Meiji, Taishō, and Early Shōwa Periods) 78
    1945: Hiroshima and Nagasaki 104
    Postwar History 109
    Okinawa, the Kurile Islands, and Sakhalin 117

BIOGRAPHICAL AND AUTOBIOGRAPHICAL ACCOUNTS 120
    Collective Biography 120
    Before the Twentieth Century 124
    Twentieth Century 131
    Westerners in Japan 143
    Biographical Dictionaries 149

Contents

POPULATION AND FAMILY PLANNING 152

MINORITIES: THE AINU, *BURAKUMIN*, AND KOREANS 154

OVERSEAS JAPANESE 158

LANGUAGE 167
 General 167
 Dictionaries 170
 Grammar 175
 Textbooks 177

RELIGION 186
 General 186
 Buddhism and Zen Buddhism 190
 Christianity 201
 Folk Religion 203
 The New Religions 206
 Shintō 209

PHILOSOPHY 212

SOCIETY AND SOCIAL CONDITIONS 216
 General 216
 Community Studies 223
 Family and Kinship 228
 Social Problems and Social Welfare 230
 Women 234

PSYCHOLOGY 239

MEDICINE AND HEALTH 244

POLITICS AND GOVERNMENT 248
 General 248
 Political Parties 258
 Prefectural and Local Government 262

FOREIGN RELATIONS 264
 General 264
 Before 1931 270
 1931-1945 (including World War II) 279
 Since 1945 294

MILITARY AND DEFENCE (Since 1945) 311

LAW AND CONSTITUTION 317
 Law 317
 Constitution 323

Contents

ECONOMY 326
    General 326
    Economic and Statistical Yearbooks and Annual Surveys 338

AGRICULTURE AND FISHING 342

BUSINESS, MARKETING, AND DOMESTIC COMMERCE 346

ENERGY 352

FINANCE AND BANKING 354

INDUSTRY 361

INTERNATIONAL TRADE AND BUSINESS 369

MANAGEMENT, LABOUR, AND EMPLOYER–EMPLOYEE
    RELATIONS 383

MULTINATIONALS AND MULTINATIONALISM 394

TRANSPORTATION AND TELECOMMUNICATIONS 398

ENVIRONMENT 400

EDUCATION 403

SCIENCE AND TECHNOLOGY 412

LITERATURE 421
    General 421
    Classical Fiction and Prose: Translations 426
    Classical Fiction and Prose: History and Criticism 435
    Modern Fiction and Prose: Translations 438
    Modern Fiction and Prose: History and Criticism 457
    Poetry: Translations 465
    Poetry: History and Criticism 475
    Drama 479
    Folklore 485

FINE ARTS 488
    General 488
    Painting and Calligraphy 502
    Prints and Drawings 511
    Photographs and Photography 519
    Pottery and Ceramics 520
    Sculpture and Netsuke 524
    Architecture 527

Contents

Gardens and Bonsai   538
Furniture   542
Textiles and Clothing   543
Other Decorative and Applied Arts   548

PERFORMING ARTS 554
General   554
Music   555
Dance   559
Theatre   560
Cinema   568

FOOD AND DRINK 574

SPORTS 579
The Martial Arts   579
Sumo and Baseball   583

RECREATION 585
General   585
Flower Arrangement (Ikebana)   587
Tea Ceremony (*Chanoyu*)   589

LIBRARIES AND MUSEUMS 592

BOOKS AND PRINTING 594

MASS MEDIA AND COMMUNICATIONS 597

PERIODICALS AND NEWSPAPERS 600
Periodicals   600
Newspapers   617

ENCYCLOPAEDIAS, DIRECTORIES, AND SUBJECT
DICTIONARIES 619

BIBLIOGRAPHIES AND RESEARCH GUIDES 630

AUTHOR INDEX 645

TITLE INDEX 669

SUBJECT INDEX 707

MAPS OF JAPAN 874

Introduction

Popularly known as the 'Land of the Rising Sun', Japan is one of the most dynamic, rapidly changing, industrialised societies in the present-day world. Over 120 million Japanese, crowded into a 3,800-kilometre (2,360-mile) long archipelago off the east coast of Asia that is just slightly smaller than the state of California or Scotland and Norway combined, are well on their way towards making Japan the most economically and technologically advanced nation of the twenty-first century and an international pace-setter in the fine and performing arts. Heirs to a civilisation whose recorded history spans more than fifteen centuries as well as to a rich artistic and literary tradition, the Japanese constitute a racially, linguistically, and culturally homogeneous population whose achievements are being increasingly appreciated in the West.

European interest in Japan predates World War II. During the nineteenth and early twentieth centuries, Japanese literature, wood-block prints (ukiyo-e), and ceramics were objects of considerable fascination among the connoisseurs of culture in Western and Central Europe, and a number of pioneering scholars wrote extensively about Japanese literature, culture, and history. War in the Pacific, in turn, provided a major impetus for the growth of Japanese studies in the United States as well as for greater attention to the country's contemporary political, economic, and social conditions.

Today, the interest of Europeans and Americans in Japanese civilisation and current affairs extends far beyond the academic realm. Japan is increasingly touching the lives of millions of people: through the manufacture and export of high-quality automobiles and consumer goods that are found in most Western households; through the popularisation of Japanese managerial techniques such as the 'quality circle' and the 'just-in-time' approach within manufacturing; through the introduction of Zen Buddhism in the West; through the diffusion of her traditional art and modern architecture; through the translated writings of the novelist Mishima Yukio, the Nobel laureate Kawabata Yasunari, and other twentieth-century authors; through the production of such films as *Rashōmon* and the *Seven Samurai* (directed by Kurosawa Akira) and such television mini-series as *Shōgun*; and through the widespread availability of such Japanese foods as tofu, tempura, and sushi. Within the United States, moreover, most four-year colleges and universities as well as a growing number of secondary schools are now regularly offering one or more courses related to Japan.

While a number of works about Japan published before the late 1950s are now considered to be 'classics', most of the noteworthy literature in English about this island nation's past and present is the product of the 1960s, the 1970s, and the 1980s. In their own time, *A selected list of books and articles on Japan in English, French, and German*, compiled by Hugh Borton, Serge Elisséeff, William W. Lockwood, and John C. Pelzel (Washington, DC: American Council of Learned Societies, 1940, 142p.; rev. & enl. ed., Cambridge, Massachusetts: Harvard University Press, 1954, 272p.) and *Japan and Korea: a critical bibliography*, by Bernard S. Silberman (Tucson, Arizona: University of Arizona Press, 1962, 120p.) were highly regarded as authoritative guides to substantial bodies of published knowledge about Japan. Each of them directed students and other interested readers to then available sources of information in several disciplines. Both of them, however, have become seriously dated, as much more has been written about Japan during the past thirty years than was published during the entire preceding century. Furthermore, this recent explosion of publications – over 300 new books, exhibition catalogues, and government reports each year during the 1980s alone – has made the identification and selection of appropriate reading material by non-specialists considerably more challenging.

The present volume aims at providing readers during the 1990s with substantial bibliographical coverage for generally accessible English-language writings about Japan. As the world enters the final decade of the twentieth century – a period when Japan will inevitably command even more attention on the international scene, and when the demands for reading material about this nation will be greater than ever before – this annotated guide should assist individuals in identifying informative and generally reliable sources which can serve many of their needs.

Japan offers a balanced selection of some 1,900 popular and academic English-language books and monographs (contained in 1,615 annotated entries) covering all major fields of knowledge: from geography, history, religion, society, politics, and foreign relations, to economics, literature, the fine and performing arts, sports and recreation, and the mass media. It does not purport to be comprehensive, but rather complements several highly specialised subject-oriented bibliographies that have appeared in recent years as well as the more extensive (but unannotated) coverage of Japan available in the annual volumes of the Association for Asian Studies' *Bibliography of Asian Studies* (q.v.) and *Doctoral Dissertations on Asia* (q.v.). Its intended audience includes college and university students who are looking for supplementary readings and information about past or present-day Japan, general readers who are seeking a broad and representative spectrum of publications, educators and scholars who wish to identify important books to read either as they begin developing an interest in Japan or as they broaden their understanding of the country and her people, librarians who wish to build or strengthen a multidisciplinary core collection about Japan or who are in need of a quick reference guide, businesspeople who must become familiar with Japanese ways and methods, and long-term Western visitors to Japan as well as proverbial 'armchair travellers'.

In accordance with the stated objectives of the Clio Press 'World Bibliographical Series' in which this volume appears, high priority has been given to the inclusion of works which one can reasonably expect to find in larger public and university libraries. Accordingly, many academic studies produced by university presses in particular have been listed in addition to the more widely available general trade imprints. Special emphasis has been placed on the inclusion of books and monographs published during the 1970s and the 1980s because of the relatively up-to-date nature of their scholarship and their coverage as well as the greater likelihood of their commercial availability. This focus on recent publications holds especially true for writings about Japan's economy and trade, politics and government, law and education, and science and technology. At the same time, the bibliography has routinely included older books whose literary merit, historical significance, or exceptional scholarly contribution have made them standard or classic works. Among these are writings by the eleventh-century court lady Murasaki Shikibu, the nineteenth-century American educator William Elliot Griffis, the prewar American anthropologist John Fee Embree, and the renowned British diplomat and historian Sir George B. Sansom. The American as well as the British imprints of monographs published on both sides of the Atlantic have normally been provided. Reprint editions and second editions are also indicated whenever possible. Books which have gone through several printings and remain commercially available, however, have not been distinguished from those which have gone out of print.

The compilation and numbering of the 1,615 annotated entries that comprise most of this volume was completed early in 1989. While efforts were made to keep the bibliography up-to-date as it progressed through the final stages of editing and production, only a limited number of newly-released titles could be incorporated through the expansion of existing annotations. Accordingly, many relevant 1989 imprints have been excluded and will have to await the appearance of some future, revised edition of this work.

Users of this bibliography will note a discernable bias in favour of publications that may have a greater appeal to British and North American audiences than to continental European, Australian, or Asian readers. Except for bilingual dictionaries, government statistical yearbooks, and Japanese-language textbooks and grammars, only books and monographs written entirely in English have been selected. In part this is because of the aforementioned outpouring of popular writing, scholarly research, and translations relating to Japan. There frequently is at least one English-language work – and at times there may be several – which can be recommended to readers with sufficiently broad subject interests.

To ensure at the same time that the views of Japanese writers and scholars are adequately represented, several hundred translations and works produced by Japanese in English (in the social sciences, history, and the fine and performing arts as well as in literature) have been included. Furthermore, English-language books brought out by major Japanese publishers – among them Kodansha International, the Japan Times, and the University of Tokyo Press – were given full consideration. The Japanese are among the most prolific publishers and the most avid readers in the world today, and much of what they have written – about themselves as well as about other societies – should be of interest to Westerners.

With a few exceptions (notably in the areas of diplomatic and military history and postwar economic and political relations), only books and monographs dealing *exclusively* with Japan or with Japanese overseas have been listed. Because of a need to limit the overall size of the bibliography, periodical articles, government and commercial reports (except for yearbooks), highly technical works, theses and dissertations, pamphlets, and unpublished documentary materials have been entirely excluded. Readers wishing to delve further into the English-language literature, however, will be directed to many thousands of other publications by the entries listed within the two reasonably comprehensive sections 'Periodicals and News-papers' (pp.600-618) and 'Bibliographies and Research Guides' (pp.630-644) as well as by individual bibliographies found in many of the books described within this volume.

A uniform bibliographic style for the Clio Press 'World Biblio-graphical Series' has dictated the nature and order of the individual bibliographical citations. Authors' personal names are given first, followed by their family names *except in the case of Japanese writers who were active before the Meiji Restoration of 1868*. Accordingly, the names of twentieth-century Japanese novelists appear in Western order, i.e. as Yasunari *Kawabata*, Yukio *Mishima*, and Junichirō *Tanizaki*, while the names of premodern authors (found particularly in the 'Classical Fiction and Prose: Translations', 'Poetry: Translations', and 'Drama' subsections of 'Literature') are entered as *Murasaki* Shikibu, *Kobayashi* Issa, and *Chikamatsu* Monzaemon. Except where they appear as the authors of subsumed titles of books, however, the names of all individual Japanese mentioned within the annotations (as well as within the subject indexes) are written in traditional Japanese order, i.e. family name first, personal name second. No information is provided in the bibliographical citations about illustrative material other than the number of maps in a book, nor is there any indication of the existence of a paperback as opposed to a clothbound edition. All Japanese words (except for *shimbun*) have been romanised according to the modified Hepburn system of transliteration. The fourth edition of *Kenkyusha's new Japanese-English dictionary* (q.v.) has served as the authority in the case of any questions. Long vowels in Japanese names and words have been indicated by macrons – e.g., Natsume Sōseki, Kyōto, Shintō, inrō – except in the case of the place name 'Tokyo' and a few Anglicised nouns such as 'Noh'. *Webster's ninth new collegiate dictionary* (Springfield, Massachusetts: Merriam-Webster, 1983) was consulted in order to determine whether a word of Japanese origin should be romanised or italicised.

Each of the numbered entries has been annotated primarily to provide readers with an overview of the scope and contents of the books and monographs selected for inclusion within this bibliography. Especially noteworthy titles are often singled out for special mention. In addition, over three hundred related works of interest are cited and frequently described within the annotations.

The arrangement of the different sections of this guide follows the general classification scheme developed for the 'World Bibliographical Series', with considerable modifications designed to allow for the expansion and refinement of the sections concerned particularly with history, biography, religion, and literature, as well as for the inclusion of such uniquely Japanese subjects as the Shintō religion, flower arrangement (ikebana), and the tea ceremony (*chanoyu*). Because of anticipated widespread interest, substantial numbers of entries have been grouped together under the headings 'Tourism and Travel Guides', 'Biographical and Autobiographical Accounts', 'Religion: Buddhism and Zen Buddhism', 'Foreign Relations: 1931-

1945 (including World War II)', 'Literature: Translations', and 'Food and Drink'. (Some of these represent aspects of Japanese life and culture that are all too often ignored in standard bibliographies.) Individual entries in nearly every section have been arranged alphabetically by author or editor. In any classification scheme there are inevitably bound to be difficulties in demarcating specific topics or in classifying works that cover two or more subject areas. A comprehensive numerical cross-referencing system has therefore been incorporated together with an index of authors that also contains translators and contributors of introductions, an index of titles that includes all of the works subsumed within the annotated entries, and a very detailed subject index that is based primarily on key terms, concepts, and names mentioned in the titles and annotations of the books.

Heartfelt thanks are due to my wife Anna, who has been supportive of this bibliographical endeavour in ever so many ways; to my friend and colleague Hans H. Wellisch, who offered invaluable editorial advice and reviewed most of the annotated entries while in draft form; to the interlibrary loan staff of the University of Maryland at College Park Libraries, who filed requests for publications not available in my extensive personal library or among the university library's holdings; and to Robert L. August, Stephen S. Large, David O. Mills, Robert G. Neville, and J. Thomas Rimer, all of whom rendered professional assistance as this volume neared completion. The Japan Foundation (Tokyo), the Suntory Foundation (Osaka), and the Great Britain-Sasakawa Foundation (London) generously subsidised some of the printing, publishing and marketing costs, thereby enabling Clio Press to bring out a work substantially larger than its companion volumes in the 'World Bibliographical Series'. The compilation and editing of this bibliography – during evenings, weekends, and vacations – was undertaken without any institutional or foundation assistance solely in my capacity as a professional bibliographer for Western-language reference works on Asia. I alone bear the responsibility for any inadvertent errors, inevitable omissions, or other possible shortcomings within this work.

Frank Joseph Shulman
College Park, Maryland
December 1989

Chronology

Historical periods and historical events referred to within the bibliography

Jōmon	before *ca.* 300 BC
Yayoi	*ca.* 300 BC–AD 300
Yamato	*ca.* 300–710
Kofun (Tumulus)	250–552
Asuka (Suiko)	552–645
Nara	710–794
Heian	794–1185
Kamakura	1185–1333
Muromachi	1333–1568
Sengoku ('Warring States')	1467–1568
Momoyama (Azuchi-Momoyama)	1568–1600
Tokugawa (Edo)	1600–1868
Genroku era	1688–1703
Meiji Restoration	1868
Meiji	1868–1912
Russo-Japanese War	1904–1905
Taishō	1912–1926
Shōwa	1926–1989
Manchurian Incident	1931
Sino-Japanese War	1937–1945
Attack on Pearl Harbor	1941
Pacific War	1941–1945
End of World War II	1945
Allied occupation of Japan	1945–1952
Heisei	1989–

The Country and Its People

1 **As the Japanese see it: past and present.**
Compiled and edited by Michiko Y. Aoki, Margaret B. Dardess.
Honolulu, Hawaii: University Press of Hawaii, 1981. 315p.

An interdisciplinary collection of thirty-one readings that portray some of the ways in which ordinary people think, act, respond to daily concerns, and view life that is going on about them. Most of the relatively brief readings date from the twentieth century; all of them have been translated from Japanese. They include folk tales, speeches, sermons, short stories, interviews, newspaper articles, and excerpts from novels and personal memoirs. Aoki and Dardess organise their selections under four headings – 'Religion', 'The Family', 'The Community', and 'The State' – and then arrange them chronologically by year of publication. This anthology is oriented towards the general reader who is interested in such facets of Japanese life as popular beliefs, marriage customs, and interpersonal relations, and who is seeking carefully selected reading material in which ordinary Japanese 'relate their ideals, goals, and expectations'. The volume should also assist teachers who are responsible for courses dealing with the history and society of Japan.

2 **Listening to Japan: a Japanese anthology.**
Edited with an introduction by Jackson H. Bailey.   New York; London: Praeger, 1973. 236p. map.

A dozen essays, one short story, and nine poems by distinguished Japanese intellectuals and writers together constitute 'a representative collection about the subjects that concern the Japanese today when they talk among themselves as if no one were listening'. This anthology – organised under the four headings of 'Culture–Ideas–Values', 'Society–Politics–Economics', 'Youth–Ideals–Education', and 'The World Scene' – brings out aspects of Japanese life which the editor feels are often readily viewed by outsiders, among them the role of tradition in Japan's formative culture, basic notions in Japanese social relations, the disharmony of form and substance in Japanese democracy, and the meaning to society of student protest in Japan.

1

3 **Water: a view from Japan.**
Bernard Barber, photographs by Dana Levy.   New York; Tokyo:
Weatherhill, 1974. 207p. map.

Nine photo-essays – covering 'natural water', 'ritual water', 'sensual water', 'awesome water', 'historical water', 'working water', 'water in gardens', 'water in art', and 'friends of water' – focus on the longstanding relationship between the Japanese people and the water which surrounds them. One hundred and seventy pages of photographs, over half of them in full colour, illustrate Barber's text and depict such subjects as Japanese landscapes filled with water, the diversity of water rituals in religious practices, the use of water in bathing and at hot springs, whirlpools, swamps and typhoons, historical scenes of warfare on the surface of the sea, and the use of water for irrigation and for the manufacturing of cloth.

4 **The Japanese and the Jews.**
Isaiah Ben-Dasan (pseud.), translated by Richard L. Gage.   Tokyo; New
York: Weatherhill, 1972. 193p. Reprinted, Weatherhill, 1981.

Almost instantly a best-seller in its original Japanese-language version, this book by the noted author and critic Yamamoto Shichihei was ostensibly written by a longtime Jewish resident of Japan for the purpose of examining the 'distinctive traits of the Japanese and the Jews'. In reality, it is a volume which uses the literary convention of comparison for intimately viewing and analysing selected aspects of the Japanese national character. Oriented specifically towards a Japanese audience, it reflects on the history, religion, values, and cultural background of the Japanese; and describes their attitudes and responses to 'such basic human concerns as food, water, spiritual freedom, physical security, government, and man's relation' to the forces of nature. As such, it provides the Western reader with an excellent example of *Nihonjinron*, the genre of books constantly being written in Japanese about the unique national identity of the Japanese people. Works that are actually concerned with relations between the Japanese and the Jews include *Wanderers and settlers in the Far East: a century of Jewish life in China and Japan*, by Herman Dicker (New York: Twayne, 1962, 207p.); Abraham Kotsuji's autobiography *From Tokyo to Jerusalem* (New York: Bernard Geis Associates, 1964, 215p.); and *Japanese, Nazis & Jews: the Jewish refugee community of Shanghai, 1938–1945*, by David Kranzler (New York: Yeshiva University Press, 1976, 644p. Reprinted, Hoboken, New Jersey: Ktav, 1988).

5 **Japan today.**
Roger Buckley.   Cambridge, England; New York: Cambridge University
Press, 1985. 139p. map. bibliog.

This introductory survey examines Japan's postwar political development and her immense economic advances against a background of social and cultural stability, and discusses the gradual changes that have occurred in Japan's international relations as her increasing economic strength has led Japanese leaders to reassess their earlier foreign and defence policies. Writing from a British perspective, Buckley shows the positive factors underlying Japan's postwar successes while also pointing out the political and social problems which have attracted less attention among Westerners. He depicts Japan as an essentially stable society which will continue to present an economic challenge to the United States and other industrialised countries and which will assume an increasingly prominent role in world affairs.

6 **Japan: a country study.**
Edited by Frederica M. Bunge. Washington, DC: American University, Foreign Area Studies; for sale by the US Government Printing Office, 1983. 4th ed. 494p. 5 maps. bibliog. (Area Handbook Series) (DA Pam 550-30)

One volume in a periodically updated series describing the economic, national security, political, and social systems and institutions of most countries in the world and analysing the interrelationships of those systems and institutions as well as the ways in which they are shaped by cultural factors. This book has eight chapters entitled 'Historical Setting', 'The Society and Its Environment', 'Education and the Arts', 'The Character and Structure of the Economy', 'International Economic Relations', 'The Political System', 'Foreign Relations', and 'National Security'. Several statistical tables and a lengthy, annotated bibliography supplement the text. This volume supersedes the third edition of *Area handbook for Japan*, by Donald P. Whitaker and others (Washington, DC: US Government Printing Office, 1974, 672p.). A fifth edition is slated for publication in 1991.

7 **Japan: a postindustrial power.**
Ardath W. Burks. Boulder, Colorado; London: Westview Press, 1984. 2nd ed. 263p. 2 maps. bibliog. (Westview Profiles. Nations of Contemporary Asia).

An overview of Japan and the Japanese, written for the general reader and the undergraduate student. Burks surveys the geography, traditions, and cultural heritage of Japan; traces the modernisation of the country since the Tokugawa period; and describes postwar politics, the postwar economy, and Japan's postindustrial society – in which the majority of the labour force is employed in the service sector. He also examines the Japanese national character under the rubric '*Kokuminsei*: Who Are the Japanese?' as well as Japan's place in the world today. A selected, annotated bibliography contains both standard and recent studies.

8 **The Japanese mind: the goliath explained.**
Robert C. Christopher. New York: Linden Press/Simon and Schuster, 1983. 352p. bibliog. Reprinted, New York: Fawcett Columbine, 1984. London: Pan Books, 1984. Rutland, Vermont; Tokyo: Tuttle, 1987.

A widely acclaimed general introduction to contemporary Japan written expressly to help Americans become more understanding and knowledgeable about Japan and thereby more responsible and intelligent in their dealings with her. Interspersing his remarks with personal anecdotes and reminiscences, Christopher (a former editor of both *Time* magazine and *Newsweek*) describes how the Japanese feel, think, act, and behave. He addresses a wide range of topics, from family life, the Japanese corporation, Japan as an information-oriented society, and automation, to the educational system, the changing role of women, Japanese habits of leisure, and the complexity of their language. His comments on the Japanese character and his analyses of the factors underlying Japan's recent economic success are particularly insightful. Christopher is convinced that America's future well-being will be directly affected by her interaction with Japan, and he recommends steps for the improvement of relations between these two powers.

The Country and Its People

9 **Perspectives on Japan: a guide for teachers.**
Edited by John J. Cogan, Donald O. Schneider, foreword by Carole L.
Hahn. Washington, DC: National Council for the Social Studies, 1983.
132p. map. bibliog. (National Council for the Social Studies Bulletin, 69).
A practical guide oriented towards American elementary and high-school teachers.
Part one – 'Japan from a Japanese Perspective' – is concerned with geography, Japan's
cultural tradition in historical retrospect, the Japanese economy, the role of women in
Japanese society, and citizenship and moral education in Japan. Part two – 'Japan from
an Outsider's Perspective' – presents Jackson H. Bailey's reflections on Japanese
religion and ethical norms, social structure and social relations, Japan's geographical
isolation, and recent Japanese history. The concluding part discusses several
recommended approaches and techniques for teaching about Japan in precollegiate
social studies programmes, and highlights a variety of resources and materials (e.g.,
films and publications) for instructional use.

10 **Japan: a comparative view.**
Edited with an introduction by Albert M. Craig. Princeton, New
Jersey; Guildford, Surrey: Princeton University Press, 1979. 437p.
Ten essays by specialists in Japanese studies offer a multidisciplinary, comparative
approach to the understanding of Japanese history, culture, and contemporary affairs.
The contributors consider the Japanese experience to be a fruitful source of valid
comparisons with China and Korea as well as with the West. They address such topics
as comparative conceptions of the city, involving Tokyo and London; the Korean and
Japanese patterns of responding to the West; nation-building in early Meiji Japan and
in post-1949 China; love and death in modern American and Japanese novels; cultural
differences between China and Japan with respect to family socialisation; pre-industrial
landholding patterns in Japan and England; and factory life in contemporary Japan and
China.

11 **Faces of Japan.**
Photographs by Bob Davis, introduction by Murray Sayle. Tokyo;
New York: Kodansha International, 1978. 108p.
An Australian photographer based in London captures the true feeling of contemporary Japanese life. His collection of eighty-eight full-page, monochrome photographs
taken between 1974 and 1978 depict a wide variety of scenes, including those of a
kimono-clad matron playing the pinball game known as *pachinko* in Tokyo, the owner
of an antique shop in Kyōto at rest, commuters on a train in Ōsaka, children playing
tag on the quay next to Itsukushima Shrine on Miyajima Island, a grandmother and
her granddaughter within a park in Nara, washday at a provincial inn in Matsue,
spectators at the start of a festival in northern Honshū, a cart selling sweet batter cakes
in Kōchi City, summer fireworks on a back street in Ashikawa City, and photographers
at dawn on the summit of Mount Fuji. The widespread existence of cultural contrasts
in postwar Japan is the focus of Sayle's introduction.

12 **Made in Japan: the methods, motivation, and culture of the Japanese,
and their influence on U.S. business and all Americans.**
Boye De Mente. Lincolnwood, Illinois: Passport Books, 1987. 176p.
A general anecdotal account that seeks to explain the basis for the deep and pervasive
influence which Japan has been having on American culture, business, and patterns of

consumption. De Mente describes both the history of United States–Japanese relations and some of the characteristic features of twentieth-century Japan, and he covers a wide range of topics including the Japanese way of life, work-style, psychology, style of competition, and Japanese business communities in the United States.

13　**Japan.**
Editors of Time-Life Books; consultants: Susan Pharr, Edwin O. Reischauer, Merry White.　Alexandria, Virginia: Time-Life Books, 1985. 160p. 2 maps. bibliog. (Library of Nations).

One in a series of popularly written, illustrated volumes describing the natural resources, peoples, histories, economies, and governments of various countries of the world. Chapters entitled 'Out of the Ashes, a New Nation', 'The Beautiful, Dangerous Land', 'People of the "Divine Wind" ', 'Art as a Way of Life', 'A Dynamo Fueled by Human Energy', and 'The Pressure to Be Japanese' introduce the physical beauty of Japan, her history and civilisation, and contemporary Japanese life. Four photo-essays describe the life of the typical middle-class salaried worker, the activities of a fisheries co-operative, some of the leading craftsmen who are regarded today as 'living national treasures', and the theme of finding peace and quiet.

14　**Facts and Figures of Japan.**
Tokyo: Foreign Press Center/Japan, 1960(?)–　. annual. (Foreign Press Center, 6th floor, Nippon Press Center Building, 2-1 Uchisaiwai-chō 2-chōme, Chiyoda-ku, Tokyo 100, Japan).

A handbook of basic factual information about present-day Japan: the land, population, government, diplomacy, defence, economy, finance, industry, trade and investment, labour, energy, transportation and communications, livelihood, welfare, housing, crime, science, education, the mass media, culture, leisure and sports. Each annual edition contains hundreds of charts, graphs, maps, and statistical tables prepared by Japanese government ministries, augmented by brief textual descriptions. Typical of the information published each year is a map indicating Japan's population density by prefecture, a table of the number of candidates elected and the voter support ratio in the House of Representatives elections by party over a 12–15 year period, graphs showing trends in Japanese direct investment overseas, an updated table of the number of schools, students and teachers, and a listing of the recent winners of major sumo tournaments.

15　**Japan: the fragile superpower.**
Frank Gibney.　New York: New American Library, 1985. 2nd rev. ed. 430p. ('A Meridian Book'). Reprinted, Rutland, Vermont; Tokyo: Tuttle, 1987.

A panoramic view of contemporary Japan and the US–Japan relationship, written by an American businessman with many years of experience in Japan. Gibney seeks to interpret the peculiar characteristics and qualities that account for Japan's modern success and that distinguish the Japanese from their counterparts in the West, as well as to show how the Japanese relate to Americans. He discusses the nature and problems of the Japanese–American relationship; the characteristics of the Japanese people and their society (including the group-oriented nature of the Japanese, their sense of honour and obligation, their method of rearing children, and their language); 'Business Japan' and its successes and problems; the educators, the press and the politicians of modern Japan; the crisis of Japan's affluent society; and the future of the country.

16 Twelve doors to Japan.
John Whitney Hall, Richard K. Beardsley, with chapters by Joseph K. Yamagiwa, B. James George, Jr.   New York; Toronto, Ontario; London: McGraw-Hill, 1965. 649p. 4 maps. bibliog.

An interdisciplinary introduction that aims at providing a basic understanding of Japanese culture and society and an acquaintance with the aims, materials, characteristic methods or viewpoints, and special features of several academic disciplines insofar as they deal with the study of Japan. The authors – specialists associated with the Center for Japanese Studies at the University of Michigan – cover the geography of Japan, the prehistoric and contemporary aspects of her cultural anthropology, the historical dimension, language as an expression of Japanese culture, literature and Japanese culture, the visual arts and Japanese culture, religion and philosophy, personality psychology, education and modern national development, Japan's political system, law in modern Japan, and aspects of Japanese economic development.

17 Japan: patterns of continuity.
Fosco Maraini.   Tokyo; Palo Alto, California: Kodansha International, 1971; London: Hamish Hamilton, 1972. 240p. 2 maps.

A perceptive and singularly original essay on the deep-rooted and powerful continuity of Japanese life and culture which underlies the chaotic surface and the contradictions of twentieth-century Japan and constitutes the source of Japan's vitality. Maraini divides his book into four parts: 'Nature and Art', 'Art and People', 'The Ideographic Space', and 'The Future of the Past'. Using over three hundred colour photographs that depict such ordinary items as water, plants, and trees as art objects, he indicates that considerable unity and continuity exist beneath the surface of change, and he shows how Japanese cultural influences of the past have blended into and shaped the life of present-day Japan. In addition, his photographs 'reveal the patterns implicit in a culture: the links between a people and its art, and between that art and every other facet of life'.

18 Through Japanese eyes.
Richard H. Minear, foreword by Leon E. Clark.   New York: Center for International Training and Education, 1987. rev. ed. 2 vols. (The CITE World Culture Series).

Written for a secondary-school audience but also generally useful as a collection of introductory readings, this work is designed 'to broaden the reader's perspective by presenting a *Japanese* view of Japan' through an edited selection of Japanese sources: autobiographies, fiction, poetry, newspaper and magazine articles, letters, diaries, and historical documents. The first volume, *The past: the road from isolation*, traces Japanese history from the seventeenth century through the late 1940s. Volume two, *The present: coping with affluence*, is primarily concerned with postwar issues and focuses on 'the personal, social, and environmental effects of Japan's current prosperity'. It also considers contemporary Japanese attitudes towards women, family life, and religion.

19 **Introducing Japan: history, way of life, creative world, seen and heard, food and wine.**
Edited by Paul Norbury.   Tenterden, Kent: Paul Norbury Publications; New York: St. Martin's Press, 1977. 192p.

A book for casual readers that presents a highly informed view of Japan and the Japanese as perceived by many Western and Japanese writers. Thirty-nine illustrated essays introduce selected topics in Tokugawa and Meiji period history; such aspects of the Japanese way of life as team spirit, Japanese shyness with foreigners, and group relationships; the folk pottery, cinema, calligraphy, music, ukiyo-e prints, and drama of the Japanese creative world; renowned tourist spots such as Kamakura and Miyajima; and the sushi, sukiyaki, tempura, saké, chopsticks, and rice that are an integral part of the Japanese culinary scene.

20 **The Japanese: a cultural portrait.**
Robert S. Ozaki.   Rutland, Vermont; Tokyo: Tuttle, 1978. 328p. bibliog.

An informative exposition of the character of modern Japan, the patterns of her culture and her interpersonal relations, and the persistence of traditional values in contemporary life. Ozaki discusses a wide range of topics including Japan's early encounters with the West, Japanese ideology and nationalism following the Meiji Restoration of 1868, law and order, Japan's system of bureaucracy, the psychology of dependence (*amae*), Japanese group orientation, the characteristic patterns of verbal and non-verbal communication, family life, the work ethic and propensity to save, consumer life, and the style of Japanese management. The author is a native of Japan who has lived and taught in the United States since his college years.

21 **Japan: the dilemmas of success.**
T. J. Pempel, foreword by Michael J. Mansfield.   New York: Foreign Policy Association, 1986. 80p. map. bibliog. (Headline Series, 277).

An introductory examination of Japan's historical background, society, politics, economy, and international role, prepared especially for use in classrooms, seminars, and community discussion groups. It includes a set of discussion questions and a brief suggested reading list.

22 **Tokyo: the city at the end of the world.**
Peter Popham, photographs by Ben Simmons.   Tokyo; New York: Kodansha International, 1985. 191p. 2 maps. bibliog.

Combining reportage and personal reflection, a longtime English resident of Japan with a particular sensitivity for architecture offers an unconventional portrait of the people and places of contemporary Tokyo: 'its monuments and shacks, its love hotels and hold-outs, its expressways and village lanes, its still center and its sprawling fringes'. Depicting Tokyo as both a challenge to accepted notions of postwar urban life and a city that succeeds in ways where many of its Western counterparts fail, Popham describes the 1923 earthquake that devastated the metropolitan area as well as some of the ongoing preparations for the inevitable next major quake, Tokyo's postwar history and development, several aspects of its urban culture, the character of some of its neighbourhoods, and its fascinating architecture. Forty-four monochrome photographs and architectural line drawings provide exterior views of some of the city's most interesting buildings.

23   **The Japanese today: change and continuity.**
Edwin O. Reischauer.   Cambridge, Massachusetts; London: Belknap Press of Harvard University Press, 1988. 426p. 3 maps. bibliog.

An eminent scholar and former US ambassador to Japan provides an authoritative introduction to the geography, history, contemporary society, political system, business organisation, and international relations of Japan. Following a brief description of the geographical setting and physical features of the country and an historical overview from the third century AD through the late 1970s, Reischauer focuses on (1) the social organisation, values, and interpersonal relationships of the Japanese people; (2) the government and politics of contemporary Japan, including the emperor, the Diet, the political parties, the elections, and the decision-making process; (3) the prewar and postwar Japanese economies as well as Japan's current employment system and business organisation; and (4) Japan's political and economic relations with other countries. He also discusses the language barrier that separates Japan from the rest of the world and the current tension between the Japanese sense of their uniqueness and the growing trend towards internationalism. An extensive revision of Reischauer's earlier work entitled *The Japanese* (Cambridge, Massachusetts: Belknap Press of Harvard University Press, 1977, 443p.), this book is one of the first titles that should be read by anyone embarking on a study of present-day Japan.

24   **Different people: pictures of some Japanese.**
Donald Richie.   Tokyo; New York: Kodansha International, 1987. 204p.

A series of forty-eight vignettes of memorable people – ranging from such famous individuals as the novelist Kawabata Yasunari and the composer Takemitsu Tōru to relatively unknown individuals such as a neighbourhood florist and the nineteen-year-old delivery boy at a local emporium – whom Richie got to know during the course of some forty years spent in Japan. Utilising a technique borrowed from the late nineteenth-century writer Kunikida Doppo, Richie outlines his feelings as well as his observations of these people in a way that sympathetically depicts the Japanese as a group of individual human beings, 'each one of whom is, being human, unique'.

25   **Introducing Japan.**
Donald Richie, foreword by Edwin O. Reischauer.   Tokyo; New York: Kodansha International, 1986. rev. ed. 72p. map.

A collection of colour photographs accompanied by extensive captions and one-page essays which introduce Japan to the general reader. Most of the volume consists of a pictorial survey of Japan's major cities – in particular, Tokyo, Kyōto, and Nara – and of several districts and regions throughout the country. Concluding sections cover a wide range of topics including the Japanese house, cuisine, crafts, martial arts, history, government, economy, religion, education, and language.

26   **A lateral view: essays on contemporary Japan.**
Donald Richie.   Tokyo: Japan Times, 1987. 208p.

A collection of twenty-three thought-provoking essays written between 1962 and 1986 that are concerned with (1) the shapes, patterns, and rhythms of Japan in general, (2) such aspects of the capital city of Tokyo as its constantly changing architecture and its 'Disneyland'-like character, (3) the languages and vocabulary of gesture, taste, and fashion in Japan as well as signs and symbols in Japanese, (4) the noh, *kyōgen*, and avant-garde theatres, (5) women in Japanese cinema, Japanese pornographic movies, and some general observations about the Japanese film, and (6) Japanese popular culture, including consideration of the images presented on television, the 'Japanese kiss', the game of *pachinko* (played on pinball machines), and the popularity of the Sony Walkman and *manga* (comic strip books) in Japanese society. A long-term resident of Tokyo, Donald Richie is well known as a critic of Japanese film, culture, and society.

27 **Japan in the 1980s: papers from a symposium on contemporary Japan held at Sheffield University, England, September 11–13, 1980.**
Rei Shiratori, general editor.   Tokyo; New York: Kodansha International, 1982. 290p.

A collection of papers – primarily by Japanese legislators, businessmen, scholars, and media people – on contemporary Japanese politics and economics. This symposium volume discusses the evolution of Japanese politics, political parties, the electoral system, foreign and national defence policies, and democracy during the 1960s and 1970s; examines contemporary Japanese economic affairs, fiscal and financial problems, energy policies, industrial reforms, Japanese foreign investment, and US–Japanese economic relations; and describes the policies and platforms of Japan's seven major political parties.

28 **A day in the life of Japan: photographed by 100 of the world's leading photojournalists on one day, June 7, 1985.**
Project directed by Rick Smolan, David Cohen.   Toronto, Ontario; New York: Collins, 1985. 236p. map.

Photographs selected from among 135,000 images taken throughout Japan on 7 June 1985. As with similar books published about Australia, Canada, Hawaii, Russia, Spain, and the United States, they capture the life of a nation during the course of one twenty-four-hour period. These photographs range from views of the early morning vegetable market in the Akihabara district of Tokyo, of sunrise over three of Japan's new skyscrapers, and of a newspaper delivery boy at 4.30 a.m., to photos of three young men staggering home after a night on the town, of squid boats anchored off the Izu Peninsula, and of a panorama of Tokyo at 11.30 p.m. Particularly prominent are pictures of people (agricultural and industrial workers, members of the Self Defence Forces, school children, funeral mourners, sales people, entertainers, and others) and of such places as Tokyo Disneyland, the Tokyo Stock Exchange, a Buddhist monastery, one small mountain village, Hiroshima, and a management training school near Mount Fuji.

29 **Japan.**
Peter Spry-Leverton, Peter Kornicki; photographs by Joel Sackett.
London: Michael O'Mara Books, 1987; New York: Facts on File, 1988. 192p. map. (A Channel Four Book).

An entertainingly written, beautifully illustrated introduction to Japan based on the television series 'Japan', produced for Channel Four by Central Independent Television in the United Kingdom and broadcast in a PBS national television series in the United States. Chapters entitled 'Through Western Eyes', 'Japan and the Outside World', 'Japan at War', 'Information and Technology', 'Town and Country', 'Domestic and Social Life', and 'International Society and Japan' offer a panorama of contemporary Japanese life, history, traditions, and character. The authors argue that

Japan's presence in the world today is too important for her to be misunderstood or ignored, and they seek to dispel many of the persisting stereotypes and myths that Westerners have had of the country and its people.

30 **Inside Japan: wealth, work and power in the new Japanese empire.**
Peter Tasker.   London: Sidgwick and Jackson, 1987; New York: E. P. Dutton; Toronto, Ontario: Fitzhenry and Whiteside, 1988. 312p. map.

Much about the 'society and institutions of Japan remains unknown, hidden behind screens of misunderstanding and cliché', in spite of her increasing influence in the West. In chapters bearing such catchy titles as 'Manufacturing Miracles', 'The Imperial Institution: At the Still Centre', and 'Japanese Leaders: "The Bulldozer" and "The Weathervane"', Tasker presents an account of contemporary Japanese life, society, economy, politics, and foreign affairs. The Japanese sense of ethnic homogeneity and isolation that has been reinforced by language as well as by history and geography; the generally strong sense of social responsibility of the Japanese; Japan's rapid postwar transformation and the consequences of her growing wealth and power; the efforts by agricultural interests, big business, the bureaucracy, and labour to influence politics; and the Japanese work ethic and concern for long-term economic gains are among the many topics which he covers at length. This book was published in the United States under the title *The Japanese: a major exploration of modern Japan*, and also reprinted under the title *The Japanese: portrait of a nation* (New York: New American Library, 1989).

31 **Shadows of the rising sun: a critical view of the 'Japanese miracle'.**
Jared Taylor, preface by Edward Seidensticker.   New York: William Morrow, 1983. 336p. Reprinted, Rutland, Vermont; Tokyo: Tuttle, 1985.

A critical commentary on contemporary patterns of Japanese thinking and behaviour and on the lifestyles of present-day Japanese by an American businessman born and raised in Japan. In contrast with many other books which portray Japan in highly admiring terms, Taylor seeks to paint a more realistic picture of Japan which includes 'glimpses of what lies in the shadows' of her recent economic success. The first half of his book describes the basic patterns of Japanese behaviour such as their narrow-mindedness and love for conformity, the rigid hierarchical structure of their society, their near reverence for self-sacrifice and submission to the group, the pervasive sexism that still exists, and their almost messianic sense of national uniqueness. The second part examines specific areas of contemporary life, among them the corporation, sex and sex roles, culture and language, and forms of recreation. Differences between life in Japan and life in the West as well as the inappropriateness of uncritically adopting Japanese practices and techniques are stressed throughout.

32 **An introduction to Japanese civilization.**
Edited by Arthur E. Tiedemann.   New York; London: Columbia University Press; Lexington, Massachusetts: D. C. Heath, 1974. 622p. 5 maps. (Companions to Asian Studies).

Eighteen essays contributed by such noted scholars as E. S. Crawcour, Donald Keene, Hugo Munsterberg, Richard Storry, and H. Paul Varley serve as an introduction to Japan for undergraduate students. A narrative history of the country, organised by period, constitutes the first half of the volume. The second half contains essays on

Japanese religion, art, literature, economic and cultural geography, the premodern and modern economies, society, modern political institutions, and law.

33 **Sources of Japanese tradition.**
Compiled by Ryūsaku Tsunoda, William Theodore de Bary, Donald Keene. New York: Columbia University Press; London: Oxford University Press, 1958. 928p. 2 maps. bibliog. (Records of Civilization: Sources and Studies) (Introduction to Oriental Civilizations, 54) (Unesco Collection of Representative Works: Japanese Series).
A standard anthology of undergraduate-level readings relating primarily to Japanese religion, philosophy, history, and culture. The authors selected and translated materials illustrating a wide range of Japanese tradition, from Early Shintō, Buddhism, and Confucianism to such modern movements as liberalism, nationalism, and socialism. The selections deal not only with religious and philosophical concerns but also with political, economic, and aesthetic questions. Introductory essays and commentary explain the historical setting and significance of each group of readings. This anthology serves as a companion volume to *Sources of Chinese tradition*, compiled by Wm. Theodore de Bary, Wing-tsit Chan, and Burton Watson (New York: Columbia University Press, 1960, 976p.) and *Sources of Indian tradition*, compiled by Wm. Theodore de Bary, Stephen N. Hay, Royal Weiler, and Andrew Yarrow (New York: Columbia University Press, 1958, 961p.)

34 **The other Japan: postwar realities.**
Edited with an introduction by E. Patricia Tsurumi for the *Bulletin of Concerned Asian Scholars*. Armonk, New York; London: M. E. Sharpe, 1988. 163p. 2 maps. (An East Gate Book).
Seventeen Western and Japanese scholars portray the 'other side of postwar Japan's remarkable story': the price which the Japanese have had to pay for their nation's political, economic, and social progress. Their analyses and literary portraits deal with 'the unresolved conflicts beneath the smooth surface of managed capitalism in Japan today', including the struggle of industrial workers to manage their own factories, the continuing legacy of the atomic bomb, the drastic changes in agriculture and rural life, the plight of the labourers of Tokyo's Sanya flophouse district, the manipulation of Zen Buddhism by Japanese capitalism, the impact of Minamata disease, and the phenomenon of subcontracted workers who regularly endanger their health in Japan's nuclear power plants.

35 **Understanding Japan.**
Tokyo: International Society for Educational Information, 1958(?)- .
(International Society for Educational Information [Kokusai Kyōiku Jōhō Sentā], Koryo Building, 18 Wakaba 1-chōme, Shinjuku-ku, Tokyo 160, Japan).
An ongoing series of educational pamphlets that seek to achieve 'mutual understanding among the peoples of the world' through the presentation and publication of accurate, up-to-date material about Japan. Each pamphlet focuses on a topic of current significance and is written by one or more Japanese specialists. Typical of the titles published through 1988 are pamphlets no. 32: *Japanese chronology*, by Tarō Sakamoto and Shigemi Kesado (1974, 73p.), an extensive chronological table of Japanese history and culture from the Jōmon period to 1972; no. 40: *New geography of Japan*, by

11

Atsuhiko Bekki (1978, 88p.), a guide to Japan's natural environment, population and its distribution, industry, agriculture, and fisheries; no. 47: *The Japanese emperor through history*, by Tarō Sakamoto (1984, 112p.); no. 50: *Japanese education*, by Shūichi Katsuta and Toshio Nakauchi (1986, 86p.), a description of present-day education with reference to the historical, political, and economic factors that have shaped its development; and no. 52: *Japan's industrial economy: recent trends and changing aspects*, by Yoshio Okuda (1987, 119p.). All pamphlets are oriented towards a broad foreign audience.

36 **Opening doors: contemporary Japan.**
United States–Japan Conference on Cultural and Educational Interchange (CULCON). Education Sub-Committee, in co-operation with the North Carolina Department of Public Instruction. Preface by Robert Leestma. New York: Asia Society, 1979. 421p. bibliog.

A resource manual for intercultural education compiled under the auspices of the American and Japanese governments. It was designed to promote mutual understanding through the curriculum at the elementary and secondary-school levels. The project involved the development of a thematic framework and associated instructional materials that would enable American students and teachers to gain better insights into their own culture, Japanese culture, and the mutual interdependence of nations. Eight curriculum 'units' (small but comprehensive packages of guidelines and materials built around basic themes) focus on the utilisation of natural and human resources; the quality of life; the role of haiku as an expression of reality; the Japanese perception of reality; decision-making in Japan; the question of identity ('Who Am I? Who Are We? And Who Are the Japanese?'); achievements, the work ethic, and education; and 'the success game'.

37 **Japanese culture.**
H. Paul Varley. Honolulu, Hawaii: University of Hawaii Press, 1984. 3rd ed. 331p. bibliog. Reprinted, Rutland, Vermont; Tokyo: Tuttle, 1986.

A reasonably comprehensive, largely descriptive survey of Japanese religion, thought, visual arts, literature, theatre, cinema, and such arts as the tea ceremony and landscape gardening that are uniquely cherished in Japan. Varley relates the formation and evolution of Japanese higher culture to concurrent political and institutional trends as he guides the reader through more than two thousand years of Japanese cultural history: from the rope-patterned pottery of the ancient Jōmon period to the world-class novels and movies produced after World War II. First published by Praeger in 1973, this new edition is oriented towards a broad audience including undergraduate students and readers seeking a solid general introduction to the history of Japanese culture.

38 **Japan as number one: lessons for America.**
Ezra F. Vogel. Cambridge, Massachusetts; London: Harvard University Press, 1979. Reprinted, New York: Harper Colophon Books; Rutland, Vermont and Tokyo: Tuttle, 1980. 272p. bibliog.

A provocative, best-selling account of the ways in which the Japanese have been remarkably successful in organising their society, managing their economic and political institutions, and resolving some of the basic problems confronting post-industrial societies. Vogel (a Harvard University professor of sociology) deals with seven major areas of national life: knowledge, the State, politics, the large company, basic education, welfare, and crime control. He describes recent Japanese accomplishments in these particular areas, and identifies some of the factors that explain their success. Among these are the group-directed quest for knowledge, Japanese workers' pride in their work and loyalty to their company, the emphasis on quality and equality in basic education, and the ability of the population to provide for its own well-being without becoming economically dependent on the State. Vogel suggests that an American understanding of Japan's recent experiences can assist the United States in rethinking its own societal difficulties. A follow-up to this book – Vogel's *Comeback: case by case: building the resurgence of American business* (New York: Simon and Schuster, 1985, 320p.) – describes four of the industries (shipbuilding, machine tools and robots, coal mining, and information) in which Japan became highly competitive and shows how American government and business leaders can work together to achieve similar kinds of success.

39 Modern Japanese organization and decision-making.
Edited by Ezra F. Vogel.   Berkeley, California; London: University of California Press, 1975. 340p. bibliog.

Thirteen essays describe and analyse the structures and the process of decision-making within Japanese governmental, business, cultural, and educational organisations. Some of the American and Japanese contributors stress the persistence of elements of Japanese tradition within these organisations; others emphasize the importance of change and contingency. Their articles are entitled: 'Functional and Dysfunctional Aspects of Government Bureaucracy'; 'Big Business and Political Influence'; 'Japanese Budget *Baransu*' [Balance]; 'A Government Ministry: The Case of the Ministry of International Trade and Industry'; 'Big Business Organization'; 'Emerging Japanese Multinational Enterprises'; 'Decision-Making in Japanese Labor Unions'; 'The Company Work Group'; 'Apprenticeship and Paternalism'; 'Economic Realities and Enterprise Strategy'; 'Intellectuals in the Decision-Making Process'; 'Competition and Conformity: An Inquiry into the Structure of Japanese Newspapers'; and 'Organizational Paralysis: The Case of Todai' [Tokyo University].

Meeting with Japan.
See item no. 70.

The Inland Sea.
See item no. 71.

The new official guide: Japan.
See item no. 82.

Introducing Tokyo.
See item no. 95.

Japanese in action: an unorthodox approach to the spoken language and the people who speak it.
See item no. 454.

The Japanese through American eyes.
See item no. 731.

Japan Statistical Yearbook = Nihon Tōkei Nenkan.
See item no. 825.

Nippon: a Charted Survey of Japan.
See item no. 826.

The East.
See item no. 1497.

East Asia: International Review of Economic, Political, and Social Development.
See item no. 1498.

Focus on Asian Studies.
See item no. 1503.

Japan Echo.
See item no. 1507.

Japan Forum.
See item no. 1508.

Japan Foundation Newsletter.
See item no. 1509.

Japan Journal.
See item no. 1510.

Japan Pictorial.
See item no. 1512.

Japan Quarterly.
See item no. 1513.

Japan Society Newsletter.
See item no. 1515.

The Japan Society Review.
See item no. 1516.

Journal of Asian Studies.
See item no. 1525.

Journal of Japanese Studies.
See item no. 1526.

Look Japan.
See item no. 1532.

PHP Intersect: Where Japan Meets Asia and the World.
See item no. 1537.

Proceedings of the British Association for Japanese Studies.
See item no. 1538.

Transactions of the Asiatic Society of Japan.
See item no. 1543.

New Japanalia: past and present.
See item no. 1551.

All-Japan: the catalogue of everything Japanese.
See item no. 1552.

Passport's Japan almanac.
See item no. 1553.

Kodansha encyclopedia of Japan.
See item no. 1556.

Discover Japan: words, customs and concepts.
See item no. 1557.

Mock Joya's things Japanese.
See item no. 1561.

Pictorial encyclopedia of Japanese culture: the soul and heritage of Japan.
See item no. 1568.

Pictorial encyclopedia of modern Japan.
See item no. 1568.

Japan today! A Westerner's guide to the people, language and culture of Japan.
See item no. 1573.

Bibliography of Asian Studies.
See item no. 1580.

Japan in film: a comprehensive annotated catalogue of documentary and theatrical films on Japan available in the United States.
See item no. 1586.

Catalogue of books in English on Japan, 1945–1981.
See item no. 1589.

Books on Japan in English: joint holdings list of ICU Library and IHJ Library, September 1983.
See item no. 1589.

A guide to reference books for Japanese studies.
See item no. 1589.

Ryukyu Islands: a bibliography.
See item no. 1591.

Japan through children's literature: an annotated bibliography.
See item no. 1596.

Japan and Korea: an annotated bibliography of doctoral dissertations in Western languages, 1877–1969.
See item no. 1607.

Doctoral dissertations on Japan and on Korea, 1969–1979: an annotated bibliography of studies in Western languages.
See item no. 1607.

Doctoral Dissertations on Asia: an Annotated Bibliographical Journal of Current International Research.
See item no. 1607.

Japan and Korea: a critical bibliography.
See item no. 1608.

Geography and Geology

General

40 **Geography of Japan.**
Edited by the Association of Japanese Geographers [Nihon Chiri
Gakkai]. Tokyo: Teikoku Shoin, 1980. 440p. maps. bibliog.
(Association of Japanese Geographers. Special Publications, 4).

Twenty-six prominent Japanese geographers discuss important aspects of Japan's
physical, historical, cultural, and socio-economic geography. They examine the
characteristics of Japan's physical nature with special reference to landforms; tephra
and its implications for the Japanese Quaternary period; seasonal and regional aspects
of Japan's weather and climate; inland water and water resources; territorial
possessions (*kuni*) in ancient Japan; the vicissitudes of village formation between the
tenth and seventeenth centuries; the growth of some castle towns between the mid-
1800s and the 1970s; the geographical distribution and historical development of rural
house types; regionalism between eastern and western Japan; regional trends in
postwar Japan's evolving agrarian structure; changes in fruit production; the formation
of industrial areas; the location of modern industry; localised industry in Japan;
urbanisation and zones of urban commerce; population distribution and movement in
the three major metropolitan areas; internal migration and population distribution;
and the regional pattern of the Japanese economy.

41 **The climate of Japan.**
Edited with an introduction by Eiichirō Fukui. Tokyo: Kodansha;
Amsterdam: Elsevier Scientific Publishing Co.; New York: Elsevier
North-Holland, 1977. 317p. 105 maps. bibliog. (Developments in
Atmospheric Science, 8).

Eight Japanese specialists in climatology and meteorology provide an overview of the
climate and weather of Japan and their effect on the activities and everyday life of the
Japanese. Their coverage includes Japan's general geographical setting, the four

seasons of the year, the dynamic and synoptic aspects of Japan's climate, the winter monsoon and such other seasonal phenomena as the *baiu* (the rainy season in early summer) and the typhoons and rains of the autumn, the heat and water balance (including air and ground temperatures, and precipitation and humidity), the flow patterns of the winds and local wind systems, and man-made climatic modifications that have come about because of air pollution. They also discuss the regional climatic characteristics and climatic divisions of the Japanese archipelago, and consider fluctuations of climate that have occurred since the Quaternary Ice Age.

42 **Land markets and land policy in a metropolitan area: a case study of Tokyo.**
Yuzuru Hanayama, foreword by Frank Schnidman.   Boston, Massachusetts: Oelgeschlager, Gunn and Hain in association with the Lincoln Institute of Land Policy, 1986. 162p. 3 maps. bibliog. (A Lincoln Institute of Land Policy Book).

Japan's metropolitan areas in general and Tokyo in particular have experienced rapidly rising land prices since the early 1960s – a phenomenon that has impeded the construction of sufficient housing and the provision of adequate urban infrastructure. After critiquing three widely-held myths about Japanese land policies and the lack of land for housing, Hanayama traces the historical evolution of the Tokyo metropolitan area and the development of its land policy, analyses the structure of Tokyo's housing land market in the 1960s and 1970s, and examines various policy instruments (e.g., land taxation rates) that can be used to improve land utilisation and control future increases in the price of land needed for residential purposes. Hanayama concludes with a proposal for integrating several policy instruments in order to resolve existing housing problems and to improve living and housing environments in Japan's major cities.

43 **Japan: geographical background to urban-industrial development.**
David Kornhauser, foreword by J. M. Houston.   Harlow, Essex: Longman Scientific and Technical; New York: John Wiley, 1982. 2nd ed. 189p. 14 maps. bibliog. (The World's Landscapes).

A non-technical introduction to the evolution of the Japanese 'landscape' (i.e., the 'total man–land complex in place and time'), with particular emphasis on the postwar urban-industrial scene. Weaving together the cultural, political, and historical factors that have influenced Japan's changing landscape patterns, Kornhauser discusses the urban and agrarian landscapes, the origins and evolution of the Japanese city with particular attention to city types during the Tokugawa period and their functional transformation after 1868, the historical development of commerce, the modernisation of commerce and industry between 1868 and 1945, and the postwar reconstruction and transformation of the Japanese landscape as a consequence of unprecedented commercial and industrial change. This is a revision and updating of Kornhauser's earlier work, *Urban Japan: its foundations and growth* (London; New York: Longman, 1976, 180p.).

44 **This land . . . this beauty: Japan's natural splendor.**
Photographs by Shinzō Maeda, translated by Ernest Richter, Matsue Richter.   Tokyo: Graphic-sha, 1987. 96p.

A collection of magnificent, full-page colour photographs taken throughout Japan that show the country's mountains, rivers, forests, and flora during the four seasons of the year. The photographs are accompanied by brief Japanese and English-language captions.

45 An industrial geography of Japan.
Edited by Kiyoji Murata, with Isamu Ota.   London: Bell and Hyman; New York: St. Martin's Press, 1980. 205p. 16 maps. (Advanced Economic Geographies).

A non-technical presentation of the development of Japan's industrial geography since World War II, oriented primarily towards geographers and economists. Murata and ten other Japanese university professors describe the industrial development and characteristics of Japan's manufacturing industries, examine the growth of the country's major industrial regions, discuss the development and distribution of Japan's most important manufacturing industries (textiles, energy, iron and steel, motor vehicles, and shipbuilding), and consider the role of the government's industrial location policy as well as the interrelationship between industrial development and environmental pollution between the 1950s and the 1970s.

46 The Japanese islands: a physical and social geography.
Jacques Pezeu-Massabuau, translated and adapted from the French by Paul C. Blum.   Rutland, Vermont; Tokyo: Tuttle, 1978. 283p. 9 maps. bibliog.

This general introduction to the geography of Japan describes the ongoing efforts of the Japanese to develop their economy in spite of inadequate natural resources, and considers the problems of pollution, overcrowding, and unequal regional development which they have sought to resolve. Pezeu-Massabuau deals not only with Japan's modern history, her 'inhospitable environment', the country's urban and rural demography, and Japanese techniques for managing their economy, but also with agriculture, fishing, energy resources, industry, communications, geographical regions, the growing megalopolis along the Pacific coast from the Tokyo Bay area to northern Kyūshū, and geographical trends as of the mid-1970s.

47 Kuroshio: physical aspects of the Japan Current.
Edited by Henry Stommel, Kōzō Yoshida.   Seattle: University of Washington Press; Tokyo: University of Tokyo Press, 1972. 517p. 221 maps. bibliog.

The Kuroshio or 'Japan Current' is a warm ocean current originating in an area east of the Philippines and flowing northward along the Ryūkyū archipelago to a point just south of Kyūshū, where it splits into two currents that continue along Japan's Pacific Ocean coast as well as into and through the Sea of Japan. It exerts considerable influence on Japan's climate during both the winter and summer. Focusing on the physical aspects of the Kuroshio, this extensive volume contains several contributions by Japanese and American scholars, among them ones concerned with the history of the Japanese Kuroshio observation programme, the bathymetry of the Kuroshio region, the characteristics of the flow of the Kuroshio, the time variation of the Kuroshio, the hydrography of the Kuroshio extension, and the Tsushima Current. A bibliography of some eight hundred publications about the oceanography of the Kuroshio is included. The book was published in Japan under the title *Kuroshio: its physical aspects*.

48 National parks of Japan.
Mary Sutherland, Dorothy Britton.   Tokyo; New York: Kodansha
International, 1980. 148p. 29 maps. bibliog.

A beautiful pictorial portrait and introduction to Japan's national park system: from Rishiri-Rebun-Sarobetsu, two islands and a marsh in the subarctic extreme north of Hokkaidō, to the mangrove swamps and coral reefs of Iriomote, one of the southernmost islands of the Ryūkyū chain. Concise descriptions and maps of each of the twenty-seven parks call attention to their outstanding scenic features, distinctive physiography, peculiar flora and/or fauna, and (in several cases) culturally significant points of interest. Westerners may be particularly familiar with Fuji-Hakone-Izu (easily accessible from Tokyo, this park comprises Mount Fuji and its environs as well as the tip of the Izu Peninsula), Nikkō (an important pilgrimage centre set in rugged mountain terrain northwest of Tokyo), Ise-Shima (the shrine to the Sun Goddess Amaterasu), and Seto Naikai (a park consisting of many parcels of land distributed among the ten prefectures bordering the Inland Sea). A history of the park system is also included.

49 Geology of Japan.
Edited by Fuyuji Takai, Tatsurō Matsumoto, Ryūzō Toriyama.   Tokyo:
University of Tokyo Press; Berkeley, California: University of California
Press, 1963. 279p. 14 maps. bibliog.

A comprehensive text about the geology of Japan, written specifically for a foreign audience, that focuses on individual geological periods: Silurian and Devonian, Carboniferous, Permian, Triassic, Jurassic, Cretaceous, Palaeocene, Neocene, and Quaternary. Several specialists survey past Japanese research on these periods, outline their stratigraphy, and present information concerning their fauna and flora and/or the distribution of their fossils and rocks. A concluding chapter deals with pre-Tertiary igneous activity, metamorphism, and metallogenesis. A revised edition of this book, edited by Toshio Kimura, Itaru Hayami, and Shizuo Yoshida, will be published by the University of Tokyo Press.

50 Japan: a geography.
Glenn T. Trewartha.   Madison, Wisconsin: University of Wisconsin
Press; London: Methuen, 1965. rev. ed. 652p. 207 maps. bibliog.

A comprehensive survey of the physical, cultural, and regional geography of Japan. Part one focuses on physical geography, analysing the country's terrain, climate, soils, native vegetation, and economically useful mineral resources. The second part is concerned with population, the cities and villages, agriculture, industry, manufacturing, transportation, and trade. Both of these parts deal with Japan in its entirety. The final part divides Japan into several regional subdivisions – Hokkaidō, Tōhoku, Tōsan and Hokuriku, Kantō, Tōkai, Kinki, Inland Sea and Shikoku, and Kyūshū – and offers detailed descriptions of these major regions. There are over two hundred well-executed maps and numerous photographs. Data in this revised edition were updated through the early 1960s, but the economic and social information is now sorely out-of-date.

51 **The landforms of Japan.**
Torao Yoshikawa, Sōhei Kaizuka, Yōko Ōta. Tokyo: University of
Tokyo Press, 1981. 222p. 79 maps. bibliog.
A systematic examination of the characteristics of Japanese landforms, with particular
emphasis on their development under variable tectonic and denudational conditions in
recent geological times. Following an outline of Japanese landforms, the authors
describe the nature and distribution of tectonic landforms; the types and distribution of
volcanoes in Japan as well as the growth features of the Fuji, Hakone, Aira and
Sakurajima volcanoes; the characteristics and growth features of Japanese mountains;
Japan's glacial and periglacial landforms; geomorphic surfaces and Quaternary
chronology, especially in the south Kantō district; the types and regional characteristics
of Japanese plains; contemporary geomorphic processes and disasters caused by
seismic and volcanic activities; and man's role in geomorphic processes in recorded
Japanese history. This book was prepared in connection with the 24th International
Geographical Congress held in Tokyo in 1984.

Water: a view from Japan
See item no. 3.

New geography of Japan.
See item no. 35.

Studies of Japan in Western languages of special interest to geographers.
See item no. 1592.

Maps and atlases

52 **Isles of gold: antique maps of Japan.**
Hugh Cortazzi.   New York; Tokyo: Weatherhill, 1983. 177p. 92 maps.
bibliog.
A selection of over ninety historically significant European and Japanese maps of
Japan, ranging from a pictorial map of a Japanese estate dated AD 756 to an 1851
British map of both Japan and Korea and an 1860 woodblock print map of the port of
Yokohama. In between are numerous cartographic reproductions, dating primarily
from the European Renaissance, the Age of Enlightenment, and the Tokugawa
period. Cortazzi, an enthusiastic map-collector and British Ambassador to Japan at the
time this book was published, depicts the encounter between the West and Japan
through the gradual process of mapping the Japanese archipelago. In both the text and
the reproductions, he emphasizes the mutual influences, borrowings, and co-operation
between European and Japanese cartographers. One section ('The Northern Islands')
briefly compares the discovery and mapping of Hokkaidō and the Kurile Islands by
Europeans and Japanese during the eighteenth century.

Geography and Geology. Maps and atlases

53 Teikoku's complete atlas of Japan.
Editorial Department of Teikoku-Shoin Co. Ltd [Teikoku Shoin
Henshūbu], with editorial collaboration of Yoshio Moriya. Tokyo:
Teikoku Shoin, 1989. 10th ed. 55p. 50 maps.

A paperback atlas of national and regional maps showing the administrative divisions,
historical development, agricultural products, geology and soils, climate, industrial and
mining areas, national parks, population, and transportation routes of Japan. Maps of
the country's physical features (drawn at a scale of 1:1,800,000) as well as enlarged
maps of the major cities – among them a map of the Tokyo transit system – are also
included. The index contains some 5,000 place-names.

54 Atlas of Japan: physical, economic and social.
Compiled by the International Society for Educational Information
[Kokusai Kyōiku Jōhō Sentā]. Tokyo: International Society for
Educational Information, 1974. 2nd ed. 64, 64p. 76 maps.

A clearly designed, detailed, large-format atlas, prepared specifically for an overseas
audience, that presents a wide range of information about the physical features and the
economic, social, and cultural aspects of Japan as a whole. Included are maps showing
Japan's topography, land classification, geology, temperature and precipitation in
January and in August respectively, population density, occupational patterns for both
primary and secondary industries, agricultural households, crops, land use, agricultural
productivity, forestry, mining, various industries (e.g., iron and steel, manufacturing,
chemical, textiles), transportation, national parks, and international trade by ports.
The maps range in scale from 1:4,000,000 to 1:8,000,000, and are accompanied by
extensive explanatory notes in English, French, and Spanish. Even though much of the
information is now dated, the atlas remains a useful reference source.

55 Old maps in Japan.
Edited by Matsutarō Nanba, Nobuo Muroga, Kazutaka Unno; preface
by Takejirō Akioka; translated by Patricia Murray. Ōsaka: Sōgensha,
1973. 204p.

Strikingly beautiful reproductions of ninety-three maps, nearly all of which were
produced during the Tokugawa period. They are arranged in eight categories: maps of
the world, complete maps of Japan, itinerary or route maps, regional maps, maps of
provinces, maps of cities and towns, maps on art objects such as folding screens and
the backs of mirrors, and a supplementary section of city maps. The reproductions are
impressive for their depiction of various panoramic views of Japan. They are also of
considerable interest as illustrations of the evolution of Japanese cartographic
knowledge in recent centuries. Two essays entitled 'The Pleasure of Collecting Old
Maps' and 'The Development of Cartography in Japan' as well as detailed notes about
the maps conclude the volume.

56 Tokyo: a bilingual atlas.
Edited by Atsushi Umeda. Tokyo: Iris Co.; distributed in the United
States by Kodansha/USA through Harper and Row, 1987. 132p.
49 maps.

An easy-to-read and easy-to-use atlas containing double-page colour maps of Tokyo
and its environs, showing the names of all localities in English and Japanese (the latter

in the *kana* syllabary as well as in Chinese characters). Thirty basic maps cover the entire Tokyo metropolitan area (including Yokohama) and provide especially detailed coverage of the city's major wards. Supplementing these are nineteen thematic maps which show the location of hotels, movie theatres, banks, embassies, sports and recreation facilities, medical facilities, major companies, government offices, shopping areas, leading tourist spots, and other buildings and places of importance to tourists and foreign residents. Also included are current maps of Tokyo's rail and subway systems and of its major roads, and a detailed bilingual index.

57 Japan: official standard names approved by the United States Board on Geographic Names.
United States. Office of Geography. Washington, DC: US Government Printing Office, 1955. 731p. (United States Board on Geographic Names, Gazetteer no. 12).

A gazetteer to approximately 28,700 entries for places and features in Japan (including the Ryūkyū Islands but excluding the Kuriles). Coverage extends to islands, reefs, inlets, harbours, shoals, channels, rivers, lakes, mountains, mountain passes, plains, plateaus, canals, volcanoes, bays, hot springs, and peninsulas as well as to cities, villages, prefectures, and various administrative subdivisions.

Tokyo city guide.
See item no. 75.

Old Kyoto: a guide to traditional shops, restaurants, and inns.
See item no. 78.

Baedeker's Japan.
See item no. 79.

The new official guide: Japan.
See item no. 82.

Japan solo: the independent traveller's passport to singular adventure.
See item no. 83.

Fodor's Japan 1989.
See item no. 86.

Historical Kyoto: with illustrations and guide maps.
See item no. 92.

Cultural atlas of Japan.
See item no. 113.

Flora and Fauna

58 **The Japanese crane: bird of happiness.**
Dorothy Britton, photographs by Tsuneo Hayashida, foreword by
S. Dillon Ripley. Tokyo; New York: Kodansha International, 1981.
64p. 2 maps. bibliog.

Japan's red-crested, black-throated, snow-white crane (*Grus japonensis*), long the symbol of eternal youth, happiness, marital fidelity and love, is an endangered species which inhabits the marshlands of southeastern Hokkaidō. Britton surveys the natural history of the bird (from its birth to its years as an adult) and its place in Japanese art, literature, and legend. Hayashida's photographs show the crane in a variety of activities including foraging, resting, dancing, and in flight.

59 **A brocade pillow: azaleas of old Japan.**
Itō Ihei, translated by Kaname Katō, introduction and commentary by
John L. Creech. New York; Tokyo: Weatherhill, 1984. 161p.

This translation of *Kinshū makura*, a classical seventeenth-century work that was the first full-length guide to azaleas and their cultivation in the world, was written by a nurseryman and authority on azaleas. It includes over 150 facsimiles of woodblock prints of flowers and foliage taken from the original Japanese-language edition, as well as a commentary on azalea culture in Japan and the West today.

60 **Fishes of Japan in color.**
Toshiji Kamohara. Tokyo: Hoikusha, 1967. 135p. 2 maps.

An illustrated guide to 312 representative species and subspecies of fish from among the approximately two thousand species currently inhabiting the rivers and lakes of Japan as well as the waters off her coast. Kamohara's description of each fish includes its scientific name, Japanese standard name, characteristics, habits, uses, size, and habitat, and is accompanied by a hand-drawn colour plate. Information about related species is also frequently provided. Yaichirō Okada's *Fishes of Japan: illustrations and descriptions of fishes of Japan* (Tokyo: Uno Shoten, 1966. rev. ed. 458, 16p.) complements this work.

61 **The flora and vegetation of Japan.**
Edited by Makoto Numata. Tokyo: Kodansha; Amsterdam: Elsevier
Scientific Publishing Co.; New York: American Elsevier, 1974. 294p.
30 maps. bibliog.

Five Japanese specialists systematically survey Japan's flora and vegetation from the
viewpoint of natural history. They emphasize the physiographic and historical
background of the flora that is found throughout the country – from northern
Hokkaidō to the southernmost islands of the Ryūkyūs – and detail its characteristics.
Nine chapters deal with the geographical background to Japan's flora and vegetation,
the origins and characteristics of Japan's flora, the forest vegetation zone, grassland
vegetation, maritime vegetation, mountain vegetation, aquatic and wetland vegetation,
volcanic vegetation, and the conservation of flora and vegetation in Japan. Numerous
monochrome photographs, tables, figures, maps, and a detailed index of species
supplement the text.

62 **Flora of Japan.**
Jisaburō Ohwi [Ōi], edited by Frederick G. Meyer, Egbert H. Walker.
Washington, DC: Smithsonian Institution, 1965. 1067p. 2 maps.
Reprinted, Washington, DC: Smithsonian Institution Press, 1984.

A detailed reference guide of permanent value to botanists, horticulturists, and
agriculturists, prepared by a member of the National Science Museum in Tokyo. It
contains a complete systematic treatment of approximately 4,500 species and varieties
of vascular plants occurring in Japan, together with indexes of Japanese plant names,
scientific names, and English names. Most of the book focuses on the phylum
Spermatophyta, but there is also extensive coverage of the phylum Pteridophyta (ferns
and fern allies). *Flora of Japan* has been complemented by Egbert H. Walker's *Flora
of Okinawa and the Southern Ryukyu Islands* (Washington, DC: Smithsonian
Institution Press, 1976, 1159p.), a detailed study of 2,080 species of plants found in the
portion of the Ryūkyū archipelago extending from Iheya Island, just north of
Okinawa, to Yonaguni Island, at the southwestern end of the Ryūkyū chain.

63 **In the shadow of Fujisan: Japan and its wildlife.**
Jo Stewart-Smith, photographs by Simon McBride. Harmondsworth,
Middlesex; New York: Viking, 1987. 208p. map.

Based on a natural history television series, this popularly written, illustrated book
examines the attitudes which the Japanese have traditionally held towards wildlife and
the world of nature, as recorded in their art, history, religion, and legends as well as in
their contemporary culture and conservation programmes. Stewart-Smith focuses on
three of the animal species which inhabit the Japanese archipelago: the Japanese
macaque monkey, the red-crowned crane (*tanchō*), and the loggerhead sea turtle,
along with such other creatures as bears and whales which share their habitats. She
describes their symbolic representations in art and literature, their cultural importance,
and their natural history; considers the equivocal attitudes of the Japanese towards
nature and their impact upon present-day conservation practices and views; and
discusses the growing efforts to save some of the endangered species which are found
in and around Japan today.

64 **Bamboo of Japan: splendor in four seasons.**
Photographs by Shinji Takama, introduction by Keiichi Itō. Tokyo:
Graphic-sha/Japan Publications; distributed in the United States by
Kodansha International, 1986. 96p.

Eighty full-colour photographs of bamboo during the four seasons of the year provide
a breathtaking view of the natural scenery of Japan, particularly in those parts of the
country that have been enriched by groves and thickets of bamboo. Takama's
photographs depict the natural history of this plant, from the emergence of fresh spring
shoots, to the tall green stalks that predominate during summer and autumn, to the
snow-laden, towering trees of the winter landscapes. A symbol of the Japanese spirit,
bamboo is 'truly the soul of the Japanese . . . . In no other part of the world is a
material so entwined with a culture even as it changes with the four seasons'.

65 **A field guide to the birds of Japan.**
Wild Bird Society of Japan [Nihon Yachō no Kai], Joseph A. Massey,
and others; illustrations by Shinji Takano; distribution maps by
Nobuyuki Monna; edited by Kōichirō Sonobe, Jane Washburn
Robinson. Tokyo; New York: Wild Bird Society of Japan and
Kodansha International, 1982. 336p. 488 maps.

Featuring 1,765 full-colour illustrations of 537 species of birds recorded throughout
Japan before 1982, this is a comprehensive field guide for bird-lovers and students of
Japanese wildlife alike. For easy reference purposes, textual information and
illustrations of each bird appear on opposite pages; and the listings of birds are
organised according to their visual and behavioural traits rather than in a taxonomic
classification scheme. Closely complementing this volume is Mark Brazil's *A
birdwatcher's guide to Japan* (Tokyo; New York: Kodansha International in
cooperation with the Wild Bird Society of Japan, 1987. 219p. 61 maps. bibliog.).
Focusing on sixty sites where bird-watchers can see a representative cross-section of
the birds, Brazil provides a general description and assessment of each site, a
comprehensive list of the birds that can be viewed there (grouped by season),
information about relevant transportation and accommodations, and a map of the site
and its environs. An updated checklist of the birds of Japan with their English,
scientific, and Japanese names is appended. Both of these highly recommended guides
are published in a convenient portable format.

This land . . . this beauty: Japan's natural splendor.
See item no. 44.

National parks of Japan.
See item no. 48.

**The Japanese flowering cherry trees of Washington, D.C.: a living symbol of
friendship.**
See item no. 663.

Birds, beasts, blossoms, and bugs: the nature of Japan.
See item no. 1221.

Hiroshige: birds and flowers.
See item no. 1257.

Black sun: the eyes of four; roots and innovation in Japanese photography.
See item no. 1275.

Japanese design through textile patterns.
See item no. 1344.

Bamboo.
See item no. 1357.

See also the sections 'Fine Arts: Gardens and Bonsai', and 'Recreation: Flower Arrangement (Ikebana)'.

Travellers' Accounts

66 **Unbeaten tracks in Japan: an account of travels on horseback in the interior, including visits to the aborigines of Yezo and the shrines of Nikkô and Isé.**
Isabella L. Bird.   London: J. Murray, 1880; New York; London: G. P. Putnam's Sons, 1881. 2 vols. map. Reprinted, with an introduction by Terence Barrow, Rutland, Vermont; Tokyo: Tuttle, 1973. 336p.; London: Virago, 1984; Boston, Massachusetts: Beacon Press, 1987.

Lively narrative of an Englishwoman's visit to Japan in 1878, written primarily in the form of a series of letters to her sister and a circle of personal friends. Bird focuses on her 1200-mile-long travels (on horseback) among the Japanese and on her observations of their mode of living in the countryside as she penetrated into northern Honshū and Hokkaidō (Yezo), 'regions unaffected by European contact'. Her wide-ranging account includes graphic descriptions of Japanese customs and dress, temples and religion, domestic life, shopping, malarial and prosperous districts, Christian missions, the treaty ports of Niigata and Hakodate, funeral ceremonies and cremation, her visit to a hospital in Akita Prefecture, a wedding ceremony, children's games, popular superstitions, hospitality among the Ainu, Ainu costume, customs and religion, her visit to the Tarumai volcano, the cities of Tokyo and Kyōto and their environs, the Ise Shrine, and the prospects for Christianity in Japan.

67 **The roads to Sata: a 2000-mile walk through Japan.**
Alan Booth.   New York; Tokyo: Weatherhill, 1985. 281p. 10 maps.

Booth, a Tokyo-based British writer and film critic, walked the entire length of Japan – from Cape Soya at the northern tip of Hokkaidō, along the seacoast and the back roads, to the southernmost tip of the island of Kyūshū – during the course of one summer and autumn. He describes the landscape and the people he encountered, recounts the conversations that he enjoyed with a wide range of individuals, and conveys his perceptive impressions about parts of Japan which Westerners tend not to visit. His perceptive account eschews many of the illusions that are popularly held in the West about Japan, for it points out some of the regrettable and negative aspects of Japanese life as well as the better-known achievements and beauties of the country.

68   Victorians in Japan: in and around the treaty ports.
Hugh Cortazzi.   London; Atlantic Highlands, New Jersey: Athlone Press, 1987. 365p. map. bibliog.

An anthology of impressions and anecdotes about the Japanese and Japan extracted from the writings of British visitors during the late Tokugawa and early Meiji periods. These published vignettes depict life in and around the seven treaty ports of Nagasaki, Hakodate, Yokohama, Edo/Tokyo, Ōsaka, Kōbe/Hyōgo, and Niigata; and they vividly convey the feeling of what it was like to be a foreigner in Japan at that time. In making his selections, Cortazzi sought out pieces which were either 'evocative of a place, an event, or a way of life' or were deliberately or unconsciously humorous. He groups these pieces under three headings: 'The Treaty Ports'; 'Some of the Places Explored around the Treaty Ports' (e.g., Kyōto, Mount Fuji, the Tōkaidō highway, Kamakura); and 'Daily Life in a Strange Land'. The latter section includes Victorian writings about language problems, the jinrikisha, brothels and mistresses, fleas and other disturbances in Japanese inns, and the mixed reactions to Japanese hot baths and Japanese food.

69   Travels in Japan.
Donald Keene.   Tokyo: Gakuseisha, 1981. 235p.

This entertaining collection of travel accounts and first-hand evaluative descriptions of places well worth visiting offers brief overviews of twelve Japanese cities and more complete narratives of the author's journeys to five additional places. Keene, an internationally renowned scholar and translator of Japanese literature who frequently visits Japan, intended this book to be 'a personal appreciation of different places' which he has visited rather than a systematic guide to Japan. Some of the places about which he writes – for example, Fukuoka, Kamakura, Kyōto, Nagasaki, and Nara – are quite famous. Others – among them Hagi, Sado, Sanuki, Shinano, and Uji – are less well known to non-Japanese. *Travels in Japan* originated as two series of articles commissioned for publication in an English-language periodical produced by Japan Air Lines and in one of Japan's leading monthly magazines.

70   Meeting with Japan.
Fosco Maraini, translated from the Italian by Eric Mosbacher.
London: Hutchinson, 1969. 2nd ed. 463p. 3 maps. bibliog.

Maraini, an Italian cultural anthropologist who lived in Japan between 1938 and 1946, discusses some of his travels, impressions, experiences, and reminiscences of Japanese life. Much of his book focuses on the two major cities of Tokyo and Kyōto, but Maraini's travels also took him to such other places as Ise, Nagoya, and Nara. His entertainingly written accounts are filled with interpretive comments and informative digressions about contemporary Japanese politics and economic affairs as well as about Japan's past history and religious, artistic and literary heritage. Many good photographs complement the book.

71 **The Inland Sea.**
Donald Richie, photographs by Yōichi Midorikawa. New York;
Tokyo: Weatherhill, 1971. 290p. map. Reprinted, London: Century,
1986.
The Inland Sea is a narrow, island-studded, nearly landlocked body of water
encompassed by three of Japan's four major islands. In this account based initially on a
journey that he made in 1962 from Kōbe to Miyajima (near Hiroshima), Donald
Richie (an American authority on Japanese films and culture) describes the islands and
communities that he visited, offers brief glimpses into the lives and views of their
inhabitants, and interprets some of their customs and folklore. The volume is much
more than a travel book. It seeks to convey a genuine feeling for the rhythm and life of
Japan as a whole and is 'part travel journal, part intimate diary, part interpretation of
the land and its people, part meditation on Eastern and Western man'.

72 **The Japan diaries of Richard Gordon Smith.**
Richard Gordon Smith, edited with an introduction by Victoria
Manthorpe. Harmondsworth, Middlesex and New York: Viking;
London: Rainbird, 1986. 224p. 2 maps.
Selections from the diaries of a seasoned traveller and sportsman who spent several
years in Japan between 1898 and the First World War. Richly illustrated by many
hand-tinted photographs, paintings commissioned from provincial Japanese artists,
wood-block prints, and the author's own drawings, the diaries record this English
gentleman's experiences, impressions, and detailed observations of Japanese life in and
around the Inland Sea (especially in the environs of Kōbe) and present his account of
Japanese reactions to the course of the Russo–Japanese War (1904–5). As Manthorpe
notes in her introduction, some readers will find Smith's views chauvinistic; but he did
find within himself 'an unexpected sympathy for the Japanese people' as well as an
admiration for their refinement and discipline – sentiments which are reflected in his
writings.

73 **Japanese pilgrimage.**
Oliver Statler. New York: Morrow; London: Pan Books, 1983. 349p.
2 maps. (Picador Original). Reprinted, Rutland, Vermont and Tokyo:
Tuttle, 1984; New York: Quill, 1985.
Kōbō Daishi (also known as Kūkai, 774-835), the founder of Shingon Buddhism, was
revered as a saint and deity by his immediate disciples. After his death they established
the tradition of encircling his home island of Shikoku, visiting its eighty-eight temples
on pilgrimages in his honour. Statler interweaves Kōbō Daishi's story with an account
of his own nine hundred-mile-long journey around Shikoku as he followed in the
footsteps of countless individuals before him. He describes the countryside, the people
he encountered, and the places he visited as he walked along the coasts of the Inland
Sea and the Pacific Ocean and ascended various mountain paths to reach the
designated temples. At the same time he explains the meaning of the Shikoku
pilgrimage, recounts the life of Kōbō Daishi, and describes some of the medieval and
modern pilgrims who followed him.

The Mikado's empire.
See item no. 114.

They came to Japan: an anthology of European reports on Japan, 1543–1640.
See item no. 133.

This island of Japan: João Rodrigues' account of 16th-century Japan.
See item no. 153

Japan diary.
See item no. 269.

The capital of the Tycoon: a narrative of a three years' residence in Japan.
See item no. 349.

As we saw them: the first Japanese embassy to the United States (1860).
See item no. 667.

Narrative of the expedition of an American squadron to the China Seas and Japan under the command of Commodore M. C. Perry, United States Navy.
See item no. 673.

Return to Tsugaru: travels of a purple tramp.
See item no. 1116.

The narrow road to the deep north and other travel sketches.
See item no. 1149.

Tourism and Travel Guides

74 **Exploring Tōhoku: a guide to Japan's back country.**
Jan Brown, with Yoko Sakakibara Kmetz. New York; Tokyo:
Weatherhill, 1982. 330p. 19 maps.

Tōhoku – the six prefectures of Aomori, Akita, Iwate, Yamagata, Miyagi, and
Fukushima that comprise the northeastern part of the island of Honshū – is 'one of the
few places left where the visitor can actually explore refreshing remnants of a pre-
Westernized, rural Japanese life style'. In this witty, personalised volume, Brown
describes the region in its many aspects, ranging from Tōhoku's colourful festivals,
local crafts, legends, and unusual cuisine, to its hamlets, temples, recreational areas,
and majestic scenic spots. She also provides a compendium of practical travel hints and
a listing of principal Tōhoku festivals and their dates. An English–Japanese finding list
(with Chinese characters [*kanji*]) that includes every place-name that is mentioned will
facilitate the use of this guide by first-time visitors to Japan.

75 **Tokyo city guide.**
Judith Connor, Mayumi Yoshida. Tokyo; New York: Ryuko Tsushin,
in co-operation with Kodansha International, 1987. rev. ed. 363p.
51 maps. bibliog.

A guide to life in contemporary Tokyo that goes far beyond what is offered in
traditional tourist itineraries. After a brief introduction to the city of Tokyo and its
many districts and neighbourhoods, this book covers accommodations, dining,
shopping (for clothing, electronics, traditional arts and crafts, accessories, antiques,
records, books, etc.), entertainment, nightlife (including bars, beer halls, live music,
and cabaret), the arts, sightseeing, health and beauty, the basics of living and getting
around Tokyo, and language. The volume concludes with fifty coloured street and
transit maps charting most of the listings found in the guide sections of the book. Each
map has a list of entries (for restaurants, shops, etc.) which are keyed to page numbers
in the text where the places are first mentioned.

76 **Exploring Kamakura: a guide for the curious traveler.**
Michael Cooper. New York; Tokyo: Weatherhill, 1979. 159p. map.
Located only one hour away by train to the southwest of Tokyo, Kamakura is a city of
numerous temples, shrines, historic sites, parks, and art treasures. It served as the
political centre of Japan between the late twelfth and early fourteenth centuries.
Cooper's guide provides some general information about Kamakura's principal places
of interest as well as about the city's local history and legends. Offering several
programmed tours in which eighty-four temples and shrines and many other points of
interest are introduced in a clearly specified order, Cooper's 'amiable companion'
enables casual visitors to explore the city on their own while benefiting from the
author's witty descriptions and personalised advice.

77 **Kyoto: seven paths to the heart of the city.**
Diane Durston. Tokyo; New York: Kodansha International, 1987.
64p. 11 maps.
An assemblage of striking colour photographs and brief essays bring to life the history,
crafts, and architectural styles of Kyōto's historic neighbourhoods and the traditions to
which they have given shelter over many centuries. Durston introduces the seven
classic old districts known as Sanneizaka (named after one of the cobblestoned streets
that leads up to the Kiyomizu Temple), Gion Shinbashi, Sagano Toriimoto (a
suburban area of thatched country houses), Kamigamo Shake-machi, Nishijin (the
centre of the traditional textile industry), Honganji-Shimabara, and Fushimi (home of
the finest saké breweries in Japan). Additional sections of her book highlight the crafts
of Kyōto, the city's cuisine, the tea ceremony, its festivals, and its shrines and temples.
Easy-to-follow maps and suggested walking itineraries enable visitors to explore the
city on their own, 'past the traditional homes, the old shops and inns, [and] the tiny
neighborhood shrines that line the narrow old streets in the heart of Kyoto'.

78 **Old Kyoto: a guide to traditional shops, restaurants, and inns.**
Diane Durston, photographs by Lucy Birmingham, foreword by Donald
Richie. Tokyo; New York: Kodansha International, 1986. 240p.
51 maps. bibliog.
A guide to the traditional arts and crafts of Kyōto is combined with an overview of the
city's history, cuisine, and housing. Durston provides concise descriptions of forty-five
Japanese-style restaurants, inns (largely *ryōkan*), and shops which she recommends
together with briefer information about an additional seventy-three shops that carry
such goods as tea utensils, hair ornaments, kimono accessories, lanterns, footwear, and
oil-papered umbrellas. Typical of these shops are the Saiun-dō, which specialises in
Japanese painting supplies; Shioyoshi-ken, famous for its Kyōto confectionery; the
Yamato Mingei Ten, a shop that offers the finest in folk crafts; and the 140-year-old
Ippō-dō store that sells green tea produced in the Uji region just south of Kyōto.
Detailed maps indicate the location of many of the places mentioned in the text.

79 **Baedeker's Japan.**
Walter Giesen, Wolfgang Hassenpflug, Karin Khan, translated from the
German by James Hogarth. Englewood Cliffs, New Jersey: Prentice-
Hall; Basingstoke(?), England: Automobile Association of the United
Kingdom and Ireland, 1983. 360p. 49 maps.
This volume in the distinguished Baedeker series of illustrated guidebooks to the

countries of the world opens with an introduction to Japan, surveying her history, culture, geography, etc. Part two – 'Japan from A to Z' – provides an alphabetically arranged guide to 106 selected cities, national parks, and other areas of tourist interest: from Abashiri, Aizu-Wakamatsu, and Akan National Park, through Yamaguchi, Yokohama, and Yoshino-Kumano National Park. Each locality's principal features of architectural, artistic, and historic interest as well as its scenic points, recommended hotels, and noteworthy restaurants are described. Considerable information of practical value to the tourist – including details of leisure activities, useful addresses (appearing in part three), and maps and street plans of Japan's major cities and towns – is also presented.

80 **A guide to Japanese hot springs.**
Anne Hotta, with Yoko Ishiguro.　Tokyo; New York: Kodansha
International, 1986. 284p. 11 maps.

A geographically organised introduction to 163 natural and man-made hot springs throughout Japan: from the vintage hot-spring area of Beppu on the island of Kyūshū to a series of thermal rock pools along the Kamuiwakka River in northeastern Hokkaidō. Each entry indicates the location of a spring and how to get there; explains the chemical properties of its waters as well as their medicinal benefits; provides information about local festivals, traditions, delicacies, and nearby tourist sites; and comments on accommodations for both high- and low-budget travellers. A brief history of Japanese hot springs, the types of baths available, tips on making travel plans, and bathing etiquette constitute the first part of the volume. Three appendixes describe the various types of mineral waters and their health benefits; provide the addresses, telephone numbers, and price ranges of all of the accommodations mentioned in the guide; and offer a 'mini-language guide' for communicating in Japanese.

81 **A guide to Japanese architecture.**
Edited by the Japan Architect; essay entitled 'Architectural Classics' by
Nobuo Itō.　Tokyo: Shinkenchikusha; distributed by The Japan
Architect, 1984. 250p. 16 maps.

A photographic guidebook to 396 architecturally outstanding postwar buildings as well as to forty traditional Japanese architectural classics. This guide is designed especially for foreign visitors who wish to see what is happening on the current architectural scene and who would benefit from an overview of Japanese architecture, both old and new. The buildings selected for illustration are located throughout Japan and are grouped together by prefecture. For each building there is a black-and-white photograph of its façade, its name and address in both English and Japanese, the date of its construction, its dimensions, the name of its architect, and a reference to the monthly issue of *Shinkenchiku* (the Japanese-language parent edition of the *Japan Architect* [q.v.]) in which additional information may be found. Indexes by type of architecture (e.g., city halls; museums and archives; office buildings and banks) and by architect are included.

82 **The new official guide: Japan.**
Compiled by the Japan National Tourist Organization [Kokusai Kankō
Shinkōkai].　Tokyo: Japan Travel Bureau, 1975. new ed. 1088p.
72 maps.

A remarkably detailed guidebook to the rural districts as well as the major cities and towns of Japan. Regarded at the time of its publication as being very authoritative and reliable, it continues to be quite useful although it is now outdated in some respects. Part one provides general information about a wide range of topics concerning Japan, including her natural features, language, history, religion, dress, food, government, economy, education, and culture. Part two, 'Travel Information', is divided into eight sections covering the different regions of Japan. (Honshū is divided into five sections while the islands of Shikoku and the Inland Sea, Kyūshū, and Hokkaidō constitute three sections.) Each section comprehensively covers the history, administration, industry and commerce, transportation, sightseeing tours, annual events, and places of interest of the region being discussed. An extensive index is also included.

83   **Japan solo: the independent traveller's passport to singular adventure.**
     Eiji Kanno, Constance O'Keefe, introduction by Shunichi Sumita.
     New York: Warner Books, 1988. rev. ed. 392p. 193 maps.
Introduced by the president of the Japan National Tourist Organization as 'the best answer to a guide book that we have ever seen', this volume provides detailed, practical information for travelling in Japan entirely on one's own. Kanno and O'Keefe suggest 135 itineraries and walking tours in Japan's major cities (Tokyo and Kyōto) and tourist sites as well as in many less frequently visited communities and regions of Honshū, Kyūshū, Hokkaidō, and Shikoku. Each chapter contains detailed maps and outlines of the most significant tourist features of the area being introduced; brief descriptions of interesting buildings and scenic spots; listings of recommended stores, restaurants, and coffee shops; suggested overnight accommodations (both Western-style hotels and Japanese-style inns known as *ryōkan*); and information on how to get there by train or by subway. Detailed train schedules, timetables for other types of inter-city transportation, bilingual conversation cards that can be detached from the book, and a variety of survival tips enable the solo traveller to devise his or her own itinerary if no English-speaking assistance is available.

84   **Good Tokyo restaurants.**
     Rick Kennedy, drawings by Ryōsuke Kami, cartoons by Akira Odagiri,
     maps by Katsusuke Konuma.   Tokyo; New York: Kodansha
     International, 1989. rev. and updated edition. 184p. 22 maps.
An entertaining and convenient guide to a wide range of eating places: from 'first-class European-style restaurants' (half of the restaurants listed specialise in Western cuisine) to 'wonderful little Japanese places of great character and charm'. Following a brief introduction to Japanese foods and saké, Kennedy groups together 108 restaurants by geographical area (e.g., 'Roppongi/Akasaka Area Restaurants') and introduces each one with a two-page overview that indicates its location, address and hours, and describes its type of menu and specialities, atmosphere, clientele, and prices. Evaluations of the cuisine tend to be very personal in nature.

85   **A guide to food buying in Japan.**
     Carolyn R. Krouse.   Rutland, Vermont; Tokyo: Tuttle, 1986. 191p.
     bibliog.
An illustrated handbook designed especially for newly arrived residents and longer-term tourists who do not read Japanese and require assistance in making informed decisions about food and household purchases. Part one – 'Before You Shop' – introduces the basic elements of reading and pronouncing Japanese, discusses the major categories of food markets as well as essential shopping procedures, and explains how to interpret price and packaging labels. Part two contains descriptions of

most basic foods and many other household needs such as detergents. It covers their appearance, where they can be found, how they differ from Western products, their names in Japanese, when they are in season, and how to use them. There are also four appendixes: counting in Japanese; weights and measures and their Western equivalents; terms used in cooking instructions; and recipes and cooking tips – together with an English–Japanese vocabulary list of words and phrases concerned with food buying.

86 **Fodor's Japan 1989.**
    Edited by David Low, introduction by Oliver Statler.   New York;
    London: Fodor's Travel Publications, 1989. 593p. 45 maps.

A popular, annually updated travel guide, created by Eugene Fodor. One in a wide-ranging series of country and area guides, this particular volume has been designed to 'enable the independent traveler to gain the widest access to – and understanding of -- Japan's scenery, religious and historical sites, entertainments, cuisine, architecture, crafts and art, and above all her people'. The 1989 edition includes special essays about Japanese history and food. A very detailed section about sightseeing, lodgings, dining, travelling, etc. in Tokyo and about one-day excursions from that city is followed by chapters covering the rest of the country; from Hokkaidō in the north to Kyūshū in the south. Practical information about selected accommodations, transportation, seasonal events and festivals, tours, museums, restaurants, children's activities, night life, parks, medical services, shopping, and places of worship may be found throughout the book. Complementing *Fodor's Japan 1989* are two directly related Fodor Travel Publications: *Fodor's great travel values: Japan*, edited by Peter Popham and Helen Brower (New York; London: Fodor's Travel Publications, 1988, 227p.) and *Fodor's Tokyo 1989*, edited by David Low (New York; London: Fodor's Travel Publications, 1989, 236p.). The latter is reprinted from *Fodor's Japan 1989*.

87 **The guide to Japanese food and restaurants.**
    Russell Marcus, Jack Plimpton.   Tokyo: Shufunotomo, 1984. 263p.
    39 maps.

A guidebook to 740 recommended restaurants in the Tokyo area. It enables tourists, businessmen, and gourmets to select from among the eighteen major types of Japanese speciality restaurants that are associated with such styles of cooking as sashimi, *tonkatsu*, *oden*, yakitori, *kaiseki*, sukiyaki, fugu, *unagi*, *nabemono*, and tempura. Marcus and Plimpton indicate where to find the best restaurants for every speciality; explain how to interpret the outside appearance and features of a restaurant in order to identify the kind of food it serves; tell what kind of décor, atmosphere, and service to expect; offer gourmet tips as well as descriptions of Japanese cuisines; describe standard menus and typical dishes; and provide bilingual menus, useful phrases, and recommendations for ordering meals. Detailed street maps with symbols indicating the locations of restaurants and identifying their specialities are also provided.

88 **The practical guide to Japanese signs. 1st part: Especially for newcomers.
    2nd part: Making life easier.**
    Tae Moriyama.   Tokyo; New York: Kodansha International, 1987.
    2 vols. bibliog.

This guidebook provides foreigners with 'a way of deciphering the myriad signs, directions, instructions, labels', etc. which they are most likely to encounter in Japan. Oriented towards short-term visitors and newly arrived residents, part one focuses on the Chinese characters (*kanji*) which are commonly used in situations involving public transportation (e.g., railway stations and trains, ticket machines, station windows, taxis, buses, and airports), public lodgings, baths, sightseeing, numbers, restaurants, post offices, banks, utilities and taxes, and a few types of highly frequented shops such as drugstores and food stores. The second part, prepared with the longer-term resident in mind, covers such situations as emergencies, house hunting, medical services, traditional Japanese food and drink, and driving.

89   **Kyoto: a contemplative guide.**
Gouverneur Mosher.   Rutland, Vermont; Tokyo: Tuttle, 1978. rev. ed. 368p. 21 maps.

Kyōto, the home of the imperial court from 794 to 1868, has long been renowned for its history, culture, and artistic beauty. Mosher's guide focuses on sixteen representative sights which the author has selected on account of their cultural and religious significance, their historical interest, and their art and architecture. Replete with photographs and maps, it contains narratives about the background, historical role, and noteworthy aspects of each location; a detailed description of each sight; and practical information (now largely outdated) on how to reach each place, how long it will take to get there, and the best time for visiting. Among the sights covered are the Phoenix Hall of the Byōdō-in (an eleventh-century Buddhist temple), the rock garden at Ryōanji, the mountain monastery temples of Enryakuji, the lavishly decorated Nijō Castle of the Tokugawas, the Ginkakuji ('Silver Pavilion') and its garden, and the old Buddhist temple known as Kiyomizudera.

90   **Japan: a traveler's companion.**
Lensey Namioka.   New York: Vanguard Press, 1979. 253p. bibliog.

A cultural guidebook that introduces many important Japanese customs and provides instructions about appropriate behaviour while staying in Japan. It is designed to help Western tourists travel on their own, eat their meals in the same way as the Japanese, stay in Japanese-style lodgings (*ryōkan*), properly use Japanese bathing facilities and restrooms, and derive greater pleasure from their sightseeing activities as well as from other types of entertainment. Part one ('Essentials') covers transportation, language, food, housing, and baths, bathrooms and toilets. Part two ('Entertainments') discusses Japanese amusements, sports, arts and crafts, castles and samurai, and churches, shrines and temples.

91   **Foot-loose in Tokyo: the curious traveler's guide to the 29 stages of the Yamanote Line.**
Jean Pearce, with Makiko Yamamoto, Fumio Ariga, illustrations by Joy Harrison, foreword by Edward Seidensticker. New York; Tokyo: Weatherhill, 1983. rev. ed. 210p. 30 maps.

Tokyo is a large city of small neighbourhoods, each with its own unique character, that are worthwhile exploring on foot. This guide can be used on walking tours around each of the twenty-nine railways stations of the Japan National Railways' Yamanote Line, which loops through the heart of Tokyo. Historic spots, gardens, distinctive restaurants, amusement areas, unusual shops, and numerous other attractions are all described in an anecdotal and knowledgeable manner. A station-by-station finding list of particularly noteworthy sights concludes this volume. *More foot-loose in Tokyo: the curious traveler's guide to Shitamachi and Narita* (New York; Tokyo: Weatherhill, 1984, 145p.), also by Pearce and her colleagues, introduces in turn the old downtown

37

districts of Tokyo (known as 'Shitamachi') and the picturesque country town of Narita (near the New Tokyo International Airport) through eleven different walking tours designed for foreign visitors and long-term visitors alike. Complementing both of these books is Gary D.'A. Walters' *Day-walks near Tokyo* (Tokyo; New York: Kodansha International, 1988, 152p.), an illustrated guide to twenty-six day-long walks through the adjacent countryside that includes information about available public transportation and descriptions of local flora and fauna.

92 **Historical Kyoto: with illustrations and guide maps.**
   Herbert E. Plutschow.   Tokyo: Japan Times, 1983. 204p. 27 maps.

The history of the imperial capital of Japan between 794 and 1868 is traced in this introduction to Kyōto's many sites and legends of the past. Plutschow combines his historical narrative with descriptions of over 150 shrines, temples, castles, and villas of note. Eighteenth-century woodblock prints illustrate his text. This book is oriented towards the experienced traveller who seeks a general, historical overview of Kyōto while spending several days sightseeing within the city and its environs. More summary background information about Kyōto may be found in Plutschow's *Introducing Kyoto* (Tokyo; New York: Kodansha International, 1979, 72p.). It contains short essays about the city's development and its renowned festivals, arts and crafts as well as eighty-seven colour photographs that depict many historical temples, gardens, and art works and portray traditional merchant houses, representative crafts, and scenes from recent festival celebrations.

93 **Historical Nara: with illustrations and guide maps.**
   Herbert E. Plutschow.   Tokyo: Japan Times, 1983. 199p. 17 maps.
   bibliog.

An historical overview of the ancient capital of Nara and a guide to the temples and shrines in and around that city. Plutschow describes early Shintō and the political and religious conditions which gave rise to the Japanese imperial family, the introduction of Buddhism in the sixth century, and the life and activities of Prince Shōtoku Taishi (574-622), as well as the history and the outstanding cultural features of fourteen important temples and shrines, among them the Kōfukuji, Tōdaiji, Murōji, and Hasedera. His book is illustrated with black-and-white photographs of famous statues and by Tokugawa period prints and drawings of local places of interest.

94 **The insider's guide to Japan.**
   Peter Popham, photographs by Nik Wheeler.   Tokyo; New York:
   Kodansha International, 1987. rev. and updated ed. 212p. 9 maps.
   bibliog.

Illustrated with many full-colour photographs, Popham's tourist guide offers practical information and personalised advice about the cities and museums, festivals and food, culture and customs, and sights and sounds of contemporary Japan. Introductory chapters briefly cover the country's history, culture, and lifestyles; much of the guide focuses on the Tokyo and Kyōto–Ōsaka areas as well as on Kyūshū; a supplementary section entitled 'Japan: Off the Beaten Track' outlines both one-day trips and longer journeys out of Tokyo; and the entire volume concludes with numerous travellers' tips concerning visas, currency, communications, etc. Popham is a free-lance British writer and journalist based in Japan.

95 **Introducing Tokyo.**
Donald Richie, photographs by Ben Simmons.   Tokyo; New York:
Kodansha International, 1987. 79p. 2 maps. bibliog.
Over 150 full-colour photographs of the cityscape and people of Tokyo accompany
Richie's descriptions of the more prominent districts of Tokyo, among them the
Imperial Palace and its grounds, the mercantile district of Shinjuku, and the Tokyo
Bay area. Also included are brief essays about the city's history, administration,
transportation, accommodations, dining, shopping, and entertainment.

96 **The Japanese inn, ryokan: a gateway to traditional Japan.**
Donald Richie, Sadao Miyamoto, photographs by Toshiaki Sakuma,
preface by Donald Richie.   Tokyo: Shufunotomo, 1985. 80p.
Staying at a traditional *ryōkan*, a lodging facility with Japanese-style architecture,
accommodations, and service, can be both an enjoyable and a rewarding experience.
This fully illustrated volume introduces the basic elements of the traditional Japanese
inn, including its architectural and spatial layout, the natural beauty of its surrounding
landscape and the views of its garden, its bathing and sleeping facilities, and its special
cuisine and amenities. A series of brief photo-essays of fifteen famous *ryōkan* is
followed by a directory of highly recommended *ryōkan* that will accommodate foreign
guests and some words of practical advice to the first-time visitor to Japan.

97 **Zen guide: where to meditate in Japan.**
Martin Roth, John Stevens.   New York; Tokyo: Weatherhill, 1985.
122p. bibliog.
Oriented in particular to Westerners interested in Zen Buddhism, this guide directs
readers to Zen masters, temples, and programmes in which they can pursue
appropriate Zen training. The core of the guide is a geographically arranged directory
to more than 150 temples, training centres, and seminar groups all over Japan.
Addresses (in both Chinese characters and romanised Japanese), telephone numbers,
and contacts for each temple are provided, along with concise descriptions and
evaluative comments. The volume is also a source of information about Buddhist
restaurants serving vegetarian food, temples with overnight accommodation, and
traditional Buddhist pilgrimage routes.

98 **A guide to the gardens of Kyoto.**
Marc Treib, Ron Herman.   Tokyo: Shufunotomo, 1980. 201p. 6 maps.
bibliog.
A handy guidebook to over fifty of Kyōto's most famous gardens. Oriented particularly
to first-time visitors, it contains two introductory essays entitled 'The Japanese Garden
and Its Cultural Context' and 'Making the Landscape of Kyoto' as well as brief listings
for the gardens of individual temples, imperial palaces, and private residences. In
addition to providing a general overview and description of each garden (including its
address, dating, attribution, history, design, special features, and recommended times
to visit), Treib and Herman comment on the types, background, and historical
evolution of these gardens and on their relationship to Kyōto's political and
environmental history.

99 **Tokyo now and then: an explorer's guide.**
Paul Waley, foreword by Edward Seidensticker.   New York; Tokyo:
Weatherhill, 1984. 502p. 25 maps. bibliog.

A lively historical guidebook to the modern city of Tokyo. Leading the reader through
forty-two areas of the metropolis, it offers both historical and practical information,
many entertaining stories about the city's past, and a four-star rating system for the
traveller which distinguishes 'between those sites with attractive stories attached but
very little of interest to see and those that include enough elements of visual appeal to
make a visit worth the while'. Far more exhaustive in its coverage than other
guidebooks, Waley's volume can be enjoyably read by the armchair traveller who is
particularly interested in the older districts of Tokyo, especially the seven inner-city
wards known as Chiyoda-ku, Chūō-ku, Taitō-ku, Kōtō-ku, Sumida-ku, Bunkyō-ku,
and Minato-ku. Illustrations are limited to a small number of black-and-white
photographs.

100 **Japan unescorted.**
James K. Weatherly.   Tokyo; New York: Kodansha International in
co-operation with Japan Air Lines, 1986. 200p. 23 maps. bibliog.

This pocket-size illustrated paperback is designed as a practical guide for adventurous
Western visitors who wish to discover Japan on their own. Introductory pages point
out some of the realities that face travellers in Japan, describe the Japanese ways of
eating and drinking, and offer suggestions on how to meet the Japanese and use the
country's extensive public transportation system. The guide then covers sixteen cities
and their environs: Tokyo, Kyōto, Nara, Uji, Ōhara, Ōsaka, Kōbe, Himeiji, Nagoya,
Takayama, Kanazawa, Kurashiki, Nagasaki, Kagoshima, Sendai, and Sapporo.
General descriptions explain what makes each city unique; worthwhile sightseeing
attractions are discussed in detail; and Weatherly's numerous listings of hotels,
Japanese-style inns (*ryōkan*), restaurants, bars, coffee parlours, and shops offer
recommendations of appropriate accommodations and places to eat. A revised edition
of this book has been announced for publication in 1990 by Kodansha International in
co-operation with Japan Air Lines.

A field guide to the birds of Japan.
See item no. 65.

A birdwatcher's guide to Japan.
See item no. 65.

Travels in Japan.
See item no. 69.

Historical Nagasaki.
See item no. 179.

Say it in Japanese.
See item no. 416.

Japanese for travellers.
See item no. 416.

Traveler's Japanese.
See item no. 446.

Everyday Japanese: a basic introduction to the Japanese language and culture.
See item no. 453.

Japanese antiques: with a guide to shops.
See item no. 1215.

The kabuki guide.
See item no. 1401.

Saké: a drinker's guide.
See item no. 1431.

Libraries in Japan.
See item no. 1474.

Roberts' guide to Japanese museums of art and archaeology.
See item no. 1475.

Japan today! A Westerner's guide to the people, language and culture of Japan.
See item no. *1573.*

Prehistory and Archaeology

101 **Prehistory of Japan.**
C. Melvin Aikens, Takayasu Higuchi. New York; London: Academic Press, 1982. 354p. 15 maps. bibliog. (Studies in Archaeology).

A well-illustrated, descriptive survey of the most important archaeological evidence of human activity in the Japanese islands between the Palaeolithic era and the expansion of the Yamato state during the fifth and sixth centuries AD. Aikens and Higuchi first discuss the physical-anthropological setting and the linguistic relationships of Japanese prehistory. They then describe in detail the most significant excavated sites dating from each of the four major prehistoric periods: Palaeolithic, Jōmon, Yayoi, and Kofun. In discussing their cultural features and artefacts, the authors provide considerable information about the establishment of agriculture, the production of ceramics, the development of military power, and the influence and contributions of Chinese and Korean culture. A concluding chapter summarises the main themes of Japanese prehistory in order to characterise the long-term evolution of Japanese culture and to suggest the basic factors which shaped its development.

102 **Protohistoric Yamato: archaeology of the first Japanese state.**
Gina L. Barnes. Ann Arbor, Michigan: Center for Japanese Studies, University of Michigan, and Museum of Anthropology, University of Michigan, 1988. 473p. 40 maps. bibliog. (Michigan Papers in Japanese Studies, 17) (Anthropological Papers, 78).

Old Yamato, or the Nara Basin, was the centre of Japan at the time of the emergence of Japanese civilisation and the formation of the early Japanese state. Barnes details the archaeological evidence in the basin in order to coordinate and evaluate the available settlement data for this area and to obtain information about the organisational changes which occurred during the protohistoric period (third–sixth centuries AD). She first studies the 'paddy field archaeology' that has taken place in the areas under wet-rice cultivation in order to reconstruct the natural topography of Nara for the protohistoric period. She then explores several aspects of its settlement archaeology, including 'territoriality, the existence of transportation routes, the identification of village sites and their placement within the general distribution of occupational materials, and the nature of special function sites in different periods'. Detailed appendixes provide data on and descriptions of all of the basin's known archaeological sites.

103 **Northeast Asia in prehistory.**
Chester S. Chard.   Madison, Wisconsin; London: University of
Wisconsin Press, 1974. 214p. 5 maps. bibliog.

An interpretive survey of the current state of knowledge about human history, adaptation, and cultural development in Northeast Asia during the Pleistocene era, in Neolithic Siberia and its near neighbours, and in Jōmon Japan, the steppes of Inner Asia, and Yayoi and Kofun Japan. During the millennia under study, this geographically coherent area was not subjected to significant Chinese influence. Nearly half of Chard's book examines changing life-styles among the Japanese as revealed by available archaeological evidence. Chard emphasizes the broader picture, focusing on long-term trends, overall patterns, and processes at work, as well as on cultural relationships and influences, human adaptation to the environment, and ecological relationships to the surrounding natural world. His study is illustrated by over 160 black-and-white photographs and figures.

104 **The beginnings of Japanese art.**
Namio Egami, with Teruya Esaka, Ken Amakasu, translated by John
Bester.   New York; Tokyo: Weatherhill/Heibonsha, 1973. 128p.
(Heibonsha Survey of Japanese Art, 2).

A survey of the development of Japanese art from the latter part of the Jōmon period (third to first millennium BC), with its hunting–gathering culture centred in Hokkaidō and the Tōhoku region of northeastern Japan, through the Tumulus or Kofun period that ended in the mid-sixth century AD. Egami studies the various types of Jōmon, Yayoi, and Tumulus period pottery (including hand-modelled earthenware vessels, ritualistic figures, and wheel-made pottery), elaborately embossed metal bells, bronze mirrors, and ceremonial weapons that are extant in Japan today. Supplementary chapters by Esaka and Amakasu deal with art before the Tumulus period and with various aspects of Yayoi and Tumulus art. More than two hundred colour and black-and-white photographs of important representative objects illustrate the text.

105 **Early Japanese art: the great tombs and treasures.**
J. Edward Kidder.   Princeton, New Jersey: Van Nostrand; London:
Thames and Hudson, 1964. 346p. 3 maps. bibliog.

A general illustrated survey of the artistic and archaeological remains of the Kofun or Protohistoric period (late third to mid-sixth centuries AD). Kidder first sketches in the background of this era and describes its Yayoi period antecedents in symbolism and style. He then groups together and discusses at greater length the types of objects produced during the Kofun period: bronze mirrors, the decorated equipment of the mounted archers (e.g., helmets, saddles, sword pommels, sword guards, and bronze horse pendants), stone figures and pottery, gold crowns, ornamented tombs, and decorated sarcophagi. Considerable attention is paid to the symbolism of the ornamented tombs found in southwestern Kyūshū. Three appendixes contain descriptive catalogues of all known ornamented tombs and decorated sarcophagi as well as a critical essay on Japanese metal workmanship.

Prehistory and Archaeology

106 **Japan before Buddhism.**
J. Edward Kidder, Jr.   London: Thames and Hudson; New York: Praeger, 1966. rev. ed. 284p. 7 maps. bibliog. (Ancient Peoples and Places, 10).

With the aid of nearly two hundred plates and figures, Kidder surveys the state of knowledge about prehistoric and protohistoric Japan as it existed in the mid-1960s. His book offers the first overview in English of the archaeological evidence for Japanese life and culture before the advent of Buddhism. It covers the Palaeolithic and Mesolithic periods; the sites, food supplies, tools and pottery, customs and symbols, and human remains of the Neolithic period; the rice-growing communities, burial methods, bronze equipment, pottery, and customs and religious practices of the Bronze–Iron age; and the communities, the use of iron, the colossal tombs (tumuli) and their contents, the tomb sculptures (*haniwa*), and the shrines of the Protohistoric or Kofun period.

107 **Prehistoric Japanese arts: Jōmon pottery.**
J. Edward Kidder, with Teruya Esaka.   Tokyo; New York: Kodansha International, 1968. 308p. 11 maps. bibliog.

The most comprehensive and representative survey available of the Neolithic 'cord-marked' earthenware of Japan's prehistoric Jōmon period (*ca.*10,000–*ca.*300 BC). Kidder, the leading Western specialist in Japanese archaeology, traces the development of Jōmon pottery (including its typology, chronology, and distribution) throughout the major stages of this culture. He discusses recent Japanese studies of this pottery and gives a complete survey of its manufacturing techniques. Seven colour plates, 439 black-and-white photographs, and detailed charts illustrate all of the major and minor Jōmon pottery types within this large, handsome volume. Also included are maps of Jōmon archaeological sites, lists of collections and carbon 14-dated sites, and a Jōmon shape development chart.

108 **Haniwa.**
Fumio Miki, translated and adapted with an introduction by Gina Lee Barnes.   New York; Tokyo: Weatherhill/Shibundō, 1974. 151p. map. bibliog. (Arts of Japan, 8).

Haniwa, the hollow clay sculptures of men, animals, and artefacts (e.g., weapons, houses, and ritual objects) that once adorned the great mounded tombs of the Kofun or Tumulus period (250-552 AD), are objects of considerable artistic interest. They also serve as important sources of information about early Japanese society. Miki studies the origins, development, and use of *haniwa*; discusses their varieties, the techniques of their manufacture, and their physical positioning on the tombs; and traces the evolution of the two major *haniwa* traditions of western and eastern Japan. Complementing this volume is Miki's earlier study, *Haniwa: the clay sculpture of proto-historic Japan* (English adaptation by Roy Andrew Miller, photographs by Yoshio Takahashi. Rutland, Vermont; Tokyo: Tuttle, 1960, 160p.). Both books abound with photographs of notable works.

109 **Windows on the Japanese past: studies in archaeology and prehistory.**
Edited by Richard J. Pearson, with Gina Lee Barnes, Karl L. Hutterer,
introduction by Richard J. Pearson, foreword by John Creighton
Campbell. Ann Arbor, Michigan: Center for Japanese Studies,
University of Michigan, 1986. 629p. 26 maps. bibliog.

Thirty-two Japanese and American scholars provide a representative sampling of work
on all of the time periods and most of the important methodological specialities
covered by Japanese archaeology. They deal with a wide range of topics including
vegetation in prehistoric Japan, the physical anthropology of the prehistoric Japanese,
mounded tombs (tumuli) in East Asia from the third to the seventh centuries AD, late
Pleistocene and early Holocene technologies, community habitation and food
gathering in prehistoric Japan, political interpretations of stone coffin production in
Protohistoric Japan, late Early Jōmon culture in the Tone River area, the structure of
Yayoi and Haji ceramic typologies, and problems concerning the preservation of
archaeological sites in Japan. The volume's 110-page glossary of place names, personal
names, site names, type names, and technical terms constitutes an important reference
aid for the field of Japanese archaeology.

The Cambridge history of Japan. Volume 1: Ancient Japan.
See item no. 115.

Early Buddhist Japan.
See item no. 143.

Kojiki.
See item no. 152.

Okinawa: the history of an island people.
See item no. 284.

**Archaeology of the Ryukyus: a regional chronology from 3000 B.C. to the
historic period.**
See item no. 284.

**Traditions of Japanese art: selections from the Kimiko and John Powers
Collection.**
See item no. 1214.

A thousand cranes: treasures of Japanese art.
See item no. 1217.

National Museum: Tokyo.
See item no. 1473.

Roberts' guide to Japanese museums of art and archaeology.
See item no. 1475.

History

General histories

110 A short economic history of modern Japan.
George Cyril Allen.   London: Macmillan; New York: St. Martin's
Press, 1981. 4th ed. 305p. bibliog.
The fruits of Allen's lifelong study of Japanese economic affairs are brought together
in this final edition of an economic history of Japan since the Meiji Restoration that
first appeared under the title *A short economic history of modern Japan, 1867–1937*
(London: Allen and Unwin; New York: Macmillan, 1947, 200p.). Part one traces the
evolution of the economy from the disintegration of the Tokugawa régime through the
industrial changes of the 1930s. Particular attention is paid to industrial and financial
developments as well as to the government's economic policy. Part two surveys the
economic developments of the 1945-79 period and analyses the causes of Japan's
postwar achievements. Over sixty updated statistical tables provide data about
population, employment, agricultural and industrial production, foreign trade, prices
and wages, national income, and gross national product.

111 The modern history of Japan.
William Gerald Beasley.   London: Weidenfeld and Nicolson; New
York: St. Martin's Press, 1981. Rutland, Vermont and Tokyo: Tuttle,
1982. 3rd rev. ed. 358p. 4 maps. bibliog.
A political, social, and economic history of Japan from the early nineteenth century
through the 1970s, written by an established British authority. Early chapters describe
the decline of Japanese feudalism, the renewal of contacts between Japan and the
West, and the fall of the Tokugawa shogunate in 1868. The rise of the Meiji
oligarchical leadership, their pursuit of modernisation and reforms in many areas, and
the beginnings of Japanese imperialist expansion bring Beasley's account to World War
I, when Japan became a world power. Subsequent chapters focus on economic and
political developments during the 1920s, the growth and consequences of Japanese

ultranationalism, and Japan's defeat in World War II. Beasley concludes with an account of postwar Japan's rapid recovery of her position in the modern world.

112 **Japan's modern century: from Perry to 1970.**
Hugh Borton. New York: Ronald Press, 1970. 2nd ed. 610p. 8 maps. bibliog.
A detailed but readable survey of Japanese history between 1850 and 1970. Borton narrates Japan's modern transformation and analyses the forces which brought it about. He covers the opening of Japan to the West (1850-68), the formation of a centralised monarchy by the early Meiji leadership (1868-90), the establishment of the Japanese empire as Japan developed into a military power (1890-1915), her leadership in a greater East Asia before World War II (1915-41), and Japan's recovery from war and defeat (1941-70). Appendixes contain the texts of the Potsdam Declaration of 1945, the 1889 and 1946 Japanese constitutions, and the US–Japan Security Treaty of 1960.

113 **Cultural atlas of Japan.**
Martin Collcutt, Marius Jansen, Isao Kumakura. Oxford, England: Phaidon; New York: Facts on File, 1988. 240p. 46 maps. bibliog. (An Equinox Book).
An authoritative overview for the general reader of Japan's rich cultural history and the physical environment in which it has developed since the Palaeolithic period. Lavishly illustrated with colour photographs of paintings, buildings, and numerous other art objects, this collaborative volume describes the geography of Japan, the archaeological origins of Japanese culture and society, the world of the ancient Japanese, the age of the Heian court, medieval culture and society, the major developments of the Tokugawa period, the Meiji Restoration (1868) and its legacy, imperial Japan, and the postwar reform and reconstruction of the country. Over thirty brief inserts in the text highlight special cultural features such as the art of the great tombs, noh drama, and the tea ceremony, as well as important sites such as the Ise Shrine, the Tōdaiji Temple at Nara, and the Zen gardens of Kyōto. A brief chronology and glossary, a table of Japanese rulers, a bibliography of suggested readings, and forty-six historical maps complement the text.

114 **The Mikado's empire.**
William Elliot Griffis. New York: Harper, 1876. 645p. map. Reprinted (8th edition), Tokyo: Jiji Press, 1971; Wilmington, Delaware: Scholarly Resources, 1973.
Griffis (1843-1928), an influential American educator and clergyman who taught in Japan between 1870 and 1874, wrote hundreds of books and articles about Meiji period Japan including his most celebrated work, *The Mikado's empire*. Book one of this work, *History of Japan, from 660 B.C. to 1872 A.D.*, presents an overview of the history of Japan, from its mythological origins through the Meiji Restoration, as it was understood in the 1870s. Book two, *Personal experiences, observations, and studies in Japan, 1870–1874*, is concerned with Griffis' years in Japan and includes chapters about his ride along the great Tōkaidō highway, the capital city of Tokyo, the sights and sounds in a 'pagan temple', his reception by his students, life in a Japanese house, household customs and superstititions, the mythical zoology of Japan, his travels through Japan, the position of women, and the 'new Japan'. *The Mikado's empire* has been reprinted more than a dozen times.

115 **The Cambridge history of Japan.**
General editors: John W. Hall, Marius B. Jansen, Madoka Kanai,
Denis Twitchett. Cambridge, England; New York: Cambridge
University Press, 1989- . 6 vols. maps. bibliog.
Expected to provide an extensive authoritative overview of the entire span of Japanese
history, this series will include interpretive and analytical essays written by seventy-two
distinguished scholars from the United States, Japan, and other countries. The six
volumes which cover Japanese history from earliest times through the late twentieth
century are entitled: *Ancient Japan*, edited by Delmer M. Brown (vol. 1); *Heian
Japan*, edited by William McCullough and Donald H. Shively (vol. 2); *Medieval Japan*,
edited by Kozo Yamamura (vol. 3); *Sengoku and Edo*, edited by John W. Hall (vol.
4); *The nineteenth century*, edited by Marius B. Jansen (vol. 5); and *The twentieth
century*, edited by Peter Duus (vol. 6). Three volumes, nearly 1000 pages each in
length, have been announced for publication in 1989. Volume 3, *Medieval Japan*,
contains thirteen essays that survey the historical events and developments in Japan's
polity, economy, society, and culture, as well as in her relations with her Asian
neighbours during the Kamakura and Muromachi periods. Volume 5, *The nineteenth
century*, offers an account of Japan's transformation from a feudal society to a modern
nation state. Its contributors discuss 'the fissures in late feudal society, the impact of
and response to the Western world, the overthrow of the shogunal government, and
the revolutionary changes that were instituted'. Volume 6, *The twentieth century*,
presents an overview of Japan's political development, external relations, economic
growth, and social and intellectual trends through the 1970s. A comparable series, the
fourteen-volume *Cambridge history of China* (under the general editorship of John K.
Fairbank and Denis Twitchett), commenced publication in 1966 and is still being
published.

116 **Japan: from prehistory to modern times.**
John Whitney Hall. New York: Delacorte Press; London: Weidenfeld
and Nicolson, 1970. 395p. 6 maps. bibliog. (Delacorte World History)
(Weidenfeld and Nicolson Universal History, 20). Reprinted, Rutland,
Vermont; Tokyo: Tuttle, 1971.
A survey of Japanese history with particular emphasis on pre-Meiji Japan. In covering
the formation of the early Japanese state, the so-called 'aristocratic' and 'feudal' ages
(the Nara through Muromachi periods), the Tokugawa period, and the century of
development since the Meiji Restoration (1868), Hall concerns himself with the
'manner in which Japan's political and social institutions have changed and diversified
over time and how this fundamentally "Eastern" culture gave rise to a modern world
power'. A brief chronology, a glossary, and a selective bibliography enhance the
overall usefulness of this standard work for the beginning student of Japanese history.

117 **A political history of Japanese capitalism.**
Jon Halliday, introduction by John W. Dower. New York: Pantheon
Books, 1975. 466p. map. (The Pantheon Asia Library). Reprinted,
New York; London: Monthly Review Press, 1975.
The first work in English to analyse the history of Japanese capitalism within a Marxist
framework. Halliday is concerned with 'the interpenetration of class structure (and
class conflict), mode of production, politics and ideology within the Japanese state; the
relationship between this structure and the global system of imperialism in which Japan
of necessity has operated; and the changes within essential structural continuity which

have characterized this dynamic configuration over time, through both the prewar and postwar periods.' This provocative study covers the entire period from the demise of Tokugawa feudalism and the rise of the Meiji state through the evolution of the postwar labour and student movements, and the growth of postwar Japanese capitalism and the ruling Liberal Democratic Party.

118 **Modern Japan: a historical survey.**
Mikiso Hane. Boulder, Colorado; London: Westview Press, 1986. 450p. 7 maps. bibliog.

A well-balanced survey of the history of Japan from the mid-nineteenth century to the early 1980s that integrates political events with the economic, social, and cultural activities of each of the periods covered. Hane opens with a summary of the early history of Japan. He then describes and interprets the fall of the Tokugawa shogunate and the establishment of the Meiji state, developments throughout the Meiji period, the era of parliamentary ascendancy (1912-32), the rise of Japanese militarism and Japan's involvement in World War II, and the reform, reconstruction and growth of Japan since the late 1940s. The author's discussion of social, cultural, and intellectual trends as well as his coverage of the lower classes sets his book apart from most other survey histories. An extensive bibliography, subdivided by chronological period and by topic, may be particularly useful for the general reader.

119 **The Japan reader. Volume 1: Imperialial Japan, 1800–1945. Volume 2: Postwar Japan, 1945 to the present.**
Edited, annotated, and with introductions by Jon Livingston, Joe Moore, Felicia Oldfather. New York: Pantheon, 1973. 2 vols. 2 maps. bibliog. (Pantheon Asia Library). Reprinted, Harmondsworth, Middlesex: Penguin, 1976.

This well-organised collection of readings for undergraduate students in modern Japanese history and culture introduces selections from important books, documents, scholarly articles, works of fiction, autobiographies, and contemporary accounts written by numerous Japanese and Westerners. Priority of coverage is given to social and economic questions. *The Japan reader* is arranged chronologically in six major sections: 'Japan's Feudal Origins: 1800–1868'; 'Meiji Japan – Foundations for Empire: 1868–1890'; 'Industrialization and Imperialism: 1890–1929'; 'Depression, Militarism, and War: 1929–1945'; 'The American Occupation, 1945–1952'; and 'Resurgent Japan: the Politics of Prosperity, 1952–1973'. Most selections have been abridged and footnotes are eliminated. The origins of this book lie in the efforts of the Committee of Concerned Asia Scholars to offer Americans new information and new – at times, even radical – approaches to the understanding of Japan.

120 **Sources of Japanese history.**
Compiled by David John Lu. New York; London: McGraw-Hill, 1974. 2 vols.

A well-balanced collection of primary source material about Japan, assembled in order to provide undergraduate students with a variety of readings in Japanese history. Lu's selection of documents emphasizes the development of Japan's social, economic, and political institutions, and his anthology contains primarily those items which 'reflected the spirit of the times and the life-styles of the people'. The first volume covers Japanese history from its mythical beginnings to the year 1800. The second volume brings that coverage up to 1968, when Kawabata Yasunari delivered an address in Stockholm upon receiving the Nobel Prize for literature. Many of the documents – among them the constitution, land tax regulations, Buddhist texts, and literary works – appear only in excerpts. Short but informative commentaries are also provided.

121 **The making of modern Japan.**
Kenneth B. Pyle. Lexington, Massachusetts; Toronto, Ontario: D. C. Heath, 1978. 196p. 3 maps. bibliog. (Civilization and Society).

Pyle's introduction to some of the principal themes in the historical development of modern Japanese society emphasizes the dynamics of historical change. His coverage extends from the unification of Japan in the late sixteenth century to the emergence of a resurgent Japan following World War II. The inclusion of several photographs and a bibliographical essay enhances the book's value for 'the person wishing a broad understanding of the emergence of Japan as a world power in modern times'.

122 **Japan: the story of a nation.**
Edwin O. Reischauer. New York: Knopf, 1981. 3rd ed. 428p. 9 maps. bibliog. Reprinted, Rutland, Vermont; Tokyo: Tuttle, 1981.

An updated classic introduction to the history of Japan. Originally published under the title *Japan: past and present* (New York: Knopf, 1946; London: Duckworth, 1947, 192p.), the 1981 edition brings her history up to 1980 and is particularly strong in its coverage of the years since World War II. Part one ('Traditional Japan') describes the land and its people and surveys their history from their early adoption of Chinese cultural and institutional patterns, through the development and growth of a feudal society, to the end of the Tokugawa period. The second part ('Modernizing Japan') focuses on Japan's transformation into an industrialised state as well as on the rise of militarism and the events which led to the Pacific War. Part three ('Postwar Japan') covers the American occupation, the nation's full economic recovery, and Japan's role in the world through the late 1970s. An extensive chronology is appended. A 4th edition of this volume has been announced for publication in 1990 by McGraw-Hill (New York).

123 **Japan: tradition and transformation.**
Edwin O. Reischauer, Albert M. Craig. Boston, Massachusetts and London: Houghton Mifflin, 1989. rev. ed. 352p. 9 maps.

This book is a reworking of the materials on Japan in the 1989 revised edition of the highly regarded textbook *East Asia: tradition and transformation*, by John K. Fairbank, Edwin O. Reischauer, and Albert M. Craig (Boston, Massachusetts: Houghton Mifflin, 1989, rev. ed., 1027p.). The larger text surveys the entire history of China, Korea, and Vietnam as well as Japan. The present volume discusses the early Japanese absorption of Chinese civilisation, the rise of Japanese feudalism, Tokugawa Japan as a centralised feudal state, Japan's response to the West during the nineteenth century, modernisation in Meiji Japan, the economy and society of imperial Japan, the growth of democracy and militarism during the first half of the twentieth century, and the new Japan that emerged from the ashes of World War II.

124 **A history of Japan.**
George B. Sansom. Stanford, California: Stanford University Press;
London: Cresset Press, 1958-63. 3 vols. 29 maps. bibliog. (Stanford
Studies in Civilizations of Eastern Asia) (The Cresset Historical Series).
Reprinted, Rutland, Vermont and Tokyo: Tuttle, 1974; Folkestone,
Kent: Dawson, 1978.

A straightforward narrative of the political and social history of Japan which Sansom
wrote during the closing years of his life. The first volume, *A history of Japan to 1334*,
covers the origins of the Japanese people, describes the emergence of an organised
state in Japan based on an imported Chinese model, traces the evolution of an efficient
system of feudal government, and concludes with the collapse of the Kamakura
shogunate in 1334. Volume two, *A history of Japan, 1334-1615*, focuses on the growth
of a new feudal hierarchy, the events of the century-long Warring States period, and
the rise of Tokugawa Ieyasu, who unified Japan under the rule of the Tokugawa
shogunate. The final volume, *A history of Japan, 1615-1867*, is less satisfying than the
others. It offers an account of the political and social development of Japan under the
Tokugawa shōguns, of Japan's relations with the West, and of the beginnings of
modern Japan up to the Meiji Restoration. Sansom's account complements his highly
acclaimed *Japan: a short cultural history* (q.v.) and in many respects supersedes James
Murdoch's detailed but outdated three-volume political history entitled *A history of
Japan* (Kobe; London, 1903-26; reprinted, London: Routledge and Kegan Paul, 1949.
3 vols.; New York: Frederick Ungar, 1964. 6 vols).

125 **Japan: a short cultural history.**
George B. Sansom. New York: Appleton-Century-Crofts, 1943. rev.
ed. 554p. 11 maps. Reprinted, London: Cresset Press, 1952; London:
Barrie and Jenkins, 1976; Stanford, California: Stanford University
Press, 1978.

First published in 1931, frequently reprinted, and widely acclaimed as one of the
classics of Western writing about Japan, this gracefully written survey introduces the
two thousand-year-long, rich cultural history that preceded the Meiji Restoration of
1868. Covering Japan's early history and the Nara, Heian, Kamakura, Muromachi,
Sengoku, and Edo (Tokugawa) periods, Sansom pays special attention to the evolution
of Japanese religion, art, and letters while offering as well an overview of the effects of
economic, social, and political conditions on the country's cultural development. This
survey is complemented by the author's three-volume *History of Japan* (q.v.), which in
turn focuses on Japan's political and social history.

126 **A brief history of Chinese and Japanese civilizations.**
Conrad Schirokauer. San Diego, California: Harcourt Brace
Jovanovich, 1989. 2nd ed. 673p. 22 maps. bibliog.

A general introduction for the undergraduate student to the political, economic, social,
artistic, cultural, and intellectual history of both traditional and modern East Asia. The
textbook offers balanced and comprehensive coverage of both China and Japan. An
extensive list of suggested readings and numerous maps and illustrations complement
the text. Readers who prefer to begin their study of East Asian history with the
modern period may prefer Schirokauer's *Modern China and Japan: a brief history*
(New York: Harcourt Brace Jovanovich, 1982, 358p.), a version of the second half of
this text.

127 **A history of modern Japan.**
Richard Storry. Harmondsworth, Middlesex; New York: Penguin
Books, 1982. rev. ed. 304p. map. bibliog.
A succinct and updated survey covering Japan's first contact with the West, the impact
of mid-nineteenth century Western pressure on the Tokugawa shogunate, the
consolidation and modernisation of the Meiji state, Japan's emergence as a world
power during the Taishō period, the events of the 1920s and the 1930s, the Pacific War,
the Allied occupation of the country, and the emergence of a new Japan following the
conclusion of the San Francisco Peace Treaty of 1951. Storry, a distinguished British
historian, emphasizes the Japanese response to intrusion by the Western world and the
interaction with the Western powers that shaped Japanese history after the mid-1800s.

128 **Japan before Perry: a short history.**
Conrad Totman. Berkeley, California; London: University of
California Press, 1981. 246p. 3 maps.
A comprehensive overview of Japanese history prior to 1853 presented within an
interpretative framework that makes use of three major chronological divisions:
'classical Japan: an age of aristocratic bureaucracy' (seventh to twelfth centuries);
'medieval Japan: an age of political fluidity' (twelfth to sixteenth centuries); and 'early-
modern Japan: an age of integral bureaucracy' (sixteenth to nineteenth centuries).
Interweaving historical facts into his interpretations of some of the major themes of
Japanese history, Totman examines the economic, political, social, and cultural
patterns that constitute the 'interconnected aspects of a single distinctive historic
whole', or 'cyclical' epoch. Throughout his essay, he stresses the unifying characteristics and developments in Japanese society and culture which are considered to have
been central to each of these three eras.

An introduction to Japanese civilization.
See item no. 32.

Japanese chronology.
See item no. 35.

The Japanese emperor through history.
See item no. 35.

A history of Japanese literature.
See item no. 999.

**Japanese history and culture from ancient to modern times: seven basic
bibliographies.**
See item no. 1583.

AD 550–1600

129 **The Christian century in Japan, 1549–1650.**
Charles R. Boxer. Berkeley, California: University of California
Press; London: Cambridge University Press, 1951. 535p. 2 maps.
bibliog. Reprinted, Berkeley, California; London: University of
California Press, 1974. (California Libraries Reprint Series Edition).
A detailed, scholarly study of the introduction, growth, and suppression of militant
Christianity in Japan between the arrival of the Jesuit missionary Francis Xavier in
1549 and the government's suppression of the Japanese Christian uprising known as
the Shimabara Rebellion in 1637-38. Boxer tells how the earliest Europeans reached
Japan, describes the organising of the first Jesuit missions there and their initial
success, discusses the impact of Christian culture on Japanese literature, art and
medicine, depicts some of the commercial activities that involved the Japanese with
various European traders, sheds light on internal political developments as they were
viewed by the Jesuits, explains why the Tokugawa shogunate decided to prohibit
Christianity, and chronicles the government's savage persecution of the missionaries
and their converts. Throughout his book, Boxer attempts to relate the Western
religious and commercial presence in Japan to the larger social and political framework
of Japan during this century.

130 **The future and the past: a translation and study of the *Gukanshō*, an
interpretive history of Japan written in 1219.**
Delmer M. Brown, Ichirō Ishida. Berkeley, California; London:
University of California Press, 1979. 479p. bibliog.
A translation of the earliest interpretive history of Japan, the *Gukanshō*, written by the
high-ranking Tendai Buddhist priest Jien (1155-1225). It describes the course of
Japanese history from the time of the country's earliest emperors through the
beginning of the thirteenth century, and seeks to demonstrate that political events were
moving 'directly and inevitably from the past into the future' along a particular course
that accorded with a divine plan created by the Japanese deities. While biased and
inaccurate in some respects, the *Gukanshō* has nevertheless come to be widely
regarded as an important historical classic. Brown and Ishida complement their
translation with three analytical essays which provide an overview of Japanese
historical writing prior to the thirteenth century, a study of Jien's life and times, and an
examination of the structure and formation of Jien's interpretation of history.

131 **Five mountains: the Rinzai Zen monastic institution in medieval Japan.**
Martin Collcutt, foreword by Edwin O. Reischauer. Cambridge,
Massachusetts: Council on East Asian Studies, Harvard University,
1981. 399p. 4 maps. bibliog. (Harvard East Asian Monographs, 85).
A scholarly study of the *gozan* ('five mountains') system of Rinzai sect Zen temples (or
monasteries) that flourished during the fourteenth and fifteenth centuries. These
religious institutions were a pervasive force in medieval Japan and are remembered
today particularly for their cultural and religious contributions to Japanese life at that
time. Focusing on their history, their political and economic roles, and their internal
organisation, Collcutt first surveys the background and development of the *gozan*
system from the early Kamakura period, when Ch'an (Zen) Buddhism as a sect was

53

introduced from China into Japan, until the rapid decline of the *gozan* system following the Ōnin War of 1467-77. In part two of his book ('The Structure of the Institution'), he examines the codification of the rules that governed monastic life, the architectural layout and physical structure of the *gozan* monasteries, their social organisation, and the economic activities of three representative temples in Kamakura and Kyōto.

132 **The southern barbarians: the first Europeans in Japan.**
Edited by Michael Cooper, introduction by Tadao Doi.   Tokyo; Palo Alto, California: Kodansha International in co-operation with Sophia University, 1976. 216p. 3 maps. bibliog.
Five articles by Ebisawa Arimichi, Michael Cooper, Fernando G. Gutiérrez, and Diego Pacheco – accompanied by 124 illustrations – provide an interpretive account of Japan's so-called 'Christian century'. They narrate the story of the Europeans who were in Japan between 1543 and 1640, show how three of them – the Jesuit missionaries João Rodrigues and Luis Frois and the English merchant Richard Cocks – viewed and described Japan in their writings, discuss the interaction of Western and Japanese cultures (with particular attention to such areas as language, education, art, and printing), and survey the genre of *nanban* ('Southern Barbarian') art that flourished during the late sixteenth and early seventeenth centuries.

133 **They came to Japan: an anthology of European reports on Japan, 1543–1640.**
Edited by Michael Cooper.   London: Thames and Hudson; Berkeley, California: University of California Press, 1965. 439p. bibliog. (Publications of the Center for Japanese and Korean Studies).
Reprinted, University of California Press, 1981.
Selections from the letters, diaries, and other writings of more than thirty Europeans who came to Japan during the so-called 'Christian century', a period which witnessed the visits of many Catholic missionaries and Western merchants. The reports that Cooper brings together offer a reasonably accurate and composite picture of Japan at that time. They contain observations about a wide range of Japanese life and civilisation including Japanese history, the Japanese people, social relations, the emperor and the nobility, castles, weapons, law and order, the Japanese language, food and drink, dress, housing, daily life and customs, art and culture, major cities, Shintō and Buddhism, temples and idols, festivals and funerals, and the persecution of the Christians during the early Tokugawa period. Among the Europeans represented are the English mariner Will Adams (1564-1620), the Portuguese Jesuit missionary Luis Frois (1532-97), and the Italian Jesuit administrator Alessandro Valignano (1539-1606).

134 **Feudalism in Japan.**
Peter Duus, introduction by Eugene Rice.   New York: Knopf, 1976. 2nd ed. 124p. map. bibliog. (Studies in World Civilization).
An introductory survey of the evolution of feudal institutions in Japan, with particular focus on feudalism as a political and social phenomenon. Duus traces the origins of feudalism back to sixth-century tribal rule and follows the course of its development to the early 1870s, when it was totally abolished by the early Meiji government. Brief comparisons of Japanese and European feudalism note some striking similarities and

major differences. This book is one in an important series of paperbacks designed to assist teachers in incorporating non-Western studies into their civilisation survey courses.

135 **Warlords, artists, and commoners: Japan in the sixteenth century.**
Edited by George Elison, Bardwell L. Smith. Honolulu, Hawaii: University Press of Hawaii, 1981. 356p. map. bibliog.

Nine American scholars examine some of the major political, cultural, and social developments of the Azuchi-Momoyama period (1568-1600). They deal specifically with the momentous institutional changes of that era; the nature of urban autonomy in the port city of Sakai; the role of Oda Nobunaga, the powerful military leader who helped to unify Japan; Kanō Eitoku's magnificent wall-paintings at Azuchi Castle and the ways in which they transformed the Japanese pictorial style; the career of Satomura Jōha, a poet of linked verse (*renga*); rice-planting folk songs and their contributions to contemporary theatrical arts (*jōruri* and kabuki); the musical culture of the era and the development of various musical instruments; the evolution of the aesthetics and culture of the tea ceremony up to the time of the great tea master Sen no Rikyū; and the efforts of Toyotomi Hideyoshi to attain political and cultural legitimacy during the course of his career.

136 **Daily life in Japan at the time of the samurai, 1185–1603.**
Louis Frédéric, translated from the French by Eileen Lowe. London: Allen and Unwin; New York: Praeger; Rutland, Vermont and Tokyo: Tuttle, 1972. 256p. bibliog. (Daily Life Series, 17).

A delightful recreation of the world of the Japanese at all levels of society during the Kamakura, Muromachi, and Momoyama periods. Frédéric vividly describes many different aspects of everyday life among the samurai, the nobility, and the commoners in both the major cities and the countryside. These aspects include love, marriage, death, the family system, housing, diet, dress, make-up, hygiene, agricultural practices, seasonal changes, medicine, commerce, military equipment, warfare, science, religious customs and beliefs, art, poetry, music, and dance. Originally published as *La vie quotidienne au Japon à l'époque des samouraï 1185–1603* (Paris: Hachette, 1968), Frédéric's book draw heavily on medieval Japanese literature and art as well as on extant historical sources.

137 **Japan's renaissance: the politics of the Muromachi bakufu.**
Kenneth Alan Grossberg. Cambridge, Massachusetts: Council on East Asian Studies, Harvard University, 1981. 207p. 6 maps. bibliog. (Harvard East Asian Monographs, 99).

Grossberg reinterprets fourteenth- and fifteenth-century Japanese politics and society in order to explain how the shōguns of the Muromachi period (1333-1568) 'presided over a synthesis of political, social, and economic changes which began the shift away from autarkic-agrarian feudal structures in Japan'. He focuses on the evolution of the shogunate (*bakufu*) as he discusses the reigns of the leading Ashikaga rulers, Muromachi economy and *bakufu* income, the *bakufu*'s bureaucratic and administrative apparatus, and the military organisation of the *bakufu* system. Grossberg argues that the Muromachi shogunate introduced most of the major political innovations for the three centuries that followed it, and he advances some comparisons between it and the states of the European Renaissance.

138 **Government and local power in Japan, 500 to 1700: a study based on Bizen Province.**
John Whitney Hall. Princeton, New Jersey: Princeton University Press, 1966. 446p. 16 maps. bibliog. Reprinted, Princeton University Press, 1980.

An influential interpretation of premodern Japanese political and institutional history based on a case-study of a province that is now part of Okayama Prefecture. Hall's detailed analysis of this microcosm of Japanese economic and sociopolitical life explains 'the fundamental institutions of political organization and social and economic structure' which underlay the government at both the local and national levels over an extended period of time. In focusing on the evolution of two sets of relationships – the 'combination of traditions and techniques by which the Japanese organized power and exercised authority', and the connections between the political power holders and the landholdings which constituted their primary source of wealth – Hall considers such subjects as 'theories of legitimacy and practices of administration, concepts of social stratification and social rights, and practices of land tenure and taxation'. By alternating at chronologically appropriate intervals chapters dealing with developments in Bizen and on the national scene respectively, he also provides a perspective that significantly enhances the reader's understanding of premodern Japanese history.

139 **Japan before Tokugawa: political consolidation and economic growth, 1500 to 1650.**
Edited by John Whitney Hall, Keiji Nagahara, Kozo Yamamura. Princeton, New Jersey; Guildford, Surrey: Princeton University Press, 1981. 392p. 4 maps.

Eleven essays by American and Japanese specialists examine several aspects of political, economic, and social history during both the era of extensive warfare among the daimyō (regional lords) and the early years of Japan's unification under the Tokugawa shogunate. These essays deal with the ways in which the Go-Hōjō and Ōuchi (two great daimyō) came into existence and held on to their extensive domains; the development of the house laws issued by the daimyō; daimyō regulation of trade; the political, social, commercial, and urban policies of Oda Nobunaga and Toyotomi Hideyoshi; the problems encountered by early Tokugawa shōguns in establishing the ideological basis of their legitimacy; the problem faced by seventeenth-century daimyō in creating a suitable political structure for exerting direct control over the samurai and the peasants; the evolution of Japanese cities; and Japan's 'agricultural revolution' and the accelerated growth of commerce, 1550-1650.

140 **Japan in the Muromachi age.**
Edited by John W. Hall, Takeshi Toyoda, introduction by John W. Hall. Berkeley, California; London: University of California Press, 1977. 376p.

A distinguished collection of essays by Japanese and American scholars that reinterpret the political, institutional, economic, social, cultural, and religious history of the Muromachi period (1334-1573). The essays are specifically concerned with Kyōto in the Muromachi age, the Muromachi power structure, the Ashikaga shōgun and the Muromachi *bakufu* administration, the *bugyōnin* system of civil administration, the provincial aspects of Muromachi politics, proprietary lordship and the structure of local power, village communities and daimyō power, the growth of commerce and the trades, the evolution of Sakai from a *shōen* (landed estate) to a port city, Japan's relations with overseas countries, social change and patronage under Shōgun Ashikaga Yoshimitsu, the concept of the 'unity of the three creeds' as a theme in fifteenth-century ink painting, the development of *shoin*-style architecture, the comic tradition in *renga* ('linked verse') poetry, medieval jongleurs and the making of a national literature, Muromachi Zen Buddhism and the *gozan* system, and Rennyo and the Shinshū (Jōdo Shin sect) religious revival.

141 **Medieval Japan: essays in institutional history.**
Edited by John W. Hall, Jeffrey P. Mass; introduction by John W. Hall. New Haven, Connecticut; London: Yale University Press, 1974. 269p. 6 maps. Reprinted, Stanford, California: Stanford University Press, 1988.

Eleven essays on the political and social institutions of Japan between the ninth and sixteenth centuries present a view of medieval Japan that is 'much more diverse and energetic' than historians had previously portrayed. Grouped together under three major headings – 'Court and Shōen in Heian Japan', '*Bakufu* versus Court', and 'The Age of Military Dominance' – these essays cover such important topics as the centuries-long history of the imperial court of Kyōto, the structure of the imperial court during the Heian period, the development of the *insei* ('cloistered') system of government, the early development of the private landed estates known as the *shōen*, the emergence of the Kamakura *bakufu* (military government, or shogunate) during the 1180s, the economic and political effects of the late thirteenth-century wars against the invading Mongols, the early Muromachi *bakufu* in Kyōto, and the *ikki* (organisations formed for military purposes) in the 1400s.

142 **Insei: abdicated sovereigns in the politics of late Heian Japan, 1086–1185.**
G. Cameron Hurst, III. New York; London: Columbia University Press, 1976. 337p. bibliog. (Studies of the East Asian Institute, Columbia University).

A thorough examination of the system of rule by retired emperors known as *insei*. Part one discusses the origins and development of abdication and explores how and why abdicated sovereigns emerged as important political forces in the imperial court. Through a detailed study of the reigns of four influential ex-emperors (Go-Sanjō, Shirakawa, Toba, and Go-Shirakawa), Hurst characterises the patterns that were common to the practice of abdication. Part two analyses the structure and function of the *in no chō*, or ex-sovereign's administrative office, which functioned essentially as a government separate from the one maintained by the reigning emperor. Oriented towards specialists in Japanese history, Hurst's study is also valuable for readers interested in the political concepts of 'legitimacy' and 'sovereignty' as well as in the study of patron–client relationships.

143 **Early Buddhist Japan.**
J. Edward Kidder. London: Thames and Hudson; New York: Praeger, 1972. 212p. 6 maps. bibliog. (Ancient Peoples and Places, 78).

A profusely illustrated introduction to Japanese history between the introduction of Buddhism in 552 AD and the end of the Nara period in 794. On the basis of a wide range of archaeological evidence, Kidder writes about the use of coins in the economy,

History. AD 550–1600

Shintō ritual sites and ceramic wares, land allotment, city planning and administration,
the military headquarters and their fortifications, several of the palaces that were built
during the seventh and eighth centuries, the development of temple architecture and
the leading temples of the Asuka and Nara periods, burial practices and the cult of
relics, and extant stone carvings and monuments. Particular attention is paid to the
archaeology of the Asuka and Nara areas, where Japan's early capitals were located.
Kidder's study constitutes a sequel to his earlier book *Japan before Buddhism* (q.v.).

144 **A chronicle of gods and sovereigns: *Jinnō Shōtōki* of Kitabatake
Chikafusa.**
Kitabatake Chikafusa, translated with an introduction by H. Paul
Varley.   New York; Guildford, Surrey: Columbia University Press,
1980. 300p. bibliog. (Translations from the Oriental Classics).
Jinnō Shōtōki ('Chronicle of the Direct Descent of Gods and Sovereigns'), a glorified
early fourteenth-century account of the history of the imperial succession, is a major
work of classical historical writing. It recounts Japan's divine origins and chronicles, in
a reign-by-reign capitulation of imperial history, the lives of the human sovereigns who
purportedly ruled over Japan between the time of Emperor Jimmu's accession to the
throne (660 BC) through the reigns of Go-Daigo and Go-Murakami in the early 1300s.
Jinnō Shōtōki was prepared as a polemical tract to win over supporters to the side of
Emperor Go-Daigo during a period of dynastic schism and civil war, and it
subsequently became 'the great catechism for loyalty to the throne' for many
generations of Japanese. Varley's extensive introduction places this work of Kitabatake
Chikafusa (1293-1354) in its historical context and assesses its significance. An analysis
of Kitabatake's political theories may be found in Varley's book *Imperial restoration in
medieval Japan* (q.v.).

145 **Buddhism and the state in sixteenth-century Japan.**
Neil McMullin.   Princeton, New Jersey; Guildford, Surrey: Princeton
University Press, 1984. 441p. map. bibliog.
Centering on the policies of the celebrated military leader Oda Nobunaga (1534-82),
this is a scholarly account of the fundamental changes that occurred in the relationship
of organised Buddhism to the Japanese state at the end of the medieval period, when
Buddhism was displaced from the central position in Japanese society that it had
enjoyed for almost a millennium. After surveying Buddhist institutional history
between the sixth and sixteenth centuries and depicting Nobunaga's rise to power as
the unifier of Japan following several decades of civil strife, McMullin details
Nobunaga's military destruction of both the political and the economic power of the
Buddhist temples and monasteries which had controlled much of the country's landed
wealth. The work concludes with an examination of the long-term effects of
Nobunaga's policies and with an assessment of Buddhism's loss of primacy as the 'main
pillar of the political ideology' that had supported the Japanese state for nearly a
thousand years.

146 **The bakufu in Japanese history.**
Edited by Jeffrey P. Mass, William B. Hauser, foreword by Marius B.
Jansen.   Stanford, California: Stanford University Press, 1985. 264p.
map.
The *bakufu* (shogunate, or military government) played a prominent role as an
institutional structure of authority during the Kamakura (1185-1333), Muromachi

(1333-1568), and Tokugawa (1600-1868) periods. In examining how warrior participation in the *bakufu* evolved over the centuries and in considering some of the administrative continuities of this form of government, the eight American specialists contributing to this volume address the following topics: the evolution of the term *bakufu*; the unanswerable questions regarding the character and nature of the Kamakura *bakufu*; the Kamakura *bakufu* and its officials; Muromachi *bakufu* rule both in Kyōto and in the regional outposts of Kyūshū and the Kantō plain; the provincial vassals of the Muromachi shōguns; the relationship between Toyotomi Hideyoshi and the daimyō; the place of Ōsaka castle in the Tokugawa political system and in *bakufu* control over western Japan; and Abe Masahiro's inadequate leadership towards the end of the Tokugawa period. This collection of essays was assembled as a tribute to John Whitney Hall, a pioneering scholar in the field of premodern Japanese history.

147 **Court and bakufu in Japan: essays in Kamakura history.**
Edited with an introduction by Jeffrey P. Mass. New Haven, Connecticut; London: Yale University Press, 1982. 322p. map. bibliog.

Eleven essays on aspects of the political, social, and institutional history of the Kamakura period (1185-1333), an era characterised by the coexistence of two centres of authority: the imperial court at Kyōto and the Hōjō military government at Kamakura. The first four essays focus on the court. They are concerned with court–*bakufu* (shogunate) relations, the imperial court as a legal authority, the fiscal fortunes of the Tōdaiji temple, and the maintenance of imperial authority in the province of Suō. Five other essays – on warrior government under the Hōjō – deal with the political ascendancy of the Hōjō family as hereditary regents of the Kamakura *bakufu*, the nature and structure of the *bakufu*, the place of the Zen monastery in Kamakura society, and late thirteenth-century banditry. Takeuchi Rizō's essay 'Old and New Approaches to Kamakura History' concludes the volume.

148 **The development of Kamakura rule, 1180–1250: a history with documents.**
Jeffrey P. Mass. Stanford, California: Stanford University Press, 1979. 312p. map. bibliog.

An in-depth examination of the judicial system that became the foundation upon which the Kamakura *bakufu* (shogunate) established its ascendancy, together with an assessment of its place in early medieval history. Mass first describes the background, nature, and consequences of the Jōkyū War of 1221, which not only affected the balance of power between the traditional aristocracy at Kyōto and the warrior government at Kamakura but also influenced Japan's administrative structure and the *bakufu*'s judicial machinery. He then focuses on the evolution of Kamakura's judicial system (from its origins to 1250) as well as on its procedures, considering such matters as the continuity of this system, the 'emergence of legal arbitration as the true centrepiece of warrior government', and the actual forms and techniques for adjudicating disputes. Both this book and the author's earlier work, *The Kamakura 'bakufu': a study in documents* (Stanford, California: Stanford University Press, 1976, 364p.), demonstrate the considerable value of documentary records (*komonjo*) for the study of medieval Japanese history. Together they contain annotated translations of over three hundred extant documents such as edicts, judicial records, and land documents that provide a fuller understanding of the workings of Japanese institutions. Summaries and annotated translations of many additional documents may be found in a classic sourcebook entitled *The documents of Iriki: illustrative of the development of the feudal institutions of Japan*, translated and edited with an introduction by Kan'ichi Asakawa (New Haven, Connecticut: Yale University Press, 1929, 442, 134p. Reprinted, Tokyo: Japan Society for the Promotion of Science, 1955; Westport, Connecticut: Greenwood Press, 1974). Some 253 documents in the possession of the southern Kyūshū feudal landholding family of Iriki-in, dating primarily from the mid-twelfth to the late fourteenth centuries, offer insights into medieval administrative and legal practices and the character of Japanese feudalism.

149 **Warrior government in early medieval Japan: a study of the Kamakura bakufu, shugo, and jitō.**

Jeffrey P. Mass. New Haven, Connecticut; London: Yale University Press, 1974. 257p. map. bibliog.

A scholarly analysis of the emergence and early development of the Kamakura *bakufu* (military government) between the 1180s and 1221, of its exercise of power in much of Japan through provincial constables (*shugo*) and estate stewards (*jitō*), and of the shift in the centre of administrative control from the imperial court in Kyōto to the warrior class led by Minamoto no Yoritomo and his successors at Kamakura. In this detailed study of a crucial period in early medieval Japanese history, Mass examines the rise of the warrior class in eastern Japan, the rivalry during the early 1180s between the Minamoto and Taira warrior houses that led to the creation of the *bakufu*, the emergent dual court–*bakufu* polity and the extension of Kamakura authority, and the origins, growth and role of the system of *shugo* and *jitō* under the new Kamakura government.

150 **The world of the shining prince: court life in ancient Japan.**

Ivan Morris. New York: Knopf; Oxford, England: Oxford University Press, 1964. 336p. bibliog. Reprinted, Harmondsworth, Middlesex: Penguin Books, 1964; Rutland, Vermont and Tokyo: Tuttle, 1978.

A vivid portrayal of court life and society between the mid-tenth and mid-eleventh centuries that can serve both as a companion volume to *The tale of Genji* (q.v.) and as a delightful introduction to the era that witnessed the flowering of Heian civilisation. Drawing heavily on *The tale of Genji*, *The pillow book of Sei Shōnagon* (q.v.), court diaries, and contemporary chronicles and journals, Morris depicts what it was like to be a member of aristocratic Heian period society. He provides an historical background; discusses the politics, society, administration, and economy of the period; and describes the religions, superstititons, the 'good people' (largely aristocrats) and their lives, the cult of beauty that became the foundation of Japanese aesthetics, and the role of women and their relations with men. Morris also devotes an entire chapter to Murasaki Shikibu, author of *The tale of Genji*, and considers selected aspects of the novel itself.

151 **A history of Japanese astronomy: Chinese background and Western impact.**

Shigeru Nakayama. Cambridge, Massachusetts: Harvard University Press, 1969. 329p. bibliog. (Harvard–Yenching Institute Monograph Series, 18).

A comprehensive history of Japanese astronomy from its Chinese origins until the 1880s, when it was thoroughly infused with Western ideas. Nakayama first examines the era of the Chinese domination of Japanese astronomy (sixth to sixteenth centuries), when the Japanese imported Chinese astrology, calender-making, and cosmology and adapted them for their own needs. He then describes the growth of Western scientific influence in East Asia; the initial Japanese reception of the cosmological schemes, mechanistic philosophies, and astronomical techniques that had been developed in Europe; and their challenge to Chinese-based astronomy in Japan (late sixteenth to early eighteenth centuries). Finally, he shows how the Japanese gradually came to recognise the supremacy of Western astronomy, particularly following the renewed importation of Western scientific books that advanced the Japanese understanding of the Copernican and Newtonian theories of astronomy.

152 **Kojiki.**
Translated with an introduction and notes by Donald L. Philippi.
Tokyo: University of Tokyo Press, 1968; Princeton, New Jersey:
Princeton University Press, 1969. 655p. bibliog.

A new translation of the *Kojiki* ('Record of Ancient Matters'), completed in 712 AD under the auspices of the imperial court. The earliest extant chronicle in Japanese history, it records the myths and legends surrounding the founding of Japan and the origins of the imperial family, and it describes the history of Japan from the time of Emperor Jimmu (the legendary first emperor) through the reign of Empress Suiko in the early seventh century. The *Kojiki* has also come to be regarded as the earliest classic of Japanese literature. Philippi's extensively annotated translation is accompanied by romanised transcriptions of the texts of the 113 songs (or poems) that appear in the *Kojiki*, as well as by an extensive glossary of place-names, names of families, individuals and deities, hereditary titles, names of selected animals and plants, and names of songs.

153 **This island of Japan: João Rodrigues' account of 16th-century Japan.**
João Rodrigues, translated and edited with an introduction by Michael Cooper. Tokyo; New York: Kodansha International, 1973. 354p. bibliog.

An introduction to a substantially longer history of Japan written by João Rodrigues (1561?-1633), a Portuguese Jesuit priest who was an astute observer and culturally sensitive man as well as an extremely influential European in late sixteenth-century Japan. Rodrigues' account deals with a wide range of topics related to Japanese art and culture including architecture, ceremonial observances and festivals, travel, food, contemporary styles of clothing and dress, New Year's customs, ritual wine drinking, the tea ceremony, traditional arts and crafts, Japanese canons of taste, and the origins and nature of the Japanese language. Cooper's presentation is an abridged translation of Part 1, Books 1 and 2 of Rodrigues' *História da Igreja do Japão*, only portions of which are extant today. For an account of Rodrigues' life, see Cooper's *Rodrigues the interpreter: an early Jesuit in Japan and China* (q.v.).

154 **The founding of the Kamakura shogunate, 1180–1185: with selected translations from the *Azuma kagami*.**
Minoru Shinoda. New York: Columbia University Press, 1960. 385p. 3 maps. bibliog. (Records of Civilization: Sources and Studies, 57).

Part one ('The Founding of the Kamakura Shogunate') offers a good overview of the background of Japan's feudal institutions and a detailed description and analysis of the political origins and establishment of the Kamakura shogunate. Particular attention is paid to the successive phases of the Gempei War, the struggle between the Taira and Minamoto clans for political supremacy. Part two consists of a translation of those sections of the *Azuma kagami* which specifically cover the years 1180-85. A strictly chronological, historical account and record of official documents and correspondence that is generally attributed to shogunal scribes and other officials, the *Azuma kagami* is valuable to historians not only for its military and political coverage of the Kamakura shogunate over a period of eighty-six years but also for its depiction of early warrior society, culture, family life, and religious practices.

155 **Japan: a history in art.**

Bradley Smith, introductions by Marius B. Jansen, Nagatake Asano. New York: Simon and Schuster; Garden City, New York: Doubleday, 1964; London: Weidenfeld and Nicolson, 1965. 295p. bibliog.

An attractively produced picture-book which allows one to view Japan's past – from prehistoric times to the end of the Meiji period (1912) – in the ways that Japanese artists recorded it. More than two hundred colour photographs of murals, sculptures, painted screens, prints, scrolls, fans, wall-paintings, and other art objects illustrate the evolution of Japanese theatre, literature, and religion, and depict the country's major political events. Smith's popularly written volume is, however, neither a serious general history of Japan nor a systematic study of her artistic heritage.

156 **The way of the samurai.**

Richard Storry, photographs by Werner Forman. London: Orbis; New York: Putnam, 1978. 128p. map. bibliog. (Echoes of the Ancient World). Reprinted, New York: Mayflower, 1981.

A British authority on Japanese history vividly presents the history, philosophy, culture, and way of life of the warrior class that dominated Japan for nearly seven full centuries. In a volume oriented towards a popular audience that combines many colourful plates with a highly readable narrative, Storry explains the 'complex and paradoxical' nature of the samurai and traces the main course of their activities from the emergence of this class in the twelfth century to their demise with the collapse of the Tokugawa shogunate in 1868. Among the photographs are many illustrations of samurai armour and weapons, imposing castles, and artists' renditions of samurai warriors engaged in fierce battle.

157 **Science and culture in traditional Japan, A.D. 600–1854.**

Masayoshi Sugimoto, David L. Swain, foreword by Nathan Sivin. Cambridge, Massachusetts; London: MIT Press, 1978. 498p. 2 maps. bibliog. (MIT East Asian Science Series, 6). Reprinted, Rutland, Vermont; Tokyo: Tuttle, 1989.

A history of the development of science in Japan within its wider social and intellectual context. Astrology and calendrical astronomy, mathematics, and medicine constitute the focus of the volume since these three scientific fields were the earliest areas of scientific endeavour in China and subsequently played a central role in the pursuit of natural knowledge and its social uses in both Japan and China. Sugimoto and Swain begin by considering the influx of Chinese learning and science into Japan between the seventh and tenth centuries, then investigate the indigenous Japanese development of science during the following five hundred years. They explore the introduction of the most sophisticated forms of Chinese culture, Confucianism, and science after 1400

AD and conclude with an examination of the shift from traditional to modern science that occurred during the latter part of the Tokugawa period. Focusing on the years 1868–1921, James R. Bartholomew's *The formation of science in Japan: building a research tradition* (New Haven, Connecticut; London: Yale University Press, 1989, 369p.) challenges the notion that Japan's feudalistic cultural inheritance obstructed the formation of a modern tradition of scientific research, as he helps carry Sugimoto and Swain's account forward. Bartholomew examines the Tokugawa period roots of Japanese science, the recruitment, training and socialisation of scientists during the Meiji era, government assistance and relations with scientific institutes, the impact of World War I on Japan's scientific community, and the development of a system for supporting scientific research.

158 **The book of the samurai: the warrior class of Japan.**
Stephen R. Turnbull. New York: Arco; London: Arms and Armour Press, 1982. 192p. 6 maps. bibliog. (A Bison Book). Reprinted, New York: Gallery Books, 1982; Leicester, England: Magna Books, 1986.
An overview of the world of the samurai between the twelfth and nineteenth centuries, written for a broad, general audience. Turnbull traces the role which these warriors played in Japanese political and social history, showing how they initially assumed power, warred with one another during the middle ages, participated in the evolution of Japanese culture, were transformed from sword-wielding warriors into sword-bearing bureaucrats during the Tokugawa period, and disappeared as an historical force shortly after the Meiji Restoration of 1868. Illustrating the text are excellent colour reproductions of woodblock prints and picture scrolls; photographs of samurai arms and armour, castles, and individuals alive during the nineteenth century; and still photographs of samurai action taken from recent Japanese movies.

159 **Imperial restoration in medieval Japan.**
H. Paul Varley. New York; London: Columbia University Press, 1971. 222p. bibliog. (Studies of the East Asian Institute, Columbia University).
An effort to explain the Kemmu Restoration of 1333-36 (Emperor Go-Daigo's attempted restoration of direct imperial rule following the overthrow of the Kamakura shogunate) as a crucial development in the transition from rule by courtiers to rule by warriors in early medieval Japan. Varley describes the circumstances leading to this restoration, including the imperial institution's loss of power and the decline of Kamakura rule; the brief period when Go-Daigo regained power from the Hōjō family (the hereditary regents of the Kamakura shogunate) but then lost it to the warlord Ashikaga Takauji, who extended his support to another member of the imperial family; and the ensuing division of the imperial court into 'northern' and 'southern' branches and the schism between them that lasted until 1392. In an historiographical study which constitutes the concluding portion of this monograph, Varley also explores the views of later generations of Japanese historians towards these particular events.

160 **The Ōnin War: history of its origins and background with a selective translation of *The chronicle of Ōnin*.**
H. Paul Varley. New York; London: Columbia University Press, 1967. 238p. map. bibliog. (Studies in Oriental Culture, 1).
Varley examines the early institutional development of the *bakufu* (shogunate)

following its inception in the late 1100s, and the civil war – fought primarily in Kyōto between 1467 and 1477 – which destroyed the balance of power between the Muromachi shogunate and its provincial military governors (the *shugo*, or 'constables') that had been established in central and western Japan. Part one surveys the institutional structure of both the Kamakura and the Muromachi *bakufu* and briefly analyses the changing relationship between them and the *shugo*. It emphasizes some of the shifts that occurred in the roles and functions of the groups that held power during the period, and describes the precipitous decline in the leadership of the Muromachi *bakufu* after 1441. Part two consists of translated selections from *The chronicle of Ōnin*, a late medieval description and reconstruction of the fighting and chaos of that great civil war.

Sources of Japanese tradition.
See item no. 33.

Kyoto: a contemplative guide.
See item no. 89.

Historical Kyoto: with illustrations and guide maps.
See item no. 92.

Historical Nara: with illustrations and guide maps.
See item no. 93.

Deus destroyed: the image of Christianity in early modern Japan.
See item no. 166.

The nobility of failure: tragic heroes in the history of Japan.
See item no. 293.

Great historical figures of Japan.
See item no. 295.

Hideyoshi.
See item no. 299.

101 letters of Hideyoshi: the private correspondence of Toyotomi Hideyoshi.
See item no. 299.

Sugawara no Michizane and the early Heian court.
See item no. 300.

The confessions of Lady Nijō.
See item no. 310.

Rodrigues the interpreter: an early Jesuit in Japan and China.
See item no. 352.

Biographical dictionary of Japanese history.
See item no. 367.

Religion in Japanese history.
See item no. 465.

Japanese Buddhism.
See item no. 475.

A history of Christianity in Japan.
See item no. 495.

Social change and the city in Japan: from earliest times through the industrial revolution.
See item no. 546.

The tale of the Soga Brothers.
See item no. 1012.

Ōkagami, the great mirror: Fujiwara Michinaga (966–1027) and his times. A study and translation.
See item no. 1017.

The Taiheiki: a chronicle of medieval Japan.
See item no. 1018.

The tale of the Heike.
See item no. 1019.

Yoshitsune: a fifteenth-century Japanese chronicle.
See item no. 1020.

A tale of flowering fortunes: annals of Japanese aristocratic life in the Heian period.
See item no. 1021.

A thousand cranes: treasures of Japanese art.
See item no. 1217.

Japan: the shaping of daimyo culture, 1185–1868.
See item no. 1218.

Japanese castles.
See item no. 1306.

Castles in Japan.
See item no. 1317.

Monumenta Nipponica: Studies in Japanese Culture.
See item no. 1534.

Legend in Japanese art: a description of historical episodes, legendary characters, folk-lore, myths, religious symbolism, illustrated in the arts of old Japan.
See item no. 1560.

The Princeton companion to classical Japanese literature.
See item no. 1566.

Early Japanese history (*c*.40 B.C.–A.D. 1167).
See item no. 1569.

1600–1868 (Tokugawa period)

161 **Peasant protest in Japan, 1590–1884.**
Herbert P. Bix. New Haven, Connecticut; London: Yale University
Press, 1986. 296p. 5 maps. bibliog.
A reconstruction of Tokugawa period social history in terms of recurring instances of
peasant and commoner revolt that seeks to explain the causes of these protests, the
ways in which they were waged, their underlying goals and values, and some of their
consequences. Bix presents a series of chronologically ordered case-studies of
representative peasant uprisings between the early eighteenth and mid-nineteenth
centuries, paying special attention to the 'relationship between particular class struggle
events and the local, regional, and "national" circumstances' of the periods during
which they occurred. He also considers the major characteristics of these revolts as
well as of the Tokugawa state itself, and examines the nature and development of
peasant consciousness (defined as 'those beliefs that are always a constituent part of
collective actions') in relation to questions of class structure, economic growth,
bureaucratic organisation, and state power. The nature and patterns of peasant protest
during the 150 years preceding the Meiji Restoration are also examined in *Peasant
protests and uprisings in Tokugawa Japan*, by Stephen Vlastos (Berkeley, California;
London: University of California Press, 1986, 184p.), and in *Social protest and popular
culture in eighteenth-century Japan*, by Anne Walthall (Tucson, Arizona: Published for
the Association for Asian Studies by the University of Arizona Press, 1986, 268p.
[Association for Asian Studies Monographs, 43]).

162 **Young Japan: Yokohama and Yedo. A narrative of the settlement and
the city from the signing of the treaties in 1858, to the close of the year
1879. With a glance at the progress of Japan during a period of twenty-
one years.**
John R. Black. Yokohama: Kelly and Walsh; London: Trubner,
1880-81; New York: Baker, Pratt, 1883. 2 vols. Reprinted, with an
introduction by Grace Fox, Tokyo; London; New York: Oxford
University Press, 1968. (Oxford in Asia Historical Reprints).
An informal history of the treaty port settlement of Yokohama and the capital city of
Edo (Tokyo) by a British newspaper editor and publisher who lived there between
1861 and 1879 and who witnessed many of the events and changes which he records.
Black describes Japan's rapid evolution from a secluded, declining feudal society to a
modernising and Westernising nation. He portrays in considerable detail the early
hostility of the Japanese towards the Westerners among them, some of the diplomatic
struggles of the period, the life of the small foreign community at Yokohama, the civil
war which resulted in the overthrow of the Tokugawa shogunate, the new government
leadership, and noteworthy political, economic and diplomatic developments of the
early Meiji period. Black's book is useful as a first-hand source of historical
information and as a representative example of Western writing about Japan during
the nineteenth century.

163   **Treasures among men: the fudai daimyo in Tokugawa Japan.**
Harold Bolitho.   New Haven, Connecticut; London: Yale University
Press, 1974. 278p. bibliog. (Yale Historical Publications, Miscellany,
101).

An interpretive study of the Tokugawa political system that focuses on the role of the
fudai daimyō, a group of hereditary feudal lords who owed personal allegiance to the
Tokugawa shōgun and who served as powerful bureaucratic administrators in the
bakufu government. Bolitho considers the structure and interests of these daimyō,
their marriage policies, their treatment by the Tokugawa, their competition for and
rewards from *bakufu* office, and their influence on international policy. He argues that
these leaders were beset by competing claims upon their feudal loyalty and their local
and regional self-interest. These claims resulted not only in their systematic opposition
to Tokugawa efforts aimed at centralising government rule but also in their failure to
provide full-fledged support to the *bakufu* during the years of conflict that immediately
preceded the Meiji Restoration of 1868.

164   **Education in Tokugawa Japan.**
Ronald P. Dore.   Berkeley, California: University of California Press,
1965. 346p. map. bibliog. (Publications of the Center for Japanese and
Korean Studies). Reprinted, with a new preface, London: Athlone
Press; Ann Arbor, Michigan: Center for Japanese Studies, University
of Michigan, 1984.

A pioneering study of both government-sponsored and private education between the
mid-1700s and the mid-1800s and of its significance in paving the way for Meiji Japan's
industrialisation and modernisation. Dore first discusses the aims of samurai education,
the organisation of the schools, the atmosphere which prevailed within them, and their
traditional curriculum. He shows how these educational institutions created social
change by promoting a respect for ability and achievement that ran counter to and
gradually undermined the principle of hereditary status. Education among the
commoners, particularly in the *terakoya* schools that served the non-samurai masses, is
also examined. A concluding chapter entitled 'The Legacy' assesses the contributions
of Tokugawa education to Japan's subsequent economic growth through the creation
of widespread popular literacy and the inculcation of the basic values of economic
efficiency, social solidarity, and ameliorative paternalism.

165   **Everyday life in traditional Japan.**
Charles J. Dunn, drawings by Laurence Broderick.   London:
Batsford; New York: Putnam, 1969. 198p. map. bibliog. Reprinted,
Rutland, Vermont; Tokyo: Tuttle, 1972.

In this illustrated survey of daily life during the Tokugawa period, Dunn describes the
food, clothing, housing, work, recreational activities, beliefs, and fears of Japan's four
social classes – the samurai, farmers, craftsmen, and merchants – and of several non-
class groups: courtiers and courtesans of the imperial court at Kyōto, Shintō and
Buddhist priests, doctors and intellectuals, actors, and outcastes and outlaws. He
concludes with a portrayal of everyday affairs in Edo (Tokyo), the capital and centre of
Tokugawa political and social life. This work was also reprinted under the title
Everyday life in imperial Japan (New York: Dorset Press, 1989).

History. AD 1600–1868 (Tokugawa period)

166 **Deus destroyed: the image of Christianity in early modern Japan.**
George Elison. Cambridge, Massachusetts: Harvard University Press, 1973. 542p. bibliog. (Harvard East Asian Series, 72). Reprinted, Council on East Asian Studies, Harvard University; distributed by Harvard University Press, 1988.

A scholarly analysis of the problems which Christianity encountered as it first sought to be accepted and was then eventually rejected by the Japanese during the late sixteenth and early seventeenth centuries. Elison explores the attitudes and procedures of the Jesuit missionaries who propagated Christianity in Japan, describes their entanglements in domestic politics (entanglements which ultimately constituted a major factor in their rejection), and shows the many levels of the Japanese response to Christianity. He discusses the ideological conflict between Christian and Japanese values which led Japanese leaders to condemn this Western religion as subversive and inimical to their interests and to forbid its continued practice. Central to Elison's study are four polemical anti-Christian tracts, published between 1620 and 1662, which are also translated.

167 **Japan: the Dutch experience.**
Grant K. Goodman. London; Dover, New Hampshire: Athlone Press, 1986. 304p. bibliog.

Dutch maritime traders were the only Europeans with whom the Japanese maintained formal contact betwen 1640 and 1853. In this revision of his earlier study *The Dutch impact on Japan* (Leiden, The Netherlands: Brill, 1967, 242p.), Goodman describes and analyses the nature of Japanese interest in Western knowledge and techniques during the Tokugawa period and the ways in which they assimilated and utilised the information that could be obtained from the West through the medium of the Dutch language. Dealing with the position of the Dutch as transmitters of Western knowledge, with the gradual spread of interest in 'Dutch learning' (*Rangaku*) throughout much of Japan (initially in such areas as medicine and astronomy and eventually in additional spheres of Western science and culture), and with the actual contents of this learning, Goodman demonstrates the nature and extent of the impact which the Dutch had on Japanese intellectual life during the two centuries that preceded the reopening of Japan to the West.

168 **Studies in the institutional history of early modern Japan.**
Edited by John Whitney Hall, Marius B. Jansen, introduction by Joseph R. Strayer. Princeton, New Jersey: Princeton University Press, 1968. 396p.

Twenty-one studies of Tokugawa institutional development collectively document the responsiveness of some of Japan's political, social, and economic institutions to changes that occurred during that era. Grouped together into three major parts – 'The Establishment of Daimyo Rule', 'Daimyo Rule in Castle Town and Village', and 'Late Tokugawa' – these essays include several case-studies of the feudal domains (*han*) of Bizen, Chōshū, Satsuma, and Tosa; studies of administration at the village level; articles about the significance of the Tokugawa period for Japan's successful modernisation after the Meiji Restoration (1868); and assessments of Tokugawa period achievements in the areas of education and law. The majority of these essays first appeared as articles published in leading historical journals of the 1950s and 1960s.

169 **Economic and demographic change in preindustrial Japan, 1600–1868.**
Susan B. Hanley, Kozo Yamamura. Princeton, New Jersey;
Guildford, Surrey: Princeton University Press, 1978. 409p. bibliog.
A reinterpretation of Tokugawa economic history through an investigation of
demographic changes and their relationship to economic change. Using a range of
national, regional, and village-level data, Hanley and Yamamura advance and test
three basic hypotheses. They suggest that the economy expanded throughout the
Tokugawa period, even though growth was slow by modern standards and uneven.
They argue that the rate of economic growth tended to exceed the rate of population
increase even in the poorer regions of Japan, thereby raising overall living standards.
Finally, they contend that a variety of family planning methods (including abortion and
infanticide) were widely used to control population growth specifically for the purpose
of maximising family income and improving per capita standards of living.

170 **Economic institutional change in Tokugawa Japan: Ōsaka and the Kinai
cotton trade.**
William B. Hauser. London; New York: Cambridge University Press,
1974. 239p. 3 maps. bibliog.
A case-study of the processes of institutional change during the eighteenth and early
nineteenth centuries in the most economically advanced area of Tokugawa Japan: the
city of Ōsaka and the three provinces of the surrounding Kinai region. Hauser opens
by describing the characteristics of Tokugawa period commercial activity, including the
expansion of trade, the growth of marketing systems, and the appearance of functional
differentiation in the mercantile community. He then details the establishment,
consolidation, and institutional decline of the Ōsaka cotton trade as he discusses such
topics as the city's role as a centre for marketing and processing cotton, and the efforts
of its merchants to establish and maintain their trade rights to this commodity. He also
examines the expansion and impact of cotton cultivation and processing in the Kinai
region, and the roles played by rural merchants and cotton cultivators as they
increasingly challenged the monopoly rights of the Ōsaka cotton merchants. Finally,
the author enumerates the implications of his study for understanding Tokugawa
period economic and social change.

171 **The revolutionary origins of modern Japan.**
Thomas M. Huber. Stanford, California: Stanford University Press,
1981. 260p. map. bibliog.
Huber challenges the popular view that the Meiji Restoration was a 'revolution from
above', and contends that it was in fact a revolt from below, carried out by a service
intelligentsia of minor administrators, priests, scholars, and village officials who
advocated the establishment of a government led by individuals selected on the basis of
merit rather than birth and feudal privilege. He focuses on the politically most active
group of Restoration leaders during the 1850s and 1860s – those who were from
Chōshū *han* – and pays particular attention to the brilliant political thinker Yoshida
Shōin and two of his disciples, Kusaka Genzui and Takasugi Shinsaku. In a sequence
of political biographies, Huber investigates their social and educational backgrounds,
their motivations and frustrations, and their intellectual and political struggles. A
different interpretation of the Chōshū *han* activists may be found in Albert M. Craig's
Chōshū in the Meiji Restoration (Cambridge, Massachusetts: Harvard University Press,
1961, 385p.), which describes Chōshū's position in the Tokugawa polity, its class and

governmental structures, its finances, and its climate of ideas before 1858, and analyses the ways in which these factors decisively influenced Chōshū's role in the Restoration movement of the 1860s.

172 Epidemics and mortality in early modern Japan.

Ann Bowman Jannetta. Princeton, New Jersey; Guildford, Surrey: Princeton University Press, 1987. 224p. 2 maps. bibliog.

A scholarly inquiry into the epidemic diseases of the Tokugawa period and their impact on population growth. Utilising contemporary medical literature, evidence from Buddhist temple death registers, and documentation left by eyewitness observers, Jannetta shows that smallpox was endemic, accounting for the deaths of many young children. Epidemics of such other major diseases as measles, dysentery, cholera, and typhus, however, were uncommon before the mid-nineteenth century, in part because of the government's strictly enforced policy of national isolation (which limited their importation from the West) and because of certain prevailing hygienic practices within the large cities. Jannetta suggests that positive measures of population control such as abortion and infanticide – rather than disease-induced widespread mortality – may well account for the stagnation of population growth during the last century and a half of Tokugawa rule.

173 The Japanese discovery of Europe, 1720–1830.

Donald Keene. Stanford, California: Stanford University Press, 1969. rev. ed. 255p. map. bibliog.

An account of the growth and uses of Western learning in Japan, with particular focus on the career and writings of the political economist and navigator Honda Toshiaki (1744-1821). Covering such topics as the activities of the Dutch in Japan, Russia's territorial expansion and its perceived threat to Japan, Honda's economic theories, and Hirata Atsutane and Western learning, Keene's book examines mid-Tokugawa period views of Europe and of European knowledge as well as the penetration of Western ideas and culture into Japan and its impact on Japanese intellectual life. An appendix contains translations of major portions of Honda's chief works: *A secret plan for managing the country* (*Keisei hisaku*) and *Tales of the West* (*Saiiki monogatari*). Keene's study was first published as *The Japanese discovery of Europe: Honda Toshiaki and other discoverers, 1720–1798* (London: Kegan Paul, 1952; New York: Grove Press, 1954, 246p.).

174 Kanazawa: a seventeenth-century Japanese castle town.

James L. McClain. New Haven, Connecticut; London: Yale University Press, 1982. 209p. 11 maps. bibliog. (Yale Historical Publications, Miscellany, 128).

A detailed study of the emergence and development of the castle town of Kanazawa, the administrative and military headquarters of the Maeda daimyō situated along the coast of the Sea of Japan, into a large and thriving city whose population rivalled that of Rome and Madrid in size. McClain describes and evaluates the interaction and contributions of the Maeda family, its samurai-staffed bureaucracy, and local merchants and artisans to Kanazawa's rapid growth between 1583 and 1700. Throughout his book, he discusses the use of space and urban planning as well as the political system and administration of the city. In addition, McClain depicts the society and culture of Kanazawa by examining such aspects of the city's life as its residential patterns, occupational activities, and forms of recreation. This account is valuable for understanding not only early Tokugawa period history but also Japan's premodern transformation into one of the most urbanised societies in the world.

175 **Conflict in modern Japanese history: the neglected tradition.**
Edited by Tetsuo Najita, J. Victor Koschmann. Princeton, New Jersey; Guildford, Surrey: Princeton University Press, 1982. 456p.

Eighteen American and Japanese scholars contend that postwar historians have generally stressed the role of consensus and harmony in modern Japanese history, and have mistakenly regarded conflict and disturbances in Japan 'as aberrations in an otherwise orderly flow of events'. In an effort to modify this view and to offer some new perspectives on the Japanese historical experience, they examine the peasant rebellions, insurrections, assassinations, suicides, urban riots, strikes, student uprisings, and coups which occurred during the 1850s and 1860s, and between the 1890s and the late 1920s. Their volume includes essays entitled 'Action as a Text: Ideology in the Tengu Insurrection'; 'The Social Background of Peasant Uprisings in Tokugawa Japan'; 'From Reformism to Transformism: Bakufu Policy, 1853-1868'; 'The Emperor and the Crowd: The Historical Significance of the Hibiya Riot'; 'Generational Conflict after the Russo-Japanese War'; 'Liberal Intellectuals and Social Conflict in Taishō Japan'; and 'In Search of Equity: Japanese Tenant Unions in the 1920s'.

176 **Visions of virtue in Tokugawa Japan: the Kaitokudō Merchant Academy of Osaka.**
Tetsuo Najita. Chicago; London: University of Chicago Press, 1987. 334p.

A major reassessment of Tokugawa social thought that focuses on the metamorphosis of merchant thinking during the eighteenth and early nineteenth centuries and on the thriving Kaitokudō Merchant Academy as a centre of scholarly learning. Najita shows how ideas of political economy and concepts of scientific inquiry which evolved at the academy came to interact broadly with new theories of knowledge, 'beginning with queries about the relevance of "virtue" to merchants and leading to larger issues: the representation of political history, the understanding of ethics through appeals to either nature or history, and the validity of general education for commoners'.

177 **Shogunal politics: Arai Hakuseki and the premises of Tokugawa rule.**
Kate Wildman Nakai. Cambridge, Massachusetts: Council on East Asian Studies, Harvard University, 1988. 427p. bibliog. (Harvard East Asian Monographs, 134).

Arai Hakuseki (1657-1725), a personal advisor to two Tokugawa shōguns, played a critical role in *bakufu* politics between 1709 and 1716 and endeavoured to transform 'the bakufu into a monarchy and the shogun into a full-fledged national sovereign'. Nakai explores the background factors that shaped Hakuseki's political perspective and aspirations, paying particular attention not only to the place of the shōgunal circle within *bakufu* politics but also to the nuances of Hakuseki's position within that circle. She examines Hakuseki's fiscal and economic policies, analyses his approach to the *bakufu*'s role in popular governance and to the structure of *bakufu* administration, and investigates his efforts to 'reshape the symbolic manifestations of shogunal authority'. Finally, Nakai considers the ways in which Hakuseki's reform programme sought to apply the norms of Chinese Confucian political theory to Tokugawa political life, examines the opposition he encountered, and discusses his arguments in defence of the policies that he strongly advocated. The bureaucratic, political, and economic aspects of a subsequent series of major Tokugawa period reform programmes – the *bakufu*'s Kansei Reforms of 1787–93 – are in turn examined in Herman Ooms' *Charismatic bureaucrat: a political biography of Matsudaira Sadanobu, 1758–1829* (Chicago; London: University of Chicago Press, 1975, 225p.).

178 Tokugawa ideology: early constructs, 1570–1680.
Herman Ooms.   Princeton, New Jersey; Guildford, Surrey: Princeton University Press, 1985. 349p. bibliog.

A scholarly study of intellectual trends during the seventeenth century which challenges prevailing views about the monolithic nature of the new ideology that was created to legitimise Tokugawa rule. Instead of being monopolised by Chu Hsi Neo-Confucianism, the official ideology of the Tokugawa shogunate is shown to have been eclectic in nature and to have been based on Shintō, Buddhism, and folk religion as well as on Confucianism. By way of illustration, Ooms surveys the writings of a wide range of thinkers from that period who were closely identified with the Tokugawa state, among them Fujiwara Seika, Hayashi Razan, Suzuki Shōsan, and Yamazaki Ansai.

179 Historical Nagasaki.
Herbert E. Plutschow.   Tokyo: Japan Times, 1983. 153p. 7 maps. bibliog.

A general history of the city of Nagasaki, illustrated with many period woodblock prints and drawings, from its founding in the late sixteenth century to Japan's opening to the West in the mid-nineteenth century. Particular attention is paid to the interaction of its residents with the Western (especially Dutch) and Chinese traders who came to this port, as well as to the government's persecution of Japanese Christians living in and around Nasgasaki in the early 1600s and to Nagasaki's subsequent role as a major source of transmission for the Western science that was introduced into Japan by the Dutch. Several guide maps identify the present location of various Catholic churches, historical residences, and other historic sites referred to in the text. Many additional illustrations of Nagasaki, its port and harbour, and its Dutch and Chinese residents during the Tokugawa period may be found in *A collection of Nagasaki colour prints and paintings: showing the influence of Chinese and European art on that of Japan*, by N. H. N. Mody (Rutland, Vermont; Tokyo: Tuttle, 1969, new ed., xii p., 250 plates).

180 Private academies of Tokugawa Japan.
Richard Rubinger.   Princeton, New Jersey; Guildford, Surrey: Princeton University Press, 1982. 282p. 7 maps. bibliog.

An examination of the role of *shijuku* (private academies of advanced studies that were open to commoners and low-ranking samurai) in preparing Japan for her modern transformation. Rubinger classifies these academies according to their areas of specialisation (e.g., Chinese studies, Dutch studies, *kokugaku* or 'national learning'), considers them in his case-studies of several representative institutions, and discusses their general characteristics, educational approaches and curricula, administration, levels of teaching, atmosphere and regulations, and student bodies. He shows how these schools tended to undermine the Tokugawa feudal order, 'strengthened the development of a more integrated "national" culture', and contributed to the education of some of Meiji Japan's early leaders.

181 **The agrarian origins of modern Japan.**
Thomas C. Smith.   Stanford, California: Stanford University Press,
1959. 250p. map. bibliog. (Stanford Studies in the Civilizations of
Eastern Asia). Reprinted, New York: Atheneum, 1966; Stanford
University Press, 1984.

A pioneering analysis of Japan's premodern agrarian village society and economy and
of the changes within it – in particular, the transition from a society based on status to
one based on contract – that came about in part because of the commercialisation of
agriculture and that contributed to Japan's rapid modernisation during the Meiji
period. Smith first examines the traditional village with respect to the land system,
agricultural servants and labour services, the small landholdings, and the organisation
of political power based on co-operative agricultural groupings with enormous power
over their members. He then traces the transformation of the village during the
Tokugawa period through studies of the growth of commercial farming, the advance of
agricultural technology and rising agricultural productivity, changes in patterns of
labour, the shift from co-operative family groups to individual farms, the emergence of
landlord–tenant relations, and intra-village political conflict.

182 **Nakahara: family farming and population in a Japanese village,
1717–1830.**
Thomas C. Smith, with Robert Y. Eng, Robert T. Lundy.   Stanford,
California: Stanford University Press, 1977. 183p. bibliog.

Smith analyses the population and tax registers of the village of Nakahara (a
pseudonymous farming community located in present-day Gifu Prefecture) in order to
reconstruct the relationship between demography and economic development during
the latter half of the Tokugawa period. He finds that both mortality and registered
fertility rates were low to moderate when compared with eighteenth-century European
rural parishes. Low registered fertility was primarily the result of sex-selective
infanticide, a commonly practised form of family planning that enabled peasants to
plan the sex composition and ultimate size of their families, maintain efficient
operation of their agrarian landholdings, and significantly increase agricultural
production and personal income on a per capita basis. Smith's lucidly written study
sheds considerable light on the economic preconditions of Japan's modern industrialisation.

183 **Native sources of Japanese industrialization, 1750–1920.**
Thomas C. Smith.   Berkeley, California; London: University of
California Press, 1988. 278p. 4 maps.

A collection of ten essays written by a distinguished historian of Japan that focus on
the factors which 'contributed to making modern Japanese society similar to but
profoundly different from Western counterparts'. Initially published between 1958 and
1986, these essays cover such topics in social history as the effect of the land tax on
Tokugawa peasants, the importance of farm family by-employment in preindustrial
Japan, peasant families and population control during the eighteenth century, the
conflict between the feudal ideal of hereditary personal service defined by rank and the
Confucian and bureaucratic ideal of meritocratic appointment to office, and the
concept of social justice ('the right to benevolence') among factory workers between
1890 and 1920.

184 **Japanese inn.**
Oliver Statler. New York: Random House; London: Secker and
Warburg, 1961. 360p. 2 maps. Reprinted, Honolulu, Hawaii: University
of Hawaii Press, 1982; London: Pan, 1985.
A delightful, literary recreation of the social history of Japan by means of a
fictionalised account of the Minaguchi-ya, an inn founded about 1582 in the coastal
village of Okitsu along the major transportation route between Edo (Tokyo) and
Kyōto known as the Tōkaidō. Operated uninterruptedly by twenty generations of the
Mochizuki family, this hotel witnesses the comings and goings of numerous travellers
and guests from the early Tokugawa period through the mid-1950s. Among them are
warriors, pilgrims and lovers, artists and poets, Dutch merchants, prominent
individuals, and even the emperor and empress. Their stories are intertwined with the
centuries-long history of the inn and its owners as well as with Japanese history.
Reproductions of old prints and drawings (many of them by the late Tokugawa period
ukiyo-e artist Katsushika Hokusai) illustrate this well-researched, best-selling work of
historical fiction.

185 **Politics in the Tokugawa bakufu, 1600–1843.**
Conrad D. Totman. Cambridge, Massachusetts: Harvard University
Press, 1967. 346p. 9 maps. bibliog. (Harvard East Asian Series, 30).
Reprinted with a new preface, Berkeley, California; London:
University of California Press, 1989.
A detailed description and analysis of the operative political organisation and
leadership of the central government of Japan as it evolved out of the Tokugawa
family's early private government into a sophisticated administrative system and
complex political instrument. Totman opens with a discussion of the early growth and
structure of the political unit known as the 'Tokugawa house' and with examinations of
its formal organisation, the Tokugawa military system, Tokugawa fiscal arrangements
and revenue sources, the physical set-up and politics of the shōguns' castle
headquarters at Edo, and the character of the major groups (the 'related daimyo',
'liege vassals' or *hatamoto* and *gokenin*, and 'vassal daimyo' or *fudai*) which played a
role in Tokugawa affairs. He then describes the 'informal, internal power structure and
the operating techniques' of the Tokugawa leadership, and concludes by tracing the
gradual evolution of *bakufu* leadership between the early seventeenth century and the
mid-1800s.

186 **The collapse of the Tokugawa bakufu, 1862–1868.**
Conrad Totman. Honolulu, Hawaii: University Press of Hawaii, 1980.
588p. 5 maps. bibliog.
A detailed investigation of the events which led to the collapse of the Tokugawa
shogunate (*bakufu*) and the destruction of the political system under which Japan had
enjoyed some 250 years of peace. Totman discusses the political, economic, and
military predicaments of the Tokugawa government during the years immediately
preceding the Meiji Restoration. He details the efforts of *bakufu* officials to respond
effectively to the constant demands that were being made by the British, the
Americans, and other foreigners during the 1860s, and he describes the civil and
military reforms which the authorities introduced in an attempt to reassert Tokugawa
hegemony over all of Japan. Totman concludes that the Tokugawa régime fell because
of the intrusion of Western imperialism and the Tokugawa inability to cope with the
ensuing political crisis.

187 **Historical development of science and technology in Japan.**
Edited by Hideomi Tuge [Tsuge]. Tokyo: Kokusai Bunka Shinkokai
(Japan Cultural Society), 1968. 200p. map. (Japanese Life and Culture
Series).

A very general survey of the historical development of geography, biology, medicine, chemistry, mathematics, astronomy, physics (including geophysics), engineering, agriculture, and geology. Primarily factual in nature and chronological in orientation, Tuge's book focuses on science and technology during the Tokugawa, Meiji, Taishō, and early Shōwa periods.

188 **The Japanese imperial institution in the Tokugawa period.**
Herschel Webb. New York; London: Columbia University Press,
1968. 296p. bibliog. (Studies of the East Asian Institute, Columbia
University).

An analysis of the character and status of the imperial institution during the Tokugawa period. Webb first surveys the evolution of this institution and its changing relationship to political power over the course of a thousand years. He then describes imperial court life and institutions in Kyōto during the 1600s and 1700s, focusing particularly on the emperors, the other members of the imperial family, and the *kuge* or hereditary court nobility. Finally, the author studies the type of Tokugawa period thought and writing known as *kinnō* or 'imperial loyalism' with its stress on the centrality of the imperial institution, and the emergence of the imperial throne in national politics during the 1840s and 1850s, as members of the court began publicly to express their views on matters of national policy and as the throne became the ideological rallying point for the opposition to the Tokugawa shogunate. Japanese attitudes towards the emperor and pre-Meiji concepts of patriotism are also examined in David Magarey Earl's *Emperor and nation in Japan: political thinkers of the Tokugawa period* (Seattle, Washington: University of Washington Press, 1964, 270p.; Reprinted, Westport, Connecticut: Greenwood Press, 1981), a work that contains a case-study of the application of loyalist and patriotic theories in the life and ideas of the mid-nineteenth century samurai scholar Yoshida Shōin.

Sources of Japanese tradition.
See item no. 33.

Victorians in Japan: in and around the treaty ports.
See item no. 68.

The Christian century in Japan, 1549–1650.
See item no. 129.

The southern barbarians: the first Europeans in Japan.
See item no. 132.

Feudalism in Japan.
See item no. 134.

Government and local power in Japan, 500 to 1700: a study based on Bizen Province.
See item no. 138.

History. AD 1600–1868 (Tokugawa period)

Japan before Tokugawa: political consolidation and economic growth, 1500 to 1650.
See item no. 139.

The bakufu in Japanese history.
See item no. 146.

A history of Japanese astronomy: Chinese background and Western impact.
See item no. 151.

Japan: a history in art.
See item no. 155.

The way of the samurai.
See item no. 156.

Science and culture in traditional Japan, A.D. 600–1854.
See item no. 157.

The book of the samurai: the warrior class of Japan.
See item no. 158.

The coming of the barbarians: a story of Western settlements in Japan, 1853–1870.
See item no. 190.

The Meiji Restoration.
See item no. 191.

Meiji ishin: restoration and revolution.
See item no. 191.

Meiji 1868: revolution and counter-revolution in Japan.
See item no. 191.

Kikkoman: company, clan, and community.
See item no. 201.

The development of Japanese business, 1600–1980.
See item no. 208.

Japan and its world: two centuries of change.
See item no. 211.

Japan in transition: from Tokugawa to Meiji.
See item no. 212.

Deference and defiance in nineteenth-century Japan.
See item no. 213.

Origins of the modern Japanese state: selected writings of E. H. Norman.
See item no. 226.

Mitsui: three centuries of Japanese business.
See item no. 231.

Japan in the Victorian mind: a study of stereotyped images of a nation 1850–80.
See item no. 251.

Personality in Japanese history.
See item no. 289.

The nobility of failure: tragic heroes in the history of Japan.
See item no. 293.

Great historical figures of Japan.
See item no. 295.

Told round a brushwood fire: the autobiography of Arai Hakuseki.
See item no. 298.

Motoori Norinaga, 1730–1801.
See item no. 309.

Tokugawa Ieyasu: shogun.
See item no. 314.

Dr. Willis in Japan, 1862–1877: British medical pioneer.
See item no. 353.

Mitford's Japan: the memoirs and recollections, 1866–1906, of Algernon Bertram Mitford, the first Lord Redesdale.
See item no. 357.

Biographical dictionary of Japanese history.
See item no. 367.

Tokugawa religion: the values of pre-industrial Japan.
See item no. 459.

Religion in Japanese history.
See item no. 465.

Japanese Buddhism.
See item no. 475.

Confucianism and Tokugawa culture.
See item no. 526.

Hagakure: the book of the samurai.
See item no. 529.

The code of the samurai.
See item no. 529.

Social change and the city in Japan: from earliest times through the industrial revolution.
See item no. 546.

Western medical pioneers in feudal Japan.
See item no. 596.

History. 1868–1945 (Meiji, Taishō, and early Shōwa periods)

A diplomat in Japan: the inner history of the critical years in the evolution of Japan when the ports were opened and the monarchy restored.
See item no. 675.

Conciliation and Japanese law: Tokugawa and modern.
See item no. 778.

Silence.
See item no. 1055.

Before the dawn.
See item no. 1094.

Musashi.
See item no. 1109.

Chūshingura: an exposition.
See item no. 1180.

Japan: the shaping of daimyo culture, 1185–1868.
See item no. 1218.

Japan: photographs, 1854–1905.
See item no. 1278.

Once upon a time: visions of old Japan.
See item no. 1278.

Ninjutsu: the art of invisibility; Japan's feudal-age espionage methods.
See item no. 1445.

Monumenta Nipponica: Studies in Japanese Culture.
See item no. 1534.

The Princeton companion to classical Japanese literature.
See item no. 1566.

1868–1945 (Meiji, Taishō, and early Shōwa periods)

189 **Foundations of constitutional government in modern Japan, 1868–1900.**
George Akita. Cambridge, Massachusetts: Harvard University Press, 1967. 292p. bibliog. (Harvard East Asian Series, 23).

A reinterpretation of the constitutional development of the Meiji state. Contending that the Meiji oligarchs were 'enlightened elitists', Akita shows that the Meiji Constitution was not forced upon them by 'public opinion' or by the participants in the movement for parliamentary government but was freely granted in the belief that constitutionalism was inextricably tied to Japan's success in becoming a strong and modern nation. He demonstrates that the Meiji leadership recognised the necessity of sharing power with the newly-created national Diet but sought to ensure that it would be 'partial, gradual, and carefully hedged' by the provisions of the constitution. Akita indicates how and why the oligarchs erroneously believed that they could control Japan's new parliamentary government; for instead of serving as their tool for legitimising authoritarianism, the Meiji Constitution became a weapon which Japan's party politicians exploited in order to weaken oligarchic control after 1890. An extensively annotated text of the Meiji Constitution may be found in Johannes Siemes' study, *Hermann Roesler and the making of the Meiji state: an examination of his background and his influence on the founders of modern Japan & the complete text of the Meiji Constitution accompanied by his personal commentaries and notes* (Tokyo: Sophia University, in co-operation with Tuttle, 1968, 252p.).

190 **The Deer Cry Pavilion: a story of Westerners in Japan 1868–1905.**
Pat Barr.   London: Macmillan, 1968; New York: Harcourt, Brace and World, 1969. 282p. 2 maps. bibliog. Reprinted, London: Penguin, 1988.

A general account of Meiji Japan viewed 'through the eyes of Westerners who were involved in its process of rapid modernisation'. Drawing upon contemporary American and European writings, Barr paints a series of vignettes in which she describes the activities and travels of such Westerners as Isabella Bird, William Elliot Griffis, Lafcadio Hearn, and Sir Ernest Satow; describes the life of the communities in which they lived and the Japanese manners and customs which they observed; and shows how the Japanese government's policy of modernisation affected their personal lives and those of the Japanese around them. This book constitutes a sequel to the author's earlier work about the opening of Japan to the West, *The coming of the barbarians: a story of Western settlements in Japan, 1853–1870* (London: Macmillan, 1967, 236p. Reprinted, Rutland, Vermont and Tokyo: Tuttle, 1972).

191 **The Meiji Restoration.**
William Gerald Beasley.   Stanford, California: Stanford University Press, 1972; London: Oxford University Press, 1973. 513p. map. bibliog.

An account and interpretation of the origins, development, and immediate aftermath of the Meiji Restoration (1868) – the biggest revolutionary change in Japanese history – which witnessed the demise of Japan's system of feudal government and the rise of a modern imperial state. Beasley explores the domestic and foreign problems that confronted the Tokugawa shogunate between the 1840s and the 1860s, details the process of the restoration itself, and discusses the initial activities and early reforms of the new Meiji government. He characterises the restoration as a 'nationalist revolution', attributing its root origins to a growing sense of national danger and national pride stimulated by Japan's early contacts with the imperialist West, rather than to contemporary economic distress or class struggle. In view of the significance of the Meiji Restoration in Japanese history, historians will also welcome the publication of *Meiji ishin: restoration and revolution*, edited by Michio Nagai and Miguel Urrutia (Tokyo: United Nations University, 1985, 225p.), which brings together the divergent views of a number of American, Chinese, Japanese, and Soviet scholars; while Paul Akamatsu's *Meiji 1868: revolution and counter-revolution in Japan*, translated from the French by Miriam Kochan (London: Allen and Unwin; New York: Harper and Row, 1972, 330p.) will particularly appeal to general readers seeking an overview of the decline of Tokugawa power and the establishment of the new Meiji government.

History. 1868–1945 (Meiji, Taishō, and early Shōwa periods)

192   The Japanese Communist Party, 1922–1945.
George M. Beckmann, Genji Ōkubo.   Stanford, California: Stanford
University Press, 1969. 453p. bibliog.
An exhaustive, chronological narrative (rather than an interpretive history) of the
prewar development of the Japanese Communist Party (JCP), focusing on the decade
between its founding in 1922 and its suppression and fragmentation in 1932. A
background chapter on the history of revolutionary socialism in Japan before the 1920s
is followed by an examination of each historical phase of the party's history. Beckmann
and Ōkubo provide a wealth of detailed information about JCP activities, leadership,
personalities, social and intellectual problems, ideas and conflicts, theoretical concerns,
political aspects, party platforms, and international relations. Appendixes contain
translations of key party documents, biographical sketches of fifty-eight leading
Communists, and a chronology of major developments between April 1921 and
January 1946. Part one of *Red flag in Japan: international communism in action,
1919–1951*, by Rodger Swearingen and Paul Langer (Cambridge, Massachusetts:
Harvard University Press, 1952, 276p. Reprinted, New York: Greenwood Press, 1968),
gives a more interpretive account of prewar JCP history, while its concluding parts
offer an analytical overview of the immediate postwar scene.

193   Parties out of power in Japan, 1931–1941.
Gordon Mark Berger.   Princeton, New Jersey; Guildford, Surrey:
Princeton University Press, 1977. 413p. bibliog.
An examination of the 'political party as a vehicle for the acquisition, allocation, and
exercise of political power in late imperial Japan'. Following an overview of the
sources of party power during the early Shōwa period, Berger studies the extent,
causes, and dynamics of the decline of the political parties as holders of power and the
concomitant rise of military influence in domestic politics during the 1930s. He also
explores the political struggle of the parties to regain influence in the late 1930s and
examines their relationship to the efforts that were under way at that time to mobilise
the entire nation for war with China. Berger concludes that the parties were able to
preserve an important share of their earlier power throughout the war years and that
they re-emerged in 1945 as experienced performers of political tasks which were vital
for Japan's postwar survival.

194   The Japanese enlightenment: a study of the writings of Fukuzawa
Yukichi.
Carmen Blacker.   Cambridge, England: Cambridge University Press,
1964. 186p. bibliog. (University of Cambridge Oriental Publications,
10).
A concise, lucid exposition of the writings of the great philosopher Fukuzawa Yukichi
(1835-1901), the 'most comprehensive exponent of the doctrines of Enlightenment'
during the Meiji period. Showing him to be a caustic critic of traditional learning,
Blacker discusses the ideological background of the era, Fukuzawa's rejection of
traditional Confucian precepts, his belief that Eastern ethics and Western science were
incompatible, and his views of the new ethical values, modern family relationships,
the new approaches to the study of history, Western political philosophy, and the
principles which governed the relations between nations. Of related interest are four
published translations of Fukuzawa's writings: *An encouragement of learning*,
translated by David A. Dilworth and Umeyo Hirano (Tokyo: Sophia University, 1969,
128p.), which criticises old ways of thought in early Meiji Japan and promotes new,

modern values; *An outline of a theory of civilization*, translated by David A. Dilworth and G. Cameron Hurst (Tokyo: Sophia University, 1973, 205p.), which inquires into the nature of civilisation in the West at a time when Western customs and institutions were attracting considerable Japanese interest; *The speeches of Fukuzawa: a translation and critical study*, by Wayne H. Oxford (Tokyo: Hokuseido Press, 1973, 281p.); and *Fukuzawa Yukichi on Japanese women: selected works*, translated and edited by Eiichi Kiyooka (Tokyo: University of Tokyo Press, 1988, 270p.).

195 **Rebellion and democracy in Meiji Japan: a study of commoners in the popular rights movement.**
Roger W. Bowen. Berkeley, California; London: University of California Press, 1980. 367p. 4 maps. bibliog.

A study at the grassroots level of both the *jiyū minken undō* ('the movement for freedom and popular rights') of the late 1870s and early 1880s and the rural-based popular uprisings that challenged the authority of the new Meiji government. Focusing on three 'incidents of intense violence' that occurred in regions north of Tokyo – the Fukushima Incident of 1882 and the Kabasan and Chichibu Incidents of 1884 – Bowen describes the dynamics of these unsuccessful rebellions and examines their historical, social, economic, and political background. He also identifies their participants and describes their socio-economic attributes; analyses the political beliefs and consciousness of their leaders and followers as well as the nature of the rural-based popular rights' societies and similar political groups to which they belonged; and assesses some of the consequences of these uprisings for subsequent democratic movements in Japan.

196 **Meiroku zasshi: journal of the Japanese enlightenment.**
Translated with an introduction by William Reynolds Braisted, assisted by Yasushi Adachi, Yūji Kikuchi. Cambridge, Massachusetts: Harvard University Press; Tokyo: University of Tokyo Press, 1976. 532p.

The *Meiroku zasshi*, a journal published between 1873 and 1875 that introduced mid-nineteenth century European and American culture into Japan, is regarded as an important contemporary source for understanding the thinking of several leading Meiji exponents of Westernisation and modernisation. The journal's contributors wrote about a wide range of concerns such as the nature of knowledge, a popularly elected assembly, the separation of church and state, economic policy, free trade, language reform, the status of women, and the concepts of 'liberty', 'freedom', and 'right'. Braisted's beautifully rendered translation makes available the views of prominent intellectuals which were vigorously promoted at that time and which influenced the nation builders of Meiji Japan in a number of significant ways.

197 **The modernizers: overseas students, foreign employees, and Meiji Japan.**
Edited with an introduction by Ardath W. Burks. Boulder, Colorado; London: Westview Press, 1985. 450p. bibliog. (A Westview Replica Edition).

A collection of essays by Japanese and Western scholars concerning early Meiji Japan's process of modernisation. The volume examines the Tokugawa historical background, the pursuit of overseas study of Japanese students, the Meiji government's employment of foreign advisers and teachers, the critical role played by education in

1868–1945 (Meiji, Taishō, and early Shōwa periods)

the modernisation of Japan, and some of the contributions made by foreign teachers and returning Japanese students. Individual essays deal with such topics as tradition and change in the feudal domains (*han*) of Fukui and Kaga, government policy towards hired foreigners, David Murray's contributions to the modernisation of school administration, William Elliot Griffis and Japan, and American–Japanese scientific and cultural contacts in the late nineteenth century. The employment of American and European educators, technicians, and financial and legal advisers by the Meiji government to assist in Japan's early modernisation is examined at greater length in *Live machines: hired foreigners and Meiji Japan*, by H. J. Jones (Vancouver, British Columbia: University of British Columbia Press, 1980, 210p.).

198 **Party rivalry and political change in Taishō Japan.**
Peter Duus. Cambridge, Massachusetts: Harvard University Press, 1968. 317p. bibliog. (Harvard East Asian Series, 35).

An examination of the gradual emergence of a two-party political system in the national Diet, 1912-27, with particular focus on Hara Kei (Seiyūkai leader and premier, 1918-21) and Katō Kōmei (Kenseikai leader and premier, 1924-26). Duus traces the growth of the political parties as respectable elements on the political scene, and analyses the tactical and policy objectives as well as the rivalry of the two major parties and their leaders within the Diet. He describes the consolidation of the parties during World War I, their maneuverings in the pursuit of power, and their respective successes as first Hara, then Katō became prime minister of Japan. Duus also considers the efforts of the Seiyūkai and the Kenseikai in dealing with the political unrest which coincided with the establishment of party cabinets as well as the ways in which inter-party rivalry affected their responses to this problem.

199 **The search for a new order: intellectuals and fascism in prewar Japan.**
William Miles Fletcher, III. Chapel Hill, North Carolina: University of North Carolina Press, 1982. 226p. bibliog.

A scholarly investigation of the thought and behaviour of three politically active intellectuals and of their role in the formulation of fascist ideas and programmes during the 1930s. Rōyama Masamichi (a distinguished political scientist; 1895-1980), Ryū Shintarō (an economist and an editor of the newspaper *Asahi Shimbun*; 1900-67), and Miki Kiyoshi (an eminent philosopher; 1895-1945) all became influential members of the Shōwa Kenkyūkai (Shōwa Research Association), an advisory body to three-times prime minister Konoe Fumimaro. Fletcher investigates their intellectual development and concerns, explores their attraction to European fascism, and examines their contributions to research studies and proposals that advocated the restructuring of the Japanese state and drastic reforms of its economic and political systems.

200 **Technology and agricultural development in pre-war Japan.**
Penelope Francks. New Haven, Connecticut; London: Yale University Press, 1984. 322p. 4 maps. bibliog.

A microeconomic study of the change brought about by innovations in irrigation technology within the rice-growing Saga Plain of northwestern Kyūshū. Francks describes how the introduction of new cultivation techniques, improved strains of rice, and, in particular, relatively cheap electric pumps which replaced the labour-intensive process of pumping water into the rice paddies from the surrounding creeks dramatically increased crop yields and roughly tripled per capita output between the 1880s and the 1930s, while reducing the demands for long-term agricultural labour. She also discusses the ways in which local social organisation as well as co-operation among local farmers and regional agricultural officials assisted in the introduction and diffusion of this new technology.

201 **Kikkoman: company, clan, and community.**
W. Mark Fruin. Cambridge, Massachusetts; London: Harvard University Press, 1983. 358p. (Harvard Studies in Business History, 35).

The history of a major industrial enterprise that has become the world's leading producer of soy sauce. Basing his microeconomic study primarily on company archives, Fruin examines Kikkoman's metamorphosis from a small-scale, family-controlled and managed business (established in the early 1660s) into a modern, diversified, multinational corporation employing new mass-production technologies, professionalised management, and an extensive labour force. He also interweaves the history of the company with the history of both the agricultural village/company town of Noda (Chiba Prefecture) in which Kikkoman was founded and remains headquartered and the clan (the interrelated Mogi and Takanishi families) which has operated it, and he shows how changes in the composition of the community and in the conception of the family brought about a transformation of the company's business practices. The growth and the problems experienced by the Noda Shōyu Corporation (as Kikkoman was known before 1964) from the early Meiji period through the 1940s are covered in detail.

202 **The state and labor in modern Japan.**
Sheldon Garon. Berkeley, California; London: University of California Press, 1988. 326p. bibliog.

An examination of the 'Japanese leadership's consideration of a series of often conflicting social policies vis-à-vis industrial labor'. Garon studies the origins of Japanese social policy (1868-1918), the immediate post-World War I crisis in relations between labour and capital, the 'social bureaucrats' of the Home Affairs Ministry and the integration of labour groups in the social policy process (1918-27), the politics of social policy between 1924 and 1929, the unsuccessful efforts of the Minseitō party and the Home Affairs Ministry to enact labour union legislation (1929-31), and the government's subsequent statist reorganisation of labour in order to maximise efficient production. By focusing on the relationship among organised labour, bureaucratic cliques, and party governments at this time, Garon 'offers a new perspective from which to judge the seemingly abrupt shifts in Japanese politics' during the late Meiji, Taishō, and early Shōwa periods.

203 **Japan's modern myths: ideology in the late Meiji period.**
Carol Gluck. Princeton, New Jersey; Guildford, Surrey: Princeton University Press, 1985. 407p. bibliog. (Studies of the East Asian Institute, Columbia University).

A sophisticated analysis of the evolution of the ideology produced in Japan between 1890 and 1915. Contending that the process whereby new civic values were formulated and inculcated among the Japanese was 'far more haphazard and inconsistent than is usually assumed', Gluck examines in depth the nature and diversity of the ideologies to which Meiji period Japanese were exposed. She concludes that such elements of ideological orthodoxy as the divine emperor system (*tennōsei*) or the mystical national polity (*kokutai*) may be less significant than the 'denaturing of politics' or the widespread belief in progress and in individual success in accounting for the course of Japanese history during the first half of the twentieth century.

204 **The evolution of labor relations in Japan: heavy industry, 1853–1955.**
Andrew Gordon. Cambridge, Massachusetts: Council on East Asian Studies, Harvard University, 1985. 524p. map. bibliog. (Harvard East Asian Monographs, 117).

This work demonstrates that the present-day Japanese labour relations system has evolved out of several decades of often bitter struggle between management and labour in which the ideas and demands of the workers played a vital role in shaping the nature of that system. Gordon examines the experiences of five heavy industrial enterprises located in Kanagawa Prefecture, just south of Tokyo. He traces the efforts of the owners and managers of those firms to control the activity of their wage-earners during the late nineteenth and early twentieth centuries; the adversary relationship that developed between management and labour as the workers sought improvements in their working conditions and working status; the intervention of government bureaucrats during World War II; and the postwar emergence of a reshaped industrial relations system – dominated by labour and characterised by permanent employment, a seniority system, and paternalistic unions – which has come to be called the 'Japanese employment system'.

205 **Peasants, rebels, and outcastes: the underside of modern Japan.**
Mikiso Hane. New York: Pantheon; London: Scolar Press, 1982. 297p. 2 maps.

Basing his account on personal testimony, contemporary writings, memoirs, diaries, and individual recollections, Hane vividly portrays the human and social costs of Japan's modernisation between 1868 and 1945. He interweaves translations of emotionally moving passages with his narrative about the 'lives and thoughts of the rural populace and of the poor who came out of the villages to enter the mines, the factories, and the brothels'. Hane depicts the impact and consequences of early Meiji government reforms on the peasants; the unrelieved misery of farming and farm life; the role of the new educational system and military conscription on peasant morals and mores; the hardships endured by rural women; the struggle of tenant farmers for survival under conditions of famine; the misery of the *burakumin* (outcastes); the working condition and lives of female textile factory employees; prostitution among impoverished women; and the suffering and exploitation of coal-miners during the early decades of the twentieth century.

206 **Farm and nation in modern Japan: agrarian nationalism, 1870–1940.**
Thomas R. H. Havens. Princeton, New Jersey; London: Princeton University Press, 1974. 358p. bibliog.

A study of agrarianist thought in Meiji and Taishō Japan that focuses on the evolution of official policy towards Japanese agriculture and the ideological background of the farm policies which the government adopted or advocated, and on some of the responses of Japanese farmers and their spokesmen to the government's pursuit of modernisation insofar as it affected Japanese agriculture and farming communities. Through a critical examination of the writings and speeches of such prominent agrarian ideologues as Gondō Seikyō, Tachibana Kōzaburō, and Katō Kanji, Havens also sheds considerable light on the ways in which agrarianist theories shaped Japanese nationalism during the early decades of the twentieth century.

207 **Valley of darkness: the Japanese people and World War Two.**
Thomas R. H. Havens. New York: Norton, 1978. 280p. bibliog.
Reprinted, Lanham, Maryland; London: University Press of America,
1986.

Havens vividly portrays the impact of the war upon Japanese society between 1937 and 1945 and the nature of daily life among ordinary civilians on the home front. As his account proceeds through the four major phases of early wartime mobilisation, consolidation and regimentation, full-scale general participation, and destruction and defeat, he focuses on the organisation of Japanese society for the war; the social changes in people's lives on account of the war; and the ravages of the war as the Japanese either fled to the countryside or struggled within their cities to endure the devastation wrought by American air raids. His accounts of the period include considerable information about the life-cycle of women, children, and the elderly; wages, prices, employment, and the role of women in various occupations; food, nutrition, and rationing; entertainment, sports, the arts, and crime; and the family, education, and health care.

208 **The development of Japanese business, 1600–1980.**
Johannes Hirschmeier, Tsunehiko Yui. London; Boston,
Massachusetts: Allen and Unwin, 1981. 2nd ed. 406p.

A description of the growth of Japanese business leadership and the evolution of its approaches towards the management of labour. Four chapters – 'The Merchants of Tokugawa Japan, 1600–1867', 'The Meiji Entrepreneurs, 1868–95', 'College Graduates as Business Leaders, 1896–1945', and 'The Organisers of Japan's Economic Miracle' – examine Japan's socio-economic conditions, leadership and business élites, business organisation and management, and the values of Japanese businessmen and their impact during clearly defined historical periods. This volume is particularly useful for its detailed description of Japanese business history since the Meiji Restoration (1868) and for its explanation of various ways in which Japanese values have shaped such modern business practices as seniority-based wages and decision by group consensus.

209 **Emperor Hirohito and his chief aide-de-camp: the Honjō diary, 1933–36.**
Shigeru Honjō, translated with an introduction by Mikiso Hane.
Tokyo: University of Tokyo Press, 1982. 263p.

A firsthand portrait of Emperor Hirohito based on diary entries kept by General Honjō Shigeru, a career army officer responsible for liaison activities between the imperial court and the Japanese military establishment between April 1933 and March 1936. Hane opens with two essays about the personalities, roles, and political behaviour of Honjō and the emperor respectively. The three-part diary (a translation of *Honjō nikki*, Tokyo, 1967) illuminates some of the internal politics in Japan during that period as well as the emperor's own views about ongoing events. It covers a range of important developments including the activities of the Kwantung Army in Manchuria, problems in north China, the London Naval Arms Limitation talks, relations with the major powers, the army's intervention in domestic Japanese politics, the dispute over the 'emperor-organ theory' of Minobe Tatsukichi, and the 26 February 1936 abortive coup d'état by radical young army officers in Tokyo.

History. 1868–1945 (Meiji, Taishō, and early Shōwa periods)

210 **Morning glory: a history of the Imperial Japanese Navy.**
Stephen Howarth. London: Hamish Hamilton; New York:
Atheneum, 1983. 398p. 5 maps. bibliog.

Published in the United States under the title *The fighting ships of the rising sun: the drama of the Imperial Japanese Navy, 1895–1945*, this book is an account of the meteoric rise and fall of the Japanese navy (at its zenith, the world's third greatest naval force) between July 1894, when three Japanese warships joined in battle with two Chinese warships off the west coast of Korea, and April 1945, when American aircraft sank the superbattleship *Yamato* off Okinawa. Howarth chronicles the major battles of the navy – Yalu Bay, Port Arthur, Tsushima, Pearl Harbor, Midway, and Leyte Gulf – and describes the 'characters and minds of the men who crewed and commanded His Imperial Majesty's ships', in particular such individuals as Tōgō Heihachirō, Katō Tomosaburō, Katō Kanji, and Yamamoto Isoroku. He also discusses the international diplomacy and politics which directly affected the course of Japan's naval history and appends a ten-page chronology to his study.

211 **Japan and its world: two centuries of change.**
Marius B. Jansen. Princeton, New Jersey; Guildford, Surrey:
Princeton University Press, 1980. 128p. bibliog. (The Brown and Haley
Lectures, 1975).

Jansen focuses on the changing views which the Japanese had of the outside world as well as of themselves between the 1770s and the 1970s. In three lectures entitled 'Challenges to the Confucian Order in the 1770's', 'Wisdom Sought throughout the World', and 'Japan's Search for Role in the Twentieth Century', he analyses the evolution of those perceptions through studies of the views and the times of three influential personalities: Sugita Genpaku (1733-1817), a pioneer in Western experimental medicine; Kume Kunitake (1839-1931), an early traveller to the West; and Matsumoto Shigeharu (1899-1989), an international journalist and a past head of the International House of Japan in Tokyo.

212 **Japan in transition: from Tokugawa to Meiji.**
Edited with an overview by Marius B. Jansen, Gilbert Rozman.
Princeton, New Jersey; Guildford, Surrey: Princeton University Press,
1986. 485p. 5 maps.

An interdisciplinary collection of seventeen essays which examine the transitional period between the 1840s and the 1880s and provide a broader picture of the context within which the Meiji Restoration and Japan's mid-nineteenth century modernisation occurred. The changes and continuities of this era are discussed in four major sections entitled 'Administration', 'Organizations', 'Cities and Population', and 'Rural Economy and Material Conditions'. Individual essays focus on the central government, the ruling class, the transition from feudal domain (*han*) to Meiji prefecture, local administration, Buddhist religious organisations, military organisations, the educational system, the press, early shipping companies, population changes, the castle towns, the city of Edo/Tokyo, the Meiji land tax reform, the rural economy, grain consumption, and material culture in general.

213 **Deference and defiance in nineteenth-century Japan.**
William W. Kelly. Princeton, New Jersey; Guildford, Surrey: Princeton University Press, 1985. 322p. 3 maps. bibliog.

On four occasions between 1840 and 1875, popular protest movements against changes in local and national government policies erupted among the inhabitants of the Shōnai Plain in northwestern Yamagata Prefecture. Each of these movements combined deference to certain conventions with an implacable defiance of government authorities. Kelly depicts the evolving character of these collective protests in the present case-study, describes their relationship to one another, and indicates how they transformed Shōnai society during this era.

214 **The self-made man in Meiji Japanese thought: from samurai to salary man.**
Earl H. Kinmonth. Berkeley, California; London: University of California Press, 1981. 385p. bibliog.

The present-day white-collar employee (or 'salary man') and his ethos in Japan have their roots in the Meiji era. Kinmonth's study of the origins of Japan's twentieth-century middle class focuses on the changes that took place during the Meiji period as the ideal of individual self-advancement through education and salaried employment, which the widely read translation of Samuel Smiles' book *Self-help* popularised among the samurai in the 1870s, came to be widely shared among the young men who became the political, business, and intellectual leaders of modern Japan.

215 **Organized workers and socialist politics in interwar Japan.**
Stephen S. Large. Cambridge, England; New York: Cambridge University Press, 1981. 326p. bibliog.

Focusing on the activities of the Nihon Rōdō Sōdōmei (Japan General Federation of Labour), the organisation which tended to dominate labour movement politics throughout the interwar period, Large chronicles the political role of organised labour and determines why the burgeoning labour movement of the 1920s stagnated during the 1930s and willingly dissolved itself in 1940. He shows how most labour union leaders rejected the more extreme views of rival Communist-influenced unions and opted for strategies that did not pose a fundamental challenge to the existing political order. They instead pursued a reform-oriented socialist policy, advocating progressive improvements on behalf of the workers through government legislation and labour-employee negotiations. Large holds these leaders partly responsible for the fragmentation of the movement for a unified Socialist party after 1925, and he is critical of their political passivity in the face of Japan's drift towards authoritarianism and militarism during the 1930s. This book is a sequel to the author's earlier study of the forerunner of the Nihon Rōdō Sōdōmei, the Yūaikai (or 'Friendly Society'): *The rise of labor in Japan: the Yūaikai, 1912–1919* (Tokyo: Sophia University, 1972, 218p.). It presents an institutional study of the Yūaikai as a labour organisation, including its leadership (particularly Suzuki Bunji, the founder of the Yūaikai), its programmes and goals, its organisational expansion, and the problems it encountered.

216 **The image of Japan: from feudal isolation to world power, 1850–1905.**
Jean-Pierre Lehmann. London; Boston, Massachusetts: Allen and Unwin, 1978. 208p. bibliog.

A study of the evolution of European and American images and attitudes towards

History. 1868–1945 (Meiji, Taishō, and early Shōwa periods)

Japan. Basing his study on contemporary writings by Lafcadio Hearn, Pierre Loti, Ernest Fenellosa, Rudyard Kipling, and other individuals who were instrumental in creating and developing popular images of Japan in the West, Lehmann portrays the transformation of Japan in the Western mind during the sixty years between the country's 'opening' to Perry in 1854 and Japan's military victory over Czarist Russia in 1905. He particularly emphasizes the Western attitudes that existed towards a *changing* Japan, as Japan rapidly modernised, industrialised, and to a certain extent Westernised, and as her increasing involvement in international politics led to a much greater interaction with the West.

217 **Human resources in Japanese industrial development.**
   Solomon B. Levine, Hisashi Kawada.   Princeton, New Jersey;
   Guildford, Surrey: Princeton University Press, 1980. 332p. bibliog.

A scholarly study of the historical evolution of the educational institutions and training systems which produced the skilled manpower needed for Japan's modern industrial- isation. Levine and Kawada first survey the historical context of Japan's economic, political, and educational development, including the despatch of hundreds of students overseas, the establishment of formal educational facilities, and the creation of informal vocational training programmes within individual enterprises. In ten detailed case-studies they then examine the relationship between education and industrialisation in the large-scale industries of steel, shipbuilding, railways, telecommunications, banking, textiles, mining, heavy machinery, electrical equipment, and chemicals. Their account focuses on the period between the mid-nineteenth and mid-twentieth centuries.

218 **The economic development of Japan c.1868–1941.**
   W. J. Macpherson, preface by L. A. Clark.   Basingstoke, Hampshire:
   Macmillan Education, 1987. 93p. bibliog. (Studies in Economic and
   Social History).

A concise account designed to survey the current state of scholarship about the prewar Japanese economy and to introduce non-specialists to the economic history of Meiji, Taishō, and early Shōwa Japan. Macpherson outlines the growth and peculiar structure of the economy, evaluates recent revisionist views about the legacy of the Tokugawa period, assesses the prominent role of the state in Japan's economic development, and analyses the contribution to economic growth of 'demand' factors such as domestic consumption, investment, and exports as well as of the 'supply' factors of land and agriculture, labour, capital, technology, and enterprise. A bibliography of 180 English- language books and articles serves as a guide for further reading. Individuals seeking a far more detailed analytical overview of the process of Japan's economic growth throughout this period – including discussions of the principal economic and technical conditions that shaped the direction of Japanese development and its rate of change (e.g., technology, capital, foreign trade, the employment of resources, and the involvement of the state in economic enterprise) – should turn in particular to William W. Lockwood's study, *The economic development of Japan: growth and structural change* (Princeton, New Jersey: Princeton University Press, 1968. expanded ed., 686p.).

219 **Capitalism and nationalism in prewar Japan: the ideology of the business elite, 1868–1941.**
Byron K. Marshall.   Stanford, California: Stanford University Press, 1967. 163p. bibliog.

An analysis of prewar business ideology that seeks to explain why Japan's business and industrial leaders explicitly rejected the major tenets of the Anglo-American capitalist creed, and instead justified their positions of wealth and authority in terms of traditional, group-oriented values. Identifying themselves with the traditional samurai, these leaders contended that their activities were motivated by devotion to their country and by a willingness to sacrifice their own best interests for the common good. Marshall clarifies the nature of this ideology and examines the difficulties of Japan's modern business élite as they attempted to reconcile the conflict between their professed values and the inherently profit-oriented nature of the institutions of private enterprise which they had created.

220 **Minobe Tatsukichi: interpreter of constitutionalism in Japan.**
Frank O. Miller.   Berkeley, California: University of California Press, 1965. 392p. bibliog. (Publications of the Center for Japanese and Korean Studies).

Minobe Tatsukichi (1873–1948), a prominent constitutional theorist and university professor, expounded the highly controversial 'emperor-organ theory' which held that sovereign power under the Imperial Meiji Constitution rested with the state and that the emperor exercised his authority only as the highest organ of the state. After outlining prewar Japanese constitutional thought and Minobe's career up to 1934, Miller systematically explains and critically analyses his constitutional theory in chapters that deal with his methodology and general theory of law and the state, his interpretation of the Imperial Constitution, and his interpretation of Meiji constitutionalism. Miller also discusses the celebrated Minobe Affair of 1935, in which he was attacked by ultranationalists and charged with lese-majesty, as well as Minobe's attitude towards the postwar constitution.

221 **Censorship in imperial Japan.**
Richard H. Mitchell.   Princeton, New Jersey; Guildford, Surrey: Princeton University Press, 1983. 424p. bibliog.

A detailed inquiry into the pervasive censorship system developed by Japan's authoritarian government between 1868 and 1945 and into the application of various methods of censorship to all forms of publishing as well as to the control of speech at public meetings, in the cinema, and on the radio. Mitchell pays particular attention to both the 'planning, drafting, enactment, application, revision, and significance' of the censorship laws and the government's effectiveness in disseminating propaganda, manipulating public opinion, and educating its citizens to censor their own thoughts internally. Complementing Mitchell's study are Gregory J. Kasza's historical narrative, *The state and the mass media in Japan, 1918–1945* (Berkeley, California; London: University of California Press, 1988, 335p.), which focuses on the relationship between two distinct types of political régimes – the relatively democratic party governments of 1918-32 and the military–bureaucratic régime of 1937-45 – and their respective policies for controlling newspapers, current events magazines, radio stations, and film companies; and Richard H. Mitchell's *Thought control in prewar Japan* (Ithaca, New

York; London: Cornell University Press, 1976, 226p.), which investigates the government's planning and enactment (in 1925) of the Peace Preservation Law and the elaborate system of thought control which was constructed upon it.

222 **Japan: the years of trial, 1919–52.**
Hyōe Murakami. Tokyo; New York: Kodansha International, 1983. 248p. 3 maps. bibliog.
A vivid personal narrative of the rise of militarism in Japan, the years of military expansion, World War II, Japan's unconditional surrender, the Allied occupation period, and the outbreak of war in Korea – all depicted from a Japanese point of view. While Murakami is critical of various aspects of Japanese policies and actions during the period that he covers, he also emphasizes such positive features of the Japanese experience as his country's liberation of those areas of Southeast Asia which had long been subjected to Western colonial rule.

223 **The Japanese colonial empire, 1895–1945.**
Edited by Ramon H. Myers, Mark R. Peattie, introduction by Mark R. Peattie. Princeton, New Jersey; Guildford, Surrey: Princeton University Press, 1984. 540p. 6 maps.
Japan acquired Taiwan in 1895, following her victory over China in the first Sino–Japanese War, and lost all of her overseas possessions at the end of World War II. This volume offers a comprehensive picture of the origins, management, and development of the Japanese colonial empire in Taiwan, Korea, Karafuto (southern Sakhalin), the Kwantung Leased Territory (in southern Manchuria), and the Japanese mandated islands of Micronesia (known as *Nan'yo*) during this fifty-year-long period. Fourteen essays deal with late Meiji period perspectives of Japanese imperialism; Japanese attitudes towards colonialism (1895-1945); the economic dimensions of Meiji imperialism in Korea; colonial rule in Micronesia; police and community control systems within the empire; attempts at integrating the empire; education in Korea and Taiwan; censorship policy in Korea; capital formation in Taiwan and Korea; agricultural development in the empire; colonialism and development in Korea, Taiwan, and Kwantung; post-1945 Japanese historiography on colonialism; the colonial legacy in Korea; and comparisons of Western and Japanese colonialism.

224 **Hara Kei in the politics of compromise, 1905–1915.**
Tetsuo Najita. Cambridge, Massachusetts: Harvard University Press, 1967. 314p. bibliog. (Harvard East Asian Series, 31).
An account of the politics underlying the sustained growth of Japan's political parties – especially the Seiyūkai under its astute leader Hara Kei (1856-1921) – between 1905 and 1915. Najita describes the steady rise of the parties as powerful élites in the political order, indicates how they penetrated the late Meiji political structure, and assesses the consequences of this development. His book first covers the period during which Hara systematically worked to spread Seiyūkai influence in the bureaucracy and among the local powerholders. It then examines the impact of this party's growth on political relationships during and after the Taishō political crisis of 1912-13. Najita attributes the Seiyūkai's success to Hara's vigilant and adroit leadership throughout this period, and he stresses the willingness of party men to abandon their attitude of uncompromising opposition to the government and to pursue realistic compromises within the governmental structure instead.

225 **Economic growth in prewar Japan.**
Takafusa Nakamura, translated by Robert A. Feldman. New Haven,
Connecticut; London: Yale University Press, 1983. 326p. bibliog.
An historical survey of Japanese economic development between the Meiji Restoration
and the outbreak of the Pacific War, accompanied by 136 statistical tables. An
overview of economic growth, 1868-1941, is followed by an analysis of Japan's
economic expansion during two consecutive time periods. Nakamura argues that the
Meiji period was an era of balanced economic growth. While the agricultural,
manufacturing, and service sectors grew at different rates, price and quantity
adjustments absorbed most changes. During the ensuing three decades, however, the
economy was characterised by imbalances. World War I resulted in an artificial scarcity
of industrial products and an excessive supply response. Throughout the 1920s and the
1930s, the government undertook major efforts (not always successfully) to balance
supply and demand, but ultimately it was forced to impose extensive wartime economic
controls in an attempt to accommodate the unrealistic demands of the military.

226 **Origins of the modern Japanese state: selected writings of E. H.
Norman.**
Egerton Herbert Norman, edited with an introduction by John W.
Dower. New York: Pantheon, 1975. 497p. bibliog. (Pantheon Asia
Library).
A reprint of Norman's classic work *Japan's emergence as a modern state: political and
economic problems of the Meiji period* (New York: Institute of Pacific Relations, 1940,
254p. [I.P.R. Inquiry Series]), an influential interpretation of the Meiji Restoration
and of Japan's political, economic, and social transformation from a feudal state to a
powerful modern nation between 1868 and the 1890s. Also included are Norman's
brief historiographical essay entitled 'The Shrine of Clio' and part of an Institute of
Pacific Relations conference paper (1945), *Feudal background of Japanese politics*, that
discusses late Tokugawa feudal society, the dominant role of the samurai in the
transitional years of the 1860s, and samurai opposition to the early Meiji government.
Dower's introductory essay, 'E. H. Norman, Japan and the Uses of History', outlines
Norman's view of history, summarises many of his writings, assesses Norman's
scholarship about Japan and its impact, considers various facets of his life and career,
and comments on postwar Western scholarly writings about Japan. For readers
interested in Norman himself, Roger Bowen's *Innocence is not enough: the life and
death of Herbert Norman* (Armonk, New York: M. E. Sharpe; Vancouver, British
Columbia: Douglas and McIntyre, 1988, 409p.) as well as Bowen's edited volume,
E. H. Norman: his life and scholarship (Toronto, Ontario; Buffalo, New York;
London: University of Toronto Press, 1984, 206p.), are highly recommended.

227 **Nan'yō: the rise and fall of the Japanese in Micronesia, 1885–1945.**
Mark R. Peattie. Honolulu, Hawaii: Center for Pacific Islands
Studies, School of Hawaiian, Asian, and Pacific Studies, University of
Hawaii; University of Hawaii Press, 1988. 382p. 28 maps. bibliog.
(Pacific Islands Monograph Series, no. 4).
A history of the appearance, activities, and ultimate expulsion of the Japanese in
Micronesia. Peattie narrates the arrival and activities of the first Japanese in
Micronesia (1885-1914), the Japanese occupation of the German-held Marianas,
Caroline and Marshall Islands in 1914, their assumption of a League of Nations
mandate over these islands after World War I, the postwar structure of Japanese

authority in Micronesia, Japanese policy towards the Micronesians, the Japanese economic development and exploitation of Micronesia, Japanese immigration to the islands during the 1920s and 1930s, the varieties of colonial life among the Japanese, the Japanese militarisation of Micronesia, and its loss to American forces during World War II. He stresses the theme of *nanshin* or 'southward advance': Japan's drive to the tropics and the role of the islands as 'stepping stones toward a greater maritime and southward dynasty'. An eyewitness report about the Japanese administration of Micronesia during the 1930s may be found in Paul Hibbert Clyde's detailed book, *Japan's Pacific mandate* (New York: Macmillan, 1935, 244p. Reprinted, Port Washington, New York: Kennikat Press, 1967).

228 **Target Tokyo: the story of the Sorge spy ring.**
Gordon W. Prange, with Donald M. Goldstein, Katherine V. Dillon.
New York: McGraw-Hill, 1984. 595p. map. bibliog. Reprinted,
London: Hodder and Stoughton, 1986. 618p.

An account of the large-scale espionage undertaken by a group of Western and Japanese nationals headed by Richard Sorge, a Russian-born, German-educated spy who became a trusted adviser and friend of the German ambassador in Tokyo. Between September 1933 and October 1941, this group transmitted significant and at times highly secret economic, political, and military intelligence from Tokyo to Moscow. Prange first describes the backgrounds of Sorge, his principal assistant Ozaki Hotsumi, and the other members of this spy ring. He then discusses their methods of operation, their various activities and notable successes, their ultimate detection by the Japanese police, and their imprisonment, trials, and fate. Interested readers should also consult Chalmers Johnson's closely related book, *An instance of treason: Ozaki Hotsumi and the Sorge spy ring* (Stanford, California: Stanford University Press, 1964, 278p.), which not only describes this espionage operation but also explores the idealism which underlay Ozaki's treason, the dilemma of the intelligentsia during the 1930s, and the influence of the Sino–Japanese War on Asian politics.

229 **Before aggression· Europeans prepare the Japanese army.**
Ernst L. Presse. .. Tucson, Arizona: Published for the Association
for Asian Studies by the University of Arizona Press, 1965. 163p.
bibliog. (Association for Asian Studies: Monographs and Papers, 21).

A study of the assistance which French and German military officers extended to the Japanese as they sought to build a modern army. Presseisen first examines the Tokugawa shogunate's employment of French military instructors in the mid-1860s, then depicts the work of French military missions during the 1870s in founding the Meiji Japanese army and in teaching the Japanese to organise, train, and command military units. The French also helped in the establishment of an officers' academy and promoted military manufacturing in Japan. The second half of Presseisen's book focuses on the work of Major Jakob Meckel, a German adviser and teacher of the Japanese army, who aided the Japanese during the 1880s in modernising their military structure and strategy, in perfecting the organisation of the Army General Staff, and in strengthening their logistic systems.

230 **The new generation in Meiji Japan: problems of cultural identity, 1885–1895.**
Kenneth B. Pyle.   Stanford, California: Stanford University Press, 1969. 240p. bibliog.

The abrupt changes that accompanied the rapid modernisation and Westernisation of Japan during the decades immediately following the Meiji Restoration had a significant impact upon the thinking of those Japanese who were raised and educated at that time. Focusing upon the first generation of Japanese to attend the new Western-oriented schools of higher learning, Pyle examines their efforts to be both modern and Japanese: their attempts to reconcile the conflicting needs of cultural borrowing from the West and of national pride during a period of intense national consciousness. The author pays particular attention to two rival groups of young intellectuals, the Minyūsha and the Seikyōsha, who debated through their respective journals questions that were concerned with defining the nature of Japan as a modern society at that time.

231 **Mitsui: three centuries of Japanese business.**
John G. Roberts, foreword by Chitoshi Yanaga.   New York; Tokyo: Weatherhill, 1989. 2nd ed. 578p. bibliog.

Mitsui, the world's oldest large-scale business enterprise, was the wealthiest merchant house of the Tokugawa period as well as Japan's largest *zaibatsu* (financial and industrial combine) before World War II. Today it is a major enterprise grouping with vast national and international holdings in such areas as banking, insurance, engineering, mining, chemicals, textiles, and heavy industry. Roberts describes the evolution of Mitsui from its founding as a small family enterprise in 1673, through its steady growth after the Meiji Restoration (1868), to its phenomenal recovery following the nearly disastrous policies of the Allied occupation of Japan. He pays particular attention to the ways in which Mitsui contributed to the building of a modern, industrialised Japanese state between the 1870s and the 1930s.

232 **Schooldays in imperial Japan: a study in the culture of a student elite.**
Donald Roden.   Berkeley, California; London: University of California Press, 1980. 300p. bibliog.

Roden describes and analyses the experiences – particularly the extracurricular life – of the men who were admitted into the university preparatory academies (the Japanese counterpart of the upper-level Gymnasium in Germany and the public schools in England) between the 1880s and the 1940s. He pays particular attention to the political and cultural socialisation of this intellectual élite – the graduates of these academies subsequently assumed positions of leadership in business, government, and academia – and to the diffusion among them of specific intellectual attitudes and behavioural norms that defined their status and honour. Roden's study examines both the pedagogical ideals of the academies' teachers and the nature of student culture with its daily customs, various rites of passage, communal dormitory life, flourishing literary and athletic activities, and fundamentally patriotic and nationalistic atmosphere.

233 **Capital formation in Japan, 1868–1940.**
Henry Rosovsky.   New York: Free Press of Glencoe, 1961. 358p. map. bibliog.

A quantitative economic analysis and critical measurement of long-term capital formation in Japan. This major work on historical trends in the prewar economy and on comparative economic development offers detailed estimates of annual capital formation in terms of non-agricultural private and government investment in construction, housing, and durable equipment. Part one contains Rosovsky's interpretation and discussion of capital formation in both the public and private sectors as well as an essay contrasting economic development in Europe and Japan. Part two (primarily of interest to specialists) explains in considerable detail the procedures by which the author derived his series of capital formation and how these data relate to previously published estimates.

234 **Memories of silk and straw: a self-portrait of small-town Japan.**
Junichi Saga, translated by Garry O. Evans, illustrated by Susumu Saga, preface by Ronald Dore. Tokyo; New York: Kodansha International, 1987. 258p. map.

Evocative portraits of daily life in the small rural community of Tsuchiura (Ibaraki Prefecture) during the first four decades of the twentieth century. Saga, a resident physician in Tsuchiura, tape-recorded his older patients' reminiscences of their youth and their recollections of experiences as young adults, and selected fifty-eight for inclusion in this volume. These personal, frequently nostalgic narratives of boatmen and fishermen, poor labourers, shopkeepers and tradesmen, gangsters, military officers, craftsmen, housewives, and geisha sensitively depict prewar rural Japan as an impoverished but, in some respects, serene society. They reveal how very different life was in Japan just one or two generations ago when compared with the relatively affluent conditions that exist today.

235 **Christian converts and social protest in Meiji Japan.**
Irwin Scheiner. Berkeley, California; London: University of California Press, 1970. 268p. bibliog.

The upheavals brought about by the Meiji Restoration destroyed much of the relevance of Confucian doctrine for the samurai, who lost their élite status in Japanese society. Some of these samurai chose to convert to Christianity out of a belief that such an action would facilitate their pursuit of a meaningful path to power in a modernising Japan. As these converts' understanding of their new faith gradually evolved into a belief that Christianity could form the basis for social change, they became infused with a sense of mission to save Japan, came into conflict with the Meiji government, and began to play a leading role in contemporary social reform movements. The views and activities of Niijima Jō and a number of other Christian converts including Ebina Danjō, Kōzaki Hiromichi, and Uemura Masahisa were particularly important in these developments, and they are discussed at length.

236 **Low city, high city: Tokyo from Edo to the earthquake.**
Edward Seidensticker. New York: Knopf; London: Lane, 1983; Rutland, Vermont and Tokyo: Tuttle, 1984; Harmondsworth, Middlesex: Penguin, 1985. 302p. 2 maps.

A portrait of the transformation of the seat of the Tokugawa shogunate into the modern metropolis of Tokyo between 1867 and the Great Kantō Earthquake of September 1923. In an anecdotal, narrative style, Seidensticker evokes the city's mood and character during the Meiji and Taishō eras as he describes the culture and life of its inhabitants, the Westernisation of its food and entertainment as well as the cityscape in general, the occurrence of such major disasters as fires, floods and earthquakes, and the general shift of wealth and influence from the Shitamachi (the 'low city' that constituted the heart of old Edo) to the Yamanote (the 'high city' that arose in the hilly region to the west and south). Seidensticker's account is profusely illustrated with reproductions of contemporary woodblock prints and photographs, but it contains relatively little political, intellectual, literary, or economic history.

237 Politics and culture in wartime Japan.
Ben-Ami Shillony. Oxford, England: Clarendon Press; New York: Oxford University Press, 1981. 238p. bibliog.

An examination of political and cultural developments on the Japanese home front. Shillony first focuses on the establishment of the cabinet of Prime Minister Tōjō Hideki in October 1941; its characteristics and the constraints under which it operated; the actions and reactions of the emperor, the bureaucrats, the Diet, and Japan's senior statesmen to Tōjō's wartime régime; Tōjō's resignation in 1944; and the activities of the Koiso and Suzuki Cabinets, 1944-45. He then examines cultural developments, particularly the collaboration of the press, the support given to the war by many scholars and writers, prevailing Japanese attitudes towards the West, and the existence of Japanese anti-Semitism. Although the wartime régime of Japan was repressive, the author contends that it differed significantly from those of other contemporary totalitarian states and pursued far more moderate policies because Japanese institutions and values resisted the imposition of an unrestrained dictatorship during the war years.

238 Revolt in Japan: the young officers and the February 26, 1936 Incident.
Ben-Ami Shillony. Princeton, New Jersey: Princeton University Press, 1973. 263p. bibliog.

A comprehensive account of the unsuccessful military rebellion of some 1,400 troops, led by junior officers, who seized control of the centre of Tokyo on 26 February 1936 in an attempted coup d'état. These young officers sought to carry out a 'Shōwa restoration' in which political and economic power was to revert to the emperor and the people, and the economy was to be controlled by the state rather than by big business. Shillony first discusses the organisational origins of the Young Officers' Movement, the backgrounds and ideologies of its leaders, the movement's connections with elements in the civilian right wing, the significance of the financial support that it received from the zaibatsu, its ties with Imperial Prince Chichibu, and the planning and preparations for the coup d'état. He then reconstructs the events of the four-day rebellion itself on the basis of published materials and interviews, and describes its suppression and aftermath.

239 Tradition and modernization in Japanese culture.
Edited by Donald H. Shively, foreword by John Whitney Hall. Princeton, New Jersey: Princeton University Press, 1971. 689p. (Studies in the Modernization of Japan, 5).

Fifteen case-studies of individual people, styles, and phenomena focus on some of the changes in Japanese culture that occurred as a result of Japan's modernisation. Essays on the Iwakura Embassy, the realistic painter Takahashi Yūichi, the Meiji educational system, and music illustrate some of the ways in which the Japanese went about borrowing from the West during the late 1800s. The interaction of modernisation and the arts, painting, music, literature, the theatre, philosophy, and language as well as the 'adjustment of the individual and the effects of progressive modernisation on culture in an increasingly complex, twentieth-century society' constitute the focus of the subsequent three parts of this volume. Included are biographical essays about the writers Natsume Sōseki, Shimazaki Tōson, Masaoka Shiki, Kobayashi Hideo (literary critic), and Fukuda Tsuneari (playwright), as well as about the philosopher Nishida Kitarō and the painter Kawakami Tōgai. This book is the penultimate volume in a series of studies about the modernisation of Japan published for the Association for Asian Studies' Conference on Modern Japan by Princeton University Press. The remaining volumes are entitled *Changing Japanese attitudes toward modernization* (edited by Marius B. Jansen, 1965, 546p.); *The state and economic enterprise in Japan: essays in the political economy of growth* (edited by William W. Lockwood, 1965, 753p.); *Aspects of social change in modern Japan* (edited by R. P. Dore, 1967, 474p.); *Political development in modern Japan* (edited by Robert E. Ward, 1968, 637p.); and *Dilemmas of growth in prewar Japan* (edited by James William Morley, 1971, 527p.).

240 **Flowers in salt: the beginnings of feminist consciousness in modern Japan.**
Sharon L. Sievers. Stanford, California: Stanford University Press, 1983. 240p.

A portrayal of the lives, personalities, and views of Meiji period women who became outspoken critics of their society and rejected the traditional roles which it assigned to them. Sievers deals with such notable individuals as Kishida Toshiko, Yajima Kajiko, and Kanno Suga as well as such groups of women as the young textile factory employees who initiated work stoppages to attain their goals and the middle-class Christian women who established the Women's Reform Society that campaigned for improvements in women's education, the abolition of licensed prostitution, and the like. Depicting these and other women against a background of economic exploitation, legal inroads on women's rights, and the political repression of women, Sievers describes and critically assesses their various struggles for economic, political, and social reforms. She supplements her account with photographs of Meiji era feminists.

241 **Japan in crisis: essays on Taishō democracy.**
Edited by Bernard S. Silberman, Harry D. Harootunian; introduction by Harry D. Harootunian. Princeton, New Jersey: Princeton University Press, 1974. 469p.

A collection of fifteen scholarly essays on the intellectual, literary, economic, diplomatic, political, and social history of Japan between the 1890s and the late 1930s, with particular focus on the Taishō period of 1912-26. Included are articles concerned with idealism in the political thought of Yoshino Sakuzō; the political thought of the renowned novelist Natsume Sōseki; the life and thought of the influential Marxist scholar Kawakami Hajime; authority and the ambiguities of intellectual choice in imperial Japan; the proletarian literary movement in Japan; the role of higher-level bureaucrats in Japanese politics; how liberalisation in the 1920s almost inevitably led to aggressive imperialism in the 1930s; the failure of Japan's 'economic diplomacy' during the 1920s; the oligopolisation of the modern sector of the economy between 1911 and 1930; incentives, productivity gaps, and agricultural growth rates in Japan and her prewar colonies; the origins of tenant unrest in the countryside; and the Noda Soy Sauce Company strike of 1927-28.

242 **Agricultural development and tenancy disputes in Japan, 1870–1940.**
Richard J. Smethurst. Princeton, New Jersey; Guildford, Surrey:
Princeton University Press, 1986. 472p. 4 maps. bibliog.

A reinterpretation of the prewar development of the Japanese countryside and of the impact which modernisation during the Meiji and Taishō periods had on the Japanese peasantry. Basing this study primarily on research conducted in Yamanashi Prefecture, Smethurst argues that the dramatic growth of a rural market economy after the Meiji Restoration resulted in a general increase in rural prosperity. By the twentieth century, even tenant farmers became small businessmen who used improved seeds, tools, fertilisers, and advanced cultivation techniques and who practised rational farm management in order to raise their standards of living. Accordingly, when landlord–tenant disputes broke out during the 1920s and 1930s, tenant farmers pragmatically joined together not to stave off poverty or to effect a radical overthrow of the landlord system but rather to secure better business conditions, increase their profits, and gain enhanced political power.

243 **A social basis for prewar Japanese militarism: the army and the rural community.**
Richard J. Smethurst. Berkeley, California; London: University of California Press, 1974. 202p. bibliog.

Through a detailed examination of four organisations (the Imperial Military Reserve Association, the Greater Japan Youth Association, the Greater Japan National Defence Women's Association, and the youth training centres) which the Japanese army utilised to develop a social basis for militarism, Smethurst describes the army's success between the early 1900s and the mid-1930s in mobilising widespread rural support for itself and in creating a strong sense of nationalism among Japan's farming population. These organisations were integrated into the life of every community, and loyalty to one's village became synonymous with loyalty to the army. In addition, by incorporating patriotic and military duties into the activities of these organisations and by disseminating nationalistic ideology, the army transformed Japan's farmers into 'national villagers' who supported military and national goals and who identified positively with both the emperor and the army, the symbols of Japan's unity.

244 **Japan's first student radicals.**
Henry DeWitt Smith, II. Cambridge, Massachusetts: Harvard University Press, 1972. 341p. bibliog. (Harvard East Asian Series, 70).

A description and analysis of the prewar student movement with particular focus on the Shinjinkai ('New Man Society'), the leading left-wing student group, between its founding at Tokyo Imperial University in late 1918 and its dissolution ten years later. Paying special attention to such problems as the relations between the student movement and the Japan Communist Party, the disputes within the student movement, student involvement in the labour movement, and the lifestyles of Japanese student radicals, Smith describes the movement's origins and evolution, the formation, structure and activities of the Shinjinkai on the University campus, its suppression in 1928, the student movement underground until 1934, and the composition of Shinjinkai membership.

History. 1868–1945 (Meiji, Taishō, and early Shōwa periods)

245 **The double patriots: a study of Japanese nationalism.**
Richard Storry. London: Chatto and Windus; Boston, Massachusetts: Houghton Mifflin, 1957. 335p. bibliog. Reprinted, Westport, Connecticut: Greenwood Press, 1973.

A study of the ideas and activities of ultranationalistic associations and groups throughout the 1930s. Focusing on political ideas, events, and trends, Storry explores the evolution and impact of Japanese nationalism through a study of the Manchurian Incident of September 1931, the political assassinations of 1932, the growth of various army factions, the attempted coup d'état of 26 February 1936, the outbreak of war with China in July 1937, Japan's interaction with Nazi Germany and Fascist Italy, and the steps that led to the attack on Pearl Harbor. The author concludes that the pervasiveness and widespread acceptance of ultranationalistic thought during the 1930s – with its promotion of the 'thesis of an urgently expanding Japan' – provided active extreme nationalists with the opportunities to exert considerable pressure on Japanese officials and politicians and, in that manner, to influence and indeed shape high-level policy even without holding any positions of governmental responsibility.

246 **Palace and politics in prewar Japan.**
David Anson Titus. New York; London: Columbia University Press, 1974. 360p. bibliog. (Studies of the East Asian Institute, Columbia University).

An analysis of the theoretical position of the imperial institution in the Japanese governing process, of the structure and style of palace politics, and of the relationship of the palace officials and the emperor to one another as well as to the political process. Titus specifically examines the concept of imperial prerogative which served as the basis for the theory of political legitimacy produced between 1868 and 1889; the creation, evolution, and composition of the palace bureaucracy as an independent governmental structure; the pluralism and competition that characterised the four key palace officials as well as the middle level of the palace bureaucracy between 1885 and 1945; the role behaviour and the communication network linking the court and the government during the 1930s (with particular focus on the patterns of association of the prominent palace official Kido Kōichi); and the policy negotiations and decision-making that privately took place among closed groups of participants.

247 **The social democratic movement in prewar Japan.**
George Oakley Totten, III. New Haven, Connecticut; London: Yale University Press, 1966. 455p. (Studies on Japan's Social Democratic Parties, vol. 1).

An analysis of the overall characteristics and role of the prewar non-communist proletarian parties and the labour, agrarian, social, national minority, and other movements which supported them. Totten first examines the antecedents of social democracy in Japan (from the 1870s to 1922), the emergence of the social democratic movement during the 1920s and the process which differentiated it from the organised communist movement, and the impact of political developments during the 1930s. He then investigates the movement's leadership, cliques, and factions, with particular focus on the Socio-Democratic clique, the Japan-Labour clique, and the Labour-Farmer faction. The author also explores the ideology, tactics, and policies of the social democrats in order to determine their views of the appropriate function of proletarian parties, and he analyses the electoral and organised support which they generally enjoyed.

248 **Imitation and innovation: the transfer of Western organizational patterns to Meiji Japan.**
D. Eleanor Westney. Cambridge, Massachusetts; London: Harvard University Press, 1987. 252p.

Systematically examines the process of transferring social technologies and social organisations from one culture to another by studying the evolution of three Meiji period organisations which were based on Western models: the police, the postal system, and the mass-circulation newspaper. In tracing Japanese patterns of imitating and emulating their European counterparts, Westney explains why Japanese decision-makers chose the models they selected, which features they observed and emulated, how and why they modified the models which were adopted, how they mobilised resources to build these three organisational systems, how and in what directions these organisations evolved over time, and in what ways they shaped and were shaped by Japan's social environment during a period of rapid change. In addition, Westney provides a good historical overview of Western-style organisations that have played a critical role in modern Japanese life.

249 **Japan examined: perspectives on modern Japanese history.**
Edited with an introduction by Harry Wray, Hilary Conroy. Honolulu, Hawaii: University of Hawaii Press, 1983. 411p. bibliog.

Forty-four North American and Japanese scholars present their differing perspectives on a range of controversial themes or 'problems' in the study of modern Japanese history. Their essays are organised around twelve topics: 'When does modern Japan begin?'; 'Have "modern" and "modernization" been overworked?'; 'The Meiji Restoration: product of gradual decay, abrupt crisis, or creative will?'; 'The Meiji government and its critics: what is best for the nation?'; 'Meiji imperialism: planned or unplanned?'; 'The Russo–Japanese War: turning point in Japanese history?'; 'How democratic was Taishō Japan?'; 'Japanese colonialism: enlightened or barbaric?'; 'The 1930s: aberration or logical outcome?'; 'Japan's foreign policy in the 1930s: search for autonomy or naked aggression?'; 'The Allied occupation: how significant was it?'; and 'Japan: East or West?'. This problems-oriented book is designed as supplementary reading for undergraduate courses and as an introduction for general readers to the various interpretations of Japanese history.

250 **Mitsubishi and the N.Y.K., 1870–1914: business strategy in the Japanese shipping industry.**
William D. Wray. Cambridge, Massachusetts: Council on East Asian Studies, Harvard University, 1984. 672p. bibliog. (Harvard East Asian Monographs, 108).

An investigation into the origins and early institutional growth of Mitsubishi (today one of Japan's largest enterprise groupings) and the Nippon Yūsen Kaisha (N.Y.K), Japan's first modern ocean-going shipping company. Wray divides his account into three parts: Mitsubishi's establishment and emergence as a major enterprise during the 1870s; the cut-throat competition between Mitsubishi and Mitsui, which resulted in the merger of Mitsubishi's shipping division with the Kyōdō Unyū Kaisha of the rival Mitsui group to form N.Y.K in 1885; and N.Y.K.'s further expansion through 1914. Utilising company records and other information sources for Meiji period business and economic history, Wray examines the N.Y.K. business strategy and practices that successfully promoted economic growth, the structure of its management, the company's close association with the government, and its involvement in overseas Japanese imperialist expansion, particularly in China.

251 **Japan in the Victorian mind: a study of stereotyped images of a nation 1850–80.**
Toshio Yokoyama.   Basingstoke, Hampshire: Macmillan, 1987. 233p. map. bibliog. (St. Antony's/Macmillan Series).

Examines the changing ideas and images which Victorian British writers had of Japan and of themselves as members of the world's most powerful empire during the three decades immediately following Japan's opening to the West. Yokoyama's focus is on some twenty monthly and quarterly reviews and magazines (among them *Blackwood's Magazine*, *Cornhill Magazine*, and *Edinburgh Review*) which enjoyed national circulation and influence and whose articles, oriented towards the general public, tended to offer background information and interpretation about Japan in a variety of areas including international relations, religion, society, economy, and the arts and crafts. Particular attention is paid to the language employed by the authors of these articles. Yokoyama demonstrates that the gap between the Japanese reality and British perceptions of Japan was often quite large, and that the images presented by British observers and writers frequently reflected their own expectations and values.

Wanderers and settlers in the Far East: a century of Jewish life in China and Japan.
See item no. 4.

Victorians in Japan: in and around the treaty ports.
See item no. 68.

The Japan diaries of Richard Gordon Smith.
See item no. 72.

Japan: a history in art.
See item no. 155.

Formation of science in Japan: building a research tradition.
See item no. 157.

Young Japan: Yokohama and Yedo. A narrative of the settlement and the city from the signing of the treaties in 1858, to the close of the year 1879. With a glance at the progress of Japan during a period of twenty-one years.
See item no. 162.

Conflict in modern Japanese history: the neglected tradition.
See item no. 175.

Native sources of Japanese industrialization, 1750–1920.
See item no. 183.

Japanese inn.
See item no. 184.

Historical development of science and technology in Japan.
See item no. 187.

History. 1868–1945 (Meiji, Taishō, and early Shōwa periods)

MITI and the Japanese miracle: the growth of industrial policy, 1925–1975.
See item no. 272.

Pacifism in Japan: the Christian and socialist tradition.
See item no. 288.

Personality in Japanese history.
See item no. 289.

Reflections on the way to the gallows: rebel women in prewar Japan.
See item no. 290.

The nobility of failure: tragic heroes in the history of Japan.
See item no. 293.

Shōwa: an inside history of Hirohito's Japan.
See item no. 294.

Great historical figures of Japan.
See item no. 295.

Five political leaders of modern Japan: Itō Hirobumi, Ōkuma Shigenobu, Hara Takashi, Inukai Tsuyoshi, and Saionji Kimmochi.
See item no. 296.

Samurai and silk: a Japanese and American heritage.
See item no. 297.

The autobiography of Yukichi Fukuzawa.
See item no. 302.

Yamagata Aritomo in the rise of modern Japan, 1838–1922.
See item no. 303.

Mori Arinori: a reconsideration.
See item no. 304.

Politics of the Meiji press: the life of Fukuchi Gen'ichirō.
See item no. 305.

Ōkubo Toshimichi: the Bismarck of Japan.
See item no. 306.

The diary of Kido Takayoshi.
See item no. 307.

Ōkuma Shigenobu: statesman of Meiji Japan.
See item no. 308.

Tokutomi Sohō, 1863–1957: a journalist for modern Japan.
See item no. 311.

Ox against the storm; a biography of Tanaka Shozo: Japan's conservationist pioneer.
See item no. 312.

History. 1868–1945 (Meiji, Taishō, and early Shōwa periods)

Japanese Marxist: a portrait of Kawakami Hajime, 1879–1946.
See item no. 318.

The emperor's adviser: Saionji Kinmochi and pre-war Japanese politics.
See item no. 323.

Facing two ways: the story of my life.
See item no. 328.

Hirohito: emperor of Japan.
See item no. 334.

Hirohito: behind the myth.
See item no. 334.

Liberalism in modern Japan: Ishibashi Tanzan and his teachers, 1905–1960.
See item no. 336.

Kōtoku Shūsui: portrait of a Japanese radical.
See item no. 337.

Noguchi and his patrons.
See item no. 343.

War criminal: the life and death of Hirota Koki.
See item no. 346.

Radical nationalist in Japan: Kita Ikki, 1883–1937.
See item no. 348.

Appointment in Japan: memories of sixty years.
See item no. 350.

Awakening Japan: the diary of a German doctor, Erwin Baelz.
See item no. 351.

Dr. Willis in Japan, 1862–1877: British medical pioneer.
See item no. 353.

A diplomat's wife in Japan: sketches at the turn of the century.
See item no. 355.

American samurai: Captain L. L. Janes and Japan.
See item no. 358.

An American teacher in early Meiji Japan.
See item no. 358.

Clara's diary: an American girl in Meiji Japan.
See item no. 363.

Biographical dictionary of Japanese history.
See item no. 367.

The population of Japan.
See item no. 371.

Imingaisha: Japanese emigration companies and Hawaii, 1894–1908.
See item no. 396.

Religion in Japanese history.
See item no. 465.

A history of Christianity in Japan.
See item no. 495.

A century of Protestant Christianity in Japan.
See item no. 496.

Social change and the city in Japan: from earliest times through the industrial revolution.
See item no. 546.

Japanese urbanism: industry and politics in Kariya, 1872–1972.
See item no. 547.

The hidden sun: women of modern Japan.
See item no. 581.

Social change and the individual: Japan before and after defeat in World War II.
See item no. 595.

When the twain meet: the rise of Western medicine in Japan.
See item no. 597.

Imperial Japan's higher civil service examinations.
See item no. 613.

Authority and the individual in Japan: citizen protest in historical perspective.
See item no. 614.

Thought and behaviour in modern Japanese politics.
See item no. 618.

I saw Tokyo burning: an eyewitness narrative from Pearl Harbor to Hiroshima.
See item no. 691.

The economic development of Japan: a quantitative study.
See item no. 803.

Patterns of Japanese economic development: a quantitative appraisal.
See item no. 808.

A century of agricultural growth in Japan: its relevance to Asian development.
See item no. 831.

Can Japanese agriculture survive? a historical and comparative approach.
See item no. 835.

The financial development of Japan, 1868–1977.
See item no. 855.

Sogo shosha: the vanguard of the Japanese economy.
See item no. 914.

Society and education in Japan.
See item no. 973.

"The factory ship" and "The absentee landlord".
See item no. 1068.

Japanese manners and customs in the Meiji era.
See item no. 1188.

The world of the Meiji print: impressions of a new civilization.
See item no. 1269.

A century of Japanese photography.
See item no. 1276.

Japan: photographs, 1854–1905.
See item no. 1278.

Once upon a time: visions of old Japan.
See item no. 1278.

Monumenta Nipponica: Studies in Japanese Culture.
See item no. 1534.

Concise dictionary of modern Japanese history.
See item no. 1555.

Asia and Oceania: a guide to archival and manuscript sources in the United States.
See item no. 1562.

The Imperial Japanese Navy.
See item no. 1572.

Japan's economy: a bibliography of its past and present.
See item no. 1614.

1945: Hiroshima and Nagasaki

252 **The Hiroshima maidens: a story of courage, compassion, and survival.**
Rodney Barker.   New York: Viking, 1985. 240p. Reprinted, New York and Harmondsworth, Middlesex: Penguin Books, 1986.

Describes the experiences of twenty-five young women who were grotesquely disfigured during the atomic bombing of Hiroshima and who were brought to New York in 1955 to undergo reconstructive surgery at Mount Sinai Hospital. Barker traces the lives of these women from the time of the atomic explosion to their hospitalisation in the United States, and then through their readjustment to life following their return to Japan.

253 **Hiroshima and Nagasaki: the physical, medical, and social effects of the atomic bombing.**
Committee for the Compilation of Materials on Damage Caused by the Atomic Bombs in Hiroshima and Nagasaki [Hiroshima-shi Nagasaki-shi Genbaku Saigaishi Henshū Iinkai], translated by Eisei Ishikawa, David L. Swain. Tokyo: Iwanami Shoten; New York: Basic Books; London: Hutchinson, 1981. 706p. 16 maps. bibliog.
The most complete one-volume account available of the overall human effects of the two atomic bombings, prepared by thirty-four Japanese physicians, physicists, and social scientists. This clearly written study summarises and analyses both published and unpublished findings about the fatalities, external wounds, burns, and physical destruction caused by the bombs at the time they were dropped as well as about their long-term medical, genetic, social, and psychological effects. The book is divided into four parts: 'Physical Aspects of Destruction'; 'Injury to the Human Body'; 'The Impact on Society and Daily Life'; and 'Toward the Abolition of Nuclear Arms'. Particularly detailed treatment is given to the physical injuries suffered in the bombings and to the overall collapse of society (including the destruction of community relationships) that accompanied the wholesale destruction of Hiroshima and Nagasaki. An abridged and updated version of this book has been published under the title *The impact of the A-bomb: Hiroshima and Nagaskai, 1945–85* (Tokyo: Iwanami Shoten, 1985, 218p.)

254 **The atomic bomb and the end of World War II.**
Herbert Feis. Princeton, New Jersey: Princeton University Press, 1966. rev. ed. 213p. bibliog.
Narrative of the plans and actions of both the American and Japanese governments during the closing months of the Pacific War. Feis outlines the political efforts that were made to induce the Japanese to accept defeat, covers the discussions that were conducted among the Allied powers at the Potsdam Conference in July, reconstructs the events and decision-making process which led to the bombing of Hiroshima, traces subsequent events and reactions in Japan (through Japan's formal surrender on 2 September 1945), and analyses the timing of the Allied efforts to persuade Japan's leaders to accept their demands for unconditional surrender as well as the decision to use the atomic bomb. Originally published under the title *Japan subdued: the atomic bomb and the end of the war in the Pacific* (Princeton, New Jersey: Princeton University Press, 1961, 199p.), this study complements Feis' earlier book, *Between war and peace: the Potsdam Conference* (Princeton, New Jersey: Princeton University Press, 1960, 367p. Reprinted, Westport, Connecticut: Greenwood Press, 1983.).

255 **Hiroshima.**
John Hersey. New York: Knopf, 1985. new ed. 196p. (A Borzoi Book). Reprinted, Harmondsworth, Middlesex: Penguin; New York and Toronto, Ontario: Bantam Books, 1986.
A new edition of a moving account about the lives of six individuals – a clerk, a widowed seamstress, a physician, a Methodist minister, a young surgeon, and a German Catholic priest – who survived the bombing of Hiroshima. Hersey tells what

these individuals were doing at 8.15 a.m. on 6 August 1945, and he follows the course of their lives, hour by hour, day by day, during the months of August and September as he details the horrors of the bombing and its immediate aftermath. *Hiroshima* was first published as an extended essay in the 31 August 1946 issue of *The New Yorker* and shortly thereafter as a book (New York: Knopf, 1946, 125p.). This new edition contains a final chapter based on Hersey's visit to Hiroshima forty years after the explosion in which he recounts what subsequently happened to the six survivors and how they have responded to the past.

256 **A place called Hiroshima.**
Betty Jean Lifton, photographs by Eikoh Hosoe.   Tokyo; New York: Kodansha International, 1985. 151p.

Photo-documentary and evocative essay about the lingering effects of the atomic bombing on the city of Hiroshima and its people. In a combination of black-and-white photographs and an essay based in part on interviews with eighteen *hibakusha* (atomic bomb victims), Lifton shows how the bomb physically, psychologically, and socially affected – and continues to affect – the lives of survivors and their families. She depicts some of their struggles to overcome their haunting memories, their social stigma, and the delayed radiation sickness from which many of them now suffer.

257 **Death in life: survivors of Hiroshima.**
Robert Jay Lifton.   New York: Random House, 1967. 594p.
Reprinted, New York: Basic Books, 1982. (Harper Colophon Books).

An American psychiatrist records the most significant psychological consequences of exposure to the atomic bombing at Hiroshima through detailed interviews with both prominent individuals and a representative cross-section of survivors, who are known in Japanese as *hibakusha*. Lifton describes and interprets the immediate and long-term responses of the *hibakusha*, including their residual concerns and fears (especially their anxiety about the delayed effects of radiation on themselves and on their children), their inner 'formulation' of their experience, and their struggle and problems with being identified as *hibakusha*. Particular emphasis is place on shared psychological and historical themes. The author shows that the dropping of the bomb 'annihilated a general sense of life's coherence as much as it did human bodies' and that the *hibakusha*'s ability to master that experience depended upon the re-establishment of the 'form within which not only the death immersion but the survivor's altered identity could be grasped and rendered significant.'

258 **The bells of Nagasaki.**
Takashi Nagai, translated with an introduction by William Johnston.
Tokyo; New York: Kodansha International, 1984. 118p.

A moving account of the nuclear destruction of Nagasaki, written in 1946 by a nuclear physicist and physician at the Nagasaki Medical School. Nagai recounts the explosion of the atomic bomb on 9 August 1945, as it was recalled by a number of survivors, and describes some of its immediate effects upon both the city and its inhabitants. He also depicts the rescue work that ensued. While Nagai's personal experiences as a survivor converted him from a nationalistic supporter of the war into a committed Christian pacifist, his book is not a polemical anti-war treatise but rather a vividly portrayed, insightful, and historically accurate eyewitness story. Nagai's book complements – and appeared just a few years after – the writings of another medical doctor, Tatsuichirō Akizuki, whose *Nagasaki 1945: the first full-length eyewitness account of the atomic bomb attack on Nagasaki*, translated by Keiichi Nagata, edited with an introduction by Gordon Honeycombe (London; New York: Quarter Books, 1981, 158p.), also powerfully depicts the destruction that was wrought on Nagasaki.

259 **Children of the A-bomb: the testament of the boys and girls of Hiroshima.**
Compiled by Arata Osada, translated by Jean Dan, Ruth Sieben-Morgen. New York: G. P. Putnam's Sons, 1963. 256p. map.
Expanded edition published under the title *Children of Hiroshima*.
Tokyo: Publishing Committee for 'Children of Hiroshima', 1980. 333p.
map. Reprinted, London: Taylor and Francis, 1981.

A collection of sixty-seven essays that were selected from among more than two thousand accounts composed by primary, middle-school, high-school, and college students between March and mid-June 1951. Originally published in Japanese later that year, these evocative writings centre on the personal experiences of these children during and immediately following the bombing of Hiroshima. In particular they depict the feelings, thoughts, and recollections of these 'guileless and sensitive boys and girls' and indicate in various ways the psychological impact of the bomb upon their lives. Other accounts by victims of Hiroshima include *Hiroshima diary: the journal of a Japanese physician, August 6–September 30, 1945*, by Michihiko Hachiya, translated and edited by Warner Wells (Chapel Hill, North Carolina: University of North Carolina Press, 1955, 238p.), and *Widows of Hiroshima: the life stories of nineteen peasant wives*, edited by Mikio Kanda, translated by Taeko Midorikawa (New York: St. Martin's Press; Basingstoke, Hampshire: Macmillan, 1989, 183p.).

260 **The day man lost: Hiroshima, 6 August 1945.**
Pacific War Research Society [Bungei Shunjū Senshi Kenkyūkai], foreword by John Toland. Tokyo; Palo Alto, California: Kodansha International, 1972. 312p. bibliog. Reprinted, Tokyo; New York: Kodansha International, 1981.

A popular account of the development, testing, and use of the atomic bomb, collectively prepared by the fourteen-member Japanese Pacific War Research Society. The authors first trace the American decision to build the bomb, and provide a year-by-year account of major developments on both sides of the Pacific between early 1941 and late 1944. Part two continues their narrative on a month-by-month basis – from 1 January to 5 August 1945 – up to the departure from Tinian of the B-29 airplane that carried the atomic bomb. The concluding part of this book chronicles the bombing mission of the *Enola Gay* and its crew over Hiroshima through a virtually minute-by-minute report of the events and emotional reactions following the release and explosion of the bomb at 8.15 a.m. on 6 August 1945.

261 **A world destroyed: the atomic bomb and the grand alliance.**
Martin J. Sherwin, foreword by Hans A. Bethe. New York: Knopf, 1975. 315p. bibliog. Reprinted, with a new introduction by the author, New York: Vintage Books, 1987. 375p.

An illuminating study of 'the assumptions and decisions . . . that governed the atomic energy policies of the United States from the discovery of nuclear fission to its military application'. Focusing on the atomic scientists who played the critical role in calling for the creation of the bomb and on the policy-makers who 'relied on principles derived from the experience of the old world in their struggle to ensure peace in the new', Sherwin critically assesses the relationship that existed between the American atomic energy and diplomatic policies that developed during World War II. He explores the motives, intentions, and policy considerations of the policy-makers who decided to drop the atomic bomb over Hiroshima and Nagasaki, and he attempts to determine the nature of the relationship that existed between the formulation of Roosevelt's wartime atomic energy policies and Truman's decision to employ the bomb on the one hand and diplomatic considerations regarding postwar relations with the Soviet Union on the other.

262　**Enola Gay.**
Gordon Thomas, Max Morgan Witts.　New York: Stein and Day, 1977. 327p. 4 maps. bibliog. Reprinted, New York: Pocket Books, 1977.

The flight of the *Enola Gay*, the B-29 which dropped the atomic bomb over Hiroshima on 6 August 1945, constitutes the climax of this dramatic account of the nine-month period between September 1944, when the United States accelerated its efforts to produce the bomb, and August 1945, when Japan unconditionally surrendered to the Allies. Particular attention is paid to the background and training of the crew members who piloted the *Enola Gay* as well as to the preparations for their historic flight and the actual bombing run over Hiroshima.

263　**Day one: before Hiroshima and after.**
Peter Wyden.　New York: Simon and Schuster, 1984. 412p. bibliog. Reprinted, New York: Warner Books, 1985.

A dramatic account of 'the start of the atomic age': of such men as J. Robert Oppenheimer, Leo Szilard, and Edward Teller who conceived and built the atomic bomb and of the initial results of their efforts. Synthesizing available literature about the events which preceded and followed the bombing of Hiroshima and drawing on numerous eyewitness interviews, Wyden deals with the early American efforts to develop the atomic bomb, the scientific breakthroughs that ensued, the initial reservations which certain scientists had of their work, the ignorance and false assumptions of the policy-makers and military personnel who supported the project, the testing of the first bomb at Alamogordo, New Mexico, the rush to select a target in Japan, the bombing and its effect on the people of Hiroshima, and some of the reactions in both the United States and Japan.

Black rain.
See item no. 1058.

Fire from the ashes: short stories about Hiroshima and Nagasaki.
See item no. 1088.

After apocalypse: four Japanese plays of Hiroshima and Nagasaki.
See item no. 1173.

Black sun: the eyes of four; roots and innovation in Japanese photography.
See item no. 1275.

Postwar history

264 **The Pacific alliance: United States foreign economic policy and Japanese trade recovery, 1947–1955.**
William S. Borden. Madison, Wisconsin; London: University of Wisconsin Press, 1984. 320p. bibliog.

This investigation into the economic basis of American postwar policy towards Japan links her with America's global hegemonic concerns and argues that Japan was viewed as the key to US policy in Asia after 1947. It discusses the reasons behind the American support for the re-industrialisation of Japan and examines how the United States actively promoted the rebuilding of her economy, the revival of her foreign trade, and her re-integration into the world market economy. It also shows how certain major decisions of American policy-makers regarding Southeast Asia were closely tied to their perception of that region as a market for Japanese exports and as a Japanese source of vital raw materials.

265 **The other Nuremberg: the untold story of the Tokyo war crimes trials.**
Arnold C. Brackman. New York: Morrow, 1987. 432p. bibliog.
Reprinted, New York: Quill, 1988; London: Collins, 1989.

A reconstruction of the 2½-year-long (1946-48) proceedings of the International Military Tribunal for the Far East, at which twenty-eight Japanese political and military leaders were tried for Japan's alleged wartime crimes. Brackman, a former United Press staff correspondent who covered the trial, recreates the atmosphere of the courtroom as he describes the course of the trial: the disagreements among the justices, the constant problems encountered by both the prosecution and the defence, the courtroom drama itself, and the final judgments. He also recounts the incidents of Japanese wartime brutality and aggression inflicted upon foreign civilians and prisoners-of-war, as well as upon the Japanese population, that were highlighted during the proceedings. While basically sympathetic to the prosecution, the author does not hesitate to point out the procedural irregularities of the trial or to comment critically on its controversial nature. Further information about this trial and other postwar prosecutions of Japanese war criminals may be found in Philip R. Piccigallo's *The Japanese on trial: Allied war crimes operations in the East, 1945–1951* (Austin, Texas; London: University of Texas Press, 1979, 292p.) and in Richard H. Minear's *Victor's justice: the Tokyo war crimes trial* (Princeton, New Jersey: Princeton University Press, 1971, 229.).

266 **Occupation diplomacy: Britain, the United States and Japan, 1945–1952.**
Roger Buckley. Cambridge, England; New York: Cambridge University Press, 1982. 294p. map. bibliog. (International Studies).

This study of the British involvement in the Allied occupation of Japan challenges the conventional view of the occupation as an exclusively American affair. It describes the role which Great Britain and the Commonwealth countries (particularly Australia) played in wartime planning for the treatment of postwar Japan, in the decision to retain the imperial institution, in constitutional and political reforms, in the military garrisoning of the Japanese home islands (through the stationing of the British Commonwealth Occupation Force in Shikoku and western Honshū), in the conduct of the war crimes trials, in economic affairs, and in the preparation and conclusion of a peace settlement with Japan. British perceptions of Japan as well as Britain's efforts to promote her own economic interests in East Asia are also discussed at length.

267 **Remaking Japan: the American occupation as New Deal.**
Theodore Cohen; edited with a foreword by Herbert Passin. New York: Free Press, 1987. 533p.

A middle-ranking civilian administrator on the staff of General Douglas MacArthur chronicles the history of the American occupation of Japan from his perspective as a major participant in some of its events and as an acute observer of the immediate postwar scene. Cohen describes many of the efforts to remake Japan in the image of New Deal America through economic democratisation. He discusses such topics as the growth of labour unionisation and collective bargaining, land reform, the enfranchisement of Japanese women, and the limited decentralisation of the *zaibatsu* holding companies. He attributes the origins of Japan's postwar development into a mass-production and mass-consumption society to the American-instigated, Japanese implemented socio-economic reforms that were achieved during the occupation period.

268 **Land reform in Japan.**
Ronald P. Dore, foreword by Seiichi Tōbata. London; New York: Oxford University Press, 1959. 510p. 2 maps. bibliog. Reprinted, London: Athlone Press, 1984; New York: Schocken Books, 1985.

An authoritative study of the extensive redistribution of agricultural land holdings which occurred during the late 1940s and the social, economic, and political consequences of this Allied-sponsored reform. Part one describes the pre-World War II tenancy system and relates agrarian unrest at that time to Japanese aggression and expansion overseas. Part two discusses the enactment and execution of the Land Reform Law itself. The final three parts characterise the impact of the land reform on rural living standards, self-help and mutual help arrangements in the villages, feelings of solidarity in various hamlets, and the hereditary status held by new and old land owners. The author also identifies some of the factors which have influenced the agricultural policies pursued by postwar political parties and the political roles of various farmers' unions and agricultural co-operative organisations.

269 **Japan diary.**
Mark Gayn. New York: Sloane, 1948. 517p. Reprinted, Rutland, Vermont; Tokyo: Tuttle, 1981.

A journalistic eyewitness report in diary form by a *Chicago Sun* correspondent stationed in Japan and Korea between December 1945 and December 1946. Capturing the atmosphere of the times, Gayn describes the interaction between the American authorities and the Japanese people in the immediate aftermath of World War II, the impact of the occupation on the daily lives of the individuals whom he interviewed or observed, various events and conditions in both the cities and the countryside, the far-reaching social and economic changes that were initiated at that time, and some of the behind-the-scenes maneuvering among the victors and the vanquished. Gayn viewed the occupation with some degree of cynicism and disillusion. He felt that a number of the efforts to democratise Japan were being severely undercut by the delegation of authority to old-style, anti-democratic leaders and by the elimination of several American 'reformers' on General Douglas MacArthur's staff.

270 **Antitrust in Japan.**
Eleanor M. Hadley.   Princeton, New Jersey: Princeton University
Press, 1970. 528p.

An account of the American efforts in 1945-48 to break up the giant family-dominated
financial and industrial combines (*zaibatsu*) which had largely controlled the prewar
Japanese economy, and a critical assessment of the results of this programme following
the passage of nearly twenty years. Hadley first describes the decision-making process
and the steps undertaken to democratise the Japanese business world by dissolving the
zaibatsu. She then discusses the sudden abandonment of this policy in 1948 and
considers the ultimate impact of this antitrust programme. She points out that *zaibatsu*
dissolution led to increased economic competition, greater investment, and enhanced
industrial performance in postwar Japan. At the same time, groups of affiliated private
enterprises (*keiretsu*) replaced some of the *zaibatsu* and the Japanese government
actively promoted market concentration and the cartelisation of business and industry
as part of its efforts to strengthen the postwar economy.

271 **Sheathing the sword: the demilitarisation of Japan.**
Meirion Harries, Susie Harries.   New York: Macmillan; London:
Hamish Hamilton, 1987. 364p. map.

An examination of the manner in which the American occupation forces brought about
the demilitarisation and reorientation of Japan and some of the ways in which the
United States and Japan have interacted with each other since the end of World War
II. The authors focus on the uprooting of militarism that occurred through
disarmament, the purge of wartime militarists, the re-education of the Japanese, and
the revision of the constitution; describe the nature, course, and outcome of the Tokyo
war crimes trial; discuss the transformation of Japan from a former enemy into a
favoured American ally; assess the subsequent American pressure on Japan to re-arm
and serve as a bulwark against communist expansion in Asia, as well as the extent to
which present-day Japan is effectively demilitarised; and argue that the US–Japan
partnership should not depend on the massive remilitarisation of a now essentially
pacifist nation.

272 **MITI and the Japanese miracle: the growth of industrial policy,
1925–1975.**
Chalmers Johnson.   Stanford, California: Stanford University Press,
1982. 393p. bibliog. Reprinted, Rutland, Vermont; Tokyo: Tuttle,
1986.

A widely acclaimed institutional study of the origins, structure, and activities of the
Ministry of International Trade and Industry (MITI) between 1925 and 1975. MITI's
role as the 'leading state actor in the economy' and its internal dynamics are examined
historically as Johnson describes the growth and evolution of its industrial policy as
well as the bureaucratic sources of that policy, the ministry's prewar successes and
failures as well as the impact of both the war (when it functioned as the Ministry of
Munitions) and the occupation, its postwar economic policy-making and its central role
in directing the collaboration of the state and private business and industry towards the
goal of rapid development, the behaviour and performance of the MITI bureaucracy,
and MITI's initial opposition to economic liberalisation and its about-face espousal of
the policy of internationalisation. Johnson concludes by contrasting the Japanese
'developmental' state with the American 'regulatory state'.

273 **Japan's American interlude.**
Kazuo Kawai. Chicago: University of Chicago Press, 1960. 257p.
bibliog. Reprinted, University of Chicago Press, 1979.
An overview and balanced assessment of the 'American interlude in the history of
Japan' (1945-52) during which the Japanese people not only were subjected to
American military occupation and political control but also were significantly affected
by American reforms in a vast number of areas. Kawai, editor-in-chief of the *Nippon
Times* (Japan's leading English-language daily newspaper) at that time, writes about
the surprisingly subservient attitude of the Japanese towards the occupation, the
character of the administration headed by General Douglas MacArthur, the
background of the occupation, constitutional revision, the new role and image of the
emperor, political reorganisation, the location of political power, various economic
reforms, labour, agriculture and the country's recovery, the introduction of basic
reforms in all sectors of education, and the process of democratisation that took place
within Japanese society.

274 **Postwar politics in Japan, 1945-1955.**
Junnosuke Masumi, translated by Lonny E. Carlile. Berkeley,
California: Center for Japanese Studies, Institute of East Asian Studies,
University of California, 1985. 420p. bibliog. (Japan Research
Monograph, 6).
A detailed portrayal of the major political events and personalities of the tumultuous
decade immediately following World War II. Masumi discusses the extensive revision
of the constitution that was mandated by the Allied occupation authorities, the factious
nature of party politics and the antagonistic relations between the conservatives and
socialists at that time, the steps leading up to the San Francisco Peace Treaty and
peace conference of 1951 (which formally ended the war in the Pacific), the evolution
and the legacy of various democratisation reforms – affecting the bureaucracy, the
zaibatsu, agriculture, and labour – which were introduced by the occupying forces, and
the realignment of the political world that resulted in the establishment of the so-called
'1955 political system' of long-term Liberal Democratic Party rule following the
collapse of the Yoshida government in 1954.

275 **Japanese workers and the struggle for power, 1945-1947.**
Joe Moore. Madison, Wisconsin; London: University of Wisconsin
Press, 1983. 305p. bibliog.
A case-study of the radical roots of Japan's present-day labour force. Moore chronicles
in detail the efforts of Japan's resurgent postwar labour movement to effect a
revolution in Japanese labour relations and to institute workers' control over
production. He also describes the response of Japanese business and government on
the one hand and the Allied occupation authorities under the command of General
Douglas MacArthur on the other hand to these radical activities, as well as the
ultimate 'surrender' of Japanese labour to MacArthur's demand that it cancel the mass
general strike which it had scheduled for 1 February 1947.

276 **Nationalism and the right wing in Japan: a study of post-war trends.**
Ivan I. Morris, introduction by Masao Maruyama. London; New
York: Issued under the auspices of the Royal Institute of International
Affairs by Oxford University Press, 1960. 476p. bibliog. Reprinted,
Westport, Connecticut: Greenwood Press, 1974.

This study of the decline and re-emergence of nationalism and right-wing nationalist
societies between 1945 and 1957 first examines the attack on organised nationalism and
the dispersal of ultranationalistic groups that occurred early during the Occupation
period. It then shows how the adverse reaction to the resurgence of communism and
the 'reverse course' in American policy towards occupied Japan led to a revival of
nationalist movements along traditional lines. Detailed analyses of nationalist trends
within the military, the student movements, and youth groups, as well as an assessment
of the strength and potential of the right-wing nationalist groups as of the mid-1950s
conclude the book. Maruyama's introductory essay surveys the traditional role of the
right wing in Japanese politics.

277 **Legal reform in occupied Japan: a participant looks back.**
Alfred C. Oppler, foreword by Kurt Steiner. Princeton, New Jersey;
Guildford, Surrey: Princeton University Press, 1976. 345p.

Oppler discusses the legal and judicial reforms that were carried out to implement the
principles of the postwar constitution. Interspersing legal and political analysis with
personal narrative, he describes the wide scope of his own activities, including the role
which he played in reorganising the courts and in rewriting the Japanese civil, criminal,
and procedural codes. During the Occupation period, Oppler served both as Chief of
the Courts and Law Division of the Government Section and as Chief of the
Legislation and Justice Division of the Legal Section under General Douglas
MacArthur.

278 **Beneath the eagle's wings: Americans in occupied Japan.**
John Curtis Perry. New York: Dodd, Mead, 1980. 253p. bibliog.

A portrait of the initial years of the occupation of Japan that focuses 'less on what the
occupiers did to the Japanese than on what the experience meant to those individual
Americans most intimately involved with it'. Perry recreates the atmosphere of that era
as he describes the arrival of the Allies in the fall of 1945, the ideological 'baggage'
which the Americans brought with them, some of their goals and programmes (among
them the demilitarisation of Japan and a concerted effort to fashion a working
democracy within the country), the character and role of General Douglas MacArthur,
American behaviour in Japan, and the conditions under which both American GIs and
civilian personnel lived and worked. Illustrating his account with many contemporary
photographs, Perry concludes that the occupation was an 'extraordinarily successful'
event despite the ethnocentrism and profound ignorance of Japanese culture and
society that characterised most Americans at that time.

279 **The American occupation of Japan: the origins of the cold war in Asia.**
Michael Schaller. Oxford, England; New York: Oxford University
Press, 1985. 351p. map. bibliog.

An inquiry into the place of the occupation within the context of overall American
East Asian diplomacy between 1945 and 1950. In contrast with many other
publications which study the internal transformation of Japan during this period,

Schaller focuses on the evolution of US policy towards Japan through an examination of the bureaucratic politics of the Truman Administration in so far as they involved Japan in particular and Asia in general, and through some consideration of the relations between Washington and General Douglas MacArthur's headquarters in Tokyo. Schaller argues that the critical turning-point occurred in 1947-48 when, in a 'reverse course' of American policy, Washington shifted the focus of its attention from China to Japan, chose to rely upon Japan as the most important country in Asia to contain the expansion of communism, and began to place a high priority on promoting Japan's postwar economic recovery.

280 **Democratizing Japan: the Allied occupation.**
Edited with an introduction by Robert E. Ward, Yoshikazu
Sakamoto. Honolulu, Hawaii: University of Hawaii Press, 1987. 456p.

Thirteen Japanese and American scholars examine the process and outcome of Allied efforts to democratise Japan's authoritarian political system during the occupation of Japan (1945-52). They discuss the pre-surrender planning for the postwar treatment of the emperor and for constitutional changes, the international context of the occupation of Japan, the policy and process of constitutional reform, the conflict between two legal traditions in making the postwar constitution, early SCAP (Supreme Commander for the Allied Powers) policy and the rehabilitation of Japan's national parliament (the Diet), the reform of the bureaucracy and the Civil Code, the politics of women's rights, the making of the postwar local government system, the occupation of Okinawa, the postwar conservative parties, early postwar reformist parties, and the formation and transformation of managerial councils.

281 **Japan's political revolution under MacArthur: a participant's account.**
Justin Williams, Sr. Athens, Georgia: University of Georgia Press;
Tokyo: University of Tokyo Press, 1979. 305p. bibliog.

Williams, Chief of the Government Section's Legislative Division during the occupation of Japan (1945-52), describes the implementation of the American policies that were designed to democratise the country. He writes at length about postwar occupation policy; the origins, nature, and adoption of the postwar constitution; the American role in restructuring the Japanese Diet; the Japanese political and parliamentary scene during the late 1940s; and various aspects of US policy towards Japan at that time. He also portrays some of the key personnel on General Douglas MacArthur's staff and appraises MacArthur's performance as the Supreme Commander for the Allied Powers. As a record of candid observations and strongly held views by a major participant in the occupation, Williams' autobiographical account is valuable for historians and political scientists.

282 **The Yoshida memoirs: the story of Japan in crisis.**
Shigeru Yoshida, translated by Kenichi Yoshida. London:
Heinemann, 1961; Boston, Massachusetts: Houghton Mifflin, 1962.
305p. Reprinted, Westport, Connecticut: Greenwood Press, 1973.

The man who headed five government cabinets between 1946 and 1954 as prime minister of Japan offers his inside account and personal assessment of the history of the Allied occupation of Japan. Yoshida describes the tragic consequences of World War II and the beginnings of the occupation, his impressions of General Douglas MacArthur and his aides, his own involvement in the governing of Japan, and several areas of occupation reforms including the revision of the constitution, the purges, education, police, agricultural and labour reforms, and the establishment of the Self-Defence Forces. In concluding chapters, Yoshida not only expresses his views about Japan's labour movement and about the communists as a destructive force but also discusses the San Francisco Peace Treaty and peace conference of 1951, the postwar disposition of Japan's territories, and the US–Japan Security Treaty and administrative agreement that terminated the occupation of Japan.

283 **Japan and the San Francisco peace settlement.**
Michael M. Yoshitsu. New York; Guildford, Surrey: Columbia University Press, 1983. 120p. (Studies of the East Asian Institute, Columbia University).

This study of the origins and policies behind Japan's early postwar relationship with the United States narrates the steps that enabled Japan to regain her independence in 1952. Concentrating on decision-making and negotiating by Japanese and American diplomats, Yoshitsu describes the early planning for a peace conference, the Yoshida initiative of the late 1940s, the security negotiations between John Foster Dulles and Prime Minister Yoshida Shigeru (1950-51), and the price that Japan had to pay in order to achieve ratification of the peace treaty. Throughout his book, the author considers the ways in which treaty planning and negotiations were influenced by perceptions of domestic political protest, Japan's economic weakness, and the cold war environment. Considerable documentation about Japanese efforts to negotiate peace settlements not only with the United States and Great Britain but also with the USSR, China, India, Korea, and the countries of Southeast Asia together with overviews of their respective attitudes towards peace-making with Japan, in turn, may be found in *Japan's postwar peace settlements*, by Rajendra Kumar Jain (Atlantic Highlands, New Jersey: Humanities Press, 1978, 399p.).

Red flag in Japan: international communism in action, 1919–1951.
See item no. 192.

Japan: the years of trial, 1919–52.
See item no. 222.

Military government in the Ryukyu Islands, 1945–1950.
See item no. 285.

Shōwa: an inside history of Hirohito's Japan.
See item no. 294.

Tojo and the coming of the war.
See item no. 321.

Empire and aftermath: Yoshida Shigeru and the Japanese experience, 1878–1954.
See item no. 324.

Hirohito: emperor of Japan.
See item no. 334.

Hirohito: behind the myth.
See item no. 334.

The years of MacArthur. Volume 3: Triumph and disaster, 1945–1964.
See item no. 356.

Encounter with Japan.
See item no. 359.

Windows for the crown prince.
See item no. 362.

Shrine Shinto after World War II.
See item no. 515.

Women against war.
See item no. 583.

Socialist parties in postwar Japan.
See item no. 630.

New frontiers in American–East Asian relations: essays presented to Dorothy Borg.
See item no. 646.

The postwar rearmament of Japanese maritime forces, 1945–71.
See item no. 759.

Japan's postwar defense policy, 1947–1968.
See item no. 770.

Conspiracy at Matsukawa.
See item no. 780.

A financial history of the new Japan.
See item no. 851.

Concise dictionary of modern Japanese history.
See item no. 1555.

Asia and Oceania: a guide to archival and manuscript sources in the United States.
See item no. 1562.

Japan and the world, 1853–1952: a bibliographic guide to Japanese scholarship in foreign relations.
See item no. 1599.

The Allied occupation of Japan, 1945–1952: an annotated bibliography of Western-language materials.
See item no. 1613.

Bibliography on the Allied occupation of Japan: a bibliography of Western-language publications from the years 1970–1980 (preliminary edition).
See item no. 1613.

Okinawa, the Kurile Islands, and Sakhalin

284 **Okinawa: the history of an island people.**
George H. Kerr. Rutland, Vermont; Tokyo: Tuttle, 1958. 542p.
6 maps. bibliog.

An authoritative history of the Ryūkyū Islands (including the main island of Okinawa) from earliest times through 1945. This account begins with a description of the legendary past of the Ryūkyūs and the rise of the kingdom of Chuzan during the fifteenth and sixteenth centuries. It then focuses on Okinawa's loss of independence in the early 1600s, its subsequent ambivalent status as both a vassal state of the powerful Japanese feudal domain (*han*) of Satsuma and a tributary state of the Ch'ing Chinese empire, and the nineteenth-century impact of the West. The concluding part ('Okinawa-ken: Frontier Province') deals with the Japanese annexation of the Ryūkyūs in 1879 and with the islands' incorporation and assimilation into Japan during the ensuing decades. Kerr's study is concerned not only with the political and diplomatic history of the Ryūkyūs but also with their economy, social structure, religion and myths, and cultural heritage. A synthesis of information about the archaeology and early culture history of the Ryūkyūs can best be found in Richard J. Pearson's *Archaeology of the Ryukyus: a regional chronology from 3000 B.C. to the historic period* (Honolulu, Hawaii: University of Hawaii Press, 1969, 210p.).

285 **The Soviet seizure of the Kuriles.**
David Rees. New York; Eastbourne, Sussex: Praeger, 1985. 182p.
4 maps. bibliog. (Praeger Special Studies) (Praeger Scientific).

The Soviet military seizure in 1945 of the strategically important Kurile island chain and the adjacent islands of Habomai and Shikotan has remained an obstruction to the normalisation of postwar Soviet–Japanese relations. Rees first outlines the course of Russo–Japanese rivalry over the Kuriles prior to World War II, then discusses the diplomatic and military developments which led to the Soviet occupation of the islands and to the Japanese government's formal renunciation of its claims to its prewar colonial empire in the San Francisco Peace Treaty of 1951. Finally the author describes the postwar Japanese campaign for the return of four disputed islands at the southern end of the Kurile chain (Japan's 'Northern Territories'), the effect of this irredentist movement on Soviet–Japanese relations, and the role of the Kuriles in current Soviet strategy. The postwar American occupation of the Ryūkyū island chain, in contrast, was peacefully terminated in 1972. Arnold G. Fisch, Jr.'s *Military government in the Ryukyu Islands, 1945–1950* (Washington, DC: Center of Military History, United States Army, 1988, 353p. [Army Historical Series]) offers an authoritative account of the US army's military government efforts on Okinawa from the first stages of planning until the beginning of the transition towards a civil administration. Akio Watanabe's *The Okinawa problem: a chapter in Japan–U.S. relations* (Clayton, Victoria: Melbourne University Press, 1970, 220p.), in turn, analyses the formation of Japanese attitudes towards Okinawa after World War II and their bearing on US–Japanese relations during the 1950s and the 1960s.

286 **The Kuril Islands: Russo–Japanese frontier in the Pacific.**
John J. Stephan. Oxford, England: Clarendon Press, 1974. 279p.
6 maps. bibliog.

A comprehensive study of the 730-mile-long chain of islands stretching between Hokkaidō and the southern tip of the Kamchatka Peninsula. Also known in Japanese as Chishima Rettō, these islands were generally administered as part of Hokkaidō (rather than as a colonial possession) from 1875, when they were formally acquired from Russia under the Treaty of St Petersburg, until summer 1945, when Soviet military forces invaded and occupied them. Stephan covers the history of the Kuriles from prehistoric times to the 1970s. He explores the Russo–Japanese dispute over them between 1750 and 1875, their subsequent development under Japan (1875-1945), and their strategic and military importance during World War II. A closing chapter focuses on the 'Northern Territories problem', the lingering dispute over the Soviet occupation of the four southernmost Kurile Islands that are claimed by the Japanese as an integral part of their homeland.

287 **Sakhalin: a history.**
John J. Stephan. Oxford, England: Clarendon Press, 1971. 240p.
6 maps. bibliog.

Sakhalin, the elongated island directly north of Hokkaidō, has been claimed as well as colonised by the Japanese in recent memory. Stephan reconstructs Sakhalin's history from prehistoric times to its incorporation into the Soviet Union after World War II. Much of his attention focuses on the Russo–Japanese rivalry over Sakhalin between 1785 and 1875, on Japan's colonial administration of the southern half of the island (known among the Japanese as Karafuto) between the end of the Russo–Japanese War in 1905 and the Soviet invasion of August 1945, and on the Japanese occupation of the northern half of the island during the early 1920s.

The Japanese colonial empire, 1895–1945.
See item no. 223.

Narrative of the expedition of an American squadron to the China Seas and Japan under the command of Commodore M. C. Perry, United States Navy.
See item no. 673.

State and diplomacy in early modern Japan: Asia in the development of the Tokugawa bakufu.
See item no. 677.

The Okinawa war.
See item no. 713.

Okinawa: the last battle.
See item no. 713.

Typhoon of steel: the battle for Okinawa.
See item no. 713.

Okinawa, 1945: gateway to Japan.
See item no. 713.

Managing an alliance: the politics of U.S.–Japanese relations.
See item no. 721.

Craft treasures of Okinawa.
See item no. 1201.

Ryukyu Islands: a bibliography.
See item no. 1591.

Ryukyu: a bibliographical guide to Okinawan studies.
See item no. 1591.

Ryukyu: an annotated bibliography.
See item no. 1591.

World War II at sea: a bibliography of sources in English. Volume II: The Pacific Theater.
See item no. 1609.

Biographical and Autobiographical Accounts

Collective biography

288 **Pacifism in Japan: the Christian and socialist tradition.**
Edited with an introduction by Nobuya Bamba, John F. Howes,
foreword by Robert N. Bellah. Vancouver, British Columbia:
University of British Columbia Press; Kyōto: Minerva Press, 1978.
300p.

A collection of essays focusing on the lives and pacifist thought of eight Japanese
Christians and socialists who were outstanding advocates of world peace during the late
nineteenth and twentieth centuries. These essays deal with the poet and essayist
Kitamura Tōkoku (1868-94), the journalist and novelist Kinoshita Naoe (1869-1937),
the religious leader and essayist Uchimura Kanzō (1861-1930), the socialist and
anarchist leader Kōtoku Shūsui (1871-1911), the educator and political leader Abe Isoo
(1865-1949), the social reformer and labour leader Kagawa Toyohiko (1888-1960), the
liberal educator and economist Yanaihara Tadao (1893-1961), and the postwar
defender of peace and the new constitution Tabata Shinobu (1902-   ).

289 **Personality in Japanese history.**
Introduced and edited by Albert M. Craig, Donald H. Shively.
Berkeley, California; London: University of California Press, 1970.
481p. (Publications of the Center for Japanese and Korean Studies).

Centring around the theme of personality as a factor in Japanese history, this
Festschrift in honour of Edwin O. Reischauer consists almost entirely of case-studies of
important figures from the Tokugawa, Meiji, and Taishō periods: the daimyō Ikeda
Mitsumasa (1609-82) of Okayama; Tokugawa Tsunayoshi (1646-1709), the Genroku
period shōgun; the farmer-scholar Ōkura Nagatsune (1768-?); the *bakufu* retainer
Ōshio Heihachirō (1793-1837), who led the rebellion known as the Tempō Uprising;
Abe Masahiro (1819-57), the *bakufu*'s chief senior councillor, and Tokugawa Nariaki
(1800-60), the daimyō of Mito; Shimazu Nariakira (1809-58), daimyō of Satsuma;
Hashimoto Sanai (1834-59), a scholar and retainer of the daimyō of Fukui; Kido Kōin

(1833-77) and Ōkubo Toshimichi (1830-78), two key Meiji statesmen; Mutsu Munemitsu (1844-97), a Meiji period foreign minister; Itō Miyoji (1857-1934), a bureaucrat and politician; the journalist Kayahara Kazan (1870-1952); the politician Nagai Ryūtarō (1881-1944); and the noted writer, Akutagawa Ryūnosuke (1892-1927).

290 **Reflections on the way to the gallows: rebel women in prewar Japan.**
Translated and edited with an introduction by Mikiso Hane.
Berkeley, California; London; University of California Press [with] Pantheon Books, 1988. 274p.

Excerpts from the memoirs, recollections, and essays of several women activists in radical movements who struggled to ensure social justice and equality for all members of society and challenged conventional customs and traditional moral principles in prewar Japan. Their writings candidly reveal their innermost thoughts and feelings and depict the 'inner workings of the family, the weight of societal pressures, and – on a more public level – the effects of political repression and the conditions of human life' at that time. Included are chapters concerned with Fukuda Hideko (1865-1927), a strong advocate of people's rights; Kanno Suga (1881-1911), an anarchist executed for treason; the women's socialist group Sekirankai ('Red Wave Society') that was prominent in the early 1920s; the labour activist and social reformer Tanno Setsu (1902-); Yamashiro Tomoe (1912-), a left-wing novelist concerned with the sufferings of rural women who was imprisoned in 1940; and Kaneko Fumiko (1903-26), a woman convicted of plotting to assassinate both Emperor Taishō and Crown Prince Hirohito.

291 **Some Japanese portraits.**
Donald Keene, illustrations by Motoichi Izawa. Tokyo; New York: Kodansha International, 1978. 228p.

Twenty-one sketches, accompanied by pen-and-ink drawings, of distinguished and lesser known literary personalities active between the fifteenth and early twentieth centuries. Keene relates these writers both to their often turbulent times and to specific literary traditions. Included are essays on the fifteenth-century Zen Buddhist poet-priest Ikkyū Sōjun, the Muromachi period noh actor and playwright Zeami Motokiyo, the sixteenth-century daimyō and *waka* poet Hosokawa Yūsai, the late Tokugawa period fiction writer Tamenaga Shunsui, the nineteenth-century *gesaku* writer Kanagaki Robun, the Meiji period *waka* and haiku poet Masaoka Shiki, and the late nineteenth-century woman novelist and poet Higuchi Ichiyō. These 'portraits' were originally written as a series of 'promenades' in Japanese literature for the popular weekly magazine *Shūkan Asahi* (Tokyo).

292 **Six lives, six deaths: portraits from modern Japan.**
Robert Jay Lifton, Shūichi Katō, Michael R. Reich. New Haven, Connecticut; London: Yale University Press, 1979. 305p. bibliog.

Biographical sketches explore the ways in which six talented writers and public figures viewed death as a universal concept and shaped their own lives in preparation for their own deaths. Nogi Maresuke (noted general of the Russo–Japanese War), Mori Ōgai (novelist and military doctor), Nakae Chōmin (liberal political theorist), Kawakami Hajime (economist and communist), Masamune Hakuchō (novelist of the naturalist school), and Mishima Yukio (right-wing author) are the subjects of this psycho-historical study of the efforts of these men to instil meaning and purpose into their lives and to manage some of the anxieties created by their knowledge of the inevitability of death.

293 **The nobility of failure: tragic heroes in the history of Japan.**
Ivan Morris. New York: Holt, Rinehart and Winston; London: Secker and Warburg, 1975. 500p. 4 maps. bibliog. Reprinted, New York: New American Library, 1976; Harmondsworth, Middlesex: Penguin, 1980; Rutland, Vermont and Tokyo: Tuttle, 1982; New York: Noonday Press, Farrar Straus Giroux, 1988.

An introduction to the lives and times of nine historic figures who, typifying the tragic hero in Japanese history, pitted themselves against overwhelming odds and failed in their various quests. These individuals included Yamato Takeru, a fourth-century imperial prince; the ninth-century government official and scholar Sugawara no Michizane; Minamoto no Yoshitsune, an immortalised twelfth-century warrior and hero of the Gempei War; the fourteenth-century warrior Kusunoki Masashige, who supported the ill-fated Kemmu Restoration; Amakusa Shirō, the seventeenth-century messianic leader of the Shimabara uprising; Ōshio Heihachirō, leader of an 1837 rebellion in Ōsaka against the Tokugawa shogunate; and the Meiji Restoration leader Saigō Takamori, who headed the Satsuma rebellion against the early Meiji government in 1877. A concluding chapter deals with the kamikaze pilots of World War II. The stories of these 'failed heroes' suggest 'the varieties of worldly defeat, the dignity it can bestow and the reasons for its particular evocative appeal in the Japanese tradition'.

294 **Shōwa: an inside history of Hirohito's Japan.**
Tessa Morris-Suzuki. London: Athlone Press, 1984; New York: Schocken Books, 1985. 330p.

An account of Japan's modern history as viewed through the eyes of two men and a woman of dissimilar backgrounds and character who were born shortly prior to the beginning of the Shōwa period (1926). Morris-Suzuki traces the lives of these three ordinary people from their childhood during the years of rampant militarism and nationalism, through the events of World War II, under the immediate postwar Allied occupation of Japan, and during the three ensuing decades when they participated – as adults with careers in business, art and politics – in Japan's spectacular 'economic miracle'. The book combines the author's narrative of the historical and social background of the Shōwa period with her subjects' own reminiscences of their personal experiences and their perspectives of the events which they witnessed between the 1930s and 1980.

295 **Great historical figures of Japan.**
Edited by Hyōe Murakami, Thomas J. Harper. Tokyo: Japan Culture Institute [Nihon Bunka Kenkyūjo], 1978. 327p. map.

A collection of chronologically arranged biographical sketches of forty-one prominent men and women who lived between the sixth and the twentieth centuries. Included are essays about Tenmu Tennō, 'an emperor who ruled as well as reigned'; Kūkai and Saichō, 'patriarchs of Heian Buddhism'; Fujiwara no Michinaga, 'regent at the peak of aristocratic prosperity'; 'Murasaki Shikibu and Sei Shōnagon, 'eminent women writers of the court'; Hōjō Masako, 'woman of power behind the Kamakura bakufu'; Shinran and Nichiren, 'innovators of Kamakura Buddhism'; Ashikaga Takauji and Ashikaga Yoshimitsu, 'insurgent warrior to supreme hegemon'; Takeda Shingen, 'daimyo in an age of strife'; Sen no Rikyū, 'tea master in a time of war'; Saikaku, Bashō, and Chikamatsu, 'creators of a new literature'; Tanuma Okitsugu, 'forerunner of the modern statesman'; Rai Sanyō, 'historian and master of Chinese verse'; Sakamoto Ryōma, 'young activist of the Meiji Restoration'; Ōkubo Toshimichi, 'architect of the modern state'; and Kawabata Yasunari, 'Nobel Prize-winning novelist'. All essays are oriented towards a general reading audience.

296 **Five political leaders of modern Japan: Itō Hirobumi, Ōkuma Shigenobu, Hara Takashi, Inukai Tsuyoshi, and Saionji Kimmochi.**
Yoshitake Oka, translated by Andrew Fraser, Patricia Murray.
Tokyo: University of Tokyo Press, 1986. 232p.

Studies the careers of five prominent politicians, each of whom wielded considerable influence in Japanese politics and served as his country's prime minister on at least one occasion between 1885 and 1932. Far more than a collection of short biographies, Oka's book constitutes a series of case-studies of political leadership, as he examines the character of these leaders and documents how and why they responded as they did to specific historical circumstances and events. Itō Hirobumi (1841-1909) is remembered as the 'father of the Meiji Constitution'; Ōkuma Shigenobu (1838-1922) as a 'champion of democracy'; Hara Takashi (1856-1921) as the 'commoner' prime minister; Inukai Tsuyoshi (1855-1932) as a politician whose career was marked by frustration, triumph, and tragedy; and Saionji Kimmochi (1849-1940) as the last of the *genrō* ('elder statesman').

297 **Samurai and silk: a Japanese and American heritage.**
Haru Matsukata Reischauer. Cambridge, Massachusetts; London: Belknap Press of Harvard University Press, 1986. 371p. map.

The wife of the noted historian and diplomat Edwin O. Reischauer recounts the story of her heritage through biographies of her two famous grandfathers and shorter accounts of some of their descendants and relatives. Her paternal grandfather, Matsukata Masayoshi (1835-1924), was a provincial farmer-samurai who rose to become a founding father of the Meiji government, a longterm minister of finance whose wide-ranging deflationary policies helped steer Japan through her first modern economic crisis, and ultimately the country's prime minister. Her maternal grandfather, Arai Ryōichirō (1855-1939), was one of Japan's first international businessmen. He played a major role in the development of direct Japanese silk exports to the United States, and settled in New York City. Reischauer depicts their lives against the backdrop of Japan's modernisation and combines her own insights with historical detail to present an engaging personalised view of modern Japanese economic history and Japanese–American relations.

A chronicle of gods and sovereigns: *Jinnō Shōtōki* **of Kitabatake Chikafusa.**
See item no. 144.

The search for a new order: intellectuals and fascism in prewar Japan.
See item no. 199.

Memories of silk and straw: a self-portrait of small-town Japan.
See item no. 234.

Tradition and modernization in Japanese culture.
See item no. 239.

Flowers in salt: the beginnings of feminist consciousness in modern Japan.
See item no. 240.

The Hiroshima maidens: a story of courage, compassion, and survival.
See item no. 252.

Hiroshima.
See item no. 255.

Women against war.
See item no. 583.

Japanese foreign policy 1869-1942: Kasumigaseki to Miyakezaka.
See item no. 654.

Japanese poetic diaries.
See item no. 1149.

Kanō Eitoku.
See item no. 1252.

Japanese film directors.
See item no. 1415.

Concise dictionary of modern Japanese history.
See item no. 1555.

Kodansha encyclopedia of Japan.
See item no. 1556.

Before the twentieth century

298　**Told round a brushwood fire: the autobiography of Arai Hakuseki.**
Arai Hakuseki, translated with an introduction and notes by Joyce
Ackroyd.　Princeton, New Jersey: Princeton University Press; Tokyo:
University of Tokyo Press, 1979. 347p. 3 maps. (Unesco Collection of
Representative Works: Japanese Series) (Princeton Library of Asian
Translations).

A translation of *Oritaku shiba no ki* (1716), the autobiography of a noted Confucian
scholar, poet, historian, and statesman (1657-1725). During his period of service to the
Tokugawa shogunate, Hakuseki initiated several significant reforms and provided
influential advice about such matters as foreign trade, currency reform, taxation, the
judicial system, and the samurai code. His autobiography is regarded as the first
Japanese literary work of this genre. It vividly recounts his childhood and youth, his
years as a *rōnin* (masterless samurai) and as a lecturer, and his work as a key adviser to
shōguns Tokugawa Ienobu and Tokugawa Ietsugu. It also portrays some of the
prominent government figures with whom Hakuseki interacted and describes the
political, economic, and social conditions of his times. Ackroyd's introduction outlines
Hakuseki's life and assesses the literary as well as historical significance of his writings.

Biographical and Autobiographical Accounts. Before the twentieth century

Hakuseki's own interpretive history of Japan from the Heian period to the early Tokugawa period, first delivered as a series of lectures to Tokugawa Ienobu, has also become available in translation as *Lessons from history: the Tokushi yoron*, translation and commentary by Joyce Ackroyd (St. Lucia, Queensland; New York: University of Queensland Press, 1982, 417p.).

299 Hideyoshi.
Mary Elizabeth Berry. Cambridge, Massachusetts; London: Harvard University Press, 1982. 293p. 3 maps. (Harvard East Asian Series, 97).

A biography of the political and military leader Toyotomi Hideyoshi (1536?-98), one of the more important figures in Japanese history. Hideyoshi completed the work of his predecessor Oda Nobunaga by reuniting Japan, reinstating the feudal order, ending a century of civil strife known as the 'Warring States period', and creating a form of government that constituted the basis for the ensuing 250 years of Tokugawa rule. Berry describes and analyses Hideyoshi's military accomplishments and the conciliatory tactics that he pursued vis-à-vis rival power holders. She discusses the various steps which he took – among them, his administrative policies and land surveys – in order to shape a new order, his relationship to the daimyō, and his pursuit of political legitimacy through the imperial court at Kyōto. Her closing chapter focuses on Hideyoshi's erratic behaviour during the 1590s, in particular his invasion of the Korean peninsula at that time. An edition of all of the extant letters which he wrote between 1574 and his death in 1598 – *101 letters of Hideyoshi: the private correspondence of Toyotomi Hideyoshi*, edited and translated with an introduction by Adriana Boscaro (Tokyo: Sophia University, 1975, 113p.) – provides firsthand news of public and private events in Hideyoshi's life, information about his normal daily routine, and a revealing portrait of this leader's character and personality.

300 Sugawara no Michizane and the early Heian court.
Robert Borgen. Cambridge, Massachusetts: Council on East Asian Studies, Harvard University, 1986. 431p. bibliog. (Harvard East Asian Monographs, 120).

A multifaceted examination of the political career, scholarly accomplishments, and literary writings of a remarkable Heian period statesman and poet (845-903). Borgen describes and analyses Michizane's work both as a governor of Sanuki Province and as a very powerful imperial court official who opposed Fujiwara family domination of the court and who was ultimately forced into exile as a result of the political scheming of his rivals. He also portrays the political, intellectual, and cultural trends and developments of the era in which Michizane lived, and presents a selection of his poems in translation.

301 A warbler's song in the dusk: the life and work of Ōtomo Yakamochi (718–785).
Paula Doe. Berkeley, California; London: University of California Press, 1982. 260p. 4 maps. bibliog.

Ōtomo no Yakamochi, the compiler of the *Manyōshū* (Japan's first anthology of poetry), is regarded as an outstanding and innovative poet as well as an arbiter of literary taste for a number of succeeding generations. Doe's biography recounts his literary career and the era in which he lived, focusing on the development of his poetic art and touching on such areas as the Chinese influence on early Japanese poetry and the use of the *chōka* as a poetic form. Most of the approximately 479 poems which

Yakamochi contributed for inclusion within the *Manyōshū* are interspersed throughout the narrative in a combination of transliterated Japanese and English translation, thereby making this book not only a valuable study of eighth-century cultural life but also an enjoyable collection of early Japanese verse.

302　**The autobiography of Yukichi Fukuzawa.**
Yukichi Fukuzawa, revised translation by Eiichi Kiyooka, preface to the 1899 edition by Kammei Ishikawa, foreword by Carmen Blacker. New York; London: Columbia University Press, 1966. 407p. (Unesco Collection of Representative Works: Japanese Series). Reprinted, New York: Schocken Books, 1972.

The standard account of a pioneering educator in Meiji Japan, presented in a translation by his grandson. Fukuzawa (1835-1901) was renowned as the founder of one of Japan's most distinguished institutions of higher learning, as a leading journalist and publisher, and as a populariser of Western culture in Japan during the 1870s and 1880s. His autobiography includes his recollections (dictated to a secretary towards the end of his life) about his childhood, his education, his visits to America and Europe, his efforts to share his first-hand knowledge of Western customs and institutions with his fellow countrymen, his establishment of Keio University, his views on business and money, and his private and family life. Carmen Blacker, who contributes a foreword briefly describing and assessing Fukuzawa's importance, is the author of a companion volume entitled *The Japanese enlightenment: a study of the writings of Fukuzawa Yukichi* (q.v.).

303　**Yamagata Aritomo in the rise of modern Japan, 1838–1922.**
Roger F. Hackett. Cambridge, Massachusetts: Harvard University Press, 1971. 377p. bibliog. (Harvard East Asian Series, 60).

Yamagata Aritomo, member of a Chōshū *han* low-ranking samurai family, rose to become both the most important military leader and the most influential political figure of Meiji and Taishō Japan. Hackett depicts the various stages of Yamagata's life and career, and assesses the nature and extent of his influence. He includes accounts of Yamagata's activities as a revolutionary loyalist during the decade preceding the Meiji Restoration of 1868; his role as the 'architect of the modern Japanese army' (Yamagata helped shape a modern military system that was based on universal conscription, and served for several years as the country's minister of war and chief of staff); his leadership as home minister (1883-90), prime minister (1889-91 and 1898-1900), and president of the Privy Council (1903-22); and his many years as a *genrō* ('elder statesman'), during which he exercised considerable authority in Japanese political affairs.

304　**Mori Arinori: a reconsideration.**
Ivan Parker Hall. Cambridge, Massachusetts: Harvard University Press, 1973. 535p. bibliog. (Harvard East Asian Series, 68).

A thorough reassessment of the career and personality of Mori Arinori (1847-89), one of early Meiji Japan's leading modernisers, who was appointed as his nation's first diplomatic envoy to Washington, founded both the Meirokusha (Japan's first modern intellectual society) and his country's first commercial college (the Shōhō Kōshūjo, now Hitotsubashi University), became the first Japanese to marry in a Western fashion, and served as the first minister of education under the Meiji cabinet system.

Biographical and Autobiographical Accounts. Before the twentieth century

Hall follows the course of Mori's life – from his boyhood and youth in the feudal domain of Satsuma through his final years as minister of education, when he restructured Japan's entire school system in ways that would enhance its ability to serve the needs of the state – and examines in some detail the evolution of his thought.

305 **Politics of the Meiji press: the life of Fukuchi Gen'ichirō.**
James L. Huffman. Honolulu, Hawaii: University Press of Hawaii, 1980. 271p. bibliog.

The life (1841-1906) and achievements of an important politician, essayist, playwright, and pioneer in the development of modern journalism. Huffman focuses on Fukuchi's career during the 1870s and 1880s as chief editor of the *Tōkyō Nichi Nichi Shimbun*, Tokyo's first daily newspaper and a forerunner of the present-day *Mainichi Shimbun*, and studies Fukuchi's utilisation of Western journalistic techniques to advocate the 'gradualist' approach of orderly, national progress toward constitutional monarchy under an enlightened government leadership. Through his editorials, Fukuchi exerted a major influence on the broad political, economic, and diplomatic movements of his times. This biography also depicts early Meiji society, the evolution of the early Japanese press, and some of the government policies adopted prior to the promulgation of the Meiji Constitution in 1888.

306 **Ōkubo Toshimichi: the Bismarck of Japan.**
Masakazu Iwata. Berkeley, California: University of California Press, 1965. 376p. bibliog. (Publications of the Center for Japanese and Korean Studies).

Ōkubo Toshimichi (1830-78), one of the central figures in the Meiji Restoration, played a prominent role in the movement to overthrow the Tokugawa shogunate (*bakufu*) and in the formation of the early Meiji state. Iwata offers the first detailed portrayal in English of Ōkubo's life, emphasizing his leadership during the 1860s and his official activities as a Meiji government policy-maker, as a staunch advocate of Westernisation and modernisation, as both a finance minister and first chief of the Home Ministry, and as the individual in charge of suppressing the domestic rebellions of 1874 and 1877. In assessing his historical influence, the author characterises Ōkubo as a shrewd, realistic statesman who succeeded in solidifying the shaky structure of the early Meiji government and in nurturing more than any other single leader the growing concept of nationalism in Japan.

307 **The diary of Kido Takayoshi.**
Takayoshi Kido, translated with an introduction and notes by Sidney DeVere Brown, Akiko Hirota. Tokyo: University of Tokyo Press, 1983-86. 3 vols. bibliog.

Kido Takayoshi (also known as Kido Kōin, 1833-77), a leading statesman in early Meiji Japan, held a number of top government positions and participated in several major government reforms. The detailed diary which he kept between April 1868 and May 1877 contains valuable information about the political events of his era and sheds considerable light on his innermost thoughts and ideas. Volume one, *1861–1871*, a colourful insider's view of early Meiji politics, focuses on the centralisation of political authority and the abolition of Tokugawa feudalism. The second volume, *1871–1874*, centring on Kido's travel to the United States and Europe as the second-ranking member of the Iwakura mission, records his observations and reactions to what he saw. The final volume, *1874–1877*, describes Kido's growing concern over the distress of the

127

Before the twentieth century

former samurai and the peasants who were being adversely affected by the government's modernisation policies, and over the resulting popular discontent.

308 **Ōkuma Shigenobou: statesman of Meiji Japan.**
Joyce C. Lebra. Canberra, ACT: Australian National University Press, 1973. 195p. bibliog.

Lebra traces the life of Ōkuma Shigenobu (1838-1922) – a brilliant Meiji political leader whom she characterises as 'a persistent champion of modernisation and parliamentary government' as well as a 'prototypal popular statesman and precursor of mass democracy in modern Japan' – in order to examine his political objectives and methods and to assess his impact on Japan's modernisation. She focuses on such highlights of Ōkuma's political life as his meteoric rise in the early Meiji bureaucracy and his contributions to government financial reforms and foreign policies during the 1870s, the so-called political crisis of 1881 which resulted in his purge from government, the rise and fall of the political party (Rikken Kaishintō) which he helped to found, and his experiences both as a cabinet minister and, twice, as prime minister.

309 **Motoori Norinaga, 1730–1801.**
Shigeru Matsumoto. Cambridge, Massachusetts: Harvard University Press, 1970. 261p. bibliog. (Harvard East Asian Series, 44).

A biography and intellectual analysis of the influential Tokugawa period scholar who played a prominent role in promoting the *kokugaku* ('national learning') movement and the revival of Shintō during the late 1700s. Matsumoto divides Norinaga's life into four major stages and examines each of them within the general context of Japan's search for cultural identity and national self-image. He shows how Norinaga's personal quest for meaning and identity was intimately related to his pioneering studies of such early Japanese texts as the *Kojiki* (q.v.) and *The tale of Genji* (q.v.), and to his rediscovery of some of the intrinsic values of ancient Japanese life embodied in classical Japanese literature.

310 **The confessions of Lady Nijō.**
Nakanoin Masatada no Musume, translated with an introduction by Karen Brazell. Garden City, New York: Anchor Books, 1973. 288p. Reprinted, London: Owen, 1975; Stanford, California: Stanford University Press, 1976; Feltham, Middlesex: Zenith, 1983.

Translation of *Towazugatari*, an autobiographical narrative of thirty-six years (1271-1306) in the life of an imperial court lady. It provides an account of Lady Nijō's life as a concubine of retired emperor Go-Fukakusa, of her love affairs with other court aristocrats, and of some of her experiences as a wandering Buddhist nun. Throughout her memoirs, Lady Nijō offers revealing descriptions of life both at the Kyōto imperial court and in the countryside. Regarded as a Japanese literary classic, this work is also a welcome historical source of information about the Kamakura period.

311 **Tokutomi Sohō, 1863–1957: a journalist for modern Japan.**
John D. Pierson. Princeton, New Jersey; London: Princeton University Press, 1980. 453p. bibliog.

An account of the thought and early experiences of an important journalist, publicist, political activist, historian, and social critic. Pierson focuses on the evolution of Sohō's ideas and ideals as he discusses his family background and childhood, his early involvement in journalism and his many other activities during the Meiji period in particular, his views about Japan's modernisation, his major publications, and his character and personality. He shows that Sohō's reformist views of how Japan should progress towards national strength and greatness (views which he developed as a youth) changed dramatically as he came to have a more realistic understanding of conditions in the West. As a result, Sohō abandoned the liberal-democratic ideals which he had initially advocated, adopted more traditional and nationalistic values, and became known as a supporter and spokesman for ultranationalism in the Japan of the 1920s and 1930s.

312 **Ox against the storm; a biography of Tanaka Shozo: Japan's conservationist pioneer.**
Kenneth Strong.   Tenterden, Kent: Paul Norbury Publications; Vancouver, British Columbia: University of British Columbia Press, 1977. 231p. bibliog.

Tanaka Shōzō (1841-1913), pioneer environmentalist, democratic statesman, and reformer, waged a lifelong campaign throughout most of the Meiji period against both the political oppression of the peasantry and industrial pollution. This narrative biography traces Shōzō's life and career from his birth as the son of a village headman in present-day Tochigi Prefecture, his frequent confrontations with government authorities, and his leadership in the Popular Rights Movement of the 1880s, to his election to the newly established national Diet in 1890, his fifteen-year-long struggle against the widespread pollution caused by the effluent from the Ashio Copper Mine as it was being developed into a world-class copper mine, his resistance to the government's creation of a reservoir that ultimately destroyed the prosperous village community of Yanaka, and his challenges to some of the Meiji government's priorities as Japan experienced a period of rapid modernisation.

313 **A daughter of the samurai. How a daughter of feudal Japan, living hundreds of years in one generation, became a modern American.**
Etsu Inagaki Sugimoto, introduction by Christopher Morley.   Garden City, New York: Doubleday, Page, 1926. 314p. Reprinted, Rutland, Vermont and Tokyo: Tuttle, 1966.

The daughter of a rural samurai family (1850-1930) recounts her childhood memories and her experiences as an adult in both Japan and the United States. Sugimoto's memoirs recreate the environment in which upper-class families lived during the late Tokugawa and early Meiji periods, and they offer many charming vignettes of traditional Japanese culture as well as anecdotes of her encounters with Americans and Japanese.

314 **Tokugawa Ieyasu: shogun.**
Conrad Totman.   San Francisco, California: Heian International, 1983. 205p. 15 maps.

This biography of the outstanding military leader who completed the unification of Japan and established the Tokugawa shogunate introduces not only Ieyasu himself but also his age and his society. Rather than presenting a straightforward chronological account of Ieyasu's life between 1543 and 1616, Totman divides his narrative into four parts – focusing on the years 1600, 1611, 1614, and 1615 – and inserts considerable background material to supplement his discussion. In spite of a poorly organised text, the volume is valuable for its information about Ieyasu's life and for its depiction of early Tokugawa society and institutions.

315 **Ueda Akinari.**
Blake Morgan Young. Vancouver, British Columbia: University of British Columbia Press, 1982. 177p. bibliog.
Ueda Akinari (1734-1809), a prolific writer of fiction, poetry and essays, is best known as the author of *Ugetsu monogatari* ('Tales of moonlight and rain'). Young's erudite study traces the course of Akinari's life and discusses his various literary works. An entire chapter is devoted to *Ugetsu monogatari* (q.v.).

The revolutionary origins of modern Japan.
See item no. 171.

The Japanese discovery of Europe, 1720–1830.
See item no. 173.

Shogunal politics: Arai Hakuseki and the premises of Tokugawa rule.
See item no. 177.

Charismatic bureaucrat: a political biography of Matsudaira Sadanobu, 1758–1829.
See item no. 177.

Admiral Togo.
See item no. 320.

Dōgen Kigen: mystical realist.
See item no. 481.

Kukai: major works, translated, with an account of his life and a study of his thought.
See item no. 482.

The gossamer years: the diary of a noblewoman of Heian Japan.
See item no. 1013.

Ōkagami, the great mirror: Fujiwara Michinaga (966–1027) and his times. A study and translation.
See item no. 1017.

Yoshitsune: a fifteenth-century Japanese chronicle.
See item no. 1020.

Murasaki Shikibu: her diary and poetic memoirs; a translation and study.
See item no. 1023.

As I crossed a bridge of dreams: recollections of a woman in eleventh-century Japan.
See item no. 1026.

Shikitei Sanba and the comic tradition in Edo fiction.
See item no. 1038.

Musashi.
See item no. 1109.

In the shade of spring leaves: the life and writings of Higuchi Ichiyō, a woman of letters in Meiji Japan.
See item no. 1111.

The poetic memoirs of Lady Daibu.
See item no. 1142.

Masaoka Shiki.
See item no. 1161.

Matsuo Bashō.
See item no. 1167.

Zeami's style: the Noh plays of Zeami Motokiyo.
See item no. 1172.

The legend of Semimaru: blind musician of Japan.
See item no. 1176.

Tall mountains and flowing waters: the arts of Uragami Gyokudō.
See item no. 1230.

Hokusai: paintings, drawings and woodcuts.
See item no. 1260.

Utamaro: colour prints and paintings.
See item no. 1262.

Twentieth century

316   **A Zen life: D. T. Suzuki remembered.**
Edited with an introduction by Masao Abe, photographs and preface by Francis Haar.   New York; Tokyo: Weatherhill, 1986. 250p. bibliog.

Daisetz Teitaro Suzuki (1870-1966) is well known for his untiring, almost single-handed efforts to introduce Zen to the West and for his numerous books and articles about Zen Buddhism, Zen culture, and the Zen tradition. Abe's memorial tribute takes the form of a few of Suzuki's autobiographical accounts, brief discussions of his work and significance, and several short reminiscences by his close friends and followers. Western contributors, among them Richard DeMartino, Erich Fromm, Christmas Humphreys, Philip Kapleau, Thomas Merton, Gary Snyder, and Alan Watts, and such eminent Japanese as Kondō Akihisa, Hisamatsu Shin'ichi, and Nishitani Keiji comment on Suzuki's personality, thought, career, and accomplishments on the basis of their past interaction and memories of him. A concise chronology of Suzuki's life, a comprehensive biography of his writings in Japanese and English, and twenty black-and-white photographs of Suzuki complement the text.

317 **The reluctant admiral: Yamamoto and the Imperial Navy.**
Hiroyuki Agawa, translated by John Bester.   Tokyo; New York:
Kodansha International, 1979. 397p.

A popular biography of Yamamoto Isoroku (1884-1943), the admiral who served as commander in chief of the combined fleet during the first half of World War II and who was widely known as the architect of both Japanese naval and air policy in the Pacific theatre and the Japanese attack on Pearl Harbor. Agawa sympathetically portrays the complex character, background, activities, and role of Yamamoto and contrasts the outlook and 'gentlemanly' traditions of the Imperial Japanese Navy with those of its rival, the Imperial Japanese Army, as he traces Yamamoto's life and career and describes the decision-making that lay behind the navy's pursuit of the specific course that it followed in the Pacific War.

318 **Japanese Marxist: a portrait of Kawakami Hajime, 1879–1946.**
Gail Lee Bernstein.   Cambridge, Massachusetts; London: Harvard
University Press, 1976. 222p. bibliog. (Harvard East Asian Series, 86).

Marxism has had a tremendous impact on the intellectual framework and political culture of twentieth-century Japanese intellectuals and has significantly shaped the evolution of modern Japanese politics as well as the Japanese conceptualisation of society. Kawakami Hajime, an influential professor of economics at Kyōto Imperial University, played a key role in introducing and popularising this ideology during the 1920s and 1930s. Bernstein's portrayal of his life, personality, and ideas traces the gradual evolution of his thought 'from patriotic nationalism to humanistic socialism and, finally, to revolutionary communism'. Her account includes descriptions and analyses of Kawakami's student years in Tokyo, his growing concern for the problems besetting Japanese society, his study of Marxism, his academic career and political activism, and his arrest and imprisonment for violating the Peace Preservation Law of 1925.

319 **Makiguchi, the value creator, revolutionary Japanese educator and founder of Soka Gakkai.**
Dayle M. Bethel.   New York; Tokyo: Weatherhill, 1973. 174p.
bibliog.

Biography of Makiguchi Tsunesaburō (1871-1944), an elementary school teacher and principal, philosopher of education, and founder of the influential Sōka Gakkai movement. Bethel discusses Makiguchi's family life and environmental influences, his professional career, his 'value-creating' pedagogy (Makiguchi's proposed system of education) and the educational philosophy out of which it emerged, Makiguchi's religious conversion to Nichiren Shōshū (a Buddhist sect) in 1928, the founding and post-World War II reconstruction of the Sōka Gakkai movement, and the important role of Makiguchi's theories in the development and growth of Sōka Gakkai.

320 **Admiral Togo.**
Georges Blond, translated from the French by Edward Hyams.   New
York: Macmillan, 1960; London: Jarrolds, 1961. 252p. 2 maps.

Published initially as *L'amiral Togo: samouraï de la mer* (Paris: Librairie Arthème Fayard, 1958), Blond's biography of Tōgō Heihachirō (1848-1934) depicts the youth, early career, and subsequent legendary heroism of Japan's 'samurai of the sea'. Much of the book centres around Tōgō's controversial actions during the Sino–Japanese War of 1894-95 and his leadership of naval operations during the Russo–Japanese War (1904-5), when he blockaded Russia's Far Eastern Fleet at Port Arthur and intercepted and destroyed her Baltic Fleet at the Battle of Tsushima.

321 **Tojo and the coming of the war.**
Robert J. C. Butow, foreword by Frederick S. Dunn. Princeton, New Jersey: Princeton University Press, 1961. 584p. bibliog. Reprinted, Stanford, California: Stanford University Press, 1969.

The life and career of Tōjō Hideki (1884-1948) are set against the background of the rise and fall of Japanese militarism during the 1930s and early 1940s. In this biographical study and historical analysis of the early Shōwa period, Butow briefly traces Tōjō's early years, examines the role of the military in affairs of state as seen through Tōjō's own career, describes the developments, events and behind-the-scenes decision-making that led Tōjō and his colleagues to embark on a course of war with the United States, considers the consequences of this action for both Tōjō as an individual and Japan as a nation, and discusses Tōjō's treatment as a class 'A' war criminal by the Allied powers and his punishment (death by hanging) at the conclusion of the Tokyo war crimes trial.

322 **Michio Ito: the dancer and his dances.**
Helen Caldwell. Berkeley, California; London: University of California Press, 1977. 184p.

An illustrated study of the career, dances, and choreographic style of Michio Ito (1892-1961), a Tokyo-born pioneer of artistic dance in the United States between 1916 and 1941. In the course of covering Ito's career in Europe and the United States, Caldwell considers some of his Japanese and Western sources of inspiration, discusses his methods of composition, and provides brief explanations of thirty-seven of the dances which he created.

323 **The emperor's adviser: Saionji Kinmochi and pre-war Japanese politics.**
Lesley Connors. London and Wolfeboro, New Hampshire: Croom Helm; Oxford, England: Nissan Institute for Japanese Studies, University of Oxford, 1987. 260p. bibliog. (Nissan Institute/Croom Helm Japanese Studies Series).

Biography of one of the most influential figures of modern Japan, a man who in his later years served as chief adviser to the emperor and as the individual responsible for recommending the appointment of each new prime minister. Connors' fresh interpretation of the political role and achievements of this aristocratic statesman (1849-1940) depicts Prince Saionji as a 'determined political leader with clearly defined objectives, a coherent political philosophy and the political sense to know when both needed to be abandoned'. She discusses and analyses Saionji's long political career and his succession to a series of high political posts, the formation of his political opinions and his principles of liberalism and internationalism, his commitment to the development of a constitutional monarchy and to the promotion of good relations with the West (particularly Great Britain and the United States), and the shifting balance of power among Japan's élites during the 1920s and 1930s.

324 **Empire and aftermath: Yoshida Shigeru and the Japanese experience, 1878–1954.**
John W. Dower. Cambridge, Massachusetts: Council on East Asian Studies, Harvard University, 1979. 618p. bibliog. (Harvard East Asian Monographs, 84). Reprinted, Council on East Asian Studies, Harvard University, 1988.

Yoshida Shigeru (1878-1967), a career diplomat and distinguished politician, rose to become ambassador to Great Britain during the 1930s and prime minister between May 1946 and October 1954. The first part of this biography traces Yoshida's career to the end of World War II and includes his involvement in Japan's China policy during the 1920s, in Anglo–Japanese relations between 1936 and 1938, and in the drafting of the Konoe Memorial in 1945. The concluding part surveys the reconsolidation and recentralisation of conservative power during the so-called Yoshida era, the strategic settlement reached between Japan and the United States that involved the restoration of Japanese sovereignty in 1952 'within a framework of rearmament and rigid cold-war partisanship', the co-operation and conflict which characterised Yoshida's relations with Washington, and his unsuccessful effort in 1954 to persuade the United States to adopt a more flexible and economically oriented policy toward Japan and non-Communist Asia. Yoshida himself wrote two books about his life and times: *The Yoshida memoirs: the story of Japan in crisis*, translated by his son Kenichi Yoshida (q.v.); and *Japan's decisive century, 1867–1967* (New York: Praeger, 1967, 110p.), a revised version of an article originally written for the 1967 *Britannica book of the year*.

325 **Fragments of rainbows: the life and poety of Saitō Mokichi, 1882–1953.**
Amy Vladeck Heinrich. New York; London: Columbia University Press, 1983. 200p. bibliog. (Studies of the East Asian Institute, Columbia University).

The first critical study of this influential poet, literary scholar, critic, and theorist. After tracing his medical and literary careers, Heinrich analyses Mokichi's choice of the thirty-one-syllable poetic form known as the tanka as his means of poetic expression, studies his poem sequence 'Ohiro', and discusses Mokichi's views of himself and of the natural world surrounding him. Representative poems (219 from more than fourteen thousand which he wrote) are presented in both romanised Japanese and English-language translation.

326 **Shinichi Suzuki: the man and his philosophy.**
Evelyn Hermann. Athens, Ohio: Ability Development Associates, 1981. 253p. bibliog.

The life and philosophy of Suzuki Shinichi (1898-), creator of the world-famous Suzuki violin method, are the focus of this popular account of one of Japan's influential educational figures. Part one ('Shinichi Suzuki: the Man') covers his family background and his life as a concert violinist and teacher. Part two focuses on his philosophy of music teaching and contains the full text or excerpts from some of his lectures, articles, and books. The explanations of Suzuki's teaching techniques that were presented between 1963 and 1980 are discussed in detail.

327 **Chronicle of my mother.**
Yasushi Inoue, translated with an introduction by Jean Oda Moy.
Tokyo; New York: Kodansha International, 1982. 164p.

An autobiographical account, written by one of Japan's foremost contemporary novelists, of the gradual ageing and mental deterioration of his mother and of its impact on himself and on other members of their family. In a series of vignettes, Inoue sensitively and compassionately depicts his observations of the events that accompanied his mother's growing senility and narrates some of the challenges that this posed for his family.

328 **Facing two ways: the story of my life.**
Shidzué Ishimoto. New York: Farrar and Rinehart, 1935. 373p.
Reprinted, with an introduction and afterword by Barbara Molony, Stanford, California: Stanford University Press, 1984. 373p.

Autobiography of a remarkable feminist and social activist, who is better known today by her married name Katō Shizue (1897-). The author describes her childhood in an upper-class Tokyo home, her education at the Peeresses' School, her first marriage to the Baron Ishimoto Keikichi and her sudden exposure to the miserable life of the mining labourers at the Mitsui coal mines in Kyūshū, her transformation into a self-supporting businesswoman as well as her emergence as a public advocate of women's rights and of birth control, her travels to the United States and Europe, and the failure of her first marriage. Throughout her book she provides glimpses into Japanese life and society during the first three decades of the twentieth century. Some years after the publication of this autobiography, Ishimoto married the socialist labour leader Katō Kanjū and was elected for several consecutive terms to a seat in the national Diet.

329 **Something like an autobiography.**
Akira Kurosawa, translated by Audie E. Bock. New York: Knopf, 1982. 205p. Reprinted, New York: Vintage Books, 1983.

Reminiscences of the highly acclaimed film director Kurosawa Akira (1910-). The autobiography covers Kurosawa's recollections of the first forty years of his life: his youth, his family, his relation to the military, and his work and techniques as both a script writer and film director during the 1940s. It also offers a first-hand glimpse of prewar urban and rural life, but concludes abruptly with the release of his film *Rashōmon* in 1950.

330 **Totto-chan: the little girl at the window.**
Tetsuko Kuroyanagi, translated by Dorothy Britton, illustrated by Chihiro Iwasaki. Tokyo; New York: Kodansha International, 1982. 195p.

An extremely popular book whose original Japanese-language version made publishing history by selling 4,500,000 copies in a single year, this is the autobiographical account of the early school years of Kuroyanagi Tetsuko, a well-known television personality and actress. Through a child's eyes, Kuroyanagi relates how an unconventional elementary school in southwestern Tokyo called Tomoe Gakuen, its highly regarded founder and headmaster Kobayashi Sosaku (1893-1963), and Kobayashi's educational methods nurtured warmth, liveliness, talent, and intelligence among its students between 1937 and 1945.

331 **Hamada, potter.**
Bernard Leach, preface by Janet Darnell Leach. Tokyo and New
York: Kodansha International; London: Thames and Hudson, 1975.
305p.

Hamada Shōji (1894-1978), Japan's most renowned twentieth-century potter and a prominent figure in the folk-crafts (*mingei*) movement, is the subject of this biography by a lifelong friend and famous British potter. In a series of recorded dialogues as well as through exchanges of conversation, Leach traces Hamada's development as an artist, while Hamada reveals his own ideas, techniques, insights, experiences, and philosophy of life. Also included are numerous photographs of Hamada at work; eighty-eight plates of his bowls, bottles, dishes, jars, teapots, and incense boxes; and sketches which Hamada has drawn of craft objects and motifs. Susan Peterson's illustrated study *Shoji Hamada: a potter's way and work* (Tokyo; New York: Kodansha International, 1974, 239p.) complements Leach's book, presenting Hamada's reflections on form, beauty, and the place of pottery and describing his techniques, working habits, and lifestyle in the town of Mashiko.

332 **Made in Japan: Akio Morita and Sony.**
Akio Morita, with Edwin M. Reingold, Mitsuko Shimomura. New
York: Dutton, 1986; London: Collins, 1987. 309p. Reprinted, London:
Fontana Paperbacks, 1987; New York: New American Library, 1988.

Autobiography of the co-founder and chairman of the Sony Corporation. Opening his account as a young man during the closing months of World War II, Morita describes how he helped establish Sony in 1946 under its original name 'Tokyo Telecommunications Engineering Corporation' and how he guided it through a period of rapid development to the prominent position that it enjoys in the world of electronics today. In the course of relating his experiences and those of his family, he also touches upon a variety of topics of interest to readers concerned with Japanese business. These include the differences between the Japanese and Western styles of management, the Japanese philosophy of lifetime employment, the importance of market research and quality control, competition and technology as factors in Japan's postwar economic success, and trade relations between Japan and the United States.

333 **Tanaka Giichi and Japan's China policy.**
William Fitch Morton. New York: St. Martin's Press; Folkestone,
Kent: Dawson, 1980. 329p. 3 maps. bibliog. (Studies of the East Asian
Institute, Columbia University).

A study and reassessment of Tanaka Giichi (army general, foreign minister, and prime minister, 1864-1929) and his controversial policies towards China. Morton examines the evolution of Japanese policy towards China before 1922, Tanaka's involvement in its formulation and execution, Japan's China policy under Foreign Minister Shidehara (1924-27), the early and later phases of the Tanaka Cabinet (1927-29) and its China policy (the heart of this study), and the course of Sino–Japanese relations down to the outbreak of war in 1937. Morton concludes that Tanaka was 'an erratic, indecisive prime minister' and that the infamous Tanaka Memorial of 1927, containing a detailed plan for the Japanese conquest of Manchuria and Mongolia (areas in which Tanaka had a special interest), has been wrongly attributed to him.

Biographical and Autobiographical Accounts. Twentieth century

334   **Hirohito: emperor of Japan.**
Leonard Mosley.   Englewood Cliffs, New Jersey: Prentice-Hall;
London: Weidenfeld and Nicolson, 1966. 371p. bibliog. Reprinted,
New York: Avon Books, 1967.

A popular but flawed and incomplete biography of Emperor Hirohito (1901-89), the eldest son of the Taishō Emperor who succeeded to the throne in December 1926 and adopted the reign name of Shōwa. Mosley's human-interest story covers Hirohito's childhood, family life, tour of Europe in 1921, marriage to Princess Nagako, accession to the throne, palace politics during the 1930s, the emperor's role in the decisions that led to the outbreak of World War II and to Japan's surrender in 1945, his public renunciation of claims to divinity in 1946, and his subsequent rule as a constitutional monarch. Interested individuals may also wish to read *Hirohito: an intimate portrait of the Japanese emperor*, by Osanaga Kanroji (Los Angeles: Gateway, 1975, 167p.), *Emperor Hirohito and his chief aide-de-camp: the Honjō diary, 1933–36*, by Shigeru Honjō (q.v.), and Edward Behr's provocative study *Hirohito: behind the myth* (New York: Villard Books; London: Hamish Hamilton, 1989, 437p.), as well as to consult *The emperor of Japan: a selected bibliography*, compiled by Margaret P. Haas (New York: Japan Society, 1975, 14p.). A more scholarly and up-to-date biographical account is now being completed by Stephen S. Large. Announced for eventual publication under the title *Emperor Hirohito and Showa Japan: a political portrait*, it will appear in the 'Nissan Institute/Routledge Japanese Studies Series' under the Routledge imprint.

335   **Mishima: a biography.**
John Nathan.   Boston, Massachusetts and Toronto, Ontario: Little,
Brown, 1974; London: Hamilton, 1975. 300p. Reprinted, Rutland,
Vermont; Tokyo: Tuttle, 1975.

Yukio Mishima (the pen name for Kimitake Hiraoka, 1925-70) was an internationally renowned author of 40 novels, 18 plays, 20 volumes of short stories, and numerous essays; a director, actor, and accomplished swordsman; and a three-time nominee for the Nobel Prize in Literature. In this account of Mishima's life, John Nathan (the translator of one of Mishima's novels) portrays his childhood, adolescence, and years as a prolific writer; examines his 'nearly superhuman personality'; analyses some of the themes which run through his life and fiction; and discusses his ultranationalistic interest in politics and the events that led up to his final act of ritual suicide in November 1970. Further information about Mishima may be found in Henry Scott-Stoke's *The life and death of Yukio Mishima* (New York: Farrar, Straus and Giroux, 1974, 344p.; London: Owen, 1975. 271p. Reprinted, New York: Ballantine Books, 1985. 305p. Harmondsworth, Middlesex: Penguin, 1985. 271p.).

336   **Liberalism in modern Japan: Ishibashi Tanzan and his teachers,
1905–1960.**
Sharon H. Nolte.   Berkeley, California; London: University of
California Press, 1987. 378p. bibliog.

An inquiry into the development and activities of three closely associated moderate liberals: the philosopher Tanaka Ōdō (1867-1932), the dramatist and critic Shimamura Hōgetsu (1871-1918), and the political economist and journalist Ishibashi Tanzan (1884-1973). Nolte examines their commitments to the freedom of the individual and to equality for women as well as their efforts to combat censorship and to promote knowledge and enlightenment among the general public. She also studies Ishibashi's

Twentieth century

career from the 1920s through 1960, during the course of which he served as both editor and president of the journal *Tōyō Keizai Shinpō* and actively participated in national politics, serving as minister in various government cabinets and as prime minister in 1956-57. Nolte's research demonstrates the continuity that existed between the liberal ideas which Ishibashi shared with Tanaka and Shimamura during the Taishō era and the policies which he implemented after World War II.

337 **Kōtoku Shūsui: portrait of a Japanese radical.**
Frederick G. Notehelfer. Cambridge, England; New York:
Cambridge University Press, 1971. 227p. bibliog.

Both a personal and a political biography of a well-known journalist, socialist, and anarchist thinker who was executed in 1911 on the charge of having led a conspiracy to assassinate the Meiji Emperor and forment a violent anarchist revolution. Notehelfer examines Kōtoku's youth, his intellectual transition from loyalism and Japanese nationalism to socialism (1899-1903), his pacifist opposition to the Russo–Japanese War, and his transition to anarchism while in the United States (1905-6), as well as his advocacy of 'direct action' by the working class, and his arrest and subsequent trial for high treason. This study is particularly concerned with determining how Kōtoku restructured his traditional values and ways of thinking in order to meet the requirements of Japan's rapidly modernising society, and with the intellectual and emotional impact which such a restructuring process had on him.

338 **Sadaharu Oh: a Zen way of baseball.**
Sadaharu Oh, David Falkner. New York: Times Books; Toronto,
Ontario: Fitzhenry and Whiteside, 1984. 279p. Reprinted, New York:
Vintage Books, 1985.

Japan's greatest baseball star recounts his personal story and secret of success. Born in Tokyo in 1940, Oh joined the Tokyo Giants (Japan's foremost major league team) and came under the tutelage of its batting coach, Arakawa Hiroshi. With Arakawa as his long-time mentor, he perfected his ability in hitting baseballs through directed training in both Zen Buddhist philosophy and the martial arts. By the time of his retirement, Oh had scored 868 home runs and had set a new world record far surpassing that of American baseball player Hank Aaron.

339 **Brush strokes: moments from my life.**
Masayoshi Ōhira, translated by Simul International. Tokyo: Foreign
Press Center, Japan, 1979. 187p.

Ōhira Masayoshi (1910-80), a leading politician in the Liberal Democratic Party and Japan's prime minister between 1978 and 1980, shares some of his views and philosophy of life. He first traces the major events of his life, among them his boyhood years and education at Hitotsubashi University, his work in the Ministry of Finance, his involvement in the postwar political scene, and his quest as foreign minister for normalised relations with the People's Republic of China as well as for a continuing stable relationship with the United States. Part two of Ōhira's book sets forth some of his 'random thoughts' about topics as diverse as administrative reform, books and Japanese culture, and the untimely death of his son Masaki. An appendix contains the official translation of Ōhira's first policy speech as prime minister, delivered to the Diet on 25 January 1979.

340 **Konoe Fumimaro: a political biography.**
Yoshitake Oka, translated by Shumpei Okamoto, Patricia Murray.
Tokyo: University of Tokyo Press, 1983. 214p.

Biographical study of Konoe Fumimaro (1891-1945), who served as Japan's prime minister three times between 1937 and 1941. It covers Konoe's youth and student days, his membership in the House of Peers, his successive premierships, Konoe's relations with the Japanese political and military élite, his efforts to achieve his goals of national unity, 'international justice' and a non-Communist East Asia, his role as a senior statesman, and his suicide shortly after World War II. Oka's depiction of Konoe is noteworthy for its portrayal of this statesman as a tragic figure who failed in his effort to prevent the outbreak of war between the United States and Japan in 1941.

341 **No surrender: my thirty-year war.**
Hiroo Onoda, translated with a foreword by Charles S. Terry. Tokyo and New York: Kodansha International, 1974; London: Andre Deutsch, 1975. 219p. map. Reprinted, London: Corgi; New York: Dell, 1976.

The autobiography of an army second lieutenant stationed in the Philippines in 1944 who skillfully outmanoeuvred the American troops, the Philippine army and police, hostile islanders, and successive Japanese search parties who tried to hunt him down during the ensuing thirty years. Characterised as an intelligent 'man of strong determination and principle', Onoda relates his early life, his training as an intelligence officer, his final assignment to Lubang Island, his retreat into the mountains following its capture by the Americans, the constant daily battle which he and a few comrades waged against their enemies as well as against the elements, his ingenuity in adapting to his primitive surroundings, and his final decision to emerge from hiding and return to Japan in the spring of 1974. For the World War II historian, Onoda's account offers important insights into the psychology of the Japanese soldiers who fought in the Pacific at that time.

342 **Ishiwara Kanji and Japan's confrontation with the West.**
Mark R. Peattie. Princeton, New Jersey; London: Princeton University Press, 1975. 430p. map. bibliog.

An analysis of the career and thought of Ishiwara Kanji (1889-1949), a military historian, staff officer, and brilliant strategist of the Imperial Japanese Army who played a prominent role in the Japanese seizure of Manchuria (1931), the Young Officers' Rebellion (1936), and the Sino–Japanese War of 1937-45. Peattie focuses on Ishiwara's perceptions of 'the nature of war, the means to prepare for it, the domestic structure of Japan, and the nation's place in Asia' as well as on his decision-making role during three specific crises. Examining the interaction of Ishiwara's ideas and activities, Peattie deals particularly with his early formulation of a theory of war and the evolution of his concept of the 'final war'; the ways in which he worked for the Japanese conquest of Manchuria while serving on the Kwantung Army Staff (1929-32); his years on the General Staff (1935-37), while at the height of his power and influence; and his activities towards the end of his career.

343 **Noguchi and his patrons.**
Isabel R. Plesset. Rutherford, New Jersey: Fairleigh Dickinson
University Press; London: Associated University Presses, 1980. 314p.
bibliog.

An account of the life, career, psychological characteristics, and motivations of
Noguchi Hideyo (1876-1928), the controversial microbiologist who isolated the
spirochaete that causes syphilis and undertook important research work on such other
diseases as rabies and yellow fever. Plesset covers Noguchi's peasant family
background and birth; a childhood accident and other factors which shaped his attitude
towards work and human relationships; his early microbiological and medical training
in Japan; his decision to pursue a career in the United States; his work at the
Rockefeller Institute for Medical Research; and his research and travels. Noguchi's
relationships with his principal Japanese and American patrons (among them his
school teacher, Kobayashi Sakae, and Simon Flexner of the Rockefeller Institute) as
well as his contributions to microbiology are thoroughly discussed.

344 **Honda: the man and his machines.**
Sol Sanders. Boston, Massachusetts; Toronto, Ontario: Little,
Brown, 1975. 208p. Reprinted, Rutland, Vermont; Tokyo: Tuttle,
1977.

A colourfully written biography of the highly innovative engineer Honda Sōichirō
(born 1906), the machines that he built, and the business enterprise that grew up
around them. Sanders depicts Honda's youth and experiences in wartime Japan, the
realisation of his dream of establishing a plant during the immediate postwar period for
the production of a newly designed motorcycle, the growth of his company, and his
success in creating a mass market for his products in the United States as well as in
Japan. Sanders also writes about Honda's introduction of the revolutionary, pollution-
controlling CVCC automobile engine in 1972 that constituted the basis for his
international success in the manufacture and sale of passenger cars. Concluding
chapters include an introduction to 'Hondaism', an assessment of Honda's future
prospects, and comments about Honda's business philosophy.

345 **Kafū the scribbler: the life and writings of Nagai Kafū, 1879-1959.**
Edward Seidensticker. Stanford, California: Stanford University
Press, 1965. 360p. bibliog. (Unesco Collection of Representative
Works: Japanese Series).

Nagai Kafū, one of Japan's most important modern novelists and essayists, is
renowned for his portrayals of late Tokugawa and Meiji period urban culture.
Seidensticker's biographical account of Kafū, together with background information
and critical remarks about his writings, is followed by translations of some of his best
stories and sketches – 'The River Sumida', 'The Peony Garden', 'Coming down with a
Cold', 'Quiet Rain', 'The Decoration', and 'The Scavengers' – and of an essay-novel,
A strange tale from east of the river (*Bokutō kitan*), as well as excerpts from three of his
other novels; *Tidings from Okubo* (*Ōkubo dayori*), *Rivalry* (*Ude kurabe*), and *The
Dancing Girl* (*Odoriko*). The city of Tokyo during the late 1800s and early 1900s serves
as the setting for many of these works.

346 **War criminal: the life and death of Hirota Koki.**
Saburō Shiroyama, translated by John Bester.   Tokyo; New York:
Kodansha International, 1977. 301p. bibliog.

Sympathetic account of Hirota Kōki (1878-1948), a career diplomat, thrice foreign minister, and prime minister of Japan during the mid-1930s, who was the only civilian to be sentenced at the Tokyo war crimes trial to death by hanging. Interweaving Hirota's life and career with those of his contemporaries and with the events of his time, Shiroyama describes Hirota's early years and connections with the ultranationalistic Genyōsha society, his work as an overseas envoy, his terms of office as foreign minister and as prime minister (during which he took steps to improve Japan's political position in China, greatly strengthened the position and resources of the army, and concluded the Anti-Comintern Pact with Germany and Italy), his role as an influential senior statesman during the war, and his behaviour while being tried by the Allied powers as a class 'A' war criminal in 1946-48.

347 **Toyota: fifty years in motion; an autobiography.**
Eiji Toyoda.   Tokyo; New York: Kodansha International, 1987. 170p.

A lively autobiography of the past president and current chairman of the Toyota Motor Corporation that interweaves the personal life history of an important executive and his family with the growth and development of one of Japan's leading automobile manufacturing companies. A graduate of Tokyo Imperial University with a degree in mechanical engineering, Toyoda recounts his childhood in Nagoya and his college years in Tokyo, the establishment of the Toyota Motor Company (in 1937) as a spin-off from the Toyoda Automatic Loom Works, the development and testing of Toyota's first motor vehicles, the successes and difficulties that were experienced during and shortly after World War II, the reorganisation and rescue of Toyota from near-bankruptcy in 1950, some of the company's postwar feats of automotive engineering and achievements in management, production and marketing, and the impressive growth of Toyota as a major corporation during the 1960s and 1970s. A complementary work, *Toyota: a history of the first 50 years* (Toyota City, Aichi Prefecture: Toyota Motor Corporation, 1988, 522p.), narrates the company's history and development in greater detail.

348 **Radical nationalist in Japan: Kita Ikki, 1883–1937.**
George M. Wilson.   Cambridge, Massachusetts: Harvard University Press, 1969. 230p. bibliog. (Harvard East Asian Series, 37).

A study of the growth of radical nationalism in prewar Japan through an examination of the life and ideas of Kita Ikki (1883-1937), one of its chief proponents, whose name has also been closely (and in some ways erroneously) associated with the abortive military coup d'état against the Japanese government of 26 February 1936. Wilson follows Kita's career and analyses the evolution of his complex thought, showing that it synthesized both a belief in the desirability of change and modernisation (based on a combination of Japanese Neo-Confucianism, Nichiren Buddhism, socialism, and other Western ideas) and an intense faith in Japan's national destiny to 'regenerate an Asia inundated by imperialist power politics'.

From Tokyo to Jerusalem.
See item no. 4.

Biographical and Autobiographical Accounts. Twentieth century

Emperor Hirohito and his chief aide-de-camp: the Honjō diary, 1933–36.
See item no. 209.

Minobe Tatsukichi: interpreter of constitutionalism in Japan.
See item no. 220.

Hara Kei in the politics of compromise, 1905–1915.
See item no. 224.

The Yoshida memoirs: the story of Japan in crisis.
See item no. 282.

Tokutomi Sohō, 1863–1957: a journalist for modern Japan.
See item no. 311.

Tokyo Rose: orphan of the Pacific.
See item no. 387.

Farewell to Manzanar: a true story of Japanese American experience during and after the World War II internment.
See item no. 391.

The Kikuchi diary: chronicle from an American concentration camp. The Tanforan journals of Charles Kikuchi.
See item no. 393.

They call me Moses Masaoka: an American saga.
See item no. 395.

American in disguise.
See item no. 398.

Nisei daughter.
See item no. 399.

Through harsh winters: the life of a Japanese immigrant woman.
See item no. 400.

Haruko's world: a Japanese farm woman and her community.
See item no. 573.

I was a kamikaze: the knights of the divine wind.
See item no. 700.

Japan and her destiny: my struggle for peace.
See item no. 708.

Entrepreneur and gentleman: a case history of a Japanese company.
See item no. 845.

Japan in the passing lane: an insider's account of life in a Japanese auto factory.
See item no. 924.

Sun and steel.
See item no. 1079.

The family.
See item no. 1096.

Literary life in Tokyo, 1885–1915: Tayama Katai's memoirs ('Thirty years in Tokyo').
See item no. 1105.

Mc ri Ōgai and the modernization of Japanese culture.
See item no. 1110.

The saga of Dazai Osamu: a critical study with translations.
See item no. 1116.

Dazai Osamu.
See item no. 1119.

Mori Ōgai.
See item no. 1121.

Akutagawa: an introduction.
See item no. 1132.

Natsume Soseki.
See item no. 1133.

Kinoshita Yūji.
See item no. 1144.

Toward a modern Japanese theatre: Kishida Kunio.
See item no. 1178.

Mizoguchi.
See item no. 1422.

Ozu: his life and films.
See item no. 1427.

Karate-dō: my way of life.
See item no. 1446.

Westerners in Japan

349 **The capital of the Tycoon: a narrative of a three years' residence in Japan.**
Rutherford Alcock.   London: Longman, Green; New York: Harper, 1863. 2 vols. 2 maps. Reprinted, New York: Greenwood Press, 1969; St. Claire Shores, Michigan: Scholarly Press, 1969.

Alcock, the first British minister to Japan, writes of his experiences and observations during a period (1859-62) in which he played a major role in promoting British interests in Japan and in pressing the Tokugawa shogunate to expand the country's

Biographical and Autobiographical Accounts. Westerners in Japan

trade with Great Britain. He records his reactions to what he saw about him, narrates the 'trials and difficulties' which he endured, details his daily life as well as the leading events of his day, provides many glimpses into the system of government at that time, and describes the character, life, manner, and customs of Japanese of all classes – 'from the Feudal Prince with his two-sworded henchmen and retainers, to the humble and peace-loving peasant'. Much of Alcock's narrative deals with his conduct of diplomatic relations and his visits to different cities and scenic spots throughout Japan.

350 **Appointment in Japan: memories of sixty years.**
George Cyril Allen. London: Athlone Press, 1983. 196p.

A British economic historian's reminiscences of his 2½-year lectureship at the Kōtō Shōgyō Gakkō (Commercial High School) in Nagoya, 1922-24, and of some of the changes that accompanied Japan's transformation during the ensuing sixty years. Allen, well known in the West as the author of numerous books and articles about the Japanese economy and its history, recounts his experiences, his friendships with individual Japanese, and his observations and impressions of Japan during the 1920s in particular. His delightfully written memoirs tell us much about Japan at that time as well as about his own efforts to understand the Japanese character. Allen returned to Japan in 1936 and again after World War II, and on the basis of his subsequent observations he also comments about the country's rapid economic development during the postwar period.

351 **Awakening Japan: the diary of a German doctor, Erwin Baelz.**
Erwin O. E. von Baelz, edited by Toku Baelz, translated from the German by Eden Paul, Cedar Paul. New York: Viking Press, 1932. 406p. Reprinted, with an introduction by George Macklin Wilson, Bloomington, Indiana; London: Indiana University Press, 1974.

Erwin von Bälz (1849-1913), a German physician who lived in Japan from 1876 to 1905, served as physician-in-waiting to the imperial household and as a professor of medicine at Tokyo University's medical school. His work brought him into contact with many high government officials and enabled him to observe Japanese life over an extended period of time. Bälz's diary, fragmentary journals, and excerpts from his published writings (dating from 1 January 1876 to 30 July 1912) record his personal experiences, sentiments, accomplishments, impressions of the Japanese, and travels within East Asia. They also contain considerable first-hand information and perceptive insights concerning domestic Japanese politics, Japanese culture and customs, contemporary personalities, and Japan's foreign relations. While Bälz is not widely remembered today, his book nevertheless remains valuable as 'an intercultural primary source for the study of Japanese history in relation to the West' during the Meiji period.

352 **Rodrigues the interpreter: an early Jesuit in Japan and China.**
Michael Cooper. New York; Tokyo: Weatherhill, 1974. 416p. bibliog.

Biography of the Portuguese Jesuit priest João Rodrigues (1561?-1633), who served as an interpreter and commercial agent for the military and political leader Toyotomi Hideyoshi and for shōgun Tokugawa Ieyasu. Cooper details Rodrigues' activities as a student, official, interpreter, missionary, diplomat, commercial agent, author, and administrator. He also portrays the evolution of contacts between Christianity and Japan through his account of the eventful years when Rodrigues was the most influential European in Japan.

353 **Dr. Willis in Japan, 1862–1877: British medical pioneer.**
Hugh Cortazzi. London; Dover, New Hampshire: Athlone Press,
1985. 273p. map. bibliog.

William Willis (1837-94), an enterprising physician and surgeon who served as medical officer to the British Legation in Edo (Tokyo) between 1862 and 1867 and as the director of Western-style hospitals and medical schools in Tokyo and Kagoshima between 1869 and 1877, witnessed some of the momentous events that occurred during a transitional period in Japanese history. This biographical account – based largely on Willis' own letters – conveys a good picture of his life in Japan. It also includes Willis' first-hand descriptions of British diplomatic activity, the bombardment of Kagoshima in 1863, life in the foreign settlement at Yokohama, the treatment of the wounded during the civil war of 1868, the fighting in northeastern Japan (1868), and his work at the hospital in Kagoshima as well as information about mid-nineteenth century Japanese medical practices and the development of Western medicine and surgery in early Meiji Japan.

354 **The Japanese thread: a life in the U.S. Foreign Service.**
John K. Emmerson. New York: Holt, Rinehart and Winston, 1978.
465p.

John K. Emmerson (1908-84) served as a distinguished foreign service officer for three decades, beginning his career in Japan during the years immediately before World War II, returning there during the Allied occupation era, and concluding his diplomatic service as Minister and Deputy Chief of Mission at the US Embassy in Tokyo between 1962 and 1966. His account is more than simply an autobiographical narrative, as it also offers insights into Japanese government attitudes, the evolution of US–Japanese relations, and the formation of American policy vis-à-vis Japan during three important periods in modern Japanese history. Emmerson was also the author of several other publications about postwar Japan's international relations and her military security, among them *Arms, yen & power: the Japanese dilemma* (New York, Dunellen, 1971, 420p.), *Will Japan rearm? a study in attitudes* (coauthored with Leonard A. Humphreys. Washington, DC: American Enterprise Institute for Public Policy Research; Stanford, California: Hoover Institution on War, Revolution and Peace, Stanford University, 1973, 165p.), and *The eagle and the rising sun: America and Japan in the twentieth century* (q.v.).

355 **A diplomat's wife in Japan: sketches at the turn of the century.**
Mary Crawford Fraser, edited by Hugh Cortazzi. New York; Tokyo:
Weatherhill, 1982. 351p. map.

A lively account of the author's five-year (1889-94) residence in Tokyo with her husband Hugh Fraser, head of the British Legation at that time. In a series of letters addressed to friends and family members that date primarily from the summer of 1889 to the summer of 1891, she describes and comments on the places she visited, the people she met, the events that occurred during her stay, and the life she experienced. Published initially under the title *A diplomatist's wife in Japan: letters from home to home* (London: Hutchinson, 1899, 2 vols.), Fraser's book offers an informative and perceptive view of mid-Meiji Japan as observed by a sympathetic Western resident.

356 **The years of MacArthur. Volume 3: Triumph and disaster, 1945–1964.**
D. Clayton James.   Boston, Massachusetts: Houghton Mifflin, 1985.
848p. 10 maps. bibliog.

The conclusion of a thoroughly researched biography of General Douglas MacArthur (1880-1964), the major American military figure who commanded US Army forces in the Far East. The first half of this volume deals with MacArthur's years in Tokyo (September 1945 to April 1951), while he served there as the Supreme Commander for the Allied Powers. Particular attention is paid to his task of overseeing the occupation of Japan and to the political and economic reforms that were carried out under his directives. James' account is far more authoritative and comprehensive than William Manchester's *American Caesar: Douglas MacArthur, 1880–1964* (Boston, Massachusetts; Toronto, Ontario: Little, Brown, 1978, 793p.). Among other published works about MacArthur, John Gunther's best-selling book, *The riddle of MacArthur: Japan, Korea and the Far East* (New York: Harper; London: Hamish Hamilton, 1951, 240p.) – published at the height of the public controversy over President Truman's dismissal of MacArthur from his command – includes an unbiased overview of the General's role in the occupation of Japan based in part on the author's interviews with both MacArthur and high-ranking members of his staff. Two biographies written by MacArthur's closest aides – *MacArthur: his rendezvous with history*, by Courtney Whitney (New York: Knopf, 1956, 547p.; Reprinted, Westport, Connecticut: Greenwood Press, 1977), and *MacArthur, 1941–1951*, by Charles A. Willoughby (New York; Toronto, Ontario; London: McGraw-Hill, 1954, 441p.) – also contain some important insights, but are marred by their highly partisan approach and their adulatory character.

357 **Mitford's Japan: the memoirs and recollections, 1866–1906, of Algernon Bertram Mitford, the first Lord Redesdale.**
Algernon Bertram Mitford, edited with an introduction by Hugh Cortazzi.   London; Dover, New Hampshire: Athlone Press, 1985. 270p. map.

Fascinating observations extracted primarily from the autobiographical writings and lectures of a diplomat-scholar (1837-1916) who served in the British Legation in Japan during the late 1860s and who revisited Tokyo four decades later. An account of Mitford's stay in Japan from 1866 to the beginning of 1870 comprises the major section of this book. It includes his meeting with Shōgun Tokugawa Keiki, his 'adventurous journey' to Kanazawa, his observations of the civil war between the Tokugawa shogunate and the imperial forces, his visit to the court of the Mikado (the young Meiji Emperor), and his reactions to changes that occurred during the early days of the newly established Meiji government. The second part of this book records Mitford's experiences and views of Japan in 1906, when he accompanied the official party sent by King Edward VII to present the emperor of Japan with the Order of the Garter.

358 **American samurai: Captain L. L. Janes and Japan.**
Frederick G. Notehelfer.   Princeton, New Jersey; Guildford, Surrey: Princeton University Press, 1985. 386p. bibliog.

A biography of Leroy Lansing Janes (1837-1909), West Point graduate and Civil War officer, who worked as a pioneering American educator in Japan. Between 1871 and 1876, Janes served as head of the Kumamoto Yōgakkō (Kumamoto School for Western Learning) in western Kyūshū. Under his influence, thirty-five students (among them Ebina Danjō, Kozaki Hiromichi, and Yokoi Tokio) were converted to

Christianity. Together they became the dominant wing of Japanese Protestantism and a driving force for modernisation in Meiji Japan. Notehelfer's study explores Janes' career in Japan as well as in the United States, and helps to shed light on the significant role which Westerners played in the transformation of Japan during the latter half of the nineteenth century. A comparable monograph, *An American teacher in early Meiji Japan* by Edward R. Beauchamp (Honolulu, Hawaii; University Press of Hawaii, 1976, 154p. [Asian Studies at Hawaii, 17]), studies William Elliot Griffis' experiences as a teacher of science in both Fukui (Echizen *han*) and Tokyo during the early 1870s as well. His experiences are instructive for the kinds of intercultural problems encountered by Westerners who went to Japan at that time.

359 **Encounter with Japan.**
Herbert Passin.   Tokyo; New York: Kodansha International, 1982.
193p.
The author, a former professor of Japanese sociology at Columbia University, describes some of his experiences between 1944 and 1947 studying Japanese at the Army Intensive Japanese Language School in Ann Arbor, Michigan, and working in Japan (with refugees in Fukuoka, with the Ainu in Hokkaidō, and as head of the Public Opinion and Sociological Research Division) during the first two years of the Allied occupation period. Mixing historical facts with personal anecdotes, Passin provides a glimpse into American attitudes towards Japan and the Japanese people at that time. His account is also useful for the information it provides about the study of the Japanese language, about the wartime training of a cadre of Americans who subsequently established the field of Japanese studies, and about some of the ways in which Americans dealt with Japan immediately after World War II.

360 **My life between Japan and America.**
Edwin O. Reischauer.   New York; London: Harper and Row, 1986.
367p.
Former US Ambassador Reischauer (1910-   ), a leading scholar in Japanese Studies, tells of his lifelong experience with Japan and the United States. He recounts his childhood growing up in Tokyo as the son of American missionary parents, his education at Oberlin College and Harvard University, his wartime service in the State Department and Army Intelligence, where he helped plan the future of Japan and supervised the processing of intercepted Japanese military and diplomatic messages, his long and illustrious career developing East Asian studies at Harvard University, his commitment to promoting better understanding and greater mutual knowledge between Japan and America, his marriage to Matsukata Haru (a Japanese of aristocratic background) following the death of his first wife, and his 5½ years (1961-66) as US Ambassador to Tokyo.

361 **Mirror in the shrine: American encounters with Meiji Japan.**
Robert A. Rosenstone.   Cambridge, Massachusetts; London: Harvard
University Press, 1988. 315p. bibliog.
Three 'biographical tales' that highlight the Japanese experience of three Americans who chose to work in Meiji Japan and 'whose lives were altered greatly by that choice, often in ways that they did not fully understand'. The missionary and educator William Elliot Griffis (1843-1928), the zoologist Edward S. Morse (1838-1925), and the writer and translator Lafcadio Hearn (1850-1904) all became widely known as interpreters of Japan to the West and were acclaimed for their many books and articles on Japanese

history, culture, society, and politics. In this well-written narrative, Rosenstone explores their efforts to understand Japan during an era when the cultural contrasts with the West were most striking. He considers the consequences of their experience living in Japan as he investigates the subtle shifts that occurred at that time in their perceptions, attitudes, and world views. In addition, Rosenstone seeks to recapture the meaning of these three lives for Americans today in an age of greatly increased cross-cultural encounters.

362 **Windows for the crown prince.**
Elizabeth Gray Vining. Philadelphia, Pennsylvania: Lippincott; London: Michael Joseph, 1952. 320p. Reprinted, Rutland, Vermont; Tokyo: Tuttle, 1989.

An intimate account of Vining's four years in Japan (October 1946 to December 1950), during which she served as tutor to Crown Prince (now Emperor) Akihito, taught English to members of the imperial family, and constantly came into contact with both the Japanese élite and American occupation personnel. While most of her narrative is on her relations with the crown prince and on his life, personality, and education, she also reminisces about some of her own activities, and offers valuable observations about Japan during the Occupation period. The title of her book is derived from Viscount Matsudaira's request that she 'open windows on to a wider world for our Crown Prince'. In her subsequent autobiography, *Quiet pilgrimage* (Philadelphia: Lippincott, 1970, 410p.), Vining elaborates on her personal experiences in Japan, describing the background to her appointment, the home in which she lived, her teaching responsibilities, her relations with and impressions of Emperor Hirohito and General Douglas MacArthur, and her summers at the mountain resort of Karuizawa.

363 **Clara's diary: an American girl in Meiji Japan.**
Clara A. N. Whitney, edited with an introduction by M. William Steele, Tamiko Ichimata. Tokyo; New York: Kodansha International, 1979. 353p. 2 maps.

An abridgement of the diary kept by a young woman in Japan between 1875 and 1884. Fifteen-year-old Clara Whitney arrived in Tokyo as the daughter of a lay missionary who had been invited to help establish Japan's first commercial college. During her years there, she became fluent in the Japanese language, grew to love and respect Japan and the Japanese, and married Kaji Umetarō, the son of a prominent Japanese statesman. Clara's diary records the incidents of both her daily life and the lives of her Japanese and Western acquaintances; her observations of Japanese society, food, dress, housing, entertainment, and ceremonies; the social changes that were taking place in early Meiji Japan; the strong sense of patriotism that characterised those years; and her own gradual adjustment to the Japanese lifestyle that she had at first rejected.

The Japan diaries of Richard Gordon Smith.
See item no. 72.

Innocence is not enough: the life and death of Herbert Norman.
See item no. 226.

E. H. Norman: his life and scholarship.
See item no. 226.

Target Tokyo: the story of the Sorge spy ring.
See item no. 228.

Before aggression: Europeans prepare the Japanese army.
See item no. 229.

Remaking Japan: the American occupation as new deal.
See item no. 267.

Legal reform in occupied Japan: a participant looks back.
See item no. 277.

Japan's political revolution under MacArthur: a participant's account.
See item no. 281.

Western medical pioneers in feudal Japan.
See item no. 596.

A diplomat in Japan: the inner history of the critical years in the evolution of Japan when the ports were opened and the monarchy restored.
See item no. 675.

The Shimoda story.
See item no. 676.

The complete journal of Townsend Harris, first American consul and minister to Japan.
See item no. 676.

Ten years in Japan: a contemporary record drawn from the diaries and private and official papers of Joseph C. Grew, United States ambassador to Japan, 1932–1942.
See item no. 690.

I saw Tokyo burning: an eyewitness narrative from Pearl Harbor to Hiroshima.
See item no. 691.

Biographical dictionaries

364 **Who's who in modern Japanese prints.**
Frances Blakemore.   New York; Tokyo: Weatherhill, 1975. 263p.
Designed as a one-volume reference work for the collector and general reader, Blakemore's survey introduces a cross-section of 105 print-makers who have been active in postwar Japan. Each entry provides brief biographical information about one individual, including the year of his or her birth, the principal medium (e.g., lithograph, woodblock, silkscreen, etching) in which he works, his background and artistic development, and his subject matter and stylistic traits. Up to five of the artist's representative prints are reproduced in black-and-white. An appendix lists some four

hundred modern Japanese print artists. This book illustrates the far-reaching diversity of materials, perceptions, styles, and techniques that characterise the modern Japanese print.

365 Biographical dictionary of Japanese literature.
Sen'ichi Hisamatsu. Tokyo; New York: Kodansha International in collaboration with the International Society for Educational Information (Tokyo), 1976. 437p. bibliog.

A reference guide to the lives and contributions of 320 individuals noteworthy in the development of Japanese literature. Each biographical entry presents the most important facts about a subject's life, describes the settings in which he or she worked as well as his literary accomplishments, and briefly evaluates his significance. Writers of prose and poetry are included; they range from the poets of the *Manyōshū* through the novelist Kawabata Yasunari and his contemporaries. The biographical entries are grouped together by major historical periods. They are followed by diagrams of important literary schools, a glossary of selected literary terms, a bibliography of the most significant Japanese-language writings about individual figures, and a subject index.

366 Who's who in Japanese government, 1988/89.
International Cultural Association, Japan; foreword by Seizaburō Satō. Tokyo: International Cultural Association, Japan, 1988. 2nd ed. 414p. (Distributed by Sanseido Co., Ltd, 1-1, Kandajinbo-chō, Chiyoda-ku, Tokyo 101, Japan).

Second edition of what is expected to become an annually updated, basic handbook to the Japanese government. In the first half of this manual, one can find a recent photograph of each of the 763 members of the Upper and Lower Houses of the Diet, together with a brief biographical sketch indicating the biographee's name, his political and factional affiliation, the prefecture he represents, the number of times he has been elected, his office and residential addresses and telephone numbers, committee or ministry assignments, party or other important posts held, university education, and date of birth. The second half contains listings of the members of the Diet's many committees, useful organisational charts of both the political parties and the legislative, administrative and judicial branches of the government, lists of party and higher-ranking government ministry and agency personnel, and the addresses and telephone numbers of the ministries and agencies, major labour unions, federations and associations, local government offices in Tokyo, special public corporations, chambers of commerce, law offices, accountants, and political party headquarters.

367 Biographical dictionary of Japanese history.
Supervising editor: Seiichi Iwao, translated by Burton Watson, foreword by Michiko Kaya. Tokyo; New York: Kodansha International in collaboration with the International Society for Educational Information (Tokyo), 1978. 655p. 2 maps. bibliog.

Brief sketches of the lives and activities of 521 major figures in the political, economic, intellectual, and religious life of Japan, from Amaterasu Ōmikami (the mythical ancestor of the Japanese imperial family) to prominent personalities following World War II. The biographical entries are grouped into four historical periods – 'ancient', 'medieval', 'early modern', and 'modern' – with nearly half of them being concerned

Biographical and Autobiographical Accounts. Biographical dictionaries

with post-1868 figures. Nineteen appendixes provide genealogies and lists of emperors, regents, shōguns, prime ministers, and their cabinets, as well as charts outlining the organisation of major systems of government, political parties and cliques. An extensive bibliography of Japanese and Western-language books about these historical figures and a subject index conclude the volume.

368 **A dictionary of Japanese artists: painting, sculpture, ceramics, prints, lacquer.**
Laurance P. Roberts, foreword by John M. Rosenfield. New York; Tokyo: Weatherhill, 1976. 299p. bibliog.
A comprehensive guide to nearly three thousand noteworthy painters, print-makers, sculptors, potters, and lacquer artists who were active up to the twentieth century. (Artists who were born after 1900 are generally excluded.) Each dictionary entry provides the original and alternate names (where appropriate) of the artist in transcription and in Chinese characters (*kanji*), brief biographical information about the artist including his years of birth and death, a list of the public collections around the world in which his work can be seen, and bibliographical references to books and other publications containing further information and illustrations. Indexes of both the artists' alternate names and their names in Chinese characters as well as a short bibliography of English, French, German, and Japanese-language publications enhance the value of this reference work for scholars and serious students of Japanese art.

369 **Biographical dictionary of Japanese art.**
Supervising editor: Yutaka Tazawa, foreword by Eishirō Saitō.
Tokyo: International Society for Educational Information in collaboration with Kodansha International, 1981. 825p. 2 maps. bibliog.
A dictionary of 863 prominent Japanese artists, from the Nara period to the twentieth century, with brief descriptive accounts of their lives and their major accomplishments. The biographical entries for these individuals are grouped together according to the types of art they produced: painting, prints, calligraphy, photography, graphic design, sculpture, utensils for the tea ceremony, architecture, landscape gardening, ceramics, swords, metalwork, textiles, and lacquer and related minor arts. Genealogies and charts of important schools, families, and art societies; a glossary; an extensive bibliography of Japanese-language books about individual artists; and a subject index enhance the value of this reference work.

Concise dictionary of modern Japanese history.
See item no. 1555.

Kabuki encyclopedia: an English-language adaptation of *Kabuki jiten*.
See item no. 1564.

Dictionary of Chinese and Japanese art.
See item no. 1567.

Who's who in Japan.
See item no. 1574.

Population and Family Planning

370   **Family planning in Japanese society: traditional birth control in a modern urban culture.**
Samuel Coleman.   Princeton, New Jersey; Guildford, Surrey: Princeton University Press, 1983. 269p. bibliog.
Most Japanese today rely heavily on two traditional contraceptive methods – the condom and the 'rhythm method' – as well as on induced abortion rather than on such modern techniques as oral contraceptives, intra-uterine devices, and contraceptive sterilisation in order to limit the size of their families. Coleman conducted anthropological field research, primarily in Tokyo during the mid-1970s, in an effort to determine why these traditional practices have persisted in an industrialised, technologically advanced society that has maintained a relatively low fertility rate since the early 1950s. He ascribes the situation to a combination of commercial, cultural, medical, legal, familial, and religious factors.

371   **The population of Japan.**
Irene B. Taeuber, foreword by Frank W. Notestein.   Princeton, New Jersey: Princeton University Press, 1958. 461p. 20 maps. bibliog.
A comprehensive demographic study of Japan from premodern times to the 1950s, which relates the author's findings to historical, political, social, and economic trends. Taeuber first summarises the growth of the Japanese population before 1920, and then concentrates on the period 1920-55. She describes the basic population changes that took place; Japan's internal migration (primarily from the countryside to the cities) and the growth of her metropolitan areas; the outward migration of Japan's population which accompanied prewar Japanese expansion overseas; the trends and effects of marriage, fertility, population control, and mortality during this period; the natural increase of population; and population-related developments during and immediately following World War II. Statistical tables (141 in all) and numerous figures supplement Taeuber's demographic analysis. A bibliography of some 1,500 Japanese and English-language books and periodical articles is also provided.

Economic and demographic change in preindustrial Japan, 1600–1868.
See item no. 169.

Epidemics and mortality in early modern Japan.
See item no. 172.

Nakahara: family farming and population in a Japanese village, 1717–1830.
See item no. 182.

Minorities: the Ainu, *Burakumin*, and Koreans

372 **Ainu life and lore: echoes of a departing race.**
John Batchelor. Tokyo: Kyobunkwan, 1927. 448p. Reprinted, New
York; London: Johnson Reprint Corporation, 1971. (Landmarks in
Anthropology).

The Ainu are an indigenous people of northern Japan who until recently were quite
distinct from the Japanese in their physical appearance, lifestyle, social organisation,
language, folklore, religious beliefs, music, and dance. John Batchelor (1854-1944), an
Anglican missionary who lived among the Ainu for more than sixty years, became
prominent for his many studies of Ainu culture and language. In this pioneering work,
he describes the history, community life, and customs of the Ainu in Hokkaidō and
recounts many of the stories and legends that had been orally transmitted from one
generation of Ainu to the next.

373 **Japan's invisible race: caste in culture and personality.**
George De Vos, Hiroshi Wagatsuma. Berkeley, California; London:
University of California Press, 1972. rev. ed. 415p. 2 maps. bibliog.

An interdisciplinary collection of writings concerned with the nature of caste
segregation and racist ideology in Japanese culture. De Vos, Wagatsuma, and eight of
their colleagues focus their attention on the *burakumin*, a pariah caste of more than
two million Japanese who have experienced a long history of discrimination and
segregation even though they have been indistinguishable in their physical appearance
from their neighbours. The authors explore the history of untouchability in Japan and
the efforts made since 1871 to improve the social and political status of these outcastes.
Several of their ethnographic studies are concerned with the ecology of special *buraku*
('outcaste communities'), the traditional urban outcaste community, the social
persistence of outcaste groups, *buraku* relations and attitudes in a progressive farming
community, the little-known minority groups of Japan, and Japanese outcastes in the
United States. In addition, a section on psychological perspectives deals with
socialisation, self-perception, and *burakumin* status; group solidarity and individual
mobility among the *burakumin*; and minority status and attitudes towards authority.

154

374 **Pariah persistence in changing Japan: a case study.**
John Donoghue, with Anna Acitelli-Donoghue, foreword by Daniel D.
Whitney. Washington, DC: University Press of America, 1978. 117p.
bibliog.

Ethnographic descriptions of a small, pseudonymous *burakumin* community ('Shin-machi') in northeastern Honshū and an assessment of social persistence and change within that community between 1954 and 1976. Following two chapters on the origins and development of pariah communities in Japan and on the theoretical parameters within which his research was conducted, Donoghue describes the institutions of kinship and marriage, education, economics, politics, religion, and associations of Shin-machi in 1954 and 1976 respectively, and indicates some of the ways in which they have evolved. He also pays considerable attention to attitudinal changes among the residents of Shin-machi towards themselves and towards the majority Japanese society, as well as to the continuing patterns of discrimination against the *burakumin* and the persistence of negative Japanese views which have been 'particularly relevant to the maintenance of caste endogamy and the mythology of the inherent inferiority of the *burakumin*'.

375 **Together with the Ainu: a vanishing people.**
M. Inez Hilger, with Chiye Sano, Midori Yamaha; introduction by
Leonard Carmichael. Norman, Oklahoma: University of Oklahoma
Press, 1971. 223p. map. bibliog.

An American cultural anthropologist and her two Japanese associates recount their experiences and observations while engaged in ethnographic fieldwork among the Ainu of Hokkaidō in 1965-66. Ainu fishing and horticulture, folklore and folk art, religious beliefs and rites, views of life after death, tattooing and weaving, family life and husband–wife relationships, infancy and child-rearing practices, and many other aspects of Ainu life are described. The authors also comment on the assimilation of the Ainu into twentieth-century Japanese culture, and illustrate this book with over fifty of their own photographs.

376 **Koreans in Japan: ethnic conflict and accommodation.**
Edited by Changsoo Lee, George De Vos, with contributions by Dae-
Gyun Chung, Thomas Rohlen, Yuzura Sasaki, Hiroshi Wagatsuma,
William O. Wetherall; foreword by Robert A. Scalapino. Berkeley,
California; London: University of California Press, 1981. 435p. bibliog.

Offering insights into the problems of race relations and discrimination within Japanese society, this volume is an interdisciplinary investigation of the historical background and present-day status of the 650,000-member Korean minority in Japan and of the legal, political, social, and economic discrimination which it has experienced. In an historical overview, the authors focus on the migration of over one million Koreans to Japan between 1910 and 1945, on the repatriation of many of them after World War II, and on the contest between North and South Korea for the allegiance of those Koreans who remained in Japan. In part two they examine the current legal status of the Korean minority, the issue of Korean ethnic education and national politics, and the educational prospects of Koreans in Japan. Finally, they present several recent case-studies of the Korean ethnic experience, among them studies concerned with community life within a Korean ghetto in Kawasaki City, with the treatment of Koreans under the Japanese judicial system, and with the maintenance of a Korean ethnic identity in Japan.

Minorities: the Ainu, *Burakumin*, and Koreans

377 **The Korean minority in Japan.**
Richard H. Mitchell. Berkeley, California: University of California Press; London: Cambridge University Press, 1967. 186p. bibliog.
Mitchell traces the history of the large Korean minority in Japan following the Japanese annexation of the Korean peninsula in 1910 and analyses the interaction between the immigrants and the Japanese over the years. He first focuses on the contributions of the Koreans in Japan to prewar Korean nationalism, on the significant Korean involvement in the Japanese Communist Party during the 1920s and 1930s, on the effect of Japan's war efforts on the Korean migrants, and on the problems of Japanese assimilation policies. In discussing developments after World War II, Mitchell deals with such topics as the legal status of the Korean minority, the tensions that existed between the Japanese government and the Koreans, the diplomacy of Korean repatriation, the activities of Korean organisations in Japan and the intensification of their political activity, and the uncertain future of this minority group as of the mid-1960s.

378 **Ainu creed and cult.**
Neil Gordon Munro, edited with a preface and an additional chapter by Brenda Z. Seligman, introduction by Hitoshi Watanabe. London: Routledge and Kegan Paul, 1962; New York: Columbia University Press, 1963. 182p. bibliog.
This synthesis of the records which Munro, a British-born physician in Japan, kept while working among the Ainu before World War II describes their religious beliefs, customs, ritual ceremonies, and practices in relation to their everyday life at that time. Munro deals with the fundamental concepts of the Ainu, the *kamui* ('gods' or 'spirits'), the *inau* (offerings to *kamui* in the form of a wooden staff with attached wood-shavings), effigies of *kamui*, the hearth and home as a place of worship, house-building rites, the house-warming ceremony (*chisei nomi*), the feast of all souls or falling tears (*shinurapa*), the exorcism of evil spirits, other rites and rituals, and the customs associated with death and burial. A concluding chapter by Seligman discusses Ainu social organisation.

379 **The Ainu: the past in the present.**
Fred C. C. Peng, Peter Geiser. Hiroshima: Bunka Hyōron, 1977. 340p. 2 maps. bibliog.
An ethnographic investigation into selected aspects of contemporary Ainu life, with particular emphasis on the persistence/disappearance of traditional forms of Ainu social organisation. Peng and Geiser survey the history of Japanese–Ainu relations, consider some of the demographic characteristics of the present-day Ainu community, examine Ainu settlement and residence patterns, study various aspects of Ainu family and social life, map out the original Ainu kinship system, and determine the extent to which Ainu kinship influences marriage patterns. They also analyse the place of the Ainu within the Japanese system of social stratification, show how education has served as an agent of social change in Ainu community life, examine the operation and modification of traditional religious concepts in order to establish an index of social change, and show how political leadership, prestige and the community power structure operate and integrate the Ainu community.

380 **Songs of gods, songs of humans: the epic tradition of the Ainu.**
Translated with an introduction by Donald L. Philippi, foreword by
Gary Snyder. Princeton, New Jersey; Guildford, Surrey: Princeton
University Press; Tokyo: University of Tokyo Press, 1979. 417p.
bibliog. Reprinted, San Francisco: North Point Press, 1982.

A collection of English translations of thirty-three representative epic songs of the
Hokkaidō Ainu, selected from the *yūkar* epics recorded by two Japanese scholars
working among female Ainu reciters before World War II. Philippi's detailed
introduction discusses the cultural history of the Ainu people, their oral literature, the
aesthetic techniques of their epic songs, and aspects of the society which are mirrored in
their folklore. The songs narrate the experiences of gods and goddesses who live apart
from the human world, of gods and goddesses who have interacted with mankind, of
Ainu culture heroes, and of Ainu men and women. All of the songs have been
translated into a sort of English free verse, reflecting the way in which they were sung
by their reciters. There are no accompanying romanised renditions of the original
Ainu-language texts.

381 **The invisible visible minority: Japan's burakumin.**
I. Roger Yoshino, Sueo Murakoshi. Ōsaka: Buraku Kaihō
Kenkyūsho, 1977. 143p. (Buraku Kaihō Kenkyūsho [Buraku Liberation
Research Institute], 1-6-12 Kuboyoshi-chō, Naniwa-ku, Ōsaka 556,
Japan).

A Japanese American researcher and the director of the Buraku Liberation Research
Institute present a sympathetic, comprehensive overview of the *burakumin* (a 'long-
suffering caste group') and of some of their ecological, social, economic, political, and
psychological problems. The authors examine the historical background of the
burakumin, the success of dominant social groups in premodern Japan in creating a
system of social stratification which condemned the *burakumin* to an inferior minority
status, the discrimination which the dominant Japanese majority has practised against
the *burakumin*, the conditions of the *burakumin* ghettoes throughout Japan, twentieth-
century *burakumin* efforts to liberate themselves by challenging discrimination at the
individual and societal levels, and the cultural and institutional deterrents to equality
which they face in postwar Japan. Short articles about recent developments affecting
the *burakumin* may be found in the bimonthly newsletter *Buraku Liberation News*
(1981-   ), published by the Buraku Liberation Research Institute.

**Unbeaten tracks in Japan: an account of travels on horseback in the interior,
including visits to the aborigines of Yezo and the shrines of Nikkô and Isé.**
See item no. 66.

Law and social change in postwar Japan.
See item no. 785.

The broken commandment.
See item no. 1095.

Textile designs of Japan. Volume 3: Okinawan, Ainu, and foreign designs.
See item no. 1347.

Overseas Japanese

382 **The enemy that never was: a history of the Japanese Canadians.**
Ken Adachi.   Toronto, Ontario: McClelland and Stewart, 1976. 456p.
map. bibliog.
Commissioned by the National Japanese Canadian Citizens Association, this book is
not a general history of the Japanese in Canada but rather a detailed account of the
racism encountered by Japanese immigrants and their descendants since the late 1800s.
The first half traces the early decades of Japanese immigration and settlement in
Canada – 'decades of prejudice and suspicions' – in order to provide the historical
background for Adachi's study of the wartime evacuation of over 20,000 Canadian
Japanese from the west coast of British Columbia in 1942. Particular attention is paid
to the formulation and consequences of the government's evacuation policy as well as
to the experiences of the evacuees and the injustices which they endured. Several
statistical tables and the texts of major documents related to the evacuation constitute
an appendix.

383 **Years of sorrow, years of shame: the story of the Japanese Canadians in
World War II.**
Barry Broadfoot.   Toronto, Ontario: Doubleday Canada; Garden
City, New York: Doubleday, 1977. 370p.
Broadfoot effectively uses oral history techniques to document the wartime experience
of some 20,000 Japanese Canadians. His subjects – mostly Canadians born in Canada
of Japanese parents, and Japanese who were naturalised citizens – recount their
reactions to the outbreak of hostilities in the Pacific, the abandonment of their homes
in British Columbia in 1942 and the confiscation of their property, their enforced
relocation to the Canadian interior and their residence in both isolated 'road camps'
and remote rural villages, their work harvesting sugar-beets and other agricultural
crops, and their efforts to re-establish themselves following the war. Twenty-four pages
of photographs illustrate this book. *Within the barbed wire fence: a Japanese man's
account of his internment in Canada*, by Takeo Uyo Nakano with Leatrice Nakano,
afterword by W. Peter Ward (Toronto, Ontario: University of Toronto Press; Seattle,

Washington: University of Washington Press, 1981, 126p.), is one of several other recently published informative accounts of this same period.

384 The bamboo people: the law and Japanese-Americans.
Frank F. Chuman, preface by Tom C. Clark. Del Mar, California: Publisher's Inc., 1976. 385p.

A legal history of the Japanese and their descendants in the United States, beginning with the arrival of the first immigrants in 1869 and extending through the late 1960s. Writing from a Japanese American perspective, Chuman chronicles both the racial discrimination that was practised against the Japanese on the US mainland and the passage of legislation that affected their legal status. Included are discussions of the San Francisco school crisis of 1906 and the 'Gentlemen's Agreement' of 1907-8 which led to voluntary government restrictions on Japanese emigration to the United States; the 'yellow peril' propaganda and the resulting alien land laws of California and Washington; the Japanese Exclusion Act of 1924; cases concerning the evacuation of Japanese Americans from the West coast in 1942; the Japanese Evacuation Claims Act of 1948; the renunciants and the restoration of their US citizenship; and the Immigration and Naturalisation Act of 1952, which eliminated race as a bar to immigration.

385 East across the Pacific: historical and sociological studies of Japanese immigration and assimilation.
Edited with a foreword by Hilary Conroy, T. Scott Miyakawa. Santa Barbara, California; Oxford, England: American Bibliographical Center-Clio Press, 1972. 322p. bibliog.

This collection of historical and sociological essays about Japanese immigration to and settlement in North America, Hawaii, and the Pacific Islands seeks to demonstrate that the Japanese assimilated and significantly contributed to American economic and cultural life. Its twelve essays are entitled: ' "First Year" Immigrants to Hawaii and Eugene Van Reed'; 'Robert Walker Irwin and Systematic Immigration to Hawaii'; 'Japanese Entrepreneurs in the Mariana, Marshall, and Caroline Islands'; 'Japanese Immigrants on a Western Frontier: the Issei in California, 1890–1940'; 'The Vancouver Riots of 1907: a Canadian Episode'; 'My Experience with the Wartime Relocation of Japanese'; 'Early New York Issei Founders of Japanese American Trade'; 'Man of Two Worlds: an Inquiry into the Value System of Inazo Nitobe (1862–1933)'; 'An Immigrant Community in America'; 'Acculturation and Childhood Accidents'; 'Assimilation of Nisei in Los Angeles'; and 'Generation and Character: the Case of the Japanese Americans'.

386 Concentration camps USA: Japanese Americans and World War II.
Roger Daniels. New York: Holt, Rinehart and Winston, 1972. 188p. map. bibliog.

An historian's examination and explanation of the US government's incarceration of the entire Japanese American population of California, Oregon, and Washington during World War II. Daniels discusses the impact of the Japanese attack on Pearl Harbor, the decision to evacuate the Japanese American population from the West Coast, the actual round-up and evacuation that took place in 1942, the question of the loyalty of the dissident minority whose opposition took the form of protest and civil disobedience, the decisions of the federal courts which reviewed the legality of the evacuation, and the return of the internees to the West Coast after the war. This period in Japanese American history has been the subject of a growing number of studies. Among several other full-length narrative histories of the internment years that are oriented towards a general audience are *America's concentration camps*, by Alan R. Bosworth (New York: Norton, 1967, 283p.); *The great betrayal: the evacuation of the Japanese-Americans during World War II*, by Audrie Girdner and Anne Loftis (New York: Macmillan; London: Collier-Macmillan, 1969, 562p.); and *Years of infamy: the untold story of America's concentration camps*, by Michi Weglyn (New York: Morrow, 1976, 351p.). Roger Daniels' book was reprinted under the title *Concentration camps: North America; Japanese in the United States and Canada during World War II* (Malabar, Florida: Robert E. Krieger, 1981, 226p.).

387 **Tokyo Rose: orphan of the Pacific.**
Masayo Duus, translated by Peter Duus, introduction by Edwin O. Reischauer. Tokyo; New York: Kodansha International, 1979. 248p.

Iva Toguri d'Aquino, a second-generation Japanese American (Nisei) woman who was caught in Japan by the outbreak of World War II, was singled out and accused of having been the English-speaking radio broadcaster of wartime Japanese propaganda to American GIs known as 'Tokyo Rose'. Duus explores the myth of the 'one and only Tokyo Rose' in this account of Toguri's life before and during the war, her conviction and imprisonment by the US government for disloyalty to the United States, her years of vilification by the press, and her eventual vindication.

388 **Issei, Nisei, war bride: three generations of Japanese American women in domestic service.**
Evelyn Nakano Glenn. Philadelphia: Temple University Press, 1986. 290p.

A sociological investigation of the relationship between the experiences of three generations of Japanese American women as domestic workers in the San Francisco Bay area, and the larger historical forces of 'the transformation of the area's economy and labor market' and 'the process of labor migration and settlement in that locale'. Glenn examines the historical and political context of Japanese settlement in northern California and describes the relationship of Japanese American women to the Bay Area's labour market, 1900-70. She then looks into these women's careers, their working conditions, their relations with their employers, their strategies for coping, and their views of their work. She also studies their struggle – at the same time as they were working – to create and maintain a family life for themselves as well as the ways in which their participation in the work-force affected the division of labour and their conjugal relations within their own families.

389 **Okage sama de: the Japanese in Hawai'i, 1885–1985.**
Dorothy Ochiai Hazama, Jane Okamoto Komeiji, foreword by Daniel K. Inouye. Honolulu, Hawaii: Bess Press, 1986. 294p. bibliog.

An historical narrative of the first one hundred years of Japanese settlement in the Hawaiian Islands. Written especially to provide Americans of Japanese ancestry in Hawaii with information about their backgrounds so that they could better appreciate their Japanese heritage, this volume recounts how and why Japanese emigrated as labourers to Hawaii during the late 1800s and early 1900s, the challenges as well as the problems of prejudice and discrimination which they faced, their efforts to create a permanent place for themselves and their families in Hawaii, their life on its plantations and the impact of World War II, the postwar growth of the community, and the nature of their contributions to Hawaii's present-day lifestyle. The book contains many excerpts from letters, memoirs, interviews, speeches, documents, and community publications in addition to over 160 black-and-white photographs.

390 **Nisei: the quiet Americans.**
Bill Hosokawa, foreword by Edwin O. Reischauer. New York: William Morrow, 1969. 522p.

A best-selling historical account of the problems and achievements of the Japanese who immigrated to the United States (the Issei) and of both the experiences and the growth of political and social consciousness among their children, the Nisei. Hosokawa first deals with the lives of the Japanese in the United States before World War II, the relocation of the West Coast Japanese American communities to the interior of the country in 1942, their lives in various internment camps, and the wartime contributions of individual Nisei to American victory in the European and Pacific theatres. Part three – 'The Years of Fulfillment' – describes the considerable social, economic, and political progress achieved by second-generation Japanese Americans since the war. The origins and activities of the Japanese American Citizens League are also discussed.

391 **Farewell to Manzanar: a true story of Japanese American experience during and after the World War II internment.**
Jeanne Wakatsuki Houston, James D. Houston. Boston, Massachusetts: Houghton Mifflin, 1973. 177p. Reprinted, New York; Toronto, Ontario; London: Bantam Books, 1974. 145p.

Jeanne Wakatsuki was a seven-year-old girl growing up in southern California when she and her family were sent to the Manzanar internment camp (in Owens Valley, California, 230 miles northeast of Los Angeles) as part of the US government's relocation of West Coast Japanese Americans following the outbreak of World War II. In one of the most eloquent accounts from that period (written thirty years after the event), Wakatsuki sensitively depicts life for herself and her family during the 3½ years which they spent at Manzanar, the problems which they experienced and their efforts to survive the indignities of forced detention, and their re-integration into American society after the camp was closed in autumn 1945. Further details about daily life at Manzanar are provided in *Manzanar*, written by John Armor and Peter Wright, with commentary by John Hersey (New York: Times Books; Toronto, Ontario: Random House of Canada, 1988, 167p.). This chronicle of the period incorporates photographs taken by Ansel Adams during the fall of 1943.

392 **The Issei: the world of the first generation Japanese immigrants, 1885–1924.**
Yuji Ichioka. New York: Free Press; London: Collier Macmillan, 1988. 317p. bibliog.

The 'history of a racial minority struggling to survive in a hostile land', Ichioka's narrative is concerned with the Japanese immigrants who sought to establish roots on the US mainland at a time when they suffered widespread racial and legal discrimination. Ichioka depicts the early migration of Japanese to the West Coast, the labour-contracting system that harshly exploited immigrant labourers, labour organising among the Japanese and the hostility of organised American labour, and the permanent settlement (particularly as farmers and businessmen) of increasing numbers of Issei in the United States. He also describes their prolonged struggle against the anti-Japanese exclusion movement which climaxed with the passage of the 1924 Immigration Act, one provision of which prohibited the admission of aliens ineligible for citizenship as immigrants and thereby abruptly halted all further Japanese immigration. For a complementary sociological study of the first-generation Japanese in Hawaii – including the process of their immigration, the formation and stabilisation of the Issei community there, their occupations, their family and social life, and the impact upon them of the First and Second World Wars – see *Issei: Japanese immigrants in Hawaii*, by Yukiko Kimura (Honolulu, Hawaii: University of Hawaii Press, 1988, 283p.).

393 **The Kikuchi diary: chronicle from an American concentration camp.**
The Tanforan journals of Charles Kikuchi.
Charles Kikuchi, edited and with an introduction by John Modell.
Urbana, Illinois; London: University of Illinois Press, 1973. 258p.
bibliog.

The edited version of the diary which Kikuchi, a second-generation Japanese American graduate student in social work, kept between December 1941 and August 1942. It perceptively recounts his experiences, observations, and sentiments while he and his family were forced to evacuate their home and to reside temporarily in a converted horse stall at Tanforan Race Track (a temporary assembly area for Japanese Americans south of San Francisco) while awaiting resettlement at the Gila Relocation Center in Arizona. Kikuchi records the daily activities of the evacuees, the gross injustices which they endured as well as the more pleasant aspects of camp life, and the overall impact of evacuation and resettlement on his family and the people around him. Modell's introduction assesses the historical significance of the diary and provides background information about Kikuchi himself.

394 **Japanese Americans: the evolution of a subculture.**
Harry H. L. Kitano, foreword by Milton M. Gordon. Englewood
Cliffs, New Jersey: Prentice-Hall, 1969. 186p. bibliog. (Ethnic Groups
in American Life Series).

A socio-psychological interpretation of the acculturation of the Japanese in the United States. Characterising the Japanese Americans as a group that has been 'effective in social organization, effective in socialization, effective in controlling deviant behavior, and effective in "becoming successful" in American terms', Kitano first presents an overview of the Japanese American experience up to and during World War II. Then, focusing on the postwar period, he describes occupational trends among Japanese Americans; their family life, family structure, and family patterns as well as their techniques of social control; the social structure of the Japanese American community, including various community institutions, religion, and community leadership; and the norms, values, and personality of Japanese American culture. Finally, Kitano considers social deviance among Japanese Americans as measured by rates of crime, delinquency, mental illness, and suicide as well as by nonconforming behaviour.

395 **They call me Moses Masaoka: an American saga.**
Mike Masaoka, with Bill Hosokawa. New York: William Morrow,
1987. 383p.

An account of the life and achievements of Mike Masaoka (1915-), a second-generation (Nisei) Japanese American who became an influential representative of the

Japanese American Citizens League (JACL) in Washington, DC. Masaoka describes his childhood and education, the steps that led to his becoming a spokesman for Japanese Americans, the wartime evacuation of Japanese Americans from the US West Coast, his own combat service in the European theatre, his successful postwar leadership of the JACL efforts to eliminate discriminatory federal naturalisation and immigration laws that applied to Asians, and the recent JACL campaign to secure some redress from the United States government for those Japanese Americans who had been forcibly evacuated from their homes and interned during World War II. A broader history of the JACL – from its founding in 1928, through the wartime internment years, to its search for monetary redress during the mid- and late-1970s – has been written by Bill Hosokawa under the title *JACL in quest of justice* (New York: William Morrow, 1982, 383p.).

396 **Imingaisha: Japanese emigration companies and Hawaii, 1894–1908.**
Alan Takeo Moriyama. Honolulu, Hawaii: University of Hawaii Press, 1985. 260p. 4 maps. bibliog.
A history of the origins and background of 125,000 early Japanese emigrants to the Hawaiian Islands, the economic and social conditions that induced them to leave their homes, the process by which they emigrated, their early experiences in Hawaii, and their contributions to the modernisation of Japan. Moriyama deals with the short period when private emigration companies (*imingaisha*) were able to control the flow of emigrants (primarily individuals seeking work on the sugar plantations) because they were the only means by which large groups of workers could secure passage to Hawaii. He also delineates the roles of the Bureau of Immigration, the Japanese consulate, and the emigration company representatives in Hawaii's immigration process; and he explains how the Japanese community in Hawaii interacted with the US and Japanese governments as well as with private institutions to obtain improved working and living conditions.

397 **Kodomo no tame ni: for the sake of the children; the Japanese American experience in Hawaii.**
Dennis M. Ogawa, with Glen Grant, foreword by Lawrence H. Fuchs, amplified by contemporaneous readings. Honolulu, Hawaii: University Press of Hawaii, 1978. 615p. bibliog.
An account of the history and cultural growth of the Japanese Americans in Hawaii, from their earliest contacts with the islands – through the years of immigration, plantation life, World War II, and the dynamic growth of the 1950s and 1960s – to the 1980s and the emergence of a 'local' Japanese American identity. Each chapter combines Ogawa's interpretation of broad social developments in Hawaii with selected readings in the form of contemporary journal articles and excerpts from books and government documents. Chapter 7 ('Shall the Japs Dominate Hawaii?'), for example, contains Ogawa's description of Hawaii during the war with four readings respectively entitled 'Pearl Harbor and Confinement', 'Report on Hawaiian Islands', 'Hawaii's 150,000 Japanese', and 'Hawaii's Loyal Japanese'. Ogawa's study also explores various aspects of the Japanese American relationship with other racial groups and their contributions to Hawaii's cultural pluralism.

398 **American in disguise.**
Daniel I. Okimoto, foreword by James A. Michener. New York;
Tokyo: Walker/Weatherhill, 1971. 206p.

A moving autobiographical account of a young Nisei's personal search for identity as a second-generation Japanese American. Okimoto writes about his parents' background, the years which he and his family spent in a World War II internment camp in Arizona, his childhood and adolescence after the war in southern California, his upbringing as a Japanese American, his years as an undergraduate student at Princeton University, and his experiences in Japan in the late 1960s, 'where he discovered that he had no real place' in his ancestral homeland. In the course of his narrative, Okimoto questions the validity of the 'lofty image of America as the great land of equality and boundless opportunity' for racial minorities and comments on some of the problems engendered by his dual identity as well as by race relations in the United States.

399 **Nisei daughter.**
Monica Sone. Boston, Massachusetts: Little, Brown, 1953. 238p. (An Atlantic Monthly Press Book). Reprinted with an introduction by S. Frank Miyamoto and a new preface, Seattle, Washington; London University of Washington Press, 1979.

The autobiographical account of a second-generation (Nisei) Japanese American woman, covering the years from 1924 (when she was six years old) to 1945. Sone first recounts her experiences as a child and adolescent while growing up in Seattle, Washington during the 1930s. She describes her relationship with her parents, with other Japanese Americans, and with white society; and she shows how she was influenced by the views and the ways of the generation of Japanese (among them her parents) who had emigrated to the United States. In the latter half of her account, Sone discusses her experiences during the years immediately following the attack on Pearl Harbor and relates how she and her family (along with 120,000 other Americans of Japanese ancestry) were forcibly uprooted from their homes and relocated to camps within the interior of the United States.

400 **Through harsh winters: the life of a Japanese immigrant woman; as told to Akemi Kikumura.**
Michiko Tanaka. Novato, California: Chandler & Sharp, 1981. 157p.

A narrative of the life of Tanaka Michiko, based on recorded interviews that were translated and edited by her daughter, Akemi Kikumura. Through her mother's life history, Kikumura not only investigates the change and continuity that occurred in Japanese American culture but also documents the experience of Japanese American immigrants to California, their encounter with racism and their internment during World War II, and their constant struggle to achieve some measure of status and a better life for themselves and their children. Tanaka's account also includes some of her Buddhist philosophical recollections.

401 **And justice for all: an oral history of the Japanese American detention camps.**
John Tateishi. New York; Toronto, Ontario: Random House, 1984. 259p. map.

Edited personal narratives of thirty Japanese Americans who were forcibly evacuated from the West Coast shortly after the outbreak of World War II and interned simply because of their Japanese racial background. These relatively brief essays by former internees at Manzanar, Topaz, Tule Lake, Minidoka, Heart Mountain, Jerome, Poston, and Rowher describe the often appalling living conditions and the individual hardships within those camps as well as their personal feelings and reactions – ranging from passive acceptance of their situation to extreme bitterness. Their accounts also convey their 'sense of personal tragedy for having experienced a nation's betrayal of a people's loyalty and faith'. In his preface, Tateishi (national redress director of the Japanese American Citizens League) indicates that these accounts are representative of the experiences of over 120,000 Japanese Americans and 'exemplify what we all went through behind barbed wire during those war years'.

402 **East to America: a history of the Japanese in the United States.**
Robert A. Wilson, Bill Hosokawa, foreword by Shigeo Wakamatsu.
New York: William Morrow, 1980. 351p. Reprinted, New York: Quill, 1982.

A history of the Japanese in the United States: from the arrival of Nakahama Manjirō and Hamada Hikozō, two late Tokugawa period castaways who were rescued by American ships, through the 1970s, when the Japanese American community began to lobby Congress for some form of compensation to cover the material loss of their basic human rights when they were interned in wartime concentration camps. Wilson and Hosokawa recount the immigration of Japanese in search of land and jobs, the growing hostility against them which culminated in the passage of legislation barring their further immigration, the success story of the Japanese who settled in Hawaii, the hardship and turmoil experienced during World War II and their struggle for justice, and the dismantling of discriminatory barriers during the late 1940s and 1950s.

403 **Transforming the past: tradition and kinship among Japanese Americans.**
Sylvia Junko Yanagisako.   Stanford, California: Stanford University Press, 1985. 289p. bibliog.

An intergenerational study of kinship change among Japanese Americans since the early 1900s which contributes to an understanding of the general process that has been central to the development of the contemporary kinship system of the United States. Basing her research on oral kinship autobiographies elicited from first- and second-generation Japanese Americans in Seattle, Washington, Yanagisako elucidates the social and symbolic processes that have shaped their kinship development and explains how they 'consciously and unconsciously moved away from their culture of origin to the culture of America'. Focusing on each of three key relationships – marriage, filial relations, and siblinghood – she shows how both generations 'conceptualize their kinship relations' in terms of a symbolic opposition between 'Japanese' and 'American', and how they have formulated a 'Japanese American synthesis' over the past several decades.

Samurai and silk: a Japanese and American heritage.
See item no. 297.

A daughter of the samurai. How a daughter of feudal Japan, living hundreds of years in one generation, became a modern American.
See item no. 313.

Noguchi and his patrons.
See item no. 343.

Overseas Japanese

Hawaii under the rising sun: Japan's plans for conquest after Pearl Harbor.
See item no. 710.

Amerasia Journal.
See item no. 1487.

Dictionary of Asian American history.
See item no. 1563.

Asians in America: a selected annotated bibliography.
See item no. 1579.

The Japanese in Hawaii: an annotated bibliography of Japanese Americans.
See item no. 1598.

Language

General

404 **The history of the Japanese written language.**
Yaeko Sato Habein.   Tokyo: University of Tokyo Press, 1984. 229p.
bibliog.

A survey history beginning with the introduction of the Chinese script before the Nara period. Habein discusses the ways in which the Japanese borrowed and adapted Chinese characters to their spoken language, and she outlines the difficulties which they encountered in writing Japanese – a language that was totally different from Chinese in phonology, syntax, and vocabulary – in a foreign script. She describes the subsequent development and evolution of Japanese-style writing (the *kana* syllabaries and a writing system combining *kana* and Chinese characters known as *kanamajiribun*), the establishment of *wakan konkōbun* (the writing style that combines *wabun* or native prose writing with *kanamajiribun*) during the Kamakura and Muromachi periods, the diversification of writing styles, and the efforts of Meiji period intellectuals to unify the written and spoken languages. Forty reading selections in Japanese, constituting the second part of this volume, exemplify the varieties of Japanese writing styles that have developed over the centuries.

405 **The Japanese language.**
Haruhiko Kindaichi, translated and annotated by Umeyo Hirano.
Rutland, Vermont; Tokyo: Tuttle, 1978. 295p.

A clarification of the nature of the Japanese language, organised under five principal headings: 'The Position of the Japanese Language', 'Aspects of Speech', 'Pronunciation', 'Vocabulary', and 'Sentence Structure'. Among the many topics discussed are the contact of Japanese with other languages over the centuries; the varieties of ordinary speech in Japanese which are directly related to the regional origin, occupation, status and sex of the speaker; the syllables, phonemes, and sound systems of Japanese; the vocabulary for nature, for human biology and emotions, and for family and society; the word and phrase arrangement of Japanese sentences; and the use of terse expressions.

406 **The unspoken way.** *Haragei*: **silence in Japanese business and society.**
Michihiro Matsumoto, introduction by Edward T. Hall. Tokyo; New York: Kodansha International, 1988. 145p. bibliog.
An explanation of one of the basic Japanese principles of interpersonal communication and traditional popular psychology: the art or practice of using *hara*, or one's 'heart, mind, soul, intuition and feeling', in order to communicate in a non-verbal manner. Matsumoto defines and analyses *haragei* ('belly play'), explains why this form of non-verbal communication has been important in Japanese society, clarifies its philosophical and religious origins, and describes how *haragei* functions in contemporary Japan.

407 **The Japanese language.**
Roy Andrew Miller. Chicago; London: University of Chicago Press, 1967. 428p. 3 maps. bibliog. (History and Structure of Languages).
Reprinted, University of Chicago Press, 1980.
A comprehensive introduction to the main features of the history and structure of Japanese, with particular consideration of the spoken language. Miller covers the historical and geographical setting of Japanese; its genetic relationships, particularly with the other major Altaic languages of Korean, Manchu, Mongolian, and Old Turkish; the history of writing systems in Japanese; the contemporary and premodern dialects of Japanese; the historical phonology of Japanese; loanwords from Western languages in Japanese as well as Japanese loanwords in other languages; 'special and notable' utterances such as the extremely complicated system for categories of speech levels generally referred to as 'honorific language' (*keigo*); and grammar and syntax. Japan's significant linguistic debt to China is stressed throughout. Miller's book presupposes no previous knowledge of Japanese language or script and may be profitably read by linguists specialising in European languages as well as by students of Japanese civilisation and history.

408 **Japan's modern myth: the language and beyond.**
Roy Andrew Miller. New York; Tokyo: Weatherhill, 1982. 298p. bibliog.
Many Japanese contend that their language is 'somehow or other unique', that it possesses a kind of spirit or soul of its own, and that it is extremely difficult for foreigners to master. Miller describes, analyses, and puts into historical perspective these and other manifestations of the 'modern myth of the Japanese language' and shows how they are closely associated with present-day Japanese concepts of their own racial and cultural identity. He also discusses the various sociocultural bases for this myth, its role in isolating the Japanese from other peoples, and its potential effect on future Japanese interaction with the rest of the world. Throughout his study, Miller attacks the validity of this myth and criticises academia and the mass media for perpetuating it. The present work is in part an expansion of the author's earlier study, *The Japanese language in contemporary Japan: some sociolinguistic observations* (Washington, DC: American Enterprise Institute for Public Policy Research; Stanford, California: Hoover Institution on War, Revolution and Peace, 1977, 105p. [AEI-Hoover Policy Studies, 22]), which deals with some of the same problems.

409 **Japanese: the spoken language in Japanese life.**
Osamu Mizutani, translated by Janet Ashby. Tokyo: Japan Times, 1981. 180p.

An examination of some of the ways in which the Japanese language is currently used in daily life. Mizutani, an experienced teacher of Japanese as a foreign language, discusses the elements of the spoken language, its special characteristics, and recent changes in the life and language of the Japanese people. Explaining the significance of selected language patterns and citing various case-studies, he devotes much of his analysis to what is said and to whom it is said, to the tendency towards maintaining or achieving harmony and unity which characterises the spoken language, and to the ongoing Japanese concern for the relative relationshps among speakers that constitutes a major part of their linguistic environment.

410 **Tense and aspect in modern colloquial Japanese.**
Matsuo Soga. Vancouver, British Columbia: University of British Columbia Press, 1983. 245p.

A comprehensive treatment of the notion of tense and aspect, the function of the so-called tense markers -*ru* and -*ta*, the semantic characteristics of verbs (e.g., stativity, non-stativity, durativity and punctuality), which are essential to the notion of aspect in verbs, and several different aspectual sub-categories and their semantic and grammatical structures.

411 **Japanese and the Japanese: words in culture.**
Takao Suzuki, translated by Akira Miura. Tokyo; New York: Kodansha International, 1978. 152p.

Language involves not only speech but also non-verbal communication (such as signs and gestures) and a set of unconscious expectations about human behaviour that are determined by one's environment and culture, In this exploration of the Japanese language as it relates to Japanese life-style, psychology, and culture, Suzuki discusses various problems that are raised by the definition of words, and he considers the kinds of misconceptions that arise when individuals use vocabulary without understanding the cultural framework. He touches upon a wide range of concerns including the meanings of words and their definitions, the use of adjectives and comparatives in Japanese, the differences between the Japanese and Indo-European languages in the use of terms to designate oneself and others, and the relationship between language and patterns of behaviour in Japan. This work was reprinted under the title *Words in context: a Japanese perspective on language and culture* (Tokyo; New York: Kodansha International, 1984. 176p.).

412 **An introduction to Japanese phonology.**
Timothy J. Vance. Albany, New York: State University of New York Press, 1987. 226p. bibliog. (SUNY Series in Linguistics).

Provides a broad overview of the phonology of modern standard Japanese (*hyōjungo*), the dialect spoken by residents of the Yamanote region of Tokyo as well as by educated speakers of Japanese throughout the rest of Japan. Among the topics covered are the articulatory setting, phonemicisation, vowels, consonants, vowel de-voicing, syllables and moras, accent, the velar nasal, sequential voicing, other morphophonemic alternatives, and verb morphology.

Getting America ready for Japanese science and technology.
See item no. 991.

The fifth generation fallacy: why Japan is betting its future on artificial intelligence.
See item no. 997.

Journal of the Association of Teachers of Japanese.
See item no. 1529.

Studies in Japanese literature and language: a bibliography of English materials.
See item no. 1615.

Dictionaries

413 **Womansword: what Japanese words say about women.**
Kittredge Cherry.   Tokyo; New York: Kodansha International, 1987.
151p.
A selection of colourful, commonly used terms to describe girls, women, and their lives in contemporary Japanese society. Over five hundred expressions pertaining to female identity, girlhood, weddings, married life, motherhood, work outside the home, sexuality, and ageing are introduced. Short, lively essays – generally containing a variety of words, phrases, and proverbs grouped around a single theme – deal with such expressions as *ofukuro* ('honourable bag', the affectionate name by which sons refer to their mothers), *otoko masari* ('male surpassers', women who excel over men in a particular way), and *urenokori* ('unsold goods', or older unmarried women). Cherry's book is designed for use as both a dictionary and a provocative interpretation of women-related aspects of present-day Japanese language and culture. For a scholarly examination of Japanese women's speech, focusing on syntactic differences in the speech of men and women, see *Japanese women's language*, by Janet S. Shibamoto (Orlando, Florida; London: Academic Press, 1985, 190p.).

414 **A dictionary of Japanese and English idiomatic equivalents.**
General editor: Charles Corwin.   Tokyo: Japan Publications Trading Co., 1968. 302p. Reprinted, Tokyo; New York: Kodansha International, 1980.
Over ten thousand of the most frequently spoken Japanese idiomatic words and expressions are grouped together under 222 'General Thought Categories' ranging from *ai* ('love') to *zokuaku* ('vulgarity') and including such other categories as *himitsu* ('secrecy'), *kiken* ('danger'), *seikō* ('success'), and *warai* ('laughter'). Each expression appears in both romanised Japanese and Chinese characters (*kanji*) together with its English-language equivalent or counterpart. A forty-page 'General Japanese Index' facilitates the location of specific terms. Corwin's dictionary is designed to serve native speakers of English as a quick guide for locating idiomatic equivalents in Japanese and

as a means for familiarising themselves with the correct use and selection of Japanese idioms.

415 A dictionary of Japanese Buddhist terms: based on references in Japanese literature.
Hisao Inagaki, Patrick Geoffrey O'Neill.   Kyōto: Nagata Bunshōdō, 1985. 2nd ed. 473p.

A dictionary of nearly 5,000 entries for Buddhist terms, names of people, ceremonies, texts, sects, and teachings that appear in Heian and Kamakura period literature. Terms related to Zen, Jōdo, Tendai, and Shingon Buddhism predominate. Each romanised entry includes the Chinese characters (*kanji*) for the specified term, its English-language definitions, and one or more references to literary passages in which the term is found. Because of the central role that Buddhism has played in Japanese history and civilisation, this specialised dictionary should be valuable to serious students of premodern history, philosophy, and art as well as of classical literature and religion.

416 Say it in Japanese.
Miwa Kai.   New York: Dover, 1984. rev. and enlarged ed. 220p. (Dover 'Say It' Series).

This compact handbook organises 2,200 entries by topics (e.g., greetings and introductions; lodgings; restaurants and food; sightseeing; post office; clothing) in order to assist travellers, students, and businessmen in expressing themselves in Japanese. Each English-language phrase or term is followed by its Japanese equivalent in both its romanised form and the Chinese characters (*kanji*) or *kana* syllabary in which it is written. All entries are numbered, and the text is fully indexed and cross-referenced for ease of use. With its coverage of '1200 phrases – 2000 useful words', *Japanese for travellers*, produced by the staff of Editions Berlitz (Lausanne, Switzerland: Berlitz, 1974, 192p.), serves many of the same functions. While it contains much practical information about travelling in Japan, however, it offers fewer words and lacks the useful indexing feature found in *Say it in Japanese*.

417 Kenkyusha's new English–Japanese dictionary.
Yoshio Koine, editor in chief.   Tokyo: Kenkyusha, 1980. 5th ed. 2477p.

The standard, comprehensive English–Japanese dictionary, containing 235,000 words. Each English term is followed by its Japanese translation (rendered in Chinese characters or the *kana* syllabary) and by occasional examples of its different meanings and usage. Since the romanised forms of the Japanese words are not provided, beginning students of the Japanese language frequently experience some difficulty in using this work. A smaller, condensed version of the dictionary, containing 55,000 words, is the fifth edition of *Kenkyusha's new little English–Japanese dictionary = Shin ritoru Ei–Wa jiten* (Tokyo: Kenkyusha, 1987, 599p.).

418 Kenkyusha's new Japanese–English dictionary.
Koh Masuda, general editor.   Tokyo: Kenkyusha, 1974. 4th ed. 2110p.

The standard, comprehensive Japanese–English dictionary. It contains 80,000 words, 160,000 compounds and phrases, and 50,000 sample sentences. All Japanese words are romanised and then listed alphabetically. Each main entry contains a word in romanised form and in Chinese characters or the *kana* syllabary, together with concise definitions or translations as well as sample sentences illustrating its use in both Japanese and English. A smaller, condensed version of this dictionary, containing 54,000 words, is the fifth edition of *Kenkyusha's new little Japanese–English dictionary* = *Shin ritoru Wa–Ei jiten* (Tokyo: Kenkyusha, 1987, 632p.).

419 **English loanwords in Japanese: a selection.**
Akira Miura. Rutland, Vermont; Tokyo: Tuttle, 1979. 192p. bibliog.

Loanwords have become a very common phenomenon in the Japanese language, especially as many thousands of English-language words and terms have been adopted by the Japanese since the end of the war. Miura presents more than 400 of these words, in particular, nouns and adjectives such as *bifuteki* ('beefsteak'), *gurīn* ('green'), *mai-kā* ('my car'), and *wan-pīsu* ('woman's dress'). He provides explanations of their meanings and their use as loanwords (*gairaigo*) in Japan as well as tips on their proper usage. In addition, he frequently discusses how these words entered the Japanese language and compares them with words of Japanese origin that have generally similar meanings but significantly different connotations. This book can be enjoyed by individuals interested in the interaction of modern Japanese culture and language as well as by Westerners learning Japanese.

420 **Japanese words and their uses.**
Akira Miura. Rutland, Vermont; Tokyo: Tuttle, 1983. 240p. bibliog.

An alphabetically arranged reference book for English-speaking students of Japanese, particularly at the elementary and intermediate levels, that concisely explains the uses and nuances of approximately three hundred hard-to-translate and commonly misused basic Japanese words and phrases such as *kanai* ('wife'), *shiru* ('to get to know'), and *mizu* ('water'). As there is no exact correspondence between the English and the Japanese for these terms, Miura clarifies their meanings, contrasts them with their English 'equivalents', explains how they should not be used as well as how they are properly used, and provides a variety of sample sentences for illustrative purposes.

421 **The modern reader's Japanese–English character dictionary.**
Andrew Nathaniel Nelson. Rutland, Vermont; Tokyo: Tuttle, 1974. 2nd rev. ed. 1109p. bibliog.

The most authoritative bilingual dictionary of Chinese characters (*kanji*) used in the modern Japanese language. It contains nearly 5,500 characters with their 11,500 current 'readings' (or pronunciations) and approximately 70,000 compounds, all with concise English definitions. The vocabulary includes terms in everyday usage together with older words still encountered in twentieth-century Japanese literature. The readings of characters used only in personal and place names (frequently different from the readings of those same characters in ordinary words) are excluded. All characters are arranged in order by their 214 traditional radicals – a system that centres around the basic elements of the characters and is used in most Chinese dictionaries to classify those characters. Appendixes contain historical tables, listings of important geographical names, a list of weights and measures, and *Tōyō Kanji* lists, as well as added information concerning the use of this dictionary. Supplementing Nelson's volume with over 47,000 entries, Mark Spahn and Wolfgang Hadamitzky's *Japanese character dictionary (with compound lookup via any kanji)* = *Kan-Ei jukugo ribāsu jiten* (Tokyo: Nichigai Associates, 1989, 1669p.) enables readers of Japanese to look up a compound word by means of any character used to construct that word, including the second, third, or fourth *kanji*.

422 Japanese business language: an essential dictionary.
Compiled by the Mitsubishi Corporation [Mitsubishi Shōji Kabushiki Kaisha], introduction by Kaori O'Connor.   London: Kegan Paul International, 1987. 221p.

A reference work of some five hundred key business terms rendered into and explained in English. All of the entries are significant words and phrases which are regularly used in business conversations but which cannot be easily translated without some accompanying clarification of the ways they are used, their background and derivation, the nuances of their meanings, and the ways in which these can change in different situations. Typical of the entries are such expressions as *chotto ippai* ('let's have a quick drink'), *dame-oshi* (the name given to the process of double-checking something), and *kabu ga agaru* ('one gains in stature'). Through its many informative descriptions, this dictionary also explains many of the concepts, customs, practices, and values of the contemporary Japanese business world.

423 Japanese names: a comprehensive index by characters and readings.
Patrick Geoffrey O'Neill.   New York; Tokyo: Weatherhill, 1972. 359p.

The problem of how to 'read' (or pronounce) Japanese personal and place names when written solely in Chinese characters (*kanji*) is a constant challenge for Japanese and Westerners alike. Many Chinese characters have special name readings that are distinct from the readings normally associated with them in everyday speech. Furthermore, virtually every character has more than one recognised name reading; some even have as many as twenty. O'Neill's dictionary provides either the correct or the most probable readings of a wide range of Japanese names appearing in Chinese characters, as well as the correct Chinese characters for many of the most common or best-known Japanese names. In two separate parts – 'From Characters to Readings' and 'From Readings to Characters' – it covers 13,500 surnames, 11,000 personal names, 6,800 literary, historical and artistic names, 4,400 place names, and 300 Japanese era names (*nengō*). O'Neill's dictionary offers far more extensive coverage of names than any other comparable reference tool, but it is far from exhaustive.

424 The Oxford–Duden pictorial English–Japanese dictionary.
English text edited by John Pheby, Japanese text edited by Akitō Miyamoto.   Oxford, England; New York: Oxford University Press, 1983. 864p.

Corresponding terms in English and Japanese that are related to a particular subject or field of activity such as photography, garden tools, winter sports, coal mines, printing, shipbuilding, and road construction are arranged together in 384 groups. These terms are linked by numbers to composite illustrations on the same or opposite page that depict the objects or the activities. These illustrations complement the translations of individual terms by enabling readers to visualise the object that is denoted by each word. In all, some 28,000 objects are represented and defined within the composite illustrations. These are supplemented by alphabetical indexes in English and Japanese. An adaptation of the famous *Oxford–Duden pictorial German–English dictionary*

(1980), this bilingual dictionary has a distinct European bias both in its general orientation and in its selection of illustrations and terms.

425 **Affective expressions in Japanese: a handbook of value-laden words in everyday Japanese.**
Ronald Suleski, Hiroko Masada.   Tokyo: Hokuseido Press, 1982. 87p.
(Distributed in the United States by Heian International, South San Francisco, California).

Affective expressions are short words or phrases which impart a particular nuance to the sentences in which they are used. The Japanese language has a large number of such frequently used expressions, among them *akumade* ('completely', 'to the last'), *masaka* ('surely not', 'impossible'), and *sekkaku* ('especially', 'purposely'). For each of the fifty-one expressions contained in this handbook, the authors explain the types of nuances which it implies, indicate its full range of English-language equivalents, and clarify the social and cultural situations in which it should be used.

426 **Romanized English–Japanese, Japanese–English dictionary.**
Morio Takahashi.   Tokyo: Taiseido, 1968. 8th ed. 457, 1226p.

One of the more comprehensive bilingual dictionaries of the modern Japanese language, this frequently reprinted reference work is organised into two parts: 'English–Japanese', with 10,000 English words and phrases; and 'Japanese–English', with 50,000 Japanese words and phrases. Takahashi's selection of the terms that are included in both sections is made on the basis of their importance in daily usage. Japanese words are written in their romanised form as well as in Chinese characters (*kanji*). A concise, pocket-sized dictionary that dispenses entirely with Chinese characters and instead presents all of its definitions solely in romanised form is the Hyōjun Rōmajikai's *All-romanized English–Japanese dictionary* (Rutland, Vermont; Tokyo: Tuttle, 1973, 732p.). Intended initially for the use of Westerners in Japan, it has also proved popular among Japanese students of English.

English–Japanese, Japanese–English dictionary of computer and data-processing terms.
See item no. 437.

Kanji and kana: a handbook and dictionary of the Japanese writing system.
See item no. 438.

Essential kanji: 2,000 basic Japanese characters systematically arranged for learning and reference.
See item no. 448.

Discover Japan: words, customs and concepts.
See item no. 1557.

Japanese art signatures: a handbook and practical guide.
See item no. 1571.

See also the section 'Encyclopedias, Directories, and Subject Dictionaries'.

Grammar

427 **Essential Japanese grammar.**
Everett F. Bleiler. New York: Dover Publications; London: Constable, 1963. 155p. Reprinted, Rutland, Vermont; Tokyo: Tuttle, 1967.
A textbook of modern colloquial Japanese grammar designed for the individual who wishes 'to express oneself orally with reasonable accuracy; to understand simple material addressed to oneself; and to be able to analyze, understand, and enlarge material in a phrase book or record set'. Bleiler presents basic grammatical information concerning nouns, personal pronouns, particles, demonstrative words, verbs, adjectives, adverbs, verbal and adjectival constructions, clauses and conjunctions, honorific forms, word order, the formation of questions, numbers and the counting of objects, and idiomatic expressions. Examples are provided for all constructions, and both word-for-word and free translations are given. All Japanese words, expressions, and sentences are written solely in romanisation.

428 **Colloquial Japanese: with important construction and grammar notes.**
Noboru Inamoto. Rutland, Vermont; Tokyo: Tuttle, 1972. 436p.
A clear presentation of the major grammatical elements in spoken Japanese together with a vocabulary of some 1,100 words in romanised form. Instead of emphasizing theoretical rules of grammar, Inamoto systematically introduces various 'patterns' of usage in order to create a grammar which beginning students can more easily assimilate. These patterns reflect contemporary colloquial usage and are accompanied by additional examples and explanations that appear in sections entitled 'Important Construction and Grammar Notes'. Each chapter also introduces important everyday expressions and includes a variety of exercises as well as drills. A comprehensive index to the grammatical points introduced throughout the text enhances its usefulness.

429 **The structure of the Japanese language.**
Susumu Kuno. Cambridge, Massachusetts; London: MIT Press, 1973. 410p. bibliog. (Current Studies in Linguistics, 3).
This descriptive and analytical study addresses several problems which have been unsatisfactorily treated in conventional grammars. Kuno explains why some sentences that should be grammatical according to explanations presented in conventional grammars are in fact ungrammatical. He also contrasts various grammatical features of Japanese with their counterparts in English, and examines the similarities and differences that exist between the two languages with respect to those features. His study includes coverage of the proper and improper use of selected particles, verbs, temporal and conditional clauses, nominal and adjectival clauses, and deictics, as well as case marking and word order in Japanese.

430 **Handbook of modern Japanese grammar: including lists of words and expressions with English equivalents for reading aid.**
Yoko Matsuoka McClain. Tokyo: Hokuseido Press, 1981. 272p. bibliog.
A comprehensive outline of Japanese grammar that covers parts of speech, verbs,

auxiliary verbs, verb-following expressions, adjectives, non-conjugative adjectives, particles, interrogative words plus particles, nouns, noun-following words and expressions, common noun-prefixes, common noun-suffixes, terms for family members and relatives, noun modifiers, pronouns, adverbs, onomatopoeic words, conjunctions, interjections, and the formal level of words and expressions. It offers concise, clearly written, non-technical explanations – primarily for the grammar of the written language. Extensive cross-references and exhaustive indexes (one for verb- and noun-following expressions, the other for grammatical parts) enhance the handbook's usefulness both as a reference book and as a reading aid. Three appendixes cover the Japanese counting system, punctuation, and the way to read a Japanese sentence.

431 **A dictionary of basic Japanese grammar.**
Seiichi Makino, Michio Tsutsui. Tokyo: Japan Times, 1986. 634p. bibliog.

Designed primarily for first- and second-year students of Japanese and for teachers of the language, this reference work introduces the major characteristics of Japanese grammar and provides – in dictionary format – extensive coverage of over 300 grammar-related expressions. Each descriptive entry for a basic grammatical term or concept includes information about its general meaning or function, its word formation rules, several sentences which illustrate its use, and detailed explanatory notes. Expressions which are semantically close to a term are frequently introduced and compared, and their differences are explained. Eight appendixes contain such information as the basic conjugations of Japanese, the rules for connecting important expressions, a list of numerals and their counters, and guidelines for improving one's reading skill by identifying an 'extended sentential unit'.

432 **A reference grammar of Japanese.**
Samuel E. Martin. New Haven, Connecticut; London: Yale University Press, 1975. 1198p. bibliog. (Yale Linguistic Series). Reprinted, Rutland, Vermont; Tokyo: Tuttle, 1988.

Widely regarded as the best and most comprehensive reference grammar in English for serious students of the Japanese language, this extensively indexed work covers virtually every style and variation of contemporary spoken and written Japanese. Entire sections are devoted to such topics as 'predicate adjuncts', 'expansion constraints', 'noun subcategorization', 'voice conversions', 'desideratives', 'negation', 'adverbializations', 'tentatives and hortatives', 'adnominalizations', 'nominalizations', 'sentence extensions', 'commands and requests', 'conjunctionalizations', 'quotations', and 'stylizations'. Throughout his book, Martin discusses and analyses the diverse examples of sentence types that are used by native speakers of Japanese. All such examples are given in romanisation only.

433 **Japanese grammar.**
Hideichi Ono. Tokyo: Hokuseido Press, 1973. 362p.

A volume intended to teach both beginning and more advanced students the essential elements of modern Japanese grammar. It contains fifty-four lessons, each consisting of a series of rules, drills, and exercises. The grammatical explanations are clearly spelled out and are accompanied by considerable illustrative material. These examples are written in a combination of the *kana* syllabaries and Chinese characters (*kanji*), in romanised Japanese, and in English translation; but the drills and exercise sections omit the romanised Japanese. The contents of the lessons are selected and arranged in a way designed to provide students with the 'well-rounded command' of the Japanese language that results from their exposure to a wide range of materials.

434 **Japanese generative grammar.**
Edited by Masayoshi Shibatani. New York; London: Academic Press, 1976. 574p. bibliog. (Syntax and Semantics, 5).
Comprehensive, in-depth studies by thirteen American and Japanese linguists that cover a wide range of topics within the area of generative grammar: subject; subject raising; reflexivisation; passivisation; causativisation; relativisation; complementation; negation; tense, aspect, and modality; nominal compounds; and honorifics.

Tense and aspect in modern colloquial Japanese.
See item no. 410.

Textbooks

435 **Japanese language patterns: a structural approach.**
Anthony Alfonso, with Yoshisuke Hirabayashi and others. Tokyo: Sophia University L. L. Center of Applied Linguistics, 1966. 2 vols.
A textbook for college students which emphasizes language learning through the mastery of language patterns that are used in standard colloquial Japanese. Each of its forty lessons includes the fundamental steps of understanding and producing new language patterns as well as thoroughly assimilating them through repetitive drill. The text's explicit grammatical analyses and linguistically-oriented explanations are accompanied by a wealth of illustrative examples. Sounds, accent, and lexical items are not analysed except when they have a bearing on Japanese language structure. All Japanese words and sentences appear only in romanised form. Teachers of elementary Japanese will also find this textbook to be a useful reference work for clarifying and explaining various grammatical points or patterns.

436 **Japanese for busy people.**
Compiled by the Association for Japanese-Language Teaching [Kokusai Nihongo Fukyū Kyōkai]; editorial consultant: Dorothy Britton. Tokyo; New York: Kodansha International, 1984. 213p.
An introductory textbook designed for tourists and businessmen who wish to acquire a basic working knowledge of spoken Japanese as it is used in everyday life. The course consists of thirty lessons containing dialogues (presented in both the Japanese *kana* syllabary and in romanisation, with translations), notes on grammar and vocabulary, exercises, and quizzes. Four 30-minute instructional cassette tapes accompany the text. A sequel – *Japanese for busy people II: intermediate level* (accompanied by six 60-minute cassette tapes) – is scheduled for publication by Kodansha International in mid-1989. Combining a series of opening dialogues, notes on grammar, usage and culture, practice sections with key sentences, exercises and short useful dialogues, and quizzes, its forty lessons are slanted towards business people but are also useful for other

individuals who seek the ability to communicate effectively on a daily conversational level.

437 **Comprehending technical Japanese.**
Edward E. Daub, R. Byron Bird, Nobuo Inoue. Madison, Wisconsin: University of Wisconsin Press; Tokyo: University of Tokyo Press, 1975. 437p.

A textbook to assist English-speaking engineers and scientists in learning to read and translate Japanese materials in the natural sciences. Designed for self-study as well as for classroom use, it consists of twenty-five graded lessons, each of which contains lists of selected vocabulary, graded readings, explanatory notes, examples of grammatical constructions, and a translation test. The authors emphasize technical vocabulary and stress the necessity of learning to recognise, read and understand five hundred essential Chinese characters (*kanji*) that are used in Japanese. They are introduced – twenty at a time – in each of the lessons. These characters have been selected on the basis of frequency counts of vocabulary appearing in physics, chemistry, and biology texts. Their mastery should enable readers to become familiar with most of the *kanji* encountered in the standard scientific literature. Individuals concerned with computers and electronic data-processing will find Gene Ferber's *English–Japanese, Japanese–English dictionary of computer and data-processing terms = Ei–Wa – Wa–Ei konpyūta-dēta shori yōgo jiten* (Cambridge, Massachusetts; London: MIT Press, 1989, 470p.) – a comprehensive dictionary of 10,000 terms organised with Westerners in mind – particularly useful.

438 **Kanji and kana: a handbook and dictionary of the Japanese writing system.**
Wolfgang Hadamitzky, Mark Spahn. Rutland, Vermont; Tokyo: Tuttle, 1981. 392p.

A systematic introduction to reading and writing Japanese that is intended primarily as a textbook but is also equally useful as a concise dictionary of the Japanese writing system. Early chapters introduce the system for transliterating Japanese; the *kana* syllabaries; punctuation; and the historical origin, form and construction, ways of reading and writing, and dictionary arrangement of Chinese characters (*kanji*). The main section of the book consists of a list of the 1,945 basic Chinese characters which the government recommended for general use in 1981. The arrangement of these *kanji* begins with the simplest and most frequently used characters and proceeds to those which are more complex and occur less often. Each *kanji* is accompanied by translations, 'readings' (i.e., romanised pronunciations), and selected compound words in which it appears. Three indexes – arranged according to radicals, stroke counts, and readings – facilitate the use of this list. The handbook is suitable for both home and classroom use. Comparable in several respects to *Kanji and kana* is the well-known and still frequently used *A guide to reading & writing Japanese: the 1,850 basic characters and the kana syllabaries*, edited by Florence Sakade (Rutland, Vermont; Tokyo: Tuttle, 1961. rev. ed. 312p.).

439 **Japanese language and culture for business and travel.**
Kyoko Hijirida, Muneo Yoshikawa, foreword by Richard K. Seymour.
Honolulu, Hawaii: University of Hawaii Press, 1987. 375p. bibliog.

A textbook targeted towards employees in the tourist industry of Hawaii that can be effectively used by anyone who is engaged in business or is travelling in Japan. It aims at developing the reader's ability in conversational Japanese. Stressing the importance of effective non-verbal as well as verbal communication, Hijirida and Yoshikawa introduce the various patterns of communication among Japanese today. In addition, they explain the cultural assumptions that form the basis of Japanese modes of thought and behaviour, integrating their explanations into the individual language lessons. Each lesson contains a set of useful expressions, a dialogue, related vocabulary, grammatical explanations, exercises, a cultural orientation, a discussion of some Japanese mode of communication, and a brief listing of suggested materials for the further study of Japanese culture.

440 **Japanese: the spoken language.**
Eleanor Harz Jorden, with Mari Noda. New Haven, Connecticut;
London: Yale University Press, 1987-90. 3 vols. map.

An introductory textbook, written entirely in romanised Japanese, that stresses one's mastery of the language as it is currently spoken in Japan. Jorden and Noda systematically introduce new core conversations, their equivalents in English, supplementary vocabulary lists, miscellaneous grammatical and linguistic notes, structural patterns, drills, and application exercises. Each core conversation covers a situation in which foreigners typically find themselves interacting with Japanese. Explanations include descriptions of how the Japanese language is used within Japanese society; they cover such topics as hierarchy, in-group/out-group differentiation, and the avoidance of confrontation. Supplementing the textbook are videotapes of the core conversations, drill videotapes which provide practice on the structural patterns of Japanese in a response drill mode, and audio cassette tape recordings. *Japanese: the spoken language* replaces Jorden's highly acclaimed *Beginning Japanese* (New Haven, Connecticut: Yale University Press, 1962-63. 2 vols.), which for twenty-five years was one of the most widely used texts for studying Japanese in the United States.

441 **Reading Japanese.**
Eleanor Harz Jorden, Hamako Ito Chaplin. New Haven, Connecticut;
London: Yale University Press, 1976. 609p. (Yale Linguistic Series).

A text designed to teach the adult foreign student of Japanese the basics of the written language even before completing a first-year course in the spoken language. Twenty-five structured lessons introduce the *katakana* and *hiragana* syllabaries and 425 Chinese characters (*kanji*). Each lesson contains 'reading lessons in context', notes on the reading section, supplementary materials, extensive and varied reading drills, and twenty-five new *kanji*. Jorden's book provides students with a 'strong awareness of the lexical and stylistic differences between spoken and written Japanese', and can be used either as a classroom text or in self-study programmes.

Language. Textbooks

442 **Let's learn hiragana.**
Lets learn katakana.
Yasuko Kosaka Mitamura.   Tokyo; New York: Kodansha
International, 1985. 2 vols.

Two companion workbooks for learning the complete *kana* syllabaries that are comparable in nature to Kodansha International's earlier publication, *Japanese kana workbook* by P. G. O'Neill (q.v.). Using pedagogical methods based on her experience in teaching Japanese to American students, Mitamura systematically introduces all of the *hiragana* and *katakana* found in present-day Japanese. Through separate series of graded lessons and exercises, readers can progress independently to the point where they develop reading and writing skills that involve not only the individual *kana* but also complete words and entire phrases written in these two syllabaries.

443 **How to be polite in Japanese.**
Osamu Mizutani, Nobuko Mizutani.   Tokyo: Japan Times, 1987.
160p.

Far more than just a listing of appropriate expressions and linguistic forms, this book explains the underlying cultural attitudes that determine politeness in Japan, indicates how to convey a feeling of proper consideration towards one's listener and be polite in both a verbal and non-verbal manner, and suggests ways for displaying verbal politeness. The Mizutanis first identify the factors which typically determine levels of politeness. They then explain how to speak politely and how to convey an attitude of politeness through body language (e.g., by bowing, and by maintaining a proper speaker–listener distance). In discussing verbal politeness, they consider the various levels of speech in Japanese and clarify the differences between the display of respect towards others, humility in regard to oneself, and reserve in developing conversations. Finally, the authors show how the Japanese use various terms and expressions to express friendliness and concern for others, and they point out some of the errors which foreign speakers commonly make in the use of 'honorific language' (*keigo*).

444 **An introduction to modern Japanese.**
Edited by Osamu Mizutani, Nobuko Mizutani.   Tokyo: Japan Times,
1977. 425p.

An elementary textbook designed to provide college students with 'a foundation in Japanese sufficient to handle everyday, practical conversations as well as discussions concerning the student's own interest or occupation'. The text consists of thirty lessons which emphasize speaking but also teach the skills of hearing, reading, and writing. Each lesson consists of six parts: a sophisticated and very natural dialogue (presented in *kana* and *kanji* as well as in romanised form and in translation); explanatory notes on the dialogue which not only clarify the grammar and vocabulary but also offer information about cultural items; structure and usage drills; pronunciation practice that stresses proper accent and intonation; reading comprehension; and aural comprehension, which calls for listening to a taped conversation and responding to the questions provided in this book. Sections entitled 'writing practice' are also incorporated into lessons 13–29.

445 **An introduction to newspaper Japanese.**
Osamu Mizutani, Nobuko Mizutani. Tokyo: Japan Times, 1981.
334p.

Designed to assist students in developing their reading comprehension of written Japanese through the study of newspaper articles, this volume consists of a selection of articles published in 1979 and 1980 that have been arranged in increasing order of difficulty and are accompanied by comprehensive explanations and exercises in both structure and vocabulary. The first part trains the reader in understanding the structure of newspaper Japanese as well as in recognising basic Chinese characters (*kanji*) and *kanji* compounds. Part two consists of excerpts of newspaper articles together with lists of vocabulary and *kanji* compounds, translations, and exercises. The concluding part reproduces newspaper articles in their entirety.

446 **Traveler's Japanese.**
Osamu Mizutani, Nobuko Mizutani. Tokyo: Japan Times, 1984.
139p.

A phrase book containing basic expressions, words and phrases; expressions which one is likely to hear as well as sample conversations; and additional expressions that will enable travellers to get the most out of their stay in Japan. This book covers situations which involve taxis, hotels, subways and buses, trains, shopping, services, restaurants, Japanese cuisine, banks and the post office, telephoning, sightseeing, the theatre, sickness and accidents, Japanese inns, coffee-shop conversation, and visits to Japanese acquaintances. Helpful tips and explanations of Japanese customs abound, and supplementary information about national holidays, signs, numbers, counting, time, dates, conversion tables, and money is also provided. With its total of some one thousand useful words and expressions but without an index, this book is designed more as a textbook for travellers than as a pocket reference work for general use.

447 **Business Japanese: a guide to improved communication.**
Business Japanese II: a second guide to improved communication.
Edited by the International Division, Nissan Motor Company [Kaigaibu, Nissan Jidōsha Kabushiki Kaisha]. Tokyo: Bonjin [vol. 1]; Tokyo: Gloview [vol. 2], 1984-85. 2 vols.

A course of thirty-five lessons, accompanied by instructional cassette tapes, that is designed to introduce Western businessmen to the basics of business communication in Japanese. Each lesson contains dialogues, vocabulary, brief explanations of grammar and syntax, lists of additional useful expressions, and background information about Japanese business practices. The dialogues simulate business situations and cover such matters as exchanging business cards (*meishi*), setting up business appointments, and conducting interviews. The business-oriented vocabulary includes practical terminology and sophisticated business expressions. Emphasis throughout is on conversational fluency and the immediate application of the lessons that have been learned.

448 **Essential kanji: 2,000 basic Japanese characters systematically arranged for learning and reference.**
Patrick Geoffrey O'Neill. New York; Tokyo: Weatherhill, 1973.
325p.

A carefully integrated course for learning to read and write the two thousand basic

Chinese characters (*kanji*) used in modern Japanese. Part one introduces these *kanji* in order of increasing difficulty. O'Neill presents three or more different forms of each character – brush, pen, and printed forms as well as old and variant forms, whenever appropriate – together with its proper stroke order, various 'readings' (pronunciations), indications of its derivation (as a mnemonic aid to character memorisation), and compound words or phrases (with meanings) that illustrate its readings. These compound readings combine the *kanji* that is being taught only with characters that have already been introduced. Part two lists all readings of the Chinese characters that appear in part one, followed in each case by the *kanji* that have those particular readings. O'Neill's book is suitable for both beginning and intermediate-level students of Japanese. It can also be used as a compact lexical reference work.

449 **Japanese kana workbook.**
Patrick Geoffrey O'Neill.   Tokyo; Palo Alto, California: Kodansha International, 1967. 128p.

Kana – phonetic symbols representing the sounds of the individual syllables in which much of the Japanese language is written – are grouped into *hiragana*, the cursively shaped symbols most commonly used for words of Japanese and Chinese origin as well as for Japanese inflectional endings and grammatical particles, and *katakana*, angularly shaped symbols in which loanwords from Western languages as well as non-Asian names normally appear. O'Neill's programmed self-instruction manual teaches students to read and write the *hiragana* and *katakana* syllabaries in as little as ten hours. Each *kana* is introduced separately and then in a number of combinations with other *kana* that have already been taught in order to familiarise the student with all of the *kana* in their proper order. Chapters 2–7 deal with *hiragana*; chapters 8–13 with *katakana*.

450 **A programmed course on respect language in modern Japanese.**
Patrick Geoffrey O'Neill.   London: English Universities Press for the School of Oriental and African Studies, University of London, 1966. 142p. Reprinted, Rutland, Vermont; Tokyo: Tuttle, 1983.

'Respect language' (*keigo*), a special style of spoken and written Japanese, is an essential part of communication among the Japanese, even in their exchanges of the simplest of greetings. It involves the use of polite and respectful words; honorific, depreciatory, and deferential verbs; and the correct imperative and adjectival forms in a manner that properly indicates the speaker's relationship to the people with whom one interacts. Designed for students who are already familiar with modern colloquial Japanese and its basic grammar, this book enables the reader to understand how respect language works, to identify its different forms accurately when they appear in conversation or in reading, and to know how to express respect in his or her own speech.

451 **A reader of handwritten Japanese.**
Patrick Geoffrey O'Neill.   Tokyo; New York: Kodansha International, 1984. 267p.

A self-study course, designed for individuals with intermediate-level ability in Japanese, that teaches one how to read the many styles of handwriting which are likely to be encountered in daily life. It contains reproductions of one hundred handwritten letters and postcards whose writing ranges from clearly written letters of high-school students to the correspondence of elderly Japanese written in a much less legible cursive script. The examples are arranged in order of increasing difficulty and are accompanied by romanised transcriptions and notes on grammatical points. The first twenty-five lessons are also translated in full. O'Neill's introduction describes various letter-writing forms and conventions.

452 Everyday Japanese characters.
Michael Pye. Tokyo: Hokuseido Press, 1977. 76p. Reprinted, London: Duckworth, 1980.

Practical information about some of the Chinese characters (*kanji*) that visitors to Japan most frequently encounter. Pye first explains the nature of the Japanese writing system. Then, in more than twenty brief lessons, he introduces and discusses the characters that are used in connection with numbers, dates, days, years, time, railway stations, trains, tobacco booths and telephones, floors or storeys of buildings, shopping, restaurants, the post office, banks, companies, shrines and temples, toilets, postal addresses, and city and other place names.

453 Everyday Japanese: a basic introduction to the Japanese language and culture.
Edward A. Schwarz, Reiko Ezawa. Lincolnwood, Illinois: Passport Books, 1985. 208p.

Designed for tourists, businessmen, and students, this volume combines an illustrated dictionary of unique Japanese terms and a phrase-book of expressions and dialogues considered useful for Westerners together with an introduction to Japan in the form of Japanese dialogues, illustrations, explanatory notes, and information of practical value. Thirty-four sections (or lessons) are organised into three basic parts. 'Getting around in Japan' covers sixteen common situations such as taking a taxi, eating and drinking Japanese-style, and making appointments. 'Only in Japan' introduces important Japanese holidays and festivals, the Japanese bath, and other things that are uniquely Japanese. 'Living in Japan' contains information about household items and repairs, gestures and counting in Japanese, and the like. Several hundred basic words in Japanese are introduced through the dialogues and the accompanying vocabulary lists that constitute an essential part of each section.

454 Japanese in action: an unorthodox approach to the spoken language and the people who speak it.
Jack Seward. New York; Tokyo: Weatherhill, 1983. rev. ed. 217p.

An entertaining and informative introduction to several important aspects of the language, behaviour, and attitudes of the Japanese people. In an anecdotal fashion, Seward covers such topics as the best ways to study Japanese, correct pronunciation, the proper use of 'yes' and 'no', sign language, introductions and names, numerals, foreign loanwords, colours in Japanese, masculine and feminine speech, polite and non-polite speech, dialects, bar talk, slang, ways to be insulting in Japanese, geisha talk, and the language of love. His selection of material is aimed at revealing the language in action and at graphically illustrating the pitfalls that one should seek to avoid. Neither a conventional textbook nor a scholarly treatise, Seward's book is replete with personal stories and with helpful vocabulary lists which pay particular attention to words and expressions appearing in the comparatively rough, everyday speech of the average Japanese male.

455 **A practical guide for teachers of elementary Japanese.**
Mutsuko Endo Simon. Ann Arbor, Michigan: Center for Japanese
Studies, University of Michigan, 1984. 111p. bibliog.

A compact handbook designed primarily for new college-level instructors that is also valuable for teachers at the high-school level. It offers information and practical advice on different aspects of teaching Japanese. Simon explains the ways to select a proper textbook and work out an appropriate course plan; how to make the most effective use of a range of teaching aids including flash cards, dittos, and videotapes; how to teach the Japanese sound system and pronunciation, the writing system, reading, writing, listening comprehension, speaking, and grammar; what types of homework to assign; how to test and grade one's students; and the steps to take in order to review course materials successfully. Her book is timely and useful in view of the rapidly growing demands on educational institutions to begin offering Japanese as a foreign language.

456 **Read Japanese today.**
Len Walsh. Rutland, Vermont; Tokyo: Tuttle, 1967. 159p.

The written Japanese language is based heavily on the Chinese writing system that was introduced during the fourth century. At that time, the Japanese began to adopt Chinese characters (*kanji*) to represent thousands of words in their native language. Walsh's entertaining book draws on this linguistic heritage to offer a pictorial mnemonic method for learning three hundred of the most common and useful Chinese characters currently found in Japan. Each character is presented with its pictorial origin, its modern meaning, its most common pronunciations, and several examples of how it is used. Clear drawings depict the evolution of individual *kanji*, noteworthy elements of the characters are highlighted, and all of the characters are arranged in an order specifically designed to facilitate their memorisation.

457 **Learn Japanese: new college text.**
John Young, Kimiko Nakajima-Okano. Honolulu, Hawaii: University
of Hawaii Press, 1984-85. rev. ed. 4 vols.

Revised edition of a popular elementary textbook, originally published in 1967, which emphasizes an integrated approach in which speaking, hearing, reading, and writing Japanese all contribute to the language-learning process. Volume 1 consists of fifteen lessons, most of which contain three or four useful expressions that are introduced at the outset, practical dialogues in romanised Japanese, pattern sentences, grammatical notes, vocabulary, *hiragana* practice, drills and exercises. This volume also introduces Japanese pronunciation and the *kana* syllabaries. Volumes 2–4 introduce additional vocabulary and grammar as well as the most important Chinese characters (*kanji*) used in the written language. The entire textbook contains an abundance of helpful drills and exercises, and provides clear explanations of Japanese grammatical points. A set of cassette tapes accompanies the text.

A guide to food buying in Japan.
See item no. 85.

The practical guide to Japanese signs. 1st part: Especially for newcomers. 2nd part: Making life easier.
See item no. 88.

English loanwords in Japanese: a selection.
See item no. 419.

Japanese words and their uses.
See item no. 420.

Affective expressions in Japanese: a handbook of value-laden words in everyday Japanese.
See item no. 425.

Essential Japanese grammar.
See item no. 427.

Colloquial Japanese: with important construction and grammar notes.
See item no. 428.

A dictionary of basic Japanese grammar.
See item no. 431.

Japanese grammar.
See item no. 433.

Religion

General

458 **History of Japanese religion: with special reference to the social and moral life of the nation.**
Masaharu Anesaki. London: Kegan Paul, Trench, Trubner, 1930. 423p. Reprinted, Rutland, Vermont; Tokyo: Tuttle, 1963.

An insightful though somewhat outdated classic survey of religion and spiritual life which tends to emphasize the 'special moral qualities' of the Japanese people. It describes (1) the general features of Shintō, Shintō mythology, and Shintō's early role in Japanese life; (2) the introduction of Buddhism and its establishment during the seventh and eighth centuries; (3) the works of Saichō and Kūkai, the growth of Shingon Buddhism, and religion and social life during the Heian period; (4) Jōdo, Nichiren and Zen Buddhism during the Kamakura and Muromachi periods, religious strife, and the introduction and subsequent suppression of Christianity; (5) religious developments during the Tokugawa period, including the flourishing of Confucianism and the revival of Shintō; and (6) religious progress and problems during the Meiji and Taishō periods, with particular focus on the impact of Western ideas, the conservative reaction, and spiritual and social unrest.

459 **Tokugawa religion: the values of pre-industrial Japan.**
Robert N. Bellah. Glencoe, Illinois: Free Press, 1957. 249p. bibliog. Reprinted, Boston, Massachusetts: Beacon Press, 1970. Reprinted with a new introduction under the title *Tokugawa religion: the cultural roots of modern Japan* (New York: Free Press; London: Collier Macmillan, 1985).

Bellah applies a Weberian sociological perspective to his explanation of how Buddhism, Confucianism, Shintō, and the Shingaku movement during the Tokugawa period fostered values and behaviour essential for Japan's subsequent modernisation. He first describes the social structure at that time as well as the basic forms of

186

Tokugawa religious belief and action. He then analyses the relation of religion to Japan's political and economic rationalisation and offers a case study of the urban-based Shingaku movement and its founder Ishida Baigan (1685-1744). Bellah concludes that a strong polity and dominant political values in Japan 'were distinctly favorable to the rise of industrial society' after the Meiji Restoration and that by 'maintaining and intensifying commitment to the central values, supplying motivation and legitimation for certain necessary political innovations and reinforcing an ethic of inner-worldly asceticism which stressed diligence and economy', religion significantly contributed to Japan's political and economic modernisation.

460 **Japanese religion: unity and diversity.**
     H. Byron Earhart.   Belmont, California: Wadsworth, 1982. 3rd ed.
     272p. map. bibliog. (The Religious Life of Man Series).
This general introduction to the history and dynamics of Japanese religion surveys the major strands of folk religion, Shintō, Buddhism, religious Taoism, Confucianism, and Christianity, and traces their development from either their origins or their introduction into Japan through the 1970s. Particular attention is devoted to six principal themes in Japanese religious history: the closeness of human beings, the gods, and nature; the religious character of the family; the significance of purification, rituals, and charms; the prominence of local festivals and individual cults; the pervasiveness of religion in everyday life; and the natural bond between religion and the nation. Lists of recommended supplementary readings accompany each chapter. The volume concludes with a set of study questions and a forty-page annotated bibliography of works on Japanese religion.

461 **Religion in the Japanese experience: sources and interpretations.**
     H. Byron Earhart, foreword by Frederick J. Streng.   Encino,
     California: Dickenson, 1974. 270p. bibliog. (The Religious Life of Man
     Series).
An anthology of fifty-two brief readings about religious life and practice in both the past and the present that seek to 'show what religion means in the Japanese experience'. Earhart's selections survey a wide range of subjects: Shintō; Buddhism; Confucianism; religious Taoism; folk religion; Christianity; syncretism in Japanese religious life; the closeness of man, the gods, and nature; the religious significance of the family, both living and dead; the importance of purification, rituals, and charms; the prominence of local festivals and individual cults; the penetration of religion into everyday life; the natural bond between religion and the state; the dilemma of organised religion in modern Japan; the New Religions; and the history and future of Japanese religion. Each reading is preceded by introductory comments in which Earhart provides historical and background information. This convenient sourcebook was initially compiled to complement the author's introductory text, *Japanese religion: unity and diversity* (q.v.).

462 **Religions of Japan: many traditions within one sacred way.**
     H. Byron Earhart.   San Francisco; London: Harper and Row, 1984.
     142p. map. bibliog. (Religious Traditions of the World).
A succinct, general introduction to Shintō, Buddhism, Christianity, Confucianism, the New Religions, and folk beliefs in Japan. Earhart opens with overviews of Japanese culture, the place of religion in that culture, and the historical evolution of Japanese

religion in terms of the objects of worship, the individuals and social groups involved in the worship activities, the places where rituals of worship are held, the times when they take place, and their relationship to normal human life. Earhart also deals with other selected aspects of Japanese religion, including traditional rural community festivals and the situation of religion in postwar Japan, and he frequently provides comparisons with religion in the West.

463 **Japanese religion: a cultural perspective.**
Robert S. Ellwood, Richard Pilgrim. Englewood Cliffs, New Jersey: Prentice-Hall, 1985. 162p. bibliog. (Prentice-Hall Series in World Religions).

An introductory textbook to the religion and religious life of the Japanese that seeks to interpret this element in both traditional and modern Japanese culture. Part one – 'A Panorama of Japanese Religion' – focuses on the history of Japan's religions. It includes a brief introduction to some of the major religious sites in Tokyo, Kamakura, Kyōto, and Nara; a survey of the evolution of Japanese religion from ancient times to the twentieth century; and descriptive information about the New Religions as well as about Shintō, Buddhism, and Christianity. Part two – 'Specific Patterns in the Religion of Japan' – deals in part with the interrelationship between religion and the arts, the conceptual worlds of Japanese religion, ritual and the practice of religion, religion and society, and religion in the rapidly changing environment of postwar Japan.

464 **On understanding Japanese religion.**
Joseph M. Kitagawa. Princeton, New Jersey; Guildford, Surrey: Princeton University Press, 1987. 343p.

The foremost scholar of Japanese religion in the West brings together nineteen articles published between 1960 and 1984 in various academic journals, conference proceedings, and edited volumes. They constitute noteworthy contributions to American and European understanding of such subjects as the prehistoric background of Japanese religion, the stages of the Japanese 'religious universe', religion and state in early Japan, the Shintō and Buddhist traditions, paradigm change in Japanese Buddhism, and the modern phase of the Japanese religious tradition.

465 **Religion in Japanese history.**
Joseph M. Kitagawa. New York; London: Columbia University Press, 1966. 475p. bibliog. (Lectures on the History of Religions, Sponsored by the American Council of Learned Societies, New Series, 7).

A delineation of the 'significance, inner logic, and patterns of religious phenomena in Japan both historically and structurally' and the intricate relationships that have existed between the country's religious system and its coeval social, political, and cultural developments. Tracing the history of religion from early Shintō to the post-World War II period, Kitagawa describes the religious leadership (the emperor, shamans, and priests) which existed among the early Japanese; religious development during the Heian period; the Pure Land (Jōdo), Nichiren, and Zen Buddhist movements in medieval Japan; the relationship between the Tokugawa shogunate and Christianity and Neo-Confucianism respectively; the religious ethos of Japan as the country rapidly modernised; and the postwar religious situation of Japan, with particular attention to the New Religions.

466 **Okinawan religion: belief, ritual, and social structure.**
William P. Lebra.   Honolulu, Hawaii: University of Hawaii Press,
1966. 241p. 2 maps. Reprinted, University of Hawaii Press, 1985.

An overview of the beliefs, practices, and organisations which constitute the indigenous religion of Okinawa (as opposed to such imported religions as Buddhism and Sectarian Shintō) together with information about the evolution of this religion and its changes between the late nineteenth century and the mid-twentieth century. Following an introduction to Okinawa and its population, Lebra explores Okinawan concepts of the supernatural, various religious practices including ritual pollution and taboos, religious organisation and specialists, and the religious system at the state, community, kin group, and household levels. His study offers many useful comparisons with mainstream Japanese indigenous religion.

467 **Japanese religion in the modern century.**
Shigeyoshi Murakami, translated by H. Byron Earhart.   Tokyo:
University of Tokyo Press, 1980. 186p. bibliog.

A survey of religious life since the Meiji Restoration (1868) that analyses the ways in which Japanese religious movements and institutions have interrelated with the economic, social, and political forces which have shaped modern Japanese history. Murakami is particularly critical of the government's suppression of religion before 1945, and is a strong advocate of freedom of religion in postwar Japan.

468 **Religion and society in modern Japan: continuity and change.**
Edward Norbeck.   Houston, Texas: Tourmaline Press, 1970. 232p.

Describes and interprets 'the state of religion in modern Japan in its relationship to social and other cultural conditions that influence its forms and functions'. Norbeck, a cultural anthropologist, assesses some of the changes that have had a major impact on Japanese religions since the Meiji Restoration (1868) and considers the various roles of religion in contemporary Japanese life. He concerns himself with four New Religions (Sōka Gakkai, Risshō Kōsei-kai, PL Kyōdan, and Seicho-no-Ie) as well as with Shintō, Buddhism, and Christianity. This volume is a reprint of the Winter 1970 issue of *Rice University Studies*.

Sources of Japanese tradition.
See item no. 33.

Japan: a short cultural history.
See item no. 125.

Biographical dictionary of Japanese history.
See item no. 367.

The challenge of Japan's internationalization: organization and culture.
See item no. 802.

Japanese Journal of Religious Studies.
See item no. 1520.

Japanese Religions.
See item no. 1523.

Monumenta Nipponica: Studies in Japanese Culture.
See item no. 1534.

Buddhism and Zen Buddhism

469   **Zen and Western thought.**
    Masao Abe, edited by William R. LaFleur, foreword by John Hick.
    London: Macmillan; Honolulu, Hawaii: University of Hawaii Press,
    1985. 308p.

Abe, the leading interpreter of Zen Buddhism to the West since the death of Daisetz
Teitarō Suzuki, presents sixteen essays which discuss the meaning and nature of Zen
and compare Buddhist and Western philosophy. Grouped together under the four
headings of 'Zen and Its Elucidation', 'Zen, Buddhism, and Western Thought', 'Three
Problems in Buddhism', and 'Religion in the Present and the Future', these essays
clarify the philosophical basis of Zen, show that the ultimate goal in both Zen and
Buddhist thought is 'emptiness', demonstrate the centrality of wisdom and compassion
in the realisation of emptiness, and discuss the significance of Buddhist self-awakening
for society and the building of community in a global age. Some familiarity with both
Buddhist and Western philosophy is essential for a full understanding of Abe's
writings.

470   **The teachings essential for rebirth: a study of Genshin's *Ōjōyōshū*.**
    Allan A. Andrews.   Tokyo: Sophia University, 1973. 133p. bibliog. (A
    Monumenta Nipponica Monograph).

Compiled by the Tendai priest Genshin (942-1017) as a manual for expounding how
ordinary people can attain rebirth in the Pure Land of Amitābha Buddha (the 'Sacred
Buddha of Eternal Life') through the invocation of the Buddha's sacred name
(*nenbutsu*), the *Ōjōyōshū* gathers together the most important scriptural passages on
the terrors of hell and the pleasures of the Pure Land, on *nenbutsu* and its cultivation,
and on the devotion necessary for one's salvation. As a doctrinal synthesis and manual
of devotions, it became one of the most widely read works in Japanese Buddhist
literature. Andrews first places the *Ōjōyōshū* in its historical and doctrinal settings by
tracing the beginning of *nenbutsu* practice and its development in China as well as the
evolution of Pure Land Buddhism in Japan before Genshin. He then investigates the
basic teachings of this religious classic and analyses the 'functions and interrelations of
its various teachings for its systematization of the theory and practice of *nenbutsu*'.

471   **Shinran's gospel of pure grace.**
    Alfred Bloom.   Tucson, Arizona: Published for the Association for
    Asian Studies by the University of Arizona Press, 1965. 97p. bibliog.
    (Association for Asian Studies: Monographs and Papers, 20).

An exposition of the cardinal ideas of Shinran (1173-1262), the founder of the Jōdo
Shin sect of Pure Land Buddhism. Bloom first summarises the basic content of the
three Mahāyāna Buddhist sutras that became the sacred texts of the Pure Land sect,
surveys the Pure Land teachers whom Shinran especially revered, and analyses his

concept of the Pure Land tradition. Then, limiting his discussion to 'those central doctrines in which Shinran's particular contribution to the Pure Land thought becomes clear', he presents those doctrines which describe the human predicament, the nature of faith, the status of the believer, the nature of religious devotion, and the final destiny of the believer. In explaining these central concepts, Bloom makes extensive use of Shinran's own words rather than relying primarily on the systems of doctrine arranged by Shinshū theologians after Shinran's death.

472 **Record of things heard from the Treasury of the Eye of the True Teaching: the Shōbōgenzō-zuimonki, talks of Zen master Dōgen, as recorded by Zen master Ejō.**
Dōgen, translated by Thomas Cleary. Boulder, Colorado: Prajñā Press, 1980. 129p.
A series of brief talks and instructions concerning the study of Zen Buddhism, expounded by the Sōtō Zen master Dōgen (1200-53) and recorded by his disciple, Ejō (1198-1280). It provides an insight into the essential requirements for the successful pursuit of a monastic life and is directed towards the beginner in Zen, as its title 'Treasury of the Eye of the True Teaching Simplified' implies. Cleary's lucid and reliable translation is considered more accurate than Reihō Masunaga's *A primer of Sōtō Zen: a translation of Dōgen's Shōbōgenzō Zuimonki* (Honolulu, Hawaii: East–West Center Press, 1971, 119p.), but both can be recommended to interested readers.

473 **Shōbōgenzō: Zen essays.**
Dōgen, translated with an introduction by Thomas Cleary. Honolulu, Hawaii: University of Hawaii Press, 1986. 123p.
Thirteen essays from a collection of sermons and commentaries on selected kōan by Dōgen (1200-53), the religious reformer and profoundly original thinker who founded the Sōtō sect of Zen Buddhism. Written in a complex, innovative style, the *Shōbōgenzō* ('Treasury of the Eye of True Teaching') is widely regarded as Dōgen's *magnum opus* as well as one of the most important Japanese philosophical texts ever written. It presents Dōgen's interpretations of several Buddhist concepts and symbols together with his views on how Zen Buddhism can be experienced, demonstrates how the mind is used in working Zen, and shows how one can use literature to foster and direct the Zen use of the mind. Cleary's annotated translation is accompanied by introductory comments to each chapter designed to clarify this text for a broad audience.

474 **A history of Zen Buddhism.**
Heinrich Dumoulin, translated from the German by Paul Peachey. New York: Pantheon; London: Faber and Faber; Boston, Massachusetts: Beacon Press, 1963. 335p. Reprinted, New York: McGraw-Hill, 1965.
Regarded by a generation of scholars as the standard work on the historical development of Zen Buddhism, this book seeks 'to put the reader into as close a contact with Zen as possible, to elucidate its inner form from history, and to make its living values apparent'. The first half is concerned with the origins of Zen Buddhism and with its development in China during the first millennium AD. Later chapters

discuss the transplanting of Zen to Japan, the flowering of Rinzai Zen during the Kamakura period, the life, work and religious metaphysics of the Zen master Dōgen, the cultural influence of Zen during the Muromachi period, the sixteenth-century encounter between Zen and Christianity, the introduction of the Ōbaku sect from China and the renewal of Zen in Tokugawa Japan, and the Zen mysticism of Hakuin. A revised and greatly expanded, two-volume edition of Dumoulin's book, translated by James W. Heisig and Paul Knitter, is being published in 1988-89 by Macmillan (New York) and Collier Macmillan (London) under the title *Zen Buddhism: a history*. Volume one deals with India and China; volume two with Japan.

475 **Japanese Buddhism.**
Charles Eliot, with a memoir of the author by Harold Parlett. London: Arnold; New York: Longman's, 1935. 449p. Reprinted, London: Routledge and Kegan Paul; New York: Barnes and Noble, 1969.

An introduction to the schools and doctrines of Japanese Buddhism as well as to their role in the history of premodern Japan. Eliot, a scholar of Asian religion and British ambassador to Japan between 1919 and 1925, opens with a survey of Buddhism on the Asian continent in which he emphasizes the continuity of Japanese Buddhism with its Indian and Chinese counterparts. He then describes the history of Buddhism in Japan from its introduction during the sixth century, through the rise of various sects during the Heian and Kamakura periods, to the crystallisation of the Buddhist church during the Tokugawa era. Finally, Eliot surveys the Tendai, Shingon, Jōdo Shinshū, Zen, and Nichiren sects and their basic doctrines. While dated and superseded by more recent scholarships in certain respects, this volume is still widely regarded as the best available book-length introduction in English to Japanese Buddhism and its history.

476 **The Zen master Hakuin: selected writings.**
Hakuin Ekaku, translated by Philip B. Yampolsky, foreword by Wm. Theodore de Bary. New York; London: Columbia University Press, 1971. 253p. bibliog. (Records of Civilization: Sources and Studies, 86) (Translations from the Oriental Classics).

Hakuin (1686-1769) is well known in Japan as the monk who revived the moribund Rinzai school of Zen Buddhism and reformed the traditions of Zen teachings during the eighteenth century. Yampolsky's annotated translations of selections from his voluminous writings offer a general introduction to this important religious leader and his works. Three of Hakuin's epistolary treatises are presented. Addressed to various acquaintances, the *Orategama*, *Yabukōji*, and *Hebiichigo* are in effect a series of sermons and lectures that present his views on such subjects as the nature and study of Zen, Zen's relationship to other schools of Buddhism, the benefits to be gained by using the kōan known as the 'Sound of the Single Hand', and the virtues of a beneficent ruler. A brief introductory account of Hakuin and Rinzai Zen as well as an appendix containing short descriptions of many of his works are also included.

477 **The sound of the one hand: 281 Zen koans with answers.**
Translated with a commentary by Yoel Hoffmann, foreword by Zen
master Hirano Sōjō, introduction by Ben-Ami Scharfstein. New
York: Basic Books, 1975. 322p. bibliog. Reprinted, London: Sheldon
Press, 1977. 303p.; St. Albans, England: Paladin, 1977. 303p.; New
York: Bantam, 1977. 366p.

A translation of a collection of kōan (catechetic questions used as an aid to meditation
and enlightenment) which the novice in the Rinzai sect of Zen Buddhism must answer
during the long course of his training as a Zen master, together with their traditional
answers. Secretly transmitted from master to pupil since the early eighteenth century,
when the Zen master Hakuin (1686-1769) created the kōan-teaching system, selected
and determined the order in which these kōan were to be presented to novices, and
composed many of their answers, these teachings were first published pseudonymously
in 1916. Hoffman's translations are rendered clearly and unencumbered by terms that
would not be understood by the Western reader who has only a limited knowledge of
Buddhism. They are accompanied by Scharfstein's essay, 'Zen: the Tactics of
Emptiness'. The title of Hoffmann's book is taken from the first kōan: 'In clapping
both hands a sound is heard; what is the sound of the one hand?'

478 **The three pillars of Zen: teaching, practice, and enlightenment.**
Compiled and edited, with translations, introductions and notes, by
Philip Kapleau; foreword by Huston Smith.   Garden City, New York:
Anchor Press; London: Rider, 1980. rev. and expanded ed. 400p.

This introductory work seeks to provide the general reader with the 'authentic
doctrines' and daily practices of Zen Buddhism. Part one contains the translated
teachings of the contemporary Sōtō Zen master Yasutani-*rōshi*, who expounds on the
aims and methods of both *shikan-taza* (the heart of Sōtō meditative discipline) and
kōan zaza (the mainstay of the Rinzai sect). The 'Dharma talk on one-mind' of the
fourteenth-century Rinzai Zen master Bassui-*zenji* and twelve letters that he addressed
to his disciples are also presented. Part two contains the accounts of eight
contemporary Japanese and Westerners who have experienced enlightenment, as well
as Iwasaki Yaeko's enlightenment letters to Harada-*rōshi* and Harada's comments in
response. The book concludes with a sequence of ten annotated illustrations known as
the 'Oxherding Pictures', several pictures of *zazen* positions accompanied by questions
and answers, and a glossary of terms and names.

479 **Zen: dawn in the West.**
Philip Kapleau, foreword by Albert Low.   Garden City, New York:
Anchor Press, 1979; London: Rider, 1980. 311p. bibliog.

A companion volume to the author's *The three pillars of Zen* (q.v.), this is a collection
of essays, dialogues, letters, encouragement talks, commentaries, and other writings
about Zen Buddhism specifically oriented towards practitioners and novices in North
America and Europe. Striking new ground by presenting Zen practices in a thoroughly
Western milieu, Kapleau's book presents questions and answers (in the form of
dialogues) on such topics as Zen and psychotherapy, and some suggested ways of
finding a teacher; offers a number of didactic lectures as well as accounts by individuals
who have experienced enlightenment; provides the translated texts of some devotional
chants; and examines the nature of moral and social responsibility in Zen Buddhism.
One of the volume's unusual features is its ability to help the reader participate

vicariously in *sesshin*, the intensive training period in seclusion that constitutes the heart of Zen discipline.

480 **Zen action/Zen person.**
Thomas Patrick Kasulis. Honolulu, Hawaii: University Press of Hawaii, 1981. 177p. bibliog.

A perceptive account of the central teaching of Zen Buddhism: what it means to become a person, to know oneself, to realise what one is. Kasulis uses both a doctrinal and a cultural–sociological approach to clarify the essence and meaning of Zen Buddhism. Paying particular attention to the writings of the Kamakura and Tokugawa period masters Dōgen and Hakuin, he explains the concepts of the Zen person and Zen action as well as the rationale behind such practices as meditation and kōan practice. Since the Zen tradition has flourished within a distinctively Japanese cultural environment, Kasulis also discusses the way in which the person is viewed in Japanese society and the Zen understanding of the person within that context.

481 **Dōgen Kigen: mystical realist.**
Hee-Jin Kim, foreword by Robert Aitken. Tucson, Arizona: University of Arizona Press, 1987. rev. ed. 324p. bibliog. (Association for Asian Studies Monograph, 29).

An analysis of the life and thought of Dōgen (1200-53), the founding figure of Sōtō Zen Buddhism. An introductory chapter deals with Dōgen's life and characterises him as a man 'who struggled to seek a mode of existence and freedom for himself and for others . . . in the midst of chaotic and tumultuous Kamakura Japan'. Concerning himself not only with the historical forces among which Dōgen's thought evolved but also with the structure of his experience and thought, Kim then examines his teachings in an historical context, explains the two basic structural elements of Dōgen's thought – meditation and wisdom – and views their nature and function in a broader context. Throughout this study, Kim discusses Dōgen's contributions as a religious thinker rather than merely as a philosopher.

482 **Kūkai: major works, translated, with an account of his life and a study of his thought.**
Kūkai, translated by Yoshito S. Hakeda, foreword by Wm. Theodore de Bary. New York; London: Columbia University Press, 1972. 303p. bibliog. (Records of Civilization: Sources and Studies, 87) (Unesco Collection of Representative Works: Japanese Series).

Kūkai (774-835), commonly known by his posthumous name of Kōbō Daishi, is remembered as the founder of Shingon or Esoteric Buddhism in Japan and remains one of the country's most respected and popular Buddhist masters. In this scholarly study, Hakeda first examines Kūkai's life and offers a summary and exegesis of the essentials of his esoteric Buddhist thought and practice. He then provides translations of eight of Kūkai's works. These include his famous *Sangō shiki*: 'Indications of the Goals of the Three Teachings'; and such other representative Shingon doctrinal writings as 'Attaining Enlightenment in This Very Existence' (*Sokushin jōbutsu gi*), 'The Precious Key to the Secret Treasury' (*Hizō hōyaku*), and 'The Meanings of Sound, Word, and Reality' (*Shōji jissō gi*).

483 **Daruma: the founder of Zen in Japanese art and popular culture.**
H. Neill McFarland. Tokyo; New York: Kodansha International,
1987. 124p. 2 maps. bibliog.
Surveys the vast range of materials in Japan relating to Bodhidharma (known in
Japanese as Bodai Daruma, or simply as Daruma), the sixth-century founder and
patriarch of Zen Buddhism in China. The Japanese regard Daruma as 'one of the most
congenial and pervasive' symbols of their society, and in addition to deifying and
greatly honouring him, they have traditionally singled him out for representation in a
wide range of arts. McFarland points out the complex interrelatedness of Daruma with
Japanese life and culture as he discusses the Daruma legend, Daruma in Zen art and
iconography, the appropriation of Daruma in Japanese folklore, folk art, and popular
art (especially sculpture, painting, and woodblock prints), and the continued vitality of
Japanese interest in Daruma in general (the so-called 'Daruma cultus'). There are 139
black-and-white photographs depicting paintings, statuettes, sculpture, papier-mâché
figures, and other representations of this celebrated figure.

484 **Foundation of Japanese Buddhism. Volume 1: The aristocratic age.**
Volume 2: The mass movement (Kamakura and Muromachi periods).
Daigan Matsunaga, Alicia Matsunaga. Los Angeles; Tokyo: Buddhist
Books International, 1974-76. 2 vols. bibliog.
A factually oriented account of the historical and sociopolitical development of
Buddhism and its institutions in Japan between the mid-sixth century AD and the
sixteenth century. The Matsunagas discuss and analyse the introduction of this religion
into Japan, the six major schools and other traditions existing within Buddhism during
the Nara period, the development of Heian Buddhism and of the Tendai and Shingon
sects, the rise of the Pure Land sects known as Jōdoshū and Jōdo Shinshū during the
Kamakura period, the beliefs of Nichiren and the emergence of the Nichiren order,
Zen Buddhism (particularly Rinzai Zen and Sōtō Zen), and the role of the older sects
during the Kamakura and Muromachi periods. One general theme of this study
revolves around the contrast between the worldly and spiritual functions of Buddhism;
a second theme centres on the efforts of new Buddhist movements during the medieval
period to overthrow the scholastic–aristocratic Buddhism of the Heian period.

485 **Buddhism: Japan's cultural identity.**
Stuart D. B. Picken, introduction by Edwin O. Reischauer. Tokyo;
New York: Kodansha International, 1982. 80p. map. bibliog.
Picken demonstrates how Buddhism first found a distinctive place for itself in Japanese
culture and then gradually merged with Shintō to take on 'the role of guarantor of
social continuity and of the unity and cultural identity of the Japanese people'. He
describes the background and Japanese transformation of this faith, its role in modern
Japanese society, the Buddhist funeral, the Buddhist concern for the dead, the
pervasive presence of Buddhism in the Japanese character, its expression in
philosophy, literature and art, the pantheon of Japanese Buddhist deities, Esoteric
Buddhism (the Tendai and Shingon sects) and *ryōbu* Shintō, and the Lotus tradition
and the New Religions of postwar Japan. Picken's work is not a scholarly treatise but
rather a beautifully illustrated account – presented at times in an oversimplified
manner – of how Buddhism remains 'a relevant and pervasive dimension of present-
day Japan'.

486 **The Zen life.**
Kōji Satō, translated by Ryōjun Victoria, photographs by Sōsei
Kuzunishi. New York; Tokyo: Weatherhill/Tankōsha, 1972. 190p.
Reprinted, Weatherhill/Tankōsha, 1977.
An introduction to monastic Zen practices that focuses on the everyday life and
routines of Zen monks at the Enpukuji Monastery near Kyōto. A 120-page photo-
essay depicts the monastery grounds, a young monk's efforts to gain admission to the
monastery, the beginning of a typical day, the recitation of the sutras, the eating of
meals in disciplined silence, the procedure of seeking guidance from the Zen master,
lectures, the tea ceremony, religious mendicancy, the monks at work, zazen
('meditation'), the religious practice of shaving one's head, bathing, and the joys of
monastic life. Kuzunishi's photographs are accompanied by Satō's comments about
various aspects of Zen life. Oriented towards an even broader audience is a
comparable, thoroughly delightful book entitled *Unsui: a diary of Zen monastic life*,
with drawings by Giei Satō, text by Eshin Nishimura, edited with an introduction by
Bardwell L. Smith (Honolulu, Hawaii: University Press of Hawaii, 1973, 114p.). Its
ninety-seven watercolour sketches – each accompanied by a brief commentary on the
event that it illustrates – depict the foibles, humour, and very human dimensions of
monastic life within a Rinzai Zen monastery.

487 **Zen training: methods and philosophy.**
Katsuki Sekida, edited with an introduction by A. V. Grimstone.
New York; Tokyo: Weatherhill, 1975. 258p.
Because zazen, the exercise in which one sits and learns to control one's body and
mind, is for Sekida 'the unquestioned basis of any serious practice of Zen', much of
this book describes the performance and effects of zazen. In clearly written practical
instructions, Sekida discusses and analyses (primarily in physiological terms) the
correct posture to adopt, the proper method of breathing, the role of the abdominal
muscles in controlling the activity of one's mind, muscle tone, and the mechanisms of
wakefulness and attention. He delineates the aims of both zazen and Zen training –
namely, the attainment of the condition of total 'stillness, or emptiness' known as
absolute *samādhi* – and stresses the importance of learning to 'live in the ordinary
world, while yet retaining the quality of one's experience of absolute samādhi'. In
addition, Sekida considers some of the theoretical and philosophical aspects of Zen
training such as pure cognition and *kenshō* ('seeing one's true nature') or *satori*
('enlightenment').

488 **A Zen forest: sayings of the masters.**
Compiled and translated with an introduction by Sōiku Shigematsu,
foreword by Gary Snyder. New York; Tokyo: Weatherhill, 1981.
177p. map. bibliog.
The distillation of Zen Buddhism is contained in about six thousand Zen words,
phrases, and verses handed down by Chinese and Japanese masters over the centuries
and collected in the *Zenrin kushū* ('Anthology of Zen Forest Sayings'). Shigematsu's
representative selection of 1,234 sayings in poetic translation is accompanied by
versions written in their original Chinese characters and in romanised Japanese. These
sayings illustrate a wide range of aspects of Zen, from the nature of *satori*
('enlightenment') to the meaning of enlightened activity in the real world.

489 **The essentials of Zen Buddhism: selected from the writings of Daisetz T. Suzuki.**
Daisetz T. Suzuki, edited with an introduction by Bernard Phillips.
New York: Dutton, 1962; London: Rider, 1963. 544p. bibliog.
Reprinted, Westport, Connecticut: Greenwood Press, 1973.

Intended as a comprehensive, one-volume introduction to Zen Buddhism, this book contains a substantial sampling of Suzuki's journal articles and essays as well as extracts from his monographic works. An introductory essay, 'Zen Buddhism as Creative Religion', is followed by a presentation of a selection of his writings under the six headings of 'The General Sense of Zen', 'The Origins of Zen', 'The Enlightenment Experience', 'The Practice and Discipline of Zen', 'The Life of Freedom in Zen', and 'Zen and Japanese Culture'. Typical selections include Suzuki's 'History of Zen Buddhism from Bodhidharma to Enō' (1927), 'The Meditation Hall and the Ideals of the Monkish Discipline' (1927), 'Zen and Swordsmanship' (1938), 'Some Aspects of Zen Buddhism' (1939), 'The Essence of Buddhism' (1948), 'Satori' (1950), and 'Human Values in Zen' (1959).

490 **An introduction to Zen Buddhism.**
Daisetz Teitarō Suzuki, foreword by C. G. Jung, editor's foreword by Christmas Humphreys.   New York: Philosophical Library, 1949. 136p. (The Complete Works of D. T. Suzuki). Reprinted, New York: Grove Press, 1954; London: Arrow Books, 1959; London: Rider, 1960; New York: Ballantine Books, 1973; New York: Causeway Books, 1974.

An introduction to the nature of Zen Buddhism and to its teachings. Suzuki brings together several articles that were originally written for the *New East* and were then published as a book in 1934 by the Eastern Buddhist Society in Kyōto. The articles are entitled 'What Is Zen?'; 'Is Zen Nihilistic?'; 'Illogical Zen'; 'Zen a Higher Affirmation'; 'Practical Zen'; 'Satori, or Acquiring a New Viewpoint'; 'The Koan'; and 'The Meditation Hall and the Monk's Life'. The 1949 edition and subsequent reprintings contain a translation of C. G. Jung's long foreword to the German edition of this work.

491 **The training of the Zen Buddhist monk.**
Daisetz Teitarō Suzuki, illustrated by Zenchū Satō.   New York: University Books, 1965. 161p. Reprinted, Berkeley, California: Wingbow Press, 1974.

Facsimile edition of a work originally published in 1934 by the Eastern Buddhist Society in Kyōto, this volume describes the rigorous training and life which Zen monks experience following their initiation into the Zen Brotherhood. It describes the life in a *Zendō* (a temple for Zen study) as a life of humility, labour, service, prayer and gratitude, and meditation; and in the course of clarifying its meaning, it relates many stories about the early Zen masters. Forty-three black-and-white drawings by another monk depict the record of his own experiences in going through all of the disciplinary measures pertaining to the life of Zen.

492 **Zen and Japanese culture.**
Daisetz T. Suzuki. Princeton, New Jersey: Princeton University
Press, 1959; London: Routledge and Kegan Paul, 1960. rev. and
enlarged 2nd ed. 478p. bibliog. (Bollingen Series, 64). Reprinted,
Princeton University Press, 1970; Rutland, Vermont and Tokyo:
Tuttle, 1988.

A series of perceptive essays which offer a restatement of the principles, meaning, and
significance of Zen Buddhism as a school of thought and a way of life, and examine its
influence on various aspects of Japanese life and art. Suzuki discusses the nature and
significance of Zen, its contributions to Japanese art culture, its role in encouraging the
study of Confucianism, its influence on samurai moral values and character, and its
impact on Japanese swordsmanship, haiku poetry, and the tea ceremony. He also
considers Zen Buddhism in relation to the Japanese love of nature, with reflections on
such aspects of nature as gardening, landscape, and weather. Appendixes to the
volume include two *mondō* (a catechistic device of Zen) from the *Hekiganshū*, and a
synopsis of the noh play *Yama-uba*. This book was first published as *Zen Buddhism
and its influence on Japanese culture* (Kyōto: Eastern Buddhist Society, 1938, 288p.).

493 **Zen mind, beginner's mind.**
Shunryū Suzuki, edited by Trudy Dixon, preface by Huston Smith,
introduction by Richard Baker. New York; Tokyo: Walker/
Weatherhill, 1970. 134p. Reprinted, New York; Tokyo: Weatherhill,
1983. 138p.

A contemporary Sōtō Zen master's introduction to the practice of Zen Buddhism, to
Zen life, and to the attitudes and understanding that make Zen practice possible.
Grouped into three sections – 'Right Practice', 'Right Attitude', and 'Right
Understanding' – Suzuki's lectures and perceptive comments offer a common-sense
approach to the practice of Zen that is specifically directed at an American audience.
They include coverage of the proper posture and breathing, the necessary mind-set and
comprehension, non-duality, emptiness, and enlightenment. This volume originated in
a series of talks which Suzuki Shunryū (1905-71) delivered before a small *zazen*
meditation group in California during the 1960s.

494 **The way of Zen.**
Alan W. Watts. New York: Pantheon, 1957; London: Thames and
Hudson, 1958. 236p. bibliog. (A Vintage Giant, 298). Reprinted,
Harmondsworth, Middlesex: Penguin, 1962. 252p. (A Pelican Book,
298). New York: Vintage Books, 1965. 236p.

An introduction to Zen Buddhism by one of its best-known Western exponents. Based
on the writings of D. T. Suzuki, the records of early Chinese Zen masters, and over
twenty years of the author's personal encounters with teachers and students of Zen, it
provides both the general reader and the serious student with a systematic survey and
description of Zen's background, history, principles, and practice. Watts first traces the
origins of Zen Buddhism to Indian and Chinese thought, and discusses the rise and
development of Zen. The second half of his book – 'Principles and Practice' – contains
four chapters entitled '"Empty and Marvellous"'; '"Sitting Quietly, Doing Nothing"';
'Za-zen and the Koan'; and 'Zen in the Arts'.

Japanese pilgrimage.
See item no. 73.

Historical Nara: with illustrations and guide maps.
See item no. 93.

Zen guide: where to meditate in Japan.
See item no. 97.

Five mountains: the Rinzai Zen monastic institution in medieval Japan.
See item no. 131.

Japan in the Muromachi age.
See item no. 140.

Early Buddhist Japan.
See item no. 143.

Buddhism and the state in sixteenth-century Japan.
See item no. 145.

A Zen life: D. T. Suzuki remembered.
See item no. 316.

A dictionary of Japanese Buddhist terms: based on references in Japanese literature.
See item no. 415.

Ancestor worship in contemporary Japan.
See item no. 505.

A Japanese New Religion: Risshō Kōsei-kai in a mountain hamlet.
See item no. 507.

Modern Japan and Shinto nationalism: a study of present-day trends in Japanese religions.
See item no. 517.

The Buddha eye: an anthology of the Kyoto school.
See item no. 521.

The karma of words: Buddhism and the literary arts in medieval Japan.
See item no. 1007.

Tales of times now past: sixty-two stories from a medieval Japanese collection.
See item no. 1032.

The temple of the golden pavilion.
See item no. 1080.

Japanese death poems: written by Zen monks and haiku poets on the verge of death.
See item no. 1138.

Ikkyū and the Crazy cloud anthology: a Zen poet of medieval Japan.
See item no. 1139.

Zen poems of the five mountains.
See item no. 1152.

Ryōkan, Zen monk-poet of Japan.
See item no. 1154.

One robe, one bowl: the Zen poems of Ryōkan.
See item no. 1154.

The Zen poems of Ryōkan.
See item no. 1154.

Zen at Daitoku-ji.
See item no. 1190.

Zen and the fine arts.
See item no. 1195.

Zen culture.
See item no. 1196.

The great eastern temple: treasures of Japanese Buddhist art from Tōdai-ji.
See item no. 1206.

Asuka Buddhist art: Horyu-ji.
See item no. 1208.

Art in Japanese esoteric Buddhism.
See item no. 1216.

Zen painting and calligraphy: an exhibition of works of art [etc.].
See item no. 1232.

Esoteric Buddhist painting.
See item no. 1237.

Pure Land Buddhist painting.
See item no. 1244.

Nara Buddhist art: Todai-ji.
See item no. 1290.

Japanese portrait sculpture.
See item no. 1292.

Sculpture of the Kamakura period.
See item no. 1293.

The great age of Japanese Buddhist sculpture, AD 600–1300.
See item no. 1295.

Classic Buddhist sculpture: the Tempyō period.
See item no. 1296.

Temples of Nara and their art.
See item no. 1316.

Early Buddhist architecture in Japan.
See item no. 1322.

The roof in Japanese Buddhist architecture.
See item no. 1322.

Good food from a Japanese temple.
See item no. 1440.

The Eastern Buddhist.
See item no. 1499.

Zen Buddhism: a bibliography of books and articles in English, 1892–1975.
See item no. 1612.

Christianity

495 **A history of Christianity in Japan.**
Richard Henry Drummond, foreword by R. Pierce Beaver.   Grand
Rapids, Michigan: William B. Eerdmans, 1971. 397p. map. bibliog.
(Christian World Mission Books).
A scholarly survey of the Christian presence in Japan from the arrival in 1549 of the
first Roman Catholic missionaries, led by Francis Xavier, through the mid-1960s.
Covering the entire Christian movement (Roman Catholic, Protestant, and Russian
Orthodox), Drummond's work represents the first comprehensive account of
Christianity and its development in Japan since the publication in 1909 of Otis Cary's
two-volume *A history of Christianity in Japan: Roman Catholic, Greek Orthodox, and
Protestant missions* (New York; London: Fleming H. Revel, 1909. Reprinted, Rutland,
Vermont and Tokyo: Tuttle, 1976). Each major branch of the church is examined in
chapters entitled 'The Early Roman Catholic Movement, 1549–1859', 'Protestantism in
Japan', 'The Roman Catholic Church from 1859', and 'The Orthodox Church'. This
work may be recommended as the first book to read for an overall understanding of
Christianity's role in Japan down to the postwar era.

496 **A century of Protestant Christianity in Japan.**
Charles W. Iglehart, foreword by Wallace C. Merwin.   Rutland,
Vermont; Tokyo: Tuttle, 1959. 384p.
A straightforward account of Protestant missionary activity and the growth of
Protestant congregations in Japan, 1859-1959, written for a general audience as part of
the 'centenary campaign' of the National Christian Council of Japan. Interweaving the
story of the Protestant Christian movement with the major changes in Japan's modern
history, Iglehart traces the beginnings of missionary activity and the early work of the
Protestant churches, the growth of the church and the problems that were encountered
as Japan modernised and became an imperial power, Christianity in Japan during
World War II and the Allied occupation period, and the renewal and advance of the
church during the 1950s.

497 **From the rising of the sun: Christians and society in contemporary Japan.**
James M. Phillips. Maryknoll, New York: Orbis Books, 1981. 307p. bibliog. (American Society of Missiology Series, 3).

A survey of Christianity in Japan since World War II – encompassing all denominations of the community including Protestants, Roman Catholics, the Orthodox churches, and Mukyōkai ('Non-Church Christianity') – that seeks to promote dialogue and understanding between church-related missiologists and secular scholars. Phillips covers the historical context of Christianity's development in Japan since 1945; Christian involvement in postwar political activities, education, and social work; Christian outreach in Japan; the role and activities of foreign missionaries; ecumenicity in Japan; Biblical studies and theology in Japan; and Christian prospects for the future. A bibliographical essay, 'On the History of Christianity in Contemporary Japan', guides readers to a selection of additional publications in both English and Japanese.

498 **Christianity and Japan: meeting, conflict, hope.**
Stuart D. B. Picken, introduction by Edwin O. Reischauer. Tokyo; New York: Kodansha International, 1983. 80p. bibliog.

Combining a concise narrative with numerous colour and black-and-white photographs, Picken traces the history of Christianity in Japan, highlights some of the past contributions of Japanese Christians, characterises the nature of Japanese Christianity, analyses its co-existence with Buddhism and Shintō in present-day Japan, and advances some of the reasons for its successes and failures. Considerable attention is paid to the spread of Christianity in Japan during the sixteenth century and its prohibition during the early decades of the Tokugawa period.

The Christian century in Japan, 1549–1650.
See item no. 129.

Deus destroyed: the image of Christianity in early modern Japan.
See item no. 166.

Christian converts and social protest in Meiji Japan.
See item no. 235.

Pacifism in Japan: the Christian and socialist tradition.
See item no. 288.

Rodrigues the interpreter: an early Jesuit in Japan and China.
See item no. 352.

Modern Japan and Shinto nationalism: a study of present-day trends in Japanese religions.
See item no. 517.

Silence.
See item no. 1055.

Japan Christian Quarterly.
See item no. 1506.

Japan Missionary Bulletin.
See item no. 1506.

A bibliography of Christianity in Japan: Protestantism in English sources (1850–1959).
See item no. 1587.

Folk religion

499 **The catalpa bow: a study of shamanistic practices in Japan.**
Carmen Blacker. London: Allen and Unwin, 1975; Totowa, New Jersey: Rowman and Littlefield, 1976. 376p. bibliog. 2nd ed., London: Allen and Unwin, 1986. 376p.

The first comprehensive study of shamans (mediums and ascetics) and shamanistic beliefs and practices in Japan. Blacker describes the benign and malevolent supernatural beings (in both Shintō and Buddhist guises) with whom the shamans directly communicate while in a state of trance, the complex geography of the other world in Japanese myth and legend, the initiatory dreams by which shamans acquire their special powers to cross the 'bridge' and interact with supernatural forces, the practices by means of which they consolidate their powers, various rites and rituals, and the shamans' techniques for dealing with the *kami* and other spiritual beings. She also depicts some of the shamans who survive in postwar Japan, among them the living goddesses of the New Religions, the blind mediums who employ many shamanistic techniques, the healing priests of Tendai, Shingon and Nichiren Buddhism, the *yamabushi* (ascetics) of Shugendō, and various healers and exorcists.

500 **Japanese rainmaking and other folk practices.**
Geoffrey Bownas, line drawings by Pauline Brown. London: Allen and Unwin, 1963. 176p.

A description and explanation of the basic forms of some Japanese folk practices and folk festivals (*matsuri*). These include the New Year and Bon celebrations (the latter being a Buddhist observance honouring the spirits of the ancestors); the Gion Festival in honour of the deity Gozu Tennō that is sponsored by the Yasaka Shrine in Kyōto; rainmaking ceremonies; and the taboos and rituals associated with births, marriages, and deaths. A concluding chapter entitled 'The Village Year' offers a general picture of the year-round activities and ceremonies of the community of Okinoshima in Shiga Prefecture.

501 **The five sacred festivals of ancient Japan: their symbolism and historical development.**
Ugo Alfonso Casal, preface by William Kostizak, Jr. Tokyo: Sophia University in co-operation with Tuttle (Rutland, Vermont and Tokyo), 1967. 114p.

A descriptive study of the most popular traditional festivals of Japan: Oshōgatsu, the New Year Festival (the most significant celebration of the year); Hinamatsuri, the

Religion. Folk religion

Girls' Festival; Tango no sekku, the Boys' Festival; Tanabata, the Star Festival (when the heavenly star-lovers meet); and Jugōya or Kiku no sekku, the Chrysanthemum Festival. Casal traces their historical evolution, religious, political and folk backgrounds, myths and traditions, symbolic elements, and the ways in which they are celebrated. He concludes that all five festivals are based on old fertility invocations and in their origins were 'days dedicated to ritual observances, purificatory and exorcising magic, with subsequent feasting'. For a good collection of photographs of these and other Japanese festivals, readers should turn to Hideo Haga's *Japanese folk festivals illustrated*, translated by Fanny Hagin Mayer (Tokyo: Miura Printing Co., 1970, 187p.). Yoshiko Yamamoto's *The Namahage: a festival in the northeast of Japan* (Philadelphia, Pennsylvania: Institute for the Study of Human Issues, 1978, 169p.), in turn, offers a detailed anthropological account of one traditional rural festival and its present-day observance in a remote community of Akita Prefecture.

502 **Gods of myth and stone: phallicism in Japanese folk religion.**
Michael Czaja, foreword by George De Vos.   New York; Tokyo:
Weatherhill, 1974. 294p. map. bibliog.

An intriguing study of the carved roadside sculptures that are the objects of Japanese folk worship, and of the religious beliefs and practices of the rural population that has produced them. Czaja first introduces the representations and worship of *Dōsojin*, a deity of agriculture and human fecundity which serves as a guardian spirit of country roads and their travellers and is represented in sculptured form as a male-and-female, husband-and-wife pair. A photo-essay of 101 black-and-white photographs of *Dōsojin* depicts each major type of this religious sculpture found in present-day Japan. This is followed by discussions of the concepts of phallic roots of folk worship. Included are Czaja's analyses of the ancient creation myths recorded in the *Kojiki* and the *Nihongi* and his investigations of selected folk festivals.

503 **Studies in Japanese folklore.**
General editor: Richard M. Dorson; advisory editors: Tōichi Mabuchi,
Tokihiko Ōtō; chief translator: Yasuyo Ishiwara.   Bloomington,
Indiana: Indiana University Press, 1963. 347p. (Indiana University
Folklore Series, 17). Reprinted, Port Washington, New York: Kennikat
Press, 1973; New York: Arno Press, 1980.

Studies concerned with Japanese folk culture and folk religion are organised into seven sections entitled 'Introduction', 'Rice Farmers', 'Fishermen', 'Ironworkers', 'Worshippers', 'Housewives', and 'Youths'. Each section contains up to five related essays by Japanese folklorists such as 'Seasonal Rituals Connected with Rice Culture'; 'The Taboos of Fishermen'; 'A Study of Yashiki-gami, the Deity of House and Grounds'; 'The Position of the Shinto Priesthood: Historical Changes and Developments'; 'Menstrual Taboos Imposed upon Women'; and 'Initiation Rites and Young Men's Organizations'. Introductions by Richard M. Dorson and Yanagita Kunio – entitled 'Bridges between Japanese and American Folklorists' and 'Opportunities for Folklore Research in Japan' – focus on the work of the contributors to this volume.

504 **Folk religion in Japan: continuity and change.**
Ichirō Hori, edited by Joseph M. Kitagawa, Alan L. Miller; foreword
by Joseph M. Kitagawa. Chicago; London: University of Chicago
Press; Tokyo: University of Tokyo Press, 1968. 278p. bibliog. (Haskell
Lectures on History of Religions, New Series, 1).

Six lectures delivered at the University of Chicago in 1965 delineate the principal
features and characteristics of Japanese folk religion. They discuss the major features
of folk religion, the popular Pure Land (Jōdo) Buddhist practice known as *nenbutsu*
within the context of folk religion, the importance of mountains for Japanese
conceptions of the other world, Japanese shamanism, and the survival of shamanistic
tendencies in the New Religions of the post-World War II era. These lectures
demonstrate how elements from Shintō, Buddhism, Confucianism, and Taoism have
been blended together on the folk level to meet the everyday spiritual needs of the
common people.

505 **Ancestor worship in contemporary Japan.**
Robert J. Smith. Stanford, California: Stanford University Press,
1974. 266p. bibliog.

An anthropological study of 'ancestor worship', a practice entailing in particular the
conduct of rites on behalf of the dead souls of a household in front of the memorial
tablets that are kept in a family's Buddhist altar. Smith first traces the historical
evolution of ancestor worship, including its transformation by Buddhism and the
impact upon it of the political and religious policies of successive central governments.
He then explores the nature of the deities, the various kinds of spirits, and the line of
demarcation between human beings and gods; describes the methods of caring for the
dead as well as the occasions and ritual practices involved in ancestor worship; shows
how the Japanese conceive of the relationship between the living and the dead; and
considers such matters as the moral authority of the ancestors and its continuing
influence. Final chapters present findings from his survey of the memorial tablets in 595
urban and rural household altars.

Ainu creed and cult.
See item no. 378.

Folk legends of Japan.
See item no. 1184.

Japanese mythology.
See item no. 1186.

Japanese ghosts & demons: art of the supernatural.
See item no. 1189.

Black sun: the eyes of four; roots and innovation in Japanese photography.
See item no. 1275.

Asian Folklore Studies.
See item no. 1490.

Legend in Japanese art: a description of historical episodes, legendary

characters, folk-lore, myths, religious symbolism, illustrated in the arts of old Japan.
See item no. 1560.

The New Religions

506   **Dojo: magic and exorcism in modern Japan.**
Winston Davis.   Stanford, California: Stanford University Press, 1980. 332p.

An ethnographic account and sociological analysis of Sūkyō Mahikari, a New Religion founded by Okada Kōtama in 1960 that employs magical amulets and ritual to exorcise the spirits which possess its members and bring about illness or misfortune. Davis, a participant-observer in this urban-based religion, particularly concerns himself with how the sect's ideas and behaviour patterns become established in the lives of its members, how people change as a result of their membership in Sūkyō Mahikari, and how social, religious and magical criteria determine the status of individual members. Davis also provides considerable firsthand evidence about the beliefs and practices of its members as well as about the sect's origins and the sources of its gospel.

507   **A Japanese New Religion: Risshō Kōsei-kai in a mountain hamlet.**
Stewart Guthrie.   Ann Arbor, Michigan: Center for Japanese Studies, University of Michigan, 1988. 245p. bibliog. (Michigan Monograph Series in Japanese Studies, 1).

An ethnographic case-study of Risshō Kōsei-kai ('Society for Virtuous Human Relations'), a Nichiren Buddhist movement of over five million adherents that has become the second largest of Japan's many New Religions. Guthrie is particularly concerned with why many people have joined this movement, what the benefits and problems of membership have been, and how it has helped them to 'interpret and influence important events in their lives'. He surveys the social organisation and economic setting of a pseudonymous mountain farming hamlet in Gunma Prefecture, discusses the continued practice of Sōtō Zen Buddhism and Shintō in many of the community's households, describes the introduction, organisation and activities of Risshō Kōsei-kai in the hamlet, and analyses the backgrounds, participation, attitudes and beliefs of six representative members of Risshō Kōsei-kai from within the community.

508   **Kurozumikyō and the New Religions of Japan.**
Helen Hardacre.   Princeton, New Jersey; Guildford, Surrey: Princeton University Press, 1986. 212p. 3 maps. bibliog.

A detailed ethnographic study of Kurozumikyō, a Shintō-derived New Religion founded by the priest Kurozumi Munetada in 1814. Through a combination of scholarly research and participant observation, Hardacre traces the origins and historical evolution of Kurozumikyō and analyses its religious organisation and activities. She describes the characteristics of its ministers and followers, depicts the religious practices of its adherents, discusses the sectarian organisation of Kurozumikyō and the relationship of its branch churches, investigates the role and involvement of women, and examines the religious mind-set of the sect's believers. Her book is also concerned with the formulation of a typology for the New Religions of Japan, which share a common world-view based on their belief that religious self-cultivation plays a basic role in determining each individual's destiny.

509 **Lay Buddhism in contemporary Japan: Reiyūkai Kyōdan.**
Helen Hardacre. Princeton, New Jersey; Guildford, Surrey: Princeton University Press, 1984. 267p. bibliog.

A conservative, middle-class, lay Buddhist movement deriving from the Nichiren tradition, Reiyūkai Kyōdan ('The Society of Friends of the Spirits') claims a current membership of three million people, and is one of the largest and most dynamic of Japan's New Religions. After tracing the history of Reiyūkai since its founding in the 1920s, Hardacre examines its contemporary activities and organisation, analyses Reiyūkai ancestor worship and veneration of the Lotus Sutra, shows how membership in Reiyūkai often assists individuals in resolving their problems (through witnessing and spiritual healing), and discusses the subordinate role of women in this movement. Throughout her book, she demonstrates how significant Reiyūkai belief and practice are in the lives of its members.

510 **The rush hour of the gods: a study of new religious movements in Japan.**
Horace Neill McFarland. New York: Macmillan; London: Collier-Macmillan, 1967. 267p. Reprinted, New York: Harper & Row, 1970. (Harper Colophon Books).

A study of the New Religions as 'a development within the religious and social history of Japan'. McFarland first defines the nature of Japan's religious heritage, sketches the record of social crisis since the seventeenth century that has given rise to the New Religions, and identifies the chief characteristics and social functions of these religious movements. He then examines the five most representative and prominent New Religions: Konkōkyō (McFarland's so-called 'functional monotheism'), PL Kyōdan ('an epicurean movement'), Seichō-no-Ie ('divine science and nationalism'), Risshō Kōsei-kai ('Buddhism of and for laymen'), and Sōka Gakkai ('a multiphasic mass movement').

511 **The history and theology of Soka Gakkai: a Japanese New Religion.**
Daniel Metraux. Lewiston, New York; Queenston, Ontario: Edwin Mellen Press, 1988. 197p. bibliog. (Studies in Asian Thought and Religion, 9).

Demonstrates how Sōka Gakkai bases its current social and political ideology and activities on its eschatological view of Japanese Buddhism and on many of the writings (in particular the famous polemical treatise *Risshō Ankokuron*) of the thirteenth-century Buddhist monk Nichiren, whom it regards as its patron. Sōka Gakkai proclaims that it is the sole force which can rescue mankind from its many afflictions, and that it can build a new and happier society – 'a peaceful and harmonious world' – that is structured on the ideas expressed by Nichiren. Metraux describes the historical development of Sōka Gakkai, traces its eschatological teachings, and analyses their impact on its leadership and on this movement's programmes. He also examines its membership and its recruitment activities, its growing success in the United States (as

Nichiren Shōshū of America), its publications, and its involvement in politics and foreign policy.

512 **Japan's new Buddhism: an objective account of Sōka Gakkai.**
Kiyoaki Murata, foreword by Daisaku Ikeda. New York; Tokyo: Walker/Weatherhill, 1969. 194p. bibliog.

A Japanese journalist and decade-long observer of Sōka Gakkai attempts to quell growing fears that this rapidly developing religious movement constitutes a threat to Japanese institutions and to the Japanese government. Murata outlines the history and doctrine of Nichiren Shōshū (a long-established Buddhist sect), the prewar history of Sōka Gakkai, the lives and contributions of Toda Jōsei and Ikeda Daisaku (the second and third presidents of Sōka Gakkai), the organisation of Sōka Gakkai, and its involvement in postwar Japanese politics. His book complements several other informative publications that were written during the late 1960s about this religious, sociological, and political phenomenon, among them *Sōka Gakkai, Japan's militant Buddhists*, by Noah S. Brannen (Richmond, Virginia: John Knox Press, 1968, 181p.); *Sōka Gakkai, builders of the third civilization: American and Japanese members*, by James Allen Dator (Seattle, Washington: University of Washington Press, 1969, 171p.); and *I denounce Soka Gakkai*, by Hirotatsu Fujiwara, translated by Worth C. Grant (Tokyo: Nishin Hodo Co., 1970, 287p.).

513 **The New Religions of Japan.**
Harry Thomsen, foreword by Olaf Hansen. Rutland, Vermont; Tokyo: Tuttle, 1963. 269p. bibliog. Reprinted, Westport, Connecticut: Greenwood Press, 1978.

Incorporating extensive source material, Thomsen provides an overview of the founding and history, headquarters, worship and practices, writings and doctrines, and future prospects of fourteen of the more influential of Japan's 'new religions'. He covers the older 'new religions': Tenrikyō, Kurozumikyō, and Konkōkyō; the 'new religions' that have a close connection with Nichiren Buddhism: Sōka Gakkai, Reiyūkai, and Risshō Kōsei-kai; the group of religious sects that is descended from Ōmotokyō: Ōmoto, Ananaikyō, Seichō-no-Ie, Sekai Kyūseikyō, and PL Kyōdan; and a few 'miscellaneous' religions, in particular Tenshō Kōtai Jingūkyō and Ittōen. Thirty-four photographs portray many of the leaders of these sects and depict some of their activities.

514 **The Sōkagakkai and mass society.**
James W. White. Stanford, California: Stanford University Press, 1970. 376p. map. bibliog. (Stanford Studies in Comparative Politics, 4).

A critical appraisal of the political significance as well as the nature of the membership and ideology of Sōka Gakkai, a rapidly growing, Nichiren Shōshū-based, new religious movement. Part one examines Sōka Gakkai's development and present state, including its background, beliefs, growth, membership patterns, the recruitment and indoctrination of new members, goals and internal government, involvement in politics, and creation of the full-fledged political party known as Kōmeitō. Part two utilises the models of the 'mass man' and the 'mass movement' developed by William Kornhauser as standards of comparison. It examines the psychological, attitudinal, and behavioural attributes of Sōka Gakkai members; the official beliefs, practices, and structures of the movement; the nature of the interaction that occurs between the members and their organisation; Sōka Gakkai's relations with its Japanese environment; and the implications of religio-political movements for both Japanese society and Japan's democratic political system.

Makiguchi, the value creator, revolutionary Japanese educator and founder of Soka Gakkai.
See item no. 319.

The New Religions of Japan: a bibliography of Western-language materials.
See item no. 1584.

Shintō bibliography in Western languages: bibliography on Shintō and religious sects, intellectual schools and movements influenced by Shintōism.
See item no. 1606.

Shintō

515 **Shrine Shinto after World War II.**
Wilhelmus H. M. Creemers. Leiden, The Netherlands: E. J. Brill, 1968. 262p. bibliog.
A detailed assessment of the position of Shrine Shintō as a postwar religious organisation. Creemers traces the historical development of Shrine Shintō and analyses the December 1945 directive of the Allied occupation authorities which terminated government control over and support of some 100,000 Shintō shrines. He discusses the manner in which this drastic separation of church and state was implemented and how a majority of shrines at the regional and local levels organised themselves as private religious institutions within the Association of Shintō Shrines. He also describes Shrine Shintō's efforts to regain some of Shintō's prewar privileges (especially the government's financial support), notes the constitutional difficulties involved in any such changes, discusses the position of the emperor and his relationship to Shrine Shintō under the postwar constitution, and considers some of the problems relating to the status of the Ise and Yasukuni Shrines. For a balanced account of Shintō prior to its disestablishment as the state religion of Japan, Daniel C. Holtom's *The national faith of Japan: a study in modern Shinto* (New York: Dutton; London: Kegan Paul, Trench, Trubner, 1938, 329p. Reprinted, New York: Paragon Book Reprint Corp., 1965) may be recommended.

516 **Shintō: at the fountain-head of Japan.**
Jean Herbert, preface by Yukitada Sasaki. New York: Stein and Day; London: Allen and Unwin, 1967. 622p. 2 maps. bibliog.
An encyclopaedic study of Shintō religious practices and mythology, based mainly on interviews conducted with hundreds of high priests between 1935 and 1964. Part one ('Religion') is concerned with the history and major subdivisions of Shintō; its metaphysics, ethics, ritual purity, spiritual discipline, and aesthetics; Shintō shrines and priests; Shintō symbolism and individual worship; and collective worship and festivals (*matsuri*). Part two ('Mythology') deals with the Shintō beliefs about the genesis of the

universe, the birth of Japan, the two joint rulers of the universe (Amaterasu Ōmikami and Susanoo), the consolidation of the land by the earthly *kami* (divinities) and its pacification by the heavenly *kami*, and the descent to earth of the heavenly grandson. It also describes the position in Shintō of the emperors and their families, the Hachiman cycle, the various *kami* (of the family, the guild, the house, food, etc.), the Japanese beliefs in the beauties and powers of nature, and Sectarian Shintō.

517 **Modern Japan and Shinto nationalism: a study of present-day trends in Japanese religions.**
Daniel C. Holtom.   Chicago: University of Chicago Press, 1947. rev. ed. 226p. Reprinted, New York: Paragon Book Reprint Corp., 1963.

A scholarly survey of the growth of State Shintō after the Meiji Restoration (1868) and of its formative role in the development of modern Japanese nationalism. The first six chapters, published initially in 1943, describe the religious foundations of the Japanese state, Shintō's contribution (as the state religion) to the process of the 'nationalistic unification' of Japan, the struggle between nationalism and the doctrines of universalism in Japan, Japanese Christianity and Shintō nationalism, Buddhism and Japanese nationalism, and the overseas expansion of State Shintō. Two supplementary chapters deal with the vastly altered status of Shintō following its disestablishment as the state religion in December 1945, and with the 'permanent values' of Shintō as a system of ethics, thought, and ritual which may enable it to contribute to the future good of Japan.

518 **Shinto: the *kami* way.**
Sokyō Ono, with William P. Woodard, foreword by Hideo Kishimoto, sketches by Sadao Sakamoto.   Tokyo; London: Bridgeway Press, 1962. 116p. Reprinted, Rutland, Vermont and Tokyo: Tuttle, 1963.

Defining Shintō as 'both a personal faith in the *kami* – the sacred spirits which are the objects of worship – and a communal way of life according to the mind of the *kami*', Ono presents a straightforward introduction to its shrines, worship and festivals and its political, social and spiritual aspects. He describes the architecture and paraphernalia of Shrine Shintō; its priests, shrine functionaries, parishes, and parishioners; its four elements of worship; the dances, music, and sacred regalia which are part of shrine worship and festivals; and the relations between Shintō and the government, the arts, economic life, other Japanese religions, and everyday customs and practices. He also examines some of the spiritual characteristics of Shintō, including the transmission of the faith, the relationship of Shintō shrines to nature, and Shintō concepts of the world, man, salvation, and death. This book initially appeared as *Bulletin* no. 8 (1960) of the International Institute for the Study of Religions in Tokyo.

519 **Shinto: Japan's spiritual roots.**
Stuart D. B. Picken, introduction by Edwin O. Reischauer.   Tokyo; New York: Kodansha International, 1980. 80p. map.

A beautifully illustrated introduction to Shintō, the 'living spiritual roots of the Japanese'. Picken briefly describes the basic national myth of Japan; the Shintō 'rites of passage' for virtually all major life transitions except for death; the Shintō seasonal community festivals, in particular the Autumn Festival of thanksgiving; the role of the Sun Goddess Amaterasu Ōmikami as the progenitor of the imperial family; the shrines and the two basic types of protective *kami* (divinities); Shintō shrine life and worship;

Shintō's contributions to such traditional arts as painting, haiku poetry, the tea ceremony, and flower-arranging; Shintō's role in such sports as sumo wrestling and the Shintō dimensions of aikidō, horse-racing, archery, and flute-playing; Shintō's relationship with Buddhism and its impact on Japanese Buddhist teachings and practices; and Shintō among the world's faiths.

520 **Shinto: the way of Japan.**
Floyd Hiatt Ross. Boston, Massachusets: Beacon Press, 1965. 187p. bibliog. Reprinted, Westport, Connecticut: Greenwood Press, 1983.
A general presentation of the 'relatively formless tradition of ancient festivals and feelings' that constitutes Shrine Shintō as it exists in contemporary Japan. Ross describes the myths and rituals of a representative shrine (Sakura-ga-ike-miya in Shizuoka Prefecture), the mythical origins of Japan, Shintō ideas of the *kami* (the 'divine'), the various festivals of Shintō and their stages, the annual Festival of New Food known as *Nii-name-sai* that involves the participation of the emperor, purification and ethical teachings in Shintō, the revival of Shintō during the Tokugawa period and its evolution between 1868 and 1945, and the status of Shrine Shintō since 1945.

Motoori Norinaga, 1730–1801.
See item no. 309.

A Japanese New Religion: Risshō Kōsei-kai in a mountain village.
See item no. 507.

The arts of Shinto.
See item no. 1199.

Shinto arts: nature, gods, and man in Japan.
See item no. 1199.

Shinzō: Hachiman imagery and its development.
See item no. 1289.

Ise: prototype of Japanese architecture.
See item no. 1323.

Shinto art: Ise and Izumo shrines.
See item no. 1325.

Shintō bibliography in Western languages: bibliography on Shintō and religious sects, intellectual schools and movements influenced by Shintōism.
See item no. 1606.

Philosophy

521 **The Buddha eye: an anthology of the Kyoto school.**
Edited with a prologue by Frederick Franck. New York: Crossroad,
1982. 235p. (Nanzan Studies in Religion and Culture, 3).
The Kyōto School of philosophy, established by Kyōto University professor Nishida
Kitarō (1870-1945), is characterised by its 'faithfulness to, and rootedness in, the
Mahāyāna Buddhist tradition, coupled with a complete openness to Western thought
and a commitment to bringing about a meeting of East and West'. This anthology
brings together seventeen essays by five prominent members of the school – Abe
Masao, Hisamatsu Shin'ichi, Nishitani Keiji, Takeuchi Yoshinori, and Ueda Shizuteru
– as well as by D. T. Suzuki and other kindred spirits. Their essays deal with the
nature of the self in the light of contemporary Buddhist thought, with Nishitani's view
of the I–Thou relationship in Zen Buddhism, with the Kyōto School's conception of
the structure of reality, and with the nature of Shin Buddhism (a major influence on
the world of ideas presented by the school).

522 **The Japanese mind: essentials of Japanese philosophy and culture.**
Edited by Charles A. Moore, with Aldyth B. Morris. Honolulu,
Hawaii: East–West Center Press, University of Hawaii Press, 1967.
357p. Reprinted, Rutland, Vermont; Tokyo: Tuttle, 1973.
Essays by Japanese scholars and thinkers clarify the philosophical, religious and social
peculiarities of the Japanese, discuss the basic characteristics of their philosophical
tradition and culture, and examine the status and role of the individual in various fields
of activity. Among the volume's many themes are the ways in which the Japanese have
adapted the diverse philosophical perspectives that have been imported from China,
India, and the West; the Japanese 'tendency to be practical, empirical, almost anti-
intellectual rather than rational and speculative'; their emphasis on immediate
experience; and the Japanese concern for harmony (*wa*) as found in their tendency to
avoid confrontation, cultivate a spirit of tolerance, and fulfill one's social obligations.
Intended for both the general reader and the specialist, this collection appeared as a

companion volume to similar books about the Chinese mind and the Indian mind edited by Charles A. Moore and published in Honolulu in 1967.

523　A history of the development of Japanese thought, from A.D. 592–1868.
Hajime Nakamura.　Tokyo: Kokusai Bunka Shinkōkai (Japan Cultural Society), 1969. 2nd ed. 2 vols. bibliog. (Japanese Life and Culture Series).

A chronologically oriented introduction to the major ideas and philosophies of different Japanese thinkers as well as to the problems considered in the history of philosophy in Japan. The first volume covers the idea of a universal state and its philosophical basis as represented in the thought of Prince Shōtoku (574-622) and his successors; the philosophical ideas of the Nara and Heian periods; medieval thought; and the controversy between Buddhism and Christianity during the sixteenth and early seventeenth centuries. Volume two examines both the general features and the specific problems of Japanese thought during the Tokugawa period, and concludes with some consideration of the problems of Japanese philosophical thought overall.

524　Fundamental problems of philosophy: the world of action and the dialectical world.
Kitarō Nishida, translated with an introduction by David A. Dilworth. Tokyo: Sophia University, 1970. 258p. (A Monumenta Nipponica Monograph).

A lucid and accurate translation of *Tetsugaku no konpon mondai* (1933–34), a mature philosophical treatise by Japan's foremost modern philosopher. Nishida Kitarō (1870-1945) elaborates on the generalised Buddhist notion of 'pure existence' (or the 'immediacy of experience') both in terms of his own Zen Buddhist experience and in terms of Western philosophy. While no book-length study of Nishida and the evolution of his philosophy is yet available in English, translations do exist of a number of his other important works, among them *A study of good*, a translation by Valdo H. Viglielmo of his *Zen no kenkyū* (Tokyo: Printing Bureau, Japanese Government, 1960, 217p.; Reprinted, New York: Greenwood Press, 1988); *Art and morality*, a translation by David A. Dilworth and Valdo H. Viglielmo of his *Geijutsu to dōtoku* (Honolulu, Hawaii: University Press of Hawaii, 1973, 216p.); and *Last writings: nothingness and the religious worldview*, a translation by David A. Dilworth of his *Bashoteki ronri to shūkyōteki sekaikan* (Honolulu, Hawaii: University of Hawaii Press, 1987, 155p.).

525　Religion and nothingness.
Keiji Nishitani, translated with an introduction by Jan Van Bragt, foreword by Winston King.　Berkeley, California; London: University of California Press, 1982. 317p. (Nanzan Studies in Religion and Culture, 2).

A translation of *Shūkyō to wa nani ka*, the most important work of a major twentieth-century Japanese philosopher. It addresses one of the deep fears of modern man – the lack of meaning of one's own life – and one's sense of nihilism. A member of the Kyōto School of Philosophy, Nishitani argues the necessity of coming to understand life from the perspective of *śūnyatā* ('absolute nothingness', or 'emptiness'), a Mahāyāna Buddhist concept which is discussed at great length. This work reveals how a modern Japanese thinker who has mastered both Eastern and Western philosophy articulates his views on some of the fundamental questions of life and death.

526   **Confucianism and Tokugawa culture.**
Edited with an introduction by Peter Nosco.   Princeton, New Jersey; Guildford, Surrey: Princeton University Press, 1984. 290p.

The proceedings of a symposium concerned with the theme of Confucianism and orthodox Neo-Confucian thought in Tokugawa Japan and with the broad range of intellectual responses and reactions to this Chinese-derived philosophical tradition. Nine American and Japanese scholars contribute essays entitled 'Neo-Confucianism and the Formation of Early Tokugawa Ideology: Contours of a Problem', 'Tokugawa Confucian Historiography: the Hayashi, Early Mito School, and Arai Hakuseki', 'The Tokugawa Peace and Popular Religion: Suzuki Shōsan, Kakugyō Tōbutsu, and Jikigyō Miroku', 'Characteristic Responses to Confucianism in Tokugawa Literature', 'Nature and Artifice in the Writings of Ogyū Sorai (1666–1728)', 'Masuho Zankō (1655–1742): a Shinto Popularizer between Nativism and National Learning', 'Jiun Sonja (1718–1804): a response to Confucianism within the Context of Buddhist Reform'. 'Neo-Confucian Thinkers in Nineteenth-Century Japan', and 'Nakae Chōmin and Confucianism'.

527   **Recent Japanese philosophical thought, 1862–1962: a survey.**
Gino K. Piovesana.   Tokyo: Sophia University, 1968; New York: St. John's University Press, 1969. rev. ed. 296p. bibliog. (Monumenta Nipponica Monograph, 29) (St. John's University. Asian Philosophical Studies, 4).

An introductory survey of the broad range of Western philosophy encountered by Japanese philosophers since the mid-1800s. Piovesana covers early empiricism, positivism, and evolutionism, 1862-85; conservatism and Anglo-German idealism, 1886-1900; individualism, pragmatism, and neo-Kantianism, 1901-25; the philosophy of Nishida Kitarō (1870-1945); the philosophy of the three leading philosophers Hatano Seiichi, Watsuji Tetsurō, and Tanabe Hajime; culturalism and Hegelianism, Marxism and world philosophy, 1926-45; and postwar philosophical trends, 1946-62. This account is designed in part to show 'something of the vitality and variegated creativity of the many Japanese philosophers who created a new heritage of philosophical thinking' within Japan. It was published in the United States (with a foreword by Paul K. T. Sih) under the title *Contemporary Japanese philosophical thought*.

528   **Confucianism in modern Japan: a study of conservatism in Japanese intellectual history.**
Warren W. Smith, Jr, foreword by Saburō Ienaga.   Tokyo: Hokuseido Press, 1973. 2nd ed. 285p.

A detailed historical overview of Confucian institutions and Confucian thought in Japan from 1868 through 1945. After briefly covering the background of Confucianism and the Tokugawa legacy, Smith discusses the decline of organised Confucianism during the early Meiji period, the efforts of Motoda Eifu, Nishimura Shigeki and others to revive it on an organised scale, and its subsequent development; the activities of the Shibunkai (a society which restored ceremonial Confucianism and propagated its doctrine) and the characteristics of the Confucian revival between 1918 and 1933; and the status of Confucianism in Japan, 1933-45, as well as its use by ultranationalistic expansionists in Japan's overseas possessions and Japanese-dominated areas. Special emphasis is paid to organised Confucianism and its interaction with the government.

529 **Hagakure: the book of the samurai.**
Yamamoto Tsunetomo, translated with an introduction by William Scott Wilson. Tokyo; New York: Kodansha International, 1979. 180p. bibliog.

A translation of selections from an early eighteenth-century guide to samurai ethics, ascribed to Yamamoto Tsunetomo (1659-1719), that contains some 1,300 short anecdotes and reflections on the qualities that make a good samurai. Considered a classic exposition of bushidō ('the way of the warrior'), this work stresses such values as uncompromising loyalty to one's lord, filial piety, bravery and readiness to die, single-mindedness, and compassion for others. An even earlier work on the ideals of behaviour that Japanese warriors were expected to cultivate is Daidōji Yūzan's *Budō shoshinshū*, translated by A. L. Sadler as *The code of the samurai* (Rutland, Vermont; Tokyo: Tuttle, 1988, 108p.). One ardent admirer of the ideals of bushidō after World War II was the novelist and playwright Mishima Yukio, among whose writings may be found *The way of the samurai: Yukio Mishima on Hagakure in modern life*, translated by Kathryn Sparling (New York: Basic Books, 1977, 166p. Reprinted, New York: Putnam, 1983).

Sources of Japanese tradition.
See item no. 33.

The Japanese enlightenment: a study of the writings of Fukuzawa Yukichi.
See item no. 194.

An encouragement of learning.
See item no. 194.

An outline of a theory of civilization.
See item no. 194.

Tradition and modernization in Japanese culture.
See item no. 239.

Zen and Western thought.
See item no. 469.

A history of Japanese literature.
See item no. 999.

The roots of Japanese architecture: a photographic quest.
See item no. 1302.

A book of five rings.
See item no. 1447.

Society and
Social Conditions

General

530 **Japan: an anthropological introduction.**
Harumi Befu. San Francisco: Chandler; New York: Harper and Row,
1971. 210p. 2 maps. bibliog. Reprinted, Rutland, Vermont; Tokyo:
Tuttle, 1981.

A wide-ranging introduction designed for individuals with only a modest background in anthropology or Japanese culture. Opening with a chapter on the cultural origins and historical background of Japan, Befu explores the evolution of the form and function of kinship, marriage, and family institutions in Japan as well as the social, economic, and political organisation and development of modern rural communities. He then considers religious beliefs and systems in both the countryside and the cities, focusing on the actual beliefs and practices of the common people – among them, folk conceptions of deities and views of pollution and purity. An analysis of how the system of social stratification changed as Japan was transformed from a traditional agrarian society to a modern industrial one is followed by an explanation of such aspects of Japanese personality as emotional interdependence; attitudes toward time, nature, and human nature; and ethical and aesthetic values. Befu concludes with a discussion of the Japanese experience of modernisation.

531 **Japanese rural society.**
Tadashi Fukutake, translated with an introduction by Ronald P. Dore.
Tokyo; London: Oxford University Press, 1967. 230p. bibliog.
Reprinted, Ithaca, New York; London: Cornell University Press, 1972.

A systematic introduction to the varieties of structural forms and cultural patterns present in rural society before the 1960s, and to the dramatic changes which rural communities were experiencing shortly after World War II. Following a survey of the Japanese agricultural and village scene, Fukutake examines Japanese kinship and family life as he focuses on the structure of the rural family, the *ie* system, and

216

patrilineal kinship groups. He deals with the nature of the 'hamlet' (small concentrations of farmers) and with its social groupings and power structure in his discussion of the structure of 'hamlet society'. He also explores the political and authority structures of Japanese villages, their development of local self-government, and the growing interrelationship between national politics and the villages. Finally, Fukutake considers village life and culture as well as some of the changing and persistent aspects of the mentality of postwar Japanese farmers.

532 **The Japanese social structure: its evolution in the modern century.**
Tadashi Fukutake, translated with a foreword by Ronald P. Dore.
Tokyo: University of Tokyo Press, 1982. 232p. bibliog.

Fukutake, an eminent sociologist, 'describes the changes and continuities in a society that has moved from feudalism to modernism in an extremely short time span, and addresses the question of whether premodern people and social relations have evolved into modern people and social relations'. He first examines prewar Japanese society, paying particular attention to the central role of the patriarchal family (*ie*) system and its emphasis on group (family, community, nation)-oriented behaviour. He then examines the postwar process of democratisation and discusses Japan's changing agrarian and employment structures, her rapid postwar industrialisation and urbanisation, the development of a mass society, and the disintegration of both the *ie* system and local communities. Finally, the author analyses Japan's postwar social structure and stresses the social imbalances that have resulted from the government's preoccupation with economic growth.

533 **Japanese society today.**
Tadashi Fukutake, translated by the Staff of the *Japan Interpreter*.
Tokyo: University of Tokyo Press, 1981. rev. ed. 165p.

Fukutake offers a comprehensive overview of contemporary Japanese society, with a focus on population and social structure, the family and socialisation, changes in rural society, urban development, industrialisation and changes in the working environment, mass society and mass culture, social ills and the destruction of the environment, economic and social development, and conservative and reform forces within the world of Japanese politics. Contending that Japan is still 'backward' in terms of her social development, he argues that the postwar emphasis on economic growth has created severe problems for the country. Among these are the deterioration of Japan's natural environment, the emergence of a distorted economy, and inadequate public spending for the creation of badly needed social facilities such as sewage disposal. Some suggestions for dealing with such problems are offered by way of conclusion.

534 **Rural society in Japan.**
Tadashi Fukutake, translated by the Staff of the *Japan Interpreter*.
Tokyo: University of Tokyo Press, 1980. 218p.

A description and analysis of the impact of socio-economic change on rural life during the 1960s and 1970s and of the magnitude of the problems confronting present-day rural society. In a work considered to be a sequel to his *Japanese rural society* (q.v.), Fukutake explores the impact of Japan's rapid economic growth on the postwar transformation of rural society at five separate levels: agriculture as a productive sector, the life of the farm family, the social structure of the hamlet, the political structure of the rural village, and the involvement of farmers in the larger national political scene. He stresses some of the changes that have occurred and critically examines current rural conditions. Rapid growth has brought farmers relative affluence and has increased their economic independence, but the traditional social and political relations which have hampered progress in the past still persist and farming remains a small-scale operation.

535 **Understanding Japanese society.**
Joy Hendry. London; New York: Croom Helm, 1987. 218p. bibliog.
(Nissan Institute/Croom Helm Japanese Studies Series).

An introduction to the world of Japanese society as it is perceived by 'someone growing up and living in Japan'. Hendry begins by discussing the foundations of Japanese identity, kinship relations and the family system, the socialisation of children, the traditional community and the modern neighbourhood, and present-day hierarchical differences within society. She then considers such aspects of daily and ceremonial life as the education system, religious influences, ritual and the life-cycle (e.g., marriage, retirement), employment opportunities and careers, and popular involvement in the arts and entertainment. Chapters about Japanese participation in politics and government, the official legal system, and the ways in which order is actually achieved conclude her account. Throughout her book, Hendry pays considerable attention to 'the symbolic aspects of Japanese behaviour, the non-verbal ways in which members of Japanese culture communicate with each other, and particularly the ritual behaviour in which they participate'.

536 **The world of sex: perspectives on Japan and the West.**
Iwao Hoshii. Woodchurch, Ashford, Kent: Paul Norbury, 1986-1987.
4 vols.

A topically arranged, comprehensive commentary on sexuality in the world today. Hoshii explores the philosophical, ethical, and legal aspects of sex as well as the development and experience of sexuality; investigates the genesis of sexual differentiation, women's liberation and social position, and the role of women in the labour market; studies the meaning of marriage and the family, discusses the position of women in marriage, and evaluates the fundamental ethical and legal norms that condition the personal character of married life; considers the ethical and legal aspects of the relations between parents and children; and surveys such topics as sexual morality, birth control, abortion, prostitution, and pornography. While dealing with sex and sexuality around the globe, Hoshii pays particular attention to Japan – providing considerable information about such matters as marriage and divorce in Japan, adoption and inheritance among the Japanese, the education of young Japanese children, traditional sex roles in Japanese society, and the educational and career opportunities for Japanese women. The work is in four volumes: Vol. 1: *Sexual equality*. Vol. 2: *Sex and marriage*. Vol. 3: *Responsible parenthood*. Vol. 4: *Sex in ethics and law*.

537 **Japanese society.**
Takeshi Ishida. New York: Random House, 1971. 145p. map.
bibliog. (Studies in Modern Societies). Reprinted, Washington, DC:
University Press of America, 1981.

A general overview which analyses the culture and social structure of contemporary Japan as they developed from traditional values, early industrialisation, and the effects of both World War II and the Allied occupation period. Particularly concerned with certain basic contradictions that are found in Japanese society – especially its 'miraculously rapid development on the one hand, and the relatively "miserable" circumstances under which the individual lives his daily life on the other' – Ishida examines the basic elements of postwar Japanese society: its values, norms, and education; the Japanese family and community; and Japanese organisations and institutions. He also considers several present-day trends and dilemmas, including the phenomenon of the 'mass age' (of mass media, mass culture, etc.), the rapid social changes which the Japanese people are experiencing, popular attitudes and opinions, and Japan's place in the world.

538 **Conflict in Japan.**
Edited by Ellis S. Krauss, Thomas P. Rohlen, Patricia G. Steinhoff.
Honolulu, Hawaii: University of Hawaii Press, 1984. 417p.
Eleven American and Japanese conferees analyse the sources, expression, and management of conflict in postwar Japan. They provide a more realistic picture of contemporary Japan by demonstrating that internal tensions and interpersonal as well as inter-group conflicts pervade Japanese society despite the widespread characterisation of the Japanese as ' "polite" people seeking the social harmony idealized in traditional culture'. Grouping their essays under three headings – 'Conflict in Interpersonal Relations', 'Conflict in Governments and Organizations', and 'Conflict in the Political Process' – they explore such topics as the appearance of conflict in a television home drama, conflict and its resolution in industrial relations and labour law, student conflict, conflict management in parliamentary politics, and policy conflict and its resolution within the Japanese governmental system.

539 **Japanese society.**
Chie Nakane.   Harmondsworth, Middlesex: Penguin, 1973. rev. ed.
162p. (Pelican Sociology). Reprinted, Rutland, Vermont; Tokyo:
Tuttle, 1984.
A provocative and highly influential analysis of the structural principles guiding contemporary Japanese society, with particular emphasis on patterns of hierarchy and group behaviour. Nakane, a prominent social anthropologist, argues that the structure of Japanese society can best be explained through the vertical (rather than horizontal) nature of the relationships which link one individual or group to another in a superior–inferior, *oyabun–kobun* ('leader–follower') type of emotionally-charged relationship. In this fashion the Japanese people have come to form a cohesive, hierarchically organised social network that is marked by commitment to the group. This group-centred, vertical orientation of society is a distinguishing feature of traditional as well as modern, rural as well as urban Japan. It is a peculiar characteristic of both personal and social relationships. Illustrations of Nakane's points are taken from a number of sectors, in particular the contemporary Japanese business firm. A summary version of this book was published under the title *Human relations in Japan* (Tokyo: Ministry of Foreign Affairs, 1972, 86p.).

540 **The honorable elders revisited: a revised cross-cultural analysis of aging in Japan.**
Erdman B. Palmore, Daisaku Maeda. Durham, North Carolina: Duke University Press, 1985. 135p. bibliog.

A revision of Palmore's *The honorable elders* (Durham, N.C.: Duke University Press, 1975, 148p.), this volume provides an overview of the current status and social integration of the elderly in Japan, accompanied by comparisons with industrialised Western societies. The authors present considerable information about the health and medical care of the aged in Japan, their family and living arrangements, their involvement in the work force and their eventual retirement, their sources of income and support, prevailing attitudes of respect for the elderly, and the activities and satisfaction of aged people in Japan.

541 **Long engagements: maturity in modern Japan.**
David W. Plath. Stanford, California: Stanford University Press, 1980. 235p.

Plath seeks to show how the Japanese have been adjusting to the process of ageing or 'maturity'. He accomplishes this by recounting the personal narratives and life-histories of four middle-aged men and women residing in the Ōsaka-Kōbe area and by pairing them with four characters from modern Japanese novels whose lives echo and supplement in fiction some of the central themes appearing in real life. He also shows 'how the qualities of the mature person evolve across the adult years' in contemporary middle-class Japanese society and 'how a person and his consociates – those who grow older along with him – sustain long engagements of interaction in which they shape the direction and pace of one another's individual development'.

542 **Work and lifecourse in Japan.**
Edited with an introduction by David W. Plath. Albany, New York: State University of New York Press, 1983. 267p. bibliog.

Ten essays examine the interrelationships that exist between the adult careers and aspirations of the members of certain occupational and professional groups and their responsibilities respectively to their families, their communities, and themselves. The first two contributors provide an overview of careers and mobility in Japan's labour markets and consider the changing employment patterns of women. The remaining chapters discuss various occupational, familial, and social aspects of the life-course of employees in both an anonymous large public corporation and the Japanese National Railways, and of physicians, city assembly members, former Imperial Army officers, female workers in a general trading company (*sōgō shōsha*), and folkcraft pottery-making households. Refuting widely held notions in the West, several of the authors show that lifetime employment exists only for certain categories of workers in present-day Japan.

543 **For harmony and strength: Japanese white-collar organization in anthropological perspective.**
Thomas P. Rohlen. Berkeley, California; London: University of California Press, 1974. 285p. bibliog.

A detailed ethnographic study of the social structure, the human relationships, and the organisational behaviour within a large regional bank. Employing a participant-observer approach, Rohlen describes and interprets organisational recruitment and 'lifelong commitment' to the bank, wages, promotions, social relationships and daily interactions among bank employees, the nature of office groups during work hours and after work, training programmes for new recruits, company ideology, labour union activities, life in company dormitories and apartments, and the relative importance of family and outside commitments. On the basis of his experience as an insider within this white-collar organisation, Rohlen offers many insights into the peculiarities of the modern Japanese business organisation and the values that pervade the Japanese work environment.

544 **Japanese society: tradition, self, and the social order.**
Robert J. Smith, foreword by Alfred Harris. Cambridge, England; New York: Cambridge University Press, 1983. 176p. bibliog. (Lewis Henry Morgan Lecture Series).

A perceptive study of the evolution of Japanese society into a mass industrial society significantly different from its Western counterparts. Smith traces the origin of these differences to Japan's historical traditions, which are based on cultural premises fundamentally unlike those of the Western world. He examines the nature and characteristics of Japan's traditional values, and shows how some of them have persisted well into the twentieth century, influencing the present-day Japanese concern for social order, harmonious interpersonal relationships, and self-discipline, as well as Japanese efforts to achieve a 'perfect society'. The difference between Japan and the West, Smith argues, 'lies less in its organization and institutions than in the way all of its history shows how the Japanese think about man and society and the relationship between the two'. An appreciation of this is essential for a proper understanding of Japan today.

545 **Classes in contemporary Japan.**
Rob Steven. Cambridge, England; New York: Cambridge University Press, 1983. 357p. bibliog.

A structural rather than an historical analysis of the structure and composition of the various social classes in Japan during the 1970s and an examination of Japan's capitalist mode of production at that time. Approaching his subject from a Marxist perspective, Steven dissects the country's remarkably persistent class divisions, revealing the tensions between traditional values and the modern industrial ideologies of competition and progress. He examines the living and working conditions, age and sex composition, relative size and potential strength, ideologies, and organisation of all of the major social classes: the bourgeoisie, petty bourgeoisie, peasantry, middle class, and working class. Steven is also concerned with the crisis in the capitalist mode of production that affected Japanese society following the 1973 oil shock.

546 **Social change and the city in Japan: from earliest times through the industrial revolution.**
Takeo Yazaki, translated with a preface by David L. Swain. Tokyo: Japan Publications, 1968. 549p. 16 maps. bibliog.

Yazaki details the growth and development of the Japanese city from its rise as a political centre during the seventh century, through each succeeding stage during the medieval and Tokugawa periods, to the emergence of the modern city following the industrialisation of Japan during the Meiji era. Employing a 'broad approach to the

Society and Social Conditions. General

structural relations of rural and urban sectors and of these to the national structure', he systematically shows that a close interrelationship existed between changes in the political and economic structure of Japanese cities and the concomitant changes in their ecological and demographic features during the most critical periods of Japanese history. Particular attention is paid to the cities of Edo/Tokyo, Ōsaka, and Kyōto.

As the Japanese see it: past and present.
See item no. 1.

The Japanese and the Jews.
See item no. 4.

Aspects of social change in modern Japan.
See item no. 239.

Japan's modern myth: the language and beyond.
See item no. 408.

Religion and society in modern Japan: continuity and change.
See item no. 468.

With respect to the Japanese: a guide for Americans.
See item no. 586.

Japanese culture and behaviour: selected readings.
See item no. 591.

Social change and the individual: Japan before and after defeat in World War II.
See item no. 595.

Illness and culture in contemporary Japan: an anthropological view.
See item no. 600.

Japanese political culture: change and continuity.
See item no. 610.

Law and society in contemporary Japan: American perspectives.
See item no. 777.

Law and social change in postwar Japan.
See item no. 785.

Inside the Japanese system: readings on contemporary society and political economy.
See item no. 809.

Japanese industrialization and its social consequences.
See item no. 812.

British factory – Japanese factory: the origins of national diversity in industrial relations.
See item no. 920.

Learning to be Japanese: selected readings on Japanese society and education.
See item no. 961.

Japanese proverbs and sayings.
See item no. 1183.

The chrysanthemum and the bat: baseball samurai style.
See item no. 1456.

You gotta have wa.
See item no. 1456.

The after hours: modern Japan and the search for enjoyment.
See item no. 1460.

AMPO: Japan-Asia Quarterly Review.
See item no. 1488.

Japan Update.
See item no. 1517.

Old age in Japan: an annotated bibliography of Western-language materials.
See item no. 1595.

Community studies

547 **Japanese urbanism: industry and politics in Kariya, 1872–1972.**
Gary D. Allinson.   Berkeley, California; London: University of
California Press, 1975. 276p. map. bibliog.
A multi-faceted analysis of the remarkably distinctive social and political consequences
of industrialisation in the thriving industrial community – southeast of the city of
Nagoya – that serves as the current headquarters of the Toyota Motor Corporation.
Allinson traces the development of the Toyota enterprise from a small textile concern
to a world-class industrial firm; describes Kariya's social, political, and economic
history during the course of its century-long transformation from a rustic country town
to an industrial satellite city; and analyses Kariya's political response to industrialism
by exploring the complex interrelationships over time between industrialisation and
political change. In addition, he sheds light on selected aspects of labour–management
relations in modern Japanese industry as well as on historical changes in the structure
and distribution of political power within this particular community.

548 **Village Japan.**
Richard K. Beardsley, John W. Hall, Robert E. Ward.   Chicago;
London: University of Chicago Press, 1959. 498p. 23 maps. Reprinted,
University of Chicago Press, 1969.
Niiike, a small rice-growing community in Okayama Prefecture, typified postwar
Japanese rural villages during the 1950s, and its inhabitants' way of life exemplified
that of millions of farmers throughout Japan, This interdisciplinary study explores the
village's geographical and historical settings, the physique and temperament of its
inhabitants, the material goods and equipment of community life, land use and

agricultural practices, the cycle of work and the variety of productive enterprises in which the villagers were engaged, income and expenditure, the household, community and kinship associations, the life-cycle, the community and local government as well as the community and the political process, and Niiike's religious institutions and concepts. The authors offer valuable descriptions and insights into the lives, problems, and attitudes of much of Japan's population during a critical period in her modern socio-economic transformation.

549   **City life in Japan: a study of a Tokyo ward.**
Ronald P. Dore.   Berkeley, California: University of California Press; London: Routledge and Kegan Paul, 1958. 472p. (International Library of Sociology and Social Construction).

A first-hand description and sociological analysis of life among the lower middle class residents of a small Tokyo ward as of 1951. Dore is concerned with what these people think and feel as well as with what they do: 'how they earn a living and run a home, how they marry, how they amuse themselves, how they treat their relatives, their neighbours, and their gods'. He first describes both the area's physical setting and the contemporary material setting for the attitudes and behaviour of its residents. He then examines the Japanese family system, household composition, the 'house' (*ie*), and husbands and wives; political attitudes, education, leisure, neighbours and friends, and the ward; and religious attitudes and practices, family rites, ideals of morality, and the relationship of the individual to society. His perspective on how Japanese values and institutions were changing during the Allied occupation period enhances both the sociological and historical importance of this classic study. A much more recent work, Theodore C. Bestor's *Neighborhood Tokyo* (Stanford, California: Stanford University Press, 1989, 347p. [Studies of the East Asian Institute, Columbia University]), presents a descriptive ethnography and analysis of the social fabric and internal dynamics of a comparable middle-class residential and commercial district in Tokyo during the late 1970s and early 1980s. Bestor's study also conveys the texture and flavour of everyday life in that community.

550   **Shinohata: a portrait of a Japanese village.**
Ronald P. Dore.   London: Allen Lane; New York: Pantheon, 1978. 322p. (Pantheon Asia Library).

A British sociologist's first-hand portrait of a farming community in central Honshū. The author visited and lived in Shinohata on several occasions between 1955 and 1975. Basing his book on field-notes, recorded conversations, and memories, he intimately depicts the hamlet, its residents, their behaviour and life-styles, their everyday activities, and their social relations. Incorporating colourful details and entertaining anecdotes into his account, he delves into such topics as the relations between husbands and wives, the changes that were occurring in farmers' and silkworm-raisers' co-operatives, and the various amusements and diversions of Shinohata's residents. Dore also describes and documents the rapid transformation of the community's economic life and its traditional values and relationships over a twenty-year period as a consequence of Japan's postwar prosperity and modernisation.

551 **Suye mura: a Japanese village.**
John F. Embree, introduction by A. R. Radcliffe-Brown. Chicago:
University of Chicago Press, 1939. 354p. 7 maps. bibliog. Reprinted,
London: Kegan Paul, Trench, Trubner, 1946. 268p; and with a
foreword by Richard K. Beardsley, Chicago: University of Chicago
Press, 1964.

A pioneering account of rural life in the southern Kyūshū village of Suye mura during
the mid-1930s. Together with his wife, Embree (the only Western anthropologist to
conduct field work in prewar Japan) spent a full year in Suye mura observing the daily
activities and behaviour of its inhabitants and gradually piecing together an integrated
social study of this remote farming community. He describes the village's organisation,
its family and household patterns, the forms of co-operation existing among the
inhabitants, its various social classes and associations, the life-history of typical
individuals, the community's formal religious beliefs and informal religious practices,
and the changes that were observable in its social organisation. Since its publication in
1939, this book has become a 'benchmark study' and has been widely used as a
standard source of information about prewar Japanese rural society.

552 **Shingū: a Japanese fishing community.**
Arne Kalland. London; Malmö, Sweden: Curzon Press, 1981. 198p.
7 maps. bibliog. (Scandinavian Institute of Asian Studies. Monograph
Series, 44).

An ethnographic study of both the socio-economic organisation of fishing and the
structure and leadership of 'net-groups' (two or more fishing crews who jointly operate
their nets) and other forms of management units in a community whose inhabitants
derive their livelihood primarily from fishing in the Sea of Japan. Based on field
research conducted in the mid-1970s, it examines Shingū's geographical setting, the
history of this northern Kyūshū community, the household and its role within the
community, the different technologies that are used and the annual cycles, the fishing
boat as a management group and the net-group as a management unit, organisational
changes in the fisheries, and the recruitment of fishermen. Kalland pays particular
attention to the control of capital, the supply of labour, fishing rights, and fish markets.
In addition, he describes the nature, organisation, and evolution of fishing between the
Tokugawa period and the 1960s.

553 **Lost innocence: folk craft potters of Onta, Japan.**
Brian Moeran. Berkeley, California; London: University of California
Press, 1984. 252p. 2 maps. bibliog.

Ontayaki ('Onta ware'), a kind of stoneware pottery produced for well over 250 years
in the northeastern Kyūshū hamlet of Sarayama, became famous when adherents of
the twentieth-century Japanese folk-crafts (*mingei*) movement began championing its
aesthetic qualities. The subsequent improvement of economic conditions in Sarayama
and changes in the working environment within this rural community, however, led to
a breakdown of communal solidarity and to the emergence of individualism among the
potters. From the perspective of the leaders of the folk-craft movement, these
economic, social, and technological changes contributed as well to a deterioration of
the overall quality of their pottery. Moeran's study focuses on the impact of these
developments on the production, marketing, and aesthetic appreciation of *Ontayaki*. It

also offers valuable insights into the social organisation and structure of villages in postwar Japan.

554 Country to city: the urbanization of a Japanese hamlet.
Edward Norbeck. Salt Lake City, Utah: University of Utah Press, 1978. 357p. 5 maps. bibliog.

Two related ethnographic studies which trace and analyse conditions in Takashima, a community along the coast of the Inland Sea that was transformed (between the early 1950s and the mid-1970s) from an isolated, impoverished fishing village into a well-integrated suburb of the growing industrial city of Kurashiki. Norbeck's first study, an account originally published under the title *Takashima: a Japanese fishing community* (University of Utah Press, 1954), examines the occupations of the village residents in 1950-51, their households and their life at home, intracommunity relations, popular beliefs and deities, the life-cycle, and the impact of Westernisation. His second study, *Takashima urbanized*, describes and discusses the same community as it existed in 1974. Particular attention is paid to changes and adjustments in daily life, familial and community organisation, relationships with the outside world, and religion that had occurred during this twenty-three-year interval. Norbeck also discusses some of the cultural continuities and discontinuities in the lives of Takashima's residents as they made the transition from rural to urban life.

555 Three decades in Shiwa: economic development and social change in a Japanese farming community.
Mitsuru Shimpō. Vancouver, British Columbia: University of British Columbia Press, 1976. 141p. 3 maps. bibliog.

A case-study that documents and analyses the changes which occurred in Shiwa (Iwate Prefecture) after World War II as agriculture within that community became mechanised, cash-based, and increasingly productive. Focusing on the introduction of new irrigation methods, the nature and impact of rapid technological change, and the role of the Shiwa Agricultural Cooperative as an agent of change, Shimpō describes the gradual transformation of the traditional economic, social, and sociopolitical organisation of this village and explains how and why its farmers chose to support the developmental thrust of their local co-operative. He also discusses the ways in which economic progress led to a significant modification of Shiwa's major social institutions, in particular, the household (*ie*) – the social unit most basic to Japanese rural communities.

556 Kurusu: the price of progress in a Japanese village, 1951–1975.
Robert J. Smith, foreword by Ronald P. Dore. Stanford, California: Stanford University Press, 1978. 269p. 4 maps. bibliog.

An anthropological account of the social and economic changes that have occurred in a typical Japanese village. Through the histories of several families in this remote Kagawa Prefecture community, Smith examines and documents the far-reaching changes that have characterised postwar rural life. These include the decline of agriculture, changes in the composition of the population, altered social relationships within the family and the community, changes in living arrangements, the introduction of wage labour and salaried work, the accompanying revolution in the standard of living, the availability of an entire range of new consumer products including television, and the decline of religious observances and social customs. Smith explores the circumstances that have led to these changes and relates them to economic developments on the national level. He also dramatically shows some of their negative consequences for traditional community values and communal solidarity.

557 **Migration in metropolitan Japan: social change and political behavior.**
James W. White. Berkeley, California: Center for Japanese Studies, Institute of East Asian Studies, University of California, 1982. 322p. 4 maps. bibliog. (Japan Research Monograph, 2).

White analyses the patterns of migration (i.e., the changes in residence from one community to another) in contemporary Japan; the social and political effects of migration on the migrants themselves and on the neighbourhoods in which they settle; and the effects which migrants' attitudes and behaviour have on the capability of those neighbourhoods to integrate, mould, and retain their new residents. The research for this study was conducted in three different neighbourhoods of Tokyo during the 1970s.

Pariah persistence in changing Japan: a case study.
See item no. 374.

Together with the Ainu: a vanishing people.
See item no. 375.

The Ainu: the past in the present.
See item no. 379.

The Namahage: a festival in the northeast of Japan.
See item no. 501.

A Japanese New Religion: Risshō Kōsei-kai in a mountain hamlet.
See item no. 507.

Japanese rural society.
See item no. 531.

Marriage in changing Japan: community and society.
See item no. 560.

Police and community in Japan.
See item no. 565.

Haruko's world: a Japanese farm woman and her community.
See item no. 573.

Urban housewives: at home and in the community.
See item no. 577.

Japanese women: constraint and fulfillment.
See item no. 579.

The women of Suye mura.
See item no. 582.

Suburban Tokyo: a comparative study in politics and social change.
See item no. 628.

Family and kinship

558 **Love match and arranged marriage: a Tokyo–Detroit comparison.**
Robert O. Blood, Jr. New York: Free Press; London: Collier-
Macmillan, 1967. 264p. bibliog.
This investigation of the Japanese ways of choosing marriage partners is based on
research conducted in Tokyo during the late 1950s. Blood discusses the traditional and
modern concepts of Japanese mate-selection and courtship; shows how marriage
partners are actually selected (regardless of how a courtship happens to get started)
and explores the marital consequences of courtship activities; and examines the
relationships between husbands and wives in order to determine whether there are any
significant differences between couples who marry out of love and couples whose
spouses are chosen on their behalf. Frequent comparisons are made with courtship and
marriage in the United States. The findings continue to be relevant for Japanese
society of the 1980s.

559 **Becoming Japanese: the world of the pre-school child.**
Joy Hendry. Honolulu, Hawaii: University of Hawaii Press;
Manchester, England: Manchester University Press, 1986. 194p.
bibliog.
Child-rearing is regarded as a very serious matter in Japan, and the training of children
for adulthood in Japanese society begins early in their lives. Hendry, a British social
anthropologist, focuses on the day-to-day life of children at home, at day nurseries,
and in kindergartens. Her non-technical study explains current Japanese methods of
child care, ways of socialisation, and the techniques used to instill in very young
children the fundamental principles of proper social behaviour which enable them to
function as adults in a wider social world. Most of Hendry's research was carried out in
the city of Tateyama (Chiba Prefecture) and the village of Kurotsuchi (Fukuoka
Prefecture).

560 **Marriage in changing Japan: community and society.**
Joy Hendry. London: Croom Helm; New York: St. Martin's Press,
1981. 274p. 9 maps. bibliog. Reprinted, Rutland, Vermont; Tokyo:
Tuttle, 1986.
An examination of the ways and extent to which marriage practices have changed in
postwar Japan and an explanation for the persistence of the traditional form of
'arranged marriage'. Basing her study on field work conducted in the northern Kyūshū
agricultural village of Kurotsuchi, Hendry opens with a broad historical background of
the Japanese family, a general ethnography of the community, and an analysis of the
household as the primary unit of village membership. She then studies the mechanics
of matchmaking; the betrothal, separation ceremonies, wedding rites, and post-
wedding celebrations of the marriage itself; and the relationship of marriage to selected
life-cycle rites and crises, annual festivals, and house-building celebrations. In her
conclusion, Hendry focuses on the 'pivotal role' of marriage, indicating that it
continues to play an important structural role in Japanese society and therefore
involves much more than a contract between two individuals. An analysis of the
relationship between the commercialisation and the symbolic content of Japanese
weddings, in turn, is provided in *Modern Japan through its weddings: gender, person,*

and society in ritual portrayal, by Walter Edwards (Stanford, California: Stanford University Press, 1989, 173p.).

561 **Kinship and economic organization in rural Japan.**
Chie Nakane. London: University of London, Athlone Press; New York: Humanities Press, 1967. 203p. map. bibliog. (London School of Economics. Monographs on Social Anthropology, 32).

A prominent social anthropologist examines the social organisation of the rural household (*ie*), the village, and local corporate groups, and analyses the role that marital relations play in forming close ties between households of similar economic and social standing. Nakane argues that the institution known as the *dōzoku* is not a patrilineal lineage but rather a corporate group of people organised together within some community structure in terms of their functional relationship to the head of a household. She also shows that social relations are in effect social adaptations to evolving economic patterns and local political power relationships. Nakane concludes that 'the primary elements which provide the frame of organisation in rural Japan are household, local corporate group and village, not family, descent group or status group'.

562 **Changing Japan.**
Edward Norbeck, foreword by George Spindler, Louise Spindler. New York: Holt, Rinehart and Winston, 1976. 2nd ed. 108p. bibliog. (Case Studies in Cultural Anthropology). Reprinted, Prospect Heights, Illinois: Waveland Press, 1984.

A brief case-study of the central process of social change in postwar Japan. Following an overview of Japanese society and culture, Norbeck describes the family members, family life, daily life, leisure activities, types of worship, friendships, and life-cycles of two closely related families: an extended family household in the rural community of Takashima (Okayama Prefecture), and a small, status-achieving urban family in Ōsaka. In this manner he contrasts the differences between Japanese rural and city life and points out some of the changes experienced by Japanese society since World War II.

563 **Letters from Sachiko: a Japanese woman's view of life in the land of the economic miracle.**
James Trager. New York: Atheneum, 1982. 218p. London: Abacus, 1984. 176p.

An entertaining and informative account of Japanese family life presented in the form of a series of letters to a Japanese woman in the United States from her immediate family in the suburbs of Tokyo. The letters are primarily concerned with everyday affairs and provide insights into the lives, thoughts, and concerns of middle-class Japanese women during the early 1980s.

564 **Japan's new middle class: the salary man and his family in a Tokyo suburb.**
Ezra F. Vogel. Berkeley, California; London: University of California Press, 1971. 2nd ed. 313p. bibliog.

An ethnographic case-study of the lives, values, and behaviour of a number of salaried workers and their families living in suburban Tokyo during the late 1950s. Vogel describes and analyses the roles of these modern 'salary men' (white-collar workers employed in business corporations and government bureaucracies) and of their wives and children. He writes about the background of these workers, their lives as husbands and fathers, the ways they provide for their families, their basic values, the decline of the traditional family system (*ie*), the division of labour within the home, authority in the family, family solidarity, and child-rearing practices. Vogel frequently highlights the changes brought about by the aftermath of World War II and Japan's rapid economic growth during the 1950s. The second edition contains a brief concluding chapter that discusses changes which occurred during the 1960s.

Chronicle of my mother.
See item no. 327.

Transforming the past: tradition and kinship among Japanese Americans.
See item no. 403.

Ancestor worship in contemporary Japan.
See item no. 505.

Heritage of endurance: family patterns and delinquency formation in urban Japan.
See item no. 571.

Japanese women: constraint and fulfillment.
See item no. 579.

The waiting years.
See item no. 1053.

The family.
See item no. 1096.

The Makioka sisters.
See item no. 1101.

Social problems and social welfare

565 **Police and community in Japan.**
Walter L. Ames. Berkeley, California; London: University of California Press, 1981. 247p. map. bibliog.

A comparative anthropological investigation of Japanese police operations in the western Tokyo suburb of Fuchū and the Okayama prefectural city of Kurashiki, and their responses to various social problems. Ames describes the organisation of the police, their daily operations, their adjustment to changing social conditions, and their ways of dealing with juvenile delinquents, radical student movements, Japan's Korean minority, the former outcaste group known as the *burakumin*, gangsters (*yakuza*), and such special problems as the investigation of crimes and the maintenance of public security. He stresses the inculcation and maintenance of the value of police solidarity and police loyalty in his examination of the recruitment, training, and socialisation of Japanese policemen. Throughout Ames shows how the police skillfully utilise the co-operation extended by their local communities in their efforts to control and fight crime.

566 **Crime control in Japan.**
William Clifford, foreword by Thorsten Sellin.   Lexington,
Massachusetts; Toronto, Ontario: Lexington Books, 1976. 200p.

An explanation of the reasons for postwar Japan's relatively low and declining crime rate and for the apparent success of the Japanese approach to crime control. Clifford first analyses the cultural factors responsible for this phenomenon, among them the Japanese concern for their self-image at home and abroad, the prevalence of toleration and dependence (*amae*) in Japanese society, Japan's tight social structure with its limits on freedom of action, and conflict and consensus. He then traces the historical evolution of the modern criminal justice system and the police and correctional services, and describes the Japanese concept of public participation in crime control and in treating and rehabilitating criminals. Clifford combines his examination of various forms of deviant conduct – juvenile delinquency, gangsterism, female crime, the use of drugs, suicide, and political offences – with descriptions of the legal and administrative institutions and measures that have been created to deal with them.

567 **The price of affluence: dilemmas of contemporary Japan.**
Rokurō Hidaka, translated and edited by Gavan McCormack and
others.   Tokyo; New York: Kodansha International, 1984. 176p.

Hidaka, a liberal intellectual and prominent sociologist, critically assesses the impact of Japan's recent economic prosperity on the lives of her citizens. In this polemical account, he singles out the problems which Japan is now facing: industrial and environmental pollution, as exemplified by the cases of mercury poisoning known as Minamata disease; political corruption; Japanese economic exploitation of the newly developing countries; and the emergence of a 'controlled' society in which individuality is being suppressed and social conscience is being replaced by self-indulgence. Arguing that Japan is paying a hidden price for her affluence, Hidaka comments on its implications for business, politics, education, civil rights, and the new militarism. This book typifies the writing of those Japanese who have recently been emphasizing the negative aspects of Japan's postwar 'economic miracle'.

568 **The thorn in the chrysanthemum: suicide and economic success in
modern Japan.**
Mamoru Iga, foreword by Edwin S. Shneidman, David K. Reynolds.
Berkeley, California; London: University of California Press, 1986.
231p.

A broad sociological study of patterns of suicide in postwar Japan, particularly among young males, based on a range of available data from the 1960s and 1970s. Analysing the cultural and social background of suicide among the Japanese, Iga focuses on the correlation between the pressure to succeed that is brought to bear upon many individuals, and the resulting stress which leads some of them to take their own lives. Considerable attention is paid to the bimodal pattern of Japanese suicide, the relatively high rate of suicide among young males, and suicide among women and among writers.

569 **Yakuza: the explosive account of Japan's criminal underworld.**
David E. Kaplan, Alec Dubro. Reading, Massachusetts: Addison-Wesley, 1986. 336p. bibliog. Reprinted, New York: Collier Books; London: Macdonald; London: Futura, 1987.

An exposé of the world of organised crime in Japan since the mid-Tokugawa period. Two award-winning journalists describe the history, organisation, major figures, culture, activities, and public image of the *yakuza*, 'Japan's own version of La Cosa Nostra'. They detail the inner workings of these groups of Japanese gangsters; discuss their involvement in such vices as prostitution, pornography, drugs, gambling, and smuggling, as well as their control of nightclubs and other entertainment industries; show how they have expanded their operations into North America as well as East and Southeast Asia; and repeatedly assert that the present-day power and influence of the *yakuza* extend to the highest levels of Japanese business and politics.

570 **The Japanese police system today: an American perspective.**
L. Craig Parker, Jr. Tokyo; New York: Kodansha International, 1984. 220p. bibliog.

A study of the history and methods of the Japanese police, their role within the framework of Japan's legal system, and their efforts to cope with various social problems. On the basis of an eight-month-long stay in Japan in 1980-81, Parker describes police work in several jurisdictions of Tokyo as well as in Hokkaidō; depicts the ways in which the police investigate crimes and the attitudes which they have towards their work; discusses their handling of family counselling, drug abuse, and crime prevention; and looks into their relations with youth and with the community. He also offers several recommendations for improved police operations in the United States.

571 **Heritage of endurance: family patterns and delinquency formation in urban Japan.**
Hiroshi Wagatsuma, George A. De Vos. Berkeley, California; London: University of California Press, 1984. 500p.

A psycho-cultural examination of the family and personality factors responsible for both the presence and absence of juvenile delinquency in Arakawa Ward, a lower-class district of Tokyo, during the late 1960s. Wagatsuma and De Vos demonstrate the significance of family cohesion and the warm and caring attitudes of parents towards one another and towards their children in inhibiting the development of juvenile delinquency at that time. This study is based on an intensive, comparative investigation of the behavioural patterns of thirty-one families with delinquent teenage sons and nineteen with non-delinquent children.

572 **The Japanese overseas: can they go home again?**
Merry White.   New York: Free Press; London: Collier-Macmillan,
1988. 179p. bibliog.
Tens of thousands of Japanese overseas employees and their families often face a
problematic and even traumatic re-entry into Japanese society. Upon returning home,
they may experience serious identity problems and be isolated within their groups as
functional but marginal members. Children's education may be disrupted as well.
White focuses on those individuals who 'must negotiate this difficult return from an
outward-looking economy to an inward-looking culture'. Her clearly written sociological study is particularly concerned with the personal and social consequences of
their foreign sojourn. She describes the experiences of a number of Japanese families,
examines the plight of the returnee child in school and the need for lessons in
readjustment, explores some of the strategies and options which mothers at home and
fathers at work pursue in order to reintegrate themselves and their families into
Japanese society, analyses the broad role of the 'border broker' in Japanese
organisations, and considers the current state and prospects of internationalisation in
Japan.

Japan's invisible race: caste in culture and personality.
See item no. 373.

Pariah persistence in changing Japan: a case study.
See item no. 374.

Koreans in Japan: ethnic conflict and accommodation.
See item no. 376.

The invisible visible minority: Japan's burakumin.
See item no. 381.

**Socialization for achievement: essays on the cultural psychology of the
Japanese.**
See item no. 588.

Japanese patterns of behavior.
See item no. 592.

Japanese criminal procedure.
See item no. 772.

Law in Japan: the legal order in a changing society.
See item no. 786.

**White Papers of Japan: Annual Abstracts of Official Reports and Statistics of
the Japanese Government.**
See item no. 829.

The Japanese tattoo.
See item no. 1372.

Women

573 **Haruko's world: a Japanese farm woman and her community.**
Gail Lee Bernstein.   Stanford, California: Stanford University Press,
1983. 199p. map.
An illuminating portrait of Japanese rural women, presented primarily through a
sensitively written study of a middle-aged farm woman. Bernstein spent six months
living with Utsunomiya Haruko and her family in a small village on the island of
Shikoku in the mid-1970s, observing and recording their daily lives and activities. She
first introduces Haruko, her family, and her environment, and narrates her life-story.
She then describes the organisation of farm work, the mechanisation of agriculture,
Haruko's own work and responsibilities, family interaction, and local education.
Focusing on the larger farming community, Bernstein also writes about social life and
social organisations, sex and drinking, and the changing patterns of life at that time.
An epilogue summarizes major changes in Haruko's life and the lives of other farm
women between 1975 and 1982.

574 **A half step behind: Japanese women of the '80s.**
Jane Condon.   New York: Dodd, Mead, 1985. 319p. bibliog.
A candid portrait of Japanese women as family members (with particular focus on
marriage, divorce, feminism, and old age), as participants in education (as 'education
mamas', teachers, and students), and as employees in the economy (as career women,
job-hunters, part-timers, 'office ladies', blue-collar workers, entertainers, and older
white-collar workers). Throughout her journalistic account, Condon comments on the
status of women in contemporary Japan, on their important contributions to Japanese
life and society, and on some of the changes currently affecting them.

575 **Women in Japan: discrimination, resistance and reform.**
Alice H. Cook, Hiroko Hayashi.   Ithaca, New York: New York State
School of Industrial and Labor Relations, Cornell University, 1980.
124p. bibliog. (Cornell International Industrial and Labor Relations
Report, 10).
A study of the exploitation and discrimination which women workers face under
Japan's present employment system and of a number of ongoing efforts to improve
their working conditions. Through a survey and analysis of court cases that have
addressed such issues as unequal pay, discriminatory retirement policies, and maternity
leave, Cook and Hayashi document the serious nature of the problems which continue
to confront women employees and record their search for legal remedies.

576 **Geisha.**
Liza Crihfield Dalby.   Berkeley, California; London: University of
California Press, 1983. 347p. map. bibliog. Reprinted, New York:
Vintage Books, 1985.
An ethnographic study of the world of the unmarried professional female entertainers
who perform traditional songs and dances, play games, engage in witty conversation,
and offer companionship to their customers. Dalby explains what it really means to be
a geisha in contemporary Japan on the basis of her year-long residence in Kyōto as a

geisha and her many interviews and questionnaires. She writes about the development of this profession since the mid-Tokugawa period, the organisation of present-day geisha communities, the place and function of geisha within Japanese society as curators of tradition and art, the artistic training which they receive, their relationships with one another as well as with their customers, the entertainment they provide at restaurant and teahouse parties, their clothing, and their fees. Dalby's intimate overview of geisha life is enlivened by numerous stories about her own experiences and those of her geisha sisters. Her earlier book – *Ko-uta: 'little songs' of the geisha world* (by Liza Crihfield. Rutland, Vermont; Tokyo: Tuttle, 1979, 100p.) – provides a good introduction to the songs which geisha sing to the accompaniment of the three-stringed plucked lute known as the shamisen and which frequently are concerned with male–female relations in the pleasure quarters.

577 **Urban housewives: at home and in the community.**
Anne E. Imamura. Honolulu, Hawaii: University of Hawaii Press, 1987. 193p. bibliog. (Studies of the East Asian Institute, Columbia University).
The first scholarly investigation into the life-style, perceived role, and community involvement of the urban, middle-class, Japanese housewife. In this sociological study, set in a western suburb of Tokyo, Imamura combines in-depth inverviews of some fifty housewives, participant observation in a community centre, and a survey of over two hundred local housewives. She explores the housewives' participation in community affairs and the specific problems related to their involvement in activities outside the home. She compares the effect that residence in five different types of housing environments (*danchi*, or 'public housing', company housing, apartments, condominiums, and privately owned homes) have on the behaviour and community perceptions of her informants. In addition, Imamura examines variations in the typical life-course of Japanese housewives as well as the expectations which some of them have of their own future.

578 **Women in changing Japan.**
Edited by Joyce Lebra, Joy Paulson, Elizabeth Powers, foreword by Kazuko Tsurumi. Boulder, Colorado: Westview Press, 1976. 322p. bibliog. (Westview Special Studies on China and East Asia). Reprinted, Stanford, California: Stanford University Press, 1978.
Essays written by twelve American women scholars about Japanese women in various occupational roles. They first examine the evolution of the Japanese feminine ideal of the wife/mother and provide a basis for assessing the extent to which women in postwar Japan have been breaking away from tradition. The authors then describe women in eleven occupational fields – agriculture, factories, offices, family businesses, service industries, nightclubs (as bar hostesses), education, the professions, the mass media, the political system, and sports – as well as patterns of suicide among women since the end of World War II.

579 **Japanese women: constraint and fulfillment.**
Takie Sugiyama Lebra. Honolulu, Hawaii: University of Hawaii Press, 1984. 348p. bibliog.
An ethnographic investigation of the life-stages and roles of fifty-seven women from various socio-economic backgrounds who resided in a small fishing and tourist-oriented

city in central Japan and ranged in age from twenty-eight to eighty years old. Basing her study on analyses of their individual and collective life-histories, Lebra describes the relationships of these women with the members of the families in which they are raised and the families in which they live after marriage, their different educational experiences, their work as participants in family businesses, as white-collar employees or professionals, and as artists or skilled craftswomen, and the changes that normally occur as they grow older. She criticises existing stereotypes and seeks to dispel erroneous generalisations about Japanese women.

580 **Political women in Japan: the search for a place in political life.**
Susan J. Pharr.   Berkeley, California; London: University of California Press, 1981. 239p. bibliog.

Drawing on interviews with one hundred young women active in a wide range of voluntary political organisations and movements, Pharr examines the origins, nature, and extent of their involvement in contemporary Japanese politics. She surveys the historical background of women's political rights in Japan; explores the evolving images and expectations that women have of themselves, of their lives, and of their role in society; investigates the effects of political socialisation on political women as well as the dynamics of change involving women who become politically active; studies the type of satisfaction which women derive from political volunteerism; and examines the psychological tensions and social costs that women experience as they seek to handle role strain. Individual case-histories of a few informants – among them a labour union leader, a Red Army activist, and a neo-traditional housewife – enliven the presentation and help document some of the findings.

581 **The hidden sun: women of modern Japan.**
Dorothy Robins-Mowry, foreword by Edwin O. Reischauer.   Boulder, Colorado: Westview Press; Epping, Essex: Bowker, 1983. 394p. bibliog.

A narrative of the history of Japanese women and their role and status in postwar society. The first part – 'Background: the Loom of History' – deals briefly with women in Japan before the Meiji period and covers in considerable detail the major women's movements between the 1870s and the Allied occupation period. Part two – 'The Fabric of Modern Times' – describes the involvement of Japanese women in society, economic affairs, and the political process during the 1950s, 1960s and 1970s, and considers their attitudes towards international problems as well as their participation in inter-cultural activities. A chronology of events concerning Japanese women and a listing of major women's organisations in Japan are among the appendixes.

582 **The women of Suye mura.**
Robert J. Smith, Ella Lury Wiswell.   Chicago; London: University of Chicago Press, 1982. 293p. map. bibliog.

Suye mura, an agricultural community in southern Kyūshū, was the object of intensive study during the mid-1930s by John Embree (Wiswell's husband) in his classic account *Suye mura: a Japanese village* (q.v.). The extensive field-notes in the form of journal entries of daily events and conversations that Wiswell in turn kept during the course of their year-long stay there form the basis of this ethnographic case-study of that village viewed from the perspective of its women. It describe the daily lives, activities, behaviour, interpersonal relations, and roles of these rural women and provides considerable information about their concerns and world-views. Smith, an authority on Japanese society, assumed responsibility for reorganising Wiswell's material into a coherent study and for providing both interpretive commentaries and introductory and concluding chapters.

583 **Women against war.**
Compiled by Women's Division of Sōka Gakkai, translated by Richard L. Gage, introduction by Richard H. Minear. Tokyo; New York: Kodansha International, 1986. 247p. 2 maps.

The personal accounts of forty Japanese women who experienced the horrors of World War II and its immediate aftermath. Among their testimonies are the stories of women trying to make their way back to Japan from Manchuria, Korea, the Philippines, and Sakhalin during the chaotic months following the end of the war; of women struggling to provide for themselves and their families in the ruins of war-devastated Japan; of victims of the atomic bombing of Hiroshima; of women who fled to the countryside from Japan's fire-bombed cities; of women who prostituted themselves to American servicemen; and of women who were widowed by the war. Selected from a twelve-volume series entitled *Heiwa e no negai o komete* ('With Hopes for Peace', published in 1981 by the Sōka Gakkai), this collection of oral histories offers a personal Japanese perspective of World War II and its impact on ordinary people.

Fukuzawa Yukichi on Japanese women: selected works.
See item no. 194.

Flowers in salt: the beginnings of feminist consciousness in modern Japan.
See item no. 240.

The Hiroshima maidens: a story of courage, compassion, and survival.
See item no. 252.

Widows of Hiroshima: the life stories of nineteen peasant wives.
See item no. 259.

Reflections on the way to the gallows: rebel women in prewar Japan.
See item no. 290.

Samurai and silk: a Japanese and American heritage.
See item no. 297.

The confessions of Lady Nijō.
See item no. 310.

A daughter of the samurai. How a daughter of feudal Japan, living hundreds of years in one generation, became a modern American.
See item no. 313.

Facing two ways: the story of my life.
See item no. 328.

Tokyo Rose: orphan of the Pacific.
See item no. 387.

Issei, Nisei, war bride: three generations of Japanese American women in domestic service.
See item no. 388.

Womansword: what Japanese words say about women.
See item no. 413.

Japanese women's language.
See item no. 413.

Work and lifecourse in Japan.
See item no. 542.

Love match and arranged marriage: a Tokyo–Detroit comparison.
See item no. 558.

Letters from Sachiko: a Japanese woman's view of life in the land of the economic miracle.
See item no. 563.

Health, illness, and medical care in Japan: cultural and social dimensions.
See item no. 599.

Law and social change in postwar Japan.
See item no. 785.

The gossamer years: the diary of a noblewoman of Heian Japan.
See item no. 1013.

A certain woman.
See item no. 1046.

The doctor's wife.
See item no. 1047.

This kind of woman: ten stories by Japanese women writers, 1960–1976.
See item no. 1098.

The mother of dreams and other short stories: portrayals of women in modern Japanese fiction.
See item no. 1106.

Shunga: the art of love in Japan.
See item no. 1259.

Suzuki Harunobu: a selection of his color prints and illustrated books.
See item no. 1261.

Utamaro: colour prints and paintings.
See item no. 1262.

Psychology

584 **Public and private self in Japan and the United States: communicative styles of two cultures.**
Dean C. Barnlund. Tokyo: Simul Press, 1975. 201p. Reprinted, Yarmouth, Maine: Intercultural Press, 1989.

A comparative study of interpersonal communication in Japan and the United States, with particular focus on the distinctiveness of Japanese patterns of interaction. Basing his research on four surveys conducted among American and Japanese college students, Barnlund examines national differences in patterns of communication and considers verbal patterns, non-verbal patterns (e.g., touching), and defensive techniques that are used when confronted with threatening interpersonal situations. He argues that the 'public self' and the 'private self' have unique relationships in both countries. Among the author's findings are the tendency of the Japanese to keep a much wider range of thoughts to themselves, the greater likelihood of their reacting passively and evasively to embarrassing questions, and the existence of a much greater difference in conversational disclosure between mothers and fathers in Japan than in the United States. A concluding chapter examines the difficulties of communication between Americans and Japanese.

585 **The chrysanthemum and the sword: patterns of Japanese culture.**
Ruth Benedict. Boston: Houghton Mifflin, 1946; London: Secker and Warburg, 1947. 324p. Reprinted, Rutland, Vermont and Tokyo: Tuttle, 1954; New York: New American Library, 1967; Cleveland, Ohio: Meridian Books, 1967; London: Routledge and Kegan Paul, 1977; (with a foreword by Ezra F. Vogel) Boston, Massachusetts: Houghton Mifflin, 1989.

A highly influential but controversial analysis of Japanese personality and behaviour, written by an American cultural anthropologist during World War II. Beginning with the observation that Japan appears to be a land of contradictions – of both the cultivation of chrysanthemums and the cult of the sword – Benedict attempts to interpret those contradictions as rational parts of a complex culture. She identifies and analyses such basic concepts as the use of hierarchy as a mechanism for assigning people's social status, the importance of reciprocal obligations in social relationships and the related code regulating the repayment of debts, the Japanese sense of shame, and the necessity of clearing one's name by avenging insults or through suicide. She also explains some of the interactions of these concepts and shows how they are related to Japanese child-rearing practices and to attitudes towards one's emotions, sensual pleasures, and self-discipline. Benedict's findings are generally more applicable to traditional Japanese society than to contemporary Japan.

586 **With respect to the Japanese: a guide for Americans.**
John C. Condon, foreword by Kohei Gōshi, preface by George W. Renwick.   Yarmouth, Maine: Intercultural Press, 1984. 92p. bibliog. (InterAct Series).

The most serious mistake Americans can make when interacting with Japanese, Condon asserts, is to be insensitive to the differences between themselves and the Japanese simply because an affluent and technologically advanced Japan seems to be so 'Westernised'. His practical guide calls attention to some of these cultural differences, to the salient features of Japanese values and behaviour that affect communication and relationships, and to the critical importance of harmony in interpersonal relations for the Japanese. It also contrasts Japanese and American managerial styles, and responds to some of the most frequently asked questions that Americans have about Japan and the Japanese.

587 **The myth of Japanese uniqueness.**
Peter Dale.   London: Croom Helm; New York: St. Martin's Press, 1986. 233p. (Nissan Institute/Croom Helm Japanese Studies Series).

Dale critically examines the tradition of thought known as *nihonjinron*: the works of cultural nationalism concerned with Japan's ostensibly 'unique' national identity and with 'what it means to be Japanese'. He explores the foundations and the assumptions of the ideological structure – the 'successive layers of thought, from linguistics, through to family structure theory, sociological concepts, and psychoanalytical notions to philosophical constructs' – that underlie the *nihonjinron*, and challenges the widely held view that the Japanese are radically different from other peoples in their cultural, social, and psychological make-up. Dale contends that this influential stream of modern Japanese thought – one that has produced a vast array of scholarly and popular writings about the national character of the Japanese and has even influenced Western scholarship and interpretations of Japan – should be regarded as a mythological system rather than as a serious contribution to science or the social sciences.

588 **Socialization for achievement: essays on the cultural psychology of the Japanese.**
George A. De Vos, with contributions by Hiroshi Wagatsuma, William Caudill, Keiichi Mizushima.   Berkeley, California; London: University of California Press, 1973. 597p. bibliog.

A collection of eighteen essays that centre on normative role behaviour, achievement motivation, and deviancy and alienation. They include studies concerned with the psychological continuities of status and role behaviour in postwar Japan; social values and personal attitudes in primary human relations in rural Japan; value attitudes towards the role behaviour of women in two villages; the psycho-cultural significance of concern over death and illness among rural Japanese; achievement orientation, social self-identity, and Japanese economic growth; the entrepreneurial mentality of lower-class urban Japanese in manufacturing industries; achievement, culture and personality among Japanese Americans; criminality and deviancy in premodern Japan; the organisation and social function of Japanese gangs; delinquency and social change in modern Japan; the minority status of the *burakumin* and delinquency among them; the nature and concept of violence in student movements; and role of narcissism and the aetiology of Japanese suicide.

589 **The anatomy of dependence.**
Takeo Doi, translated with a foreword by John Bester. Tokyo; New York: Kodansha International, 1973. 170p. bibliog.

A leading psychiatrist and scholar's interpretation of interpersonal relations and emotional dependence among present-day Japanese. Doi examines the concept of *amae* ('the indulging, passive love which surrounds and supports the individual in a group, whether the family, neighbourhood or the world at large') in Japanese psychology and argues that a Japanese infant's natural feelings of dependence continue to be nurtured during childhood and evolve into an adult's reliance upon other individuals for goodwill and emotional support. These basic attitudes influence the Japanese outlook on life and the overall organisation of Japanese society. Doi also shows how *amae* can be identified in a wide range of activities, examines the psychological structure implied by the term *amae*, discusses its relationship to Japan's spiritual culture, describes such abnormal forms of behaviour as the fear of other people and the sense of injury into which *amae* sometimes is transformed, and considers certain contemporary social problems from the viewpoint of *amae*.

590 **The anatomy of self: the individual versus society.**
Takeo Doi, translated by Mark A. Harbison, foreword by Edward Hall. Tokyo; New York: Kodansha International, 1986. 163p.

A sequel to *The anatomy of dependence*, this book seeks to explain the relationship between individual psyche and group-oriented behaviour among the Japanese. Doi analyses the dyadic concepts of *omote/ura* (equivalent to 'outer appearance'/'inner reality') and of *tatemae/honne* ('collective norm'/'personal motive'), and suggests that the dualistic structures represented by these dyadic oppositions are profoundly related to the psychology of *amae*. Throughout this book, he discusses the roles of *omote* and *ura* in self-awareness, communication, and human relations. He examines, for example, the role of secrets in personal relations, and – arguing that the ideal state of the heart is one in which the individual is able to keep secrets – explains how the secret of an attractive personality is ultimately related to the existence of something secret in that personality. While his focus is primarily on Japanese psychology and culture, Doi also frequently offers comparisons with Western culture.

591 **Japanese culture and behavior: selected readings.**
Edited by Takie Sugiyama Lebra, William P. Lebra. Honolulu, Hawaii: University of Hawaii Press, 1986. rev. ed. 428p. bibliog.

An introductory text that addresses both the cultural context of Japanese behaviour and the behavioural manifestations of Japanese culture in an effort to present an updated, integrated portrait of the Japanese. This collection of essays stresses the complexity, conflict, and dynamism inherent in contemporary Japanese culture as it presents a wide range of readings – primarily by Japanese and Western specialists in the areas of anthropology, linguistics, psychiatry, and psychology – which focus on dominant, normative, and deviant behaviour. Dinner entertainment, child-rearing patterns, male chauvinism and love in marriage, domestic violence, morality and shared values, and patterns of social interaction are among the many topics that are explored in some depth.

592 **Japanese patterns of behavior.**
Takie Sugiyama Lebra. Honolulu, Hawaii: University Press of Hawaii, 1976. 295p. bibliog. (An East-West Center Book).
An interdisciplinary description and analysis of the seemingly contradictory aspects of contemporary Japanese behaviour. Lebra examines some of the most commonly held beliefs and values of the postwar generation, stresses the great importance which harmonious social interaction and social relationships have for them, and shows how this concern for proper social behaviour constitutes an important means for understanding Japanese behavioural patterns. In her explanation of the factors that influence behaviour in Japan, she discusses belongingness, empathy, dependency, the concept of occupying the proper place, reciprocity, early socialisation, selfhood, organised delinquency, and suicide as well as three selected types of therapy: the Naikan method of culturally based moral rehabilitation, Morita psychotherapy and *shinkeishitsu* (a type of neuroses), and spirit possession in a Japanese healing-cult.

593 **Mirror, sword and jewel: a study of Japanese characteristics.**
Kurt Singer, edited with an introduction by Richard Storry. London: Croom Helm; New York: Braziller, 1973. 174p.
Insightful reflections about Japan and the Japanese distilled from the personal observations and experiences of a German Jew who taught in Japan during the 1930s. Singer interprets some of the essential characteristics and patterns of Japanese society and psychology, among them the close bonds between man and nature; the 'fidelity of Japanese instinctive feelings'; the Japanese preoccupation with the ways of 'wrapping up ideas, things, feelings'; the value of the Japanese system of ritual customs in transforming ordinary daily life into a 'harmonious flow'; the importance of social harmony; the significance of the age group and patron–client relationships; the 'law of inescapable change and universal impermanence' that governs the psychological world of the Japanese; and the central role in Japanese life of movement, action, and inspired spontaneity. This work was reprinted under the title *Mirror, sword and jewel: the geometry of Japanese life* (Tokyo; New York: Kodansha International, 1981).

594 **Child development and education in Japan.**
Edited by Harold Stevenson, Hiroshi Azuma, Kenji Hakuta. New York: Freeman, 1986. 315p.
American and Japanese psychologists, educators, sociologists, and anthropologists depict the rearing and education of children in contemporary Japan. Eight essays that constitute a 'background' section cover such topics as the social and cultural background of child development, the special characteristics of the Japanese conception of the child, child-rearing concepts as a belief-value system of both society and the individual, the privatisation of family life in Japan, and the history and contemporary status of Japanese school education. These are followed by seven

empirical studies, including those concerned with the family influences on school readiness and achievement, the personality development of adolescents, the social development of children, Japanese achievement in mathematics, and the process of learning to read Japanese. A concluding section deals primarily with conceptual issues.

595 Social change and the individual: Japan before and after defeat in World War II.
Kazuko Tsurumi, foreword by Silvan S. Tomkins. Princeton, New Jersey: Princeton University Press, 1970. 441p. bibliog.

Tsurumi analyses the process of socialisation throughout an individual's lifetime from a theoretical point of view, contrasts the patterns of adult socialisation in Japanese society during the periods 1931-45 and 1945 to the 1960s respectively, examines the relationship between societal change and personality development, and shows the effects that major economic and social trends in postwar Japan have had on the attitudes and roles of various segments of the population. Her essays deal specifically with such topics as ideological conversion (*tenkō*) during the 1930s, moral education and socialisation in the prewar Japanese school and in the army, the efforts during the Tokyo war crimes trial (1946-48) to redirect the Japanese towards peace, socialisation through informal study groups among textile workers, the impact of the war on women, the changing roles of women as mothers and as wives, and the patterns of socialisation implemented by student movement organisations.

The Japanese and the Jews.
See item no. 4.

Death in life: survivors of Hiroshima.
See item no. 257.

Personality in Japanese history.
See item no. 289.

Six lives, six deaths: portraits from modern Japan.
See item no. 292.

Japan's invisible race: caste in culture and personality.
See item no. 373.

The unspoken way. *Haragei*: silence in Japanese business and society.
See item no. 406.

Heritage of endurance: family patterns and delinquency formation in urban Japan.
See item no. 571.

The psychological world of Natsume Sōseki.
See item no. 1112.

Crisis in identity and contemporary Japanese novels.
See item no. 1115.

A book of five rings.
See item no. 1447.

Medicine and Health

596 **Western medical pioneers in feudal Japan.**
John Z. Bowers. Baltimore, Maryland; London: Published for the
Josiah Macy, Jr., Foundation by Johns Hopkins Press, 1970. 245p.
bibliog.

Traces the evolution of Japanese knowledge of Western medicine during the
Tokugawa period by focusing on the lives and accomplishments of five physician-
explorers who were stationed at the Dutch trading post on the island of Deshima and
who served as intermediaries between Japanese and Western culture: Willem Ten
Rhijne (1647-1700), the first doctor at Deshima to describe Japanese medicine and
culture to the West; Engelbert Kaempfer (1651-1716), the German physician who
wrote the monumental *History of Japan*; Carl Pieter Thunberg (1743-1828), a Swede
who introduced the science of botany to Japan and wrote extensively about Japanese
flora; Philipp Franz von Siebold (1796-1866), the German physician who taught
Western medicine in Nagasaki and introduced many Japanese trees and plants to
Europe; and J. L. C. Pompe van Meerdervoort (1829-1908), the Dutch naval medical
officer who was invited by the Tokugawa shogunate to teach medicine in Nagasaki and
who founded Japan's first modern Western-style hospital and medical school.

597 **When the twain meet: the rise of Western medicine in Japan.**
John Z. Bowers. Baltimore, Maryland; London: Johns Hopkins
University Press, 1980. 173p. bibliog. (The Henry E. Sigerist
Supplements to the Bulletin of the History of Medicine; New Series, 5).

A sequel to Bowers' *Western medical pioneers in feudal Japan*, this book deals with the
growing influence of German medicine in Japan during the mid-nineteenth century and
the government's decision in the 1870s to adopt the German rather than the English
system of medical education. Bowers discusses the activities of Otto Mohnike, the
German physician who introduced smallpox vaccination and the stethoscope into
Japan; William Willis, a British physician who introduced techniques of military
surgery and methods of public hygiene; the German professor Erwin von Baelz, who
taught at the Tokyo Medical School; and other German, British, and American

physicians who played important roles in introducing Western medical practices into Japan and whose students became the country's medical leaders during the Meiji period.

598 **East Asian medicine in urban Japan: varieties of medical experience.**
Margaret M. Lock. Berkeley, California; London: University of California Press, 1980. 311p. bibliog. (Comparative Studies of Health Systems and Medical Care, 4).

The postwar urban medical scene has been characterised by the revival of a widespread interest in 'East Asian medicine'. Better known as *kanpō*, this type of medicine was introduced from China during the sixth century, was adapted to Japanese cultural conditions, and currently involves the use of a vast array of Chinese herbs as well as the techniques of acupuncture, moxibustion, and massage. Lock's ethnographic account about the varieties of medical beliefs and practices found in the city of Kyōto studies the philosophical foundations and historical development of *kanpō*; Japanese attitudes towards health, illness and the human body; the use of herbal medicine and the clinical practice of acupuncture, moxibustion, and *shiatsu* and *anma* (two types of massage); the schools that teach *kanpō*; the place of 'holism' in *kanpō*; and some of the problems inherent in the practice of Western-style medicine.

599 **Health, illness, and medical care in Japan: cultural and social dimensions.**
Edited by Edward Norbeck, Margaret Lock, foreword by Robert J. Smith, introduction by Margaret Lock. Honolulu, Hawaii: University of Hawaii Press, 1987. 202p. bibliog.

Six essays entitled 'The Japanese State of Health: a Political-Economic Perspective', 'Health Care Providers: Technology, Policy, and Professional Dominance', 'Care of the Aged in Japan', 'Japanese Models of Psychotherapy', 'Protests of a Good Wife and Wise Mother: the Medicalization of Distress in Japan', and 'Productivity, Sexuality, and Ideologies of Menopausal Problems in Japan'. The authors consider present-day medical care in Japan to be a 'culturally shaped part of a specific historical and social tradition' rather than a value-free scientific endeavour. They explore the effects of social, political, and cultural variables on contemporary Japanese ideas about health, illness, and medical care, and show how culturally constituted values and beliefs are integral to the experience of illness as well as to its interpretation and care.

600 **Illness and culture in contemporary Japan: an anthropological view.**
Emiko Ohnuki-Tierney. Cambridge, England; New York: Cambridge University Press, 1984. 242p. bibliog.

An account of the cultural meaning of health care in urban Japan. Ohnuki-Tierney examines everyday hygienic practices and beliefs; Japanese attitudes towards illness, the body and death, and the causes of illness; and the existence of a pluralistic system of medicine and health care encompassing traditional Japanese medicine of Chinese origin (*kanpō*), Western-derived biomedicine, and a belief in the ability of religious deities to cure illness. Her descriptions of the ways in which this pluralistic system functions and her investigations of such matters as family involvement in the care of the sick, the transformed nature of the profession of biomedical doctor, and the omnipresent nature of *kanpō* show that contemporary Japanese concepts and behaviour regarding health, illness, and health care are to a large extent culturally patterned.

601 **Morita psychotherapy.**
David K. Reynolds. Berkeley, California; London: University of California Press, 1976. 243p. bibliog.

Introduction to a Buddhist-based Japanese form of psychotherapy for the treatment of neuroses that was developed in the early twentieth century by Morita Shōma and is still being successfully practised in Japan. Reynolds studies both the theory and practice of this therapy. He presents a broad perspective of Morita psychotherapy and of its various styles; a detailed analysis of its practice at a hospital in Tokyo; a generalised discussion of selected aspects of the Japanese character that are relevant to an understanding of neuroses and their treatment in Japan; some consideration of the changes which have occurred in Morita therapy over a fifty-year period and their relationship to concomitant developments in Japanese culture; and comparisons of Morita therapy with other Japanese and Western forms of therapy designed to induce behavioural change.

602 **The quiet therapies: Japanese pathways to personal growth.**
David K. Reynolds, afterword by George De Vos. Honolulu, Hawaii: University Press of Hawaii, 1980. 135p. bibliog.

A brief introduction for the general reader to five forms of Japanese psychotherapy: Morita therapy (named after the professor of psychiatry who developed it), *naikan* ('introspection therapy'), *shadan* ('isolation therapy'), *seiza* ('quiet-sitting therapy'), and zen ('meditation therapy'). Reynolds describes each form of therapy from the perspective of a patient undergoing treatment, and offers some assessment of their methods as well as occasional short case-histories. All five Buddhist-based psychotherapies have a history of clinical success in treating neuroses in Japan.

603 **Health and illness in changing Japanese society.**
Kyōichi Sonoda. Tokyo: University of Tokyo Press, 1988. 170p. bibliog.

A collection of ten papers, oriented towards both the lay reader and the scholar, that focus on some of the problems of physical and mental health which have resulted from the rapid changes in life-styles and living environments accompanying Japan's postwar industrialisation and urbanisation. These papers are entitled: 'Urbanization and Health: Problems and Solutions'; 'Change in the Family and Community: the Quest for New Solidarity'; 'Health Trends and Problems of Medical Care'; 'Health Care for the Elderly in Japan: a Comparison with Developments in the United States'; 'Community Health and Medicine'; 'Traditional Medicine and Methods of Treatment'; 'SMON [Subacute Myelo Optico Neuropathy] and Other Socially Induced Diseases in Japan'; 'Three Medical Sociological Studies: Women Smokers, Health Checkups, and Reliance on Medications'; 'The Role of CATV [Cable Television] and Other Communications Media in Health Education'; and 'Review and Future Prospects of Health and Medical Sociology in Japan'.

604   **Doctors in politics: the political life of the Japan Medical Association.**
William E. Steslicke.   New York: Praeger, 1973. 302p. bibliog.
(Studies of the East Asian Institute, Columbia University) (Praeger
Special Studies in International Politics and Government).
A detailed case-study of pressure group politics involving the Japan Medical
Association (JMA), a nationwide professional organisation of nearly 100,000 practising
doctors which has exerted considerable influence on government medical policies
throughout most of the postwar period. Steslicke describes and analyses a year-long
(1960-61) campaign of the JMA – directed in particular at the Cabinet, the government
bureaucracy, and government party leaders – and the specific issues and controversies
involved in its effort to secure favourable government action on four points related to
Japan's system of health insurance.

The other Japan: postwar realities.
See item no. 34.

A guide to Japanese hot springs.
See item no. 80.

Epidemics and mortality in early modern Japan.
See item no. 172.

Hiroshima and Nagasaki: the physical, medical, and social effects of the atomic bombing.
See item no. 253.

Hiroshima diary: the journal of a Japanese physician, August 6–September 30, 1945.
See item no. 259.

Chronicle of my mother.
See item no. 327.

Noguchi and his patrons.
See item no. 343.

Dr. Willis in Japan, 1862–1877: British medical pioneer.
See item no. 353.

The honorable elders revisited: a revised cross-cultural analysis of aging in Japan.
See item no. 540.

Island of dreams: environmental crisis in Japan.
See item no. 957.

Minamata.
See item no. 959.

Furo: the Japanese bath.
See item no. 1457.

Politics and
Government

General

605 **Organization of the government of Japan.**
Edited by the Administrative Management Bureau, Administrative
Management Agency, Prime Minister's Office [Gyōsei Kanri Kyoku,
Gyōsei Kanrichō, Sōrifu]. Tokyo: Institute of Administrative
Management [Gyōsei Kanri Kenkyū Sentā], 1977- . *ca*.142p. annual.
(Gyōsei Kanri Kenkyū Sentā, 1-1 Higashi-Ikebukuro 3-chōme,
Toshima-ku, Tokyo 170, Japan).
An introductory overview with descriptions of the functions and purposes of individual
government bodies, charts summarising their organisational structure, and listings of
their addresses. Coverage is provided for the Prime Minister's Office and its various
agencies; the Ministries of Justice, Foreign Affairs, Finance, Education, Health and
Welfare, Agriculture, Forestry and Fisheries, International Trade and Industry,
Transport, Post and Telecommunications, Labour, Construction, and Home Affairs;
the Board of Audit; and public corporations. Also included are translations of the
Constitution, the Cabinet Law, and the National Government Organisation Law.

606 **Against the state: politics and social protest in Japan.**
David E. Apter, Nagayo Sawa. Cambridge, Massachusetts; London:
Harvard University Press, 1984. 271p.
A case-study of the large-scale protest movement against government construction of
the New Tokyo International Airport in the Sanrizuka area of Narita City, Chiba
Prefecture. Apter and Sawa describe the background of the movement, depict and
chronicle its development during the late 1960s and throughout the 1970s, and analyse
the motivations and viewpoints of the farmers, the militants, and the government
officials and politicians who were directly involved. These protests were characterised
by violent battles in which the Sanrizuka farmers who faced the loss of their land and
groups of militant leftists who supported their struggle for ideological reasons

248

confronted the Japanese riot police who were assigned to protect the construction area and the airport facilities following their completion.

607 **Japan's parliament: an introduction.**
Hans H. Baerwald. London; New York: Cambridge University Press, 1974. 155p. bibliog.
A brief but authoritative study of Japan's bicameral legislature, the national Diet. Baerwald is particularly concerned with (1) the prewar origins and historical evolution of the Diet as well as the impact of this heritage on its place in contemporary Japanese politics; (2) those features of Japan's political parties – especially the central role of personal factions and factionalism in intra-party politics and the character of the postwar electoral system – which significantly influence their manner of operation within the Diet; (3) the internal organisation of the Diet (including the standing committee system of the Diet and the powers of the presiding officers of both houses) and the ways in which the Diet's rules of procedure affect its ability to serve as Japan's constitutionally mandated supreme legislative organ; and (4) the confrontational politics and periodic turmoil which tend to characterise the proceedings of the Diet as well as the ideological, structural, and value-oriented factors that have promoted such scenes of confrontation.

608 **Contemporary Japanese budget politics.**
John Creighton Campbell. Berkeley, California; London: University of California Press, 1977. 308p. bibliog. (Studies of the East Asian Institute, Columbia University).
A detailed examination of the process of budget-making in postwar Japan that focuses on the 'annual cycle of strategies and tactics' involved in compiling the General Account budget between 1954 and 1974. Campbell indicates that budgeting has become central to Japanese politics since 'most domestic policy matters are determined during the annual compilation process, and accordingly are conditioned by the intricate formal and informal rules of the budgetary game'. He then describes and analyses the behaviour of the primary actors in the budgetary system: the spending ministries and agencies which strive to increase their share of the budget, the Budget Bureau and some other Ministry of Finance staff who determine the desirable levels of government expenditures and revenues and seek to coordinate them with a wide range of policies, and certain organs of the governing Liberal Democratic Party which try to ensure that the final budget adequately accommodates the party's political needs.

609 **The politics of labor legislation in Japan: national–international interaction.**
Ehud Harari. Berkeley, California; London: University of California Press, 1973. 221p. bibliog.
A study of the complex policy-making process in Japan with particular emphasis on the area of labour policy. Harari investigates the interrelationship of politics at the local-prefectural, national, and international levels as witnessed in Japanese labour's efforts to pressure the Diet into both ratifying ILO (International Labour Organisation) Convention no. 87 ('Freedom of Association and Protection of the Right to Organise') and undertaking concomitant revision of several restrictive Japanese labour laws. He traces the history of the struggle for the right to organise and strike by public employees in both prewar and postwar Japan; explains why Japanese labour union

leaders appealed to the ILO in 1957 for assistance in pressuring the Japanese government to act positively on what was essentially a domestic issue; indicates the domestic and international considerations that affected the government's response; and explains why this issue has not yet been fully resolved.

610 **Japanese political culture: change and continuity.**
Takeshi Ishida. New Brunswick, New Jersey; London: Transaction Books, 1983. 173p. bibliog.

Ishida, a leading Japanese social scientist, investigates the essential features of the modern Japanese value system and organisational structure, both of which combine traditional and innovative elements. In this collection of eight general articles, he deals with the integration of conformity and competition in Japanese society and culture, the interpretations of Max Weber that have been advanced by Japanese scholars, the problem of East and West, the elements of tradition and 'renovation' in Japan between the late 1920s and 1945, Japan's traditional concept of peace compared with the meaning of the word 'peace' in other cultures, the changing Japanese images of Mahatma Gandhi, and the importance of non-violent direct action as a means of realising justice through social change.

611 **Japanese politics – an inside view: readings from Japan.**
Edited and translated with introductions by Hiroshi Itoh. Ithaca, New York; London: Cornell University Press, 1973. 248p. bibliog.

A collection of nine representative empirical studies, written by Japanese scholars, that are concerned with various aspects of policy-making at the national and local levels, with public opinion and voting behaviour, and with the formulation of foreign policy. These articles are entitled: 'An Outline of the Policy-making Process in Japan'; 'The Small and Medium-Sized Enterprises Organization Law'; 'Interest Groups in the Legislative Process'; 'Electoral Behavior in a Conservative Stronghold: a Case Study of the Ishikawa Prefecture'; 'The Voting Behavior and Party Preference of Labor'; 'Consciousness of Human Rights and Problems of Equality'; 'Leadership and Power Structure in Local Politics'; 'Japan's Voting Behavior in the United Nations'; and 'Consciousness of Peace and National Security'.

612 **Japan's public policy companies.**
Chalmers Johnson. Washington, DC: American Enterprise Institute for Public Policy Research; Stanford, California: Hoover Institution on War, Revolution and Peace, Stanford University, 1978. 173p. (AEI-Hoover Policy Studies, 24) (Hoover Institution Studies, 60).

The Japan External Trade Organisation (JETRO), the Japan Foundation, the Japanese National Railways, the Nippon Telegraph and Telephone Public Corporation, and the Overseas Economic Cooperation Fund are among the public corporations and public–private enterprises which constitute an important sector of the government's economic bureaucracy and serve a variety of state purposes. Johnson describes the entire range of these public policy companies, their prewar origins and the impact of the Allied occupation period, their financing and control, the practice (known as *amakudari*) of employing retired government officials as chief executives or board members of public and private corporations, the history and role of government corporations in the energy sector, and the issue of bureaucratism. An appendix provides tabular information about 157 past and present public companies, including the percentage of fixed capital supplied by the government, and the ministries (or agencies) which control them.

613 **Japan's civil service system: its structure, personnel, and politics.**
Paul S. Kim. New York; London: Greenwood Press, 1988. 193p.
bibliog. (Contributions in Political Science, 202).

An introduction to the structure, personnel, and policy-making processes of the civil service system. An examination of the administrative structure through which the National Personnel Authority and the Management and Coordination Agency co-ordinate and control the operation of the bureaucracy is followed by a description of the systems for recruiting and retiring higher civil servants and by a profile of the background and career development of a typical bureaucrat. Japan's local public administration is also considered. Finally Kim presents two case-studies of the bureaucratic decision-making process as it applied to the history textbook controversy of the early 1980s and to the involvement of higher civil servants in the national defence policy-making process. For an earlier, complementary study of the Japanese bureaucracy, see Akira Kubota's *Higher civil servants in postwar Japan: their social origins, educational backgrounds, and career patterns* (Princeton, New Jersey: Princeton University Press, 1969, 197p.), which surveys a sample of 1,353 civil servants who held the rank of section chief or above. Robert M. Spaulding, Jr.'s *Imperial Japan's higher civil service examinations* (Princeton, New Jersey: Princeton University Press, 1967, 416p.), in turn, studies the origins and evolution of the modern Japanese method of selecting higher civil servants through an analysis of the examination system which regulated access to the inner civil bureaucracy in prewar Japan and shaped its political outlook.

614 **Authority and the individual in Japan: citizen protest in historical perspective.**
Edited with an introduction by J. Victor Koschmann. Tokyo:
University of Tokyo Press, 1978. 318p.

Twelve prominent Japanese scholars and critics discuss political authority in Japan and patterns of obedience and disobedience before and after World War II. Part one – 'The Individual as Subject: Prewar Japan' – deals with the structure and dynamics of centralised rule under the imperial state and analyses some aspects of the resistance against that rule waged in the name of Christianity, Marxism, and liberalism. Part two – 'The Individual as Citizen: Postwar Japan' – focuses on the ethos, behaviour, and political significance of citizen protest in postwar society. It also highlights two contrasting views of the basis for civic action: one emphasizing individual action by concerned citizens, the other stressing communal resistance and political action. Many of the essays are interpretive in nature and polemical in their approach.

615 **The political dynamics of Japan.**
Junichi Kyōgoku, translated by Nobutaka Ike. Tokyo: University of
Tokyo Press, 1987. 239p. bibliog.

An abridged translation of a work that analyses contemporary Japanese politics, indicates how the political process functions on a daily basis, and points out a number of basic problems and current trends. In the course of his presentation, Kyōgoku discusses the role of religion, mass media, personal connections, and group ethics within a political context. He shows how Japanese politics represent a combination of political institutions such as parliamentary democracy that have been imported from the West or patterned after Western institutions, and traditional and social institutions, Japanese cultural values, and religious beliefs that heavily influence the political behaviour of political leaders and the electorate.

616 **Democracy in contemporary Japan.**
Edited with an introduction by Gavan McCormack, Yoshio Sugimoto. Armonk, New York; London: M. E. Sharpe; Sydney, New South Wales: Hale and Iremonger, 1986. 272p.

A collection of essays by thirteen Australian and Japanese scholars who are concerned with the 'gradual erosion of local autonomy and reestablishment of central, bureaucratic authority' in postwar Japan. Regarding this process as inimical to popular democracy, they explore the degree to which 'responsibilities, initiative and, above all, power have been devolved to the grass roots level' and seek to determine the extent to which democracy 'as a participatory process' is operative in Japan today. Their essays generally assume the form of critical commentaries about the state, society, education, labour, citizens' movements, women, human rights, and science. Typical are articles entitled 'The Manipulative Bases of "Consensus" in Japan', 'Sources of Conflict in the "Information Society"', 'Educational Democracy versus State Control', 'Class Struggle in Postwar Japan', 'The Reality of Enterprise Unionism', 'Democracy Derailed: Citizens' Movements in Historical Perspective', and 'Crime, Confession, and Control'.

617 **Politics and government in Japan.**
Theodore H. McNelly. Lanham, Maryland; London: University Press of America, 1984. 3rd ed. 274p. 2 maps. bibliog.

This description of Japan's political institutions and processes in both historical and comparative perspective emphasizes the fundamental changes that have been occurring in the Japanese polity. Designed primarily as a textbook, it covers the political development of Japan, the Allied occupation period (1945-52) and the introduction of democratic reforms, contemporary Japanese interest groups, political parties, the legislature and the courts, the emperor system and the cabinet, local government, Japanese foreign relations, and the future prospects of democracy in Japan. A list of suggested readings follows each chapter and the text of the postwar constitution is included.

618 **Thought and behaviour in modern Japanese politics.**
Masao Maruyama, edited by Ivan Morris, translations by Ivan Morris and others. London; New York: Oxford University Press, 1969. expanded ed. 407p. bibliog. (Oxford in Asia College Textbooks).

This classic work offers a challenging introduction to twentieth-century Japanese intellectual and political history. Some of Maruyama's essays deal with general questions like political power, but most of them focus on the Japanese political scene and are concerned with such subjects as the theory and psychology of ultra-nationalism in Japan during the 1930s and 1940s, the ideology and dynamism of prewar Japanese fascism, the thought and behavioural patterns of Japan's wartime leaders, the theoretical background and prospects of nationalism in Japan, and politics as a science in Japan. Maruyama examines modern Japanese politics in terms of Japan's general cultural context and the pattern of interpersonal relationships, paying particular attention to the 'impact of non-political behaviour and activities in politics'. He also defines the underlying value-systems of the Japanese and shows how they affected the country's political leadership and their decision-making process.

619 **Policy and politics in Japan: creative conservatism.**
T. J. Pempel.   Philadelphia: Temple University Press, 1982. 330p. bibliog. (Policy and Politics in Industrial States).
An explanation of the particular mix of consensus and conflict that has characterised Japanese policy-making processes during the post-World War II period and the blend of success and failure in policy outcomes pursued by the ruling Liberal Democratic Party (LDP). Pempel deals with the LDP's creative but conservative responses to changing conditions in the six areas of economic policy, labour–management relations, social welfare, higher education, environmental protection, and administrative reform. For each of these areas, he analyses the context of the policy problem, considers the agenda set out for the problem, and traces the consequences of policy for official objectives, for the distribution of power within the area, and for other policies. He also provides illustrative readings drawn principally from government documents, interpretations or critiques of policy, and politically informed analysis.

620 **Policymaking in contemporary Japan.**
Edited with an introduction by T. J. Pempel.   Ithaca, New York; London: Cornell University Press, 1977. 345p. bibliog.
Essays by American and Japanese scholars describe and analyse 'policymaking within diverse but representative political contexts in contemporary Japan'. A broad overview of the published literature of Japanese policy-making is followed by in-depth case-studies dealing with the government's decision to have Prime Minister Tanaka Kakuei visit Peking in 1972, interest-group politics and the government's payment of compensation to repatriated Japanese for their loss of overseas assets at the end of World War II, the long-term policy of subsidising the price of rice produced by Japanese farmers, the government's responses to the problem of high levels of industrial pollution, and the resolution of different higher educational issues through dramatically different policy-making procedures. One essay – 'Policymaking in Japan: an Organizing Perspective' – demonstrates the wide variation that occurs in the process of policy-making and the positions of policy-makers over the course of a single year. Several other scholarly essays concerned with the effectiveness and responsiveness of political decision-making ('effectiveness, in the sense of the ability of the system to achieve goals, and responsiveness, meaning the extent to which both internal and external pressures are reacted to rather than ignored or resisted') can be found in *Dynamic and immobilist politics in Japan* by J. A. A. Stockwin and others (London: Macmillan; Honolulu, Hawaii: University of Hawaii Press, 1988, 342p.). These essays focus on Japan's political parties, her government bureaucracy, various interest groups, the economy, and the financial system.

621 **The political culture of Japan.**
Bradley M. Richardson.   Berkeley, California; London: University of California Press, 1974. 271p. bibliog.
A study of popular political culture, or mass political attitudes, during the 1950s and 1960s that is based primarily on the findings of nearly three hundred public opinion surveys conducted over a period of several years. Richardson examines four kinds of attitudes – mass involvement in politics, popular evaluations of the quality and

potential of public affairs, attitudes towards one's role as an active participant in the political process, and voting-choice behaviour and voting attitudes – and relates them to urban–rural residence and to the ages of the individuals surveyed. He also seeks to ascertain the degree and scope of attitudinal change among the Japanese that have resulted from postwar political reforms.

622   **Politics in Japan.**
Bradley M. Richardson, Scott C. Flanagan.   Boston, Massachusetts; Toronto, Ontario: Little, Brown, 1984. 459p. (The Little, Brown Series in Comparative Politics. A Country Study).
Employing a structural-functional approach to politics, Richardson and Flanagan study the performance of Japanese political structures and examine the interaction between politics and society during the 1960s and 1970s. The first half of their book focuses on Japan's social and political setting and on the patterns of Japanese political behaviour. It covers Japan's historical background, her postwar reforms and political structure, the contemporary context of political competition and the parties which structure that competition, Japan's distinctive cultural tradition, and the ways in which that tradition has influenced contemporary political attitudes and behaviour on both the mass and élite levels. The concluding half focuses on three central process functions – political recruitment, interest articulation and aggregation, and policy-making – and analyses the outputs, outcomes, and capabilities of the Japanese political system.

623   **The challenge of China and Japan: politics and development in East Asia.**
Edited with an introduction by Susan L. Shirk, with Kevin Kennedy. New York; Eastbourne, Sussex: Praeger, 1985. 533p. bibliog. (Praeger Special Studies) (Praeger Scientific).
The primary textbook for a course developed by the Global Understanding Project at National Public Radio, this anthology of sixty-two readings seeks 'to introduce the reader to the political and economic institutions of China and Japan and to explore the different ways these two countries have approached similar problems of public policy'. The first half surveys the differences between China and Japan, describes the cultural and historical patterns that shape the context of their contemporary politics, and examines their respective political parties, political leadership, government–business relationships, and bureaucracies. The second half shows how these political institutions have responded to problems which they share in common. The contributors focus on Chinese and Japanese industrial policy, foreign trade policy, agricultural policy, energy policy, education policy, social welfare policy, military defence policy, and foreign policy. All readings have been drawn from a variety of scholarly, popular, and government sources, most of them written by leading American specialists.

624   **Japan: divided politics in a growth economy.**
James Arthur Ainscow Stockwin.   London: Weidenfeld and Nicolson; New York: Norton, 1982. 2nd ed. 333p. 2 maps. bibliog. (Modern Governments).
This is the substantially revised and enlarged version of a 1975 introductory text to contemporary Japanese politics in which the close interrelationship between government and business is emphasized. The work covers the historical, social and political background of present-day Japan, the national Diet and the parliamentary elections,

the Liberal Democratic Party, the structure and process of the central government, the politics of opposition, some problems involving the postwar constitution, domestic political issues, and issues of foreign policy and defence. Institutional descriptions are balanced with analyses of Japan's political process. The Japanese political world is portrayed as remaining fundamentally divided over several basic issues even though successive governments since 1955 have provided the country with an extended period of stable conservative rule.

625 **Public administration in Japan.**
Edited by Kiyoaki Tsuji. Tokyo: University of Tokyo Press, 1984. 271p.
Prepared explicitly for foreign readers, this volume introduces and outlines the basic structure and operations of Japanese public administration at both the national and local levels. The contributors (Japanese scholars and government officials) specifically write about the legal framework of public administration; the Cabinet and administrative organisation; public corporations (the Japanese National Railways and Nippon Telegraph and Telephone); the civil service system; the mechanisms for controlling the number of staff in national public service; local administration and finance; the relations between the national and local governments; problems of local administration exemplified in the case of the Tokyo Metropolitan Government; legislative review; the budgetary system; administrative inspection; the state audit system; 'administrative guidance' (*gyōsei shidō*); administrative and judicial remedies against administrative actions; administrative counselling; and data-processing within the government.

626 **The Japanese Diet and the U.S. Congress.**
Edited by Francis R. Valeo, Charles E. Morrison; foreword by Jed Johnson, Jr; introduction by Francis R. Valeo, Tadashi Yamamoto. Boulder, Colorado: Westview Press, 1983. 212p. (A Westview Special Study). Reprinted, Epping, Essex: Bowker, 1985.
Twelve conference papers concerning the nature and role of the national legislative bodies of Japan and the United States provide a comparative study of these two institutions. The Diet and the Congress are first portrayed in the light of their respective histories and the places they occupy in their respective constitutional structures. The authors then discuss the organisation and distribution of power between and within each bicameral body, investigate the process by which laws are actually made, describe the nature of the tasks and the roles of the individual members of these two legislatures, and examine the complex procedures of budgeting and finance. Final chapters explore the role of these two institutions in matters relating to defence, trade, and foreign policy.

627 **Japan's political system.**
Robert E. Ward. Englewood Cliffs, New Jersey: Prentice-Hall, 1978. 2nd ed. 253p. 2 maps. bibliog. (Comparative Asian Governments Series).
An introductory study of the postwar political system with particular emphasis on the government's performance in allocating its attention, funds, and resources among appropriate spheres of political concern and activity; and on its ability to cope with long-term problems of political development and modernisation. In order 'to

illuminate the functioning and performance of the Japanese political system', Ward both surveys and analyses Japan's political history and ecology, her social structure and political culture, present-day political interest groups, political parties, elections, the leadership and organs of government, and governmental performance in both domestic affairs and foreign relations. The texts of the 1947 Constitution and the 1960 Treaty of Mutual Cooperation and Security between the United States and Japan appear within the appendixes.

Modern Japanese organization and decision-making.
See item no. 39.

Political development in modern Japan.
See item no. 239.

Postwar politics in Japan, 1945-1955.
See item no. 274.

Nationalism and the right wing in Japan: a study of post-war trends.
See item no. 276.

Democratizing Japan: the Allied occupation.
See item no. 280.

Japan's political revolution under MacArthur: a participant's account.
See item no. 281.

Brush strokes: moments from my life.
See item no. 339.

Who's who in Japanese government, 1988/89.
See item no. 366.

Conflict in Japan.
See item no. 538.

Japanese urbanism: industry and politics in Kariya, 1872–1972.
See item no. 547.

Migration in metropolitan Japan: social change and political behavior.
See item no. 557.

Political women in Japan: the search for a place in political life.
See item no. 580.

Doctors in politics: the political life of the Japan Medical Association.
See item no. 604.

America versus Japan: a comparative study of business–government relations conducted at the Harvard Business School.
See item no. 801.

Inside the Japanese system: readings on contemporary society and political economy.
See item no. 809.

The political economy of Japan. Volume 1: The domestic transformation.
See item no. 817.

Big business in Japanese politics.
See item no. 846.

The business of the Japanese state: energy markets in comparative and historical perspective.
See item no. 850.

Japan, disincorporated: the economic liberalization process.
See item no. 856.

Japan's financial markets: conflict and consensus in policymaking.
See item no. 857.

Government policy towards industry in the United States and Japan.
See item no. 884.

Environmental protest and citizen politics in Japan.
See item no. 958.

Japan's militant teachers: a history of the left-wing teachers' movement.
See item no. 967.

Japanese radicals revisited: student protest in postwar Japan.
See item no. 969.

Patterns of Japanese policymaking: experiences from higher education.
See item no. 974.

Teachers and politics in Japan.
See item no. 977.

The political character of the Japanese press.
See item no. 1485.

AMPO: Japan-Asia Quarterly Review.
See item no. 1488.

Far Eastern Economic Review.
See item no. 1501.

Pacific Affairs.
See item no. 1536.

Who's who in Japan.
See item no. 1574.

An introduction to Japanese government publications.
See item no. 1593.

Japanese national government publications in the Library of Congress: a bibliography.
See item no. 1602.

See also the sections under 'History' for political history.

Political parties

628 **Suburban Tokyo: a comparative study in politics and social change.**
Gary D. Allinson. Berkeley, California; London: University of
California Press, 1979. 258p. 3 maps. bibliog.

A comparative, cross-disciplinary study of the growth of opposition party strength in
the western Tokyo suburbs of Musashino and Fuchū. Allinson describes the social,
economic, and demographic processes of these two communities as they developed
into densely populated cities between the 1920s and the 1970s. He analyses the political
changes which have ensued, showing how these processes have been interrelated with
long-term trends in electoral politics characterised by a shift among voters away from
support for such conservative parties as the Liberal Democratic Party and towards the
opposition Socialist parties. In addition, Allinson investigates the impact on political
behaviour of such variables as the mobilisation of voters, the recruitment of leaders,
local administrative policies, and the political activities of voluntary organisations and
pressure groups.

629 **Party politics in Japan.**
Hans H. Baerwald. London; Boston, Massachusetts: Allen and
Unwin, 1986. 204p. bibliog.

An introduction for the general reader to Japanese party politics, especially since the
mid-1970s. Baerwald first describes the structure and operation of the party system
between 1955 and 1985, paying particular attention to factionalism within the Liberal
Democratic Party (LDP), and analyses the nature of the postwar electoral systems. He
then discusses the national Diet's operations and its internal governance, the strategies
of the parties within this legislative body, rivalry among LDP factions in the Diet, and
the changing relationship between the governing and opposition parties, as well as such
questions as whether the Diet has fulfilled its constitutional mandate, whether it is a
truly representative assembly, and what its future is likely to be. An epilogue covers
the 6 July 1986 election and the Third Nakasone Cabinet.

630 **Socialist parties in postwar Japan.**
Allan B. Cole, George O. Totten, Cecil H. Uyehara, with a
contributed chapter by Ronald P. Dore. New Haven, Connecticut;
London: Yale University Press, 1966. 490p. bibliog. (Studies on Japan's
Social Democratic Parties, vol. 2).

A comprehensive examination of the evolution of Japan's non-communist socialist
parties between their revival in 1945 and the early 1960s. While these parties never
gained full control of the government through national elections, they nevertheless
constituted a significant political force within the Diet and were the main opposition
throughout to the conservative parties of Japan. This study opens with a short history
of the postwar socialist movement in terms of the major events and controversies in
which it was involved. Part two deals with the principles and theories of the socialist
parties, their political tactics, some of the major issues confronting them, and their
economic and foreign policies. The third part presents an account of the party organs
and their functions as well as of their leaders and factions. Finally the authors analyse
the socialists' electoral and organisational support among organised labour, the
farmers, and Japan's growing urban middle class.

631 **Election campaigning Japanese style.**
Gerald L. Curtis. New York; London: Columbia University Press,
1971. 275p. map. bibliog. (Studies of the East Asian Institute,
Columbia University). Reprinted, Tokyo; New York: Kodansha
International, 1983.
A first-hand account of how Satō Bunsei, a non-incumbent member of the Liberal
Democratic Party, successfully organised the campaign which resulted in his January
1967 election to the Lower House of the national Diet as the representative for a semi-
rural district in Ōita Prefecture of northeastern Kyūshū. Curtis examines the politics
involved in this conservative candidate's efforts to secure party endorsement, Satō's
campaign strategy, his campaign organisation in both the rural and metropolitan areas
of his district, the restrictions imposed by the Election Law and the ways in which they
could be circumvented, the intermixture of traditional methods and new practices, the
use of the *kōenkai* (a mass membership organisation) to mobilise support, and Satō's
formal and informal campaign. In addition to providing insights into campaign
practices and the electoral process within a single voting district, this study illuminates
various aspects of Japan's postwar electoral system and the country's political
processes.

632 **The Japanese way of politics.**
Gerald L. Curtis. New York; London: Columbia University Press,
1988. 301p. bibliog. (Studies of the East Asian Institute, Columbia
University).
Drawing heavily on information derived from extended discussions with Japanese
political leaders, this book focuses on the evolution of Japanese politics during the
more than three decades of Liberal Democratic Party (LDP) rule. As the story of how
the political system has absorbed, reacted to, and helped promote and channel the
momentous economic and social changes which have occurred since World War II, it is
an account of 'the dynamics of a political system that has combined stability in terms of
party power with a remarkable capacity for flexibility and change'. Curtis considers the
transformation of the postwar political party system; the 'perpetuating dominance' of
the LDP as well as its organisation of political power; the Japan Socialist Party as a
perpetual opposition party; campaigns, financing and the modern party; and the
changing Japanese voter. An epilogue sums up some of the author's views about the
Japanese way of politics.

633 **Party in power: the Japanese Liberal-Democrats and policy-making.**
Haruhiro Fukui. Berkeley, California: University of California Press;
Canberra, ACT: Australian National University Press, 1970. 301p.
bibliog. (Publications of the Center for Japanese and Korean Studies).
A detailed description and analysis of the behaviour of the Liberal Democratic Party
(LDP) in various decision-making situations during the 1950s and 1960s. Fukui focuses
on 'the processes involved in the formulation of policies over issues of a more or less
controversial character, as interpreted in terms of the organisational framework and
the interaction of persons and of groups, rather than of doctrinal or ideological
factors'. His book presents (1) a discussion of the historical background of the basic
organisational framework and characteristics of conservative party politics in
contemporary Japan; (2) an examination of four selected factors underlying LDP
policy-making: party membership, party organisation, intra-party factionalism, and

connections with influential external groups which provide support (especially votes and funds); and (3) three case-studies – of government compensation to former landlords, constitutional revision, and relations with the People's Republic of China – which document and illustrate the LDP's policy-making processes.

634 **The Japanese party system: from one-party rule to coalition government.**
Ronald J. Hrebenar, with contributions by J. A. A. Stockwin, Peter Berton, Nobuo Tomita, Akira Nakamura. Boulder, Colorado; London: Westview Press, 1986. 330p. bibliog.

An introduction to the Japanese political party system and to the major and minor parties which presently exist at the national level: the Japan Socialist Party and the Japan Communist Party (the two long-term, leftist-oriented opposition parties), the Kōmeitō ('Clean Government Party'), the Democratic Socialist Party, the New Liberal Club and the mini-parties that have emerged in recent years, and the dominant Liberal Democratic Party (LDP). Hrebenar pays particular attention to party structures, electoral processes, factional and personal organisational identity, and the numerous functions of Japanese political recruitment and leadership. In addition, he surveys the major patterns of change in the postwar party system, analyses the impact of the electoral system on Japanese parties, discusses the money base of Japanese politics, and comments on the prospects for the LDP-centred coalition government in the years ahead.

635 **Communism in Japan: a case of political naturalization.**
Paul F. Langer, introduction by Jan. F. Triska. Stanford, California: Hoover Institution Press, 1972. 112p. bibliog. (Hoover Institution Studies, 30) (Comparative Communist Party Politics).

The Japan Communist Party (JCP) has remained a leading opposition party ever since its legalisation shortly after World War II. Following an overview of the prewar emergence and evolution of the JCP, Langer describes its postwar political role and status; party leadership and membership, and organisational structure; the domestic and international environments in which it operates; JCP doctrine, political strategy, and electoral record; the dualities in the Japanese Communist leadership; the role of peripheral organisations; the JCP's relations with the major ruling Communist parties; its reaction to the Sino–Soviet conflict of the 1960s; and the major national and cross-national determinants of JCP behaviour. Also included is a chronology of the communist movement in Japan between April 1921 and July 1970. For a more detailed study of the JCP after the war, see *The Japanese communist movement, 1920–1966*, by Robert A. Scalapino (Berkeley, California: University of California Press; London: Cambridge University Press, 1967, 412p.), which is concerned primarily with the activities of the party during the early 1960s.

636 **Political leadership in contemporary Japan.**
Edited with an introduction by Terry Edward MacDougall. Ann Arbor, Michigan: Center for Japanese Studies, University of Michigan, 1982. 145p. bibliog. (Michigan Papers in Japanese Studies, 1).

Six American scholars analyse the style and structure of political leadership on the national and local levels in essays entitled '*Kanryō* vs. *shomin*: Contrasting Dynamics of Conservative Political Leadership in Postwar Japan'; 'Liberal Democrats in Disarray: Intergenerational Conflict in the Conservative Camp'; 'Asukata Ichio and Some Dilemmas of Socialist Leadership in Japan'; 'Japanese Parties and Parliament: Changing Leadership Roles and Role Conflict'; 'Mayoral Leadership in Japan: What's in a Sewer Pipe?'; and 'Power behind the Throne'. Each of these essays focuses on one or more political leaders, among them Fukuda Takeo, Tanaka Kakuei, Kōno Yōhei, Suzuki Heizaburō, and Matsunaga Yasuzaemon. By showing that these individuals are characterised by a variety of leadership styles, goals, and skills, this volume helps put to rest the stereotypical view of a uniform managerial style of political leadership in present-day Japan.

637 **The Japanese Socialist Party and neutralism: a study of a political party and its foreign policy.**
James Arthur Ainscow Stockwin. Clayton, Victoria: Melbourne University Press; London: Cambridge University Press, 1968. 197p. bibliog.

A carefully documented, balanced presentation of the political and ideological history of the Japan Socialist Party (JSP), the major opponent of Liberal Democratic Party rule, and of the fluctuations that occurred in this party's avowed policy of 'neutralism' during the two decades following World War II. In seeking to understand 'what Japanese socialists mean when they talk of neutralism, and what kind of party it is that puts forward this particular set of policies', Stockwin explores several topics including the complex factional divisions within the JSP and its relations with both left-wing and right-wing elements; the relationship between personal and factional politics and the evolution of the party's foreign policy; the debates within its leadership concerning neutralism; and JSP attitudes towards US–Japanese relations, nuclear weapons, and comparable foreign policy issues.

638 **How the conservatives rule Japan.**
Nathaniel B. Thayer. Princeton, New Jersey: Princeton University Press, 1969. 349p. bibliog. (Studies of the East Asian Institute, Columbia University).

A detailed analysis of the organisation, internal structure, and operation of the Liberal Democratic Party (LDP), the political party that has governed Japan uninterruptedly since its formation in 1955. Thayer, a press attaché at the US Embassy in Tokyo from 1962 to 1966, explores the realities of the LDP's operation; the critical role of party factions; the LDP's relations with business and industrial interests; the organisation and financing of local and general elections, particularly the elections for the lower house of the Diet; the selection of a party president; the formation of a new government cabinet; policy formulation and decision-making within the LDP; and the process of running the party. Because the LDP is 'an amalgam of personal power lodged in the factions and institutional power lodged in the party organs', the balance between the two constitutes a major focus of this study.

Japan in the 1980s: papers from a symposium on contemporary Japan held at Sheffield University, England, September 11–13, 1980.
See item no. 27.

The Japanese Communist Party, 1922–1945.
See item no. 192.

Red flag in Japan: international communism in action.
See item no. 192.

Parties out of power in Japan, 1931–1941.
See item no. 193.

Party rivalry and political change in Taishō Japan.
See item no. 198.

Hara Kei in the politics of compromise, 1905–1915.
See item no. 224.

The social democratic movement in prewar Japan.
See item no. 247.

The Sōkagakkai and mass society.
See item no. 514.

Japan's parliament: an introduction.
See item no. 607.

Japanese politics – an inside view: readings from Japan.
See item no. 611.

Prefectural and local government

639 **Japanese prefectures and policymaking.**
Steven R. Reed.   Pittsburgh, Pennsylvania: University of Pittsburgh Press, 1986. 197p. bibliog. (Pitt Series in Policy and Institutional Studies).

Reed offers a fresh perspective on relations between the central government and local administrations through his case-studies of recent policy-making in Chiba, Saga, and Saitama, three of Japan's forty-seven prefectures. He compares the records of their respective governments in the critical policy areas of pollution control, the provision of publicly financed housing, and access to good high-school education. Examining the links between various levels of government, he identifies the circumstances under which local governments have adopted independent policies as well as the circumstances under which the central government has influenced local policy-making. The once-clear dichotomy between national and local spheres of responsibility is found to have disappeared, in part because of the significant increases in local innovation that occurred during the late 1960s and the early 1970s.

640 **The politics of regional policy in Japan: localities incorporated?**
Richard J. Samuels.   Princeton, New Jersey; Guildford, Surrey:
Princeton University Press, 1983. 290p.

This study of the participation of local governments in regional policy-making,
particularly during the 1970s, modifies a number of widely held perceptions about the
centralised nature of the postwar Japanese state, the role of political leadership, and
the formation of political coalitions in Japan. It describes the mechanisms available to
Japanese local governments for jointly implementing desirable policies, and discusses
the horizontal relationships which exist among local autonomous bodies. It also
chronicles the largely unsuccessful schemes that the Ministry of Home Affairs has
pursued in recent decades for amalgamating prefectures or otherwise creating large
regional administrations, and presents a case-study of the policies and politics that
were involved in planning for the construction of a major bridge across Tokyo Bay.

641 **Local government in Japan.**
Kurt Steiner.   Stanford, California: Stanford University Press, 1965.
564p. bibliog.

A comprehensive introduction to Japanese local government covering activities from
the prefectural and metropolitan levels down to the ward level. An historical survey of
the institutions and processes which shaped the modern local governmental system as it
evolved between 1871 and 1952 constitutes the first part of this study. Part two seeks to
determine the degree to which local autonomy existed both in law and in reality as of
the early 1960s. Steiner describes and analyses the constitutional provisions for local
autonomy, the future of the prefectures, the municipalities and special local public
bodies, the informal rural and urban neighbourhood associations, the distribution of
administrative functions among the various levels of government, the financial basis of
local government, relations between the national and local governments, the
organisation of local entities, and the nature of citizen participation in local
government.

642 **Political opposition and local politics in Japan.**
Edited by Kurt Steiner, Ellis S. Krauss, Scott C. Flanagan, introduction
by Kurt Steiner.   Princeton, New Jersey; Guildford, Surrey: Princeton
University Press, 1980. 486p.

Nine American scholars describe and analyse the role of political opposition in
Japanese local politics during the 1960s and 1970s. Grouped together under the three
main headings of 'Electoral Trends', 'Citizens' Movements', and 'Progressive Local
Administrations', their essays deal with electoral change in Japan, political opposition
and big city elections (1947-75), opposition in the suburbs, cross-level linkages and
correlates of change in national and local voting trends, the growth and impact of
environmental protest in Japan, political socialisation through citizens' movements,
citizens' movements and the politics of the environment in Mishima City, local public
policy and local–national relations, political choice and policy change in medium-sized
cities (1962-74), and the development and maintenance of leftist government in Kyōto
Prefecture. The study also contributes to theory-building in the field of comparative
local politics by broadening the scope of that field to include the case of Japan.

Foreign Relations

General

643 **Pacific rivals: a Japanese view of Japanese–American relations.**
Asahi Shimbun. Staff, foreword by Edwin O. Reischauer. New York; Tokyo: Weatherhill/Asahi, 1972. 431p.

The English-language version of a popular series of 135 topically oriented articles that originally appeared in Japan's largest newspaper, the *Asahi Shinbun*. Presenting the Japanese perspective of the evolution of US–Japanese relations between 1853 and the 1970s, they portray some of the prominent individuals involved in these relations, chronologically survey important developments up through 1945, provide a variegated picture of the postwar American occupation, discuss binational efforts to facilitate Japan's re-entry into the world of nations during the 1950s, describe the new image of Japan that emerged in the United States by the 1960s, and investigate some of the political, military, economic, social, and cultural problems that were troubling the US–Japanese relationship as of the 1970s. The articles are generally brief (many of them take the form of vignettes), and are written in a factual, anecdotal manner.

644 **Japanese imperialism, 1894–1945.**
William G. Beasley. Oxford, England: Clarendon Press; New York: Oxford University Press, 1987. 279p. 2 maps. bibliog.

An examination of the origins and nature of Japanese imperialism during the half century following the outbreak of the Sino–Japanese War of 1894-95. Beasley contends that there was a close relationship between Japan's success in building up her industrial economy and her rapid growth into a formidable imperial power. Rather than remaining static, Japanese imperialism evolved over time. Japan's early objectives, heavily influenced by her experience of nineteenth-century Western imperialism, changed as external circumstances changed and as Japan's economic and military capacity grew. During the 1930s, Japanese leaders devised a new pattern of imperialism, the 'Greater East Asia Co-Prosperity Sphere', which sought to ensure Japan's political and economic control over East and Southeast Asia but collapsed with the end of World War II. This is a highly recommended book by a distinguished British scholar of modern Japanese history.

645 **Japanese international negotiating style.**
Michael Blaker. New York; Guildford, Surrey: Columbia University Press, 1977. 253p. bibliog. (Studies of the East Asian Institute, Columbia University).

Basing his study on an examination of eighteen cases of Japanese diplomatic negotiations – from the negotiations for the Treaty of Shimonoseki that concluded the Sino–Japanese War of 1894-95 to the US–Japan negotiations in 1941 immediately preceding Pearl Harbor – Blaker identifies a distinctive and remarkably consistent style of prewar Japanese negotiating behaviour. He notes the ways in which Japanese negotiators determined their goals, outlines the handicaps (e.g., cumbersome policy-making processes, bureaucratic rivalries, limited discretionary latitude) which impeded their efforts, and explains how and why they usually met with success. Blaker credits Japanese negotiators with an unusual tenacity and commitment to positions that supported national goals, and argues that they negotiated in good faith and honoured the understandings which were reached.

646 **New frontiers in American–East Asian relations: essays presented to Dorothy Borg.**
Edited with an introduction by Warren I. Cohen. New York; Guildford, Surrey: Columbia University Press, 1983. 294p. (Studies of the East Asian Institute, Columbia University).

Eight historiographical essays that constitute a state-of-the-art survey and analysis of American cultural, economic, military, and political relations with China, Japan, and Korea during the nineteenth and twentieth centuries. Particular attention is paid to the scholarship of the 1970s. While only one chapter – 'Entangling Illusions: Japanese and American Views of the Occupation' (by Carol Gluck) – deals exclusively with Japan, US–Japanese relations are also examined very extensively in essays by Michael H. Hunt, Akira Iriye, Waldo Heinrichs, and Ernest R. May on various aspects of US–East Asian relations as a whole. This volume is a sequel to *American–East Asian relations: a survey*, edited by Ernest R. May and James C. Thomson, Jr. (Cambridge, Massachusetts: Harvard University Press, 1972, 425p.). The latter, an historiographical survey of American diplomatic, commercial, and military relations with East Asia from 1784 to 1970, contains seventeen essays covering the scholarly literature in this field on a period-by-period basis. In both volumes, the contributors emphasize the writings of American scholars, although Gluck's excellent survey does cover Japanese-language scholarship about the Allied occupation period as well.

647 **China and Japan: search for balance since World War I.**
Edited by Alvin D. Coox, Hilary Conroy, introduction by Robert A. Scalapino. Santa Barbara, California: ABC-Clio; Oxford, England: European Bibliographical Centre-Clio Press, 1978. 468p.

A collection of seventeen essays about Sino–Japanese relations between 1915 and the early 1970s. Written by American, Chinese, and Japanese scholars, they deal with a range of topics including Japan's intervention in Shantung during World War I, the beginnings of China's diplomacy of resistance against Japan, the portrayal of China in Japanese textbooks, the Chinese Communist Party and the anti-Japanese movement in

Manchuria during the 1930s, Doihara Kenji and the North China Autonomy Movement in 1935-36, the Sino–Japanese War of 1937-45, terminating the state of war between Japan and the Republic of China (Taiwan) in 1952, and the mechanics of the Tanaka Government's decision to establish diplomatic relations with Peking in 1972.

648 **A history of the Japanese secret service.**
Richard Deacon. London: Muller, 1982; New York: Beaufort Books, 1983. 306p. bibliog. Reprinted, New York: Berkley Books, 1985.

An entertaining account of the development of the Japanese secret service from its inception under Hideyoshi in the late 1500s through the events of the 1970s. Writing for the general reader, Deacon recounts numerous intriguing cases of Japanese espionage in China, Russia, Southeast Asia, and the United States, particularly as Japan was seeking to increase her influence as a world power and to expand her overseas empire. The work was published in the United States under the title *Kempei tai: a history of the Japanese secret service*.

649 **Across the Pacific: an inner history of American–East Asian relations.**
Akira Iriye, introduction by John K. Fairbank. New York: Harcourt, Brace and World, 1967. 361p. bibliog.

An illuminating analysis of the successive images or stereotypes which Americans, Chinese, and Japanese have had of one another since the late eighteenth century as well as an account of the major phases and incidents of US relations with both China and Japan. Iriye focuses on the ways in which policy-makers and educated people in these three countries have viewed each other, the changing world about them, and the problems that they have had in common. Similarly, he relates their respective responses and reactions – what he describes as 'the crude reality of misunderstanding, misperception, and miscalculation' – to their historical experiences and to the evolution of their countries' foreign policies. Paying particular attention to the period between the 1890s and the 1960s, Iriye's narrative is organised into four chronologically oriented sections entitled 'The Initial Encounter, 1780–1880', 'Imperialism, Nationalism, Racism', 'Sino–American Co-operation against Japan', and 'The Sino–American Crisis'.

650 **The Chinese and the Japanese: essays in political and cultural interactions.**
Edited with an introduction by Akira Iriye. Princeton, New Jersey; Guildford, Surrey: Princeton University Press, 1979. 368p.

Reconsidering the political and cultural relationship that existed between China and Japan from 1800 through 1945, sixteen scholarly essays explore several points of contact between the ideas, institutions and individuals of these two countries as well as their interaction at the government level. Among the topics covered are the functions of China in Tokugawa period thought, the nature of the Chinese community in early Meiji Japan, Chinese attitudes towards Japan at the time of the Sino–Japanese War of 1894–95, Chinese leaders and Japanese aid during the early Chinese Republican period (the decade of the 1910s), the intellectual biographies of five individuals – Konoe Atsumaro, Naitō Konan, Ishibashi Tanzan, Ugaki Kazushige, and Ts'ao Ju-lin – who actively shaped Japanese and Chinese perceptions of each other, and Chinese collaboration and Japanese atrocities during the Sino–Japanese War of 1937-45.

651 **Mutual images: essays in American–Japanese relations.**
Edited with an introduction by Akira Iriye, foreword by Takeo
Kuwabara. Cambridge, Massachusetts; London: Harvard University
Press, 1975. 304p. (Harvard Studies in American–East Asian
Relations, 7).
A series of empirical essays about Japanese and American views of each other since
the 1850s. These essays examine the images projected by Japanese participation in
American fairs between 1876 and 1904; the images of America in nineteenth-century
Japan; the American image of Japan as a competitor in trade and immigration, 1895-
1917; images of the United States as a hypothetical enemy in Japanese books published
before World War II; the images of war with the United States that were held by the
army, navy, policy-makers, and other Japanese groups; the evolution of the American
image of Japan after 1945; postwar Japanese education and the United States;
Japanese travellers' views of America since the Meiji period; the postwar images of
Japan held by members of the American élite; and the images of Japan held by
Japanese Americans in Los Angeles. All of the essays seek to contribute to the study
of images by examining the sources, ranges, uses, and constituencies of these images.

652 **Japan and China: from war to peace, 1894–1972.**
Marius B. Jansen. Chicago: Rand McNally, 1975. 547p. 6 maps.
bibliog. (Rand McNally History Series).
Twelve interpretive essays centre around the evolution of relations between China and
Japan 'within the setting of the responses both societies made to the challenge of
modern times'. These essays chronologically proceed from the Sino–Japanese War and
the 1895 Treaty of Shimonoseki to the conclusion of the 1972 agreement by Premier
Chou En-lai and Prime Minister Tanaka Kakuei to normalise relations between the
People's Republic of China and Japan. Jansen's account offers a scholarly introduction
to modern East Asian history as well as a general overview of the important dimension
of Sino–Japanese relations set within a broadly conceived framework. His detailed
bibliographical essay is designed to lead the reader into the growing literature on the
history of both modern China and Japan.

653 **The troubled encounter: the United States and Japan.**
Charles E. Neu, foreword by Robert A. Divine. New York; London:
Wiley, 1975. 257p. bibliog. (America and the World). Reprinted,
Huntington, New York: R. E. Krieger, 1979.
A concise exploration of the evolution of American political relations with Japan,
based on extensive research in available English-language sources. Focusing on the
period between 1890 and 1941, Neu explains many of the facets of both American and
Japanese government policies at that time and explores 'the intellectual assumptions,
bureaucratic perspectives, domestic political currents, and national aspirations that
fused together to form official decisions'. Particular attention is paid to the conflict and
the crises – the 'troubled encounter' – that increasingly upset this relationship.

Foreign Relations. General

654 **Japanese foreign policy 1869–1942: Kasumigaseki to Miyakezaka.**
Ian Nish. London; Boston, Massachusetts: Routledge and Kegan Paul, 1977. 346p. 2 maps. bibliog. (Foreign Policies of the Great Powers).
An interpretation of the evolution of Japan's foreign policy from the founding of the Foreign Ministry in 1869 through the Japanese attack on Pearl Harbor and Japan's military successes during the early months of 1942. Organising his presentation around analyses of the personalities and actions of twelve foreign ministers – from Iwakura Tomomi through Matsuoka Yōsuke – Nish charts the gradual shift in the control of foreign policy-making from the Foreign Ministry to the general staff of the Imperial Japanese Army, headquartered at Miyakezaka. In showing how Japanese foreign relations progressed through three consecutive stages in which Japan first sought equality and then partnership with the Western powers and finally autonomy as one of the great powers, Nish emphasizes the human dimension of Japanese foreign policy formulation.

655 **Neighbors across the Pacific: Canadian–Japanese relations 1870–1982.**
Klaus H. Pringsheim. Westport, Connecticut: Greenwood Press; Oakville, Ontario: Mosaic Press, 1983. 241p. bibliog. (Contributions in Political Science, 90).
A comprehensive analysis of the evolution of economic and political relations between Canada and Japan. Pringsheim's account is divided into five periods: the early years (1877-1929), when relations were established and political problems developed as a result of increased Japanese immigration to British Columbia; the establishment of legations in Ottawa and Tokyo and the development of Canadian–Japanese relations up to the outbreak of World War II; the war years, which were marked by the Canadian government's internment of most Japanese Canadians, and Canada's participation in the Allied occupation of Japan; the resumption of diplomatic relations and the building of a flourishing trade partnership between the two countries (1952-68); and the quest for a more diverse relationship under Prime Minister Pierre Elliott Trudeau (1968-78).

656 **Japan and the decline of the West in Asia 1894–1943.**
Richard Storry. London: Macmillan; New York: St. Martin's Press, 1979. 186p. bibliog. (The Making of the 20th Century).
A general description and interpretation of Japan's rise to world power between 1894 and 1943 and of some of the consequences of this development for the nations of the West – especially Great Britain and the United States – with vested interests in Asia at that time. Storry's book broadly covers the evolution of Japanese foreign policy and foreign relations between the outbreak of the first Sino–Japanese War and the midpoint of the Pacific War. Britain's interaction with Japan and contemporary British reactions to Japanese policy and imperialism are frequently highlighted.

657 **Sentimental imperialists: the American experience in East Asia.**
James C. Thomson, Jr, Peter W. Stanley, John Curtis Perry; foreword by John King Fairbank. New York: Harper and Row, 1981. 323p. 3 maps. Reprinted, Harper and Row, 1985. (Harper Torchbooks).
Three experts on the American–East Asian experience offer a broad-based picture of

268

US involvement in China, Japan, Korea, the Philippines, and Vietnam. Their interpretive essays trace the evolution of these relations between the mid-1780s and the early 1980s, and emphasize the role of sentimentality and illusions in the formulation of American policies. Much of their book examines the nature of American activities in nineteenth-century Japan, the American reaction to the emergence of imperial Japan, the deterioration of the US–Japan relationship in the early twentieth century, World War II in the Pacific, the Allied occupation and reorientation of Japan during the late 1940s, and US–Japanese relations after 1960.

The Japan reader.
See item no. 119.

Morning glory: a history of the imperial Japanese navy.
See item no. 210.

Japan and its world: two centuries of change.
See item no. 211.

The Japanese colonial empire, 1895–1945.
See item no. 223.

Nan'yō: the rise and fall of the Japanese in Micronesia, 1885–1945.
See item no. 227.

Japan examined: perspectives on modern Japanese history.
See item no. 249.

Okinawa: the history of an island people.
See item no. 284.

The Kuril Islands: Russo–Japanese frontier in the Pacific.
See item no. 286.

Sakhalin: a history.
See item no. 287.

Japan versus Europe: a history of misunderstanding.
See item no. 755.

Asia and Oceania: a guide to archival and manuscript sources in the United States.
See item no. 1562.

The United States in East Asia: a historical bibliography.
See item no. 1575.

Japanese history & culture from ancient to modern times: seven basic bibliographies.
See item no. 1583.

Japan and Korea: an annotated bibliography of doctoral dissertations in Western languages, 1877–1969.
See item no. 1607.

Before 1931

658 Great Britain and the opening of Japan, 1834–1858.
William G. Beasley. London: Luzac, 1951. 227p. 2 maps. bibliog.
An account of official British policy towards Japan, 1834-58, with particular attention to government motives, plans, and negotiations during that period. Contending that China played an important part in both British policy towards Japan and Japanese policy towards Britain, Beasley is chiefly concerned with the activities of the British Foreign Office and its representatives in China and, to a lesser extent, with the Admiralty and the commanders of the East Indies Station. He devotes much of his book to studying the impact of the Opium War on Anglo–Japanese relations, the Anglo–Japanese Convention negotiated at Nagasaki by Sir James Stirling (1854-55), the activities of Sir John Bowring and the Foreign Office (1854-57), and the mission of Lord Elgin to Edo that concluded with the signing of a full commercial treaty (1857-58). Contrasting Japan's situation with that of China at various points in time, Beasley concludes that there was 'no policy of *deliberate* British political and territorial expansion in Japan before 1858'.

659 Theodore Roosevelt and Japan.
Raymond A. Esthus.   Seattle, Washington; London: University of Washington Press, 1966. 329p. bibliog.
A comprehensive account of US–Japanese relations during the first decade of the twentieth century. Particular attention is paid to President Roosevelt's mediation in the Portsmouth Peace Conference (1905), which concluded the Russo–Japanese War; the growing Japanese–American economic rivalry over Manchuria in an era when the US government was promoting its open door policy in China; the increase of Japanese immigration to the United States; and the anti-Japanese prejudice on the US West Coast (manifested by school segregation, riots, and anti-Japanese legislation in California) that led to the Gentlemen's Agreement of 1907-8 severely limiting further Japanese immigration to the continental United States.

660 Britain and Japan, 1858–1883.
Grace Fox.   Oxford, England: Clarendon Press, 1969. 627p. 3 maps. bibliog.
A scholarly account, written from the British point of view, of the relationship between Great Britain and Japan during a critical, formative period in the history of modern Japan. The first part narrates the course of diplomatic relations between the two countries, with particular emphasis on the British pressures which forced Japan to open her ports to foreign commerce and on British policy during the years immediately preceding the Meiji Restoration of 1868. Part two investigates British involvement in Japanese economic and technological development, especially in the areas of trade, industry, and finance. The concluding part offers a detailed review of British influence on Japanese culture, notably in the areas of the press, science and medicine, and religious toleration.

661 **After imperialism: the search for a new order in the Far East, 1921–1931.**
Akira Iriye. Cambridge, Massachusetts: Harvard University Press, 1965. 375p. map. bibliog. (Harvard East Asian Series, 22). Reprinted, New York: Atheneum, 1973. (Atheneum College Edition, 147).

A systematic analysis of the foreign policies of Japan in particular but also of those of the United States, the Soviet Union, China, and Great Britain, following the collapse of the diplomacy of imperialism as a mechanism of power politics, as efforts were made to promote a new basis for stability in East Asia. Part one focuses on the failure of the powers to solidify the new system of international relations based on the Washington Conference treaties of 1921-22, the active anti-imperialist campaign of the Soviet Union between 1922 and 1927, and the diplomatic response of the powers to the Northern Expedition in China. Part two deals with the short-lived Japanese initiative to create a 'new era of Sino–Japanese co-prosperity as a guarantee for protecting Japanese interests in China and Manchuria'. Part three advances Iriye's account from 1928 to the eve of the Manchurian Incident (1931), as a unified China pursued its own concept of a new order in East Asia while Japanese efforts to devise a new comprehensive policy towards China suffered from the growing rift between the civilian and military conceptions of that policy.

662 **Pacific estrangement: Japanese and American expansion, 1897–1911.**
Akira Iriye. Cambridge, Massachusetts: Harvard University Press, 1972. 290p. bibliog. (Harvard Studies in American–East Asian Relations, 2).

Recounts the history of Japanese and American overseas expansion and interaction at the turn of the twentieth century by tracing the ways in which emerging feelings of international tension and estrangement across the Pacific were related to the parallel development of these two nations as new world powers. Iriye examines the origins, nature, evolution, and practice of each country's imperialist ideology and activity as he discusses the various kinds of expansion – economic and cultural as well as political and military – which they pursued in China, Manchuria, Korea, Hawaii, and the US West Coast and as he focuses on the problematic relationship that arose between the United States and Japan as a consequence of their competition and growing confrontation. Throughout his book, Iriye characterises US expansionism as being essentially ideological in nature, mission-oriented, and racially inclined, while Japanese expansionism is depicted as being oriented primarily towards economic growth and overseas settlement.

663 **The Japanese flowering cherry trees of Washington, D.C.: a living symbol of friendship.**
Roland M. Jefferson, Alan E. Fusonie, foreword by John L. Creech. Washington, DC: Agricultural Research Service, US Department of Agriculture, 1977. 66p. bibliog. (National Arboretum Contribution, 4).

An illustrated historical narrative of the origin, development, introduction, and planting of the world famous Japanese flowering cherry trees along the Tidal Basin in Washington, DC. These trees constituted a gift of friendship from the people of Japan to the United States between 1909 and 1912. Their story entailed international diplomacy and protocol as well as the involvement of high-ranking Americans and

Japanese such as the wife of President William Howard Taft and the mayor of Tokyo, Ozaki Yukio.

664 **The Russian push toward Japan: Russo–Japanese relations, 1697–1875.**
George Alexander Lensen.   Princeton, New Jersey: Princeton
University Press, 1959. 553p. 16 maps. bibliog. Reprinted, New York:
Octagon Books, 1971.

A comprehensive, narrative history of the early period of Russo–Japanese relations: from the first recorded encounter between a Russian explorer and a Japanese castaway on Kamchatka (in 1697) to the delineation of the Russo–Japanese frontier by means of the Treaty of St. Petersburg (1875) in which Japan ceded her claims to southern Sakhalin in exchange for Russia's recognition of Japanese sovereignty over the entire Kurile Island chain. Lensen vividly describes the course of these early relations and, in particular, the experiences of such individuals as Adam Erikovich Laxman, Nikolai Petrovich Rezanov, Vasilii Mikhailovich Golovnin, and Evfimii Vasil'evich Putiatin, who sought to establish commercial relations with Tokugawa Japan during the country's period of national seclusion. He also covers the reactions and activities of minor Japanese officials, traders, and castaways at that time. The period of treaty-making during the 1850s is examined in even greater detail in Lensen's earlier book, *Russia's Japan expedition of 1852 to 1855* (Gainesville, Florida: University of Florida Press, 1955, 208p.).

665 **New Zealand and Japan 1900–1941.**
M. P. Lissington.   Wellington, New Zealand: A. R. Shearer, 1972.
206p. map. bibliog.

An examination of the origins and evolution of prewar relations between Japan and New Zealand, culminating with the outbreak of World War II in the Pacific. Lissington discusses these relations within the larger context of New Zealand's relations with Great Britain and her gradual development of an independent foreign policy. She attributes the growth and direction of that policy in part to New Zealand's increasing preoccupation with Japan during the 1930s as a potential threat to the country's national security. Based heavily on New Zealand government documents, published official sources, and the local press, her account depicts primarily the New Zealand side of the relationship.

666 **Great Britain and Japan, 1911–15: a study of British Far Eastern policy.**
Peter Lowe.   London: Macmillan; New York: St. Martin's Press,
1969. 343p. 4 maps. bibliog.

This study of the role and significance of the Anglo–Japanese alliance in the formulation of British Far Eastern policy traces the development of that alliance 'from a position of close cordiality to one of growing conflict', particularly with regard to the situation in China. Lowe argues that this increasing disharmony was a direct consequence of Great Britain's relative decline as a world power and Japan's desire to continue expanding her influence and position in East Asia. He covers the revision and renewal of the alliance in 1911, British policy towards the Chinese revolution of 1911 and subsequent British and Japanese ties to the new Chinese republic, British policy and loans to China (1911-14), Britain's rejection of Japanese efforts to engage her in co-operative railway development in the Yangtze River valley (1913-14), the Anglo–Japanese alliance and the negotiations over Japan's entry into World War I,

Japan's 'Twenty-One Demands' on the Chinese government in 1915 and the resulting crisis, and the generally hostile attitudes of the British Dominions and India towards Japan throughout this period.

667 **As we saw them: the first Japanese embassy to the United States (1860).**
Masao Miyoshi.   Berkeley, California; London: University of
California Press, 1979. 232p.

An illustrated account of the journey of the Japanese embassy that was entrusted with presenting government officials in Washington with the instrument of ratification of the Treaty of Kanagawa, Japan's first treaty of friendship with the United States. Miyoshi's study is concerned with the views and opinions about Americans (particularly their comments on race, women, and democracy) which the members of this embassy expressed in their diaries, travelogues, and memoirs; the 'minds' of these travellers as they sought to comprehend the meaning of what 'they were observing and experiencing; and the lives of some of the more prominent members of the embassy following their return to Japan.

668 **Kenkenroku: a diplomatic record of the Sino–Japanese War, 1894–95.**
Munemitsu Mutsu, edited and translated with historical notes by
Gordon Mark Berger.   Tokyo: University of Tokyo Press; Princeton,
New Jersey: University of Tokyo Press, 1982. 318p. map. bibliog.
(Princeton Library of Asian Translations).

These memoirs of Mutsu Munemitsu (1844-97), foreign minister of Japan during and immediately after the Sino–Japanese War, constitute an insider's account about the decision-making of the Meiji government and the diplomatic manoeuvring that occurred in 1894–95. They were written to explain as well as to defend the Japanese government's decision to return to China the Liaotung Peninsula (which China had ceded to Japan) as a result of the diplomatic pressure exerted upon Tokyo by Russia, Germany, and France during the weeks immediately following the end of the war. Mutsu's account focuses on the Tonghak Rebellion in Korea, the outbreak of Sino–Japanese hostilities, the peace negotiations between China and Japan that led to the signing of the Treaty of Shimonoseki, and the ensuing 'Triple Intervention'. The memoirs are based heavily on various interchanges between Mutsu and Prime Minister Itō Hirobumi as well as on official papers of the Japanese Foreign Ministry.

669 **The Anglo–Japanese alliance: the diplomacy of two island empires, 1894–1907.**
Ian Nish.   London; Dover, New Hampshire: Athlone Press, 1985.
2nd ed. 420p. 2 maps. bibliog. (University of London Historical
Studies, 18).

The Anglo–Japanese alliance, concluded in 1902 and kept in force until 1923, was one factor underlying Japan's emergence as a major power in Asia. This book is the most thorough and detailed account available of the developments which led to the conclusion of that alliance and to its renewal in 1905. Nish demonstrates how Great Britain and Japan, both individually and collectively, responded to Russia's expansionist policy in China at the turn of the twentieth century. He also assesses some of the considerations behind London and Tokyo's decision to enter into this unprecedented political and defensive agreement. An appendix contains translations of important Japanese documents that illustrate the motives underlying Japanese government policy as well as the alternatives which were open to it.

670   **Alliance in decline: a study in Anglo–Japanese relations, 1908–23.**
Ian H. Nish.   London: Athlone Press, 1972. 424p. 3 maps. bibliog.
(University of London Historical Studies, 33).
A detailed account of the negotiations that culminated in the renewal of the Anglo–Japanese alliance in 1911, and of the working relationship between Great Britain and Japan that linked these two nations until the replacement of the alliance in 1923 by the Washington Treaties. Characterising the story of the alliance during this period as one of 'decline, disappointment and disillusion rather than one of abrupt disruption', Nish's chronologically organised study includes extensive coverage of the factors which affected the formulation of Japanese and British policy towards one another and which helped to sustain the alliance, the mutual benefits of the alliance during World War I, the disharmony which became visible in their relations at all levels but especially in their differences of policy over China, and the impact of this relationship of growing Anglo–American co-operation in Asia and the Pacific. This book is a companion volume to Nish's earlier work, *The Anglo–Japanese alliance* (q.v.).

671   **The origins of the Russo–Japanese War.**
Ian Nish, foreword by Harry Hearder.   London; New York:
Longman, 1985. 274p. 3 maps. bibliog. (Origins of Modern Wars).
A scholarly reassessment of the origins of Japan's first war (1904-5) with a European power. Nish traces the causes of the war back to Russia's efforts to exploit China's weakness following her defeat in the Sino–Japanese War of 1894-95, and he examines the tensions that arose when Russia actively pursued an expansionist policy in Manchuria. Beyond exploring the military and strategic considerations that were of concern to both the Japanese and Russian leadership, he also discusses the personalities, beliefs, and shortcomings of the Japanese and Russian officials whose actions influenced the policy-making processes that ultimately led to the outbreak of the Russo–Japanese War.

672   **The Japanese oligarchy and the Russo–Japanese War.**
Shumpei Okamoto.   New York; London: Columbia University Press,
1970. 358p. bibliog. (Studies of the East Asian Institute, Columbia
University).
An examination of the formulation and execution of Japan's foreign policy during the Russo–Japanese War (1904-5), and an assessment of the strengths, weaknesses, and effects of oligarchic control of that policy. Okamoto opens with a discussion of the constitutional structure and components of Meiji period foreign policy in the early 1900s and of the dichotomy which existed between the attitudes of the ruling oligarchy and the country's political activists. He explains the decision of the oligarchs to go to war against Imperial Russia and indicates how the activities and attitudes of the political activists affected their decision-making process. He also shows how both the oligarchs and the political activists followed the progress of the war, what each group expected of the war, and how they prepared for its termination. Finally, Okamoto studies the domestic reaction – in particular, the mass rioting that took place in Tokyo – to the conclusion of the Portsmouth Peace Conference and the signing of a peace

treaty with Russia. The conference itself, including the negotiations that led first to the conference table and then to the conclusion of a peaceful settlement, and the important mediating role of President Theodore Roosevelt, are described in Eugene P. Trani's *The Treaty of Portsmouth: an adventure in American diplomacy* (Lexington, Kentucky: University of Kentucky Press, 1969, 194p.).

673 **Narrative of the expedition of an American squadron to the China Seas and Japan under the command of Commodore M. C. Perry, United States Navy.**
Matthew C. Perry, compiled by Francis L. Hawks, abridged and edited by Sidney Wallach. New York: Coward-McCann; London: MacDonald Press, 1952. 305p.

Compiled under Perry's supervision from official correspondence, notes, and journals, the original three-volume edition of this work (Washington, DC: Nicholson, 1856; Reprinted, New York: AMS Press, 1967) served as the commodore's official report to the US government about his efforts to open diplomatic and commercial relations between Japan and the United States. This abridged edition records the events of the expedition in China, Lew Chew (the Ryūkyū Islands), the Bonin Islands, and Japan in 1853-54. In addition, it contains considerable descriptive information about Japanese life and customs, the Japanese countryside, and the Japanese people whom Perry and his crew encountered during their two separate visits. The daily journal which Perry kept during these years, in turn, offers insights into his own attitudes and character, describes his observations of life in both China and Japan, and records his conduct of treaty negotiations with the Japanese government in 1854. Entitled *The Japan expedition, 1852–1854: the personal journal of Commodore Matthew C. Perry* and edited by Roger Pineau (Washington, DC: Smithsonian Institution Press, 1968, 241p.), it is augmented by reproductions of colour sketches and lithographs of drawings made during the expedition. For a standard scholarly history of the expedition and its background that is based not only on Perry's own accounts but also on diaries kept by other crew members as well as on selected Japanese sources of information, see *Black ships off Japan: the story of Commodore Perry's expedition* by Arthur Walworth (New York: Knopf, 1946, 277p. Reprinted, Hamden, Connecticut: Archon Books, 1966).

674 **The Western world and Japan: a study in the interaction of European and Asiatic cultures.**
George B. Sansom. New York: Knopf, 1950. 504p. 2 maps.
Reprinted, New York: Vintage Books, 1973; Rutland, Vermont and Tokyo: Tuttle, 1977.

An authoritative analysis of the cultural influence of the West upon Japan between 1600 and the outbreak of the Sino–Japanese War in 1894 as well as a study of the process by which Western civilisations influenced the civilisations of Asia in general and of Japan in particular. Sansom first surveys the early cultural relations between Europe and Asia. He then indicates how Japan responded to Western influence during the Tokugawa period. Finally, in four chapters devoted to a description and assessment of the impact of the West on Japan during the first half of the Meiji period, Sansom shows 'how Japanese tradition fought against new doctrine and how, beneath a "modern" surface, many features of earlier Japanese political life survived without substantial change'. These chapters also constitute in effect a continuation of the author's earlier book, *Japan: a short cultural history* (q.v.).

675 **A diplomat in Japan: the inner history of the critical years in the evolution of Japan when the ports were opened and the monarchy restored, recorded by a diplomatist who took an active part in the events of the time, with an account of his personal experiences during that period.**
Ernest Satow. London: Seeley, Service; Philadelphia, Pennsylvania: Lippincott, 1921. 427p. 2 maps. Reprinted, with an introduction by Gordon Daniels, Tokyo; New York: Oxford University Press, 1969. (Oxford in Asia Historical Reprints). Also reprinted under the title *A diplomat in Japan: an inner history of the critical years in the evolution of Japan* (Rutland, Vermont; Tokyo: Tuttle, 1983).

Basing his work on diary notes kept throughout his term of service in Japan, Satow – a diplomat, linguist, and scholar who served first as interpreter and then as secretary to the English legation during the 1860s – recounts the critical years which led to the overthrow of the Tokugawa shogunate, the restoration in 1868 of direct imperial rule, and the emergence of a new Japan. Combining his astute insight and personal observations with a first-hand knowledge of such events as the Richardson affair (1862), the Allied bombardment of the city of Kagoshima in 1863 and naval operations against the forts at Shimonoseki in 1864, the imperial ratification of the Ansei Treaties, the outbreak of the civil war, the massacre of French sailors at Sakai, and the entry of a triumphant emperor into Edo (Tokyo) in 1868, he provides a detailed account of Anglo–Japanese relations and of Japanese political history during this critical transitional period.

676 **The Shimoda story.**
Oliver Statler. New York: Random House, 1969. 627p. 4 maps. bibliog. Reprinted, Honolulu, Hawaii: University of Hawaii Press, 1986.

An embellished but thoroughly researched account of Townsend Harris (1804-78), America's first consul-general to Japan, and his sixteenth-month stay (1856-58) in the town of Shimoda while he negotiated a full commercial treaty between Japan and the United States. Interweaving historical fact and recorded events with colourful descriptions and anecdotal stories, Statler writes about Harris' personal life in Shimoda, the lives of some of the port's inhabitants which were directly or indirected affected by his presence, and his protracted negotiations with the Japanese government. Excellent depictions of local history and late Tokugawa rural society together with rich and intimate portrayals of townspeople and government officials as well as of Harris himself help make *The Shimoda story* an enjoyable and informative book. Harris' own record of his stay in Shimoda is available in *The complete journal of Townsend Harris, first American consul and minister to Japan*, introduction and notes by Mario Emilio Cosenza (Garden City, New York: Doubleday, Doran, 1930, 616p. Reprinted with a preface by Douglas MacArthur, II, Rutland, Vermont; Tokyo: Tuttle, 1959).

677 **State and diplomacy in early modern Japan: Asia in the development of the Tokugawa bakufu.**
Ronald P. Toby.   Princeton, New Jersey; Guildford, Surrey: Princeton University Press, 1984. 309p. 2 maps. bibliog. (Studies of the East Asian Institute, Columbia University).

Challenging the Eurocentric view of Japan as a totally isolated country during most of the seventeenth century, Toby argues that the early Tokugawa leaders regarded the maintenance of relations with neighbouring states as a matter of political and strategic importance. He examines the Tokugawa restoration of diplomatic ties with Korea and the Ryūkyūs, the shogunate's policy vis-à-vis the Manchu assumption of power in China, and the various avenues of Sino–Japanese contact. Toby shows that the shogunate made use of the rituals of diplomacy and the principles of Confucian interstate relations to legitimise and enhance its domestic political prestige as well as to preserve Japan's security during an era of international and civil war in East Asia. In addition, it had ideological pretensions which aimed at creating a Japan-centred world order in East Asia, and carried on trade with the Ryūkyūs, China, and Korea as well as with the Dutch.

678 **Russia against Japan, 1904–05: a new look at the Russo–Japanese War.**
John N. Westwood.   Basingstoke, Hampshire: Macmillan; Albany, New York: State University of New York Press, 1986. 183p. map. bibliog.

A scholarly narrative and analysis of the Russo–Japanese War, based heavily on Russian-language sources. Initial chapters depict the diplomatic and strategic origins and background of the conflict, while succeeding chapters examine the war itself: Admiral Tōgō Heihachirō's surprise attack of 8 February 1904 on the Russian naval fleet at Port Arthur, the subsequent fighting in Manchuria, the Japanese destruction of the Russian squadron, the siege of Port Arthur, the battle of Mukden, and the May 1905 sinking of the Russian Baltic fleet in the Tsushima Strait. A concluding chapter focuses on the negotiation of the Treaty of Portsmouth, which formally ended the war, and on the treaty's reception in both Russia and Japan. Westwood's complementary work, *The illustrated history of the Russo–Japanese War* (London: Sidgwick and Jackson, 1973; Chicago: Henry Regnery, 1974, 126p.), contains numerous wartime photographs and artistic depictions.

Victorians in Japan: in and around the treaty ports.
See item no. 68.

The Christian century in Japan, 1549–1650.
See item no. 129.

They came to Japan: an anthology of European reports on Japan, 1543–1640.
See item no. 133.

Deus destroyed: the image of Christianity in early modern Japan.
See item no. 166.

Japan: the Dutch experience.
See item no. 167.

Foreign Relations. Before 1931

The Japanese discovery of Europe, 1720–1830.
See item no. 173.

Historical Nagasaki.
See item no. 179.

The collapse of the Tokugawa bakufu, 1862–1868.
See item no. 186.

The Deer Cry Pavilion: a story of Westerners in Japan 1868–1905.
See item no. 190.

The Meiji Restoration.
See item no. 191.

The modernizers: overseas students, foreign employees, and Meiji Japan.
See item no. 197.

The image of Japan: from feudal isolation to world power, 1850–1905.
See item no. 216.

Japan in the Victorian mind: a study of stereotyped images of a nation 1850–80.
See item no. 251.

Admiral Togo.
See item no. 320.

Tanaka Giichi and Japan's China policy.
See item no. 333.

The capital of the Tycoon: a narrative of a three years' residence in Japan.
See item no. 349.

Mirror in the shrine: American encounters with Meiji Japan.
See item no. 361.

East across the Pacific: historical and sociological studies of Japanese immigration and assimilation.
See item no. 385.

The samurai.
See item no. 1054.

Warships of the Imperial Japanese Navy, 1869–1945.
See item no. 1572.

Japan's foreign policy, 1868–1941: a research guide.
See item no. 1599.

Japan and the world, 1853–1952: a bibliographic guide to Japanese scholarship in foreign relations.
See item no. 1599.

1931–1945 (including World War II)

679   Japan prepares for total war: the search for economic security, 1919–1941.
Michael A. Barnhart.   Ithaca, New York; London: Cornell University Press, 1987. 290p. 2 maps. bibliog. (Cornell Studies in Security Affairs).

A scholarly account of Japan's search for economic self-sufficiency and of the transformation of that quest into an aggressive effort to expand her empire on the Asian mainland – an action which ultimately provoked American economic pressure on Tokyo and led directly to the outbreak of the Pacific War. Most of the study focuses on diplomatic, economic, and military activities between 1937 and 1941 (from the China Incident through Pearl Harbor), with particular attention to the bitter rivalry between the Japanese army and navy for control over the direction of Japanese policy, and to the gradual deterioration of US–Japanese relations during that period.

680   Titans of the seas: the development and operations of Japanese and American carrier task forces during World War II.
James H. Belote, William M. Belote.   New York; London: Harper and Row, 1975. 336p. 5 maps. bibliog.

Following an historical overview of the Japanese and American aircraft carrier task forces before World War II, the Belotes trace the planning and execution of Japan's surprise attack on Pearl Harbor, the subsequent Japanese sweep of the southwest Pacific and Indian Oceans, the great carrier battles of the Coral Sea, Midway, the Eastern Solomons, and Santa Cruz that took place in 1942, the American task force attacks on Japanese bases in 1943, and the climactic Battle of the Philippine Sea in June 1944, which witnessed the virtual destruction of Japan's remaining carrier power. Numerous descriptions of aircraft and carrier types as well as detailed accounts of individual battles enliven the narrative for the general audience.

681   Silent victory: the U.S. submarine war against Japan.
Clay Blair, Jr.   Philadelphia: Lippincott, 1975. 1071p. 37 maps. bibliog.

An historical account of the US submarine offensive against the Japanese merchant marine and the Imperial Japanese Navy during World War II. Blair depicts the 'little known war-within-a-war' whereby a comparatively small number of American submarines succeeded in sinking more than one thousand Japanese merchant ships as well as numerous naval vessels, among them one battleship, eight aircraft carriers, three heavy cruisers, and eight light cruisers. He details the various submarine patrols and their attacks on enemy shipping, and assesses their significant contributions to America's victory in the Pacific. Some of the twelve appendixes provide information about Japanese losses.

Foreign Relations. 1931–1945 (including World War II)

682 **Pearl Harbor as history: Japanese–American relations, 1931–1941.**
Edited with an introduction by Dorothy Borg, Shumpei Okamoto, with
Dale K. A. Finlayson. New York; London: Columbia University
Press, 1973. 801p. (Studies of the East Asian Institute, Columbia
University).

An award-winning collection of twenty-six scholarly conference papers by American
and Japanese historians who adopt an institutional approach in their examination of
the foreign policy decision-making that shaped US–Japanese relations during the
1930s. Particular attention is paid to the roles of several government ministries (e.g.,
the Finance and Foreign Ministries) and departments (e.g., the State and War
Departments), the American and Japanese armies and navies, Congress and the Diet,
political parties, and such non-governmental entities as business and pressure groups
and the press. The contributors deal with such questions as 'how the various
institutions were organized, what the characteristics were of the people who kept them
functioning, who the key individuals were and how they related to each other, how
complex international issues were defined, and whether the institutions themselves had
weaknesses which played a significant role in the ultimate Japanese–American
confrontation'. Also included are historiographical essays that assess American and
Japanese scholarship about prewar Japanese–American relations.

683 **Japan's decision to surrender.**
Robert J. C. Butow, foreword by Edwin O. Reischauer. Stanford,
California: Stanford University Press, 1954. 259p. bibliog. (Hoover
Institution Studies).

An authoritative analysis of Japan's decision to surrender unconditionally to the Allied
powers in mid-August 1945. Butow narrates and clarifies the activities and efforts of
those Japanese who sought to save their country from total destruction in a war which
they knew was lost. Focusing on the months between July 1944 (the fall of the Tōjō
Cabinet) and August 1945, he describes the decision-making process, the events, and
the moves which the Japanese made towards their final acceptance of defeat. These
included peace feelers to Washington through the so-called Dulles organisation,
Japanese overtures to the Kremlin, and the imperial conference at which the emperor
insisted on surrender and termination of the war.

684 **Nomonhan: Japan against Russia, 1939.**
Alvin D. Coox. Stanford, California: Stanford University Press, 1985.
2 vols. 8 maps. bibliog.

A richly detailed and exhaustively documented account of a fierce, undeclared five-
month war waged between Japan and the Soviet Union on the steppes of Mongolia
throughout the summer of 1939. This war involved tens of thousands of troops as well
as many tanks and aeroplanes, engaged in full-scale conflict over a poorly demarcated
boundary between Manchoukuo (as Manchuria under Japanese rule was then known)
and Mongolia. It culminated in a decisive Soviet victory, demonstrated that the
Japanese Kwantung Army was far from invincible, and led to a momentous
reorientation of military planning and strategy among Japan's highest leaders. For
other accounts of Soviet–Japanese relations between the end of World War I and the
early 1940s, see in particular James William Morley's *The Japanese thrust into Siberia,
1918* (New York: Columbia University Press; London: Oxford University Press, 1957,
395p. [Studies of the Russian Institute, Columbia University]); George Alexander

Lensen's two books *The damned inheritance: the Soviet Union and the Manchurian crises, 1924–1935* (Tallahassee, Florida: Diplomatic Press, 1974, 533p.) and *The strange neutrality: Soviet–Japanese relations during the Second World War, 1941–1945* (Tallahassee, Florida: Diplomatic Press, 1972, 332p.); and David Rees' *The Soviet seizure of the Kuriles* (q.v.).

685 **Japan's quest for autonomy: national security and foreign policy, 1930–1938.**
James B. Crowley. Princeton, New Jersey: Princeton University Press, 1966. 428p. bibliog.

Crowley explains the process by which Japan's military and political leaders became convinced of the need for, and accordingly the propriety of, an 'autonomous national defence' and a 'self-sufficient' economy that were to be achieved through Japanese hegemony in East Asia. Focusing on the relationship between their concepts of national security and the formulation of foreign policy as well as on the changing nature of policy-making within the Japanese government, he examines the attitudes, opinions, and policies which ministers of state, responsible officials of the war, naval and foreign ministries, and senior officers of the two general staffs articulated during the 1930s. His study includes appraisals of the military discontent with the London Naval Treaty of 1930, the crisis created by the Japanese Kwantung Army's seizure of Manchuria following the Mukden Incident of 1931, Japan's decision to withdraw from membership in the League of Nations, the 26 February 1936 attempted coup d'état, and Konoe Fumimaro's role in the decision to launch a full-scale war with China.

686 **War without mercy: race and power in the Pacific War.**
John W. Dower. New York: Pantheon; London and Boston, Massachusetts: Faber and Faber; Toronto, Ontario: Random House of Canada, 1986. 398p. bibliog.

A comparative historical study which examines the racist stereotypes of World War II that predominated in American, English, and Japanese propaganda films, songs, cartoons, slogans, and battlefield epithets as well as in official documents, secret reports, and scholarly writings. The Americans are said to have viewed their enemies as apes, children, vermin, and neurotic savages, while the Japanese emphasized their racial uniqueness and superiority and denigrated enemy forces. Dower recreates the ethos which underlay the attitudes and actions of the wartime combatants and indicates how racist thinking and distorted mutual perceptions 'contributed to poor military intelligence and planning, atrocious behaviour, and the adoption of exterminationist policies'. He also shows how the 'kill or be killed' nature of combat and the kamikaze and Western traditions of sacrifice were linked to centuries-old patterns of racist thought in this 'war without mercy' in the Pacific.

687 **A battle history of the Imperial Japanese Navy (1941–1945).**
Paul S. Dull, foreword by Dean C. Allard. Annapolis, Maryland: Naval Institute Press, 1978. 402p. 42 maps. bibliog.

The Japanese navy's involvement in World War II viewed through the eyes of Japanese commanders. Limited in scope to describing the principal surface and carrier engagements of the war, this narrative is essentially a history of Japanese ships and naval units from the attack on Pearl Harbor (December 1941) to the sinking of the super-battleship *Yamato* (April 1945). In between Dull covers many other events including the Japanese capture of Southeast Asia and New Guinea, naval raids in the Indian Ocean, the battles of the Coral Sea and Midway, the Japanese seizure of two Aleutian Islands, Guadalcanal, three battles of the Solomons Seas, engagements in the Philippines, and the final defeat of the Imperial Japanese Navy during the closing year of the war. Dull's account is complemented by his appraisals of Japanese naval leadership, intelligence, strategy, tactics, and weapons.

688 **The Japanese navy in World War II: in the words of former Japanese naval officers.**
Edited and translated by David C. Evans, introduction and commentary by Raymond O'Connor. Annapolis, Maryland: Naval Institute Press, 1986. 2nd ed. 568p. 19 maps.

First published as *The Japanese navy in World War II: an anthology of articles by former officers of the Imperial Japanese Navy and Air Defence Force*, edited by Raymond O'Connor (Annapolis, Maryland: US Naval Institute, 1969), this is an expanded edition of seventeen essays that offer first-hand accounts of Japanese wartime strategy, tactics, and operations as well as insights into the motivations and personalities of selected Japanese naval leaders. Among its articles are 'The Hawaii Operations'; 'The Air Attack on Pearl Harbor'; 'The Opening Air Offensive against the Philippines'; 'The Battle of Midway'; 'The Struggle for Guadalcanal'; 'The Withdrawal from Kiska'; 'The Air Battle off Taiwan'; 'The Battle of Leyte Gulf'; 'Why Japan's Antisubmarine Warfare Failed'; 'The Kamikaze Attack Corps'; 'Kamikazes in the Okinawa Campaign'; 'The Sinking of the *Yamato*'; and 'Thoughts on Japan's Naval Defeat'.

689 **Japanese aircraft of the Pacific War.**
René J. Francillon, technical illustrations by J. B. Roberts. London: Putnam, 1979. new ed. 570p. Reprinted, Annapolis, Maryland: Naval Institute Press, 1987.

A comprehensive guide to the more than one hundred types of aircraft operated by or designed for the Imperial Japanese Army and Navy. Francillon opens with short histories of the Japanese aircraft industry and of the army and navy airforces, as well as with descriptions of the military aircraft designation systems and of the fundamental camouflage and marking systems. The heart of his book consists of descriptions, technical data, black-and-white photographs, and multi-view drawings of the most important operational and experimental types of wartime aircraft such as the well-known Mitsubishi Ki-67 Hiryu bomber and the Nakajima Ki-84 Hayate fighter-plane. Entries for these and other aircraft are arranged chronologically under the abbreviated names of the manufacturers (e.g., Kawanishi, Kokusai, Mitsubishi, Nakajima, Tachikawa, Yokosuka), which in turn are divided into two major sections covering the aircraft of the army and navy respectively. Descriptions of less important aircraft types, information about Japanese aero-engines and aircraft weapons, and a section about foreign-designed aircraft that contributed to Japan's prewar aircraft development constitute some of the book's six appendixes.

690 **Ten years in Japan: a contemporary record drawn from the diaries and private and official papers of Joseph C. Grew, United States ambassador to Japan, 1932–1942.**
Joseph C. Grew. New York: Simon and Schuster, 1944. 554p; London: Hammond, 1944. 480p. Reprinted, New York: Arno Press, 1972. 554p.; Westport, Connecticut: Greenwood Press, 1973. 554p.

Excerpts from the thirteen large typewritten volumes constituting the day-to-day diaries which Grew kept during his decade of diplomatic service in Tokyo are combined with material drawn from his personal and official correspondence as well as from his despatches to the US State Department to form a narrative of the evolution of American–Japanese relations between May 1932 and May 1942. Grew sketches in the background and depicts such developments as the growth of militarism in Japan, the 26 February 1936 abortive coup d'état, Japanese efforts to vanquish China, and the negotiations and manoeuvrings that preceded the outbreak of war between the USA and Japan. He also portrays the diplomatic orbit in which he moved and some of the ways in which he sought to carry out his diplomatic assignments. Grew's account complements his earlier book, *Report from Tokyo: a message to the American people* (New York; Simon and Schuster, 1942, 88p.), in which he tried to alert Americans to the 'formidable character of the Japanese military machine' and to correct a number of misconceptions prevalent about the Japanese at that time. The full texts of many of the official documents relating to US–Japanese relations during this period may be found in *Papers relating to the foreign relations of the United States; Japan: 1931–1941*, compiled and edited by the US Department of State (Washington, DC: US Government Printing Office, 1943, 2 vols.).

691 **I saw Tokyo burning: an eyewitness narrative from Pearl Harbor to Hiroshima.**
Robert Guillain, translated from the French by William Byron. Garden City, New York: Doubleday; London: J. Murray, 1981. 298p. Reprinted, New York: Playboy Paperbacks, 1982.

A first-hand account of Japan at war by a French correspondent who remained in Tokyo from 1938 to 1945. First published in French in 1946, it describes the reactions of the home front to the major wartime events which directly affected the people living in Japan. In particular, it offers detailed and picturesque descriptions of the fire-bombing of Tokyo, the desperate efforts to defend the country through the use of kamikaze pilots, and the Japanese response to news about Hiroshima and their nation's surrender to the Allies.

692 **Kōgun: the Japanese army in the Pacific War.**
Saburō Hayashi, with Alvin D. Coox. Quantico, Virginia: Marine Corps Association, 1959. 249p. 11 maps. Reprinted, Westport, Connecticut: Greenwood Press, 1978.

A former member of the Imperial General Staff candidly chronicles the actions of the Army High Command during World War II. Hayashi focuses on the ways in which the High Command estimated each of the situations confronting it during the war, on the thinking which served as the basis for its various plans of operation, and on its actual conduct and implementation of important wartime plans. He outlines the progress of operations in each major campaign – from the 'Southern Operations' of winter 1941/42 that secured Southeast Asia for Japan through the defeat of the Kwantung Army in

Foreign Relations. 1931–1945 (including World War II)

Manchuria by Soviet armed forces in August 1945 – and he critically assesses their conduct. First written for a Japanese audience, the text of *Kōgun* was extensively annotated for this English-language edition and is accompanied by Coox's appendix presenting biographical digests of the careers of ninety-one high-ranking officers.

693 **Japan's decision for war: records of the 1941 policy conferences.**
Translated, edited, and with an introduction by Nobutaka Ike.
Stanford, California: Stanford University Press, 1967. 306p. map.
bibliog.

A translation of the detailed notes kept by Sugiyama Hajime (Army Chief of Staff who was also known as Sugiyama Gen) of the deliberations of the fifty-seven Liaison Conferences and the five Imperial Conferences held in Tokyo between 18 April and 4 December 1941. These Liaison Conferences between representatives of the Cabinet and the Army and Navy entailed discussions of foreign policy, in particular, developments affecting US–Japanese relations. The Imperial Conferences involved the emperor's ratification of key decisions of the Liaison Conferences. Altogether these records provide direct access to the thinking and planning of Japan's top leadership during the months preceding the attack on Pearl Harbor, and show what actually transpired in the highest decision-making organs of Japan at that time. Ike provides introductory remarks to each of the translated records as well as a general introductory essay.

694 **The origins of the Second World War in Asia and the Pacific.**
Akira Iriye, foreword by Harry Hearder. London; New York:
Longman, 1987. 202p. 2 maps. bibliog. (Origins of Modern Wars).

Iriye traces the course of international relations in East Asia from September 1931, when the post-World War I international system of affairs (exemplified by the Washington Conference treaties) was challenged by the Japanese Kwantung Army's seizure of control in Manchuria, to Japan's surprise attack against the United States, Great Britain, and the Netherlands in early December 1941. As he describes and analyses the evolving international frameworks which provided the setting for the foreign policies not only of Japan but also of China, the United States, Great Britain, the Soviet Union, and Germany, he explains how Japanese actions during the late 1930s helped to precipitate a realignment of the powers in Asia and why Japan ultimately decided to embark on a full-scale war against the Western allies even though she had not yet defeated the isolated and divided forces of China.

695 **Power and culture: the Japanese–American war, 1941–1945.**
Akira Iriye. Cambridge, Massachusetts; London: Harvard University
Press, 1981. 304p. map. bibliog.

An inquiry into the meaning of World War II in the Pacific from the perspective of its two major combatants. Focusing on the interplay between culture and international relations, Iriye examines the wartime objectives that were enunciated by the Japanese and by the Americans, their respective policies toward China and Southeast Asia, and the visions of a postwar Asia and a postwar world which each side developed. Contrasting the military and symbolic aspects of this bitter and protracted struggle, he seeks to use the Japanese–American war as a case-study for understanding the multifaceted nature of modern international relations. Iriye argues that instead of being merely a ruthless pursuit of power, the war represented a search by both sides for the type of international environment which each one considered 'most conducive to compatibility among different power and cultural systems'.

696 Thirty seconds over Tokyo.
Ted W. Lawson, edited by Robert Considine.   New York: Random House, 1943. 221p. Reprinted, Random House, 1953. 186p. (Landmark Books, 35).

An American pilot's first-hand account of the background, implementation, and aftermath of the Doolittle raid of 18 April 1942. On that day, sixteen medium land-bombers led by Lieutenant Colonel James H. Doolittle bombed Tokyo and three other Japanese cities, inflicting only slight physical damage but significantly affecting both American and Japanese morale. Lawson's 'classic' book subsequently served as the basis for a popular American wartime movie. Caroll V. Glines' *The Doolittle raid: America's daring first strike against Japan* (New York: Orion Books, 1988, 258p.) expands on Lawson's account by offering a fuller, retrospective narrative based on available documents and the author's interviews with many of the raid's eighty participants.

697 Great Britain and the origins of the Pacific War: a study of British policy in East Asia, 1937–1941.
Peter Lowe.   Oxford, England: Clarendon Press, 1977. 318p. 2 maps. bibliog.

An examination of Great Britain's involvement in the origins of the Pacific War and of British policy towards Japan between the outbreak of the Sino–Japanese War in July 1937 and the Japanese attack on Pearl Harbor in December 1941. Lowe covers the early months of Japanese aggression in northern and eastern China, the continued Japanese imperialist expansion in China, the summer 1939 crisis over Tientsin that brought Great Britain and Japan to the verge of conflict, the repercussions of the outbreak of war in Europe on Anglo–Japanese relations, the Burma Road crisis, British efforts to assist the nationalist Chinese against Japan, and Anglo–Japanese diplomacy and the views of British policy-makers during the summer and fall of 1941. The author shows that the British underestimated Japan's economic and military potential as well as her ability to wage a large-scale war for a protracted period. This book is a continuation of Ann Trotter's study *Britain and East Asia, 1933–1937* (London; New York: Cambridge University Press, 1975, 277p.). It also supersedes in a number of respects Bradford A. Lee's *Britain and the Sino–Japanese War: a study in the dilemmas of British decline* (Stanford, California: Stanford University Press, 1973, 319p.), and complements several studies on relations between the United States and East Asia during the 1930s.

698 Old friends, new enemies: the Royal Navy and the Imperial Japanese Navy; strategic illusions 1936–1941.
Arthur J. Marder.   Oxford, England: Clarendon Press, 1981. 533p. 3 maps.

A vivid portrayal of the roles which the Royal and Imperial Japanese Navies played in their respective governments' decisions for war, of their mutual images, and of the decisive 10 December 1941 battle between these two navies off the coast of Malaya. Part one ('Collision Course') describes the evolution of British and Japanese policies (1936-41) that ultimately led to war. Part two ('Comparisons and Images') depicts the education and spirit of the men and officers of the Imperial Japanese Navy, their *matériel*, tactics and strategy, and the images which the British and Japanese had of one another. Part three ('The Saga of Force Z') narrates and analyses the naval battle in which Saigon-based aircraft of the Japanese navy torpedoed and sank the battleship *Prince of Wales* and the battle-cruiser *Repulse*.

699 **The Pacific War remembered: an oral history collection.**
Edited by John T. Mason, Jr.   Annapolis, Maryland: Naval Institute
Press, 1986. 373p. 16 maps. bibliog.

Excerpts from a substantial collection of personal and poignant interviews about the war against Japan that were conducted with American naval personnel, in particular admirals, rear-admirals, and vice-admirals. Thirty individuals recount their involvement in such aspects of World War II as the Japanese attack on Pearl Harbor, the secret planning for Jimmy Doolittle's April 1942 raid over Tokyo, the struggle for Guadalcanal, the downing of Admiral Yamamoto Isoroku's aircraft by American fighter-planes over Bougainville, the preparations for the assault on Saipan, the conquest of Tinian, the battle for Leyte Gulf, the landing at Iwo Jima, and the Japanese surrender ceremony on the USS *Missouri*. Each interview is preceded by a preface orienting the reader to the battle, the operation, or the period during which the narrated event occurred.

700 **I was a kamikaze: the knights of the divine wind.**
Ryūji Nagatsuka, translated from the French by Nina Rootes,
introduction by Robert Leckie.   London: Abelard-Schuman, 1973;
New York: Macmillan, 1974. 212p.

Nagatsuka describes the background, training, motivations, and emotions of the kamikaze pilots who crashed their aeroplanes on to the decks of American warships during the closing months of World War II; their day-to-day life in their training camps; their early flying experiences; the planes which they flew; and one of the suicidal missions which was carried out in a desperate effort to save Japan from invasion and defeat. These men, Leckie argues in his brief introduction, 'were neither coerced nor brainwashed into volunteering for kamikaze missions'. They all volunteered in order to save their families and homeland during a time of national crisis. The subject of the kamikaze is one of long-standing fascination to Westerners, and Nagatsuka's account is well supplemented by such other books as *The divine wind: Japan's kamikaze force in World War II*, by Rikihei Inoguchi, Tadashi Nakajima, with Roger Pineau (Annapolis, Maryland: US Naval Institute, 1958, 240p. Reprinted, New York: Bantam Books, 1960); *Divine thunder: the life and death of the kamikaze*, by Bernard Millot, translated by Lowell Bair (London: Macdonald, 1971, 243p.); and *Thunder gods: the kamikaze pilots tell their story*, by Hatsuho Naitō, translated by Mayumi Ichikawa, foreword by James Michener (Tokyo; New York: Kodansha International, 1989, 215p.).

701 **Anglo–Japanese alienation 1919–1952: papers of the Anglo–Japanese Conference on the History of the Second World War.**
Edited by Ian Nish.   Cambridge, England; New York: Cambridge
University Press, 1982. 305p. (International Studies).

A collection of fourteen papers dealing with the deterioration of relations between Great Britain and Japan during the 1920s and 1930s; their military and political confrontation during World War II and their planning for the postwar period; and relations immediately following the war. Distinguished British, Japanese, and American scholars examine such topics as Britain and the United States in Japan's views of the international system, 1919-37 and 1937-41; Japanese and British strategy during the Pacific War, 1941-45; Japan's views of the United Kingdom, 1945-52; and Britain's view of postwar Japan, 1945-49. The volume re-examines the view that the war – in its origins, execution, and aftermath – was largely an American–Japanese affair, and provides a more balanced perspective which accounts for Britain's frequently overlooked role during this era.

702 **Defiance in Manchuria: the making of Japanese foreign policy, 1931–1932.**
Sadako N. Ogata. Berkeley, California: University of California Press, 1964. 259p. map. bibliog. (Publications of the Center for Japanese and Korean Studies). Reprinted, Westport, Connecticut: Greenwood Press, 1984.

A lucid, scholarly reconstruction of the step-by-step decision-making of the Manchurian Affair, an historic event which is widely regarded as the prelude to an era of Japanese imperialist expansion throughout East and Southeast Asia. Ogata focuses her study on the policy statements and programmes of the Japanese Kwantung Army, whose middle- and lower-grade officers defied central army and government authorities and whose actions and objectives between the outbreak of the Mukden Incident (September 1931) and the establishment of the so-called independent state of Manchoukuo (February 1932) significantly shaped Japanese foreign policy during that period. Ogata's examination of the Manchurian Affair, her analysis of 'military radicalism' within the officer corps, and her inquiry into the process of policy formulation (1931-32) as well as into the effects of the Affair reveal how the Japanese 'political power structure changed during the military action, and how the emerging structure affected policy formulation'. Other scholarly studies about Sino–Japanese relations during the 1930s include *The United States and the Far Eastern crisis of 1933–1938: from the Manchurian Incident through the initial stage of the undeclared Sino–Japanese War*, by Dorothy Borg (Cambridge, Massachusetts: Harvard University Press, 1964, 674p. [Harvard East Asian Series, 14]); *China and Japan at war, 1937–1945: the politics of collaboration*, by John Hunter Boyle (Stanford, California: Stanford University Press, 1972, 430p.); *The peace conspiracy: Wang Ching-wei and the China War, 1937–1941*, by Gerald E. Bunker (Cambridge, Massachusetts: Harvard University Press, 1972, 327p. [Harvard East Asian Series, 67]); and *The Japanese army in North China, 1937–1941: problems of political and economic control*, by Lincoln Li (Tokyo; London; New York: Oxford University Press, 1975, 278p.).

703 **Japan's longest day.**
Compiled by the Pacific War Research Society [Bungei Shunjū Senshi Kenkyūkai], foreword by Kazutoshi Hando. Tokyo; Palo Alto, California: Kodansha International, 1968. 339p.

An hour-by-hour account of the dramatic events in Tokyo during the day which immediately preceded Emperor Hirohito's nationwide broadcast informing the Japanese people of their country's unconditional surrender. Based on the eyewitness testimony of seventy-nine participants as well as on available documentation, the book reconstructs the actions, emotions, and states of mind of the participants – from the Imperial Conference on 14 August 1945 (at which the final decision to surrender to the

Allied Powers was made), through the abortive coup d'état of some young army officers who took over the Imperial Household Guard, to the broadcast itself at twelve noon on 15 August 1945.

704   **Race to Pearl Harbor: the failure of the Second London Naval Conference and the onset of World War II.**
Stephen E. Pelz.   Cambridge, Massachusetts: Harvard University Press, 1974. 268p. map. bibliog. (Harvard Studies in American–East Asian Relations, 5).

Demonstrates how the breakdown of naval disarmament negotiations among Japan, the United States, and Great Britain led to a spiral of armament building during the 1930s that culminated in the Japanese attack on Pearl Harbor. Pelz details the progression of events as Japan adopted a more belligerent foreign policy and as her naval leaders – supported by most civilian authorities – pressed for abandoning the existing system of naval limitation imposed by the naval disarmament agreements of 1922 and 1930. He also shows how Japan embarked on a major programme of naval expansion, how British economic weakness led His Majesty's government to sacrifice the defence of Britain's Asian empire in the face of Nazi Germany's military challenge, and how the Roosevelt administration encountered difficulties in its efforts to pursue a determined and consistent policy vis-à-vis Japan.

705   **At dawn we slept: the untold story of Pearl Harbor.**
Gordon W. Prange, with Donald M. Goldstein, Katherine V. Dillon. New York: McGraw-Hill, 1981; London: Joseph, 1982; Harmondsworth, Middlesex and New York: Penguin Books, 1982. 873p. 7 maps. bibliog. Reprinted, Norwalk, Connecticut: Easton Press, 1988. (Leather-bound Library of Military History).

The first volume of a trilogy about Japan's surprise attack on US naval installations and the Pacific Fleet at Pearl Harbor. Prange recounts the Japanese planning that went on between January and October 1941, the subsequent course of events that culminated in the attack on 7 December, the reactions on the Hawaiian island of Oahu, in Washington, and within the Japanese naval task force following the attack, and the emotions and thoughts of all of the major participants, both American and Japanese. Prange's second volume, *Pearl Harbor: the verdict of history* (New York: McGraw-Hill, 1986, 699p.), offers an in-depth study of the actions and responsibilities of numerous US government officials and military leaders as well as less important individuals in order to determine who really was to blame for America's military débâcle at Pearl Harbor and whether it could have been prevented. *December 7, 1941: the day the Japanese attacked Pearl Harbor* (New York: McGraw-Hill; London: Harrap, 1988, 493p.), also by Gordon W. Prange, provides a richly detailed, chronological account of 7 December itself – primarily at the major installations on Oahu. Together these three volumes constitute (at least for the present time) the definitive story of a major turning-point in the history of US–Japanese relations. Many other popular and academic books have been written about Pearl Harbor because of the event's historical significance and its enduring interest to a wide range of readers. Among the better-known works are Walter Lord's *Day of infamy* (New York: Henry Holt, 1957, 243p.), Roberta Wohlstetter's *Pearl Harbor: warning and decision* (Stanford, California: Stanford University Press, 1962, 426p.), and John Toland's *Infamy: Pearl Harbor and its aftermath* (Garden City, New York: Doubleday, 1982, 366p.).

706   **Miracle at Midway.**
Gordon W. Prange, with Donald M. Goldstein, Katherine V. Dillon.
New York: McGraw-Hill, 1982; Harmondsworth, Middlesex and New
York: Penguin Books, 1983. 469p. 6 maps. bibliog. Reprinted,
Norwalk, Connecticut: Easton Press, 1986. (Leather-bound Library of
Military History).

In his sequel to *At dawn we slept*, Prange uses eyewitness accounts and the findings of
his extensive archival research to detail the strategies, planning, and decision-making
that concluded in a decisive US naval victory at Midway in early June 1942. Engaging a
large and powerful fleet under the command of Admiral Yamamoto Isoroku, the
smaller US naval force under Admiral Chester Nimitz dealt a crushing defeat to the
Japanese and thwarted their plans to seize control of the island of Midway. This
American 'miracle' marked a turning-point in the Pacific War, for it constituted a
severe setback for the Japanese and cost them the initiative in the struggle for naval
dominance in the Pacific theatre.

707   **Tarawa: the story of a battle.**
Robert Sherrod.   New York: Duell, Sloan and Pearce, 1944. 183p. 5
maps. Reprinted, Fredericksburg, Texas: Admiral Nimitz Foundation,
1973. 206p. New York: Bantam Books, 1983. 192p. (The Bantam War
Book Series).

The battle for heavily defended Tarawa Atoll of the Gilbert Islands in late November
1943 opened a series of amphibious operations in the Central Pacific that aimed
ultimately at the invasion of Japan. US Marines suffered over 3,000 casualties – and an
estimated 4,690 Japanese soldiers were killed – during the ground fighting and the
accompanying air, naval, and artillery bombardments. Relying entirely upon his
memory of what had happened and upon the notebooks which he filled during the
course of the battle, Sherrod (a war correspondent) vividly describes the prelude to the
assault, the Marines who were involved and their feelings, the four days of fighting,
and the devastation and carnage that he witnessed. In his 'Afterthoughts', he contrasts
the stark realities of the war with the relatively insipid American press reports being
published at that time.

708   **Japan and her destiny: my struggle for peace.**
Mamoru Shigemitsu, edited by F. S. G. Piggott, translated with an
introduction by Oswald White.   London: Hutchinson; New York:
Dutton, 1958. 392p.

Shigemitsu Mamoru (1887-1957), a career diplomat who served as Japan's Vice-
Minister and Minister for Foreign Affairs as well as ambassador to Great Britain and
the Soviet Union, reflects on the course of Japanese foreign policy between 1931 and
1945. Presenting his personal (and at times inconsistent) interpretation of the
progression of historical events, he endeavours to explain and frequently defend
Japan's alleged policy of maintaining 'peace and stability' in East Asia as he describes
the inner workings of Japanese politics and graphically recounts such important events
as the Manchurian Incident of 1931-32, the 26 February 1936 attempted coup d'état,
the debates over the direction of Japan's military expansion, the outbreak and progress
of the Sino–Japanese War, the creation of the Tokyo–Berlin–Rome axis, the 'War of
Greater East Asia' (1941-45), and Japan's eventual surrender. Shigemitsu's subjective

account is particularly useful for its revelations of the complex mental processes and world-view of one of Japan's most prominent statesmen of the 1930s and early 1940s.

709 **Eagle against the sun: the American war with Japan.**
Ronald H. Spector.   New York: Free Press; New York: Vintage
Books; New York and Harmondsworth, Middlesex: Viking, 1985.
589p. bibliog. Reprinted, Harmondsworth, Middlesex: Penguin, 1987.

A comprehensive history of the American–Japanese conflict during World War II, based on a synthesis of Allied and Japanese official accounts, memoirs, oral histories, biographies, battle studies, and other secondary literature. Spector writes about the policy, strategy, and operations of the war – primarily from the American point of view – and vividly recreates its major battles and lesser-known campaigns. He focuses in part on the inability of the US army and navy to co-operate fully with one another, on the ongoing debates over the allocation of resources as well as on the internecine quarrels among the Allies, on the nature of the Pacific War as a war of attrition, and on some of the strengths and weaknesses of American leadership. The author concludes that the war was won largely on the basis of 'superior American industrial power and organizational ability'.

710 **Hawaii under the rising sun: Japan's plans for conquest after Pearl Harbor.**
John J. Stephan.   Honolulu, Hawaii: University of Hawaii Press, 1984.
228p. 2 maps. bibliog.

An account of Japanese planning for the invasion and occupation of the Hawaiian Islands. Stephan describes the growth of Japanese interest in Hawaii, showing how the Imperial Navy became increasingly sensitive to Hawaii's strategic importance and how officers on the staff of Admiral Yamamoto Isoroku first conceived of the invasion of the islands and then convinced the army and navy general staffs of its necessity. He argues that the Japanese would have conquered Hawaii early in the war if they had not been decisively defeated at the battle of Midway in June 1942. He also investigates the relationship of the Japanese American community in Hawaii to Japan and the United States respectively, and discusses the role which the Hawaiian Japanese were expected to play in the invasion, occupation, and subsequent development of the islands as part of Japan's Greater East Asia Co-Prosperity Sphere.

711 **Allies of a kind: the United States, Britain and the war against Japan, 1941–1945.**
Christopher Thorne.   London: Hamish Hamilton; New York: Oxford
University Press, 1978. 772p. bibliog. 3 maps.

Embracing not only the United States and Great Britain but also France, the Netherlands, Australia, and New Zealand, this study investigates both the strategic and military aspects and the political elements of their protracted struggle against Japan in Asia and the Pacific. Thorne begins by examining the setting before Pearl Harbor and the Anglo-American relationship between 1939 and 1941. He then divides his account into four major periods – Pearl Harbor to Casablanca (December 1941–January 1943), Casablanca to Cairo (January–December 1943), Cairo to the Second Quebec Conference (December 1943–September 1944), and the Second Quebec Conference to the Japanese Surrender (September 1944–August 1945) – and describes the foreign policy developments as well as the strategic and military aspects of each period as he covers the war against Japan, Anglo-American relations with China and India respectively, the debates and discussions over the future of the European colonial empires in Southeast Asia, and developments in Australasia and the Southwest Pacific. Particular attention throughout is paid to Britain's involvement in the war and to her policies, concerns, and relations with the United States. This book constitutes a sequel to the author's *The limits of foreign policy: the West, the League, and the Far Eastern crisis of 1931–1933* (London: Hamish Hamilton, 1972; New York: Putnam, 1973, 442p. Reprinted, New York: Capricorn Books, 1973). It is in turn complemented by Thorne's *The issue of war: states, societies, and the Far Eastern conflict of 1941–1945* (London: Hamish Hamilton; New York: Oxford University Press, 1985, 364p.).

712 **The rising sun: the decline and fall of the Japanese empire, 1936–1945.**
John Toland. New York: Random House, 1970. 954p. 8 maps. bibliog. Reprinted, London: Cassell, 1971. 954p. New York: Bantam Books, 1971. 1072p.

A Pulitzer Prize author's narrative of the entire course of the Pacific War, preceded by his extended examination of developments between the 26 February 1936 attempted coup d'état in Tokyo and Japan's preparations for her attack on Pearl Harbor. Writing with a sympathetic understanding of Japan, Toland dramatically presents many of the events and decisions of the war from the Japanese perspective – in part to account for Japanese behaviour and plans of action at that time. For this purpose, he utilises numerous documents produced by the Japanese as well as information obtained from his interviews with hundreds of Japanese military and civilian leaders, lower-ranking army and navy personnel, and ordinary individuals.

713 **The Okinawa war.**
Gordon Warner, foreword by James L. Day. Naha, Okinawa: Ikemiya Shokai, 1987. 2nd ed. 214p. 46 maps. bibliog.

The battle for Okinawa, 1 April–23 June 1945, was the single bloodiest battle of the Pacific War, resulting in the death of over 200,000 people, nearly half of whom were Okinawan civilians. Warner's account centres on the capture of the island by US armed forces. Containing large numbers of battlefield photographs and detailed maps, it depicts what was happening not only on the front lines but also with the combat support and service support units. Information about Japanese resistance is provided as well. Since the end of the war, the battle of Okinawa has also been the focus of many other publications, among them *Okinawa: the last battle*, by Roy E. Appleman, James M. Burns, Russell A. Gugeler, and John Stevens (Washington, DC: Historical Division, Department of the Army, 1948, 529p. Reprinted, Rutland, Vermont and Tokyo: Tuttle, 1960. [United States Army in World War II Series]); *Typhoon of steel: the battle for Okinawa*, by James H. Belote and William M. Belote (New York; London: Harper and Row, 1970, 384p.); and *Okinawa, 1945: gateway to Japan*, by Ian Gow (Garden City, New York: Doubleday, 1985; London: Grub Street, 1986, 224p.). Their accounts are more detailed than Warner's but contain substantially fewer illustrations.

714 **Iwo.**
Richard Wheeler. New York: Lippincott and Crowell, 1980. 243p.
New York: Kensington, 1980. 348p. 3 maps. bibliog.

An illustrated narrative of the battle for the small island of Iwo Jima (situated 600 nautical miles south of Tokyo) in February and March 1945. Wheeler, a member of the company that raised the American flag atop Mount Suribachi, depicts the ferocious fighting which raged for weeks between the US marines who invaded and eventually captured this strategic island and the Japanese soldiers who heroically defended it. A vivid, day-by-day picture of the progress of the battle is presented as are some of the feelings and experiences of the combatants. For other accounts of the battle of Iwo Jima, consult the listings under 'Iwo Jima' in *World War II at sea: a bibliography of sources in English. Volume II: The Pacific theater*, by Myron J. Smith, Jr. (q.v.) as well as more recently published accounts such as *Iwo Jima: legacy of valor*, by Bill D. Ross (New York: Vanguard Press, 1985, 376p.).

715 **World War II (Series).**
Alexandria, Virginia: Time-Life Books, 1977-83.

A thirty-nine-volume series of vividly written, popular accounts of World War II in which nine volumes focus specifically on Japan and the war within the Pacific theatre: *The rising sun*, by Arthur Zich (1977, vol. 4); *China–Burma–India*, by Don Moser (1978, vol. 9); *Island fighting*, by Rafael Steinberg (1978, vol. 10); *Return to the Philippines*, by Rafael Steinberg (1979, vol. 15); *The road to Tokyo*, by Keith Wheeler and the Editors of Time-Life Books (1979, vol. 19); *War under the Pacific*, by Keith Wheeler (1980, vol. 23); *Japan at war*, by the Editors of Time-Life Books (1980, vol. 26); *Bombers over Japan*, by Keith Wheeler (1982, vol. 34); and *The fall of Japan*, by Keith Wheeler (1983, vol. 37). The text of each of these 208-page-long books is accompanied by up to ten black-and-white photo-essays, various maps, and a brief bibliography. Altogether the series not only graphically records the major events of the war but also evocatively depicts the human experience at home as well as at the front.

716 **Requiem for battleship Yamato.**
Mitsuru Yoshida, translated with an introduction by Richard H.
Minear. Seattle, Washington; London: University of Washington
Press, 1985. 152p. map.

In April 1945, the supposedly unsinkable super-battleship *Yamato* set sail for Okinawa in a desperate effort to assist Japanese forces engaged in defending that island against American invaders. Attacked by waves of carrier-based American aeroplanes, the ship was sunk off the southwestern coast of Kyūshū with a tremendous loss of life. Yoshida's prose-poem recounts the author's own experiences, observations, thoughts, and reflections as an assistant radar officer aboard the *Yamato* during that fateful voyage and during the final battle itself. Yoshida's ultimate concern was less with bombs and bullets than with human nature, less with death than with life. The *Requiem* is considered by many Japanese today to be a minor literary classic. For American accounts of the sinking of the *Yamato* and of a sister ship, *Shinano*, readers should turn to Russell Spurr's *A glorious way to die: the kamikaze mission of the battleship* Yamato, *April 1945* (New York: Newmarket Press, 1981, 341p.) and to Joseph F. Enright's *Shinano! The sinking of Japan's secret supership* (with James W. Ryan. New York: St. Martin's Press, 1987; London: Bodley Head, 250p.). The latter details the successful attack against this 72,000-ton aircraft carrier that Commander Enright's submarine *Archer-Fish* carried out during the night of 28/29 November 1944.

Japanese, Nazis & Jews: the Jewish refugee community of Shanghai, 1938–1945.
See item no. 4.

Emperor Hirohito and his chief aide-de-camp: the Honjō diary, 1933–36.
See item no. 209.

Target Tokyo: the story of the Sorge spy ring.
See item no. 228.

The atomic bomb and the end of World War II.
See item no. 254.

The other Nuremberg: the untold story of the Tokyo war crimes trials.
See item no. 265.

The reluctant admiral: Yamamoto and the Imperial Navy.
See item no. 317.

Tojo and the coming of the war.
See item no. 321.

Empire and aftermath: Yoshida Shigeru and the Japanese experience, 1878–1954.
See item no. 324.

Konoe Fumimaro: a political biography.
See item no. 340.

No surrender: my thirty-year war.
See item no. 341.

Ishiwara Kanji and Japan's confrontation with the West.
See item no. 342.

War criminal: the life and death of Hirota Koki.
See item no. 346.

The Japanese thread: a life in the U.S. Foreign Service.
See item no. 354.

Tokyo Rose: orphan of the Pacific.
See item no. 387.

Women against war.
See item no. 583.

New Zealand and Japan 1900–1941.
See item no. 665.

Anglo–Japanese trade rivalry in the Middle East in the inter-war period.
See item no. 758.

Fires on the plain.
See item no. 1091.

Harp of Burma.
See item no. 1097.

The Imperial Japanese Navy.
See item no. 1572.

Warships of the Imperial Japanese Navy, 1869–1945.
See item no. 1572.

Japan's foreign policy, 1868–1941: a research guide.
See item no. 1599.

Japan and the world, 1853–1952: a bibliographic guide to Japanese scholarship in foreign relations.
See item no. 1599.

World War II at sea: a bibliography of sources in English. Volume II: The Pacific theater.
See item no. 1609.

See also the section 'History: 1945: Hiroshima and Nagasaki'.

Since 1945

717 **Japan in global ocean politics.**
Tsuneo Akaha. Honolulu, Hawaii: University of Hawaii Press and Law of the Sea Institute, University of Hawaii, 1985. 224p. 2 maps. bibliog.
Examines Japan's reaction to an important global trend of the 1970s: the shift away from the traditional ocean régime based on the principle of the freedom of the seas to the emergence of a new economic and political order characterised by the decision of nation-states to claim territorial jurisdiction over the ocean areas bordering their coastlines and to exert control over their fisheries, mineral rights, and other natural resources. Akaha describes and evaluates Japan's initial opposition to this development and her ultimately successful adjustment to the new ocean order through a detailed analysis of the ocean-policy problems confronting Japan, her participation in the United Nations Conference on the Law of the Sea, her behaviour in bilateral fishery negotiations with other Pacific rim states, and the accommodations that she made amid competing domestic and international pressures.

718 **Japan and the United States: challenges and opportunities.**
Edited by William J. Barnds. New York: New York University Press, 1979; London: Macmillan, 1980. 286p. (A Council on Foreign Relations Book).
A collection of six articles resulting from a series of discussions at the Council of Foreign Relations (New York City) about new developments in Japan and in the American position in East Asia and about their implications for the 1980s and beyond. Written by such American specialists as David MacEachron, Gerald L. Curtis, and I. M. Destler, they are entitled 'New Challenges to a Successful Relationship',

Foreign Relations. Since 1945

'Domestic Politics and Japanese Foreign Policy', 'Japan's Economic Strategy and Prospects', 'Trends in Japanese Foreign and Defense Policies', 'U.S.–Japanese Relations and the American Trade Initiative of 1977: Was This Trip Necessary?', and 'The United States and Japan in Asian Affairs'.

719 **Korea and Japan in world politics.**
Edited by Chin-Wee Chung, Ky-Moon Ohm, Suk-Ryul Yu, Dal-Joong Chang. Seoul: Korean Association of International Relations, 1985. 335p.

Seventeen essays that were first presented at an international conference in Seoul offer an up-to-date overview and assessment of Korean–Japanese relations. Analyses of the evolution of this relationship from both the Korean and Japanese perspectives precede an exploration of the ways in which each country's domestic political trends have affected their bilateral relations. In part three, the contributors describe some of the developing structural problems of Korean–Japanese trade, and consider their implications for the future. Part four focuses on American, European, and Southeast Asian views of selected aspects of the Korean–Japanese relationship; and is followed by an examination of the ways in which the People's Republic of China, the Soviet Union, and Japan's Two-Korea policy have affected these relations. The volume concludes by analysing the issues which Korea and Japan face in the area of Pacific regional co-operation.

720 **Europe and Japan: changing relationships since 1945.**
Edited by Gordon Daniels, Reinhard Drifte. Ashford, Kent: Paul Norbury, 1986. 123p.

A collection of eight essays by British, German, and Japanese scholars which analyse the recent past, present, and future of European–Japanese relations. They are entitled: 'Japan in the Post-war World: between Europe and the United States', 'Political Development, Decision-making and Foreign Policy in Modern Japan', 'The Economic and Non-economic Dimensions of Euro–Japanese Relations', 'Psychological Aspects of Euro–Japanese Trade Frictions: a Japanese Viewpoint', 'Japanese Security Policy and European Security', 'Japanese–Soviet Relations in the Contemporary World', 'Regional Policies in Europe and East Asia', and 'Euro–Japanese Relations: Realities and Prospects'.

721 **Managing an alliance: the politics of U.S.–Japanese relations.**
I. M. Destler, Priscilla Clapp, Hideo Satō, Haruhiro Fukui; foreword by Gilbert Y. Steiner. Washington, DC: Brookings Institution, 1976. 209p. bibliog.

A perceptive examination of the politics and bureaucratic processes that have influenced postwar US–Japanese relations. The authors examine the national political and bureaucratic institutions in Japan and the United States through which policy decisions and actions are taken; consider how officials in each government tend to perceive actions taken by the other; study the interplay between the two governments (for example, the resolution of issues); and offer policy recommendations for managing future US–Japanese relations. To illustrate various points, they draw heavily on three significant episodes: the revision of the bilateral Security Treaty in 1960, the negotiation of the 1969 agreement for the reversion of Okinawa to Japan, and the 1969-71 dispute over Japanese textile exports to the United States.

295

722 **The textile wrangle: conflict in Japanese–American relations, 1969–1971.**
I. M. Destler, Haruhiro Fukui, Hideo Satō. Ithaca, New York;
London: Cornell University Press, 1979. 394p. bibliog.

A study in international relations which details the controversial efforts of the Nixon
administration to pressure the Japanese government into enforcing comprehensive
controls over the export of synthetic and wool textile products to the American
market. Treating the 'textile wrangle' as a political rather than economic issue, the
authors examine the evolution and final outcome of this dispute and indicate how
internal politics in both Japan and the United States impeded its settlement. They also
show 'how and why this particular trade dispute generated a broader political crisis' in
US–Japanese relations and, through an analysis of policy-making within various
ministries, departments, and other governmental bodies, seek to determine how
comparable crises can be avoided in the future.

723 **Japan & Australia: two societies and their interaction.**
Edited by Peter Drysdale, Hironobu Kitaoji, introduction by Peter
Drysdale. Canberra, ACT; London; Miami, Florida: Australian
National University Press, 1981. 447p.

A co-operative undertaking among Australian and Japanese scholars to produce a
fuller picture of both Australian–Japanese relations and the 'societal, institutional, and
political factors which underpin the superstructure of economic, political and cultural
contacts between the two countries'. The volume covers the historical background of
this relationship; important features of both nations' social structure (including
demographic history, social stratification and mobility, family systems, education, and
constitutions); the roles and activities of major social and political interest groups such
as Japan's nationwide farmers' group (Nōkyō), and both Australia's and Japan's labour
unions and bureaucracies; and contemporary interactions between these two societies:
the cultural and social factors in Australian–Japanese relations, the impact of the Cold
War on both nations, and their bilateral economic relationship.

724 **Japan and the Pacific quadrille: the major powers in East Asia.**
Edited with an introduction by Herbert J. Ellison. Boulder,
Colorado; London: Westview Press, 1987. 252p. (A Special Study of
the Kennan Institute for Advanced Russian Studies).

Since the early 1970s, there has been a dramatic transformation in the relationships of
China, Japan, the Soviet Union, and the United States with one another as well as with
the smaller Asian powers. Focusing on Japan as the 'center of the dynamic process of
change in East Asia', the ten American and Japanese contributors to this conference
volume discuss the background and current pattern of relations among these four
nations, the geopolitics of East and Southeast Asia, Japan's central role in East Asia's
economic expansion, the general background of Japan's foreign policy, Japanese–
Chinese relations (1952-82), patterns and prospects of Japanese–Soviet relations, the
economic and security dimensions of Japanese–American relations in the 1980s, and
the changing conceptions among the Japanese of Japan's international role.

725 **The eagle and the rising sun: America and Japan in the twentieth century.**
John K. Emmerson, Harrison M. Holland.   Stanford, California:
Stanford Alumni Association, 1987; Reading, Massachusetts: Addison-
Wesley, 1988. 199p. bibliog. (A Portable Stanford Book).

Two career diplomats who served as foreign service officers in Japan offer a general survey and assessment of the US–Japan relationship. They seek to clear up some of the misunderstandings about the respective roles and responsibilities of the United States and Japan that have arisen in recent years, particularly over trade and defence. Emmerson and Holland trace Japan's modern development and the evolution of US–Japan relations; examine the critical and controversial trade and security issues; comment on Japan's current relations with the Soviet Union, the People's Republic of China, and the Republic of Korea as well as their impact on her relations with the United States; and discuss Japanese intentions to increase their role in international affairs. Barring an economic upheaval, the economic interdependence of Japan and the USA will continue to grow, and their bilateral alliance will survive despite their divergent national interests.

726 **For richer, for poorer: the new U.S.–Japan relationship.**
Ellen L. Frost.   New York: Council on Foreign Relations, 1987. 199p.
bibliog.

A specialist in government and business attributes the current tensions between the United States and Japan to the recent transformation of the US–Japan relationship that has accompanied the rapid shift in the relative wealth of these two countries. In analysing the emotional and political core of this relationship, Frost examines present-day images of wealth and poverty, recent trends in the Japanese economy, the differences in patterns of social behaviour and in styles of leadership and communication between Americans and Japanese, the current nature of Japanese society and politics, and the adjustment which Tokyo and Washington must make to Japan's new world role. Because their two nations are so closely intertwined, it is essential that Americans and Japanese understand both their differences and their similarities and that they work harder – through quiet constructive pressure and a coalition strategy of like-minded groups of Americans and Japanese – to manage their vital partnership.

727 **Fire across the sea: the Vietnam War and Japan, 1965–1975.**
Thomas R. H. Havens.   Princeton, New Jersey; Guildford, Surrey:
Princeton University Press, 1987. 329p. bibliog.

An account of Japan's involvement in the Vietnam War and its impact on Japanese politics, foreign relations, trade, society, and culture during the 1960s and early 1970s. Havens describes the adverse reactions of the Japanese people and the deterioration of their once favourable image of the United States, examines in considerable detail the growth of civilian anti-war activism and the activities of the Beheiren anti-war movement, and discusses the continued support provided by the government of Prime Minister Satō Eisaku in accordance with its treaty obligations. He suggests that Japan traded its non-military support of the war for the reversion of Okinawa to Japanese sovereignty in 1972, and points out how Japan profited economically from the conflict as she emerged as the leading economic power in Southeast Asia. For other writings about Japan's postwar relations with Southeast Asia, see in particular Masashi Nishihara's *The Japanese and Sukarno's Indonesia: Tokyo–Jakarta relations, 1951–1966*

(Honolulu, Hawaii: University Press of Hawaii, 1976, 244p. [Monographs of the Center for Southeast Asian Studies, Kyoto University: English Language Series, 8]), Kunio Yoshihara's *Japanese investment in Southeast Asia* (Honolulu, Hawaii: University Press of Hawaii, 1978, 230p. [Monographs of the Center for Southeast Asian Studies, Kyoto University: English Language Series, 11]), and *Japan and Southeast Asia: a bibliography of historical, economic and political relations*, compiled by Ikuo Iwasaki and issued under the auspices of the Institute of Southeast Asian Studies in Singapore (Tokyo: Library, Institute of Developing Economies, 1983, 176p.).

728   **Japanese foreign policy and domestic politics: the peace agreement with the Soviet Union.**
Donald C. Hellmann.   Berkeley, California; London: University of California Press, 1969. 202p. bibliog. (Publications of the Center for Japanese and Korean Studies).

A comprehensive examination of the dynamics of the Japanese foreign policy-making process and its interrelationship with domestic politics as seen in a case-study of the Soviet–Japanese peace agreement of 1956. Hellmann first sketches the characteristics of this process and the history of Soviet–Japanese negotiations between 1954 and 1956. He then describes the roles played by the Liberal Democratic Party (LDP), public opinion, 'articulate opinion' (the views of senior diplomats, businessmen, policy and issue groups, and the press), business interest groups (especially employers' associations and the fishing industry), and both the Ministry of Foreign Affairs and the national Diet. The most striking feature of these negotiations was the extent to which the control of policy was concentrated in the hands of the LDP. A more descriptive, broader overview of the diplomatic context within which this peace agreement was concluded may be found in *Normalization of Japanese–Soviet relations, 1945–1970*, by Savitri Vishwanathan (Tallahassee, Florida: Diplomatic Press, 1973, 190p.).

729   **Managing diplomacy: the United States and Japan.**
Harrison M. Holland, foreword by John K. Emmerson.   Stanford, California: Hoover Institution Press, 1984. 251p. bibliog. (Hoover Press Publication, 300).

A former foreign service officer compares the differences between Japan and the United States in the management of their respective foreign services. Holland concerns himself with 'the types of persons entrusted with the management of diplomacy: their professionalism, their career expectations and frustrations, their roles as negotiators and decision-makers, their place in the bureaucracy of the national government, and the image they project to the public they serve'. His critical study encompasses the organisation and administration of the Japanese Ministry of Foreign Affairs and the US State Department, the operations of their respective personnel systems (including recruitment, training, assignment procedures, and promotions), the limitations of authority faced by their foreign service officers, their difficulties in staffing, and the public image of these two government entities.

730 **China and Japan, 1949–1980.**
Rajendra Kumar Jain.   Oxford, England: Martin Robertson; Atlantic
Highlands, New Jersey: Humanities Press, 1981. rev. 2nd ed. 339p.
bibliog.
An analysis of the economic, political, and strategic dimensions of postwar
Sino–Japanese relations within the context of the Sino–Soviet dispute, Sino–American
rapprochement, and the new alignment among China, Japan, and the United States.
Jain specifically examines the evolution of Sino–Japanese relations with particular
focus on the normalisation of these relations in 1972, the conclusion of the
China–Japan Peace and Friendship Treaty of 1978, the dispute over the Senkaku
Islands, and recent Sino–Japanese interaction in the economic, political, and energy
spheres. His analysis is accompanied by the full texts or relevant extracts of eighty-
seven bilateral treaties, agreements, joint communiqués, important interviews and
statements by government dignitaries, and press commentaries and editorials. This
book is a revised edition of Jain's *China and Japan, 1949–1976* (London: Martin
Robertson; Atlantic Highlands, New Jersey: Humanities Press, 1977, 336p.).

731 **The Japanese through American eyes.**
Sheila K. Johnson.   Stanford, California: Stanford University Press,
1988. 191p.
A perceptive examination of the evolution of American attitudes and stereotypes
about Japan from the early 1940s through the late 1980s. Basing her analysis primarily
on a study of popular writings – best-selling novels and works of non-fiction such as
James Clavell's *Shōgun* (1975) – and John Hersey's *Hiroshima* (1946), magazine articles,
newspaper and magazine cartoons, movies, and television shows – Johnson reveals
how American perceptions of Japan have changed over the years and how certain
stereotypes about Japan and the Japanese, 'though mutually contradictory, stubbornly
persist'. She discusses some of the major events and developments that have shaped
American images of Japan, among them World War II, the Allied occupation period,
the developing American infatuation with Japanese culture, and Japan's recent
emergence as a powerful, high-tech, industrialised society. In conclusion, Johnson
suggests that the promotion and publicising of a multiplicity of stereotypes about Japan
may benefit the future course of US–Japanese relations.

732 **Japan's new world role.**
Edited by Joshua D. Katz, Tilly C. Friedman-Lichtschein.   Boulder,
Colorado; London: Westview Press, 1985. 190p.
Fifteen Japanese and American government officials, businessmen, and scholars
present their views of Japan's potential for an expanded world role and Japan's
concomitant responsibilities and policy choices. Topics specifically addressed include
the implications for Japan of global security in East Asia, the improvement of
US–Japanese economic relations, Japan's changing role in the United Nations,
evolving Sino–Japanese relations, the Soviet proposal on confidence-building measures
and the Japanese response, the politics of trade liberalisation in Japan, the wider
dimensions of the relationship between the European Economic Community and
Japan, and increased Japanese responsibility for maintaining their own security in the
1980s. This volume is a reprint of the Summer 1983 issue of the *Journal of International
Affairs*.

733 **Between friends: Japanese diplomats look at Japan–U.S. relations.**
Hiroshi Kitamura, Ryōhei Murata, Hisahiko Okazaki, translated by
Daniel R. Zoll, foreword by Angier Biddle Duke. New York; Tokyo:
Weatherhill, 1985. 220p.

Three senior diplomats, all of them with years of experience in US–Japanese relations,
candidly comment on the current state of these relations. Presenting their views in the
form of a round-table discussion, they discuss what they perceive to be some of the
noteworthy economic and political changes in the United States, the differences
between the American and Japanese government and commercial systems, the 'natural
alliance' that exists between the two countries, and Japanese–American relations from
an East–West perspective. They also consider the issue of Japanese defence, growing
bilateral economic friction (with particular focus on the emergence of Japan as an
American scapegoat and on some of the solutions to current economic problems
plaguing their relationship), and the need for communicating ways in which Japan and
the United States can benefit from their mutual co-operation.

734 **The politics of Canadian–Japanese economic relations, 1952–1983.**
Frank Langdon. Vancouver, British Columbia: University of British
Columbia Press, 1983. 180p.

A descriptive account of major issues in the economic sphere that have affected
postwar Canadian relations with Japan. Following a brief review of trade relations and
controversies before World War II, Langdon describes the Canadian commercial
agreement of 1954 that sought to insure entrée to the Japanese market for Canadian
natural resources, the efforts to limit the inroads of Japan's manufactures, Canada's
participation in the North Pacific Fisheries Convention in order to restrain competition
from Japanese fishermen, the problem of securing a foothold in the Japanese market
for Canadian-manufactured and high-technology goods, Canadian actions regarding
uranium exports to Japan and the ultimately unsuccessful sale of a CANDU reactor,
and the activities of Japanese firms investing in Canada. The study concludes with a
summary of major Canadian government policies towards Japan and an assessment of
future prospects.

735 **China and Japan: new economic diplomacy.**
Chae-Jin Lee. Stanford, California: Hoover Institution Press, 1984.
174p. 2 maps. bibliog. (Hoover Press Publication, 297).

This analysis of Sino–Japanese economic diplomacy between the early 1970s and the
early 1980s focuses on how China and Japan conducted their economic negotiations,
what they accomplished and failed to achieve, why problems and difficulties arose in
their relationship, and how they searched for various solutions. Lee first traces the
historical evolution of Sino–Japanese economic relations after 1949. He then focuses
on three prominent examples of economic diplomacy: the collaborative construction of
the multibillion-dollar integrated Baoshan steel complex in a suburb of Shanghai, the
long-term joint offshore Bohai Sea petroleum development projects, and the Japanese
government's economic assistance for several of China's important construction
programmes. He concludes with a brief but broad policy assessment.

736   **Japan faces China: political and economic relations in the postwar era.**
Chae-Jin Lee.   Baltimore, Maryland; London: Johns Hopkins
University Press, 1976. 242p. map.
A detailed investigation of the evolution of relations between Japan and the People's
Republic of China from the establishment of the People's Republic in late 1949
through the inauguration of formal diplomatic relations in 1972. Since the pattern of
Sino–Japanese relations during these two decades fluctuated widely from political,
diplomatic, and strategic differences to bilateral economic and cultural contacts, Lee
focuses on the issues of political confrontation, diplomatic relations, and economic co-
operation. He describes the broad pattern of relations during this era; discusses the
'politics of linkages that Japan's political and economic groups, especially the ruling
Liberal-Democratic Party and the opposition Socialist Party, maintained with China';
and assesses the impact of this inter-party competition and certain other factors upon
the evolution of these relations.

737   **Japan and Korea: the political dimension.**
Chong-Sik Lee.   Stanford, California: Hoover Institution Press, 1985.
234p. map. (Hoover Press Publication, 318).
An analysis of relations between Japan and the Republic of Korea since World War II
that focuses on their political, psychological, and economic differences. Following a
brief discussion of the legacies of the Japanese colonial occupation of Korea, Lee
examines the evolution of their postwar bilateral relations, paying particular attention
to such major issues as the normalisation of relations during the 1960s, the negotiations
over Japanese loans to Korea in 1981-83, and a controversy over the portrayal of
World War II in Japanese textbooks that erupted in 1982. He also considers some of
the efforts to improve relations between these two countries.

738   **Issues in Japan's China policy.**
Wolf Mendl.   London: Macmillan; New York: Oxford University
Press, 1978. 178p. map. bibliog.
An account of Japanese attitudes and policies towards China between 1945 and 1976.
Focusing on four themes that dominated Sino–Japanese relations – trade, the 'two
Chinas' policy, the problem of security and of the international environment, and the
role of the China question in Japanese domestic politics – Mendl traces the evolution
of these relations, discusses the normalisation of Japan's ties with the People's
Republic of China in 1972, examines various aspects of Japan's China problem in the
mid-1970s, and considers the outlook for Japanese policy towards China.

739   **Western Europe and Japan: between the super powers.**
Wolf Mendl.   London: Croom Helm; New York: St. Martin's Press,
1984. 181p.
In light of the changing international environment, Mendl advocates that Japan,
France, West Germany, and the United Kingdom pursue policies which would modify
or limit their present security relationship with the United States and increase their
'business-like relations' with the Soviet Union. While these four nations are too heavily
involved in global affairs to adopt a neutralist or non-aligned stance, they should
nevertheless disassociate themselves from the East–West ideological struggle. Their
own common national interests would be best served if they were to seek a more
independent security policy, contribute to multinational economic assistance and

development projects through the United Nations and other international organisations, and maintain peaceful relations with both of the superpowers.

740 **Japan in the global community: its role and contribution on the eve of the 21st century.**
Edited by Yasusuke Murakami, Yutaka Kōsai. Tokyo: Round Table Discussions on Japan in the Global Community, distributed by the University of Tokyo Press, 1986. 129, 37p.
Twenty-six participants in a series of round-table discussions sponsored by Japan's Ministry of International Trade and Industry collectively present their views on how Japan should be contributing culturally, economically, and politically to the global community during the decades immediately ahead. They assert that Japan's new status as one of the world's major economic powers compels her to play an important role in the newly emerging multipolar international order. The Japanese must become more internationally minded, make some fundamental changes in their economy and society, and strive to eliminate current tensions (particularly in the area of international trade) which threaten the increasingly interconnected and interdependent global system.

741 **Trilateralism in Asia: problems and prospects in U.S.–Japan–ASEAN relations.**
Edited by K. S. Nathan, M. Pathmanathan, foreword by Khoo Kay Kim. Kuala Lumpur: Antara Book Company, 1986. 205p.
An examination of the political, economic, and strategic linkages which exist among the United States, Japan, and the Association of Southeast Asian Nations (ASEAN) and of current areas of convergence and divergence in their relationships. Written primarily by Southeast Asian scholars, several chapters deal with topics that focus on Japan. These include 'Japan's Role in the Pacific Region in the 1980's', 'U.S.–Soviet Relations in Asia: their Impact upon ASEAN and Japan', 'ASEAN Regionalism: Indonesian Perspectives on the Role of the U.S. & Japan', 'Malaysia–Japan Relations in Historical and Regional Perspective', 'Japan's Defence Policy in the Context of Asian Trilateralism', and 'Strategic Issues in the Trilateral Relations of U.S., Japan, and ASEAN'. For an American perspective on these same interrelationships, see *Japan, the United States and a changing Southeast Asia*, by Charles E. Morrison (Lanham, Maryland and London: University Press of America; New York: Asia Society, 1985, 69p. [Asian Agenda Report, 1]).

742 **Japan in postwar Asia.**
Laurence Olson. New York; London: Published for the Council on Foreign Relations by Praeger, 1970. 292p. bibliog.
Olson traces Japan's attitudes, actions, and policies vis-à-vis East, Southeast, and South Asia from the signing of the San Francisco Peace Treaty (1952) to 1964, when she pursued a low-key policy in Asia, and then from 1964 to 1969, when Japanese activities became increasingly visible within the region. He first surveys Japan's efforts to atone for her activities in World War II, to overcome the wartime legacy of hatred and distrust among her Asian neighbours, and to create a new network of economic relationships in Asia. He also examines Japanese efforts to resume relations and conduct trade with both the People's Republic of China and the Republic of Korea. Olson then focuses on the key elements of two major policy debates which have engaged Japanese foreign policy-makers since the mid-1960s: the question of Japan's

security and how it could be affected by developments in China, and the optimal level and nature of Japanese economic and technical assistance to the developing world. He concludes by considering the scope of Japanese involvement in the non-Communist countries of Asia during the 1960s and Japan's future policy options there.

743 **Japan's foreign relations: a global search for economic security.**
Edited with an introduction by Robert S. Ozaki, Walter Arnold.
Boulder, Colorado; London: Westview, 1985. 240p. (Westview Special Studies on East Asia).

A well-integrated investigation of how Japan's postwar economic growth has affected the nature of her recent foreign relations, and of the ways and extent to which economic principles have had to be compromised because of political, legal, cultural, or ideological reasons. The contributors analyse Japan's relations with North America, the European Community, Oceania, the USSR, the COMECON (economic association of Communist) countries, China, the Association of Southeast Asian Nations (ASEAN), the Middle East, Latin America, Africa, Korea, and Taiwan, focusing on developments during the 1970s and predicting likely trends in the 1980s. They frequently show that various trends and issues in Japan's foreign relations have been overshadowed by the problems which she has encountered in the process of integrating her domestic economy with the world market.

744 **Protest in Tokyo: the Security Treaty crisis of 1960.**
George R. Packard, III.   Princeton, New Jersey: Princeton University Press, 1966. 423p. bibliog. Reprinted, Westport, Connecticut: Greenwood Press, 1978.

The revision of the US–Japan Security Treaty became the focal point of a bitter political struggle in May–June 1960. It was characterised by anti-treaty riots and demonstrations, and led to the cancellation of President Eisenhower's scheduled visit to Japan as well as to the resignation of Prime Minister Kishi Nobusuke. Focusing upon the Japanese political process, Packard describes and analyses the background of the treaty revision issue, the support for treaty negotiations among the conservatives and the vigorous opposition manifested by the political left (especially the socialists, communists, Sōhyō, and the Zengakuren student federation), the organisation of the protests and the tactics of the opposition, the counter-tactics of the government, the succession of events between the storming of the Diet on 27 November 1959 and Kishi's announcement of his intended resignation on 23 June 1960, and the aftermath of the crisis. Packard shows that the crisis did not derive from one single cause but rather 'resulted from the convergence of international and domestic forces'.

745 **Coming to terms: the politics of Australia's trade with Japan, 1945–57.**
Alan Rix.   Sydney, New South Wales; London: Allen and Unwin, 1986. 267p. bibliog.

An examination of the several stages and mechanisms involved in the process of postwar rapprochement between Australia and Japan. Rix opens with an assessment of Australian wartime planning for postwar trade, particularly as it related to Japan, and with a study of Australia's initial policies towards the Occupation and her early steps in determining the potential of trade with Japan. He then focuses on the arrangements that were made for financing trade in essential goods, the renewal of private trade with Japan, the role and impact of the sterling payments arrangements that boosted bilateral trade, international efforts to gain entry for Japan into GATT (General Agreement on Tariffs and Trade), the 1951 peace treaty, and Australia's eventual acceptance of most-favoured-nation treatment for Japan. Finally Rix considers the impact of market pressures upon the Australian government during the 1950s, Japanese interests in trading with Australia, the gradual dismantling of Australian trade barriers against Japan, and Australia's agreement to the trade negotiations that led to the bilateral Commerce Agreement of 1957.

746 **Japan's economic aid: policy-making and politics.**
Alan Rix. London: Croom Helm; New York: St. Martin's Press, 1980. 286p. bibliog.

This examination of postwar Japan's foreign aid decision-making process demonstrates that 'bureaucratic interests were the main determinants of the articulation of Japan's aid and economic cooperation policies'. Rix first traces the growth of Japanese interest in extending economic assistance to other countries, and details the creation of the Japan International Cooperation Agency in 1974. He then outlines the various elements of Japan's domestic aid system, describes the decision-making involved in allocating four major types of development aid, and analyses the politics of the budgetary process for aid. Finally, Rix discusses the interaction of the agencies which implement the foreign aid programmes, the activities of private firms, and the recipient nations; shows how the patterns of Japanese aid policy have been maintained by persisting emphasis on certain key bilateral relationships; and considers recent patterns of growth and change in Japan's foreign aid programme.

747 **Soviet policy towards Japan: an analysis of trends in the 1970s and 1980s.**
Myles L. C. Robertson. Cambridge, England; New York: Cambridge University Press, 1988. 234p. bibliog. (Cambridge Studies in International Relations, 1).

A close examination, primarily from a Soviet viewpoint, of Soviet–Japanese relations between the early 1970s and 1985. Four major sections focus on (1) the influence of ideology on Soviet policy and Soviet ideological views of Japan at the global level, at the regional (Pacific) level, and as a social-political structure; (2) the Soviet–Japanese economic relationship and the politics of Soviet–Japanese trade, with consideration of such matters as the concentration of trade on energy-related materials and on the development of Siberia; (3) Soviet strategy in northeast Asia and the Pacific, Soviet military policy in operation within that region, and the problems created for Japan as a result of the growth of Soviet military strength; and (4) Soviet perceptions of the Sino–Japanese and American–Japanese relationships as well as an assessment of the extent to which the Soviets comprehend Japanese politics and policy processes.

748 **The foreign policy of modern Japan.**
Edited by Robert A. Scalapino, foreword by Edwin O. Reischauer. Berkeley, California; London: University of California Press, 1977. 426p.

Thirteen American and Japanese scholars share their views on a wide range of subjects relating to Japanese foreign policy. These include policy-making within the Japanese Foreign Ministry, the relatively impotent role of the Diet in foreign policy-making, the Japanese 'tactical style' of negotiating internationally, Japanese public opinion and foreign affairs between 1964 and 1973, Japanese foreign policy-making and the Tyumen oil development project in Siberia, the involvement of the Japanese business community in the normalisation of Japan's relations with the People's Republic of China, the international economic policy developed by the Ministry of International Trade and Industry, Japanese security and postwar Japanese foreign policy, basic trends in Japan's security policies, and the foundations of modern Japanese foreign policy. Altogether these essays constitute a broadly based explanation of the processes and institutions involved in the making of Japan's foreign policy during the 1960s and the early 1970s.

749 **Japan and the Asian Pacific region: profile of change.**
Masahide Shibusawa. London: Croom Helm; New York: St. Martin's Press, 1984. 196p. map. bibliog.
Shibusawa traces the major political and economic changes that have occurred in East and Southeast Asia since World War II and examines the response of Japan and her neighbours to these developments. Against this backdrop he studies four major events which shook Japan during the 1970s – changes in Sino–Japanese relations, discord in US–Japanese relations, anti-Japanese movements in Southeast Asia, and the oil shock of 1973 – and explains how she successfully maintained her balance and momentum during that era. Finally, the author surveys the recent growth of the economies of the Asian Pacific region, examines their interdependence with Japan, and considers Japan's evolving role there as well as in the world in general. In accounting for the nature of Japan's postwar involvement in Asia, he emphasizes such themes as her concerted efforts to develop her economy, her concern for economic security, and her contributions to Asian regional stability.

750 **Tokyo and Washington: dilemmas of a mature alliance.**
Frederick L. Shiels. Lexington, Massachusetts; Toronto, Ontario: Lexington Books, 1980. 202p. 3 maps. bibliog.
An examination of the nature of the important alliance that exists between Japan and the United States and the ways in which it functioned between 1952 and 1980. Shiels is particularly concerned with how leadership styles and bureaucratic politics in both countries have shaped the policies and critical decisions that significantly influenced the course of this bilateral relationship. He discusses the evolution of a close relationship before 1972 as well as the subsequent emergence of problems of communication and gaps in mutual understanding. Finally, he examines developments under the Nixon, Ford, and Carter administrations, including the strains that occurred in US–Japanese mutual security ties and the growing bilateral trade friction.

751 **Japan and Australia in the seventies.**
Edited with a preface by James Arthur Ainscow Stockwin. Sydney, New South Wales; London: Angus and Robertson in association with the Australian Institute of International Affairs, 1972. 223p.
A collection of conference papers, commentaries, and edited discussion concerning Japan's economy, politics, and defence policies as well as her postwar relations with Australia. Essays focusing on the Australian–Japanese relationship during the 1960s include 'Australia's Economic Relations with Japan: Dependence or Partnership?', 'Educational and Cultural Aspects of Australian–Japanese Relations', 'Japan in Australia's Future', and 'Immigration in Australian–Japanese Relations'.

752 **The Soviet Union and postwar Japan: escalating challenge and response.**
Rodger Swearingen, foreword by Edwin O. Reischauer. Stanford,
California: Hoover Institution Press, 1978. 340p. 2 maps. (Hoover
Institution Publication, 197).

In this detailed account of Soviet–Japanese relations, 1945-78, Swearingen examines
Soviet policy and practice in occupied Japan, Soviet indoctrination of repatriated
Japanese prisoners-of-war, Moscow's ties with the Japan Communist Party, Soviet
intentions and techniques in the process of normalising diplomatic relations with
Japan, and Japanese public opinion towards the USSR and the ways in which it has
been influenced by the press. He also discusses the joint economic ventures that have
taken place in Siberia, the growth of bilateral trade, and the lingering diplomatic and
strategic problems of Japanese fishing rights off the Siberian coasts, the unresolved
territorial dispute over the southern Kurile Islands (Japan's 'Northern Territories'),
and various security concerns. The texts of thirty-eight postwar treaties and agreements
appear in full or in summary form within an appendix.

753 **The United States and Japan: a troubled partnership.**
William Watts. Cambridge, Massachusetts: Ballinger, 1984. 118p.

Drawing upon extensive public opinion surveys conducted in Japan and the United
States in 1982-83 as well as upon his own experience and expertise, Watts explores the
differing views, attitudes, and perceptions which Japanese and Americans have of one
another. He examines the realities and images of US–Japanese economic relations as
well as related economic issues and problems; evaluates the state of the bilateral
security alliance; considers the effect of one's age on public opinion in both countries;
and interprets important trends and identifies areas of contention and misunderstanding. Characterising the US–Japan relationship as 'both remarkably strong and yet
weak', Watts urges Americans to 'cool the rhetoric, open fully and strengthen the lines
of communication' with Japan, and make a more concerted effort to work
harmoniously with the Japanese.

754 **An empire in eclipse: Japan in the postwar American alliance system; a**
study in the interaction of domestic politics and foreign policy.
John Welfield. London; Atlantic Highlands, New Jersey: Athlone
Press, 1988. 513p. bibliog.

A scholarly examination of Japanese politics and diplomacy between the closing
months of World War II and the collapse of Soviet–American *détente* in 1978. Welfield
attempts to demonstrate the essential continuity of postwar Japan's foreign relations –
in particular, her extremely close and special relationship with the United States – by
'exploring the roots of the Japanese diplomatic tradition, examining the background
and objectives of Japan's postwar leaders, tracing the movement of public opinion, and
carefully analysing the interaction between domestic politics and foreign policy'. His
chronologically organised study is concerned in part with Japan and the US Pacific
alliance system; Japan, the United States and China; Japanese rearmament, the Self-
Defence Forces, and defence policy decision-making; the 1960 Security Treaty crisis;
domestic politics, foreign policy, and the reversion of Okinawa; Japan's nuclear
policies and the non-proliferation treaty; and Japanese foreign policy in the age of
détente.

755 **Japan versus Europe: a history of misunderstanding.**
Endymion Wilkinson. Harmondsworth, Middlesex; New York:
Penguin Books, 1983. 288p. 3 maps.

A discussion of relations between Japan and the European Community within their broader cultural and historical context. Part one – 'The Upside-down Land: Japan as Seen by the Europeans' – examines the evolution of the European image of Japan from 'aesthetic vogue' and 'military and colonial power' to 'world economic power' and a nation of 'paradoxical people'. Part two – 'The Cultural Museum: Europe as Seen by the Japanese' – traces Japanese attitudes towards the West and the formation of their images of Europe. Wilkinson argues that the Japanese have a more accurate understanding of Europe than do Europeans of Japan. Part three focuses on Japan's rise as an economic power, on Europe's relative decline, and on the economic and trade frictions between them during the late 1970s and the early 1980s. In part four, the author suggests various measures for improving bilateral relations and communications. This book is a revised edition of Wilkinson's *Misunderstanding: Europe vs. Japan* (Tokyo: Chūōkōron-sha, 1981, 293p.).

756 **Japan and the Asian Development Bank.**
Dennis T. Yasutomo. New York: Praeger, 1983. 210p. bibliog.
(Studies of the East Asian Institute, Columbia University).

Japan has played a very active and pivotal role since the early 1960s in the establishment, administration, and expansion of the Manila-based Asian Development Bank, an international organisation that promotes the funding and execution of development projects throughout Asia. Yasutomo describes the history and dimensions of Japanese involvement in the Bank from its inception through 1982. He casts his analysis in terms of Japanese initiative and activities; shows how the Japanese 'moved from ambivalence and hesitation toward a regional bank scheme to their most intimate relationship with any international organization'; and pays special attention to politics (e.g., the decision to reject Tokyo as the site of the Bank's headquarters), personnel issues (among them the Japanese participation in the Bank's staffing and management), and the interplay of various national interests.

757 **The manner of giving: strategic aid and Japanese foreign policy.**
Dennis T. Yasutomo. Lexington, Massachusetts; Toronto, Ontario:
Lexington Books, 1986. 139p. bibliog. (Studies of the East Asian
Institute, Columbia University).

An analysis of Japanese foreign aid policy and, in particular, the recent emergence of strategic aid as a political tool in Japan's relations with the Third World. Yasutomo points out that Japanese foreign aid is no longer simply a matter of economics but has instead become 'a foreign policy tool for achieving political and security objectives as well as economic benefits'. It has in fact become the central pillar of Japan's overall diplomacy, especially her broadly conceived national security policy. Yasutomo investigates this politicisation of Japan's strategic aid policy as well as its globalisation by studying such matters as its origins and evolution, the amount of public support that it enjoys, its effect on Japan's traditionally regional aid focus, its reflection of Japan's peculiar national interests as well as her lack of a world-class army and navy, and its role in Japan's foreign policy and her relations with the United States.

758   **Caught in the Middle East: Japan's diplomacy in transition.**
      Michael M. Yoshitsu.   Lexington, Massachusetts; Toronto, Ontario:
      Lexington Books, 1984. 113p. bibliog.

An analysis of the transformation of Japanese policies towards the Middle East
between the early 1970s and the early 1980s. Yoshitsu focuses on five major events and
developments: Japan's new Middle East diplomacy in the wake of the oil embargo that
accompanied the 1973 Arab–Israeli war, the emergence of Japanese relations with the
Palestine Liberation Organisation, the crisis surrounding the Iranian seizure of
hostages at the American Embassy in Teheran in 1979-80, the Soviet military invasion
of Afghanistan, and the outbreak of the Iran–Iraq War. The author examines Japan's
diplomatic response to each development and shows how Tokyo increasingly adopted
foreign policy initiatives that were at variance with the policies of the United States.
Japanese economic relations with the Arab World and North Africa during the 1920s
and the 1930s, in turn, are examined in Hiroshi Shimizu's *Anglo-Japanese trade rivalry
in the Middle East in the inter-war period* (London: Published for the Middle East
Centre, St. Antony's College, Oxford by Ithaca Press, 1986, 302p. [St. Antony's
Middle East Monographs, 17]).

**The Pacific alliance: United States foreign economy policy and Japanese trade
recovery, 1945–1955.**
See item no. 264.

Occupation diplomacy: Britain, the United States and Japan, 1945–1952.
See item no. 266.

The American occupation of Japan: the origins of the cold war in Asia.
See item no. 279.

Japan and the San Francisco peace settlement.
See item no. 283.

Japan's postwar peace settlements.
See item no. 283.

The Soviet seizure of the Kuriles.
See item no. 285.

The Okinawa problem: a chapter in Japan–U.S. relations.
See item no. 285.

The Japanese thread: a life in the U.S. Foreign Service.
See item no. 354.

My life between Japan and America.
See item no. 360.

The politics of labor legislation in Japan: national–international interaction.
See item no. 609.

Policymaking in contemporary Japan.
See item no. 620.

Party in power: the Japanese Liberal-Democrats and policy-making.
See item no. 633.

The Japanese Socialist Party and neutralism: a study of a political party and its foreign policy.
See item no. 637.

Anglo–Japanese alienation 1919–1952: papers of the Anglo–Japanese Conference on the History of the Second World War.
See item no. 701.

Japan's quest for comprehensive security: defence – diplomacy – dependence.
See item no. 762.

The common security interests of Japan, the United States, and NATO.
See item no. 765.

Japan re-armed.
See item no. 766.

U.S.–Japanese security relations: a historical perspective.
See item no. 768.

Japan and the new ocean regime.
See item no. 796.

The political economy of Japan. Volume 2: The changing international context.
See item no. 817.

U.S.–Japanese energy relations: cooperation and competition.
See item no. 847.

The politics of Japan's energy strategy: resources – diplomacy – security.
See item no. 849.

Partners in prosperity: strategic industries for the United States and Japan.
See item no. 873.

Coping with U.S.–Japanese economic conflicts.
See item no. 892.

Japan and Western Europe: conflict and cooperation.
See item no. 910.

Asian Survey.
See item no. 1491.

Japan Review of International Affairs.
See item no. 1514.

JEI Report.
See item no. 1524.

Journal of Northeast Asian Studies.
See item no. 1528.

Pacific Affairs.
See item no. 1536.

Foreign Relations. Since 1945

Speaking of Japan.
See item no. 1540.

Technology and Development.
See item no. 1541.

Japan and Korea: an annotated bibliography of doctoral dissertations in Western languages, 1877–1969.
See item no. 1607.

Doctoral dissertations on Japan and on Korea, 1969–1979: an annotated bibliography of studies in Western languages.
See item no. 1607.

The Allied occupation of Japan, 1945–1952: an annotated bibliography of Western-language materials.
See item no. 1613.

Military and Defence (since 1945)

759 **The postwar rearmament of Japanese maritime forces, 1945–71.**
James E. Auer, foreword by Arleigh Burke. New York; London:
Praeger, 1973. 345p. 4 maps. bibliog. (Praeger Special Studies in
International Politics and Government).

An investigation of the early history of Japan's postwar naval forces and some of the
problems which they faced during the 1950s and 1960s. Auer first discusses the
historical background of the postwar navy and the demobilisation and continuation of
naval activities during the Allied occupation of Japan (1945-52). He then traces the
role and development of the Japanese Maritime Self-Defence Force from 1953 through
1971, and examines its problems in recruiting, retaining, educating, and training
qualified personnel as well as its difficulties in securing up-to-date technology,
weaponry, and adequate logistical support.

760 **Beyond war: Japan's concept of comprehensive national security.**
Robert W. Barnett. Washington, DC: Pergamon-Brassey's
International Defense Publishers, 1984. 154p.

An inquiry into how the Japanese believe they 'should help to forestall, to prevent, or
to limit war'. Barnett opens with a translation of the official summary of a report on
comprehensive national security that was prepared by a task force headed by Inoki
Masamichi and submitted to the Japanese government in 1980, and with his own
evaluation of that report. He then provides an account of the views that were
expressed by over fifty informed Americans, Japanese, and other Asians when they
candidly discussed the origins of the report, its meaning and operational significance,
and its implications for Japan's role in the security arrangements of the Pacific region.
This account was based on Barnett's private conversations in Washington, Tokyo, and
elsewhere with defence specialists, high government officials, foreign service officers,
economists, journalists, and scholars.

761 **The modern Japanese military system.**
Edited with an introduction by James H. Buck. Beverly Hills,
California; London: Sage Publications, 1975. 253p. bibliog. (Sage
Research Progress Series on War, Revolution, and Peacekeeping, 5).

Nine American scholars discuss the historical background and institutional charac-
teristics of Japan's Self-Defence Forces as well as civilian–military relations and
security policy in contemporary Japan. Their essays are entitled 'The Japanese Military
Tradition'; 'The Evolution of the Japan Self-Defense Forces'; 'Recruitment and
Training in the SDF' [Self-Defence Forces]; 'The Constitutionality of Japan's Defense
Establishment'; 'Defense Policy and the Business Community: the Keidanren Defense
Production Committee'; 'Public Views of the Japanese Defense System'; 'Power,
Politics, and Defense'; 'National Security Perspectives: Japan and Asia'; and 'The
Japanese Military in the 1980s'. Five appendixes to this collection provide the text of
the United States–Japan Security Treaty (1960) and statistical information about
defence expenditures and military manpower.

762 **Japan's quest for comprehensive security:**
defence – diplomacy – dependence.
John W. M. Chapman, Reinhard Drifte, Ian T. M. Gow. London:
Frances Pinter; New York: St. Martin's Press, 1982. 259p. bibliog.

An examination of some of the military, diplomatic, and economic aspects of Japan's
comprehensive national security policy, viewed from an explicitly European perspective. Gow studies the political environment within which defence policy is formulated,
the military elements (e.g., the Self-Defence Forces) in Japan's postwar defence, the
key actors within the Japanese defence establishment, and the development of Japan's
defence policy and her defence plans. Drifte analyses Japan's foreign policy system as a
pillar of her comprehensive security policy, the changing strategic environment of
Japan within East Asia, and the disarmament and arms control measures that
constitute an integral part of Japan's concept of comprehensive national security.
Finally, Chapman considers the economic importance of Japan's metal-processing
industries and their dependence on a continuous flow of imported minerals, the
Japanese concern for ensuring themselves stable and secure supplies of energy and
foodstuffs, and the increasingly close Japanese ties with the countries of the Pacific
region.

763 **Arms production in Japan: the military applications of civilian**
technology.
Reinhard Drifte. Boulder, Colorado; London: Westview Press, 1986.
134p. bibliog. (Westview Special Studies on East Asia).

Recent changes in Japan's domestic and international environment have encouraged
her leaders not only to strengthen their country's national defence but also to expand
Japanese involvement in the development and production of modern weapons systems.
Drifte surveys the evolution and present-day situation of Japan's arms production
capabilities, and studies the nature of research and development in Japan, the
shipbuilding industry, aircraft production, the space and missile industry, and arms
exports. He points out that Japan's growing Self-Defence Forces rely primarily on
domestic production to meet their needs and that some of the research carried out
within the civilian sector could be adapted for military use. Appendixes to his book

contain the texts of the US–Japan Exchange of Technology Agreements of 1983 and the Detailed Arrangement for Exchange of Military Technologies of 1985.

764 **Managing defense: Japan's dilemma.**
Harrison M. Holland. Lanham, Maryland; London: University Press of America, 1988. 134p. 2 maps. bibliog.

Explores the role of Japanese bureaucrats and politicians in the decision-making directly related to their country's defence policy. Holland focuses on Japan's defence budget; on the defence charter that is known as the National Defence Programme Outline (NDPO); and on the Mid-Term Planning Estimate (MTPE), the Japan Defence Agency's annual review of defence policy. He examines how the preparation of the annual defence budget is affected by conflicting domestic and foreign pressures and shows how the NDPO and MTPE have been interpreted by government officials and politicians as they have sought to steer a middle course between the demands of the Japanese public, which has generally opposed a greater defence effort because of its nervousness over military spending and its fear of resurgent militarism, and the demands of the United States government, which has been expressing its impatience with the slow growth in Japanese defence capabilities and Japan's inadequate defence 'burden-sharing'. A case-study of the 1985 defence budget and translations of the Defence Agency Establishment Law, the NDPO, and the MTPE for 1985 are included.

765 **The common security interests of Japan, the United States, and NATO.**
Joint Working Group of the Atlantic Council of the United States and the Research Institute for Peace and Security, Tokyo; U. Alexis Johnson, chairman; George R. Packard, rapporteur; foreword by Kenneth Rush, Masamichi Inoki. Cambridge, Massachusetts: Ballinger, 1981. 232p. map.

Over fifty members of a binational research project identify the common security interests and problem areas of Japan, the USA, and NATO (North Atlantic Treaty Organization), and recommend policies for future co-operative action. They focus on Japan's role in the Western alliance and on its consequences for East Asian security, relations with China and the Soviet Union, and Japan's self-defence strategies. A policy paper summarising their discussions is followed by ten individual studies. Among these are two papers that present the American and Japanese perspectives on the balance of power in East Asia and the Western Pacific in the 1980s, and four essays respectively entitled: 'Japan's Foreign Policy and Areas of Common Interest, Possible Cooperation, and Potential Friction among Japan, the United States, and Other Western Countries'; 'The U.S.–Japan Alliance: Overview and Outlook'; 'U.S.–Japan Relations in Retrospect and Future Challenges'; and 'Japan's Self-Defense Requirements and Capabilities'.

766 **Japan re-armed.**
Malcolm McIntosh. London: Frances Pinter; New York: St. Martin's Press, 1986. 169p. map. bibliog.

A critique of Japan's current policy of rearmament. McIntosh's historical overview is followed by a picture of how Japan has been rearming at an alarming rate in recent years. He discusses Japan's security treaty with the United States, the origins and nature of her Self-Defence Forces, the perceived as well as the real threats confronting Japan, her relations with the superpowers, and some of the determinants of her

313

external relations as well as the pressures upon her to build up her military strength. Concluding with an examination of certain ongoing changes in Japan that have resulted from the rise of the political right wing and the country's 'growing militarism', McIntosh expresses the hope that Japan will reject the dictates of American foreign policy and instead adopt a policy of neutrality which will enable her to play a leading role in the creation of a nuclear-free Pacific Ocean region.

767 U.S.–Japan strategic reciprocity: a neo-internationalist view.

Edward A. Olsen. Stanford, California: Hoover Institution Press, 1985. 194p. (Hoover Press Publication, 307).

Olsen sketches the history of postwar US–Japanese security ties, describes the mutuality and conflict which characterise their security interests, considers their significantly different perceptions of the threats facing Japan, and reviews the recent evolution of their bilateral economic relations. In addition, he critically assesses how both countries differ in their respective levels of defence preparedness as well as in the commitments which they have made to the burden of defence burden-sharing, discusses Japanese strategic thinking, and recommends ways for the United States to develop unequivocal ideas of what it expects of Japan and of how to guide Japan most effectively. Olsen concludes by strongly advocating that both nations strive towards 'the sort of strategic and economic interdependence that will put U.S.–Japan relations on a firm footing in the 1990s' and beyond.

768 U.S.–Japanese security relations: a historical perspective.

Richard L. Sneider. New York: East Asian Institute, Columbia University, 1982. 117p. (Occasional Papers of the East Asian Institute).

A prominent US government official with many years of experience in East Asian affairs considers the past, present, and future of Japanese security relations with the United States. Sneider argues that American policy towards Japan must be based on a sound and realistic assessment of the debates going on within Japan over the scale and future direction of the Japanese defence effort. With this in mind, he examines the element of continuity in the past history of US–Japan security relations, the changing defence scene and the ensuing controversies over Japan's appropriate defence posture, present-day public and political attitudes towards defence in Japan, current Japanese government defence and security policies, and the policy dilemmas facing both Japan and the United States in the security defence area.

769 Japanese policy and East Asian security.

Taketsugu Tsurutani. New York: Praeger, 1981. 208p. bibliog. (Praeger Special Studies) (Praeger Scientific).

An inquiry into Japanese defence policy and Japan's role in promoting and maintaining effective arrangements for regional security in East Asia in the 1980s. Tsurutani opens with a discussion of Japan's new security predicament and of her status as a 'fragile superpower' – a highly industrialised democracy and island nation that is extremely dependent on foreign trade and increasingly sensitive to regional instability. He then provides a synoptic description and analysis of changes in East Asian regional security during the 1970s and examines the status of Japan's national defence, the major features of the security debate within Japan, and various aspects of present-day Japan–US security arrangements. Finally, Tsurutani considers the character, motivation, and dynamics of Japanese politics and foreign policy and offers a series of recommendations concerning the direction of the country's defence policy and the nature of her growing responsibility for security within East Asia.

770   **Japan's postwar defense policy, 1947–1968.**
      Martin E. Weinstein.   New York; London: Columbia University
      Press, 1971. 160p. bibliog. (Studies of the East Asian Institute,
      Columbia University).

The first serious study of the sources and early development of Japan's postwar defence policy. Weinstein begins by discussing the origins and basic conception of this policy during the early years of the Allied occupation period. He then traces its evolution through the Korean War era and its modification through the 1951 and 1960 security treaties with the United States. He also analyses the growth of Japan's Self-Defence Forces (the armed forces designed to protect the country against foreign aggression) and examines their role in her defence policy during the 1950s and 1960s. Weinstein contends that Japan's conservative government leaders consistently adhered to a carefully defined defence policy which was based on their own strategic views and was not simply 'a response to American initiatives and to pacifist, antirearmament opinion' in Japan.

Sheathing the sword: the demilitarisation of Japan.
See item no. 271.

Arms, yen & power: the Japanese dilemma.
See item no. 354.

Will Japan rearm? a study in attitudes.
See item no. 354.

Managing an alliance: the politics of U.S.–Japanese relations.
See item no. 721.

Western Europe and Japan: between the super powers.
See item no. 739.

Protest in Tokyo: the Security Treaty crisis of 1960.
See item no. 744.

Soviet policy towards Japan: an analysis of trends in the 1970s and 1980s.
See item no. 747.

The foreign policy of modern Japan.
See item no. 748.

Tokyo and Washington: dilemmas of a mature alliance.
See item no. 750.

Japan and Australia in the seventies.
See item no. 751.

The United States and Japan: a troubled partnership.
See item no. 753.

An empire in eclipse: Japan in the postwar American alliance system; a study

Military and Defence (since 1945)

in the interaction of domestic politics and foreign policy.
See item no. 754.

The manner of giving: strategic aid and Japanese foreign policy.
See item no. 757.

White Papers of Japan: Annual Abstracts of Official Reports and Statistics of the Japanese Government.
See item no. 829.

AMPO: Japan-Asia Quarterly Review.
See item no. 1488.

Asian Survey.
See item no. 1491.

Journal of Northeast Asian Studies.
See item no. 1528.

Pacific Affairs.
See item no. 1536.

Law and Constitution

Law

771 **Freedom of expression in Japan: a study in comparative law, politics, and society.**
Lawrence Ward Beer, foreword by Masami Itō. Tokyo; New York: Kodansha International, 1984. 415p.

Beer opens with discussions of the Japanese legal system, the evolution of freedom in Japan between the 1860s and the 1980s, Japanese social patterns and the freedom of expression, and official regulations and the promotion of freedom throughout Japan. Then, in part two ('Some Legal Questions on Freedom of Expression'), he proceeds to 'shed new light on the mind, sociopolitical life, and law of Japan through the multifaceted prism of freedom of expression'. He examines various legal issues and significant court decisions including the freedoms of assembly and association; the rights of workers (especially public employees); freedom of information; freedom of expression in the mass media; the issues of media defamation and invasion of privacy; the question of obscenity; relationships among publishing, education, ideology, and freedom of expression; freedom of advertising; and freedom of expression during election campaigns.

772 **Japanese criminal procedure.**
Shigemitsu Dandō, translated by B. J. George, Jr.   South Hackensack, New Jersey: Fred B. Rothman, 1965. 663p. (Publications of the Comparative Criminal Law Project, New York University, 4).

A scholarly introduction to the Japanese law of criminal procedure. Dandō discusses its forms and essential nature; the mechanisms of criminal proceedings, with particular focus on the courts and the parties; the basic elements of criminal proceedings, including the development of the prosecution and the termination of the proceedings; and such aspects of criminal proceedings as compulsory measures, investigation, trial in the first instance, appeal, extraordinary proceedings in review, and the criminal compensation law.

773 **The intellectual property law of Japan.**
Teruo Doi. Alphen aan den Rijn, The Netherlands; Germantown, Maryland: Sijthoff & Noordhoff, 1980. 335p.

A comprehensive treatise written for foreign investors, authors, businessmen, lawyers, and patent agents who seek protection for intellectual property in Japan. Doi covers the substantive and procedural aspects of the patent system, the Utility Model Law, the protection of unpatented technical know-how and trade secrets, the substantive and procedural aspects of the protection of industrial designs under the Design Law, the essential features of the Trademark Law, the law to prevent unfair competition, the main provisions of the Copyright Law, and the regulation of various types of licensing agreements under the Antimonopoly Law. His text frequently explains important court decisions and statutory provisions, and it contains a very extensive table of statutes, ordinances, regulations, and treaties.

774 **Patent and know-how licensing in Japan and the United States.**
Edited by Teruo Doi, Warren L. Shattuck. Seattle, Washington; London: University of Washington Press, 1977. 430p. (Asian Law Series, 5).

Eighteen American and Japanese attorneys, lawyers, and university professors offer basic information about the substantive and procedural aspects of the Japanese and American patent systems. In particular, they discuss the legal protection of know-how, the law governing remedies, antitrust, taxation, and the fundamentals of licensing agreements. The seven chapters focusing on Japan are entitled 'A Comparative Study of the Patent Laws of the United States and Japan', 'The Protection of Unpatented Know-how and Trade Secrets in the United States and Japan', 'Patent Office and Court Procedures in Japan', 'Drafting License Agreements in Japan and in the United States', 'Remedies for Breach of License Agreements', 'Regulation of International Licensing Agreements under the Japanese Antimonopoly Law', and 'Japanese Taxation of Patent and Know-how Licensing'. Appendixes provide the texts of several agreements.

775 **Environmental law in Japan.**
Julian Gresser, Kōichirō Fujikura, Akio Morishima. Cambridge, Massachusetts; London: MIT Press, 1981. 525p. (Harvard Studies in East Asian Law).

This comprehensive assessment of the development and implementation of Japan's environmental law and policy begins by surveying Japan's legal response to environmental problems from an historical perspective and by showing how many Japanese came to view pollution in moral terms as they found their health endangered by the pollution that accompanied postwar economic growth. By recognising new rights and remedies, Japanese courts helped articulate and legitimise such new values as the sanctity of human life, individual dignity, and the integrity of local communities which emerged during the 1960s and 1970s. The authors then discuss recent Japanese environmental protection legislation and its administration, including the incentives used to induce industry's compliance with environmental policies. They also analyse Japan's compensation system for pollution-related health injuries and the uses of conciliation, mediation, and arbitration in the settlement of environmental disputes. The volume concludes by placing Japan's environmental law and policy in international perspective.

776 **Japanese business law and the legal system.**
Elliott J. Hahn. Westport, Connecticut; London: Quorum Books,
1984. 168p. bibliog.

Intended as a 'primer on the workings of the Japanese business law system for the
American lawyer or businessman who needs to understand the major aspects of the
system and how to work within it'. For this purpose, Hahn discusses the role of
lawyers, legal education, quasi-lawyers, and the court system of Japan; the appropriate
ways for negotiating with the Japanese; the ways of doing business in Japan; the legal
aspects of doing business in Japan; the role of the government in the Japanese business
law system; and antitrust in Japan. Throughout he points out various cultural,
sociological, and economic differences between the United States and Japan, and
stresses the importance of being sensitive to the 'beliefs, customs, modes of behavior,
and values' embodied within the Japanese business law system.

777 **Law and society in contemporary Japan: American perspectives.**
Edited with an introduction by John O. Haley. Dubuque, Iowa:
Kendall/Hunt, 1988. 313p. bibliog.

Thirteen essays reflecting current American scholarship on Japanese law collectively
'provide important insights into the function and limits of law as an instrument for
social ordering in contemporary Japan'. They discuss Japan's constitutional system and
its judicial interpretation, Japanese administrative law, the role of administrative
guidance during the oil crisis of 1973-74, the oil cartel criminal cases, the doctrinal
adaptation of administrative guidance in the courts, declining public ownership of
Japanese industry as a case of regulatory failure, the 1973 Japanese law for the
compensation of pollution-related health damage, public and private responses to a
chemical disaster in Japan, the legal framework of Japanese approaches to equal rights
for women, legal obstacles to marital dissolution and their impact, the use and non-use
of contract law in Japan, the discretionary authority of public prosecutors in Japan,
and the Buraku Liberation League's use of violence as an instrument of social change.

778 **Conciliation and Japanese law: Tokugawa and modern.**
Dan Fenno Henderson. Seattle, Washington: University of
Washington Press; Tokyo: University of Tokyo Press, 1964. 2 vols.
bibliog. (Association for Asian Studies. Monographs and Papers, 13).

An investigation of the use of conciliation (or mediation) in Japanese society between
the 1740s and 1964. It explores the political implications of various kinds of Japanese
techniques for resolving private civil disputes, particularly as they 'affect the
enforcement of rights and popular right-consciousness essential to democratic
government and rational industrial society'. Henderson presents an overview of
traditional conciliation and the concept and role of law in Tokugawa society; examines
the nature of Tokugawa courts and their jurisdiction, the hierarchy of procedural
protection in the shogunal courts, and settlement by conciliation in Tokugawa civil
trials; discusses the modern analogies to Tokugawa conciliatory practices; and
describes as well as evaluates modern practices of mediating disputes as they have been
formalised in procedural law under Japan's postwar constitution. The concluding one
hundred pages of the second volume comprise a bibliography of sources and writings
on Tokugawa and modern Japanese law.

Law and Constitution. Law

779 **Foreign enterprise in Japan: laws and policies.**
Dan Fenno Henderson, foreword by Stephen M. Schwebel.   Chapel
Hill, North Carolina: University of North Carolina Press, 1973. 574p.
bibliog. (The American Society of International Law. Studies in
Foreign Investment and Economic Development).

Henderson's authoritative treatment of the general environment and the legal
problems of foreign enterprises in Japan as of the early 1970s opens with an historical
survey and detailed descriptions of the country's political climate, the scope and
dynamics of the Japanese economy, the business environment, and the legal
environment for foreign enterprise. Part three, 'Legal Problems of Foreign Enterprises'
– the core of this study – critically examines the legal institutions which govern the
introduction and participation of foreign capital and technology in the Japanese
economy. It describes the economic ministries, 'administrative guidance', and laws that
are concerned with the administration and entry of foreign enterprises; Japan's capital
liberalisation and counter-liberalisation measures; contracts and contractual problems
between Japanese and foreign enterprises; and the use of arbitration to settle disputes.

780 **Conspiracy at Matsukawa.**
Chalmers Johnson.   Berkeley, California; London: University of
California Press, 1972. 460p. 2 maps. bibliog. (Publications of the
Center for Japanese and Korean Studies).

In August 1949, a passenger train was allegedly sabotaged by communists and trade
union leaders at Matsukawa in Fukushima Prefecture. The resulting investigations and
trials continued until the complete exoneration of the defendants in 1970. Johnson uses
this exhaustive study of the Matsukawa case to examine the functioning of the postwar
Japanese procuratorial and judicial system, to analyse American efforts to introduce
Anglo-American adversary proceedings and certain other reforms into Japanese
criminal trials, to consider various changes in American policy during the latter half of
the Allied occupation period, and to discuss the role of Japan's trade unions in the
country's postwar economic development. He also evaluates the impact which the
American-initiated reforms had upon the Matsukawa case in particular and generally
upon the administration of justice in Japan after World War II.

781 **Japanese securities regulation.**
Edited by Louis Loss, Makoto Yazawa, Barbara Ann Banoff.   Tokyo:
University of Tokyo Press; Boston, Massachusetts: Little, Brown, 1983.
420p. bibliog.

A comprehensive overview of securities regulation in Japan during the early 1980s,
prepared by a committee of fifty-six scholars, government officials, and members of the
securities industry chaired by Suzuki Takeo. The volume first offers synopses of
securities regulation in the United States and Japan respectively. It then examines the
Japanese disclosure system and the regulation of the distribution of securities; the
coverage of the disclosure system; international securities transactions; the regulation
of broker-dealers; the regulation of exchange markets; the relations between securities
corporations and their customers; proxy regulation, tender offers, and insider trading;
civil liabilities; and investment trusts. Appendixes contain the translated texts of the
Securities and Exchange Law, the Law on Foreign Securities Firms, the Securities
Investment Trust Law, and the Banking Law.

782 **Introduction to Japanese law.**
Yoshiyuki Noda, translated and edited by Anthony H. Angelo.
Tokyo: University of Tokyo Press, 1976. 253p.

Noda first sketches the historical evolution of Japanese law and provides a detailed outline of the postwar legal system and its structure in which he covers the emperor, the legislature, the executive, the courts, the legal profession, the judiciary, and legislative statutes. In a section entitled 'Japanese and the Law' he analyses a number of commonly held Japanese attitudes towards law and stresses the importance of such extra-legal factors as Japanese customs and the rules of social obligation or duty that are known as *giri*. A section on the sources of Japanese law concludes the volume.

783 **Law and trade issues of the Japanese economy: American and Japanese perspectives.**
Edited with an introduction by Gary R. Saxonhouse, Kozo
Yamamura, foreword by Glenn Campbell. Seattle, Washington
London: University of Washington Press; Tokyo: University of Tokyo
Press, 1986. 290p.

Nine essays by Japanese and American officials, lawyers, and economists examine the legal institutions surrounding US–Japanese economic relations. Part one, 'Japanese Legal Framework and Domestic Economy Institutions', discusses the existence and the enforcement of Japanese laws that affect the practices and behaviour of individuals, firms, and the government. These include economic laws which influence household savings behaviour, antitrust and industrial policy, product liability rules, and the government's administrative guidance. The second part, 'Japan's Legal Framework and Foreign Access to the Japanese Market', examines selected aspects of Japanese foreign exchange controls and banking law which affect American access to the Japanese market as well as the role of intellectual property law in US–Japanese licensing transactions. The concluding part of this volume studies the role of American laws in US–Japanese economic relations, with particular focus on antitrust matters, the National Security Clause of the Trade Expansion Act of 1962, and the alleged dumping of Japanese television sets.

784 **The Japanese legal system: introductory cases and materials.**
Edited by Hideo Tanaka, with Malcolm D. H. Smith. Tokyo:
University of Tokyo Press; Berkeley, California: University of
California Press, 1976. 954p. bibliog.

This comprehensive introduction to Japanese law, legal structure, and legal procedures – taking essentially the form of a casebook for law students – provides extensive excerpts from published legal decisions, scholarly articles, and other relevant sources. The authors present the complete texts of the Meiji and postwar constitutions, describe Japan's constitutional system and her legal institutions, and discuss the so-called 'legal process' in Japan, the post-1867 development of Japanese law, the role of law and lawyers in Japanese society, courts and procedure, the nature of the legal profession, Japanese constitutional history since the Meiji Restoration, judicial review, the 'renunciation of war' clause (Article 9) in the postwar constitution, and the constitutional guarantee of human rights. A closing chapter outlines the procedures for undertaking research in Japanese legal materials.

785 **Law and social change in postwar Japan.**
Frank K. Upham. Cambridge, Massachusetts; London: Harvard
University Press, 1987. 269p.

Investigates the ways in which political élites have used legal rules and institutions to manage and direct the course of social conflict and change. Focusing on the legal framework within which social conflict develops and evolves, Upham analyses the evolution of the anti-pollution movement and the development of the government's industrial pollution control policy; the struggle of the *burakumin* (an outcaste group) to overcome and eliminate social discrimination; the elimination of discrimination against women in working conditions, wages, and personnel practices; and the formation and implementation of economic policy by the Ministry of International Trade and Industry. The author studies each aggrieved party's choice of litigation, mediation, or violent self-help, and how their options were broadened or narrowed by legal doctrine or government policy. He also examines the government's response to both their tactics and their substantive grievances. Throughout Upham looks at the social role of the courts and legal doctrine and shows how the government has manipulated the legal environment.

786 **Law in Japan: the legal order in a changing society.**
Edited by Arthur Taylor von Mehren. Cambridge, Massachusetts:
Harvard University Press; Tokyo: Tuttle, 1963. 706p.

Seventeen Japanese legal scholars write about various aspects of law in postwar Japan. Their essays deal with the development of Japanese law between 1868 and 1961, dispute resolution in postwar Japan, the process of litigation, the historical development and current state of the legal profession, the education of the legal profession, constitutional development, the judicial review of administrative actions, some aspects of Japanese criminal law, the administration of criminal justice, therapeutic and preventive aspects of criminal justice, the individualistic premise and modern Japanese family law, the treatment of motor-vehicle accidents, labour relations law, the law of unfair competition and the control of monopoly power, commercial law, shareholder–management relations under Japanese law, and the computation of income in Japanese income taxation.

The development of Kamakura rule, 1180–1250: a history with documents.
See item no. 148.

The other Nuremberg: the untold story of the Tokyo war crimes trial.
See item no. 265.

Legal reform in occupied Japan: a participant looks back.
See item no. 277.

The bamboo people: the law and Japanese–Americans.
See item no. 384.

Women in Japan: discrimination, resistance and reform.
See item no. 575.

The politics of labor legislation in Japan: national–international interaction.
See item no. 609.

Japan in global ocean politics.
See item no. 717.

Law in Japan: an Annual.
See item no. 1531.

An index to Japanese law: a bibliography of Western language materials, 1867–1973.
See item no. 1582.

Constitution

787 **The constitution of Japan: its first twenty years, 1947–1967.**
Edited with an introduction by Dan Fenno Henderson. Seattle, Washington; London: University of Washington Press, 1968. 323p. (Asian Law Series, 1).

Several American and Japanese authorities review the achievements and problems of Japan's postwar constitution in this symposium volume. Their essays are entitled: 'The Japanese Constitutional Style'; 'Twenty Years of Revisionism'; 'Some Reminiscences of Japan's Commission on the Constitution'; 'Appendix: Opinion on Some Constitutional Problems – the Rule of Law'; 'Japanese Judicial Review of Legislation: the First Twenty Years'; 'Political Questions and Judicial Review: a Comparison'; 'Judicial Review of Administrative Actions in Japan'; 'The Public Welfare Standard and Freedom of Expression in Japan'; 'Protection of Property Rights and Due Process of Law in the Japanese Constitution'; and 'The "Right of Silence" in Japanese Law'. John M. Maki's article 'The Documents of Japan's Commission on the Constitution' and the text of the postwar constitution are also reprinted.

788 **The constitutional case law of Japan: selected Supreme Court decisions, 1961–70.**
Compiled and translated with an introduction by Hiroshi Itoh, Lawrence Ward Beer. Seattle, Washington; London: University of Washington Press, 1978. 283p. map. bibliog. (Asian Law Series, 6).

A presentation of thirty-two noteworthy Supreme Court decisions. These cases covered a wide range of issues including the constitutionality of the Income Tax Law and of a police law, the validity of a Diet election, the right of resident aliens to visit their ancestral home (North Korea) and re-enter Japan, the rights of public employees, the state's lack of any obligation to provide students with free textbooks under the compulsory education system, the right to participate in election politics, the inadmissibility of evidence obtained from a criminal suspect under duress, restrictions on business advertising, the right to distribute politically inflammatory pamphlets, the permissibility of limiting academic freedom under the public welfare doctrine, and the regulation of poster displays on telephone poles. While this volume does not analyse the legal, socio-economic, or political significance of these cases, the introductory chapter explains Japan's judicial system and the major trends in constitutional law during the early postwar era.

789   **Japan's Commission on the Constitution: the final report.**
Japan. Kempō Chōsakai [Commission on the Constitution], translated
and edited with an introduction by John M. Maki.   Seattle,
Washington; London: University of Washington Press, 1980. 413p.
bibliog. (Asian Law Series, 7).

The final report of the government commission which between 1957 and 1964
investigated a wide range of issues related to Japan's postwar constitution, including
the unusual circumstances of its enactment, problems arising from its application,
interpretations of each article, and the possibilities of its revision. The report is divided
into four parts: 'The Establishment and Organization of the Commission'; 'Duties,
Organization, and Operation of the Commission'; 'The Investigations and Deliberations of the Commission'; and 'The Opinions of the Commissioners'. Maki's brief
introduction evaluates the commission's contribution to the study of the constitution
from the perspective of the late 1970s.

790   **Court and constitution in Japan: selected Supreme Court decisions,
1948–60.**
John M. Maki, translated by Masaaki Ikeda, David C. S. Sissons, Kurt
Steiner.   Seattle, Washington: University of Washington Press, 1964.
445p. bibliog. (University of Washington Publications on Asia).

Translations of twenty-six representative constitutional decisions of the Supreme
Court, selected on the basis of their importance, the nature of the issues with which
they dealt, and their ability to illuminate the opinions of the Court and the individual
justices. They include decisions concerned with obscenity and freedom of expression;
the licensing of public gatherings; filial piety, patricide, and equality under the law; the
constitutionality of the death penalty; the admission of confessions made under duress;
denial of an application for a writ of habeus corpus; 'just compensation' in Article 29
and the land reform of the Allied occupation period; the constitutionality under Article
9 of United States military bases in Japan; the Supreme Court and constitutional
review; the power of the Cabinet to dissolve the House of Representatives; and local
autonomy, the Prime Minister, and the courts.

Foundations of constitutional government in modern Japan, 1868–1900.
See item no. 189.

**Hermann Roesler and the making of the Meiji state: an examination of his
background and his influence on the founders of modern Japan & the
complete text of the Meiji Constitution accompanied by his personal
commentaries and notes.**
See item no. 189.

Minobe Tatsukichi: interpreter of constitutionalism in Japan.
See item no. 220.

Democratizing Japan: the Allied occupation.
See item no. 280.

Japan's political revolution under MacArthur: a participant's account.
See item no. 281.

Party in power: the Japanese Liberal-Democrats and policy-making.
See item no. 633.

The Japanese legal system: introductory cases and materials.
See item no. 784.

An index to Japanese law: a bibliography of Western language materials, 1867–1973.
See item no. 1582.

The Allied occupation of Japan, 1945–1952: an annotated bibliography of Western-language materials.
See item no. 1613.

Economy

General

791　**The Japanese economy.**
George Cyril Allen.　New York: St. Martin's Press; London: Weidenfeld and Nicolson, 1981. 226p. bibliog.

A survey that not only describes the state of the postwar economy but also analyses the operations of its various sectors. Following an overview of major developments before 1945, Allen surveys the recovery and expansion of the economy after World War II as well as the economic functions of both the central and local governments, in particular the relations between their respective bureaucracies and private industry. Japan's financial system and monetary policy, agriculture, manufacturing industry (including its management and capital, evolving structure, organisation, technology, and policies), industrial relations system, and foreign trade and investment are each examined at length. Allen continually emphasizes the contribution of Japan's social and political institutions to the country's phenomenal economic success, and concludes with a summation of Japan's achievements as well as the factors responsible for them.

792　**Japan: an economic survey, 1953–1973.**
Andrea Boltho.　London; New York: Oxford University Press, 1975. 204p. map. bibliog. (Economies of the World).

A description and discussion of the phenomenal growth of the Japanese economy during the years when Japan surged ahead to become one of the world's leading economic powers. Part one provides an overview of the most important postwar trends of the economy, its structural features, and the economy's actual performance. The second half of the book examines those factors which contributed the most to Japan's economic growth: capital formation, labour supply, the role of government economic policies, foreign trade, and income distribution.

793 **How Japan's economy grew so fast: the sources of postwar expansion.**
Edward F. Denison, William K. Chung, foreword by Gilbert Y.
Steiner. Washington, DC: Brookings Institution, 1976. 267p.

A quantitative analysis of the determinants of economic growth in Japan between 1953
and 1971, with frequent comparisons between Japan and ten Western countries.
Denison and Chung first compare Japan's levels of output and consumption in 1970
with five other industrial nations, briefly describe Japan's record of postwar economic
growth, and present estimates of the sources of that growth. They then discuss the
individual determinants of her economic growth: the increase in labour employment,
the increase in the stock of private capital, the reallocation of labour from agriculture
and self-employment, the incorporation of improved technology into production, and
the adoption of economies of scale. The authors also analyse the sources of differences
in the level of output per person employed and conclude with some predictions about
Japan's future economic growth rate. Several appendixes describe in detail the data
sources and estimation procedures employed in this study.

794 **Flexible rigidities: industrial policy and structural adjustment in the
Japanese economy, 1970–80.**
Ronald Dore. Stanford, California: Stanford University Press,
London: Athlone Press, 1986. 278p. bibliog.

Dore seeks to establish how and why Japan, 'an economy which almost flaunts its
rigidities as a matter of principle', successfully met three major economic challenges
during the 1970s: absorbing the rise in the price of imported oil, controlling inflationary
pressures, and decisively shifting the weight of its industrial structure away from
declining to competitive industries. He examines the ability of businessmen, labourers
and their unions, and the government to adapt to changing economic circumstances, to
co-operate in stimulating innovation and growth, and to adjust the structure of the
Japanese economy. Through a detailed case-study he also documents the adjustment
and modernisation which actually occurred in the textile and clothing industries at that
time.

795 **Taking Japan seriously: a Confucian perspective on leading economic
issues.**
Ronald Dore. London: Athlone Press; Stanford, California: Stanford
University Press, 1987. 264p. bibliog.

Japan's growing economic prowess and competitive strength are a result in part of her
successful response to the technological and organisational opportunities and
requirements of the late twentieth century. The Japanese can be emulated in many
ways that would improve economic efficiency and social justice as well as enhance
social cohesion in the West, and Japanese methods and institutions – among them the
practice of lifetime employment of workers with flexible if specialist skills, the
emphasis on 'meritocracy' (a system in which educational merit constitutes a major
criterion of 'worker quality'), and the increasing intervention of the state in the
development of the country's international competitiveness (a practice known as
'industrial policy') – should be studied very seriously. Emphasizing the 'economic and
social importance of a concern for fairness and compromise', Dore also argues for the
adoption – as the Japanese have done – of conventions, precedents, and norms which
would improve the quality of interpersonal relationships and prevent market forces
alone from determining the allocation either of resources or of rewards.

796 **Japan and the new ocean regime.**
Robert L. Friedheim, George O. Totten, III, Haruhiro Fukui, Tsuneo
Akaha, Masayuki Takeyama, Mamoru Koga, Hiroyuki Nakahara.
Boulder, Colorado: Westview Press; Epping, Essex: Bowker, 1984.
383p. 5 maps. (Westview Special Studies in Ocean Science and Policy).

On Japan's response to the need for developing a modern ocean policy that would be
in accord with decisions reached at the United Nations Conference on the Law of the
Sea. The volume opens with an assessment of general trends in ocean management and
with discussions of government structures for handling ocean policy. Several case-
studies then examine the decision-making processes and the contents of specific ocean-
related policies in recent years. These involve fundamental changes in the Japanese
shipbuilding industry, Japan's fisheries policy, the development of a manganese nodule
policy, Japanese–Korean negotiations over offshore petroleum development, and the
siting of a nuclear power generating plant along the coast at Onagawa, Miyagi
Prefecture (in northeastern Honshū).

797 **Miracle by design: the real reasons behind Japan's economic success.**
Frank Gibney. New York: Times Books; Toronto, Ontario: Fitzhenry
& Whiteside, 1982. 239p.

Gibney, a journalist, businessman and scholar, explores the reasons for Japan's
'miraculous' recovery from the defeat and destruction of World War II and for her
phenomenal economic growth in more recent years. He delves into the basic elements
of Japanese business including the Japanese work ethic, the people-centred orientation
of Japanese management, the Japanese concern for the integrity of the company, the
company unions that work, the use of consultation and consensus to resolve problems
together with the rejection of the adversary method as a way to settle disputes, the
close, co-operative relationship between business and government, and the intense
pursuit of quality control. Japan's success is attributed to her ability to combine
traditional Japanese values and the Confucian work ethic with capitalist business know-
how acquired from the United States. Numerous comparisons with current American
practices and the author's concluding chapter suggest ways in which Americans can
profit from the Japanese example.

798 **The internationalization of the Japanese economy.**
Chikara Higashi, G. Peter Lauter. Boston, Massachusetts; Lancaster,
England: Kluwer Academic Publishers, 1987. 273p. bibliog.

Japan's recent decision and current efforts to 'internationalise' her economy by shifting
from export-led growth to domestic demand-led growth constitute the focus of this
study. Paying particular attention to the 1985 Action Program and the 1986 Maekawa
Commission Report, Higashi and Lauter explore the key issues surrounding the
domestic and international economic policy alternatives available to the Japanese
government. They discuss the major events which exerted pressure upon the Japanese
to change their economic ways, among them the recent conflicts in US–Japan trade
relations and Japan's success in accumulating large current and trade account
surpluses. They also examine the controversies within Japan surrounding the
internationalisation process, some of the potential constraints on internationalisation,
trends and changes already under way in 1986, and both the domestic policy and
international policy options (e.g., tax reform, privatisation, reduced working hours,
increased foreign direct investment) open to the Japanese.

799   **The era of high-speed growth: notes on the postwar Japanese economy.**
Yutaka Kōsai, translated by Jacqueline Kaminski.   Tokyo: University
of Tokyo Press, 1986. 223p.

Kōsai, a member of Japan's Economic Planning Agency during the 1960s and 1970s,
recounts the history of Japan's phenomenal postwar economic recovery and growth.
He divides the postwar economy into three eras: the period of reconstruction (from
1945 to 1955); the ensuing period of rapid growth (through 1970); and the adjustment
period of the 1970s and early 1980s, which was characterised by a general movement
towards stable growth. He then traces the roots of Japan's 'economic miracle' to the
fiscal and monetary policies of the immediate postwar decade and analyses the
economic and political record of the years when Japan's economy grew at the high
annual rate of nearly ten percent.

800   **Japan: facing economic maturity.**
Edward J. Lincoln, foreword by Bruce K. MacLaury.   Washington,
DC: Brookings Institution, 1988. 298p.

A study of macroeconomic developments in Japan since the oil crisis of 1973 and their
implications for US–Japanese economic relations as well as for the domestic Japanese
economy. Lincoln discusses the declining rate of economic growth that came with
economic maturity in the 1970s as well as the complex interplay of forces that brought
about an unprecedented imbalance between continued high levels of savings and the
need for only moderate levels of investment. Financial deregulation as an outgrowth of
these shifts is also considered. He analyses the role of government deficit spending in
absorbing the savings–investment imbalance in the 1970s, and the enormous rise of
Japan's current-account surplus with the world in absorbing it in the 1980s. Lincoln
emphasizes the need for macroeconomic issues and developments to be part of the
bilateral US–Japan agenda, and concludes with a presentation of Japan's options for
stimulating domestic demand through reducing private-sector savings, increasing
investment, and raising government spending.

801   **America versus Japan: a comparative study of business–government
relations conducted at the Harvard Business School.**
Edited by Thomas K. McCraw.   Boston, Massachusetts: Harvard
Business School Press, 1986. 463p.

The similarities and differences between Japan and the United States in the realm of
business policy-making as well as the nature and problems of their current bilateral
economic relationship constitute the focus of this well-integrated study. Fourteen
largely non-Japan specialists associated with the Harvard Business School contribute
essays concerned with trade and the protection of world export markets, cross-
investment in Japan and the United States, their respective production and distribution
structures, agriculture, energy markets and policy, environmental pollution and
regulation, financial institutions, and fiscal and disinvestment policies. This volume is
addressed to a broad American audience for whom it seeks to elucidate the present-
day interaction of business and government within the two major economic powers of
the non-communist world.

802 **The challenge of Japan's internationalization: organization and culture.**
Edited by Hiroshi Mannari, Harumi Befu. Nishinomiya, Hyōgo,
Japan: Kwansei Gakuin University; Tokyo and New York: Kodansha
International, 1983. 308p. bibliog.

With Japan's emergence as a global power, the concept of 'internationalisation'
(*kokusaika*) has become a potent force in Japan. In these international conference
proceedings, sixteen Japanese and Western scholars assess the impact of internationalisation on the Japanese economy, corporate management, politics, religion, and
personal values. The contributors deal with such topics as the consequences of the
close relationship between the government and industry for the internationalisation of
the Japanese economy, the internationalisation of management in Japanese multinational corporations, the effect of the postwar democratisation of Japan and
internationalisation on the corporate management of the Kikkoman Corporation, the
management of high technology in Japan and the United States, Japanese work-related
values as reflected in the attitudes of Japanese employees of a multinational
corporation, the national and international dimensions of religion in Japan, the
secularisation of Japanese civil religion, and internationalisation as an ideology in
Japanese society.

803 **The economic development of Japan: a quantitative study.**
Ryōshin Minami, translated by Ralph Thompson, Ryōshin Minami,
with the assistance of David Merriman. London: Macmillan; New
York: St. Martin's Press, 1986. 487p. map. bibliog. (Studies in the
Modern Japanese Economy).

A detailed structural, quantitative, and overall analysis of a century of economic
growth between the early Meiji period and 1980, replete with over two hundred
statistical tables and figures. The subjects covered in this study include Japan's
readiness for modern economic growth, the growth rate during modern economic
growth, agriculture during industrialisation, industrialisation itself, capital formation
and its sources, foreign trade, population and labour supply, labour market and dual
structure, public finance and the financial system, prices and living standards, and the
future prospects of economic growth. Three major themes are emphasized: why Japan
was able to achieve modern economic growth initially; why she could achieve a more
rapid rate of economic growth than other developed countries; and what the probable
future of her economy might be. International comparisons are frequently provided in
order to offer a better perspective of Japan's economic experiences.

804 **Why has Japan 'succeeded'? Western technology and the Japanese
ethos.**
Michio Morishima. Cambridge, England; New York: Cambridge
University Press, 1982. 207p. map.

In a series of lectures first delivered at Cambridge University in 1981, Morishima
attempts to interpret the factors unique to Japan's history and culture which account
for the nature and degree of her economic success. Writing in the tradition of Max
Weber, he uses economic, sociological, religious, and historical forces to describe
Japan's rapid development since the Meiji period and to isolate the most significant
causes for the remarkably strong performance of the Japanese economy during the
1960s and 1970s.

805   **The postwar Japanese economy: its development and structure.**
Takafusa Nakamura, translated by Jacqueline Kaminski.   Tokyo:
University of Tokyo Press, 1981. 277p.
Nakamura, a leading economist, describes the evolution and inner workings of the
Japanese economy since World War II. He opens with an historical account of the
legacy of Japan's wartime economic patterns, the changes introduced under the Allied
occupation, and the period of rapid growth that ensued. He then examines from a
structural point of view several aspects of the postwar economy including the
mechanism and policies for its growth, the economy's 'dual structure' (with its large
modern-sector firms and small traditional-sector entrepreneurial firms), changes in
agriculture, government participation in economic affairs, the banking and monetary
systems, Japanese foreign trade and economic relations with the rest of the world, and
the major economic developments of the 1970s – among them the adjustments that
occurred in the wake of the abandonment of the 360 yen-to-the-dollar exchange rate,
the oil crisis of 1973-74, and Japan's emergence as the new economic 'superpower'.
Covering the period 1868-1941, Nakamura's *Economic growth in prewar Japan* (q.v.)
offers a more historical perspective on this subject.

806   **Japan and the developing countries: a comparative analysis.**
Edited with an introduction by Kazushi Ohkawa, Gustav Ranis, with
Larry Meissner.   Oxford, England: New York: Basil Blackwell, 1985.
456p. bibliog.
Eighteen essays seek to determine which elements in the basic Japanese historical
pattern of development are 'peculiar to Japan, which are relevant only to less
developed countries that are culturally related to Japan, and which are more generally
transferable'. These essays are grouped into five parts – 'Initial Conditions',
'Agricultural Development', 'Technology Choice in Industry', 'Intersectoral Resource
Flows and Finance', and 'Foreign Trade and Development' – and frequently involve in-
depth comparisons between the Japanese historical experience and the more recent
experiences of such countries as India, Korea, the Philippines, the Republic of China
(Taiwan), and Thailand. Typical essays include 'Supply and Demand for Quality
Workers in Cotton Spinning in Japan and India', 'Government Credit to the Banking
System: Rural Banks in 19th-Century Japan and the Postwar Philippines', and 'Trading
Companies and the Expansion of Foreign Trade: Japan, Korea, and Thailand'.
Lectures on developing economies: Japan's experience and its relevance (Tokyo:
University of Tokyo Press, 1989, 340p.), by Kazushi Ohkawa and Hirohisa Kohama, is
among the editors' other writings about Third World development and Japan.

807   **Japanese economic growth: trend acceleration in the twentieth century.**
Kazushi Ohkawa, Henry Rosovsky.   Stanford, California: Stanford
University Press; London: Oxford University Press, 1973. 327p.
(Studies of Economic Growth in Industrialized Countries).
Fitting Japan's experience into an historical growth model of the type familiar to
economists, Ohkawa and Rosovsky attempt to explain not only why the Japanese
economy grew between the early 1900s and the mid-1960s but also why it grew at a
dramatically increasing rate, particularly after World War II. Following a brief
historical introduction, they establish the basic pattern of twentieth-century growth
with an analysis of long swings and trend acceleration in private capital formation and
a variety of other aggregate economic measures. Chapters 3–7 consider factor inputs
and aggregate productivity, sectoral growth patterns and intersectoral relations, the

demand and supply for labour in a dualistic economy, aggregate demand and resource allocation, and the impact of foreign trade on Japanese growth. The concluding chapters outline an historical model to explain certain trends, analyse institutional innovation and Japan's rising social capability to import advanced technology, and assess Japan's economic future.

808 **Patterns of Japanese economic development: a quantitative appraisal.**
Edited with an introduction by Kazushi Ohkawa, Miyohei Shinohara, with Larry Meissner, foreword by Hugh Patrick.   New Haven, Connecticut; London: Yale University Press, 1979. 411p. bibliog. (A Publication of the Economic Growth Center, Yale University, and the Council on East Asian Studies, Yale University).

This invaluable reference work presents the most important series of long-term statistical data available for studying the overall patterns of Japan's economic growth; her production (in agriculture, manufacturing, and the service sector) and trade; product allocation (including consumption, capital formation and capital stock, and government expenditures and revenues); and factor incomes and shares, prices, wages, population and labour force. These series are based on research in Japan designed to produce complete and accurate sets of long-term economic statistics for the years since the Meiji Restoration of 1868. The text provides a summary of the patterns in the data and describes some of the analysis done on Japanese economic development. Fifty-four detailed statistical tables in the appendix bear such titles as 'Gross National Expenditures in Current Prices, 1885–1940', 'Agriculture: Production and Output in Current Prices at the Farm Gate, 1874–1940 and 1950–71', 'Exports of Major Commodity Groups in Constant Prices 1874–1939 and 1953–70', and 'Government Revenues, 1868–1970'.

809 **Inside the Japanese system: readings on contemporary society and political economy.**
Edited by Daniel I. Okimoto, Thomas P. Rohlen.   Stanford, California: Stanford University Press, 1988. 286p.

A selection of fifty-five readings about Japan's complex industrial system, extracted in most cases from recently published works. These brief essays initially constituted part of a broad introduction to the structure and inner workings of the Japanese system organised for a series of executive seminars on Japan held at the Aspen Institute for Humanistic Studies in Colorado. The readings are grouped into five major parts: 'Culture and Society', 'The Economy', 'The Company Pattern', 'Government Institutions and Policy Making', and 'Issues for the Future'. Topics covered include the element of hierarchy in Japanese society, dependence in human relationships, the Japanese bond and stock markets, the Japan–United States savings-rate gap, a training programme for Japanese bank employees, permanent employment policies in times of recession, the near-bankruptcy and subsequent turnabout of Mazda Motors, ex-bureaucrats in the Liberal Democratic Party, the costs of Japanese industrial policy, and the impact of the ageing of Japan's population.

810 **The developing economies and Japan: lessons in growth.**
Saburō Ōkita.   Tokyo: University of Tokyo Press, 1980. 284p.

A collection of thirteen speeches, papers, and essays written primarily during the 1970s by a leading Japanese economist. They address the question of how various countries can initiate and promote economic development without threatening their national integrity and traditions. Grouped into three parts – 'Developing Countries in the World Economy', 'The Japanese Example', and 'Japan's Relations with the Developing World' – the essays are concerned with such matters as the causes of rapid growth in postwar Japan and their implications for newly developing countries, the relations between population and development as seen in the case of Japan, the Japanese experience of economic planning, and the Japan–ASEAN (Association of Southeast Asian Nations) relationship. Altogether they convey the essence of Ōkita's views as they reflect his long involvement in economic planning and research both nationally and internationally.

811 **Asia's new giant: how the Japanese economy works.**
Edited by Hugh Patrick, Henry Rosovsky, foreword by Kermit Gordon.   Washington, DC: Brookings Institution, 1976. 943p.

Twenty-three American and Japanese scholars explain how the Japanese managed their economy during the 1950s and the 1960s, and assess Japan's economic prospects both domestically and internationally following the 'oil shock' of 1973-74. In detailed, self-contained essays, they first provide an overview of Japan's economic performance. Then they discuss Japan's postwar economic growth and its sources; her fiscal, monetary, and other macroeconomic policies; capital formation, the banking system, and the securities market; taxation and the tax system; Japan's relations with the world economy (particularly her international trade and finance); the organisation of Japanese industry; the distinctive characteristics of Japan's postwar technological development; the Japanese labour market (including wages, the employment and bargaining systems, and trade unions and management); urbanisation and urban problems; postwar party politics, government administration, and economic growth; the social and cultural factors that have contributed to Japanese economic growth; and the prospects for Japan's economic future.

812 **Japanese industrialization and its social consequences.**
Edited with an introductory overview by Hugh Patrick, with Larry Meissner.   Berkeley, California; London: University of California Press, 1976. 505p. bibliog.

An analysis of the interrelationships between Japanese industrialisation and its social consequences over the past one hundred years. Twelve essays focus on the evolving sociological and economic characteristics of Japanese industrial workers, the micro-patterns of industrial development and issues associated with selected features of Japanese industrial firms, and the major social consequences of the industrial process. Case-studies cover such topics as Japan's changing occupational structure and its significance; the Japanese shipbuilding industry; the origins and growth of general trading companies; the evolution of the dualistic wage structure; the introduction of electric power and its impact on smaller-scale manufacturing plants; the demographic transition in the process of Japanese industrialisation; the perceptions and realities of poverty in modern Japan; and welfare, environment and the postindustrial society.

813 **The competition: dealing with Japan.**
Thomas Pepper, Merit E. Janow, Jimmy W. Wheeler, foreword by Henry Rosovsky.   New York; Eastbourne, Sussex: Praeger, 1985. 374p.

An examination of the evolution of Japan's economy and the changes in her economic position vis-à-vis the United States since the end of World War II. Following a brief historical overview, the authors describe how Japanese economic development – particularly the role of the government's industrial policies which have targeted industrial development in specially designated areas – has dramatically evolved. They probe into recent changes in the structure of the Japanese financial system, investigate the emergence of new industries (especially computers, electronics, and telecommunications), and examine the decline in competitiveness of basic manufacturing industries such as shipbuilding and petrochemicals. They conclude with a discussion of the business and policy implications of Japan's changing economy for both the United States and Japan as they suggest the directions in which her economy and government policy are heading.

814 **Industrial growth, trade, and dynamic patterns in the Japanese economy.**
Miyohei Shinohara.   Tokyo: University of Tokyo Press, 1982. 243p.

A policy-oriented study of the major factors contributing to Japan's postwar economic development: the role of the Ministry of International Trade and Industry (MITI) in formulating the country's industrial policy; Japan's export policies and trading relationships; and the savings and investment cycles which affect growth. Shinohara first demonstrates that MITI's policies promoted efficiency and technological innovation rather than monopoly and stagnation. He then explores the important changes in Japan's trade structure and trading relationships, the problems that have beset her trade with other industrialised nations, and the implications of Japanese economic growth for Australia. Finally he discusses the role in Japan's economy of her citizens' high rate of savings, the Kondratieff cycle, the medium-term investment cycle, and the short-term inventory cycle.

815 **Japan's postwar economy: an insider's view of its history and its future.**
Tatsurō Uchino, translated by Mark A. Harbison.   Tokyo; New York: Kodansha International, 1983. 286p.

A non-technical account of the development and implementation of the economic policies which led to Japan's emergence as an economic superpower. Uchino argues that Japan's economic growth between the 1950s and the early 1980s should be primarily attributed to the government's careful analyses of the country's economic needs and to its formulation and adoption of such strategies as a monetary policy which stressed exports and the attainment of a positive balance of payments, the National Income-Doubling Plan of the 1960s which emphasized the development of human resources and widespread consumerism, and a national policy for eliminating the dual structure of the economy. The author was one of the economic planners within the government who helped draft the 'white papers' (reports released by government ministries and agencies which express official policy) that served as a basis for Japan's postwar economic policies.

816 **Policy and trade issues of the Japanese economy: American and Japanese perspectives.**
Edited with an introduction by Kozo Yamamura.   Seattle, Washington: University of Washington Press; Tokyo: University of Tokyo Press, 1982. 332p. (Publications of the Henry M. Jackson School of International Studies, 36).

Ten leading Japanese and American scholars analyse Japan's economy and the

US–Japanese trade relationship during the 1970s. Focusing on government policies and the behaviour of firms and individuals, the first seven essays deal with the socio-institutional explanations of Japan's recent economic performance; Japan's changing industrial structure and Japanese–American industrial relations; administrative guidance and Japan's pro-cartel policies; Japanese entrepreneurial behaviour and economic policy; the government–business relationship; Japan's high level of household savings; and the economy's response to the oil crises of 1973 and 1979. The remaining essays, centring on Japan's foreign economic relationships, are concerned with the political economy of US–Japanese trade in steel; evolving comparative advantage and Japan's imports of manufactures; policy interactions and the US–Japan exchange rate; and the policy determinants (in both the United States and Japan) of the yen–dollar exchange rate.

817 **The political economy of Japan. Volume 1: The domestic transformation.**
Edited with an introduction by Kozo Yamamura, Yasukichi Yasuba, preface by Yasusuke Murakami, Hugh T. Patrick.   Stanford, California: Stanford University Press, 1987. 666p.
The first volume in a trilogy designed to 'evaluate the political economy of Japan as it approaches the 1990s'. Particular issues considered include the changes in institutions, performance, behaviour patterns, and other significant aspects of the Japanese polity and economy that have occurred since 1945, the factors which account for the performance of Japan's postwar political economy, and the directions in which Japan is heading as well as her future prospects and problems. Nineteen (mostly Japanese) contributors cover the following topics: the Japanese model of political economy, economic welfare, saving and investment, public finance, the political economy of the financial market, the Japanese firm in transition, human resource development and labour–management relations, small-scale family enterprises, technology and the future of the economy, the future of industrial policy, industrial organisation since the 1970s, the development of planned pluralism, and the politics of economic management. The second volume, entitled *The political economy of Japan. Volume 2: The changing international context*, edited by Takashi Inoguchi and Daniel I. Okimoto (Stanford University Press, 1988, 566p.), analyses 'the impact of international forces on the emerging shape of Japan's domestic political economy, and examines the ramifications of Japan's development for the changing structure of the international system'. Its American and Japanese contributors discuss such subjects as Japan's growing involvement in the international monetary régime, her international trade and trade policy between 1955 and 1984, the impact of Japanese domestic politics on Japanese foreign policy, the prospects for stability in the US–Japan relationship, and the evolution of Japan's regional role in Southeast Asia. The final publication in this trilogy, edited by Shumpei Kumon and Henry Rosovsky and scheduled to appear in 1990, will be entitled *The political economy of Japan. Volume 3: Cultural and social dynamics.*

818 **Japanese economic development: a short introduction.**
Kunio Yoshihara.   Tokyo; Oxford, England; New York: Oxford University Press, 1979. 153p. bibliog.
This introductory volume on the economic growth of modern Japan views the country's major development issues within a general framework of modern economic development, instead of focusing on peculiarly Japanese problems. An overview of Japan's economic growth from 1868 to 1973 is followed by a discussion of its major

characteristics. Yoshihara then considers the ways in which trade patterns evolved after the Meiji Restoration (1868), the reasons for the changes which occurred, and the extent to which international trade stimulated Japanese growth. He examines the initial conditions of development and contrasts Japan's 'preparedness for modernization' with that of Thailand and China. In addition, he discusses the institutional reforms of both the early Meiji era and the Allied occupation period in so far as they deeply affected Japan's economic development. His closing chapter focuses on the pathological aspects of Japanese development and assesses the appropriateness of the Japanese experience as a model for other countries.

Modern Japanese organization and decision-making.
See item no. 39.

Land markets and land policy in a metropolitan area: a case study of Tokyo.
See item no. 42.

A short economic history of modern Japan.
See item no. 110.

The economic development of Japan *c.*1868–1941.
See item no. 218.

The economic development of Japan: growth and structural change.
See item no. 218.

Mitsui: three centuries of Japanese business.
See item no. 231.

The state and economic enterprise in Japan: essays in the political economy of growth.
See item no. 239.

MITI and the Japanese miracle: the growth of industrial policy, 1925–1975.
See item no. 272.

Kinship and economic organization in rural Japan.
See item no. 561.

The price of affluence: dilemmas of contemporary Japan.
See item no. 567.

Japan's public policy companies.
See item no. 612.

The challenge of China and Japan: politics and development in East Asia.
See item no. 623.

Law in Japan: the legal order in a changing society.
See item no. 786.

Japan's economy: coping with change in the international environment.
See item no. 903.

Japan Inc.: an introduction to Japanese economics (the comic book).
See item no. 1480.

AMPO: Japan-Asia Quarterly Review.
See item no. 1488.

Asian Survey.
See item no. 1491.

Economic Eye: a Quarterly Digest of Views from Japan.
See item no. 1500.

Far Eastern Economic Review.
See item no. 1501.

Japan Update.
See item no. 1517.

Japanese Economic Studies.
See item no. 1518.

JEI Report.
See item no. 1524.

Journal of the Japanese and International Economies.
See item no. 1530.

Pacific Affairs.
See item no. 1536.

Speaking of Japan.
See item no. 1540.

Tokyo Business Today: a Monthly Magazine of Japan's Business and Finance.
See item no. 1542.

Japan Economic Journal.
See item no. 1548.

Who's who in Japan.
See item no. 1574.

Japan's economic challenge: a bibliographic sourcebook.
See item no. 1590.

East Asian economies: a guide to information sources.
See item no. 1594.

Japanese national government publications in the Library of Congress: a bibliography.
See item no. 1602.

Japan's economy: a bibliography of its past and present.
See item no. 1614.

See also the sections under 'History' for economic history.

Economic and statistical yearbooks and annual surveys

819 **Economic Statistics Annual = Keizai Tōkei Nenpō.**
Nihon Ginkō. Tōkeikyoku [Bank of Japan, Statistical Bureau].
Tokyo: Nihon Ginkō. Tōkeikyoku, 1967- . annual.

An authoritative yearbook with many statistical tables covering Japan's money and banking, public finance, foreign trade, foreign exchange and balance of payments, industry, labour, prices, national accounts, and economic prospects. Comparable in format to the *Japan Statistical Yearbook* (q.v.), the text as well as the headings appear in both English and Japanese.

820 **Economic Survey of Japan.**
Economic Planning Agency [Keizai Kikakuchō].   Tokyo: Printing Bureau, Ministry of Finance, 1951- . annual.

Official translation of the 'White Paper on the Economy', the government's annual economic report which analyses the performance of the economy during the immediately preceding year and identifies the medium- to long-term problems that lie ahead. Each volume generally singles out a major theme. The 1983-84 volume, subtitled 'Japanese Economy Coping with New Internationalization', is concerned with trends in Japan's current-account balance, with the transition in Japan's industrial structure, and with progress in the liberalisation/internationalisation of finance. The 1984-85 volume, subtitled 'New Growth and Its Issues', deals with the era of new growth as well as with Japan's ageing society and her economic vitality. The 1985-86 volume, in turn, is subtitled 'Japanese Economy Seeking International Harmony' and focuses on the economic impact of the upward revaluation of the yen, the trends for new industrial development, and the problem of stock enrichment. Over two hundred authoritative charts and statistical tables accompany each year's report.

821 **Economic Surveys: Japan.**
Organisation for Economic Co-operation and Development.   Paris: Organisation for Economic Co-operation and Development, 1964- . annual.

An authoritative survey (at the aggregate level) of major economic developments in Japan, prepared each year by the Economic and Development Review Committee of the OECD (Organisation for Economic Co-operation and Development). Each volume surveys recent economic trends, economic policies, and short-term economic prospects. In addition, many annual volumes feature discussions and analyses of such other areas of concern as the liberalisation of the Japanese financial market and the basic features of an economic recession. A brief statistical appendix concludes each survey. The OECD is also well known for its many other special studies and periodic reports about the Japanese economy, among them volumes entitled *Agricultural policy in Japan*, *The industrial policy of Japan*, *Manpower policy in Japan*, and *Monetary policy in Japan*.

822 **Japan Company Handbook.**
Tokyo: Oriental Economist [Tōyō Keizai Shinpōsha], 1936- . semi-
annual.

A convenient guide to basic management and financial information for over 1,100
corporations listed on the First Sections of the Tokyo, Ōsaka, and Nagoya stock
exchanges. The synopsis of a company that is provided in each one-page entry covers
such items as its history, management strategy, overseas policy, short- and long-term
prospects, earnings, sales, profits and losses, stock price movements and turnover
during a 4½-year period, major stockholders, principal methods of procuring funds,
assets and liabilities, investment in facilities, dates of establishment and registration as
a joint-stock company, principal office and address, overseas offices, number of
employees, and names of its chairman and president. Among the many companies
included in this handbook are Sony and Kenwood (in consumer electronics), Nissan
Motor and Toyota Motor (in automobiles and trucks), and Osaka Soda and Nippon
Sanso (in chemicals).

823 **Japan Economic Almanac.**
Japan Economic Journal [Nihon Keizai Shimbun]. Tokyo: Nihon
Keizai Shimbun, 1985- . annual. (Nihon Keizai Shimbun, Inc., 1-9-5
Ōtemachi, Chiyoda-ku, Tokyo 100, Japan. For subscribers in the
United States: OCS America, Inc., P.O. Box 1654, Long Island City,
NY 11101).

Published from 1956 to 1984 under the title *Industrial Review of Japan*, this
authoritative reference work provides updated analytical overviews of many areas of
Japanese business and industrial activity. Through a series of concise reports, it
comments on such topics as government finance, Japan's balance of payments, foreign
trade, overseas investment, prices and consumption, banking and insurance, bond
markets, industrial policy, and tax reform. It also summarises (on an industry-by-
industry basis) present conditions and current trends in every major industrial and
business sector such as electronics, computers, telecommunications, automobiles,
robotics, chemicals, machinery, textiles, agriculture, construction, advertising, fashion,
and restaurants. The concluding pages of each annual volume contain a chronology of
major economic events during the preceding year, a 'who's who' of over three hundred
of Japan's most prominent businessmen, and a selected directory and statistical
information.

824 **Japan 1990: an international comparison.**
Yoichi Anzai, Editor in Chief. Tokyo: Keizai Kōhō Center [Japan
Institute for Social and Economic Affairs], 1988. 98p. map. (Keizai
Kōhō Center, 6-1 Ōtemachi 1-chōme, Chiyoda-ku, Tokyo 100, Japan).

A paperback booklet containing a wealth of statistical information about Japan's
population, area, and national income; agriculture and food supply; industry and
services; foreign trade; balance of payments and foreign exchange rates; development
assistance and overseas investment; energy and resources; wages, employment, and
productivity; prices, interest rates, and financial markets; taxes, public finance, and
defence; and Japan's society and culture. Most of the tables compare Japan statistically
with one or more other countries such as the United States, the Federal Republic of
Germany, France, the United Kingdom, Italy, Canada, Australia, the Republic of
Korea, China, and Israel. This booklet has been updated and published annually by
the Keizai Kōhō Center for the past several years.

825 **Japan Statistical Yearbook = Nihon Tōkei Nenkan.**
Edited by Statistics Bureau, Prime Minister's Office [Sōrifu,
Tōkeikyoku]. Tokyo: Sōrifu, Tōkeikyoku, 1949- . annual.

The most comprehensive, single-volume source of basic statistical information about Japan. Each yearbook contains authoritative statistical tables covering a wide range of subjects including agriculture, banking, business enterprises, climate, construction, education, elections, fisheries, forestry, health, household finances, housing, justice, labour, land, manufacturing, mining, population, prices, public finance, religion, science, social security, technology, trade, transportation, and wages. Captions appearing both in English and in Japanese facilitate its use by a wide readership. This yearbook continues the prewar (1868-1940) series entitled *Statistical Year Book of the Empire of Japan*, published between 1882 and 1948.

826 **Nippon: a Charted Survey of Japan.**
Edited by the Tsuneta Yano Memorial Society [Yano Tsuneta
Kinenkai]. Tokyo: Kokuseisha, 1936- . annual. (Kokuseisha
Corporation, Daiichi-Seimei Building, 19-3 Nishi-Gotanda 2-chōme,
Shinagawa-ku, Tokyo 141, Japan).

An easy-to-read statistical reference book, combining introductory essays with annually updated tables and charts, that provides information about the geography, economy, industries, and social life and welfare of contemporary Japan. Individual chapters focus on such specific subjects as climate, foreign trade, commodity prices, the chemical industry, transportation, national livelihood, health and medical care, and environmental pollution. The published data usually lag two to three years behind. The statistical tables within the volume for 1987/88, for example, contain statistics which date largely from 1985 and earlier years.

827 **Statistical Handbook of Japan.**
Edited by the Statistics Bureau, Prime Minister's Office [Sōrifu.
Tōkeikyoku]. Tokyo: Statistics Bureau, Prime Minister's Office,
1964- . annual. (Available from the Japan Statistical Association,
19-1 Wakamatsu-chō, Shinjuku-ku, Tokyo 162, Japan).

A concise overview of present-day conditions in Japan through brief descriptions and numerous statistical tables, charts, and photographs. Each annual handbook constitutes an up-to-date introduction to Japan's history, land and climate, population, economic development, agriculture, forestry, fisheries, energy, manufacturing, construction, transportation, communications, domestic and foreign commerce, finance and banking, labour, household economy and prices, social security and health, education, culture, science, foreign aid, and government. This publication is intended for the general reader. More detailed statistical information may be found in individual volumes of the *Japan Statistical Yearbook* (q.v.).

828 **White Paper on International Trade.**
Ministry of International Trade and Industry [Tsūshō Sangyōshō].
Tokyo: Japan External Trade Organization (JETRO), 1972- . annual.

An abridged translation of *Tsūshō hakusho*, a report prepared by the Ministry of International Trade and Industry. Each yearly analysis of Japan's international trade provides detailed information about the world economy in relation to Japan, describes developments concerning Japan's overseas economic activities, and offers statistics for Japan's foreign trade by region, country, and commodity. This annual report continues *Foreign Trade of Japan*, published between 1950 and 1971 by the Ministry of International Trade and Industry and the Japan Export Trade Promotion Agency.

829 **White Papers of Japan: Annual Abstract of Official Reports and Statistics of the Japanese Government.**
Edited by the Japan Institute of International Affairs [Nihon Kokusai Mondai Kenkyūjo]. Tokyo: Japan Institute of International Affairs [Nihon Kokusai Mondai Kenkyūjo], 1969- . annual. (Japan Institute of International Affairs, No. 19 Mori Building, 2-20 Toranomon 1-chōme, Minato-ku, Tokyo 105, Japan).

Valuable summaries of the 'white papers' (annual reports expressing official policy) issued by the more important Japanese government ministries and agencies. These reports cover foreign policy, defence, the economy, international trade, economic co-operation, small and medium enterprise, labour, transportation, agriculture, fisheries, the environment, crime, atomic energy, and science and technology. Each report is accompanied by statistical tables and figures. These annual volumes of abstracts constitute a convenient source of information about current government policies and government perceptions of issues that concern the Japanese people.

Facts and Figures of Japan.
See item no. 14.

Agriculture and
Fishing

830 **The one-straw revolution: an introduction to natural farming.**
Masanobu Fukuoka, translated by Chris Pearce, Tsune Kurosawa,
Larry Korn, edited by Larry Korn, preface by Wendell Berry.
Emmaus, Pennsylvania: Rodale Press, 1978. 181p. Reprinted, Toronto,
Ontario; New York: Bantam Books, 1985. 155p.

Since World War II, Fukuoka Masanobu has developed some unique methods of
natural farming on the land he owns overlooking Matsuyama Bay (Shikoku Island),
and he has taught these methods to thousands of other Japanese. His personal
testament describes the events which led him to develop natural farming methods
through a refinement of traditional Japanese agricultural practices, discusses these
methods and the basic principles underlying them, and explains the advantages of
natural farming, particularly in minimising the disruption of nature. Indicating that he
considers the purification of the human spirit and the healing of land which has
degenerated over the years to be essentially the same process, Fukuoka also discusses
the connections between natural farming and human physical and spiritual health.

831 **A century of agricultural growth in Japan: its relevance to Asian**
development.
Yūjirō Hayami, with Masakatsu Akino, Masahiko Shintani, Saburō
Yamada. Minneapolis, Minnesota: University of Minnesota Press;
Tokyo: University of Tokyo Press, 1975. 248p. map.

An economic analysis of the long-term growth of Japanese agriculture that assesses
both the significance of agricultural development in Japan during a century of modern
economic growth and the relevance of the Japanese experience for Asian farmers
today. Part one presents a chronology of agricultural developments between 1880 and
1973, with particular emphasis on trends in output, inputs, and productivities as well as
on the institutional aspects of agricultural development. Part two explores the sources
of long-term productivity growth in agriculture. Part three analyses the process by
which public resource allocations to agricultural research and investments in such
improvements of land infrastructure as irrigation and drainage have enabled Japanese

agriculture to enjoy sustained growth. The concluding part discusses the implications of the Japanese experience for agricultural development strategies in contemporary Asia.

832 **Japanese agriculture under siege: the political economy of agricultural policies.**
Yūjirō Hayami, foreword by Malcolm Falkus. New York: St. Martin's Press; London: Macmillan, 1988. 145p. bibliog. (Studies in the Modern Japanese Economy).

Originally prepared as an additional chapter to the author's anticipated revision of *A Century of agricultural growth in Japan* (q.v.), this book analyses the interactions between economy and politics within the Japanese agricultural sector. While less than ten percent of the population is currently engaged in farming, the agrarian sector retains considerable political influence and continues to push hard for severe restrictions on agricultural imports. In exploring recent changes and present dilemmas confronting Japanese agriculture, Hayami discusses the roots of Japan's present-day agricultural trade friction, the changing nature of the agricultural problem, the structure of agricultural protection, the failure of structural policies under the Agricultural Basic Law, and new prospects for structural adjustment. He concludes with a set of recommendations for restructuring Japanese agriculture into a viable economic sector.

833 **Beef in Japan: politics, production, marketing and trade.**
John W. Longworth. St. Lucia, Queensland; New York: University of Queensland Press, 1983. 327p. map. bibliog.

A detailed case-study of the economics of the Japanese livestock industry. Its wide-ranging coverage includes the consumer demand for beef in Japan, the post-World War II changes in the domestic production of food and grain, the politics behind the formulation and administration of government policies with regard to the production and import of beef, the traditional breeding (*wagyū*) and new dairy beef sectors, and the slaughtering, distribution and marketing of beef within Japan. Also considered are the control of Japanese beef imports, American and Australian pressures on the Japanese government to eliminate trade restrictions, the raising and supply of feeder cattle, and the issues surrounding the import of food for Japanese livestock and related feedstuff policies.

834 **The lonely furrow: farming in the United States, Japan and India.**
Kusum Nair. Ann Arbor, Michigan: University of Michigan Press; Don Mills, Ontario: Longmans Canada, 1969. 314p. 3 maps.

This examination of the attitudes, beliefs, and behaviours of farmers in Japan and the United States (with a much briefer look at the Indian situation) tries to determine why farmers work and produce the way that they do, and what will induce them to seek ways of becoming even more efficient in the future. Nair focuses on the past and present responses of Japanese and American farmers to emerging opportunities and available resources, and on their role in the development of agriculture within their respective countries. She deals with such economic variables as land, capital, prices and profits, and technology only to the extent that they provide substantive background information for her sociologically oriented investigation. Her historical concerns also centre on the events and actions of individuals engaged in agriculture.

835 **Can Japanese agriculture survive? a historical and comparative approach.**
Takekazu Ogura.   Tokyo: Agricultural Policy Research Center, 1982. 3rd ed. 880p. map.

A comprehensive study of agricultural development, policy, structure, and organisation from the early Meiji period through the late 1970s. Ogura covers the development of basic Japanese ideas about agricultural policy, the evolution of Japanese agriculture between the 1870s and the 1940s, Japan's decline in food self-sufficiency, the growth of agricultural co-operatives, the postwar transformation of rural society and agricultural administrative organisation, the rural land reforms of both the Meiji and the Allied occupation periods and their related agricultural policies, the enactment of the Agricultural Basic Law in 1961 and its aftermath, and the structure of Japanese agriculture in the 1970s. He concludes with some proposals for Japan's future agricultural policy. The inclusion of over 125 pages of statistics and figures, a chronology of agricultural developments between 1859 and 1978, and numerous illustrations make this volume a valuable reference work.

The agrarian origins of modern Japan.
See item no. 181.

Nakahara: family farming and population in a Japanese village, 1717–1830.
See item no. 182

Technology and agricultural development in pre-war Japan.
See item no. 200.

Farm and nation in modern Japan: agrarian nationalism, 1870–1940.
See item no. 206.

Agricultural development and tenancy disputes in Japan, 1870–1940.
See item no. 242.

Land reform in Japan.
See item no. 268.

Japanese rural society.
See item no. 531.

Rural society in Japan.
See item no. 534.

Village Japan.
See item no. 548.

Shinohata: a portrait of a Japanese village.
See item no. 550.

Suye mura: a Japanese village.
See item no. 551.

Shingū: a Japanese fishing community.
See item no. 552.

Country to city: the urbanization of a Japanese hamlet.
See item no. 554.

Three decades in Shiwa: economic development and social change in a Japanese farming community.
See item no. 555.

Kurusu: the price of progress in a Japanese village, 1951–1975.
See item no. 556.

Haruko's world: a Japanese farm woman and her community.
See item no. 573.

Against the state: politics and social protest in Japan.
See item no. 606.

Policymaking in contemporary Japan.
See item no. 620.

Japan in global ocean politics.
See item no. 717.

Japan and the new ocean regime.
See item no. 796.

Japan's economic security.
See item no. 885.

U.S.–Japanese agricultural trade relations.
See item no. 888.

"The factory ship" and "The absentee landlord".
See item no. 1068.

Farming Japan.
See item no. 1502.

Japan Economic Journal.
See item no. 1548.

East Asian economies: a guide to information sources.
See item no. 1594.

The Allied occupation of Japan, 1945–1952: an annotated bibliography of Western-language materials.
See item no. 1613.

Business, Marketing, and Domestic Commerce

836 *Kaisha*: the Japanese corporation.
James C. Abegglen, George Stalk, Jr.   New York: Basic Books, 1985.
309p. bibliog.

A description and assessment of 'how marketing, money, and manpower strategy, not management style, make the Japanese world pace-setters' in international business. Abegglen and Stalk, senior members of the Tokyo office of the Boston Consulting Group, present a wealth of empirical information about the inner workings and behaviour of Japanese business corporations (*kaisha*), including their pursuit of competitive advantage in manufacturing, their 'just-in-time' production practices, their drive for technological leadership, their research and development programmes, their financial practices entailing close co-operation with banks and stockholders, and their increasingly multinational character. The authors conclude that many of the traits of Japanese corporations which account for their success are transferable to Western companies that are willing to study and adopt Japanese manufacturing and financial methods, employment practices, technological innovations, corporate objectives, and corporate planning. This book was reprinted under the title *Kaisha, the Japanese corporation: the new competitors in world business* (London: Tauris, 1986).

837 The strategy of Japanese business.
James C. Abegglen.   Cambridge, Massachusetts: Ballinger, 1984.
227p. (An Abt Books/Ballinger Publication).

A consultant and scholar in the field of Japanese business brings together fifteen articles and speeches written between 1978 and 1983 that analyse selected aspects of Japan's recent economic growth and the Japanese challenge in world business and trade. Abegglen groups his writings into four parts: 'Trade with Japan', 'Japanese Management', 'Foreign Companies in Japan', and 'Research and Development in Japan'. They specifically deal with such topics as US–Japanese trade competition in the 1980s, America's need to face up to the trade gap with Japan, the efficiency of Japanese-style management, Japan's industrial policy, acquisitions in Japan by foreign companies, and the dynamics driving Japan's technological advances. Based upon empirical analysis combined with the author's thirty years of practical experience, this volume is valuable for understanding the Japanese business world today.

838 **The Japanese company.**
Rodney Clark.   New Haven, Connecticut; London: Yale University Press, 1979. 282p. bibliog. Reprinted, Rutland, Vermont; Tokyo: Tuttle, 1987.

Combining his anthropological training with fourteen months of first-hand work experience in Japan, Clark explores the nature and location of authority in Japanese industry and the effect of Japanese industrial and commercial organisation upon the distribution of wealth and power. He first provides a broad discussion of the historical background of present-day Japanese business and of the company's role as the elementary unit of Japanese industry. Then he examines the case of a single company (an anonymous, medium-sized manufacturing enterprise) and considers its organisation and management, the ways in which its managers are chosen and assigned their tasks, the recruitment and resignation of company workers, the nature and quality of the relationship between the company and its employee, and the company's influence on society.

839 **Japan's market: the distribution system.**
Michael R. Czinkota, Jon Woronoff, foreword by William E. Brock. New York; London: Praeger, 1986. 141p. bibliog. (Praeger Special Studies) (Praeger Scientific).

An introduction to the intricacies of Japan's present-day distribution system which explains how this complex and restrictive system functions and how large foreign companies can penetrate the Japanese market and successfully operate within it. Czinkota and Woronoff first focus their attention on the three types of Japanese business groupings known as *keiretsu*, and explain both the consequences of their 'insider/outsider mentality' and the nature of their long-standing cultural and business influence. In covering the distribution system within the retail and the wholesale sectors, they trace the origins and development of the system, describe the close ties that exist among the business groups engaged in wholesaling, discuss the types of intermediaries involved in retailing, and point out some of the changes now under way within these two sectors. A concluding chapter, 'Toward a Level Playing Field', calls for improved foreign access to the Japanese market for the sake of enhanced US–Japanese economic relations. A more sophisticated – but now somewhat outdated – analysis of marketing in Japan is Michael Y. Yoshino's *The Japanese marketing system: adaptations and innovations* (Cambridge, Massachusetts; London: MIT Press, 1971, 319p.), which focuses on the dynamic process of change that was occurring within the Japanese marketing system during the mid- and late 1960s.

840 **Japanese etiquette & ethics in business.**
Boye De Mente.   Lincolnwood, Illinois: Passport Books, 1987. 5th ed. 182p.

Advertised as 'a penetrating analysis of the morals and values that shape the Japanese business personality', this is an introduction to several different aspects of the Japanese business world (including its hierarchical nature, its emphasis on peace and harmony, and its characteristic techniques of management) and a description of 'how concepts from Japanese daily life extend to dealings in business, and how loyalty within the family and nation applies to their professional relationships as well'. Throughout the book, De Mente offers advice to the Western businessman on how to conduct business with the Japanese, and he suggests ways for establishing 'lines of communication' within Japanese companies. A forty-page appendix provides a glossary of useful business-related terms. This volume is a completely revised and updated edition of the author's *Japanese manners and ethics in business*, first published in Tokyo in 1960.

841　**From bonsai to levi's. When West meets East: an insider's surprising account of how the Japanese live.**
George Fields.　New York: Macmillan, 1983. 213p. Reprinted, London: Futura, 1985. 213p. New York: New American Library, 1985. 247p.

An American marketing research expert who grew up in Japan and spent many years there promoting the sale of Western products explains how Japanese cultural patterns and business practices influence the buying habits of Japanese consumers. Writing in an entertaining and at times anecdotal manner, Fields provides a knowledgeable introduction to 'the inscrutable Japanese consumer' and shows how the Japanese and the Western markets for an identical product frequently differ from one another. He covers a wide range of topics including the Japanese style of advertising, the differing roles of the housewife in Japanese society as revealed in her shopping behaviour, brand preferences among the Japanese, and the relationship between Japanese management–labour negotiations and consumer behaviour. While not intended as a primer for marketing in Japan, the book nevertheless has much to offer Western businessmen. George Fields is also the author of *Gucci on the Ginza: Japan's new consumer generation* (Tokyo; New York: Kodansha International, 1989, 267p.), a work that focuses on the cultural idiosyncrasies of consumers in the late 1980s, the means for effectively communicating with them, the emerging role of a 'new' Japanese consumer, and the domestic and international forces which affect Japan's new consumer market.

842　**The mind of the strategist: the art of Japanese business.**
Kenichi Ohmae, foreword by Andrall E. Pearson.　New York; London: McGraw-Hill, 1982. 283p.

A director of the international consulting firm of McKinsey and Company presents some of the concepts and fundamentals involved in the process of strategic planning. He discusses the directions to pursue in quest of innovative strategies; explains how different kinds of strategies develop as one takes into account the corporation itself, the customer, and the competition; and examines the environmental factors which bear on strategic thinking and strategy formulation, the realities of Japanese business strategy, and the nature of strategic foresight. Ohmae argues that successful business strategies result from a particular state of mind in which 'insight and a consequent drive for achievement, often amounting to a sense of mission, fuel a thought process which is basically creative and intuitive rather than rational'. Many examples from the Japanese business world illustrate his points. This book is based primarily on several highly acclaimed works on strategy-related topics which the author published in Japanese during the 1970s and early 1980s.

Business, Marketing, and Domestic Commerce

843 Business and society in Japan: fundamentals for businessmen.
Edited by Bradley M. Richardson, Taizō Ueda, foreword by Michihiro Nishida. New York: Praeger, 1981. 334p. bibliog. (Praeger Special Studies) (Praeger Scientific).

The product of a joint project between the Honda Motor Company of Japan and the East Asian Studies Program of the Ohio State University, this general introduction offers Western businessmen practical information about the Japanese business scene and about trade with Japan. It deals with Japanese business organisation, labour, economic growth, trade competitiveness, income distribution, purchasing power and the market for consumer goods, law, the political environment, socio-historic trends, society and culture, the ways of entering the Japanese market, social relations and business practices, and the impact of modernisation on Japan. Each chapter was written by an American academic specialist and includes brief listings of suggested additional reading. While some of the data and factual information are now outdated on account of Japan's continued economic progress during the 1980s, the 'fundamentals' stressed by the authors remain essentially valid.

844 Japan, the hungry guest: Japanese business ethics vs. those of the U.S.
Jack Seward, Howard Van Zandt. Tokyo: Lotus Press, 1985. 295p.

Oriented in particular towards a broad US business audience, this study analyses and compares the ethical basis for American and Japanese business practices. Instead of focusing narrowly on specific ethical codes, Seward and Van Zandt consider the 'provenance of business ethics: the morality, traditions, and even the history' of these two societies. They write about the background of Japanese ethics, morality in present-day America, business ethics and codes, the influence of religion on Japanese business ethics, the work ethic in both Japan and the United States, the controversial issue of foreign trade, corporate management practices, the ethics of elected and non-elected government officials, the ethics of legal action, business negotiations, conferences and contracts, ethics in advertising, and corruption, bribery and scandals. Through their inquiry, the authors seek to address some of the perceptions among Americans that 'the Japanese are not playing the game of trade fairly' and to identify activities which are truly unethical and worthy of corrective action.

845 Entrepreneur and gentleman: a case history of a Japanese company.
Akira Sueno, translated by Neal Donner, foreword by Ernest D. Frawley. Rutland, Vermont; Tokyo: Tuttle, 1977. 249p.

This chronicle of the evolution of a packaging enterprise known as Shōwa Bōeki offers a glimpse into the world of the small Japanese businessman. Sueno, the founder and president of the company, tells of its origins and growth between the early 1950s and the late 1960s, explains his managerial attitudes and philosophy of life, and presents his views on a wide range of subjects including education, non-monetary compensation, company wives, international travel and business, recreation, and the proper methods for building a company of committed employees.

846 Big business in Japanese politics.
Chitoshi Yanaga. New Haven, Connecticut; London: Yale University Press, 1968. 371p. bibliog. (Yale Studies in Political Science, 22).

Yanaga shows how Japan's re-emergence as a great industrial and trading nation during the 1950s and early 1960s was achieved through the close co-operation of organised business and the government. After surveying the setting, framework, and style of Japanese politics and the character, structure, and functions of organised business, he details the numerous ways in which big business participated in government and indicates how the bureaucratic leadership provided an important supporting role. He also demonstrates the role of organised business in political and economic decision-making as he considers the modification and relaxation of the government's postwar anti-monopoly policy, the development of Japan's atomic energy policy, her reparations agreements with Southeast Asia, the merger of the conservative political parties, the creation of a political and economic relationship with the United States, and the attainment of military security under the US–Japan Mutual Security Treaty of 1960.

Economic institutional change in Tokugawa Japan: Ōsaka and the Kinai cotton trade.
See item no. 170.

Kikkoman: company, clan, and community.
See item no. 201.

The development of Japanese business, 1600–1980.
See item no. 208.

Capitalism and nationalism in prewar Japan: the ideology of the business elite, 1868–1941.
See item no. 219.

Mitsui: three centuries of Japanese business.
See item no. 231.

Japanese business language: an essential dictionary.
See item no. 422.

Business Japanese: a guide to improved communication.
See item no. 447.

Japan Company Handbook.
See item no. 822.

Industry and business in Japan.
See item no. 883.

How to do business with the Japanese: a complete guide to Japanese customs and business practices.
See item no. 891.

Hidden differences: doing business with the Japanese.
See item no. 894.

Business in Japan: a guide to Japanese business practice and procedure.
See item no. 901.

The anatomy of Japanese business.
See item no. 935.

Business Japan.
See item no. 1494.

Business Tokyo.
See item no. 1495.

Journal of Japanese Trade & Industry.
See item no. 1527.

Tokyo Business Today: a Monthly Magazine of Japan's Business and Finance.
See item no. 1542.

Japan Economic Journal.
See item no. 1548.

East Asian economies: a guide to information sources.
See item no. 1594.

Japan's economy: a bibliography of its past and present.
See item no. 1614.

See also the section 'Management, Labour, and Employer–Employee Relations'.

Energy

847　**U.S.–Japanese energy relations: cooperation and competition.**
Edited with an introduction by Charles K. Ebinger, Ronald A.
Morse.　Boulder, Colorado; London: Westview Press, 1984. 239p.
4 maps. (A Westview Replica Edition).

Twelve analytical essays highlight the major problems and challenges confronting
US–Japanese energy relations during the mid-1980s. The contributors discuss the
bilateral and multilateral aspects of energy co-operation as well as the changing
character of US–Japanese energy relations; examine the politics of US crude oil
exports to Japan and other Asian nations; and explore the prospects for co-operation
in the areas of nuclear energy, coal, and liquefied natural gas as well as in connection
with research and development projects that are concerned with alternative sources of
energy. In addition, they consider the competition between the United States and
Japan for the world photovoltaic market, their respective petroleum investment
strategies, and the prospects for conflict between Washington and Tokyo over the issue
of Soviet–Japanese energy co-operation in eastern Siberia.

848　**Nuclear energy and nuclear proliferation: Japanese and American views.**
Ryūkichi Imai, Henry S. Rowen, foreword by Joseph S. Nye, preface
by Franklin B. Weinstein.　Boulder, Colorado: Westview Press, 1980.
194p. (Westview Special Studies in International Relations).

This pair of studies pinpoints major differences in the way Japanese and Americans
during the 1970s were perceiving problems related to 'the complex interplay between
civilian nuclear power production and the development of a military nuclear capacity'.
Imai and Rowen analyse the range of political, technical, and economic issues which
must be considered in order to ensure that legitimate concerns about the future of
nuclear energy production and the spread of nuclear weapons are met. One of the
central themes of Imai's presentation is that countries like Japan which in the past have
supported nuclear non-proliferation as a matter of principle are now debating the
wisdom of remaining dependent on the United States for their nuclear technology and
fuel supplies and are questioning whether they can continue to comply with American

requirements. Considerable information about Japan's own nuclear power programme is included.

849   **The politics of Japan's energy strategy: resources – diplomacy – security.**
Edited with an introduction by Ronald A. Morse, foreword by Henry D. Jacoby.   Berkeley, California: Institute of East Asian Studies, University of California, 1981. 166p. 4 maps. bibliog. (Research Papers and Policy Studies, 3).

Six experts analyse the interrelationships between the formulation of energy strategies on the domestic scene and the Japanese concern with insulating their economy from any future 'oil shocks' and with ensuring their country's long-term economic prosperity. They consider recent Japanese efforts to reduce the demand for energy and to diversify their sources of energy supply through close co-operation between the government and the business sector. Examined in particular are Japan's strategy for financing her foreign purchases of high-cost energy, the country's national security strategy as it relates to energy, Japan's oil diplomacy and the dilemmas of her dependence on overseas sources of petroleum, the role of the Tokyo Electric Power Company in shaping Japan's coal and liquefied natural gas policies, the technological promise of nuclear power and the social and political limitations of its development, and the politics of alternative energy research and development in Japan.

850   **The business of the Japanese state: energy markets in comparative and historical perspective.**
Richard J. Samuels.   Ithaca, New York; London: Cornell University Press, 1987. 359p. bibliog. (Cornell Studies in Political Economy).

An investigation of the ways in which businessmen and bureaucrats in general, and the Japanese in particular, have sought to organise their economies. Samuels reconstructs the modern political histories that have defined present-day Japanese markets for coal, petroleum, electricity, and alternative energies. Refuting the view that Japan's economic bureaucracy has intentionally adopted particular policies in order to anticipate and conform to the demands of the market, he emphasizes the constraints under which the government has had to operate. He contends that the Japanese state does not participate directly in the market-place to ensure the continuous supply of energy and that it 'negotiates more than it leads' in so far as its relations with private industry and the country's energy markets are concerned.

China and Japan: new economic diplomacy.
See item no. 735.

Japan's economic security.
See item no. 885.

Two hungry giants: the United States and Japan in the quest for oil and ores.
See item no. 913.

Finance and Banking

851 **A financial history of the new Japan.**

Thomas Francis Morton Adams, Iwao Hoshii.   Tokyo; Palo Alto,
California: Kodansha International, 1972. 547p.

A comprehensive history and analysis of Japanese finance, 1945-71, written for
economists and businessmen alike. Part one, covering the economy during the Allied
occupation period and the Korean War, describes the conditions and practical
measures which led to Japan's rapid postwar recovery. Part two ('Institutional
Developments') offers detailed accounts of the banking system, the securities
companies, the stock exchanges, and the insurance companies during the 1950s and
1960s. Part three covers economic developments, fiscal and monetary policies, the
capital market, the call money market, consumer credit, leasing, and the financial role
of trading companies during the same two decades. Finally, part four ('The Era of
Internationalization') analyses Japan's position in the international community during
the early 1970s, her role in international finance, the foreign business of Japanese
banks, Japan's balance of payments, and the 1971 revaluation of the yen.

852 **The financial behavior of Japanese corporations.**

Robert J. Ballon, Iwao Tomita.   Tokyo; New York: Kodansha
International, 1988. 268p. bibliog.

A non-technical introduction to the ways in which Japanese managers perceive and
handle the financial dimensions of their corporate activities, and to some of the
fundamental cultural and organisational differences between Japanese and Western
accounting practices. Ballon and Tomita initially focus on the constant interaction
between government authorities and business organisations, among companies, and
within companies themselves that is characteristic of Japanese society. They then
examine corporate financing – in particular, debt financing, equity financing, and
internal sources of funds – and show how the Japanese are becoming 'much more
strategically savvy and bold'. They also detail the world of corporate accountants,
accounting practices, and independent audits. The authors conclude by describing the
major forms of Japanese financial reporting and by indicating the major peculiarities of
Japanese reporting practices which Westerners should bear in mind when reviewing the

disclosure and financial statements and evaluating the performance of Japanese companies.

853 **Yen! Japan's new financial empire and its threat to America.**

Daniel Burstein.   New York; London: Simon and Schuster, 1988. 335p.

An alarming yet convincingly depicted portrayal of Japan's recent emergence as a financial superpower and of the implications of her increasing control over money, 'the global economy's most strategic single resource'. Extremely critical of America's budget deficits, stagnant productivity, trade imbalances, and lack of strategic economic objectives, Burstein describes how Reaganomics has eroded America's economic strength and how the decision to double the value of the yen has been 'vastly enriching Japan while providing only short-term aid to American companies'. He describes some of the successes of the Nomura Securities Company, outlines selected aspects of Japan's financial culture and financial institutions, and describes current Japanese inroads into the US financial services sector. Unless the USA redresses the present situation and regains its financial independence, Burstein predicts an era of declining American living standards and reduced American influence: a twenty-first century in which, for example, the yen will become the world's key currency and Tokyo the leading global financial centre.

854 **The Japanese money market.**

Robert F. Emery.   Lexington, Massachusetts; Toronto, Ontario: Lexington Books, 1984. 143p. bibliog.

A description of the postwar growth of the Japanese money market together with a detailed analysis of its major components, in particular its organisation, primary participants, the types of instruments used, and significant postwar developments. Two introductory chapters are followed by Emery's studies of the bill discount market, the yen call money market, the *gensaki* ('bond repurchase') market, the Tokyo dollar call market, and the market in negotiable certificates of deposit. Concluding chapters examine the government's control of the money market and the market's interest rate structure, and provide an assessment of some of its strengths and weaknesses.

855 **The financial development of Japan, 1868–1977.**

Raymond W. Goldsmith.   New Haven, Connecticut; London: Yale University Press, 1983. 231p. bibliog.

A study of the financial structure and development of Japan during the periods 1868-85, 1886-1913, 1914-31, 1932-45, 1946-53, and 1954-75. Within each time period, Goldsmith examines the changes that occurred in Japan's infrastructure, money and prices, capital formation and savings, financial institutions, financing for the major non-financial sectors, the financial superstructure as a whole, and the national balance sheet. His book contains 105 statistical tables, over half of which are for the post-World War II period. This study was undertaken as part of a project comprising parallel volumes on India and Japan and a shorter volume comparing both countries with the United States: *The financial development of India, Japan, and the United States: a trilateral institutional, statistical, and analytical comparison* (New Haven, Connecticut; London: Yale University Press, 1973, 120p.).

Finance and Banking

856 **Japan, disincorporated: the economic liberalization process.**
Leon Hollerman. Stanford, California: Hoover Institution Press,
1988. 185p. bibliog. (Hoover Press Publication, 363).

Focusing on the interval between 1980 and 1984, when Japan's liberalisation process
rapidly moved ahead, Hollerman examines the relationship between domestic and
external liberalisation, the institutional nature of policy-making within the Ministry of
Finance, and the inter-ministerial rivalry, bureaucratic in-fighting, and conflict between
government and business over liberalisation at that time. Following a description of the
decision-making process of Japan's economic policy and an explanation of how
economic liberalisation created a dilemma for the bureaucracy, he details the
conflicting interests of the Ministry of Finance and the Bank of Japan within the
context of financial liberalisation. He then studies the role of administrative reform in
Japan's emergence as a 'headquarters country'. Throughout much of his book,
Hollerman contends that this liberalisation process – which centred on Japan's money
markets, capital markets, and capital movements – was essentially 'the result of a
compromise among bureaucrats and businessmen in response to pressures on their
respective interests and the national interests of Japan'.

857 **Japan's financial markets: conflict and consensus in policymaking.**
James Horne. Sydney, New South Wales; London: Allen and Unwin,
in association with the Australia–Japan Research Centre, Australian
National University, 1985. 271p.

An analysis of the major issues in, and the structure of, the regulatory policy-making
processes that conditioned the development of Japanese financial markets during the
1970s and early 1980s. Horne examines the conflict which occurred among different
parts of the Japanese élite over the formulation of policies in the government bond
market, the establishment of the certificates of deposit market, and intra-ministerial
policy-making concerning the issue of trading in government bonds. He also discusses
the inter-ministerial conflict over the postal savings system and the new foreign
exchange law, the foreign influences upon policy-making in the yen bond market, and
the influence of career and retirement patterns on policy-making within the Ministry of
Finance. Horne focuses throughout on political interaction among the government
ministries and their departments, the ruling Liberal Democratic Party, and the
financial institutions rather than on contemporary financial activities and legislation.

858 **Securities market in Japan 1988.**
Japan Securities Research Institute [Nihon Shōken Keizai
Kenkyūjo]. Tokyo: Japan Securities Research Institute, 1988. 237p.
(Japan Securities Research Institute, Tōkyō Shōken Kaikan, 1-5-8
Nihonbashi, Kayabachō, Chūō-ku, Tokyo 103, Japan).

The latest edition of a biennially updated overview of the Japanese securities market
that provides an introductory explanation for the generalist as well as 'the necessary
data and materials' needed by the specialist. First published in 1973, its thirteen
chapters trace the postwar development of the Japanese securities market and offer
authoritative information about the stock market, the bond market, the stock
exchange, Japanese securities companies, the investment trust, securities investment
advisers, the disclosure system of Japanese corporations, securities credit, the
internationalisation of the securities market, securities taxation, and securities
administration. Statistical tables, graphs, and charts present such data as the

organisation of the Tokyo Stock Exchange and recent changes in the total net asset value of open-end trusts.

859 **Japanese and U.S. inflation: a comparative analysis.**
Ching-yuan Lin.   Lexington, Massachusetts; Toronto, Ontario: Lexington Books, 1984. 157p. bibliog.

Focusing on the interaction between government policy and the evolution of the economy, Lin analyses the causes for the divergence in price stabilisation in Japan and the United States during the 1970s. He presents an overview of inflation and the process of price stabilisation between 1965 and 1980; examines the management of monetary and fiscal policy in response to the two oil shocks of the 1970s; considers the movements of wage rate, unit labour costs, and finished goods prices in manufacturing and discusses the factors underlying divergent wage behaviour in Japan and the United States; investigates the principal factors underlying the contrasting productivity trends in these two countries both before and after 1974; and studies the differences in Japanese and American saving and investment behaviour as well as the Japanese government's role in the financial intermediation of saving and investment.

860 **Japan and the United States today: exchange rates, macroeconomic policies, and financial market innovations.**
Edited with an introduction by Hugh T. Patrick, Ryūichirō Tachi. New York: Center on Japanese Economy and Business, Columbia University, 1986. 234p. bibliog.

The proceedings of a 1986 conference of Japanese and American officials, businessmen, and scholars that probed the most recent changes in exchange rates, macroeconomic policy, and the financial markets affecting both Japan and the United States. Emphasizing present conditions and implications for the future, the volume includes up-to-date analyses as well as several papers entitled 'Prospects for Japan's Current-Account Surplus'; 'Internationalization of the Yen: its Implications for the U.S.–Japan Relationship'; 'Recent Developments in the Yen–Dollar Exchange-Rate Relationship'; 'Japan's Financial Market: Present Conditions and Outlook'; and 'Comparative Studies of Financial Innovation, Deregulation, and Reform in Japan and the United States'.

861 **Japanese finance: a guide to banking in Japan.**
Andreas R. Prindl.   New York; Chichester, Sussex: Wiley, 1981. 137p. bibliog.

A somewhat dated but still very informative study based on the author's four years of experience as the general manager of the Tokyo office of Morgan Guaranty Trust. Part one examines the historical background of Japanese banking, the regulatory environment as of the early 1980s (with particular focus on the Ministry of Finance and the Bank of Japan), the structure of Japan's banking system, and the prospects (as of 1981) for internationalising the yen, liberalising the domestic money markets, and developing Tokyo into a major 'world financial centre'. Part two offers practical information on ways to use the Japanese banking system to secure credit, discusses the role of foreign banks in Japan and of Japanese bank lending abroad, examines the floating of the so-called 'samurai bonds' by non-residents within the local yen market, and considers cash management, foreign exchange exposure management, and the financial management of subsidiaries and joint ventures in Japan.

862   **Tokyo: a world financial centre.**
Brian Robins, historical introduction by Fumimasa Hamada.   London:
Euromoney Publications, 1987. 285p.

An overview of the world of Japanese finance as of 1987 that covers the outlook for
deregulation, the Ministry of Finance, the Bank of Japan, the city banks, the long-term
credit banks, the specialised banks, the regional banks, corporate finance, the stock
markets, Japan's securities houses, foreign banks, foreign securities houses, Japan's
bond markets, the short-term money markets, the foreign exchange markets, and
Japan's offshore market. Also discussed are the management of funds, general
insurance, life insurance, pension funds, law and regulation in Japan and its financial
markets, taxation and accounting requirements for the foreign investor, and Tokyo's
potential as a financial centre. This book underscores the significance of Japan's
emergence during the 1980s as the largest provider of capital in the world and Tokyo's
increased stature as an international financial centre comparable in many respects to
both New York and London.

863   **Public finance in Japan.**
Edited by Tokue Shibata.   Tokyo: University of Tokyo Press, 1986.
195p. map. bibliog.

A collection of ten essays by Japanese scholars and government officials that
introduces the basic features of Japan's public finance system and enhances an
understanding of the role which Japanese financial policies have been playing in the
country's postwar economic growth. The volume covers the historical development and
general administration of public finance, the role of the public sector in the national
economy, the administration of national finance, the general account budget, the
government credit programme and its assistance to public enterprises, the national tax
system, the development and use of government bonds, the local public finance
system, and the financial relations between the national and local governments. Also
included are a glossary of English-language terms related to finance and the names of
corporate bodies and laws with their Japanese equivalents.

864   **The Japanese financial system.**
Edited by Yoshio Suzuki.   Oxford, England; New York: Oxford
University Press, 1987. 358p. bibliog.

An English-language version of an authoritative study of the Japanese financial system
prepared by the staff of the Institute for Monetary and Economic Studies of the Bank
of Japan. Largely descriptive in nature, this comprehensive work was explicitly
intended for a broad audience. Part one – 'Overview: the Financial Structure and the
Financial System' – outlines the postwar development of the Japanese economy and
examines the tremendous changes which the financial system was experiencing during
the mid-1980s. Part two – 'Details of the Financial System' – offers in-depth
descriptions of (1) the financial assets available in Japan and their uses, (2) the existing
types of money markets, foreign exchange markets, and securities markets and the
determinants of their interest rates, (3) Japan's financial institutions (commercial
banks, long-term credit banks, securities companies, etc.), and (4) the role of the Bank
of Japan and its monetary policy.

865 **Money and banking in contemporary Japan: the theoretical setting and its application.**
Yoshio Suzuki, translated by John G. Greenwood, foreword by James Tobin, Hugh Patrick. New Haven, Connecticut; London: Yale University Press, 1980. 256p. bibliog.

An analysis and basic introduction to the structure and monetary instruments of the Japanese financial system between the late 1950s and the early 1970s, when the first oil shock and the transition to a floating exchange rate system fundamentally altered Japan's postwar economic history. Suzuki, a senior staff economist of the Bank of Japan, examines the distinctive features of Japan's financial structure and shows how the Japanese monetary mechanism was functioning during this decade and a half of rapid economic growth. In addition, he explains the operations of the instruments of Japanese monetary policy, indicates their effects on the banking system, and explores the role of the Bank of Japan in implementing national monetary policy.

866 **Money, finance, and macroeconomic performance in Japan.**
Yoshio Suzuki, translated by Robert Alan Feldman. New Haven, Connecticut; London: Yale University Press, 1986. 218p. bibliog.

Analyses changes in Japan's monetary policy and financial institutions and Japan's monetary macroeconomic performance during the decade following the oil crisis of 1973. Part one ('Evolution of the Financial System') sketches the postwar historical background, presents statistical analyses of recent changes in the accumulation and selection of financial assets and of the resultant changes in the flow of funds, discusses the impact of financial changes on the implementation of monetary policy, and studies interest rate decontrol and the effectiveness of monetary policy. Part two ('Money and Monetary Performance') surveys the debate over inflation in Japan as well as the successes and failures of price stabilisation, explores the potential explanations for the improvement of Japan's macroeconomic performance since 1973, analyses yen exchange rate movements since the transition to a floating rate régime, and examines the Bank of Japan's money-focused monetary policy. In several respects, this book is a sequel to the author's *Money and banking in contemporary Japan* (q.v.).

867 **The emerging power of Japanese money.**
Aron Viner. Homewood, Illinois: Dow Jones-Irwin; London: Kogan Page, 1988. 254p. bibliog.

Viner, a former vice-president of the Yamaichi Capital Management Company, first examines the current trends in Japan's foreign economic relations and considers the opposing Japanese and Western views of some of the major trade issues that have involved her in disputes with other nations. He then focuses on several recent changes in global finance – among them, Japan's rise to the status of the world's largest creditor nation – and their long-term implications. In a chapter entitled 'Japan versus World Finance', he describes current Japanese approaches to finance and corporate structure within the context of international investment. Finally, the author assesses Japan's dominant role in the new world of international finance that is emerging in the late 1980s. This work was published in the United Kingdom under the title *The financial samurai: the emerging power of Japanese money.*

868 **Inside Japanese financial markets.**
Aron Viner. London: Economist Publications, 1987. 274p.
Homewood, Illinois: Dow Jones-Irwin, 1988. 364p. bibliog.

Focusing on the securities market rather than on the money markets or the market in
foreign exchange, Viner provides the Western investor with a non-technical overview
of the Japanese financial system and an explanation of its postwar evolution. He
assesses the government's role in shaping the structure and function of securities
companies, banks, and regulations governing the stock exchange, and he explains how
the investment climate in Japan has been shaped by the interplay of these financial
forces. In addition, Viner discusses such topics as insider trading, hostile corporate
takeovers, and greenmail in Japan, and examines the Japanese socio-economic
structure and value system in order to reveal how they influence Japanese investors.
This book was published in the United Kingdom under the title *Inside Japan's financial
markets*.

Capital formation in Japan, 1868–1940.
See item no. 233.

Contemporary Japanese budget politics.
See item no. 608.

Japan and the Asian Development Bank.
See item no. 756.

Japanese securities regulation.
See item no. 781.

Japan: facing economic maturity.
See item no. 800.

Government policy towards industry in the United States and Japan.
See item no. 884.

Japan's response to crisis and change in the world economy.
See item no. 909.

Japanese Finance and Industry: Quarterly Survey.
See item no. 1519.

Tokyo Business Today: a Monthly Magazine of Japan's Business and Finance.
See item no. 1542.

Japan Economic Journal.
See item no. 1548.

East Asian economies: a guide to information sources.
See item no. 1594.

Japan's economy: a bibliography of its past and present.
See item no. 1614.

Industry

869 **Industrial organization in Japan.**
Richard E. Caves, Masu Uekusa, foreword by Gilbert Y. Steiner.
Washington, DC: Brookings Institution, 1976. 169p.

The first sequel to Patrick and Rosovsky's *Asia's new giant: how the Japanese economy works* (q.v.), this volume offers a sophisticated analysis of Japanese economic growth since the 1950s with particular focus on Japan's industrial economy. Caves and Uekusa examine the institutions of business and industry in Japan, the structure of industry, patterns of competition, the role of intermarket groups, allocative and technical efficiency, the relationship between imported technology and industrial progress, and the government's industrial policy. They conclude that such distinctively Japanese institutions as the industrial groups, the practice of permanent employment, and the prevalence of small enterprises have had a measurable influence on the performance of the Japanese economy, but that the economic forces at work in Japan as well as the consequences of Japanese industrial policy are similar in many respects to those found in Western industrialised countries.

870 **The American and Japanese auto industries in transition: report of the Joint U.S.–Japan Automobile Study.**
Edited with an introduction by Robert E. Cole, Taizō Yakushiji, conducted under the general direction of research chairmen Paul W. McCracken, Keichi Oshima. Ann Arbor, Michigan: Center for Japanese Studies, University of Michigan; Tokyo: Technova, 1984. 223p.

A comprehensive examination of the Japanese and US automobile industries which covers the following topics: the evolution and internationalisation of the industries; trade relations, market factors, and public policy; manufacturing cost differences; product and process evolution and manufacturer–supplier relations; and human resource development among both blue- and white-collar workers. This volume is complemented by the proceedings of several joint US–Japan Automotive Industry Conferences held at the University of Michigan, also published by the University's

Industry

Center for Japanese Studies. They include *The Japanese automobile industry: model and challenge for the future?*, edited by Robert E. Cole (1981); *Industry at the crossroads*, edited by Robert E. Cole (1982); *Automobiles and the future: competition, cooperation, and change*, edited by Robert E. Cole (1983); *Entrepreneurship in a 'mature industry'*, edited by John Creighton Campbell (1986); and *The Japanese competition: phase 2*, edited by Peter J. Arnesen (1987).

871 **The Japanese automobile industry: technology and management at Nissan and Toyota.**

Michael A. Cusumano.   Cambridge, Massachusetts: Council on East Asian Studies, Harvard University, 1985. 487p. bibliog. (Harvard East Asian Monographs, 122).

A comprehensive study of the growth of Nissan and Toyota, two of Japan's leading automobile manufacturing companies, between the 1930s and the mid-1980s. In seeking to explain how Japan began to manufacture motor vehicles and eventually surpassed the United States in productivity while matching the Europeans in small-car design, Cusumano pays particular attention to the different methods by which these two rivals acquired and improved sophisticated foreign technology. He examines their adaptation of modern manufacturing techniques to Japanese conditions, their development of new products and new systems of production management and organisation, and the character of postwar management–labour relations. Also discussed in some detail are the widely admired inventory control and quality control systems of these two firms, and the ways in which managerial and technical skills, Japanese government policy, and such historical circumstances as the outbreak of the Korean War contributed to their success.

872 **The misunderstood miracle: industrial development and political change in Japan.**

David Friedman.   Ithaca, New York; London: Cornell University Press, 1988. 265p. (Cornell Studies in Political Economy).

An inquiry into the reasons for the spectacular postwar growth of Japan's manufacturing industry, focusing on the evolution of the machine tool industry from the 1930s to the early 1980s. Friedman examines government attempts to regulate the prewar and wartime production of the machine tool industry, the postwar bureaucratic efforts to direct Japanese firms toward high-profit markets, the dramatic expansion and predominance of small-scale flexible manufacturing firms throughout the economy, and the impact of the growth of flexible manufacturing opportunities upon the rapid development and adoption of computer-guided machinery. He contends that 'often overlooked or misinterpreted political and industrial developments' enabled small-scale producers to implement more flexible manufacturing strategies than those which were possible for firms that pursued mass production alone as a means for greater efficiency. Because of flexible manufacturing, these producers could introduce rapid and extensive product changes more easily and thereby gain a significant advantage over their competitors.

873 **Partners in prosperity: strategic industries for the United States and Japan.**
Julian Gresser. New York; Toronto, Ontario: McGraw-Hill, 1984. 427p.

Gresser is concerned with the problem of stimulating US industrial growth and improving US–Japanese relations. He begins by describing some of the basic characteristics of 'strategic industries' (industries which are 'the primary cause of economic growth in a given time and place'), identifies their historic role, and depicts the present-day dilemma of America's high-tech industry. He then discusses the theory of industrial development in Japan in historical perspective and explains how postwar Japan has targeted automobiles, semiconductors, computers, and other strategic industries in order to sustain rapid economic development. He also suggests how the USA should identify and promote her own strategic industries for the sake of a national industrial recovery. Finally, after lamenting the recent deterioration of the US–Japan relationship, Gresser advances a set of proposals calling for 'joint economic growth' in order to 'increase productivity and output and stimulate innovation simultaneously' in both nations.

874 **The reckoning.**
David Halberstam. New York: Morrow, 1986; London: Bloomsbury, 1987. 752p. Reprinted, New York: Avon Books; London: Bantam, 1987. 786p.

A Pulitzer Prize-winning author chronicles the recent ascent of Japan as an economic superpower and the industrial decline of US industrial supremacy through detailed comparisons of the number two automobile manufacturers of each nation: Nissan and Ford. Halberstam compares their origins, growth, philosophies, management styles, responses to labour problems, and leadership – particularly in the form of mini-biographies of such individuals as Nissan president Kawamata Katsuji and labour organiser Masuda Tetsuo. A good picture of the operations and values of modern Japanese industry emerges from his descriptions of the Japanese corporate and labour worlds. A complementary account – *Car wars: the untold story*, by Robert Sobel (New York: E. P. Dutton; Toronto, Ontario: Fitzhenry & Whiteside, 1984, 371p.) – depicts the postwar struggle of the great Japanese, American, and European car-makers for global supremacy and the success of Japanese producers in securing a significant share of the American automobile market.

875 **Tough words for American industry.**
Hajime Karatsu, foreword by Norman Bodek. Cambridge, Massachusetts; Norwalk, Connecticut: Productivity Press, 1987. 157p.

Karatsu examines the hidden patterns behind US–Japanese trade friction, attributes the gradual decline of American industry to the single-minded obsession of Americans with short-term profits, discusses the factors that have enabled Japan to become pre-eminent in the area of manufacturing, emphasizes the critical role of productivity in her postwar industrial achievements, advances four principles of human productivity, reviews Japan's recent advances in the realm of industrial technology, and urges the Japanese to export their successful management practices and expertise to other parts of the world in order to reduce current trade friction and contribute to global prosperity. He constantly stresses the need for his American readers to learn from the Japanese example, to concern themselves with matters of productivity and quality, and to stop blaming the Japanese for America's faltering economy and trade deficits.

876 **Industrial policy of Japan.**
Edited by Ryūtarō Komiya, Masahiro Okuno, Kōtarō Suzumura;
translated under the supervision of Kazuo Satō. Tokyo: Academic
Press Japan; San Diego, California and London: Academic Press, 1988.
590p.

The results of a two-year-long research project undertaken by several Japanese
scholars in order 'to investigate and analyze Japanese industrial policy from an
economic perspective and to provide a comprehensive, quantitative evaluation of its
significance and impact'. Their publication formulates a standard economic-theoretical
framework for the analysis of industrial policy, examines the changing features of
industrial policy in Japan between the 1950s and the 1980s, studies policy interventions
in each of several major industrial sectors from the viewpoint of Japan's industrial
policy, and analyses and evaluates the impact of industrial promotion policies,
industrial adjustment policies, and industrial organisation policies on national
economic welfare. Case-studies which investigate the content and effectiveness of
policy interventions respectively in the steel, automobile, computer, textile, shipbuilding, and aluminium-refining industries are included.

877 **The Sony vision.**
Nick Lyons. New York: Crown, 1976. 235p. bibliog.

A 'rags-to-riches' story that vividly recounts the dynamic postwar growth of Sony, Inc.,
a company which evolved into a major multinational corporation in the area of
consumer electronics by exploiting technological innovations and timely changes in the
international market. It provides glimpses into the creativity, marketing philosophy,
strategic planning, decision-making, and orientation towards long-term growth that
have characterised some of Japan's postwar entrepreneurs. Lyons' book complements
the autobiography of Morita Akio, co-founder of Sony, entitled *Made in Japan: Akio
Morita and Sony* (q.v.).

878 **The Japanese industrial system.**
Charles J. McMillan. Berlin; New York: de Gruyter, 1985. 2nd rev.
ed. 356p. bibliog. (De Gruyter Studies in Organization, 1).

A description and analysis of the institutional framework of the Japanese industrial
economy and of Japanese management strategies at the national, industry (or
sectoral), and organisational (or corporate) levels in the 1980s. The book comprehensively covers the many aspects of Japan's complex industrial system including
business–government relations, industrial planning, technology and knowledge intensification, education and management recruitment, management strategy and organisation, human resource strategies and work, production and operations management,
marketing, Japanese management abroad, and money and banking. McMillan plays
down Japan's unique social values and institutions as well as the 'superhuman' nature
of the Japanese and, instead, attributes their economic success primarily to their ability
to 'apply textbook management principles in everyday work life'.

879 **Japanese industrial policy: a descriptive account of postwar
developments with case studies of selected industries.**
Ira C. Magaziner, Thomas M. Hout. London: Policy Studies
Institute, 1980. 90p.

A succinct analysis of Japan's industrial policy (defined as the 'application of government resources and influence to industrial affairs') combined with case-studies of its implementation. Magaziner and Hout trace the historical evolution and economic background of Japanese industrial policy, discuss past strategies of selected Japanese companies, and describe how industrial policy is made, the form it takes, the pressures exerted by various parties (including the Ministry of International Trade and Industry), and the range of measures which the government employs in its execution. Three pairs of case-studies of industrial policy in the steel and automobile, aluminium and shipbuilding, and industrial machinery and information electronics industries are then presented. These studies show how the course of industrial policy is influenced by, and changes with, the stages of an industry's business cycle. This work was reprinted under the title *Japanese industrial policy* (Berkeley, California: Institute of International Studies, University of California, 1981).

880 **Competitive edge: the semiconductor industry in the U.S. and Japan.**
Edited by Daniel I. Okimoto, Takuo Sugano, Franklin B. Weinstein.
Stanford, California: Stanford University Press, 1984. 275p. (ISIS Studies in International Policy).

The product of a binational, multidisciplinary effort to assess the dynamics of US–Japanese industrial competition in one critical sector of high technology. This book describes the development and analyses the relative strengths and weaknesses of the semiconductor industry in both Japan and the United States during the early 1980s. Three major areas are examined: 'technological innovation; the role of government not only in specific policies directed towards the semiconductor industry, but also in the broader context of industrial policy, government–business relations, and the two political systems; and the influence of financial institutions, ties between banks and businesses, and corporate financing'. The volume evaluates the significance of these factors for the ability of each country's industry to compete successfully in world markets, and concludes that there are opportunities for both sides to prosper in the foreseeable future. A more recent study by Daniel Okimoto, *Between MITI and the market: Japanese industrial policy for high technology* (Stanford, California: Stanford University Press, 1989, 267p.), analyses the relative effectiveness of Japanese industrial policy in high technology by studying the attitudes of Japanese leaders toward state intervention in the market-place, the efforts of MITI (Ministry of International Trade and Industry) in advancing the development of high technology, the organisation of the private sector and its impact on MITI's capacity for effective intervention, and the elements that enable Japan's industrial policy-making to be insulated politically from the demands of interest-group politics.

881 **Japan's high technology industries: lessons and limitations of industrial policy.**
Edited with an introduction by Hugh Patrick, with Larry Meissner.
Seattle, Washington: University of Washington Press; Tokyo: University of Tokyo Press, 1986. 277p. bibliog.

Leading American and Japanese scholars analyse and evaluate Japan's high-tech industrial policy and its relevance for the United States in the 1980s. An overview of the evolving industrial policies which Japan has pursued to promote her high-technology industries is followed by in-depth case-studies of the information industry, biotechnology, and the full range of high-technology industries. A description and evaluation of the contrasting Japanese and American approaches to joint research projects involving the co-operation of large, competing firms in the same industry

365

points out how the Japanese government has encouraged rival companies to co-operate in a number of key sectors. A chapter entitled 'Technology in Transition: Two Perspectives on Industrial Policy' argues that Japan is just entering into a new era of technological advancement. The volume concludes with a comparison of the specific American and Japanese policies that make up their respective industrial policies and with a discussion of what the United States can learn from Japanese government support of high-technology industries.

882 Honda Motor: the men, the management, the machines.

Tetsuo Sakiya, translated by Kiyoshi Ikemi, adapted by Timothy Porter.   Tokyo; New York: Kodansha International, 1982. 242p.

Case-history of the Honda Motor Company, a firm established in 1946 that became a leading manufacturer and exporter of motorcycles, automobiles, and industrial engines. Sakiya depicts the two entrepreneurs (Honda Sōichirō and Fujisawa Takeo) who were responsible for the growth and success of the company; analyses Honda Motor's corporate management system and its strategies within the framework of twentieth-century Japanese politics, economics, culture, and psychology; traces the company's history following Honda and Fujisawa's retirement in 1973; and describes as well as explains some of Honda's research and technological innovations. In the course of his narrative, Sakiya also delineates some of the historical forces that shaped not only Honda Motors but also Japan's postwar economic policies.

883 Industry and business in Japan.

Edited with an introduction by Kazuo Satō.   White Plains, New York: M. E. Sharpe; London: Croom Helm, 1980. 465p. bibliog.

Twelve essays by leading Japanese specialists in the field of industrial organisation analyse the structure, organisation, competition, and co-operation of Japanese business and industry between the 1950s and the early 1970s. They cover such topics as postwar industrial growth, the dual structure of the Japanese economy, industrial policy, big business and business groups, and capital concentration. Specific papers range from 'The Dual Structure of the Japanese Economy and Its Growth Pattern', 'The Automobile Industry of Japan', and 'The Japanese-Type Structure of Big Business', to 'The Concentration and Evaluation of Japanese Industrial Policy' and 'The Measurement of Interfirm Relationships'. Eight of the essays first appeared in the quarterly journal *Japanese Economic Studies*.

884 Government policy towards industry in the United States and Japan: Proceedings of a conference co-organized by Chikashi Moriguchi and John B. Shoven and sponsored by the Center for Economic Policy Research of Stanford University and the Suntory Foundation of Japan.

Edited with an editor's summary by John B. Shoven.   Cambridge, England; New York: Cambridge University Press, 1988. 354p. bibliog.

Eleven essays present some of the latest thinking among American and Japanese scholars about significant issues related to government policy towards industry in their respective national economies. The contributors are concerned with the comparative cost of capital in Japan and the United States, the taxation of income from capital in Japan, corporate tax burdens and tax incentives in Japan, present-day savings rates and investment in the USA and Japan, the Japanese current-account surplus and fiscal policy in both countries, the prospects for rectifying their current bilateral trade imbalance through internationally co-ordinated tax policies, public policy towards declining industries in Japan, corporate capital structure in the USA as well as Japan and the implications of financial deregulation, the role of the Japanese bureaucracy in economic administration, developments in Japan's energy policy during the 1970s, and industrial structure and government policies directed towards the American and Japanese integrated-circuit industries.

Japan's industrial economy: recent trends and changing aspects.
See item no. 35.

Comeback: case by case: building the resurgence of American business.
See item no. 38.

An industrial geography of Japan.
See item no. 45.

Kikkoman: company, clan, and community.
See item no. 201.

Human resources in Japanese industrial development.
See item no. 217.

Antitrust in Japan.
See item no. 270.

Made in Japan: Akio Morita and Sony.
See item no. 332.

Honda: the man and his machines.
See item no. 344.

Toyota: fifty years in motion; an autobiography.
See item no. 347.

Japanese urbanism: industry and politics in Kariya, 1872–1972.
See item no. 547.

Flexible rigidities: industrial policy and structural adjustment in the Japanese economy, 1970–80.
See item no. 794.

Japanese industrialization and its social consequences.
See item no. 812.

Japan Company Handbook.
See item no. 822.

Trade war: greed, power, and industrial policy on opposite sides of the Pacific.
See item no. 908.

Strategy and structure of Japanese enterprises.
See item no. 926.

Japanese manufacturing techniques: nine hidden lessons in simplicity.
See item no. 936.

Science and technology in Japan.
See item no. 980.

The amazing race: winning the technorivalry with Japan.
See item no. 981.

Japanese electronics technology: enterprise and innovation.
See item no. 985.

Flexible automation in Japan.
See item no. 986.

How Japan innovates: a comparison with the U.S. in the case of oxygen steelmaking.
See item no. 989.

Applied artificial intelligence in Japan: current status, key research and development performers, strategic focus.
See item no. 994.

Japanese Finance and Industry: Quarterly Survey.
See item no. 1519.

Journal of Japanese Trade & Industry.
See item no. 1527.

The Wheel Extended.
See item no. 1545.

Japan Economic Journal.
See item no. 1548.

Postwar industrial policy in Japan: an annotated bibliography.
See item no. 1581.

East Asian economies: a guide to information sources.
See item no. 1594.

Japan's economy: a bibliography of its past and present.
See item no. 1614.

See also the section 'Management, Labour, and Employer–Employee Relations'.

International Trade and Business

885 **Japan's economic security.**
Edited with an introduction by Nobutoshi Akao. New York: St.
Martin's Press; Aldershot, Hampshire: Gower, 1983. 279p.

In this book, published in the United Kingdom under the title *Japan's economic
security: resources as a factor in foreign policy*, nine Australian, British, and Japanese
contributors analyse Japan's economic dependence on overseas supplies of raw
materials and food, particularly during the 1970s. They examine the security
implications of this dependence; the policies being pursued to lessen Japan's
vulnerability; Japan's heavy reliance on the Middle East for oil and its impact on the
government's Middle East policy; Japanese efforts to diversify their supplies of energy
and to secure alternative energy sources in the form of coal (particularly coal imported
from Australia), liquefied natural gas, and nuclear power; Japan's food procurement
policies and the related problem of ensuring uninterrupted imports of food; the
potential and actual roles of Soviet Siberia and the People's Republic of China as
suppliers of important raw materials and fuels for the Japanese economy; and Japan's
quest for economic security.

886 **The United States–Japan economic problem.**
C. Fred Bergsten, William R. Cline. Washington, DC: Institute for
International Economics, 1987. 2nd ed. 180p. bibliog. (Policy Analyses
in International Economics, 13).

An assessment of major aspects of the complex US–Japan economic relationship,
including the composition of Japan's external accounts and her trade imbalance with
the United States; the structural elements of the Japanese and American economies,
particularly their significantly different rates of national savings and investment; the
roles of monetary and macroeconomic influences, among them the yen–dollar
exchange rate and sector-specific factors which have been generating Japan's huge
trade surpluses; and the nature, levels, and impact of trade restrictions and trade
barriers, including such intangible practices in Japan as industrial targeting and the
keiretsu system of oligopoly trading. The authors attribute the rapidly growing bilateral

trade imbalance to the different macroeconomic (particularly fiscal) policies pursued by the two countries. They conclude with a series of recommended policy actions for alleviating current economic conflicts between the United States and Japan and for averting a systemic breakdown in their relations.

887 **Japanese private economic diplomacy: an analysis of business–government linkages.**
William E. Bryant. New York; London: Praeger, 1975. 138p. bibliog.
(Praeger Special Studies in International Politics and Government).

An examination of some of the ways in which the government has sought to create and maintain a favourable economic climate that would enhance the possibilities for overseas trade, investment, and sales and lead to improved bilateral and multilateral relations. Analysing the linkages between Japanese business and government as well as between domestic and international politics, Bryant shows how the government has utilised private businessmen in economic missions, joint economic committees, and international conferences as well as in the role of roving ambassadors in order to represent their country's economic interests.

888 **U.S.–Japanese agricultural trade relations.**
Edited with an introduction by Emery N. Castle, Kenzō Hemmi, with Sally A. Skillings. Tokyo: University of Tokyo Press; Washington, DC: Resources for the Future, Inc., distributed by Johns Hopkins University Press, 1982. 436p. bibliog.

A scholarly examination of agriculture and agricultural policies in the United States and Japan, including consideration of the domestic and external political conditions under which these policies have been developed. The contributors describe the historical background and current nature of US–Japanese agricultural trade relations, discuss agriculture and agricultural policy and their interrelationships in both countries, indicate some of the similarities and differences between the United States and Japan in the ways that agricultural policy is made, and analyse the interdependence of the US and Japanese agricultural economies. The authors demonstrate how their respective nations' trade relations have been significantly affected by the nature of their postwar agricultural industries.

889 **Second to none: American companies in Japan.**
Robert C. Christopher. New York: Crown, 1986. 258p. bibliog.
Reprinted, Rutland, Vermont and Tokyo: Tuttle, 1987; New York: Fawcett Columbine, 1987.

Christopher refutes the widespread contention that American companies have been systematically denied the opportunity to compete in the Japanese market. He argues that many US entrepreneurs have indeed been able to establish successful operations in Japan in the face of competition from the Japanese themselves. He notes the experiences of such companies as Max Factor, IBM, Johnson & Johnson, Coca Cola, Texas Instruments, and McDonald's, pointing out how they overcame various problems and adjusted to the Japanese environment. He repeatedly indicates that there are a number of keys to being successful in Japan, and argues the importance of responding promptly and innovatively to changing social and economic patterns, providing first-rate products to quality-conscious consumers, understanding the

Japanese ways of doing business, and pursuing long-term rather than short-term business strategies.

890 **Uneasy partnership: competition and conflict in U.S.–Japanese trade relations.**
Stephen D. Cohen.   Cambridge, Massachusetts: Ballinger, 1985. 228p. bibliog.

A balanced examination of the evolution of US–Japanese trade relations and an analysis of the nature, scope, and significance of the problems besetting this bilateral relationship in the 1980s. Cohen argues that the current long-term competitive disequilibrium originated in the 1960s and 1970s, when Japan aggressively expanded her worldwide export markets while pursuing policies designed to protect her home markets. The United States, at the same time, remained economically complacent. American managerial philosophy continued to emphasize short-term economic gains and did not adequately stress productivity and improvement of the quality of the work force. Repeated efforts to correct the unbalanced relationship on a piecemeal basis have failed. Bilateral trade friction – characterised by charges and countercharges – has intensified instead. The study concludes with a set of recommendations for improving US–Japanese trade relations.

891 **How to do business with the Japanese: a complete guide to Japanese customs and business practices.**
Boye De Mente.   Lincolnwood, Illinois: NTC Business Books, 1987. 269p.

De Mente discusses the problems confronting Westerners who do business with the Japanese, the characteristics of the Japanese businessman, the areas of friction between Japanese and Western businessmen, Japanese consumer attitudes and their image of foreign products, the communications barrier, joint ventures and their special problems, the ways to find, hire and retain employees, the peculiarities of Japanese unions, the make-up of Japan's consumer market, Japan's distribution network, the Japanese method of selling goods, the Japanese way of advertising, and the importance of good public relations. He also deals with three other topics important to foreign businessmen: the practical problems of living in Japan, the nature of Japan's business world, and the question of Japan's future prospects.

892 **Coping with U.S.–Japanese economic conflicts.**
Edited by I. M. Destler, Hideo Satō.   Lexington, Massachusetts; Toronto, Ontario: Lexington Books, 1982. 293p. bibliog.

Case-studies of the policy-making and negotiations involved in five politically sensitive economic controversies between 1977 and 1981. These were concerned with the efforts to limit Japanese exports of steel and automobiles to the United States, American endeavours to increase the export of beef and citrus fruit to Japan, US insistence that foreign firms be permitted to compete for all of Nippon Telegraph and Telephone's future procurement, and macroeconomic policy co-ordination policies that arose from American pressures on the Japanese government to appreciate the value of the yen and to stimulate the domestic economy. The contributors (both Americans and Japanese) explain how and why these conflicts emerged, analyse the issues involved, present the viewpoints of both sides, and describe the ways in which the conflicts were handled and resolved. A concluding chapter advances some recommendations for managing and containing future US–Japanese economic conflicts.

893 **Smart bargaining: doing business with the Japanese.**
John L. Graham, Yoshihiro Sano. Cambridge, Massachusetts: Ballinger, 1989. rev. ed. 212p.

Directing their remarks towards an audience of American businessmen, Graham and Sano contend that Americans who wish to deal with prospective clients or partners in Japan must be prepared to handle their negotiations in a manner different from the one they are accustomed to at home. The authors first survey American and Japanese negotiating styles and show how the Japanese have a style of bargaining that is distinctly their own. They then guide the reader step by step through the process of successful cross-cultural bargaining: the selection of negotiating teams and team assignments, the preliminaries to negotiations, the conduct of negotiations at face-to-face meetings, the procedures to follow after negotiating, and some of the major cultural and personality issues involved. They also present the experiences of four American companies, offer a summary list of recommendations for Americans bargaining in Japan, and conclude with a chapter entitled 'Prescriptions for Japanese Traveling in the United States'.

894 **Hidden differences: doing business with the Japanese.**
Edward T. Hall, Mildred Reed Hall. Garden City, New York: Anchor Press/Doubleday, 1987. 172p. bibliog.

Aimed at American business executives interacting with the Japanese, this book seeks to clarify Japanese psychology and behaviour in the business world as well as some of the hidden differences between American and Japanese cultures. The authors present some conceptual tools to help readers understand the 'complex and unspoken messages of Japanese culture', and explain selected elements of Japanese thought and behaviour. They then identify some of the major contrasts between American and Japanese behaviour within the broader context of their cultural differences. Part three describes Japanese corporate philosophy, the typical relationship between employees and their company, the organisation of individual companies, and the ways in which business decisions are made. Finally, in part four ('The American Company in Japan'), the authors outline some of the essentials for American business success in Japan, including the proper ways for starting a business there and the basic elements of communicating and negotiating with the Japanese.

895 **Canadian perspectives on economic relations with Japan: proceedings of a conference sponsored by the University of Toronto–York University Joint Centre on Modern East Asia and the Institute for Research on Public Policy, Toronto, May 1979.**
Edited by Keith A. J. Hay, foreword by Gordon Robertson.
Montreal, Quebec: Institute for Research on Public Policy, 1980. 383p.

Eleven papers consider issues related to Canada's rapidly expanding economic relations with Japan. They discuss the development of prewar and wartime Canadian–Japanese relations, the problems of Canadian–Japanese economic diplomacy during the 1960s and 1970s, the impact of the Law of the Sea on Japanese–Canadian relations, multilateral trade negotiations, and human resource policies, labour markets and unions. They also examine the role of the multinational enterprise in Canadian–Japanese relations, foreign investment between the two nations, the impact of Japanese imports on Canadian manufacturers, the marketing of Canadian products through the Japanese distribution system, corporate strategies and productivity performance in Japan's manufacturing industries, and Canadian–Japanese agricultural trade. The volume provides a good background for understanding Canadian–Japanese economic relations during the 1980s.

896 **Japanese trade policy formulation.**
Chikara Higashi, forewords by Yasuhiro Nakasone, Michio Watanabe.   New York: Praeger, 1983. 179p. bibliog. (Praeger Special Studies).
A former high official of the Ministry of Finance addresses some misconceptions of the current Japanese trade policy formulation process. These have come about in part because Japan's trade policies have only recently undergone a rapid, fundamental shift from a restrictive to a liberal orientation. Higashi discusses the international and domestic economic environment of trade policy formulation in Japan, clarifies the institutional aspects of its formulation, and illustrates in three case-studies some of the problems encountered in US–Japanese trade negotiations. He particularly stresses the 'bottom-up' participatory style of decision-making among Japanese bureaucrats and Japanese organisations that are involved in the policy formulation process.

897 **Japan and the United States: economic and political adversaries.**
Edited with an introduction by Leon Hollerman.   Boulder, Colorado: Westview Press, 1980. 224p. (Westview Special Studies in International Economics and Business).
Nine American and Japanese scholars, government officials, and business executives contribute their views to the ongoing discussion about the postwar origins, current nature, and future prospects of the US–Japan economic relationship. Included are articles about Japan's growing technological superiority, binational relations in science and technology, the Japan factor in US trade problems, Japan's foreign trade policy, the relations of the Association of Southeast Asian Nations (ASEAN) with Japan and the United States, the future of Japanese–American trade relations, the evolution of US–Japan relations, the US–Japan alliance, Japanese views of US protectionism, and the politics of US–Japanese economic relations. Most of the authors predict a more outward-looking Japan that will increasingly diversify its export markets and contribute to development efforts in the Third World.

898 **Japan's economic strategy in Brazil: challenge for the United States.**
Leon Hollerman.   Lexington, Massachusetts; Toronto, Ontario: Lexington Books, 1988. 284p.
Brazil's relations with both Japan and the United States are strategically important in view of her size, resource endowment, and leadership potential. Focusing on relations during the 1970s and early 1980s, Hollerman first outlines Japan's foreign economic policies, Brazil's place in the Japanese strategy, the US policy predicament, and Brazil's own economic strategy. He then describes and contrasts the Brazilian and Japanese approaches towards one another, covering such topics as the milieu and nature of capital inflow into Brazil, the Brazilian view of Japan, and the Japanese government's role in promoting economic co-operation with Brazil. The Japanese experience in Brazil – including its successes and difficulties and the *sōgō shōsha*

(general trading company) transition – as well as the US and Japanese responses to the challenge posed by Brazil's massive foreign debt are examined. Finally, Hollerman compares both Japanese and American investment in and trade with Brazil, and assesses the implications of that country's economic programmes.

899 **Organizing business: trade associations in America and Japan.**
Leonard H. Lynn, Timothy J. McKeown, foreword by Claude E. Barfield, Jr. Washington, DC: American Enterprise Institute for Public Policy Research, 1988. 191p. (AEI Studies, 459).

A comparative analysis of the role which such industry trade associations as the Japan Iron and Steel Federation and the Japan Machine Tool Builders Association play in the co-ordination of economic and political activity in Japan and the United States. Focusing on the trade associations within the iron and steel and the machine tools/robotics sectors, Lynn and McKeown trace the historical development of trade associations, compare the American and Japanese antitrust environments, detail how trade associations are structured to influence their respective governments, compare governmental interaction with these associations, and examine their involvement in tv ɔ areas central to the issue of international competitiveness: foreign trade and i:.dustrial research. Much of their study highlights the differences between Japan and the United States in how information is exchanged and how influence flows between firms and trade associations, between trade associations and other business groups within their industrial sectors, and between trade associations and government.

900 **Japan's role in Soviet economic growth: transfer of technology since 1965.**
Raymond S. Mathieson. New York; London: Praeger, 1979. 277p. 14 maps. bibliog. (Praeger Special Studies).

Since the mid-1960s, Japan has participated in the exploitation of Siberia's vast mineral resources and in the development of the Soviet Union's industrial infrastructure. Mathieson describes the Japanese involvement in Soviet civil engineering projects, the modernisation of forest processing industries, the development of vast energy resources (coal, oil, and natural gas), and the growth and modernisation of the Soviet chemical, metal manufacturing, heavy engineering, and precision manufacturing industries. Several of the problems encountered by the Japanese are discussed, and the author demonstrates how the Japanese export of sophisticated plants, highly modern machinery, automated equipment, and industrial technology has not only contributed to the Soviet Union's industrial expansion but also has enabled her to acquire valuable foreign technology at a relatively small cost.

901 **Business in Japan: a guide to Japanese business practice and procedure.**
Edited by Paul Norbury, Geoffrey Bownas, foreword by Endymion Wilkinson. Boulder, Colorado: Westview Press; London: Macmillan, 1980. rev. ed. 210p. bibliog.

Containing analyses of Japan's 'business culture' and much shrewd advice on how to penetrate the Japanese market, this book covers the major practical elements of doing business with the Japanese. Following a brief introductory section entitled 'Understanding the Japanese', the twenty-one contributors discuss the new industrial policies of Japan, various approaches to the Japanese market, finance and the banks, aspects of business strategy and management, and the ways of adjusting to Japan. They also write about such specific concerns of Western businessmen as the value of market research in Japan, the services which are provided by Japanese banks, the relationship of the Japanese legal system to business and commercial transactions, the best way for individuals or organisations to set up small liaison-offices in Tokyo, and the basics of proper Japanese etiquette and behaviour.

902   **Triad power: the coming shape of global competition.**
Kenichi Ohmae.   New York: Free Press; London: Collier Macmillan, 1985. 220p.

Ohmae, a well-known management consultant and director of McKinsey Japan & Co., surveys the revolutionary changes that have been reshaping the global economy and creating a business world dominated by Japan, the United States, and Europe (the 'triad'). He outlines the forces of change (capital-intensive operations, the accelerating tempo of technology, the universal consumer, and neo-protectionism); describes the current realities of global competition; assesses the activities of Japanese companies in the United States and Europe and the operations of Western corporations in Japan; and indicates how a business corporation can become a 'triad power'. Stressing the strategic significance of Japan, the United States, and Europe as the world's major markets and the source of new technologies and new competitors, he argues that 'the prime objective of every corporation must be to become a true insider in all three regions'. Ohmae's views on international business are also found in two of his other books: *The mind of the strategist: the art of Japanese business* (q.v.), and *Beyond national borders: reflections on Japan and the world* (Homewood, Illinois: Dow Jones-Irwin, 1987. 128p. Reprinted, Tokyo: Kodansha, 1988).

903   **Japan's economy: coping with change in the international environment.**
Edited with an introduction by Daniel I. Okimoto. Boulder, Colorado: Westview Press, 1982. 304p. (Westview Special Studies on East Asia).

A thought-provoking treatment of Japan's need to modify her successful postwar economic policies in order to adapt to the dramatically changing international environment occasioned by the increase in oil prices after 1973. The seven contributors examine the formidable problems and challenges that face Japan and analyse some of her initial responses. They specifically discuss the momentous changes which occurred in the world economic environment during the 1970s, Japan's heavy dependence on overseas energy supplies and the ways in which she has already coped with the 'oil shocks', the forces of change in Japan's financial system, the character of the macroeconomic interdependence between the Japanese and US economies and its bilateral implications, the economic dimensions of the US–Japan alliance, the growing trade conflict between Japan and the United States, and the interrelationship of economic and military security in Japan.

904   **Trading places: how we allowed Japan to take the lead.**
Clyde V. Prestowitz, Jr.   New York: Basic Books; Rutland, Vermont and Tokyo: Tuttle, 1988. 365p. bibliog.

Prestowitz, the Counselor for Japan Affairs to the US Secretary of Commerce between 1983 and 1986, describes how the United States has yielded her economically and technologically pre-eminent position in the world to the Japanese. Focusing upon the early and mid-1980s, he outlines the nature of Japan's challenge to American power; depicts how the Japanese have displaced not only the US semiconductor industry but also the critically important equipment and materials manufacturers who supply it;

analyses the character of Japan's highly structured society, her postwar industry policy, and present-day Japanese ways of doing business; contrasts this with the mismanagement of US industrial and economic policy and with the decline of US economic power; considers the conflict between US non-interventionist free-trade policies and the US commitment to national security; and reviews the problematic pattern of US–Japanese trade negotiations. Prestowitz concludes with some recommendations on how the United States and Japan should reorder their future priorities and integrate their economies.

905 **Fragile interdependence: economic issues in U.S.–Japanese trade and investment.**
Edited by Thomas A. Pugel, with Robert G. Hawkins, introduction by Thomas A. Pugel.   Lexington, Massachusetts; Toronto, Ontario: Lexington Books, 1986. 276p. bibliog.

The growing economic interdependence between Japan and the United States has not only brought substantial benefits to the two largest economies in the free world but has also created considerable stress and strain in their bilateral economic relationship. The Japanese and American contributors to this volume focus on the three major issue areas of: (1) foreign access to Japan's large industrial and consumer markets, (2) international investment resulting from the growth of significant flows of two-way foreign direct investment and from financial interdependence, and (3) international technological competition and the impact of government policies on the competitiveness of each country's high-technology industries. Japan's invisible trade barriers, Japanese policy toward foreign multinationals, and Japan's technological catch-up and leadership are among the topics which are examined in depth.

906 **Economic diplomacy between the European Community and Japan 1959–1981.**
Albrecht Rothacher.   Aldershot, Hampshire: Gower, 1983. 377p. bibliog.

A detailed study in the area of political economy of the relations between the European Community (EC) and Japan. Part one examines the institutional framework for foreign economic policy decisions within both the EC and Japan and shows that they were characterised by 'a structural bias towards complex and slow bureaucratic decision making oriented primarily at achieving domestic consensus'. Part two offers a longitudinal policy analysis of the development of bilateral economic relations and trade policies. Emphasizing the underlying structural conditions for inter-administrative compromises, bilateral negotiations, and policy results, Rothacher covers Japan's diplomatic endeavours to achieve international recognition and to secure greater access to the European market, 1955-63; the EC's efforts to initiate a common trade agreement with Japan and the concurrent liberalisation of imports in Japan, 1969-75; and the cyclical bilateral crises and 'high politics cooperation' of 1976-80.

907 **Trade friction and economic policy: problems and prospects for Japan and the United States.**
Edited by Ryūzō Satō, Paul Wachtel, foreword by Richard R. West, introduction by Paul Wachtel.   Cambridge, England; New York: Cambridge University Press, 1987. 243p.

The complex, multidimensional problem of trade friction between Japan and the

United States is examined from the perspectives of both countries. Ten essays consider in particular the sources of this bilateral trade friction, the appropriate American and Japanese macroeconomic policy responses, and the appropriate trade policy responses. Typical of their essays are chapters entitled 'Industrial Policy in Japan: Overview and Evaluation'; 'Japanese–U.S. Current Accounts and Exchange Rates before and after the G5 Agreement'; and 'Limits of Trade Policy toward High Technology Industries: the Case of Semiconductors'. Wachtel points out that there is a consensus among the authors that restrictive trade policies would not constitute a worthwhile means of reducing the current Japanese–US trade deficit.

908   **Trade war: greed, power, and industrial policy on opposite sides of the Pacific.**
Steven Schlossstein.   New York: Congdon and Weed, 1984. 296p.
bibliog.

A study of Japan's growth as an industrial and exporting power and the concurrent decline of America's international industrial competitiveness. Schlossstein, a former vice-president of the Morgan Guaranty Trust Company, analyses Japan's co-ordinated industrial policy – from its nineteenth-century origins to its remarkable postwar successes – and ridicules the charges levelled by various critics that this policy is unfair. He praises postwar Japan's economic strategies and the Japanese emphasis on both productivity and quality control. Instead of allowing 'free market forces' to determine its economic fate, he argues that the United States should realize that it is now engaged in a trade war with Japan, study the Japanese example, and adopt as well as pursue a coherent industrial policy of its own.

909   **Japan's response to crisis and change in the world economy.**
Edited with an introduction by Michèle Schmiegelow.   Armonk, New York; London: M. E. Sharpe, 1986. 309p.

Different aspects of Japan's economy which directly affect her involvement in the world economy constitute the focus of this publication of the Institute of Asian Affairs in Hamburg, West Germany. Its fourteen essays are concerned with the reform of Japan's foreign exchange and foreign trade control laws; her exchange rate policy; the foreign exchange market in Japan; the internationalisation of Japan's financial markets; Japanese direct investment in Western Europe; the external safeguard of domestic monetary and fiscal policies; the impact of Japanese banks and securities companies on international capital flows; deficiencies in Japanese infrastructure and their relationship to budgetary policy and capital flows; the links between the foreign sector and the macroeconomic performance of the economy; the impact of labour policies on export competitiveness; industrial policy in Japan; the relationship between the domestic marketing system and imports from abroad; and changes in government policy towards cartels.

910   **Japan and Western Europe: conflict and cooperation.**
Edited by Loukas Tsoukalis, Maureen White.   London: Frances Pinter; New York: St. Martin's Press, 1982. 222p. (Studies in International Political Economy).

The problems and prospects of Japanese relations with the European Economic Community (EEC) are the focus of this collection of conference papers oriented towards a broad European audience. Part one briefly reviews the historical origins of these relations. Part two ('The Japanese Dimension') describes Japan's economic, industrial, and foreign economic policies as well as the changing nature of Japanese involvement in world politics. Part three examines the major bilateral economic issues: the trade imbalance between Japan and Western Europe, bilateral perceptions and reactions to this imbalance, the impact of Japanese exports on European manufacturing industries, the process of economic adjustment and the role of industrial policies in Europe, and the prospects and implications of Japanese direct investment in Europe. The concluding part ('From Conflict to Cooperation') explores the possibilities of broadening European–Japanese co-operation in both the political and economic spheres.

911 **Business negotiations with the Japanese.**
Rosalie L. Tung. Lexington, Massachusetts; Toronto, Ontario: Lexington Books, 1984. 250p. bibliog.
An examination of Japanese attitudes and values regarding business negotiations and of the dynamics of some recent US–Japanese business dealings. Tung studies the mechanics of these business negotiations, the ways in which US firms prepare for their negotiations, the factors accounting for the success or failure of such negotiations, the manner by which US firms organise for trade with Japan, and how six US firms – in the computer, aircraft production, pharmaceuticals, and automotive chemicals industries – have negotiated with Japanese companies to establish joint-venture arrangements or other forms of economic co-operation, and their subsequent experiences. A concluding chapter, entitled 'The Dos and Don'ts of Business Negotiations with the Japanese', offers some practical guidelines. This study is based on a survey of 114 firms that have entered into various types of negotiations with the Japanese and on in-depth interviews with a limited number of them.

912 **Industrial collaboration with Japan.**
Louis Turner, foreword by Hiroshi Takeuchi. London; New York: Routledge and Kegan Paul, 1987. 117p. (Chatham House Papers, 34).
Stressing the value of industrial collaboration, a team of American, British, German, and Japanese researchers summarises the results of its investigation of the experiences of American and European firms that have collaborated with their Japanese competitors in the consumer electronics, automotive, and information technology sectors as well as in aerospace. Companies such as Fujitsu and Amdahl (in the computer industry) and Toyota and General Motors have formed joint ventures, co-operatively designed numerous products, and pursued complementary marketing strategies. The team's spokesman, Louis Turner, traces the history of Japanese–Western collaboration, considers the ways it has been perceived, and analyses industrial collaboration during the 1970s and 1980s on the basis of several case-studies. He also outlines some of the issues which corporate strategists should consider and urges government officials to come to terms with the realities of Japanese multinational investment and with Western demands for access to the Japanese market.

913 **Two hungry giants: the United States and Japan in the quest for oil and ores.**
Raymond Vernon. Cambridge, Massachusetts; London: Harvard University Press, 1983. 161p.
In their efforts to secure dependable supplies of critically needed raw materials for

their burgeoning economies, the United States and Japan have come to dominate the world's raw materials markets. Focusing on the quest of these two industrial giants for oil and oil products, iron ore, bauxite, and copper ore, Vernon explores the nature of their competitive relationship and of their respective policies as he describes the changing world markets in oil, minerals and metals, the principles and practices involved in each country's resource strategy, and the possible prospects for the future. Compared to their American counterparts, Japanese leaders are shown to have pursued a more flexible and innovative policy in helping their industries acquire raw materials from abroad and in responding to the economic needs of their country.

914   **Sogo shosha: the vanguard of the Japanese economy.**
Kunio Yoshihara.   Tokyo; Oxford, England; New York: Oxford University Press, 1982. 358p. bibliog.

An account of the evolution, role, and organisation of the large and diversified Japanese trading companies known as *sōgō shōsha* that handle the import and export of numerous commodities on a worldwide basis. Yoshihara first traces the development (since the nineteenth century) of several of these trading companies – especially Mitsui Bussan, Mitsubishi Shōji, C. Itoh, Marubeni, Tōyō Menka, Nichimen, Gosho, Iwai, Ataka, Nisshō, and Sumitomo Shōji – and accounts for their success. He then analyses the cultural and economic background for the growth of *sōgō shōsha* in Japan and examines the role of these companies as marketing and financial intermediaries in Japan's industrialisation. He concludes by describing the people and organisational structure of present-day *sōgō shōsha* as well as the types of involvement in postwar Japanese politics that have drawn criticism from journalists, intellectuals, leftist politicians, and the government's Fair Trade Commission.

915   **The invisible link: Japan's sogo shosha and the organization of trade.**
Michael Y. Yoshino, Thomas B. Lifson.   Cambridge, Massachusetts; London: MIT Press, 1986. 291p. bibliog.

An institutional investigation that focuses on the six largest *sōgō shōsha*, the general trading companies which co-ordinate a wide range of business activities including the purchase of raw materials, the production of finished goods, and their sale both at home and abroad. Yoshino and Lifson explore the historical evolution of the *sōgō shōsha*; their dynamics and strategy, culture and organisation, administrative structures and processes, personnel practices, sectional and network organisation, and inter-unit and inter-firm co-ordination; and the challenges facing them with the continuing transformation of the Japanese economy. The six major companies – C. Itoh, Marubeni, Mitsubishi, Mitsui, Nisshō-Iwai, and Sumitomo – are uniquely Japanese institutions that differ from other types of business firms in their strategy, operations, and organisation. They are a key element of the present-day Japanese economy.

916   **How to do business with the Japanese.**
Mark Zimmerman, foreword by Mike Mansfield.   New York: Random House, 1985. 316p. London: Allen and Unwin, 1985. 320p.

A former US corporate executive and leader of the American business community in Tokyo argues that the best strategy for successful business dealing in Japan lies in the development of close personal relationships with the Japanese. Seeking to show 'what competing, negotiating, or working with the Japanese is all about', Zimmerman discusses Japanese culture, etiquette, language, social values, and above all the concept of *ningen kankei* ('human relations'). He also offers ways for negotiating and concluding a business deal; discusses how the Japanese conduct business at home and abroad and how Western companies can compete as well as respond to their marketing challenges; and describes various ways of co-operation (e.g., through joint ventures and by employment in Japanese firms). This book, published in the United Kingdom under the title *Dealing with the Japanese*, is recommended as a practical guide for both Western businessmen and general readers interested in Japanese social and business behaviour.

The Pacific alliance: United States foreign economic policy and Japanese trade recovery, 1945–1955.
See item no. 264.

The Japanese overseas: can they go home again?
See item no. 572.

Neighbors across the Pacific: Canadian–Japanese relations 1870–1982.
See item no. 655.

Japan and the United States: challenges and opportunities.
See item no. 718.

Europe and Japan: changing relationships since 1945.
See item no. 720.

Managing an alliance: the politics of U.S.–Japanese relations.
See item no. 721.

The textile wrangle: conflict in Japanese–American relations, 1969–1971.
See item no. 722.

Japanese investment in Southeast Asia.
See item no. 727.

Japan and Southeast Asia: a bibliography of historical, economic and political relations.
See item no. 727.

Japan's new world role.
See item no. 732.

The politics of Canadian–Japanese economic relations, 1952–1983.
See item no. 734.

China and Japan: new economic diplomacy.
See item no. 735.

Japan's foreign relations: a global search for economic security.
See item no. 743.

Coming to terms: the politics of Australia's trade with Japan, 1945–57.
See item no. 745.

Japan's economic aid: policy-making and politics.
See item no. 746.

Soviet policy towards Japan: an analysis of trends in the 1970s and 1980s.
See item no. 747.

The foreign policy of modern Japan.
See item no. 748.

Japan and Australia in the seventies.
See item no. 751.

The United States and Japan: a troubled partnership.
See item no. 753.

Japanese business law and the legal system.
See item no. 776.

Foreign enterprise in Japan: laws and policies.
See item no. 779.

Law and trade issues of the Japanese economy: American and Japanese perspectives.
See item no. 783.

The internationalization of the Japanese economy.
See item no. 798.

The developing economies and Japan: lessons in growth.
See item no. 810.

Policy and trade issues of the Japanese economy: American and Japanese perspectives.
See item no. 816.

White Paper on International Trade.
See item no. 828.

Beef in Japan: politics, production, marketing and trade.
See item no. 833.

The strategy of Japanese business.
See item no. 837.

Japan's market: the distribution system.
See item no. 839.

Japanese etiquette & ethics in business.
See item no. 840.

From bonsai to levi's. When West meets East: an insider's surprising account of how the Japanese live.
See item no. 841.

Business and society in Japan: fundamentals for businessmen.
See item no. 843.

Japan, the hungry guest: Japanese business ethics vs. those of the U.S.
See item no. 844.

U.S.–Japanese energy relations: cooperation and competition.
See item no. 847.

Yen! Japan's new financial empire and its threat to America.
See item no. 853.

Japan, disincorporated: the economic liberalization process.
See item no. 856.

Car wars: the untold story.
See item no. 874.

Tough words for American industry.
See item no. 875.

Japan's technological challenge to the West, 1950–1974: motivation and accomplishment.
See item no. 993.

AMPO: Japan-Asia Quarterly Review.
See item no. 1488.

Asian Survey.
See item no. 1491.

JEI Report.
See item no. 1524.

Japan Economic Survey: a Monthly Review of U.S.–Japan Economic Relations.
See item no. 1524.

Speaking of Japan.
See item no. 1540.

Venture Japan: the Journal of Global Opportunity.
See item no. 1544.

Japan Economic Journal.
See item no. 1548.

Information gathering on Japan: a primer.
See item no. 1570.

Japan's economic challenge: a bibliographic sourcebook.
See item no. 1590.

U.S./Japan foreign trade: an annotated bibliography of socioeconomic perspectives.
See item no. 1600.

Japan's economy: a bibliography of its past and present.
See item no. 1614.

See also the section 'Multinationals and Multinationalism'.

Management, Labour, and Employer–Employee Relations

917 **Management and worker: the Japanese solution.**
James C. Abegglen, introduction by Henry Rosovsky.   Tokyo: Sophia
University in co-operation with Kodansha International, 1973. 200p.

An updated version of the author's classic work, *The Japanese factory: aspects of its social organization* (Glencoe, Illinois: Free Press, 1958), supplemented by two new studies. Part one describes and analyses the nature, consequences, and prospects of Japan's employment system in the 1970s. Part two – 'The Japanese Factory, 1956' – contains most of Abegglen's earlier study, a report based on his investigations into the organisation and personnel practices of large companies in the mid-1950s. It covers such areas as lifetime employment, the recruitment of personnel, the system of rewards and incentives employed in the factory, the basic relationship between employee and firm, and the nature and extent of the firm's involvement in the life of its employees. Abegglen argues that the Japanese organisation of labour resources differs significantly from the Western pattern but is generally consistent with broader social patterns unique to Japanese society. A concluding report compares organisational methods in Japanese companies in 1966 with those of a decade earlier.

918 **Japanese blue collar: the changing tradition.**
Robert E. Cole.   Berkeley, California; London: University of
California Press, 1971. 300p. bibliog.

A sociological investigation of the working conditions, everyday activities, behaviour, and attitudes of Japanese blue-collar workers, based in part on the author's first-hand observations while employed in a Tokyo die-casting factory and in a rural automobile parts company. Cole studies the wage structure and the effects of the prevailing wage systems among blue-collar employees, the workers' search for advancement and security, various elements of unity and cleavage that exist among these workers, the Japanese-style paternalism that characterises worker–company relations, the autonomy and ideology of labour unions, and the changing characteristics of blue-collar employees. Even though his study is based on data collected during the mid-1960s, Cole's book remains important today for understanding the motivations and concerns of Japanese labourers, the life-styles of production workers, and the nature and functioning of the Japanese labour system.

919 **Work, mobility, and participation: a comparative study of American and Japanese industry.**
Robert E. Cole. Berkeley, California; London: University of California Press, 1979. 302p. bibliog.

A sociological comparison of the labour conditions and working habits of Japanese and American blue-collar workers. Cole begins by investigating the question of permanent employment and its consequences, as well as job mobility patterns within and between individual companies. His findings suggest that the two most significant factors influencing the nature of job mobility are the size of a particular firm and the workers' level of education. He also examines the formation and operation of quality control circles in one large Japanese company, inquires into related in-company career development activities for its employees, and discusses the comparative strength of the work ethic among Japanese and Americans. This study is based on a comparative investigation of some six hundred male workers each in Yokohama and Detroit, Michigan in 1970-71, and on a case-study of quality control circles and career development in a Toyota assembly plant near Nagoya.

920 **British factory – Japanese factory: the origins of national diversity in industrial relations.**
Ronald Dore. London: Allen and Unwin; Berkeley, California: University of California Press, 1973. 432p. Reprinted with a new afterword by the author, University of California Press, 1990.

A comparison of the patterns of social organisation in Britain and Japan and an explanation of their significant differences. Much of this sociological study, based on intensive research in two matched pairs of factories owned by the electrical engineering firms English Electric and Hitachi, is a detailed description of the economic and social structures of those factories. It includes coverage of their recruitment and training of workers, wage systems, labour union membership and organisation, industrial relations, the Japanese 'enterprise as a community', and the hierarchy of authority and function. After showing that Hitachi is a reasonably typical large Japanese firm, Dore challenges the 'convergence' thesis as he assesses trends of change in both the British and Japanese employment systems. Finally, he traces the historical evolution of the Japanese system and analyses the reasons for the existence of a market-oriented British employment system and an organisation-centred Japanese system.

921 **Labor relations in Japan today.**
Tadashi Hanami. Tokyo; New York: Kodansha International, 1979. 253p. bibliog. Reprinted, London: John Martin, 1980.

A prominent Tokyo labour lawyer surveys industrial relations in postwar Japan, the extent and the nature of labour conflict during the 1970s, and Japanese ways of resolving labour disputes. He focuses on the traditional and modern features of Japan's system of industrial relations, the importance of personal relations in industrial relations, the legal right of Japanese labour unions to organise, labour union practices, enterprise unionism on a nationwide basis, the characteristics of labour disputes, strikes and other types of labour unrest such as the act of pasting up posters and union take-overs, violence in industrial relations, and the role of third parties in settling disputes.

922   **Japanese-style management: an insider's analysis.**
Keitarō Hasegawa.   Tokyo; New York: Kodansha International, 1986.
162p. bibliog.
An examination of the methods, successes, and weaknesses of Japanese-style management. Hasegawa discusses the people-centred nature of Japanese management, the importance of consensus and harmony in Japanese business relations, the contributions of middle-level managers, the unique role of *de facto* leaders, Japanese methods of establishing priorities, the emphasis on quality, Japanese personnel management, and Japanese attitudes towards research and development. In addition, he investigates the ways in which large trading companies (*sōgō shōsha*) operate and how Japanese corporations are financed, and he suggests ways in which Western businessmen can adopt and adapt Japanese management techniques.

923   **The Japanese working man: what choice? what reward?**
Ernest van Helvoort.   Tenterden, Kent: Paul Norbury; Vancouver,
British Columbia: University of British Columbia Press, 1979. 158p.
bibliog.
An introduction to personnel management principles and practices, particularly as of the late 1970s. Helvoort outlines the basic features of the Japanese employment system, including lifetime employment, the 'regular employee', working women, home-workers and handicapped employees, older workers, formal education, the recruitment of employees, training, job hierarchy, cash rewards, compulsory and voluntary welfare benefits, informal relationships, and organised labour. He also deals with such related matters as the ways in which workers are motivated, Japanese methods of decision-making and communication, and the ways in which quality control and safety practices are realised.

924   **Japan in the passing lane: an insider's account of life in a Japanese auto
factory.**
Satoshi Kamata, translated and edited by Tatsuru Akimoto,
introduction by Ronald Dore.   New York: Pantheon; London: Allen
and Unwin, 1983. 211p. Reprinted, London: Unwin Paperbacks, 1984.
A free-lance journalist's chronicle (presented in the form of a diary) of his six months in 1972-73 as a seasonal worker on a Toyota automobile assembly line. Kamata depicts the tedious nature of the work, the dehumanising impact of the assembly-line technology, management's overwhelming preoccupation with meeting production schedules, the frequent obligation of employees to put in overtime, the numerous unreported accidents, and in general the adverse working conditions of a mass production factory system. The author's exposé is openly critical of Toyota and of the company's labour–management relations. At the same time, the Toyota employees are shown to have a deep sense of commitment to their company and a general willingness to accept the onerous working conditions despite their many complaints. This stirring indictment is preceded by an introduction that places Kamata's story into a broader perspective and points out that the conditions which he describes are not common to most Japanese firms.

925 **Understanding industrial relations in modern Japan.**
Kazuo Koike, translated by Mary Saso. Basingstoke, Hampshire:
Macmillan; New York: St. Martin's Press, 1988. 306p. bibliog. (Studies
in the Modern Japanese Economy).

Koike rejects the argument that the Japanese system of industrial relations –
characterised by permanent employment, seniority-based wages, and enterprise-based
labour unions – is culturally unique. He suggests that the high morale of the Japanese
industrial work force and its critical contributions to postwar Japan's economic
performance result from a situation in which skilled employees work against a
background of high technology. The ability of manual workers to acquire a broad
understanding of their company's production processes through on-the-job training and
experience and, consequently, to possess wide-ranging technical and intellectual skills
constitutes the 'real essence of white-collarization' in Japan. This phenomenon has
served as the foundation for high morale among factory employees and has enabled the
Japanese economy to be more responsive to ongoing economic and technical change.

926 **Strategy and structure of Japanese enterprises.**
Toyohiro Kōno, foreword by Malcolm Falkus. London: Macmillan;
Armonk, New York: M. E. Sharpe, 1984. 352p. bibliog.

An analysis of the product-market strategy, organisational structure, and strategic
decision-making of relatively large and successful Japanese companies. Basing his
investigation on a study of 102 large manufacturing corporations (four of which –
Toyota Motor, Hitachi, Matsushita Electric, and Canon – were selected for intensive
analysis), Kōno stresses the innovative, competition-oriented, and centralised nature of
their strategic management practices. Most aspects of Japanese management behaviour
are covered: the general patterns of top management, organisational goals, product
mix and diversification, vertical integration, multinational management, competition
strategy, new-product development, long-range planning, organisational structure and
resource structure, and personnel management systems. Comparisons are frequently
made with American and British companies.

927 **Japanese management: cultural and environmental considerations.**
Edited by Sang M. Lee, Gary Schwendiman. New York: Praeger,
1982. 302p. bibliog. (Praeger Special Studies).

A collection of the best empirical and conceptual studies presented at the
Japan–United States Business Conference (University of Nebraska) in October 1981.
Four key issues essential for understanding Japanese management systems are
emphasized: (1) what Americans can learn from the Japanese; (2) sociocultural aspects
of Japanese management; (3) the Japanese management environment; and (4) the
relationship between the United States and Japan. Representative contributions
include articles entitled 'Japanese Values and Management Processes'; 'Mindscapes,
Workers, and Management: Japan and the U.S.A.'; 'Japanese Management Success:
Implications for the Field of Organizational Development'; and 'Differences in
Japanese and American Corporate Tax Incentives and Their Investment Implications'.
The editors stress the transferability of Japanese management approaches to US
corporations.

928 **Inside corporate Japan: the art of fumble-free management.**
David J. Lu, foreword by Norman Bodek.   Stanford, Connecticut;
Cambridge, Massachusetts: Productivity Press, 1987. 249p. map.
bibliog.

Equating corporate success in the global market-place with a football team's victory on
the playing-field, Lu shows how the Japanese have organised and developed the
world's leading corporations. He describes the three basic regional approaches to
industrial management that shape Japan's successful companies; the recruitment and
training methods which ensure that employees become good team players; the
corporate philosophy and values that maintain a family-like atmosphere and reinforce
Japan's record of labour peace; the ways in which representative companies structure
their operations to maximise productivity; the all-encompassing, genuine commitment
to total quality control; and the community-, employee- and consumer-oriented nature
of successful Japanese businesses. Lu also relates how two American companies – IBM
Japan and Coca Cola – have done well in Japan. An appendix entitled 'A Common
Sense Approach to Japanese Etiquette' presents some simple rules designed to make
an American businessman's stay in Japan more enjoyable and rewarding.

929 **Modernization and the Japanese factory.**
Robert M. Marsh, Hiroshi Mannari.   Princeton, New Jersey; London:
Princeton University Press, 1976. 437p. bibliog.

Two sociologists argue that the popularly accepted 'paternalism–lifetime commitment
model' of Japanese factories exaggerates the uniformity, traditionalism, and distinctly
Japanese character of those firms, that the most successful firms in the postwar era
have in fact moved in the direction of a more modern organisational structure which is
based on the Western model of company–employee relations, and that the firms which
are not moving in this direction will suffer significant organisational strains. Marsh and
Mannari base their contentions on the results of field-work undertaken within an
electrical appliance factory, a shipyard, and a saké brewery (where they studied the
attitudes and behaviour of company management and company employees) as well as
on systematic comparisons across firms. The authors disagree with the views of those
individuals (e.g., James C. Abegglen and Ronald Dore) who have asserted that to the
extent organisations vary, they do so on account of their national cultural settings, i.e.,
because they are Japanese or British or American. A closely related work by Marsh
and Mannari is their more recently published study entitled *Organizational change in
Japanese factories* (Greenwich, Connecticut: JAI Press, 1988, 313p. [Monographs in
organizational behaviour and industrial relations, 9]).

930 **The labor market in Japan: selected readings.**
Edited by Shunsaku Nishikawa, translated by Ross Mouer.   Tokyo:
University of Tokyo Press, 1980. 277p. bibliog.

Fifteen essays, most of them behavioural in approach, are concerned with the labour
market and the determination of wages in Japan. Focusing on the Japanese labour
market in its broader socio-economic setting, the contributors write about such topics
as the structure of the postwar labour force and related patterns of mobility, the effect
of reductions in working hours on productivity, the future of the fixed-age retirement
system, employment and unemployment during the early 1970s, postwar changes in the
Japanese wage system, the seniority-wage system in Japan, intra-firm wage differentials,
and the economic impact of labour disputes in the public sector. While most of the
authors make extensive use of quantitative analysis, their essays contain much

information that can be readily used by students of Japanese studies in general as well as by labour economists.

931   **Workers and employers in Japan: the Japanese employment relations system.**
Edited by Kazuo Ōkōchi, Bernard Karsh, Solomon B. Levine.
Tokyo: University of Tokyo Press, 1973; Princeton, New Jersey:
Princeton University Press, 1974. 538p.

A collaborative volume of twelve essays by leading Japanese specialists that focus on industrial relations in Japan, particularly during the two decades immediately following World War II. Their contributions cover four broad categories: (1) the context of the industrial relations system, particularly the economic, political, social, and legal arrangements from which industrialisation proceeded; (2) the managers, workers, and government (the leading actors within the system) and the processes of interaction among them, especially in collective bargaining and in the settlement of labour disputes; (3) the substantive rules themselves and their administration at the plant and public agency levels (including rewards and benefits for work, personnel administration, and social security for the workers); and (4) a comparative overview of the industrial relations system by which employees are managed in Japan.

932   **Theory Z: how American business can meet the Japanese challenge.**
William G. Ouchi.   Reading, Massachusetts: Addison-Wesley, 1981.
283p. bibliog. Reprinted, New York: Avon, 1982. 244p.

Ouchi identifies some of the fundamental differences between Japanese and American management styles, and seeks to 'address the practicalities of applying an understanding of Japanese management to the American setting'. Because involved workers are the key to increased productivity, he argues that American managers must learn how to manage people in ways that will promote effective interaction if they are to resolve the problem of productivity. Part one – 'Learning from Japan' – describes some of the managerial techniques that Americans can learn from Japan, investigates the workings of the typical Japanese corporation, compares Japanese with American companies, and discusses the so-called 'Z organisation'. Part two – 'Making Theory Z Work' – sets forth several steps and procedures for applying Theory Z in American organisations and presents case-histories of American companies which have evolved Japanese-like management on their own. Ouchi constantly urges American businessmen to create an atmosphere of trust, subtlety, and intimacy within their respective organisations.

933   **The art of Japanese management: applications for American executives.**
Richard Tanner Pascale, Anthony G. Athos, introduction by D.
Ronald Daniel.   New York: Simon and Schuster, 1981; London: Allen
Lane, 1982. 221p. Reprinted, Harmondsworth, Middlesex: Penguin
Books, 1982; London: Sidgwick and Jackson, 1986. (The Library of
Management Classics).

Focusing on intra-firm relations, Pascale and Athos assert that much of the recent success which Japanese management has enjoyed can be attributed to strategies which Americans should study and selectively apply. The authors compare the personnel policies of the Matsushita Electric Company (which has maintained an entrepreneurial spirit among its employees in part by utilising managerial tools common in the West) and of IT&T (International Telephone and Telegraph). They examine the subtleties of Japanese management style – for example, the use of ambiguity and implicit communication rather than forced directness, and the emphasis on co-ordinated interdependence and harmonious human relationships rather than on competitive individualism – and they demonstrate how the differences in Japanese and American managerial approaches can be overcome to create a system that combines the strengths of both cultures.

934 **Japan vs. the West: implications for management.**
C. Carl Pegels.   Boston, Massachusetts; The Hague: Kluwer-Nijhoff, 1984. 219p. bibliog. (International Series in Management Science/Operations Research).

Pegels introduces the world of Japanese management practices and stresses their transferability to the West. He opens with an overview of Japanese industry and an explanation of the role of industrial strategy in Japan's postwar economic success. Part two, an overview of Japanese management, discusses the concept of *wa* ('harmony, unity, and cooperation') and the pervasiveness of harmonious relationships between large Japanese firms and the subcontractors and parts suppliers on which they depend. Directly related to this discussion is the author's explanation of the Toyota Motor Corporation's production system and its *kanban* ('just-in-time') inventory management system. Part three considers the effects of Japanese influence on Western management practices, the experiences of several Western firms with Japanese-style managements, and the Japanese management technique known as the 'quality circle'. Pegels frequently indicates how Western managers can adopt or adapt Japanese practices in order to increase their companies' productivity and effectiveness.

935 **The anatomy of Japanese business.**
Edited with an introduction by Kazuo Satō, Yasuo Hoshino. Armonk, New York: M. E. Sharpe; London: Croom Helm, 1984. 371p. bibliog.

A collection of eleven essays (most of them originally published in Japanese) which analyse various aspects of Japanese management and business style. The four parts – 'Management', 'Business Groups', 'Production Systems', and 'Strategy' – deal with such topics as the adaptive patterns of American and Japanese firms, the structure of managerial control in Japanese businesses, inter-firm relations in the Mitsubishi enterprise group, the creation of the Toyota production system, quality control at Fuji Xerox, the grand strategy of Japanese business, and the financial characteristics of merging and non-merging firms in Japan.

936 **Japanese manufacturing techniques: nine hidden lessons in simplicity.**
Richard J. Schonberger.   New York: Free Press; London: Collier Macmillan, 1982. 260p. bibliog.

American 'industry is ready to change its ways, and now we know what to do: simplify and reduce, simplify and integrate, simplify and expect results'. Emphasizing this theme throughout, Schonberger explains the principles of the Japanese system of production and quality management, and advocates their adoption by US industry. In 'nine lessons in simplicity', he provides American managers with informative overviews of industrial management in Japan; just-in-time production with total quality; total quality control; the début of just-in-time production in the United States; plant configurations; production-line management; just-in-time purchasing; quality circles, work improvement, and specialisation; and US prospects for catching up with Japan. Also included are several case-studies and an appendix explaining the Toyota Motor Corporation's *kanban* ('just-in-time') inventory management system.

937 **Contemporary industrial relations in Japan.**
Edited by Taishirō Shirai, foreword by Solomon B. Levine. Madison, Wisconsin; London: University of Wisconsin Press, 1983. 421p. bibliog.

A collection of articles concerning industrial relations in Japan, primarily during the 1970s. Nine Japanese contributors cover such aspects of contemporary industrial relations as the quality of working life in Japanese factories, the situation of workers in small firms and of women in industry, trade union finance and administration, the function of the law in Japanese industrial relations, conflict resolution in Japanese industrial relations, the development of collective bargaining in postwar Japan, labour relations in public enterprises and among civil servants, the links between labour unions and politics, and the characteristics of Japanese management with regard to labour relations.

938 **Economic development and the labor market in Japan.**
Kōji Taira. New York; London: Columbia University Press, 1970. 280p. bibliog. (Studies of the East Asian Institute, Columbia University).

An examination of the working of the Japanese labour market during the one hundred years following the Meiji Restoration. Taira first analyses two well-known hypotheses – the secular narrowing of wage differentials, and the responsiveness of wage differentials to business cycles – in the case of Japan. He then discusses several institutional characteristics of the Japanese economic system including the structure of the labour market, the responsiveness of employers to market conditions, the labour movement and trade unions, and the power of big business and government. He concludes that the Japanese labour market 'has always exhibited a surprising degree of efficiency in the allocation of human resources and the adjustment of relative wages' and that the emergence and institutionalisation of such practices as permanent employment and seniority-based promotion arose out of economic necessity and not on account of Japan's unique cultural heritage.

939 **The management challenge: Japanese views.**
Edited with an introduction by Lester C. Thurow. Cambridge, Massachusetts; London: MIT Press, 1985. 237p.

A collection of essays by eleven Japanese scholars and businessmen. They cover the subjects of motivation and productivity, the impact of Japanese culture on management, the perceptions and reality of Japanese industrial relations, the firm and the market in Japan, the past, present and future of the Japanese financial system, product diversification, Japanese strategies for overseas markets, competition and co-operation among Japanese corporations, Japan's industrial policy, economic planning in Japan, and trends in the Japanese economy. At the conclusion of each chapter, Thurow contributes a postscript in which he analyses the applicability of the Japanese experience as a source of new ideas for improving the inputs into the American blend of economic practices and institutions.

940 **Industrial relations in transition: the cases of Japan and the Federal Republic of Germany.**
Edited by Shigeyoshi Tokunaga, Joachim Bergmann. Tokyo: University of Tokyo Press, 1984. 302p.

The proceedings of a 1982 conference concerned with recent changes in the system of industrial relations in Japan and West Germany. Particular attention is paid to labour markets, managerial strategies and labour management, workers' organisations (including trade unions and work councils), and the policies of those organisations with respect to rationalisation. The presentations by Japanese participants include papers entitled: 'The Structure of the Japanese Labour Market'; 'Seniority Wages and Labour Management: Japanese Employers' Wage Policy'; 'Technological Changes and Rationalization in Japanese Industry since the Oil Crisis: Characteristics of Management Strategies'; 'Labour–Management Consultation as a Japanese Type of Participation'; 'The Japanese Enterprise Union and Its Functions'; and 'Japanese Trade Unions' Responses to Microelectronization'.

941 **Japan's reluctant multinationals: Japanese management at home and abroad.**
Malcolm Trevor, foreword by Michael Isherwood. London: Frances Pinter; New York: St. Martin's Press, 1983. 223p. bibliog.

An examination, from the viewpoint of industrial relations, of the structure and managerial methods of large Japanese enterprises. Following his discussion of the basic concepts of Japanese managerial systems and the problems of multinationalisation, Trevor contrasts managerial policies and practices within Japan with those in the United Kingdom. Key areas of managerial activity such as staff recruitment and selection, training and promotion, decision-making processes, and employee relations and communication are treated in some detail. Finally Trevor examines Japanese management in its British context and suggests that 'the environment has very little Westernizing influence'. He also considers why Japanese companies have been reluctant to adopt Western management styles. Trevor's study is based on a comprehensive survey of Japanese companies in the United Kingdom.

942 **Key to Japan's economic strength: human power.**
Rosalie L. Tung. Lexington, Massachusetts; Toronto, Ontario: Lexington Books, 1984. 219p. bibliog.

Tung compares and contrasts the selection criteria and training programmes of a number of Japanese and American multinational corporations that are concerned with preparing their employees for overseas assignments; investigates some of the factors that explain why the managers of Japanese multinational corporations in the United States are more successful than their American counterparts abroad; and suggests some of the applicable lessons for US multinational corporations in this regard. She attributes the Japanese success rate to better education and selection of managers, greater employee commitment to their companies, a corporate overseas support system, and longer overseas assignments. Tung's presentation includes analytical case-studies of personnel practices in Japanese trading companies (Marubeni and Mitsui), financial institutions (Nomura Securities and Bank of Yokohama), manufacturers of electrical machinery (Sony and Canon), and corporations within the heavy industrial sector (Nissan Motor and Nippon Steel).

943 **Japan's managerial system: tradition and innovation.**
Michael Y. Yoshino.   Cambridge, Massachusetts; London: MIT Press,
1968. 292p. bibliog.

An analysis of Japan's modern industrial and managerial system viewed in terms of her
socio-economic and political environment, together with an examination of the ways in
which leading firms have sought to modernise their managerial practices and the
problems which they have encountered. Yoshino discusses Japan's Tokugawa heritage
and her modernisation after the Meiji Restoration of 1868, the entrepreneurial and
paternalistic ideologies of the prewar business élite as well as the ideologies and
background of the postwar business leadership, the organisation of Japanese industries
and their intercorporate relationships before and after the war, the competitive
behaviour of large Japanese firms in the postwar era and the challenges of international
competition that emerged in the 1960s, and three areas of managerial practices:
organisational structure and practices, personnel practices and policies, and the
decision-making process. This study is based on interviews with the executives of
twenty major industrial corporations.

The state and labor in modern Japan.
See item no. 202.

The evolution of labor relations in Japan: heavy industry, 1853–1955.
See item no. 204.

The development of Japanese business, 1600–1980.
See item no. 208.

Organized workers and socialist politics in interwar Japan.
See item no. 215.

The rise of labor in Japan: the Yūaikai, 1912–1919.
See item no. 215.

Human resources in Japanese industrial development.
See item no. 217.

Japanese workers and the struggle for power, 1945–1947.
See item no. 275.

Work and lifecourse in Japan.
See item no. 542.

**For harmony and strength: Japanese white-collar organization in
anthropological perspective.**
See item no. 543.

Women in Japan: discrimination, resistance and reform.
See item no. 575.

Women in changing Japan.
See item no. 578.

The politics of labor legislation in Japan: national–international interaction.
See item no. 609.

The Japanese automobile industry: technology and management at Nissan and Toyota.
See item no. 871.

The Japanese industrial system.
See item no. 878.

Honda Motor: the men, the management, the machines.
See item no. 882.

Japan's emerging multinationals: an international comparison of policies and practices.
See item no. 947.

The internationalization of Japanese business: European and Japanese perspectives.
See item no. 948.

The Japanese management development system: generalists and specialists in Japanese companies abroad.
See item no. 949.

Under Japanese management: the experience of British workers.
See item no. 950.

Educational choice and labor markets in Japan.
See item no. 962.

The Japanese school: lessons for industrial America.
See item no. 966.

Japan Labor Bulletin.
See item no. 1511.

Japanese Economic Studies.
See item no. 1518.

Management Japan.
See item no. 1533.

Japan Economic Journal.
See item no. 1548.

Japan's economic challenge: a bibliographic sourcebook.
See item no. 1590.

East Asian economies: a guide to information sources.
See item no. 1594.

Japan's economy: a bibliography of its past and present.
See item no. 1614.

Multinationals and Multinationalism

944 **Japanese participation in British industry.**
John H. Dunning. London; Dover, New Hampshire: Croom Helm, 1986. 207p. bibliog. (The Croom Helm Series in International Business).
A detailed study containing the results of a field survey of Japanese manufacturing affiliates in the United Kingdom (UK) conducted in 1983-84. Dunning describes the extent, shape, and motivations of Japanese participation in British industry; examines some organisational relationships between the affiliates and their parent companies; presents some data about the affiliates' performance vis-à-vis both their parent companies and their British competitors; and reviews some of the ways in which the Japanese presence in the UK has had an impact on its economy. Particular attention is paid to the extent to which direct investment by Japanese manufacturing enterprises in the UK has assisted in the transfer of desirable Japanese management styles and technologies to that country's economy.

945 **The threat of Japanese multinationals: how the West can respond.**
Lawrence G. Franko, foreword by Terutomo Ozawa. Chichester, Sussex; New York: Wiley, 1983. 148p. bibliog. (Wiley/IRM Series on Multinationals).
A concise survey of the industrial strengths, strategies, and weaknesses of Japanese multinational corporations together with comparative overviews of some of their American and Western counterparts. Franko reviews Western perceptions of the threat of Japanese multinationals in the world markets, critically assesses various myths regarding Japan's high labour productivity, long working hours, low labour costs, government industrial targeting, and Japan's dependence on the West for trade and investment; describes how Japanese multinational companies manage their production and marketing strategies; and discusses some of the distinctive features of Japanese multinationalism. He illustrates his book with four case-studies of Japanese, American, and European competition in the colour television, semiconductor, steel, and synthetic

fibre industries. Franko concludes that the successful response of Western firms to the Japanese threat will depend on the quality of their managers and their strategies.

946 **Multinationalism, Japanese style: the political economy of outward dependency.**
Terutomo Ozawa, foreword by Peter B. Kenen.   Princeton, New Jersey; Guildford, Surrey: Princeton University Press, 1979. 289p. bibliog.

A description and analysis of the forces which accounted for the growth of Japanese direct overseas production during the 1970s and a preliminary assessment of the problems and successes of Japanese multinationalism. Ozawa shows how such factors as the appreciation of the yen, rising domestic labour and energy costs, concerns about the environment, shortage of industrial sites, and a desire for secure, stable supplies of raw materials led many Japanese firms to relocate some of their production facilities abroad. They were encouraged and assisted by the governments of both Japan and the developing 'host' countries (which were anxious to attract Japanese capital and technology) as well as by Japanese trading companies. As one factor, Ozawa singles out the important connections between the Japanese government's programmes of overseas economic and technical assistance and its domestic programmes for assisting local business firms.

947 **Japan's emerging multinationals: an international comparison of policies and practices.**
Edited by Susumu Takamiya, Keith Thurley, foreword by Herbert A. Simon.   Tokyo: University of Tokyo Press, 1985. 287p. bibliog.

Reports the early findings from a cross-cultural research study of personnel practices and worker perceptions and performance. Part one – 'Multinational Corporations: Theoretical Perspectives and Previous Research' – deals essentially with non-Japanese firms. Part two focuses on the similarities and differences in personnel management, personnel policy, and employee job satisfaction among one British, one American-owned, and two Japanese-owned colour television manufacturing plants in the United Kingdom. The authors find that the Japanese subsidiaries are particularly effective in creating an organisational environment which encourages smooth co-operative relationships between individuals, sections, and departments. Part three, limited to Japanese multinational corporations, emphasizes both the industrial relations implications of the overseas expansion of Japanese companies since the early 1970s and the changing style of management in Japanese multinationals in the 1980s.

948 **The internationalization of Japanese business: European and Japanese perspectives.**
Edited with an introduction by Malcolm Trevor.   Frankfurt-am-Main: Campus Verlag; Boulder, Colorado: Westview Press, 1987. 209p.

These proceedings of the 1985 London conference of the Euro–Japanese Management Studies Association analyse Japanese efforts to learn about international business operations and to apply that new knowledge to internationalising their own industries. The seventeen contributors cover such topics as the growth of Japanese companies in the United Kingdom, Japanese direct investment and subsidiaries in the Federal Republic of Germany, the overseas market strategies of the Japanese electronics industry, the comparative values of Japanese and British managers, the internationalisation of Japanese financial industries, the personnel policies of Japanese subsidiaries in Germany, innovations in collective bargaining through the multinationalisation of Japanese automobile companies, the recruitment, selection and job satisfaction of expatriate managers in Japanese and German multinational corporations, and Japanese direct foreign investment in the Netherlands.

949 **The Japanese management development system: generalists and specialists in Japanese companies abroad.**
Malcolm Trevor, Jochen Schendel, Bernhard Wilpert. London; Wolfeboro, New Hampshire: Frances Pinter, 1986. 278p. bibliog.

An empirical study of the managerial behaviour of both generalists and specialists assigned to Japanese branch operations within the United Kingdom and the Federal Republic of Germany, the two principal locations of Japanese investment and manufacturing in Europe. Through a series of semi-structured interviews, the authors investigate the managerial approaches of these individuals in the production, marketing, commercial, and financial sectors of precision engineering, light engineering, electronics, general trading, banking, and transportation companies. Trevor, Schendel and Wilpert are particularly concerned with comparing the Japanese experience within the British and the West German environments, but they also contrast the Japanese with the British and German styles of management and evaluate some of the differences that can be found among them.

950 **Under Japanese management: the experience of British workers.**
Michael White, Malcolm Trevor, foreword by John Pinder. London: Heinemann, 1983. 162p. (Policy Studies Institute Series).

A non-technical assessment of Japanese management methods as applied in Great Britain. Through a community survey and six case-studies, White and Trevor examine the personnel and working practices of three Japanese manufacturing subsidiaries and three Japanese financial subsidiaries (two banks and a trading company) in Britain. Many of the employment practices common in Japan (such as lifetime employment and company unions) have not been applied in Great Britain; there are no systematic differences between the levels of satisfaction of industrial workers in Japanese-owned manufacturing companies and those in British-owned firms; the Japanese subsidiaries are characterised by a greater emphasis on detail; and those firms tend to be distinguished by a high degree of leadership by example.

951 **Japanese direct manufacturing investment in the United States.**
Mamoru Yoshida, foreword by Duane Kujawa. New York; London: Praeger, 1987. 220p. bibliog.

An examination of the investment decision-making processes and control systems of Japanese companies, and a study of the character of Japan's industrial policies in so far as they appear to influence the overseas business strategies of Japanese firms. Using primary data collected in 1984, Yoshida first examines the investment decision-making processes of fifteen high-tech companies, among them Canon, Hitachi, NEC, Sony, and Toshiba. He then investigates some of the parent company–subsidiary linkages in the international management area and explains how these Japan-based firms administer the manufacturing activities of their subsidiaries in the United States. Finally, he traces the gradual changes that have occurred in the Japanese government–business relationship and indicates how these changes help to account for the sharp rise in Japan's overseas direct manufacturing investment since the 1970s.

952   **Japan's multinational enterprises.**
Michael Y. Yoshino, introduction by Raymond Vernon.   Cambridge, Massachusetts; London: Harvard University Press, 1976. 191p.

An analysis of the process by which Japanese enterprises evolved their multinational strategies and adapted the structure of their business management to changing circumstances and different environments. Yoshino first accounts for the historical forces that prompted Japanese companies to pursue a strategy of multinationalisation and industrial investment abroad. He then discusses some of their efforts to assure themselves of a stable supply of raw materials (particularly oil) from abroad; their investment in overseas manufacturing, especially in Southeast Asia, in order to secure foreign markets for manufactured goods; the involvement of the *sōgō shōsha* (trading companies) in the multinationalisation of Japanese firms and the ways in which the *sōgō shōsha* have functioned as multinational enterprises in their own right; the organisational problems arising within Japanese enterprises in connection with the management of overseas subsidiaries; and the transformation of internal managerial practices that has been necessitated by the multinationalisation process.

Industrial collaboration with Japan.
See item no. 912.

Japan's reluctant multinationals: Japanese management at home and abroad.
See item no. 941.

Key to Japan's economic strength: human power.
See item no. 942.

Japan Economic Journal.
See item no. 1548.

Transportation and Telecommunications

953 Deregulating telecoms: competition and control in the United States, Japan and Britain.
Jill Hills.   London: Frances Pinter; Westport, Connecticut: Quorum Books, 1986. 220p. bibliog.

An investigation of the recent deregulation of telecommunications transmission in the United States and its spread to Great Britain and Japan in the form of privatisation and liberalisation. In the Japanese case, telecommunications transmission moved from the status of dual monopolies of the Nippon Telegraph and Telephone Public Corporation and the Kokusai Denshin Denwa Company to one of ostensible competition. Hills compares the process of deregulation in the United States, Japan and Britain, and determines the beneficiaries of that process. She concludes that the deregulation and privatisation of the telecommunications market have been a primary mechanism of industrial policy in all three countries and that the increased domination of the market for international communications constitutes a major objective.

954 The lure of Japan's railways.
Naotaka Hirota.   Tokyo: Japan Times, 1969. 1 vol. (largely unpaginated). map.

A professional photographer's photo-essay of Japanese trains and railroads illustrates some of the conditions that existed during the 1960s. Grouping them together in sections bearing such lyrical titles as 'Mammoths through the Snow', 'Rails through History', and 'Moving the Millions', Hirota presents 104 largely black-and-white photographs that depict an express diesel speeding through Hokkaidō in the dead of winter, an old electric locomotive hauling goods in the Tokyo area, suburban electric trains emanating from Kyōto, a class 9600 locomotive in the marshalling yard at Wakkanai, and other similar subjects. A sixteen-page outline of Japan's railways describes their development since the 1870s and their principal operations following World War II.

955   **The information explosion: the new electronic media in Japan and Europe.**
Edited by Mick McLean.   London: Frances Pinter; Westport, Connecticut: Greenwood Press, 1985. 130p. (Emerging Patterns of Work and Communications in an Information Age, 3).

Brings together the views presented by eleven Japanese and European experts at a seminar sponsored by Technova, a Tokyo-based research promotion organisation in the area of advanced technology development. The essays focusing on Japan deal with the prospects for Japan's socio-economic development by the year 2000, the socio-economic role of the new electronic media, Japanese family life in the new media era, Nippon Telegraph and Telephone's long-term plans to create the infrastructure for the new media, the ways in which private Japanese companies expect to create their own information networks, the development of a practical automatic translation system utilising computer and communication technologies, and satellite broadcasting in Japan.

Mitsubishi and the N.Y.K., 1870–1914: business strategy in the Japanese shipping industry.
See item no. 250.

Against the state: politics and social protest in Japan.
See item no. 606.

The competition: dealing with Japan.
See item no. 813.

Coping with U.S.–Japanese economic conflicts.
See item no. 892.

Japanese electronics technology: enterprise and innovation.
See item no. 985.

Japanese Philately.
See item no. 1522.

Environment

956 **Garbage management in Japan: leading the way.**
Allen Hershkowitz, Eugene Salerni, preface by Maurice D. Hinchey.
New York: INFORM, 1987. 131p. map.

On the basis of their investigation of Japan's well-developed municipal solid waste
management programmes and practices, Hershkowitz and Salerni demonstrate that the
solutions to current problems of waste management in the United States are
fundamentally political and cultural rather than technical in nature. The authors
describe the laws and strategies for solid waste management in Japan, the existing
procedures for separating and collecting discarded waste materials, the recycling of
paper, glass and metals and the special handling of plastics, batteries and tyres, the
importance given to incinerating non-recyclable materials, and the limited use of
landfills. Far more environmentally conscious than Americans, the Japanese are
currently recycling about 50 per cent of their solid wastes, incinerating about 34 per
cent, and disposing in landfills and in other ways only the remaining 16 per cent.

957 **Island of dreams: environmental crisis in Japan.**
Norie Huddle, Michael Reich, with Nahum Stiskin; foreword by Paul
R. Ehrlich, afterword by Ralph Nader.   New York; Tokyo: Autumn
Press, 1975. 351p. 3 maps. bibliog. Reprinted with a new introduction,
Cambridge, Massachusetts: Schenkman Books, 1987.

An introduction to the severe environmental problems that have accompanied Japan's
economic growth, especially since the 1950s. The authors discuss the Ashio Mine
copper poisoning incident, Yokkaichi 'asthma' (a type of air pollution), the incidents of
organic mercury poisoning known as Minamata disease, a massive outbreak of human
PCB poisoning (the Kanemi Rice Oil poisoning case), 'itai-itai' disease, the 'red tides'
of the Inland Sea that were caused by the discharge of industrial wastes into its waters,
Japan's lack of an adequate sewage system, and Tokyo's 'garbage war', automobile
congestion, photochemical smog, and contamination of its waterways. The book's
multi-causal interpretation of this environmental crisis takes into account such factors
as the inadequate development of technology for preventing pollution, the collusion of

governmental and industrial leaders, and the tendency of the Japanese to endure intolerable conditions without complaining. Recent efforts by citizens' and victims' groups to rectify this situation are described in a chapter entitled 'The Drive for Citizenship'.

958 **Environmental protest and citizen politics in Japan.**
Margaret A. McKean. Berkeley, California; London: University of California Press, 1981. 291p. bibliog.

A study of the widespread protest movements against environmental pollution which mobilised millions of Japanese during the 1970s and led to significant changes in local politics and policy at that time. McKean first discusses the major environmental lawsuits of the period and recounts the histories and accomplishments of fourteen different citizens' movements. She then investigates the mobilisation, structure, and tactics of those movements; the information, beliefs, and experience in politics of individuals who were active within them; and the impact of the citizens' movement experience on partisanship, general patterns of belief change, and voting behaviour among activist members. She also assesses the ways in which these anti-pollution movements affected the participants, their surrounding communities, and Japanese politics as a whole.

959 **Minamata.**
W. Eugene Smith, Aileen M. Smith. New York; Toronto, Ontario: Holt, Rinehart and Winston; London: Chatto and Windus, 1975. 192p. 6 maps. ('An Alskorg-Sensorium Book').

A passionately written book, illustrated by over one hundred striking and frequently evocative photographs, about the disaster which befell the fishing and farming town of Minamata (Kumamoto Prefecture, Kyūshū) during the 1950s. Many of the community's residents became afflicted by 'Minamata disease' (a disease of the central nervous system) as a result of widespread methyl-mercury poisoning caused by industrial wastes discharged from the Chisso Corporation's local chemical factory. Moving back and forth between various human stories and happenings which they recount, the Smiths document the appearance and impact of this disease, the ways in which the citizens of Minamata and the management of the Chisso Corporation responded, and the ultimately successful crusade to compel both industry and government to assume responsibility for the poisoning of the environment. Both the concluding section of this book – 'Minamata Disease: a Medical Report', by Masazumi Harada – and *Minamata disease: methylmercury poisoning in Minamata and Niigata, Japan*, edited by Tadao Tsubaki and Katsuro Irukayama (Tokyo: Kodansha; Amsterdam: Elsevier Scientific, 1977, 317p.) provide further technical information.

Ox against the storm; a biography of Tanaka Shozo: Japan's conservationist pioneer.
See item no. 312.

Policymaking in contemporary Japan.
See item no. 620.

Japanese prefectures and policymaking.
See item no. 639.

Environment

Political opposition and local politics in Japan.
See item no. 642.

Environmental law in Japan.
See item no. 775.

Law and social change in postwar Japan.
See item no. 785.

America versus Japan: a comparative study of business–government relations conducted at the Harvard Business School.
See item no. 801.

White Papers of Japan: Annual Abstracts of Official Reports and Statistics of the Japanese Government.
See item no. 829.

The one–straw revolution: an introduction to natural farming.
See item no. 830.

New Japanese photography.
See item no. 1277.

Education

960 **Education in Japan: a century of modern development.**
Ronald S. Anderson, foreword by Robert Leestma, preface by John
Whitney Hall. Washington, DC: US Department of Health,
Education, and Welfare, Office of Education; for sale by the
Superintendent of Documents, US Government Printing Office, 1975.
412p. map. bibliog. (DHEW Publication, no.(OE)74-19110).
A longtime observer of and participant in the Japanese educational scene discusses
some of the issues confronting Japanese education following a century of modern
development. Part one of this comprehensive study describes the evolution of Japanese
education from feudal to modern times, the prewar educational system, the
introduction of major reforms during the Allied occupation period, and important
developments after 1952. Part two details the nature of contemporary education
(including its structure and the curriculum) in kindergartens and elementary schools,
junior and senior high-schools, and higher education respectively. Part three focuses
on problem areas involving teacher status, power, and preparation; the administration,
supervision, and finance of Japanese education; instructional media and special
programmes; and student power. This volume revises and updates Anderson's earlier
work, *Japan: three epochs of modern education* (Washington, DC: US Department of
Health, Education, and Welfare, 1959, 219p.).

961 **Learning to be Japanese: selected readings on Japanese society and
education.**
Edited by Edward R. Beauchamp. Hamden, Connecticut: Linnet
Books, 1978. 408p. bibliog.
A collection of articles and chapters of books concerning the history and nature of
formal education in Japan and the ways in which people learn to be Japanese. It is
divided into three parts covering the historical roots of present-day education, various
dimensions of contemporary education, and future directions of Japanese education.
Representative articles include: 'Inoue Kowashi, 1843–1895, and the Formation of
Modern Japan'; 'The Processes of Army Socialization' (during World War II); 'Japan:

under American Occupation' (on curriculum reform); 'The Textbook Controversy'; 'Education: an Agent of Social Change in Ainu Community Life'; 'The Sociology of a Student Movement: a Japanese Case Study'; 'The Conservatives Reform Higher Education'; and 'Changing Styles of University Life in Japan'.

962 **Educational choice and labor markets in Japan.**
Mary Jean Bowman, with Hideo Ikeda, Yasumasa Tomoda.   Chicago; London: University of Chicago Press, 1981. 367p. bibliog.

Utilising data from a survey of 7,000 male high-school students and their fathers, the authors analyse the ways in which Japanese students have made some of the vital decisions that affect their future education and their career options. They identify the key influences on these students as they selected the schools which they attended and the curricula which they pursued. They consider such socio-economic factors as career aspirations, family background, geographical location, self-ability assessments, earning prospects, family income levels, and the costs of higher education. The authors also discuss student and parental perceptions of labour market structures and employment opportunities, and they show how their choices and perceptions changed as rapid postwar economic growth brought about a dramatic socio-economic transformation of modern Japan.

963 **Changes in the Japanese university: a comparative perspective.**
Edited with an introduction by William K. Cummings, Ikuo Amano, Kazuyuki Kitamura; foreword by Michio Nagai.   New York: Praeger, 1979. 261p. bibliog. (Praeger Special Studies Series in Comparative Education).

A collection of essays by leading Japanese and American scholars who describe and analyse changes in Japanese higher education during the 1970s. They address such subjects as continuity and change in the structure of higher education, the financing of higher education, Japanese students and the labour market, the changing role of Japanese professors, the productivity of Japanese scholars, the internationalisation of Japanese higher education, the organisation and administration of Japanese universities, Japan's postmodern student movement, and the Japanese system of higher education viewed in a comparative perspective.

964 **Education and equality in Japan.**
William K. Cummings.   Princeton, New Jersey; Guildford, Surrey: Princeton University Press, 1980. 305p. bibliog.

Studies Japan's postwar educational system and the egalitarian reform which it has been promoting within Japanese society. Cummings first analyses the historical, political, and social background of Japanese education since the 1940s. Then, on the basis of a case-study of primary and secondary school life in Kyōto, he reports on the surprising degree of equality found among schoolchildren in the area of cognitive achievement and shows how egalitarianism has come to pervade the curriculum, pedagogy, and the teacher–pupil relationship in Japanese schools. He also explores how Japanese youth with their egalitarian, individuated, and participatory values are contributing to the gradual transformation of contemporary Japanese society.

965 **Educational policies in crisis: Japanese and American perspectives.**
Edited by William K. Cummings, Edward R. Beauchamp, Shōgo
Ichikawa, Victor N. Kobayashi, Morikazu Ushiogi. New York;
London: Praeger in association with the East-West Center (Honolulu,
Hawaii), 1986. 308p. bibliog. (Praeger Special Studies Series in
Comparative Education).

Fourteen American and Japanese scholars discuss and compare their respective educational systems on the elementary, secondary, and university levels in such areas as curriculum, academic achievement, and educational reform. The papers dealing with Japan include: 'Reform Traditions in the United States and Japan'; 'Educational Crisis in Japan'; 'Japanese and U.S. Curricula Compared'; 'Patterns of Academic Achievement in Japan and the United States'; 'The Decline and Reform of Education in Japan'; 'Transition from School to Work: the Japanese Case'; 'American Perceptions of Japanese Education'; and 'American Images of Japanese Secondary and Higher Education'.

966 **The Japanese school: lessons for industrial America.**
Benjamin Duke; forewords by Clark Kerr, James M. Hestor, Michio
Nagai; introduction by Edwin Reischauer. New York; London:
Praeger, 1986. 242p.

Duke explores the ways in which the Japanese classroom produces loyal, literate, competent, and diligent workers who master a complex written language, attain high standards in mathematics, and are imbued with the spirit of perseverance. His highly informative picture of Japanese education today stresses three points in particular: (1) much of postwar Japan's economic success should be directly attributed to the accomplishments of her educational system; (2) there are many ways in which the United States should seek to learn from the Japanese experience; and (3) the Japanese educational system too has its share of shortcomings and problems. The author asserts that the challenge to industrial America lies more in the Japanese classroom than in the factory, for it is the contemporary Japanese school which provides the basic training of the highly productive Japanese work force.

967 **Japan's militant teachers: a history of the left-wing teachers' movement.**
Benjamin C. Duke, foreword by Tetsuya Kobayashi. Honolulu,
Hawaii: University Press of Hawaii, 1973. 236p. (An East-West Center
Book).

A comprehensive analysis of the origins, development, and activities of the Nihon Kyōshokuin Kumiai (or Nikkyōso), the left-wing Japan Teachers Union whose membership encompasses the majority of public-school teachers. Ever since its formation in 1947, Nikkyōso has maintained a hostile relationship with the Japanese Ministry of Education and has pursued policies of opposition and resistance involving peaceful strikes and sit-ins as well as violent demonstrations and confrontations with government authorities. Duke first studies the evolution of the left-wing teachers' movement in Japan from 1919 to 1947. He then examines Nikkyōso's record of militancy between 1947 and 1967, focusing on the periodic confrontations between the militant teachers and the Japanese government over economic, educational, and ideological issues. He concludes with a study of the union's left-wing leadership by briefly reviewing the careers of some of its members.

968 **Public policy and private education in Japan.**
Estelle James, Gail Benjamin. New York: St. Martin's Press;
Basingstoke, Hampshire: Macmillan, 1988. 218p. bibliog.

A systematic study of Japan's private and public school systems and the ways in which they interact to provide some of the highest educational achievement indices in the world. Part one ('Education in Japanese Culture') describes the historical, social, and cultural setting of modern education and surveys major issues and non-issues on the contemporary educational scene. Part two focuses on the role of the private sector and contrasts it with the public sector, especially at the high-school and university levels. James and Benjamin deal particularly with the founding and funding of private schools; the important differences between the private and public sectors in terms of clientele, benefits, prestige, quality, costs, efficiency, and the socio-economic distribution and redistributional effects of education; the differences among prefectures in the size and nature of the private sector; the government's attempt in the 1960s to make public education more uniform; and the institution of government subsidies to private schools in the 1970s.

969 **Japanese radicals revisited: student protest in postwar Japan.**
Ellis S. Krauss. Berkeley, California; London: University of
California Press, 1974. 192p. bibliog.

A case-study of the process of political socialisation and the sources of student protest during the 1950s and the 1960s that is based primarily on research conducted among a sample of fifty-three former students, most of whom had participated in the 1960 protest movement against the US–Japan Security Treaty which led to the resignation of the cabinet of Prime Minister Kishi Nobusuke. Krauss focuses on two related questions concerning this particular generation of students: the ways in which they developed their left-wing, radical beliefs, Marxist ideology, and activist behaviour; and the extent to which their experiences following graduation, once they entered adult society, affected their radicalism and activism. The role of the family in political socialisation and the influence of education, peer group, political and social climate, and work-place on the author's sample of informants are explained in detail.

970 **Japanese education today: a report from the U.S. study of education in
Japan.**
Prepared by a special task force of the OERI [Office of Educational
Research and Improvement] Japan Study Team: Robert Leestma,
Robert L. August, Betty George, Lois Peak, with contributions by
Nobuo Shimahara, William K. Cummings, Nevzer G. Stacey, and with
an epilogue, Implications for American education, by William J.
Bennett; foreword by Chester E. Finn, Jr.; edited by Cynthia Hearn
Dorfman. Washington, DC: US Department of Education, for sale by
the US Government Printing Office, 1987. 95p. map. bibliog.

This report, part of a larger bilateral (US–Japan) study on education, provides a concise overview of the nature, dynamics, and accomplishments of the Japanese educational system. It discusses the *juku* ('private schools'), the teaching profession, pre-elementary education, compulsory education (grades 1–9), upper secondary education (grades 10–12), higher education, education and employment, and educational reform. Concerned with understanding Japanese education in its cultural context, the authors took into account the home environment of Japanese students and the responsibilities of their families, relationships between the home and the school, unofficial education programmes outside of the school, and the relationship between industry and education.

971 **Educational achievement in Japan: lessons for the West.**
Richard Lynn. London: Macmillan; Armonk, New York: M. E. Sharpe, 1988. 157p. bibliog.

This analysis of the Japanese educational system accounts for its high educational standards and suggests certain steps by which the West can adopt some of the system's exemplary features. Lynn first delineates current educational standards in Japan, considers the extent to which Japanese schoolchildren are ahead of their European and American contemporaries, and describes the school system itself. Then, as he discusses the intelligence of Japanese children, motivation and incentives for educational achievement, the intrinsic motivation of schoolchildren, and the contribution of teachers and schools to educational achievement, he analyses the factors responsible for Japan's high educational standards. In particular they include the core curriculum that is laid down by the government, the significantly longer school year required of Japanese children, the strong incentives for academic achievement that take the form of competitive entrance examinations to senior high-schools and universities, and the incentives for teachers to work efficiently.

972 **Higher education in Japan: its take-off and crash.**
Michio Nagai, translated by Jerry Dusenbury. Tokyo: University of Tokyo Press, 1971. 264p. bibliog.

Two works combined into one book by an American-educated Japanese minister of education. Part one ('University and Society in Modern Japan') describes the chaotic state of higher education during the late 1960s, when Japanese universities were disrupted by extensive student rioting, and analyses the roots of this situation by examining the historical development of modern Japanese universities. Nagai also discusses the challenges facing Japanese higher education as of 1970 and proposes a number of steps for its reform and reconstruction. The second part, six essays written between 1954 and 1970 about the problems of educational development in Japan, is concerned with the uncritical adoption of the ideas of the nineteenth-century English philosopher Herbert Spencer, the educational policies of Mori Arinori during the 1880s, the university and the intellectual, the problematic development of Japanese education in the twentieth century, and the causes underlying student unrest in the late 1960s.

973 **Society and education in Japan.**
Herbert Passin. New York: Teachers College Press and East Asian Institute, Columbia University, 1965. 347p. bibliog. (Teachers College. Columbia University. Comparative Education Studies) (Studies of the East Asian Institute, Columbia University). Reprinted, Tokyo and New York: Kodansha International, 1983.

A classic study of the role of education in the modernisation of Japan. Passin first examines the late Tokugawa period educational system and the problems of building a modern school system during the decades immediately following the Meiji Restoration of 1868. He then looks at Japan as an advanced industrial society. His main concern is with the development of education from the 1930s through the 1950s, particularly the government's systematic use of the schools to propagate political ideology and the ways in which the educational system facilitated social mobility. Nearly half of the book consists of a collection of forty-three primary documents on Japanese education dating from the 1615 Tokugawa 'Laws governing the military households' (a compendium of regulations and instructions that dealt in part with learning and scholarship' to Morito Tatsuo's June 1947 appeal to teachers to support the postwar educational reform programme.

974 **Patterns of Japanese policymaking: experiences from higher education.**
T. J. Pempel. Boulder, Colorado: Westview Press, 1978. 248p.
(Studies of the East Asian Institute, Columbia University) (A Westview Replica Edition).

Pempel argues that the prevailing perceptions of postwar Japanese policy-making are inadequate. He suggests that at least three distinct patterns of policy-making can be identified within Japan's current system of hegemonic pluralism: 'policymaking by camp conflict, policymaking by incrementalism, and pressure group policymaking'. He examines these patterns both theoretically and empirically and tests them in detailed studies of the ways in which the government has formulated public policy in three specific areas of higher education: the 'control of political activities and disruptions on campus; the shift from general and humanistic educational context to specialized and technical education; and the expansion in the overall number of students enrolled in higher educational institutions'.

975 **Japan's high schools.**
Thomas P. Rohlen. Berkeley, California; London: University of California Press, 1983. 363p. bibliog.

Basing his book on his observations of five representative secondary schools located in the industrial port city of Kōbe, Rohlen (an anthropologist) considers the social context of high school education in Japan today, describes and analyses the fundamental patterns of high schooling, and assesses its strengths and weaknesses. He presents an excellent picture of school organisation, classroom instruction, teacher and union politics, textbooks, adolescent peer relations, and extracurricular activities. He also examines the impact of the fiercely competitive university entrance examinations, twentieth-century modernisation and nationalism, the postwar American occupation reforms, and the differences in student social background upon the educational system. This book, the first comprehensive study in English of Japanese high schools, offers an insightful introduction to the ways in which postwar Japan's educational system has produced a well-trained, highly disciplined, group-oriented work force.

976 **Adaptation and education in Japan.**
Nobuo K. Shimahara. New York: Praeger, 1979. 190p. bibliog.
(Praeger Special Studies Series in Comparative Education).

A sociological examination of Japanese education from the standpoint of its adaptive qualities. Following a discussion of the group-oriented nature of Japanese society and of its major consequences for education, Shimahara traces the evolution of Japanese education from the Tokugawa period to the post-World War II era. He investigates the role and significance of the college entrance examination system and shows how education has responded to the needs of Japan's social, economic, and political institutions. The author concludes that formal education in Japan is 'a function of political and economic institutions. While it may enhance personal interest in one way or another, its primary goals are to mold individuals so as to promote organizational imperatives'.

977 **Teachers and politics in Japan.**
Donald R. Thurston. Princeton, New Jersey: Princeton University Press, 1973. 337p. bibliog. (Studies of the East Asian Institute, Columbia University).

A description and assessment of the Japan Teachers Union (Nikkyōso) as a renovationist interest group in postwar Japanese politics. This broad cross-sectional case-study evaluates the union's influence on its own members and on the formulation and implementation of a wide range of governmental policies dealing with teachers and education. Thurston examines the historical background, postwar origins, and major struggles (between 1947 and 1972) of Nikkyōso, as well as its ideology and objectives, its organisational structure and union consciousness, the claims and demands which it has made on the educational bureaucracy in the Ministry of Education, and its influence on elections and legislation. He concludes that Nikkyōso has been much more effective at the local and prefectural levels, where educational policies are implemented and changed in the course of their implementation, than at the national level, where policy is formulated.

978 **The Japanese educational challenge: a commitment to children.**
Merry White. New York: Free Press; London: Collier Macmillan, 1987. 210p. bibliog.

A penetrating analysis of Japan's educational system that focuses on the environment in which Japanese children are reared and educated. Part one ('A Society Mobilized for Education') demonstrates how committed all levels of Japanese society and all Japanese institutions are to children and their education. The history of Japanese education is briefly discussed along with the nature of Japanese schools today; mothers and teachers are shown to be the sources of motivation and incentive among children; and the training, role, and practices of teachers are examined. Part two ('The Experience of Childhood') shows how children begin their formal schooling, advance through elementary and secondary school, and experience the anxiety-producing examination system. Part three compares educational objectives and the needs for reform in Japan and the West, and points out the problems of transferring practices from one society to another, particularly since the success of Japanese schooling is partly due to deep-rooted psychological and cultural conditions peculiar to Japan.

979 **A guide to teaching English in Japan.**
Compiled and edited by Charles B. Wordell. Tokyo: Japan Times, 1985. 343p. bibliog.

Written primarily for native speakers of English who are either practising or prospective teachers of English in Japan, this collection of essays by seventeen experienced teachers describes a variety of 'job situations (contexts) and teaching techniques (strategies) for language instruction' to Japanese. The volume covers several instructional environments: children's classrooms, junior and senior highschools, universities, private language-schools, private lessons, and teaching as employees of Japanese corporations. The essays frequently recommend practical techniques, among them child-centred language acquisition approaches, various ways for teaching oral

Education

English in large classes, professionalising methods and materials for teaching English at large companies, and one contributor's personal technique for training students to monitor and improve their English and conversational ability. Constantly recurring problems are also covered in depth.

Perspectives on Japan: a guide for teachers.
See item no. 9.

Japanese education.
See item no. 35.

Education in Tokugawa Japan.
See item no. 164.

Visions of virtue in Tokugawa Japan: the Kaitokudō Merchant Academy of Osaka.
See item no. 176.

Private academies of the Tokugawa period.
See item no. 180.

The modernizers: overseas students, foreign employees, and Meiji Japan.
See item no. 197.

Human resources in Japanese industrial development.
See item no. 217.

Schooldays in imperial Japan: a study in the culture of a student elite.
See item no. 232.

Japan's first student radicals.
See item no. 244.

Mori Arinori: a reconsideration.
See item no. 304.

Makiguchi, the value creator, revolutionary Japanese educator and founder of Soka Gakkai.
See item no. 319.

Shinichi Suzuki: the man and his philosophy.
See item no. 326.

Totto-chan: the little girl at the window.
See item no. 330.

Windows for the crown prince.
See item no. 362.

Becoming Japanese: the world of the pre-school child.
See item no. 559.

The Japanese overseas: can they go home again?
See item no. 572.

Child development and education in Japan.
See item no. 594.

Policymaking in contemporary Japan.
See item no. 620.

Japanese prefectures and policymaking.
See item no. 639.

101 favorite songs taught in Japanese schools.
See item no. 1386.

Japanese colleges and universities 1989: a guide to institutions of higher education in Japan.
See item no. 1550.

Overseas Japanese studies institutions = Kaigai Nihon kenkyū kikan yōran.
See item no. 1554.

Japanese studies in Europe [etc.].
See item no. 1559.

Bibliography on Japanese education: postwar publications in Western languages.
See item no. 1610.

Japanese education: a bibliography of materials in the English language.
See item no. 1610.

Education in Japan: a source book.
See item no. 1610.

Science and Technology

980 **Science and technology in Japan.**
Alun M. Anderson.   Harlow, Essex: Longman, 1984. 421p. 7 maps.
(Longman Guide to World Science and Technology, 4).

A comprehensive description of Japan's major government–industry research projects
and of current Japanese efforts to stimulate basic research. Introductory chapters
about the state of Japanese science and technology, government science policy and
decision-making, the government ministries and their major scientific programmes,
education and academic research, and industrial research and development are
followed by detailed discussions of the work of the major research institutes in
agriculture, medicine, the life sciences, biotechnology, energy, aerospace, aviation,
railways, electronics, industry, earthquake and disaster prevention, environmental
protection, the earth sciences, marine science and technology, and defence. Anderson
also describes Japan's learned and professional societies and associations, the postwar
development of a 'science city' at Tsukuba, national co-operation in the area of
scientific and technical information, and international scientific and technological
co-operation. A directory of major Japanese research establishments constitutes a
valuable appendix to the volume.

981 **The amazing race: winning the technorivalry with Japan.**
William H. Davidson.   New York; Chichester, Sussex: Wiley, 1984.
270p.

Japan and the United States are engaged in an 'intense and complex race' for global
supremacy in the area of information technology, and America's continued military
and industrial leadership as well as Japan's efforts to attain a 'position of leadership,
pride and prestige in the Western world' are at stake. Davidson describes the effect of
this competition on developments in the information technology sector (including
computers, communication equipment, and software) and on broader economic and
social conditions. He focuses on the origins of postwar Japanese industrial strategy, the
nature of the Japanese economic system, and the US response between 1959 and 1979;
the state and nature of the information technology sector in the early 1980s; and
current Japanese initiatives and American responses in this area.

982　The fifth generation: artificial intelligence and Japan's computer
challenge to the world.
Edward A. Feigenbaum, Pamela McCorduck.　Reading,
Massachusetts: Addison-Wesley, 1983. 275p. bibliog. Reprinted,
London: Pan, 1984. 378p. Revised and updated edition, New York:
New American Library, 1984. 334p.

Japan intends to develop and market the 'fifth generation' of computers: artificially
intelligent machines that can reason, draw conclusions, make judgements, and even
understand the written and spoken word. Feigenbaum and McCorduck, two American
authorities on artificial intelligence, claim that the Japanese have already formulated
their strategy and are currently making a concerted effort to attain leadership in the
world's computer industry by the late 1990s because of that industry's critical
importance for their nation's economic future. The authors explain the nature and
significance of this new computer technology, point out its roots in American and
British research, and discuss the current plans and objectives of the Japanese. They
warn Americans that a complacent response to this Japanese challenge could well
result in their becoming knowledge-dependent on Japan during the years ahead.
Robert M. Sobel's *IBM vs. Japan: the struggle for the future* (New York: Stein and
Day, 1986, 262p.) complements this study with its discussion of the origins and growth
of IBM and the ongoing Japanese efforts to challenge that company's dominant
position in the world computer industry.

983　**Technology policy and economic performance: lessons from Japan.**
Christopher Freeman.　London; New York: Pinter, 1987. 155p.
bibliog.

A study of the postwar development of an institutionalised 'national system of
innovation/diffusion' in Japan. Freeman first compares the long-term trends in national
levels of scientific and technological research and development activity in Japan, the
United States, and Western Europe. He then describes some of the characteristics of
the Japanese system of innovation, among them the role of company research and
development strategy in creating new production systems, and 'the development of an
industrial structure particularly favourable to long-term strategic investment in
marketing, training and technological activities'. After analysing the experience of the
Japanese in identifying, promoting, and efficiently diffusing new information and
communication technologies throughout their economy, Freeman points to some of the
problems that are arising out of Japan's growing technological lead. He concludes with
an examination of national technology policies in the OECD (Organization for
Economic Co-operation and Development) countries, particularly the United Kingdom,
in view of the technology gap that is opening up between Japan and the industrialised
West.

984　**Gaining ground: Japan's strides in science and technology.**
George Gamota, Wendy Frieman.　Cambridge, Massachusetts:
Ballinger, 1988. 180p.

Written in order to raise the level of consciousness of American scientists, engineers,
and corporate R & D (research and development) managers with regard to the
seriousness of the Japanese challenge in science and technology, this book offers the
first systematic comparative assessment of Japanese and American work in a number
of scientific fields. It consists of the summaries of six volumes of assessments in the

Science and Technology

areas of computer science, opto- and micro-electronics, advanced polymers, mecha-tronics, telecommunications, and biotechnology, as well as an executive summary of a seventh volume concerned with advanced computing. Begun in 1983 and continuing through 1988, these studies have been sponsored by the US Department of Commerce, the National Science Foundation, and the Defense Advanced Research Projects Agency. Each chapter concludes with a diagram comparing the status of US and Japanese science and technology in subcategories of each field. The full texts of these seven reports – known collectively as the *JTECH panel reports* [*on computer science*, etc.] and produced under contract by the Science Applications International Corporation – are available from the National Technical Information Service (US Department of Commerce, Springfield, Virginia 22161).

985 **Japanese electronics technology: enterprise and innovation.**
Gene Gregory. Tokyo: Japan Times; Chichester, Sussex, and New York: Wiley, 1986. 2nd ed. 458p.

A collection of articles written between 1979 and the mid-1980s which record and analyse recent developments in the major sectors of the Japanese electronics industry. These articles, many of which first appeared in the *Far Eastern Economic Review* (q.v.), examine the inner workings of the industry and the forces which have enabled it to capture a large share of the world's markets. They also discuss the role of invention and innovation in consumer electronics, semiconductors, computers, software, factory automation (including robotics), and telecommunications. While many of the articles were journalistic in nature and are now outdated, the volume remains a useful source of information.

986 **Flexible automation in Japan.**
John Hartley, foreword by Brian Rooks. Kempston, Bedford: IFS Publications; Berlin: Springer-Verlag, 1984. 264p.

A resident of Japan during the early 1980s describes and assesses current developments in Japan involving advanced manufacturing technology. Forty-three concise articles and case-studies constitute Hartley's most significant contributions on the subject of flexible automation to four IFS magazines: *The Industrial Robot, Assembly Automation, Sensor Review*, and *The FMS Magazine*. Eleven other articles were written by leading authorities on new technology in Japanese manufacturing industry. They focus on robotics on the Japanese scene; the assembly of automotive products, precision mechanical products, electrical parts, and electronics; flexible manufacturing systems (FMS); and Japanese R & D (research and development).

987 **Evaluating applied research: lessons from Japan.**
John Irvine, foreword by Philip Hills. London; New York: Pinter, 1988. 103p. bibliog.

Commissioned by the British Department of Trade and Industry (DTI), this study seeks to determine exactly 'what experience exists in Japan with the assessment of government-funded applied research, and whether any lessons might be drawn for the use of evaluation methods and techniques in the UK'. Irvine's report covers recent developments in R & D evaluation; the evaluation of applied research by the Science and Technology Agency as well as in MITI's (Ministry of International Trade and Industry) Agency of Industrial Science and Technology; and the evaluation of applied research by five major business companies: Hitachi, Mitsubishi Electric Corp., NEC

Corp., Sharp Corp., and Toray Industries. Among its many findings, the report shows that the Japanese government in recent years has begun to place great emphasis on achieving 'value-for-money' in its expenditure on research, and that the Japanese have 'developed a highly effective system for planning, managing and evaluating research intended to make incremental contributions to science and technology'.

988   **Japanese electronics: a worm's-eye view of its evolution.**
Makoto Kikuchi, translated by Simul International.   Tokyo: Simul Press, 1983. 208p.

A scientist who became the director for research at the Sony Corporation in 1974 presents his 'accumulation of seemingly random and disordered real-life experiences' in order to trace the phenomenal growth of electronics in postwar Japan and to demonstrate that the competence of the Japanese in various areas of modern technology has attained a level enabling them to make significant contributions to the world scene. Kikuchi comments on such matters as the ways in which Japan has been able to catch up with the West in just thirty years, the differences between research practices and research in Japan and the United States, and the consequences of Japan's remarkable technological progress for US–Japanese relations.

989   **How Japan innovates: a comparison with the U.S. in the case of oxygen steelmaking.**
Leonard H. Lynn.   Boulder, Colorado: Westview Press, 1982. 211p. bibliog. (A Westview Replica Edition).

An explanation of postwar Japan's successful and rapid adoption of a new industrial technology that significantly enhanced the international competitiveness of the Japanese steel industry and contributed to the country's phenomenal economic growth. Lynn compares the introduction of a major steelmaking process – the basic oxygen furnace – into both Japan and the United States following its development by a small Austrian firm. He first discusses the adoption of this efficient technology by Japanese steelmakers, then compares their record with that of American manufacturers. He concludes that it was 'the nature of interorganizational relations – among steel firms, trading companies, and the government' – rather than internal decision-making patterns that contributed most to profitable innovation within the Japanese steel industry, and that Japanese industry is apparently better structured than its American counterpart to exploit new technologies efficiently.

990   **Japanese technology: getting the best for the least.**
Masanori Moritani, translated by Simul International.   Tokyo: Simul Press, 1982. 237p. bibliog.

Because Japan's great technological capacity has been partly responsible for her economic success, Moritani seeks to track down – from a comparative technology perspective – the 'secret behind Japan's ability to produce outstanding industrial products at astonishingly low cost'. Orienting his discussion towards the general reader, he examines such factors as the priority given to the production line, the importance of quality control circles, the pervasive feeling of group accomplishment, industry's response to consumer demands for flawless products, and the relationship of Japanese-style management to research and development. He contends that Japan's traditional culture remains 'inseparably linked to the nature of contemporary Japanese technology' and is fostering an environment that encourages hard work, high performance, and group-oriented production.

991 **Getting America ready for Japanese science and technology.**
Edited with an introduction by Ronald A. Morse, Richard J.
Samuels. Lanham, Maryland; London: University Press of America,
1986. 196p.

Americans must address the serious problem of their technical illiteracy in the area of
Japanese science and technology and develop the linguistic capability to seek out more
knowledge and utilise Japanese scientific and technological information if the United
States wishes to be truly competitive with Japan and enjoy a balanced bilateral
scientific relationship. In this conference volume jointly sponsored by the Asia
Program of the Woodrow Wilson International Center for Scholars and the MIT–Japan
Science and Technology Program, several specialists explore the current situation and
the challenges involved in training a new generation of scientists and engineers to read
Japanese. They also examine the immediate problem of gaining access to Japanese
technical data, the failure of US national language policies, the development and long-
term prospects of machine translation, and the 'medium-term solution' of utilising new
language technologies in the form of computer-assisted instruction to teach Japanese.

992 **Science and society in modern Japan: selected historical sources.**
Edited by Shigeru Nakayama, David L. Swain, Eri Yagi, forewords by
Nathan Sivin, Yuasa Mitsutomo, introduction by David L. Swain.
Tokyo: University of Tokyo Press; Cambridge, Massachusetts: MIT
Press, 1974. 337p. (MIT East Asian Science Series, 5).

Essays by prominent Japanese historians of science discuss emergent ideologies of
science as defined by some of its primary participants and present a selection of
representative postwar writings including Ōya Shin'ichi's 'Reflections on the History of
Science in Japan' and Yagi Eri's 'Statistical Approaches to the History of Science'. The
seven essays concluding this volume focus on the concern of these historians with their
social environments and on some of the movements they have organised to express
that concern. Among these are Kaneseki Yoshinori's 'The Elementary Particle Theory
Group' and Nakayama Shigeru's 'Grass-roots Geology: Ijiri Shōji and the Chindanken'.
Also included is an annotated bibliography of English-language works on the social
history of modern Japanese science by James Bartholomew.

993 **Japan's technological challenge to the West, 1950–1974: motivation and
accomplishment.**
Terutomo Ozawa. Cambridge, Massachusetts; London: MIT Press,
1974. 162p.

Ozawa analyses Japan's postwar economic experience largely in terms of the inflow
and outflow of technology. He argues that Japan's postwar industrial growth was
closely tied to her ability to acquire vital Western technological know-how, to
assimilate and continuously modify imported industrial techniques, and to develop
technological innovations through increased investment in research and development.
By facilitating imports of Western technology while restricting foreign investment in
Japanese industry, the government greatly assisted Japanese firms in becoming
competitive in world markets. Furthermore, by the late 1960s, Japan developed the
ability to export industrial technology, particularly to the developing Asian countries.
This new dimension in the transfer of technology, frequently undertaken in connection
with Japanese direct overseas investment, counterbalanced those countries' increasing

resistance to Japanese commodity exports and provided Japanese companies with access to more foreign markets.

994 **Applied artificial intelligence in Japan: current status, key research and development performers, strategic focus.**
Bruce Rubinger. New York: Hemisphere, 1988. 256p.

Artificial intelligence (AI) has been aggressively embraced by Japanese industry in recent years and has been transformed into a competitive factor designed to improve product utility, reduce costs in manufacturing, and enhance corporate decision-making. Rubinger's source-book provides an introduction to the AI market; a guide to AI professional societies, research organisations, study groups, AI-related exhibitions, and key AI publications; and detailed directories to twenty-seven major organisations engaged in AI research, development, and utilisation (e.g., Fujitsu, IBM-Japan, Nissan Motor, Toppan Printing, Toyota) as well as to the leading experts in the AI community. Each entry for a Japanese organisation includes an overview of its general R & D (research and development) structure, a description of its activities, achievements, plans and areas of primary emphasis in applied AI, and an indication where reports about its projects and research are published and/or disclosed.

995 **Inside the robot kingdom: Japan, mechatronics, and the coming robotopia.**
Frederik L. Schodt.   Tokyo; New York: Kodansha International, 1988. 256p. bibliog.

A provocative examination of technology and culture in Japan that centres on how the Japanese have assumed world leadership in robotic technology and the development of applied robots. In clear, non-technical language Schodt writes about the historical and social roots of Japan's success at robotics, demonstrates how robots have developed a friendly and useful image in feature films and comic books as well as in the Japanese toy industry, considers the broad public acceptance of robotisation at all levels of Japanese society, describes the current role of robots in industry and manufacturing as well as the impact of the robotics industry in the Japanese economy of the 1980s, identifies some of the research in robotics being undertaken by government and university institutes, and reveals some of the robot-related labour problems that have emerged in recent years.

996 **The technopolis strategy: Japan, high technology, and the control of the twenty-first century.**
Sheridan Tatsuno.   New York: Prentice Hall Press, 1986. 298p. 8 maps. bibliog. ("A Brady Book").

An informed overview of current Japanese strategies for developing key sectors of the country's high technology industry in a nationwide network of nineteen moderate-sized hi-tech towns, or technopolises. These technopolises will become the focal point for much advanced research in science and technology and are expected to become the engines for Japan's economic growth into the twenty-first century. Tatsuno reviews Japan's postwar technological and economic growth, documents the 'national obsession' with quality, and discusses the blueprint of Japan's Ministry of International Trade and Industry (MITI) for advancing Japanese technological capabilities. He argues that Japan is already moving ahead of the West in technological innovativeness and creativity – not only in product development but also in basic research – in one field after another. He concludes with a recommendation of possible American responses to this Japanese challenge.

997 **The fifth generation fallacy: why Japan is betting its future on artificial intelligence.**
J. Marshall Unger.   New York; Oxford, England: Oxford University Press, 1987. 230p. bibliog.

Noting that the current commitment of the Japanese to research in the area of artificial intelligence is very closely related to the nature of their writing system, Unger argues that the traditional Japanese script – with its reliance on Chinese characters – is basically incompatible with modern data-processing technology. Its continued use in computer environments will create intolerable inefficiencies as the scope and number of computer applications grow unless a new, fundamentally different type of computer can be built. Unger first describes the nature of the Japanese writing system, the ways it affects many areas of daily life, and the current sources of resistance to script reform. Contending that 'very modest innovations in orthography for purposes of data processing' could correct the present situation, he then explains why computers cannot solve the problems posed by the traditional Japanese script, how the Japanese are attempting to avoid a script reform compromise in data processing, and what role the 'fifth generation' of computers may well play in this 'losing battle'.

998 **U.S.–Japan science and technology exchange: patterns of interdependence.**
Edited by Cecil H. Uyehara.   Boulder, Colorado; London: Westview Press in co-operation with the Japan-America Society of Washington, 1988. 279p. bibliog. (Westview Special Studies in International Economics and Business).

Since the early 1980s, rapid Japanese advances in science and technology have resulted in an intensified two-way, competitive relationship between Japan and the United States in areas which the USA had previously dominated. This volume first offers a comparative assessment of science and technology in the United States and Japan and evaluates the management of innovation in both countries. It then analyses the evolving nature of this bilateral relationship, utilising case-studies from the four areas of biotechnology, mechatronics, computers and communications, and new materials. The contributors conclude by exploring the impact of this changing relationship on corporate strategies for co-operation and competition and by offering suggestions for broadening and strengthening US–Japan science and technology relations during the years immediately ahead.

A history of Japanese astronomy: Chinese background and Western impact.
See item no. 151.

Science and culture in traditional Japan, A.D. 600–1854.
See item no. 157.

Formation of science in Japan: building a research tradition.
See item no. 157.

Japan: the Dutch experience.
See item no. 167.

Historical development of science and technology in Japan.
See item no. 187.

Technology and agricultural development in pre-war Japan.
See item no. 200.

Comprehending technical Japanese.
See item no. 437.

English–Japanese, Japanese–English dictionary of computer and data-processing terms.
See item no. 437.

The intellectual property law of Japan.
See item no. 773.

Patent and know-how licensing in Japan and the United States.
See item no. 774.

White Papers of Japan: Annual Abstracts of Official Reports and Statistics of the Japanese Government.
See item no. 829.

The Japanese automobile industry: technology and management at Nissan and Toyota.
See item no. 871.

Competitive edge: the semiconductor industry in the U.S. and Japan.
See item no. 880.

Between MITI and the market: Japanese industrial policy for high technology.
See item no. 880.

Japan's high technology industries: lessons and limitations of industrial policy.
See item no. 881.

Japan and the United States: economic and political adversaries.
See item no. 897.

Japan's role in Soviet economic growth: transfer of technology since 1965.
See item no. 900.

Fragile interdependence: economic issues in U.S.–Japanese trade and investment.
See item no. 905.

Business Japan.
See item no. 1494.

Science & Technology in Japan.
See item no. 1539.

Science and Technology

Technology and Development.
See item no. 1541.

Venture Japan: the Journal of Global Opportunity.
See item no. 1544.

The Wheel Extended.
See item no. 1545.

Postwar industrial policy in Japan: an annotated bibliography.
See item no. 1581.

Literature

General

999 A history of Japanese literature.
Shūichi Katō, translated by David Chibbett [volume 1], Don Sanderson [volumes 2–3], forewords by Ronald Dore, René Etiemble, Edwin McClellan.   London: Macmillan; Tokyo and New York: Kodansha International, 1979-83. 3 vols. bibliog.
A distinguished critic and scholar's interpretive essay about Japanese literature as an aspect of intellectual history. Katō relates the evolution of Japanese literature in its widest sense – criticism, journalism, philosophy, and history as well as prose, poetry, and drama – to developments in Japanese history and society. He also examines the role and contributions of individual writers to Japanese culture. Volume one, *The first thousand years*, studies the literature produced between the age of the *Manyōshū* (eighth century) and the age of noh and *kyōgen* (Muromachi period). Volume two, *The years of isolation*, focuses on the Tokugawa period and is in part concerned with the activities of such prominent thinkers as Ogyū Sorai and Arai Hakuseki as well as with such writers as Ihara Saikaku and Ueda Akinari. The final volume, *The modern years*, deals with the writings of many of the intellectuals who played an important role in the development of modern Japanese thought and literature during the century following the Meiji Restoration (1868) and examines their responses to Western ideas and literary trends.

1000 Anthology of Japanese literature. Volume 1: From the earliest era to the mid-nineteenth century. Volume 2: Modern Japanese literature.
Compiled and edited with introductions by Donald Keene.   New York: Grove Press; London: Allen and Unwin, 1955-56. 2 vols. bibliog. (Unesco Collection of Representative Works: Japanese Series). Reprinted, Rutland, Vermont; Tokyo: Tuttle, 1956.
The first and still the best English-language anthology of poetry, prose, and drama

from classical and modern times. Keene selects some of the most representative literary works produced in Japan and presents them in their entirety or as excerpts together with brief introductions about their significance and background and with occasional explanatory notes. Volume one groups forty-nine translations chronologically under five major periods: Ancient, Heian, Kamakura, Muromachi, and Tokugawa. Volume two brings together translations of thirty-six works that originally appeared between 1871 and 1949. Every important genre and style is represented, including excerpts from celebrated noh plays, selections from Heian period diaries, poetry and prose written during the Tokugawa period in Chinese, and tales composed by twentieth-century short-story writers. The translations are by several Americans, Europeans, and Japanese as well as by the editor himself.

1001 **Dawn to the West: Japanese literature of the modern era.**
Volume 1: Fiction. Volume 2: Poetry, drama, criticism.
Donald Keene. New York: Holt, Rinehart and Winston, 1984.
2 vols. bibliog. Reprinted, New York: H. Holt, 1987.

A sequel to *World within walls: Japanese literature of the pre-modern era, 1600–1867* (q.v.), these two volumes constitute the concluding sections of an eminent scholar's comprehensive history of Japanese literature. They provide straightforward, almost encyclopaedic coverage of the novels, short stories, poetry, drama, and literary criticism written between the Meiji Restoration of 1868 and the 1940s. Living authors, however, are generally excluded. In volume one, *Fiction*, Keene structures most of his account around individual authors – from Tsubouchi Shōyō, Futabatei Shimei, Kōda Rohan, and Higuchi Ichiyō through Tanizaki Junichirō, Kawabata Yasunari, Dazai Osamu, and Mishima Yukio – focusing on both their lives and their literary contributions. Individual works are described in some detail; plot summaries, character analyses, and evaluative comments are provided. In volume two, *Poetry, drama, criticism*, he organises his study into four parts according to literary format: poetry in traditional forms; poetry in new forms; the modern drama (modern kabuki, *shinpa*, and *shingeki*); and modern criticism. Keene's descriptions and interpretations are very informative as well as insightful, and his entire multi-volume history should be regarded as essential reading for anyone interested in Japanese literature.

1002 **Japanese literature: an introduction for Western readers.**
Donald Keene. London: John Murray, 1953. 114p. bibliog. (The Wisdom of the East Series). Reprinted, New York: Grove Press; Rutland, Vermont and Tokyo: Tuttle, 1955.

An introduction to Japanese literature through a discussion of several representative works. In chapters dealing with Japanese poetry, the Japanese theatre, the Japanese novel, and Japanese literature under Western influence, Keene provides both a concise historical overview of Japan's literary achievements and a guide to the critical understanding of a selected number of writings, among them the haiku of Bashō, noh drama, the puppet plays of Chikamatsu Monzaemon, *The tale of Genji* by Murasaki Shikibu, Shimazaki Tōson's novel *The broken commandment* (*Hakai*), and Tanizaki Junichirō's *The thin snow* (also known as *The Makioka sisters*, or *Sasameyuki*).

1003 **Landscapes and portraits: appreciations of Japanese culture.**
Donald Keene. Tokyo; Palo Alto, California: Kodansha
International, 1971; London: Secker and Warburg, 1972. 343p.
bibliog.

A collection of twenty critical essays written over a period of several years by an
eminent American scholar and translator of Japanese literature. Keene's essays are
concerned with Japanese aesthetics, feminine sensibility in Heian period literature,
realism and unreality in Japanese drama, seventeenth-century *haikai* poetry, the
creation of modern Japanese poetry, the three modern novelists Tanizaki Junichirō,
Dazai Osamu and Mishima Yukio, some Japanese 'eccentrics' such as Ikkyū Sōjun and
Fujimoto Kizan, the impact of the Sino–Japanese War of 1894-95 and World War II on
Japanese culture and Japanese writers, and the problems and experience of translating
Japanese literature into English. This work was reprinted under the title *Appreciations
of Japanese culture* (Tokyo; New York: Kodansha International, 1981).

1004 **The pleasures of Japanese literature.**
Donald Keene. New York; Guildford, Surrey: Columbia University
Press, 1988. 133p. bibliog. (Companions to Asian Studies).

An introduction for the general reader to the world of Japanese aesthetics, poetry,
fiction, and drama prior to the mid-nineteenth century. Keene describes some of the
characteristics of Japanese taste in terms of Yoshida Kenkō's book *Essays in idleness*
(*Tsurezuregusa*), discusses the poetry of the *Manyōshū* and the *Kokinshū*, explores
some of the distinctive uses made of poetry in Japan over the centuries, talks about the
pre-modern tradition of Japanese fiction with particular focus on such works as the
Taketori monogatari ('The Tale of the Bamboo Cutter'), *The tales of Ise* (*Ise
monogatari*), *The tale of Genji* and the novels of Ihara Saikaku, and comments on the
various types of traditional Japanese theatre including the noh plays of Zeami
Motokiyo and the kabuki and bunraku of the Tokugawa period. In a number of
respects this volume complements Keene's much earlier work, *Japanese literature: an
introduction for Western readers* (q.v.).

1005 **World within walls: Japanese literature of the pre-modern era,
1600–1867.**
Donald Keene. New York: Holt, Rinehart and Winston; London:
Secker and Warburg, 1976. 606p. bibliog. Reprinted, New York:
Grove Press, 1978; Rutland, Vermont and Tokyo: Tuttle, 1978.

A wide-ranging, comprehensive study, organised primarily by literary genre, of the
literature that flourished while Japan was largely isolated from the rest of the world.
Dividing his narrative into two major parts – 'Literature from 1600–1770' (when Kyōto
and Ōsaka formed the centre of literary production) and 'Literature from 1770–1867'
(when the centre shifted to Edo, or Tokyo) – Keene discusses the major literary forms
and authors of the Tokugawa period. He introduces the *haikai* poetry, fiction, drama,
and *waka* poetry of that era, devoting entire chapters to such authors as Matsuo
Bashō, Ihara Saikaku, Chikamatsu Monzaemon, and Ueda Akinari, as well as to such
types of literature as *kana zōshi*, *jōruri*, *gesaku* fiction, and nineteenth-century kabuki.
He also intersperses his account with many translated poems and prose passages, and
concludes with a survey of the poetry and prose that were written by Japanese authors
in Chinese. This book is the second in Keene's projected four-volume history of

Japanese literature, and is continued by his *Dawn to the West: Japanese literature of the modern era* (q.v.).

1006 **A history of Japanese literature.**
Jin'ichi Konishi, translated by Aileen Gatten, Nicholas Teele, edited by Earl Miner.   Princeton, New Jersey; Guildford, Surrey: Princeton University Press, 1984- . 5 vols. maps. bibliog.
A distinguished scholar's highly interpretive history of Japanese literature from its earliest stages through the death of Mishima Yukio in 1970. Konishi's major objective is not the orderly presentation of basic factual information but rather the 'systematic delineation of the special qualities of Japanese literature'. The first volume, *The archaic and ancient ages*, opens with Konishi's general introduction, which explicates his approach and summarises the principal characteristics of Japanese literature. The ensuing chapters cover the earliest recorded poetry through the composition of *waka* and *setsuwa* during the eighth century. Volume two, *The early middle ages*, analyses the literature of the ninth, tenth, and eleventh centuries. Whenever appropriate, Konishi examines the influence of Chinese, Korean, and other Asian literatures as well as Western culture on Japanese writers, and he compares Japanese with Okinawan, Ainu, Chinese, and Korean poetry and prose. This projected five-volume history (vols. 3–5 have yet to appear) differs from Donald Keene's four-volume history of Japanese literature (q.v.) not only on account of its different methodological approach and Konishi's personal and at times unusual interpretations but also because of its orientation towards a more scholarly audience.

1007 **The karma of words: Buddhism and the literary arts in medieval Japan.**
William R. LaFleur.   Berkeley, California; London: University of California Press, 1983. 204p. bibliog.
A highly acclaimed scholarly study in the field of Japanese literature and religion that reconstructs the ways in which the medieval Japanese perceived their environment and identifies as well as explains the intellectual and religious assumptions of the Buddhist writers of that period. LaFleur's analysis is based on a study of several important literary works including the *Nihon ryōiki* of the eighth-century monk Kyōkai, the *Hōjōki* of Kamo no Chōmei, the poetry of the twelfth-century Buddhist priest Saigyō, the *Korai fūteishō* of Fujiwara no Shunzei, the noh plays of Zeami, the *kyōgen* of the Muromachi period, and *Oku no hosomichi* of the early Tokugawa period poet Matsuo Bashō.

1008 **Modern Japanese fiction and its traditions: an introduction.**
J. Thomas Rimer.   Princeton, New Jersey; Guildford, Surrey: Princeton University Press, 1978. 313p. bibliog.
This explanation of the background, structural principles, and development of both pre-modern and modern Japanese fiction discusses a wide range of literary works that are readily accessible in translation to the general reader. Rimer analyses such traditional classics as *The tale of Genji*, the *Tale of the Heike*, and *The tales of Ise*, as well as representative novels and short stories by such modern authors as Tanizaki Junichirō, Natsume Sōseki, Kawabata Yasunari, Endō Shūsaku, and Ibuse Masuji. Using each of these works as his point of departure, he cites other literary and critical texts and shows how 'Japanese tradition, as it developed, produced a close interplay of

thematic and narrative structures, an interplay that in turn came to represent the central element in a highly coherent literary aesthetic, with its carefully wrought sanctions of thought and expression'. Rimer's emphasis on persistent elements of style, subject and presentation in Japan's literary tradition offers an insightful approach to understanding Japanese literature as a whole.

1009 **A reader's guide to Japanese literature.**
J. Thomas Rimer.   Tokyo; New York: Kodansha International, 1988. 208p.

A selection of twenty classical and thirty modern literary works by a noted translator, author, critic and teacher that are considered representative, 'in the largest sense of the word, of the Japanese tradition of excellence in literature'. All are currently available in translation. Ranging in genre from fiction and poetry to essays and dramatic texts, these works include such masterpieces as *The tale of Genji*, Natsume Sōseki's novel *Kokoro*, and Hagiwara Sakutarō's collection of poetry *Howling at the moon*. Each work is introduced in an essay that provides selected background information, an outline of its plot, a sketch of the life of its author, a number of Rimer's critical insights, and comments on its translation into English and on the translation of related literary works. This guide is intended to offer 'simple and practical advice' to general readers who wish to identify some literary works admired by the Japanese themselves which they can read for pleasure.

1010 **Japanese literature in Chinese. Volume 1: Poetry & prose in Chinese by Japanese writers of the early period. Volume 2: Poetry & prose in Chinese by Japanese writers of the later period.**
Translated with introductions by Burton Watson.   New York; London: Columbia University Press, 1975-76. 2 vols. (Translations from the Oriental Classics).

An anthology of selected works in classical Chinese by writers, scholars, and officials active between the mid-seventh century and the early twentieth century. Known as *kanshi* ('Chinese poetry') and *kanbun* ('Chinese prose'), these writings have constituted an integral part of the Japanese literary experience. The first volume (covering the mid-600s to 1185) contains translations of ten poems from the *Kaifusō* (compiled in 751), four tales from the *Nihon ryōiki*, fourteen poems from a variety of Heian period collections, Yoshishige no Yasutane's 'Record of the pond pavilion', and a selection of poems and prose of Sugawara no Michizane (845-903). The second volume, focusing on the period 1780-1916, contains 135 poems in *shih* form and four prose writings, among them sizeable selections from the works of the Zen monk Ryōkan (1758-1831), the historian Rai Sanyō (1781-1832), and the novelist Natsume Sōseki (1867-1916), as well as a sampling of poetry by other medieval and Tokugawa period writers.

Tradition and modernization in Japanese culture.
See item no. 239.

Some Japanese portraits.
See item no. 291.

Biographical dictionary of Japanese literature.
See item no. 365.

A dictionary of Japanese Buddhist terms: based on references in Japanese literature.
See item no. 415.

Multiple meanings: the written word in Japan – past, present, and future.
See item no. 1231.

Chanoyu Quarterly: Tea and the Arts of Japan.
See item no. 1496.

Japanese Literature Today.
See item no. 1521.

Journal of the Association of Teachers of Japanese.
See item no. 1529.

Monumenta Nipponica: Studies in Japanese Culture.
See item no. 1534.

Japan through children's literature: an annotated bibliography.
See item no. 1596.

Guide to Japanese prose.
See item no. 1597.

Studies in Japanese literature and language: a bibliography of English materials.
See item no. 1615.

Classical fiction and prose: translations

1011 **The riverside counselor's stories: vernacular fiction of late Heian Japan.**
Translated with an introduction and notes by Robert L. Backus.
Stanford, California: Stanford University Press, 1985. 234p. bibliog.

A new rendition into English of the ten short stories dating from the eleventh to the thirteenth century that were collected under the title *Tsutsumi Chūnagon monogatari*. These entertaining examples of late Heian period vernacular fiction, attributed primarily to women of the Japanese aristocracy, describe amorous relationships in and about the imperial court. They have such titles as 'The Lady Who Admired Vermin', 'Courtship at Different Levels', 'The Shell-matching Contest', 'The Lieutenants Who Lodged in Unexpected Quarters', and 'The Flower Ladies'. Each story is preceded by a brief analytical introduction. Backus' graceful literary translations in this anthology are far superior to those produced by Edwin O. Reischauer and Joseph K. Yamagiwa in their *Translations from early Japanese literature* (Cambridge, Massachusetts: Harvard University Press, 1951, 467p.) and compare favourably with Arthur Waley's rendition of *The lady who loved insects* (London: Blackmore, 1929, 35p.).

1012 **The tale of the Soga Brothers.**
Translated with an introduction and notes by Thomas J. Cogan.
Tokyo: University of Tokyo Press, 1987. 336p.

A fifteenth-century historical narrative, filled with intrigue and adventure, of the lifelong quest of two brothers to avenge the death of their father by slaying his murderer. Set in the late twelfth century, this tale vividly portrays the customs, values, ideals, and practices (e.g., filial piety, honour, self-sacrifice, courage, and tenacity) of medieval warrior society. The *Soga monogatari* also served as a major source of themes and motifs for the drama and literature that were written during the Muromachi and Tokugawa periods.

1013 **The gossamer years: the diary of a noblewoman of Heian Japan.**
Fujiwara Michitsuna no haha, translated with an introduction by
Edward Seidensticker. Rutland, Vermont; Tokyo: Tuttle, 1964.
201p. map. (Unesco Collection of Representative Works: Japanese
Series).

The autobiographical diary of a mid-tenth century Fujiwara noblewoman known today simply as the 'mother of Fujiwara Michitsuna'. Filled with tanka poetry, these memoirs are a remarkably frank confession of the author's unhappy marriage to the statesman Fujiwara Kaneie and her bitterness at her husband's marital infidelities. The diary concludes in the year 974 with her complete estrangement from her husband. Translation of *Kagerō nikki*.

1014 **The life of an amorous man.**
Ihara Saikaku, translated by Kengi Hamada, illustrations by Masakazu
Kuwata. Rutland, Vermont; Tokyo: Tuttle, 1964. 233p. (Library of
Japanese Literature).

Saikaku's first major work of prose depicts in picaresque fashion the pursuits and follies of Yonosuke (or, 'man of the world'), a hero whom he creates out of a composite of the many wealthy commoners who indulged in the free and easy life of the pleasure districts of late seventeenth-century urban Japan. Saikaku follows Yonosuke from his precocious childhood to the end of his amatory career, describing his many romances and his travels, delineating his personality and the characters of those with whom he came into contact, and presenting a realistic picture of selected aspects of contemporary Japanese life and customs. The work is a translation of *Kōshoku ichidai otoko*.

1015 **The life of an amorous woman, and other writings.**
Ihara Saikaku, edited and translated with an introduction by Ivan
Morris. London: Chapman and Hall; New York: New Directions,
1963. 403p. bibliog. (Unesco Collection of Representative Literary
Works: Japanese Series).

An annotated collection of popular and frequently erotic stories written for late seventeenth-century townsmen. These tales of sexual love and of money-making tend to reflect the atmosphere of the Genroku period, an era characterised by prosperity, extravagance, and self-indulgence. The anthology consists of translated extracts from four of Saikaku's works: *Kōshoku gonin onna* ('Five Women Who Chose Love'), *Kōshoku ichidai onna* ('The Life of an Amorous Woman'), *Nihon eitaigura* ('The

Literature. Classical fiction and prose: translations

Eternal Storehouse of Japan'), and *Seken munesanyo* ('Reckonings That Carry Men through the World'). These translations are preceded by a lengthy introduction about the period, the author, Saikaku's writings and literary style, the illustrations in the volume, and Saikaku's place in literature. A complete translation of *Kōshoku gonin onna*, prepared by Wm. Theodore de Bary, appeared under the title *Five women who loved love* (Rutland, Vermont; Tokyo: Tuttle, 1956, 264p.).

1016   **Shanks' mare; being a translation of the Tokaido volumes of Hizakurige, Japan's great comic novel of travel and ribaldry.**
Jippensha Ikku, translated by Thomas Satchell.   Rutland, Vermont; Tokyo: Tuttle, 1960. rev. ed. 414p. (Unesco Collection of Representative Works: Japanese Series).

A chronicle of the comic adventures of two amiable scoundrels, Yajirobei and Kitahachi, during their journey by foot from Edo (Tokyo) to Kyōto along the Tōkaidō highway, the major road connecting eastern and western Japan during the Tokugawa period. The *Hizakurige* was first published in 1802 by the humorist, fiction writer, and playwright Jippensha Ikku (1765-1831), and it attained instant popular success. Satchell's highly entertaining translation of *Tōkaidōchū Hizakurige* first appeared in a limited edition under the title *Hizakurige (Tōkaidō circuit)* (Kōbe: Chronicle Press, 1929, 430p.).

1017   **Ōkagami, the great mirror: Fujiwara Michinaga (966–1027) and his times. A study and translation.**
Helen Craig McCullough.   Princeton, New Jersey; Guildford, Surrey: Princeton University Press; Tokyo: University of Tokyo Press, 1980. 381p. 4 maps. bibliog. (Princeton Library of Asian Translations).

A complete translation of the anonymous, late eleventh-century historical tale that focuses on the career of the great statesman Fujiwara no Michinaga (966-1027) and on the lives and families of the powerful Fujiwara regents and chancellors between 850 and 1025. The *Ōkagami* is composed of five parts: a preface; the 'Imperial Annals', which outline the history of fourteen emperors from Montoku through Go-Ichijō; the 'Biographies' of twenty Fujiwara ministers of state, among them Michinaga; the 'Tales of the Fujiwara Family', their leaders and their religious establishments; and the 'Tales of the Past', stories which deal with festival origins, poems and poets, elegant events and strange happenings, emperors of the past, members of the rival Minamoto family, and Buddhist preachers. McCullough's authoritative translation is accompanied by a long introduction and four appendixes, among them a listing of the people and places mentioned in the text and a chronology of the *Ōkagami* period.

1018   **The Taiheiki: a chronicle of medieval Japan.**
Translated with an introduction and notes by Helen Craig McCullough.   New York: Columbia University Press; London: Oxford University Press, 1959. 401p. (Records of Civilization: Sources and Studies, 59). Reprinted, Westport, Connecticut: Greenwood Press, 1976; Rutland, Vermont and Tokyo: Tuttle, 1979.

The partial translation of a classic work in the literary genre known as *gunki monogatari*, or 'war tales'. Rich in intrigue and in scenes of battles, the *Taiheiki* vividly recounts the origins and course of the fourteenth-century conflict between Japan's two rival imperial courts. McCullough's translation is limited to the first twelve of the forty chapters of this important chronicle. They cover Emperor Go-Daigo's accession to the throne in 1318, his early efforts to overthrow the Hōjō family who controlled the Kamakura shogunate, his own deposition and exile, the legendary exploits of Kusonoki Masashige and his other generals, the emperor's triumphant return from exile in 1333, and the subsequent brief restoration of imperial power known as the Kemmu Restoration. The translator's scholarly introduction provides an historical frame of reference for this tale and evaluates the significance of the events which took place during that period.

1019 **The tale of the Heike.**
Translated with an introduction by Helen Craig McCullough.
Stanford, California: Stanford University Press, 1988. 489p. 2 maps.

The *Heike monogatari*, the most important work in the medieval literary genre known as *gunki monogatari* ('war tales'), narrates the rise and especially the fall of the Taira family (also known as the Heike clan) and its defeat at the hands of the powerful Minamoto (Genji) clan before and during the Gempei War of 1180-85. This tale is replete with accounts of fierce battles, detailed descriptions of the heroic conduct of individual warriors, and stories about women who suffered at that time. McCullough's annotated translation of the *Heike* is the third rendition into English of this literary classic, following those by Arthur L. Sadler (in *Transactions of the Asiatic Society of Japan*, 1918 and 1921) and by Hiroshi Kitagawa and Bruce T. Tsuchida (Tokyo: University of Tokyo Press, 1975, 807p.). Intended for both a general and a scholarly audience, it includes three appendixes that provide background information, a chronology, and an evaluation of the *Heike* as literature.

1020 **Yoshitsune: a fifteenth-century Japanese chronicle.**
Translated with an introduction by Helen Craig McCullough.   Tokyo: University of Tokyo Press; Stanford, California: Stanford University Press, 1966. 367p. (Unesco Collection of Representative Works: Japanese Series).

A fictional biography, based on a large body of popular legends, of Japan's foremost military hero: Minamoto no Yoshitsune (1159-89). His military defeat of the Taira clan in 1185 paved the way for the establishment of the Kamakura shogunate by his brother, the first shōgun, Minamoto no Yoritomo. Yoshitsune subsequently became estranged from his brother, and was forced to commit suicide with his wife and daughter after being hunted down as an outlaw. This tragic story has served as a rich source for countless noh and kabuki plays, novels and stories, poems and motion pictures. Translation of *Gikeiki*.

1021 **A tale of flowering fortunes: annals of Japanese aristocratic life in the Heian period.**
Translated with an introduction and notes by William H. McCullough, Helen Craig McCullough.   Stanford, California: Stanford University Press, 1980. 910p. bibliog.

An annotated translation of the first thirty (out of forty) chapters of the *Eiga monogatari*, an embellished account of mid-Heian period historical figures and events attributed to the eleventh-century court lady Akazome Emon. This classic work of the *rekishi monogatari* ('historical tale') genre focuses on the life and times of the great courtier and statesman Fujiwara no Michinaga (966-1028) and on the glory of the Fujiwara family at the Heian court under his leadership. It depicts a wide range of events including births, romances, marriages, deaths, parties, and ceremonies. The introduction analyses the origins of this tale, its authorship, special qualities, and contributions to Japanese historiography. The extensive annotations, supplementary notes, tables, and appended descriptions of the imperial palace and Heian government ranks and offices are invaluable for their detailed coverage of Heian court life and aristocratic culture.

1022 **A collection of tales from Uji: a study and translation of Uji shūi monogatari.**
Douglas Edgar Mills. Cambridge, England; New York: Cambridge University Press, 1970. 459p. bibliog. (University of Cambridge Oriental Publications, 15) (Unesco Collection of Representative Literary Works: Japanese Series).

A scholarly study and complete translation of an anonymous collection of 197 short tales (from the genre of *setsuwa bungaku*, or 'anecdotal literature') believed to have been compiled in its present form early in the thirteenth century. These Buddhist and secular tales include stories about deceitful begging priests, temple novices, festival musicians, image-making, magical cures, flying begging-bowls, the miracles wrought by Kannon, everyday peasant life, and the like. Many of them are filled with ribald humour and will immediately appeal to the general reader. Mills' introduction outlines the development and problems of *setsuwa bungaku*; discusses the content, style, and literary qualities of the *Uji shūi monogatari*; considers its parallels with other works as well as Japanese views on its date and on its relationship with other collections of tales, especially the *Konjaku monogatari* (q.v.); and sets forth the translator's personal observations on its date, structure, and position in the history of Japanese literature.

1023 **Murasaki Shikibu: her diary and poetic memoirs; a translation and study.**
Murasaki Shikibu, translation and study by Richard Bowring. Princeton, New Jersey; Guildford, Surrey: Princeton University Press, 1982. 290p. 8 maps. bibliog. (Princeton Library of Asian Translations).

Extensively annotated translations of both the diary and the autobiographical poems written by the author of *The tale of Genji* are preceded by brief introductory studies of Murasaki Shikibu's life, her literary accomplishments, and the background and structure of these two texts. The diary, in actuality 'a series of reminiscences and records of memorable scenes interspersed with personal reflections recalled later in tranquility', sheds considerable light on life and culture at the Heian imperial court early in the eleventh century. The anthology of autobiographical, poetic memoirs (*Murasaki Shikibu shū*) is of more literary than biographical value.

1024 **The tale of Genji.**
Murasaki Shikibu, translated with an introduction by Edward G.
Seidensticker. New York: Knopf; London: Secker and Warburg,
1976. 2 vols. (Unesco Collection of Representative Works: Japanese
Series). Reprinted, Rutland, Vermont and Tokyo: Tuttle, 1978;
Harmondsworth, Middlesex: Penguin, 1981; New York: Vintage
Books, 1985.

Japan's greatest literary masterpiece, written in the early eleventh century by the
celebrated court lady Murasaki Shikibu (978-?1016). In a succession of episodes
focusing on a Japanese prince named Genji, this lengthy novel describes Genji's life,
his many amorous adventures, his political career, his preoccupation with the arts that
flourished during the Heian period, and the less successful love affairs of Genji's son
and grandson following his death. The *Genji monogatari* is renowned for its graceful
poetic style, emotional and psychological subtlety, and aesthetic sensitivity. It is widely
considered one of the great works of world literature. Like the writings of Shakespeare
and Goethe in the West, *The tale of Genji* has exerted a tremendous influence in Japan
– on literature, drama, and art – up to the very present. Seidensticker's scholarly and
highly acclaimed rendition is the first complete translation of this novel into English,
succeeding but not replacing a slightly less complete but masterly version by Arthur
Waley (London: Allen and Unwin; Boston, Massachusetts: Houghton Mifflin, 1935,
1135p. Reprinted many times).

1025 **The pillow book of Sei Shōnagon.**
Sei Shōnagon, translated and edited by Ivan Morris, foreword by Wm.
Theodore de Bary. New York: Columbia University Press; London:
Oxford University Press, 1967. 2 vols. 7 maps. bibliog. (Records of
Civilization: Sources and Studies, 77) (Unesco Collection of
Representative Works: Japanese Series). Reprinted, Baltimore,
Maryland; Harmondsworth, Middlesex: Penguin, 1970. 411p.

Sei Shōnagon, a talented late tenth-century imperial court lady, recorded life around
her in the form of character sketches, anecdotes, diary entries, short eyewitness
narratives, casual essays, poetry exchanges, conversations, and lists of things and
places that she liked or disliked. Writing with great humour, insight, and stylistic
refinement, she created a literary masterpiece and established a new literary genre
known as *zuihitsu* ('random essay', or 'loose collection of jottings'). The first volume
presents a complete translation of Sei Shōnagon's *Pillow book*. Volume two contains
nearly two hundred pages of notes and commentaries, ten appendixes, and a very
detailed index-glossary. Only about one-quarter of this literary work appeared in
Arthur Waley's abridged translation, published in 1928 under the same title (London:
George Allen and Unwin, 1928; Boston, Massachusetts: Houghton Mifflin, 1929, 162p.
Reprinted, London: Allen and Unwin, 1957). This book is a translation of *Makura no
sōshi*.

1026   **As I crossed a bridge of dreams: recollections of a woman in eleventh-century Japan.**
Sugawara Takasue no musume, translated with an introduction by
Ivan Morris.   New York: Dial Press; London: Oxford University
Press, 1971. 159p. 3 maps. Reprinted, Harmondsworth, Middlesex:
Penguin, 1975.

The literary memoirs of an anonymous court lady known simply as Takasue no
musume ('Takasue's daughter') or as Lady Sarashina (from the title given to her
book). Kept between 1020 and 1059, this diary candidly records Lady Sarashina's
innermost thoughts and feelings, her dreams, and her observations of the world in
which she lived, as well as some of the events in her life and her associations with
people around her. Morris' annotated translation of the *Sarashina nikki* is
accompanied by an introduction to Lady Sarashina's life, an assessment of her work,
woodblock prints which suggest how people dressed, lived and travelled during the
mid-Heian period, and photographs of her favourite temples in and around Kyōto.

1027   **A tale of eleventh-century Japan: *Hamamatsu Chūnagon monogatari*.**
Sugawara Takasue no musume, introduction and translation by
Thomas H. Rohlich.   Princeton, New Jersey; Guildford, Surrey:
Princeton University Press, 1983. 247p. bibliog. (Princeton Library of
Asian Translations).

A complete, annotated translation of the 'Tale of the Hamamatsu Middle Counselor',
a highly regarded late Heian period story about the romantic entanglements of a
Japanese nobleman in China and Japan. It describes the prince's amorous relationships
with his step-sister and a half-Japanese consort of the Chinese emperor, among others;
and portrays the psychological suffering incurred in his ill-fated love affairs. Sequences
of dreams figure prominently within the narrative. Rohlich's introductory essay focuses
on the authorship, composition, and history of this literary work as well as on its
motifs, its parallels with *The tale of Genji* (q.v.), and its use of dreams.

1028   **Tales of Yamato: a tenth-century poem-tale.**
Translated with an introduction by Mildred M. Tahara, foreword by
Donald Keene.   Honolulu, Hawaii: University of Hawaii Press, 1980.
318p. bibliog.

A complete, annotated translation of the *Yamato monogatari*, an important tenth-
century anthology of 173 'poem-tales' (*uta monogatari*). They centre around early
Heian period courtiers, court ladies, emperors, and priests, but also deal at times with
common people. Written in a combination of prose and poetry, these stories generally
depict love affairs, romances, and other episodes that occurred around the Heian court
as well as some of the customs and beliefs of that era. Tahara's concluding essay
surveys the development of poetry and prose during the early Heian period and
discusses the authorship, dating, literary significance, literary influence, and extant
texts of the *Tales of Yamato*.

1029   **Japanese tales.**
Selected, edited, and translated with an introduction by Royall
Tyler.   New York: Pantheon Books; Toronto, Ontario: Random
House, 1987. 341p. (Pantheon Fairy Tale and Folklore Library).
These 220 tales are selected from medieval collections of 'tale literature' (*setsuwa
bungaku*) that were compiled between the ninth and fourteenth centuries. More than
two-thirds of them are taken from two masterpieces of this genre: the *Konjaku
monogatari shū* and the *Uji shūi monogatari*. Tyler includes stories dealing with
Buddhist topics and with the imperial court and its world, as well as numerous legends
and popular folktales. His translations are not 'studiously faithful' versions but rather
renditions in modern, natural-sounding prose that will appeal to the general reader
while retaining their basic form and nature.

1030   **Tales of the spring rain: Harusame monogatari.**
Ueda Akinari, translated with an introduction by Barry Jackman.
Tokyo: Japan Foundation; Tokyo: University of Tokyo Press, 1975.
249p. bibliog. (Japan Foundation Translation Series).
Translation of a collection of ten tales which were published shortly before Ueda
Akinari's death in 1809. They cover a wide range of subjects and may be regarded as
'historical or critical essays cast in a fiction mold' that reveal the author's philosophical
and moral outlook. Jackman's translation is accompanied by an introduction to
Akinari's life and work and by perceptive commentaries on the individual stories.

1031   **Ugetsu monogatari: tales of moonlight and rain. A complete English
version of the eighteenth-century Japanese collection of tales of the
supernatural.**
Ueda Akinari, translated and edited by Leon M. Zolbrod.   London:
Allen and Unwin; Vancouver, British Columbia: University of British
Columbia Press, 1974. 280p. map. bibliog. (Unesco Collection of
Representative Works: Japanese Series). Reprinted, Rutland,
Vermont; Tokyo: Tuttle, 1977.
A scholarly, annotated translation of nine evocative tales, each set in times past, that
together constitute one of the great masterpieces of Tokugawa period fiction. First
published in 1776, these tales depict the world of the supernatural as they recount such
stories as the tale of a jealous wife who returns from the dead to avenge herself on her
faithless husband, and the tale of a poet who confronts the ghost of a former emperor.
Zolbrod's rendition is accompanied by an introduction to the literary background,
style, and nature of Ueda's work. A second translation – *Tales of moonlight and rain:
Japanese gothic tales*, prepared by Kengi Hamada (Tokyo: University of Tokyo Press,
1971; New York: Columbia University Press, 1972, 150p.) – will appeal to a general
audience on account of its readability but is not faithful to the original Japanese in
terms of its structure, style, and literary technique.

Literature. Classical fiction and prose: translations

1032 **Tales of times now past: sixty-two stories from a medieval Japanese collection.**
Translated with an introduction by Marian Ury. Berkeley, California; London: University of California Press, 1979. 199p. bibliog.

Translations of sixty-two representative stories from an anonymous twelfth-century collection of more than one thousand brief tales. Following an introduction which explains the internal arrangement of the *Konjaku monogatari*, the nature and style of its tales, and the sources of its legends, Ury presents her selection of tales under four headings: 'Tales of India', 'Tales of China', 'Tales of Buddhism in Japan', and 'Secular Tales of Japan'. Many of them concern the Buddha, Buddhism, or important practitioners of Buddhism; others deal with such varied subjects as famous warriors, criminals, or ghosts. As her translations are meant for the general reader, Ury's annotations are kept to a minimum. An earlier published collection of translations from this same work, prepared by Susan W. Jones, is entitled *Ages ago: thirty-seven tales from the Konjaku monogatari collection* (Cambridge, Massachusetts: Harvard University Press, 1959, 175p.). Jones' selection excludes all of the Japanese Buddhist stories, however, and her translations are less precise.

1033 **Ochikubo monogatari, or the tale of the Lady Ochikubo: a tenth century Japanese novel.**
Translated by Wilfrid Whitehouse, Eizo Yanagisawa. Tokyo: Hokuseido Press, 1965. rev. ed. 287p. (Unesco Collection of Representative Works: Japanese Series).

The translation of an anonymous late tenth-century tale which centres around a young girl who suffers at the hands of her wicked stepmother, secretly marries a young hero who rises to the highest ranks of officialdom, and escapes from her home. It also narrates her husband's many acts of revenge on those who have harmed her, and his eventual change of heart in response to the pleadings of his wife. Comparable to the Cinderella stories popular in the West, *Ochikubo monogatari* has enjoyed considerable popularity among Japanese audiences over the centuries. Two appendixes briefly discuss the tale's title, authorship, and date; its place in Heian literature; and the political organisation of Japan during the tenth century. This work has been reprinted under the title *The tale of the Lady Ochikubo: a tenth century Japanese novel* (London: Owen, 1970; Garden City, New York: Doubleday, 1971; London: Arena, 1985).

1034 **Essays in idleness: the *Tsurezuregusa* of Kenkō.**
Yoshida Kenkō, translated with an introduction by Donald Keene, foreword by Wm. Theodore de Bary. New York; London: Columbia University Press, 1967. 213p. bibliog. (Unesco Collection of Representative Works: Japanese Series) (Records of Civilization: Sources and Studies, no. 78). Reprinted, Rutland, Vermont; Tokyo: Tuttle, 1981.

A collection of 243 essays, ranging in length from a single sentence to a few pages, that were written between 1330 and 1332 by a perceptive Buddhist monk and former court official. This influential literary classic records Kenkō's scattered thoughts, observations, opinions, and reminiscences; his views about peculiarly Japanese aesthetics and appropriate behaviour; and his accounts of customs and ceremonials. Kenkō also sets forth his ideas about such matters as the ideal qualities of a friend; presents various anecdotes that he found amusing or instructive; and records several queries on factual matters. His obsession with the beauty of nature and the impermanence of worldly things permeates much of his book. Keene's brief introduction comments on Kenkō's life and on the structure and nature of his essays.

Kojiki.
See item no. 152.

The confessions of Lady Nijō.
See item no. 310.

The floating world in Japanese fiction.
See item no. 1036.

Shikitei Sanba and the comic tradition in Edo fiction.
See item no. 1038.

Tales of Ise: lyrical episodes from tenth-century Japan.
See item no. 1148.

Japanese literature in European languages: a bibliography.
See item no. 1588.

Guide to Japanese prose.
See item no. 1597.

Classical fiction and prose: history and criticism

1035 **Murasaki Shikibu: the tale of Genji.**
Richard Bowring.   Cambridge, England; New York: Cambridge University Press, 1988. 111p. bibliog. (Landmarks of World Literature).

This introductory guide seeks to 'summarise, encapsulate and create a foundation for a deeper understanding' of the most important work in Japanese literature, one that is often thought of as the world's first novel. A sketch of the cultural background of the *Genji* covering contemporary politics and religion, the use of language, and the literary expression of sexual relations is followed by a series of lengthy summaries of the entire work which outline the plot and discuss its major points. The guide then analyses the language and style of the *Genji* and critically compares the translations into English that have been produced by Arthur Waley and Edward G. Seidensticker (q.v.). Finally, Bowring considers the impact, influence, and reception of *The tale of Genji* over the course of nine centuries of cultural change, and provides a nine-page 'guide to further reading' that will particularly interest scholars and students of classical Japanese literature.

1036 **The floating world in Japanese fiction.**
Howard Hibbett. London; New York: Oxford University Press,
1959. 232p. Reprinted, New York: Grove Press, 1960; Freeport, New
York: Books for Libraries Press, 1970; Rutland, Vermont and Tokyo:
Tuttle, 1975.

A study and translation of popular tales written during the late seventeenth and early
eighteenth centuries which reflect the manners, customs, art, and lively culture of
Ōsaka, Kyōto, and Edo (Tokyo). Hibbett first introduces the world of the *ukiyo-zōshi*
('tales of the floating world') through a discussion of the Genroku era, its pleasure-
seeking atmosphere, its two leading writers Ihara Saikaku (1642-93) and Ejima Kiseki
(1666-1735), ukiyo-e prints and Genroku period fiction, and the special characteristics
of the tales known as *ukiyo-zōshi*. He then provides selections from Kiseki's *Characters
of worldly young women* (*Seken musume katagi*) and *Characters of worldly young men*
(*Seken musuko katagi*) as well as ten stories from Saikaku's *The woman who spent her
life in love* (*Kōshoku ichidai onna*). Twenty-four woodblock illustrations depict the
floating world through the eyes of contemporary artists.

1037 **Konjaku monogatari-shū.**
W. Michael Kelsey. Boston, Massachusetts: Twayne, 1982. 174p.
bibliog. (Twayne's World Authors Series: TWAS, 621).

An introductory study of the *Konjaku monogatari*, an encyclopaedic work of over one
thousand tales 'compiled primarily for the betterment – both spiritual and social – of its
audience'. Kelsey begins with a consideration of the anonymous compiler of this
literary collection (probably a late Heian period Buddhist monk) and of his times,
examines its relationship to the genre of *setsuwa* ('tales') literature in order to identify
its unique characteristics, and elucidates its contents, organisational structure, sources,
and language through discussions of selected tales. He then critically evaluates this
collection and compares it with other Japanese literary works in an effort to see how it
fits into the overall picture of Japanese literature. Translations of a good selection of
stories from the *Konjaku monogatari* may be found in Marian Ury's *Tales of times now
past: sixty-two stories from a medieval Japanese collection* (q.v.).

1038 **Shikitei Sanba and the comic tradition in Edo fiction.**
Robert W. Leutner. Cambridge, Massachusetts: Council on East
Asian Studies, Harvard University, and the Harvard-Yenching
Institute, distributed by the Harvard University Press, 1985. 232p.
bibliog. (Harvard-Yenching Institute Monograph Series, 25).

On the private life and literary career of Shikitei Sanba (1776-1822), a noted writer of
the humorous fiction known as *gesaku*. Leutner characterises Sanba as a representative
writer of his era as he describes his childhood, early career, and professional
accomplishments. He also examines two of his most popular works, *Ukiyoburo* ('The
Bathhouse of the Floating World') and *Ukiyodoko* ('The Barbershop of the Floating
World'), providing a fully annotated translation of two long excerpts from the former.
Beyond serving as a study of Sanba, this book is an introduction to the world of the
Tokugawa period author, to the values and social and economic forces which shaped
the fiction of that time, and to life among the townspeople of Edo (Tokyo) as depicted
in contemporary literature.

1039 **Ukifune: love in *The tale of Genji*.**
Edited with an introduction by Andrew Pekarik.   New York;
Guildford, Surrey: Columbia University Press, 1982. 278p.
(Companions to Asian Studies).

Ten essays by scholars of classical Japanese literature focus on chapter 51 ('Ukifune')
of *The tale of Genji*. It describes the pursuit of the heroine Ukifune by two powerful
suitors and her decision to drown herself in desperation. The essays in this pioneering
collection of Western literary scholarship cover a range of topics including the
operation of the lyrical mode in the *Genji monogatari*, the role of poetry in 'Ukifune',
the development of an iconographic tradition in illustrations for this tale, and some of
the principles governing the proper conduct of love affairs during the Heian period.

1040 **The bridge of dreams: a poetics of 'The tale of Genji'.**
Haruo Shirane.   Stanford, California: Stanford University Press,
1987. 276p. bibliog.

A diachronic and synchronic analysis of different aspects of the *Genji*, focusing on the
political, social, and religious concerns that persist over a number of sequences and
stages of this narrative. Each of these topics is 'analyzed in relationship to prior
discourse, to political, social, and religious history, as well as to preexistent literary
forms, topoi, metaphors, and conventions'. Shirane also shows how these particular
concerns are developed, subverted, or otherwise transformed as the chapters of the
Genji unfold, new characters are introduced, and the author (Murasaki Shikibu)
recasts earlier sequences and episodes of her narrative in a significantly different light.

The world of the shining prince: court life in ancient Japan.
See item no. 150.

Ueda Akinari.
See item no. 315.

A collection of tales from Uji: a study and translation of Uji shūi monogatari.
See item no. 1022.

A tale of eleventh-century Japan: *Hamamatsu Chūnagon monogatari*.
See item no. 1027.

Ugetsu monogatari: tales of moonlight and rain.
See item no. 1031.

Iconography of The tale of Genji: Genji monogatari ekotoba.
See item no. 1241.

Tanrokubon: rare books of seventeenth-century Japan.
See item no. 1481.

The Princeton companion to classical Japanese literature.
See item no. 1566.

Guide to The tale of Genji by Murasaki Shikibu.
See item no. 1604.

Modern fiction and prose: translations

1041 The box man.

Kōbō Abe, translated by E. Dale Saunders. New York: Knopf,
1974; Rutland, Vermont and Tokyo: Tuttle, 1975. 178p. Reprinted,
New York: Berkley, 1975; New York: Putnam Perigee, 1981.

A fantastic and chilling novel of the narrator in his new home: a large, empty box, with
a peephole cut into it but without any external markings, in which he wanders about
once it has been placed over his head. This work is a translation of *Hako otoko*.

1042 The ruined map.

Kōbō Abe, translated by E. Dale Saunders. New York: Knopf,
1969; Rutland, Vermont and Tokyo: Tuttle, 1970; London: Cape,
1972. 299p. Reprinted, New York: Putnam Perigee, 1980.

Translation of *Moetsukita chizu*, a psychological drama – narrated in the form of a
mystery story – which centres around the experiences and feelings of a private
detective who has been hired to investigate the disappearance of a man called Nemuro.
The detective's pursuit leads him deep into the underworld of Tokyo, and as his search
progresses, he finds his own identity and personality dissolving as 'his own map of his
once familiar world and self blur with that of the lost man'.

1043 The woman in the dunes.

Kōbō Abe, translated by E. Dale Saunders, drawings by Machi Abe.
New York: Knopf, 1964; London: Secker and Warburg, 1965;
Rutland, Vermont and Tokyo: Tuttle, 1965. 241p. (Unesco Collection
of Contemporary Works: Asian Series). Reprinted, London: Sphere,
1967; New York: Vintage Books, 1972; Oxford, England: Oxford
University Press, 1987.

A scientist collecting insects in a remote seaside area finds himself helplessly trapped
together with a solitary young woman at the bottom of a large sand-pit. The details of
his daily life, his relationship with the woman, and his eventual acceptance of his fate
are narrated as the two of them struggle, day after day, to dig out the sand which
continually threatens to inundate them. This novel – a translation of *Suna no onna* – is
widely considered to be Abe's most representative work.

1044 Kappa; a novel.

Ryūnosuke Akutagawa, translated by Geoffrey Bownas, introduction
by G. H. Healey. London: Peter Owen, 1970; Rutland, Vermont
and Tokyo: Tuttle, 1971. 141p.

A Japanese version of Jonathan Swift's *Gulliver's travels* in which Akutagawa satirizes
prewar Japanese intellectual, political, and social life as he recounts the experiences of
a mentally ill patient who has spent some time in the land of the *kappas* (amphibious
supernatural creatures who allegedly inhabit the rivers and lakes of Japan). First
available to English readers in a now-superseded translation by Seiichi Shiojiri (rev.
ed. Tokyo: Hokuseido Press, 1949, 136p. Reprinted, Westport, Connecticut:

Greenwood Press, 1970), this novel remains one of the author's most widely known literary works. Translation of *Kappa*.

1045 Rashomon and other stories.

Ryūnosuke Akutagawa, translated by Takashi Kojima, introduction by Howard Hibbett. Rutland, Vermont; Tokyo: Tuttle, 1954. 2nd ed. 102p. (Unesco Collection of Representative Works: Japanese Series). Reprinted, New York: Bantam Books, 1959; New York: Liveright, 1970.

The finest of several collections of the work of this early twentieth-century master storyteller. It contains six of Akutagawa's most representative short stories: 'In a Grove' (the story on which the film director Kurosawa Akira based his prize-winning movie *Rashōmon*), 'Rashomon', 'Yam Gruel', 'The Martyr', 'Kesa and Moritō', and 'The Dragon'. A second collection of Akutagawa's writings – *Japanese short stories*, translated by Takashi Kojima (New York: Liveright, 1961, 224p.) – contains his masterpiece 'Hell Screen' (the story of a talented artist who paints a large screen depicting the suffering of people who are condemned to hell) as well as nine of his other short stories. A third Akutagawa anthology (and the most extensive volume to appear so far) is *Exotic Japanese stories: the beautiful and the grotesque; 16 unusual tales and unforgettable images*, translated by Takashi Kojima and John McVittie (New York: Liveright, 1964, 431p.). It includes such works as 'The Robbers', 'The Dog', and 'Withered Fields'. The most recently published collection – *Hell screen, Cogwheels, A fool's life* (Hygiene, Colorado: Eridanos Press, 1987, 145p.) – reprints the translations of three important stories and contains a foreword by Jorge Luis Borges.

1046 A certain woman.

Takeo Arishima, translated with an introduction by Kenneth Strong. Tokyo: University of Tokyo Press, 1978. 382p. (Unesco Collection of Representative Works: Japanese Series).

A novel, first published in 1919 under the title *Aru onna*, that depicts the life of an independent woman named Yōko, who 'struggles against the ethical oppression of the male-dominated society of Japan' and feels free to violate the social conventions of marriage and chastity in order to pursue one love affair after another until she falls ill and dies. Arishima's remarkable psychological portrait of this female character calls to mind such European counterparts as Gustave Flaubert's *Madame Bovary*.

1047 The doctor's wife.

Sawako Ariyoshi, translated with an introduction by Wakako Hironaka, Ann Siller Kostant. Tokyo; New York: Kodansha International, 1978. 174p.

Based on the life of Hanaoka Seishū (1760-1835), the physician who developed a general anesthetic from herbal medicine for use in major surgery, Ariyoshi's novel depicts the sacrifices of the two women in Seishū's life – his strong-willed wife Kae and his assertive mother Otsugi – and their ongoing competition for his affections 'in an atmosphere of perpetual tension'. While a work of fiction, this translation of *Hanaoka Seishū no tsuma* vividly illuminates important aspects of the role of women in traditional Japanese society.

1048 **Rabbits, crabs, etc.: stories by Japanese women.**
Translated with an introduction by Phyllis Birnbaum. Honolulu,
Hawaii: University of Hawaii Press, 1982. 147p.

Translations of five short stories and one novella by widely recognised twentieth-
century authors: 'Rabbits ('Usagi'), by Kanai Mieko; 'Fuji', by Sono Ayako; 'A Bond
for Two Lifetimes – Gleanings' ('Nisei no en shūi'), by Enchi Fumiko; 'A Mother's
Love' ('Boshi jojō'), by Okamoto Kanoko; 'Crabs' ('Kani'), by Kōno Taeko; and
'Happiness' ('Kōfuku'), by Uno Chiyo.

1049 **No longer human.**
Osamu Dazai, translated with an introduction by Donald Keene.
London: Peter Owen, 1957. 154p. Reprinted, Norfolk, Connecticut:
New Directions, 1958; Rutland, Vermont and Tokyo: Tuttle, 1981.

Yozo, a man who views himself as being 'disqualified from life as a human being',
narrates his predicaments and his life of dissipation in three notebooks which are
discovered following his disappearance and possible death. This translation of *Ningen
Shikkaku* is an effective evocation of the kind of nihilism that has been found among
modern Japanese intellectuals.

1050 **The setting sun.**
Osamu Dazai, translated with an introduction by Donald Keene.
Norfolk, Connecticut: New Directions, 1956; London: Peter Owen,
1958. 175p. Reprinted, Rutland, Vermont and Tokyo: Tuttle, 1981.

Centring around the lives of three members of an aristocratic family who have moved
to the countryside from Tokyo in the aftermath of World War II, Dazai's novel
portrays the decline of Japan's traditional aristocracy and her transition from a feudal
to an industrial society. The Japanese title of this work is *Shayō*.

1051 **A late chrysanthemum: twenty-one stories from the Japanese.**
Translated by Lane Dunlop, with etchings by Ryōhei Tanaka. San
Francisco: North Point Press, 1986. 178p.

An anthology of short stories composed during the first half of the twentieth century by
seven well-known authors: Shiga Naoya, Ozaki Shirō, Kawabata Yasunari, Shimaki
Kensaku, Hayashi Fumiko, Dazai Osamu, and Abe Kōbō.

1052 **Masks.**
Fumiko Enchi, translated by Juliet Winters Carpenter. New York:
Knopf, 1983. 141p. Reprinted, New York: Vintage Books; Rutland,
Vermont and Tokyo: Tuttle; London: Arena, 1985.

A novel about seduction and infidelity in contemporary Japan and about the
destructive force of feminine jealousy and resentment. Enchi, one of Japan's most
important twentieth-century female novelists, narrates the story of a cultivated older
woman (Togano Mieko) who manipulates the relationship between her widowed
daughter-in-law and the two men in love with her. Translation of *Onna-men*.

1053 **The waiting years.**
Fumiko Enchi, translated by John Bester. Tokyo; Palo Alto,
California: Kodansha International, 1971. 203p.

Evocative of the human relationships and feelings within one upper-class family during
the Meiji period, Enchi's award-winning novel depicts the struggles of Shirakawa
Tomo, a long-suffering wife, as she stoically endures until just before her death the
abuse and philandering of her self-indulgent husband. Translation of *Onnazaka*.

1054 **The samurai.**
Shūsaku Endō, translated by Van C. Gessel. Tokyo; New York:
Kodansha International; London: Peter Owen, 1982. 272p. (Unesco
Collection of Representative Works: Japanese Series). Reprinted,
New York: Vintage Books, 1984; Harmondsworth, Middlesex:
Penguin Books, 1984; Toronto, Ontario: Lester & Orpen Dennys,
1984.

Set in the early seventeenth century, this highly acclaimed novel tells of four low-
ranking samurai, accompanied by a Franciscan missionary priest, who journey from
Japan to Rome via Mexico and Spain in an effort to establish trade relations with Spain
and her Pacific Ocean colonies and to facilitate the conversion of Japan to Catholicism.
Their mission concludes in failure, however, and both the priest and one of the
samurai suffer martyrdom following their return to Japan. Translation of *Samurai*.

1055 **Silence.**
Shūsaku Endō, translated with a preface by William Johnston.
Tokyo: Sophia University, in co-operation with Tuttle (Rutland,
Vermont and Tokyo), 1969. 306p. Reprinted, London: Owen, 1976;
London: Quartet Books, 1978; New York: Taplinger, 1979; Tokyo
and New York: Kodansha International, 1982; Harmondsworth,
Middlesex: Penguin, 1988.

A moving novel – *Chinmoku* in Japanese – about the conflict between East and West
as depicted in the tale of two early seventeenth-century Portuguese Jesuit priests in
Japan, Sebastian Rodrigues and Christavão Ferreira, at a time when both European
missionaries and their Japanese converts were being increasingly persecuted by the
Japanese government. Johnston's preface discusses the historical background of the
novel as well as the controversial reception accorded it following its publication.

1056 **The Shōwa anthology: modern Japanese short stories. Volume 1:
1929–1961. Volume 2: 1961–1984.**
Edited with an introduction by Van C. Gessel, Tomone Matsumoto.
Tokyo; New York: Kodansha International, 1985. 2 vols.

Translations of twenty-five stories – ranging from 'Kuchisuke's Valley' by Ibuse Masuji
(1929) through 'The Immortal' by Nakagami Kenji (1984) – written during the reign
(Shōwa period) of Emperor Hirohito. Eighteen of the stories are first-person narratives
(*watakushi shōsetsu*), but otherwise they vary considerably in their style, technique,
and subject-matter. While not all of the authors represented in this anthology are well
known in the West, they all are highly regarded in Japan. Each story is introduced by a
biographical sketch of its author.

1057 **Contemporary Japanese literature: an anthology of fiction, film, and other writing since 1945.**
Edited with an introduction by Howard Hibbett.   New York: Knopf, 1977. 468p. Reprinted, Rutland, Vermont; Tokyo: Tuttle, 1978.

A representative selection of literary writings from the late 1940s through the early 1970s. Included are stories written by fourteen noted authors, among them Yasuoka Shōtarō, Kojima Nobuo, Takeda Taijun, Mishima Yukio, Kawabata Yasunari, Abe Akira, Tanizaki Junichirō, Yoshiyuki Junnosuke, and Ōe Kenzaburō; the film scripts of *Ikiru* by Kurosawa Akira and *Tokyo Story* (*Tōkyō monogatari*) by Ozu Yasujirō; poetry by Kaneko Mitsuharu, Sekine Hiroshi, Tamura Ryūichi, Kanai Mieko, and Yoshioka Minoru; and the play *Friends* (*Tomodachi*) of Abe Kōbō. The anthology opens with a brief general introduction, and each translation is accompanied by a biographical sketch of its author.

1058 **Black rain.**
Masuji Ibuse, translated with a preface by John Bester.   Tokyo; Palo Alto, California: Kodansha International, 1969; London: Secker and Warburg, 1971. 300p. Reprinted, New York: Bantam Books, 1985.

Translation of *Kuroi ame*, a realistic, award-winning novel centred on the story of a young girl named Yasuko and her uncle, Shigematsu Shizuma, who were caught in the radioactive 'black rain' that fell after the atomic bombing of Hiroshima in August 1945. The material for Ibuse's skillfully narrated account was drawn from actual records and interviews with various atomic bomb survivors. A critical analysis of this novel and an examination of the pervasive themes, images and motifs that characterise Ibuse's writings may be found in John Whittier Treat's *Pools of water, pillars of fire: the literature of Ibuse Masuji* (Seattle, Washington; London: University of Washington Press, 1988, 294p.).

1059 **Lieutenant Lookeast, and other stories.**
Masuji Ibuse, translated by John Bester.   Tokyo; Palo Alto, California: Kodansha International; London: Secker and Warburg, 1971. 247p. Abridged edition, Tokyo; New York: Kodansha International, 1981. 134p.

Translations of ten short stories by the award-winning novelist, short-story writer, and essayist Ibuse Masuji (1898-): 'Plum Blossom by Night' ('Yofuke to ume no hana'), 'Lieutenant Lookeast' ('Yōhai taichō'), 'Pilgrim's Inn' ('Henrō yado'), 'Salamander' ('Sanshōuo'), 'Old Ushitora' ('Ushitora jiisan'), 'Carp' ('Koi'), 'Life at Mr. Tange's' ('Tange shi tei'), 'Yosaku the Settler' ('Kaikon mura no Yosaku'), 'Savan on the Roof' ('Yane no ue no sawan'), and 'Tajinko Village' ('Tajinko mura'). These stories range from literary and intellectual pieces with a strong element of fantasy to semi-autobiographical stories and a group of stories on historical themes. An abridged edition was reprinted in 1981 under the title *Salamander, and other stories*. It excludes Ibuse's last major prewar work, 'Tajinko Village'.

1060 **The counterfeiter, and other stories.**
Yasushi Inoue, translated with an introduction by Leon Picon.
Rutland, Vermont; Tokyo: Tuttle, 1965. 124p. (Unesco Collection of
Representative Works: Japanese Series). Reprinted, London: Peter
Owen, 1989.

Three stories by a distinguished postwar novelist and storywriter. 'The Counterfeiter'
('Aru gisakka no shōgai') relates the narrator's fascination with a man who produced
forgeries of the work of an artist whose biography he had been commissioned to write.
'Obasute' concerns an individual's obsession with legends about abandoning the elderly
on Mount Obasute and the way they influenced his interpretation of the actions of his
own family members. 'The Full Moon' ('Mangetsu'), the story of the rise and fall of a
company president, is told largely through the incidents at annual company parties.

1061 **The roof tile of Tempyō.**
Yasushi Inoue, translated with an introduction by James T. Araki.
Tokyo: University of Tokyo Press, 1975. 140p. (Unesco Collection of
Representative Works: Japanese Series). Reprinted, University of
Tokyo Press, 1981.

Translation of *Tempyō no iroka*, an historical novel that recounts the journey of four
Japanese Buddhist monks to China during the Nara period. They are in search of
religious texts and seek a learned Chinese Buddhist priest to interpret their teachings.
Also set in premodern China is a second novel of Inoue entitled *Tun-huang* (Japanese:
Tonkō), translated with an introduction by Jean Oda Moy (Tokyo; New York:
Kodansha International, 1978, 201p.).

1062 **Into a black sun.**
Takeshi Kaikō, translated by Cecilia Segawa Seigle.   Tokyo; New
York: Kodansha International, 1980. 214p.

Translation of *Kagayakeru yami*, a sensitively rendered account of a Japanese
reporter's first-hand experiences of the atrocities of war, presented in the form of a
novel. Kaikō relates the points of view of American GIs, Vietnamese civilians, and
other individuals who were caught up in the Vietnam conflict during the mid-1960s,
while evoking for the reader some of the sights, sounds, and smells of that era.

1063 **Beauty and sadness.**
Yasunari Kawabata, translated by Howard Hibbett.   New York:
Knopf, 1975; London: Secker & Warburg, 1975; Rutland, Vermont
and Tokyo, 1976. 206p. Reprinted, New York: Berkley, 1976;
Harmondsworth, Middlesex, 1979; New York: Putnam Perigee, 1981.

This translation of *Utsukushisa to kanashimi to* tells the story of a successful, middle-
aged novelist (Oki Toshio), his tragic love affair with a young girl named Otoko, and
the desire of her lover (Keiko) to avenge the humiliating behaviour that Otoko had
been subjected to on Oki's account.

1064 **The master of *go*.**
Yasunari Kawabata, translated with an introduction by Edward G.
Seidensticker.   New York: Knopf, 1972; London: Secker and
Warburg, 1973; Rutland, Vermont and Tokyo: Tuttle, 1973. 188p.
Reprinted, New York: Berkley, 1974; Harmondsworth, Middlesex:
Penguin, 1976; New York: Putnam Perigee, 1981.

Narrative of a single game of go (a Japanese game played with 'stones' on a square
board), played over a six-month period, between the hitherto invincible master and his
younger, more modern challenger. Kawabata regarded this novel of complex human
emotions and of the contest between traditional ways and the forces of change as his
finest work. Translation of *Meijin*.

1065 **Snow country.**
Yasunari Kawabata, translated with an introduction by Edward G.
Seidensticker.   New York: Knopf, 1956. 175p. London: Secker and
Warburg, 1957. 188p. (Unesco Collection of Contemporary Works:
Japanese Series). Reprinted, Rutland, Vermont and Tokyo: Tuttle,
1957; New York: Berkley, 1960; New York: Putnam Perigee, 1981.

The story of the love affair, doomed from the outset, between a wealthy dilettante
from Tokyo (Shimamura) and a young country geisha (Komako). Set at a hot-spring
mountain resort in the 'snow country' of Japan (an area along the western coast of the
island of Honshū), *Yukiguni* is one of the two novels for which Kawabata was awarded
the Nobel Prize for Literature in 1968.

1066 **The sound of the mountain.**
Yasunari Kawabata, translated by Edward G. Seidensticker.   New
York: Knopf; London: Peter Owen; Rutland, Vermont and Tokyo:
Tuttle, 1970. 276p. Reprinted, Harmondsworth, Middlesex: Penguin,
1974; New York: Putnam Perigee, 1981.

This novel – entitled *Yama no oto* in Japanese – describes the anxieties and desires of
an elderly man named Shingo who lives with his family in a suburb of Tokyo. The
protagonist seeks to cope with the increasing tensions in his relations with his wife, son
and daughter, with the death of close friends, and with the affection that he feels for
his own daughter-in-law. The form of this book, combining contemporary psychology
and traditional haiku-like writing technique, makes this work one of the most
innovative of Kawabata's novels.

1067 **Thousand cranes.**
Yasunari Kawabata, translated by Edward G. Seidensticker.   New
York: Knopf; London: Secker and Warburg, 1959; Rutland, Vermont
and Tokyo: Tuttle, 1960. 147p. Reprinted, New York: Berkley, 1964;
New York: Putnam Perigee, 1981.

Senbazuru is one of the two short novels for which Kawabata was awarded the 1968
Nobel Prize for Literature. Within the setting of the tea ceremony, a stylised way of
preparing and serving tea from water heated over a charcoal hearth, a young man
named Kikuji becomes involved with the two mistresses of his late father and with the
daughter of one of them.

1068 **"The factory ship" and "The absentee landlord".**
Takiji Kobayashi, translated with an introduction by Frank
Motofuji.   Seattle, Washington: University of Washington Press;
Tokyo: University of Tokyo Press, 1973. 184p. (Unesco Collection of
Representative Works: Japanese Series).

These translations of 'Kani kōsen' and 'Fuzai jinushi' respectively are two fictionalised
accounts of political struggles which Kobayashi (1903-33), the foremost writer of the
proletarian school in Japan, witnessed during the mid-1920s. In 'The Factory Ship',
Kobayashi narrates the plight of fishermen and factory-hands working on the *Hakkō
Maru*, a floating crab-cannery off the coast of Kamchatka. In 'The Absentee
Landlord', he sympathetically portrays the lives of impoverished and exploited tenant
farmers on the northern island of Hokkaidō. Both novellas dramatise and publicise the
oppression of the working class by rampant Japanese capitalism before World War II.

1069 **Pagoda, skull and samurai: three stories.**
Rohan Kōda, translated with an introduction and notes by Chieko Irie
Mulhern.   Ithaca, New York: China–Japan Program, Cornell
University, 1982. 213p. (Cornell University East Asia Papers, 26).
Reprinted, Rutland, Vermont; Tokyo: Tuttle, 1985. 280p.

Translations of 'Gojū no tō', ('The Five-Storied Pagoda'), in which a divinely inspired
carpenter-architect constructs a Buddhist pagoda in defiance of Tokugawa period codes
of behaviour; 'Tai dokuro' ('Encounter with a Skull'), the story of the chance
encounter between a traveller and the spirit of a beautiful dead woman; and 'Higetoku'
('The Bearded Samurai'), a historical narrative which portrays the Battle of Nagashino
(1575) primarily as a conflict of personalities and moral principles and in which the
main fictional characters display differing attitudes toward loyalty and death.
Mulhern's introduction outlines Rohan's background and literary philosophy. More
biographical information about this writer, a chronological discussion of his major
works, and an exploration of the complex idealism underlying these and others of his
stories can be found in Mulhern's *Kōda Rohan* (Boston, Massachusetts: Twayne, 1977,
178p. [Twayne's World Authors Series, TWAS 432, Japan]).

1070 **River mist, and other stories.**
Doppo Kunikida, translated with an introduction by David G.
Chibbett.   Tokyo; New York: Kodansha International, 1983;
Tenterden, Kent: Paul Norbury, 1983. 151p. (Unesco Collection of
Representative Works: Japanese Series).

Twelve of the most widely admired short stories of Kunikida Doppo (1861-1908):
'River Mist' ('Kawagiri'), 'Old Gen' ('Gen oji'), 'The Deer Hunt' ('Shikagari'), 'Those
Unforgettable People' ('Wasureenu hitobito'), 'Third Party' ('Daisansha'), 'Woman
Trouble' ('Jonan'), 'Phantoms' ('Maboroshi'), 'Musashino' ('Musashino'), 'The Self-
Made Man' ('Hibon naru bonjin'), 'Letter from Yugahara' ('Yugahara yori'), 'Bird of
Spring' ('Haru no tori'), and 'Meat and Potatoes' ('Gyūniku to bareishō'). Together
with these are translations of three prose poems: 'The Bonfire' ('Tabiki'), 'Stars'
('Hoshi'), and 'Poetic Images' ('Shisō'). Chibbett's introduction outlines Doppo's life
and briefly analyses his fiction and some of the thematic elements in his writings.

1071 **Stories by contemporary Japanese women writers.**
Translated and edited with an introduction by Noriko Mizuta Lippit,
Kyoko Iriye Selden. Armonk, New York; London: M. E. Sharpe,
1982. 221p.

An anthology of twelve short stories by Enchi Fumiko, Hayashi Fumiko, Hayashi
Kyōko, Hirabayashi Taiko, Kōno Taeko, Miyamoto Yuriko, Nogami Yaeko, Ohba
Minako, Sata Ineko, Takahashi Takako, Tomioka Taeko, and Uno Chiyo that were
written between 1938 and 1977. They were selected for inclusion in order to indicate
the range and degree of their authors' participation in twentieth-century Japanese life
as well as the intellectual and aesthetic development of the era. The stories also
illustrate the 'consciousness and views characteristic of women writers'. A brief
introduction summarises the role of women as authors in Japanese literary history.

1072 **After the banquet.**
Yukio Mishima, translated by Donald Keene. New York: Knopf;
London: Secker and Warburg; Rutland, Vermont and Tokyo: Tuttle,
1963. 270p. Reprinted, New York: Berkley, 1971; New York: Putnam
Perigee, 1980.

This translation of *Utage no ato* presents a witty account of the marriage of an ageing
liberal politician named Noguchi with the attractive proprietress of a fashionable
Tokyo restaurant (Kazu), their joint efforts in a political campaign in which Noguchi
runs unsuccessfully for election to the governorship of Tokyo, and the subsequent
disintegration of their relationship.

1073 **Confessions of a mask.**
Yukio Mishima, translated by Meredith Weatherby. New York:
New Directions, 1958. 254p. Reprinted, London: Peter Owen, 1960;
New York: New Directions, 1968; Rutland, Vermont and Tokyo:
Tuttle, 1970; London: Panther, 1972.

A novel set during the closing years of World War II and its immediate aftermath in
which the youthful protagonist describes his sadistic homosexual yearnings and
loneliness in a straightforward manner, and comes to hide his true identity behind a
mask of propriety. The publication of this novel – as *Kamen no kokuhaku* in Japanese
– is said to have firmly established Mishima's reputation as a leading young writer.

1074 **Death in midsummer, and other stories.**
Yukio Mishima, translated by Donald Keene, Ivan Morris, Geoffrey
Sargent, Edward Seidensticker. New York: New Directions, 1966.
181p.; London: Secker and Warburg, 1967. 224p. Reprinted,
Harmondsworth, Middlesex: Penguin, 1971; Rutland, Vermont and
Tokyo: Tuttle, 1987.

A collection of nine of Mishima's finest short stories: 'Death in Midsummer' ('Manatsu
no shi'), 'Three Million Yen' ('Hyakuman'en senbei'), 'Thermos Bottles' ('Mahōbin'),
'The Priest of Shiga Temple and His Love' ('Shigadera shōnin no koi'), 'The Seven
Bridges' ('Hashi zukushi'), 'Patriotism' ('Yūkoku'), 'Onnagata', 'The Pearl' ('Shinju'),
and 'Swaddling Clothes' ('Shinbungami'). Also included is one of Mishima's modern
noh plays, *Dōjōji*. The story entitled 'Patriotism' formed the basis for a celebrated

short film starring Mishima himself and is a powerful statement of the author's view of the relationship between love and death.

1075 **Forbidden colors.**
Yukio Mishima, translated by Alfred H. Marks. New York: Knopf; London: Secker and Warburg, 1968. Rutland, Vermont and Tokyo: Tuttle, 1969. 403p. Reprinted, Harmondsworth, Middlesex: Penguin, 1976; New York: Putnam Perigee, 1980.

One of Mishima's masterpieces, *Kinjiki* is the moving story of Minami Yuichi, a handsome young married man with bisexual inclinations, and of Hinoki Shunsuke, an ageing heterosexual writer who uses Yuichi to entrap women on his behalf.

1076 **The sailor who fell from grace with the sea.**
Yukio Mishima, translated by John Nathan. New York: Knopf, 1965. 181p.; London: Secker and Warburg, 1966. 150p. Reprinted, Rutland, Vermont and Tokyo: Tuttle, 1967; New York: Berkley, 1971; Harmondsworth, Middlesex: Penguin, 1976; New York: Putnam Perigee, 1980.

This translation of *Gogo no eikō* narrates the love affair between the widowed mother of a thirteen-year-old boy and a ship's officer named Ryuji, and its shattering effect on her adolescent son, whose initial admiration for Ryuji turns into disdain and a desire to kill and dissect him.

1077 **The sea of fertility: a cycle of four novels.**
Volume 1: Spring snow. Volume 2: Runaway horses. Volume 3: The temple of dawn. Volume 4: The decay of the angel.
Yukio Mishima, translated by Michael Gallagher [volumes 1–2], E. Dale Saunders, Cecilia Segawa Seigle [volume 3], Edward G. Seidensticker [volume 4]. New York: Knopf; London: Secker and Warburg; Rutland, Vermont and Tokyo: Tuttle, 1972-74. 4 vols. (Unesco Collection of Representative Works: Japanese Series).

An epic saga of the Japanese experience in the twentieth century, containing complex plots and themes that are set in the years between 1912-13 and the late 1960s. The activities and experiences of Honda Shigekuni – as a young law student, a respected judge, a philosopher-voyeur, and an aged and wealthy man – provide the thread of continuity through these four novels, originally entitled *Haru no yuki*, *Homma*, *Akatsuki no tera*, and *Tennin gosui*.

1078 **The sound of waves.**
Yukio Mishima, translated by Meredith Weatherby. New York: Knopf; Rutland, Vermont and Tokyo: Tuttle, 1956; London: Secker and Warburg, 1957. 182p. (Unesco Collection of Representative Works: Japanese Series). Reprinted, New York: Berkley, 1961; New York: Putnam Perigee, 1980.

Shiosai, a story of first love inspired by the tale of Daphnis and Chloë, is set in a

447

fishing village on a remote island in the Gulf of Ise. Mishima lyrically portrays the relationship that develops between Shinji, an eighteen-year-old fisherman, and Hatsue, the daughter of a prosperous villager who dives for abalone, as well as the obstacles which they eventually overcome in their efforts to become engaged.

1079 **Sun and steel.**
Yukio Mishima, translated by John Bester. Tokyo; Palo Alto, California: Kodansha International; New York: Grove Press, 1970; London: Secker and Warburg, 1971. 104p.

Written towards the end of his life, *Taiyō to tetsu* is an autobiographical, literary essay in which Mishima reflects philosophically on his physical transformation – with the aid of 'sun and steel' (sunbathing and weight-lifting) – and accounts for his 'search for identity and self-integration' as well as for his quest to become a tragic hero.

1080 **The temple of the golden pavilion.**
Yukio Mishima, translated by Ivan Morris, introduction by Nancy Wilson Ross. New York: Knopf; London: Secker and Warburg; Rutland, Vermont and Tokyo: Tuttle, 1959. 262p. (Unesco Collection of Representative Works: Japanese Series). Reprinted, New York: Berkley, 1971; New York: Putnam Perigee, 1980; Harmondsworth, Middlesex: Penguin, 1987.

Translation of *Kinkakuji*, a novel which probes deeply into the life of a young Zen Buddhist priest who is so obsessed by the beauty of the temple in which he serves as an acolyte and by his own alienation from the world that he destroys himself and all that he loves by setting that temple on fire. This masterpiece is based on an incident in 1950 when an unhappy and unbalanced Zen acolyte actually burned down the 500-year-old Kinkakuji ('Golden Pavilion') Temple in Kyōto.

1081 **The historical literature of Mori Ōgai. Volume 1: The incident at Sakai and other stories. Volume 2: Saiki kōi and other stories.**
Ōgai Mori, edited with introductions by David Dilworth, J. Thomas Rimer, translated by the editors and others. Honolulu, Hawaii: University Press of Hawaii, 1977. 2 vols. (Unesco Collection of Representative Works: Japanese Series).

Eighteen stories on historical themes set principally in the Tokugawa period. Written between 1912 and 1918, they afforded Ōgai with the means for dealing artistically with a number of contemporary moral and philosophical problems. The editors' introductory essays discuss both the nature and the significance of this literature.

1082 **The wild geese.**
Ōgai Mori, translated by Kingo Ochiai, Sanford Goldstein. Rutland, Vermont; Tokyo: Tuttle, 1959. 119p. (Library of Japanese Literature, 1).

A poignant love story, set in Tokyo during the 1880s, of a beautiful young girl named Otama who is forced by poverty to become the mistress of a moneylender, and of a lonely medical student (Okada) who passes by her home on his daily walks, develops a liking for her, but fails to get to know her before leaving for Germany in pursuit of his medical studies. This novel – entitled *Gan* in Japanese – has become the most popular of Ōgai's longer works.

1083 Modern Japanese stories: an anthology.

Edited with an introduction by Ivan Morris, translated by Edward Seidensticker, George Saitō, Geoffrey Sargent, Ivan Morris. London: Eyre and Spottiswoode, 1961. 527p.; Rutland, Vermont and Tokyo: Tuttle, 1962. 512p. bibliog. (Unesco Collection of Representative Works: Japanese Series).

An excellent collection of representative short stories by twenty-five established writers. These stories reflect several different styles of writing and illustrate the directions which Japanese literature has taken during the twentieth century. The editor's introductory essay surveys the course of modern Japanese literature. Notes about the individual authors provide both biographical information and critical assessments of their works. The stories selected for this anthology range from 'Under Reconstruction' by the late nineteenth-century writer Mori Ōgai to 'The Priest of Shiga Temple and His Love' by the postwar author Mishima Yukio, and include such other writings as 'The Victim' (Tanizaki Junichirō), 'An Autumn Mountain' (Akutagawa Ryūnosuke), 'The Moon on the Water' (Kawabata Yasunari), 'Tokyo' (Hayashi Fumiko), and 'A Visitor' (Dazai Osamu).

1084 Botchan.

Sōseki Natsume, translated by Alan Turney. Tokyo; Palo Alto, California: Kodansha International, 1972. 173p. London: Peter Owen, 1973. 176p.

Translation of *Botchan*, a warm and humorous narrative of the misadventures of a nonconformist. Botchan, the younger son of a middle-class Tokyo family, secures employment as a mathematics teacher in a middle school in Shikoku, where he constantly encounters difficulties in his relations with his landlord, his fellow teachers, and his students.

1085 I am a cat.

Sōseki Natsume, translated by Aiko Itō, Graeme Wilson. Rutland, Vermont; Tokyo: Tuttle, 1972-85. 3 vols.

Wagahai wa neko de aru is one of the novels for which Sōseki is most remembered. First published in 1905-7, it is a loosely organised, humorous narrative of Japanese life around the turn of the century as viewed through the eyes of an anonymous narrator, a cat belonging to the family of an English teacher named Kushami. The cat tells about his daily life in the home of that schoolteacher, about several of Kushami's friends and neighbours, and about many of the long conversations which he happens to overhear. This engaging novel is also available in a translation by Katsue Shibata and Motonari Kai published under the same title (Tokyo: Kenkyusha, 1961; London: Peter Owen, 1971, 431p.).

Literature. Modern fiction and prose: translations

1086 **Kokoro.**
Sōseki Natsume, translated with a foreword by Edwin McClellan.
Chicago: Henry Regnery, 1957. 248p. (Unesco Collection of
Representative Works: Japanese Series). Reprinted, London: Peter
Owen; Rutland, Vermont and Tokyo: Tuttle, 1969; London: Arena,
1984; Chicago: Regnery Gateway, 1985.

A story within a story, told throughout in the first person, of the experiences of a
young and admiring student (the narrator) who seeks out the friendship of an older,
remote man whom he calls Sensei ('teacher'), and of Sensei's own story (recounted in a
long suicide note addresssed to the narrator) of his disillusionment with humanity and
the failure of his own relationships with a young man whom he simply calls K as well as
with the daughter of his landlady (Ojōsan). Written in 1914, at the peak of Sōseki's
career, this novel focuses on the theme of man's loneliness in the modern world.
Translation of *Kokoro* ('the heart of things').

1087 **Sanshiro: a novel.**
Sōseki Natsume, translated with a critical essay by Jay Rubin.
Tokyo: University of Tokyo Press; Seattle, Washington: University of
Washington Press, 1977. 248p. Reprinted, New York: Putnam, 1982.

Written in 1908, the novel *Sanshirō* depicts the experiences of a twenty-three-year-old
student from the quiet countryside who arrives in Tokyo for the first time in his life to
encounter both the 'real world' of the metropolis and the impersonal environment of
Tokyo Imperial University. A critical essay on *Sanshirō* and its place among Sōseki's
writings provides a framework for better understanding the work.

1088 **Fire from the ashes: short stories about Hiroshima and Nagasaki.**
Edited with an introduction by Kenzaburō Ōe. London: Readers
International; New York: Grove Press, 1985. 204p.

Translations of nine short stories that are regarded not only as literary expressions of
what happened at Hiroshima and Nagasaki but also as 'a means for stirring our
imaginative powers to consider the fundamental conditions of human existence'. The
stories are entitled 'The Crazy Iris' ('Kakitsubata'), by Ibuse Masuji; 'Summer Flower'
('Natsu no hana') and 'The Land of Heart's Desire' ('Shingan no kuni'), by Hara
Tamiki; 'Human Ashes' ('Ningen no hai'), by Oda Katsuzō; 'Fireflies' ('Hotaru'), by
Ōta Yōko; 'The Colorless Paintings' ('Iro no nai e'), by Sata Ineko; 'The Empty Can'
('Akikan'), by Hayashi Kyōko; 'The House of Hands' ('Te no ie'), by Inoue
Mitsuharu; and 'The Rite' ('Gishiki'), by Takenishi Hiroko. In his introduction, Ōe
(one of Japan's leading contemporary writers) comments on each of the authors
represented in this anthology and on Japanese A-bomb literature in general. The work
was published in the United States under the title *The crazy iris and other stories of the
atomic aftermath*.

1089 **A personal matter.**
Kenzaburō Ōe, translated by John Nathan. New York: Grove Press,
1968; London: Weidenfeld and Nicolson, 1969. 214p. Reprinted,
Rutland, Vermont and Tokyo: Tuttle, 1969.

Translation of *Kojinteki na taiken*, an existentialist novel that chronicles the reactions –
particularly anguish and despair – of an alienated young man named Bird to the birth
of his abnormally formed child.

450

1090 **The silent cry.**
Kenzaburō Ōe, translated with an introduction by John Bester.
Tokyo; New York: Kodansha International, 1974. 274p. Reprinted,
London: Serpent's Tail, 1988.

Man'en gannen no futtōbōro narrates the story of the dramatic and tragic conflict that occurs between two brothers, Mitsusaburō and Takashi, following their return to the village of their birth. This novel is considered to be Ōe's most ambitious work to date.

1091 **Fires on the plain.**
Shōhei Ōoka, translated by Ivan Morris. New York: Knopf, 1957.
246p. London: Secker and Warburg, 1957. 212p. Reprinted, Rutland,
Vermont and Tokyo: Tuttle, 1967; Harmondsworth, Middlesex:
Penguin Books, 1969; London: Corgi, 1975; Westport, Connecticut:
Greenwood Press, 1978.

This horrifying novel, a translation of *Nobi*, is about war and the physical and mental anguish which war occasions. Tamura, a private in the Imperial Japanese Army stationed in the Philippines during World War II, becomes separated from his unit, wanders about the countryside in his search for food and safety, and finds himself resorting to cannibalism in order to survive.

1092 **Homecoming.**
Jirō Osaragi, translated by Brewster Horwitz, introduction by Harold
Strauss. New York: Knopf, 1954; London: Secker and Warburg,
1955; Rutland, Vermont and Tokyo: Tuttle, 1955. 303p. (Unesco
Collection of Representative Works: Japanese Series). Reprinted,
Westport, Connecticut: Greenwood Press, 1977.

Moriya Kyōgo, an expatriate who was betrayed by an avaricious woman named Takano Saeko and imprisoned in Singapore during World War II, returns to a devastated Japan out of an overwhelming desire to see what has happened to his homeland. He establishes contact with his daughter Tomoko and once again encounters Saeko, but sensitive to the difficulties that his homecoming would create for his former wife and her family, he resolves (in a mood of self-sacrifice) to resume his wanderings abroad. Translation of *Kikyō*.

1093 **A dark night's passing.**
Naoya Shiga, translated by Edwin McClellan. Tokyo; New York:
Kodansha International, 1976. 408p. (Unesco Collection of
Representative Works: Japanese Series).

Anya kōro, 'an intensely private and self-centered novel', was written between 1921 and 1937 and established Shiga Naoya (1883-1971) as one of Japan's leading prose writers. It movingly portrays the experiences and feelings of the protagonist (Kensaku) as he grows up, passes through a series of emotional incidents and crises that expose his self-doubts and his lack of confidence, discovers the true circumstances of his birth, marries, encounters further difficulties (particularly after his wife is seduced by his best friend), and finally – in the course of a pilgrimage to Mount Daisen – comes to terms with both nature and human nature.

1094 **Before the dawn.**
Tōson Shimazaki, translated with an introduction by William E.
Naff. Honolulu, Hawaii: University of Hawaii Press, 1987. 798p.
3 maps. bibliog.

A classic historical novel that focuses on the life of the Kiso Road (the great highway which runs through the Kiso District of central Japan), on the people of the village of Magome which one of Tōson's forefathers had established, and on the life of the idealistic Aoyama Hanzō (a recreation of Tōson's own father) during the three decades following the arrival, in 1853, of Commodore Matthew E. Perry's fleet off the coast of Japan. A mixture of fiction and history, *Before the dawn* – *Yoakemae* in Japanese – reconstructs the world of Tōson's immediate ancestors and depicts some of the historical forces, including Westernisation, that resulted in a new, non-feudalistic order. The novel also sympathetically reveals the human dimension of an era that had vanished by Tōson's own lifetime.

1095 **The broken commandment.**
Tōson Shimazaki, translated with an introduction by Kenneth
Strong. Tokyo: University of Tokyo Press, 1974. 249p. (Unesco
Collection of Representative Books: Japanese Series) (Japan
Foundation Translation Series).

Published in 1906, the novel *Hakai* describes the efforts of a young schoolteacher to conceal his origins as a member of the outcaste class known as *eta* (or *burakumin*), until his secret is finally disclosed and he is forced to resign from his teaching position. Tōson's work is, in effect, a protest against the discrimination and prejudice that existed within Japanese society during the author's lifetime.

1096 **The family.**
Tōson Shimazaki, translated with an introduction by Cecilia Segawa
Seigle. Tokyo: University of Tokyo Press, 1976. 311p. (Unesco
Collection of Representative Works: Japanese Series).

One of Japan's greatest naturalist authors chronicles the degeneration and financial disintegration of the Koizumi and Hashimoto families over the twelve-year period 1898-1910. Much of the novel is in reality an autobiographical account of Tōson's own life and the lives of many of his immediate relatives – the two families are those of Tōson and of his married elder sister Takase Sonoko – and it offers an excellent literary depiction of the structure, character, and obligations of traditional Japanese family life. Translation of *Ie*.

1097 **Harp of Burma.**
Michio Takeyama, translated by Howard Hibbett. Rutland,
Vermont; Tokyo: Tuttle, 1966. 132p. (Unesco Collection of
Contemporary Works) (Library of Japanese Literature).

Hibbett's translation of *Biruma no tategoto* sympathetically portrays a group of young Japanese soldiers in Burma during and after the closing days of World War II, and the eventual decision of one of them – Mizushima, a talented harp player – to remain there as a Buddhist monk in order to bury the scattered bones of his dead countrymen.

1098   **This kind of woman: ten stories by Japanese women writers, 1960–1976.**
Edited with an introduction by Yukiko Tanaka, Elizabeth Hanson, translated by Mona Nagai and others.   Stanford, California: Stanford University Press, 1982. 287p. Reprinted, New York: Putnam Perigee, 1984.

This anthology of ten outstanding works of fiction, each by a different writer, constitutes a representative selection of stories not only by women but also about women. The stories portray the experiences, thoughts, and feelings of single mothers, housewives in conventional marriages, and other types of women who are living in a changing world. Initially published between 1960 and 1976, they are entitled 'Partei' (by Kurahashi Yumiko), 'Lingering Affection' (Setouchi Harumi), 'The Last Time' (Kōno Taeko), 'Boxcar of Chrysanthemums' (Enchi Fumiko), 'The Three Crabs' (Ōba Minako), 'Luminous Watch' (Tsumura Setsuko), 'Family in Hell' (Tomioka Taeko), 'The Man Who Cut the Grass' (Yamamoto Michiko), 'Doll Love' (Takahashi Takako), and 'A Bed of Grass' (Tsushima Yūko).

1099   **Diary of a mad old man.**
Junichirō Tanizaki, translated by Howard Hibbett.   New York: Knopf, 1965. 177p. London: Secker and Warburg, 1966. 203p. (Unesco Collection of Representative Works: Japanese Series). Reprinted, Rutland, Vermont and Tokyo: Tuttle, 1967; New York: Berkley, 1971; New York: Putnam Perigee, 1981; Oxford, England and New York: Oxford University Press, 1988.

Written in the form of a diary, this translation of *Fūten rōjin no nikki* vividly depicts the development of an amorous relationship between a refined, seventy-seven-year-old man and his beautiful, cosmopolitan daughter-in-law with whom he becomes infatuated at a time when he experiences increasingly poor health.

1100   **The key.**
Junichirō Tanizaki, translated by Howard Hibbett.   New York: Knopf; London: Secker and Warburg, 1961. 183p. Rutland, Vermont and Tokyo: Tuttle, 1962. 176p. Reprinted, New York: Berkley, 1971; New York: Putnam Perigee, 1981; London: Flamingo, 1985.

The entries in two diaries, kept by a middle-aged man and his wife Ikuko, are interwoven in this account of their personal relationship and their sexual lives. Ikuko's account concludes shortly after her husband's fatal heart attack as a consequence of his uninhibited passion. Translation of *Kagi*.

1101 **The Makioka sisters.**
Junichirō Tanizaki, translated by Edward G. Seidensticker. New York: Knopf, 1957; London: Secker and Warburg; Rutland, Vermont and Tokyo: Tuttle, 1958. 530p. (Unesco Collection of Representative Works: Japanese Series). Reprinted, New York: Grosset & Dunlap, 1966; New York: Berkley, 1975; London: Pan Books in association with Secker and Warburg, 1983.

Translation of *Sasameyuki*, a family chronicle of four sisters living near Ōsaka during the 1930s. Generally recognised as Tanizaki's masterpiece, this long novel focuses on the relationships of these sisters as they seek in particular to find a suitable husband for one of them, Yukiko, through a series of *miai* (arranged meetings with a view to marriage).

1102 **The secret history of the lord of Musashi, and Arrowroot.**
Junichirō Tanizaki, translated with an introduction by Anthony H. Chambers. New York: Knopf, 1982; London: Secker and Warburg, 1983. 199p. Reprinted, New York: Putnam Perigee, 1983; Rutland, Vermont and Tokyo: Tuttle, 1984.

Translations of two very different novellas. *The secret history* (*Bushūkō no hiwa*), a pseudo-historic reconstruction of past events based on 'secret documents', is a comic novel about the bizarre private life of a renowned sixteenth-century warrior. *Arrowroot* (*Yoshino kuzu*), a novel in the form of a memoir-essay, deals with three interrelated journeys: one by foot into the mountainous interior along the Yoshino River, another back into the historical past of the Yoshino region of Yamato, and a search for information about a 'long-dead mother' who was a native of this myth-filled region. *Naomi*, Chambers' most recent translation of a Tanizaki novel (New York: Knopf, 1985; London: Secker and Warburg, 1986, 237p.), satirically portrays the love affair between a timid Japanese gentleman and a young Tokyo waitress typical of the 1920s flapper era.

1103 **Seven Japanese tales.**
Junichirō Tanizaki, translated with an introduction by Howard Hibbett. New York: Knopf, 1963. 298p. Reprinted, New York: Berkley, 1965; Rutland, Vermont and Tokyo: Tuttle, 1967; New York: Putnam Perigee, 1981.

An anthology of seven novellas or short stories about sexual and psychological obsessions which Tanizaki wrote during the course of his long and distinguished literary career: 'A Portrait of Shunkin' ('Shunkinsho', 1933); 'Terror' ('Kyōfu', 1913); 'The Bridge of Dreams' ('Yume no ukihashi', 1959); 'The Tattooer' ('Shisei', 1910); 'The Thief' ('Watakushi', 1921); 'Aguri' ('Aoi hana', 1922); and 'A Blind Man's Tale' (Mōmoku monogatari', 1931).

1104 **Some prefer nettles.**
Junichirō Tanizaki, translated with an introduction by Edward G.
Seidensticker. New York: Knopf, 1955; London: Secker and
Warburg; Rutland, Vermont and Tokyo: Tuttle, 1956. 202p. (Library
of Japanese Literature). Reprinted, New York: Berkley, 1965;
Harmondsworth, Middlesex: Penguin, 1970; New York: Putnam
Perigee, 1981.

Story of the impending dissolution of the marriage of a modern bourgeois, Kaname,
and his wife Misako, and of Kaname's growing attachment to the traditional Japanese
arts, particularly the puppet theatre (bunraku) of Ōsaka. The novel also deals
thematically with the clash between the new and the old, between imported Western
influences and classical tradition, in Japan during the 1920s. Translation of *Tade kuu
mushi*.

1105 **The quilt, and other stories by Tayama Katai.**
Katai Tayama, translated with an introduction by Kenneth G.
Henshall. Tokyo: University of Tokyo Press, 1981. 204p. (Unesco
Collection of Representative Works: Japanese Series).

Tayama Katai (1872-1930), the author of more than twenty novels and hundreds of
novelettes, short stories, and critical articles, was the chief representative of the
naturalist movement in Japan. After introducing his life, writings, European
influences, and views of nature and society, Henshall presents translations of Katai's
best-known work – 'Futon' ('The Quilt') – and seven other stories which illustrate his
views of nature as well as his literary technique. They are entitled 'The End of Jūemon'
('Jūemon no saigo'), 'One Soldier' ('Ippeisotsu'), 'The Girl Watcher' ('Shōjobyō'),
'The Railway Track' ('Senro'), 'The Photograph' ('Shashin'), 'The Sound of Wheels'
('Kuruma no oto'), and 'One Cold Morning' ('Aru samui asa'). Henshall has also
produced a fully annotated translation of Katai's reminiscences – *Literary life in
Tokyo, 1885–1915: Tayama Katai's memoirs ('Thirty years in Tokyo')* (Leiden, The
Netherlands; New York: E. J. Brill, 1987, 292p.) – which is especially valuable for
readers interested in the Meiji literary world and Meiji period society as well as in
Katai himself.

1106 **The mother of dreams and other short stories: portrayals of women in
modern Japanese fiction.**
Edited with an introduction by Makoto Ueda. Tokyo; New York:
Kodansha International, 1986. 277p.

An anthology of short stories by sixteen leading writers (among them Kawabata
Yasunari, Inoue Yasushi, Dazai Osamu, Matsumoto Seichō, Enchi Fumiko, Ōoka
Shōhei, Abe Kōbō, and Ariyoshi Sawako) that portray Japanese women according to
their five traditionally designated roles: the maiden, the mistress, the wife, the mother,
and the working woman. Undertaken primarily by students of Makoto Ueda at
Stanford University, the translations are accompanied by biographical sketches of their
respective authors.

1107 A view by the sea.
Shōtarō Yasuoka, translated with an introduction by Kären Wigen
Lewis, foreword by Van C. Gessel. New York; Guildford, Surrey:
Columbia University Press, 1984. 196p. (Modern Asian Literature
Series).
Translations of a novella – 'Umikibe no kōkei' – and five short stories by a
contemporary novelist who writes in the autobiographical style of the 'I-novel' and
whose stories in this collection are characterised by a generally sombre mood. Written
during the 1950s, the stories are entitled 'Bad Company' ('Warui nakama'), 'Thick the
New Leaves' ('Aoba shigereru'), 'The Moth' ('Ga'), 'Gloomy Pleasures' ('Inki na
tanoshimi'), and 'Rain' ('Ame').

1108 " 'Love' " and other stories of Yokomitsu Riichi.
Riichi Yokomitsu, translated with an introduction by Dennis Keene.
Tokyo: University of Tokyo Press, 1974. 266p. bibliog. (The Japan
Foundation Translation Series).
Eleven short stories by a major writer of the 1920s and 1930s: ' "Love" ' ('Onmi'),
'The Child Who Was Laughed at' ('Warawareta ko'), 'The Defeated Husand' ('Maketa
otto'), 'After Picking up a Blue Stone' ('Aoi ishi o hirotte kara'), 'The Pale Captain'
('Aoi taii'), 'The Depths of the Town' ('Machi no soko'), 'Spring Riding in a Carriage'
('Haru wa basha ni notte'), 'Ideas of a Flower Garden' ('Hanasono no shisō'), 'The
Machine' ('Kikai'), 'The Carriage' ('Basha'), and 'Smile' ('Bishō'). Keene's brief
introduction traces Yokomitsu's life and literary career and comments on his historical
importance. Yokomitsu is also the focus of Keene's scholarly study, *Yokomitsu Riichi:
modernist* (q.v.).

1109 Musashi.
Eiji Yoshikawa, translated by Charles S. Terry, foreword by Edwin O.
Reischauer. New York: Harper and Row/Kodansha International,
1981. 970p. Reprinted, New York: Pocket Books, 1989.
Characterised as a 'dashing tale of swashbuckling adventure and a subdued story of
love, Japanese style', this long historical novel offers a romanticised account of the
early life of the master swordsman, Miyamoto Musashi (1584-1645). It tells how this
young, reckless warrior survived the battle of Sekigahara, trained his mind and
disciplined his spirit, set out to become the greatest swordsman in Japan, travelled
throughout the country, and ultimately vanquished his most valiant of adversaries.
Published first in serialised form in Japan's prestigious newspaper, the *Asahi Shimbun*,
Yoshikawa's popular novel is representative of the twentieth-century fiction that is
based on the world of the samurai. Translation of *Musashi*.

Kafu the scribbler: the life and writings of Nagai Kafu, 1879–1959.
See item no. 345.

The way of the samurai: Yukio Mishima on Hagakure in modern life.
See item no. 529.

Requiem for battleship Yamato.
See item no. 716.

In the shade of spring leaves: the life and writings of Higuchi Ichiyō, a woman of letters in Meiji Japan.
See item no. 1111.

The saga of Dazai Osamu: a critical study with translations.
See item no. 1116.

Return to Tsugaru: travels of a purple tramp.
See item no. 1116.

Japan's first modern novel: Ukigumo of Futabatei Shimei.
See item no. 1124.

The Shiga hero.
See item no. 1125.

Romaji diary and Sad toys.
See item no. 1140.

In praise of shadows.
See item no. 1225.

Modern Japanese literature in translation: a bibliography.
See item no. 1588.

Guide to Japanese prose.
See item no. 1597.

Modern fiction and prose: history and criticism

1110 **Mori Ōgai and the modernization of Japanese culture.**
Richard John Bowring. Cambridge, England; New York: Cambridge University Press, 1979. 297p. bibliog. (University of Cambridge Oriental Publications, no. 28).

A richly documented account of the life, contributions, and place in modern Japanese intellectual and cultural history of Mori Ōgai (1862-1922), a prolific poet, translator, novelist, playwright, literary critic, essayist, philosopher, medical officer, and military bureaucrat. Concerned with Ōgai as both an intellectual and an author, and seeking to define his role within the wider context of the modernisation that took place during the late Meiji and early Taishō periods, Bowring addresses a range of subjects including Ōgai's use of German aesthetic theory, his deep sense of mission, his dedication and self-sacrifice to the cultural welfare of Japan, his 'literature of ideas', his relationship to the contemporary literary scene, his attitude towards history, and the position of autobiographical and historical themes in his works. An appendix lists all of the poems, stories, and plays which he translated into Japanese.

1111　**In the shade of spring leaves: the life and writings of Higuchi Ichiyō, a woman of letters in Meiji Japan.**
Robert Lyons Danly.　New Haven, Connecticut; London: Yale University Press, 1981. 355p. 2 maps. bibliog.

An authoritative biography of Japan's first modern woman writer of stature (1872-96) combined with an anthology of some of her best-known short stories. Relying heavily upon the multi-volume diary which Ichiyō kept, Danly first describes her education, her development as a writer, the relationship which she had with her mentor (the novelist Nakarai Tōsui), the impact of her family's financial difficulties, and her role within her family. He then provides award-winning translations of nine of Ichiyō's most representative stories, all of which are discussed within the biography: 'Flowers at Dusk', 'A Snowy Day', 'The Sound of the Koto', 'Encounters on a Dark Night', 'On the Last Day of the Year', 'Troubled Waters', 'The Thirteenth Night', 'Child's Play', and 'Separate Ways'.

1112　**The psychological world of Natsume Sōseki.**
Takeo Doi, translated with an introduction and synopses by William Jefferson Tyler, preface by Albert M. Craig, Ezra F. Vogel.
Cambridge, Massachusetts: East Asian Research Center, Harvard University, 1976. 161p. (Harvard East Asian Monographs, 68).

Essays by an eminent Japanese psychiatrist who has long been interested in the writings of Natsume Sōseki (1867-1916) both as literary works and as novels whose central characters provide material for psychoanalytical study. Doi focuses on the behaviour and attitudes of the protagonists in ten of Sōseki's major novels – Botchan, Kōfu ('The Miner'), Sanshirō, Sorekara ('And Then'), Mon ('The Gate'), Higan sugi made ('By after the Equinox'), Kōjin ('The Wayfarer'), Kokoro ('The Human Heart'), Michikusa ('Grass on the Wayside'), and Meian ('Light and Darkness') – and offers insights into the human psyche and Japanese society that are latent within those works. A synopsis of each novel precedes each essay.

1113　**The rhetoric of confession: shishōsetsu in early twentieth-century Japanese fiction.**
Edward Fowler.　Berkeley, California; London: University of California Press, 1988. 333p. bibliog.

A scholarly analysis of the autobiographical form of narrative fiction known as the shishōsetsu (frequently translated as 'I-novel') that flourished in early twentieth-century Japan. Fowler clarifies the nature and focus of this particular type of literature and stresses the basic characteristics which distinguish it from classical Western narrative. He first traces the roots of shishōsetsu, then explores the impact which literary tradition, the naturalist movement, and the realities of Taishō period journalism had on the writing of Japanese autobiographical fiction. Finally, he examines the writings of three diverse authors – Chikamatsu Shūkō (1876-1944), Shiga Naoya (1883-1971), and Kasai Zenzō (1887-1928) – who were particularly instrumental figures in the development of shishōsetsu.

1114   **Yokomitsu Riichi: modernist.**
Dennis Keene.   New York: Columbia University Press; Guildford,
Surrey: Columbia University Press, 1980. 226p. bibliog. (Modern
Asian Literature Series).
Yokomitsu Riichi (1898-1947), a central figure in the Japanese literary world during
the interwar period, is best known as the 'only serious counterpart in modern Japanese
prose literature to the experimental, "modernist" writing that existed in Europe' at
that time. Keene critically analyses Yokomitsu's early modernist works, documents the
impact of a European literary movement on Japanese literature, and shows how
Yokomitsu and other members of the literary group known as the Shinkankakuha
responded to that movement and introduced Western modernism through symbolic
techniques into their own writings. Keene's book complements his earlier translation,
'Love' and other stories of Yokomitsu Riichi (q.v.), in a number of respects.

1115   **Crisis in identity and contemporary Japanese novels.**
Arthur G. Kimball.   Rutland, Vermont; Tokyo: Tuttle, 1973. 190p.
bibliog.
The problem of identity, a prominent concern of contemporary Japanese writers, is
often stressed in the postwar novel. Kimball examines this quest for identity in ten
readily available translated works: *Fires on the plain* (*Nobi*), by Ōoka Shōhei;
Luminous moss (*Hikari goke*), by Takeda Taijun; *No requiem* (*Raguna ko no kita*), by
Moriya Tadashi; *Black rain* (*Kuroi ame*), by Ibuse Masuji; *Homecoming* (*Kikyō*), by
Osaragi Jirō; *The temple of the golden pavilion* (*Kinkakuji*), by Mishima Yukio; *House
of the sleeping beauties* (*Nemureru bijo*), by Kawabata Yasunari; *Diary of a mad old
man* (*Fūten rōjin no nikki*), by Tanizaki Junichirō; *The woman in the dunes* (*Suna no
onna*), by Abe Kōbō; and *A personal matter* (*Kojinteki na taiken*), by Ōe Kenzaburō.
In order to encourage the study and appreciation of contemporary Japanese fiction,
Kimball's book also contains a syllabus and a twelve-week suggested reading course in
the postwar novel.

1116   **The saga of Dazai Osamu: a critical study with translations.**
Phyllis I. Lyons.   Stanford, California: Stanford University Press,
1985. 410p. bibliog.
The intensely personal and autobiographically oriented writings of Dazai Osamu (1909-
48) are well known for their insights into Japanese society and character. Lyons depicts
Dazai's childhood and adolescence as well as his fifteen years as a writer, and examines
some of the psychological problems which beset him throughout most of his life. She
also shows how his autobiographical stories and novels constitute the so-called 'Osamu
Saga', the literary character which Dazai created of himself. Her book concludes with
award-winning translations of five short stories – 'Recollections' ('Omoide'), 'Eight
Views of Tokyo' ('Tōkyō hakkei'), 'Going Home' ('Kikyōrai'), 'Hometown' ('Kokyō'),
and 'An Almanac of Pain' ('Kunō no nenkan') – and of *Tsugaru*, a 'nonfiction novel'
about the author's return as an adult to his childhood home in the Tsugaru Peninsula
of northernmost Honshū. A translation of *Tsugaru* by James Westerhoven has also
appeared under the title *Return to Tsugaru: travels of a purple tramp* (Tokyo; New
York: Kodansha International, 1985, 189p.).

1117 **Two Japanese novelists: Sōseki and Tōson.**
Edwin McClellan. Chicago; London: University of Chicago Press, 1969. 168p. bibliog.

An introduction to the lives and particularly the writings of two outstanding pioneers of realism in Japanese literature who established the autobiographical novel as a major literary form in Japan: Natsume Sōseki (1867-1916) and Shimazaki Tōson (1872–1943). In his essay about Sōseki, McClellan outlines his career and provides short synopses and analyses of ten of his major works: *I am a cat*, *Little master*, *Pillow of grass*, *Autumn wind*, *Sanshirō*, *And then*, *The gate*, *The wanderer*, *The heart*, and *Grass on the wayside*. Similar coverage of Tōson's life and writings focuses on his most important novels: *Broken commandment*, *Spring*, *The house*, *A new life*, and *Before the dawn*.

1118 **Accomplices of silence: the modern Japanese novel.**
Masao Miyoshi. Berkeley, California; London: University of California Press, 1974. 194p.

A series of lively and penetrating essays, intended primarily for the general reader, about four basic aspects of the modern Japanese novel: the narrative situation, the characters, the plot, and language. These essays focus on six leading writers who 'represented the landmark achievements as well as the difficulties and failures of Japanese fiction': Futabatei Shimei, Mori Ōgai, Natsume Sōseki, Kawabata Yasunari, Dazai Osamu, and Mishima Yukio. Miyoshi critically analyses either one or two of each of their works (all are available in English translation), contrasts them with selected Western novels, and shows how they reflect the unique culture and society of Japan in a number of important ways.

1119 **Dazai Osamu.**
James A. O'Brien. Boston, Massachusetts: Twayne, 1975. 179p. bibliog. (Twayne's World Authors Series, TWAS 348: Japan).

A well-documented introduction to the life and work of Dazai Osamu (1909-1948). Dividing Dazai's life into five periods, O'Brien focuses on the series of self-images that emerge in this author's writings. He offers a brief biographical sketch of Dazai, a critical discussion (with plot summaries) of his better-known works, and some consideration of the basis of Dazai's appeal, his role as a 'writer invoking his past', his ambivalence and its literary effects, and Dazai's suicide in 1948.

1120 **Writers and society in modern Japan.**
Irena Powell. London: Macmillan; Tokyo and New York: Kodansha International, 1983. 149p. bibliog. (St. Antony's Macmillan Series).

A study of the social context of modern Japanese literature which focuses on the emergence, development, and decline of the *bundan* (the literary élite or literary establishment) between the 1890s and the 1940s. Through an examination of the modes of thought and the behaviour of Japanese writers belonging to the *bundan*, Powell indicates the close relationship which existed between the views of the world which they expressed in their literary writings and the social and historical reality of *bundan* life. Akutagawa Ryūnosuke, Dazai Osamu, and Shiga Naoya were among the more prominent members of this élite.

Literature. Modern fiction and prose: history and criticism

1121 Mori Ōgai.
J. Thomas Rimer. Boston, Massachusetts: Twayne, 1975. 135p.
bibliog. (Twayne's World Authors Series, TWAS 355: Japan).
An introduction to the life and especially the major literary accomplishments of this leading novelist, critic, translator, and medical scientist. Rimer begins with a brief account of Mori Ōgai's life (1862-1922), then discusses his most representative works (fiction as well as drama and poetry) in relation to his literary career and his views. Many illustrative passages translated from Ōgai's works appear throughout the book, as Rimer seeks to indicate some of the intellectual and spiritual continuities within the author's writings and account for his reputation among the Japanese as a major figure in twentieth-century cultural and artistic history. Rimer's study is complemented by his two-volume translation of Ōgai's stories entitled *The historical literature of Mori Ōgai* (q.v.).

1122 Injurious to public morals: writers and the Meiji state.
Jay Rubin. Seattle, Washington; London: University of Washington Press, 1984. 331p. bibliog.
An examination of the development and deployment of the Meiji government's system of censorship and a detailed study of the rise of the modern Japanese novel and the government's efforts to eliminate its subversive moral influence, especially during the period 1906-13. Particular attention is paid to the emergence of naturalism and its portrayal of human experience in an open, honest manner; to the writers (among them Natsume Sōseki, Ishikawa Takuboku, Mori Ōgai, and Nagai Kafū) who opposed the government's policies; to the reactions of several writers to the trial of Kōtoku Shūsui and other socialists on charges of high treason; and to various abortive government efforts to co-opt Meiji period writers.

1123 The development of realism in the fiction of Tsubouchi Shōyō.
Marleigh Grayer Ryan. Seattle, Washington; London: University of Washington Press, 1975. 133p.
Tsubouchi Shōyō (1859-1935) was a pioneer in the modernisation of Japanese literature. His critical essay *Shōsetsu shinzui* ('The Essence of the Novel', 1885) set forth his influential ideals about incorporating Western literary techniques into modern Japanese writing. Ryan discusses the literary milieu of the 1870s and 1880s as well as of Tsubouchi's early years, and evaluates his short career as a writer of fiction through a detailed presentation and critical assessment of the four novels which he wrote during the 1880s: *Tōsei shosei katagi* ('The Character of Present-day Students'), *Imotose kagami* ('A Mirror of Marriage'), *Matsu no uchi* (a term referring to the first seven days of the New Year), and *Saikun* ('The Wife'). Through her study Ryan demonstrates that Tsubouchi made successful use of the psychological realism of Western literature that he had espoused in his own critical essay.

1124 **Japan's first modern novel: *Ukigumo* of Futabatei Shimei.**
Translation and critical commentary by Marleigh Grayer Ryan. New
York; London: Columbia University Press, 1967. 381p. bibliog.
(Studies of the East Asian Institute, Columbia University) (Unesco
Collection of Representative Works: Japanese Series). Reprinted,
Westport, Connecticut: Greenwood Press, 1983.
A study and translation of *Ukigumo* ('Drifting Clouds'), a work published between
1887 and 1889 that is regarded as Japan's first modern novel. Written in colloquial
Japanese, it narrates the story of Bunzō, a young Meiji bureaucrat, and of Osei, the
woman whom he had intended to marry. This realistic novel was specifically designed
to reveal the psychology of these and two other characters. The translation is preceded
by Ryan's detailed study of Futabatei's life and education; the friendship which he
enjoyed with Tsubouchi Shōyō, a well-established novelist, translator and critic who
influenced and assisted him in his work; Futabatei's experiences and feelings as he was
writing *Ukigumo* and simultaneously translating the Russian novelist Ivan Turgenev
into Japanese; and the influence of nineteenth-century Russian literature on
Futabatei's portrayal of Bunzō as a 'superfluous hero'.

1125 **The Shiga hero.**
William F. Sibley. Chicago; London: University of Chicago Press,
1979. 221p. bibliog.
A literary analysis of the one fully developed character in the writings of Shiga Naoya
(1883-1971) who may be associated, in varying degrees, with the author himself. In
four interpretive essays Sibley reconstructs the biography of this fictional hero, thereby
unifying Shiga's fragmented narratives and establishing a close psychological link
between Shiga and his hero. He also translates ten of the author's short stories. Shiga
Naoya enjoyed considerable literary success as both a novelist and short-story writer
and was regarded as a foremost writer of autobiographical fiction.

1126 **Approaches to the modern Japanese short story.**
Edited by Thomas E. Swann, Kinya Tsuruta, introduction by Thomas
E. Swann. Tokyo: Waseda University Press, 1982. 341p.
Brief essays discuss and interpret thirty-four short stories by fifteen of Japan's most
important twentieth-century authors: Abe Kōbō, Akutagawa Ryūnosuke, Dazai
Osamu, Hayashi Fumiko, Higuchi Ichiyō, Ibuse Masuji, Kawabata Yasunari, Kunikida
Doppo, Mishima Yukio, Mori Ōgai, Nagai Kafū, Natsume Sōseki, Ōe Kenzaburō,
Shiga Naoya, and Tanizaki Junichirō. Each of the stories is available in English
translation. This guide serves as a companion volume to the editors' *Approaches to the
modern Japanese novel* (q.v.).

1127 **Approaches to the modern Japanese novel.**
Edited by Kinya Tsuruta, Thomas E. Swann. Tokyo: Sophia
University, 1976. 244p.
Specialists in Japanese literature discuss some of the major works of ten modern
authors in this collection of pedagogically oriented essays. They examine in some detail
the plots, themes, symbols, imagery, and characterisation of fifteen novels that were
accessible to the study of Japanese literature in translation as well as to the general
reader in 1975. The analyses cover *The woman in the dunes* (by Abe Kōbō), *The setting*

sun and *No longer human* (Dazai Osamu), *Black rain* (Ibuse Masuji), *Snow country*, *The sound of the mountain* and *The master of go* (Kawabata Yasunari), *Confessions of a mask* (Mishima Yukio), *The wild geese* (Mori Ōgai), *Botchan* and *Kokoro* (Natsume Sōseki), *A personal matter* (Ōe Kenzaburō), *Fires on the plain* (Ōoka Shōhei), and *The key* and *The Makioka sisters* (Tanizaki Junichirō).

1128 **Modern Japanese writers and the nature of literature.**
Makoto Ueda. Stanford, California: Stanford University Press, 1976. 292p. bibliog.

This study of eight prominent novelists – Natsume Sōseki, Nagai Kafū, Tanizaki Junichirō, Shiga Naoya, Akutagawa Ryūnosuke, Dazai Osamu, Kawabata Yasunari, and Mishima Yukio – examines some of their views of the nature of literature and assists the general reader towards a better understanding and appreciation of their work. Ueda systematically surveys and interprets each writer's concept of literature in terms of five basic issues in literary theory: art versus nature, the literary work and the author, the literary work and the reader, structure and style, and the purpose of literature. He bases his analysis on their literary and autobiographical essays, critical reviews, prefaces and postscripts, diaries, and letters as well as on a reading of their novels and short stories. All eight writers have been extensively translated into English. A companion study appeared in 1983 under the title *Modern Japanese poets and the nature of literature* (q.v.).

1129 **The Japanese novel of the Meiji period and the ideal of individualism.**
Janet A. Walker. Princeton, New Jersey; Guildford, Surrey: Princeton University Press, 1979. 315p. bibliog.

The Western ideal of individualism exerted an important influence on the development of the novel during the Meiji period. Walker shows how this ideal formed the core of the essays of Kitamura Tōkoku as well as of some of the novels written by Futabatei Shimei (*Ukigumo*), Tayama Katai (*Futon*), and Shimazaki Tōson (*Hakai* and *Shinsei*). She also demonstrates how these four writers contributed to the growth of a type of literature which made the depiction of the modern Japanese individual its primary objective. Because Tōson was the writer most influenced by the ideal of individualism, the entire second half of the study is devoted to discussions of his development of a personal ideal of selfhood and to analyses of two of his major novels.

1130 **The search for authenticity in modern Japanese literature.**
Hisaaki Yamanouchi. Cambridge, England; New York: Cambridge University Press, 1978. 214p. bibliog.

Seven essays on Japanese literature since the Meiji Restoration (1868) which focus on twelve important representative writers: Tsubouchi Shōyō, Futabatei Shimei, Kitamura Tōkoku, Shimazaki Tōson, Natsume Sōseki, Shiga Naoya, Akutagawa Ryūnosuke, Tanizaki Junichirō, Kawabata Yasunari, Mishima Yukio, Abe Kōbō, and Ōe Kenzaburō. Yamanouchi explores the ways in which these authors addressed their personal, social, and intellectual concerns and sought (not always successfully) to portray their experiences in an authentic, artistic manner. He also discusses those aspects of their personal lives and cultural identity which influenced their literary development and orientation.

1131 **Mishima: a vision of the void.**
Marguerite Yourcenar, translated from the French by Alberto
Manguel with Marguerite Yourcenar. New York: Farrar, Straus and
Giroux; Henley-on-Thames, Oxfordshire: Ellis, 1986. 151p.

A sympathetic, interpretive essay about Mishima Yukio's life and work which focuses
on some of the essential elements in his writings. Yourcenar discusses Mishima's
principal novels, in particular his *Confessions of a mask*, the *Temple of the golden
pavilion*, and his tetralogy, *The sea of fertility*. She also examines Mishima's suicide in
1970 and some of the events preceding it.

1132 **Akutagawa: an introduction.**
Beongcheon Yu. Detroit, Michigan: Wayne State University Press;
Toronto, Ontario: Copp Clark, 1972. 148p. bibliog.

The first critical study of the entire literary career of Akutagawa Ryūnosuke (1892-
1927), the author of the short story upon which Kurosawa Akira's film *Rashōmon* is
based, as well as the writer of numerous critical essays and over 150 tales and stories.
After depicting Akutagawa's early years, Yu traces three major periods in his career,
introducing his writings, analysing his literary techniques and his works, and indicating
his critical reaction to the literary questions of his era. Finally Yu places Akutagawa
and his art in a perspective designed to enhance an appreciation of his contributions. A
brief biographical chronology and a listing of Akutagawa's stories in English
translation, arranged by translator, are appended.

1133 **Natsume Soseki.**
Beongcheon Yu. New York: Twayne, 1969. 192p. bibliog.
(Twayne's World Author Series, TWAS 99: Japan).

An informative study of the literary accomplishments of Natsume Sōseki (1867-1916),
a major novelist, essayist, critic, and haiku poet. Interweaving pertinent details about
Sōseki's life into his discussion, Yu first places him within the intellectual and cultural
milieu of the Meiji period. He then discusses his novels, grouping them according to
their thematic and structural development. Yu relates each work to its predecessors,
summarises its plot, and comments on its themes and techniques. In addition, he
assesses Sōseki's significance as the first professional novelist in modern Japan, as a
major contributor to the development of modern Japanese literature, and as 'an
exemplary case of the impact of Western literature on the creative spirit of modern
Japan'.

Mishima: a biography.
See item no. 335.

Kafu the scribbler: the life and writings of Nagai Kafu, 1879–1959.
See item no. 345.

Long engagements: maturity in modern Japan.
See item no. 541.

Pools of water, pillars of fire: the literature of Ibuse Masuji.
See item no. 1058.

Kōda Rohan.
See item no. 1069.

Sanshiro: a novel.
See item no. 1087.

The quilt and other stories by Tayama Katai.
See item no. 1105.

Literary life in Tokyo, 1885–1915: Tayama Katai's memoirs ('Thirty Years in Tokyo').
See item no. 1105.

Poetry: translations

1134 **The Penguin book of Japanese verse.**
Translated by Geoffrey Bownas, Anthony Thwaite, with an introduction by Geoffrey Bownas. Harmondsworth, Middlesex; Baltimore, Maryland: Penguin Books, 1964. 242p. (Penguin Poets, D77) (Unesco Collection of Representative Works: Japanese Series).

A carefully selected anthology encompassing the full range of Japanese poetry, from the verse composed by members of the imperial family before the eighth century to the poems written after World War II by well-established contemporary authors. The poems are grouped together by period and then by author. They appear only in English translation. Bownas' introduction explores the relationship between the language and poetry of Japan, and surveys the development of subjects and styles in Japanese poetry. This very popular anthology has been reprinted every two or three years since its initial publication.

1135 **Fujiwara Teika's Superior poems of our time: a thirteenth-century poetic treatise and sequence.**
Fujiwara Sadaie, translated with an introduction and notes by Robert H. Brower, Earl Miner. Stanford, California: Stanford University Press; Tokyo: University of Tokyo Press, 1967. 148p. bibliog. (Unesco Collection of Representative Works: Japanese Series).

A fully annotated translation of the *Kindai shūka* of Fujiwara Sadaie (or Teika) (1162-1241). It consists of Teika's short critical essay on the nature of Japanese poetry and its state during the early thirteenth century, and a carefully arranged sequence of eighty-three tanka written by thirty-seven known poets during the previous three centuries in particular that Teika highly regarded. These poems appear both in romanised Japanese and English translation. The translators' introduction offers an overview of the life and times of this great poet, critic, and teacher; discusses Teika's prefatory essay and the poems which he selected; and considers his poetic sequence as an integrated whole.

1136   **Howling at the moon: poems of Hagiwara Sakutarō.**
Sakutarō Hagiwara, translated with an introduction by Hiroaki Sato.
Tokyo: University of Tokyo Press, 1978. 142p.

Translations of two well-known, epoch-making collections of poetry composed in modern colloquial Japanese by Hagiwara Sakutarō (1886-1942): *Tsuki ni hoeru* ('Howling at the Moon') and *Aoneko* ('Blue Cat'). Reproductions of the illustrations that appeared in the 1917 edition of *Tsuki ni hoeru* are included with Sato's translations. A different approach to the translation of Hagiwara's free-style poetry is taken by Graeme Wilson in his rendition of the forty poems that appear in *Face at the bottom of the world, and other poems*, by Sakutarō Hagiwara (Rutland, Vermont; Tokyo: Tuttle, 1969, 83p. [Unesco Collection of Representative Works: Japanese Series]).

1137   **An introduction to haiku: an anthology of poems and poets from Bashō to Shiki.**
Harold G. Henderson.   Garden City, New York: Doubleday, 1958.
190p. (Doubleday Anchor Books).

A delightful and informative survey of the characteristics and historical evolution of haiku, the popular seventeen-syllable poem which flourished during the seventeenth and eighteenth centuries in particular. Accompanying this are renditions of several hundred haiku in polished translations, in romanised Japanese, and in literal word-for-word translations. Henderson pays considerable attention to the four greatest haiku masters: Matsuo Bashō, Taniguchi (Yosa) Buson, Kobayashi Issa, and Masaoka Shiki. Other chapters cover early haiku written before the time of Bashō, the haiku of Bashō's disciples and other early eighteenth-century poets, and the haiku of Buson's contemporaries. This popular introduction has become a widely recognised classic in its field.

1138   **Japanese death poems: written by Zen monks and haiku poets on the verge of death.**
Compiled with an introduction and commentary by Yoel Hoffmann.
Rutland, Vermont; Tokyo: Tuttle, 1986. 366p. bibliog.

An anthology of several hundred *jisei*, or poems composed as their authors lay dying, accompanied by individual commentaries explaining the circumstances of each poet's death. Hoffmann shows that *jisei* have been written over the centuries by a wide range of people. His detailed introduction (part one) explains the tradition of writing death poems and discusses both the beliefs of the Japanese about death and the role of death and its poetry in Japan's cultural history. The second and third parts are collections of death poems by Zen monks and haiku poets respectively, alphabetically arranged according to the name of each author. Poems in parts one and three appear in English translation and romanised Japanese. Those in part two, translated from the Chinese, appear in English only.

1139 **Ikkyū and the Crazy cloud anthology: a Zen poet of medieval Japan.**
Ikkyū Sōjun, translated with an introduction by Sonja Arntzen,
foreword by Shūichi Katō.   Tokyo: University of Tokyo Press, 1986.
197p. bibliog. (Unesco Collection of Representative Works: Japanese
Series).

Ikkyū Sōjun (1394-1481), an eccentric Zen monk and an unconventional poet, created
a body of poetry, written in classical Chinese, that is among the most original verse in
the Zen Buddhist tradition. The poems from the *Kyōunshū* or 'Crazy Cloud
Anthology', Ikkyū's major collection, deal with both religious and secular themes.
Arntzen's translations of 144 poems (about one-sixth of the entire anthology) are
accompanied by their original Chinese texts, full explanatory notes, an introduction to
Ikkyū's life, and an analysis of his poetic techniques.

1140 **Romaji diary and Sad toys.**
Takuboku Ishikawa, translated with an introduction by Sanford
Goldstein, Seishi Shinoda.   West Lafayette, Indiana: Purdue
University Press, 1977. 198p. Reprinted, Rutland, Vermont; Tokyo:
Tuttle, 1985. 279p.

Translations of two works by a fine poet and novelist. *Romaji diary* (*Rōmaji nikki*), a
kind of naturalistic novel, candidly records Takuboku's lifestyle and environment in
Tokyo as well as the emotional conflict that he experienced in 1909. *Sad toys*
(*Kanashiki gangu*) is a collection of 194 tanka poems written in 1910-11 that express
with an intensity of feeling the private world of his inner thoughts shortly before his
death. Fifty-nine tanka from *Sad toys* together with a selection of tanka from other
works by Takuboku also appear in *Takuboku: poems to eat*, translated with an
introduction by Carl Sesar (Tokyo; Palo Alto, California: Kodansha International,
1966, 168p.).

1141 **The modern Japanese prose poem: an anthology of six poets.**
Translated with an introduction by Dennis Keene.   Princeton, New
Jersey; Guildford, Surrey: Princeton University Press, 1980. 187p.

The prose poem (*sanbunshi*), in its origins a nineteenth-century French literary genre,
occupies an important place in twentieth-century Japanese literature. Keene's
introduction discusses the French prose poem, traces the development of modern
Japanese poetry, and introduces the six poets covered in this volume. The anthology
presents a selection of the works of Miyoshi Tatsuji and Anzai Fuyue, representing the
'New Prose Poem Movement' of the 1920s; Tamura Ryūichi and Yoshioka Minoru,
representing the postwar modernism of the late 1950s; and Tanikawa Shuntarō and
Inoue Yasushi, showing aspects of the present-day poetic scene. The translations of
their poems are not accompanied by parallel transliterations, but biographies of the six
poets are provided.

1142 **The poetic memoirs of Lady Daibu.**
Kenreimon'in Ukyō no Daibu, translated with an introduction by
Phillip Tudor Harries.   Stanford, California: Stanford University
Press, 1980. 324p. bibliog.

An annotated translation of *Kenreimon'in Ukyō no Daibu shū*, a collection of 358 five-
line tanka poems arranged in chronological order and frequently preceded by passages

Literature. Poetry: translations

of narrative prose. As a whole, this work constitutes a short lyrical autobiography reflecting the experiences and emotions of Lady Daibu between 1175 and 1212. Some of the poems are concerned with love affairs that were carried on with Fujiwara no Takanobu and Taira no Sukemori. Others depict her feelings of grief and nostalgia occasioned by the events of her time, among them the Minamoto defeat of the Taira family in 1185. Harries' introduction presents a general political and economic history of the era in which Lady Daibu lived, a discussion and structural analysis of the work, and a critical assessment of her writings. The texts of the poems appear in romanised Japanese as well as in translation.

1143 **The poetry of postwar Japan.**
Edited by Hajime Kijima, foreword by Paul Engle, Hualing Nieh Engle. Iowa City, Iowa: University of Iowa Press, 1975. 267p. (Iowa Translations).

Translations of representative poems of thirty-one contemporary authors, among them Ayukawa Nobuo, Iwata Hiroshi, Kijima Hajime, Kuroda Kio, Shiraishi Kazuko, Tamura Ryūichi, Tanikawa Shuntarō, Tomioka Taeko, and Yoshimasu Gōzō. Each poet contributed between three and twelve of his works to this anthology. Brief biographical sketches of these poets accompany the translations that were prepared by several American and Japanese specialists. Also included are two introductory essays entitled 'On Postwar Japanese Poetry' (by Kijima Hajime) and 'Hadaka no Gengo: the Naked Language of Postwar Japanese Poetry' (by Roy Andrew Miller). This volume is the fourth in a translation series that seeks to present translations of poetry from several lesser-known world languages as a result of activities undertaken within the International Writing Program at the University of Iowa.

1144 **Treelike: the poetry of Kinoshita Yūji.**
Yūji Kinoshita, translated with an introduction by Robert Epp, preface by Makoto Ōoka. Rochester, Michigan: Oakland University, Katydid Books, published in association with the Center for Japanese Studies, University of Michigan, 1982. 272p. (Asian Poetry in Translation, 4) (Michigan Papers in Japanese Studies, 8) (Unesco Collection of Representative Works: Japanese Series).

Award-winning translations of the poetry of a man who wrote free verse while working as a pharmacist in a village in eastern Hiroshima Prefecture. Epp's anthology contains 111 poems (approximately one-quarter of Kinoshita's entire literary output) – both in Japanese and in English-language translation – arranged according to the period of their publication. Epp's biography of this poet (1914-65), *Kinoshita Yūji* (Boston, Massachusetts: Twayne, 1982, 145p.), is a companion volume which explores the major themes within Kinoshita's poetry.

1145 **Modern Japanese poetry.**
Translated by James Kirkup, edited and introduced by A. R. Davis. St. Lucia, Queensland, Australia: University of Queensland Press, 1978; Milton Keynes, England: Open University Press, 1979. 323p. bibliog. (Asian and Pacific Writing, 9).

A brief introductory essay about the history and development of modern Japanese poetry is followed by an anthology of 227 poems written during the late nineteenth and twentieth centuries. Most of the eighty-three poets are represented by only a small selection of their poetry, but Kirkup (himself a poet who has lived in Japan) has included well over a dozen poems by Miyoshi Tatsuji (1900-64) and Murano Shirō (1901-75) respectively. All poems appear solely in English-language translation. Biographical notes about the poets are grouped together towards the end of the book.

1146 **The year of my life: a translation of Issa's** *Oraga haru*.
Kobayashi Issa, translated with an introduction by Nobuyuki Yuasa. Berkeley, California; London: University of California Press, 1972. 2nd ed. 142p.

A translation of the best-known work of the prominent haiku poet Kobayashi Issa (1763-1827): the evocative, poetic diary which he wrote in *haibun* (haiku mixed with prose passages) in 1819. Issa records what he did, felt, and heard over the course of that year as he lived with his family in the small mountain village of Kashiwabara (Nagano Prefecture). Yuasa's introduction sketches Issa's life, considers his poetic aims and accomplishments, gauges his literary significance, and describes the overall structure of *Oraga haru*. A much broader range of Issa's poetry may be found in *The autumn wind: a selection from the poems of Issa*, translated by Lewis Mackenzie (Tokyo; New York: Kodansha International, 1984. rev. ed., 137p.), which offers selections of his haiku from several periods in his life.

1147 **The ten thousand leaves: a translation of the** *Man'yōshū*, **Japan's premier anthology of classical poetry.**
Translated with an introduction by Ian Hideo Levy. Princeton, New Jersey: Princeton University Press; Tokyo: University of Tokyo Press, 1981- . 4 vols. (Princeton Library of Asian Translations) (Unesco Collection of Representative Works: Japanese Series).

The earliest extant collection of Japanese poetry, the *Manyōshū* ('Collection of Ten Thousand Leaves') is a monumental anthology of 4,516 numbered tanka and *chōka* poems composed by many hundreds of people during the seventh and eighth centuries. These poems range from 'the elegant banquet verse of aristocrats to the "poems of the frontier guardsmen" and the rustic "poems of the Eastland" in provincial dialect'. Levy's first volume contains an introductory essay and a comprehensive translation of Books One to Five of the *Manyōshū*. It does not include, however, any transliterated texts. Following the publication of the remaining three volumes, this definitive translation is expected to replace the Nippon Gakujutsu Shinkōkai's 1940 edition (reprinted in 1965 by Columbia University Press) of the *Manyōshū*, whose translations are limited to a selection of about 1,000 poems chosen from all twenty books of this collection. Levy's work was published in Japan under the title *Man'yōshū: a translation of Japan's premier anthology of classical poetry*.

1148 **Tales of Ise: lyrical episodes from tenth-century Japan.**
Translated with an introduction and notes by Helen Craig McCullough. Stanford, California: Stanford University Press; Tokyo: University of Tokyo Press, 1968. 277p. bibliog.

A translation of an anonymous tenth-century collection of some 125 brief prose narratives built around 209 *waka* poems, known as the *Ise monogatari*, that has been traditionally esteemed as a handbook for the study of poetry and is regarded as the epitome of Heian court literature. The poems deal with several literary topics, in particular the theme of love. Among them are many of the surviving works of the famous poet Ariwara no Narihira (825-80). McCullough's lengthy introduction discusses the intellectual, political, and social background of the Japanese poetic tradition and pays special attention to the interplay between Chinese and Japanese influence and to Narihira's life and role in this collection. Two other available translations of the *Ise monogatari* are *A study of the Ise-monogatari: with the text according to the Den-Teika-hippon and an annotated translation*, by Frits Vos (The Hague: Mouton, 1957, 2 vols.) and *The tales of Ise*, translated by H. Jay Harris (Rutland, Vermont; Tokyo: Tuttle, 1972, 247p.).

1149 **Japanese poetic diaries.**
Selected and translated, with an introduction, by Earl Miner.
Berkeley, California; London: University of California Press, 1969.
211p. 2 maps. bibliog. (Publications of the Center for Japanese and Korean Studies).

Translations and brief analyses of four major diaries written in combinations of prose and verse during four different periods: *The Tosa diary* (*Tosa nikki*) by Ki no Tsurayuki (*ca.* 868-945), *The diary of Izumi Shikibu* (*Izumi Shikibu nikki*) attributed to Izumi Shikibu (eleventh century), *The narrow road through the provinces* (*Oku no hosomichi*) by Matsuo Bashō (1644-94), and the short *Verse record of my peonies* (*Botan kuroku*) by Masaoka Shiki (1867-1902). In his introduction, Miner discusses the background, literary techniques, and themes of these four works; illuminates some of the special characteristics of the literary genre of poetic diaries; and expounds his thesis that 'these diaries are not only members of a genre but also part of a unified tradition that is one of the main currents of Japanese literary history'. Readers should also note the exhaustively annotated translation by Edward A. Cranston entitled *The Izumi Shikibu diary: a romance of the Heian court* (Cambridge, Massachusetts: Harvard University Press, 1969, 332p.) as well as the appearance of several versions of Bashō's diary, most notably Nobuyuki Yuasa's fine translation entitled *The narrow road to the deep north and other travel sketches* (Harmondsworth, Middlesex; Baltimore, Maryland: Penguin, 1966, 167p.), and the magnificently illustrated, freer translation *A haiku journey: Bashō's 'The narrow road to the far north' and selected haiku*, translated and introduced by Dorothy Britton with photographs by Dennis Stock (Tokyo; New York: Kodansha International, 1974, 111p.).

1150 **The monkey's straw raincoat and other poetry of the Bashō school.**
Translated with an introduction by Earl Miner, Hiroko Odagiri.
Princeton, New Jersey; Guildford, Surrey: Princeton University Press, 1981. 394p. 3 maps. bibliog. (Princeton Library of Asian Translations).

An introduction to the emergence and development of the seventeen-syllable *haikai* poem, a complete translation of *The monkey's straw raincoat* (*Sarumino*, 1693), the most esteemed of several collections of poetry by Matsuo Bashō (1644-94) and his disciples, and a selection of some of their other poetry. Each poem appears in both romanised Japanese and English translation, together with a brief annotation. Indexes containing definitions of technical terminology and biographical sketches of the poets represented in this collection conclude the volume.

1151　**A play of mirrors: eight major poets of modern Japan.**
Edited by Makoto Ōoka, Thomas Fitzsimmons, translated by Toshio
Akai and others.　Rochester, Michigan: Katydid Books, Oakland
University, 1987. 311p. (Asian Poetry in Translation: Japan, no. 7).

An anthology of long selections from the work of Yoshioka Minoru, Tamura Ryūichi,
Iijima Kōichi, Tada Chimako, Ōoka Makoto, Tanikawa Shuntarō, Shiraishi Kazuko,
and Yoshimasu Gōzō. Accompanying the translated poetry of these eight writers are
introductions about their careers and the nature of their poetry as well as an opening
essay by Ōoka Makoto entitled 'Modern Japanese Poetry: Realities and Challenges'.

1152　**Zen poems of the five mountains.**
David Pollack.　New York: Crossroad; Decatur, Georgia: Scholars
Press, 1985. 166p. (American Academy of Religion. Studies in
Religion, 37).

This volume on *Gozan bungaku* ('literature of the Five Mountains') poetry seeks to
convey through both an introductory essay and annotated translations 'something of
how a Zen monk in Japan between 1200 and 1500 might have perceived his world and
felt about it'. Over two hundred poems written in Chinese by twenty-seven Rinzai Zen
poets – among them Gidō Shūshin (1325-88), Zekkai Chūshin (1336-1405), Kisei
Reigen (1403-88), and Keijo Shūrin (1440-1518) – are arranged topically into sections
('Meditation and Daily Practice', 'Living in Hermitage', 'Nature', 'Weather and the
Changing Seasons', etc.) that reflect the variety of experiences encountered by these
Zen priests. Each section is prefaced by a brief discussion of the issues raised by the
poetry, and biographies of all of the poets conclude the book.

1153　**Kokinshū: a collection of poems ancient and modern.**
Translated and annotated by Laurel Rasplica Rodd, with Mary
Catherine Henkenius; including a study of Chinese influences on the
Kokinshū prefaces by John Timothy Wixted, and an annotated
translation of the Chinese preface by Leonard Grzanka.　Princeton,
New Jersey; Guildford, Surrey: Princeton University Press, 1984.
442p. bibliog. (Princeton Library of Asian Translations) (Unesco
Collection of Representative Works: Japanese Series).

The *Kokinshū*, or *Kokinwakashū* ('Collection of Ancient and Modern Poems',
compiled by Ki no Tsurayuki and others, *ca.* 920 AD), was the first in a series of
twenty-one imperially commissioned anthologies of Japanese-language poetry. Most of
its 1,111 poems, written in the dominant thirty-one-syllable form known as the *waka*,
are concerned with the seasons, travel, qualities of experience, and such types of lyrical
expression as love and grief. They are grouped together by topic rather than by author.
Rodd's translation is accompanied by an introductory essay outlining the background,
compilation, aesthetics, and arrangement of the *Kokinshū*; by author and subject
indexes and brief biographies of *Kokinshū* poets; and by an index of first lines of
poems in this anthology. A second translation of this literary classic, published
together with English-language renditions of two other mid-tenth-century collections of
poetry, has appeared under the title *Kokin wakashū: the first imperial anthology of
Japanese poetry; with Tosa nikki and Shinsen waka* (Stanford, California: Stanford
University Press, 1985, 388p.). Prepared by Helen Craig McCullough, it is
accompanied by a companion volume – *Brocade by night: 'Kokin wakashū' and the*

court style in Japanese classical poetry (Stanford, California: Stanford University Press, 1985, 591p.) – in which she provides an analysis of the *Kokinshū*'s Chinese heritage and Japanese antecedents as well as detailed, scholarly information about its composition, style, and other significant literary features.

1154 **Ryōkan, Zen monk-poet of Japan.**
Ryōkan, translated with an introduction by Burton Watson. New York; Guildford, Surrey: Columbia University Press, 1977. 126p. (Translations from the Oriental Classics).

Translations of a representative selection of eighty-three Japanese and forty-three Chinese-language poems written by the celebrated Sōtō Zen monk, poet, and master calligrapher, Ryōkan (1758-1831). The Japanese poetry, appearing in parallel translations and transliterations, includes both thirty-one-syllable tanka poems and the longer *chōka*. The selection concludes with a prose piece translated from Chinese, 'Statement on Begging for Food', in which Ryōkan discusses the Buddhist practice of begging for alms. Watson's brief introduction sketches the life of this 'writer of unusual and highly personal poetry' and assesses his religious views and poetic practices. Two other readily available anthologies of Ryōkan's poetry are *One robe, one bowl: the Zen poems of Ryōkan*, translated with an introduction by John Stevens (New York; Tokyo: Weatherhill, 1977, 85p.), and *The Zen poems of Ryōkan*, selected and translated by Nobuyuki Yuasa (Princeton, New Jersey; Guildford, Surrey: Princeton University Press, 1981, 218p.).

1155 **Mirror for the moon: a selection of poems.**
Saigyō, translated with an introduction by William R. LaFleur, foreword by Gary Snyder. New York: New Directions, 1978. 100p. bibliog. (A New Directions Book).

A selection of 163 *waka* by the renowned Buddhist monk Saigyō (1118-90), taken from his major anthology, the *Sankashū*. Arranged by such topics as the seasons of the year and love, these poems appear both in romanised Japanese and in free translations which frequently seek to provide explicit renditions of some of the nuances in the original Japanese. LaFleur's introduction outlines Saigyō's career and relates his work to both its historical setting and the evolution of Japanese poetry. The volume concludes with an index to the first lines of all of the poems.

1156 **From the country of eight islands: an anthology of Japanese poetry.**
Edited and translated by Hiroaki Sato, Burton Watson; with an introduction by Thomas Rimer; Robert Fagan, associate editor. Seattle, Washington: University of Washington Press; Garden City, New York: Anchor Press, 1981. 652p. bibliog.

The contents of this widely acclaimed anthology by two prominent translators range from the songs of the *Kojiki* (seventh century) to the poetry of the contemporary poet, Takahashi Mutsuo. Their translations include numerous selections of most types of Japanese verse – *chōka*, tanka, *renga*, *haibun*, haiku, *hokku*, *kanshi*, *senryū*, songs, free verse, even the noh play *Teika* written in poetry – grouped into five historical periods and then arranged according to author. The poems appear only in English translation; not even the sources of the original texts are identified. Rimer's introduction briefly discusses the history, language, forms, and aesthetic ideals of

Japanese poetry. He also contributes a concise glossary, biographical sketches about the major poets in the anthology, and a selected bibliography of English-language writings about and translations of Japanese poetry.

1157 **Anthology of modern Japanese poetry.**
Compiled and translated with an introduction by Edith Marcombe Shiffert, Yūki Sawa.   Rutland, Vermont; Tokyo: Tuttle, 1972. 195p. bibliog.

Forty-nine noted poets are represented in this collection of free verse, tanka, and haiku. Appearing in translation only, the poetry is accompanied by an introduction which traces the evolution of Japanese poetry since the Meiji Restoration (1868) and by brief biographical notes about the authors themselves. Shiffert and Sawa indicate that they have felt free 'to choose what they particularly found significant and amenable to translation' and that the anthology seeks to supplement other published collections rather than to provide a comprehensive overview of modern Japanese verse.

1158 **Chieko and other poems of Takamura Kōtarō.**
Kōtarō Takamura, translated with an introduction and notes by Hiroaki Sato.   Honolulu, Hawaii: University Press of Hawaii, 1980. 164p.

Takamura Kōtarō (1883-1956), one of Japan's most widely read modern poets, is best known for the poetry he wrote in a new, freer form called *shi* that was characterised by 'a pristine vigor and straightforwardness'. Translations of about one-seventh of his poetic oeuvre are accompanied by a brief biographical introduction. Part one, 'The Journey', is a selection of fifty-eight chronologically arranged pieces chosen from the poet's writings throughout his life. Part two, 'Chieko', contains twenty-six of the poems that Takamura wrote to or about his wife, Chieko. Part three, 'A Brief History of Imbecility', offers a complete translation of the twenty autobiographical poems that he composed shortly after World War II.

1159 **Modern Japanese haiku: an anthology.**
Compiled and translated with an introduction by Makoto Ueda.
Toronto, Ontario; Buffalo, New York: University of Toronto Press, 1976. 265p.

Twenty haiku by each of twenty writers active since the Meiji Restoration (1868), among them Masaoka Shiki, Ozaki Hōsai, Akutagawa Ryūnosuke, Natsume Sōseki, Hino Sōjō, and Kaneko Tōta. Each poem appears in romanised Japanese and a word-by-word literal English translation. The anthology begins with an introduction to the evolution of the modern haiku and to the activities of various groups and individual poets, while the poems and translations are accompanied by concise biographical sketches of the respective writers. Ueda's approach results not only in a readable collection of modern haiku but also in a deeper understanding of the haiku as a poetic form.

1160   **Tangled hair: selected tanka from** *Midaregami*.
Akiko Yosano, translated with an introduction by Sanford Goldstein,
Seishi Shinoda.   Lafayette, Indiana: Purdue University Studies, 1971.
165p. Reprinted, Rutland, Vermont; Tokyo: Tuttle, 1987.

The highly gifted feminist poet Yosano Akiko (1878-1942) created a sensation in the
Japanese literary world in 1901 when she published her first volume of emotionally
charged poetry, *Midaregami* ('Tangled Hair'). Reshaping the tanka form into an
intensely personal and dramatic vehicle for expressing such feelings as suffering, love,
hatred, and pity, Akiko infused the classical tanka with a new spirit and a new subject-
matter. Goldstein and Shinoda's lengthy introduction – presenting information about
Akiko's personal life and about the background of her poetic achievements – is
combined with a graceful translation of 165 selected tanka and the texts of those poems
in both their original Japanese and their romanised form. Notes about individual
poems conclude the volume.

**A warbler's song in the dusk: the life and work of Ōtomo Yakamochi
(718–785).**
See item no. 301.

Fragments of rainbows: the life and poetry of Saitō Mokichi, 1882–1953.
See item no. 325.

A Zen forest: sayings of the masters.
See item no. 488.

Requiem for battleship Yamato.
See item no. 716.

Murasaki Shikibu: her diary and poetic memoirs; a translation and study.
See item no. 1023.

Tales of Yamato: a tenth-century poem-tale.
See item no. 1028.

**Contemporary Japanese literature: an anthology of fiction, film, and other
writing since 1945.**
See item no. 1057.

Masaoka Shiki.
See item no. 1161.

Hitomaro and the birth of Japanese lyricism.
See item no. 1163.

An introduction to Japanese court poetry.
See item no. 1164.

Japanese court poetry.
See item no. 1164.

**Japanese linked poetry: an account with translations of renga and haikai
sequences.**
See item no. 1165.

The road to Komatsubara: a classical reading of the renga hyakuin.
See item no. 1165.

One hundred frogs: from renga to haiku in English.
See item no. 1166.

Matsuo Bashō.
See item no. 1167.

Modern Japanese literature in translation: a bibliography.
See item no. 1588.

Japanese literature in European languages: a bibliography.
See item no. 1588.

Haiku in Western languages: an annotated bibliography (with some reference to senryu).
See item no. 1588.

Guide to Japanese poetry.
See item no. 1605.

Poetry: history and criticism

1161 **Masaoka Shiki.**
Janine Beichman.   Boston, Massachusetts: Twayne, 1982. 174p.
bibliog. (Twayne's World Authors Series, TWAS 661: Japan).
Reprinted, Tokyo; New York: Kodansha International, 1986.
The 'father of modern haiku', Masaoka Shiki (1867-1902) is regarded as a man of
vision and great energy who was responsible for introducing a new realism and
directness into Japanese poetry during the latter half of the Meiji period. Beichman's
critical study of this poet and literary critic surveys Shiki's short life and career,
considers the influence of earlier haiku poets upon his writings, examines the
development of his literary theories and standards, discusses and analyses his
composition not only of haiku and tanka but also of prose writings and diaries, and
assesses some of his efforts at reforming and revitalising two of the traditional forms of
poetry: haiku and tanka. Numerous translations of Shiki's poetry and prose are
included.

1162 **The haiku handbook: how to write, share, and teach haiku.**
William J. Higginson, with Penny Harter.   New York; Toronto,
Ontario: McGraw-Hill, 1985. 331p. bibliog.
A poet and past editor of *Haiku* magazine presents a comprehensive compendium of
the essentials of haiku including its nature, uses, and history. The first part ('Haiku Old
and New') surveys the development of haiku in Japan since the Tokugawa period and
the more recent rise of the haiku movement in the West. Part two ('Art of Haiku')
centres on the use of nature in haiku, its form and craft, and the sharing of haiku. This

is followed by a section about teaching haiku to children which includes 'a lesson plan that works'. Finally, in part four ('Before and Beyond Haiku'), Higginson offers a survey of tanka and *renga* (the precursors of haiku), *senryū* and haiku sequences (genres related to haiku), and *haibun* (haiku prose); and discusses some of the many uses of haiku. His handbook concludes with a reference section containing a season-word list that collects six hundred 'season words' (*kigo*) which poets have used to incorporate 'seasonal topics' (*kidai*) in traditional poetry, a glossary of haiku-related terms, and an annotated bibliography.

1163　**Hitomaro and the birth of Japanese lyricism.**
Ian Hideo Levy.　Princeton, New Jersey; Guildford, Surrey:
Princeton University Press, 1984. 174p. map. bibliog.

The poetry of Kakinomoto no Hitomaro (flourished *ca.* 685-705), the author of the most celebrated poems in the *Manyōshū* (q.v.), is the focus of this critical examination of the development of Japanese lyric verse during the late seventh century. Levy explores the ritual origins of Japanese poetry, the impact of Chinese and Korean literary influence, the conscious deification of the imperial family in Hitomaro's verse, and Hitomaro's lasting poetic achievements. English translations and Japanese transliterations of his poems appear throughout his study.

1164　**An introduction to Japanese court poetry.**
Earl Miner, with translations by Earl Miner, Robert H. Brower.
Stanford, California: Stanford University Press, 1968. 173p.

A general introduction to the poetry composed by members of the imperial court and by other individuals who followed their example between 500 and 1500 AD. The central part of the book surveys the major court poets and their work, beginning with Hitomaro, the greatest poet represented in the *Manyōshū*, and continuing through the Buddhist poet-priest Sōgi (1421-1502), master of the linked-verse known as *renga*. Over 150 poems in both romanised Japanese and English translation are included. Other chapters discuss the human and cultural values of this poetic tradition as well as its major themes, forms, and conventions. This work is a condensation, a reorganisation, and an extension (from the year 1350 to 1500) of *Japanese court poetry*, by Robert H. Brower and Earl Miner (Stanford, California: Stanford University Press, 1961; London: Cresset Press, 1962, 527p. [Stanford Studies in the Civilizations of Eastern Asia]). The latter is widely regarded as the standard, scholarly examination of the nature, ideals, practice, development, aesthetics, and tradition of Japanese court poetry before the Muromachi period.

1165　**Japanese linked poetry: an account with translations of renga and haikai sequences.**
Earl Miner.　Princeton, New Jersey; Guildford, Surrey: Princeton
University Press, 1979. 376p.

A comprehensive study of *renga* and *haikai*, two forms of linked verse that flourished during the fifteenth and sixteenth centuries and the seventeenth and eighteenth centuries respectively. Composed by two or three poets, each stanza is linked to the stanzas which immediately precede and follow it. Part one of Miner's study examines the historical evolution, principal poets, canons, and distinctive features of linked verse. The second and third parts present two *renga* sequences – *One hundred stanzas by three poets at Minase* (*Minase sangin hyakuin*), by Sōgi, Shōhaku, and Sōchō, and *A hundred stanzas related to "person" by Sōgi alone* (*Sōgi dokugin nanibito hyakuin*) – and four *haikai* sequences, composed by six renowned poets including Bashō and Buson. The texts of these poems appear in both Japanese transliteration and English translation and are accompanied by critical commentaries. An annotated translation of *Sōgi dokugin nanibito hyakuin* – preceded by extended discussions of the evolution of linked verse as a poetic genre, the various conventions of *renga*, and other basic elements important for understanding this poetry – also appears in Steven D. Carter's *The road to Komatsubara: a classical reading of the renga hyakuin* (Cambridge, Massachusetts: Council on East Asian Studies, Harvard University, 1987, 291p. [Harvard East Asian Monographs, 124]).

1166 **One hundred frogs: from renga to haiku to English.**
Hiroaki Sato. New York; Tokyo: Weatherhill, 1983. 241p. bibliog.
An historical survey, description, and presentation of the *renga*, hokku, and haiku forms of poetry. Part one (comprising over one-half of the volume) discusses the early history, conventions, and aesthetic characteristics of *renga* ('linked-verse'), the composition of *renga* by the seventeenth-century poet Matsuo Bashō and his disciples, and the evolution of the *renga* into hokku and haiku. In part two, Sato explains his own principles of translation and illustrates many other possible approaches through the compilation of one hundred different translations and adaptations of Bashō's famous hokku on a frog in an old pond. The concluding part consists of selections of *renga* and haiku by contemporary Western poets in English. This book is particularly valuable for its insights into the techniques of translating Japanese poetry. At the same time, it offers a clear, concise, and very enjoyable introduction to traditional Japanese poetry.

1167 **Matsuo Bashō.**
Makoto Ueda. New York: Twayne, 1970. 202p. map. bibliog.
(Twayne's World Authors Series, 102: Japan). Reprinted, Tokyo;
New York: Kodansha International, 1983.
The first book in English to provide a comprehensive account of the works of Matsuo Bashō (1644-94), Japan's foremost haiku poet. Ueda presents an overview of Bashō's life; discusses and analyses his haiku, *renku* (the linked verse out of which haiku evolved), prose writings (including short poetic essays and travel journals), and literary criticism; and comments briefly on Bashō's influence on subsequent Japanese literature. The texts of about 160 haiku, two complete *renku*, and excerpts from his prose writings appear in both romanised Japanese and English translation.

1168 **Modern Japanese poets and the nature of literature.**
Makoto Ueda. Stanford, California: Stanford University Press, 1983.
451p. bibliog.
An examination of the ideas about poetry that were held by eight important poets: Masaoka Shiki, Yosano Akiko, Ishikawa Takuboku, Hagiwara Sakutarō, Miyazawa Kenji, Takamura Kōtarō, Ogiwara Seisensui, and Takahashi Shinkichi. Ueda first summarises the historical development of Japanese poetry between the eighth century and the Meiji Restoration of 1868. He then explores their individual views about the relationship between art and nature, the creative process, the poem–reader relationship, the intrinsic elements of poetry, and the use of poetry. Based not only on their poems but also on their diaries, letters, essays, and published criticism, this

volume offers a wealth of information about these eight poets, all of whom have been extensively translated into English, as well as insights into the nature of modern Japanese poetry in general. A companion study, *Modern Japanese writers and the nature of literature* (q.v.), appeared in 1976.

Warlords, artists, and commoners: Japan in the sixteenth century.
See item no. 135.

Japan in the Muromachi age.
See item no. 140.

Sugawara no Michizane and the early Heian court.
See item no. 300.

A warbler's song in the dusk: the life and work of Ōtomo Yakamochi (718–785).
See item no. 301.

Fragments of rainbows: the life and poetry of Saitō Mokichi, 1882–1953.
See item no. 325.

Fujiwara Teika's Superior poems of our time: a thirteenth-century poetic treatise and sequence.
See item no. 1135.

Japanese death poems: written by Zen monks and haiku poets on the verge of death.
See item no. 1138.

The modern Japanese prose poem: an anthology of six poets.
See item no. 1141.

Kinoshita Yūji.
See item no. 1144.

A study of the Ise-monogatari: with the text according to the Den-Teika-hippon and an annotated translation.
See item no. 1148.

Kokinshū: a collection of poems ancient and modern.
See item no. 1153.

Brocade by night: 'Kokin wakashū' and the court style in Japanese classical poetry.
See item no. 1153.

Tall mountains and flowing waters: the arts of Uragami Gyokudō.
See item no. 1230.

Mountain storm, pine breeze: folk song in Japan.
See item no. 1381.

The Princeton companion to classical Japanese literature.
See item no. 1566.

Haiku in Western languages: an annotated bibliography (with some references to senryu).
See item no. 1588.

Guide to Japanese poetry.
See item no. 1605.

Drama

1169 **The ballad-drama of medieval Japan.**
James T. Araki. Berkeley, California: University of California Press, 1964. 289p. bibliog. (Publications of the Center for Japanese and Korean Studies).

A detailed, scholarly account of the *kōwaka*, a ballad-drama that was created and widely performed under samurai patronage during the sixteenth century. Its stories are drawn primarily from the early medieval period and narrate the dramatic highlights of stirring martial adventures, especially various episodes associated with the struggle for power between the Genji and Heike clans. Part one of Araki's study examines the *kōwaka* as a performing art and discusses the influence which *gagaku*, noh, *bugaku*, and various dances had upon its development. Particular attention is paid to its historical antecedents and evolution as well as to its present-day performance. Part two, a study of the librettos of *kōwaka*, discusses *kōwaka*'s narrative structure, literary characteristics, and style; summarises the plots of fifty surviving ballad-dramas; and provides the complete, annotated translations of two representative works: *Atsumori* (a prose narrative) and *Izumi's fortress* (a libretto written for recitation in a performance).

1170 **Major plays of Chikamatsu.**
Chikamatsu Monzaemon, translated with an introduction by Donald Keene, foreword by Wm. Theodore de Bary. New York; London: Columbia University Press, 1961. 485p. bibliog. (Records of Civilization: Sources and Studies, 66) (Unesco Collection of Representative Works: Japanese Series).

Complete, annotated translation of eleven of the 130 plays written by Japan's greatest playwright of the bunraku and kabuki theatres, Chikamatsu Monzaemon (1653-1724), whose plays were extremely popular among Tokugawa audiences and continue to be performed today. The introduction surveys Chikamatsu's career, the age in which he lived, his plays (including their subjects, characters, and structure), and their literary value. Four of Keene's translations – *The Love Suicides at Sonezaki*, *The Battles of Coxinga*, *The Uprooted Pine*, and *The Love Suicides at Amijima* – also subsequently appeared in an abbreviated edition entitled *Four major plays of Chikamatsu* (New York; London: Columbia University Press, 1964, 220p.). The other plays in this collection are *The Drum of the Waves of Horikawa*, *Yosaku from Tamba*, *The Love Suicides in the Women's Temple*, *The Courier for Hell*, *Gonza the Lancer*, *The Girls from Hakata, or Love at Sea*, and *The Woman-killer and the Hell of Oil*. Nearly all of the plays are 'domestic tragedies' (*sewamono*) dealing with love, adultery, murder, and double suicide.

1171   **Japanese drama and culture in the 1960s: the return of the gods.**
David G. Goodman.   Armonk, New York; London: M. E. Sharpe, 1988. 363p. (An East Gate Book).

A translation of five representative plays from the post-realistic theatre of the culturally turbulent 1960s – *Find Hakamadare!* (by Fukuda Yoshiyuki); *Kaison the Priest of Hitachi* (Akimoto Matsuyo); *My Beatles* (Satoh Makoto); *John Silver: The Beggar of Love* (Kara Jūrō); and *The Dance of Angels Who Burn Their Own Wings* (Satoh Makoto et al.) – accompanied by analytical commentaries which indicate how they were related to their psycho-historical context and at the same time also revealed it. These five plays are set within the broader contexts of both modern Japanese cultural history and contemporary world theatre movements. Goodman's study relates the political movement of Japanese New Left youth during the 1960s – 'protesting equally against the shadow of the atomic bombings, Stalinism, and the restoration of ruling-class hierarchies in the Vietnam War period' – to their quest for personal and collective meaning. A postscript about how Japanese theatre of the 1960s influenced subsequent developments in Japanese drama concludes the work.

1172   **Zeami's style: the Noh plays of Zeami Motokiyo.**
Thomas Blenman Hare.   Stanford, California: Stanford University Press, 1986. 319p. bibliog.

This comprehensive study of Zeami Motokiyo (1363-1443), the greatest playwright of classical noh theatre, investigates the characteristics which distinguish him from his fellow Muromachi period playwrights. It offers a documentary biography of Zeami; an explanation of various technical aspects of the structure and performance of Zeami's noh drama; detailed examinations of three of his most celebrated plays about old men, women, and warriors respectively – *Takasago*, *Izutsu*, and *Tadanori* – accompanied by their texts in transliterated Japanese and English translation; and a discussion of Zeami's style and the relationship between his dramatic theory and his plays.

1173   **After apocalypse: four Japanese plays of Hiroshima and Nagasaki.**
Kiyomi Hotta, Chikao Tanaka, Minoru Betsuyaku, Makoto Satoh; selected, translated and introduced by David G. Goodman.   New York; Guildford, Surrey: Columbia University Press, 1986. 325p.

Deeply moving plays by four of Japan's leading playwrights that range in style from realism to verse drama and offer distinctly different perspectives on the atomic bombing of Hiroshima and Nagasaki. *The Island* (by Hotta Kiyomi, 1955) realistically depicts the impact of Hiroshima on one family. *The Head of Mary* (Tanaka Chikao, 1958) deals with the bombing of Nagasaki within the context of Catholic theology as a manifestation of God's will in history. *The Elephant* (Betsuyaku Minoru, 1962) is an existentialist drama that portrays the anguish of survivors who have been ostracised by society. *Nezumi kozō: the Rat* (Satoh Makoto, 1969) interprets the atomic bomb as a manifestation of man's impulse for self-destruction.

1174 **Sugawara and the secrets of calligraphy.**
Edited and translated with an introduction by Stanleigh H. Jones, Jr.
New York; Guildford, Surrey: Columbia University Press, 1985. 288p.
bibliog. (Translations from the Oriental Classics).

A complete, annotated translation of one of the three most famous plays in the repertoire of both the bunraku and kabuki theatres. *Sugawara denju tenarai kagami* was written by Takeda Izumo II and two other playwrights and was first presented as a bunraku performance in 1746. It is based on the facts and legends surrounding the life of the ninth-century statesman, scholar, and poet Sugawara no Michizane. In his introduction Jones deals with the general background of the play, its authorship, and its adaptation for the kabuki theatre. He treats the play as both a literary work and a performance piece, faithfully translating the bunraku version of the text into a highly readable literary work while also providing related stage directions and performance notes. An appendix shows the construction and manipulation of the bunraku puppets.

1175 **Twenty plays of the nō theater.**
Edited with an introduction by Donald Keene, assisted by Royall
Tyler, illustrated with drawings by Tanrō Fukami and from the Hōshō
texts, foreword by Wm. Theodore de Bary. New York; London:
Columbia University Press, 1970. 336p. bibliog. (Records of
Civilization: Sources and Studies, 85) (Unesco Collection of
Representative Works: Japanese Series).

A representative selection in English translation of twenty plays in the active noh repertory, dating from the late fourteenth through the late sixteenth century. Among these are several plays by Kan'ami, Zeami, and Zenchiku (the chief noh dramatists) as well as works of unknown authorship. A complete 'program' of five plays – one from each of the traditional five categories of 'god plays', 'warrior plays', 'woman plays', 'realistic plays', and 'demon plays' – concludes the set of annotated translations prepared by Donald Keene and several collaborators. The introduction to the volume outlines some of the major conventions of noh drama together with its history. Line drawings in the margins, illustrating various movements of the actors as well as props and scenes from the plays, are interspersed throughout the texts.

1176 **The legend of Semimaru: blind musician of Japan.**
Susan Matisoff. New York; Guildford, Surrey: Columbia University
Press, 1978. 290p. bibliog. (Studies in Oriental Culture, 14).

A detailed study of the growth and transformation of the stories surrounding a legendary, tenth-century, blind *biwa* (lute)-playing musician named Semimaru of Ausaka. Matisoff begins by examining the historical background and character of this legendary figure. She analyses the literature of the legend of Semimaru – including the poetry ascribed to him – as well as Zeami's noh plays *Semimaru* and *Ausaka madman* (which deal with the theme of his life) and subsequent Tokugawa period reinterpretations of the Semimaru legend. The second half of her book translates in full the literary works associated with Semimaru, among them Zeami's two noh plays and Chikamatsu's puppet play *Semimaru*.

1177 **Five modern nō plays.**
Yukio Mishima, translated with an introduction by Donald Keene.
New York: Knopf, 1957. 198p. Reprinted, Rutland, Vermont and
Tokyo: Tuttle, 1967. New York: Vintage Books, 1973.

Five works adapted from well-known, centuries-old noh plays that blend dramatic
themes and plots of the past with contemporary theatrical forms and realism of feeling.
Written between 1950 and 1955, these five plays are entitled: *Sotoba Komachi, The
Damask Drum, Kantan, The Lady Aoi,* and *Hanjo.*

1178 **Toward a modern Japanese theatre: Kishida Kunio.**
J. Thomas Rimer.   Princeton, New Jersey: Princeton University
Press, 1974. 306p. bibliog.

An examination of the *shingeki,* or the 'New Theatre' movement in Japan, through the
career of Kishida Kunio (1890-1954), a playwright, critic, director, and teacher whose
writings and activities made him the most significant figure in the theatre of the 1930s.
Rimer begins his study with an overview of the efforts by the first generation of writers
of *shingeki* to modernise Japanese drama. He then describes and assesses Kishida's
work and his impact after he returned from France with the ambitious goal of
promoting the growth of a theatre dedicated to literary and humanistic ideals. Critical
discussions and detailed summaries of Kishida's plays are provided, and an appendix
briefly describes the New Theatre movement after 1939. Translations of *Kami fūsen*
('Paper Balloon'), *Shūu* ('Cloudburst'), *Ochiba nikki* ('A Diary of Fallen Leaves'),
Sawa-shi no futari musume ('The Two Daughters of Mr. Sawa'), and *Nyonin katsugō*
('Adoration') – a representative sampling of Kishida's nearly sixty plays – appear in
Five plays by Kishida Kunio, edited with an introduction by David G. Goodman,
translations by David G. Goodman, Richard McKinnon, and J. Thomas Rimer
(Ithaca, New York: East Asia Program, Cornell University, 1989, 143p. [Cornell
University East Asia Papers, 51]).

1179 **Modern Japanese drama: an anthology.**
Edited and translated with an introduction by Ted T. Takaya.   New
York; Guildford, Surrey: Columbia University Press, 1979. 277p.
bibliog. (Modern Asian Literature Series).

Translation of five plays written by some of Japan's leading postwar playwrights: *You,
Too, Are Guilty* (Abe Kōbō); *Yoroboshi: the Blind Young Man* (Mishima Yukio);
Hokusai Sketchbooks (Yashiro Seiichi); *The Boat is a Sailboat* (Yamazaki Masakazu);
and *The Move* (Betsuyaku Minoru). As a group, these *shingeki* drama are
representative of hundreds of plays which constitute the rapidly expanding repertory of
the modern Japanese theatre. Takaya's introduction outlines the evolution of the
modern theatre movement in Japan and briefly discusses the achievements of some of
its founders and playwrights. The plays selected for this anthology were produced
during the 1960s and 1970s.

1180 **Chūshingura (the treasury of loyal retainers): a puppet play.**
Takeda Izumo II, Miyoshi Shōraku, Namiki Senryū, translated with
an introduction by Donald Keene, foreword by Wm. Theodore de
Bary. New York; London: Columbia University Press, 1971. 183p.
bibliog. (Translations from the Oriental Classics) (Unesco Collection
of Representative Works: Japanese Series).

A complete translation of the original text (written in 1748) of the most popular work
in the bunraku and kabuki repertoires. This gripping play dramatises the story of the
forty-seven *rōnin* (masterless samurai): the revenge exacted in 1703 by the former
retainers of Asano Naganori, the daimyō of Akō, on the feudal lord (Kira
Kōzukenosuke) who had brought about his untimely death. Focusing on the theme of
devotion and loyalty, the play highlights one of the paramount principles of samurai
conduct during the Tokugawa period. Takaya's introduction discusses the historical
background, authorship, characters, and style of the play; the kabuki versions of
Chūshingura; and the play's theatrical reputation. A more detailed presentation of the
historical background of this dramatic masterpiece appears in *Chūshingura: an
exposition*, by Shioya Sakae, illustrated with Hiroshige's coloured plates (Tokyo:
Hokuseido Press, 1965. 2nd ed., 236p.).

1181 **The nō plays of Japan.**
Edited, translated and introduced by Arthur Waley. London: Allen
and Unwin, 1921; New York: Knopf, 1922. 270p. Reprinted, New
York: Grove Press, 1957. 319p.; Rutland, Vermont and Tokyo:
Tuttle, 1976. 270p.; London: Unwin Paperbacks, 1988. 319p.

Translations of nineteen important noh plays – among them *Atsumori*, *Sotoba
Komachi*, *Hagoromo*, and *Haku rakuten* – and of one *kyōgen* interlude together with
summaries of sixteen additional plays. Many of these texts are by the famous
playwrights Zeami Motokiyo and Komparu Zenchiku (also known as Zenchiku
Ujinobu). Waley's introductory essay discusses the background and historical
development of noh drama; its basic theatrical elements such as costumes, music, and
stage properties; and the texts of the noh plays. This volume helped to establish noh
drama as an important Japanese literary genre in the view of Western readers well
before World War II.

1182 **Mask and sword: two plays for the contemporary Japanese theater.**
Masakazu Yamazaki, translated with an introduction by J. Thomas
Rimer. New York; Guildford, Surrey: Columbia University Press;
Tokyo: University of Tokyo Press, 1980. 221p. (Modern Asian
Literature Series).

Complete translations of *Zeami* and *Sanetomo*, two plays by a contemporary
playwright, teacher, and literary critic. Dealing with historical incidents in the lives of
the noh actor Zeami Motokiyo (1364-1443) and the shōgun and accomplished poet
Minamoto Sanetomo (1192-1219), these plays illuminate such modern 'psychological
and philosophical concerns' as the conflict between an individual's vocation and his
self-identity. Rimer's extended interview with Yamazaki Masakazu about his own
career and philosophy, the development of modern Japanese theatre, and theatrical
conditions and problems in Japan during the 1970s is appended as a source of
additional information for the study of *shingeki* drama.

Literature. Drama

Contemporary Japanese literature: an anthology of fiction, film, and other writing since 1945.
See item no. 1057.

Japanese theatre.
See item no. 1394.

Kabuki: five classic plays.
See item no. 1396.

The kabuki guide.
See item no. 1401.

The kabuki handbook: a guide to understanding and appreciation, with summaries of favourite plays, explanatory notes, and illustrations.
See item no. 1401.

Kyōgen.
See item no. 1402.

A guide to kyōgen.
See item no. 1402.

Japanese folk plays: the Ink-smeared lady and other kyōgen.
See item no. 1402.

The art of kabuki: famous plays in performance.
See item no. 1407.

Early nō drama: its background, character, and development, 1300–1450.
See item no. 1409.

The puppet theatre of Japan.
See item no. 1411.

Kabuki encyclopedia: an English-language adaptation of *Kabuki jiten*.
See item no. 1564.

The Princeton companion to classical Japanese literature.
See item no. 1566.

Modern Japanese literature in translation: a bibliography.
See item no. 1588.

Japanese literature in European languages: a bibliography.
See item no. 1588.

Guide to Japanese drama.
See item no. 1603.

Folklore

1183 **Japanese proverbs and sayings.**
Compiled and edited by Daniel Crump Buchanan. Norman,
Oklahoma: University of Oklahoma Press, 1965. 280p.

Some 2,500 proverbs and idiomatic sayings in romanised Japanese and English translation are grouped together under fifty-six categories designed to illustrate such aspects of the Japanese character as amorousness, class consciousness, deceit, discipline, honour, patience, pessimism, shame, superstition, and thrift. Under the category of 'learning', for example, one can find the saying *Shomotsu wa hozon-sareta kokoro nari*: 'Books are preserved minds'. Buchanan frequently adds brief comments about the history or etymological derivation of a proverb, together with a parallel saying in English (if one exists), to help clarify its meaning. A subject index helps readers to locate proverbs and sayings on specific topics.

1184 **Folk legends of Japan.**
Richard M. Dorson, illustrated by Yoshie Noguchi. Rutland,
Vermont; Tokyo: Tuttle, 1962. 256p. bibliog.

An anthology of 123 representative folk legends about priests, temples and shrines, monsters, spirits, transformations, heroes and strong men, *chōja* (rich peasants), knaves, and places. Each legend is prefaced by a brief explanation of its nature and meaning as well as by an indication of its sources.

1185 **Ancient tales in modern Japan: an anthology of Japanese folk tales.**
Selected and translated with an introduction by Fanny Hagin Mayer.
Bloomington, Indiana: Indiana University Press, 1985. 360p. bibliog.

A comprehensive representation of Japanese folk-tale types is offered in this collection of 347 folk tales. Divided into two categories (tales in complete form, and derived tales), these tales deal with such themes and subjects as success in finding treasure, the ability to overcome evil, the receipt of help from animals, cleverness at work, and unpromising marriages that turn into happy ones. Also included are ghost stories, humorous stories, stories about destiny, and tales about birds, beasts, plants, and trees. Fanny Hagin Mayer, a pioneer Western scholar in the field of folklore, selected and in many cases translated these tales.

1186 **Japanese mythology.**
Juliet Piggott. London: Hamlyn, 1982; New York: Peter Bedrick
Books, 1983. rev. ed. 144p. map. bibliog. (Library of the World's
Myths and Legends).

A profusely illustrated presentation and general interpretation of Japanese myths, legends, folk tales, and folklore, divided into seven sections: 'The Country and Its Creation', 'A Historical Survey', 'The Beliefs and Deities of Japan', 'Creatures and Spirits', 'Heroes and Heroines', 'Men and Animals', and 'Stories of Old and New'. Piggott introduces and summarises many of the myths and stories that have been derived from the Buddhist and Shintō religious traditions as well as from other sources, and shows how indigenous stories about the gods and other supernatural beings, men and women, and animals appear in various forms within Japanese literature and culture.

1187 **Folktales of Japan.**
Edited with an introduction by Keigo Seki, translated by Robert J. Adams, foreword by Richard M. Dorson. Chicago: University of Chicago Press; London: Routledge and Kegan Paul, 1963. 221p. bibliog. (Folktales of the World).

Sixty-three representative tales chosen from a selection of 240 stories that were collected by the noted folklorist Seki Keigo and published in his three-volume work *Nihon no mukashi-banashi* (Tokyo, 1956-57). Adams' translations are thematically grouped into six sections: 'Animal Tales', 'Ogres', 'Supernatural Husbands and Wives', 'Kindness Rewarded and Evil Punished', 'Good Fortune', and 'Cleverness and Stupidity'. The Aarne–Thompson tale-type number, the motif, and a brief translator's note appear at the beginning of each tale.

1188 **The legends of Tōno.**
Kunio Yanagita, translated with an introduction by Ronald A. Morse, foreword by Richard M. Dorson. Tokyo: Japan Foundation, 1975. 90p. 3 maps. (Japan Foundation Translation Series).

In 1910, the noted folklorist and scholar Yanagita Kunio (1875-1962) published a collection of 119 legends which had been recorded in conversations with a storyteller from the remote mountain village of Tōno (Iwate Prefecture). These brief tales describe the comings and goings of a wide variety of spirits such as demons, goblins, and *kappa* (amphibious supernatural creatures), and they are intimately bound up with the daily life of that village. *Tōno monogatari* ('The legends of Tōno') subsequently became the most widely read of Yanagita's many works and is now considered a modern classic of Japanese folklore and literature. *Japanese folk tales: a revised selection*, translated by Fanny Hagin Mayer (Tokyo: Tokyo News Service, 1966, 190p.), *Japanese manners and customs in the Meiji era*, translated and adapted by Charles S. Terry (Tokyo: Ōbunsha, 1957, 335p. [Centenary Cultural Council. Japanese Culture in the Meiji Era, 4.] Reprinted, Tokyo: Toyo Bunko, 1969), and *The Yanagita Kunio guide to the Japanese folk tale*, translated and edited by Fanny Hagin Mayer (Bloomington, Indiana: Indiana University Press, 1986, 363p.) are among Yanagita's other books currently available in English.

Ainu life and lore: echoes of a departing race.
See item no. 372.

Songs of gods, songs of humans: the epic tradition of the Ainu.
See item no. 380.

Daruma: the founder of Zen in Japanese art and popular culture.
See item no. 483.

Studies in Japanese folklore.
See item no. 503.

Japanese tales.
See item no. 1029.

Japanese ghosts & demons: art of the supernatural.
See item no. 1189.

Asian Folklore Studies.
See item no. 1490.

Legend in Japanese art: a description of historical episodes, legendary characters, folk-lore, myths, religious symbolism, illustrated in the arts of old Japan.
See item no. 1560.

Mock Joya's things Japanese.
See item no. 1561.

Japanese folk literature: a core collection and reference guide.
See item no. 1577.

Fine Arts

General

1189 **Japanese ghosts & demons: art of the supernatural.**
Edited by Stephen Addiss, preface by Jay Gates, introduction by
Akira Y. Yamamoto. New York: Braziller; Lawrence, Kansas:
Spencer Museum of Art, University of Kansas, 1985. 192p. bibliog.

An exhibition catalogue, organised by subject, which focuses upon the theme of the
supernatural in Japanese art and culture. It contains photographs of ninety-nine
Tokugawa and Meiji period artworks including woodblock prints, woodblock-printed
books, paintings and screens, netsuke and inrō, and wood sculptures produced by
Tsukioka Yoshitoshi, Utagawa Kuniyoshi, and other imaginative artists. Ten essays
about the major sections of the exhibition define the most vital areas of supernatural
folk beliefs in Japan and discuss the aesthetic, biographical, historical, and social
aspects of these artworks. These essays bear the titles 'One Hundred Demons and One
Hundred Supernatural Tales', '*Yūrei*: Tales of Female Ghosts', 'The Male Ghost in
Kabuki and Ukiyo-e', '*Sennin*: the Immortals of Taoism', '*Shōki* the Demon Queller',
'*Oni*: the Japanese Demon', '*Tengu*, the Mountain Goblin', 'The Trickster in Japan:
Tanuki and *Kitsune*', 'Snakes, Serpents, and Humans', and 'Two and a Half Worlds:
Humans, Animals, and In-between'.

1190 **Zen at Daitoku-ji.**
Jon Covell, Sōbin Yamada. Tokyo; New York: Kodansha
International, 1974. 203p. 3 maps.

The Daitokuji ('The Temple of Great Virtue'), a large temple complex of the Rinzai
Zen Buddhist sect in Kyōto, was established in the early fourteenth century and has
since been patronised by major historical figures. It houses many priceless works of art,
among them ten paintings by the Sung period Chinese artist Mu Ch'i, and is world-
famous for some of its gardens. Covell (an American specialist in Japanese art history)
and Yamada Sōbin (the twenty-sixth abbot of the Shinju-an sub-temple of the
Daitokuji) write about the Zen-influenced art and daily life at Daitokuji, illustrating

their text with 102 photographs, many in full colour. They focus on the temple's celebrated history, its six-centuries-long tradition of the tea ceremony, its gardens, the Chinese and Japanese paintings found within its precincts, and daily life at the temple during the early 1970s.

1191 **The elements of Japanese design: a handbook of family crests, heraldry & symbolism.**
John W. Dower, crests drawn by Kiyoshi Kawamoto.   New York; Tokyo: Walker/Weatherhill, 1971. 170p. bibliog.

Mon or *monshō* – the 'heraldic emblems of Japan' – were initially used by medieval warriors as a means of identification on the battlefield. These designs subsequently developed familial associations and were adopted first by the samurai class to indicate lineage and then also by commoners as an element of popular fashion. Dower begins by tracing the history and social significance of heraldic design and practice in Japan. Informative commentaries accompany his classified presentation of over 2,700 precisely drawn crests. Six major sections (entitled 'Heaven and Earth', 'Plants, Flowers, and Trees', 'Birds, Beasts, and Insects', 'Man-made Objects', 'Patterns and Designs', and 'Symbols and Ideographs') categorise these crests according to their dominant design motifs, e.g., mountain, pine, goose, amulet, stripe, incense symbols. The book provides a comprehensive and detailed overview which a wide range of readers – from artists to social historians – can readily appreciate.

1192 **Heian temples: Byodo-in and Chuson-ji.**
Toshio Fukuyama, translated by Ronald K. Jones.   New York; Tokyo: Weatherhill/Heibonsha, 1976. 168p. 13 maps. (Heibonsha Survey of Japanese Art, 9).

The paintings, sculpture, interior decoration, and architecture of Pure Land (Jōdo) Buddhism, a sect which flourished during the Heian period, are depicted in this heavily illustrated study that centres on two major extant temples: the Byōdōin at Uji, near Kyōto, and the Chūsonji in Iwate Prefecture. Fukuyama covers the origins and subsequent development of the Pure Land Buddhist art of this period, several of the temples that were built by the Fujiwara aristocracy and by the retired emperors in and around the capital city of Kyōto, the extension and manifestations of Pure Land Buddhist art in northern and western Japan, and the artistic world of the mandala in Pure Land Buddhism.

1193 **Folk traditions in Japanese art.**
Introduction and catalogue by Victor Hauge, Takako Hauge.
Tokyo; New York: Kodansha International in co-operation with the International Exhibitions Foundation and the Japan Foundation, 1978. 272p. bibliog.

Commemorates the first major travelling exhibition in North America of representative Japanese folk art objects – paintings, prints, sculpture, textiles, ceramics, lacquerware, furniture, bambooware, basketry, metalwork, and religious objects – dating from the years 1600 to 1930. In 230 photographs, each accompanied by a short commentary about the object's cultural background and special characteristics, the catalogue documents the beauty, strength and vitality of the true folk art of Japan, conveys a picture of the history and way of life of the common people, and explains the ways in which these objects were produced and used.

1194 **The silk road and the Shoso-in.**
Ryōichi Hayashi, translated by Robert Ricketts.   New York; Tokyo:
Weatherhill/Heibonsha, 1975. 181p. map. (Heibonsha Survey of
Japanese Art, 6).

The Shōsōin, a huge wooden storehouse on the grounds of the Tōdaiji temple in Nara,
contains several thousand rare ornamental and fine-art objects dating from the eighth
century. Its fabulous collection of paintings, musical instruments, chests, mirrors,
masks, Buddhist altar fittings, calligraphy, furniture, dance costumes, brocades,
ceramics, metalwork, official documents, medicines, weapons, textiles, sculpture,
stationery, and similar objects has been almost perfectly preserved for over 1,200
years. Some of these works came to Japan over the 'silk road', the great trade route
between Byzantium and Persia in the West and T'ang China in the East. Hayashi
discusses the general background of both the imported and domestically produced
objects, analyses many of these works, and illustrates selected items in some two
hundred photographs.

1195 **Zen and the fine arts.**
Shin'ichi Hisamatsu, translated by Gishin Tokiwa.   Tokyo; Palo
Alto, California: Kodansha International, 1971. 400p. Reprinted,
Tokyo; New York: Kodansha International, 1982.

A description of the tradition and spiritual impact of Zen Buddhism on Japanese art
and culture, particularly during the fifteenth, sixteenth, and seventeenth centuries. The
first sixty pages survey the fine arts of Zen in both China and Japan, discuss Zen
aesthetics, consider the basic characteristics of Zen Buddhism, and present Hisamatsu's
'appreciations' (commentaries) on a number of the photographic plates which the
author has selected to illustrate many of his points. The remainder of the book consists
of 275 largely monochromatic plates of representative paintings, calligraphy,
architecture, gardens, costumes, masks, stage properties, tea bowls, and other ceramic
pieces associated with the noh theatre.

1196 **Zen culture.**
Thomas Hoover.   New York: Random House, 1977; London:
Routledge and Kegan Paul, 1978; New York: Vintage Books, 1978.
262p. bibliog. Reprinted, London: Routledge, 1988.

Traces the historical development and characteristics of Zen Buddhism from early to
modern times, and introduces the Zen culture which found expression in archery and
swordsmanship, landscape gardening, stone gardens, monochrome ink painting,
calligraphy, architecture, the noh theatre, the tea ceremony, haiku poetry, flower
arrangement, ceramics, and the aesthetics of Japanese cuisine. Hoover shows how
these individual art forms originated in early Japanese (especially Heian period)
culture and were subsequently influenced by Zen in ways that led to the creation of a
uniquely Japanese set of aesthetics.

1197 **The heritage of Japanese art.**
Masao Ishizawa (et al.).   Tokyo; New York: Kodansha International,
1982. 208p. map. bibliog.

An overview of the major constituents of traditional Japanese art – from prehistoric
times through the Tokugawa period – is presented in a brief but authoritative textual

survey and 161 captioned, full-colour plates. Included are illustrations of paintings, scrolls, folding screens, ancient figurines, tea bowls, jars, masks, bronze and wooden statues, textiles, woodblock prints, lacquerware, swords, and mirrors. Many of these objects have been designated as 'national treasures' and are housed in the Tokyo National Museum and in various temples and museums of the Kyōto–Nara area. The text and captions of this book were adapted from *Art treasures of Japan*, edited by Yukio Yashiro (Tokyo: Kokusai Bunka Shinkōkai, 1960, 2 vols.).

1198 **Forms, textures, images: traditional Japanese craftsmanship in everyday life. A photo-essay.**
Takeji Iwamiya, edited and introduced by Mitsukuni Yoshida, with an appreciation by Richard L. Gage, translated by Susan Carol Barberi.
New York; Tokyo: Weatherhill/Tankosha, 1979. 303p.

This magnificently produced, folio-size volume is an attempt 'to fix in photographs the forms of some of the objects that the Japanese people of the past devised from natural materials and passed on to' succeeding generations. Under the headings of 'wood', 'bamboo', 'paper', 'metal', 'clay', 'stone', and 'symbols', Iwamiya presents a photographic survey of traditional Japanese handicrafts that are grouped together according to the material of their manufacture. Some three hundred full-page pictures illustrate the aesthetic qualities of kitchen utensils, ritual objects, musical instruments, clothing accessories, architectural features, flower containers, kites and children's toys, and a variety of other objects typically found in the past. Yoshida's introduction, 'Aspects of Form in Japan', and Gage's appreciation, 'The Myriad-Fragment Mirror', comment on the evolution and importance of forms in Japanese cultural life and discuss the objects that are depicted from the viewpoints of colour, material, and function.

1199 **The arts of Shinto.**
Haruki Kageyama, translated and adapted with an introduction by Christine Guth. New York; Tokyo: Weatherhill/Shibundo, 1973. 143p. bibliog. (Arts of Japan, 4).

An illustrated guide through the complexities of Shintō art which examines this indigenously Japanese art in its religious rather than art-historical context. Specifically discussed are the special characteristics of Shintō art, the treasures of a number of shrines, Shintō sculpture, paintings of various Shintō deities, and the art of four Shintō cults: Kasuga, Hachiman, Sannō, and Kumano. Complementing Kageyama's book is a collaborative volume of Haruki Kageyama and Christine Guth Kanda entitled *Shinto arts: nature, gods, and man in Japan* (New York: Japan Society, 1976, 169p.), which served as a catalogue for fifty Shintō art works on display at the Japan House Gallery (New York City) and the Seattle (Washington) Art Museum.

1200 **Form, style, tradition: reflections on Japanese art and society.**
Shūichi Katō, translated by John Bester. Berkeley, California; London: University of California Press, 1971. 216p. bibliog. Reprinted, Tokyo; New York: Kodansha International, 1982.

A collection of eight essays dealing with a wide range of Japanese art that are united by Katō's concern with the position of the artist in society and with the historical and social determinants of style. Through an analysis of such themes as social values and the artist, the alienation of the artist, and the impact of technological change upon art, and through his discussions of style in Buddhist sculpture, the '*Tale of Genji* picture scroll', the style of the school of Sōtatsu, and the tea ceremony, Katō tries to identify the traditional elements of Japanese culture and the universal elements of human expression that are found in contemporary Japanese art. His final essay, 'Artistic Creativity Today', makes use of the Japanese case to show the kinds of difficulties which can confront an artist in a situation of culture conflict.

1201 **Craft treasures of Okinawa.**
Michiaki Kawakita, Seikō Hokama, Yoshinobu Tokugawa, Hirokazu Arakawa, Yoshitarō Kamakura, translated and adapted by Erika Kaneko. Tokyo; New York: Kodansha International, 1978. 294p. map. bibliog.

A magnificent, visual record of the first major exhibition of handicrafts from the Ryūkyū Islands, held at the National Museum of Modern Art in Kyōto in 1974. Two hundred full-size illustrations show the range, scope, and beauty of Okinawan ceramics, musical instruments, lacquerware, and textiles. Most of the volume consists of colour plates of the objects that were selected for display, accompanied by notes providing basic information about them. In addition, five Japanese specialists contribute a sequence of brief essays about the history of the Ryūkyūs and the production there of fine handicraft work since the fifteenth century.

1202 **Forms in Japan.**
Yūichirō Kōjiro, translated by Kenneth Yasuda, photographs by Yukio Futagawa. Honolulu, Hawaii: East-West Center Press, 1965. 184p.

A noted architectural critic systematically describes, analyses, and classifies a set of Japanese aesthetic principles regarding the various forms which exist within the Japanese universe. Kōjiro classifies these forms into four major categories – 'forms of unity', 'forms of force', 'forms of adaptation', and 'forms of change' – and further subdivides each of these categories as he presents representations of individual forms. Over one hundred superb black-and-white photographs taken primarily of Japanese architecture, art, and handicrafts accompany the text.

1203 **The contemporary artist in Japan.**
David Kung. Honolulu, Hawaii: East-West Center Press; Sydney, New South Wales: Angus & Robertson; Tokyo: Bijutsu Shuppansha, 1966. 187p.

An introduction to a wide range of techniques and styles current among such painters, sculptors, print-makers, and calligraphy artists as Fukuzawa Ichirō, Kumagai Morikazu, Munakata Shikō, Shinoda Morio, and Yamaguchi Takeo. Using their own words, Kung presents some of the views which thirty-five contemporary artists have of the objects they have created and of Japanese art in general. This is supplemented by over one hundred black-and-white and twenty-four colour illustrations of their work, brief biographies and photographs of the artists, Imaizumi Atsuo's short essay on the background of modern Japanese painting, and the author's interview with Takoguchi Shūzō, a poet who has followed the development of modern culture in Japan since the 1930s.

1204　**The genius of Japanese design.**
Sherman E. Lee.　Tokyo; New York: Kodansha International, 1981.
203p. bibliog.

A brief introductory essay surveys the historical evolution and aesthetic conception of Japanese design and seeks to explain why 'so much Japanese art looks so different from Chinese art'. Lee's comments are then substantiated through the presentation of several hundred examples of design motifs and techniques found in traditional Japanese (largely Tokugawa period) paintings, prints, textiles, ceramics, lacquerware, metalwork, and garden design as well as in family crests. The largely monochrome photographs and illustrations of these objects are grouped together according to subject and motif, e.g., cherry blossoms, spring grasses, chrysanthemums, grape vines, bamboo, birds and insects, animals, water, implements, and geometric patterns.

1205　**Reflections of reality in Japanese art.**
Sherman E. Lee, catalogue by Michael R. Cunningham with James T. Ulak.　Cleveland, Ohio: Cleveland Museum of Art in co-operation with Indiana University Press (Bloomington, Indiana), 1983. 292p. bibliog.

The catalogue of an exhibition organised by the world-renowned director and chief curator of Oriental art at the Cleveland Museum of Art shortly before his retirement. Lee's discussion of realism in style, method, and subject-matter as a reflection of Japanese society, history, and beliefs is illustrated by 138 examples of Japanese painting and sculpture. Detailed information is provided about each subject. Sherman Lee is also well known for his copiously illustrated survey textbook, *A history of Far Eastern art* (Englewood Cliffs, New Jersey: Prentice-Hall and Harry N. Abrams [New York], 1982. 4th ed. 548p.), which offers a general introduction to the visual arts of Asia from Pakistan to Japan and Southeast Asia between the fifth millennium BC and 1850 AD, with particular focus on the artistic traditions of China, India, and Japan and their interrelationships.

1206　**The great eastern temple: treasures of Japanese Buddhist art from Tōdai-ji.**
Organized by Yutaka Mino, with contributions from John M. Rosenfield, William H. Coaldrake, Samuel C. Morse, Christine M. E. Guth; foreword by James N. Wood.　Chicago: Art Institute of Chicago in association with Indiana University Press (Bloomington, Indiana), 1986. 180p. bibliog.

An exhibition catalogue of eighty-one important sculptures, theatrical masks, illustrated handscrolls, hanging scrolls, screens, examples of calligraphy, and decorative and ritual art objects (including seals, mirrors, bowls, bells, lanterns, and reliquaries) from the monastic complex known as the Tōdaiji ('The Great Eastern Temple') in Nara. These works of Buddhist art, acquired by that temple over a thousand-year-long period, constitute some of its most prized possessions. They were on exhibit at the Art Institute of Chicago during the summer of 1986. Introducing the catalogue are four illustrated essays entitled 'Tōdai-ji in Japanese History and Art', 'The Architecture of Tōdai-ji', 'Sculpture at Tōdai-ji', and 'Painting at Tōdai-ji'.

Fine Arts. General

1207 **Design motifs.**
Saburō Mizoguchi, translated and adapted by Louise Allison Cort.
New York; Tokyo: Weatherhill/Shibundo, 1973. 143p. (Arts of
Japan, 1).

A concise survey of the evolution of traditional Japanese decorative motifs from
Neolithic and Jōmon times through the nineteenth century. These motifs appeared on
a wide range of objects including textiles, furniture, ceramics, weapons, lacquerware,
paper scrolls, musical instruments, and sword guards. Mizoguchi's fully illustrated
account discusses the origins, variations, and aesthetic uses of the most representative
motifs of each period. It also examines Yūsoku textile patterns and family crests.

1208 **Asuka Buddhist art: Horyu-ji.**
Seiichi Mizuno, translated by Richard L. Gage. New York; Tokyo:
Weatherhill/Heibonsha, 1974. 172p. 2 maps. (Heibonsha Survey of
Japanese Art, 4).

The Hōryūji, a monastery-temple complex near Nara that was first built in the early
seventh century, owns one of the finest collections of Buddhist art in Japan and is
unsurpassed for its holdings from the Asuka period. It is particularly renowned for
housing the oldest wooden buildings in the world today and for possessing such works
of art as the Buddha Shaka triad in the Golden Hall, the Amida triad of Lady
Tachibana's Shrine, the statues of the Kudara Kannon and the Chuguji Miroku
Bosatsu, and the Tamamushi Shrine, all of which are discussed and depicted in some
detail. Mizuno's richly illustrated text describes the beginnings of Buddhist art in
Japan, the masterpieces of Asuka and early Hakuhō period sculpture, the
reconstruction and architectural features of the Hōryūji following its destruction by a
conflagration in 670 AD, the celebrated murals and sculpture of this complex, and the
origins and sources of Japanese Buddhist sculpture.

1209 **The art of modern Japan: from the Meiji Restoration to the Meiji
centennial, 1868–1968.**
Hugo Munsterberg. New York: Hacker Art Books, 1978. 159p.
bibliog.

An illustrated overview of the extraordinary changes and developments that occurred
in Japanese painting, print-making, sculpture, architecture, and crafts during a
comparatively brief period in Japanese history: the one hundred years following the
Meiji Restoration. Munsterberg traces in particular some of the interaction between
Western art forms and techniques and traditional Japanese art which characterised this
era.

1210 **Folk arts and crafts of Japan.**
Kageo Muraoka, Kichiemon Okamura, translated by Daphne S.
Stegmaier. New York; Tokyo: Weatherhill/Heibonsha, 1973. 164p.
(Heibonsha Survey of Japanese Art, 26).

A general introduction to the world of Japanese folk arts, viewed within the context of
Japanese life. Muraoka and Okamura introduce the full range of folk-craft products –
ceramics, textiles, woodwork, metalwork, and folk pictures – and discuss their
appreciation, characteristics, beauty, and history. They conclude with an examination
of past influences on the development of folk crafts and with an analysis of its present-

494

day state. The 160 photographs (30 of them in colour) illustrate such objects as bowls, chests, curtains, plates, funerary urns, pipes, stationery boxes, rugs, and the jars used for storing tea.

1211 **The arts of Japan. Volume 1: Ancient and medieval. Volume 2: Late medieval to modern.**
Seiroku Noma, translated and adapted with a foreword and a preface by John Rosenfield, Glenn T. Webb, photographs by Bin Takahashi. Tokyo; New York: Kodansha International, 1978. 1st standard ed. 2 vols. 5 maps. bibliog.

A very extensively illustrated survey of the history of the visual arts: sculpture, painting, ceramics, architecture, woodblock prints, textiles, garden design, lacquerware, and swords. Examining the historical, political, social, and religious circumstances that fostered various schools and styles as well as the aesthetic aspects of Japan's artistic accomplishments, Noma presents a contextual overview of Japanese art while authoritatively commenting on those representative works which 'seem to evoke the aesthetic, spiritual, and even social ideals of their original setting'. Volume one follows the evolution of Japanese art from the pottery and tomb artefacts of prehistoric Japan through the Buddhist and secular arts of Nara, Kyōto, and Kamakura. Volume two topically covers such artistic developments as castle architecture and ukiyo–e woodblock prints between the late sixteenth and mid-twentieth centuries. The bibliographies found in an earlier, deluxe edition of this work (published by Kodansha International in 1966-67) have been revised and updated.

1212 **The art and architecture of Japan.**
Robert Treat Paine, Alexander Soper. Part 1 brought up to date by David B. Waterhouse, part 2 brought up to date by Bunji Kobayashi, with revisions and updated notes and bibliography to part 1 by David B. Waterhouse. Harmondsworth, Middlesex; Baltimore, Maryland: Penguin Books, 1981. 3rd ed. 524p. 2 maps. bibliog. (Pelican History of Art).

A thoroughly researched introduction to the art and architecture of Japan, presented as part of a major series on the history of world art. In part one, Paine provides an historical analysis of painting and sculpture from the Archaic period through the Buddhist art of the Heian and Kamakura periods, the decorative arts of the Muromachi era, and the ukiyo-e paintings and prints of the Tokugawa period. In part two, Soper examines the evolution of architecture from the Shintō shrines and tombs of the pre-Buddhist age through the secular and Buddhist architecture of the Heian period to the secular and religious architecture of the Muromachi, Momoyama, and Tokugawa periods. Numerous monochrome photographs and architectural drawings are included.

1213 **Yō no bi: the beauty of Japanese folk art.**
William Jay Rathbun, with contributions by Michael Knight, foreword by Henry Trubner, Arnold Jolles. Seattle, Washington: Seattle Art Museum and University of Washington Press, 1983. 133p. map. bibliog.

Yō no bi means 'beauty in function' and refers to the 'natural grace that inhabits works

Fine Arts. General

made in specific, though perhaps unconscious, response to human needs'. This catalogue of folk art drawn from collections in the northwestern part of the United States that was exhibited at the Seattle Art Museum in 1983 shows many fine examples of sculpture and wood-carving, furniture (*tansu* and lanterns), metalwork, lacquerware, bamboo and basketry, textiles (primarily kimono and coats), painting and shop signs, and ceramics dating principally from the Tokugawa and Meiji periods. The largely black-and-white photographs of the 148 objects on display are accompanied by detailed descriptions of their origins, character, use, and significance.

1214 **Traditions of Japanese art: selections from the Kimiko and John Powers Collection.**
John M. Rosenfield, Shūjirō Shimada, foreword by Agnes Mongan. Cambridge, Massachusetts: Fogg Art Museum, Harvard University, 1970. 393p.

Reflecting most major aspects of Japanese art from prehistoric times through the Tokugawa period, the collection of Kimiko and John Powers is particularly strong in its holdings of painting, sculpture, calligraphy, archaeological material, and Buddhist ritual implements. The 153 objects selected for exhibition at Harvard University, Princeton University, and the Seattle (Washington) Art Museum are grouped together under the main headings 'Japanese Buddhist Arts', 'Arts Related to the Zen Sect', 'Kōetsu, Sōtatsu and Their Tradition', 'Bunjin-ga' (paintings of the literary men), 'Genre Themes in Painting and the Decorative Arts', and 'Archaeological Material'. The authors describe each object in both historical and aesthetic terms, relate it to the larger patterns and traditions of Japanese culture, and depict it in one or more black-and-white photographs.

1215 **Japanese antiques: with a guide to shops.**
Patricia Salmon. Tokyo: Art International Publishers [distributed outside Japan by the University of Hawaii Press], 1985. rev. ed. 256p. 8 maps. bibliog.

An illustrated guidebook and directory to a very wide range of currently available antiques, including fans, netsuke, lacquerware, chests, *gagaku* and noh masks, hanging scrolls, screens, woodblock prints, several kinds of porcelain, incense burners, sword guards, writing-boxes, stone lanterns, tea kettles, kimonos, dolls, and shop signs. Salmon briefly describes each type of antique, indicates when and how they were created, and comments on both their traditonal use and the ways in which they can now be used. She also includes an annotated directory (with maps) to antique shops and dealers in the Tokyo, Kamakura, and Kyōto areas; information about how to recognise, select, and preserve antiques; and a glossary of Japanese antique terms.

1216 **Art in Japanese esoteric Buddhism.**
Takaaki Sawa, translated by Richard L. Gage. New York; Tokyo: Weatherhill/Heibonsha, 1972. 151p. (Heibonsha Survey of Japanese Art, 8).

A lavishly illustrated survey of the temples, mandalas, paintings, and sculptures of esoteric Buddhism (Mikkyō), dating primarily from the seventh through the thirteenth centuries. Sawa presents the most outstanding, surviving examples of the artworks which the adherents of this Buddhist faith produced. He also discusses their aesthetic values, their religious connotations, and some of their historical origins.

496

1217 **A thousand cranes: treasures of Japanese art.**
Seattle Art Museum, foreword by Henry Trubner, Bonnie Pitman-
Gelles, preface by William Jay Rathbun. Seattle, Washington:
Seattle Art Museum; San Francisco: Chronicle Books, 1987. 239p.
map. bibliog.

Provides an attractive overview of pre-modern Japanese art, particularly as it relates to
the rich holdings of the Seattle Art Museum. Opening this volume are five broad
essays by prominent North American scholars – 'Archaeological Perspectives on
Japan's Oldest Art', 'Buddhism in Japan', 'Heian Aristocratic Society and Civilization',
'Chūsei: the Medieval Age', and 'Kinsei: Early Modern Japan' – which enhance the
reader's understanding of Japan's social and political history as well as the cultural
milieu in which various objects were created. Illustrations of ninety archaeological
objects, paintings, folding screens, statues, masks, lacquerware, ceramics, and kimono
that constitute the museum's treasures of Japanese art are accompanied by extensive
commentaries describing the environments in which these pieces were produced, their
creators, their subjects, and the works themselves.

1218 **Japan: the shaping of daimyo culture, 1185–1868.**
Edited by Yoshiaki Shimizu; forewords by J. Carter Brown, Hiroshi
Ueki, Yasue Katori; translations by Kyoko Selden. New York:
George Braziller; Washington, DC: National Gallery of Art, 1988.
402p. bibliog.

A beautifully illustrated *catalogue raisonné* that chronicles the artistic and cultural
contributions of the hereditary feudal lords known as the daimyō from the early
Kamakura period through the late Tokugawa era. It is based on an exhibition of 333
works of art (among them many objects that have been designated as 'national
treasures', 'important cultural properties', or 'important art objects') from over one
hundred public and private Japanese collections that was held in 1988-89 at the
National Gallery of Art in Washington, DC. These art treasures are grouped together
into ten major categories: portraiture, calligraphy, religious sculpture, painting, arms
and armour, lacquer, ceramics, textiles, tea ceremony utensils, and works related to
the noh theatre. Martin Collcutt's essay 'Daimyo and Daimyo Culture' provides a basic
introduction to seven centuries of Japanese history and is supplemented by Shimizu's
briefer essay entitled 'Daimyo and the Arts'. Detailed descriptions and commentaries
accompany all of the illustrations.

1219 **The Shogun Age Exhibition: from the Tokugawa Art Museum, Japan.**
Compiled by the Shogun Age Exhibition Executive Committee,
introductory essays by Shinzaburō Ōishi, Yoshinobu Tokugawa.
Tokyo: Shogun Age Exhibition Executive Committee, 1983; Seattle,
Washington: University of Washington Press, 1984. 279p. map.

A lavishly illustrated catalogue of 273 of the some 20,000 items in the collection of the
Tokugawa Art Museum (Nagoya) that were on exhibition in four American and
European cities between December 1983 and May 1985. The exhibit was designed to
indicate the nature of the artworks owned by the Tokugawa shōguns and to illustrate
how they were used and appreciated. It also provided an informative introduction to
Japan's pre-modern samurai culture. The objects on display included swords, saddles
and stirrups; beautiful interior furnishings such as paintings, folding screens,
handscrolls, lacquerware, and incense, tea and calligraphy utensils; noh masks and noh

robes; and such accessories of daily life as cabinets, boxes, clothing, musical instruments, and a palanquin. Detailed commentaries accompanying the photographs within the catalogue discuss each object's manufacture, history, usage, and acquisition.

1220 **Japanese art.**
Joan Stanley-Baker. London; New York: Thames and Hudson, 1984. 216p. 2 maps. bibliog. (World of Art).

A general introduction to 'some of the most significant artistic innovations made on Japanese soil'. Nearly all aspects of Japanese art – architecture, calligraphy, ceramics, gardens, painting, sculpture, textiles, and woodblock prints – are covered from prehistoric times through the 1970s. Photographs of over 150 selected art objects illustrate the text.

1221 **Birds, beasts, blossoms, and bugs: the nature of Japan.**
Harold P. Stern. New York: Abrams, 1976. 196p. bibliog.

This catalogue of an exhibition held at the University of California in Los Angeles records the creatures of nature whom various Japanese artists have preserved in their works. Concentrating on outstanding art objects available in American collections, Stern displays representative works of a wide variety of materials, a considerable span of time, and a range of artists which demonstrate the importance of nature in the arts throughout Japanese history. Among the 140 objects dating from as early as the twelfth century and particularly from the late Momoyama and Tokugawa periods are bronzes, pairs of screens, hanging scrolls (kakemono), handscrolls, porcelain bottles and dishes, sword guards (*tsuba*), lacquered medicine boxes (inrō), netsuke, inkstone writing-cases, incense boxes, and stencils. Each object is depicted in one or more illustrations which are accompanied by Stern's eloquently written commentary about its background, subject, artist, style, and manner of portraying nature.

1222 **Living crafts of Okinawa.**
Photographs by Tsune Sugimura, text by Hisao Suzuki, translated and adapted by Patricia Murray and the staff of Weatherhill. New York; Tokyo: Weatherhill, 1973. 235p. map.

Full-page monochrome and colour photographs – 164 altogether – reveal the diversity of Okinawan folk art and portray some of the talented craftsmen who have preserved much of the artistic heritage of the Ryūkyū Islands. These photographs are grouped together into eight major sections: 'Carpentry and Stonemasonry', 'Textile Crafts on Okinawa Island', 'Textile Crafts on the Outer Islands', 'Pottery and Ceramic Roof Tiles', 'Lacquerware', 'Musical Instruments', 'Miscellaneous Crafts' (e.g., toys of papier-mâché, various wooden objects, glassware, and bamboo baskets and hats), and 'Shipbuilding'. Each section is preceded by a brief overview of the lives and traditions of these artisans as well as of the materials and technical aspects of their crafts. A general introduction to the entire volume sketches the history of Okinawa's centuries-old folk art traditions. Sugimura's photographs also constitute the heart of a related earlier book, *The enduring crafts of Japan: 33 living national treasures*, with text by Masataka Ogawa (New York; Tokyo: Walker/Weatherhill, 1968, 229p.).

1223   **A concise history of Japanese art.**
Peter C. Swann.   Tokyo; New York: Kodansha International, 1979.
332p. map. bibliog.
An excellent survey of the traditional arts of Japan that completely updates the author's earlier work, *An introduction to the arts of Japan* (New York: Praeger, 1958, 220p.). Published in pocket-size format, with new illustrations and an expanded bibliography, Swann's book consists of nine individual chapters covering Japan's artistic achievements up to the sixth century and during the Asuka or Suiko, Nara, early Heian, late Heian or Fujiwara, Kamakura, Ashikaga or Muromachi, Momoyama, and Tokugawa or Edo periods.

1224   **Japan design: the four seasons in design.**
Edited by Ikko Tanaka, Kazuko Koike, editorial supervision by
Mitsukuni Yoshida, translated by Lynne E. Riggs, Ken Frankel.
Tokyo: Libro Port Co., 1984. 142p. San Francisco: Chronicle Books,
1984. 130p.
A presentation of 109 full-page, captioned colour photographs, grouped together according to the four seasons of the year, that depict the design of both traditional and modern objects such as clothing, furniture, accessories, dishes, toys, vehicles, and musical instruments. This volume is based on a catalogue prepared for the exhibition 'Japan Design: Traditional and Modern', which was organised in 1984 by the Seibu Museum of Art and the USSR Ministry of Culture. The plates are preceded by Yoshida Mitsukuni's brief essay 'The Heritage of Japanese Design'.

1225   **In praise of shadows.**
Junichirō Tanizaki, translated by Thomas J. Harper, Edward G.
Seidensticker, foreword by Charles Moore, afterword by Thomas J.
Harper.   New Haven, Connecticut: Leete's Island Books, 1977. 48p.
An eminent novelist's eloquent essay about his ideals of beauty in life and in art. Written in 1933, this celebrated work expresses Tanizaki's 'deep, even scholarly interest in the traditional culture of Japan'. Wandering almost erratically from topic to topic – architecture, toilets, electric lighting, lacquerware, cuisine, kabuki drama, noh costumes, feminine beauty, skin colour, etc. – he comments on various aspects of pre-modern aesthetic sensibility and compares Japanese ideals of beauty with their Western counterparts. Tanizaki makes it clear that he prefers 'the softer, quieter, more shadowy, older aesthetic tradition' of his native land that developed during the Tokugawa period. In his conclusion, moreover, he indicates that he intended to call back through his literary writings the 'world of shadows' which was being lost at a time when Japan was undergoing rapid change with the introduction of Western technology and with increasing modernisation.

1226   **The enduring art of Japan.**
Langdon Warner.   Cambridge, Massachusetts: Harvard University
Press, 1952. 113p. bibliog. Reprinted, New York: Grove Press;
London: Evergreen Books, 1958; New York: Grove Press, 1988.
A charming, illustrated introduction to Japanese art, artists, and traditions by a past authority on East Asian art and a former curator of the Oriental collection at Harvard University's Fogg Art Museum. Paying particular attention to the common denominators

of Japanese art, Warner (1881-1955) first surveys the history, personalities, culture, and religion of Japan on a period-by-period basis: from the beginnings of Shintō and Buddhism through the mid-Tokugawa period. He then offers his interpretations of Japanese folk art, the development of the shorthand convention in painting, and the transcendental force of Zen Buddhism and its expression in the layout of Japanese gardens and in the tea ceremony. This book originated in a series of lectures which Warner delivered on behalf of the Lowell Institute in Boston. It has since become a classic in its field.

1227 **The Great Japan Exhibition: art of the Edo period 1600–1868.**
Edited by William Watson; prefaces by Kentarō Hayashi, Hugh Casson, foreword by Nicolas Wolfers, essays by W. G. Beasley, Masahide Bitō, William Watson.   London: Royal Academy of Arts; New York: Alpine Fine Arts Collection, 1981. 365p. map. bibliog.

Catalogue raisonné of a remarkable exhibition covering the decorative and fine arts of the age of the Tokugawa shōguns that was held at the Royal Academy of Arts in 1981-82. All 412 items on display (from both private and public collections in Japan as well as from three British museums) are illustrated in a combination of colour and monochrome reproductions accompanied by brief descriptive notes. The catalogue encompasses a broad range of Tokugawa period painting, calligraphy, woodblock prints, woodblock books and albums, lacquer, ceramics, armour, sword blades and sword mounts, sculpture, netsuke, and textiles. Three brief essays – 'Edo Japan: Politics and Foreign Relations' (Beasley), 'Society and Economy in the Edo Period' (Bitō), and 'Art in Momoyama and Edo' (Watson) – offer introductory background reading for a general audience unfamiliar with Japanese history.

1228 **The unknown craftsman: a Japanese insight into beauty.**
Sōetsu Yanagi, adapted by Bernard Leach, foreword by Shōji Hamada.   Tokyo; New York: Kodansha International, 1972. 230p.

A selection and adaptation of the extensive writings of Yanagi Sōetsu (also known as Yanagi Muneyoshi, 1889-1961), the father of the Japanese folk-crafts (*mingei*) movement and a prolific author on all aspects of aesthetics. His writings are addressed primarily 'to Oriental craftsmen and lovers of craftsmanship, but they are concerned with the very nature of human life and work'. An introduction by Leach outlines Yanagi's life and philosophy. The eleven essays about traditional Japanese aesthetics which follow are entitled 'Towards a Standard of Beauty', 'Seeing and Knowing', 'Pattern', 'The Beauty of Irregularity', 'The Buddhist Idea of Beauty', 'Crafts of Okinawa', 'Hakeme', 'The Way of Tea', 'The Kizaemon Tea-Bowl', 'The Way of Craftsmanship', and 'The Responsibility of the Craftsman'.

1229 **Imperial Japan: the art of the Meiji era (1868–1912).**
Exhibition organized by Martie W. Young, catalogue and introduction by Frederick Baekeland, preface by Thomas W. Leavitt.   Ithaca, New York: Herbert F. Johnson Museum of Art, Cornell University, 1980. 232p. bibliog.

Catalogue of the first large-scale exhibition of Meiji period art held in the United States since the Louisiana Purchase Exposition (St. Louis, Missouri) of 1904. Containing a range of objects which represent all major forms of the traditional visual arts of that era, the volume offers a comprehensive overview of painting, calligraphy, woodblock prints and illustrated books, ivory and wood sculpture, metalwork, cloisonné, ceramics, and lacquerware. Each of the 148 black-and-white illustrations is accompanied by a short descriptive entry, and each major section of the catalogue is preceded by an introductory essay about the form of art on display. Only those artists who spent at least half of their working careers during the Meiji era are represented within the exhibition. Artists who pursued purely Western-style art are entirely excluded.

Old Kyoto: a guide to traditional shops, restaurants, and inns.
See item no. 78.

The beginnings of Japanese art.
See item no. 104.

Early Japanese art: the great tombs and treasures.
See item no. 105.

Cultural atlas of Japan.
See item no. 113.

Japan: a short cultural history.
See item no. 125.

Japan in the Muromachi age.
See item no. 140.

Japan: a history in art.
See item no. 155.

A dictionary of Japanese artists: painting, sculpture, ceramics, prints, lacquer.
See item no. 368.

Biographical dictionary of Japanese art.
See item no. 369.

Daruma: the founder of Zen in Japanese art and popular culture.
See item no. 483.

Zen and Japanese culture.
See item no. 492.

The Freer Gallery of Art. II. Japan.
See item no. 1250.

Artist and patron in postwar Japan: dance, music, theater, and the visual arts, 1955–1980.
See item no. 1376.

The way of tea.
See item no. 1467.

Tea ceremony utensils.
See item no. 1468.

Chanoyu: Japanese tea ceremony.
See item no. 1469.

National Museum: Tokyo.
See item no. 1473.

Roberts' guide to Japanese museums of art and archaeology.
See item no. 1475.

Arts of Asia.
See item no. 1489.

Chanoyu Quarterly: Tea and the Arts of Japan.
See item no. 1496.

Monumenta Nipponica: Studies in Japanese Culture.
See item no. 1534.

Orientations: the Monthly Magazine for Collectors and Connoisseurs of Oriental Art.
See item no. 1535.

Legend in Japanese art: a description of historical episodes, legendary characters, folk-lore, myths, religious symbolism, illustrated in the arts of old Japan.
See item no. 1560.

Dictionary of Chinese and Japanese art.
See item no. 1567.

Japanese art signatures: a handbook and practical guide.
See item no. 1571.

Painting and calligraphy

1230 **Tall mountains and flowing waters: the arts of Uragami Gyokudō.**
Stephen Addiss.   Honolulu, Hawaii: University of Hawaii Press, 1987. 163p. bibliog.

An illustrated study of the artistic accomplishments and career of Uragami Gyokudō (1745-1820), 'one of the most individualistic painters the world has yet seen' and a talented calligrapher, poet, and musician. Addiss traces Gyokudō's life, discusses the music he composed and performed on the seven-string *ch'in*, evaluates the Chinese-style poetry in which he expressed his ideals most clearly and directly, examines the calligraphy he wrote in the Chinese clerical and running scripts, and describes the masterpieces of landscape painting which he produced as well as his standing in the Nanga school of art. A short appendix contains reproductions of twenty-two of Gyokudō's signatures and seals.

1231 **Words in motion: modern Japanese calligraphy.**
Essays by San'u Aoyama, Stephen Addiss, Barbara Rose, Taiun
Yanagida. Tokyo: Yomiuri Shimbun, 1984. 187p.

The creativity of Aoyama San'u, Kuwata Sasafune, Miyamoto Chikukei, Yanagida
Taiun, and eight other outstanding calligraphers is illustrated by nearly one hundred
works of art assembled by the Yomiuri Shimbun for exhibit at the Library of Congress
(Washington, DC) in 1984. Complementing this was a special display of some fifty
examples of calligraphy from the Library's own collections. The catalogue of this joint
exhibition consists primarily of black-and-white reproductions, grouped by calligrapher,
together with brief descriptions of their art and short biographical statements. Four
introductory essays discuss the Japanese approach to calligraphy, the role of
calligraphy in Japanese society, and its impact on American abstract expressionism. A
companion volume, *Multiple meanings: the written word in Japan – past, present, and
future*, edited by J. Thomas Rimer (Washington, DC: Library of Congress, 1986,
111p.), contains papers from both the Library's 1984 symposium 'Calligraphy and the
Japanese Word' and its 1979 symposium 'Japanese Literature in Translation'.

1232 **Zen painting & calligraphy: an exhibition of works of art lent by
temples, private collectors, and public and private museums in Japan,
organized in collaboration with the Agency for Cultural Affairs of the
Japanese Government.**
Jan Fontein, Money L. Hickman, foreword by Hidemi Kohn, preface
by Perry Townsend Rathbone. Boston, Massachusetts: Museum of
Fine Arts; distributed by New York Graphic Society (Greenwich,
Connecticut), 1970. 173p.

This is the catalogue of the first exhibition ever held in the West of Zen-inspired
painting and calligraphy. The exhibitors sought to display a wide range of
representative works from public and private Japanese collections in order to illustrate
the broad scope and distinctive characteristics of Ch'an Buddhist art in China (dating
from the Sung and Yüan periods) and Zen Buddhist art in Japan (from the Kamakura,
Muromachi, and Tokugawa periods). Included were *chinsō* portraits of Ch'an and Zen
masters; paintings of patriarchs and eccentrics as well as of landscapes, animals, birds,
and plants; and calligraphy by eminent monks. The introduction to the catalogue
surveys the history of contemplative or meditative (Ch'an/Zen) Buddhism in East Asia
and discusses the associated art forms. The authoritatively written text offers detailed
descriptions of the seventy-one works on display; provides information about their
background, their subjects, and the artists who painted them; and includes translations
of the texts, colophons, and encomiums that appear within some of them.

1233 **Japanese fan paintings from Western collections.**
Selection and introductory essay by Kurt A. Gitter, notes to the plates
by Pat Fister. New Orleans, Louisiana: New Orleans Museum of
Art, 1985. 136p. bibliog.

The catalogue of an exhibition held at the New Orleans Museum of Art and the Asian
Art Museum of San Francisco in 1985-86. Illustrated in beautiful colour plates is a
selection of fifty-three folding fans and circular fans as well as screens with fan-shaped
paintings that were painted during the Tokugawa period by such well-known artists of
the Rimpa, Nanga, and Shijō schools as Ike no Taiga, Nakamura Hōchū, Ogata Kōrin,
Shibata Zeshin, and Uragami Gyokudō. Gitter's short essay surveys the entire history

of Japanese fan painting with particular reference to the Tokugawa era. The volume is intended to enhance the general reader's perception and appreciation of a type of art that reached its zenith during the eighteenth and nineteenth centuries.

1234 **The art of the Japanese screen.**
Elise Grilli. New York; Tokyo: Walker/Weatherhill in collaboration with Bijutsu Shuppansha (Tokyo), 1970. 276p.

This quarto-sized volume examines the Japanese folding screen (*byōbu*) as an artform within an art-historical and aesthetic context. Part one introduces six of the most celebrated masterpieces of screen painting – among them works by Sōtatsu and Kōrin – produced between 1598 and 1712. They are discussed in considerable detail and are illustrated by over fifty full-size colour plates. Part two, 'The Screen as a Medium in Japanese Art', focuses on the thematic content, decorative elements, construction, design, and function of folding screens in Japanese homes. A concise historical overview of Japanese screens, from the Nara period into the twentieth century, concludes this lavishly illustrated book.

1235 **Meiji Western painting.**
Minoru Harada, translated by Akiko Murakata, adapted and introduced by Bonnie F. Abiko. New York; Tokyo: Weatherhill/Shibundo, 1974. 143p. bibliog. (Arts of Japan, 6).

A survey of the development of Western-style painting that focuses on the ways in which the Western artform of oil-painting evolved in Meiji Japan and on the effects which this new art style had on the ideas and attitudes of Japanese painters. Harada reviews the work of Western-influenced pioneering artists such as Kawakami Tōgai and Takahashi Yūichi; discusses *yōga* ('Western-style painting') and its practitioners between 1877 and 1887; examines the work of Asai Chū in connection with the newly established Meiji Art Society; studies the painting of Kuroda Seiki and his introduction of the *plein-air* technique; considers the emergence of the Impressionist *plein-air* movement and the achievements of such artists as Aoki Shigeru and Fujishima Takeji; and concludes with an examination of the government-sponsored Bunten organisation. Both colour and monochrome plates of representative paintings illustrate the text.

1236 **Painting in the Yamato style.**
Saburō Ienaga, translated by John M. Shields. New York; Tokyo: Weatherhill/Heibonsha, 1973. 162p. (Heibonsha Survey of Japanese Art, 10).

An introduction to current views about the origin and nature of *yamato-e* ('Japanese style') painting during the late Heian and Kamakura periods. Instead of producing paintings based on Chinese landscapes, personages, and legends, Japanese artists at that time created works which depicted scenes of famous Japanese landscapes, subjects linked with contemporary Japanese literature, and themes involving the four seasons of the year. Ienaga describes the evolution of *yamato-e* painting, indicates how it differed in concept and realisation from its Chinese counterparts, describes some of the extant Kamakura period screens and illustrated handscrolls that are most closely associated with this genre, analyses the influence of *yamato-e* on later Japanese art forms, and concludes with a detailed study of this genre of painting. Ienaga's text is illustrated with 158 photographs (43 in full colour).

1237 **Esoteric Buddhist painting.**
Hisatoyo Ishida, translated and adapted with an introduction by
E. Dale Saunders.   Tokyo; New York: Kodansha International and
Shibundo, 1987. 204p. bibliog. (Japanese Arts Library, 15).
An extensive, illustrated overview of the history of esoteric Buddhism (Mikkyō) in
Japan and its influence on Japanese painting. Ishida opens with an examination of
mandalas (graphic representations composed of many painted images, which constitute
the very essence of esoteric Buddhist painting), focusing in particular on the two major
mandalas of Japanese Tantrism and their variations. He then discusses the iconography
and transmission of esoteric Buddhism from India through Tibet and China to Japan,
the changes which occurred in Japanese Tantric paintings between the ninth and
fourteenth centuries, the assimilation of Shintō deities into esoteric Buddhist
iconography, and the absorption of elements of esoteric Buddhist painting by the Pure
Land (Jōdo) and Kegon sects of Buddhism.

1238 **Modern currents in Japanese art.**
Michiaki Kawakita, translated and adapted by Charles S. Terry.
New York; Tokyo: Weatherhill/Heibonsha, 1974. 159p. (Heibonsha
Survey of Japanese Art, 24).
This survey of artistic developments between the Meiji Restoration of 1868 and the
early 1950s discusses the Tokugawa antecedents of modern Japanese art, the
impressionist school in Japan, the development of the art derived from the traditional
schools of painting which came to be known as *nihonga* and was favoured by Okakura
Tenshin, the impact of post-impressionism and fauvism on artists during the Taishō
period, and the evolution of Japanese art through the immediate post-World War II
era. With the exception of one chapter that summarises developments in sculpture and
in architecture, Kawakita's account is devoted entirely to painting.

1239 **Ink painting.**
Takaaki Matsushita, translated and adapted with an introduction by
Martin Collcutt.   New York; Tokyo: Weatherhill/Shibundo, 1974.
143p. bibliog. (Arts of Japan, 7).
An illustrated survey of five centuries of monochrome ink painting (*suibokuga*) in
Japan: from its introduction from China in the twelfth century to the major changes in
ink painting that occurred during the Tokugawa period. Matsushita describes the
Chinese origins of this artistic genre and its close relationship with Zen Buddhism. His
presentation of *suibokuga* painters deals with several artists who were associated with
the Shōkokuji and Daitokuji Buddhist monasteries in Kyōto, with the Ami group of
painters, and with the Kamakura, Kanō, and Edo schools of painting. Matsushita not
only provides biographical information about such artists as Josetsu, Shūbun, and
Sesshū, but also discusses the various iconographic themes and the stylistic evolution of
this genre.

1240 **Edo painting: Sotatsu and Korin.**
Hiroshi Mizuo, translated by John M. Shields.   New York; Tokyo:
Weatherhill/Heibonsha, 1972. 162p. (Heibonsha Survey of Japanese
Art, 18).
A general survey of the Rimpa or 'Decorative' school of Tokugawa art, including its

antecedents and successors. Mizuo devotes most of his book to the four masters of the decorative style – Hon'ami Kōetsu, Tawaraya Sōtatsu, Ogata Kōrin, and Ogata Kenzan – examining the ink and fan painting, calligraphy, screens and wall panels, scrolls and books, ceramics, and lacquerware which they produced. He pays particular attention to the historical setting in which these artists and their contemporaries worked, and explains how the Rimpa school embodied 'the very essence of what is Japanese in Japanese art'. Over 150 illustrations (many in full colour) and two charts showing Sōtatsu and Kōrin's methods of composition complement the text.

1241   **Iconography of The tale of Genji: Genji monogatari ekotoba.**
Miyeko Murase.   New York; Tokyo: Weatherhill, 1983. 351p.
bibliog.

An illustrated translation of a fifteenth-century manual (in its late sixteenth-century manuscript version) that was intended for illustrators of the great literary classic, *The tale of Genji* (q.v.). The *Genji* was a perennial source of inspiration to Japanese painters. Depictions of scenes from this work appeared in paintings, screens, and narrative picture scrolls, and the style and the artistic representation of various aspects and motifs of the novel gradually became codified into a formal iconography. The *Genji monogatari ekotoba*, one of the earliest practical manuals, contains descriptions of the elements that were to be depicted in illustrating each of the 282 episodes of the *Genji* together with textual quotations that could accompany those illustrations. Murase also provides a brief overview of the history of *Genji* painting and tries to identify the sources of the illustrations which may have been available to the author of this manual.

1242   **The art of Japanese calligraphy.**
Yūjirō Nakata, translated by Alan Woodhull, Armins Nikovskis.
New York; Tokyo: Weatherhill/Heibonsha, 1973. 172p. (Heibonsha Survey of Japanese Art, 27).

The first substantive study in English on Japanese calligraphy, an important artform because of 'the flexibility of the materials used and the graphic possibilities inherent in the scripts'. Nakata begins by comparing the origins and basic styles of Chinese and Japanese calligraphy in order to identify their differences. He then describes in some detail each of the major styles of Japanese calligraphic script: *tensho* ('seal script'), *reisho* ('scribe's script'), *zattaisho* ('ornamental styles'), *gakuji* ('plaque inscriptions'), *kaisho* ('block script'), *gyōsho* ('semi-cursive script'), and *sōsho* ('cursive script'). In addition, Nakata deals with the evolution of the *hiragana* phonetic script, the history of *karayō* ('Chinese script') between the Yamato and Asuka periods and the twentieth century, and the emergence of a uniquely Japanese calligraphic style known as *wayō*. There are 187 illustrations, several of them in colour, which provide numerous examples of calligraphy in Japan over the centuries.

1243   **The Namban art of Japan.**
Yoshitomo Okamoto, translated by Ronald K. Jones. New York;
Tokyo: Weatherhill/Heibonsha, 1972. 156p. map. (Heibonsha Survey of Japanese Art, 19).

Nanban ('Southern barbarian') art, a unique genre of Japanese art which flourished between the mid-1500s and the early 1600s, was influenced by European materials and techniques and generally depicted the European traders and missionaries who came to

Japan at that time as well as their unusual-looking ships, their customs and manners, and the imagery of the Christian religion. With its 36 colour and 106 black-and-white illustrations, Okamoto's survey of *nanban* art offers an overview of the background and development of *nanban* culture, an introduction to Japanese Christian art, and a brief assessment of *nanban* art during the Momoyama period.

1244 **Pure Land Buddhist painting.**
Jōji Okazaki, translated and adapted with an introduction by Elizabeth ten Grotenhuis. Tokyo; New York: Kodansha International and Shibundo, 1977. 201p. bibliog. (Japanese Arts Library, 4).

An illustrated, historical survey of Japanese Pure Land (Jōdo) Buddhist painting up to the end of the thirteenth century. Okazaki discusses the Chinese antecedents and prototypes of this painting; details the various types and the rich imagery that occurred in Pure Land mandalas and in the depictions of Amitābha Buddha descending to welcome the faithful to Paradise; and examines the variety of paintings from the eleventh century onwards dealing with Amida, Maitreya, and Kannon that were made in response to religious and social demands at that time. Ten Grotenhuis' introduction focuses on the genesis and development of the Pure Land Buddhist faith.

1245 **Narrative picture scrolls.**
Hideo Okudaira, translated and adapted with an introduction by Elizabeth ten Grotenhuis. New York; Tokyo: Weatherhill/Shibundo, 1974. 151p. bibliog. (Arts of Japan, 5).

An introduction to the narrative picture-scrolls known as *emaki* that were painted in large numbers between the twelfth and sixteenth centuries in order to illustrate Buddhist sutras, contemporary literary works, military histories, narrative accounts, *waka* poetry, folk tales, and legends. Okudaira first discusses the historical evolution of these scrolls, then focuses on *emaki* as an artform and as a reflection of Japanese history. He introduces the major formal and technical characteristics of these picture-scrolls and identifies both their major themes and the subjects which they depict. A closing chapter presents pertinent material about selected individual *emaki*. The volume is illustrated throughout.

1246 **Song of the brush: Japanese paintings from the Sansō Collection.**
Edited by John M. Rosenfield, preface by Henry Trubner, essay by Peter F. Drucker, contributions by William J. Rathbun, Fumiko E. Cranston, translation by Fumiko E. Cranston. Seattle, Washington: Seattle Art Museum, 1979. 167p. map. bibliog.

Sixty-three works mounted on hanging scrolls are represented in this exhibition catalogue focusing on three important schools of painting: the *suibokuga* ('ink painting') of the Muromachi and Momoyama periods, the paintings by Zen Buddhist monks (*Zenga*) of the Tokugawa period, and the paintings by masters of the Nanga school that flourished during the eighteenth and nineteenth centuries. The reproductions, many of them depictions of landscapes, are accompanied by highly informative commentaries. The concluding essay, 'A View of Japan through Japanese Art', comments on a number of Japanese characteristics including the capacity for pure enjoyment, the tension between conformity and spontaneity, and the perceptual nature of the Japanese.

1247 **The art of sumi-e: appreciation, techniques, and application.**
Shōzō Satō, with Thomas A. Heenan.   Tokyo; New York: Kodansha International, 1984. 329p. bibliog.

A comprehensive introduction and instruction manual for general readers and art specialists alike to the philosophical, aesthetic, and technical aspects of *sumi-e*, the classical monochrome ink painting most frequently associated with Zen Buddhism. Copiously illustrated with some four hundred examples and sketches, Satō's book begins with an historical survey of *sumi-e* that highlights selected Chinese and Japanese masterpieces, and continues with a discussion of the use of line and space, paper, brushes and inks, and basic brush strokes. Excerpts from *The mustard seed garden manual on painting*, a classic seventeenth-century Chinese work, show how to paint such standard subjects as mountains, bamboo, rocks, and birds. Accompanying these excerpts are instructions for employing the same techniques in painting modern subject-matter. A brief overview of contemporary *sumi-e* artists concludes the book.

1248 **Japanese ink paintings: from American collections – the Muromachi period; an exhibition in honor of Shūjirō Shimada.**
Edited with an introduction by Yoshiaki Shimizu, Carolyn Wheelwright.   Princeton, New Jersey: Art Museum, Princeton University, 1976. 300p. map. bibliog.

Focusing on ink paintings owned by private American collectors and selected American museums which were assembled for an exhibit at the Princeton University Art Museum, this illustrated volume is a study in connoisseurship that analyses thirty-seven works and provides an introduction to the artistic styles and cultural milieu of the Muromachi period. Each of the paintings (by such artists as Kantei, Sesson Shūkei, Shikibu, Sōami, and Tesshū Tokusai) is described and placed within an art-historical context; its sources of inspiration are identified; it is compared with other works; its composition, brushwork, and technical characteristics are analysed; and its special features are noted. Photographs of the entire painting as well as of some of its details are included. Helmut Brinker, Sarah Handler, John Rosenfield, David Sensabaugh, Richard Stanley-Baker, and Ann Yonemura joined with the editors in contributing the thirty-seven essays in this volume.

1249 **Masters of calligraphy, 8th–19th century.**
Yoshiaki Shimizu, John M. Rosenfield.   New York: Asia Society Galleries; Japan House Gallery, 1984. 340p. bibliog.

Catalogue of a comprehensive exhibition of Japanese calligraphy organised in 1984-85. Eight chapters, each one organised according to a basic unifying principle, cover most of the essential phases in the historical development of calligraphy in Japan from its early maturity until the Meiji Restoration: the Buddhist texts of the eighth century; the distinctive aristocratic scripts (*wayō*) of the tenth century; the Shōren-in tradition; the immortal poets (*kasen*) as depicted in portraits accompanied by calligraphy; the calligraphy by the Zen Buddhist masters of Sung Chinese writing-styles in Japan; the brushwork of such masters of the tea ceremony as Sen no Rikyū; the sumptuous calligraphies of sixteenth- and seventeenth-century Kyōto; and the calligraphy of the literati, or men of letters. Reproductions of 135 works of art from American collections, accompanied by extensive, scholarly notes, provide an excellent overview of the range, writing styles, various schools, and aesthetic traditions of traditional Japanese calligraphy.

1250   **Freer Gallery of Art fiftieth anniversary exhibition: 1. Ukiyo-e painting.**
        Harold P. Stern.   Washington, DC: Smithsonian Institution, 1973.
        319p. bibliog.

The fully illustrated catalogue of a special exhibition of ukiyo-e paintings from the collection of the Freer Gallery of Art in Washington, DC. Depicting primarily the people, costumes, and customs of the Tokugawa world in which they were created are 118 representative paintings by such artists as Hishikawa Moroyasu, Miyagawa Chōshun, Nishikawa Sukenobu, Katsukawa Shunshō, and Katsushika Hokusai. Accompanying commentaries describe their subject-matter, analyse their composition, evaluate their artistic significance, and provide background information about their artists. Stern's easy-going mode of exposition helps to orient this catalogue towards a broad audience of art collectors and students. Among the other publications also prepared in celebration of the Gallery's fiftieth anniversay is *The Freer Gallery of Art. II: Japan*, by Harold P. Stern and Thomas Lawton (Tokyo: Kodansha, 1971. 184p.). This selection of important paintings, works of sculpture, and decorative art objects, accompanied by brief explanatory statements, provides a general introduction to one of the major collections of Japanese art in the West.

1251   **Paris in Japan: the Japanese encounter with European painting.**
        Shūji Takashina, J. Thomas Rimer, with Gerald D. Bolas, forewords
        by Shoji Satō, Gerald D. Bolas.   Tokyo: Japan Foundation;
        St. Louis, Missouri: Washington University, 1987. 287p. bibliog.

Combining scholarly essays, biographies, and a lavishly illustrated exhibition catalogue, this volume offers the first systematic overview of the impact which both the city of Paris and the paintings introduced through Paris had on Japanese artists between 1890 and 1930. It opens with four essays that respectively examine the American responses to Western-style Japanese painting, Eastern and Western dynamics in the development of Western-style oil-painting during the Meiji era, the significance of the French experience and the French example in the growth of modern Japanese art, and the most salient characteristics of the paintings by Yorozu Tetsugorō, Koide Narashige, and Kishida Ryūsei. Biographical sketches of the twenty-six painters represented in the exhibition are then followed by seventy-seven fully annotated colour plates of exhibited paintings, in particular the works of Fujishima Takeji, Fujita Tsuguji, Kishida Ryūsei, Koide Narashige, Kuroda Seiki, Nakamura Tsune, Saeki Yūzō, Sakamoto Hanjirō, Umehara Ryūzaburō, Yasui Sōtarō, and Yorozu Tetsugorō.

1252   **Kanō Eitoku.**
        Tsuneo Takeda, translated and adapted by H. Mack Horton,
        Catherine Kaputa, introduction by Catherine Kaputa.   Tokyo; New
        York: Kodansha International and Shibundo, 1977. 178p. bibliog.
        (Japanese Arts Library, 3).

Examines the lives and works of Kanō Eitoku (a painter renowned for his screen and wall paintings, 1543-90) and his immediate associates: his father Shōei, his brother Sōshū, and his son Mitsunobu. Takeda surveys the origins of the famous Kanō school of painting; discusses Eitoku's career and his monumental style of painting, characterised by broad, sweeping, colourful brushwork against backgrounds of shining gold; and examines the accomplishments of other important members of the Kanō school. Numerous colour and black-and-white plates as well as a genealogy of the Kanō school supplement the text.

1253 **Japanese ink painting: Shubun to Sesshu.**
Ichimatsu Tanaka, translated by Bruce Darling. New York; Tokyo: Weatherhill/Heibonsha, 1972. 174p. (Heibonsha Survey of Japanese Art, 12).

A profusely illustrated historical overview of the development of Japanese monochrome ink painting, with particular emphasis on the works of the fifteenth-century masters Shūbun and Sesshū and on their artistic and social milieu. After tracing the evolution of Nara, Heian, and Kamakura period painting, Tanaka considers the major academy painters of the early fifteenth century (among them Josetsu and Shūbun) and examines the career and painting style of Sesshū, the first Japanese artist to have worked as an independent painter. Tanaka concludes with studies of the members of the Unkoku and Soga schools and of other artists who were active in the late Muromachi period as well as with commentaries on the major works of art reproduced in this volume.

1254 **Complete sumi-e techniques: complete instructions for painting over 200 subjects including flowers, trees, animals, fish, and landscapes.**
Sadami Yamada, translated by Transearch under the direction of Charles Pomeroy. Tokyo; Elmsford, New York: Japan Publications Trading Company, 1966. 151p.

Sumi-e, a type of painting executed in monochrome ink on pure white paper, is a traditional form of artistic expression that attained initial widespread popularity among Zen artists of the Muromachi period and is distinguished by its 'simplicity, lucidity and elegance of style'. Yamada (president of the Japan *Sumi-e* Association) first introduces the basics of *sumi-e*, including its materials and implements, the proper procedures for preparing the ink and for holding the brush, basic *sumi-e* techniques and brushwork, brush and painting practice, and composition. He then describes and illustrates the techniques of painting flowers, animals, and landscapes, offering precise and easy-to-follow instructions in a manner most suitable for beginning artists.

1255 **Japanese painting in the literati style.**
Yoshiho Yonezawa, Chū Yoshizawa, translated and adapted by Betty Iverson Monroe. New York; Tokyo: Weatherhill/Heibonsha, 1974. 190p. (Heibonsha Survey of Japanese Art, 23).

A profusely illustrated introduction to the entire range of Nanga ('Southern School') painting that flourished between the early 1700s and the mid-1800s: its history, its relationship with the literati painting of Ming and Ch'ing China, its theories and ideals, its subject-matter and techniques, and its outstanding artists. Yonezawa and Yoshizawa first introduce this genre of painting, discuss its pioneers and masters (especially Ikeno Taiga and Yosa Buson), and trace its spread within Japan. Then, in order to explain its background, they discuss the Chinese sources for Nanga painting (including the Chinese painters who lived in Japan), introduce and assess the influence of some of the printed Chinese painting manuals that appeared in Tokugawa period printed editions, and indicate how and why Japanese literati painting differed from its Chinese antecedents. James Cahill's *Scholar painters of Japan: the Nanga school* (New York: Asia House, 1972, 135p.), a highly acclaimed catalogue accompanying an exhibition of the works of twenty-two Nanga artists, is a good companion volume to this book.

Warlords, artists, and commoners: Japan in the sixteenth century.
See item no. 135.

A collection of Nagasaki colour prints and paintings: showing the influence of Chinese and European art on that of Japan.
See item no. 179.

Tradition and modernization in Japanese culture.
See item no. 239.

Hokusai: paintings, drawings and woodcuts.
See item no. 1260.

Utamaro: colour prints and paintings.
See item no. 1262.

Masters of the Japanese print: their world and their work.
See item no. 1267.

Prints and drawings

1256 **One hundred famous views of Edo.**
Andō Hiroshige, introductory essays by Henry D. Smith, II and Amy G. Poster, commentaries on the plates by Henry D. Smith, preface by Robert Buck. New York: George Braziller; London: Thames and Hudson, 1986. 256p. map. bibliog.

Splendid colour reproductions of the celebrated series of 118 woodblock landscapes and genre scenes of mid-nineteenth century Edo (Tokyo) which the ukiyo-e print master Hiroshige produced between 1856 and 1858 under the title *Meisho Edo Hyakkei*, or *One Hundred Famous Views of Edo*. A map of the city indicates the location of each scene, and detailed commentaries accompany the full-sized, vertically formatted reproductions. The essays by Smith and Poster discuss Hiroshige's life, the places he depicted as well as local customs and cultures, the influence of artistic prototypes, Hiroshige's artistic style, his woodblock print techniques, the provenance and dating of the set of prints belonging to the Brooklyn (New York) Museum which are reproduced, and their connoisseurship. Smith also provides an erudite introduction and commentaries on the plates of Katsushika Hokusai's *One hundred views of Mt. Fuji* (New York: George Braziller; London: Thames and Hudson, 1988, 224p.), first published in the 1830s in monochrome black and grey.

1257 **Hiroshige: birds and flowers.**
Introduction by Cynthea J. Bogel, commentaries on the plates by
Israel Goldman, poetry translated by Alfred H. Marks, foreword by
Maggie Bickford, preface by Franklin Robinson. New York: George
Braziller in association with the Rhode Island School of Design, 1988.
192p. bibliog.

The genre of 'bird and flower' painting (*kachō-ga*), developed in China during the
Northern Sung era, was transformed from a courtly painting tradition into a popular
graphic mode and distinctive Japanese artform during the Muromachi and Tokugawa
periods. Basing their presentation on a selection of the finest prints found within the
Abby Aldrich Rockefeller Collection in Providence, Rhode Island, the authors
reproduce in full colour ninety-one meticulously drawn woodblock prints from among
the large number of bird and flower studies which the ukiyo-e master Andō Hiroshige
(1797-1858) produced during his career. Bogel's introductory essay, 'Hiroshige and the
Bird and Flower Tradition in Edo Japan', places Hiroshige's prints within their art-
historical and cultural context. Many of the birds and flowers which are depicted as
well as referred to in the accompanying poetry – among them the sparrow, the
swallow, the chrysanthemum, and the peony – are long-standing favourites of the
Japanese people.

1258 **The drawings of Hokusai.**
Theodore Bowie. Bloomington, Indiana: Indiana University Press,
1964. 190p. bibliog. Reprinted, Westport, Connecticut: Greenwood
Press, 1979.

This detailed description of the graphic technique and style of Katsushika Hokusai
(1760-1849) seeks to acquaint readers with 'the rich variety of work – sketches, drafts,
preparatory materials – left by one of the world's great draftsmen'. Bowie describes
and illustrates some of Hokusai's cutters' transparencies, watercolour washes in red
with corrections in black, copying or study sheets with sketches, and carefully drafted
line drawings. He compares a number of them with his completed woodblock prints,
while also considering Hokusai's instructional drawing books and his pedagogical
techniques. Closely complementing this study is James A. Michener's *The Hokusai
sketchbooks: selections from the Manga* (Rutland, Vermont; Tokyo: Tuttle, 1958,
286p.). It contains an introductory essay, explanatory notes, and reproductions of 187
three-coloured, woodblock-printed pages with Hokusai's random sketches of different
types of people, animal life, flowers, grasses and trees, landscape scenes, historical and
mythological characters, grotesque aspects of life, ghosts, technical matters, and
architecture.

1259 **Shunga: the art of love in Japan.**
Tom Evans, Mary Anne Evans. London; New York: Paddington
Press, 1975. 284p. bibliog. Reprinted, New York: Bookthrift, (n.d.).

The best and most complete work available on the subject of *shunga* ('spring
drawings'), the generic name given to the overtly erotic series of woodblock prints,
illustrated books, and paintings produced throughout the Tokugawa period. Executed
with considerable skill and imagination by such well-known artists as Katsushika
Hokusai, Kitagawa Utamaro, Suzuki Harunobu, and Utagawa Kuniyoshi, they portray
'the sexual practices and conventions of a lively, uninhibited society'. The authors first
place *shunga* in their cultural context as they write about the classes of Tokugawa

Fine Arts. Prints and drawings

society, the culture of the 'floating world', sexual attitudes and behaviour in Japanese society, and women as workers, wives, lovers and courtesans. The two major sections of their book – 'The Shunga and the Growth of Ukiyo-e' and 'The Shunga: Maturity and Decay' – in turn deal with *shunga* as works of popular art and focus on their major artistic developments and on their artists. Reproductions (largely black-and-white) of some two hundred representative *shunga* are included.

1260 **Hokusai: paintings, drawings and woodcuts.**
Jack Hillier.   Oxford, England; New York: Phaidon, 1978. 3rd ed. 136p. bibliog.

An authoritative, illustrated introduction to the life and work of Katsushika Hokusai (1760-1849), organised into chapters dealing with individual periods of his life. Hillier discusses Hokusai's upbringing as an ukiyo-e artist (1760-95); his work as a designer of *surimono* (1796-1800); his broadsheet series based on the famous kabuki play *Chūshingura* and his illustrations to the kyōka poets (1798-1806); his book illustrations, particularly the *Manga* and the *Shashin gafu* (1807-19); the production of his great landscapes and *kachō* ('bird and flower') prints (1820-32); his paintings and drawings; and some of the series of prints that he created during the closing decades of his life, among them the *One Hundred Views of Mount Fuji* and *One Hundred Poems Explained by the Nurse*. An appendix provides a chronological list of books that were illustrated by Hokusai throughout his career.

1261 **Suzuki Harunobu: a selection of his color prints and illustrated books.**
Jack Hillier, foreword by Evan H. Turner.   Boston, Massachusetts: David R. Godine in association with the Philadelphia Museum of Art, 1970. 239p. bibliog.

An exhibition catalogue of 150 ukiyo-e woodblock prints created by Suzuki Harunobu (1725?-70), published on the bicentenary of his death. Harunobu is renowned for having been the first major print artist to produce full-colour woodcuts using the new multiple-block colour-printmaking technique. Hillier, an eminent authority on Japanese prints and drawings, contributes an introductory essay entitled 'The Colour-Prints of Suzuki Harunobu' as well as commentaries for the prints that are reproduced. Most of them depict courtesans, beauties, and other women of mid-eighteenth century Edo (Tokyo). Of related interest is David B. Waterhouse's *Harunobu and his age: the development of colour printing in Japan* (London: Trustees of the British Museum, 1964, 326p.), a scholarly catalogue (with 124 plates) of the British Museum's exhibition in commemoration of the 200th anniversary of the invention of polychrome printing in Japan.

1262 **Utamaro: colour prints and paintings.**
Jack Hillier.   Oxford, England: Phaidon, 1979. 2nd ed. 160p. bibliog.

The best of several publications about Kitagawa Utamaro (1753-1806), one of the most creative and influential woodblock print artists and painters of the Tokugawa period. Utamaro is especially well known for his distinctive and accomplished portrayals of feminine beauty: colourful depictions of elegant women from the teahouses, shops, and pleasure quarters of Edo (Tokyo) in both vertically and horizontally-oriented formats. Aided by reproductions of over one hundred prints and colour plates, Hillier traces Utamaro's life and career from his earliest known works – illustrations produced in 1775 for various kinds of inexpensive popular literature (e.g., theatre books) –

through such series as *The Forms of Feminine Physiognomy* and *The Twelve-Sheet Print of Silk-Worm Culture* that he created shortly before his death. Hillier's text describes Utamaro's work in some detail and indicates his significance within the ukiyo-e tradition.

1263 **Surimono: privately published Japanese prints in the Spencer Museum of Art.**
Roger Keyes, preface by Elizabeth Broun.   Tokyo; New York:
Published for the Spencer Museum of Art by Kodansha International,
1984. 199p. bibliog.

Surimono – a type of privately published, usually coloured, woodblock print containing a poetic verse – were especially popular during the late 1700s and early 1800s. Some *surimono* were distributed to commemorate personal events such as birthdays or to announce musical performances; others were commissioned by poets as gifts for their friends to celebrate the new year or other seasonal occurrences. Keyes' comprehensive catalogue of the 268 *surimono* in the Spencer Museum at the University of Kansas provides an excellent overview of this artistic genre. Each reproduction (including sixty in full colour) is accompanied by a commentary or notes focusing on the subject it depicts. An introductory essay covers the background of *surimono*, their production, colours, formats, calligraphers, subjects, styles, and poetry. Thirty-three additional *surimono* are reproduced in *Japanese woodblock prints in miniature: the genre of surimono*, by Kurt Meissner (Rutland, Vermont; Tokyo: Tuttle, 1970, 143p.); while Keyes's scholarly two-volume work entitled *The art of surimono: privately published Japanese woodblock prints and books in the Chester Beatty Library, Dublin* (London: Published for Sotheby Publications by Philip Wilson, 1985) offers the most extensive study in English available to date of this traditional form of art.

1264 **The theatrical world of Osaka prints: a collection of eighteenth and nineteenth century Japanese woodblock prints in the Philadelphia Museum of Art.**
Roger S. Keyes, Keiko Mizushima; curator's preface by Kneeland
McNulty.   Philadelphia, Pennsylvania: Philadelphia Museum of Art,
1973. 334p. 2 maps. bibliog.

A detailed exhibition catalogue of the woodcuts and drawings of actors and scenes from the kabuki stage that a little-known school of artists in Ōsaka produced during the first half of the nineteenth century. Two introductory essays – 'The Social Setting of the Japanese Woodblock Print' and 'The Kabuki Theater' – survey the differences between print-making in Ōsaka and Edo (Tokyo), briefly describe the history of the Ōsaka style, and clarify the relationship between the kabuki theatre and the Ōsaka prints. Eighty full-size plates and accompanying historical and critical commentaries describe the evolution of this artistic school and suggest 'the particular excellence of the Osaka style'. Many additional illustrations are found among the concluding one hundred pages of the catalogue, which together with extensive technical material, lists of artists and actors, a table of facsimiles of artists' signatures, and a concordance of the names of artists, engravers and publishers constitute a valuable reference guide for specialists.

1265 **The fifty-three stages of the Tokaido by Hiroshige.**
The thirty-six views of Mount Fuji by Hokusai.
Ichitarō Kondō, English adaptation by Charles S. Terry. Honolulu,
Hawaii: East-West Center Press, 1965-66. 2 vols. 2 maps.
Companion volumes reproducing two celebrated series of atmospheric landscape prints
produced during the 1820s and 1830s. Andō Hiroshige's *Fifty-three Stages of the
Tōkaidō* portrays scenes at the fifty-three stations or stopping points (where lodgings
and refreshments were available) along the national highway connecting Edo (Tokyo)
with Kyōto and the western provinces. Katsushika Hokusai's *Thirty-six Views of Mount
Fuji* is actually a collection of forty-six prints with Mount Fuji viewed from various
locations. About half of them depict life in or around Edo; the remainder are set at
points much closer to the mountain. The full-colour reproductions in these two
volumes accurately capture the character of the original prints and are accompanied by
explanatory notes that provide geographical and artistic information about the scenes
being depicted. Kondō's brief introductory essays touch upon the respective artists'
lives, their artistic careers, and the creation of these two print series. All of the texts
appear in both English and Japanese.

1266 **Images from the floating world: the Japanese print; including an
illustrated dictionary of ukiyo-e.**
Richard Lane.   New York: Putnam; Secaucus, New Jersey: Chartwell
Books, 1978. 364p. 3 maps. bibliog.
Dividing his account into four major sections – 'Early Genre Painting and the Rise of
Ukiyo-e', 'The Primitives and the First Century of Ukiyo-e, 1660–1765', 'The Golden
Age of the Color Print, 1765–1810', and 'Hokusai, Hiroshige and the Japanese
Landscape, 1810–1880' – Lane offers a highly informative treatment of the evolution of
Japanese woodblock prints that focuses on the lives of the ukiyo-e masters and on
various innovations in their respective styles and techniques. He also provides a very
extensive, illustrated dictionary of ukiyo-e that contains cross-referenced entries for
artists, schools, and techniques as well as for relevant geographical, historical, literary,
and theatrical terms. Over nine hundred drawings (some in colour) illustrate the
volume.

1267 **Masters of the Japanese print.**
Richard Lane.   Garden City, New York: Doubleday; London:
Thames and Hudson, 1962. 319p. (World of Art Series).
An informally written, illustrated introduction to ukiyo-e prints and painting. Tracing
the development of this art from the rise of genre-painting and the production of the
earliest ukiyo-e prints in the seventeenth century through the landscape prints created
by Hokusai and Hiroshige, Lane covers not only such well-known masters as
Harunobu, Kiyonobu, Sharaku, and Utamaro but also such artists as Kaigetsudō Ando
and Miyagawa Chōshun, who devoted their careers to painting ukiyo-e masterpieces
but refused to permit the printing of their work for popular consumption. Lane's
informative treatment of ukiyo-e paintings and the technical development of
woodblock printing together with his skilful integration into the text of 148 captioned
reproductions of the work of nearly seventy artists help make this book a good
overview for the general reader.

Fine Arts. Prints and drawings

1268 **Primitive ukiyo-e from the James A. Michener Collection in the
Honolulu Academy of Arts.**
Howard A. Link, with Jūzō Suzuki, Roger S. Keyes; preface by James
W. Foster, Jr.   Honolulu, Hawaii: Published for the Honolulu
Academy of Arts by the University Press of Hawaii, 1980. 322p.
bibliog.

Catalogue of representative woodblock prints dating from the 1670s to the 1760s, a
period of technical experimentation which witnessed the evolution of the art of
woodblock printing from simple black-and-white to complex full-colour prints. Prints
by Torii Kiyomasu II, Okumura Masanobu, Nishimura Shigenaga, Ishikawa Toyonobu,
Torii Kiyomitsu I and others – 281 in all – are arranged by artist in chronological
sequence. For each work of art, Link provides a half-page reproduction together with
such particulars as its title, date, size, publisher, condition, and provenance, as well as
a commentary elucidating the subject of the design, its background, and special
problems of identification or attribution. Most of the prints depict city life during the
first half of the Tokugawa period, in particular the world of the kabuki theatre, the
courtesan, and the samurai warrior.

1269 **The world of the Meiji print: impressions of a new civilization.**
Julia Meech-Pekarik, foreword by Edward Seidensticker.   New
York; Tokyo: Weatherhill, 1986. 259p. bibliog.

A lively and extensively illustrated account of Meiji woodblock prints – characterised
in part by bright new pigments and a new realism in perspective and shading – that
depict Japan's rapid modernisation after 1860, the predominant wave of Western
cultural influence, and some of the country's foreign residents. Meech-Pekarik
examines the cultural context within which the Meiji print evolved as she discusses the
'Yokohama' prints of the early 1860s, the 'enlightenment' prints of the 1870s and 1880s
and their promotion of a modernised and Westernised civilisation, prints illustrating
the emperor, the empress and their family and entourage, satirical prints and cartoons,
prints depicting the Sino–Japanese War of 1894-95, and frontispiece prints in late Meiji
period novels. She alternates between a general overview of Meiji history and a
detailed analysis of specific prints, including their settings, the clothing styles they
depict, and their revelation of contemporary tastes and values.

1270 **The floating world.**
James A. Michener.   New York: Random House; London: Secker
and Warburg, 1954. 403p. bibliog. Reprinted, with a commentary by
Howard A. Link, Honolulu, Hawaii: University of Hawaii Press,
1983. 453p.

Michener, a longtime collector and connoisseur of Japanese prints as well as an
accomplished novelist, provides considerable information about ukiyo-e artists and
their subject-matter, the woodblock prints which they produced, and their print-
making techniques as he seeks to demonstrate that the prints of the Tokugawa period
constitute a form of art equal in their own right to some of the art created by major
schools of traditional European painting. The result is a pioneering study filled with
many insights that now contains some outmoded and misleading representations of the
history and aesthetics of ukiyo-e. In his commentary to the 1983 reprint edition, Link
offers a corrective to this account as he discusses the contributions of some thirty years
of scholarship about ukiyo-e following the first publication of Michener's widely read

book. Michener is also the author of two other informative publications about Japanese prints, both of which are oriented towards a broad audience: *Japanese prints from the early masters to the modern*, with notes on the prints by Richard Lane (Rutland, Vermont; Tokyo: Tuttle, 1959, 287p.), and *The modern Japanese print: an appreciation* (Rutland, Vermont; Tokyo: Tuttle, 1968, 57p.). These books contain many personal and interpretive comments which reflect Michener's intimate knowledge of the artists and their prints and supplement the information available in more scholarly writings.

1271   **The Japanese print: a historical guide.**
Hugo Munsterberg.   New York; Tokyo: Weatherhill, 1982. 220p. bibliog.

An introduction for beginning students and new collectors that spans the entire chronology of print-making in Japan: from the Buddhist prints of the medieval period through the prints produced after World War II. Munsterberg begins with an introductory chapter on the 'discovery and appreciation' of the Japanese print in the West. In almost encyclopaedia-like fashion, he then presents a survey of Japan's leading print artists, especially of the Tokugawa period. Short, illustrated chapters bearing such titles as 'Moronobu and the Origins of Ukiyo-e', 'Shunshō, Bunchō, and the Actor Print', 'Utamaro, His Contemporaries, and His Followers', 'Hokusai, the Old Man Mad with Painting', and 'Woodblock Prints outside of Edo' discuss the aesthetics of Japanese prints, the lives of their creators, and some of the highlights of their work. Munsterberg concludes with an overview about the collecting and care of Japanese prints as well as with an annotated bibliography of important books.

1272   **The Japanese print: its evolution and essence.**
Muneshige Narazaki, English adaptation by C. H. Mitchell.   Tokyo; Palo Alto, California: Kodansha International, 1966. 274p. bibliog. Reprinted, Tokyo; New York: Kodansha International, 1982.

The first full presentation in English of an eminent Japanese scholar's study of the traditional Japanese print. Dividing his sophisticated discussion into three major parts ('The Early Prints', 'The Full-Color Prints', and 'Later Prints'), Narazaki seeks to provide a broad, historical understanding of the popular culture and world of aesthetics within which the Japanese print evolved as he advances his presentation from a consideration of the earliest prints of the seventeenth century to an examination of some of the prints produced shortly after the Meiji Restoration (1868). Mounted colour plates reproduce 107 outstanding prints, in particular works by Suzuki Harunobu, Torii Kiyonaga, Kitagawa Utamaro, Tōshūsai Sharaku, Katsushika Hokusai, Utagawa Kunisada, and Andō Hiroshige. Each reproduction is accompanied by a full description and critical comments. Also included is a chapter on collecting Japanese prints.

1273   **Evolving techniques in Japanese woodblock prints.**
Gaston Petit, Amadio Arboleda.   Tokyo; New York: Kodansha International, 1977. 175p. bibliog.

A step-by-step look at how six contemporary print-makers creatively use new materials and apply new techniques to the production of multicoloured woodblock prints. Petit and Arboleda first describe the traditional process of making a multicoloured print. They then focus on the evolving approaches of postwar artists who have utilised various types of wood when making the printing blocks and have created special effects through carving the blocks, using various pigments, and adopting new methods of printing. The radical techniques of six print-makers – Morozumi Osamu, Miyashita Tokio, Noda Tetsuya, Funasaka Yoshisuke, Yoshida Hodaka, and Matsumoto Akira – are examined in detail. Nearly three hundred photographs depict the actual production of prints and offer a sequential view of several techniques which the artists employ in their own studios. A short appendix deals with Japanese handmade paper.

1274 **Modern Japanese prints: an art reborn.**
Oliver Statler, introduction by James A. Michener.   Rutland,
Vermont; Tokyo: Tuttle, 1956. 209p.

An illustrated account of modern Japanese creative prints (*sōsaku hanga*) written by an American who studied with several of the artists and who championed their work. Confining his attention almost entirely to a representative and diversified selection of twenty-nine artists who were active during the early 1950s, Statler tells something about their lives, their thinking, their ways of working, and the background of their woodblock prints. He does not, however, attempt a critical analysis of their art because he feels that 'the prints speak for themselves'. Among the individuals covered are Yamamoto Kanae, Onchi Kōshirō, Hiratsuka Un'ichi, Maekawa Senpan, Saitō Kiyoshi, Sekino Junichirō, Shinagawa Takumi, and Munakata Shikō. One hundred plates and illustrations (fourteen of them in colour) are included, together with some general and technical information about each print. In a number of respects, Statler's volume served as a follow-up to James A. Michener's *The floating world* (q.v.) at the time of its publication.

Old maps in Japan.
See item no. 55.

A brocade pillow: azaleas of old Japan.
See item no. 59.

A collection of Nagasaki colour prints and paintings: showing the influence of Chinese and European art on that of Japan.
See item no. 179.

Who's who in modern Japanese prints.
See item no. 364.

The floating world in Japanese fiction.
See item no. 1036.

The history of Japanese printing and book illustration.
See item no. 1477.

The art of Hokusai in book illustration.
See item no. 1478.

Tanrokubon: rare books of seventeenth-century Japan.
See item no. 1481.

The history and practice of Japanese printmaking: a selectively annotated bibliography of English language materials.
See item no. 1576.

Photographs and photography

1275 **Black sun: the eyes of four; roots and innovation in Japanese photography.**
Mark Holborn. New York: Aperture, 1986. 80p.
A selection of black-and-white photographs by four contemporary masters of photography – Hosoe Eikoe, Tōmatsu Shōmei, Fukase Masahisa, and Moriyama Daidō – accompanied by Holborn's essays about these photographers and their work. Most of the photographs depict the demonic imagery of Kamaitachi as dramatised by a dancer in the villages and rice fields of the far north, the effects of the 1945 Nagasaki atomic bombing, the crows (symbols of ill omen) inhabiting Hokkaidō and other areas of Japan, and the still-life abstractions found in the alleys and backstreets of an urban environment (Tokyo). This publication was prepared to accompany a travelling exhibition, 'Black Sun: The Eyes of Four', organised by the Alfred Stieglitz Center of the Philadelphia Museum of Art, the Museum of Modern Art in Oxford, and the Arts Council of Great Britain.

1276 **A century of Japanese photography.**
Japan Photographers Association [Nihon Shashinka Kyōkai], introduction by John W. Dower. New York: Pantheon, 1980. 385p. bibliog.
These 514 photographs comprehensively illustrate the development of photography in Japan and provide a visual record of her history between 1840 and 1945. Taken by Japanese photographers, they graphically depict many scenes from the recent past as well as Japanese customs, individual portraits, and historic and lesser-known buildings. The photographs are grouped into nine sections – 'Dawn', 'The Period of Enlightenment', 'Commercial Photography', 'Records of War, I', 'Art Photography', 'The Epoch of Development', 'The Camera's Eye', 'Advertisements and Propaganda', and 'Records of War, II' – and are supplemented by an introductory essay entitled 'Ways of Seeing, Ways of Remembering: the Photography of Prewar Japan'.

1277 **New Japanese photography.**
Edited with introductions by John Szarkowski, Shōji Yamagishi.
New York: Museum of Modern Art; distributed by the New York Graphic Society (Greenwich, Connecticut), 1974. 111p.
The first extensive English-language survey of contemporary Japanese photography, based on an exhibition held at New York's Museum of Modern Art. Organised as a series of one-man shows which identifies the central concerns of each of fifteen postwar photographers, the exhibition did not attempt to present the many features indigenous to Japanese photography but rather sought to answer the question: 'How does Japanese photography relate to the contemporary concerns of the entire photographic community?' The editors' selection of black-and-white photographs focuses on such subjects as Buddhist images in the Murōji Temple southeast of Nara, the aftermath of the atomic bombing of Nagasaki, analyses of people, everyday life in contemporary Japan, the eroticism of the Japanese, and the devastation of the human environment.

1278   **Japan: photographs, 1854–1905.**
       Edited with a historical text by Clark Worswick, introduction by Jan
       Morris.   New York: Knopf, 1979; London: H. Hamilton, 1980. 151p.
       bibliog. (A Pennwick Book).

These 120 photographs depict the people (actors, pedlars, priests, sumo wrestlers,
etc.), professions, clothing, customs, rural and urban landscapes, buildings (e.g.,
Buddhist temples and the residences of the feudal lords), interiors of Japanese homes,
and gardens of the late Tokugawa and Meiji periods. They were taken by several
European and Japanese photographers, in particular Felix Beato, Ogawa Isshin,
Kusakabe Kinbei, and Baron Raimund von Stillfried. Worswick's brief text,
'Photography in Nineteenth-Century Japan', surveys the photographers who were
active during that era and their photographic techniques and styles. Seventy-two hand-
coloured photographs by Beato and Stillfried have also been reproduced in *Once upon
a time: visions of old Japan*, photographs by Felice Beato and Baron Raimund von
Stillfried, words by Pierre Loti, introduction by Chantal Edel, translated by Linda
Coverdale (New York: Friendly Press, 1986, 112p.).

Faces of Japan.
See item no. 11.

**A day in the life of Japan: photographed by 100 of the world's leading
photojournalists on one day, June 7, 1985.**
See item no. 28.

This land . . . this beauty: Japan's natural splendor.
See item no. 44.

Bamboo of Japan: splendor in four seasons.
See item no. 64.

The lure of Japan's railways.
See item no. 954.

Living crafts of Okinawa.
See item no. 1222.

The roots of Japanese architecture: a photographic quest.
See item no. 1302.

Imperial gardens of Japan: Sento Gosho, Katsura, Shugaku-in.
See item no. 1334.

Pottery and ceramics

1279   **Karatsu ware: a tradition of diversity.**
       Johanna Becker.   Tokyo; New York: Kodansha International, 1986.
       220p. map. bibliog.

The history and stylistic analysis of a popular style of stoneware produced in northwestern Kyūshū since the late sixteenth century. Throughout the Tokugawa period and well into the present century, Karatsu ware has been highly prized by connoisseurs and practitioners of the tea ceremony on account of the beauty of its tea utensils, and an excellent collection of these ceramics can be seen at the Idemitsu Art Museum in Tokyo. Dividing her study into four chapters – 'History', 'Examples, Influence, Problems', 'Kilns and Techniques', and 'The Karatsu Style' – Becker writes about the origins, evolution and nature of this ceramic style; the materials, kilns and technical processes involved in its production; and the individual objects which she has studied. Many of them are depicted in 234 accompanying photographs.

1280 **Shigaraki, potters' valley.**
Louise Allison Cort. Tokyo; New York: Kodansha International, 1979. 428p. 4 maps. bibliog.

An intimate account of the stoneware produced since the thirteenth century by farmer-potters dwelling in the Shigaraki Valley southeast of Kyōto. Paying particular attention to the constraints imposed by Shigaraki's singular clays and to the influence of pottery makers and pottery markets outside the valley, Cort studies the stylistic development of this pottery and describes the throwing, glazing, firing, and kiln-building involved in its production. Individual chapters discuss each major group of products: beginning with medieval utilitarian wares and covering tea-storage jars, tea ceremony utensils, official tea jars, and present-day glazed domestic wares. The special relationship which has existed between Shigaraki and the former imperial capital of Kyōto is also examined. More than three hundred photographs illustrate both the great variety of Shigaraki ware and the techniques and processes that are in use today.

1281 **Famous ceramics of Japan.**
Tokyo; New York: Kodansha International, 1981-84. 39–45p. per volume. maps.

A series of folio-sized volumes covering major types of Japanese ceramics. Each volume contains a brief introductory essay, 50–75 full-colour plates, moderately detailed notes about the plates, and maps of various kiln sites. The twelve publications are: *Nabeshima*, by Motosuke Imaizumi (vol. 1, 1981); *Agano and Takatori*, by Gen Kōzuru (vol. 2, 1981); *Folk kilns I*, by Hiroshi Mizuo (vol. 3, 1981); *Folk kilns II*, by Kichiemon Okamura (vol. 4, 1981); *Kakiemon*, by Takeshi Nagatake (vol. 5, 1981); *Imari*, by Takeshi Nagatake (vol. 6, 1982); *Tokoname*, by Yoshiharu Sawada (vol. 7, 1982); *Oribe*, by Takeshi Murayama (vol. 8, 1982); *Karatsu*, by Tarōemon Nakazato (vol. 9, 1983); *Kiseto and Setoguro*, by Shōsaku Furukawa (vol. 10, 1983); *Hagi*, by Ryōsuke Kawano (vol. 11, 1983); and *Shino*, by Ryōji Kuroda (vol. 12, 1984).

1282 **Shino and Oribe ceramics.**
Ryōichi Fujioka, translated and adapted with an introduction by Samuel Crowell Morse. Tokyo; New York: Kodansha International and Shibundo, 1977. 178p. map. bibliog. (Japanese Arts Library, 1).

A comprehensive, illustrated survey of two classic tea wares that were introduced into the tea ceremony during its formative stages in the late sixteenth century, influenced the aesthetic development of that ceremony, and 'revolutionized Japanese ceramic methods at a time when pottery in Japan was developing from purely utilitarian forms into works of art created for their inherent beauty'. Fujioka writes about the origins, characteristics (colours, forms, glazes, decoration), and types of Shino and Oribe ceramics; discusses their methods of production, their kilns (located in present-day western Gifu Prefecture), and their kiln marks; and briefly comments on the connoisseurship of these ceramics.

1283 **Japanese pottery.**
Soame Jenyns, foreword by Harry M. Garner. London: Faber and Faber; New York: Praeger, 1971. 380p. map. bibliog.

A scholarly examination of Japanese pottery from prehistoric times up to the late Tokugawa period, illustrated by black-and-white plates of 256 selected objects. It discusses the prehistoric and protohistoric unglazed tomb wares dating from the Jōmon period through the seventh century, pottery produced during the Nara and Heian periods, the seven old kilns of Japan (Seto, Echizen, Tokoname, Bizen, Tamba, Shigaraki, and Iga), the rise of the pottery associated with the tea ceremony, the Mino wares, the pottery produced by the kilns founded by sixteenth-century Korean immigrants (e.g., Karatsu, Satsuma, and Hagi), the pottery of Yamashiro, the work of selected minor potters and kilns, and the problems involved in dating and attributing Japanese pottery. This volume is a companion to the author's earlier book, *Japanese porcelain* (London: Faber and Faber; New York: Praeger, 1965, 351p.), which details the making of porcelain in Japan from its seventeenth-century beginnings to the mid-1800s.

1284 **Kutani ware.**
Sensaku Nakagawa, translated and adapted by John Bester, introduction by Louise Allison Cort. Tokyo; New York: Kodansha International and Shibundo, 1979. 181p. 2 maps. bibliog. (Japanese Arts Library, 7).

Kutani ware, one of the better-known types of Japanese ceramics in the West, is famous for its bold decorations in richly coloured overglaze enamels. In this study, Nakagawa examines both the Old Kutani ware that flourished during the late 1600s and the newer style of Kutani ware that has been produced since the early nineteenth century. He first discusses in detail the production, clays, forms, glazes, decorations, motifs, and inscriptions of Old Kutani ware. Then he turns to the newer Kutani ware, focusing on the production of several specified kilns and their potters. Nakagawa's presentation is illustrated by nearly two hundred captioned photographs, particularly of shallow bowls currently found within the collections of the Ishikawa Prefecture Art Museum.

1285 **Japanese painted porcelain: modern masterpieces in overglaze enamel.**
Edited by the National Museum of Modern Art, Tokyo [Tōkyō Kokuritsu Kindai Bijutsukan], translated by Richard L. Gage, foreword by Kenji Adachi, introduction by Mitsuhiko Hasebe. New York; Tokyo; Kyōto: Weatherhill/Tankōsha, 1980. 245p.

Based upon the catalogue of an exhibition held at the Museum in 1979, this splendidly illustrated volume introduces the works of fourteen twentieth-century ceramic artists, with particular focus on the porcelains produced by Tomimoto Kenkichi (1886-1963), Katō Hajime (1900-68), and Kitaōji Rosanjin (1883-1959). The 189 full-page colour plates illustrate several kinds of multicolour overglaze-decorated porcelains ranging from plates, bowls, square and octagonal dishes, and lidded jars, to vases, incense burners, cups, and boxes. Detailed commentaries on individual pieces and biographical sketches of the artists conclude the book.

1286 **Tamba pottery: the timeless art of a Japanese village.**
Daniel Rhodes. Tokyo; New York: Kodansha International, 1970. 180p. bibliog. Reprinted, Kodansha International, 1982.
An illustrated study of the ceramics produced in the mountainous Tamba area of eastern Hyōgo Prefecture, presented primarily through an historical survey and present-day examination of the kilns at Tachikui, the one village in the region where pottery is still being made. Rhodes describes the older Tamba ware (first made during the Kamakura period) and then traces its historical and technical evolution through the Momoyama and Tokugawa periods into the twentieth century. He explains the technical processes involved in its production as well as the pottery's distinctive characteristics. Rhodes concludes with a brief chapter contrasting Tamba ware with the ceramics from the five other 'ancient kilns' of Echizen, Tokoname, Seto, Shigaraki, and Bizen.

1287 **The world of Japanese ceramics.**
Herbert H. Sanders, with Kenkichi Tomimoto, introductory notes by Shōji Hamada, Bernard Leach. Tokyo; Palo Alto, California: Kodansha International, 1967. 267p. map. Reprinted, Tokyo; New York: Kodansha International, 1982.
On the basis of interviews with over one hundred potters, Sanders provides detailed information about the basic techniques of pottery production in postwar Japan and about the origins and historical development of Japanese pottery. He describes the tools and materials used by contemporary craftsmen, the processes they employ for forming pottery and for decoration, and their various underglazes, glazes and overglaze enamels. The concluding chapter contains technical information about the composition of Japanese glazes in particular. Many photographs, some in colour, illustrate representative types of pottery, kilns and tools, and depict individual potters at work. A map indicates the location of one hundred kilns and kiln sites, from Hirosaki in northern Honshū to Tateno in southern Kyūshū.

Prehistoric Japanese arts: Jōmon pottery.
See item no. 107.

Hamada, potter.
See item no. 331.

Lost innocence: folk craft potters of Onta, Japan.
See item no. 553.

A feast for the eyes: the Japanese art of food arrangement.
See item no. 1435.

Sculpture and netsuke

1288 Collectors' netsuke.
Raymond Bushell. New York; Tokyo: Weatherhill, 1971. 199p. bibliog.

Netsuke are miniature carvings made of a large variety of materials, especially wood, ivory, bone, and lacquer, that were worn during the Tokugawa period as attachments to one's purse, pouch, or lacquer box. Writing for the sophisticated collector in particular, Bushell discusses the netsuke of seventy-nine prominent carvers – from Yoshimura Shūzan (died 1776) through Nakamura Tokisada (best known by his artist name, Masatoshi, 1915-) – and deals with such matters as their signatures, schools, copies, commercialism, age, and authentication. Seven hundred photographs (half of them in full colour) illustrate his account. Readers seeking fuller explanations of the fundamentals and basic terms associated with netsuke may also wish to consult Bushell's *An introduction to netsuke* (Rutland, Vermont; Tokyo: Tuttle, 1971, 78p.), which deals with the nature, origin, development, and materials of netsuke; Ueda Reikichi's *The netsuke handbook*, adapted by Raymond Bushell (Rutland, Vermont; Tokyo: Tuttle, 1961, 325p.); and Frederick Meinertzhagen's *The art of the netsuke carver* (London: Routledge and Kegan Paul, 1956, 80p. Reprinted, Hollywood, Florida: Kurstin-Schneider, 1975). Many additional books and articles may be identified through a perusal of *Netsuke: a bibliography*, by Cornelius Van S. Roosevelt (Washington, DC: privately published, 1978, 105p.).

1289 Shinzō: Hachiman imagery and its development.
Christine Guth Kanda. Cambridge, Massachusetts: Council on East Asian Studies, Harvard University, 1985. 135p. bibliog. (Harvard East Asian Monographs, 119).

Among the diverse representational arts associated with Shintō, *shinzō* (wooden statues of Shintō deities) have long commanded great reverence among Japanese worshippers. Kanda's scholarly, illustrated examination of the stylistic and iconographic evolution of *shinzō* between the ninth and fourteenth centuries focuses on the images of the popular deity known as Hachiman. Part one is a general introduction that pays particular attention to the genesis of anthropomorphic imagery in Japan, the formal development of *shinzō*, the function, patronage and devotional practices pertaining to *shinzō*, and the evolution of the Hachiman cult and image. Detailed case-studies of three major statues of Hachiman – in the Tōji, Yakushiji, and Tōdaiji temples of Kyōto and Nara – and briefer discussions of other portrayals of Hachiman constitute part two. Kanda's book also offers a good overview of the development of Shintō aesthetic attitudes and their relationship to Buddhist influences.

1290 Nara Buddhist art: Todai-ji.
Takeshi Kobayashi, translated and adapted by Richard L. Gage. New York; Tokyo: Weatherhill/Heibonsha, 1975. 157p. map. (Heibonsha Survey of Japanese Art, 5).

The Tōdaiji, an immense monastery-temple complex belonging to the Kegon sect of Buddhism, was built under imperial sponsorship during the eighth century in the capital city of Nara. Its principal image, a colossal sculpture of the Buddha cast in gilded bronze, is housed in the largest wooden building in the world. The temple and its Great Buddha together constitute the focus of Kobayashi's study of Nara period religious sculpture. Kobayashi also discusses other major works in the Tōdaiji – among them the images of the Four Celestial Guardians in the Kaidanin and the Fukukenjaku Kannon in the Sangatsudō – as well as such sculptures as the Yakushi Triad (at the Yakushiji) that are found elsewhere in the city. A discussion of Buddhism as a unifying force introduces this beautifully illustrated volume, and separate chapters examine the Tōdaiji school of sculpture and the special quality of Nara sculpture in general.

1291   **Art of netsuke carving.**
Masatoshi [Tokisada Nakamura], as told by Raymond Bushell.
Tokyo; New York: Kodansha International, 1981. 236p. bibliog.

A top-ranking, twentieth-century carver of netsuke recounts his training as an apprentice, the influences which moulded his craftsmanship, the ways in which he has made and used his tools, the effect of his concern for quality and suitability upon his selection of materials, his various carving techniques, his procedures for polishing, colouring, and staining his netsuke, the sources of the ideas he has for subjects, the ways he works out his decisions, and his adoption of a range of styles and techniques. Bushell's complementary catalogue of 356 netsuke that Masatoshi carved between the 1940s and the late 1970s (constituting 'the major part of his lifework') contains larger-than-life-size colour illustrations which depict such figures and objects as kabuki actors, birds, insects, supernatural animals, gods and sages, masks and heads, fish, subjects from ukiyo-e, toys and dolls, frogs, and weird beings.

1292   **Japanese portrait sculpture.**
Hisashi Mōri, translated and adapted with an introduction by W. Chië Ishibashi.   Tokyo; New York: Kodansha International and Shibundo, 1977. 150p. bibliog. (Japanese Arts Library, 2).

A comprehensive illustrated study of the sculpture of both religious personages and lay people produced between the eighth and sixteenth centuries. Many of these statues depict Buddhist subjects such as famous monks and founders of sects, and have been venerated as objects of worship. Mōri considers the intimate relationship between Buddhism and portrait sculpture, examines the statues of both imaginary beings and historical individuals, and discusses their historical and stylistic development.

1293   **Sculpture of the Kamakura period.**
Hisashi Mōri, translated by Katherine Eickmann.   New York; Tokyo: Weatherhill/Heibonsha, 1974. 174p. map. (Heibonsha Survey of Japanese Art, 11).

The popularisation of Buddhism and the political ascendancy of the military class during the twelfth and thirteenth centuries were accompanied by the tendency of contemporary religious and portrait sculpture to display an originality, a realism, and a dramatic vigour that set it apart from its Heian period antecedents. Mōri's examination of the full range of Kamakura period sculpture first covers its historical and social background, then focuses on the achievements of the noted sculptors Kōkei (flourished late 1100s), Unkei (died 1223), and Kaikei (late 1100s to early 1200s). In discussing their work, Mōri considers their innovative sculptural styles and techniques as well as their motivations and intentions.

Fine Arts. Sculpture and netsuke

1294 **Bugaku masks.**
Kyōtarō Nishikawa, translated and adapted with an introduction by
Monica Bethe.   Tokyo; New York: Kodansha International and
Shibundo, 1978. 194p. bibliog. (Japanese Arts Library, 5).

An illustrated study of the highly stylised carved masks worn by performers of *bugaku*,
a dance-drama which flourished between the ninth and twelfth centuries at the imperial
court in Kyōto. Nishikawa begins with an account of the historical background to
bugaku masks and the dance-drama in which they were used. A detailed description of
the different types of masks is followed by overviews of the masks that were carved
outside Kyōto and of the technical aspects of their manufacture. He concludes with a
discussion of the carvers of *bugaku* masks and their inscriptions, and with appendixes
listing (1) places to see performers and masks today, (2) datable masks, and (3) *bugaku*
masks in Japan.

1295 **The great age of Japanese Buddhist sculpture, AD 600–1300.**
Kyōtarō Nishikawa, Emily J. Sano, preface by Edmund P. Pillsbury,
Rand Castile, foreword by Bunichirō Sano, introduction by Emily J.
Sano.   Fort Worth, Texas; Kimbell Art Museum; New York: Japan
Society; distributed by the University of Washington Press (Seattle,
Washington), 1982. 151p. bibliog.

A beautifully produced catalogue of an exhibition of fifty-two masterpieces of bronze,
wooden, and dry-lacquer statues drawn from several temples and museums in Japan.
Opening with an Asuka period gilt bronze statue of Kannon from the Hōryūji in Nara
and closing with Kamakura period polychromed wood statues of five great Myōō
('Wisdom Buddhas') from the Enryakuji, this book seeks to demonstrate how stylistic
developments progressed over a period of seven hundred years from an initial reliance
on the forms and techniques of Chinese art to the creation of the realistic sculpture of
the thirteenth century, and how art styles were influenced by changing patronage and
the advancement of Buddhist thought. Full-page colour photographs of each object are
supplemented by substantial catalogue entries. Nishikawa's long introductory essay
covers the introduction of Buddhism into Japan, surveys its evolution, discusses the
iconography of Buddhist sculpture, and describes the techniques of Buddhist image-
making.

1296 **Japanese sculpture of the Tempyo period: masterpieces of the eighth
century.**
Langdon Warner, edited and arranged with an introduction by James
Marshal Plumer.   Cambridge, Massachusetts: Harvard University
Press, 1964. 165p. 2 maps. bibliog.

The reissued, one-volume edition of an account of Tempyō period (710-94) art which
Harvard University Press originally published as a two-volume work in 1959. The first
part of Warner's lifelong study introduces the Tempyō period by surveying its society,
craftsmen, beliefs, Buddhism and the arts, the influence of T'ang Chinese culture, the
Abbot Ganjin, lacquer sculpture, the masks of the *gigaku* drama, and the essentials of
image-making. The second part consists of approximately one hundred separate
commentaries that accompany 217 black-and-white plates devoted to individual or
groups of sculpture. These are arranged in several sections according to material:
'Bronze (Hakuho Period, 645–710)', 'Tempyo Temple Interior', 'Bronze (Tempyo
Period: 710–794)', 'Clay', 'Hollow Lacquer', 'Hollow Lacquer with Lattice Support',

'Lacquered Wood Core', 'Lacquered Carved Wood', and 'Wood (Tempyo and Post-Tempyo)'. Concluding the volume is a section on *gigaku* masks, which Warner regarded as true sculpture rather than as mere faces. *Classic Buddhist sculpture: the Tempyō period*, by Jirō Sugiyama, translated and adapted by Samuel Crowell Morse (Tokyo; New York: Kodansha International, 1982, 230p. [Japanese Arts Library, 11]), examines the key monuments of eighth-century sculpture and relates them to their historical and religious background. It incorporates the findings of recent Japanese scholarship but does not supersede Warner's distinguished work.

Haniwa.
See item no. 108.

Haniwa: the clay sculpture of proto-historic Japan.
See item no. 108.

Gods of myth and stone: phallicism in Japanese folk religion.
See item no. 502.

Temples of Nara and their art.
See item no. 1316.

The inrō handbook: studies of netsuke, inrō, and lacquer.
See item no. 1360.

Architecture

1297 **Contemporary Japanese architecture: its development and challenge.**
Botond Bognar, foreword by Arata Isozaki. New York: Van Nostrand Reinhold, 1985. 363p. bibliog.

Paying particular attention to developments since the 1960s, Bognar reviews the entire spectrum of postwar Japanese architecture and seeks to demonstrate how it has drawn its inspiration from Japanese cultural traditions even as it has assimilated a variety of Western influences. Five chapters entitled 'First Impressions', 'Cultural Traditions', 'Modern Japanese Architecture', 'New Directions in the 1960s: Early Departures from Modern Architecture', and 'Japanese Architecture Today: Pluralism' – illustrated with hundreds of photographs and floor plans – provide an excellent overview of postwar trends, the accomplishments of individual architects, and some of the basic principles found in contemporary architecture. Bognar argues that Japanese architecture now has the capability of exerting a positive influence on the Western world and that the time has come for the West to assimilate the Japanese example.

1298 **New directions in Japanese architecture.**
Robin Boyd. New York: Braziller; London: Studio Vista, 1968. 128p. (New Directions in Architecture).

An introduction to the 'Architects' Modern', or the 'New Japan Style', of postwar Japanese architecture, illustrated by numerous black-and-white photographs and floor plans. Boyd first considers some of the factors influencing this architecture, among

Fine Arts. Architecture

them the problems of inadequate space in Japan and the country's position geographically, culturally, and politically between East and West. He then briefly describes and analyses some of the work of fourteen architects, starting with the Metabolist generation, continuing on to the anti-Metabolists and to the older men who have remained influential, and concluding with Tange Kenzō, a leader of modern world architecture. Kikutake Kiyonari, Kurokawa Noriaki, Maki Fumihiko, Isozaki Arata, Yokoyama Kimio, Ashihara Yoshinobu, Sakakura Junzō, and Maekawa Kunio are among the other architects whom he studies.

1299　**The architecture of Arata Isozaki.**
Philip Drew.　London: Granada; New York: Harper and Row, 1982. 206p. bibliog.

A full presentation of the work of the 'foremost creative personality in Japanese architecture', Isozaki Arata, between 1960 and 1980. Drew is particularly concerned with depicting Isozaki as a 'type of Mannerist reacting to modern architecture in much the same way that a Raphael . . . reacted to the High Renaissance'. He discusses his search for solutions to a number of problems besetting world architects, his values and the sources of his inspiration, the stylistic shifts in his architecture during this twenty-year period, and the buildings he designed – among them banks, schools, office buildings, museums and exhibition halls, medical clinics, town halls, country clubhouses, libraries, and houses. Also included are 163 photographs and architectural plans and drawings, a translation of Isozaki's brief essay (1978) 'An Architecture of Quotation and Metaphor', a biographical note, and a list of his works.

1300　**The Japanese house: a tradition for contemporary architecture.**
Heinrich Engel, introduction by Walter Gropius.　Rutland, Vermont; Tokyo: Tuttle, 1964. 495p. bibliog.

An award-winning, comprehensive study of traditional domestic architecture and its basic principles. Engel (a professional architect) describes the evolution of ordinary Japanese residential architecture, highlights some of its special characteristics and qualities, and singles out a number of values or principles which can be incorporated into contemporary Western architectural design. The four parts of the book – 'Structure', 'Organism', 'Environment', and 'Aesthetics' – are illustrated by over two hundred line drawings, plans, and black-and-white photographs. A two-chapter (149p.) excerpt, containing many of these illustrations, was published by Tuttle in 1985 under the title *Measure and construction of the Japanese house*. It not only presents the qualities of space, form, and structure in Japanese construction but also provides a useful guide to ways in which Westerners can adapt or replicate Japanese architectural achievements in their own homes.

1301　**The essential Japanese house: craftsmanship, function, and style in town and country.**
Photographs by Yukio Futagawa, text and commentaries by Teiji Itoh. Tokyo: Weatherhill and Bijutsu Shuppansha, 1967. 419p. 11 maps.

An extended photographic essay and brief discussion of the *minka* (traditional-style houses of farmers, landowners, merchants, and public servants) that were built largely during the Tokugawa period. Futagawa, an architectural photographer, reproduces 320 of his black-and-white photographs in order to present regional surveys of the *minka* still found in the Kyōto area, in Nara and Ōsaka, along the Inland Sea, on the islands

528

of Shikoku and Kyūshū, in northern Honshū, within the Tokyo Bay area, deep in the Japanese Alps, along the Sea of Japan, and within the Hida District. Itoh's text comments on the architectural tradition and craftsmanship of this type of home and examines its architectural functions and styles. Both authors highlight the variations in structure and style which resulted from local geographical conditions, the availability of different types of structural material, the social code of the times in which they were built, and the particular requirements of their residents.

1302 **The roots of Japanese architecture: a photographic quest.**
Yukio Futagawa, text and commentaries by Teiji Itoh, translated by Paul Konya, foreword by Isamu Noguchi. New York; London: Harper and Row, 1963. 207p.
Through 128 full-page black-and-white photographs in particular, Futagawa and Itoh record their search for the roots of Japanese architecture. They concern themselves with the philosophical concepts which have inspired Japan's architectural heritage rather than with its specific techniques. Their photographs and commentaries are arranged into ten broad categories entitled 'Wood, Stone, Earth', 'Setting Limits to Infinity', 'Dynamic Space', 'The Garden as a Miniature Universe', 'Linking Nature and Architecture', 'The Pillar and the Mat', 'Of Tea, Bamboo, and More Pillars', 'Borrowing Space', 'Rhythms of the Vertical Plane', and 'The Roof as Symbol'.

1303 **Traditional Japanese houses.**
Edited and photographed by Yukio Futagawa, introduction and text by Teiji Itoh, translated by Richard L. Gage. New York: Rizzoli, 1983. 356p. map.
Ninety-six *minka* (traditional-style houses) – grouped by region from the Tōhoku area in the north to Okinawa in the far south – are depicted in this photographic survey. Futagawa's numerous duotones and twelve colour photographs illustrate the range and types of farmhouses, storehouses, urban residences, and even shrines that were built by the common people before the twentieth century. They depict both the interiors and exteriors of these buildings, frequently show details of individual rooms, and provide an understanding of regional influences, traits, and materials. Itoh's commentary briefly discusses the background and some of the details of these *minka*, but his illustrated book *Traditional domestic architecture of Japan*, translated by Richard L. Gage (New York; Tokyo: Weatherhill/Heibonsha, 1972, 150p. [Heibonsha Survey of Japanese Art, 21]), contains a much more comprehensive text about this architectural style. It surveys the place of the *minka* in Japanese architectural history (especially during the Tokugawa period) as well as its method of design, considers the development of special *minka* characteristics such as its roof-truss structures, explores the variations in the structure and the style of these dwellings that were determined by their owners as well as their adaptation to differing environmental conditions, and comments on their functional and aesthetic values.

1304 **Space and spirit in modern Japan.**
Text and photographs by Barrie B. Greenbie. New Haven, Connecticut; London: Yale University Press, 1988. map. bibliog. 195p.
A collection of personal observations on the imaginative use of private and public space in Japan and the extraordinary capacity of the Japanese 'to absorb the cultural

and technical ways of other peoples without giving up their own traditions'. Illustrating his account with some three hundred black-and-white photographs, Greenbie depicts Japan's urban and rural landscape as he searches for some general principles of human experience that are expressed in characteristic Japanese ways. He explores the traditional Japanese homes with their walled-in gardens and 'ambience of privacy and security' as well as various types of public space in major urban centres and the country's parks and agricultural lands. In addition to studying the ways in which the Japanese perceive and interact with the space about them, he examines their current efforts to preserve public 'green space' in both their cities and their rural surroundings.

1305 **Katsura: tradition and creation in Japanese architecture.**
Walter Gropius, Kenzō Tange, photographs by Yasuhiro Ishimoto.
New Haven, Connecticut: Yale University Press; Tokyo: Zokeisha
Publications, 1960. 36p., 148 pages of illustrations. 6 maps.

The Katsura Detached Palace west of Kyōto, built during the years 1620-47 as a country villa for Imperial Prince Toshihito of the Hachijō no Miya family, is well known as a masterpiece of traditional Japanese architecture and as an important influence on modern Japanese architecture. This collection of monochromatic photographs of the palace complex and its individual buildings – 'a visual record of the living Katsura as it exists in the minds of an architect and a photographer' – concentrates on the architectural elements of form and space. Brief essays by Walter Gropius on architecture in Japan in relation to other world architectures, and by Tange Kenzō on creation and tradition in Japanese architecture as exemplified in this villa serve as an introduction. A complementary work is Akira Naitō's *Katsura: a princely retreat*, translated by Charles S. Terry, photographs by Takeshi Nishikawa (Tokyo; New York: Kodansha International, 1977, 182p.). This commentary on the cultural and architectural history of the Katsura and its gardens is illustrated by numerous colour and black-and-white plates, architectural drawings, and a fold-out site plan.

1306 **Japanese castles.**
Motoo Hinago, translated and adapted with an introduction by
William H. Coaldrake. Tokyo; New York: Kodansha International
and Shibundo, 1986. 200p. 7 maps. bibliog. (Japanese Arts Library,
14).

With its emphasis on fortification technology and the histories of individual castles, this profusely illustrated study complements Kiyoshi Hirai's *Feudal architecture of Japan* (q.v.) as it traces the evolution of fortification techniques from their origins in primitive mountain fortresses, through the 'golden age' (late sixteenth and early seventeenth centuries) of castle-building, to the construction of the renowned Himeji Castle. Hinago describes the technical, logistical, engineering, and design aspects of traditional castle buildings, while examining the stone walls, towers, and gateways which constitute their primary architectural components. He also singles out two castles – at Azuchi and Himeji – for particularly detailed descriptions. Coaldrake enhances Hinago's study with a comparison of European and Japanese castles, a discussion of recent discoveries about the development of castle design, two appendixes, and a glossary of technical terms.

1307 **Feudal architecture of Japan.**
Kiyoshi Hirai, translated by Hiroaki Sato, Jeannine Ciliotta.   New
York; Tokyo: Weatherhill/Heibonsha, 1973. 166p. (Heibonsha Survey
of Japanese Art, 13).

An introduction to the architecture of late sixteenth- and early seventeenth-century
castles and to the *shoin*-style mansions found within them. Paying particular attention
to both their exterior structural features and their interior décor, Hirai describes a
number of castles and residences, traces the evolution of the *shoin* style of architecture
(with particular focus on traditional standards of residential design and on the
arrangement and use of castle rooms), and singles out for special consideration Nijō
Castle in Kyōto, the Ōsaka Castle complex, and the castle at Edo (Tokyo) that served
as the seat of the Tokugawa shōguns. He highlights the important role of castles and
shoin as symbols of power among the Tokugawa ruling class, and surveys various
aspects of daily life within these walled compounds. Numerous photographs, old prints
of castles, and detailed building plans illustrate the account.

1308 **Space in Japanese architecture.**
Mitsuo Inoue, translated by Hiroshi Watanabe.   New York; Tokyo:
Weatherhill, 1985. 210p. bibliog.

A sophisticated analysis of the evolving treatment of both interior and exterior space in
Japanese architecture through a study of the process of the development of Japanese
architecture between the Asuka and Tokugawa periods. Inoue investigates large-scale
religious as well as secular architecture – the architecture associated with shrines and
temple complexes as well as with the residential compounds of Japan's aristocracy –
primarily through a study of site arrangements and building plans revealed in original
architectural drawings, scroll paintings, and literary descriptions, and through an
examination of several extant buildings. He sees the Japanese conception of space as
having progressed through a number of major stages, and focuses on three of them:
the 'sculptural' (Asuka period), the 'pictorial' (Nara and Heian periods), and the
'architectural' (Kamakura to Edo or Tokugawa periods).

1309 **The classic tradition in Japanese architecture: modern versions of the
Sukiya style.**
Teiji Itoh, translated by Richard L. Gage, photographs by Yukio
Futagawa.   New York; Tokyo: Weatherhill/Tankōsha, 1972. 279p.

For educated Japanese, the word *sukiya* 'evokes a world of associations with buildings
in which the ancient and traditional fondness for natural materials, simplicity, and
closeness to nature dominates every detail of the composition'. Itoh explores *sukiya*
architecture as it is being employed in postwar Japan, probes the reasons for the
survival of the *sukiya* style since the late sixteenth century, shows how five outstanding
architects with fundamentally Western backgrounds are reviving *sukiya* architecture,
and demonstrates the adaptability of this style by indicating how it is being
incorporated into modern steel-and-concrete buildings. Itoh's text is organised into
four parts: 'The Background of the Modern Sukiya Style', 'Four Modern Sukiya
Types', 'Elements of the Modern Sukiya Structure', and 'Sukiya Components in
Modern Buildings'. Over 250 photographs and architectural drawings illustrate houses,
museums, restaurants, teahouses, and other buildings, the majority of which date from
the 1960s.

1310 **The elegant Japanese house: traditional sukiya architecture.**
Teiji Itoh, translated and adapted by the staff of John Weatherhill,
Inc., under the editorship of Ralph Friedrich, photographs by Yukio
Futagawa. New York; Tokyo: Walker/Weatherhill, 1969. 218p.

This examination of one of the major traditional styles surviving in contemporary
domestic architecture deals with the *sukiya* in two different forms: as a separately built
teahouse and as a structure built in teahouse form. Itoh first describes the residence of
Kitamura Kinjirō in Kyōto (a modern structure in *sukiya* style) in order to provide a
basic understanding of this style. He then traces the history of the *sukiya* style – its
origins date back to the tea master Sen no Rikyū (1521-91) and his house at Jurakudai
– and considers the style's essential characteristics. Finally Itoh details the most typical
features of the *sukiya* style – a diagonal-line approach, conciseness of statement and
composition, 'pivotal space', and an interior that can be adapted to a number of
purposes and spatial patterns – and their role in creating the total atmosphere of the
sukiya-style building. This extensively illustrated book is intended as a companion
volume to the author's *Essential Japanese house: craftsmanship, function, and style in
town and country* (q.v.).

1311 **Kura: design and tradition of the Japanese storehouse.**
Teiji Itoh, adapted by Charles S. Terry, photographs by Kiyoshi
Takai. Tokyo; New York: Kodansha International in co-operation
with Tankōsha (Kyōto), 1973. 251p. map. Abridged ed., Seattle,
Washington: Madrona Publishers, 1980. 187p.

Kura ('storehouses') date back to the prehistoric late Jōmon period and continue to
serve as repositories for rice and many types of valuables requiring protection against
Japan's damp climate, rodents, and fire. *Kura* have also frequently been used as small
factories, warehouses, shops, family residences, and even as temples. This handsome
volume, written by a noted architectural historian, examines all structural types of *kura*
including board-wall storehouses, intersecting-board storehouses, clay storehouses,
raised-floor storehouses, and *dozō*, or storehouses with heavy plaster walls. Itoh
describes their historical and cultural characteristics, their architectural styles in
relation to their regional requirements, and the nature of their construction. Takai's
165 full-page photographs and seventeen architectural drawings demonstrate the
beauty of these buildings and clarify their architectural features.

1312 **Minka: traditional houses of rural Japan.**
Chūji Kawashima, translated by Lynne E. Riggs. Tokyo; New York:
Kodansha International, 1986. 260p.

A comprehensive study of the traditional-style houses known as *minka* that were once
found throughout Japan. Kawashima describes the materials with which they are
constructed, their basic external and internal features, the evolution of their floor
plans, and their structure (the foundation, floor, posts and framework, beam system,
and roof truss). He also discusses in great detail the diverse regional styles (in
particular, the different types of roofs) which evolved over the centuries in response to
the differing climates, terrains, and types of economy that characterise the Japanese
islands. There are 120 drawings and floor plans and three hundred black-and-white
photographs, reproduced largely from museums and reconstructed exhibition villages,
to illustrate this account. Kawashima's book complements *The essential Japanese*

house, by Yukio Futagawa and Teiji Itoh (q.v.), which contains a wealth of original photographs of *minka* but a substantially smaller text.

1313   **Kenzo Tange, 1946–1969: architecture and urban design.**
Edited with an introduction by Udo Kultermann, preface by Kenzō Tange.   New York: Praeger; London: Pall Mall Press, 1970. 304p. bibliog.

Illustrated international edition (with parallel texts in English, French, and German) of a descriptive study of the buildings designed by the renowned architect Tange Kenzō (born 1913) and his associates over a twenty-five-year period. It covers some thirty projects, among them the Peace Centre in Hiroshima, the architect's home in Tokyo, town halls in Shimizu, Kurayoshi, Imabori, and Kurashiki, the Sogetsu Art Centre in Tokyo, a housing project in Takamatsu, St. Mary's Cathedral in Tokyo, the Olympic arenas (Tokyo), and the office building of the Shizuoka Newspaper and Broadcasting Corporation in Tokyo. In addition, this volume includes four of Tange's essays: 'A Plan for Tokyo, 1960: toward a Structural Reorganization'; 'Tokaido-Megalopolis: the Japanese Archipelago in the Future'; 'Function, Structure and Symbol, 1966'; and 'The Expo '70 Master Plan and Master Design'.

1314   **What is Japanese architecture?**
Kazuo Nishi, Kazuo Hozumi, translated, adapted, and with an introduction by H. Mack Horton.   Tokyo; New York: Kodansha International, 1985. 144p. map. bibliog.

A highly compressed historical survey of the entire range of Japanese architecture (temples, shrines, palaces, castles, teahouses, theatres) up to the mid-nineteenth century. In four distinct parts, dealing respectively with the architecture of worship, of daily life, of battle, and of entertainment, Nishi explains the evolution of various types of buildings, relates architectural planning and design to historical events and social change, and elucidates Japanese construction methods and architectural styles. Hozumi's 350 superb line drawings enhance the value and appeal of this volume. They depict the buildings mentioned in the text and in many cases also highlight important architectural details and recreate images of the buildings in actual use. An address list of sites that are referred to and an annotated bibliography are provided as well.

1315   **Edo architecture: Katsura and Nikko.**
Naomi Ōkawa, photographs by Chūji Hirayama, translated by Alan Woodhull, Akitō Miyamoto.   New York; Tokyo: Weatherhill/Heibonsha, 1975. 162p. 6 maps. (Heibonsha Survey of Japanese Art, 20).

The Katsura Detached Palace in Kyōto (which served as the country villa of the Hachijō no Miya family) and the Tōshōgū Shrine at Nikkō (which houses the remains of Tokugawa Ieyasu, the first Tokugawa period shōgun) constitute two major architectural complexes of the seventeenth century. Ōkawa introduces these two architectural undertakings, discusses their origins, describes their respective designs, provides an account of their architects and their ideas, and shows how both the Katsura and Nikkō share a common spirit of synthesis of style and experimentation despite their radically different appearance.

Fine Arts. Architecture

1316 **Temples of Nara and their art.**
Minoru Ōoka, translated by Dennis Lishka. New York; Tokyo:
Weatherhill/Heibonsha, 1973. 184p. (Heibonsha Survey of Japanese
Art, 7).
Nara, the eighth-century capital of Japan and the centre of Japanese Buddhist activity
at that time, is the site of some of the country's best-preserved Buddhist temples.
Concerning himself primarily with the temple architecture of this city and its environs,
Ōoka describes such major places of worship as the Kōfukuji, the Yakushiji, and the
Tōdaiji as they evolved between the Nara and Kamakura periods. Illustrating his
account with over two hundred photographs and drawings, he discusses both the
structure and the architectural styles of these temples and the important art treasures –
masterpieces of sculpture in particular – which they now contain.

1317 **Castles in Japan.**
Morton S. Schmorleitz. Rutland, Vermont; Tokyo: Tuttle, 1974.
188p. 4 maps. bibliog.
A vivid presentation of the architectural features and historical background of more
than eighty castles together with information about their current physical state. Aided
by detailed maps, diagrams, and black-and-white photographs, Schmorleitz discusses
the historical evolution of castle construction (particularly during the sixteenth
century), investigates the anatomy of the typical Japanese castle, and presents
descriptions, background information, and little-known facts about the four major
castles of Azuchi, Ōsaka, Nijō, and Fushimi; the historically important castles of
Odawara, Edo, Mito, and Kumamoto; and many of the country's other noteworthy
castles from Matsumae on the northern island of Hokkaidō to Kagoshima in southern
Kyūshū. Each of the castles examined is treated as an architectural entity.

1318 **The art of Japanese joinery.**
Kiyosi Seike, translated and adapted with an introduction by Yuriko
Yobuko, Rebecca M. Davis. New York; Tokyo; Kyōto:
Weatherhill/Tankōsha, 1977. 126p.
An introduction to the Japanese techniques of joining two or more pieces of wood
together in the course of constructing a building or creating some smaller wooden
object. Seike first provides an overview of the origins, history, and development of
Japanese carpentry. He then discusses the function of Japanese joinery and presents
forty-eight joints (among them the equivalents of the cross lap joint, the common
dovetail joint, and the bevelled shoulder mortise and tenon) which he has selected
from among the several hundred distinctly different joints that are still commonly used
in Japan. Particular attention is paid to two major types of joints: *tsugite* ('splicing
joints'), which splice shorter timbers together to create longer beams and posts; and
shiguchi ('connecting joints'), which connect timbers at an angle, rather than end to
end. Fifty-seven excellent black-and-white photographs and seventeen clear isometric
projections of selected joints illustrate the text.

1319 **Japanese style.**
Suzanne Slesin, Stafford Cliff, Daniel Rozensztroch; photographs by
Gilles de Chabaneix. New York: Clarkson N. Potter, 1987. 287p.
Nearly eight hundred full-colour photographs capture the diversity of Japanese interior

Fine Arts. Architecture

decoration in a wide range of traditional and modern houses and apartments. Entire
rooms as well as sections of individual rooms are depicted as the authors explore such
topics as the inspiration of the past, the influence of the Japanese craft tradition, the
choice of the materials that are incorporated into interior design, the influence of the
Western way of life on Japanese home design, and the ways in which city-dwellers
make the most of a small space. Included within the volume are photographs of a four-
storey residence in Tokyo by the architect Isozaki Arata, the country house where the
renowned potter Hamada Shōji lived and worked, a fashion designer's luxurious
Tokyo duplex, and the Tawaraya Inn in Kyōto.

1320   **The making of a modern Japanese architecture: 1868 to the present.**
David B. Stewart.   Tokyo; New York: Kodansha International, 1987.
304p. bibliog.

An in-depth look at the development of modern Japanese architecture from its
Victorian foundations to post-modernism. Stewart begins with an examination of the
impact of Western cultural influences, particularly with regard to façade design,
massing, and ornamentation. He then traces the evolution of architectural styles that
developed out of the interaction of Western practices and Japanese tradition, and
devotes an entire chapter to Frank Lloyd Wright and the Imperial Hotel in Tokyo.
Following extended discussions of architectural trends during the 1930s (including the
Japanese wing of the International Style) and the postwar period, Stewart concludes by
focusing on the most important architects of the 1960s onwards – Shinohara Kazuo and
Isozaki Arata – examining their approaches to the problems of urban development and
architecture as well as the ideas embodied in Isozaki's 'space of darkness' and
Shinohara's 'Japanese space'. Some four hundred black-and-white photographs and
plans illustrate the book.

1321   **Contemporary architecture of Japan 1958–1984.**
Hiroyuki Suzuki, Reyner Banham, Katsuhiro Kobayashi.   New
York: Rizzoli, 1985. 224p.

An introduction to ninety-two representative office and government buildings, private
residences, hotels, cultural and sports centres, and religious structures designed by
fifty-nine important postwar architects. Grouping these buildings together according to
four phases in the development of modern Japanese architecture, the authors provide a
brief description, selected floor plans, and three or more excellent monochrome
photographs of each of the buildings under review. Among these are the Tokyo
Metropolitan Art Museum designed by Maekawa Kunio (1975), the Shinjuku NS
Building (Tokyo) by Hayashi Shōji (1982), the Matsuo Shrine in Kamimuta (Kyūshū)
by Kijima Yasufumi (1975), and the Akasaka Prince Hotel in Tokyo by Tange Kenzō
(1983). Suzuki Hiroyuki's essay 'Contemporary Architecture of Japan' and Reyner
Banham's 'The Japonization of World Architecture' open the volume. Appended
biographical sketches of all of the architects enhance the reference value of this work.

1322   **Early Buddhist architecture in Japan.**
Kakichi Suzuki, translated and adapted by Mary Neighbour Parent,
Nancy Shatzman Steinhardt, with an introduction by Mary Neighbour
Parent.   Tokyo; New York: Kodansha International and Shibundo,
1980. 238p. bibliog. (Japanese Arts Library, 9).

A systematic survey, illustrated by numerous photographs and architectural drawings, of the evolution of Buddhist architecture from its introduction in the sixth century to the inception of the Main Halls of the Kamakura period (around 1200 AD). Focusing on the structural elements of their construction, Suzuki examines and analyses the architecture of representative temples and monasteries in the Nara and Kyōto areas, in particular the Asukadera, Kawaradera, Hōryūji, Yakushiji, Tōshōdaiji, Murōji, Daigoji, Byōdōin, and Chūsonji. He indicates how each stage in the development of Japanese Buddhist architecture corresponded to parallel developments in religion, and shows how the international Buddhist architectural style became fully assimilated. Mary Neighbour Parent, the translator of Suzuki's study, is herself the author of a complementary work, *The roof in Japanese Buddhist architecture* (New York; Tokyo: Weatherhill; Tokyo: Kajima Institute, 1983, 348p.), a book that exhaustively investigates the development of the form and structure of the roof in Japanese architecture between the seventh and the fifteenth centuries.

1323 **Ise: prototype of Japanese architecture.**

Kenzō Tange, Noboru Kawazoe, photographs by Yoshio Watanabe, introduction by John Burchard. Cambridge, Massachusetts: MIT Press, 1965. 212p. 5 maps. bibliog.

The Ise Shrine, allegedly dating from 685 AD or earlier and enshrining the mythical ancestress of the Japanese imperial family Amaterasu Ōmikami, is considered to be a major architectural achievement. The first essay, by the internationally recognised architect Tange Kenzō, introduces the shrine through discussions of its form, its religious symbols, space and architecture, its mythological background and history, its special characteristics, and its significance. Kawazoe's essay, 'The Ise Shrine and Its Cultural Context', focuses on the roots of Japanese religious symbolism and on shrine architecture and its background. Watanabe's outstanding black-and-white photographs depict both the inner and outer precincts of Ise and document the architectural characteristics of this important religious complex.

1324 **New Japanese architecture.**

Egon Tempel, translated from the German by E. Rockwell.

London: Thames and Hudson; New York: Praeger, 1969. 220p.

A bilingual (English and German) introduction to postwar architecture with particular focus on fifty-seven buildings constructed between the late 1950s and the late 1960s. Tempel covers summer houses and single-family homes, multi-family dwellings and housing developments, hotels, sports and leisure-time centres, kindergartens, schools and universities, religious buildings, museums and exhibition pavilions, theatres and festival halls, cultural centres, town halls and administration buildings, office buildings, industrial buildings, and town planning. Each building is briefly described and illustrated with black-and-white photographs and floor plans. An introductory essay by Nishimura Norio and Egon Tempel outlines Japanese architectural development up to 1945, the reorientation of Japanese architecture shortly after the war, the inception and consolidation of a new architectural style in the 1950s, and the work of a group known as the 'Metabolists' during the 1960s.

1325 **Shinto art: Ise and Izumo shrines.**
Yasutada Watanabe, translated by Robert Ricketts. New York; Tokyo: Weatherhill/Heibonsha, 1974. 190p. 2 maps. (Heibonsha Survey of Japanese Art, 3).

Two of the most important Shintō shrines, originating in the fifth century or earlier, are described in detail and illustrated by nearly two hundred photographs and drawings. Watanabe illuminates the evolution of early Japanese architecture in general and Shintō architecture in particular as he discusses the origins of the Ise and Izumo shrines in the Kofun or Tumulus period, their prototypes in early Japanese architecture, the emergence and gradual development of a distinctive shrine style, and the historical diversification of Shintō shrine types.

1326 **A Japanese touch for your home.**
Koji Yagi, translated by Mark B. Williams, photographs by Ryō Hata. Tokyo; New York: Kodansha International, 1982. 84p. bibliog.

An introduction to the basic elements of Japanese interior design and a practical guide to their application and use in American homes and apartments. Illustrating his text with 121 colour photographs of private homes as well as numerous detailed drawings, Yagi first describes the intermediate space in Japanese homes that is occupied by a formal entrance way, a veranda, and various screening devices used in place of Western-style doors and windows. He then focuses on the elements of interior space – among them tatami mats, translucent and opaque sliding doors, portable partitions, alcoves, lighting techniques, and the bath – and shows how to incorporate them into American residences. A section on 'do-it-yourself projects' explains how to make hanging *shōji* ('sliding screens'), *shōji* lampshades, floor lamps with paper shades, and *chōchin* ('paper lanterns').

Tokyo: the city at the end of the world.
See item no. 22.

A guide to Japanese architecture.
See item no. 81.

Kyoto: a contemplative guide.
See item no. 89.

The Japanese inn, ryokan: a gateway to traditional Japan.
See item no. 96.

Five mountains: the Rinzai Zen monastic institution in medieval Japan.
See item no. 131.

The art and architecture of Japan.
See item no. 1212.

Japan Architect.
See item no. 1505.

Gardens and bonsai

1327 **Japanese gardens: design and meaning.**
Mitchell Bring, Josse Wayembergh. New York: McGraw Hill, 1981.
214p. maps. bibliog. (McGraw-Hill Series in Landscape and
Landscape Architecture).

Written especially for landscape architects unfamiliar with Japanese culture but also valuable for people concerned with East Asian studies in general, this volume introduces ten masterworks of Japanese gardening through sets of plans, sections, conceptual drawings, classic woodblock renderings, maps of elevations, and photographs which enable readers to visualise the overall design and specific details of these gardens. The gardens in Kyōto selected for study – Saihōji, Kinkakuji, Ginkakuji, Ryōanji, Daisenin, Sanbōin, Shōdenji, Entsuji, Shisendō, and Kohōan – 'illustrate a broad range of designs yet are close enough in spirit to demonstrate some general principles'. The authors deal with the Chinese and Japanese sources for these gardens, present details about their construction and maintenance, and discuss several general principles regarding their visual and spatial design.

1328 **The masters' book of bonsai.**
Compiled by Directors of the Japan Bonsai Association [Nippon
Bonsai Kyōkai]: Nobukichi Koide, Saburō Katō, Fusazō Takeyama.
Tokyo; Palo Alto, California: Kodansha International, 1967; London;
New York: Collinridge, 1968. 144p. Reprinted, Tokyo; New York:
Kodansha International, 1983.

Three experts in the cultivation of bonsai (miniaturised trees or plants that 'entirely express the beauty and volume of trees grown in a natural environment') present a compendium of recommended techniques for Western enthusiasts of this traditional Japanese art. Their instruction manual covers the growing of bonsai from seed, the ways to collect plants from nature, the procedures for growing cuttings, the principal methods of grafting, the special methods of layering and dividing bonsai in order to develop new trees, the care of bonsai, the group planting of bonsai, rock-grown bonsai, and appropriate tools and equipment. Full-colour plates of selected bonsai as well as numerous black-and-white photographs illustrate various techniques and procedures. The Japan Bonsai Association has also published through Kodansha a lavishly illustrated guide to the history, aesthetics, and appreciation of this centuries-old form of gardening. Containing two hundred full-colour and black-and-white photographs (with detailed captions) of bonsai masterpieces, ranging in age from fifteen to seven hundred years, it is entitled *Classic bonsai of Japan* (by the Nippon Bonsai Association, translated by John Bester, introduction by John Naka, foreword by Hideo Aragaki. Tokyo and New York: Kodansha International, 1989, 188p.).

1329 **The garden art of Japan.**
Masao Hayakawa, translated by Richard L. Gage. New York;
Tokyo: Weatherhill/Heibonsha, 1973. 173p. (Heibonsha Survey of
Japanese Art, 28).

An illustrated history which traces the evolution of Japanese gardens from their beginnings, through the Buddhist gardens of the medieval age, to the world of the

Zen-influenced dry-landscape garden and the gardens of the Momoyama, Tokugawa, and Meiji periods. Introductory and concluding chapters briefly discuss the basic concepts of the Japanese garden and describe its use of space and form.

1330 **Bonkei: tray landscapes.**
Jōzan Hirota, photographs by Yoshikazu Ezaki. Tokyo; New York: Kodansha International, 1970. 128p. Reprinted, Kodansha International, 1981.

An introduction and manual for the creation of *bonkei*, the three-dimensional miniature landscapes set within the confines of shallow trays that are frequently placed in the *tokonoma* ('alcoves') of Japanese homes. These landscapes may be based on such themes as fields and mountains, fantastically shaped rocks, rivers and waterfalls, or the sea and the shore. Step-by-step instructions on the composition of *bonkei* set forth some of its basic principles. Hirota describes the tools (especially the spatula) and the materials used in this traditional art, indicates the general rules for creating bodies of water out of sand, and discusses some of the subjects for *bonkei*, the types of *bonkei*, and the use of both bonsai and artificial trees. The principles and techniques described in this guide can easily be mastered.

1331 **The gardens of Japan.**
Teiji Itoh. Tokyo; New York: Kodansha International, 1984. 228p. 11 maps. bibliog.

Illustrated with full-colour photographs and numerous black-and-white pictures, this handsomely designed, oversized volume introduces the evolving forms of the Japanese garden and their history, its consistent use of combinations of stones, water and plants, its success in 'celebrating nature and offering a space for man's creative work and relaxation', the characteristic features of modern gardens, and the elements of design, the materials of creation, and the philosophy of Japanese gardens. Itoh's commentary guides the reader through some of Japan's finest gardens, both large and small, and highlights a few of them, including the 'Moss Temple' ('Kokedera', the name popularly given to the Saihōji Temple in Kyōto) and the Zen garden of Shinjuan in the Daitokuji (also in Kyōto). A special section, intended for readers who plan to visit Japan, describes fifty selected gardens that are generally open to the public and provides information about their hours, special features, and historical past.

1332 **The Japanese garden: an approach to nature.**
Teiji Itoh, photographs by Takeji Iwamiya, design by Yusaku Kamekura, English version by Donald Richie. New Haven, Connecticut: Yale University Press; Tokyo: Zokeisha, 1972. 205p.

An inquiry into the historical evolution of the Japanese approach to nature: from their early concept of the garden as a place of religious meditation to their more recent view of the garden as a place for aesthetic enjoyment. The volume describes the various phases of Japanese gardening throughout history and the ways in which Japanese attitudes toward their natural environment have affected the kinds of gardens which they have built. The 105 full-page photographs (some in colour) illustrate several types of gardens in the Kyōto area, among them rock arrangements in the Ryōanji stone garden, the grounds of the Katsura Detached Palace, and the dry gardens of the Daitokuji and Myōshinji temples. A second edition was published under the title *The Japanese garden* (Tokyo: Zokeisha, 1978, 178p).

1333　**Space and illusion in the Japanese garden.**
Teiji Itoh, photographs by Sōsei Kuzunishi, translated and adapted by
Ralph Friedrich, Masajirō Shimamura.　New York; Tokyo; Kyōto:
Weatherhill/Tankōsha, 1973. 229p.

Itoh explores the fundamental concepts of Japanese garden design known as 'borrowed
scenery' (*shakkei*) and 'the great within the small' in dealing primarily with two
distinctive types of gardens: 'the borrowed-landscape garden, which incorporates
distant scenery as part of its design', and the small, enclosed courtyard garden, which
'suggests a corner of a great, outdoor space and thereby produces an illusion of more
than can be seen'. Through his discussion of the historical evolution, special
characteristics, essential components, and spatial effects of both *shakkei* and courtyard
gardens, he shows how these two aesthetic principles have been incorporated within a
range of gardens in Kyōto that belong to private residences, temples and shrines,
restaurants, and inns as well as to the Kyōto Imperial Palace. There are 103 full-page,
largely black-and-white photographs to illustrate some of these garden settings.

1334　**Imperial gardens of Japan: Sento Gosho, Katsura, Shugaku-in.**
Photographs by Takeji Iwamiya, introduction and commentaries on
the photographs by Teiji Itoh; essays by Yukio Mishima, Yasushi
Inoue, Jirō Osaragi; translated and adapted by Richard L. Gage,
Akira Furuta; foreword by Loraine Kuck.　New York; Tokyo:
Walker/Weatherhill in collaboration with Tankōsha (Kyōto),
1970. 290p. 3 maps.

An award-winning collection of large colour photographs of the suburban estate of the
Katsura Detached Palace, the city garden of the Sentō Imperial Palace, and the
mountain retreat of the Shūgakuin Detached Palace – all of them built in the Kyōto
area during the seventeenth century. Itoh's introduction and commentaries sketch the
historical background and significance of these three celebrated gardens, call attention
to details of their construction and design, and explain some of their noteworthy
features. Essays by three of Japan's foremost novelists – 'Sojourn in a Region of
Repose' (Mishima), 'The Villa, the Garden, and the Prince' (Inoue), and 'A Fantasy in
Space and Time' (Osaragi) – respectively convey their impressions of the Sentō,
Katsura, and Shūgakuin gardens. The photographs frequently focus on such things as
ground covers and paving, the colour and juxtaposition of flat stones, and the many
kinds of moss in the course of depicting a wide range of views – among them, stone-
paved walks, teahouses, ponds and waterfalls, bridges, and broad panoramas.

1335　**The world of the Japanese garden: from Chinese origins to modern
landscape art.**
Loraine Kuck, colour photographs by Takeji Iwamiya.　New York;
Tokyo: Walker/Weatherhill, 1968. 414p. bibliog. Reprinted, New
York; Tokyo: Weatherhill, 1980.

An extensively illustrated, non-technical study of the Japanese garden as a unique and
major artform. After surveying the early development of gardens in China, Kuck
traces the evolution of the gardens of Japan from the eighth-century copies of Chinese
gardens to the magnificent gardens of the fifteenth and sixteenth centuries. She writes
extensively about the gardens of the Kinkakuji and the Ginkakuji (the 'Gold' and
'Silver Pavilions'), the Ryōanji Temple, and the Katsura and Shūgakuin imperial

estates in the Kyōto area, as well as about Momoyama period tea gardens. She also briefly discusses the gardens of both the Tokugawa era and the twentieth century. The aesthetic and philosophical principles which found expression in the art of garden-making in Japan are considered throughout.

1336 **Bonsai: the complete guide to art and technique.**
Paul Lesniewicz, translated by Susan Simpson. Poole, Dorset: Blandford Press, 1984. 194p.

A lavishly illustrated, comprehensive introduction to the forms and techniques of raising bonsai, the miniaturised trees grown in dishes that resemble in every detail except size their large counterparts in nature. Following a brief introduction to the history of bonsai, Lesniewicz discusses the various styles of bonsai; their cultivation from seeds, from cuttings, and by other techniques; the pruning, wiring techniques, and other methods involved in bonsai training; the general care of bonsai, including their protection against pests and diseases; Chinese bonsai; and indoor bonsai. Appendixes include lists of important Japanese terms and English–Japanese plant names; a guide to the care and training of bonsai plants; and a seasonal guide to their cultivation.

1337 **A Japanese touch for your garden.**
Kiyoshi Seike, Masanobu Kudō, with David H. Engel; photographs by Haruzō Ōhashi. Tokyo; New York: Kodansha International, 1980. 80p. bibliog.

A brief, practical introduction to the materials and techniques involved in creating Japanese-style courtyard, rock, and tree–water gardens. The authors describe the basic elements of Japanese gardening principles and traditions; introduce the materials and elements of design of Japanese gardens including rock formations, stepping-stones, pathways, sand patterns, water basins, lanterns, fences, and gates; offer various schematic layout plans; and provide notes on the care of bamboo, moss, and grass as well as the names of North American plants and trees which can be substituted for Japanese varieties. The 130 colour photographs of both old and new, traditional and modern gardens in Japan complement the text.

1338 **Secret teachings in the art of Japanese gardens: design principles, aesthetic values.**
David A. Slawson. Tokyo; New York: Kodansha International, 1987. 220p. bibliog.

Slawson contends that the aesthetic principles which underlie classical Japanese garden design are ones which can be shared with the West. After explaining how the art of Japanese gardening was transmitted over the centuries, he groups these principles together according to 'natural categories of human perception' (in sections entitled 'The Art We See: Scenic Effects', 'The Art We See: Sensory Effects', and 'The Art We See: Cultural Values') and discusses each of them in some detail. His investigations contain numerous references to the so-called 'secret teachings' about Japanese garden design that appear within the two oldest extant Japanese garden manuals: *Sakuteiki* ('Notes on Garden Making') by Tachibana no Toshitsuna, and a fifteenth-century manuscript first compiled by the Priest Zōen, *Senzui narabi ni yagyō no zu* ('Illustrations for Designing Mountain, Water, and Hillside Field Landscapes'). Slawson's translation of the latter work constitutes the second part of his book.

1339 **Japanese gardens revisited.**
Gisei Takakuwa, photographs by Kiichi Asano, English adaptation by
Frank Davies, Hirokuni Kobatake.   Rutland, Vermont; Tokyo:
Tuttle, 1973. 165p. 2 maps.

Over one hundred colour photographs, accompanied by Takakuwa's commentary,
provide a general overview of Japanese gardens and gardening techniques. Part one
depicts the natural beauty of pond gardens and the appeal of dry-landscape gardens.
Part two ('Garden-Planning as an Art') explores the use of stones, the harmony of
gardens and buildings, the paths to teahouses, the concepts of 'miniature scenery' and
'distant scenery', and the beauty derived from the inclusion of trees and colouring
leaves. In their concluding part ('Materials and the Sense of Beauty'), the authors
focus on the trimming of shrubs, the use of waterfalls and streams, and the function of
garden bridges, stepping-stones, pavements and paths, sand patterns, moss and lawns,
fences and gates, stone water-basins, stone lanterns, and such other adornments as
pine needles.

Kyoto: a contemplative guide.
See item no. 89.

A guide to the gardens of Kyoto.
See item no. 98.

The Japanese art of stone appreciation: suiseki and its use with bonsai.
See item no. 1362.

Furniture

1340 **Antique Japanese furniture: a guide to evaluating and restoring.**
Rosy Clarke.   New York; Tokyo: Weatherhill, 1983. 150p. bibliog.

Focusing on *tansu* (cabinetry constructed of wood and designed for storage) because of
their popularity but also covering such other items as tobacco boxes, sewing chests,
hibachi, trunks, and vanities, Clarke provides a general introduction to the
identification, evaluation, purchase, restoration, and care for a wide range of
traditional Japanese furniture. As she describes how to evaluate and select antique
furniture, she seeks to assist Westerners who are seriously considering the purchase of
a *tansu*. She likewise presents an easy-to-follow, twenty-three-step restoration
procedure (employing supplies and tools available in both the United States and
Japan) for those individuals who wish to restore Japanese furniture on their own.
Appendixes list antique shops, fairs, and flea markets in the Tokyo area.

1341 **Tansu: traditional Japanese cabinetry.**
Ty Heineken, Kiyoko Heineken, foreword by Hugo Munsterberg.
New York; Tokyo: Weatherhill, 1981. 247p. 2 maps. bibliog.

An illustrated guide to the history, appreciation, and care of the traditional wooden
chests known as *tansu* that allow for mobility by either structural design or hardware.
The first half of this book is concerned with the origins and early development of *tansu*,

the *funa-dansu* ('sea chests') produced during the Tokugawa period for use on merchant ships plying the Sea of Japan and the Inland Sea, the Meiji era *tansu* and their regional characteristics, and the mass production of these chests in the twentieth century. Part two details the techniques associated with *tansu* cabinetry: the types of wood from which *tansu* were made, the range of joints employed by *tansu* craftsmen, their metal hardware (locks, drawer pulls and handles, hinges, and surface plating), the dry and lacquer finishes for the surfaces of these chests, and the ideal and practical methods for conserving *tansu* in both Japan and the West today.

1342 **Traditional Japanese furniture.**
Kazuko Koizumi, translated by Alfred Birnbaum.   Tokyo; New York: Kodansha International, 1986. 223p. map.

An extensively illustrated, broad-survey volume focusing on the traditional furniture that reached its highest level of perfection and craftsmanship during the Tokugawa and Meiji periods. Koizumi first presents an overview of the types of hand-worked furniture that were developed and used at that time: cabinetry (especially chests and trunks), partition devices such as screens and curtains, floor coverings, seating and bedding, lighting and heating devices, writing and study furnishings, toilette and bathing accessories, and mealtime and kitchen furnishings. In discussing the historical development of Japanese furniture, she then provides a perspective on the intricate and changing relationships between architecture and furnishings in Japan from ancient times to the twentieth century. Finally, Koizumi discusses the types of woods that were used, examines the techniques of wood joinery and wood finishing, and describes the procedures for lacquering, metal fitting, and metalworking. Several hundred photographs and line drawings illustrate the text.

1343 **Japanese woodworking tools: their tradition, spirit and use.**
Toshio Ōdate.   Newtown, Connecticut: Taunton Press, 1984. 189p.

A Japanese-born craftsman and sculptor describes in some depth the range of woodworking tools that have traditionally been used by Japanese artisans. Following a brief overview of the workshop, he writes about Japanese marking tools, saws, chisels, planes, sharpening-stones, adzes and axes, hammers, gimlets, knives, nail pullers, oil pots, and clamps. Ōdate also conveys something of the spiritual relationship which skilled craftsmen are expected to have with their tools as well as with the objects they produce. Numerous photographs and line drawings illustrate the text.

The art of Japanese joinery.
See item no. 1318.

Textiles and clothing

1344 **Japanese design through textile patterns.**
Frances Blakemore.   New York; Tokyo: Weatherhill, 1978. 272p.

Blakemore illustrates Japanese design and design concepts through the medium of the *katagami*, the handmade paper stencils used for dyeing the fabrics which were traditionally produced for making handcrafted kimonos. Black-and-white reproductions of 198 stencil patterns and fifty photographs of woodblock prints showing the patterns used in both men's and women's clothing during the Tokugawa period are grouped together according to pattern type: water-related patterns (e.g., dew, waves, irises, fish, rain, seashells, etc.); sky-related patterns (e.g., geese, cranes, clouds, butterflies, etc.); abstract patterns; flower patterns (e.g., orchids, peonies, cherries, lilies, etc.); tree and leaf patterns (e.g., ivy, pine, honeysuckle, bamboo, etc.); garden-related patterns (e.g., landscapes, flora, fauna, fans, fish, etc.); and chrysanthemum patterns. Brief commentaries accompany these illustrations.

1345   **Country textiles of Japan: the art of tsutsugaki.**
Reiko Mochinaga Brandon.   New York; Tokyo: Weatherhill, 1986.
151p. bibliog.

This introduction to a type of hand-dyed, indigo-coloured, cotton textiles produced in the countryside was written to accompany an exhibition of *tsutsugaki* cloths on display at the Honolulu Academy of Arts. It discusses the sociological backgrounds and function of selected *tsutsugaki* fabrics, their various motifs and designs, the techniques involved in their production, the traditional process of ginning, fluffing, spinning, and weaving the cotton cloth that is then dyed to produce these textiles, and the manufacture of the indigo dye itself. Photographs of forty-eight *tsutsugaki* pieces, among them jackets, *noren* ('shop-curtains'), and cloth used in making Japanese quilts, illustrate the text.

1346   **Tsujigahana: the flower of Japanese textile art.**
Toshiko Itō, translated with an introduction by Monica Bethe.
Tokyo; New York: Kodansha International, 1985. 1st standard ed.
202p.

The term *tsujigahana* refers to cloth dyed with a particular combination of tie-dyeing and hand-painting whose production flourished between the fifteenth and early seventeenth centuries. Itō describes the origins, flowering, and demise of this textile tradition. She begins with a brief historical survey of *tsujigahana* and a discussion of tie-dyeing, the art most basic to the production of this type of cloth. She then discusses *tsujigahana* textiles by technique: tie-dyeing and painting; tie-dyeing with painting and gold- or silver-leaf imprint; and tie-dyeing with embroidery, gold- or silver-leaf imprint, and painting. Many of her illustrations are of *tsujigahana* garments and fragments of *tsujigahana* fabrics that are now regarded as 'important cultural properties'.

1347   **Textile designs of Japan.**
Compiled by the Japan Textile Color Design Center [Nihon Sen'i Ishō Sentā, Ōsaka], preface by Osamu Uno.   Tokyo; New York:
Kodansha International, 1980-81. rev. ed. 3 vols.

A richly illustrated, authoritative compendium of traditional textile designs – principally from the Muromachi, Momoyama, and Tokugawa periods – that reveals some of the special characteristics of Japanese textile design. An introductory essay in volume one, *Free-style designs*, entitled 'The Development and Characteristics of Japanese Textile Designs' examines their evolution through the mid-nineteenth century and is followed by a discussion of free-style designs and a presentation of 771 colour and black-and-white photographs. Volume two, *Geometric designs*, contains essays about Japanese geometric designs and *komon* (a class of extremely fine small-scale patterns) together with 929 additional photographs. Accompanied by 615 photographs, volume three, *Okinawan, Ainu, and foreign designs*, focuses on the distinctive designs produced in the Ryūkyū Islands and by the Ainu as well as on the foreign designs (especially from China) that have strongly influenced Japanese textiles. The notes to each colour plate describe the design of the item that is depicted, indicate the composition of its material (silk, ramie, etc.), and note its origin and date.

1348 **New fashion Japan.**
Leonard Koren. Tokyo; New York: Kodansha International, 1984. 176p.
A profusely illustrated guide to 'the new world of Japanese fashion', focusing on leading designers and featuring scenes of Tokyo streets and people, displays of fabrics and clothing, pictures showing the influence of traditional Japanese attire, pages reproduced from lively fashion magazines, and 'brief discussions connecting the emerging look of urban culture and the Japanese revolution in clothesmaking'. With over two hundred photographs, collages, and drawings, Koren's book graphically reveals some of the new styles that were coming out of Japan during the late 1970s and early 1980s, and includes interviews with seven avant-garde fashion designers: Miyake Issey, Yamamoto Yohji, Yamamoto Kansai, Kawakubo Rei, Kikuchi Takeo, Hosokawa Shin, and Jürgen Lehl.

1349 **Japanese costume and the makers of its elegant tradition.**
Helen Benton Minnich, with Shōjirō Nomura. Rutland, Vermont; Tokyo: Tuttle, 1963. 374p. bibliog. Reprinted, Tuttle, 1986.
An overview of the evolution of costume design and fabric manufacture between the seventh and twentieth centuries, viewed in the light of their craftsmen and artists, the eras in which they were active, and the dyeing and weaving methods which they employed. Minnich pays particular attention to aspects of colour and design rather than to costume structure or construction, and illustrates her account with nearly 150 photographs and colour plates.

1350 **Japanese stencil dyeing: paste-resist techniques.**
Eisha Nakano, with Barbara B. Stephan. New York; Tokyo: Weatherhill, 1982. 143p. bibliog.
A practical introduction to *katazome*, or 'stencil dyeing'. Utilising a variety of traditional materials and modern substitutes, Nakano and Stephan explain the multi-stepped processes involved in this textile handicraft, among them the methods of designing and cutting the stencil, preparing the paste, preparing and sizing the fabric, selecting the dyes, and dyeing the fabric. Over 260 photographs illustrating various tools and techniques are complemented by tables explaining the use of natural pigments, the preparation and use of natural dyes, and the applicability of various dyes to *katazome*. An appendix contains directory information about worldwide suppliers of appropriate materials.

1351 **Japanese costume and textile arts.**
Seiroku Noma, translated by Armins Nikovskis. New York; Tokyo:
Weatherhill/Heibonsha, 1974. 168p. (Heibonsha Survey of Japanese
Art, 16).

A comprehensive, illustrated survey of the development of Japanese costume and
textile design – in particular, the *kosode* and the costumes of the noh theatre – from
the Kamakura through the Tokugawa period. Noma first discusses the kimono and its
setting, the evolution of the *kosode* (an undergarment which evolved over the centuries
into the beautifully decorated outer garment known today as the kimono), and the
various types of costume that were developed for the noh, *kyōgen*, and kabuki
theatres. He examines the impact of changing tastes and techniques on textile design,
and concludes with some coverage of the basic dyeing, weaving, tie-dyeing,
embroidery, and printing techniques of Japanese textiles as well as of the use of hand-
painted designs, colours, and abstract and figurative motifs.

1352 **Kabuki costume.**
Ruth M. Shaver, illustrated by Akira Sōma, Gakō Ōta. Rutland,
Vermont; Tokyo: Tuttle, 1966. 396p. bibliog.

A lavishly illustrated presentation of the array of splendid costumes worn by the actors
in kabuki. Shaver first summarises the historical background of the kabuki theatre and
the evolution of its conventions in acting, staging, and costume design. She then
describes and analyses the attire of actors impersonating feudal lords, warriors, priests,
courtesans, geisha, farmers, townspeople, and other period figures. Particular attention
is paid to the costumes worn by men and by female impersonators in *jidaimono*
('history plays') and *sewamono* ('domestic plays'). Shaver also examines armour and
battle costumes, costume patterns and colour, heraldic crests (*mon*), head bands,
headgear, hand towels (*tengui*), fans, swords, wigs, stylised make-up, ways of pulling
up the hem of a kimono, and quick changes of costume on stage. Throughout there are
revealing glimpses of backstage life, of the influence of famous actors on costume
development, and of the mechanics of costuming kabuki productions.

1353 **Kosode: 16th–19th century textiles from the Nomura Collection.**
Amanda Mayer Stinchecum, with essays by Monica Bethe, Margot
Paul, photographs by Takeshi Nishikawa. Tokyo; New York:
Kodansha International and the Japan Society, 1984. 234p. bibliog.

The simple one-piece style of kimono with relatively short sleeves that attained
popularity in the sixteenth century and, as the prototype of the modern kimono,
became the principal form of clothing for women up to the twentieth century is known
as the *kosode*. Through its numerous illustrations and essays, this exhibition catalogue
provides a survey of this particular type of Momoyama and Tokugawa period costume
as it is found within the collection of Nomura Shōjirō (1879-1943). The catalogue
specifically introduces Nomura's life and work; presents a wide-ranging overview of the
kosode textiles on display through discussions of costume evolution, design, weave
structures, the techniques of textile decoration, and the history of the Japanese
weaving industry; and investigates the use of colours and dyes in *kosode* fabrics.

1354 **Japanese ikat weaving: the techniques of kasuri.**
Jun Tomita, Norika Tomita. London; Boston, Massachusetts:
Routledge and Kegan Paul, 1982. 88p. map. bibliog.

Ikat weaving, known as *kasuri* in Japan, is the technique by which lengths of yarn are tied and dyed before being woven together. Orienting their volume to hand-weavers in the West who wish to make use of *kasuri* techniques in their work, the Tomitas concentrate on explaining and adapting the most important of these techniques. They classify *kasuri* by colour, technique, place of production, and design as well as by the direction in which the tied and dyed yarn is applied; describe the uses of *kasuri* material; present step-by-step instructions for making both weft *kasuri* and warp *kasuri*; and introduce the methods for dyeing cotton and wool with indigo. Numerous line drawings, diagrams, and black-and-white photographs illustrate their account.

1355 **Shibori: the inventive art of Japanese shaped resist dyeing: tradition, techniques, innovation.**
Yoshiko Wada, Mary Kellogg Rice, Jane Burton. Tokyo; New York: Kodansha International, 1983. 303p. bibliog.

Shibori, a term used to designate a particular group of resist-dyed textiles, is the 'Japanese word for a variety of ways of embellishing textiles by shaping cloth and securing it before dyeing. . . . Rather than treating cloth as a two-dimensional surface, with *shibori* it is given a three-dimensional form by folding, crumpling, stitching, plaiting, or plucking and twisting'. This comprehensive study surveys the evolution of *shibori* techniques and processes from the Asuka and Nara periods through the mid-twentieth century; offers a detailed, illustrated discussion of the binding, stitching, folding, and pole-wrapping techniques that are involved in the production of these textiles; considers some of the contemporary innovations in this art and some of the Japanese and American artists responsible for these changes; and presents a gallery of traditional and modern examples of *shibori* through hundreds of full-colour and black-and-white photographs.

1356 **The book of kimono.**
Norio Yamanaka. Tokyo; New York: Kodansha International, 1982. 139p.

The word 'kimono' usually refers to the traditional wrap-around garment with rectangular sleeves that is made of vertical panels of cloth stitched together and bound with an elaborate sash known as the *obi*. Yamanaka's practical guide briefly traces the historical evolution of Japanese dress; describes the weaving, dyeing, parts, and standard size of the kimono; introduces the outer garments, undergarments, footwear, and accessories that are normally worn with kimono; discusses the development as well as the various kinds of *obi*; and explains how both the kimono and *obi* are properly put on. In addition, Yamanaka offers tips on the cleaning and folding of kimono that will help in their preservation and discusses the proper posture and movements when walking as well as sitting and dining. Many full-colour plates, black-and-white photographs, and diagrams of kimono for both men and women illustrate this account.

Living crafts of Okinawa.
See item no. 1222.

The Tokugawa Collection: nō robes and masks.
See item no. 1412.

Other decorative and applied arts

1357 **Bamboo.**
Robert Austin, Kōichirō Ueda, photographs by Dana Levy. New York; Tokyo: Weatherhill, 1970. 215p. bibliog.
A study of the cultural, aesthetic, and technical aspects of a plant which the Japanese have long associated with the natural landscape of their home islands. Austin examines the lore and versatility of bamboo; its beauty and uses in nature, in gardens and homes, in everyday life, and in the arts and crafts; and the growth and cultivation of this plant. There are 162 pages of photographs (many in full colour) which show bamboo as a part of nature, as a building material for fences and walls, as the material that is used to make everyday articles such as cups, baskets, tea whisks, and writing brushes, and as the material out of which skilled craftsmen fashion such beautiful objects as fans, flutes, and brush holders.

1358 **Japanese papermaking: traditions, tools, and techniques.**
Timothy Barrett, with an appendix by Winifred Lutz. New York; Tokyo: Weatherhill, 1983. 317p. bibliog.
An American who was apprenticed with Japanese paper-makers during the 1970s combines an introduction to the art of Japanese paper-making with a step-by-step instruction manual for producing *washi* (Japanese handmade paper). In part one, Barrett narrates some of his experiences in Japan as he discusses the cultivation, harvesting, stripping, cooking, washing, cleaning, and beating of the paper-making bark fibres. He also details the procedures for forming, pressing, and drying the finished sheets of paper. In part two, an illustrated instructional guide for producing Japanese-style paper in the West, Barrett writes about the proper tools and equipment (including their construction) as well as about the requisite materials and their preparation. He sets forth two methods for making *washi* – the traditional technique for the experienced paper-maker, and a simplified version for the novice – and briefly presents some procedural variations. Lutz's appendix offers both scholarly and practical information about the use of non-Japanese fibres in Japanese-style paper-making.

1359 **A history of glass in Japan.**
Dorothy Blair, foreword by Paul N. Perrot. Tokyo; New York: Kodansha International and the Corning Museum of Glass, 1973. 479p. 2 maps. bibliog. (A Corning Museum of Glass Monograph).
A detailed study of the manufacturing, artistry, and use of glass in Japan, organised by historical period. Blair discusses the evolution of glass from its beginnings during the Jōmon period, through the introduction of foreign manufacturing techniques and the spread of glass-making during the Tokugawa period, to the establishment of new glass industries in the late nineteenth and twentieth centuries. Nearly 250 plates, all of them

accompanied by precise identifications and informative commentaries, illustrate the book.

1360   **The inrō handbook: studies of netsuke, inrō, and lacquer.**
Raymond Bushell.   New York; Tokyo: Weatherhill, 1979. 263p. bibliog.

A detailed study of the sophisticated techniques, time-consuming manufacturing processes, materials, decorative effects, and lacquer artists' signatures of the elegant inrō – compartmentalised boxes or cases worn suspended by cords from men's *obi*, or sashes – that were produced between the Tokugawa period and the 1930s. Oriented towards the collector of inrō, netsuke, and other forms of miniature Japanese art, this book focuses on the many different types of inrō which currently exist. It also reproduces several hundred photographs of selected inrō and netsuke as well as enlargements of lacquer artists' signatures.

1361   **Japanese cloisonné: history, technique, and appreciation.**
Lawrence A. Coben, Dorothy C. Ferster.   New York; Tokyo: Weatherhill, 1982. 323p. map. bibliog.

Cloisonné consists of a multicoloured decoration in which enamel glass is poured into the divided areas of an artistic design outlined by fine wires or metal strips secured to a metal object. Focusing on its production in Japan during the nineteenth and twentieth centuries, this illustrated survey traces the historical evolution of Japanese enamelling technology, describes the development of Japanese cloisonné design and aesthetic expression, and discusses (with collectors particularly in mind) the dating and identification of individual pieces of Japanese cloisonné.

1362   **The Japanese art of stone appreciation: suiseki and its use with bonsai.**
Vincent T. Covello, Yūji Yoshimura.   Rutland, Vermont; Tokyo: Tuttle, 1984. 166p. map.

Suiseki are small, naturally formed stones selected for their shape, balance, and beauty and widely admired for their power to suggest a scene from nature such as distant mountains and waterfalls or an object closely associated with nature. These stones are traditionally exhibited on carved wooden bases or are placed in shallow tray settings enhanced by bonsai surroundings of miniature trees. Covello and Yoshimura describe the historical background of the art of *suiseki*, the characteristics and aesthetic qualities of high-quality *suiseki*, the various sytems of stone classification, and the best ways for displaying these stones. They also introduce the art of combining *suiseki* with bonsai either as rock plantings or as tray landscapes, and discuss present-day *suiseki* collecting in both Japan and the United States. There are 156 photographs (seventy-one in full colour) which display prized *suiseki* in both public and private collections.

1363   **Japanese antique dolls.**
Jill Gribbin, David Gribbin, photographs by Masami Shimoda, foreword by Ronald F. Thomas.   New York; Tokyo: Weatherhill, 1984. 172p. map. bibliog.

The first detailed introduction to all of the major types of antique dolls found in Japan today. The authors trace the historical development of Japanese dolls and in succeeding chapters focus on the categories of festival dolls, classic dolls, play dolls

Fine Arts. Other decorative and applied arts

(including puppets), and clay dolls. Throughout the volume (and especially in the closing chapter entitled 'Collecting and Caring for Japanese Dolls') they provide helpful information for the collector on the identification and evaluation of Japanese dolls as well as on their care and restoration. Fifty full-colour plates of dolls in both museum and private collections illustrate some of the finest examples of doll-making from the Tokugawa and Meiji periods.

1364 **The world of origami.**
Isao Honda, translated by Richard L. Gage, photographs by Yūtarō Tsutsumi. London: Blanford Press; Tokyo and Rutland, Vermont: Japan Publications Trading Company, 1965. 264p. bibliog. Abridged popular edition: Tokyo; Elmsford, New York: Japan Publications Trading Company, 1976. 182p.

Honda opens with overviews of the origins of the Japanese art of paper folding, the origami tradition in Japan, the basic folds and constructions which comprise origami, and the fundamental forms of this handicraft. The remainder of his book presents easy-to-follow directions for producing 157, largely traditional, origami figures, using different sizes and shapes of paper as well as a variety of folding techniques.

1365 **Washi: the world of Japanese paper.**
Sukey Hughes, foreword by Isamu Noguchi. Tokyo; New York: Kodansha International, 1978. 360p. 2 maps. bibliog.

A detailed description of the evolution of Japanese handmade paper (*washi*), the techniques of paper-making, the people who make *washi*, its aesthetics, some of the different types of paper, and the future outlook for *washi* in Japan. Hughes' explanations and accounts are based in part on the first-hand knowledge and experience she gained by studying with and observing the work of three noted paper-makers, in particular Gotō Seikichirō. There are 236 photographs, 60 line drawings, and a glossary to enhance the usefulness of this informative introduction and guide. A deluxe 456-page edition of this book includes over one hundred samples of *washi*.

1366 **Japanese teapots.**
Noritake Kanzaki, photographs by Kiyomi Suganuma. Tokyo; New York: Kodansha International, 1981. 73p. (Form and Function Series, 5).

The fifth in a series of books about the beauty of everyday objects in contemporary Japanese culture. Consisting essentially of sketches and black-and-white photographs, this volume indicates the range of design and quality of handmade objects whose form is closely allied with their function. Other titles in the Form and Function series include *Japanese brushes*, introduction and photographs by Masao Usui (no. 1, 1979, 80p.); *Japanese knives*, introduction by Yoshio Akioka, photographs by Masao Usui (no. 2, 1979, 79p.); *Japanese spoons and ladles*, introduction by Yoshio Akioka, photographs by Masao Usui (no. 3, 1979, 78p.); and *Japanese bamboo baskets*, introduction by Kazuyoshi Kudō, photographs by Kiyomi Suganuma (no. 4, 1980, 88p.).

1367 **Creative origami.**
Kunihiko Kasahara.   Tokyo: Japan Publications, 1967. 179p.
Reprinted, London: Pitman, 1970.
An instruction manual for origami, the art of folding a single sheet of paper to produce
a range of figures and objects. Kasahara provides precise directions, accompanied by
clearly drawn diagrams and photographs, for creating one hundred types of origami in
the shape of birds, animals, other fauna and flora, masks, and people. He enables both
the origami beginner and the long-time fan to develop a greater appreciation for this
eight hundred-year-old Japanese craft while gaining a greater understanding of the
basic folds in origami that will enable them to develop new origami of their own. The
concluding chapter explains the creative processes used in each of the origami types.

1368 **Kanban: shop signs of Japan.**
Photographs and design by Dana Levy, commentaries by Lea Sneider,
introductory essay by Frank B. Gibney, preface by Letitia Burns
O'Connor.   New York; Tokyo: Weatherhill, 1983. 167p. bibliog.
A pictorial essay and catalogue of the Tokugawa, Meiji, and Taishō period shop signs
(or sign boards) which the authors selected for inclusion in an exhibition held under
the sponsorship of the Japan Society of New York and the American Federation of
Arts. Gibney's introductory essay, 'The Marks of a Japanese Merchant', sketches the
history of kanban ('shop signs') and outlines some of the factors which influenced the
nature, style, and evolution of this traditional, functional art. Over a hundred full-page
illustrations of shop signs are then grouped together according to the types of business
which they advertise: food and drink, tobacco and related objects, household goods,
clothes and accessories, the martial arts, money and banking, medical services, and
arts and leisure. Commentaries identify the subject-matter, size, historical period,
materials, and function and meaning of each sign.

1369 **Japanese crafts.**
John Lowe, photographs by Mark Lowe.   London: John Murray;
New York: Van Nostrand Reinhold, 1983. 175p. bibliog.
An illustrated general introduction to fourteen traditional handicrafts and to their
present-day craftsmanship: floor mats (tatami), kitchen knives (hōcho), brooms (hōki),
folding fans (sensu), carrying cloths (furoshiki), wooden combs (kushi), paper umbrellas
(karakasa), writing and painting brushes (fude), seal-engraving (tenkoku), incense
(ko), paper lanterns (chōchin), bamboo flutes (shakuhachi), sweetmeats (o-kashi), and
raw fish (sushi). Each chapter briefly traces the history of the craft, discusses its place
in Japanese life, describes and illustrates the craft process, and offers a short 'practical
note' for Western craftsmen and craft teachers.

1370 **Japanese lacquer art: modern masterpieces.**
Edited by the National Museum of Modern Art, Tokyo [Tōkyō
Kokuritsu Kindai Bijutsukan], foreword by Kenji Adachi,
introduction by Jō Okada, essay by Masami Shiraishi, translated by
Richard L. Gage.   New York; Tokyo: Weatherhill; Kyōto:
Tankōsha, 1982. 299p.
A handsomely produced, folio-sized guide to 152 works by thirty-seven leading artists
that were on exhibition at the National Museum of Modern Art (Tokyo) in 1979. The

246 large colour plates, accompanied by detailed commentaries, depict a wide range of objects including folding screens, incense boxes, and cabinets. A separate section of 230 colour photographs illustrates various processes and techniques of lacquerwork as well as a variety of design patterns. Shiraishi's historical essay traces the transformation of Japanese lacquerwork from a traditional art before the Meiji Restoration (1868) into a modern craft. Brief biographies of the artists are provided.

1371 **How to wrap five more eggs: traditional Japanese packaging.**
Hideyuki Oka, photographs by Michikazu Sakai. New York; Tokyo:
Weatherhill, 1975. 215p.

Issued in conjunction with an exhibition held at the Japan House Gallery, New York, in 1975, this volume traces the evolution of various forms of Japanese packaging and presents artistically photographed views of over two hundred objects, ranging from straw wrappers for dried fish to elegant wrappings for gifts of food. Commentaries on Sakai's photographs describe the provenance, function, and symbolic references of each item. This publication complements Oka's earlier work, *How to wrap five eggs: Japanese design in traditional packaging*, with photographs by Michikazu Sakai (New York: Weatherhill; Tokyo: Bijutsu Shuppansha, 1967, 203p.).

1372 **The Japanese tattoo.**
Donald Richie, photographs by Ian Buruma, foreword by Horibun II
(Shōtarō Yamada). New York; Tokyo: Weatherhill, 1980. 115p.
bibliog.

A richly illustrated book presenting the two hundred-year history of the Japanese tattoo, investigating its iconography, discussing the social psychology of tattooing, and describing the traditional methods of this craft. The Japanese tattoo flourished during the late Tokugawa period, when it was heavily influenced by ukiyo-e woodblock prints, but it was subsequently subjected to widespread social disapproval and is now frequently associated with gangsters as well as with labourers and artisans.

1373 **The Japanese sword.**
Kanzan Satō, translated and adapted with an introduction by Joe
Earle. Tokyo; New York: Kodansha International and Shibundo,
1983. 210p. bibliog. (Japanese Arts Library, 12).

A comprehensive introduction to the history and appreciation of the Japanese sword as a work of art and traditional technology. Satō details the historical development of the Japanese sword from before the Nara period, examines over a dozen of Japan's most famous blades and explains what has made them so highly appreciated by succeeding generations of Japanese, describes the sword mounts and metal guards (*tsuba*) of Japanese swords, and briefly discusses how Japanese swords are forged, professionally appraised, and properly cared for. Numerous illustrations and a glossary of technical terms enhance the value of this volume. The exhibition catalogue *Nippon-tō: art swords of Japan: the Walter A. Compton Collection*, by Walter A. Compton and others (New York: Japan Society, 1976, 134p.), and Basil William Robinson's *Japanese sword-fittings and associated metalwork: the Bauer Collection* (Geneva: Collections Baur, 1980, 444p.) complement this work with their many additional photographs.

1374   **A history of Japanese lacquerwork.**
Beatrix von Ragué, translated from the German by Annie R. de
Wassermann.   Toronto, Ontario: University of Toronto Press, 1976.
303p. map. bibliog.
Illustrating her book with many photographs of important examples of Japanese
lacquerwork, von Ragué presents an interpretive study of the stylistic development of
this distinctive Japanese craft from the fourth century AD to the mid-1960s. She
synthesizes available information about dated pieces, stylistic traits, changes of style,
varying shapes, techniques, and influences from abroad to present a comprehensive
historical account. She also discusses nearly two hundred individual pieces of
lacquerwork in some detail and shows how such other applied arts as ceramics,
metalwork, and textiles have influenced Japanese lacquerwork and design. The English
edition is a translation of the author's *Geschichte der japanischen Lackkunst* (Berlin:
Walter de Gruyter, 1967, 380p.).

1375   **The samurai sword: a handbook.**
John M. Yumoto.   Rutland, Vermont; Tokyo: Tuttle, 1958. 191p.
bibliog.
The first handbook in English about the traditional samurai swords, many of which
were beautifully crafted by skilled swordsmiths for use by the samurai class. Yumoto's
extensively illustrated guide deals with the origins and historical development of
Japanese swords, their various types, the shapes of their blades, the differences in their
construction, their grain, the ways in which they were made, their inscriptions and
their readings, the problems of care and maintenance, and their identification and
appraisal. A bibliography of selected English and Japanese publications and a useful
glossary of terms conclude the volume.

The Tokugawa Collection: nō robes and masks.
See item no. 1412.

The art of the Japanese kite.
See item no. 1461.

Japanese bookbinding: instructions from a master craftsman.
See item no. 1479.

Performing Arts

General

1376 **Artist and patron in postwar Japan: dance, music, theater, and the visual arts, 1955–1980.**
Thomas R. H. Havens.   Princeton, New Jersey; Guildford, Surrey: Princeton University Press, 1982. 324p. bibliog.

A study of Japanese patronage of the choreographic, musical, dramatic, and visual arts (especially painting, sculpture, and print-making) in postwar Japan, with particular focus on the relatively narrow non-profit sector of the art industry 'where the greatest risks, both of innovation and revival, are taken in the name of art'. Havens describes the social context and organisation of the arts in Japan, examines the support which both government institutions and private sources (primarily businessmen and corporations) have provided, describes the marketing of art through museums and galleries, and discusses the accomplishments and difficulties faced by individuals and groups engaged in music, theatre, and dance. In showing how and why the Japanese have supported the arts in recent years, Havens makes it clear that the success enjoyed by contemporary artists may be partly attributed to the ways in which their art has served the cultural needs of society.

1377 **Gagaku: court music and dance.**
Masatarō Togi, translated by Don Kenny, with an introduction by William P. Malm.   New York; Tokyo: Walker/Weatherhill in collaboration with Tankōsha (Kyōto), 1971. 207p. (Performing Arts of Japan, 5).

A comprehensive introduction to *gagaku*, the ceremonial music and dance of the imperial court, presented from the vantage point of contemporary practice. Following Malm's essay entitled 'The Special Characteristics of Gagaku', Togi explains the classifications, instruments, techniques, songs, dances, masks, costumes, and aesthetics of *gagaku*; traces its history from the seventh century through the Tokugawa period;

and describes the renovation, reorganisation, and performance of *gagaku* in present-day Japan. There are 220 photographs depicting various musicians, dancers, masks, costumes, musical instruments, and scenes from *gagaku* performances.

Warlords, artists, and commoners: Japan in the sixteenth century.
See item no. 135.

Music

1378   **The kumiuta and danmono traditions of Japanese koto music.**
Willem Adriaansz.   Berkeley, California; London: University of California Press, 1973. 493p. bibliog.

A scholarly investigation of the two earliest forms of music composed for the thirteen-stringed plucked zither known as the koto: *kumiuta*, or vocal suite for koto and song, and *danmono*, the first purely instrumental form of koto music. Adriaansz introduces the sources of koto music and traces its historical evolution up to the seventeenth century. He also discusses the principles of musical aesthetics that underlie this music, and systematically analyses *kumiuta* and *danmono* compositions in terms of their structure, phrases, thematic organisation, functional degrees, rhythmical patterns, playing techniques, and ornamentations. Adriaansz concludes with transcriptions of ten *kumiuta* and three *danmono* pieces, accompanied by transliterations and translations into English of the texts of the songs.

1379   **Music of a thousand autumns: the Tōgaku style of Japanese court music.**
Robert Garfias.   Berkeley, California; London: University of California Press, 1975. 322p. bibliog.

A scholarly investigation of the style of imperial court music that was imported from China during the eighth and ninth centuries. Garfias first deals with the historical background of *Tōgaku*, the instruments of the *Tōgaku* ensemble, its traditional theory and notation system, the performance and musical forms of its repertory, its rhythmic and melodic structure, Tōgaku ornamentation technique and its earlier variants, and the placement of ornamentation in relation to modal practice. He also analyses two compositions and discusses the continuous evolution of the *Tōgaku* style. Garfias continues in part two with Western musical transcriptions of melodic passages to harmonic clusters for the mouth organ (*sho*), one of the important instruments of the *Tōgaku* ensemble, as well as with transcriptions of eleven pieces and seven preludes in the basic six modes of *Tōgaku*.

1380   **A history of Japanese music.**
Eta Harich-Schneider.   London; New York: Oxford University Press, 1973. 720p. map. bibliog.

A chronological, almost encyclopaedic survey of the long history of musical activity in Japan, based on a wide range of available evidence. Harich-Schneider deals with such topics as the instruments and ceremonies of the Jōmon, Yayoi, and Kofun periods; the music, musical instruments, and dances of the Heian period as depicted in handscrolls of that era; the Kamakura and Muromachi period musical manuscripts that constitute the most important written records of the Middle Ages; the introduction of Western music into Japan during the late sixteenth century and its reintroduction following the Meiji Restoration (1868); and the survival of *gagaku*, Shintō and Buddhist music, traditional theatrical music, *zokugaku* instrumental music, and folk songs after World War II. The various musical phenomena of each period are generally presented in their proper social and political climate.

1381 **Mountain storm, pine breeze: folk song in Japan.**
Patia R. Isaku. Tucson, Arizona: University of Arizona Press, 1981. 126p. bibliog.

A concise introduction to several aspects of Japanese folk songs, the songs which are 'performed at traditional local and national folk festivals' and are recognised for their authenticity by modern scholars. Included are discussions of their historical background, their associations with traditional beliefs and practices, folk-song poetry, the custom of alluding to older poems within folk-song poetry, the various types of Japanese folk songs, the musical accompaniment for these songs, and the present-day musical mixture of new popular songs and dance. A discography lists recordings of the songs that are cited. Many of them have been recorded on more than one occasion. An annotated collection of seventy-one folk songs with lyrics in both Japanese and English, compiled by Ryūtarō Hattori with the assistance of Masao Shinohara and Iwao Matsuhara, may be found in *Traditional folksongs of Japan: with piano accompaniment* (Tokyo: Ongaku-no-Tomo Sha, 1966, 223p.).

1382 **The traditional music of Japan.**
Shigeo Kishibe. Tokyo: Japan Foundation, 1982. 2nd ed. 92p. 2 maps. bibliog.

Kishibe briefly describes the various genres of traditional Japanese music and places them in their appropriate historical and aesthetic contexts. An outline of eight musical genres – *gagaku* ('court music'), *shōmyō* ('Buddhist chanting'), *biwa* music, noh, *sōkyoku* ('koto music'), the shamisen music of the kabuki and bunraku plays, *shakuhachi* flute music, and folk songs and folk music – is supplemented by numerous figures of musical notations and instruments as well as by photographs of those instruments and their performers.

1383 **Japanese music and musical instruments.**
William P. Malm. Rutland, Vermont; Tokyo: Tuttle, 1959. 299p. bibliog.

The standard general survey of the history of Japanese music, the construction of Japanese musical instruments, and the music itself, illustrated by eighty-nine plates and accompanied by some musical notations. Malm writes about the role of music over the centuries; the music of Japan's three major religions: Shintō, Buddhism, and Christianity; *gagaku*, the court music of Japan; the music of the noh drama and the kabuki theatre; four major instruments – the *biwa* (a short-necked plucked lute), *shakuhachi* (an end-blown flute), koto (a thirteen-stringed plucked zither), and shamisen (a three-stringed plucked lute) – and their music; and the folk musical arts. While some of the appendixes as well as the bibliography and discography are now outdated, the outline of Japanese music notation systems in appendix two and the glossary of musical terms remain useful for musicologists and laymen alike.

1384 **Nagauta: the heart of kabuki music.**
William P. Malm.   Rutland, Vermont; Tokyo: Tuttle, 1963. 344p. bibliog.

An introduction to *nagauta*, a major form of lyrical song accompanied by the music of the three-stringed plucked lute known as the shamisen that constitutes a major element in the kabuki theatre. Written for a variety of audiences, including musicians and theatre devotees, the study commences with a short history of *nagauta* and a discussion of several forms in *nagauta*. Part two ('Music and Instruments') focuses on the playing techniques of the instruments which accompany the vocal line as well as on their interrelationships. It describes *nagauta* singing, the shamisen (the central instrumental component of the *nagauta* ensemble) and its music, the drums and flutes of the *hayashi* ensemble, and the off-stage ensemble and its music. Of particular interest to musicologists are analyses of *Tsuru-kame*, the first noh-derived *nagauta* composition, and *Gorō Tokimune*, a kabuki dance piece. Both were composed in the mid-1800s. Complete transcriptions of these two *nagauta* pieces in Western musical notation are provided as a special insert.

1385 **Six hidden views of Japanese music.**
William P. Malm.   Berkeley, California; London: University of California Press, 1986. 222p.

A series of studies concerned with Japanese musical composition and performance that deal with (1) the art of constructing the small, hourglass-shaped drums with two lashed heads that are known as *ko tsuzumi*; (2) the process of learning to play drums, which Malm contends is 'ritually and intellectually structured in such a way that its ultimate goal may be spiritual rather than musical'; (3) a comparison of the music performed in the noh and kabuki versions of one story, *Shakkyō*; (4) the ways in which shamisen and festival music are combined in *Kanda matsuri*, a *nagauta* piece; (5) four different performance interpretations of the *nagauta* composition *Hōrai*; and (6) a comparison of the musical techniques involved in both the noh play *Sumidagawa* and Benjamin Britten's opera *Curlew River*, which was closely based upon it. An 'interlude' entitled 'General Principles of Japanese Music' is also included.

1386 **101 favorite songs taught in Japanese schools.**
Essay and translations by Ichirō Nakano, illustrations by Sachiko Higuchi.   Tokyo: Japan Times, 1983. 274p.

A collection of European-style songs, composed primarily for children between the 1870s and the 1940s, that have been taught in both primary and middle school for many years. All of them are well known throughout Japan. The volume contains the Western musical notation of these songs, their lyrics in both English and Japanese, and the translator's brief commentaries on their origins and special characteristics. 'Sakura, Sakura', 'Edoko mori uta' ('Lullaby in Edo'), 'Kono michi' ('Tis the Road'), and 'Hi no maru no hata' ('The Sun Flag') are among the songs included.

1387 **The musical structure of nō.**
Akira Tamba, translated by Patricia Matoré. Tokyo: Tokai
University Press, 1981. 242p. bibliog.

A study of the complex musical system of the noh theatre that was developed during the medieval period. An introductory chapter surveys the historical background, staging, categories, structure, and performers of noh drama. Tamba then explores in some depth the vocal techniques in noh, especially vocal emission, peculiarities of pronunciation, the tonal system in the noh song and the process of its evolution, melody cells and rhythm in the noh song, the system of notation in the noh score, and the classification of noh songs. He examines the four instruments – the noh flute, shoulder drum, side drum, and drum played with sticks – which together with the chorus of vocalists structure the music of each noh play. Finally, a reconstitution of the structure of the instrumental part of noh music through Tamba's investigation into the composition of the flute and drum cells as well as their juxtaposition and superimposition is followed by a brief consideration of the rhythmic organisation of noh plays.

Shinichi Suzuki: the man and his philosophy.
See item no. 326.

Geisha.
See item no. 576.

Ko-uta: 'little songs' of the geisha world.
See item no. 576.

The ballad-drama of medieval Japan.
See item no. 1169.

The legend of Semimaru: blind musician of Japan.
See item no. 1176.

Craft treasures of Okinawa.
See item no. 1201.

Tall mountains and flowing waters: the arts of Uragami Gyokudō.
See item no. 1230.

Dance in the nō theatre.
See item no. 1389.

Chūshingura: studies in kabuki and the puppet theatre.
See item no. 1395.

Studies in kabuki: its acting, music, and historical context.
See item no. 1397.

Circles of fantasy: convention in the plays of Chikamatsu.
See item no. 1399.

Early nō drama: its background, character and development, 1300–1450.
See item no. 1409.

Japanese music: an annotated bibliography.
See item no. 1611.

Dance

1388 **The Japanese dance.**
Eiryo [Hidesato] Ashihara.   Tokyo: Japan Travel Bureau, 1964.
164p. bibliog. (Tourist Library, 29). Reprinted, New York: Books for
Libraries, 1980. (Books for Libraries Collection: Dance).

A general explanation of the characteristics and essence of the classical Japanese dance
with some indication of how it differs from Western dance, especially ballet. Ashihara
first traces the evolution of Japanese dance from the seventh century to the origins of
the kabuki dance in the Tokugawa period. Devoting the remainder of his book to an
explanation of the kabuki dance, he then discusses its basic elements, outlines its
composition, and comments on the kabuki dance stage, the folding fan and Japanese
towel that serve as the major dance accessories, the musical accompaniment and
costuming, and the *suodori* (dances without special costuming). Some introductory
notes on the twelve most popular kabuki dance dramas are given in an appendix.

1389 **Dance in the nō theater.**
Monica Bethe, Karen Brazell.   Ithaca, New York: China–Japan
Program, Cornell University, 1982. 3 vols. bibliog. (Cornell University
East Asia Papers, 29).

A detailed, analytical study of dance in traditional noh drama. Volume one, *Dance
analysis*, presents the basic system of noh dance, describes its major dance movements
or dance patterns in very generalised terms, describes the noh stage and explains how
noh performances are affected by its design and construction, and analyses the
relationship of dance to verbal meaning, props, costumes, masks, and instrumental
music. The second volume, *Plays and scores*, provides the scores of the dances which
are used as illustrations in volume one and are recorded on five accompanying video
cassettes. It also discusses dance in seven noh plays that are representative of the five
traditional categories of plays within this theatrical genre, and analyses several types of
dance, among them dances performed to song, and long instrumental dances
performed to drum and flute music. The third volume, *Dance patterns*, contains
detailed descriptions and hundreds of step-by-step photographs which document the
basic patterns in noh drama, e.g., foot patterns, fan-centred patterns, and patterns
involving props and costumes. It also compares the traditional dance patterns of the
Kita and Kanze schools of noh actors, indicating some of the subtle differences
between them.

1390 **Buyo: the classical dance.**
Masakatsu Gunji, translated by Don Kenny, with an introduction by
James R. Brandon.   New York: Tokyo: Walker/Weatherhill in
collaboration with Tankōsha (Kyōto), 1970. 207p. (Performing Arts of
Japan, 3).

Buyō, the classical dance of Japan, is described and visually presented in this study of
the aesthetics and history of Japanese dance. Following Brandon's essay 'Kabuki
Dance: a View from the Outside' (an informative, personal account of *buyō* and its
performance on the kabuki stage), Gunji discusses the basic terminology and concepts
pertinent to an understanding of Japanese dance, traces the general development of

buyō from the seventh century onwards, explains its techniques, interprets its aesthetics, recreates the atmosphere in which it is performed, examines the problems currently faced by the *buyō* movement, and critically considers the teaching of Japanese dance today. There are 153 photographs (some in colour) depicting a variety of dances and dance themes, including scenes from famous dance pieces, notable performers, and paintings and prints from Japanese dance history.

Michio Ito: the dancer and his dances.
See item no. 322.

Bugaku masks.
See item no. 1294.

Theatre

1391   **Backstage at bunraku: a behind-the-scenes look at Japan's traditional puppet theatre.**
Barbara C. Adachi, photographs by Joel Sackett, foreword by Donald Keene.   New York; Tokyo: Weatherhill, 1985. 192p.
A revealing portrait of the behind-the-scenes world of the famed Ōsaka Bunraku Troupe. Through a combination of narrative and interviews, fifty-six photographs, and stage diagrams, Adachi introduces the puppeteers, narrators, shamisen players, off-stage musicians, the carver and the repairer of the puppet heads, the wig master, the costume maker, the prop masters, and the various stage assistants who constitute the human dimension of Japan's puppet theatre. Each of these artists and craftsmen explains the nature of his work and shows how it contributes to the creation of a bunraku puppet performance. Altogether they present a comprehensive picture of their training, their workshops and studios, rehearsals, and performances. Adachi's book revises her earlier study, *The voices and hands of bunraku* (Tokyo; New York: Kodansha International, 1978, 145p.), but it lacks its seventy large-size photographs.

1392   **Bunraku: the puppet theater.**
Tsuruo Andō, translated and adapted by Don Kenny, with an introduction by Charles Dunn.   New York; Tokyo: Walker/Weatherhill in collaboration with Tankōsha (Kyōto), 1970. 222p. (Performing Arts of Japan, 1).
This overview of Japan's traditional puppet theatre traces the evolution of bunraku from the early Tokugawa period to the 1960s. Its coverage extends to the development of *jōruri* (a form of dramatic narrative chanting accompanied by shamisen music), the plays written by Chikamatsu Monzaemon, the puppeteers and performances at the Takemoto-za playhouse in Ōsaka between 1684 and 1767, and bunraku artists of the Meiji, Taishō and Shōwa periods. The 173 photographs depict scenes from celebrated plays, a wide range of puppet heads, Tokugawa period paintings and drawings of bunraku, and puppeteers and narrators in actual performance. A concise chronology is also provided. Dunn's introduction examines the major elements of the bunraku

performance, discusses the function of its puppets, and briefly considers the position of bunraku in relation to other theatrical arts.

1393 **The theatres of Japan.**
Peter D. Arnott.   London: Macmillan; New York: St. Martin's Press; Rutland, Vermont and Tokyo: Tuttle, 1969. 319p. bibliog.

A general introduction to the classical forms of the Japanese theatre, their development, and their influence on twentieth-century productions. Arnott discusses the origins of Japan's theatrical arts, focusing on early dances and festivals; examines the history, performances, forms and structures, aesthetics, stage techniques, and theatrical conventions of noh, kabuki, and bunraku; and provides descriptions of a number of plays. In addition, he surveys the twentieth-century theatre, particularly through a series of reviews of individual productions. Appendixes compare productions of the play *Shunkan* in its noh, kabuki, and bunraku versions; consider the influence of traditional drama on the modern Japanese cinema; and comment on the influence which the noh theatre has had on the work of the Irish playwright William Butler Yeats and the British composer Benjamin Britten.

1394 **Japanese theatre.**
Faubion Bowers, foreword by Joshua Logan.   New York: Hermitage House, 1952. 294p. Reprinted, London: Peter Owen, 1954; New York: Hill and Wang, 1959; Rutland, Vermont and Tokyo: Tuttle, 1974; Westport, Connecticut: Greenwood Press, 1976.

An introduction to the kabuki theatre with much briefer historical analyses of Japanese drama before the emergence of kabuki, following the Meiji Restoration of 1868, and during the twentieth century. Bowers identifies and examines the major types of kabuki; their development around the time of the Genroku era (1688–1704); the contribution of historical kabuki to twentieth-century kabuki with respect to role-types, actors, the stage, plots, major emphases, and types of dramatic forms; and the aesthetics of kabuki: colour, motion, and reality versus unreality. He also provides translations of *Tsuchigumo*, *Gappo ga Tsuji*, and *Sukeroku Yukari no Edo zakura* as well as brief synopses of many other kabuki plays.

1395 **Chūshingura: studies in kabuki and the puppet theater.**
Edited by James R. Brandon.   Honolulu, Hawaii: University of Hawaii Press, 1982. 231p.

Leading scholars examine the most famous play in the kabuki and bunraku repertoires: *Chūshingura* (q.v.), a mid-eighteenth century drama about the revenge taken by the forty-seven loyal retainers of Lord Asano, the daimyō of Akō, against the Tokugawa official who had caused his death. Donald Keene describes how this historical vendetta became the basis of numerous plays during the decades following its occurrence. In his essay 'Tokugawa Plays on Forbidden Topics', Donald H. Shively shows how theatrical managers and actors succeeded in circumventing severe government censorship in order to stage this drama. William P. Malm discusses the musical accompaniment to the bunraku version of *Chūshingura*. James R. Brandon examines the transformation of the original puppet play into a kabuki play and compares the two versions in some detail. The volume concludes with a complete translation of the kabuki version of *Chūshingura*, adapted for live performance at the University of Hawaii in 1979, accompanied by photographs and stage directions.

1396 **Kabuki: five classic plays.**
Translated with an introduction by James R. Brandon. Cambridge,
Massachusetts; London: Harvard University Press, 1975. 378p.
bibliog. (Unesco Collection of Representative Works: Japanese
Series).

Recreates five plays from the standard kabuki repertory that were written between
1712 and 1817: *Sukeroku: flower of Edo* (*Sukeroku Yukari no Edo zakura*); *Saint
Narukami and the god Fudō* (*Narukami Fudō Kitayama zakura*); *Chronicle of the battle
of Ichinotani* (*Ichinotani futaba gunki*); *Love letter from the licensed quarter* (*Kuruwa
bunshō*); and *The scarlet princess of Edo* (*Sakura Hime Azuma bunshō*). The
translations of these plays were prepared on the basis of taped theatrical performances
and are accompanied by simultaneous commentary, stage directions, and over one
hundred black-and-white production photographs. Brandon's introduction describes
the history of kabuki, its playwriting system, religious background, themes, languages,
and performance conventions. Appendixes providing information about various sound
effects (*ki* and *tsuke* patterns) as well as about musical cues in performance are
supplemented by a concise glossary of specialised terms.

1397 **Studies in kabuki: its acting, music, and historical context.**
James R. Brandon, William P. Malm, Donald H. Shively. Honolulu,
Hawaii: University Press of Hawaii, 1978. 183p. bibliog. (A Culture
Learning Institute Monograph).

A collection of three essays that enhance one's understanding of the socio-historical,
technical, and musical features of kabuki. 'The Social Environment of Tokugawa
Kabuki' (by Shively) discusses the socio-economic conditions that nurtured kabuki's
early development and describes the relationship between kabuki and the world of
public entertainment. 'Forms in Kabuki Acting' (by Brandon) examines the acting
forms (*kata*), performance style, and performance techniques which predominate in
this theatrical genre. And in 'Music in the Kabuki Theater', Malm looks at the history
of kabuki music and examines its instruments, melodies, and rhythmic patterns as well
as the music itself.

1398 **The kabuki theatre.**
Earle Ernst. London: Secker and Warburg; New York: Oxford
University Press, 1956. 296p. bibliog. Reprinted, Honolulu, Hawaii:
University Press of Hawaii, 1974.

A comprehensive, illustrated overview of the kabuki theatre written particularly for
the general reader but also invaluable for specialists in Japanese drama. Following an
introduction to the historical and social context within which kabuki flourished, it
discusses in considerable detail many facets of this theatre, including the development
of its physical layout and the evolution of the kabuki stage; the audience and its
attitudes; the nature and role of the *hanamichi*, the passageway through the kabuki
auditorium on which important entrances and exits are made; the major elements of
the performance, among them musical sound effects and the stage properties; the
stage; the actors; the plays and their characters; and twentieth-century Western
influences on kabuki. Frequent points of reference and comparisons with the Western
theatre are designed to enhance one's understanding of kabuki.

1399 **Circles of fantasy: convention in the plays of Chikamatsu.**
C. Andrew Gerstle. Cambridge, Massachusetts: Council on East
Asian Studies, Harvard University, 1986. 248p. bibliog. (Harvard East
Asian Monographs, 116).

A delineation of two fundamental conventions in the *jidaimono* ('history' or 'period'),
shinjū ('love suicide'), and *sewamono* ('contemporary life') puppet plays of Chikamatsu
Monzaemon (1653-1725), the foremost playwright of popular Japanese drama. Gerstle
examines the musical structure of these plays and shows how a combination of chant-
like narration and the playing of stringed shamisen instruments supplements their plots
and 'expresses a dramatized action or emotion through complex changes in pitch,
tempo, and style of delivery'. He also studies the cyclical movement within the plays,
as it has been influenced by Buddhist tradition. Glossaries of theatrical forms, major
musical notation, and structural units of *jōruri* plays are included.

1400 **Kabuki.**
Masakatsu Gunji, photographs by Chiaki Yoshida, introduction by
Donald Keene. Tokyo; New York: Kodansha International, 1985.
new ed. 223p. bibliog.

Concisely describes the historical evolution of kabuki from its sixteenth-century origins
to the present day, the principal actors of the kabuki stage, its plays and playwrights,
the production and performances of its plays, its theatre and stage machinery, and the
audiences and performances of this type of drama. Hundreds of colour and
monochrome photographs depicting famous stage scenes, specialised techniques used
in kabuki, and the settings and history of this theatre constitute the core of this folio-
sized volume. Also serving as an extensively illustrated, general introduction to kabuki
is *Kabuki: the popular theater*, by Yasuji Toita, translated by Don Kenny (New York;
Tokyo; Kyōto: Weatherhill/Tankōsha, 1970, 245p. [Performing Arts of Japan, 2]). It
deals with various idiosyncracies of this classical theatre – including the roles of its
actors, the use of hand-properties, and costume colour – as well as with its origins and
history and its popularity in postwar Japan.

1401 **The kabuki guide.**
Masakatsu Gunji, translated by Christopher Holmes, photographs by
Chiaki Yoshida. Tokyo; New York: Kodansha International, 1987.
144p.

A concise, illustrated guide for the novice and occasional theatregoer that presents a
basic overview of kabuki and synopses of the most frequently performed plays.
Following a very brief survey of the development of kabuki, Gunji describes the typical
kabuki theatre and discusses the different types of kabuki plays, their make-up,
costumes and acting, their actors, and the colours and musical sounds of this traditional
theatrical art. The core of Gunji's guidebook are synopses and highlights (together
with brief background information) of thirty-six major plays, all written during the
eighteenth and nineteenth century. Information on where to see kabuki in Japan and
how to obtain tickets is also provided. Regular playgoers and connoisseurs of the
kabuki may prefer to avail themselves of an earlier manual, *The kabuki handbook: a
guide to understanding and appreciation, with summaries of favourite plays, explanatory
notes, and illustrations*, by Aubrey S. Halford and Giovanna M. Halford (Rutland,
Vermont; Tokyo: Tuttle, 1956, 487p.), which contains more detailed synopses for
nearly one hundred plays together with some notes explaining kabuki conventions and
customs.

Performing Arts. Theatre

1402 **Kyōgen.**
Hisashi Hata, translated and edited by Don Kenny, photographs by
Tatsuo Yoshikoshi. Tokyo: Hoikusha, 1982. 124p. (Hoikusha Color
Books).

This extensively illustrated, compact guide assists readers in enjoying *kyōgen*
performances by introducing and describing a form of comic drama which first
flourished during the fourteenth century and is traditionally performed between two
noh plays. Hata covers the historical origins and evolution of *kyōgen*, its scripts and the
categories of plays found within the *kyōgen* repertory, various aspects of *kyōgen*
humour, and such elements of *kyōgen* acting and dramaturgy as the use of time and
space, dialogue and gesture, and masks and properties. Helpful synopses of all of the
plays of the *kyōgen* repertory can be found in Kenny's *A guide to kyōgen* (Tokyo:
Hinoki Shoten, 1968, 303p.; rev. ed., 1980). The most extensive collection of
translations of *kyōgen* remains Shio Sakanishi's *Japanese folk plays: the Ink-smeared
lady and other kyōgen* (Boston, Massachusetts: Marshall Jones, 1938, 150p.; reprinted,
Rutland, Vermont and Tokyo: Tuttle, 1980).

1403 **The traditional theater of Japan.**
Yoshinobu Inoura, Toshio Kawatake. New York; Tokyo:
Weatherhill in collaboration with the Japan Foundation, 1981. 259p.

An illustrated survey of the historical development of the traditional theatre.
Beginning with *kagura* (simple plays that originated in Shintō religious rites), part one
discusses several of Japan's early theatrical forms: *gigaku* (dances and dramas
associated with Buddhist religious services), *gagaku* and *bugaku* (Chinese-derived
Heian court music and dance), *sarugaku* and other prototypes of noh, and the noh
theatre in both its early phases (*ennen noh, sarugaku noh, dengaku noh*, and *shūgen
noh*) and its true classical form. The comic interludes between noh plays known as
kyōgen are also dealt with. Part two focuses on the bunraku and kabuki theatre of the
Tokugawa period and considers their origins and history, stylistic beauty, common
characteristics, and drama. This book was first publ'shed as a two-volume study
entitled *A history of Japanese theater* (Tokyo: Kokusai Bunka Shinkōkai, 1971).

1404 **Bunraku: the art of the Japanese puppet theatre.**
Donald Keene, photographs by Hiroshi Kaneko, introduction by
Junichirō Tanizaki. Tokyo; New York: Kodansha International,
1965. 287p. bibliog. Revised paperback edition, Tokyo; New York:
Kodansha International, 1973. 88p.

A description and recreation in 360 photographs of the heads, puppets, and
performances of a traditional theatrical art in which large, elaborately carved and
costumed puppets are manipulated by operators standing beside and behind them.
Keene describes the pleasures of watching performances of bunraku, its historical
development, the literary texts that are used and the individuals who chant them, the
accompanying shamisen instruments and their players, the puppets and the people who
operate them, and the various gestures of the bunraku puppets on stage. The
photographs, which constitute the major part of this volume, reveal the visual appeal
of the bunraku theatre.

1405 **Nō: the classical theatre of Japan.**
Donald Keene, photographs by Hiroshi Kaneko, introduction by Jun Ishikawa. Tokyo; Palo Alto, California: Kodansha International, 1966. 311p. bibliog. Revised paperback edition, Tokyo; New York: Kodansha International, 1973. 112p.

A comprehensive survey of the most important aspects of both the noh theatre and the comic interlude known as *kyōgen*. Keene covers their historical development since the Heian period, the literary content of their texts, the training of various actors, the schools of noh, noh masks and costumes, the music and dance associated with the plays, and the noh stage and its properties. Over four hundred photographs show details of the stage, the props, the musical instruments and costumes, and dramatic scenes from major noh and *kyōgen* plays. This folio-sized book is a companion volume to Donald Keene's study of bunraku (q.v.) and Gunji Masakatsu's work on kabuki (q.v.).

1406 **The noh theater: principles and perspectives.**
Kunio Komparu, foreword by Michio Sakurama, translated by Jane Corddry, Stephen Comee. New York; Tokyo; Kyōto: Weatherhill/Tankōsha, 1983. 376p.

A comprehensive explanation and authoritative analysis of the principles of noh, written by a direct successor of the fifteenth-century playwright Zeami Motokiyo. Komparu discusses the characteristics which distinguish noh as a theatrical art and explains its basic principles; examines the many elements of noh, including the noh stage, plots, performers, music, movement (or dance) patterns, *nohmen* (face masks), costumes, and stage and personal properties; shows how these elements are combined in the noh theatre; and analyses the performance of two plays, *Nonomiya* and *Shunkan*, both of which are translated in full. Three appendixes briefly discuss Zeami's life and thought, and list the current noh repertoire as well as the principal noh theatres in Japan. Numerous photographs, tables, sketches, and diagrams enhance this volume's usefulness as a reference work.

1407 **The art of kabuki: famous plays in performance.**
Translated with commentary and an introduction by Samuel L. Leiter. Berkeley, California; London: University of California Press, 1979. 298p. bibliog.

Performance-oriented translations of famous scenes and acts from four popular kabuki plays: *Benten Kōzō* and *Naozamurai*, by Kawatake Mokuami; and *Sugawara denju tenarai kagami* and *Shunkan*, kabuki adaptations of puppet plays by Miyoshi Shōraku, Namiki Senryū and Takeda Izumo II, and by Chikamatsu Monzaemon respectively. Accompanying the translations are descriptions of their stage movements and information about their scenic appurtenances, types of costume and make-up used, wigs, acting style, musical accompaniment, etc. that are based on observations of theatrical performances in Tokyo. Leiter's extensive introductions to the individual plays comment on their background, outline their plots, discuss the *kata* (or 'forms') which determine the interpretations of leading roles, and briefly introduce their playwrights. Several black-and-white photographs illustrating the settings as well as important actions of major characters follow the text of each play.

1408 **Noh: the classical theater.**
Yasuo Nakamura, translated by Don Kenny, introduction by Earle
Ernst. New York; Tokyo: Walker/Weatherhill in collaboration with
Tankōsha (Kyōto), 1971. 248p. (Performing Arts of Japan, 4).
A general introduction to noh that begins by describing selected aspects of its
performance and continues with a survey of the origins, evolution, and formalisation of
noh through the centuries down to the 1960s. Particular consideration is given to the
many changes and innovations which occurred in noh following its development under
the playwright and actor Zeami Motokiyo. A good overview of noh in present-day
Japan – with a focus on the training of actors, masks, costumes, stage properties,
music, stage movements, and performance – is also provided. Complementing the text
are a concise chronology of the history of this theatrical art and 161 largely
monochrome photographs that depict scenes from noh plays, the basic poses and
movements in noh drama, the antecedent dance and theatrical forms of noh, and
representative masks and costumes.

1409 **Early nō drama: its background, character and development,
1300–1450.**
Patrick Geoffrey O'Neill. London: Lund Humphries, 1958. 223p.
bibliog. Reprinted, Westport, Connecticut: Greenwood Press, 1974.
A carefully documented study that describes the role which *sarugaku* and *dengaku noh*
plays as well as the *kusemai* song-and-dance form played in the evolution of noh
drama. In order to provide a coherent account of the most important period in the
history of noh and to offer a basis for understanding the artistic theories of the noh
actor and playwright Zeami Motokiyo, O'Neill discusses the troupes, organisation,
popularity, patrons, and players of *sarugaku* and *dengaku noh*; *kusemai* music and
songs and the role which they came to assume in *sarugaku noh*; the religious and
subscription performances of noh plays and their content; *sarugaku noh* plays before
the time of Zeami as well as the plays which Zeami himself wrote; *dengaku noh* plays;
and artistic standards in noh performances. Four appendixes contain translations of
selected *kusemai* and *dengaku noh* plays as well as lists of noh plays by Zeami and his
predecessors.

1410 **Audience and actors: a study of their interaction in the Japanese
traditional theatre.**
Jacob Raz. Leiden, The Netherlands: Brill, 1983. 307p. bibliog.
A history of the critical relationship between actors and their audiences in the Japanese
theatre. Raz analyses the ways in which the theatre and its performers were affected by
the behaviour, expectations, and demands of their audiences as he examines the
theatre's origins in early Japanese folk festivals; the medieval audiences of *gigaku*,
bugaku, *sarugaku noh*, and *dengaku noh*; the patronage of the noh theatre; the kabuki
theatre of the Tokugawa period and its enthusiastic fans; and the audiences for the
performance of classical Japanese drama since the mid-1800s

1411 **The puppet theatre of Japan.**
Adolphe Clarence Scott. Rutland, Vermont; Tokyo: Tuttle, 1963.
173p. map. Reprinted, Tuttle, 1973.
Synopses of frequently performed puppet plays are preceded by a general history of
bunraku since the seventeenth century; consideration of the roles of the puppeteers,

narrators, and shamisen players; descriptions of both the puppet stage and the construction of the puppets; and a discussion of some of the themes, historical settings, and ideals of the puppet theatre as well as of the characteristics of Tokugawa society and Japanese life that are reflected in its plays. Nearly half of the volume consists of plot summaries (accompanied by brief critical remarks) of ten plays which are best known to generations of theatregoers by their popular titles: *Yoshidaya, Numazu, Horikawa, Tsubosaka, Hinomi, Kagamijishi. Domomata, Sendai Hagi, Gappo,* and *Yari no Gonza kasane katabira.*

1412 **The Tokugawa Collection: nō robes and masks.**
Yoshinobu Tokugawa, Sadao Ōkōchi, translated and adapted by
Louise Allison Cort, Monica Bethe, foreword by Rand Castile. New
York: Japan Society, 1977. 277p. bibliog.

Exhibition catalogue of robes, masks, and such accessories as sashes and caps that were commissioned by the Tokugawa family and used in noh drama performances on its own stages. Housed today within the Tokugawa Art Museum in Nagoya, the majority of these garments and masks were produced in the seventeeenth and eighteenth centuries, an era when the noh wardrobe reached a peak of elegance and luxury. The catalogue contains captioned illustrations of each of the 145 objects that were on display in the United States, together with essays which discuss the relationship of the Owari Tokugawa House to noh and describe the noh costumes in the Tokugawa Art Museum.

1413 **On the art of the nō drama: the major treatises of Zeami.**
Zeami Motokiyo, translated, introduced and annotated by J. Thomas
Rimer, Masakazu Yamazaki, foreword by Wallace Chappell.
Princeton, New Jersey; Guildford, Surrey: Princeton University Press,
1984. 298p. bibliog. (Princeton Library of Asian Translations).

Annotated translations of the nine major treatises on the principles of the noh theatre produced by the noted actor and playwright Zeami Motokiyo (1363-1443) at different times in his career. These secret writings were originally shared only among the members of the Kanze school of noh and were intended for transmission from one generation to the next. They cover a wide range of topics including Zeami's views of the fundamentals of acting, his instruction in basic performance skills, his explanation of the levels of performance, his ideas about the proper methods of composing a noh text, and his views on the nature of ensemble acting. Introductory essays discuss the historical background of these treatises and the basic characteristics of Zeami's artistic theories.

The theatrical world of Osaka prints: a collection of eighteenth and nineteenth century Japanese woodblock prints in the Philadelphia Museum of Art.
See item no. 1264.

Japanese costume and textile arts.
See item no. 1351.

Kabuki costume.
See item no. 1352.

Nagauta: the heart of kabuki music.
See item no. 1384.

Six hidden views of Japanese music.
See item no. 1385.

The musical structure of nō.
See item no. 1387.

The Japanese dance.
See item no. 1388.

Dance in the nō theatre.
See item no. 1389.

Asian Theatre Journal.
See item no. 1492.

Kabuki encyclopedia: an English-language adaptation of *Kabuki jiten*.
See item no. 1564.

Japanese music: an annotated bibliography.
See item no. 1611.

Cinema

1414 **The Japanese film: art and industry.**
Joseph L. Anderson, Donald Richie, foreword by Akira Kurosawa.
Princeton, New Jersey; Guildford, Surrey: Princeton University Press,
1982. expanded ed. 526p. bibliog.

A detailed history and authoritative critique of the Japanese cinema. Part one
('Background') offers a period-by-period study of the cinema's development from 1896
(when the first Edison Kinetoscope was imported into Japan), through the golden age
of Japanese film-making, to 1959. Part two ('Foreground') analyses the distinctive
content, technique, directors, actors, theatres, and audiences of Japanese movies. Two
brief essays update the authors' coverage of the cinema through the early 1980s and
consider such topics as the peculiar qualities of the *jidai-geki* genre and the rise of
television. Also included are 168 still photographs, a chart outlining the teacher–pupil
relationships which traditionally lead to entrance into the ranks of feature film
directors, and a chart tracing the chronological development of major film production
companies.

1415 **Japanese film directors.**
Audie Bock, foreword by Tatsuya Nakadai, preface by Donald
Richie.   Tokyo; New York: Kodansha International, 1985. updated
ed. 378p. bibliog.

A series of in-depth essays about ten prewar, postwar, and 'New Wave-and-After' film-
makers who 'represent the most consistently high achievements of Japanese cinematic
art': Mizoguchi Kenji, Ozu Yasujirō, Naruse Mikio, Kurosawa Akira, Kinoshita
Keisuke, Ichikawa Kon, Kobayashi Masaki, Imamura Shōhei, Ōshima Nagisa, and
Shinoda Masahiro. Bock presents brief biographical overviews of their careers;

discusses their main interests, themes, visual styles, and the technical qualities of their work; analyses some of their most representative films; and provides complete annotated filmographies which contain succinct plot summaries and critical appraisals of their productions as well as notes on the availability of prints in Japan and the United States. The inclusion of over one hundred stills of various films enhances the value of this book as both an introduction to the Japanese cinema and a reference work.

1416 **Ozu and the poetics of cinema.**
David Bordwell. London: British Film Institute; Princeton, New Jersey: Princeton University Press, 1988. 406p. bibliog.
This detailed study of the cinematography of Ozu Yasujirō (1903-63) argues that Ozu's films are far more varied in subject and theme and far less concerned with psychological verisimilitude than critics generally suggest. Employing an historical poetics of cinema as his frame of reference, Bordwell begins by surveying this film director's career, analysing the materials and formal processes of his work, and discussing some of the social and historical functions of his movies. Part two offers a chronologically ordered series of succinct critical essays of fifty-five films. Each essay highlights only one or two issues about the film under review, such as 'a stylistic strategy, a narrational approach, an important treatment of a subject or theme, [or] a pattern of ideological tensions'. Over five hundred stills from Ozu's movies are included.

1417 **To the distant observer: form and meaning in the Japanese cinema.**
Noël Burch, revised and edited by Annette Michelson. Berkeley, California: University of California Press; London: Scolar Press, 1979. 387p. bibliog.
An insightful and extensively illustrated examination of early Japanese cinematography, particularly between 1917 and 1945. Burch's major concern is 'with the *modes of representation* common to, and distinctive of, most Japanese films within given periods, and with the highly refined styles generated by those modes in the work of a handful' of producers. He shows how the early decades of the twentieth century were not ones of stagnation and 'underdevelopment' but instead constituted a preparatory period for the 1930-45 'golden age' of Japanese cinema, during which Ozu Yasujirō, Mizoguchi Kenji, and other lesser-known masters such as Naruse Mikio, Yamanaka Sadao, Ishida Tamizo, and Shimizu Hiroshi produced their most distinguished movies. Burch views the post-1945 era of 'democratisation' as 'one of regression in cinema', especially in the works of Ozu and Mizoguchi. His concluding chapters focus on the accomplishments of Kurosawa Akira and Ōshima Nagisa.

1418 **The making of James Clavell's Shōgun.**
Foreword by James Clavell. New York: Dell, 1980. 224p. (A Delta Book).
Shōgun (New York: Atheneum; London: Hodder and Stoughton, 1975, 802p.), James Clavell's historical novel about an English navigator who went to Japan around 1600, dealt with the leading warlords of his day, and achieved samurai status, enjoyed a tremendous readership in the West. In 1979–80 it was made into a twelve-hour-long television mini-series for NBC. Starring Richard Chamberlain, Mifune Toshirō, and Shimada Yōko, this adventure drama caught the imagination of millions of viewers, created a new popular image of Japan, and stimulated greater interest in Japanese

history and culture. This profusely illustrated book recounts how *Shōgun* the novel was converted into *Shōgun* the film, and explains what was involved in shooting the movie entirely on location in Japan. Because this was the first time that foreigners had gone there to make such a movie, and because they used Japanese actors, film-makers and facilities extensively, the book provides unusual insights into Japanese movie-making and graphically describes some of the intercultural encounters between *Shōgun*'s American producers and the Japanese at that time.

1419 **Eros plus massacre: an introduction to the Japanese New Wave cinema.**
David Desser. Bloomington, Indiana: Indiana University Press,
1988. 239p. bibliog. (A Midland Book).
An examination of the major motifs and cultural concerns of the 'New Wave' of Japanese films that were produced during the 1960s. Focusing on several influential directors – especially Ōshima Nagisa, Shinoda Masahiro, Imamura Shōhei, Suzuki Seijun, and Yoshida Yoshishige – Desser discusses the emergence of this new cinematic movement; examines its concern with themes such as youth and Japanese identity, the problem of women and women's problems, and the issue of prejudice and discrimination; and investigates the links between the New Wave cinema and the post-Shingeki theatre. He also explores the cinematic contributions of these directors – in particular, the ways in which they handled the same set of issues and motifs – and demonstrates that the New Wave was a movement (rather than simply a group) of film-makers whose works posed a challenge to cinematic traditions and Japanese culture at large.

1420 **The samurai films of Akira Kurosawa.**
David Desser. Ann Arbor, Michigan: UMI Research Press; Epping,
Essex: Bowker, 1983. 164p. bibliog. (Studies in Cinema, 23).
Explores the most widely known genre of postwar Japanese cinematography in the West: the films set in Japan's feudal past, particularly the Tokugawa period, when the warrior class held political power. Desser explores the idea of the mythicisation of history, isolates four different sub-genres of samurai film (nostalgic samurai drama; anti-feudal drama; Zen fighters; sword films), and argues that the samurai film, like the Western in the United States, is an amorphous cinematographic form which has evolved over time. Much of the work offers a detailed analysis of five of Kurosawa's most famous movies: *Seven Samurai*, *The Hidden Fortress*, *Yōjimbō*, *Sanjūrō*, and *Kagemusha*. While Desser's presentation is marred by factual errors and other inaccuracies in its coverage of Japanese history, his book nevertheless can be profitably read by aficionados of Kurosawa and his samurai films. Alain Silver's closely related work, *The samurai film* (Woodstock, New York: Overlook Press, 1983. rev. updated ed., 242p.), also deals extensively with Kurosawa, but it provides broader coverage of this cinematic genre through its treatment of the films of such additional directors as Inagaki Hiroshi, Okamoto Kihachi, Gosha Hideo, and Shinoda Masahiro.

1421 **Cinema east: a critical study of major Japanese films.**
Keiko I. McDonald. Rutherford, New Jersey: Fairleigh Dickinson
University Press, 1983. 279p. bibliog.
A collection of essays concerning twelve major films that offers Western audiences an enhanced understanding of the ways in which they can best be viewed. It provides detailed summaries of the plots or structures of these films as well as commentary about their symbolism, character types, use of space, time, narrative mode, camera

techniques, and rhetoric or audience manipulation. Among the films examined are Kurosawa Akira's *Rashōmon* and *Red Beard*, Teshigahara Hiroshi's *Woman in the Dunes*, Shinoda Masahiro's *Double Suicide*, Ichikawa Kon's *Harp of Burma*, Mizoguchi Kenji's *Ugetsu*, Kinoshita Keisuke's *Twenty-four Eyes*, Ōshima Nagisa's *Death by Hanging*, and Ozu Yasujirō's *Tokyo Story*.

1422 **Mizoguchi.**
Keiko McDonald, foreword by Warren French. Boston, Massachusetts: Twayne, 1984. 187p. bibliog. (Twayne's Filmmakers Series).

A critical study of Mizoguchi Kenji (1898-1956), the eminent director of more than eighty feature films including *Women of the Night*, *Ugetsu monogatari*, *Sanshō the Bailiff*, and *The Life of Oharu*. McDonald portrays Mizoguchi's life and describes his evolving cinematic style, summarises his plots and appraises many of his movies, examines the close interaction of his thematic and aesthetic aims, illuminates his dedication of themes connected with women, explores his 'progressively more universal conception of human existence', considers the autobiographical elements in his various films, and assesses Mizoguchi's achievements as a whole. Readers seeking further information about Mizoguchi and his work may wish to consult Dudley and Paul Andrew's *Kenji Mizoguchi: a guide to references and resources* (q.v.).

1423 **Voices from the Japanese cinema.**
Joan Mellen. New York: Liveright, 1975. 295p.

Fifteen important film directors, artists, and distributors share their views about their techniques and activities as well as about the postwar cinema in general. The interviews conducted by Joan Mellen, an American specialist in the study of feminist films, focus on films and film-making and are preceded by introductions to each of the interviewees and their work. Mellen's subjects are the film directors Itō Daisuke, Kurosawa Akira, Shindō Kaneto, Imai Tadashi, Ichikawa Kon, Kobayashi Masaki, Teshigahara Hiroshi, Hani Susumu, Shinoda Masahiro, Ōshima Nagisa, and Terayama Shūji; the film distributor and curator Kawakita Kashiko; the set designer Asakura Setsu; the film star and director Hidari Sachiko; and the cinematographer Narushima Tōichirō. Photographs of these individuals and stills from various movies illustrate the book.

1424 **The waves at Genji's door: Japan through its cinema.**
Joan Mellen. New York: Pantheon, 1976. 463p. (Pantheon Asia Library).

Mellen places the Japanese film in its historical, social, and political context in order to enhance Western understanding and appreciation of the Japanese cinema. She examines the evolution of the Japanese film, specifically focusing on those directors (Naruse Mikio, Mizoguchi Kenji, Ozu Yasujirō, Kurosawa Akira, Ōshima Nagisa, and Shinoda Masahiro, among others) whose films are preoccupied with the 'spiritual fate of Japan' and with the Japanese 'quest of national and self-discovery'. In addition, she explores the Japanese cinematic portrayal of the Second World War and its aftermath, the role of Japanese women in society, and changes in the traditional Japanese family. Still photographs of scenes from nearly one hundred movies illustrate the book.

1425 **The films of Akira Kurosawa.**
Donald Richie, with additional material by Joan Mellen. Berkeley,
California; London: University of California Press, 1984. rev. ed.
255p. bibliog.
A critical examination of twenty-six films made by the internationally renowned
director Akira Kurosawa (1910-   ). Among these are *Sugata Sanshirō*, *Rashōmon*,
Ikiru, *Seven Samurai*, *Throne of Blood*, *Yōjimbō*, *Red Beard*, *Dodesukaden*, and
Kagemusha. Richie discusses the background of each film, summarises its plot in some
detail and frequently includes excerpts from its script, and analyses it in terms of
characterisation, treatment, production, and use of camera. A separate chapter focuses
on Kurosawa's cinematographic methods, techniques, and style. Dozens of film stills
throughout the text present notable scenes from these movies. A complete filmography
and a selective bibliography are also included.

1426 **The Japanese movie: an illustrated history.**
Donald Richie, preface by Teinosuke Kinugasa. Tokyo; New York:
Kodansha International, 1982. rev. ed. 212p.
Pictures and text covering a span of over eighty years recreate the history of the film in
Japan. While this volume is less scholarly than *The Japanese film: art and industry*
(q.v.), it nevertheless offers an excellent descriptive and evaluative introduction to the
Japanese cinema and illustrates that with nearly five hundred stills of scenes from
hundreds of movies as well as with numerous photographs of film directors in action.

1427 **Ozu: his life and films.**
Donald Richie. Berkeley, California; London: University of
California Press, 1974. 275p. bibliog.
A critical study of Ozu Yasujirō (1903-63), the 'most Japanese' of Japan's greatest film
directors. Richie begins with a discussion of the subjects and themes of Ozu's films as
well as of the similarities among his pictures and the limitations of the 'Ozu world'. He
then traces the development of Ozu's films from their beginnings through scriptwriting,
shooting, and editing. He also explains and interprets the artistic strategies and
implications of his work. An extensive, chronologically organised, biographical
filmography covers each film, indicating the circumstances of its production and placing
it within the context of this director's entire career. Numerous black-and-white stills
illustrate the book. A special portfolio section reproduces Ozu's sketches, notebook
entries, and shooting scripts for a number of his films.

1428 **Currents in Japanese cinema: essays by Tadao Sato.**
Tadao Satō, translated with an introduction by Gregory Barrett.
Tokyo; New York: Kodansha International, 1982. 288p.
A collection of essays by an extremely popular and prolific film critic. Reflecting Satō's
anti-feudalistic stance, his interest in the sentiments of the average man, and his own
belief in human progress, these essays deal with such topics as the influence of foreign
films on Japanese cinema, the depiction of film heroines, Japanese war films, the
meaning of life in the movies of Kurosawa Akira, films about the family and about the
villain respectively, the cinematic techniques of Mizoguchi Kenji, Ozu Yasujirō and
Naruse Mikio, the portrayal of American–Japanese relations in Japanese films, and
film developments during the 1960s. Most of Satō's essays are taken from his widely
acclaimed book *Nihon eiga shisōshi* ('The Intellectual History of the Japanese Film';

Tokyo, 1970), a publication which altered the course of film criticism by introducing a new approach that judged movies more on the basis of the sentiments which they expressed than on their ideology or conformity to aesthetic standards.

A lateral view: essays on contemporary Japan.
See item no. 26.

Censorship in imperial Japan.
See item no. 221.

Something like an autobiography.
See item no. 329.

War without mercy: race and power in the Pacific War.
See item no. 686.

Contemporary Japanese literature: an anthology of fiction, film, and other writing since 1945.
See item no. 1057.

All-Japan: the catalogue of everything Japanese.
See item no. 1552.

Kenji Mizoguchi: a guide to references and resources.
See item no. 1578.

Akira Kurosawa: a guide to references and resources.
See item no. 1585.

Japan: a comprehensive annotated catalogue of documentary and theatrical films on Japan available in the United States.
See item no. 1586.

Food and Drink

1429   **At home with Japanese cooking.**
Elizabeth Andoh.   New York: Knopf, 1980. 254p.

An American who was apprenticed at the Yanagihara School of Classical Japanese Cooking shares the kind of home cooking that she came to know and enjoy during her many years in Japan. Andoh describes the techniques and equipment of the typical Japanese kitchen; discusses the incorporation of Japanese cuisine into everyday meals and meal planning; provides recipes for soups, rice, noodles, braised and simmered foods, grilled and skillet-grilled foods, deep-fried foods, steamed foods, mixed, sauced and tossed foods, pickles, sweet things, and beverages; and lists the basic foodstuffs used in Japanese cooking together with information about their purchase, storage, and nutritional value. Many of the recipes are accompanied by instructive black-and-white drawings.

1430   **Cook Japanese.**
Masaru Doi, photographs by Yoshikatsu Saeki.   Tokyo; Palo Alto, California: Kodansha International, 1970. 2nd ed. 129p.

Sixty-four recipes, each accompanied by a full-page colour photograph of the finished dish arranged in serving plates, bowls, and containers that enhance their visual appeal, are grouped together under the headings 'party food', 'appetizers', 'egg dishes', 'rice dishes', 'fish', 'chicken', 'beef', 'pork', 'ground meat', and 'desserts'. Prepared especially for the American household, each easy-to-follow recipe includes a listing of ingredients, an indication of its appropriate cooking utensils and equipment, the method of preparation and cooking, and variations of the dish itself.

1431   *Saké*: **a drinker's guide.**
Hiroshi Kondō, foreword by George Plimpton.   Tokyo; New York: Kodansha International, 1984. 128p.

This illustrated history and guide to the world of Japan's national drink begins with a discussion of the history and lore of saké and an explanation of the process by which this alcoholic beverage is brewed from fermented rice. Part two – 'Principles of

574

Food and Drink

Connoisseurship' – introduces the special vocabulary for describing the attributes of saké, identifies the varieties and the best brands, explains the etiquette and utensils associated with drinking saké, indicates the seasonal foods to order or serve with this drink, and lists the fifty best public drinking places in Tokyo and elsewhere in Japan together with the types of food which they serve.

1432   **The book of sushi.**
Kinjirō Ōmae, Yuzuru Tachibana, foreword by Jean-Pierre Rampal.
Tokyo; New York: Kodansha International, 1981. 127p. map.
Reprinted, Kodansha International, 1988.
A beautifully illustrated guide to the world of sushi, an assortment of many colourful varieties of raw fish and other ingredients combined with vinegar-flavoured boiled rice. Ōmae and Tachibana discuss the nature and operations of the typical sushi shop, the various types and ways of making sushi, Tokyo's famed Tsukiji fish market and the buying and selling of seafood, the apprenticeship and training of the sushi chef, the ways that sushi can be arranged on serving dishes, sushi's nutritional value, its history, and its regional variations. In addition, they include such useful information as the proper manner of ordering and eating sushi at a sushi shop and the ways for making and serving this dish on one's own.

1433   **A taste of Japan: food fact and fable; what the people eat; customs and etiquette.**
Donald Richie.   Tokyo; New York: Kodansha International, 1985.
112p.
This illustrated exploration of everyday Japanese cuisine, its history, and its place in Japanese life should enable Western readers to view Japanese foods as the Japanese themselves do. Richie describes several popular dishes – among them sushi, sukiyaki, tempura, tofu, *tonkatsu* ('pork cutlets'), *unagi* ('charcoal-broiled eels'), *onigiri* ('rice balls'), *tsukemono* ('pickles'), *okashi* ('sweets'), saké, and *ocha* ('green tea') – and indicates how they should be eaten. He also introduces some of the customs and etiquette of Japanese cuisine, and explains various facets of Japan's food culture such as why rice is considered basic to every meal, why the Japanese insist so much that food be fresh and natural-looking, and why saké is normally served hot. Richie does not, however, discuss how dishes should be prepared nor does he provide any recipes.

1434   **Japanese cooking.**
Jon Spayde, introduction by Kazuko Emi.   Secaucus, New Jersey:
Chartwell Books; London: Century, 1984. 223p. map.
A wide range of authentic recipes from basic dishes to regional variations are accompanied by background information about the land, history, and people of Japan. Dividing his book into three major sections – 'The Fundamentals' (utensils, ingredients, preparing fish, preparing vegetables, cooking techniques, beverages, cooking at home); 'Basic Dishes' (soups, sashimi, broiling and pan-frying, steaming, simmering, deep-frying, one-pot cooking, rice, salads); and 'Regional Dishes' – Spayde shows in both words and numerous full-colour photographs many of the elements that are involved in preparing and serving contemporary Japanese cuisine. Nearly one hundred often beautifully illustrated recipes are included.

575

1435   A feast for the eyes: the Japanese art of food arrangement.
Yoshio Tsuchiya, with Masaru Yamamoto, photographs by Eiji Kōri,
translated by Juliet Winters Carpenter.   Tokyo; New York:
Kodansha International, 1985. 165p.

Central to the aesthetics of Japanese cooking is the art of serving food in dishes which enhance its appeal and attractiveness. This lavishly illustrated volume is not a cookbook but rather a guide to the ways of arranging food that is already prepared. Numerous photographs depicting seasonal food arrangements are followed by an extended discussion of the art of food arrangement. Readers are shown how to use dishes of contrasting shapes and sizes, how to present food aesthetically, and how to harmonise the elements of a meal through the proper placement of food in its serving vessels. An historical perspective is provided through surveys of the function and beauty of lacquerware and ceramics as well as of food and service vessels in Japan from ancient times to the twentieth century.

1436   Sushi made easy.
Nobuko Tsuda, foreword by Donald Richie.   New York; Tokyo:
Weatherhill, 1982. 128p.

Easy-to-follow instructions for the preparation of sushi, a very popular assortment of pieces of raw fish and/or vegetables together with vinegar-flavoured boiled rice. After introducing the ingredients (vegetables, dried foods, liquids, fish, and shellfish) and utensils for making sushi, Tsuda offers directions for cleaning and filleting twenty-one kinds of fish; explains the principles of sushi-making; and provides forty-two illustrated recipes for making *nigiri-zushi* ('finger sushi'), *nori maki* ('rolled sushi'), *chirashi-zushi* ('scattered sushi'), *hako-zushi* ('box sushi'), *oshi-zushi* ('pressed sushi'), and other varieties of sushi at home. Serving suggestions, guidelines for selecting beverages when eating sushi, six recipes for soups, and a list of North American suppliers of Japanese foods supplement the text.

1437   Kaiseki: Zen tastes in Japanese cooking.
Kaichi Tsuji, foreword by Yasunari Kawabata, introductions by
Sōshitsu Sen, Seizō Hayashiya, photographs by Muneori Kuzunishi,
Yoshihiro Matsuda, adapted by Akiko Sugawara.   Kyōto: Tankōsha;
Tokyo; Palo Alto, California: Kodansha International, 1972. 207p.

Kaiseki cooking is a refined type of cuisine associated with the world of the tea ceremony. It seeks to blend aroma, taste, colour, texture, and serving utensils with the season, the guests, and the particular occasion. This work surveys the historical background of *kaiseki* cooking, discusses the pottery and utensils that are most appropriate, describes full-course *kaiseki* meals for tea gatherings during each month of the year, and examines each of the elements in a *kaiseki* meal. Ninety-six full-colour photographs illustrate the serving utensils and the food which they contain in order to suggest the aesthetics of *kaiseki* as well as to depict the meals themselves. The cursory manner in which recipes and lists of ingredients are presented limits the book's usefulness as a practical cookbook.

1438   Japanese cooking: a simple art.
Shizuo Tsuji, with Mary Sutherland, introduction by M. F. K.
Fisher.   Tokyo; New York: Kodansha International, 1980. 517p.

Reportedly Kodansha's all-time best-seller, this encyclopaedic volume first introduces the basic elements of the Japanese meal, the ingredients of Japanese cooking, the proper utensils and knives, and the procedures for selecting and cutting fish, chicken and vegetables. All of the basic methods and principal types of prepared foods are then presented: bonito stock (dashi), making soups, slicing and serving sashimi, grilling and pan-frying, steaming, simmering, deep-frying, Japanese salads, 'one-pot cooking' (*nabemono*), rice, varieties of sushi, noodles, pickled vegetables (*tsukemono*), sweets and confections (*okashi*), and tea and saké. Part two provides 130 additional recipes, ranging from simple daily meals to dishes prepared for banquets. Colour plates and line drawings illustrate suggested arrangements of some of the foods as well as their cooking techniques. Tsuji, the proprietor of the largest school for training professional chefs in Japan, has also co-authored with Koichirō Hata an illustrated cookbook entitled *Practical Japanese cooking: easy and elegant* (Tokyo; New York: Kodansha International, 1986, 151p.), which offers over one hundred more recipes (using ingredients readily available in the West) for appetizers, soups, fish, seafood, beef and pork, chicken, egg, tofu, vegetables, rice, sushi, noodles, one-pot dishes, and 'other delectables'.

1439　**A first book of Japanese cooking.**
Masako Yamaoka.　Tokyo; New York: Kodansha International, 1984. 154p.

A longtime teacher of homestyle Japanese cooking presents one hundred recipes using ingredients readily found in a growing number of supermarkets and Oriental food stores in the United States. These recipes cover the entire range of basic Japanese cuisine: from soups, appetizers, vegetables, and chicken, to tofu dishes, sushi, yakitori, and tempura. Several of the recipes – including ones for salmon and *shiitake* mushroom sushi and for chicken-stuffed squash balls – are not frequently served in Japan but appear to have been included in order to increase the book's appeal to American readers. Suggested menus for cocktails, sushi, yakitori, tempura, and mixed grill parties are also provided.

1440　**Good food from a Japanese temple.**
Soei Yoneda, with Koei Hoshino, translated by Kim Schuefftan, introduction by Robert Farrar Capon.　Tokyo; New York: Kodansha International, 1982. 224p.

An introduction and guide to the six hundred-year-old Zen Buddhist tradition of *shōjin ryōri*, a type of vegetarian cooking that entirely excludes meat, fish, eggs, and dairy products in accordance with the Buddhist injunction against killing. Soei Yoneda, the abbess of the Sankoin temple in Tokyo, describes the basic steps for preparing this type of food and provides over two hundred recipes for a wide range of dishes, grouped together largely by the season of the year. She also includes a short chapter about how this vegetarian style of cooking developed, a glossary, an explanatory list of ingredients (which indicates the differences between the American and Japanese varieties of certain ingredients), and information about appropriate cookware and traditional methods of presenting dishes that are ready to be served.

Old Kyoto: a guide to traditional shops, restaurants, and inns.
See item no. 78.

Good Tokyo restaurants.
See item no. 84.

Food and Drink

A guide to food buying in Japan.
See item no. 85.

The guide to Japanese food and restaurants.
See item no. 87.

Zen guide: where to meditate in Japan.
See item no. 97.

Japanese crafts.
See item no. 1369.

New Japanalia: past and present.
See item no. 1551.

All-Japan: the catalogue of everything Japanese.
See item no. 1552.

Mock Joya's things Japanese.
See item no. 1561.

See also the section 'Recreation: Tea Ceremony (*Chanoyu*)'.

Sports

The martial arts

1441 **Iai-jitsu: the art of drawing the sword.**
Darrell Craig. Tokyo: Lotus Press, 1981. 257p. bibliog. Reprinted as
Iai-jitsu: center of the circle, Rutland, Vermont and Tokyo: Tuttle,
1988. 257p.

Iai-jutsu or *iaidō*, the technique of swordsmanship that includes the skill of cutting
one's opponent on the draw or by a vertical cut through the head, consists of four
movements: drawing the sword (*nukitsuke*), cutting (*kiritsuke*), removing the blood
from the sword (*chinburi*), and returning the sword to its scabbard (*notō*). Focusing on
the seven *kata* ('forms') of *iaidō* of the All-Japan Kendō Federation as well as on the
basic styles of the Mu Gai Ryū, Craig introduces the basic characteristics of the
Japanese sword, the proper sword procedures, the basic movements and philosophy of
iaidō, sword testing, the styles of Mu Gai Ryū, and the *kata* of kendō. Many line
drawings illustrate his explanations.

1442 **Classical budo.**
Donn F. Draeger. New York; Tokyo: Weatherhill, 1973. 127p. (The
Martial Arts and Ways of Japan, 2).

The classical *budō* ('martial ways') are 'first and foremost spiritual disciplines whose
ultimate goal, achieved through rigorous and systematic physical training, is [the
cultivation of] self-realization and self-perfection in the Zen sense'. Oriented towards a
general audience, this volume traces the development of the classical *budō* during the
Tokugawa period; examines their underlying concepts, rationales, and methods of
training; discusses the evolution and salient characteristics of the classical *budō* systems
that involve the use of weapons (e.g., kendō and *iaidō*) as well as those systems that do
not (known collectively as judo); and briefly considers the status and practice of the
classical *budō* in present-day Japan. Throughout his text Draeger shows how Zen
concepts and attitudes permeate all of the classical *budō* disciplines. A combination of

traditional woodblock prints and black-and-white photographs of modern masters in action illustrate the development and techniques of the classical *budō*.

1443 **Classical bujutsu.**
Donn F. Draeger. New York; Tokyo: Weatherhill, 1973. 109p. (The Martial Arts and Ways of Japan, 1).

Bujutsu in pre-modern times taught the warrior how to use his weapons with a 'perfect unity of thought and action' and prepared him both technically and psychologically to 'confront death at any moment while remaining in full control of himself'. This illustrated general history and exploration of Japan's traditional systems for training in the martial arts begins with overviews of Japan's martial tradition, the historical development of the warrior class, and the growth of *bujutsu*. Part two describes sixteen major martial arts – among them *kenjutsu* ('use of the sword'), *kyūjutsu* ('archery'), *bajutsu* ('horsemanship'), *suiei-jutsu* ('combat swimming'), and *yoroi kumi-uchi* ('grappling in armour') – that entail the use of a variety of weapons including swords, halberds, hardwood staffs, spears, bows and arrows, iron bars, and sickles and chains. The volume concludes with an epilogue entitled 'Classical Bujutsu Today'.

1444 **Modern bujutsu and budo.**
Donn F. Draeger. New York; Tokyo: Weatherhill, 1974. 190p. (The Martial Arts and Ways of Japan, 3).

Draeger discusses the general nature and scope of the martial arts (*bujutsu*) and martial ways (*budō*) since the Meiji Restoration of 1868. He elucidates the historical background, fundamental characteristics, aims, techniques, and training methods of fifteen major martial arts including *battō-jutsu* ('the art of drawing the sword'), *keijo-jutsu* ('the art of using the police stick'), *keibō-sōhō* ('the use of the patrolman's short wooden club'), kendō, jūdō, *karate-dō* ('the way of karate'), aikidō, and *naginata-dō* ('the way of the halberd'). He also indicates how these modern disciplines have evolved, establishes their relationships with classical *bujutsu* and *budō*, and comments on their technical and spiritual natures and on their popularity around the world.

1445 **Ninjutsu: the art of invisibility; Japan's feudal-age espionage methods.**
Donn F. Draeger, introduction by Jack Seward. Tokyo: Lotus Press, 1977; distributed in the United States by Phoenix Books (Phoenix, Arizona). 118p.

A basic introduction to *ninjutsu* (literally, 'the art of stealthy movement'), a martial art that entails making oneself 'invisible' by artifice or stratagem in order to avoid detection. Practised by the *ninja* ('secret agents'), it was especially used for the purpose of espionage, theft, arson, and assassination during the Tokugawa period. Draeger discusses the history and organisation of *ninjutsu*; its training methods and the skills which the *ninja* were expected to master; various operating techniques; the *ninja*'s standard costume, tools, and weapons; their tactics, ruses, and feats; and the facts and legends surrounding both *ninjutsu* and the *ninja*.

1446 **Karate-dō kyōhan: the master text.**
Gichin Funakoshi, translated by Tsutomu Ohshima. Tokyo; New York: Kodansha International, 1973. 256p.

In this well-known manual, first published in Japanese in 1936 and revised in 1958, Funakoshi discusses the development, philosophy, and techniques of karate; describes its fundamental elements and basic training; and portrays and explains at length nineteen formal karate exercises or *kata*. He also briefly comments on engagement matches, the vital points of the human body, and maxims for the trainee. Illustrated by more than 1,200 photographs of various movements, forms, and postures in karate, the author's detailed explanations and figures are designed to help students attain substantial proficiency in karate through self-study as well as through group instruction. Information about the life (1868-1957) of this great master of karate as well as about his personality and his way of thinking may be found in his memoirs, *Karate-dō: my way of life* (Tokyo; New York: Kodansha International, 1975, 127p.).

1447 **A book of five rings.**
Miyamoto Musashi, translated with an introduction by Victor Harris. Woodstock, New York: Overlook Press; London: Allison and Busby, 1974. 95p. map. Reprinted, Toronto, Ontario; New York: Bantam Books, 1982. 107p. Woodstock, New York: Overlook Press, 1982. 95p. London: Flamingo, 1984. 112p.

Miyamoto Musashi (1584-1645), a master swordsman and painter of the early Tokugawa period, formulates his philosophy of the 'way of the sword' in this classic work on swordsmanship. Allegedly transmitted to a disciple on Miyamoto's deathbed, *Gorin no sho (Book of five rings)* is not a thesis on battle strategy but rather a very perceptive and psychologically-oriented 'guide for men who want to learn strategy'. Its underlying philosophy – influenced by Zen Buddhism, Shintō, and Confucianism – is applicable to business, sport, and many other areas of life as well as to the martial arts. The book is considered to be one of the most essential works for individuals seeking to master any of the martial arts. It is also useful for illuminating a traditional Japanese approach to life and has become quite popular among American businessmen.

1448 **Karate training: the samurai legacy and modern practice.**
Robin L. Rielly, foreword by Teruyuki Okazaki. Rutland, Vermont; Tokyo: Tuttle, 1985. 238p. bibliog.

Rielly details the history of karate, samurai ethos and traditions, and the influences which changes in those traditions have had on the practice of karate in Japan. In addition, he provides a profusely illustrated manual that features presentations about *kumite* or sparring techniques ('a variety of karate training drills designed to give the practitioners experience in using diverse techniques against an actual opponent') and explanations of selected *kata* (exercises in the form of 'predetermined sets of movements that represent the motions of blocking, striking, punching, and kicking against imaginary opponents') in karate. The manual is designed particularly for students who have advanced beyond the beginning stages of this martial art. Readers interested in a more general history of the development of karate throughout East and Southeast Asia as well as in the United States will find Bruce A. Haines' *Karate's history and traditions* (Rutland, Vermont; Tokyo: Tuttle, 1968, 192p.) both informative and reliable.

1449 **This is kendo: the art of Japanese fencing.**
Junzō Sasamori, Gordon Warner, foreword by Juichi Tsushima. Rutland, Vermont; Tokyo: Tuttle, 1964. 159p. bibliog.

This fully illustrated introduction to the essential nature and basic techniques of the traditional art of Japanese fencing surveys the origins and history of kendō and describes and analyses this martial art. Major subjects presented include the equipment, fundamental procedures and techniques of kendō, the physical and psychological aspects of kendō, the relationship between kendō and Zen Buddhism, and the traditions governing kendō etiquette and techniques. Descriptions of the most important strikes, offensive and defensive positions, and training exercises are also provided.

1450   **Aikido: the way of harmony.**
John Stevens, under the direction of Rinjirō Shirata, foreword by
Yoshimi Hanzawa. Boulder, Colorado; London: Shambhala, 1984.
198p.
An introductory guide to aikidō, a system of self-defence that employs immobilising holds and twisting throws which enable a practitioner to make use of his opponent's own strength and momentum in order to defeat him. The book begins with a biographical account of Ueshiba Morihei (1883-1969), the founder of aikidō; an overview of the history of this martial art; and some brief comments about its essence and training. Most of the volume consists of black-and-white photo sequences illustrating 'breath meditation' (*kokyū-hō*) and the performance of such techniques as *shihō-nage* ('four directions throw'), *irimi-nage* ('entering throw'), *kaiten* ('open and throw'), *taninsu-gake* ('multiple attack'), *osae waza* ('pinning techniques'), and *ushiro waza* ('rear techniques').

1451   **The spirit of aikidō.**
Kisshōmaru Ueshiba, translated with a foreword by Taitetsu Unno.
Tokyo; New York: Kodansha International, 1984. 126p.
Ueshiba, the chairman of the Aikikai Foundation (the principal aikidō organisation in Japan) and the third son and heir of the founder of aikidō, sets forth the basic philosophy and ideals of this martial art in an effort to dispel a number of misconceptions regarding both its nature and its objectives. He explains the underlying principles and physical movements of aikidō; emphasizes the importance of understanding the philosophy of aikidō in order to master one's mind, develop one's character, and cultivate its proper techniques; indicates how each individual can realise 'a dynamic life based on the unity of universal and personal *ki*' through training and practice; and concludes with a brief history of aikidō and its internationalisation. Sixteen pages of black-and-white photographs depict the history of aikidō and illustrate some representative techniques.

1452   **Japanese swordsmanship: technique and practice.**
Gordon Warner, Donn F. Draeger.   New York; Tokyo: Weatherhill,
1982. 296p. bibliog.
The non-combative physical and mental discipline of modern Japanese swordsmanship known as *iaidō* involves the techniques of drawing, cutting with, and returning the Japanese sword to its scabbard. It may be the most philosophically oriented of all martial arts. This authoritative introduction focuses first on the evolution of the Japanese sword, swordsmanship and classical warrior education, and the moral precepts of classical warriors. It then discusses the background, development, and essence of *iaidō*; the choice, nomenclature, care, and maintenance of the Japanese sword; the proper costume for *iaidō* as well as its formal etiquette; and the ten basic *seitei-gata* techniques which comprise the modern *iaidō* curriculum. Hundreds of

sequential photographs and other illustrations depict the fundamental procedures involved in the making of a skilful swordsman.

The Japanese sword.
See item no. 1373.

The samurai sword: a handbook.
See item no. 1375.

Sumo and baseball

1453 **Sumo: from rite to sport.**
Patricia Lee Cuyler, revised by Doreen Simmons. New York; Tokyo: Weatherhill, 1985. rev. ed. 230p. bibliog.
An examination of a unique two thousand-year-old form of wrestling that is regarded as Japan's national sport. Cuyler details the historical evolution of sumo from its prehistoric, religious origins to its current status as an extremely popular spectator sport. She also explains the complexities of present-day sumo, including its rules and rituals, ranking system, forms of training and practice, fighting techniques, management, and the stables in which the sumo wrestlers live and train.

1454 **The book of sumo: sport, spectacle, and ritual.**
Doug Kenrick. New York; Tokyo: Walker/Weatherhill, 1969. 171p. bibliog.
A detailed account of Japan's national sport, written by the sumo columnist for Tokyo's *Asahi Evening News*. Kenrick describes the rules and ranking of sumo; the places and ways to view this popular spectator sport; the wrestlers, recruits, and their accoutrements; the stables which house, train, and manage sumo wrestlers; the *yokozuna* ('grand champions') of sumo and, in particular, the champion of the 1960s, Taiho the Great; the past and present-day techniques of sumo wrestling; the staging and ritual of sumo tournaments; the referees, judges, and adminstrators of sumo; the remuneration and recognition which sumo wrestlers receive; non-Japanese wrestlers and sumo wrestling abroad; the historical background of sumo; and the sumo wrestlers of 1968. A combined glossary-index facilitates the use of this volume as a reference work.

1455 **Rikishi: the men of sumo.**
Joel Sackett, text by Wes Benson. New York; Tokyo: Weatherhill, 1986. 182p.
Some 148 photographs vividly document the lifestyle and activities (in 1985) of one group of sumo wrestlers (*rikishi*), men who may weigh up to five hundred pounds and tower well over six feet in height but whose success in the sumo ring is measured more by technique and strength than by size. Scenes of early morning training sessions, mid-morning meals, dressing for bouts, signing autographs, the tense moments before a tournament match, the *rikishi* in times of relaxation, touring the countryside within the

Hokuriku region, and the ceremonial retirement of a *rikishi* are all recorded by the documentary photographer Joel Sackett. Benson's introductory essay outlines a day in a *rikishi*'s life and provides an insider's view of the sumo world and the champions who populate it.

1456   **The chrysanthemum and the bat: baseball samurai style.**
         Robert Whiting.   New York: Dodd, Mead; Tokyo: Permanent Press,
         1977. 247p.   Reprinted, New York: Avon Press, 1983.
Whiting demonstrates that baseball in Japan differs in several key respects from the game played in the United States. He recounts numerous events in the history of this sport since its introduction into Japan and describes the organisation and management of Japanese teams, the ways in which the games are played, the experiences of some of its famous players, and the growing Japanese enthusiasm for baseball. He also shows how such Japanese social values as the emphasis on group identity, co-operation, hard work, respect for age, seniority, and 'face' have permeated almost every facet of this sport and have modified its basic character. For a complementary study of the history of baseball in Japan, see Robert Obojski's *The rise of Japanese baseball power* (Radnor, Pennsylvania: Chilton Book Co., 1975, 230p.). Robert Whiting's latest book – *You gotta have wa* (New York: Macmillan; London: Collier Macmillan, 1989, 339p.) – in turn presents an anecdotal and informative account of Japanese-style baseball during the 1980s, and describes some of the difficulties that imported American baseball players faced in getting along with the Japanese because of major cultural gaps.

Sadaharu Oh: a Zen way of baseball.
See item no. 338.

Recreation

General

1457　**Furo: the Japanese bath.**
Peter Grilli, photographs by Dana Levy, foreword by Isamu
Noguchi.　Tokyo; New York: Kodansha International, 1985. 191p.
5 maps.

The high regard in which the Japanese have traditionally held bathing as a pleasurable experience as well as a way for getting clean is depicted in this beautifully illustrated volume on the *furo* ('Japanese bath'). Grilli traces the history of the bath from early Shintō purification rites, through the rise of public bath-houses, which during the seventeenth century became places to socialise as well as to bathe, to the emergence of the private bath in modern times. He also explores some of Japan's numerous hot springs (*onsen*) and appends an annotated guide to more than one hundred of these popular resorts. Many forms of the bath today are surveyed, including the sauna, spa, handicrafted tubs in luxurious Japanese inns, and mass-produced metal or plastic tubs in lower-class homes. Forty-eight pages of colour photographs and eighty duotone illustrations show the *furo* in its various forms.

1458　**Go for beginners.**
Kaoru Iwamoto.　Berkeley, California; Tokyo: Ishi Press, 1972.
151p.　Reprinted in a slightly expanded and updated version, with an
introduction by John C. Stephenson, New York: Pantheon Books,
1976. 148p. bibliog.

Go, a game for two players in which black and white stones are alternately placed at the intersections of lines on a board with the object of capturing the stones of one's opponent and gaining control over the open spaces on the board, originated in China and came to Japan around the fifth century AD. Iwamoto provides an introduction to go, a brief demonstration game, an explanation of the rules of go, illustrations of the simplest techniques, and illustrations of many easy and some more difficult problems which go players encounter. The appendixes include a concise list of rules, a glossary of the more common technical go terms, and a list of go organisations. Other available books about go include *Stepping stones to go: a game of strategy*, by Shigemi Kishikawa (Rutland, Vermont; Tokyo: Tuttle, 1965, 159p.), and *Go: a guide to the game*, by David B. Pritchard (London: Faber and Faber; Harrisburg, Pennsylvania: Stackpole Books, 1973, 216p.).

1459 **Shogi, Japan's game of strategy.**
Trevor Leggett. Rutland, Vermont; Tokyo: Tuttle, 1966. 99p.

Step-by-step instructions, clearly illustrated by diagrams, explain how to play the game of *shōgi*. Frequently referred to as 'Japanese chess', it makes use of a square board with a grid of eighty-one squares and forty flat wooden pieces of an elongated irregular pentagon shape which are distinguished by Chinese characters written on each side. This book describes the layout of the *shōgi* board and the moves of each of the pieces, the strategies for effectively using the pieces during the course of a game, the use of those pieces which are captured from one's opponent, the novices' games, the various possible openings and their results, and a few game positions that show how to deal with various *shōgi* situations. A stiff paper *shōgi* board is bound into the book, together with shōgi pieces that can be punched out from an accompanying sheet.

1460 **The after hours: modern Japan and the search for enjoyment.**
David W. Plath. Berkeley, California: University of California Press, 1964. 222p. Reprinted, Westport, Connecticut: Greenwood Press, 1984.

This ethnographic inquiry into the impact of modernisation upon the Japanese focuses on how three representative families have adjusted to the increase in leisure time which has accompanied Japan's postwar prosperity. Plath first sketches the modernisation that has occurred in the city of Matsumoto and the village of Ariake within the Anchiku region of central Honshū. He then depicts the social and physical work-setting and home environments of a salary-earner, a grocer, and a farmer (three occupational types) and their families during the late 1950s. In the course of his study, Plath examines their attitudes towards work and leisure, considers some of the alternatives open to them in their choice of activities, and discusses the history of schedules and time patterns in Japan. A glimpse of the emerging Japanese image of the 'after-hours man' concludes the book.

1461 **The art of the Japanese kite.**
Tal Streeter. New York; Tokyo: Weatherhill, 1974. 181p. bibliog.

A well-illustrated general introduction to the history, varieties, manufacturing techniques, and decorations of Japanese kites. Streeter, an American sculptor who spent two years in Japan studying kites and the art of kite-making, introduces six master kite-makers and one kite collector, describes the workmanship involved in making fine kites, and portrays several kite-flying events including the annual kite festivals held at Shirone and Hamamatsu. He also surveys the history of Oriental kites, and offers brief directions on how to make and fly one's own Japanese kite.

A guide to Japanese hot springs.
See item no. 80.

Zen and Japanese culture.
See item no. 492.

Yakuza: the explosive account of Japan's criminal underworld.
See item no. 569.

Geisha.
See item no. 576.

The master of *go***.**
See item no. 1064.

Zen culture.
See item no. 1196.

The world of origami.
See item no. 1364.

Creative origami.
See item no. 1367.

Manga! manga! the world of Japanese comic books.
See item no. 1480.

Japanese Philately.
See item no. 1522.

Flower arrangement (ikebana)

1462 **Ikebana: a practical and philosophical guide to Japanese flower arrangement.**
Stella Coe, edited by Mary L. Stewart, foreword by Hiroshi Teshigahara.   Woodstock, New York: Overlook Press; London: Century, 1984. 176p. Reprinted, London: Octopus, 1986.

An illustrated presentation of the basic arrangements of the Sōgetsu School of ikebana in the sequence in which they should be studied: from the simplest arrangements to those which 'require greater dexterity and deeper understanding'. Coe first discusses the orgins of ikebana and its various schools, and the materials, containers and tools used in Japanese flower arrangement. She then focuses on the principles and fundamentals of two basic styles used in Sōgetsu School ikebana – *moribana* and *nagaire* (arrangements made in low, shallow containers and in tall containers respectively) – and on advanced arrangements (usually called 'free-style', 'abstract', and 'avant-garde') as well as on the ways in which a wide variety of materials can be used in arrangements that are attuned to the four seasons of the year. A concluding chapter, 'Ikebana as a Way of Life', introduces a number of Zen themes popular with ikebana students.

1463 **Ikebana: spirit and technique.**
Shusui Komoda, Horst Pointner, translated by Eileen Baum.   Poole, Dorset: Blandford Press, 1980. 184p. bibliog.

This textbook to the art of arranging flowers opens with brief explanations of traditional Japanese aesthetics, the Japanese love of flowers, the concept of ikebana,

Recreation. Flower arrangement (ikebana)

the history of its several styles, and the technique of ikebana. Ninety-two concise lessons 'prepared and tested in accordance with the knowledge and skills which the authors assume a European or non-Japanese can bring to the art of ikebana' begin with the *moribana* style and work their way through *nageire* and modern and classical *shōka* to *rikka* and the free style of ikebana. Over five hundred diagrams, sketches, full-colour plates, and monochrome photographs facilitate the use of this book as a self-study course by both beginning and advanced students.

1464 **Flower arrangement: the ikebana way.**
Minobu Ohi, Senei Ikenobō, Hōun Ohara, Sōfū Teshigahara; translated by Seiko Aoyama, Yoshimasa Ichikawa, Ruth Dillon, Fukiko Yamaguchi, Hisako Komine; edited by William C. Steere. Tokyo: Shufunotomo; New York: Grosset and Dunlap; London: Souvenir Press, 1972. 286p.
The headmasters of three of the most important schools of ikebana in Japan – Ikenobō Senei (Ikenobō School), Ohara Hōun (Ohara School), and Teshigahara Sōfū (Sōgetsu School) – provide 'a sense of the seriousness, the creativity, the great flexibility of symbolism and ritualism, and the underlying communication of emotion' that is inherent in the art of Japanese flower arranging. They discuss the philosophy, fundamental form, and evolution of ikebana; present the basic rules and practices of their respective schools; and illustrate (by means of some 450 photographs) various ikebana methods, forms, and styles. Ohi's introductory essay, 'The History of Ikebana', surveys the origins and evolution of floral art in Japan up to the present day.

1465 **The masters' book of ikebana: background and principles of Japanese flower arrangement.**
Edited by Donald Richie, Meredith Weatherby, with lessons by Sen'ei Ikenobō, Hōun Ohara, Sōfū Teshigahara; background essay by Donald Richie, foreword by Haru Reischauer. Tokyo: Bijutsu Shuppansha; London: Thames and Hudson, 1966. 272p. bibliog.
Concerned with elucidating the philosophy and place of ikebana in Japanese life and in Japanese homes, this oversized, extensively illustrated volume aims at providing 'an authoritative guide to Japanese flower arrangement in all its many aspects – practical, historical, philosophical, aesthetic, visual, and sheerly pleasurable'. Richie's background essay entitled 'Ikebana in Japanese Life' traces the history of ikebana from its medieval origins as floral arrangements used only for religious purposes, through its evolution as a secular art, to its continuing role as a 'living and meaningful art' in postwar Japan. 'Ikebana in the Home' (part two) contains general introductions to the Ikenobō, Ohara, and Sōgetsu Schools together with explanations of their basic principles through lessons prepared by their headmasters. A concluding section covering the basic techniques of ikebana briefly discusses the selection of containers, the cutting, trimming and bending of flowers, the way to fix them in place, and recommended procedures for preserving plant material.

1466 **Japanese flower arrangement: classical and modern.**
Norman J. Sparnon, photography by Miki Takagi, forewords by Sōfū Teshigahara, Tadao Yamamoto. Rutland, Vermont; Tokyo: Tuttle; New York: Greystone Press, 1960. 264p. bibliog.
An authority in the art of flower arrangement introduces a broad range of classical and

modern floral arrangements as exemplified by the Sōgetsu and Ikenobō Schools of ikebana. Following an historical summary and overview of present-day ikebana, Sparnon presents a series of lessons in the basic styles of these two schools, focusing first on the *rikka* and *shōka* forms and then on free-style arrangements. One hundred colour plates and 115 figures illustrate the basic lessons and many different arrangements. Sparnon has also written a briefer guide to the principles of classical and modern flower arranging as expressed in the *moribana, nageire, shōka,* and *rikka* styles: *A guide to Japanese flower arrangement* (Tokyo: Shufunotomo, 1969, 78p. Reprinted, New York: Hippocrene Books, 1974). That volume includes several photographs of representative arrangements for each of these four styles.

Tea ceremony (*chanoyu*)

1467   The way of tea.
Rand Castile, foreword by Sen no Sōshitsu.   New York; Tokyo: Weatherhill, 1971. 329p. bibliog.

Intended for the student of *chadō* ('the way of tea') as well as for the general reader 'who wishes to learn about one of the fundamental shaping forces of Japanese culture', this is a comprehensive examination of the nature, practice, and meaning of the traditional Japanese tea ceremony. Castile traces the history of the ceremony from the time of its medieval origins; studies the gardens and architecture which constitute the ceremonial setting; introduces the major and minor tea utensils and comments on their production, attributes and other selected features; and describes and compares the non-professional and professional study of the tea ceremony. There are 159 monochrome photographs and illustrations (largely from Tokugawa period books) to accompany the text. Complementing this volume is the first major English-language history of *chanoyu: Tea in Japan: essays on the history of 'chanoyu'* (Honolulu, Hawaii: University of Hawaii Press, 1989, 285p.). Edited by Paul Varley and Isao Kumakura, it traces that history from the introduction of tea in the early ninth century, through the career of the great sixteenth-century tea master Sen no Rikyū and the reinterpretation of Rikyū's formulation of *chanoyu* by subsequent generations, to the mid-1800s. Also included is an essay about *wabi*, the central aesthetic form of *chanoyu* that evolved from various artistic tastes and philosophical and religious values.

1468   Tea ceremony utensils.
Ryōichi Fujioka, with Masaki Nakano, Hirokazu Arakawa, Seizō Hayashiya, translated and adapted with an introduction by Louise Allison Cort.   New York; Tokyo: Weatherhill/Shibundo, 1973. 142p. (Arts of Japan, 3).

An illustrated introduction to the historical background, aesthetic values, and role of the types of utensils used in the tea ceremony: the tea bowl, tea caddy and tea-leaf jar, tea scoop, kettle and lid rest, fresh-water and waste-water jars, flower container, incense and hearth utensils, utensils for the *kaiseki* meal, and boxes for tea ceremony utensils. Each object is described as a work of art attuned to the season and to the spirit of the occasion; but its practical function within the centuries-old tea ceremony is indicated as well.

Recreation. Tea ceremony (*chanoyu*)

1469 **Chanoyu: Japanese tea ceremony.**
Seizō Hayashiya, foreword by Sōshitsu Sen, preface by Noboru Gotō, catalogue adapted and translated by Emily J. Sano, essays by H. Paul Varley, Louise Allison Cort, Rand Castile, Sondra Castile. New York: Japan Society, 1979. 187p. bibliog.

The catalogue of a spring 1979 exhibition organised by the Japan House Gallery (New York) in co-operation with the Urasenke Foundation (Kyōto) and the Gotō Museum (Tokyo). Illustrations of one hundred outstanding Japanese, Chinese, and Korean utensils used in the tea ceremony are grouped together in ten sections covering painting, calligraphy, flower containers, incense and charcoal containers, kettles and braziers, tea containers, tea scoops, water jars, tea bowls, and serving bowls. Brief essays discuss the evolution of the Japanese tea ceremony from its origins to the late sixteenth century and from the late 1500s to the present day, depict the setting and aesthetics of the tea ceremony, and describe each of the categories of tea ceremony utensils that were on display.

1470 **The book of tea.**
Kakuzō Okakura, foreword and biographical sketch by Elise Grilli. Rutland, Vermont; Tokyo: Tuttle, 1956. 133p.

Long regarded as a classic introduction to the tea ceremony, this sentimental but very popular account of the philosophical underpinnings of tea (Okakura's 'cup of humanity') has been characterised by Elise Grilli as a work which reveals 'to the West a unified concept of art and life, of nature and art blended in a world anxious to find a way out from the maze of complexities into which it has blundered'. First published in 1906, the book consists of seven brief essays which discuss the tea ceremony and some of its formalities, the various schools of tea and their beliefs, Taoist and Zen Buddhist influences on the tea ceremony, the tea room and its atmosphere, the appreciation of art, the importance of flowers and floral arrangements, and some of the great tea masters of the past. Okakura Kakuzō (1862-1913) was an art critic, art historian, and philosopher whose writings brought him fame as an interpreter of Japan and strongly coloured Western perceptions of Japanese culture during the first half of the twentieth century. This work is also available in a number of other editions including one edited and introduced by Everett F. Bleiler (New York: Dover, 1964, 76p.), one published with an introduction and notes by Hiroshi Muraoka (Tokyo: Kenkyusha, 1948, 117p.) and one containing a foreword and afterword by Sōshitsu Sen XV that is scheduled for publication by Kodansha International (Tokyo and New York) in winter 1989-90.

1471 **Chado: the Japanese way of tea.**
Sōshitsu Sen, translated and edited by Masuo Yamaguchi and others. New York; Tokyo; Kyōto: Weatherhill/Tankōsha, 1979. 186p.

An adaptation of two books by the Grand Master of the Urasenke School of Tea concerning the tradition and practice of *chadō* ('the way of tea'). After briefly discussing its meaning and history, Sōshitsu Sen introduces the structures and garden which together constitute the surroundings for the tea ceremony; the utensils and decorations which form part of the ceremony; and the refreshments which are served. With the aid of hundreds of sequential black-and-white photographs, he describes a standard tea gathering in terms of its setting, utensils, cuisine, and step-by-step procedures from the arrival of the guest all the way through his or her departure for home. The author also explains the proper etiquette and manners that are associated with the tea ceremony, among them the appropriate ways of bowing, opening and closing sliding doors, examining a tea whisk, and partaking of various sweets as well as thin and thick tea.

1472 **The tea ceremony.**
Sen'ō Tanaka, photographs by Takeshi Nishikawa, foreword by Edwin O. Reischauer, preface by Yasushi Inoue.   Tokyo; New York: Kodansha International, 1973. 214p.   Reprinted, New York: Harmony Books, 1977.

A contemporary tea master's account of the tea ceremony and his explanation of the rationale behind its ritualised actions and behaviour. Tanaka traces the history of *chanoyu* ('the tea ceremony') from its twelfth-century origins to the present day, introduces the outstanding tea masters of the past and their individual styles, accompanies the reader through the performance of a tea ceremony, explains the aesthetics of *chanoyu* as well as the etiquette of preparing and serving tea, and shows how the teahouse and its landscape garden setting together with the tea utensils, flower arrangement, hanging scroll, incense, food, dress, and stylised actions of the tea master and his guests contribute to the overall atmosphere. Illustrated by eighty-four photographs, this book captures the aesthetic spirit that is the essence of *chanoyu* and provides the visitor in advance with an explanation of the proper behaviour to be displayed both before and during the ceremony itself.

Warlords, artists, and commoners: Japan in the sixteenth century.
See item no. 135.

Zen at Daitoku-ji.
See item no. 1190.

Zen culture.
See item no. 1196.

The enduring art of Japan.
See item no. 1226.

The unknown craftsman: a Japanese insight into beauty.
See item no. 1228.

Shigaraki, potters' valley.
See item no. 1280.

Shino and Oribe ceramics.
See item no. 1282.

Kaiseki: Zen tastes in Japanese cooking.
See item no. 1437.

Chanoyu Quarterly: Tea and the Arts of Japan.
See item no. 1496.

Libraries and
Museums

1473 **National Museum: Tokyo.**
Alberto Giuganimo, Adolfo Tamburello, translated from Italian,
foreword by Nagatake Asano, preface by Jō Okada.   New York:
Newsweek, 1968; London: Hamlyn, 1969. 171p. bibliog. (Great
Museums of the World).

The holdings of Japanese art and archaeology within the Tokyo National Museum,
founded in 1871, are the finest and most extensive of their kind. The museum is also
renowned for its excellent collections of Chinese and Korean art and owns several
important works of art from other parts of the world. This introduction to a selection
of the more than 90,000 objects in the museum as of the mid-1960s concentrates on its
masterpieces of East Asian painting and calligraphy but also includes various examples
of ancient bronzes, sculptures, metalwork, ceramics, lacquerware, textiles, and
archaeological finds. The text consists largely of commentaries to the book's many full-
colour illustrations.

1474 **Libraries in Japan.**
Edited by the Japan Library Association [Nihon Toshokan Kyōkai],
International Exchange Committee.   Tokyo: Japan Library
Association, 1980. new ed. 48p. 29 maps.

A directory of twenty-six of the most important and representative libraries in Japan,
prepared as a 'guide-book for foreign librarians visiting Japanese libraries'. A short
essay describes the current status of libraries in Japan, the nature of education for
librarianship, and the organisational structure and activities of the Japan Library
Association. Concise entries for the National Diet Library, Tōyō Bunko, University of
Tokyo General Library, Hibiya Municipal High School Library, the National Institute
of Japanese Literature, and other similar institutions provide brief histories of these
libraries, listings of their special collections, information about their holdings, opening
hours and services, photographs of their buildings, and street maps showing their
location. Also included are the full text of the Library Law of 1950 and an address list
of related library associations.

1475 **Roberts' guide to Japanese museums of art and archaeology.**
Laurance P. Roberts. Tokyo: Simul Press, 1987. 384p. map.
An informative guide to the collections of Japanese, Chinese, Korean, and Western art and archaeological finds available in 347 public, private, and institutional museums. Only those museums which are of interest to foreigners and are reasonably accessible are included. Each museum entry (entered under its official English name) contains directory information, a succinct description of its collections, critical comments on the quality of its holdings and on its displays, an indication of its regularly scheduled hours, and directions for reaching the museum by public transportation and by foot. Indexes by the museums' Japanese names (where they differ from the English), by branch museums and other collections, by prefectures, and by types of collection facilitate the use of this guide. Now in its third, completely revised and expanded edition, this book has been published under the auspices of the International House of Japan and the Japan Foundation.

1476 **Toshokan: libraries in Japanese society.**
Theodore F. Welch. London: Clive Bingley; Chicago: American Library Association, 1976. 306p. map. bibliog.
A comprehensive survey of contemporary Japanese libraries and librarianship. Following an overview of the traditional setting of libraries in Japan, Welch discusses the current setting of Japanese public libraries, the basic characteristics of library employees, postwar laws and public support for libraries, education for librarianship and Japan's professional library associations, the role of the National Diet Library (the counterpart of the British Library and the Library of Congress), and the concern of librarians for standardised tools to facilitate the technical processing of library materials. This study covers most types of libraries including those operating on the prefectural, municipal and village levels, university and research libraries, and school and special libraries. Among the six appendixes are a detailed chronology of major events relating to Japanese libraries and librarianship (1868-1968) and translations of the Library Law of 1950 and the 1955 revision of the 1948 National Diet Library Law.

Directory of information sources in Japan, 1986.
See item no. 1558.

Scholars' guide to Washington, D.C. for East Asian studies (China, Japan, Korea, and Mongolia).
See item no. 1562.

Books and Printing

1477 **The history of Japanese printing and book illustration.**
David Chibbett. Tokyo; New York: Kodansha International, 1977.
264p. bibliog.

Part one of this overview – which is oriented towards the general reader as well as the bibliophile – offers an essentially chronological account of the development of Japanese printing. It includes the introduction of block printing and colour printing techniques from China, the growth of printing in Nara and Kyōto under Buddhist and imperial court patronage, the influence exerted by the Jesuit Mission Press and the introduction of movable type from Korea during the late 1500s, and the expansion of the publishing industry during the seventeenth and eighteenth centuries. A more extensive second part is concerned with the history of printed book illustrations, primarily during the Tokugawa period. Chibbett surveys the Tosa, Ukiyo-e, Kanō, Kōrin (or Rimpa), Nanga, Maruyama, Shijō, and Kishi schools of art; considers their influence on the various styles of book illustration that appeared in publications oriented towards a mass urban readership; and writes about the most important contemporary illustrators and their most celebrated works.

1478 **The art of Hokusai in book illustration.**
Jack Ronald Hillier. Berkeley, California: University of California Press; London: Sotheby Parke Bernet, 1980. 288p. bibliog.

A beautifully designed, authoritative study of both the numerous books and albums of woodblock prints produced by the graphic artist Katsushika Hokusai (1760-1849) and the incidental illustrations which he contributed to various books of fiction and poetry. Hillier describes the historical background of book illustration in Japan and the manner in which books of woodblock prints were produced. He identifies and describes the 272 publications – among them novelettes, books of poetry, *yomihon* novels, Hokusai's celebrated series of picture books known as the *Manga*, albums of erotic prints (*shunga*), and his *One hundred views of Mount Fuji* – which Hokusai illustrated or to which he contributed designs during the course of his life. The book is illustrated by over two hundred reproductions.

594

1479 **Japanese bookbinding: instructions from a master craftsman.**
Kōjirō Ikegami, adapted by Barbara B. Stephan. New York; Tokyo:
Weatherhill, 1986. 127p. bibliog.

Easy-to-follow instructions for making all of the major historically important styles of Japanese bookbindings and traditional cases for books. This beautifully illustrated work by one of Japan's leading professional bookbinders covers the historical development and structure of Japanese books, the tools, paper and materials used, the basic binding procedure, four-hole binding variations (including Chinese-style binding and Yamato binding), accordion books, ledgers, book cases, and book repair. Ikegami's study has been adapted and expanded for a Western audience. Listings of American and Japanese suppliers of traditional tools and materials are included, as are explanations about Japanese handmade paper and wheat paste papers.

1480 **Manga! manga! the world of Japanese comic books.**
Frederik L. Schodt, foreword by Osamu Tezuka. Tokyo; New York:
Kodansha International, 1983. 260p. bibliog.

Explores the various kinds of narrative comic strip books that are found in Japan today: from sports and romance comics written for boys and for girls to mahjong and erotic comics for adult readers. Schodt offers a wide-ranging introduction to the role of comics in Japanese history as well as to their themes, their contents, their artists, and their appeal. He notes the extreme popularity of comic strip books in postwar Japan and points out that they have created a multi-billion dollar publishing industry which caters to a variety of needs including that of providing readers with 'an instant escape into a fantasy world'. This account is illustrated with full-colour pages of representative comics, 185 monochrome plates, and ninety-six pages of sample narrative comic strips in English translation. For an excellent example of the type of comic strip book described, readers may wish to turn to *Japan Inc.: an introduction to Japanese economics (the comic book)*, by Shōtarō Ishinomori, translated by Betsey Scheiner and with an introduction by Peter Duus (Berkeley, California; London: University of California Press, 1988, 313p.). The translation of a best-seller that was published by Japan's leading business newspaper (the *Nihon Keizai Shimbun*) and illustrated by the country's leading comic book artist, this work offers an informative and enjoyable portrait of the Japanese economy and of its relationship to the world economy as perceived by present-day Japanese.

1481 **Tanrokubon: rare books of seventeenth-century Japan.**
Kogorō Yoshida, foreword and synopses by Ryūshin Matsumoto,
translated and adapted by Mark A. Harbison. Tokyo; New York:
Kodansha International, 1984. 228p. bibliog.

A beautifully produced account of the development of *tanrokubon*, woodblock print editions of medieval literary works containing hand-coloured illustrations which flourished during the first part of the seventeenth century and were noteworthy predecessors of ukiyo-e woodblock printing. Yoshida, a prominent collector of *tanrokubon*, first surveys the history of this genre of early Tokugawa period book printing. With Matsumoto he then presents reproductions of representative *tanrokubon* illustrations together with detailed narrative synopses of the literary works from which they are taken.

Censorship in imperial Japan.
See item no. 221.

Books and Printing

Suzuki Harunobu: a selection of his color prints and illustrated books.
See item no. 1261.

Harunobu and his age: the development of colour printing in Japan.
See item no. 1261.

The art of surimono: privately published Japanese woodblock prints and books in the Chester Beatty Library, Dublin.
See item no. 1263.

Japanese papermaking: traditions, tools, and techniques.
See item no. 1358.

An introduction to Japanese government publications.
See item no. 1593.

Mass Media and Communications

1482 **Broadcasting in Japan.**
Masami Itō, with a study group on the Japanese broadcasting system; foreword by Asa Briggs.   London; Boston, Massachusetts: Routledge and Kegan Paul in association with the International Institute of Communications, 1978. 125p. (Case Studies on Broadcasting Systems).

This study is part of a series of monographs on the origins, historical development, and future of the broadcasting structures of several industrialised and Third World countries. Itō outlines the nature of the broadcasting environment in Japan; traces the evolution of broadcasting from its inception in 1925 through 1970; describes the present broadcasting structure, the laws and regulations governing broadcasting, and the existing state of broadcasting services; discusses the structure, administration, programmes, and relations of the Japan Broadcasting Corporation (Nippon Hōsō Kyōkai); explores the establishment, growth, structure, and activities of commercial broadcasting services; and comments on the future of broadcasting in Japan. Several brief statistical appendixes cover the postwar revenues and expenditures of the Japanese broadcasting industry.

1483 **The Japanese Press.**
Edited by the Japan Newspaper Publishers and Editors Association [Nihon Shimbun Kyōkai].   Tokyo: Nihon Shimbun Kyōkai [Japan Newspaper Publishers and Editors Association], 1949- . annual. (Nihon Shimbun Kyōkai, Nippon Press Center Building, 2-1 Uchisaiwai-chō 2-chōme, Chiyoda-ku, Tokyo 100, Japan).

Each annual summary of general trends in the newspaper industry – covering editorial problems, news reporting and editorials, newspaper production techniques, management, sales and circulation, and advertising – is followed by two special feature articles, e.g., 'The Development of Japanese Newspapers' (1985) and 'Newspapers in the Year 2000 as Envisaged by Newspapermen' (1986). The editors also briefly describe the activities of the Nippon Kisha Club and the Foreign Press Centre (two newspaper-related organisations) as well as the organisation and activities of the Japan Newspaper Publishers and Editors Association. Several statistical tables about Japanese newspaper operations and an updated directory of Japanese newspapers, news agencies, broadcasting stations, and overseas Japanese correspondents round out each year's coverage.

1484   **Japanese journalists and their world.**

Young C. Kim.   Charlottesville, Virginia: University Press of Virginia, 1981. 226p.

An inquiry into the background, career patterns, role orientations, news-gathering and news-processing activities, and newspaper articles of Japanese reporters. Kim first discusses the major characteristics of Japanese newspapers and their readership, the recruitment and career patterns of Japanese journalists, the organisational factors involved in the gathering and processing of news, the differing orientations of reporters and government officials, and the legal aspects of newspaper publishing. He then analyses the contents of Japanese newspaper articles, paying special attention to press coverage of the Vietnam War, reporting about China, government attempts to influence news reporting, and the impact of ideology and such journalistic norms as objectivity and neutrality on actual reporting. The study deals largely with four of Japan's leading newspapers: the *Asahi*, *Mainichi*, *Sankei*, and *Yomiuri*.

1485   **The political character of the Japanese press.**

Jung Bock Lee, foreword by Kyong-Dong Kim.   Seoul: Seoul National University Press, 1985. 198p. bibliog. (Institute of Social Sciences International Studies Series, 6).

Lee analyses the origins, historical development, structure, and attitudinal inclinations of the Japanese press in an effort to determine whether the press should properly be considered as 'anti-government' and 'leftist' or as 'pro-government' and 'conservative' in character. Focusing on the *Asahi*, *Mainichi*, and *Yomiuri* (the three dominant national papers), he investigates the professional and political attitudes of Japanese newspapermen and examines the professional and economic structure of the newspaper industry. He also provides a case-study of the political behaviour of the press during the US–Japan Security Treaty crisis of 1960. Lee shows that Japan's major newspapers have been largely independent of the government since the mid-Meiji period. Stressing their common political character rather than their differences, he argues that they generally take positions which lie somewhere in between full support for the government and consistent support for the left-wing opposition parties.

1486   **50 years of Japanese broadcasting.**

Edited by the Nippon Hōsō Kyōkai. Radio and TV Culture Research Institute. History Compilation Room [Nippon Hōsō Kyōkai. Sōgō Hōsō Bunka Kenkyūjo], with the Mainichi Newspapers; preface by Tomokazu Sakamoto.   Tokyo: NHK Radio and TV Culture Research Institute, 1977. 429p. 3 maps.

This account of radio and television broadcasting between 1925 and 1975 describes the development and activities of both the Japan Broadcasting Corporation – the national public broadcasting system known as Nippon Hōsō Kyōkai (NHK) – and Japanese commercial broadcasting interests. It covers the origins of radio broadcasting and programming, the establishment and expansion of nationwide radio service, broadcasting during the Pacific War, the impact of the Allied occupation of Japan, NHK's fresh start as a public broadcasting enterprise in 1950, the dawn of the television era, the rapid growth and nature of television broadcasting, and television programming during the 1960s and 1970s. Appendixes include extensive excerpts from the Broadcast Law and a detailed chronology of broadcasting in Japan.

Meiroku zasshi: journal of the Japanese enlightenment.
See item no. 196.

Censorship in imperial Japan.
See item no. 221.

The State and the mass media in Japan, 1918–1945.
See item no. 221.

Imitation and innovation: the transfer of Western organizational patterns to Meiji Japan.
See item no. 248.

Politics of the Meiji press: the life of Fukuchi Gen'ichirō.
See item no. 305.

Tokutomi Sohō, 1863-1957: a journalist for modern Japan.
See item no. 311.

An introduction to newspaper Japanese.
See item no. 445.

The information explosion: the new electronic media in Japan and Europe.
See item no. 955.

Periodicals and Newspapers

Periodicals

1487 **Amerasia Journal.**
Los Angeles, California: Asian American Studies Center, University
of California, 1971- . semi-annual. (Asian American Studies Center,
3232 Campbell Hall, University of California, Los Angeles, CA 90024-
1546 USA).

An interdisciplinary journal of critical scholarship, opinion, and creative literature
concerned with Japanese and other Asian and Pacific island ethnic minorities in the
United States and Canada. Each issue includes a series of articles, resource notes, and
book reviews; and every other issue also contains an 'annual selected bibliography',
which lists English-language books, articles, dissertations, and theses completed during
the preceding year. Japanese American responses to race relations, Japanese
immigrants and organised American labour in 1915-16, and Japanese American
contributions to US counter-intelligence activities during World War II are some of the
subjects which have been discussed at length in this periodical.

1488 **AMPO: Japan-Asia Quarterly Review.**
Tokyo: Pacific-Asia Resource Centre, 1969- . quarterly. (Pacific-Asia
Resource Centre, P.O. Box 5250 Tokyo International, Japan).

A leftwing journal offering critical analyses of the postwar Japanese economy,
government, and society. Each issue contains articles which 'unmask the real face of
Japan' and present both views and information about Japan that do not regularly
appear in mainstream Western periodicals. Typical issues have dealt with the 'Japanese
farmers' struggle to preserve their way of life', 'the challenges facing Japanese women',
the remilitarisation of Japan, and 'Japanese monopoly capital's economic aggression
overseas'.

600

1489   **Arts of Asia.**
Kowloon, Hong Kong: Arts of Asia Publications, 1971- . bimonthly.
(Arts of Asia Publications Ltd., 1309 Kowloon Centre, 29-39 Ashley
Road, Kowloon, Hong Kong).
A beautifully illustrated magazine on the art, culture, and art-related history of East,
Southeast, and South Asia, with contributions by art collectors, museum specialists,
and students of Asian art. General issues containing a wide range of articles of interest
to collectors alternate with special numbers featuring an Asian country or a particular
museum. Articles about Japanese art are frequently published, along with entire issues
devoted to such subjects as the Japanese decorative arts.

1490   **Asian Folklore Studies.**
Nagoya: Anthropological Institute, Nanzan University, 1942- . semi-
annual. (Asian Folklore Studies, Nanzan University, 18 Yamazato-
chō, Shōwa-ku, Nagoya 466, Japan).
A journal of scholarly research and news about the folklore of East, Southeast, and
South Asia – including the literary and oral traditions, beliefs and myths, medical
practices, art, and customs of those regions. Among its many published studies of
Japan are articles entitled '*Mura-zakai*: the Japanese Village Boundary and its
Symbolic Interpretation', 'Yasukuni-Jinja and Folk Religion: the Problem of Vengeful
Spirits', 'The Swan-Maiden Revisited: Religious Significance of 'Divine-Wife' Folktales
with Special Reference to Japan', 'The Impact of Tourism on Japanese *Kyōgen*: Two
Case Studies', and 'Miyako Theology: Shamans' Interpretation of Traditional Beliefs'.

1491   **Asian Survey: a Monthly Review of Contemporary Asian Affairs.**
Berkeley, California: University of California Press, 1961- . monthly.
A journal of informed opinions and analyses of political, economic, military, social,
and diplomatic developments in the countries of East, Southeast, and South Asia.
Contributed largely by scholars and researchers, the articles are oriented towards both
a general and an academic audience and bear such titles as 'Japanese–Soviet Relations
in the Early Gorbachev Era', 'Japanese Capital Markets and Financial Liberalization',
'Japan's United Nations Policy in the 1980s', 'The Japanese System of Human
Resource Management: Transferability to the Indian Industrial Environment', and
'North Korea's Relations with Japan: the Legacy of War'.

1492   **Asian Theatre Journal.**
Honolulu, Hawaii: University of Hawaii Press, 1984- . semi-annual.
The official publication of the Association for Asian Performance, this periodical
contains scholarly articles, field research reports, translations of documents and plays,
and book reviews that are concerned with the performing arts of Asia in both their
traditional and modern forms. Among its articles on Japan are 'Flowers of Edo:
Eighteenth-Century *Kabuki* and its Patrons', 'Children's Theatre in Japan', 'Time and
Tradition in Modern Japanese Theatre', and 'Shamanism in the Origins of the *Nō*
Theatre'.

Periodicals and Newspapers. Periodicals

1493 **Bulletin of Concerned Asian Scholars.**
Boulder, Colorado, 1968- . quarterly. (3239 9th Street, Boulder, CO
80302-2112, USA).
A journal concerned with the modern history, politics, society, economy, international
relations, and literature of East, Southeast, and South Asia. Representative articles
about Japan include 'Class Conflict in Rural Japan: an Historical Methodology',
'Problem Consciousness and Modern Japanese History: Female Textile Workers of
Meiji and Taisho', 'Nuclear Power Plant Gypsies in High-Tech Society', and
'Productivity First: Japanese Management Methods in Singapore'. Selected articles
about Japan have been reprinted in the anthology *The other Japan: postwar realities*,
edited by E. Patricia Tsurumi (q.v.).

1494 **Business Japan.**
Tokyo: Nihon Kōgyō Shimbun, 1971- . monthly. (Nihon Kōgyō
Shimbun, 7-2 Ōtemachi 1-chōme, Chiyoda-ku, Tokyo 100, Japan).
Published by a major Japanese newspaper company, *Business Japan* offers up-to-date
information about Japanese business news and business trends together with special
reports, interviews, industry studies, economic reviews, reports on books, and wide-
ranging feature articles. Many of the articles are concerned with developments in
Japanese industrial technology or with the operations (at home or abroad) of Japanese
companies. The contributors are largely Japanese scholars, businessmen and the
journal's own staff.

1495 **Business Tokyo.**
Tokyo: Keizaikai Co. Ltd., 1987- . monthly. (Keizaikai Co. Ltd.,
2-13-18 Minami Aoyama, Minato-ku, Tokyo 107, Japan. For
subscribers in the United States: Keizaikai USA, Inc., 1270 Avenue of
the Americas, Suite 2720, New York, NY 10020).
Billed as 'Japan's only English-language magazine that tells you all you need to know
about Japanese business anywhere in the world', *Business Tokyo* contains a range of
feature articles aimed at a general business audience together with interviews with
leading businessmen, a section entitled 'News from Nippon', and information about
business trends. Covering Japanese technology, politics, finance, marketing, and
business, the feature articles examine such specific topics as character processing in
Japanese using electronic word-processors, changes in Japanese methods of doing
business, obstacles to the growth of a cost-competitive domestic defence industry in
Japan, the impact of the appreciation of the yen on the Japanese economy, the
simplification of Japanese automobile insurance, and the marketing of cleaning
materials and houseware products.

1496 **Chanoyu Quarterly: Tea and the Arts of Japan.**
Kyōto: Urasenke Foundation; New York: Urasenke Chanoyu Center,
1970- . quarterly. (Urasenke Foundation, Ogawa Teranouchi agaru,
Kamikyō-ku, Kyōto 602, Japan. For subscribers in the United States:
Urasenke Chanoyu Center, 153 East 69th St., New York, NY 10021).
Concerned with the Japanese tea ceremony (*chanoyu*) and with related etiquette,
utensils, paintings, furnishings, fabrics, philosophy, and literature. Many issues contain
sequences of black-and-white photographs that illustrate the progression of a tea

ceremony. Articles are generally contributed by Japanese specialists in the area of Japanese culture and by practitioners of *chanoyu*.

1497 **The East.**
Tokyo: The East Publications, 1964- . bimonthly. (The East Publications, Inc., 19-7-101 Minami-Azabu 3-chōme, Minato-ku, Tokyo 106, Japan. For subscribers in the United States: The East Publications, Inc., P.O.B. 2640, Grand Central Station, New York, NY 10164-9990).

A general-interest magazine with illustrated articles about a wide range of subjects concerning Japan, both past and present, written in an anecdotal style. Many of the topics – for example, the natural beauty of certain small islands west of Hokkaidō, and the make-up methods and utensils of Tokugawa period women – are not normally covered anywhere else in English.

1498 **East Asia: International Review of Economic, Political, and Social Development.**
Frankfurt am Main, FRG: Campus Verlag; Boulder, Colorado: Westview Press, 1983- . annual.

Edited by members of the East Asia Seminar at the Free University of Berlin, this annual focuses on the economic, institutional, ideological, and cultural determinants of development in postwar China, Japan, and Korea; the region's prospects for and problems of development; intra- and interregional co-operation and conflict in East Asia; the human factor in the development process and its role in economic and social development; and the economic and political impact of development within East Asia upon neighbouring countries. Japan has frequently been featured in its volumes. Volume 2 (1984) centred on the theme 'Japan as a Model for the First and/or Third World' (with a dozen articles on Japan's political development, industrial relations, labour market, new technology, foreign and defence policy, economic co-operation, and development strategy). Other annual volumes have published groups of articles under such headings as 'Japan: Problems of a Post-Industrial Society' and 'Japan and Intra- and Interregional Cooperation'.

1499 **The Eastern Buddhist.**
Kyōto: Eastern Buddhist Society [Tōhō Bukkyō Kyōkai], Ōtani University, 1921- ; new series, 1965- . semi-annual. (Eastern Buddhist Society, Ōtani University, Koyama, Kita-ku, Kyōto 603, Japan. For subscribers in the United States and Canada: Scholars Press, P.O. Box 1608, Decatur, GA 30031).

A non-sectarian journal devoted to the critical study of all aspects of Mahāyāna Buddhism, especially within its Japanese context. It contains articles, 'dialogues', translations of Buddhist texts, and book reviews contributed both by Japanese and Westerners. Typical articles include 'Seeking Enlightenment in the Last Age: *Mappō* Thought in Kamakura Buddhism', 'Buddhism and the Fine Arts in Kyoto', 'Kiyozawa Manshi and the Meaning of Buddhist Ethics', 'Nothingness and Death in Heidegger and Zen Buddhism', 'The Religious Worldview of Nishida Kitarō', 'Conversations with D.T. Suzuki' (a dialogue), and 'Talks by Hakuin Introductory to Lectures on the Records of Old Sokkō' (a translation of *Sokkō-roku kaien fusetsu*).

1500   **Economic Eye: a Quarterly Digest of Views from Japan.**
Tokyo: Keizai Kōhō Center [Japan Institute for Social and Economic
Affairs], 1980- . quarterly. (Keizai Kōhō Center, 6-1 Ōtemachi
1-chōme, Chiyoda-ku, Tokyo 100, Japan).
A magazine featuring full or partial translations of important Japanese periodical
articles on economic topics that are deemed to be of interest to foreign readers. They
generally deal with trends in the Japanese economy, Japan's international economic
policy, and the country's industry and technology, management and labour, and
finance. Typical of the magazine contents are the following items that appeared in
some 1987 and 1988 issues: 'Strategies to Balance Japan–U.S. Trade'; 'Korean
Products: a Threat to Japan?'; 'Hard Times for Tokyo's Shopkeepers'; 'A Tax Solution
to High Land Prices'; 'A Pause in the Rental Housing Boom'; 'Changing Japan's
Corporate Behavior'; 'Five Myths about Japanese Agriculture'; 'Labor's Retreat in the
Shadow of Unemployment'; and 'The Retooling of Traditional Industry'. A collection
of twenty-eight articles from early volumes of *Economic Eye* has been published as
Economic views from Japan: selections from Economic Eye (Tokyo: Keizai Kōhō
Center, 1986, 247p.).

1501   **Far Eastern Economic Review.**
Hong Kong: Far Eastern Economic Review, Ltd., 1946- . weekly.
(Far Eastern Economic Review, P.O. Box 160, General Post Office,
Hong Kong).
A news magazine dealing with regional, business, and political affairs throughout East,
Southeast, and South Asia. Each issue also carries book reviews, stock market news,
current economic indicators, and other regional features. Japan is routinely covered in
depth in view of her prominence on the Asian scene. She is also periodically featured
within the section known as 'Focus', which brings together articles centring around a
common topic such as Japanese banking, finance, and investment.

1502   **Farming Japan.**
Tokyo: Farming Japan Co. Ltd., 1967- . bimonthly. (Farming Japan
Co. Ltd., 5-4 Uchikanda 1-chōme, Chiyoda-ku, Tokyo 101, Japan).
A periodical for both general readers and specialists interested in the agriculture,
forestry, and fisheries of present-day Japan as well as in Japanese technical co-
operation with the developing countries of the Third World. Each issue features one
broad subject such as the development and management of irrigation and drainage, the
utilisation of wood as a source of energy, the current status and prospects of the
Japanese flower industry, the production and use of soybeans, the growth and activities
of agricultural co-operatives, medical care for Japan's rural population, the development of information networks for farming areas, the control of infectious diseases
among domestic animals, agricultural extension activities, and the processing of fish,
shellfish and seaweed. Most issues also contain a column entitled 'New Highlights in
Agriculture, Forestry and Fisheries', discuss some topic related to Japanese
agricultural technology, and report on an activity involving overseas Japanese co-
operation activities.

1503 **Focus on Asian Studies.**
New York: Asia Society, 1981- . three times a year. (Asia Society,
725 Park Avenue, New York, NY 10021, USA).
Published in conjunction with the Association for Asian Studies and the Committee on
Teaching about Asia, this journal seeks to bring both general and specific information
about East, Southeast, and South Asia to the attention of educators on the
precollegiate level. Individual issues contain articles covering such thematic subjects as
women in Asia, modern Asian leadership, Asian crafts, and contemporary Asian
literature; columns about curriculum materials and resources which can be used by
area specialists, non-specialists, and educators at all levels of education; calendars of
major Asia-related events across the United States; book reviews; and briefly
annotated announcements of new books and multi-media materials.

1504 **Harvard Journal of Asiatic Studies.**
Cambridge, Massachusetts: Harvard-Yenching Institute, 1936- . semi-
annual. (Harvard-Yenching Institute, 2 Divinity Avenue, Cambridge,
MA 02138, USA).
A scholarly periodical concerned particularly with China and to a lesser extent Japan
that contains important articles and critical book reviews in the areas of history,
literature, religion, and philosophy. Emphasis is on the premodern period.

1505 **Japan Architect: International Edition of Shinkenchiku.**
Tokyo: Shinkenchikusha, 1956- . monthly. (Japan Architect Co. Ltd.,
31-2 Yushima 2-chōme, Bunkyō-ku, Tokyo 113, Japan).
An illustrated journal on contemporary Japanese architecture which features articles
by architects and critics about new buildings, projects, and design competitions and
which occasionally devotes entire monthly issues to the work of individual architects
such as Andō Tadao and Itō Tōyō. Most of the buildings and projects are in Japan, but
architectural developments in Asia and elsewhere undertaken by Japanese architects
are also described. Representative articles published in 1988 include 'Iwasaki Art
Museum Annex', 'Minakami Highlands Prince Hotel', 'Mito Municipal Culture
Center', 'House under Fallen Snow', 'Tokyo Institute of Technology Centennial Hall',
'Ochanomizu Square', and 'Shinkenchiku Residential Design Competition 1987'. Like
most other articles in this magazine, they were translated from Japanese-language
versions prepared for publication in the journal *Shinkenchiku*.

1506 **Japan Christian Quarterly.**
Tokyo: Christian Literature Society [Kyō Bun Kwan], 1926- .
quarterly. (Kyō Bun Kwan, 4-5-1 Ginza, Chūō-ku, Tokyo 104, Japan.
For subscribers outside Japan: Japan Publications Trading Company,
Box 5030 Tokyo International, Tokyo 100-31, Japan).
An independent journal of Christian thought and opinion sponsored by the Fellowship
of Christian Missionaries in Japan. It covers a wide range of topics such as Christ in
Japanese Christian thought, problems in the history of Japanese Bible translation, the
influence of Christianity on the writings of Meiji period intellectuals, the cultural
conflict between Japanese polytheism and Biblical monotheism, the peace movement
of postwar Japanese Christians, Japanese women and the Church, the missionary in
rural evangelisation, Japanese attitudes towards disabled people, the 'emperor system'
and Christian responsibility, and the ways in which contemporary Japanese novelists

depict Jesus. Interested readers should also be aware of the *Japan Missionary Bulletin* (Tokyo: Oriens Institute for Religious Research [2-28-5 Matsubara, Setagaya-ku, Tokyo 156, Japan], 1947-), a Catholic-sponsored monthly with articles in both English and Japanese covering various aspects of Christian work in Japan.

1507 **Japan Echo.**
Tokyo: Japan Echo, Inc., 1974- . quarterly. (Japan Echo, Inc., Moto Akasaka Building, 1-7-10 Moto Akasaka, Minato-ku, Tokyo 107, Japan).

This journal enables Western readers to sample the contents of Japan's more serious general-interest magazines. It contains full or partial translations of articles by prominent commentators on a wide range of topics of current interest shortly after they first appear in leading Japanese periodicals. The articles within individual issues tend to centre around a handful of themes such as 'political realignment', 'history and national sensibilities', 'tackling tax reform', 'nationalism and racism', and 'farm policy under fire'.

1508 **Japan Forum.**
Oxford, England: Oxford University Press for the British Association for Japanese Studies, 1989- . semi-annual.

This European-based, multidisciplinary journal of Japanese studies contains articles and research notes on all aspects of Japanese culture and society, a section entitled 'Professional Notes' that highlights important academic developments, and review articles on recent developments in the arts, humanities and social sciences as well as reviews of significant publications in Japanese and European languages. Articles appearing in the first issue include 'The Political Mechanisms of Consensus in the Industrial Policy Process: the Shipbuilding Industry in the Face of Crisis, 1973–1978', 'Convergence Theory and the Development of the British and Japanese Steel Industries, 1960–1988', 'Japan and Nuclear Proliferation in East Asia', ' "In the Beginning Woman was the Sun": Autobiographies of Modern Japanese Women Writers', and 'The Japanese Attempt to Secure Racial Equality in 1919'.

1509 **Japan Foundation Newsletter.**
Tokyo: Japan Foundation, 1973- . bimonthly. (Japan Foundation, Park Building, 3-6 Kioi-chō, Chiyoda-ku, Tokyo 102, Japan).

The Japan Foundation, a special corporation established by the Japanese government in 1972, is charged with promoting international understanding of Japan through its programmes of educational and cultural exchange. It sponsors conferences, symposia, art exhibitions, and cultural performances; financially assists overseas Japanese studies programmes and the teaching of the Japanese language; supports the exchange of people by bringing scholars, students, and other individuals to Japan and by sending Japanese specialists abroad; and prepares and distributes cultural materials about Japan while also subsidising new publications about Japan. Its newsletter (distributed free of charge) reports on Foundation activities, includes news about cultural topics in Japan, publishes reviews of selected new books, and contains scholarly articles about Japanese culture (e.g., 'Japan and the Avant-garde'; 'Shinto and Buddhism in Japanese Culture') and about Japanese studies abroad.

1510   **Japan Journal.**
Tokyo: Cross Cultural Communications, Inc., 1987- . monthly. (Cross
Cultural Communications, Inc., MSD 15 Building, 3F, 3-7-4
Sendagaya, Shibuya-ku, Tokyo 151, Japan. For subscribers in the
United States: Cross Cultural Media, Inc., Westchester Financial
Center, Suite 1000, 50 Main St., White Plains, NY 10606.)
The international edition of *Tokyo Journal* (Tokyo, 1981-), this magazine offers
broad general coverage of contemporary Japanese affairs. Each issue carries several
feature stories on such diverse topics as Japan's 'peace corps', nursing homes in Tokyo,
the country's space programme, and the 'Japanization of America'. A 50- to 80-page
centre insert entitled 'Cityscope' provides a comprehensive guide to the latest
developments within Tokyo in the worlds of art, film, music, the performing arts,
festivals and events. Also appearing regularly are monthly columns concerned with art,
new books, business, food, the international marketplace, Japanalia, the martial arts,
new products, profiles of important personalities, and travel and leisure.

1511   **Japan Labor Bulletin.**
Tokyo: Japan Institute of Labor, 1962- . monthly. (Japan Institute of
Labor, Chutaikin Building, 7-6 Shibakōen 1-chōme, Minato-ku,
Tokyo, Japan).
A bulletin with regular coverage of the Japanese economy in general, working
conditions and the labour market, labour disputes and trade unions, public policy, and
Japanese labour's involvement in international relations. Each issue also examines a
'special topic' such as 'the process of job creation and job destruction in Japanese
industry' and the search for a new industrial relations system.

1512   **Japan Pictorial.**
Tokyo: Japan Graphic, Inc., 1978- . quarterly. (Japan Graphic, Inc.,
Palaceside Building, 1-1 Hitotsubashi 1-chōme, Chiyoda-ku, Tokyo
100, Japan).
A general-interest periodical, illustrated by numerous colour photographs, that
introduces foreigners to contemporary Japanese life. Its articles often highlight
changing Japanese life-styles and cover a wide range of topics, among them the
transformation of the port city of Hakodate on the island of Hokkaidō, the activities of
the elderly on a small island southwest of Hiroshima, and the world of elementary
school students in Tokyo.

1513   **Japan Quarterly.**
Tokyo: Asahi Shimbun, 1954- . quarterly. (Asahi Shimbun Publishing
Co., 5-3-2 Tsukiji, Chūō-ku, Tokyo 104-11, Japan).
Keeps both the general reader and the specialist up-to-date on important trends and
concerns in Japan through articles dealing with contemporary Japanese life, in
particular political and social issues. Also included are translated excerpts of
contemporary Japanese literature, feature articles about significant personalities, book
reviews, concisely annotated listings of recently published Western-language books on
Japan, and a chronology of events in Japan during the preceding three months. Most
contributors to this journal are Japanese.

1514 **Japan Review of International Affairs.**
Tokyo: Japan Institute of International Affairs, 1987- . semi-annual.
(Japan Institute of International Affairs, 19th Mori Building, 1-2-20
Toranomon, Minato-ku, Tokyo 105, Japan).
A journal of informed opinion by leading Japanese statesmen and scholars on a broad
range of topics related to international affairs, among them the evolution of Japan's
United Nations policy, arms control and disarmament today (a Japanese view), the
US–Japan relationship, and the expansion of domestic demand in Japan in response to
pressure from abroad.

1515 **Japan Society Newsletter.**
New York: Japan Society, 1953- . monthly. (Japan Society, Inc., 333
East 47th St., New York, NY 10017, USA).
News about the activities of the Society, feature articles on Japan by leading scholars
and public figures, and a monthly calendar of general and art-related events in the New
York metropolitan area and elsewhere in the United States combine to make this the
most informative of the more than one dozen newsletters published by various Japan
Societies across the country. Typical of its many articles are: 'An Ambassador's Job'
(on Edwin Reischauer's diplomatic assignment in Japan), 'The Middle-aged Japanese
Woman', 'Farm Life in a Japanese Village', 'Zen and the Art of Dying', 'U.S.–Japan
Economic Relations: Adapting to Changing Realities', and 'Victorians in Kobe: Some
Early Impressions by Westerners'. A 108-page history of the Society, *Japan Society
1907–1982: 75 years of partnership across the Pacific* by Edwin O. Reischauer, was
published by the Japan Society in 1982.

1516 **The Japan Society Review.**
London: Japan Society, 1950- . three times a year. (Japan Society of
London, Room 331, 162-168 Regent St., London W1R 5TB, UK).
Founded in 1891 as the Japan Society of London and now serving the entire United
Kingdom, the Society seeks to promote the study and understanding of Japan within
the UK and contribute to the further development of friendly relations between Britain
and Japan. It organises regular lectures about the history, culture, and institutions of
Japan as well as various periodic functions. The *Review* (until 1985, the *Japan Society
of London Bulletin*) contains news about the activities and members of the Society,
information of interest to its readership, brief contributions by members (e.g.,
'Changing Seasons in Japan', 'Old Shizuoka: the Experiences of some Foreign
Visitors'), and reviews of new books. The Society also publishes annual *Proceedings*
that contain the texts of lectures and material of lasting interest. Representative
articles in the *Proceedings* that appeared during the mid-1980s include 'Some Early
British Connections with Satsuma', 'Japanese Entrepreneurs in the 1980s', and 'Japan
and English Literature'.

1517 **Japan Update.**
Tokyo: Keizai Kōhō Center [Japan Institute for Social and Economic
Affairs], 1986- . quarterly. (Keizai Kōhō Center, 6-1, Ōtemachi
1-chōme, Chiyoda-ku, Tokyo 100, Japan).
A magazine designed to improve worldwide understanding of Japan by disseminating
up-to-date information about her society and economy. Selected articles dealing with
education, life-style, society, industry, business, labour, communication, technology,

regional and urban development, and Japanese tradition are reprinted from the publications of a number of Japanese companies and economic institutes, among them *Age of Tomorrow*, *Honda Today*, *Nippon Steel Forum*, *Sumitomo Corporation News*, and *Tokyo Financial Review*.

1518 **Japanese Economic Studies.**
Armonk, New York: M. E. Sharpe, 1972- . quarterly. (M. E. Sharpe, Inc., 80 Business Park Drive, Armonk, NY 10504, USA).
Consisting of translated materials from Japanese academic books and periodicals, this is an important ongoing source of information in English about the Japanese economy and Japanese management. Wage flexibility and employment changes, the corporate network in Japan, competition in Japan's securities industry, new developments in Japan's public debt management, and the deregulation and reorganisation of Japan's financial system are among the subjects covered by this magazine in 1987 and 1988.

1519 **Japanese Finance and Industry: Quarterly Survey.**
Tokyo: Industrial Bank of Japan [Nihon Kōgyō Ginkō], 1949- . quarterly. (Nihon Kōgyō Ginkō, 3-3 Marunouchi 1-chōme, Chiyoda-ku, Tokyo 100, Japan).
Offers sophisticated analyses of trends and issues affecting such major Japanese industries as electronics, automobiles, shipbuilding, iron and steel, petrochemicals, shipping, real estate, and leasing. Representative articles include 'Medium-term Prospects for the Japanese Economy', 'Rationalization of Physical Distribution and the Response of the Warehousing Industry', 'Holography: the Beginnings of a Full-fledged Technology', 'Carbon Fibers: the Rush for Higher Performance', and 'The Collapse of Crude Oil Prices and its Impact on Japan's Oil Industry'.

1520 **Japanese Journal of Religious Studies.**
Nagoya: Nanzan Institute for Religion and Culture, 1974- . quarterly. (Nanzan Institute for Religion and Culture, 18 Yamazato-chō, Shōwa-ku, Nagoya 466, Japan).
A continuation of *Contemporary Religions in Japan* (Tokyo: International Institute for the Study of Religions, 1960-74), this journal of theoretical and descriptive scholarly articles seeks to 'advance interreligious understanding and further the pursuit of knowledge in the study of religion, particularly Japanese religion'. Representative articles contributed by both Japanese and Westerners in 1986-87 include 'Buddhism in Noh', 'Continuity and Change: Funeral Customs in Modern Japan', 'The Enryaku-ji and the Gion Shrine-temple Complex in the Mid-Heian Period', 'The Goal of Meditation', 'The Influence of the Buddhist Practice of *Sange* on Literary Form: Revelatory Tales', and 'Religious Rites in a Japanese Factory'. A special double issue is devoted each summer to a particular theme such as 'women and religion in Japan', 'religious ideas in Japan', and 'Tendai Buddhism in Japan'.

1521 **Japanese Literature Today.**
Tokyo: Japan P.E.N. Club, 1976- . annual. (Japan P.E.N. Club, 265 Shuwa Residential Hotel, 9-1-7 Akasaka, Minato-ku, Tokyo, Japan).
Each annual issue contains a survey of modern Japanese literature published during the preceding calendar year; a translation of one new short story; synopses of a few new novels; and a bibliography entitled 'Japanese Literature in Foreign Languages'

that provides full bibliographical details about newly published translations in European languages (including English), Chinese, and Korean.

1522 **Japanese Philately.**
Silver Spring, Maryland: International Society for Japanese Philately, 1946- . bimonthly. (Japanese Philately, 2233 Countryside Drive, Silver Spring, MD 20904-4520, USA).
A periodical of interest to serious collectors of postage stamps as well as to historians of modern Japan. Each issue contains feature articles, news stories, and other information about regular and special philatelic issues, postal stationery, postal markings, and the postal history of Japan, her past colonies, areas occupied during World War II, the Ryūkyū Islands, and Manchoukuo. The International Society for Japanese Philately has also published several specialised monographs, among them *A concordance: the stamps of Japan, Ryukyus, and Manchoukuo 1871–1979*, by Sune Johnson (1981).

1523 **Japanese Religions.**
Kyōto: NCC Center for the Study of Japanese Religions, 1959- . semi-annual. (NCC Center for the Study of Japanese Religions, Karasuma-Shimotachiuri, Kamikyo-ku, Kyōto 602, Japan).
For many years, the NCC Center has been undertaking studies of Japanese religiousness 'from a perspective which is both pastoral and academic in scope'. In its efforts to contribute to the life of the Christian church in Japan, the Center engages in dialogue with its Japanese religious environment and promotes ongoing research about religion in Japan. Its semi-annual magazine publishes some of the results of this research. These include articles entitled 'Shinran's View of the Human Predicament and the Christian Concept of Sin', 'Transformations and Changes in the Teachings of the Sōtō Zen Buddhist Sect', 'Japan's Roman Catholic Church and Ancestor Veneration', 'Formative Elements in the Emergence and Growth of the New Religions in Japan', 'An Unhappy Dialogue: Problems of Reversibility and Irreversibility in Buddhist–Christian Discussions', and 'Japanese Civil Religion and the Yasukuni Shrine'.

1524 **JEI Report.**
Washington, DC: Japan Economic Institute of America, 1981- . weekly. (Japan Economic Institute of America, 1000 Connecticut Avenue, N.W., Suite 211, Washington, DC 20036, USA).
Prepared on the basis of information gleaned from a multitude of news sources, this two-part report provides up-to-date information and analyses about economic, business, and political developments in Japan and about current Japan–US economic and political relations. Typical of its coverage are stories about Japan's monetary policy, capital market liberalisation in Japan, the impact of foreign exchange rates on trade, US exports to and imports from Japan, US–Japanese competition in various areas of trade, Japanese direct investment in the United States, Japan's new materials industry, US Congressional activities affecting Japan, Japan's foreign aid programme, trends in Japanese defence policy, and Japan's political relations with the countries of East and Southeast Asia. A complementary publication of the Institute, *Japan Economic Survey: a Monthly Review of U.S.–Japan Economic Relations* (1967-), highlights developments within the Japanese economy and those affecting this bilateral

relationship. The Japan Economic Institute of America is a US research organisation funded by Japan's Ministry of Foreign Affairs that was founded in 1957 as the United States–Japan Trade Council.

1525 **Journal of Asian Studies.**
Ann Arbor, Michigan: Association for Asian Studies, 1941- . quarterly. (Association for Asian Studies, 1 Lane Hall, University of Michigan, Ann Arbor, MI 48109, USA).

The leading academic journal in the field of Asian studies, published by the largest association in the West of specialists interested in East, Southeast, and South Asia. Each issue contains a range of articles and book reviews in the humanities and the social sciences, many of which concern Japan. Representative articles include 'Universities and Students in Wartime Japan', 'Democracy and the Founding of Japanese Public Radio', 'Japan and America: the Dynamics of Partnership', and 'The Imperial Bureaucracy and Labor Policy in Postwar Japan'. Between 1941 and 1956, this periodical appeared under the title *Far Eastern Quarterly*. The Association for Asian Studies also issues an informative bulletin entitled *Asian Studies Newsletter*. Appearing five times each year, it carries news about the association, notices of fellowships, grants and conferences, information concerning new publications, films and exhibits, and a professional employment personnel registry.

1526 **Journal of Japanese Studies.**
Seattle, Washington: Society for Japanese Studies, University of Washington, 1974- . semi-annual. (Journal of Japanese Studies, Thomson Hall, DR-05, University of Washington, Seattle, WA 98195, USA).

An interdisciplinary periodical featuring original research articles and in-depth reviews of books in the fields of history, government, economy, society, religion, and literature. The journal strives 'to serve as a vehicle for scholarly communication within the field of Japanese studies' by publishing articles which present specialised research results in some detail, analytical articles summarising the 'state of the argument' on a particular theme of scholarly debate and contributing further to that debate, bibliographical articles and essays, translations of articles and edited excerpts from major works by leading Japanese scholars, substantial book reviews and critical review articles, and conference or symposia papers organised around a specific theme such as the medieval economy of Japan, modern Japanese society, or the United States–Japan trade crisis in the 1980s.

1527 **Journal of Japanese Trade & Industry.**
Tokyo: Japan Economic Foundation [Kokusai Keizai Kōryū Zaidan], 1982- . bimonthly. (Japan Economic Foundation, 11th floor, Fukoku Seimei Building, 2-2 Uchisaiwai-chō 2-chōme, Chiyoda-ku, Tokyo 100, Japan. For subscribers in the United States and Canada: Elsevier Science Publishers, Journal Information Center, 52 Vanderbilt Avenue, New York, NY 10017).

A magazine oriented towards Western businessmen, containing articles about various aspects of the Japanese business world including Japan's industrial policy, new developments in Japanese industry, and current Japanese business trends. These are

Periodicals and Newspapers. Periodicals

supplemented by in-depth cover stories focusing on such topics as housing in Japan, changing life-styles among the Japanese, Japan's distribution industry, restructuring within the Japanese economy, and Japanese overseas investment. The journal also carries regular interviews with government and business officials, profiles of foreign business companies in Japan as well as of leading Japanese corporate figures, reviews of new English-language books published in Japan, and a section of current economic indicators.

1528 **Journal of Northeast Asian Studies.**
Washington, DC: Institute for Sino-Soviet Studies, George Washington University, 1982- . quarterly.

Presents analyses of social, political, economic, and military developments in northeastern Asia since World War II as well as studies of external factors likely to have a significant impact on China, Japan, and Korea. 'Japan's Search for an Independent Foreign Policy: an American Perspective', 'History and Politics in Japanese–Korean Relations: the Textbook Controversy and Beyond', and 'Japan's Defense Policy and the May 1981 Summit' are typical of the articles that it publishes.

1529 **Journal of the Association of Teachers of Japanese.**
Madison, Wisconsin: Association of Teachers of Japanese, 1964- . semi-annual. (Association of Teachers of Japanese, c/o Department of East Asian Languages and Literature, University of Wisconsin, Madison, WI 53706, USA).

The Association of Teachers of Japanese is a professional organisation of North American scholars and teachers concerned with Japanese language, linguistics, and literature. Its journal publishes articles on such topics as sequential predicates in Japanese, the status of native and non-native instructors of Japanese, and creative literature about the bombing of Hiroshima; translations of poetry and fiction; numerous book reviews; and an annotated bibliographical column of recently completed dissertations and theses in fields of interest to its readership.

1530 **Journal of the Japanese and International Economies.**
Duluth, Minnesota: Academic Press, 1987- . quarterly. (Editorial and subscription offices: Academic Press, Inc., Journals Division, 1250 Sixth Ave., San Diego, CA 92101, USA).

Published in co-operation with the Tokyo Center for Economic Research (Tōkyō Keizai Kenkyū Sentā), this periodical contains analyses of the interdependence between the Japanese and Western economies, reviews of other international issues related to the Japanese economy and the economies of the Pacific basin, studies of the Japanese perspective in contemporary economic issues, and theoretical, empirical and comparative analyses of Japanese markets and institutions. Typical of its coverage are articles entitled 'Japan–U.S. Industry-level Productivity Comparisons, 1960–1979', 'Bonuses and Employment in Japan', 'Short-term and Long-term Expectations of the Yen/Dollar Exchange Rate', 'Japanese Firms, Chinese Firms: Problems for Economic Reform in China', and 'Savings and Growth: Experiences of Korea and Japan'.

1531 **Law in Japan: an Annual.**
Edited by the Japanese American Society for Legal Studies. Tokyo: University of Tokyo Press, 1967- . annual. (For subscribers in the United States: Asian Law Program, School of Law, JB-20, University of Washington, Seattle, WA 98195).

Offers scholarly analyses of Japanese law (including articles translated from Japanese) as well as commentaries on judicial cases written by Japanese and Western scholars. Typical of its contents are contributions entitled 'The Internationalization of the Japanese Economy and Corporate Reorganization Procedures: the Iwazawa Group and Sapporo Toyopet Failures', 'A Comparative View of Legal Culture in Japan and the United States', '*Gyōsei shido* [administrative guidance] and the Antimonopoly Law', 'The Limits of Administrative Authority in Japan: the Oil Cartel Criminal Cases and the Reaction of MITI and the FTC', and 'Americanization of Japanese Family Law, 1945–1975'.

1532 **Look Japan.**
Tokyo: Look Japan, Ltd., 1956- . monthly. (Look Japan, Ltd., 2-2 Kanda-Ogawamachi, Chiyoda-ku, Tokyo 101, Japan).

Short news stories and brief feature articles offer coverage of recent developments and current trends in Japan. Stories are grouped together by broad subject under eight headings: 'Opinion', 'Economics', 'Business', 'Sci-Tech', 'People', 'Everyday', 'Culture', and 'Others'. Each monthly issue also features a cover story with such titles as 'Where the Money Goes' (on direct and indirect overseas Japanese investment), 'Marital Strife' (on Japan–US economic relations), and 'JNR Jr.' (on the privatisation of the Japanese National Railways).

1533 **Management Japan.**
Tokyo: International Management Association of Japan [Sekai Keiei Kyōgikai], 1967- . semi-annual. (Sekai Keiei Kyōgikai, No. 10 Mori Building, 18-1 Toranomon 1-chōme, Minato-ku, Tokyo 105, Japan).

Concerned with the management techniques and problems facing Japanese management, among them matters relating to industrial expansion, business trends, the administration of business, and foreign investment. Articles comparing Japanese management with management abroad are also included.

1534 **Monumenta Nipponica: Studies in Japanese Culture.**
Tokyo: Sophia University, 1938-43, 1951- . quarterly. (Monumenta Nipponica, Sophia University, 7-1 Kioi-chō, Chiyoda-ku, Tokyo 102, Japan).

A journal of scholarly articles, occasional translations, and numerous book reviews dealing with the study of Japanese literature, history, culture, and religion. Representative articles have been concerned with musical instruction in Meiji period education, the rise of sectarian identity in Jōdo Shinshū Buddhism, the transformation of Japanese foreign policy attitudes between 1853 and 1868, secret teachings in medieval calligraphy, the philosophical dimensions of human nature in Natsume Sōseki's novel *Kokoro*, the standardisation of the written language as a factor in Japan's modernisation, and sacral kingship and confederacy in Izumo Province before the ninth century AD.

1535 **Orientations: the Monthly Magazine for Collectors and Connoisseurs of Oriental Art.**
Hong Kong: Orientations Magazine, Ltd., 1970- . monthly.
(Orientations Magazine, Ltd., 14th floor, 200 Lockhart Road, Hong Kong).

A richly illustrated journal devoted to the visual arts of China, Japan, Korea, and the countries of South and Southeast Asia. *Orientations* contains informed articles on all aspects of Asian art including ceramics, paintings, lacquerware, sculpture, metalwork, calligraphy, and netsuke as well as monthly calendars of important exhibitions, symposia, and conferences around the world; regular reports about activities at major auctions in London, New York, Hong Kong, and other cities that analyse the latest price and collecting trends; special reports about new museum acquisitions and exhibitions; and occasional book reviews. 'Japan through an Artist's Eyes: the True-View Pictures of Yamamoto Baiitsu', 'Modern Japanese Studio Ceramics: the Revolt against Tradition', '*Bijin* Paintings from the Harari Collection', and 'The Tradition of Temple Fund Raising: Treasures of Japanese Art from Todai-ji' are typical of the Japan-related articles that have appeared within its pages.

1536 **Pacific Affairs.**
Vancouver, British Columbia: University of British Columbia, 1928- . quarterly. (Pacific Affairs, 2029 West Mall, University of British Columbia, Vancouver, British Columbia V6T 1W5, Canada).

A well-established scholarly journal concerned with the contemporary social, economic, and political affairs of the countries of East, Southeast, and South Asia, Australasia, and the western Pacific. Containing numerous book reviews as well as frequent articles about Japan, it has published such pieces as 'The Security Debate in Japan', 'The Road to Becoming a Regional Leader: Japanese Attempts in Southeast Asia, 1975–1980', 'The Patterns of Japanese Relations with China, 1952–1982', 'Japan's Response to Threats of Shipping Disruptions in Southeast Asia and the Middle East', and 'Japan's Keidanren and Its New Leadership'.

1537 **PHP Intersect: Where Japan Meets Asia and the World.**
Tokyo: PHP Institute, Inc., 1985- . monthly. (PHP Institute, Inc., 3-10 Sanbanchō, Chiyoda-ku, Tokyo 102, Japan).

A general-interest magazine which contains a wide range of articles about modern Japan as well as photo-essays and regular columns about news, art, family life, business, traditional culture, and new books. Each issue also explores in depth a particular theme such as changing Japanese tastes in fast foods, impediments in US–Japanese relations, old age in Japan, the diversification of Japanese business, and Japanese gods. The PHP Institute was established in 1946 by Matsushita Kōnosuke, the founder of the Matsushita Electric Industrial Company, at the time that he launched his PHP ('Peace and Happiness through Prosperity') movement.

1538 **Proceedings of the British Association for Japanese Studies.**
Sheffield, England: Centre of Japanese Studies, University of Sheffield, 1976- . annual.

The proceedings of the annual meetings of the Association, edited over the years by several of its members including Gordon Daniels, John Chapman, Ian Gow, Peter Lowe, and David Steeds. The Association was founded in 1974 with the intention of fostering interest in all aspects of Japanese culture including history, international relations, economy, politics, society, art, and literature. Typical of the papers appearing in the 1984 and 1985 proceedings are: 'Great Britain, Japan and the Korean War, 1950–51', 'Discrimination in Japan: the Post-war Debate', 'Religious Rites in a Japanese Factory', 'Recruitment in the Japanese Silk Reeling and Cotton Spinning Industries, 1870s–1930s', 'Japan, Japanese and Information Technology', and 'Images of Japan in Late Nineteenth Century Western Art'.

1539 **Science & Technology in Japan.**
Tokyo: Three "I" Publications, Ltd., 1982- . quarterly. (Three "I" Publications, Ltd., Yamaguchi Building, 2-8-5 Uchikanda, Chiyoda-ku, Tokyo 101, Japan).

Offers up-to-date, reliable information about the world of Japanese science and technology, including feature articles that provide in-depth analyses of current developments in such fields as nuclear energy, information science, biotechnology, materials science, and space technology; descriptions of new technologies and discoveries ('R & D Highlights'); practical information about the organisation, budgets, and R & D interests of research institutes in both the private and government sectors; special articles on newsworthy topics; and interviews with important Japanese personalities.

1540 **Speaking of Japan.**
Tokyo: Keizai Kōhō Center [Japan Institute for Social and Economic Affairs], 1981- . monthly. (Keizai Kōhō Center, 6-1 Ōtemachi 1-chōme, Chiyoda-ku, Tokyo 100, Japan).

A magazine containing speeches delivered by such distinguished Japanese and foreign politicians, businessmen, and academic specialists as Prime Minister Nakasone Yasuhiro, US Ambassador Mike Mansfield, Sony Corporation Chairman Morita Akio, Interallianz Bank Zürich President Peter V. Huggler, and Hebrew University professor Ben-Ami Shillony. Most speeches are presented in their original, unabridged versions. They generally focus on Japanese foreign economic and political relations, and on Japanese economic activities and business practices. Typical of speeches published in 1988 are: 'Adjusting to Interdependence: the Challenges Ahead for Europe–Japan Relations'; 'Burden Sharing: Japan's Contribution to Collective Security'; 'Painful Progress: Restructuring the Japanese and U.S. Economies'; 'Expert Consumers: Trends in Japanese Purchasing and Lifestyles'; and 'A New Partnership: U.S.–Japan Bilateral Cooperation in the Multilateral Context'.

1541 **Technology and Development.**
Tokyo: Institute for International Cooperation, Japan International Cooperation Agency, 1988- . annual. (Institute for International Cooperation, Japan International Cooperation Agency, International Cooperation Center Building, 10-5 Ichigaya-Honmura-chō, Shinjuku-ku, Tokyo 162, Japan).

A selection of articles and case-studies translated from the Institute's semi-annual periodical *Kokusai kyōryoku kenkyū* that focus on Japan's rapidly growing technical co-operation with the developing countries of the world. Among the items appearing within the inaugural issue of this magazine were articles dealing with the contributions that Japan can make to controlling malaria in the Third World, Japan's technical assistance to Sri Lanka in order to promote industrial development in that country's agricultural villages, a village improvement programme in Malaysia carried out by an organisation known as Japan Overseas Cooperation Volunteers, and the audiovisual technology courses offered to overseas students at the Okinawa International Center in the Ryūkyūs.

1542 **Tokyo Business Today: a Monthly Magazine of Japan's Business and Finance.**
Tokyo: Tōyō Keizai Shinposha (The Oriental Economist), 1986- . monthly. (Tōyō Keizai Shinposha, 1-2-1 Nihonbashi Hongokuchō, Chūō-ku, Tokyo 103, Japan).

Publishes reliable reports, carefully reasoned analyses, and feature stories about Japan's economy, industry, and politics, as well as news about some of the major issues affecting Japanese business. Among its regular features are columns by widely respected experts including James C. Abegglen and Okawara Yoshio, book reviews, a section entitled 'Corporate Information', and economic and financial indicators. This journal is the successor to *The Oriental Economist*, one of Japan's most prestigious English-language periodicals between 1934 and 1985.

1543 **Transactions of the Asiatic Society of Japan.**
Tokyo: Asiatic Society of Japan. Series 1: 1872/73-1922; Series 2: 1924-40; Series 3: 1948-85; Series 4: 1986- . annual. (Asiatic Society of Japan, Central Post Office Box 592, Tokyo, Japan).

The Asiatic Society of Japan, founded in 1872, was established for the purpose of promoting and recording scholarly knowledge about 'all manner of aspects of Japan'. Since 1874 it has published four series of annual transactions. Each volume consists of up to six original research articles – generally dealing with Japanese history, literature, thought, language, art, and culture as well as with the activities of Westerners who have lived in Japan or who have had some special interest in Japan – together with information about the Society's activities and its membership. A comprehensive history of the first one hundred years of the Society, written by Douglas Moore Kenrick, appeared in December 1978 as volume 14 in the third series of the *Transactions*. The Society also publishes a monthly bulletin which contains detailed summaries of scholarly lectures presented at its membership meetings.

1544 **Venture Japan: the Journal of Global Opportunity.**
San Francisco: Asia Pacific Communications, Inc., 1988- . quarterly. (Asia Pacific Communications, Inc., 110 Sutter St., Suite 708, San Francisco, CA 94104, USA).

Targeted towards corporate executives, investors, and international associations, this journal focuses on contemporary US–Japanese relations in the areas of trade, technology, and investment. Short articles deal with such subjects as Japanese venture capital firms, Japan's new tax system, US–Japanese technological partnering and trends, Japanese mergers and acquisitions activity in the United States, trade barriers and the ongoing US–Japan trade dispute, and the efforts of American firms to gain a competitive edge in Japan. Each issue also carries a special report – e.g., 'Top 100 Japanese Firms in the U.S.', and 'Japanese Language Schools in New York City' – as well as book reviews and information sources.

1545 **The Wheel Extended.**
Tokyo: Toyota Motor Corporation, 1971- . quarterly. (Toyota Motor Corporation, Public Affairs Department, 4-18 Kōraku 1-chōme, Bunkyo-ku, Tokyo 112, Japan).
An illustrated general-interest magazine containing, in particular, articles dealing with important social issues in Japan and with various aspects of Japanese industry and technology. A number of issues appearing during the mid-1980s focused on present-day Tokyo, high technology in Japan, the Pan-Pacific era, education in Japan, the growth of the Japanese automobile industry, the impact of television broadcasting, and the relationship between science/technology and human culture.

Buraku Liberation News.
See item no. 381.

Summaries of Selected Japanese Magazines.
See item no. 1547.

Japanese periodicals and newspapers in Western languages: an international union list.
See item no. 1601.

Doctoral Dissertations on Asia: an Annotated Bibliographical Journal of Current International Research.
See item no. 1607.

Newspapers

1546 **Asahi Evening News.**
Tokyo: Asahi Evening News, 1954- . daily. (Asahi Evening News, 8-5 Tsukiji 7-chōme, Chūō-ku, Tokyo 104, Japan).
International news is featured in Japan's only English-language evening newspaper, a publication which also offers good coverage of national, local, business, financial, entertainment, and sports news of interest to its readers. Because the editorial page regularly carries translations of material that first appears in the *Asahi Shimbun*, one of Japan's leading daily newspapers, it is particularly informative about Japanese views on current events.

1547 **Daily Summary of Japanese Press.**
Tokyo: Office of Translation Services, Political Section, US Embassy, 1952- . daily (except weekends and holidays).
Translations and synopses of significant articles and editorials about contemporary affairs in Japan – especially Japan's economy, business world, international trade, government and politics, foreign relations, and military defence – appearing in the country's leading newspapers: *Asahi*, *Mainichi*, *Nihon Keizai*, *Sankei*, *Tōkyō Shimbun*, and *Yomiuri*. Similiar in scope is the American Embassy's *Summaries of Selected Japanese Magazines* (1952-), which contains full translations of particularly important

`magazine articles, summaries of all major articles appearing in *Bungei Shunjū* and *Chūō Kōron*, and the tables of contents in translation of the monthly issues of *Sekai*, *Seiron*, *Jiyū*, *Kankai*, *Shokun*, and *Seikai Ōrai*. Both publications are issued in mimeographed format and are distributed to research libraries and selected government agencies, particularly in the United States.

1548 **Japan Economic Journal.**
Tokyo; New York: Nihon Keizai Shimbun, 1963- . weekly. (Nihon Keizai Shimbun, 9-5 Ōtemachi 1-chōme, Chiyoda-ku, Tokyo 100-66, Japan. For subscribers in the United States: JEJ Subscription Department, c/o OCS America, Inc., P.O.B. 1654, Long Island City, NY 11101).

The weekly English-language edition of the *Nihon Keizai Shimbun* (the '*Wall Street Journal* of Japan'), Japan's leading economic and business newspaper. Each issue contains over 250 news reports and analytical feature articles about the Japanese economy in general, overall business trends, the industrial sector (e.g., electronics, computers, machinery, textiles), marketing, finance, trade (particularly with the United States), industrial innovations, and government policies. Topical features on personalities in the world of business and finance offer insights into some of the people responsible for Japan's recent transformation into a major economic and financial power, while a new product highlight section focuses attention on advances of particular interest to the world of commerce. Tables of leading economic indicators and the weekly transactions of the Tokyo Stock Exchange are also included. Editions of the *Japan Economic Journal* are printed in Tokyo, New York, and San Francisco on the same day.

1549 **Japan Times.**
Tokyo: Japan Times, 1897- . daily. (Japan Times, Ltd., 5-4 Shibaura 4-chōme, Minato-ku, Tokyo 108; C.P.O. Box 144, Tokyo 100-91, Japan).

The largest circulating English-language daily newspaper in Japan, offering widespread coverage of domestic, international, political, social, business, and cultural news from a moderate and internationalist perspective. Sports, entertainment, and editorial pages as well as a large classified advertisements section are also included. Since its establishment in 1897, the *Japan Times* has also appeared under three other names: *Japan Times and Mail* (1918-40), *Japan Times and Advertiser* (1940-42), and *Nippon Times* (1943-56). The 'Weekly Overseas Edition' of the *Japan Times* (1961-) – an edition which contains the week's top national news, the editorials and columns of the daily *Japan Times*, and several additional features – may be of particular interest to people overseas who wish to keep themselves informed of major developments in Japan and of the Japanese perspective on world events.

Japanese periodicals and newspapers in Western languages: an international union list.
See item no. 1601.

Encyclopaedias, Directories, and Subject Dictionaries

1550 **Japanese colleges and universities 1989: a guide to institutions of higher education in Japan.**
Compiled and edited by the Association of International Education, Japan [Nihon Kokusai Kyōiku Kyōkai] in collaboration with the Association of National Universities [Kokuritsu Daigaku Kyōkai], the Association of Public Universities [Kōritsu Daigaku Kyōkai], the Federation of Japanese Private Colleges and Universities Associations [Shiritsu Daigaku Dantai Rengokai]; supervised by the Monbushō [Ministry of Education, Science, and Culture]; prefaces by Hiroshi Ueki, Tsuneaki Kawamura.   Tokyo: Maruzen, 1989. 731p.
The expanded and updated third edition of a comprehensive guide to Japan's world of higher education: 95 national, 36 local public, and 334 private four-year colleges and universities. Oriented towards foreign students wishing to study in Japan, it provides informative descriptions (2-6 pages in length) of each institution – covering its history, location, characteristics, size, libraries, undergraduate and graduate programmes, research institutes and centres, foreign student admission requirements and procedures, facilities for foreign students, and special programmes for students from abroad – together with addresses from which additional information can be secured. Other helpful features include an index by subject majors, lists of school fees, listings of government and university scholarships and fellowships, and information about Japanese language courses.

1551 **New Japanalia: past and present.**
Lewis Bush.   Tokyo: Japan Times, 1977. 272p.
A selection of brief articles about Japan and the Japanese which Bush compiled from his popular newspaper column in the *Japan Times* (q.v.). They are grouped under thirteen headings: 'The Zodiac', 'Festivals, Celebrations', 'Annual Events', 'Holidays, Anniversaries', 'Gods, Goblins', 'Birds, Flowers, Trees, Insects', 'Food, Drink, Tobacco', 'Land of the Gods', 'The Old Highways', 'Early Overseas Ventures',

Encyclopaedias, Directories, and Subject Dictionaries

'Personalities', 'Dawn of Modern Japan', and 'Miscellany'. Encompassing a wide range of subjects, these articles offer insightful and frequently amusing views of Japan's past and present. Interested readers may also wish to consult some of the author's earlier volumes on 'things Japanese', among them his *Japanalia: a concise cyclopaedia* (Tokyo: Tokyo News Service, 1965. 6th rev. and enlarged ed., 420p.).

1552 **All-Japan: the catalogue of everything Japanese.**
Liza Dalby (et al.), introduction by Oliver Statler. New York: William Morrow; Bromley, Kent: Columbus Books, 1984. 224p. bibliog.

A richly illustrated guide to many facets of Japanese culture (both past and present) ranging from architecture, beer and whiskey, and bunraku, to traditional and folk medicine, wooden crafts, and the pleasure quarter in Tokyo known as the Yoshiwara. These are covered in over one hundred brief essays and more than 250 photographs that are grouped together under sixteen topical headings: 'Crafts', 'Design'. 'Visual Arts', 'Literature and Film', 'The Bath', 'The Tea Ceremony', 'Food and Drink', 'Music', 'Medicine', 'Sports', 'Religion', 'Theatre', 'Travel', 'Child's Play', 'After Hours', and 'Language'. Address listings of such 'sources' of things Japanese as bookstores, gift shops, language schools, etc. in Canada, the United Kingdom, and the United States provide supplementary information. The catalogue was produced by eight experts on Japan for a wide general audience.

1553 **Passport's Japan almanac.**
Boye De Mente. Lincolnwood, Illinois: Passport Books, 1987. 319p. map.

A profusely illustrated general compendium of nearly one thousand terms relating to Japan, the Japanese people, and various aspects of Japanese civilisation, Japanese customs, and contemporary Japanese life. Both things that are uniquely Japanese (e.g., bushidō, the Ginza, kamikaze pilots, Shin Kanmon Tunnel, wooden clogs) and things that are universal in nature but have a special Japanese quality about them (e.g., dolls, hotels, medical care, newspapers, trains, unlucky numbers) are presented. Arranged in alphabetical sequence from 'abacus' to 'Zushi' (the name of a popular seaside resort south of Yokohama), all of the entries are accompanied by explanations ranging from one or two paragraphs to a few pages in length as well as by their equivalent in Japanese and their phonetic pronunciation in English.

1554 **Overseas Japanese studies institutions = Kaigai Nihon kenkyū kikan yōran.**
Fukuoka Unesco Association [Fukuoka Yunesuko Kyōkai], foreword by Takeshi Hashimoto. Fukuoka: Fukuoka Unesco Association, 1984. 182p.

A comprehensive directory to 221 universities and research organisations with programmes in Japanese studies that are located in thirty-nine countries other than Japan. These institutions are grouped together under their respective countries. Within each entry the compilers generally provide the institution's name, address, year it was established, subsections into which it is organisationally divided, director's name, number of research personnel and students in Japanese studies, research fields, special research programmes, publications, and library holdings, as well as the names and specialities of the institution's research personnel. A new edition is due for publication by early 1990.

1555 **Concise dictionary of modern Japanese history.**
Compiled by Janet E. Hunter. Berkeley, California; London: University of California Press, 1984. 347p. 3 maps. bibliog.

A reliable reference guide to individuals, places, events, organisations, and ideas of significance in Japan between 1853 and 1980. The 650 relatively brief entries present the most salient facts and summarise current interpretations about political, economic, and social developments in modern Japan. Short bibliographies following most of the entries guide the reader to generally accessible sources of more detailed information in English. There are appendixes for the names and dates of eras and emperor's reigns, Japan's modern population growth (1872-1977), the development of modern political parties, and the names and dates of office for all Cabinet members from the introduction of the Cabinet system in 1885 through the Suzuki Zenkō Cabinet of 1980. The dictionary is aimed primarily at non-specialists, undergraduate students, and professionals in business and government.

1556 **Kodansha encyclopedia of Japan.**
Gen Itasaka, editor-in-chief; executive editors: Alan Campbell, Gyō Furuta, Takeshi Kokubo; introduction by Edwin O. Reischauer, foreword by Koremichi Noma. Tokyo; New York: Kodansha, 1983. 9 vols. maps. bibliog. Supplement, first edition. Tokyo; New York: Kodansha, 1986. 59p.

This monumental reference work is the consummation of a ten-year joint effort by 680 Japanese and 524 non-Japanese scholars 'to provide an up-to-date and sophisticated compilation of knowledge about Japan to the English-speaking world'. The first eight volumes contain 9,417 entries of varying length that cover virtually every important topic and personality related to Japan. Broad introductory or summary articles for most of the major areas into which Japanese culture can be divided are included. The encyclopaedia places its greatest emphasis on history, geography, the fine and performing arts, and literature, while also according considerable attention to economic and business affairs. Many entries are followed by suggestions for further reading. Numerous black-and-white photographs, tables, charts, drawings, graphs, and maps accompany the text. The ninth volume consists of the index to the entire set. The encyclopaedia was written with a wide audience of students, scholars, diplomats, businessmen, and the general public in mind. While an abbreviated one-volume edition is due to be published in 1990, the present nine-volume set is unlikely to be superseded for many years to come.

1557 **Discover Japan: words, customs and concepts.**
Japan Culture Institute [Nihon Bunka Kenkyūjo]. Tokyo; New York: Kodansha International, 1982-83. 2 vols.

Brief illustrated essays offer informative and entertaining descriptions of selected words, ideas, and customs in order to enhance the foreigner's understanding of contemporary Japanese culture and society. The essays cover a broad range of topics: from *kangeiko* (midwinter training for those in the martial arts), *omiyage* (a souvenir, usually in the form of a present or gift), *koinobori* (carp-shaped streamers traditionally flown by Japanese families on the holiday known as Boy's Day), and *omiai* (an interview or meeting with a view to marriage), to sushi (sliced, usually raw seafood over rice-balls), *yukimizake* (drinking saké while enjoying views of the snow), *sakura* (Japanese cherry trees or their blossoms), and *omawari-san* (the friendly patrolman in one's neighbourhood). All of the contributors are foreigners who have lived in Japan. The two volumes of this set were first published by the Japan Culture Institute under the titles *A hundred things Japanese* (1975) and *A hundred more things Japanese* (1980).

1558 **Directory of information sources in Japan, 1986.**
Edited by the Japan Special Libraries Association [Senmon Toshokan Kyōgikai], Committee of Statistical Survey and Research; preface by Norobu Gotoh. Tokyo: Nichigai Associates, 1986. 378p.
Revised edition of a directory to libraries and other specialised information centres or sources of informational materials that are available in government agencies, research institutes, and similar types of institutions on the national level, as well as in public corporations and government organisations, local governments, universities and colleges, learned societies and independent organisations, private enterprises, international organisations, and foreign diplomatic establishments. Consisting principally of a classified listing of 1,778 sources of information, indexed by their names in both English and romanised Japanese, the directory provides such basic information for each entry as the full name of a library or information centre, its address and telephone number, the size of its staff, its book budget, monograph and serial holdings, subject specialties, special collections, and the names of any periodicals that it publishes.

1559 **Japanese studies in Europe.** Tokyo: Japan Foundation, 1985. 427p.
(Directory Series, 7).
Directory of Japan specialists in Australia. Tokyo: Japan
Foundation, 1986. rev. ed. 61p. (Directory Series, 8).
Japanese studies in Southeast Asia. Tokyo: Japan Foundation, 1987.
204p. (Directory Series, 11).
Japanese studies in the United Kingdom. Tokyo: Japan Foundation,
1988. 285p. (Japanese Studies Series, 15).
Japan studies in Canada: 1987. Tokyo: Japan Foundation, 1988.
354p. (Japanese Studies Series, 16).
Japanese studies in the United States. Part 1: History and present condition. Compiled and edited by Marius B. Jansen. Part 2: Directory of Japan specialists and Japanese studies institutions in the United States and Canada. Edited by Patricia G. Steinhoff. Ann Arbor, Michigan: Association for Asian Studies, 1988-89. 3 vols. (Japanese Studies Series, 17–18).
(Japan Foundation [Kokusai Kōryū Kikin], Park Building, 3-6 Kioi-chō, Chiyoda-ku, Tokyo 102, Japan).
Since 1981, the Japan Foundation has been producing a series of periodically revised directories and survey reports for Japanese studies abroad that provide detailed information about all levels of Japanese studies within a particular country or region and help promote closer contacts among individuals engaged in studying and teaching about Japan. While these directories and reports vary among themselves in terms of

their scope, comprehensiveness, and even language (some are written in Japanese or Spanish), they generally contain the following types of information: (1) descriptive reports about the historical background, development, and current state of Japanese studies within a particular country or region, and (2) directories of institutions and individual specialists – including their addresses, academic affiliation, area of specialisation and current research interests, and major publications about Japan.

1560 **Legend in Japanese art: a description of historical episodes, legendary characters, folk-lore, myths, religious symbolism, illustrated in the arts of old Japan.**
Henri L. Joly.   London; New York: John Lane, 1908. 543p. bibliog. Reprinted, Rutland, Vermont and Tokyo: Tuttle; London: Kegan Paul, Trench, Trubner, 1967. 623p.
An encyclopaedic guide covering many of the legends, traditional customs, popular beliefs, and historical incidents that are embodied as subjects and themes in such types of art as netsuke, inrō, *tsuba* ('metal sword-fittings'), woodblock prints, and painting. From 'Abe no Yasuna' (the folk figure who married a white fox that had assumed the shape of a beautiful woman to bewitch him) to 'Zuire' (a son of Benten, the goddess of learning and speech, whose attributes are the draught ox and the horse), 1,120 entries identify and describe numerous deities, personages, animals, plants, types of amusement, temples, etc. which were familiar to traditional Japanese artists and were depicted in the objects they created. Initially published to assist collectors and admirers of Japanese art objects, this volume is also useful for students of Japanese art in general.

1561 **Mock Joya's things Japanese.**
Mock Jōya.   Tokyo: Japan Times, 1985. new ed. 728p.
Slightly more than one thousand articles covering a wide range of subjects – from lanterns, smallpox, fugu (a globefish), and blackened teeth, to tattooing, the wedding ceremony, archery, and new year's cards – constitute an encyclopaedic overview of Japanese life, culture, tradition, and customs. These articles (250 to 3,000 words in length) are grouped into chapters entitled: 'Apparel and Utensils', 'Cures and Medicines', 'Dwelling Houses and other Buildings', 'Fetes and Festivals', 'Fish, Birds and Animals', 'Folk Tales', 'Food, Saké and Tobacco', 'Living Habits', 'Marriage, Funerals and Memorials', 'Natural Phenomena', 'Plants and Flowers', 'Popular Beliefs and Traditions', 'Recreation and Entertainment', 'Religious Rites', 'Social Customs', 'Historical Tales and Relics', and 'Miscellaneous'. Oriented towards the general reader but also valuable for the student of Japanese society, this volume (like Lewish Bush's comparable work, *New Japanalia: past and present*, q.v.) originated in a series of articles written for publication in the *Japan Times* (q.v.).

1562 **Scholars' guide to Washington, D.C. for East Asian studies (China, Japan, Korea, and Mongolia).**
Hong N. Kim; consultants: Frank Joseph Shulman, Warren M. Tsuneishi; series editor: Zdeněk V. David; foreword by James H. Billington.   Washington, DC: Smithsonian Institution Press, 1979. 413p. bibliog. (Scholars' Guide to Washington, D.C., 3).
Prepared as part of a series of scholarly guidebooks sponsored by the Woodrow Wilson International Center for Scholars, this volume presents descriptive and evaluative

surveys of Washington-area resources that are concerned in large measure with Japan and the Japanese. Part one surveys the holdings of local research libraries; archives and manuscript repositories; museums, galleries, and art collections; music, map, film and still-picture collections; and data banks. Part two covers the pertinent activities of both public and private Washington-based organisations including academic, cultural, and professional associations; cultural exchange organisations; US government agencies; foreign government agencies and international organisations; research centres and academic programmes and departments; and publications and media. More exhaustive, itemised inventories of source material about Japan in Washington, DC as well as as elsewhere in the United States may be found in *Asia and Oceania: a guide to archival and manuscript sources in the United States*, edited by G. Raymond Nunn, with contributions from Alberta Freidus, Walter Pierson and the Center for Asian and Pacific Studies, University of Hawaii (London; New York: Mansell, 1985, 5 vols.).

1563 **Dictionary of Asian American history.**
Edited by Hyung-Chan Kim. Westport, Connecticut; London: Greenwood Press, 1986. 627p. bibliog.

A reference work concerning the experiences of major Asian groups in the United States. The volume opens with fifteen introductory essays on individual Asian groups – in particular, the Chinese, Japanese, Koreans, Filipinos, and Indians – as well as on Asian Americans and their involvement in American immigration law, justice, politics, economy, education, mental health, popular culture, and literature. The remainder of the dictionary consists largely of some eight hundred entries for 'major events, persons, places, and concepts that have left indelible marks on the collective experience of Asian and Pacific Americans'. Japanese Americans are the focus of many of these entries, as in the case of 'Inoue, Daniel Ken' (a senator from Hawaii), 'Japanese Federation of Labor', '*Tanomoshi*' (a form of rotating credit association), and '442nd Regimental Combat Unit' (a World War II military unit made up of Nisei volunteers).

1564 **Kabuki encyclopedia: an English-language adaptation of *Kabuki jiten*.**
Samuel L. Leiter. Westport, Connecticut; London: Greenwood Press, 1979. 572p. bibliog.

This adaptation of a standard Japanese reference work is designed to make the traditional kabuki theatre more accessible to non-Japanese theatre lovers. Several hundred concise entries deal with the actors, texts and playwrights, plays, acting and staging, costumes and make-up, theatrical architecture, décor and props, music, dance schools, and other historical and technical terms relating to kabuki. Synopses of over two hundred plays accompanied by information about their original casts, their premières, and their backgrounds and performance methods are provided. Appendixes offer a brief chronological survey of kabuki, a list of all major plays within the kabuki repertoire, a list of all major variant and popularised play and act titles, and the genealogies of all prominent acting families.

1565 **Japan information resources in the United States, 1985.**
Edited by Toshio Matsuoka, with Makito Noda, Pamela J. Noda.
Tokyo: Keizai Kōhō Center [Japan Institute for Social and Economic
Affairs], 1985. 128p. (Keizai Kōhō Center, 6-1, Ōtemachi 1-chōme,
Chiyoda-ku, Tokyo 100, Japan).

Compiled to promote the widespread use and development of information sources
about Japan in the United States, this directory identifies pertinent Japanese and US
government organisations, Japanese trade centres and chambers of commerce,
Japanese industry associations, Japan Societies (which seek to promote friendly
relations between the USA and Japan and to disseminate information about Japan
within the United States), non-profit organisations (e.g., the Association of Teachers
of Japanese, and the U.S.–Japan Culture Center), university programmes and research
institutes, and academic and public libraries. For each organisation, the authors
provide full address and telephone information, a listing of key personnel, and either a
description of its major activities and programmes or a statement about its history and
objectives.

1566 **The Princeton companion to classical Japanese literature.**
Earl Miner, Hiroko Odagiri, Robert E. Morrell.   Princeton, New
Jersey; Guildford, Surrey: Princeton University Press, 1985. 570p.
7 maps.

An indispensable handbook to Japanese literature from its beginnings through the end
of the Tokugawa period (1868). It opens with four essays on literary history and on
poetics as well as several brief chronologies. It continues with a dictionary listing of 435
major authors and significant literary works; a glossary of literary terms; essays on the
history, structure, conventions, and terminology of the six major dramatic forms – noh,
kyōgen, *mibu kyōgen*, *kōwakamai*, *jōruri*, and kabuki; a section entitled 'Collections,
Kinds, Criticism: Buddhism and Confucianism; Dictionaries'; and lists, tables and
descriptions of time, directions, related symbolism, and annual celebrations as they are
depicted in classical literature. Also covered are geography, maps, and poetic place
names; and imperial and bureaucratic ranks, offices, and some of the incumbents of
those offices. The concluding part contains annotated illustrations of architecture,
clothing, armour and arms, as well as samples of illustrated popular books and other
genre representations.

1567 **Dictionary of Chinese and Japanese art.**
Hugo Munsterberg.   New York: Hacker Books, 1981. 354p. bibliog.

A dictionary of approximately two thousand terms associated with the fine arts, in
particular painting, print-making, ceramics, lacquerware, and architecture. The entries
are oriented towards the beginning student and art collector. They cover artists'
names, place names, motifs, artistic processes and techniques, and the deities, animals,
and other beings that are depicted in Chinese and Japanese art. Representative terms
include 'Adachigahara' (a legendary figure), '*chawan*' (tea bowls), 'Furukawa Genshin'
(eighteenth-century maker of sword guards), '*kirigane*' (a form of decoration utilising
rectangular pieces of gold foil), 'Ohara' (village north of Kyōto), 'Shidoro' (a
traditional type of pottery), and '*zogan-nuri*' (a Japanese lacquer technique).

1568   **Pictorial encyclopedia of Japanese culture: the soul and heritage of Japan.**
Tokyo: Gakken, 1987. 130p. (Distributed in the United States by Kodansha International).

Five hundred photographs and illustrations, mostly in full colour, offer a broad overview (with brief textual information) of the culture, history, and society of Japan. The encyclopaedia is designed as an easy-to-use reference aid for general readers seeking introductory material about the origins and myths of Japan; her religions, rituals, temples, and shrines; Japanese traditions, festivals, and other seasonal events; and such artistic achievements and architectural accomplishments as noh drama, ukiyo-e prints, traditional houses and gardens, and mediaeval castles. This book is a companion volume to the *Pictorial encyclopedia of modern Japan* (Tokyo: Gakken, 1986, 136p.), a profusely illustrated work that focuses on the wide range of industries found in postwar Japan, among them automobiles, computers, cameras, fine ceramics, steel, and textiles. It also deals extensively with the everyday life of the Japanese people, including their demographics, standard of living, and types of employment.

1569   **Early Japanese history (*c*.40 B.C.–A.D. 1167).**
Robert Karl Reischauer.   Princeton, New Jersey: Princeton University Press, 1937. 2 vols. 18 maps. Reprinted, Gloucester, Massachusetts: Peter Smith, 1967.

A pioneering but now somewhat outdated reference guide that contains chronological listings of era names, emperors, and high officials; diagrams and tables showing the organisation of the government between 592 and 1167; a detailed chronology of events from mythological times to 1167, based on original chronicles; a selection of maps of ancient Japan; and several genealogical tables. A very detailed index and glossary conclude the second volume.

1570   **Information gathering on Japan: a primer.**
Search Associates, Inc.   Washington, DC: Search Associates, Inc., 1988. rev. ed. 89p. bibliog. (Search Associates, Inc., International Research, 3422 Q Street, N.W., Washington, DC 20007, USA).

This compendium of sources offers the business researcher in particular 'a framework within which to find leads for information on Japan'. The primer lists many of the offices and agencies of the US Department of Commerce; identifies the offices and people throughout the United States government that work on Japan-related issues and projects; points out who in the US Congress and its support groups is concerned with the US–Japan relationship; and introduces the research world of think tanks and universities. It also examines the growing Japanese corporate and governmental presence in the United States; briefly introduces selected resources in Japan, including business and research associations; identifies helpful publications and databases which focus on Japan; points out some of the American business and trade associations which are becoming increasingly interested in Japan; touches upon Japanese lobbying in the United States; identifies some available consultants and translators; lists various information sources about Japan found elsewhere in the West; and concludes with a list of recommended books and articles for further reading. The present edition is not indexed.

1571 **Japanese art signatures: a handbook and practical guide.**
James Self, Nobuko Hirose; foreword by Jack Hillier. London:
Bamboo Publishing; Rutland, Vermont and Tokyo: Tuttle, 1987.
399p. bibliog.

This comprehensive research aid assists both laymen and scholars in deciphering and
reading the names which painters, print-designers, metalworkers, swordsmiths, lacquer
artists, netsuke carvers, and potters have inscribed on their works. Self and Hirose
present 'a simplified approach to this complex subject' by means of a dictionary of
nearly 1,700 commonly encountered, handwritten Chinese characters (*kanji*), a
catalogue of more than 11,000 names used by artists and craftsmen (all cross-
referenced to the character dictionary), and a lexicon of character variations in the
readings of names that are difficult to relate to the standard dictionary entry. Other
distinctive features of the handbook include a catalogue of provincial, town, and place
names; a guide to dates in Japanese and how to read them; and a section which lists
over three hundred facsimile signatures found on woodblock prints. The grouping and
classification of Chinese characters adopted throughout the handbook is based on
standard Chinese–Japanese dictionaries.

1572 **The Imperial Japanese Navy.**
Anthony J. Watts, Brian G. Gordon. London: Macdonald; Garden
City, New York: Doubleday, 1971. 529p.

An encyclopaedic reference book as well as a detailed historical narrative about the
Imperial Japanese Navy from its inception in the 1870s, through its rapid growth and
development before World War II, to its total destruction in spring 1945. Nearly every
type of warship is covered: capital ships; cruisers; aircraft carriers; destroyers and
torpedo boats; submarines; escorts, gunboats, and despatch vessels; minesweepers,
minelayers, and cable vessels; and coastal forces, amphibious warfare vessels, and fleet
support ships. The authors provide a summary of the history and background of each
ship, including information about its construction, the action which it saw, and its fate;
details about its dimensions, machinery, bunkers and radius, protection, armament,
and complement; and a photograph or line drawing. Complementing this volume is a
similarly comprehensive and authoritative reference work – *Warships of the Imperial
Japanese Navy, 1869–1945*, by Hansgeorg Jentschura, Dieter Jung, and Peter Mickel,
translated by Anthony Preston and J. D. Brown (London: Arms and Armour Press;
Annapolis, Maryland: Naval Institute Press, 1977, 284p.) – which contains hundreds of
photographs and drawings as well as extensive details, measurements, and histories for
every type of naval combat vessel and fleet support ship as well as for submarine depot
ships, hospital ships, icebreakers, tugboats, and training ships.

1573 **Japan today! A Westerner's guide to the people, language and culture
of Japan.**
Theodore F. Welch, Hiroki Kato. Lincolnwood, Illinois: Passport
Books, 1986. 115p. map. bibliog.

This guide offers travellers, businessmen, and educators paragraph-long factual
presentations about Japan and the Japanese, explanations of Japanese terms and
customs as well as of various subjects of a cross-cultural nature, and useful information
on travel, accommodation, and the best use of one's free time. Typical of the nearly
three hundred topics covered are: *amae* ('dependence'), bookstores, *budō* ('martial
arts'), currency, customs duties, dating and marriage, festivals, gestures, gifts and
giving, Kyōto, *meishi* ('business cards'), national holidays, origami, police, prefectures,

sex roles, shopping, taxis, trains, vertical society, and 'yes' and 'no' in Japanese. A section on the Japanese language, a selected bibliography, and an appendix with information for travelling in Japan are also included.

1574 **Who's who in Japan.**
Hong Kong: International Culture Institute, 1984- . biennial.
(International Culture Institute, 13th floor, Jubilee Commercial
Building, 42-46 Gloucester Road, Hong Kong).

A series of comprehensive, short-entry directories to leading figures in Japanese society (especially businessmen) and to noteworthy companies, businesses, and government offices. The first volume (1984-85) contains biographical data about 42,000 prominent Japanese in the areas of government, commerce and industry, medicine, journalism, the visual and performing arts, literature, and education. A typical entry provides the individual's name, his education, current and previous positions, date of birth, honours, memberships, wife's name, hobbies, address, and telephone number. The second volume (1987-88) is a classified directory to some 15,000 national and local government offices as well as commercial and industrial enterprises in such fields as chemicals, construction and housing, electrical appliances, and textiles. Each entry includes the company or office's name, address, telephone number, president or director, and (for companies only) date of founding and level of capitalisation.

Japanese chronology.
See item no. 35.

Fishes of Japan in color.
See item no. 60.

Flora of Japan.
See item no. 62.

A field guide to the birds of Japan.
See item no. 65.

Windows on the Japanese past: studies in archaeology and prehistory.
See item no. 109.

Who's who in Japanese government, 1988/89.
See item no. 366.

Organisation of the government of Japan.
See item no. 605.

Japanese aircraft of the Pacific War.
See item no. 689.

Japan Company Handbook.
See item no. 822.

Science and technology in Japan.
See item no. 980.

Applied artificial intelligence in Japan: current status, key research and development performers, strategic focus.
See item no. 994.

Japanese antiques: with a guide to shops.
See item no. 1215.

Images from the floating world: the Japanese print; including an illustrated dictionary of ukiyo-e.
See item no. 1266.

Bibliographies and Research Guides

1575 The United States in East Asia: a historical bibliography.
Compiled by editors at ABC-Clio Information Services, introduction
by Jessica S. Brown. Santa Barbara, California: ABC-Clio
Information Services; Oxford, England: Clio Press, 1985. 298p.
(ABC-Clio Research Guides, 14).

An annotated bibliography of 1,176 periodical articles – published in hundreds of
American, European, and Asian journals between 1973 and 1984 – that are concerned
with the history of diplomatic, political, economic, and cultural relations between the
United States and the countries of East Asia, particularly during the twentieth century.
Chapter one ('General') encompasses those articles which discuss multilateral relations
among the United States and two or more countries in East Asia, or with the region as
a whole. Chapter four, containing over one-third of the entries, deals just with Japan.
Detailed subject and author indexes conclude the volume. All of the bibliographical
citations have been compiled from a vast computerised history database maintained by
ABC-Clio Information Services.

**1576 The history and practice of Japanese printmaking: a selectively
annotated bibliography of English language materials.**
Leslie E. Abrams. Westport, Connecticut; London: Greenwood
Press, 1984. 197p. (Art Reference Collection, 5).

The first book-length bibliographical guide to English-language publications concerned
with the entire history of Japanese print-making, the wide range of subjects (e.g.
nature, contemporary personalities, traditional theatre, Buddhist and cultural themes)
portrayed in both traditional and modern prints, the various types of prints (from
'almanac prints' through 'pillar prints' to 'Yokohama prints'), the techniques employed
in creating prints, the cross-cultural influences of print-making, seals and symbols on
prints, the collecting and connoisseurship of prints, permanent collections and special
exhibitions of Japanese prints in Japan as well as in the West, and the lives and careers
of noteworthy print-makers since the early Tokugawa period. Citations to 1,231 books,
periodical articles, exhibition and sales catalogues, illustrated works, and dissertations

published between 1861 and 1980 are classified into thirteen chapters. A majority of the monographs have been annotated, and there are author and detailed subject indexes.

1577 **Japanese folk literature: a core collection and reference guide.**
Joanne P. Algarin. New York; London: Bowker, 1982. 226p.
An annotated bibliography of English-language books and articles about Japanese folk tales, myths, legends, and fairy tales from premodern times to the twentieth century. Algarin's introductory overview of the development of Japanese folk literature is followed by her three-part bibliography of sixty-three scholarly books and articles concerned with Japanese folklore, by descriptions and evaluations of forty-eight anthologies which present approximately one thousand individual folk tales in English translation, and by synopses of twenty-seven classic folk tales. This is an important guide for educators and storytellers as well as for folklorists and librarians.

1578 **Kenji Mizoguchi: a guide to references and resources.**
Dudley Andrew, Paul Andrew. Boston, Massachusetts: G. K. Hall, 1981. 333p. bibliog. (A Reference Publication in Film).
A comprehensive reference guide to the life and films of one of Japan's greatest film directors. It contains a brief biographical sketch of Mizoguchi Kenji (1898-1956) as well as a critical survey of his work and cinematic style, a filmography that provides detailed synopses and credits for each of his eighty-five films (among them *Women of the Night* and *The Life of Oharu*), and an annotated bibliography of publications about Mizoguchi written primarily in English and Japanese.

1579 **Asians in America: a selected annotated bibliography.**
Asian American Studies, University of California, Davis; introduction by George Kagiwada. expanded and rev. ed. Davis, California: Asian American Studies, University of California, 1983. 292p.
A guide to English-language books, articles, theses, and dissertations about the Asian experience on the US mainland and about the accomplishments of Asians in the United States. Each chapter deals with one specific ethnic group – the Chinese, Japanese, Filipinos, Koreans, and East Indians respectively – and within individual chapters the entries are classified under the broad subject areas of history, economic and political aspects, communities, social and psychological processes, and education. Of the 1,528 entries, 550 focus on the Japanese in America and on Japanese Americans. More current (but unannotated) listings of publications about the Japanese in the United States may be found in the annual bibliographies appearing within *Amerasia Journal* (q.v.).

1580 **Bibliography of Asian Studies.**
Ann Arbor, Michigan: Association for Asian Studies, 1941- . annual.
The single most comprehensive, annual bibliography of new Western-language scholarly publications about Japan (as well as about other Asian countries) in the humanities and the social sciences. Each volume contains 1,200 to 2,400 unannotated entries for books, periodical articles, and contributions to symposia and conference proceedings that are specifically concerned with Japan. These entries are classified by subject under numerous headings such as agriculture, elementary education, international relations, linguistics, local history, management of industry, philosophy

and religion, and rural conditions. Most citations are to publications in English, but there is also considerable coverage of European-language scholarship. Annual volumes of the *Bibliography of Asian Studies* generally appear three to four years after their year of coverage; the 1984 volume, for example, was published in early 1989. Entries in bibliographies dating from the years 1941-65 and from 1966-70 have been cumulated and published by G. K. Hall (Boston, Massachusetts) in two major sets of author and subject bibliographies.

1581 **Postwar industrial policy in Japan: an annotated bibliography.**
Karl Boger.   Metuchen, New Jersey; London: Scarecrow Press, 1988.
208p.

A fully annotated bibliography of 520 English-language books, short monographs, United States government documents, Japanese government reports, and periodical articles bearing directly on Japan's industrial policy and its role in the postwar performance of her economy. Most of the publications address the question of industrial policy in Japan from a US perspective and date from the 1970s and 1980s. All entries are classified under eight headings: 'Japanese Industrial Policy'; 'Japan's Economic Development'; 'International Competition and Industrial Policy: Japan and the United States'; 'International Economic Relations'; 'Technology and Industrial Policy' (covering technological innovations and industrial policies geared towards promoting technological development); 'Finance and Financial Organization'; 'Management, Industrial Organization, and the Firm'; and 'Productivity and Labor Relations'. There are separate author, title, and abbreviated subject indexes.

1582 **An index to Japanese law: a bibliography of Western language materials, 1867–1973.**
Compiled by Rex Coleman, John Owen Haley.   Tokyo: University of Tokyo Press, 1975. 167p. (Law in Japan: An Annual, Special Issue, 1975).

A comprehensive, unannotated, classified guide to nearly 4,000 books, pamphlets, articles, and essays in English, French, and German that have been published since the early Meiji period, among them numerous Western-language translations of Japanese statutes and regulatory materials. All aspects of Japanese law are covered, including constitutional law, administrative law, the administration of justice, civil law and procedure, commercial law, criminal law and procedure, labour law, social law, laws relating to agriculture, industry and commerce, energy, banking and securities regulation, insurance, and transportation and communication, anti-monopoly law, industrial property and copyright law, foreign investment and foreign trade law, public finance and tax law, and public and private international law. There is no author index. Supplementary bibliographical listings appear in the volumes of *Law in Japan: an Annual* (q.v.).

1583 **Japanese history & culture from ancient to modern times: seven basic bibliographies.**
John W. Dower.   New York: Markus Wiener; Manchester, England: Manchester University Press, 1986. 232p.

Originating in reading lists prepared for the author's students, this volume serves as a practical working guide to the large number of English-language books, journal articles, microforms, and reference works that were available as of 1985 for the study of Japanese history. The first five unannotated bibliographies are entitled 'Ancient & Medieval Japan from Earliest Times through the Sixteenth Century'; 'Early Modern & Modern Japan, 1600–1945'; 'Japan Abroad: Foreign Relations, Empire, & War from the Restoration to 1945'; 'Japan & the Crisis in Asia, 1931–1945: "Primary" Materials in English'; and 'Occupied Japan & the Cold War in Asia'. They are supplemented by two short listings of bibliographies and research guides, and of journals and other serial publications. The volume lacks an author index.

1584 **The New Religions of Japan: a bibliography of Western-language materials.**
H. Byron Earhart.   Ann Arbor, Michigan: Center for Japanese Studies, University of Michigan, 1983. 2nd ed. 213p. (Michigan Papers in Japanese Studies, 9).

An authoritative indexed guide containing nearly 1,500 citations to primary and secondary materials – books, articles, and dissertations – about fifty-six New Religions. Earhart's coverage of Sōka Gakkai and Tenrikyō is particularly extensive, but much valuable material about such other New Religions as Ananaikyō, Gedatsu-kai, Konkōkyō, PL Kyōdan, Reiyūkai, Risshō Kōseikai, Sekai Kyūseikyō, Tenshō-Kōtai-Jingūkyō, and Ittōen is also included. All entries are grouped into two major parts: 'General Bibliography' (arranged by author, and briefly annotated) and 'Bibliography of Individual New Religions' (arranged by the name of each religion).

1585 **Akira Kurosawa: a guide to references and resources.**
Patricia Erens.   Boston, Massachusetts: G. K. Hall, 1979. 135p. (A Reference Publication in Film).

Kurosawa (1910-), one of postwar Japan's foremost film directors, has produced such world-famous movies as *Rashōmon*, the *Seven Samurai*, and *Yojimbo*. Erens provides a brief biographical background of Kurosawa, a critical survey of his works, an exhaustive listing of his films (with synopses, credits, and notes), and an unannotated listing of nearly five hundred scholarly and popular, English- and French-language publications about him that appeared between 1951 and 1977. Her volume is a basic reference work for readers interested in the Japanese cinema.

1586 **Japan in film: a comprehensive annotated catalogue of documentary and theatrical films on Japan available in the United States.**
Edited by Peter Grilli, introduction by Timothy Plummer, Meredith Waddell.   New York: Japan Society, 1984. 122p.

A critical guide to 516 documentary or educational films about Japan as well as to 130 full-length theatrical films produced in Japan since the 1930s. Each entry contains such basic information as the title, format, credits, running time, and distributor; a brief synopsis of the film's contents or plot; and brief evaluative information representing the views of American specialists on Japan. All of these films were available in 16-mm format for use in American classrooms as of 1984. An introductory essay, 'Teaching Japan through Film', offers the reader practical advice for evaluating the educational quality and suitability of films about Japan. A comprehensive subject index and information about the distributors enhance the usefulness of the catalogue. In 1988 the Japan Society issued a fourteen-page supplement which lists fifty new titles added to the catalogue and provides updated directory information about film distributors in the United States.

1587 **A bibliography of Christianity in Japan: Protestantism in English sources (1859–1959).**
Compiled by Fujio Ikado, James R. McGovern; foreword by Nobushige Ukai, preface by Kiyoko Takeda Cho. Tokyo: Committee on Asian Cultural Studies, International Christian University, 1966. 125p.

A partially annotated guide to 891 books and pamphlets, 286 periodical articles, and 52 dissertations and theses about the introduction of Protestant Christianity into Japan, the activities of Western missionaries, and the Japanese adoption of Christianity. The bibliography is informative but requires updating.

1588 **Modern Japanese literature in translation: a bibliography.**
Compiled by the International House of Japan Library [Kokusai Bunka Kaikan. Toshoshitsu], introduction by Yukio Fujino. Tokyo; New York: Kodansha International, 1979. 311p.

A compendium of nearly nine thousand citations to translations of Japanese literary works – primarily fiction, drama, poetry, and essays – written by nearly 1,500 authors between 1868 and the mid-1970s. Translations published in periodicals and anthologies as well as in full-length books have been included. Many of them are in English. Entries are arranged alphabetically by the Japanese author's romanised name, then alphabetically by the romanised title of the original work and chronologically by the translation's date of publication. There are indexes by translator and by the original Japanese title but not by the translated title. Even though numerous new translations have appeared since the time it was published, this bibliography remains an invaluable resource. Similarly, while it is very much out-of-date, the Japan P.E.N. Club's *Japanese literature in European languages: a bibliography* (Tokyo: Japan P.E.N. Club, 1961. 2nd ed., 98p.) – the predecessor to this guide – remains the only available bibliography comprehensively covering the translations of classical Japanese literature. Numerous citations to general and scholarly writings about classical and modern haiku, to translations into Western languages, and to haiku poetry composed in English, Spanish, Portuguese, Italian, French, and German may be found in *Haiku in Western languages: an annotated bibliography (with some reference to senryu)*, by Gary L. Brower, with David William Foster (Metuchen, New Jersey: Scarecrow Press, 1972, 133p.).

1589 **Catalogue of books in English on Japan, 1945–1981 = Eibun Nihon kankei tosho mokuroku 1945–1981.**
Compiled by the Japan Foundation [Kokusai Kōryū Kikin]. Tokyo: Japan Foundation, 1986. 726p.

A classified, subject-oriented catalogue of approximately nine thousand books about Japan selected from materials available in the collections of the National Diet Library and the Japan Foundation (Tokyo) as well as from publications listed in the annual volumes of the *Bibliography of Asian Studies* (q.v.). Coverage is limited primarily to the humanities, the social sciences, and the fine arts. The main listing is supplemented by author and title indexes. This catalogue – currently the most extensive single-volume work of its kind – is based on an extensive database that is expected to be further developed through the accumulation of additional information into a comprehensive reference tool. The more than six thousand English-language books and pamphlets on Japan housed within the libraries of the International Christian

University and the International House of Japan (both in Tokyo), in turn, are listed in *Books on Japan in English: joint holdings list of ICU Library and IHJ Library, September 1983*, compiled by the International Christian University Library [Kokusai Kirisutokyō Daigaku. Toshokan] and the International House of Japan Library [Kokusai Bunka Kaikan. Toshoshitsu] (Mitaka-shi, Tokyo: International Christian University Library, 1984, 683p.). This classified, indexed, and more up-to-date volume likewise serves as a valuable guide to a wide range of publications likely to be found at major institutional libraries in the West. For a selection of over nine hundred English and Japanese-language reference tools in the humanities and the social sciences published during the 1970s and 1980s in particular, see *A guide to reference books for Japanese studies = Nihon kenkyū no tame no sankōtosho*, compiled by the International House of Japan Library (Tokyo: International House of Japan Library, 1989. 37, 156p.).

1590 **Japan's economic challenge: a bibliographic sourcebook.**
Michael Keresztesi, Gary R. Cocozzoli.   New York; London:
Garland, 1988. 440p. (Garland Reference Library of Social Science,
425).

A classified, unannotated bibliography of over three thousand English-language books and periodical articles dealing with Japan's historical background and foreign relations; the background to the Japanese economy; Japan's industrial policy; her trade and trade relations; labour, social policy, employment, and women; the Japanese corporate world; Japanese management; productivity, quality, and quality control; the dimensions and consideration of the Japanese economic challenge; and the response to the Japanese economic challenge. The majority of the entries cite scholarly, professional, trade, technical, and journalistic publications that appeared between the late 1970s and the mid-1980s. A 'topical locator' in the front of the volume assists readers in conducting narrowly defined subject searches. An author index is also provided.

1591 **Ryukyu Islands: a bibliography.**
Norman D. King.   Washington, DC: Department of the Army, 1967.
105p. (Department of the Army Pamphlet 550-4).

A classified bibliography of 2,108 entries comprising nearly all known English-language books, pamphlets, periodical articles, reports, documents, and theses pertaining to the six hundred-mile-long Ryūkyū island chain, including Okinawa. At the time the volume was being prepared, the Ryūkyūs were still under postwar US military occupation. King covers all subject areas, from agriculture and forestry, economics, and education, to political aspects and religion, US government publications, and the 'World War II period'. He includes many items that are translations from Japanese, and annotates the more important publications. Other available reference works about these islands include *Ryukyu: a bibliographical guide to Okinawan studies*, by Shunzō Sakamaki (Honolulu, Hawaii: University of Hawaii Press, 1963, 353p.) and *Ryukyu: an annotated bibliography*, by Masato Matsui, Tomoyoshi Kurokawa, and Minako I. Song (Honolulu, Hawaii: Center for Asian and Pacific Studies, Council for Japanese Studies, University of Hawaii, 1981, 345p.).

1592 **Studies of Japan in Western languages of special interest to geographers.**
Compiled and edited by David H. Kornhauser, preface by Hiroshi Ishida. Tokyo: Kokon-Shoin, 1984. 99p. 2 maps.
A classified, unannotated listing of English, French, German, and Russian-language books, journal articles, published reports, and dissertations concerned with geographical studies in particular and social science research in general. Part one covers the landforms, climate, hydrology, and economic and geographical resources of Japan. It is followed by sections dealing with population, ethnography, history, economy, land use, agriculture, industry, settlement, environment, and politics. Regional studies of Japan and a selection of broader geographical studies constitute the focus of the concluding parts. Only a small number of works by Japanese scholars are listed since most of their writings have never appeared in translation.

1593 **An introduction to Japanese government publications.**
Tsutomu Kuroki, translated by Masako Kishi, annotated bibliography by Chine Hayeshi. Oxford, England; New York: Pergamon Press, 1981. 204p. bibliog. (Guides to Official Publications, 10).
The first book to offer a systematic introduction to Japanese government imprints, many of which are basic for understanding current developments in such areas as politics, economic and social conditions, and education. The manual defines and discusses the types and characteristics of present-day government publications; elucidates their authorship and their method of production; describes the ways in which they are published and distributed; and addresses the question of their accessibility to interested readers. It also contains an informative, annotated guide to government periodicals, 'white papers', investigations, statistics, and reports.

1594 **East Asian economies: a guide to information sources.**
Molly Kyung Sook Chang Lee. Detroit, Michigan: Gale, 1979. 326p. (Economics Information Guide Series, 1).
A selected, annotated, classified bibliography of English-language books, government documents, dissertations, and statistical reports prepared by financial institutions. One-third of the volume is devoted to the twentieth-century Japanese economy. It covers agriculture and natural resources; commerce, industry, and technological change; economic growth, development, planning, and fluctuations; capital formation; international economics and trade; manpower, labour, population, social security, and management; and monetary and fiscal theory and institutions. While periodical articles have been entirely excluded, a concluding section lists the major journals and serial publications focusing on the economies of East Asia.

1595 **Old age in Japan: an annotated bibliography of Western-language materials.**
Edited with an introduction by Sepp Linhart, Fleur Wöss. Wien (Austria): Institüt für Japanologie, Universität Wien, 1984. 231p. (Beiträge zur Japanologie, 20).
Old age has become a major focus of concern in contemporary Japanese society. This descriptively annotated, classified guide to 397 English- and German-language books, articles, and reports offers a comprehensive overview of the available publications

related to social gerontology. Demographic trends and life expectancy, the stages of life, work in old age, retirement and *inkyo* (abdication of the headship of a family), the family, women, leisure and social participation, psychic problems, income and pensions, public policies for the aged, health and medical treatment, old people's homes, and the portrayal of old people in Japanese literature are among the topics prominently covered. Works on ancestor worship and folktales dealing with old people as well as purely medical articles about old age in Japan have been omitted, but social science-oriented medical research is included.

1596 **Japan through children's literature: an annotated bibliography.**
Compiled by Yasuko Makino, with Roberta K. Gumport. Westport, Connecticut; London: Greenwood Press, 1985. enlarged 2nd ed. 144p.

Expanded edition of a classified bibliography designed to 'help young Americans acquire an accurate image and understanding' of Japan. With the goal of assisting teachers and librarians to identify appropriate reading material, Makino's guide evaluates 450 trade books about Japan published in English primarily between the mid-1960s and the early 1980s that are oriented towards the elementary and secondary school levels. Each publication is described and critically evaluated in terms of its content and accuracy in portraying Japanese culture and the Japanese people. A suggested grade level is also indicated for each work. Books on Japanese Americans are excluded.

1597 **Guide to Japanese prose.**
Alfred H. Marks, Barry D. Bort. Boston, Massachusetts: G. K. Hall, 1984. 2nd ed. 186p. (Asian Literature Bibliography Series).

A selective guide to 174 masterpieces of Japanese prose (novels, diaries, anthologies of short stories, *monogatari*), written between the early eighth century and the 1970s, that are available in English translation. Each title is accompanied by a full bibliographical description as well as by a lengthy annotation that presents a synopsis of the work, discusses its significance in the history of Japanese literature, and offers some critical comments on the translated version. The annotated bibliography is preceded by an introductory survey of the history of Japanese prose and is followed by a selected listing of works of Japanese literary criticism. This is a convenient guide for the individual who wishes to identify some recommended literary works in translation either for general reading or for a more serious introduction to Japanese literature.

1598 **The Japanese in Hawaii: an annotated bibliography of Japanese Americans.**
Mitsugu Matsuda, revised by Dennis M. Ogawa and Jerry Y. Fujioka. Honolulu, Hawaii: Social Sciences and Linguistics Institute, University of Hawaii, 1975. 304p. (Hawaii Series, 5).

Japanese Americans constitute a significant percentage of the population of Hawaii. This bibliography covers all aspects of their experience in the Hawaiian Islands from 1868 to the mid-1970s. Its listings of published and unpublished materials range from scholarly works to literature found in newspapers, novels, and general periodicals which have historical, biographical, or general descriptive value. The main listing of 764 English-language publications is particularly oriented towards an undergraduate student audience. It is supplemented by an appendix of 378 Japanese-language entries (of interest primarily to researchers) reprinted from Matsuda's *The Japanese in Hawaii:*

1868–1967: a bibliography of the first hundred years (Honolulu, Hawaii: Social Science Research Institute, University of Hawaii, 1968, 222p.).

1599 **Japan's foreign policy, 1868–1941: a research guide.**
Edited with an introduction by James William Morley.   New York;
London: Columbia University Press, 1974. 618p. bibliog. (Studies of
the East Asian Institute, Columbia University).
Divided into two parts – 'Critical Essays' and 'Bibliography of Japan's Foreign Policy, 1868–1941' – this research guide is intended for graduate students and specialists but has also proved useful for advanced undergraduates. Eight detailed critical essays discuss Japan's foreign policies in the military, economic, and cultural spheres, and review her policies towards Great Britain, China, Germany, Russia, and the United States. Each essay takes the form of an analytical and, at times, comprehensive historical survey that incorporates relevant bibliographical citations and listings. The second part of the research guide contains a 101-page listing of 'standard works', which provides full bibliographical citations of the monographs, essays, and articles mentioned within the eight critical essays; and a supplementary listing of selected works published between 1963 and 1971. While the majority of bibliographical references are to Japanese-language materials, many publications in English are included as well. *Japan and the world, 1853-1952: a bibliographic guide to Japanese scholarship in foreign relations*, edited by Sadao Asada (New York; Oxford, England: Columbia University Press, 1989, 462p. [Studies of the East Asian Institute, Columbia University]), complements and updates this volume.

1600 **U.S./Japan foreign trade: an annotated bibliography of socioeconomic
perspectives.**
Rita E. Neri.   New York; London: Garland, 1988. 306p. (Garland
Reference Library of Social Science, 403).
A selective, annotated bibliography of English-language books and journal articles concerned with the socio-economic aspects of Japanese society as well as the general and economic dynamics of trade relations between Japan and the United States. The 965 entries are classified under twelve main headings: 'History and General Works'; 'Culture and Society'; 'Science, Technology and Environment'; 'Law and Politics'; 'General Works on the Economy'; 'Economic Planning'; 'Finance'; 'Commerce, Business and Industry'; 'Industrial Management, Organization and Productivity'; 'Industrial Relations'; 'U.S.–Japan Relations (General)'; and 'U.S.–Japan Economic Relations'. Most of these publications appeared between 1970 and 1987. Works which present the Japanese perspective are emphasized. Separate author, title, and subject indexes are provided.

1601 **Japanese periodicals and newspapers in Western languages: an
international union list.**
Compiled by G. Raymond Nunn.   London: Mansell, 1979. 235p.
Serial publications have become an essential source of information not only for understanding the history of Japan but also for studying her economic, literary, intellectual, human, and scientific development. This comprehensive catalogue contains some 3,500 Western-language (primarily English) titles of magazines, newspapers, society transactions, bulletins, reports, directories, trade guides, handbooks, and yearbooks published in Japan between the 1860s and 1978. Typical of these are *A & U: Architecture and Urbanism*, *Contemporary Japan*, *Geochemical Journal*,

Japanese Journal of Veterinary Research, *Mainichi Daily News*, *Report of the Bank of Japan*, *Science and Engineering Review of Doshisha University*, *Waseda Political Studies*, and *Zosen Year Book*. All entries contain basic bibliographical data as well as information about the library holdings for these publications in over eight hundred American, British, Canadian, and Japanese institutions.

1602 **Japanese national government publications in the Library of Congress: a bibliography.**
Compiled by Thaddeus Y. Ohta, foreword by Richard C. Howard.
Washington, DC: Library of Congress; for sale by the Superintendent of Documents, US Government Printing Office, 1981. 402p.

The legislative, executive, and judicial branches of the Japanese government, the commercial publishers serving the different government ministries and agencies, and such quasi-governmental bodies as the Bank of Japan, the Japan Broadcasting Corporation (NHK), and the Japan External Trade Organisation (JETRO) issue a voluminous number of valuable publications each year. Their serial publications, catalogues, directories, guidebooks, handbooks, statistical surveys, census reports, and white papers document the political, social, and economic life of the Japanese. Ohta's guide comprehensively lists the 3,376 titles housed in the Japanese Collection of the Library of Congress (the major depository of Japanese government documents in the United States) as of 1977. Of these titles, 350 are either bilingual or entirely in English.

1603 **Guide to Japanese drama.**
Leonard C. Pronko. Boston, Massachusetts: G. K. Hall, 1984. 2nd ed. 149p. (Asian Literature Bibliography Series).

This guide contains a brief essay on the historical evolution of Japanese drama, a concise chronology of Japanese history and theatre, and a critically annotated bibliography of 105 significant English-language books. The bibliography is divided by type of drama, and is concerned with both the texts of various plays in translation and related works of literary criticism. It focuses on *noh*, *kyōgen*, kabuki, bunraku, and *shingeki* (modern theatre) but also includes citations to other traditional forms of drama ranging from the aristocratic *bugaku* to country festival presentations. Most of the entries are for books published between the early 1950s and the late 1970s.

1604 **Guide to The tale of Genji by Murasaki Shikibu.**
William J. Puette. Rutland, Vermont; Tokyo: Tuttle, 1983. 196p. 4 maps. bibliog.

A valuable reader's guide to the translations of the *Genji* by Arthur Waley and Edward G. Seidensticker (q.v.). Part one ('The World of Genji') contains brief essays on the historical, philosophical, and cultural features of the novel, including daily life at the Heian court, the basic Shintō and Buddhist tenets of the Heian era, and the subtle aesthetics of *aware* ('pathos') and Heian period poetics. It also provides a brief biography of Murasaki Shikibu and an assessment of the strengths and weaknesses of the Waley and Seidensticker translations. Part two offers detailed chapter précis with commentaries of chapters 1–9 of the *Genji* and brief summaries of chapters 10–54. Part three – 'Notes on the Structure of the Novel' and 'Critical Questions for Study' – is particularly useful for classroom teaching. Appendixes list the names, titles and sobriquets of the novel's many characters, and provide comparative age charts of its leading figures as well as maps of the places which are mentioned.

1605 **Guide to Japanese poetry.**
J. Thomas Rimer, Robert E. Morrell. Boston, Massachusett: G. K.
Hall, 1984. 2nd ed. 189p. (Asian Literature Bibliography Series).
A well-organised guide to a selected body of translations and critical writings about the
entire range of classical and modern Japanese poetry, including haiku, *waka*, *renga*,
tanka, comic verse, and free verse. The volume includes an historical sketch of the
evolution of Japanese poetry, a bibliographical outline to the poetry that has become
available in English, and an extensively annotated bibliography of translations of
poetic texts, anthologies, journals, general studies, and literary criticism. The
arrangement of this bibliography is by literary period within which the works are
organised topically whenever possible and in order of their usefulness.

1606 **Shintō bibliography in Western languages: bibliography of Shintō and
religious sects, intellectual schools and movements influenced by
Shintōism.**
Arcadio Schwade. Leiden, The Netherlands: Brill, 1986. 124p.
Monographs, essays, and periodical articles dealing directly or indirectly with Shintō in
its various forms are listed alphabetically by author in this extensive but unannotated
bibliography. Most of the 2,006 entries are for works written in English, French, and
German. A topical index offers a subject approach to the main listing of publications
about this indigenous religious tradition and its sects.

1607 **Japan and Korea: an annotated bibliography of doctoral dissertations
in Western languages, 1877–1969.**
Compiled and edited by Frank Joseph Shulman, foreword by Roger F.
Hackett. Chicago: American Library Association; London: Frank
Cass, 1970. 340p.
An annotated, classified guide to doctoral-level research dealing in whole or in part
with Japan, Korea, and their overseas ethnic communities. It includes entries for 2,077
dissertations on Japan – indexed by author, degree-awarding institution, and selected
subjects – that were accepted by institutions of higher learning in North America,
Europe, Australia, India, and the Philippines. Virtually all academic subjects are
covered, ranging from anthropology, economics, and political science to history,
literature, and the natural sciences. For each dissertation cited there is full
bibliographical information including details about its availability and about the
publication of a book-length manuscript and/or periodical articles based on or closely
related to it. The coverage of this volume has been kept up-to-date through the
publication of Shulman's subsequent guide, *Doctoral dissertations on Japan and on
Korea, 1969–1979: an annotated bibliography of studies in Western languages* (Seattle,
Washington; London: University of Washington Press, 1982, 473p.), a comprehensive
listing of 2,537 studies that are concerned in whole or in part with Japan; and through
the annual volumes of his journal *Doctoral Dissertations on Asia: an Annotated
Bibliographical Journal of Current International Research* (Ann Arbor, Michigan:
Association for Asian Studies, 1975-).

1608   **Japan and Korea: a critical bibliography.**
Bernard S. Silberman.   Tucson, Arizona: University of Arizona
Press, 1962. 120p. Reprinted, Westport, Connecticut: Greenwood
Press, 1982.

A highly selective, classified, but now considerably outdated guide to over 1,600 books
and articles about Japan and over 300 publications about Korea. Covering a wide
range of subjects – among them geography, language, history, religion and philosophy,
art, literature, political patterns, social organisation and structure, education,
economic patterns, and population – its entries are critically annotated and graded
according to the two-fold criteria of authoritativeness and availability. Companion
volumes for China (by Charles Hucker, 1962), India (by J. Michael Mahar, 1964), and
Southeast Asia (by Kennedy G. Tregonning, 1969) were also published under the
University of Arizona Press imprint.

1609   **World War II at sea: a bibliography of sources in English. Volume II:
The Pacific theater.**
Myron J. Smith, Jr, forewords by E. H. Simmons, Edward L.
Beach.   Metuchen, New Jersey: Scarecrow Press, 1976. 427p.

The operations of the Japanese and Allied naval forces (including the marines, the
coast guards, and amphibious and special units) during World War II continue to be a
subject of widespread interest. This comprehensive guide contains nearly 3,200 entries
for books, scholarly papers, periodical articles, government documents, dissertations
and theses, and publications of the various armed services that were published up to
December 1973. It covers all aspects of naval warfare, among them the Japanese attack
on Pearl Harbor, the epic of Midway, and the fighting in the central and south Pacific
(including Guadalcanal, New Guinea, Tarawa, Saipan, the Palaus, Leyte Gulf, the
Philippines, Iwo Jima, and Okinawa). An annotated listing of nearly 185 Japanese-
language monographs about the Pacific War written during the late 1940s by former
officers of the Imperial Japanese Army and Navy constitutes a valuable scholarly
appendix.

1610   **Bibliography on Japanese education = Bibliographie zum japanischen
Erziehungswesen: postwar publications in Western languages.**
Ulrich Teichler, Friedrich Voss, preface by Dietrich Goldschmidt.
Pullach bei München, FRG: Verlag Dokumentation, 1974. 294p.

A classified but unannotated bibliography of 2,658 books, articles, and reports written
primarily in English (and to a lesser extent in German and French) and published
between 1945 and 1973. While all aspects of Japan's educational system such as
vocational education, Christian education, social education, correspondence education,
international education, and women's education are covered, nearly half of the entries
focus on just two subjects: 'elementary and secondary education', and 'higher
education and students'. In many respects, this volume supersedes Herbert Passin's
Japanese education: a bibliography of materials in the English language (New York:
Teachers College Press, 1970, 135p.), which cites over 1,500 titles that appeared
between the 1870s and the late 1960s. Supplementing and updating both of these works
is *Education in Japan: a source book*, by Edward R. Beauchamp and Richard
Rubinger (New York; London: Garland, 1989, 300p. [Reference Books in International Education, 5] [Garland Reference Library of Social Science, 329]). A partially
annotated, classified, and indexed guide to nearly one thousand English-language
books, articles and dissertations produced since 1970, it covers both the history of

Japanese education up to 1952 and various problems and issues relating to contemporary Japanese education.

1611 Japanese music: an annotated bibliography.
Gen'ichi Tsuge. New York; London: Garland, 1986. 161p. (Garland Bibliographies in Ethnomusicology, 2) (Garland Reference Library of the Humanities, 472).

A briefly annotated bibliography listing 881 scholarly books, articles, review essays, theses, dissertations, bibliographies, and discographies in English, French, and German that are concerned with all phases and types of Japanese music as well as with Japanese musical history. Included are translations of song-texts, libretti, and synopses of dance-dramas as well as numerous publications concerned with the performing arts (kabuki, *kyōgen*, noh, etc.) that include some information about music. Concert programme notes, record album jacket notes, reviews, and journalistic writings of an introductory nature are, however, excluded.

1612 Zen Buddhism: a bibliography of books and articles in English, 1892–1975.
Patricia Armstrong Vessie. Ann Arbor, Michigan: University Microfilms International, 1976. 81p. (Monograph Publishing on Demand, Sponsor Series).

This unannotated guide is a classified listing of 762 books, periodicals, and journal articles grouped together under fifteen subject categories. It lists writings which explain Zen Buddhism not only as a product of Chinese and Japanese civilisation but also as a human experience. Part one includes general works, texts and commentaries, and publications about the historical development of Zen as well as about the Rinzai and Sōtō Zen sects. Part two deals with Zen in relation to archery, the arts, Christianity, food, philosophy, psychology, science, training, and the West.

1613 The Allied occupation of Japan, 1945–1952: an annotated bibliography of Western-language materials.
Compiled and edited by Robert E. Ward, Frank Joseph Shulman, with Masashi Nishihara, Mary Tobin Espey; foreword by John Richardson, Jr. Chicago: American Library Association, 1974. 867p. Reprinted, Tokyo: Nihon Tosho Center, 1990.

The Allied occupation of Japan witnessed the revision of the Japanese constitution; changes in Japan's legal system, her judiciary, and the organisation of her government; a series of war crimes trials; land reform; the *zaibatsu* deconcentration programme; and major reforms in Japan's educational system. These and many other topics such as wartime planning among the Allied powers for the postwar treatment of Japan and the successive steps that led to the signing of both a peace treaty and the US–Japan Security Treaty in 1951 are extensively covered in this definitive bibliography of 3,167 books, periodical articles, dissertations, government publications, and collections of archival materials. An appendix contains a classified list of high-ranking occupation personnel as well as organisation charts of the headquarters of the Supreme Commander for the Allied Powers (General Douglas MacArthur). This is an essential reference work for the study of modern Japanese history and postwar US–Japanese relations. It is supplemented by *Bibliography on the Allied occupation of Japan: a bibliography of Western-language publications from the years 1970–1980 (preliminary edition)*, compiled and edited by Frank Joseph Shulman, with Ellen Anne Nollman (College Park, Maryland: University of Maryland, McKeldin Library, East Asia Collection, 1980, 47p.).

1614 **Japan's economy: a bibliography of its past and present.**
William D. Wray. New York: Markus Wiener, 1989. 303p.
An extensive, classified guide to English-language monographs, periodical articles, and chapters of books about the Japanese economy, from the Tokugawa period through the 1980s. The citations are grouped chronologically under six major headings: 'Early Modern Japan: the Tokugawa Period', 'The Restoration Era', 'The Modern Period (1868–1945)', 'World War II', 'The Occupation', and 'Postwar and Contemporary Japan'. This work provides a good bibliographical overview of what has been written in English about such topics as economic thought, industrial development, government economic policy, money and banking, Japan's colonial economy, management (including company organisation, postwar enterprise groups, and labour relations), employment, industrial structure and industrial policy, manufacturing (textiles, steel, automobile industry, electrical industry, computers, and robots), services, resources and communications (including food, energy, and transportation), market access, and Japan's international economic relations (by topic and by area). There is no author index.

1615 **Studies in Japanese literature and language: a bibliography of English materials.**
Compiled by Yasuhiro Yoshizaki. Tokyo: Nichigai Associates, 1979. 451p.
This bibliography of over 3,750 entries lists most of the scholarly and critical writings about Japanese literature and language that were available in English as of 1977. The first part, 'Studies in Japanese Literature', is concerned with writings about individual authors and their works; with general studies of poetry, drama, and modern literature; with Japanese literature abroad and its influence on Western literature; and with foreign literatures in Japan and their influence on Japanese literature. Part two – 'Studies in Japanese Language' – focuses on English-language scholarship about Japanese dictionaries, lexical studies and dialectology, phonology and grammatical studies, and language pedagogy and textbooks. The volume concludes with lists of bibliographies, journals, and anthologies of translations of Japanese literature that can be used for obtaining further information as well as with directories of both Western institutions and scholars interested in Japanese literature and language.

New frontiers in American–East Asian relations: essays presented to Dorothy Borg.
See item no. 646.

American–East Asian relations: a survey.
See item no. 646.

Japanese aircraft of the Pacific War.
See item no. 689.

Japan and Southeast Asia: a bibliography of historical, economic and political relations.
See item no. 727.

A reader's guide to Japanese literature.
See item no. 1009.

The Yanagita Kunio guide to the Japanese folk tale.
See item no. 1188.

Netsuke: a bibliography.
See item no. 1288.

Amerasia Journal.
See item no. 1487.

Japan Quarterly.
See item no. 1513.

Japanese Literature Today.
See item no. 1521.

Journal of the Association of Teachers of Japanese.
See item no. 1529.

Indexes

The following indexes consist of three separate listings: authors (personal and corporate); titles; and subjects. Title entries are italicized and refer either to the main titles, or to other works cited in the annotations. Similarly, author entries refer both to the authors of main items and to the authors mentioned in the annotations. The numbers refer to bibliographic entries rather than page numbers. Individual index entries are arranged in alphabetical sequence.

Index of Authors

A

ABC-Clio Information Services 1575
Abe, Akira 1057
Abe, Kōbō 1041-1043, 1051, 1057, 1106, 1179
Abé, Machi 1043
Abe, Masao 316, 469, 521
Abegglen, James C. 836-837, 917
Abiko, Bonnie F. 1235
Abrams, Leslie A. 1576
Acitelli-Donoghue, Anna 374
Ackroyd, Joyce 298
Adachi, Barbara C. 1391
Adachi, Ken 382
Adachi, Yasushi 196
Adams, Robert J. 1187
Adams, Thomas Francis Morton 851
Addiss, Stephen 1189, 1230-1231
Administrative Management Bureau. Administrative Management Agency. Prime Minister's Office 605
Adriaansz, Willem 1378
Agawa, Hiroyuki 317
Aikens, C. Melvin 101
Akaha, Tsuneo 717, 796
Akai, Toshio 1151
Akamatsu, Paul 191
Akao, Nobutoshi 885
Akazome Emon 1021
Akimoto, Matsuyo 1171
Akimoto, Tatsuru 924
Akinari, *see* Ueda Akinari 1030-1031
Akino, Masakatsu 831
Akioka, Yoshio 1366

Akita, George 189
Akizuki, Tatsuichirō 258
Akutagawa, Ryūnosuke 1044-1045, 1083, 1159
Alcock, Rutherford 349
Alfonso, Anthony 435
Algarin, Joanne P. 1577
Allen, George Cyril 110, 350, 791
Allinson, Gary D. 547, 628
Amakasu, Ken 104
Amano, Ikuo 963
Ames, Walter L. 565
Anderson, Alun M. 980
Anderson, Joseph L. 1414
Anderson, Ronald S. 960
Andō Hiroshige 1256
Andō, Tsuruo 1392
Andoh, Elizabeth 1429
Andrew, Dudley 1578
Andrew, Paul 1578
Andrews, Allan A. 470
Anesaki, Masaharu 458
Angelo, Anthony H. 782
Anzai, Yoichi 824
Aoki, Michiko Y. 1
Aoyama, San'u 1231
Aoyama, Seiko 1464
Appleman, Roy E. 713
Apter, David E. 606
Arai Hakuseki 298
Arakawa, Hirokazu 1201, 1468
Araki, James T. 1061, 1169
Arboleda, Amadio 1273
Ariga, Fumio 91

Arimichi, Ebisawa 132
Arishima, Takeo 1046
Ariyoshi, Sawako 1047, 1106
Armor, John 391
Arnesen, Peter J. 870
Arnold, Walter 743
Arnott, Peter D. 1393
Arntzen, Sonja 1139
Asada, Sadao 1599
Asahi Shimbun. Staff 643
Asakawa, Kan'ichi 148
Asano, Kiichi 1339
Asano, Nagatake 155
Ashby, Janet 409
Ashihara, Eiryo 1388
Ashihara, Hidesato 1388
Asian American Studies. University of
   California, Davis 1579
Association for Japanese-Language
   Teaching 436
Association of international Education,
   Japan 1550
Association of Japanese Geographers 40
Association of National Universities
   1550
Association of Public Universities 1550
Athos, Anthony G. 933
Atlantic Council of the United States
   765
Auer, James E. 759
August, Robert L. 970
Austin, Robert 1357
Ayukawa, Nobuo 1143
Azuma, Hiroshi 594

B
Backus, Robert L. 1011
Baekeland, Frederick 1229
Baelz, Toku 351
Baerwald, Hans H. 607, 629
Bailey, Jackson H. 2, 9
Bair, Lowell 700
Baker, Richard 493
Ballon, Robert J. 852
Bamba, Nobuya 288
Banham, Reyner 1321
Bank of Japan. Statistical Bureau 819
Banoff, Barbara Ann 781
Barber, Bernard 3
Barberi, Susan Carol 1198
Barker, Rodney 252
Barnds, William J. 718

Barnes, Gina Lee 102, 108-109
Barnett, Robert W. 760
Barnhart, Michael A. 679
Barnlund, Dean C. 584
Barr, Pat 190
Barrett, Gregory 1428
Barrett, Timothy 1358
Barrow, Terence 66
Bartholomew, James R. 157
Barton, Jane 1355
Bashō, *see* Matsuo Bashō 1149-1150
Batchelor, John 372
Baum, Eileen 1463
Beardsley, Richard K. 16, 548
Beasley, William Gerald, 111, 191, 644,
   658, 1227
Beato, Felice 1278
Beauchamp, Edward R. 358, 961, 965,
   1610
Becker, Johanna 1279
Beckmann, George M. 192
Beer, Lawrence Ward 771, 788
Befu, Harumi 530, 802
Behr, Edward 334
Beichman, Janine 1161
Bekki, Atsuhiko 35
Bellah, Robert N. 459
Belote, James H. 680, 713
Belote, William M. 680, 713
Ben-Dasan, Isaiah 4
Benedict, Ruth 585
Benjamin, Gail 968
Bennett, William J. 970
Benson, Wes 1455
Berger, Gordon Mark 193, 668
Bergmann, Joachim 940
Bergsten, C. Fred 886
Bernstein, Gail Lee 318, 573
Berry, Mary Elizabeth 299
Berton, Peter 634
Bester, John 104, 317, 346, 589, 1053,
   1058-1059, 1079, 1090, 1200, 1284,
   1328
Bestor, Theodore C. 549
Bethe, Monica 1294, 1346, 1353, 1389
Bethel, Dayle M. 319
Betsuyaku, Minoru 1173, 1179
Bird, Isabella L. 66
Bird, R. Byron 437
Birmingham, Lucy 78
Birnbaum, Alfred 1342
Birnbaum, Phyllis 1048
Bitō, Masahide 1227

Bix, Herbert P. 161
Black, John R. 162
Blacker, Carmen 194, 499
Blair, Clay, Jr. 681
Blair, Dorothy 1359
Blakemore, Frances 364, 1344
Blaker, Michael 645
Bleiler, Everett F. 427, 1470
Blond, Georges 320
Blood, Robert O., Jr. 558
Bloom, Alfred 471
Blum, Paul C. 46
Bock, Audie E. 329, 1415
Bogel, Cynthea J. 1257
Boger, Karl 1581
Bognar, Botond 1297
Bolas, Gerald D. 1251
Bolitho, Harold 163
Boltho, Andrea 792
Booth, Alan 67
Borden, William S. 264
Bordwell, David 1416
Borg, Dorothy 682, 702
Borgen, Robert 300
Bort, Barry D. 1597
Borton, Hugh 112
Boscaro, Adriana 299
Bosworth, Alan R. 386
Bowen, Roger W. 195, 226
Bowers, Faubion 1394
Bowers, John Z. 596-597
Bowie, Theodore 1258
Bowman, Mary Jean 962
Bownas, Geoffrey 500, 901, 1044, 1134
Bowring, Richard 1023, 1035, 1110
Boxer, Charles R. 129
Boyd, Robin 1298
Boyle, John Hunter 702
Brackman, Arnold C. 265
Bragt, Jan Van 525
Braisted, William Reynolds 196
Brandon, James R. 1390, 1395-1397
Brandon, Reiko Mochinaga 1345
Brannen, Noah S. 512
Brazell, Karen 310, 1389
Brazil, Mark 65
Bring, Mitchell 1327
Britton, Dorothy 48, 58, 330, 436, 1149
Broadfoot, Barry 383
Broderick, Laurence 165
Brower, Gary L. 1588
Brower, Helen 86
Brower, Robert H. 1135, 1164

Brown, Delmer M. 115, 130
Brown, J. D. 1572
Brown, Jan 74
Brown, Jessica S. 1575
Brown, Pauline 500
Brown, Sidney DeVere 307
Bryant, William E. 887
Buchanan, Daniel Crump 1183
Buck, James H. 761
Buckley, Roger 5, 266
Bunge, Frederica M. 6
Bungei Shunjū Senshi Kenkyūkai 260, 703
Bunker, Gerald E. 702
Burch, Noël 1417
Burchard, John 1323
Burks, Ardath W. 7, 197
Burns, James M. 713
Burstein, Daniel 853
Buruma, Ian 1372
Bush, Lewis 1551
Bushell, Raymond 1288, 1291, 1360
Butow, Robert J. C. 321, 683
Byron, William 691

C

Cahill, James 1255
Caldwell, Helen 322
Campbell, Alan 1556
Campbell, John Creighton 608, 870
Capon, Robert Farrar 1440
Carlile, Lonny E. 274
Carmichael, Leonard 375
Carpenter, Juliet Winters 1052
Carter, Steven D. 1165
Cary, Otis 495
Casal, Ugo Alfonso 501
Castile, Rand 1467, 1469
Castile, Sondra 1469
Castle, Emery N. 888
Caudill, William 588
Caves, Richard E. 869
Chambers, Anthony H. 1102
Chang, Dal-Joong 719
Chaplin, Hamako Ito 441
Chapman, John W. M. 762
Chard, Chester S. 103
Cherry, Kittredge 413
Chibbett, David G. 999, 1070, 1477
Chikafusa Kitabatake, *see* Kitabatake Chikafusa 144
Chikamatsu Monzaemon 1170, 1407
Christopher, Robert C. 8, 889

Chuman, Frank F. 384
Chung, Chin-Wee 719
Chung, Dae-Gyun 376
Chung, William K. 793
Ciliotta, Jeannine 1307
Clapp, Priscilla 721
Clark, Rodney 838
Clarke, Rosy 1340
Clavell, James 1418
Cleary, Thomas 472-473
Cliff, Stafford 1319
Clifford, William 566
Cline, William R. 886
Clyde, Paul Hibbert 227
Coaldrake, William H. 1206, 1306
Coben, Lawrence A. 1361
Cocozzoli, Gary R. 1590
Coe, Stella 1462
Cogan, John J. 9
Cogan, Thomas J. 1012
Cohen, David 28
Cohen, Stephen D. 890
Cohen, Theodore 267
Cohen, Warren I. 646
Cole, Allan B. 630
Cole, Robert E. 870, 918-919
Coleman, Rex 1582
Coleman, Samuel 370
Collcutt, Martin 113, 131, 1218, 1239
Comee, Stephen 1406
Commission on the Constitution 789
Committee for the Compilation of
    Materials on Damage Caused by the
    Atomic Bombs in Hiroshima and
    Nagasaki 253
Compton, Walter A. 1373
Condon, Jane 574
Condon, John C. 586
Connor, Judith 75
Connors, Lesley 323
Conroy, Hilary 249, 385, 647
Considine, Robert 696
Cook, Alice H. 575
Cooper, Michael 76, 132-133, 153, 352
Coox, Alvin D. 647, 684, 692
Corddry, Jane 1406
Cort, Louise Allison 1207, 1280, 1284,
    1412, 1468-1469
Cortazzi, Hugh 52, 68, 353, 355, 357
Corwin, Charles 414
Cosenza, Mario Emilio 676
Covell, Jon 1190
Covello, Vincent T. 1362

Coverdale, Linda 1278
Craig, Albert M. 10, 123, 171, 289
Craig, Darrell 1441
Cranston, Edward A. 1149
Cranston, Fumiko F. 1246
Crawcour, E. S. 32
Creech, John L. 59
Creemers, Wilhelmus H. M. 515
Crihfield, Liza 576
Crowley, James B. 685
CULCON 36
Cummings, William K. 963-965, 970
Cunningham, Michael R. 1205
Curtis, Gerald L. 631-632
Cusumano, Michael A. 871
Cuyler, Patricia Lee 1453
Czaja, Michael 502
Czinkota, Michael R. 839

D

Daibu, Lady 1142
Daidōji Yūzan 529
Dalby, Liza Crihfield 576, 1552
Dale, Peter 587
Dan, Jean 259
Dandō, Shigemitsu 772
Daniel, D. Ronald 933
Daniels, Gordon 675, 720
Daniels, Roger 386
Danly, Robert Lyons 1111
Dardess, Margaret B. 1
Darling, Bruce 1253
Dator, James Allen 512
Daub, Edward E. 437
David, Zdeněk V. 1562
Davidson, William H. 981
Davies, Frank 1339
Davis, A. R. 1145
Davis, Bob 11
Davis, Rebecca M. 1318
Davis, Winston 506
Dazai, Osamu 1049-1051, 1083, 1106,
    1116
de Bary, William Theodore 33, 1015
de Chabaneix, Gilles 1319
De Mente, Boye 12, 840, 891, 1553
De Vos, George A. 373, 376, 571, 588
de Wassermann, Annie R. 1374
Deacon, Richard 648
Denison, Edward F. 793
Desser, David 1419-1420
Destler, I. M. 721-722, 892
Dicker, Herman 4

Dillon, Katherine V. 228, 705-706
Dillon, Ruth 1464
Dilworth, David A. 194, 524, 1081
Directors of the Japan Bonsai
   Association 1328
Dixon, Trudy 493
Doe, Paula 301
Dōgen 472-473
Doi, Masaru 1430
Doi, Tadao 132
Doi, Takeo 589-590, 1112
Doi, Teruo 773-774
Donner, Neal 845
Donoghue, John 374
Dore, Ronald P. 164, 239, 268, 531-532,
   549-550, 630, 794-795, 920, 924
Dorfman, Cynthia Hearn 970
Dorson, Richard M. 503, 1184
Dower, John W. 117, 226, 324, 686,
   1191, 1276, 1583
Draeger, Donn F. 1442-1445, 1452
Drew, Philip 1299
Drifte, Reinhard 720, 762-763
Drucker, Peter F. 1246
Drummond, Richard Henry 495
Drysdale, Peter 723
Dubro, Alec 569
Duke, Benjamin C. 966-967
Dull, Paul S. 687
Dumoulin, Heinrich 474
Dunlop, Lane 1051
Dunn, Charles J. 165, 1392
Dunning, John H. 944
Durston, Diane 77-78
Dusenbury, Jerry 972
Duus, Masayo 387
Duus, Peter 115, 134, 198, 387, 1480

E

Earhart, H. Byron 460-462, 467, 1584
Earl, David Magarey 188
Earle, Joe 1373
Ebinger, Charles K. 847
Economic Planning Agency 820
Edel, Chantal 1278
Editions Berlitz 416
Editorial Department of Teikoku-Shoin
   Co. Ltd 53
Editors of Time-Life Books 13, 715
Edwards, Walter 560
Egami, Namio 104
Eickmann, Katherine 1293
Eliot, Charles 475

Elison, George 135, 166
Ellison, Herbert J. 724
Ellwood, Robert S. 463
Embree, John F. 551
Emery, Robert F. 854
Emi, Kazuko 1434
Emmerson, John K. 354, 725
Enchi, Fumiko 1048, 1052-1053, 1071,
   1098, 1106
Endō, Shūsaku 1054-1055
Eng, Robert Y. 182
Engel, David H. 1337
Engel, Heinrich 1300
Enright, Joseph F. 716
Epp, Robert 1144
Erens, Patricia 1585
Ernst, Earle 1398, 1408
Esaka, Teruya 104, 107
Espey, Mary Tobin 1613
Esthus, Raymond A. 659
Evans, David C. 688
Evans, Garry O. 234
Evans, Mary Anne 1259
Evans, Tom 1259
Ezaki, Yoshikazu 1330
Ezawa, Reiko 453

F

Fagan, Robert 1156
Fairbank, John King 123, 649
Falkner, David 338
Federation of Japanese Private Colleges
   and Universities Associations 1550
Feigenbaum, Edward A. 982
Feis, Herbert 254
Feldman, Robert A. 225, 866
Ferber, Gene 437
Ferster, Dorothy C. 1361
Fields, George 841
Finlayson, Dale K. A. 682
Fisch, Arnold G., Jr. 285
Fisher, M. F. K. 1438
Fister, Pat 1233
Fitzsimmons, Thomas 1151
Flanagan, Scott C. 622, 642
Fletcher, William Miles, III 199
Fontein, Jan 1232
Forman, Werner 156
Foster, David William 1588
Fowler, Edward 1113
Fox, Grace 162, 660
Francillon, René J. 689
Franck, Frederick 521

Francks, Penelope 200
Frankel, Ken 1224
Franko, Lawrence G. 945
Fraser, Andrew 296
Fraser, Mary Crawford 355
Frédéric, Louis 136
Freeman, Christopher 983
Freidus, Alberta 1562
Friedheim, Robert L. 796
Friedman, David 872
Friedman-Lichtschein, Tilly C. 732
Friedrich, Ralph 1310, 1333
Frieman, Wendy 984
Frost, Ellen L. 726
Fruin, W. Mark 201
Fujikura, Kōichirō 775
Fujino, Yukio 1588
Fujioka, Jerry Y. 1598
Fujioka, Ryōichi 1282, 1468
Fujiwara, Hirotatsu 512
Fujiwara Michitsuna no haha 1013
Fujiwara Sadaie 1135
Fujiwara Teika 1135
Fukami, Tanrō 1175
Fukuda, Yoshiyuki 1171
Fukui, Eiichirō 41
Fukui, Haruhiro 633, 721-722, 796
Fukuoka, Masanobu 830
Fukuoka UNESCO Association 1554
Fukuoka Yunesuko Kyōkai 1554
Fukutake, Tadashi 531-534
Fukuyama, Toshio 1192
Fukuzawa, Yukichi 194, 302
Funakoshi, Gichin 1446
Furukawa, Shōsaku 1281
Furuta, Akira 1334
Furuta, Gyō 1556
Fusonie, Alan E. 663
Futabatei, Shimei 1124
Futagawa, Yukio 1202, 1301-1303, 1309-1310

G
Gage, Richard L. 4, 583, 1198, 1208, 1216, 1285, 1290, 1303, 1309, 1329, 1334, 1364, 1370
Gallagher, Michael 1077
Gamota, George 984
Garfias, Robert 1379
Garon, Sheldon 202
Gatten, Aileen 1006
Gayn, Mark 269
Geiser, Peter 379

George, B. James, Jr. 16, 772
George, Betty 970
Gerstle, C. Andrew 1399
Gessel, Van C. 1054, 1056
Gibney, Frank B. 15, 797, 1368
Gidō Shūshin 1152
Giesen, Walter 79
Girdner, Audrie 386
Gitter, Kurt A. 1233
Giuganimo, Alberto 1473
Glenn, Evelyn Nakano 388
Glines, C. V. 696
Gluck, Carol 203, 646
Goldman, Israel 1257
Goldsmith, Raymond W. 855
Goldstein, Donald M. 228, 705-706
Goldstein, Sanford 1082, 1160
Goodman, David G. 1171, 1173, 1178
Goodman, Grant K. 167
Gordon, Andrew 204
Gordon, Brian G. 1572
Gow, Ian T. M. 713, 762
Graham, John L. 893
Grant, Glen 397
Grant, Worth C. 512
Greenbie, Barrie B. 1304
Greenwood, John G. 865
Gregory, Gene 985
Gresser, Julian 775, 873
Grew, Joseph C. 690
Gribbin, David 1363
Gribbin, Jill 1363
Griffis, William Elliot 114
Grilli, Elise 1234, 1470
Grilli, Peter 1457, 1586
Grimstone, A. V. 487
Gropius, Walter 1300, 1305
Grossberg, Kenneth Alan 137
Grzanka, Leonard 1153
Gugeler, Russell A. 713
Guillain, Robert 691
Gumport, Roberta K. 1596
Gunji, Masakatsu 1390, 1400-1401
Gunther, John 356
Guth, Christine M. E. 1199, 1206; see also Kanda, Christine Guth 1289
Guthrie, Stewart 507
Gutiérrez, Fernando G. 132
Gyōsei Kanri Kyoku. Gyōsei Kanrichō. Sōrifu. 605

H
Haar, Francis 316

Haas, Margaret P. 334
Habein, Yaeko Sato 404
Hachiya, Michihiko 259
Hackett, Roger F. 303
Hadamitzky, Wolfgang 421, 438
Hadley, Eleanor M. 270
Haga, Hideo 501
Hagiwara, Sakutarō 1136
Hahn, Elliott J. 776
Haines, Bruce A. 1448
Hakeda, Yoshito S. 482
Hakuin Ekaku 476
Hakuseki, *see* Arai Hakuseki 298
Hakuta, Kenji 594
Halberstam, David 874
Haley, John O. 777, 1582
Halford, Aubrey S. 1401
Halford, Giovanna M. 1401
Hall, Edward T. 406, 894
Hall, Ivan Parker 304
Hall, John Whitney 16, 115-116, 138-141, 168, 548
Hall, Mildred Reed 894
Halliday, Jon 117
Hamada, Fumimasa 862
Hamada, Kengi 1014, 1031
Hamada, Shōji 1287
Hanami, Tadashi 921
Hanayama, Yuzuru 42
Hane, Mikiso 118, 205, 209, 290
Hanley, Susan B. 169
Hanson, Elizabeth 1098
Hara, Tamiki 1088
Harada, Masazumi 959
Harada, Minoru 1235
Harari, Ehud 609
Harbison, Mark A. 590, 815, 1481
Hardacre, Helen 508-509
Hare, Thomas Blenman 1172
Harich-Schneider, Eta 1380
Harootunian, Harry D. 241
Harper, Thomas J. 295, 1225
Harries, Meirion 271
Harries, Phillip Tudor 1142
Harries, Susie 271
Harris, H. Jay 1148
Harris, Townsend 676
Harris, Victor 1447
Harrison, Joy 91
Harter, Penny 1162
Hartley, John 986
Hasebe, Mitsuhiko 1285
Hasegawa, Keitarō 922

Hassenpflug, Wolfgang 79
Hata, Hisashi 1402
Hata, Koichirō 1438
Hata, Ryō 1326
Hattori, Ryūtarō 1381
Hauge, Takako 1193
Hauge, Victor 1193
Hauser, William B. 146, 170
Havens, Thomas R. H. 206-207, 727, 1376
Hawkins, Robert G. 905
Hawks, Francis L. 673
Hay, Keith A. J. 895
Hayakawa, Masao 1329
Hayami, Yūjirō 831-832
Hayashi, Fumiko 1051, 1071, 1083
Hayashi, Hiroko 575
Hayashi, Kyokō 1071, 1088
Hayashi, Ryōichi 1194
Hayashi, Saburō 692
Hayashida, Tsuneo 58
Hayashiya, Seizō 1437, 1468-1469
Hayeshi, Chine 1593
Hazama, Dorothy Ochiai 389
Heenan, Thomas A. 1247
Heineken, Kiyoko 1341
Heineken, Ty 1341
Heinrich, Amy Vladeck 325
Heisig, James W. 474
Hellmann, Donald C. 728
Hemmi, Kenzō 888
Henderson, Dan Fenno 778-779, 787
Henderson, Harold G. 1137
Hendry, Joy 535, 559-560
Henkenius, Mary Catherine 1153
Henshall, Kenneth G. 1105
Herbert, Jean 516
Herman, Ron 98
Hermann, Evelyn 326
Hersey, John 255, 391
Hershkowitz, Allen 956
Hibbett, Howard 1036, 1045, 1057, 1063, 1097, 1099-1100, 1103
Hickman, Money L. 1232
Hidaka, Rokurō 567
Hideyoshi, *see* Toyotomi Hideyoshi 299
Higashi, Chikara 798, 896
Higginson, William J. 1162
Higuchi, Ichiyō 1111
Higuchi, Sachiko 1386
Higuchi, Takayasu 101
Hijirida, Kyoko 439
Hilger, M. Inez 375

Hillier, Jack Ronald 1260-1262, 1478
Hills, Jill 953
Hinago, Motoo 1306
Hino, Sōjō 1159
Hirabayashi, Taiko 1071
Hirabayashi, Yoshisuke 435
Hirai, Kiyoshi 1307
Hirano, Umeyo 194, 405
Hirayama, Chūji 1315
Hironaka, Wakako 1047
Hirose, Nobuko 1571
Hiroshige, see Andō Hiroshige 1256
Hiroshima-shi Nagasaki-shi Genbaku
    Saigaishi Henshū Iinkai 253
Hirota, Akiko 307
Hirota, Jōzan 1330
Hirota, Naotaka 954
Hirschmeier, Johannes 208
Hisamatsu, Sen'ichi 365
Hisamatsu, Shin'ichi 521, 1195
Hoffmann, Yoel 477, 1138
Hogarth, James 79
Hokama, Seikō 1201
Hokusai, see Katsushika Hokusai 1256
Holborn, Mark 1275
Holland, Harrison M. 725, 729, 764
Hollerman, Leon 856, 897-898
Holmes, Christopher 1401
Holtom, Daniel C. 515, 517
Honda, Isao 1364
Honda Toshiaki 173
Honeycombe, Gordon 258
Honjō, Shigeru 209, 334
Hoover, Thomas 1196
Hori, Ichirō 504
Horne, James 857
Horton, H. Mack 1252, 1314
Horwitz, Brewster 1092
Hoshii, Iwao 536, 851
Hoshino, Koei 1440
Hoshino, Yasuo 935
Hosoe, Eikoh 256
Hosokawa, Bill 390, 395, 402
Hotta, Anne 80
Hotta, Kiyomi 1173
Houston, James D. 391
Houston, Jeanne Wakatsuki 391
Hout, Thomas M. 879
Howarth, Stephen 210
Howes, John F. 288
Hozumi, Kazuo 1314
Hrebenar, Ronald J. 634
Huber, Thomas M. 171

Huddle, Norie 957
Huffman, James L. 305
Hughes, Sukey 1365
Humphreys, Leonard A. 354
Hunter, Janet E. 1555
Hurst, G. Cameron, III 142, 194
Hutterer, Karl L. 109
Hyams, Edward 320
Hyōjun Rōmajikai 426

I

Ibuse, Masuji 1056, 1058-1059, 1088
Ichikawa, Mayumi 700
Ichikawa, Shōgo 965
Ichikawa, Yoshimasa 1464
Ichimata, Tamiko 363
Ichioka, Yuji 392
Ienaga, Saburō 1236
Iga, Mamoru 568
Iglehart, Charles W. 496
Ihara Saikaku 1014-1015
Ihei Itō see Itō Ihei 59
Iijima, Kōichi 1151
Ikado, Fujio 1587
Ike, Nobutaka 615, 693
Ikeda, Hideo 962
Ikeda, Masaaki 790
Ikegami, Kōjirō 1479
Ikemi, Kiyoshi 882
Ikenobō, Sen'ei 1464-1465
Ikku Jippensha, see Jippensha Ikku 1016
Ikkyū Sōjun 1139
Imai, Ryūkichi 848
Imaizumi, Motosuke 1281
Imamura, Anne E. 577
Inagaki, Hisao 415
Inamoto, Noboru 428
Inoguchi, Rikihei 700
Inoguchi, Takashi 817
Inoue, Mitsuharu 1088
Inoue, Mitsuo 1308
Inoue, Nobuo 437
Inoue, Yasushi 327, 1060-1061, 1106,
    1334
Inoura, Yoshinobu 1403
International Christian University
    Library 1589
International Cultural Association,
    Japan 366
International Division. Nissan Motor
    Company 447
International House of Japan Library
    1588-1589

International Society for Educational Information 54
Iriye, Akira 649-651, 661-662, 694-695
Irukayama, Katsurō 959
Irvine, John 987
Isaku, Patia R. 1381
Ishibashi, W. Chië 1292
Ishida, Hisatoyo 1237·
Ishida, Ichirō 130
Ishida, Takeshi 537, 610
Ishiguro, Yoko 80
Ishikawa, Eisei 253
Ishikawa, Jun 1405
Ishikawa, Takuboku 1140
Ishimoto, Shidzué 328
Ishimoto, Yasuhiro 1305
Ishinomori, Shōtarō 1480
Ishiwara, Yasuyo 503
Ishizawa, Masao 1197
Itasaka, Gen 1556
Itō, Aiko 1085
Itō Ihei 59
Itō, Keiichi 64
Itō, Masami 1482
Itō, Nobuo 81
Itō, Toshiko 1346
Itoh, Hiroshi 611, 788
Itoh, Teiji 1301-1303, 1309-1311, 1331-1334
Iwamiya, Takeji 1198, 1332, 1334-1335
Iwamoto, Kaoru 1458
Iwao, Seiichi 367
Iwasaki, Chihiro 330
Iwasaki, Ikuo 727
Iwata, Hiroshi 1143
Iwata, Masakazu 306
Izawa, Motoichi 291
Izumi Shikibu 1149

J
Jackman, Barry 1030
Jain, Rajendra Kumar 283, 730
James, D. Clayton 356
James, Estelle 968
Jannetta, Ann Bowman 172
Janow, Merit E. 813
Jansen, Marius B. 113, 115, 155, 168, 211-212, 239, 652, 1559
Japan Architect 81
Japan Bonsai Association. Directors 1328
Japan Culture Institute 1557
Japan Economic Journal 823

Japan Foundation 1559, 1589
Japan Institute of International Affairs 829
Japan Interpreter. Staff 533-534
Japan Library Association. International Exchange Committee 1474
Japan National Tourist Organization 82
Japan Newspaper Publishers and Editors Association 1483
Japan P. E. N. Club 1588
Japan Photographers Association 1276
Japan Securities Research Institute 858
Japan Special Libraries Association. Committee of Statistical Survey and Research 1558
Japan Textile Color Design Center 1347
Japan. Commission on the Constitution 789
Japan. Keizai Kikakuchō, 820
Japan. Kempō Chōsakai 789
Japan. Sōrifu Gyōsei Kanrichō. Gyōsei Kanri Kyoku 605
Japan. Sōrifu. Tōkeikyoku 825, 827
Japan. Tsūshō Sangyōshō 828
Jefferson, Roland M. 663
Jentschura, Hansgeorg 1572
Jenyns, Soame 1283
Jien 130
Jippensha Ikku 1016
Johnson, Chalmers 228, 272, 612, 780
Johnson, Sheila K. 731
Johnson, Sune 1522
Johnson, U. Alexis 765
Johnston, William 258, 1055
Joint Working Group of the Atlantic Council of the United States & the Research Institute for Peace and Security, Tokyo 765
Joly, Henri L. 1560
Jones, H. J. 197
Jones, Ronald K. 1192, 1243
Jones, Stanleigh H., Jr. 1174
Jones, Susan W. 1032
Jorden, Eleanor Harz 440-441
Jōya, Mock 1561
Jung, Dieter 1572

K
Kageyama, Haruki 1199
Kagiwada, George 1579
Kai, Miwa 416
Kai, Motonari 1085
Kaikō, Takeshi 1062

Kaizuka, Sōhei 51
Kalland, Arne 552
Kamakura, Yoshitarō 1201
Kamata, Satoshi 924
Kami, Ryōsuke 84
Kaminski, Jacqueline 799, 805
Kamohara, Toshiji 60
Kanai, Madoka 115
Kanai, Mieko 1048, 1057
Kanda, Christine Guth 1199, 1289; see
 also Guth, Christine M. E. 1199, 1206
Kanda, Mikio 259
Kaneko, Erika 1201
Kaneko, Hiroshi 1404-1405
Kaneko, Mitsuharu 1057
Kaneko, Tōta 1159
Kanno, Eiji 83
Kanroji, Osanaga 334
Kanzaki, Noritake 1366
Kaplan, David E. 569
Kapleau, Philip 478-479
Kaputa, Catherine 1252
Kara, Jūrō 1171
Karatsu, Hajime 875
Karsh, Bernard 931
Kasahara, Kunihiko 1367
Kasulis, Thomas Patrick 480
Kasza, Gregory J. 221
Kato, Hiroki 1573
Katō, Kaname 59
Katō, Saburō 1328
Katō Shizue 328
Katō, Shūichi 292, 999, 1200
Katsushika Hokusai 1256
Katsuta, Shūichi 35
Katz, Joshua D. 732
Kawabata, Yasunari 1051, 1057, 1063-
 1067, 1083, 1106
Kawada, Hisashi 217
Kawai, Kazuo 273
Kawakita, Michiaki 1201, 1238
Kawamoto, Kiyoshi 1191
Kawano, Ryōsuke 1281
Kawashima, Chūji 1312
Kawatake, Mokuami 1407
Kawatake, Toshio 1403
Kawazoe, Noboru 1323
Keene, Dennis 1108, 1114, 1141
Keene, Donald 32-33, 69, 173, 291,
 1000-1005, 1034, 1049-1050, 1072,
 1074, 1170, 1175, 1177, 1180, 1395,
 1400, 1404-1405
Keijo Shūrin 1152

Keizai Kikakuchō 820
Kelly, William W. 213
Kelsey, W. Michael 1037
Kempō Chōsakai 789
Kenko, see Yoshida Kenkō 1034
Kennedy, Kevin 623
Kennedy, Rick 84
Kenny, Don, 1377, 1390, 1392, 1400,
 1402, 1408
Kenreimon'in Ukyō no Daibu 1142
Kenrick, Doug 1454
Keresztesi, Michael 1590
Kerr, George H. 284
Kesado, Shigemi 35
Keyes, Roger S. 1263-1264, 1268
Khan, Karin 79
Ki no Tsurayuki 1149
Kidder, J. Edward, Jr. 105-107, 143
Kido, Kōin 307
Kido, Takayoshi 307
Kijima, Hajime 1143
Kikuchi, Charles 393
Kikuchi, Makoto 988
Kikuchi, Yūji 196
Kikumura, Akemi 400
Kim, Hee-Jin 481
Kim, Hong N. 1562
Kim, Hyung-Chan 1563
Kim, Paul S. 613
Kim, Young C. 1484
Kimball, Arthur G. 1115
Kimura, Yukiko 392
Kindaichi, Haruhiko 405
King, Norman D. 1591
Kinmonth, Earl H. 214
Kinoshita, Yūji 1144
Kirkup, James 1145
Kisei Reigen 1152
Kishi, Masako 1593
Kishibe, Shigeo 1382
Kishikawa, Shigemi 1458
Kitabatake Chikafusa 144
Kitagawa, Hiroshi 1019
Kitagawa, Joseph M. 464-465, 504
Kitamura, Hiroshi 733
Kitamura, Kazuyuki 963
Kitano, Harry H. L. 394
Kitaoji, Hironobu 723
Kiyooka, Eiichi 194, 302
Kmetz, Yoko Sakakibara 74
Knight, Michael 1213
Knitter, Paul 474
Kobayashi, Bunji 1212

Kobayashi Issa 1146
Kobayashi, Katsuhiro 1321
Kobayashi, Takeshi 1290
Kobayashi, Takiji 1068
Kobayashi, Victor N. 965
Kōbō Daishi 482
Kochan, Miriam 191
Kōda, Rohan 1069
Koga, Mamoru 796
Kohama, Hirohisa 806
Koide, Nobukichi 1328
Koike, Kazuko 1224
Koike, Kazuo 925
Koine, Yoshio 417
Koizumi, Kazuko 1342
Kojima, Nobuo 1057
Kojima, Takashi 1045
Kōjiro, Yūichirō 1202
Kokubo, Takeshi 1556
Kokuritsu Daigaku Kyōkai 1550
Kokusai Bunka Kaikan. Toshoshitsu
  1588-1589
Kokusai Kankō Shinkōkai 82
Kokusai Kirisutokyō Daigaku. Toshokan
  1589
Kokusai Kōryū Kikin 1559, 1589
Kokusai Kyōiku Jōhō Sentā 54
Kokusai Nihongo Fukyū Kyōkai 436
Komeiji, Jane Okamoto 389
Komine, Hisako 1464
Komiya, Ryūtarō 876
Komoda, Shusui 1463
Komparu, Kunio 1406
Komparu Zenchiku 1181
Kondō Hiroshi 1431
Kondō, Ichitarō 1265
Konishi, Jin'ichi 1006
Kōno, Taeko 1048, 1071, 1098
Kōno, Toyohiro 926
Konuma, Katsusuke 84
Konya, Paul 1302
Koren, Leonard 1348
Kōri, Eiji 1435
Koritsu Daigaku Kyōkai 1550
Korn, Larry 830
Kornhauser, David H. 43, 1592
Kornicki, Peter 29
Kōsai, Yutaka 740, 799
Koschmann, J. Victor 175, 614
Kostant, Ann Siller 1047
Kotsuji, Abraham 4
Kōzuru, Gen 1281
Kranzler, David 4

Krauss, Ellis S. 538, 642, 969
Krouse, Carolyn R. 85
Kubota, Akira 613
Kuck, Loraine 1335
Kudō, Kazuyoshi 1366
Kudō, Masanobu 1337
Kūkai 482
Kultermann, Udo 1313
Kumakura, Isao 113, 1467
Kumon, Shumpei 817
Kung, David 1203
Kunikida, Doppo 1070
Kuno, Susumu 429
Kurahashi, Yumiko 1098
Kuroda, Kio 1143
Kuroda, Ryōji 1281
Kurokawa, Tomoyoshi 1591
Kuroki, Tsutomu 1593
Kurosawa, Akira 329, 1057
Kuroyanagi, Tetsuko 330
Kuwata, Masakazu 1014
Kuzunishi, Muneori 1437
Kuzunishi, Sōsei 486, 1333
Kyōgoku, Junichi 615

L
LaFleur, William R. 469, 1007, 1155
Lane, Richard 1266-1267, 1270
Langdon, Frank 734
Langer, Paul F. 192, 635
Large, Stephen S. 215, 334
Lauter, G. Peter 798
Lawson, Ted W. 696
Lawton, Thomas 1250
Leach, Bernard 331, 1228, 1287
Lebra, Joyce C. 308, 578
Lebra, Takie Sugiyama 579, 591-592
Lebra, William P. 466, 591
Leckie, Robert 700
Lee, Bradford A. 697
Lee, Chae-Jin 735-736
Lee, Changsoo 376
Lee, Chong-Sik 737
Lee, Jung Bock 1485
Lee, Molly Kyung Sook Chang 1594
Lee, Sang M. 927
Lee, Sherman E. 1204-1205
Leestma, Robert 970
Leggett, Trevor 1459
Lehmann, Jean-Pierre 216
Leiter, Samuel L. 1407, 1564
Lensen, George Alexander 664, 684
Lesniewicz, Paul 1336

Leutner, Robert W. 1038
Levine, Solomon B. 217, 931
Levy, Dana 3, 1357, 1368, 1457
Levy, Ian Hideo 1147, 1163
Lewis, Kären Wigen 1107
Li, Lincoln 702
Lifson, Thomas B. 915
Lifton, Betty Jean 256
Lifton, Robert Jay 257, 292
Lin, Ching-yuan 859
Lincoln, Edward J. 800
Linhart, Sepp 1595
Link, Howard A. 1268, 1270
Lippit, Noriko Mizuta 1071
Lishka, Dennis 1316
Lissington, M. P. 665
Livingston, Jon 119
Lock, Margaret M. 598-599
Lockwood, William W. 218, 239
Loftis, Anne 386
Longworth, John W. 833
Lord, Walter 705
Loss, Louis 781
Loti, Pierre 1278
Low, David 86
Lowe, Eileen 136
Lowe, John 1369
Lowe, Mark 1369
Lowe, Peter 666, 697
Lu, David John 120, 928
Lundy, Robert T. 182
Lutz, Winifred 1358
Lynn, Leonard H. 899, 989
Lynn, Richard 971
Lyons, Nick 877
Lyons, Phyllis I. 1116

M
Mabuchi, Tōichi 503
McBride, Simon 63
McClain, James L. 174
McClain, Yoko Matsuoka 430
McClellan, Edwin 1086, 1093, 1117
McCorduck, Pamela 982
McCormack, Gavan 567, 616
McCraw, Thomas K. 801
McCullough, Helen Craig 1017-1021,
   1148, 1153
McCullough, William H. 115, 1021
McDonald, Keiko I. 1421-1422
MacDougall, Terry Edward 636
McFarland, Horace Neill 483, 510
McGovern, James R. 1587

McIntosh, Malcolm 766
McKean, Margaret A. 958
Mackenzie, Lewis 1146
McKeown, Timothy J. 899
McKinnon, Richard 1178
McLean, Mick 955
McMillan, Charles J. 878
McMullin, Neil 145
McNelly, Theodore H. 617
Macpherson, W. J. 218
McVittie, John 1045
Maeda, Daisaku 540
Maeda, Shinzō 44
Magaziner, Ira C. 879
Maki, John M. 787, 789-790
Makino, Seiichi 431
Makino, Yasuko 1596
Malm, William P. 1377, 1383-1385, 1395,
   1397
Manchester, William 356
Manguel, Alberto 1131
Mannari, Hiroshi 802, 929
Manthorpe, Victoria 72
Maraini, Fosco 17, 70
Marcus, Russell 87
Marder, Arthur J. 698
Marks, Alfred H. 1075, 1257, 1597
Marsh, Robert M. 929
Marshall, Byron K. 219
Martin, Samuel E. 432
Maruyama, Masao 276, 618
Masada, Hiroko 425
Masaoka, Mike 395
Masaoka, Shiki 1149, 1159
Masatoshi 1291
Mason, John T., Jr. 699
Mass, Jeffrey P. 141, 146-149
Massey, Joseph A. 65
Masuda, Koh 418
Masumi, Junnosuke 274
Masunaga, Reihō 472
Mathieson, Raymond S. 900
Matisoff, Susan 1176
Matoré, Patricia 1387
Matsuda, Mitsugu 1598
Matsuda, Yoshihiro 1437
Matsuhara, Iwao 1381
Matsui, Masato 1591
Matsumoto, Michihiro 406
Matsumoto, Ryūshin 1481
Matsumoto, Seichō 1106
Matsumoto, Shigeru 309
Matsumoto, Tatsurō 49

Matsumoto, Tomone 1056
Matsunaga, Alicia 484
Matsunaga, Daigan 484
Matsuo Bashō 1149-1150
Matsuoka, Toshio 1565
Matsushita, Takaaki 1239
May, Ernest R. 646
Mayer, Fanny Hagin 501, 1185, 1188
Meech-Pekarik, Julia 1269
Meinertzhagen, Frederick 1288
Meissner, Kurt 1263
Meissner, Larry 806, 808, 812, 881
Mellen, Joan 1423-1425
Mendl, Wolf 738-739
Merriman, David 803
Metraux, Daniel 511
Meyer, Frederick G. 62
Michelson, Annette 1417
Michener, James A. 1258, 1270, 1274
Mickel, Peter 1572
Midorikawa, Taeko 259
Midorikawa, Yōichi 71
Miki, Fumio 108
Miller, Alan L. 504
Miller, Frank O. 220
Miller, Roy Andrew 108, 407-408, 1143
Millot, Bernard 700
Mills, Douglas Edgar 1022
Minami, Ryōshin 803
Minear, Richard H. 18, 265, 583, 716
Miner, Earl 1006, 1135, 1149-1150, 1164-
  1165, 1566
Ministry of International Trade and
  Industry 828
Minnich, Helen Benton 1349
Mino, Yutaka 1206
Mishima, Yukio 529, 1057, 1072-1080,
  1083, 1177, 1179, 1334
Mitamura, Yasuko Kosaka 442
Mitchell, C. H. 1272
Mitchell, Richard H. 221, 377
Mitford, Algernon Bertram 357
Mitsubishi Corporation 422
Mitsubishi Shōji Kabushiki Kaisha 422
Miura, Akira 411, 419-420
Miyakawa, T. Scott 385
Miyamoto, Akitō 424, 1315
Miyamoto Musashi 1447
Miyamoto, S. Frank 399
Miyamoto, Sadao 96
Miyamoto, Yuriko 1071
Miyoshi, Masao 667, 1118
Miyoshi Shōraku 1180, 1407

Miyoshi, Tatsuji 1145
Mizoguchi, Saburō 1207
Mizuno, Seiichi 1208
Mizuo, Hiroshi 1240, 1281
Mizushima, Keiichi 588
Mizushima, Keiko 1264
Mizutani, Nobuko 443-446
Mizutani, Osamu 409, 443-446
Modell, John 393
Mody, N. H. N. 179
Moeran Brian 553
Molony, Barbara 328
Monna, Nobuyuki 65
Monroe, Betty Iverson 1255
Moore, Charles A. 522
Moore, Joe 119, 275
Mōri, Hisashi 1292-1293
Mori, Ōgai 1081-1083
Morishima, Akio 775
Morishima, Michio 804
Morita, Akio 332
Moritani, Masanori 990
Moriya, Yoshio 53
Moriyama, Alan Takeo 396
Moriyama, Tae 88
Morley, James William 239, 684, 1599
Morrell, Robert E. 1566, 1605
Morris, Aldyth B. 522
Morris, Ivan 150, 276, 293, 618, 1015,
  1025-1026, 1074, 1080, 1083, 1091
Morris, Jan 1278
Morris-Suzuki, Tessa 294
Morrison, Charles E. 626, 741
Morse, Ronald A. 847, 849, 991, 1188
Morse, Samuel C. 1206, 1282, 1296
Morton, William Fitch 333
Mosbacher, Eric 70
Moser, Don 715
Mosher, Gouverneur 89
Mosley, Leonard 334
Motofuji, Frank 1068
Mouer, Ross 930
Moy, Jean Oda 327, 1061
Mulhern, Chieko Irie 1069
Munro, Neil Gordon 378
Munsterberg, Hugo 32, 1209, 1271, 1567
Murakami, Hyōe 222, 295
Murakami, Shigeyoshi 467
Murakami, Yasusuke 740
Murakata, Akiko 1235
Murakoshi, Sueo 381
Murano, Shirō 1145
Muraoka, Hiroshi 1470

Muraoka, Kageo 1210
Murasaki Shikibu 1023-1024
Murase, Miyeko 1241
Murata, Kiyoaki 512
Murata, Kiyoji 45
Murata, Ryōhei 733
Murayama, Takeshi 1281
Murdoch, James 124
Muroga, Nobuo 55
Murray, Patricia 55, 296, 340, 1222
Mutsu, Munemitsu 668
Myers, Ramon H. 223

N
Naff, William E. 1094
Nagahara, Keiji 139
Nagai, Michio 191, 972
Nagai, Mona 1098
Nagai, Takashi 258
Nagata, Keiichi 258
Nagatake, Takeshi 1281
Nagatsuka, Ryūji 700
Nair, Kusum 834
Naitō, Akira 1305
Naitō, Hatsuho 700
Najita, Tetsuo 175-176, 224
Naka, John 1328
Nakagami, Kenji 1056
Nakagawa, Sensaku 1284
Nakahara, Hiroyuki 796
Nakai, Kate Wildman 177
Nakajima, Tadashi 700
Nakajima-Okano, Kimiko 457
Nakamura, Akira 634
Nakamura, Hajime 523
Nakamura, Takafusa 225, 805
Nakamura, Tokisada 1291
Nakamura, Yasuo 1408
Nakane, Chie 539, 561
Nakano, Eisha 1350
Nakano, Ichirō 1386
Nakano, Leatrice 383
Nakano, Masaki 1468
Nakano, Takeo Uyo 383
Nakanoin Masatada no Musume 310
Nakata, Yūjirō 1242
Nakauchi, Toshio 35
Nakayama, Shigeru 151, 992
Nakazato, Tarōemon 1281
Namiki Senryū 1180, 1407
Namioka, Lensey 90
Nanba, Matsutarō 55
Narazaki, Muneshige 1272

Nathan, John 335, 1076, 1089
Nathan, K. S. 741
National Museum of Modern Art,
   Tokyo 1285, 1370
Natsume, Sōseki 1084-1087, 1159
Nelson, Andrew Nathaniel 421
Neri, Rita E. 1600
Neu, Charles E. 653
Nihon Bonsai Kyōkai. Directors 1328
Nihon Bunka Kenkyūjo 1557
Nihon Chiri Gakkai 40
Nihon Ginkō. Tōkeikyoku 819
Nihon Keizai Shimbun 823
Nihon Kokusai Kyōiku Kyōkai 1550
Nihon Kokusai Mondai Kenkyūjo 829
Nihon Sen'i Ishō Sentā, Ōsaka 1347
Nihon Shashinka Kyōkai 1276
Nihon Shimbun Kyōkai 1483
Nihon Shōken Keizai Kenkyūjo 858
Nihon Toshokan Kyōkai 1474
Nihon Yachō no Kai 65
Nijō, Lady 310
Nikovskis, Armins 1242, 1351
Nippon Bonsai Kyōkai. Directors 1328
Nippon Hōsō Kyōkai. Radio and TV
   Culture Research Institute. History
   Compilation Room 1486
Nippon Hōsō Kyōkai. Sōgō Bunka
   Kenkyūjo 1486
Nish, Ian 654, 669-671, 701
Nishi, Kazuo 1314
Nishida, Kitarō 524
Nishihara, Masashi 727, 1613
Nishikawa, Kyōtarō 1294-1295
Nishikawa, Shunsaku 930
Nishikawa, Takeshi 1305, 1353, 1472
Nishimura, Eshin 486
Nishitani, Keiji 521 525
Nissan Jidōsha Kabushiki Kaisha.
   Kaigaibu 447
Nissan Motor Compariy. International
   Division 447
Noda, Makito 1565
Noda, Mari 440
Noda, Pamela J. 1565
Noda, Yoshiyuki 782
Nogami, Yaeko 1071
Noguchi, Yoshie 1184
Nollman, Ellen Anne 1613
Nolte, Sharon H. 336
Noma, Seiroku 1211, 1351
Nomura, Shōjirō 1349
Norbeck, Edward 468, 554, 562, 599

Norbury, Paul 19, 901
Norman, Egerton Herbert 226
North Carolina Department of Public
    Instruction 36
Nosco, Peter 526
Notehelfer, Frederick G. 337, 358
Numata, Makoto 61
Nunn, G. Raymond 1562, 1601

O
Ōba, Minako 1071, 1098
Obojski, Robert 1456
O'Brien, James A. 1119
Ochiai, Kingo 1082
O'Connor, Kaori 422
O'Connor, Raymond 688
Oda, Katsuzō 1088
Odagiri, Akira 84
Odagiri, Hiroko 1150, 1566
Ōdate, Toshio 1343
Ōe, Kenzaburō 1057, 1088-1090
OECD, see Organisation for Economic
    Co-operation and Development 821
OERI [Office of Educational Research
    and Improvement] Japan Study Team
    970
Ōgai, see Mori, Ōgai 1081-1083
Ogata, Sadako N. 702
Ogawa, Dennis M. 397, 1598
Ogawa, Masataka 1222
Ogura, Takekazu 835
Oh, Sadaharu 338
Ohara, Hōun 1464-1465
Ōhashi, Haruzō 1337
Ohba, Minako, see Ōba, Minako 1071,
    1098
Ohi, Minobu 1464
Ōhira, Masayoshi 339
Ohkawa, Kazushi 806-808
Ohm, Ky-Moon 719
Ohmae, Kenichi 842, 902
Ohnuki-Tierney, Emiko 600
Ohshima, Tsutomu 1446
Ohta, Thaddeus Y. 1602
Ohwi, Jisaburō 62
Ōi, Jisaburō 62
Oishi, Shinzaburō 1219
Oka, Hideyuki 1371
Oka, Yoshitake 296, 340
Okada, Jō 1370
Okada, Yaichirō 60
Okakura, Kakuzō 1470
Okamoto, Kanoko 1048

Okamoto, Shumpei 340, 672, 682
Okamoto, Yoshitomo 1243
Okamura, Kichiemon 1210, 1281
Ōkawa, Kazushi, see Ohkawa, Kazushi
    806-808
Ōkawa, Naomi 1315
Okazaki, Hisahiko 733
Okazaki, Jōji 1244
O'Keefe, Constance 83
Okimoto, Daniel I. 398, 809, 817, 880,
    903
Ōkita, Saburō 810
Ōkōchi, Kazuo 931
Ōkōchi, Sadao 1412
Ōkubo, Genji 192
Okuda, Yoshio 35
Okudaira, Hideo 1245
Okuno, Masahiro 876
Oldfather, Felicia 119
Olsen, Edward A. 767
Olson, Laurence 742
Ōmae, Kenichi, see Ohmae, Kenichi
    842, 902
Ōmae, Kinjirō 1432
O'Neill, Patrick Geoffrey 415, 423, 448-
    451, 1409
Ono, Hideichi 433
Ono, Sokyō 518
Onoda, Hiroo 341
Ōoka, Makoto 1151
Ōoka, Minoru 1316
Ōoka, Shōhei 1091, 1106
Ooms, Herman 177-178
Oppler, Alfred C. 277
Organisation for Economic Co-operation
    and Development 821
Osada, Arata 259
Osaragi, Jirō 1092, 1334
Ōshima, Tsutomu, see Ohshima,
    Tsutomu 1446
Ōta, Gakō 1352
Ota, Isamu 45
Ōta, Yoko 51, 1088
Ōtō, Tokihiko 503
Ouchi, William G. 932
Oxford, Wayne H. 194
Ozaki, Hōsai 1159
Ozaki, Robert S. 20, 743
Ozaki, Shirō 1051
Ozawa, Terutomo 946, 993
Ozu, Yasujirō 1057

P

Pacheco, Diego 132
Pacific War Research Society 260, 703
Packard, George R., III 744, 765
Paine, Robert Treat 1212
Palmore, Erdman B. 540
Parent, Mary Neighbour 1322
Parker, L. Craig, Jr. 570
Parlett, Harold 475
Pascale, Richard Tanner 933
Passin, Herbert 267, 359, 973, 1610
Pathmanathan, M. 741
Patrick, Hugh T. 811-812, 860, 881
Paul, Cedar 351
Paul, Eden Paul 351
Paul, Margot 1353
Paulson, Joy 578
Peachey, Paul 474
Peak, Lois 970
Pearce, Jean 91
Pearson, Richard J. 109, 284
Peattie, Mark R. 223, 227, 342
Pegels, C. Carl 934
Pekarik, Andrew 1039
Pelz, Stephen E. 704
Pempel, T. J. 21, 619-620, 974
Peng, Fred C. C. 379
Pepper, Thomas 813
Perry, John Curtis 278, 657
Perry, Matthew C. 673
Peterson, Susan 331
Petit, Gaston 1273
Pezeu-Massabuau, Jacques 46
Pharr, Susan J. 13, 580
Pheby, John 424
Philippi, Donald L. 152, 380
Phillips, Bernard 489
Phillips, James M. 497
Piccigallo, Philip R. 265
Picken, Stuart D. B. 485, 498, 519
Picon, Leon 1060
Pierson, John D. 311
Pierson, Walter 1562
Piggott, F. S. G. 708
Piggott, Juliet 1186
Pilgrim, Richard 463
Pineau, Roger 673, 700
Piovesana, Gino K. 527
Plath, David W. 541-542, 1460
Plesset, Isabel R. 343
Plimpton, Jack 87
Plumer, James Marshal 1296
Plummer, Timothy 1586

Plutschow, Herbert E. 92-93, 179
Pointner, Horst 1463
Pollack, David 1152
Pomeroy, Charles 1254
Popham, Peter 22, 86, 94
Porter, Timothy 882
Poster, Amy G. 1256
Powell, Irena 1120
Powers, Elizabeth 578
Prange, Gordon W. 228, 705-706
Presseisen, Ernst L. 229
Preston, Anthony 1572
Prestowitz, Clyde V., Jr. 904
Prime Minister's Office. Administrative
    Management Agency. Administrative
    Management Bureau 605
Prime Minister's Office. Statistics
    Bureau 825, 827
Prindl, Andreas R. 861
Pringsheim, Klaus H. 655
Pritchard, David B. 1458
Pronko, Leonard C. 1603
Puette, William J. 1604
Pugel, Thomas A. 905
Pye, Michael 452
Pyle, Kenneth B. 121, 230

R

Radcliffe-Brown, A. R 551
Ranis, Gustav 806
Rathbun, William Jay 1213, 1246
Raz, Jacob 1410
Reed, Steven R. 639
Rees, David 285
Reich, Michael R. 292, 957
Reingold, Edwin M. 332
Reischauer, Edwin O. 13, 23, 122-123,
    360, 387, 485, 498, 519, 966, 1011,
    1515, 1556
Reischauer, Haru Matsukata 297
Reischauer, Robert Karl 1569
Research Institute for Peace and
    Security, Tokyo 765
Reynolds, David K. 601-602
Rhodes, Daniel 1286
Rice, Eugene 134
Rice, Mary Kellogg 1355
Richardson, Bradley M. 621-622, 843
Richie, Donald 24-26, 71, 95-96, 1332,
    1372, 1414, 1425-1427, 1433, 1465
Richter, Ernest 44
Richter, Matsue 44
Ricketts, Robert 1194, 1325

Rielly, Robin L. 1448
Riggs, Lynne E. 1224, 1312
Rimer, J. Thomas 1008-1009, 1081,
    1121, 1156, 1178, 1182, 1231, 1251,
    1413, 1605
Rix, Alan 745-746
Roberts, J. B. 689
Roberts, John G. 231
Roberts, Laurance P. 368, 1475
Robertson, Myles L. C. 747
Robins, Brian 862
Robins-Mowry, Dorothy 581
Robinson, Basil William 1373
Robinson, Jane Washburn 65
Rockwell, E. 1324
Rodd, Laurel Rasplica 1153
Roden, Donald 232
Rodrigues, João 153
Roesler, Hermann 189
Rohlen, Thomas P. 376, 538, 543, 809,
    975
Rohlich, Thomas H. 1027
Roosevelt, Cornelius Van S. 1288
Rootes, Nina 700
Rose, Barbara 1231
Rosenfield, John M. 1206, 1211, 1214,
    1246, 1249
Rosenstone, Robert A. 361
Rosovsky, Henry 233, 807, 811, 817, 917
Ross, Bill D. 714
Ross, Floyd Hiatt 520
Ross, Nancy Wilson 1080
Roth, Martin 97
Rothacher, Albrecht 906
Rowen, Henry S. 848
Rozensztroch, Daniel 1319
Rozman, Gilbert 212
Rubin, Jay 1087, 1122
Rubinger, Bruce 994
Rubinger, Richard 180
Ryan, Marleigh Grayer 1123-1124
Ryōkan 1154

                    S
Sackett, Joel 29, 1391, 1455
Sadler, Arthur L. 529, 1019
Saeki, Yoshikatsu 1430
Saga, Junichi 234
Saga, Susumu 234
Saigyō 1155
Saikaku, see Ihara Saikaku 1014-1015
Saito, George 1083
Sakade, Florence 438

Sakae, Shioya 1180
Sakai, Michikazu 1371
Sakamaki, Shunzō 1591
Sakamoto, Sadao 518
Sakamoto, Tarō 35
Sakamoto, Yoshikazu 280
Sakanishi, Shio 1402
Sakiya, Tetsuo 882
Sakuma, Toshiaki 96
Sakurama, Michio 1406
Salerni, Eugene 956
Salmon, Patricia 1215
Samuels, Richard J. 640, 850, 991
Sanders, Herbert H. 1287
Sanders, Sol 344
Sanderson, Don 999
Sano, Chiye 375
Sano, Emily J. 1295, 1469
Sano, Yoshihiro 893
Sansom, George B. 124-125, 674
Sargent, Geoffrey 1074, 1083
Sasaki, Yuzura 376
Sasamori, Junzō 1449
Saso, Mary 925
Sata, Ineko 1071, 1088
Satchell, Thomas 1016
Satō, Giei 486
Satō, Hideo 721-722, 892
Sato, Hiroaki 1136, 1156, 1158, 1166,
    1307
Satō, Kanzan 1373
Satō, Kazuo 876, 883, 935
Satō, Kōji 486
Satō, Ryūzō 907
Satō, Shōzō 1247
Satō, Tadao 1428
Satō, Zenchū 491
Satoh, Makoto 1171, 1173
Satow, Ernest 675
Saunders, E. Dale 1041-1043, 1077, 1237
Sawa, Nagayo 606
Sawa, Takaaki 1216
Sawa, Yūki 1157
Sawada, Yoshiharu 1281
Saxonhouse, Gary R. 783
Sayle, Murray 11
Scalapino, Robert A. 635, 647, 748
Schaller, Michael 279
Scharfstein, Ben-Ami 477
Scheiner, Betsey 1480
Scheiner, Irwin 235
Schendel, Jochen 949
Schirokauer, Conrad 126

Schlossstein, Steven 908
Schmiegelow, Michèle 909
Schmorleitz, Morton S. 1317
Schneider, Donald O. 9
Schodt, Frederik L. 995, 1480
Schonberger, Richard J. 936
Schuefftan, Kim 1440
Schwade, Arcadio 1606
Schwarz, Edward A. 453
Schwendiman, Gary 927
Scott, Adolphe Clarence 1411
Scott-Stoke, Henry 335
Search Associates, Inc. 1570
Seattle Art Museum 1217
Sei Shōnagon 1025
Seidensticker, Edward G. 236, 345,
   1013, 1024, 1064-1067, 1074, 1077,
   1083, 1101, 1104, 1225
Seigle, Cecilia Segawa 1062, 1077, 1096
Seike, Kiyoshi 1318, 1337
Seki, Keigo 1187
Sekida, Katsuki 487
Sekine, Hiroshi 1057
Selden, Kyoko Iriye 1071, 1218
Self, James 1571
Seligman, Brenda Z. 378
Sen, Sōshitsu 1437, 1470-1471
Senmon Toshokan Kyōgikai 1558
Sesar, Carl 1140
Setouchi, Harumi 1098
Seward, Jack 454, 844, 1445
Shattuck, Warren L. 774
Shaver, Ruth M. 1352
Sherrod, Robert 707
Sherwin, Martin J. 261
Shibamoto, Janet S. 413
Shibata, Katsue 1085
Shibata, Tokue 863
Shibatani, Masayoshi 434
Shibusawa, Masahide 749
Shields, John M. 1236, 1240
Shiels, Frederick L. 750
Shiffert, Edith Marcombe 1157
Shiga, Naoya 1051, 1093
Shigematsu, Sōiku 488
Shigemitsu, Mamoru 708
Shillony, Ben-Ami 237-238
Shimada, Shūjiro 1214
Shimahara, Nobuo K. 970, 976
Shimaki, Kensaku 1051
Shimamura, Masajirō 1333
Shimazaki, Tōson 1094-1096
Shimizu, Hiroshi 758

Shimizu, Yoshiaki 1218, 1248-1249
Shimoda, Masami 1363
Shimomura, Mitsuko 332
Shimpō, Mitsuru 555
Shinoda, Minoru 154
Shinoda, Seishi 1160
Shinohara, Masao 1381
Shinohara, Miyohei 808, 814
Shintani, Masahiko 831
Shiojiri, Seiichi 1044
Shirai, Taishirō 937
Shiraishi, Kazuko 1143, 1151
Shiraishi, Masami 1370
Shirane, Haruo 1040
Shirata, Rinjirō 1450
Shiratori, Rei 27
Shiritsu Daigaku Dantai Rengokai 1550
Shirk, Susan L. 623
Shiroyama, Saburō 346
Shively, Donald H. 115, 239, 289, 1395,
   1397
Shogun Age Exhibition Executive
   Committee 1219
Shoven, John B. 884
Shulman, Frank Joseph 1562, 1607, 1613
Sibley, William F. 1125
Sieben-Morgen, Ruth 259
Siemes, Johannes 189
Sievers, Sharon L. 240
Silberman, Bernard S. 241, 1608
Silver, Alain 1420
Simmons, Ben 22, 95
Simmons, Doreen 1453
Simon, Mutsuko Endo 455
Simpson, Susan 1336
Simul International 339, 988, 990
Singer, Kurt 593
Sissons, David C. S. 790
Skillings, Sally A. 888
Slawson, David A. 1338
Slesin, Suzanne 1319
Smethurst, Richard J. 242-243
Smith, Aileen M. 959
Smith, Bardwell L. 135, 486
Smith, Bradley 155
Smith, Henry DeWitt, II 244, 1256
Smith, Malcolm D. H. 784
Smith, Myron J., Jr. 1609
Smith, Richard Gordon 72
Smith, Robert J. 505, 544, 556, 582
Smith, Thomas C. 181-183
Smith, W. Eugene 959
Smith, Warren W., Jr. 528

Smolan, Rick 28
Sneider, Lea 1368
Sneider, Richard L. 768
Sobel, Robert 874, 982
Soga, Matsuo 410
Sōka Gakkai. Women's Division 583
Sōma, Akira 1352
Sone, Monica 399
Song, Minako I. 1591
Sono, Ayako 1048
Sonobe, Kōichirō 65
Sonoda, Kyōichi 603
Soper, Alexander 1212
Sōrifu. Gyōsei Kanrichō. Gyōsei Kanri Kyoku 605
Sōrifu. Tōkeikyoku 825, 827
Sōseki see Natsume, Sōseki 1084-1087, 1159
Spahn, Mark 421, 438
Sparling, Kathryn 529
Sparnon, Norman J. 1466
Spaulding, Robert M., Jr. 613
Spayde, Jon 1434
Spector, Ronald H. 709
Spry-Leverton, Peter 29
Spurr, Russell 716
Stacey, Nevzer G. 970
Stalk, George, Jr. 836
Stanley, Peter W. 657
Stanley-Baker, Joan 1220
Statistics Bureau. Prime Minister's Office 825, 827
Statler, Oliver 73, 86, 184, 676, 1274, 1552
Steele, M. William 363
Steere, William C. 1464
Stegmaier, Daphne S. 1210
Steinberg, Rafael 715
Steiner, Kurt 641-642, 790
Steinhardt, Nancy Shatzman 1322
Steinhoff, Patricia G. 538, 1559
Stephan, Barbara B. 1350, 1479
Stephan, John J. 286-287, 710
Stephenson, John C. 1458
Stern, Harold P. 1221, 1250
Steslicke, William E. 604
Steven, Rob 545
Stevens, John 97, 713, 1154, 1450
Stevenson, Harold 594
Stewart, David B. 1320
Stewart, Mary L. 1462
Stewart-Smith, Jo 63
Stinchecum, Amanda Mayer 1353

Stiskin, Nahum 957
Stock, Dennis 1149
Stockwin, J. A. A. 620, 624, 634, 637, 751
Stommel, Henry 47
Storry, Richard 32, 127, 156, 245, 593, 656
Strauss, Harold 1092
Strayer, Joseph R. 168
Streeter, Tal 1461
Strong, Kenneth 312, 1046, 1095
Sueno, Akira 845
Sugano, Takuo 880
Suganuma, Kiyomi 1366
Sugawara, Akiko 1437
Sugawara Takasue no musume 1026-1027
Sugimoto, Etsu Inagaki 313
Sugimoto, Masayoshi 157
Sugimoto, Yoshio 616
Sugimura, Tsune 1222
Sugiyama, Hajime 693
Sugiyama, Jirō 1296
Suleski, Ronald 425
Sumita, Shunichi 83
Sutherland, Mary 48, 1438
Suzuki, Daisetz T. 489-492, 521
Suzuki, Hiroyuki 1321
Suzuki, Hisao 1222
Suzuki, Jūzō 1268
Suzuki, Kakichi 1322
Suzuki, Shunryū 493
Suzuki, Takao 411
Suzuki, Yoshio 864-866
Suzumura, Kōtarō 876
Swain, David L. 157, 253, 546, 992
Swann, Peter C. 1223
Swann, Thomas E. 1126-1127
Swearingen, Rodger 192, 752
Szarkowski, John 1277

T
Tachi, Ryūichirō 860
Tachibana, Yuzuru 1432
Tada, Chimako 1151
Taeuber, Irene B. 371
Tahara, Mildred M. 1028
Taira, Kōji 938
Takagi, Miki 1466
Takahashi, Bin 1211
Takahashi, Morio 426
Takahashi, Takako 1071, 1098
Takahashi, Yoshio 108

Takai, Fuyuji 49
Takai, Kiyoshi 1311
Takakuwa, Gisei 1339
Takama, Shinji 64
Takamiya, Susumu 947
Takamura, Kōtarō 1158
Takano, Shinji 65
Takashina, Shūji 1251
Takaya, Ted T. 1179
Takeda Izumo 1180, 1407
Takeda Izumo II 1174
Takeda, Taijun 1057
Takeda, Tsuneo 1252
Takenishi, Hiroko 1088
Takeuchi, Rizō 147
Takeuchi, Yoshinori 521
Takeyama, Fusazō 1328
Takeyama, Masayuki 796
Takeyama, Michio 1097
Tamba, Akira 1387
Tamburello, Adolfo 1473
Tamura, Ryūichi 1057, 1143, 1151
Tanaka, Chikao 1173
Tanaka, Hideo 784
Tanaka, Ichimatsu 1253
Tanaka, Ikko 1224
Tanaka, Michiko 400
Tanaka, Ryōhei 1051
Tanaka, Sen'ō 1472
Tanaka, Yukiko 1098
Tange, Kenzō 1305, 1323
Tanikawa, Shuntarō 1143, 1151
Tanizaki, Junichirō 1057, 1083, 1099-
    1104, 1225, 1404
Tasker, Peter 30
Tateishi, John 401
Tatsuno, Sheridan 996
Tayama, Katai 1105
Taylor, Jared 31
Tazawa, Yutaka 369
Teele, Nicholas 1006
Teichler, Ulrich 1610
Teika, see Fujiwara Teika 1135
Teikoku Shoin Henshūbu 53
Tempel, Egon 1324
ten Grotenhuis, Elizabeth 1244-1245
Terry, Charles S. 341, 1109, 1188, 1238,
    1265, 1305, 1311
Teshigahara, Sōfū 1464-1465
Thayer, Nathaniel B. 638
Thomas, Gordon 262
Thompson, Ralph 803
Thomsen, Harry 513

Thomson, James C., Jr. 646, 657
Thorne, Christopher 711
Thurley, Keith 947
Thurow, Lester C. 939
Thurston, Donald R. 977
Thwaite, Anthony 1134
Tiedemann, Arthur E. 32
Time-Life Books. Editors 13, 715
Titus, David Anson 246
Toby, Ronald P. 677
Togi, Masatō 1377
Toita, Yasuji 1400
Tokiwa, Gishin 1195
Tokugawa, Yoshinobu 1201, 1219, 1412
Tokunaga, Shigeyoshi 940
Tōkyō Kokuritsu Kindai Bijutsukan
    1285, 1370
Toland, John 705, 712
Tomimoto, Kenkichi 1287
Tomioka, Taeko 1071, 1098, 1143
Tomita, Iwao 852
Tomita, Jun 1354
Tomita, Nobuo 634
Tomita, Norika 1354
Tomoda, Yasumasa 962
Toriyama, Ryūzō 49
Totman, Conrad D. 128, 185-186, 314
Totten, George Oakley, III 247, 630,
    796
Toyoda, Eiji 347
Toyoda, Takeshi 140
Toyotomi Hideyoshi 299
Trager, James 563
Trani, Eugene P. 672
Treat, John Whittier 1058
Treib, Marc 98
Trevor, Malcolm 941, 948-950
Trewartha, Glenn T. 50
Triska, Jan F. 635
Trotter, Ann 697
Tsoukalis, Loukas 910
Tsubaki, Tadao 959
Tsuchida, Bruce T. 1019
Tsuchiya, Yoshio 1435
Tsuda, Nobuko 1436
Tsuge, Gen'ichi 1611
Tsuge, Hideomi 187
Tsuji, Kaichi 1437
Tsuji, Kiyoaki 625
Tsuji, Shizuo 1438
Tsumura, Setsuko 1098
Tsuneishi, Warren M. 1562
Tsuneta Yano Memorial Society 826

Tsunoda, Ryūsaku 33
Tsurumi, E. Patricia 34
Tsurumi, Kazuko, 595
Tsuruta, Kinya 1126-1127
Tsurutani, Taketsugu 769
Tsushima, Yūko 1098
Tsūshō Sangyōshō 828
Tsutsui, Michio 431
Tsutsumi, Yūtarō 1364
Tuge, Hideomi 187
Tung, Rosalie L. 911, 942
Turnbull, Stephen R. 158
Turner, Louis 912
Turney, Alan 1084
Twitchett, Denis 115
Tyler, Royall 1029, 1175
Tyler, William Jefferson 1112

U
Uchino, Tatsurō 815
Ueda Akinari 1030-1031
Ueda, Kōichirō 1357
Ueda, Makoto 1106, 1128, 1159, 1167-
  1168
Ueda, Reikichi 1288
Ueda, Shizuteru 521
Ueda, Taizō 843
Uekusa, Masu 869
Ueshiba, Kisshōmaru 1451
Ulak, James T. 1205
Umeda, Atsushi 56
Unger, J. Marshall 997
United States-Japan Conference on
  Cultural and Educational Interchange
  (CULCON). Education
  Sub-Committee 36
United States. Department of State 690
United States. Office of Geography 57
University of California, Davis. Asian
  American Studies 1579
Unno, Kazutaka 55
Unno, Taitetsu 1451
Uno, Chiyo 1048, 1071
Upham, Frank K. 785
Urrutia, Miguel 191
Ury, Marian 1032
Ushiogi, Morikazu 965
Usui, Masao 1366
Uyehara, Cecil H. 630, 998

V
Valeo, Francis R. 626
Van Bragt, Jan 525

van Helvoort, Ernest 923
Van Zandt, Howard 844
Vance, Timothy J. 412
Varley, H. Paul 32, 37, 144, 159-160,
  1467, 1469
Vernon, Raymond 913, 952
Vessie, Patricia Armstrong 1612
Victoria, Ryōjun 486
Viglielmo, Valdo H. 524
Viner, Aron 867-868
Vining, Elizabeth Gray 362
Vishwanathan, Savitri 728
Vlastos, Stephen 161
Vogel, Ezra F. 38-39, 564
von Baelz, Erwin O. E. 351
von Mehren, Arthur Taylor 786
von Ragué, Beatrix 1374
von Stillfried, Raimund 1278
Vos, Frits 1148
Voss, Friedrich 1610

W
Wachtel, Paul 907
Wada, Yoshiko 1355
Waddell, Meredith 1586
Wagatsuma, Hiroshi 373, 376, 571, 588
Waley, Arthur 1011, 1024-1025, 1181
Waley, Paul 99
Walker, Egbert H. 62
Walker, Janet A. 1129
Wallach, Sidney 673
Walsh, Len 456
Walters, Gary D.'A. 91
Walthall, Anne 161
Walworth, Arthur 673
Ward, Robert E. 239, 280, 548, 627,
  1613
Warner, Gordon 713, 1449, 1452
Warner, Langdon 1226, 1296
Watanabe, Akio 285
Watanabe, Hiroshi 1308
Watanabe, Hitoshi 378
Watanabe, Yasutada 1325
Watanabe, Yoshio 1323
Waterhouse, David B. 1212, 1261
Watson, Burton 367, 1010, 1154, 1156
Watson, William 1227
Watts, Alan W. 494
Watts, Anthony J. 1572
Watts, William 753
Wayembergh, Josse 1327
Weatherby, Meredith 1073, 1078, 1465
Weatherly, James K. 100

Webb, Glenn T. 1211
Webb, Herschel 188
Weglyn, Michi 386
Weinstein, Franklin B. 880
Weinstein, Martin E. 770
Welch, Theodore F. 1476, 1573
Welfield, John 754
Wells, Warner 259
Westerhoven, James 1116
Westney, D. Eleanor 248
Westwood, John N. 678
Wetherall, William O. 376
Wheeler, Jimmy W. 813
Wheeler, Keith 715
Wheeler, Nik 94
Wheeler, Richard 714
Wheelwright, Carolyn 1248
Whitaker, Donald P. 6
White, James W. 514, 557
White, Maureen 910
White, Merry 13, 572, 978
White, Michael 950
White, Oswald 708
Whitehouse, Wilfrid 1033
Whiting, Robert 1456
Whitney, Clara A. N. 363
Whitney, Courtney 356
Wild Bird Society of Japan 65
Wilkinson, Endymion 755
Williams, Justin, Sr. 281
Williams, Mark B. 1326
Willoughby, Charles A. 356
Wilpert, Bernhard 949
Wilson, George M. 348, 351
Wilson, Graeme 1085, 1136
Wilson, Robert A. 402
Wilson, William Scott 529
Wiswell, Ella Lury 582
Witts, Max Morgan 262
Wixted, John Timothy 1153
Wöss, Fleur 1595
Wohlstetter, Roberta 705
Women's Division of Sōka Gakkai 583
Woodard, William P. 518
Woodhull, Alan 1242, 1315
Wordell, Charles B. 979
Woronoff, Jon 839
Worswick, Clark 1278
Wray, Harry 249
Wray, William D. 250, 1614
Wright, Peter 391
Wyden, Peter 263

Y

Yagi, Eri 992
Yagi, Koji 1326
Yakushiji, Taizō 870
Yamada, Saburō 831
Yamada, Sadami 1254
Yamada, Sōbin 1190
Yamagishi, Shōji 1277
Yamagiwa, Joseph K. 16, 1011
Yamaguchi, Fukiko 1464
Yamaguchi, Masuo 1471
Yamaha, Midori 375
Yamamoto, Akira Y. 1189
Yamamoto, Makiko 91
Yamamoto, Masaru 1435
Yamamoto, Michiko 1098
Yamamoto, Shichihei 4
Yamamoto, Tadashi 626
Yamamoto Tsunetomo 529
Yamamoto, Yoshiko 501
Yamamura, Kozo 115, 139, 169, 783,
  816-817
Yamanaka, Norio 1356
Yamanouchi, Hisaaki 1130
Yamaoka, Masako 1439
Yamazaki, Masakazu 1179, 1182, 1413
Yampolsky, Philip B. 476
Yanaga, Chitoshi 846
Yanagi, Muneyoshi 1228
Yanagi, Sōetsu 1228
Yanagida, Taiun 1231
Yanagisako, Sylvia Junko 403
Yanagisawa, Eizo 1033
Yanagita, Kunio 503, 1188
Yano Tsuneta Kinenkai 826
Yashiro, Seiichi 1179
Yashiro, Yukio 1197
Yasuba, Yasukichi 817
Yasuda, Kenneth 1202
Yasuoka, Shōtarō 1057, 1107
Yasutomo, Dennis T. 756-757
Yazaki, Takeo 546
Yazawa, Makoto 781
Yobuko, Yuriko 1318
Yokomitsu, Riichi 1108
Yokoyama, Toshio 251
Yoneda, Soei 1440
Yonezawa, Yoshiho 1255
Yosano, Akiko 1160
Yoshida, Chiaki, 1400
Yoshida, Kenichi 282
Yoshida Kenkō 1034
Yoshida, Kogorō 1481

Yoshida, Kōzō 47
Yoshida, Mamoru 951
Yoshida, Mayumi 75
Yoshida, Mitsukuni 1198, 1224
Yoshida, Mitsuru 716
Yoshida, Shigeru 282, 324
Yoshihara, Kunio 727, 818, 914
Yoshikawa, Eiji 1109
Yoshikawa, Muneo 439
Yoshikawa, Torao 51
Yoshikoshi, Tatsuo 1402
Yoshimasu, Gōzō 1143
Yoshimura, Yūji 1362
Yoshino, I. Roger 381
Yoshino, Michael Y. 839, 915, 943, 952
Yoshioka, Minoru, 1057, 1151
Yoshitsu, Michael M. 283, 758
Yoshiyuki, Junnosuke 1057
Yoshizaki, Yasuhiro 1615
Yoshizawa, Chū 1255

Young, Blake Morgan 315
Young, John 457
Young, Martie W. 1229
Yourcenar, Marguerite 1131
Yu, Beongcheon 1132-1133
Yu, Suk-Ryul 719
Yuasa, Nobuyuki 1146, 1149, 1154
Yui, Tsunehiko 208
Yumoto, John M. 1375
Yūzan Daidōji, see Daidōji Yūzan 529

Z
Zeami Motokiyo 1181, 1413
Zekkai Chūshin 1152
Zenchiku Ujinobu 1181
Zich, Arthur 715
Zimmerman, M. 916
Zolbrod, Leon M. 1031
Zoll, Daniel R. 733

Index of Titles

A

Accomplices of silence: the modern Japanese novel 1118

Across the Pacific: an inner history of American-East Asian relations 649

Adaptation and education in Japan 976

Admiral Togo 320

Affective expressions in Japanese: a handbook of value-laden words in everyday Japanese 425

After apocalypse: four Japanese plays of Hiroshima and Nagasaki 1173

After hours: modern Japan and the search for enjoyment 1460

After imperialism: the search for a new order in the Far East, 1921-1931 661

After the banquet 1072

Against the state: politics and social protest in Japan 606

Agano and Takatori [Famous ceramics of Japan] 1281

Ages ago: thirty-seven tales from the Konjaku monogatari collection 1032

Agrarian origins of modern Japan 181

Agricultural development and tenancy disputes in Japan, 1870-1940 242

Agricultural policy in Japan 821

Aikido: the way of harmony 1450

Ainu creed and cult 378

Ainu life and lore: echoes of a departing race 372

Ainu: the past in the present 379

Akatsuki no tera 1077

Akira Kurosawa: a guide to references and resources 1585

Akutagawa: an introduction 1132

All-Japan: the catalogue of everything Japanese 1552

All-romanized English-Japanese dictionary 426

Alliance in decline: a study in Anglo-Japanese relations, 1908-23 670

Allied occupation of Japan, 1945-1952: an annotated bibliography of Western-language materials 1613

Allies of a kind: the United States, Britain and the war against Japan, 1941-1945 711

Amazing race: winning the technorivalry with Japan 981

Amerasia Journal 1487

America versus Japan: a comparative study of business-government relations conducted at the Harvard Business School 801

American and Japanese auto industries in transition: report of the Joint U.S.-Japan Automobile Study 870

American Caesar: Douglas MacArthur, 1880-1964 356

American-East Asian relations: a survey 646

American in disguise 398

American occupation of Japan: the origins of the cold war in Asia 279

American samurai: Captain L. L. Janes and Japan 358

American teacher in early Meiji Japan 358

America's concentration camps 386

AMPO: Japan-Asia Quarterly Review 1488

Anatomy of dependence 589

Anatomy of Japanese business 935

Anatomy of self: the individual versus society 590

Ancestor worship in contemporary Japan 505

Ancient Japan [Cambridge history of Japan] 115

Ancient tales in modern Japan: an anthology of Japanese folk tales 1185

And justice for all: an oral history of the Japanese American detention camps 401

Anglo-Japanese alienation 1919-1952: papers of the Anglo-Japanese Conference on the History of the Second World War 701

Anglo-Japanese alliance: the diplomacy of two island empires, 1894-1907 669

Anglo-Japanese trade rivalry in the Middle East in the inter-war period 758

Anthology of Japanese literature. Volume 1: From the earliest era to the mid-nineteenth century 1000

Anthology of Japanese literature. Volume 2: Modern Japanese literature 1000

Anthology of modern Japanese poetry 1157

Antique Japanese furniture: a guide to
evaluating and restoring 1340
Antitrust in Japan 270
Anya kōro 1093
Aoneko 1136
Applied artificial intelligence in Japan:
current status, key research and
development performers, strategic
focus 994
Appointment in Japan: memories of sixty
years 350
Appreciations of Japanese culture 1003
Approaches to the modern Japanese
novel 1127
Approaches to the modern Japanese short
story 1126
Archaeology of the Ryukyus: a regional
chronology from 3000 B.C. to the
historic period 284
Architecture of Arata Isozaki 1299
Area handbook for Japan 6
Arms production in Japan: the military
applications of civilian technology 763
Arms, yen & power: the Japanese
dilemma 354
Arrowroot 1102
Art and architecture of Japan 1212
Art and morality 524
Art in Japanese esoteric Buddhism 1216
Art of Hokusai in book illustration 1478
Art of Japanese calligraphy 1242
Art of Japanese joinery 1318
Art of Japanese management:
applications for American executives
933
Art of kabuki: famous plays in
performance 1407
Art of modern Japan: from the Meiji
Restoration to the Meiji centennial,
1868-1968 1209
Art of netsuke carving 1291
Art of sumi-e: appreciation, techniques,
and application 1247
Art of surimono: privately published
Japanese woodblock prints and books
in the Chester Beatty Library, Dublin
1263
Art of the Japanese kite 1461
Art of the Japanese screen 1234
Art of the netsuke carver 1288
Art treasures of Japan 1197
Artist and patron in postwar Japan:
dance, music, theater, and the visual

arts, 1955-1980 1376
Arts of Asia 1489
Arts of Japan. Volume 1: Ancient and
medieval 1211
Arts of Japan. Volume 2: Late medieval
to modern 1211
Arts of Shinto 1199
Aru onna 1046
As I crossed a bridge of dreams:
recollections of a woman in eleventh-
century Japan 1026
As the Japanese see it: past and present 1
As we saw them: the first Japanese
embassy to the United States (1860) 667
Asahi Evening News 1546
Asia and Oceania: a guide to archival &
manuscript sources in the United States
1562
Asian Folklore Studies 1490
Asian Studies Newsletter 1525
Asian Survey: a Monthly Review of
Contemporary Asian Affairs 1491
Asian Theatre Journal 1492
Asians in America: a selected annotated
bibliography 1579
Asia's new giant: how the Japanese
economy works 811
Asiatic Society of Japan. Transactions
1543
Aspects of social change in modern
Japan 239
Association of Teachers of Japanese.
Journal 1529
Asuka Buddhist art: Horyu-ji 1208
At dawn we slept: the untold story of
Pearl Harbor 705
At home with Japanese cooking 1429
Atlas of Japan: physical, economic and
social 54
Atomic bomb and the end of World War
II 254
Audience and actors: a study of their
interaction in the Japanese traditional
theatre 1410
Authority and the individual in Japan:
citizen protest in historical perspective
614
Autobiography of Yukichi Fukuzawa 302
Automobiles and the future:
competition, cooperation, and change
870
Autumn wind: a selection from the poems
of Issa 1146

Awakening Japan: the diary of a German
  doctor, Erwin Baelz 351
Azuma kagami 154

B

Backstage at bunraku: a
  behind-the-scenes look at Japan's
  traditional puppet theatre 1391
Baedeker's Japan 79
Bakufu in Japanese history 146
Ballad-drama of medieval Japan 1169
Bamboo 1357
Bamboo of Japan: splendor in four
  seasons 64
Bamboo people: the law and Japanese-
  Americans 384
Bashoteki ronri to shūkyōteki sekaikan
  524
Battle history of the Imperial Japanese
  Navy (1941-1945) 687
Beauty and sadness 1063
Becoming Japanese: the world of the pre-
  school child 559
Beef in Japan: politics, production,
  marketing and trade 833
Before aggression: Europeans prepare
  the Japanese army 229
Before the dawn 1094
Beginning Japanese 440
Beginnings of Japanese art 104
Bells of Nagasaki 258
Beneath the eagle's wings: Americans in
  occupied Japan 278
Between friends: Japanese diplomats look
  at Japan-U.S. relations 733
Between MITI and the market: Japanese
  industrial policy for high technology
  880
Between war and peace: the Potsdam
  Conference 254
Beyond national borders: reflections on
  Japan and the world 902
Beyond war: Japan's concept of
  comprehensive national security 760
Bibliographie zum japanischen
  Erziehungswesen: postwar publications
  in Western languages 1610
Bibliography of Asian Studies 1580
Bibliography of Christianity in Japan:
  Protestantism in English sources (1859-
  1959) 1587
Bibliography on Japanese education =
  Bibliographie zum japanischen

Erziehungswesen: postwar publications
  in Western languages 1610
Bibliography on the Allied occupation of
  Japan: a bibliography of
  Western-language publications from
  the years 1970-1980 (preliminary
  edition) 1613
Big business in Japanese politics 846
Biographical dictionary of Japanese art
  369
Biographical dictionary of Japanese
  history 367
Biographical dictionary of Japanese
  literature 365
Birds, beasts, blossoms, and bugs: the
  nature of Japan 1221
Birdwatcher's guide to Japan 65
Biruma no tategoto 1097
Black rain 1058
Black ships off Japan: the story of
  Commodore Perry's expedition 673
Black sun: the eyes of four; roots and
  innovation in Japanese photography
  1275
Bombers over Japan 715
Bonkei: tray landscapes 1330
Bonsai: the complete guide to art and
  technique 1336
Book of five rings 1447
Book of kimono 1356
Book of sumo: sport, spectacle, and
  ritual 1454
Book of sushi 1432
Book of tea 1470
Book of the samurai: the warrior class of
  Japan 158
Books on Japan in English: joint
  holdings list of ICU Library and IHJ
  Library, September 1983 1589
Botchan 1084
Box man 1041
Bridge of dreams: a poetics of 'The tale
  of Genji' 1040
Brief history of Chinese and Japanese
  civilizations 126
Britain and East Asia, 1933-1937 697
Britain and Japan, 1858-1883 660
Britain and the Sino-Japanese War: a
  study in the dilemmas of British decline
  697
British Association for Japanese Studies.
  Proceedings 1538
British factory – Japanese factory: the

origins of national diversity in industrial relations 920
Broadcasting in Japan 1482
Brocade by night: 'Kokin wakashū' and the court style in Japanese classical poetry 1153
Brocade pillow: azaleas of old Japan 59
Broken commandment 1095
Brush strokes: moments from my life 339
Buddha eye: an anthology of the Kyoto school 521
Buddhism and the state in sixteenth-century Japan 145
Buddhism: Japan's cultural identity 485
Budō shoshinshū 529
Bugaku masks 1294
Bulletin of Concerned Asian Scholars 1493
Bunraku: the art of the Japanese puppet theatre 1404
Bunraku: the puppet theater 1392
Buraku Liberation News 381
Bushūkō no hiwa 1102
Business and society in Japan: fundamentals for businessmen 843
Business in Japan: a guide to Japanese business practice and procedure 901
Business Japan 1494
Business Japanese: a guide to improved communication 447
Business Japanese II: a second guide to improved communication 447
Business negotiations with the Japanese 911
Business of the Japanese state: energy markets in comparative and historical perspective 850
Business Tokyo 1495
Buyo: the classical dance 1390

C

Cambridge history of Japan 115
Can Japanese agriculture survive? a historical and comparative approach 835
Canadian perspectives on economic relations with Japan: proceedings of a conference sponsored by the University of Toronto-York University Joint Centre on Modern East Asia and the Institute for Research on Public Policy, Toronto, May 1979 895

Capital formation in Japan, 1868-1940 233
Capital of the Tycoon: a narrative of a three years' residence in Japan 349
Capitalism and nationalism in prewar Japan: the ideology of the business elite, 1868-1941 219
Car wars: the untold story 874
Castles in Japan 1317
Catalogue of books in English on Japan, 1945-1981 = Eibun Nihon kankei tosho mokuroku 1945-1981 1589
Catalpa bow: a study of shamanistic practices in Japan 499
Caught in the Middle East: Japan's diplomacy in transition 758
Censorship in imperial Japan 221
Century of agricultural growth in Japan: its relevance to Asian development 831
Century of Japanese photography 1276
Century of Protestant Christianity in Japan 496
Certain woman 1046
Chado: the Japanese way of tea 1471
Challenge of China and Japan: politics and development in East Asia 623
Challenge of Japan's internationalization: organization and culture 802
Changes in the Japanese university: a comparative perspective 963
Changing Japan 562
Changing Japanese attitudes toward modernization 239
Chanoyu: Japanese tea ceremony 1469
Chanoyu Quarterly: Tea and the Arts of Japan 1496
Charismatic bureaucrat: a political biography of Matsudaira Sadanobu, 1758-1829 177
Chieko and other poems of Takamura Kōtarō 1158
Child development and education in Japan 594
Children of Hiroshima 259
Children of the A-bomb: the testament of the boys and girls of Hiroshima 259
China and Japan at war, 1937-1945: the politics of collaboration 702
China and Japan: new economic diplomacy 735
China and Japan, 1949-1976 730
China and Japan, 1949-1980 730
China and Japan: search for balance

since World War I 647
China-Burma-India 715
Chinese and the Japanese: essays in political and cultural interactions 650
Chinmoku 1055
Chōshū in the Meiji Restoration 171
Christian century in Japan, 1549-1650 129
Christian converts and social protest in Meiji Japan 235
Christianity and Japan: meeting, conflict, hope 498
Chronicle of gods and sovereigns: 'Jinnō Shōtōki' of Kitabatake Chikafusa 144
Chronicle of my mother 327
Chrysanthemum and the bat: baseball samurai style 1456
Chrysanthemum and the sword: patterns of Japanese culture 585
Chūshingura: an exposition 1180
Chūshingura: studies in kabuki and the puppet theater 1395
Chūshingura (the treasury of loyal retainers): a puppet play 1180
Cinema east: a critical study of major Japanese films 1421
Circles of fantasy: convention in the plays of Chikamatsu 1399
City life in Japan: a study of a Tokyo ward 549
Clara's diary: an American girl in Meiji Japan 363
Classes in contemporary Japan 545
Classic bonsai of Japan 1328
Classic Buddhist sculpture: the Tempyō period 1296
Classic tradition in Japanese architecture: modern versions of the Sukiya style 1309
Classical budo 1442
Classical bujutsu 1443
Climate of Japan 41
Code of the samurai 529
Collapse of the Tokugawa bakufu, 1862-1868 186
Collection of Nagasaki colour prints and drawings: showing the influence of Chinese and Japanese art on that of Japan 179
Collection of tales from Uji: a study and translation of Uji shūi monogatari 1022
Collectors' netsuke 1288
Colloquial Japanese: with important construction and grammar notes 428
Comeback: case by case: building the resurgence of American business 38
Coming of the barbarians: a story of Western settlements in Japan, 1853-1870 190
Coming to terms: the politics of Australia's trade with Japan, 1945-57 745
Common security interests of Japan, the United States, and NATO 765
Communism in Japan: a case of political naturalization 635
Competition: dealing with Japan 813
Competitive edge: the semiconductor industry in the U.S. and Japan 880
Complete journal of Townsend Harris, first American consul and minister to Japan 676
Complete sumi-e techniques: complete instructions for painting over 200 subjects including flowers, trees, animals, fish, and landscapes 1254
Comprehending technical Japanese 437
Concentration camps USA: Japanese Americans and World War II 386
Conciliation and Japanese law: Tokugawa and modern 778
Concise dictionary of modern Japanese history 1555
Concise history of Japanese art 1223
Concordance: the stamps of Japan, Ryukyus, and Manchoukuo 1871-1979 1522
Confessions of a mask 1073
Confessions of Lady Nijō 310
Conflict in Japan 538
Conflict in modern Japanese history: the neglected tradition 175
Confucianism and Tokugawa culture 526
Confucianism in modern Japan: a study of conservatism in Japanese intellectual history 528
Conspiracy at Matsukawa 780
Constitution of Japan: its first twenty years, 1947-1967 787
Constitutional case law of Japan: selected Supreme Court decisions, 1961-70 788
Contemporary architecture of Japan 1958-1984 1321
Contemporary artist in Japan 1203
Contemporary industrial relations in Japan 937

673

Contemporary Japanese architecture: its development and challenge 1297
Contemporary Japanese budget politics 608
Contemporary Japanese literature: an anthology of fiction, film, and other writing since 1945 1057
Contemporary Japanese philosophical thought 527
Contemporary Religions in Japan 1520
Cook Japanese 1430
Coping with U.S-Japanese economic conflicts 892
Counterfeiter, and other stories 1060
Country textiles of Japan: the art of tsutsugaki 1345
Country to city: the urbanization of a Japanese hamlet 554
Court and bakufu in Japan: essays in Kamakura history 147
Court and constitution in Japan: selected Supreme Court decisions, 1948-60 790
Craft treasures of Okinawa 1201
Crazy iris and other stories of the atomic aftermath 1088
Creative origami 1367
Crime control in Japan 566
Crisis in identity and contemporary Japanese novels 1115
Cultural atlas of Japan 113
Currents in Japanese cinema: essays by Tadao Sato 1428

D
Daily life in Japan at the time of the samurai, 1185-1603 136
Daily Summary of Japanese Press 1547
Damned inheritance: the Soviet Union and the Manchurian crises, 1924-1935 684
Dance in the nō theatre. Volume 1: Dance analysis 1389
Dance in the nō theatre. Volume 2: Plays and scores 1389
Dance in the nō theater. Volume 3: Dance patterns 1389
Dark night's passing 1093
Daruma: the founder of Zen in Japanese art and popular culture 483
Daughter of the samurai. How a daughter of feudal Japan, living hundreds of years in one generation, became a modern American 313
Dawn to the West: Japanese literature of the modern era. Volume 1: Fiction 1001
Dawn to the West: Japanese literature of the modern era. Volume 2: Poetry, drama, criticism 1001
Day in the life of Japan: photographed by 100 of the world's leading photojournalists on one day, June 7, 1985 28
Day man lost: Hiroshima, 6 August 1945 260
Day of infamy 705
Day one: before Hiroshima and after 263
Day-walks near Tokyo 91
Dazai Osamu 1119
Dealing with the Japanese 916
Death in life: survivors of Hiroshima 257
Death in midsummer, and other stories 1074
Decay of the angel 1077
December 7, 1941: the day the Japanese attacked Pearl Harbor 705
Deer Cry Pavilion: a story of Westerners in Japan 1868-1905 190
Deference and defiance in nineteenth-century Japan 213
Defiance in Manchuria: the making of Japanese foreign policy, 1931-1932 702
Democracy in contemporary Japan 616
Democratizing Japan: the Allied occupation 280
Deregulating telecoms: competition and control in the United States, Japan and Britain 953
Design motifs 1207
Deus destroyed: the image of Christianity in early modern Japan 166
Developing economies and Japan: lessons in growth 810
Development of Japanese business, 1600-1980 208
Development of Kamakura rule, 1180-1250: a history with documents 148
Development of realism in the fiction of Tsubouchi Shōyō 1123
Diary of a mad old man 1099
Diary of Kido Takayoshi 307
Dictionary of Asian American history 1563
Dictionary of basic Japanese grammar 431

Dictionary of Chinese and Japanese art 1567
Dictionary of Japanese and English idiomatic equivalents 414
Dictionary of Japanese artists: painting, sculpture, ceramics, prints, lacquer 368
Dictionary of Japanese Buddhist terms: based on references in Japanese literature 415
Different people: pictures of some Japanese 24
Dilemmas of growth in prewar Japan 239
Diplomat in Japan: the inner history of the critical years in the evolution of Japan when the ports were opened and the monarchy restored, recorded by a diplomatist who took an active part in the events of the time, with an account of his personal experiences during that period 675
Diplomatist's wife in Japan: letters from home to home 355
Diplomat's wife in Japan: sketches at the turn of the century 355
Directory of information sources in Japan, 1986 1558
Directory of Japan specialists in Australia 1559
Directory of Japanese specialists and Japanese study institutions in the United States and Canada 1559
Discover Japan: words, customs and concepts 1557
Divine thunder: the life and death of the kamikaze 700
Divine wind: Japan's kamikaze force in World War II 700
Doctoral Dissertations on Asia: an Annotated Bibliographical Journal of Current International Research 1607
Doctoral dissertations on Japan and on Korea, 1969-1979: an annotated bibliography of studies in Western languages 1607
Doctors in politics: the political life of the Japan Medical Association 604
Doctor's wife 1047
Documents of Iriki: illustrative of the development of the feudal institutions of Japan 148
Dōgen Kigen: mystical realist 481
Dojo: magic and exorcism in modern Japan 506

Doolittle raid: America's daring first strike against Japan 696
Double patriots: a study of Japanese nationalism 245
Dr. Willis in Japan, 1862-1877: British medical pioneer 353
Drawings of Hokusai 1258
Dutch impact on Japan 167
Dynamic and immobilist politics in Japan 620

E
E. H. Norman: his life and scholarship 226
Eagle against the sun: the American war with Japan 709
Eagle and the rising sun: America and Japan in the twentieth century 725
Early Buddhist architecture in Japan 1322
Early Buddhist Japan 143
Early Japanese art: the great tombs and treasures 105
Early Japanese history (c.40 B.C.-A.D. 1167) 1569
Early nō drama: its background, character and development, 1300-1450 1409
East 1497
East across the Pacific: historical and sociological studies of Japanese immigration and assimilation 385
East Asia: International Review of Economic, Political, and Social Development 1498
East Asia: tradition and transformation 123
East Asian economies: a guide to information sources 1594
East Asian medicine in urban Japan: varieties of medical experience 598
East to America: a history of the Japanese in the United States 402
Eastern Buddhist 1499
Economic and demographic change in preindustrial Japan, 1600-1868 169
Economic development and the labor market in Japan 938
Economic development of Japan: a quantitative study 803
Economic development of Japan c. 1868-1941 218
Economic development of Japan: growth

and structural change 218
Economic diplomacy between the European Community and Japan 1959-1981 906
Economic Eye: a Quarterly Digest of Views from Japan 1500
Economic growth in prewar Japan 225
Economic institutional change in Tokugawa Japan: Ōsaka and the Kinai cotton trade 170
Economic Statistics Annual 819
Economic Survey of Japan 820
Economic surveys: Japan 821
Edo architecture: Katsura and Nikko 1315
Edo painting: Sotatsu and Korin 1240
Education and equality in Japan 964
Education in Japan: a century of modern development 960
Education in Japan: a source book 1610
Education in Tokugawa Japan 164
Educational achievement in Japan: lessons for the West 971
Educational choice and labor markets in Japan 962
Educational policies in crisis: Japanese and American perspectives 965
Ei-Wa – Wa-Ei konpyūta-dēta shori yōgo jiten 437
Eibun Nihon kankei tosho mokuroku 1945-1981 1589
Eiga monogatari 1021
Election campaigning Japanese style 631
Elegant Japanese house: traditional sukiya architecture 1310
Elements of Japanese design: a handbook of family crests, heraldry & symbolism 1191
Emerging power of Japanese money 867
Emperor and nation in Japan: political thinkers of the Tokugawa period 188
Emperor Hirohito and his chief aide-de-camp: the Honjō diary, 1933-36 209
Emperor Hirohito and Showa Japan: a political portrait 334
Emperor of Japan: a selected bibliography 334
Emperor's adviser; Saionji Kinmochi and pre-war Japanese politics 323
Empire and aftermath: Yoshida Shigeru and the Japanese experience, 1878-1954 324
Empire in eclipse: Japan in the postwar

American alliance system; a study in the interaction of domestic politics and foreign policy 754
Encounter with Japan 359
Encouragement of learning 194
Enduring art of Japan 1226
Enduring crafts of Japan: 33 living national treasures 1222
Enemy that never was: a history of the Japanese Canadians 382
English-Japanese, Japanese-English dictionary of computer and data-processing terms 437
English loanwords in Japanese: a selection 419
Enola Gay 262
Entrepreneur and gentleman: a case history of a Japanese company 845
Entrepreneurship in a 'mature industry' 870
Environmental law in Japan 775
Environmental protest and citizen politics in Japan 958
Epidemics and mortality in early modern Japan 172
Era of high-speed growth: notes on the postwar Japanese economy 799
Eros plus massacre: an introduction to the Japanese New Wave cinema 1419
Esoteric Buddhist painting 1237
Essays in idleness: the 'Tsurezuregusa' of Kenkō 1034
Essential Japanese grammar 427
Essential Japanese house: craftsmanship, function, and style in town and country 1301
Essential kanji: 2,000 basic Japanese characters systematically arranged for learning and reference 448
Essentials of Zen Buddhism: selected from the writings of Daisetz T. Suzuki 489
Europe and Japan: changing relationships since 1945 720
Evaluating applied research: lessons from Japan 987
Everyday Japanese: a basic introduction to the Japanese language & culture 453
Everyday Japanese characters 452
Everyday life in traditional Japan 165
Evolution of labor relations in Japan: heavy industry, 1853-1955 204
Evolving techniques in Japanese

676

woodblock prints 1273
Exotic Japanese stories: the beautiful and the grotesque; 16 unusual tales and unforgettable images 1045
Exploring Kamakura: a guide for the curious traveler 76
Exploring Tōhoku: a guide to Japan's back country 74

F
Face at the bottom of the world, and other poems 1136
Faces of Japan 11
Facing two ways: the story of my life 328
"Factory ship" and "The absentee landlord" 1068
Facts and Figures of Japan 14
Fall of Japan 715
Family 1096
Family planning in Japanese society: traditional birth control in a modern urban culture 3
Famous ceramics of Japan 1281
Far Eastern Economic Review 1501
Far Eastern Quarterly 1525
Farewell to Manzanar: a true story of Japanese American experience during and after the World War II internment 391
Farm and nation in modern Japan: agrarian nationalism, 1870-1940 206
Farming Japan 1502
Feast for the eyes: the Japanese art of food arrangement 1435
Feudal architecture of Japan 1307
Feudal background of Japanese politics 226
Feudalism in Japan 134
Field guide to the birds of Japan 65
Fifth generation: artificial intelligence and Japan's computer challenge to the world 982
Fifth generation fallacy: why Japan is betting its future on artificial intelligence 997
50 years of Japanese broadcasting 1486
Fifty-three stages of the Tokaido by Hiroshige 1265
Fighting ships of the rising sun: the drama of the Imperial Japanese Navy, 1895-1945 210
Films of Akira Kurosawa 1425
Financial behavior of Japanese

corporations 852
Financial development of India, Japan, and the United States: a trilateral institutional, statistical, and analytical comparison 855
Financial development of Japan, 1868-1977 855
Financial history of the new Japan 851
Financial samurai: the emerging power of Japanese money 867
Fire across the sea: the Vietnam War and Japan, 1965-1975 727
Fire from the ashes: short stories about Hiroshima and Nagasaki 1088
Fires on the plain 1091
First book of Japanese cooking 1439
Fishes of Japan: illustrations and descriptions of fishes of Japan 60
Fishes of Japan in color 60
Five modern nō plays 1177
Five mountains: the Rinzai Zen monastic institution in medieval Japan 131
Five plays by Kishida Kunio 1178
Five political leaders of modern Japan: Itō Hirobumi, Ōkuma Shigenobu, Hara Takashi, Inukai Tsuyoshi, and Saionji Kimmochi 296
Five sacred festivals of ancient Japan: their symbolism and historical development 501
Five women who loved love 1015
Flexible automation in Japan 986
Flexible rigidities: industrial policy and structural adjustment in the Japanese economy, 1970-80 794
Floating world 1270
Floating world in Japanese fiction 1036
Flora and vegetation of Japan 61
Flora of Japan 62
Flora of Okinawa and the Southern Ryukyu Islands 62
Flower arrangement: the ikebana way 1464
Flowers in salt: the beginnings of feminist consciousness in modern Japan 240
Focus on Asian Studies 1503
Fodor's great travel values: Japan 86
Fodor's Japan 1989 86
Fodor's Tokyo 1989 86
Folk arts and crafts of Japan 1210
Folk kilns I [Famous ceramics of Japan] 1281
Folk kilns II [Famous ceramics of Japan] 1281

Folk legends of Japan 1184
Folk religion in Japan: continuity and change 504
Folk traditions in Japanese art 1193
Folktales of Japan 1187
Foot-loose in Tokyo: the curious traveler's guide to the 29 stages of the Yamanote Line 91
For harmony and strength: Japanese white-collar organization in anthropological perspective 543
For richer, for poorer: the new U.S.-Japan relationship 726
Forbidden colors 1075
Foreign enterprise in Japan: laws and policies 779
Foreign policy of modern Japan 748
Foreign Trade of Japan 828
Form, style, tradition: reflections on Japanese art and society 1200
Formation of science in Japan: building a research tradition 157
Forms in Japan 1202
Forms, textures, images: traditional Japanese craftsmanship in everyday life. A photo-essay 1198
Foundation of Japanese Buddhism. Volume 1: The aristocratic age 484
Foundation of Japanese Buddhism. Volume 2: The mass movement (Kamakura and Muromachi periods) 484
Foundations of constitutional government in modern Japan, 1868-1900 189
Founding of the Kamakura shogunate, 1180-1185: with selected translations from the 'Azuma kagami' 154
Four major plays of Chikamatsu 1170
Fragile interdependence: economic issues in U.S.-Japanese trade and investment 905
Fragments of rainbows: the life and poetry of Saitō Mokichi, 1882-1953 325
Freedom of expression in Japan: a study in comparative law, politics, and society 771
Freer Gallery of Art fiftieth anniversary exhibition: I. Ukiyo-e painting 1250
Freer Gallery of Art. II: Japan 1250
From bonsai to levi's. When West meets East: an insider's surprising account of how the Japanese live 841
From the country of eight islands: an anthology of Japanese poetry 1156
From the rising of the sun: Christians and society in contemporary Japan 497
From Tokyo to Jerusalem 4
Fujiwara Teika's Superior poems of our time: a thirteenth-century poetic treatise and sequence 1135
Fukuzawa Yukichi on Japanese women: selected works 194
Fundamental problems of philosophy: the world of action and the dialectical world 524
Furo: the Japanese bath 1457
Fūten rōjin no nikki 1099
Future and the past: a translation and study of the 'Gukanshō', an interpretive history of Japan written in 1219 130
'Fuzai jinushi' 1068

G

Gagaku: court music and dance 1377
Gaining ground: Japan's strides in science and technology 984
Gan 1082
Garbage management in Japan: leading the way 956
Garden art of Japan 1329
Gardens of Japan 1331
Geijutsu to dōtoku 524
Geisha 576
Genius of Japanese design 1204
Genji monogatari 1024
Geography of Japan 40
Geology of Japan 49
Getting America ready for Japanese science and technology 991
Gikeiki 1020
Glorious way to die: the kamikaze mission of the battleship 'Yamato', April 1945 716
Go: a guide to the game 1458
Go for beginners 1458
Gods of myth and stone: phallicism in Japanese folk religion 502
Gogo no eikō 1076
Good food from a Japanese temple 1440
Good Tokyo restaurants 84
Gorin no sho 1447
Gossamer years: the diary of a noblewoman of Heian Japan 1013
Government and local power in Japan, 500 to 1700: a study based on Bizen

Province 138
Government policy towards industry in
the United States and Japan:
proceedings of a conference
co-organized by Chikashi Moriguchi
and John B. Shoven and sponsored by
the Center for Economic Policy
Research of Stanford University and
the Suntory Foundation of Japan 884
Great age of Japanese Buddhist
sculpture, AD 600-1300 1295
Great betrayal: the evacuation of the
Japanese-Americans during World War
II 386
Great Britain and Japan, 1911-15: a
study of British Far Eastern policy 666
Great Britain and the opening of Japan,
1834-1858 658
Great Britain and the origins of the
Pacific War: a study of British policy in
East Asia, 1937-1941 697
Great eastern temple: treasures of
Japanese Buddhist art from Tōdai-ji
1206
Great historical figures of Japan 295
Great Japan Exhibition: art of the Edo
period 1600-1868 1227
Gucci on the Ginza: Japan's new
consumer generation 841
Guide to food buying in Japan 85
Guide to Japanese architecture 81
Guide to Japanese drama 1603
Guide to Japanese flower arrangement
1466
Guide to Japanese food and restaurants
87
Guide to Japanese hot springs 80
Guide to Japanese poetry 1605
Guide to Japanese prose 1597
Guide to kyōgen 1402
Guide to reading & writing Japanese: the
1,850 basic characters and the kana
syllabaries 438
Guide to reference books for Japanese
studies = Nihon kenkyū no tame no
sankōtosho 1589
Guide to teaching English in Japan 979
Guide to the gardens of Kyoto 98
Guide to The tale of Genji by Murasaki
Shikibu 1604
Gukanshō 130

H
Hagakure: the book of the samurai 529
Hagi [Famous ceramics of Japan] 1281
Haiku handbook: how to write, share,
and teach haiku 1162
Haiku in Western languages: an
annotated bibliography (with some
reference to senryu) 1588
Haiku journey: Bashō's 'The narrow
road to the far north' and selected
haiku 1149
Hakai 1095
Hako otoko 1041
Half step behind: Japanese women of the
'80s 574
Hamada, potter 331
Hamamatsu Chūnagon monogatari 1027
Hanaoka Seishū no tsuma 1047
Handbook of modern Japanese
grammar: including lists of words and
expressions with English equivalents
for reading aid 430
Haniwa 108
Haniwa: the clay sculpture of proto-
historic Japan 108
Hara Kei in the politics of compromise,
1905-1915 224
Harp of Burma 1097
Haru no yuki 1077
Haruko's world: a Japanese farm woman
and her community 573
Harunobu and his age: the development
of colour printing in Japan 1261
Harusame monogatari 1030
Harvard Journal of Asiatic Studies 1504
Hawaii under the rising sun: Japan's
plans for conquest after Pearl Harbor
710
Health and illness in changing Japanese
society 603
Health, illness, and medical care in
Japan: cultural and social dimensions
599
Heian Japan [Cambridge history of
Japan] 115
Heian temples: Byodo-in and Chuson-ji
1192
Heike monogatari 1019
Hell screen, Cogwheels, A fool's life 1045
Heritage of endurance: family patterns
and delinquency formation in urban
Japan 571
Heritage of Japanese art 1197

Hermann Roesler and the making of the Meiji state: an examination of his background and his influence on the founders of modern Japan and the complete text of the Meiji Constitution accompanied by his personal commentaries and notes 189

Hidden differences: doing business with the Japanese 894

Hidden sun: women of modern Japan 581

Hideyoshi 299

Higher civil servants in postwar Japan: their social origins, educational backgrounds, and career patterns 613

Higher education in Japan: its take-off and crash 972

Hirohito: an intimate portrait of the Japanese emperor 334

Hirohito: behind the myth 334

Hirohito: emperor of Japan 334

Hiroshige: birds and flowers 1257

Hiroshima 255

Hiroshima and Nagasaki: the physical, medical, and social effects of the atomic bombing 253

Hiroshima diary: the journal of a Japanese physician, August 6 – September 30, 1945 259

Hiroshima maidens: a story of courage, compassion, and survival 252

História da Igreja do Japão 153

Historical development of science and technology in Japan 187

Historical Kyoto: with illustrations and guide maps 92

Historical literature of Mori Ōgai. Volume 1: The incident at Sakai and other stories 108

Historical literature of Mori Ōgai. Volume 2: Saiki kōi and other stories 1081

Historical Nagasaki 179

Historical Nara: with illustrations and guide maps 93

History and practice of Japanese printmaking: a selectively annotated bibliography of English language materials 1576

History and theology of Soka Gakkai: a Japanese New Religion 511

History of Christianity in Japan 495

History of Christianity in Japan: Roman Catholic, Greek Orthodox, and Protestant missions 495

History of Far Eastern art 1205

History of glass in Japan 1359

History of Japan [Murdoch] 124

History of Japan. Volume 1: A history of Japan to 1334 124

History of Japan. Volume 2: A history of Japan 1334-1615 124

History of Japan. Volume 3: A history of Japan 1615-1867 124

History of Japanese astronomy: Chinese background and Western impact 151

History of Japanese lacquerwork 1374

History of Japanese literature [Katō] 999

History of Japanese literature [Konishi] 1006

History of Japanese literature. Volume 1: The archaic and ancient ages 1006

History of Japanese literature. Volume 1: The first thousand years 999

History of Japanese literature. Volume 2: The early middle ages 1006

History of Japanese literature. Volume 2: The years of isolation 999

History of Japanese literature. Volume 3: The modern years 999

History of Japanese music 1380

History of Japanese printing and book illustration 1477

History of Japanese religion: with special reference to the social and moral life of the nation 458

History of Japanese theater 1403

History of modern Japan 127

History of the development of Japanese thought, from A.D. 592-1868 523

History of the Japanese secret service 648

History of the Japanese written language 404

History of Zen Buddhism 474

Hitomaro and the birth of Japanese lyricism 1163

Hizakurige (Tōkaidō circuit) 1016

Hokusai: paintings, drawings and woodcuts 1260

Hokusai sketchbooks: selections from the Manga 1258

Homecoming 1092

Homma 1077

Honda Motor: the men, the management, the machines 882

Honda: the man and his machines 344

Honjō nikki 209
*Honorable elders revisited: a revised
cross-cultural analysis of aging in
Japan* 540
*How Japan innovates: a comparison with
the U.S. in the case of oxygen
steelmaking* 989
*How Japan's economy grew so fast: the
sources of postwar expansion* 793
How the conservatives rule Japan 638
How to be polite in Japanese 443
How to do business with the Japanese 916
*How to do business with the Japanese: a
complete guide to Japanese customs
and business practices* 891
*How to wrap five eggs: Japanese design
in traditional packaging* 1371
*How to wrap five more eggs: traditional
Japanese packaging* 1371
*Howling at the moon: poems of
Hagiwara Sakutarō* 1136
Human relations in Japan 539
*Human resources in Japanese industrial
development* 217
Hundred more things Japanese 1557
Hundred things Japanese 1557

I

I am a cat 1085
I denounce Soka Gakkai 512
*I saw Tokyo burning: an eyewitness
narrative from Pearl Harbor to
Hiroshima* 691
*I was a kamikaze: the knights of the
divine wind* 700
Iai-jitsu: center of the circle 1441
Iai-jitsu: the art of drawing the sword
1441
IBM vs. Japan: the struggle for the future
982
*Iconography of The tale of Genji: Genji
monogatari ekotoba* 1241
Ie 1096
*Ikebana: a practical and philosophical
guide to Japanese flower arrangement*
1462
Ikebana: spirit and technique 1463
*Ikkyū and the Crazy cloud anthology: a
Zen poet of medieval Japan* 1139
*Illness and culture in contemporary
Japan: an anthropological view* 600
*Illustrated history of the Russo-Japanese
War* 678

*Image of Japan: from feudal isolation to
world power, 1850-1905* 216
*Images from the floating world: the
Japanese print; including an illustrated
dictionary of ukiyo-e* 1266
Imari [Famous ceramics of Japan] 1281
*Imingaisha: Japanese emigration
companies and Hawaii, 1894-1908* 396
*Imitation and innovation: the transfer of
Western organizational patterns to
Meiji Japan* 248
*Impact of the A-bomb: Hiroshima and
Nagasaki, 1945-85* 253
*Imperial gardens of Japan: Sento Gosho,
Katsura, Shugaku-in* 1334
*Imperial Japan: the art of the Meiji era
(1868-1912)* 1229
Imperial Japanese navy 1572
*Imperial Japan's higher civil service
examinations* 613
Imperial restoration in medieval Japan
159
In praise of shadows 1225
*In the shade of spring leaves: the life and
writings of Higuchi Ichiyō, a woman of
letters in Meiji Japan* 1111
*In the shadow of Fujisan: Japan and its
wildlife* 63
Incident at Sakai and other stories 1081
*Index to Japanese law: a bibliography of
Western language materials, 1867-1973*
1582
Industrial collaboration with Japan 912
Industrial geography of Japan 45
*Industrial growth, trade, and dynamic
patterns in the Japanese economy* 814
Industrial organization in Japan 869
Industrial policy of Japan [Komiya] 876
Industrial policy of Japan [OECD] 821
*Industrial relations in transition: the cases
of Japan and the Federal Republic of
Germany* 940
Industrial Review of Japan 823
Industry and business in Japan 883
Industry at the crossroads 870
Infamy: Pearl Harbor and its aftermath
705
*Information explosion: the new electronic
media in Japan and Europe* 955
Information gathering on Japan: a primer
1570
*Injurious to public morals: writers and
the Meiji state* 1122

Ink painting 1239
Inland Sea 71
Innocence is not enough: the life and
    death of Herbert Norman 226
Inrō handbook: studies of netsuke, inrō,
    and lacquer 1360
Insei: abdicated sovereigns in the politics
    of late Heian Japan, 1086-1185 142
Inside corporate Japan: the art of fumble-
    free management 928
Inside Japan: wealth, work and power in
    the new Japanese empire 30
Inside Japanese financial markets 868
Inside Japan's financial markets 868
Inside the Japanese system: readings on
    contemporary society and political
    economy 809
Inside the robot kingdom: Japan,
    mechatronics, and the coming
    robotopia 995
Insider's guide to Japan 94
Instance of treason: Ozaki Hotsumi and
    the Sorge spy ring 228
Intellectual property law of Japan 773
Internationalization of Japanese business:
    European and Japanese perspectives
    948
Internationalization of the Japanese
    economy 798
Into a black sun 1062
Introducing Japan 25
Introducing Japan: history, way of life,
    creative world, seen and heard, food
    and wine 19
Introducing Kyoto 92
Introducing Tokyo 95
Introduction to haiku: an anthology of
    poems and poets from Bashō to Shiki
    1137
Introduction to Japanese civilization 32
Introduction to Japanese court poetry
    1164
Introduction to Japanese government
    publications 1593
Introduction to Japanese law 782
Introduction to Japanese phonology 412
Introduction to modern Japanese 444
Introduction to netsuke 1288
Introduction to newspaper Japanese 445
Introduction to the arts of Japan 1223
Introduction to Zen Buddhism 490
Invisible link: Japan's sogo shosha and
    the organization of trade 915

Invisible visible minority: Japan's
    burakumin 381
Ise monogatari 1148
Ise: prototype of Japanese architecture
    1323
Ishiwara Kanji and Japan's confrontation
    with the West 342
Island fighting 715
Island of dreams: environmental crisis in
    Japan 957
Isles of gold: antique maps of Japan 52
Issei: Japanese immigrants in Hawaii 392
Issei, Nisei, war bride: three generations
    of Japanese American women in
    domestic service 388
Issei: the world of the first generation
    Japanese immigrants, 1885-1924 392
Issue of war: states, societies, and the Far
    Eastern conflict of 1941-1945 711
Issues in Japan's China policy 738
Iwo 714
Iwo Jima: legacy of valor 714
Izumi Shikibu diary: a romance of the
    Heian court 1149

J

JACL in quest of justice 395
Japan [Editors of Time-Life Books] 13
Japan [Spry-Leverton] 29
Japan: a comparative view 10
Japan: a country study 6
Japan: a geography 50
Japan: a history in art 155
Japan: a postindustrial power 7
Japan: a short cultural history 125
Japan: a traveler's companion 90
Japan: an anthropological introduction
    530
Japan: an economic survey, 1953-1973
    792
Japan and Australia in the seventies 751
Japan & Australia: two societies and their
    interaction 723
Japan and China: from war to peace,
    1894-1972 652
Japan and her destiny: my struggle for
    peace 708
Japan and its world: two centuries of
    change 211
Japan and Korea: a critical bibliography
    1608
Japan and Korea: an annotated
    bibliography of doctoral dissertations

in Western languages, 1877-1969 1607
Japan and Korea: the political dimension 737
Japan and Southeast Asia: a bibliography of historical, economic and political relations 727
Japan and the Asian Development Bank 756
Japan and the Asian Pacific region: profile of change 749
Japan and the decline of the West in Asia 1894-1943 656
Japan and the developing countries: a comparative analysis 806
Japan and the new ocean regime 796
Japan and the Pacific quadrille: the major powers in East Asia 724
Japan and the San Francisco peace settlement 283
Japan and the United States: challenges and opportunities 718
Japan and the United States: economic and political adversaries 897
Japan and the United States today: exchange rates, macroeconomic policies, and financial market innovations 860
Japan and the world, 1853-1952: a bibliographic guide to Japanese scholarship in foreign relations 1599
Japan and Western Europe: conflict and cooperation 910
Japan Architect: International Edition of Shinkenchiku 1505
Japan as number one: lessons for America 38
Japan at war 715
Japan before Buddhism 106
Japan before Perry: a short history 128
Japan before Tokugawa: political consolidation and economic growth, 1500 to 1650 139
Japan Christian Quarterly 1506
Japan Company Handbook 822
Japan design: the four seasons in design 1224
Japan diaries of Richard Gordon Smith 72
Japan diary 269
Japan, disincorporated: the economic liberalization process 856
Japan: divided politics in a growth economy 624

Japan Echo 1507
Japan Economic Almanac 823
Japan Economic Journal 1548
Japan Economic Survey: a Monthly Review of U.S.-Japan Economic Relations 1524
Japan examined: perspectives on modern Japanese history 249
Japan expedition, 1852-1854: the personal journal of Commodore Matthew C. Perry 673
Japan faces China: political and economic relations in the postwar era 736
Japan: facing economic maturity 800
Japan Forum 1508
Japan Foundation Newsletter 1509
Japan: from prehistory to modern times 116
Japan: geographical background to urban-industrial development 43
Japan in crisis: essays on Taishō democracy 241
Japan in film: a comprehensive annotated catalogue of documentary and theatrical films on Japan available in the United States 1586
Japan in global ocean politics 717
Japan in postwar Asia 742
Japan in the global community: its role and contribution on the eve of the 21st century 740
Japan in the Muromachi age 140
Japan in the 1980s: papers from a symposium on contemporary Japan held at Sheffield University, England, September 11-13, 1980 27
Japan in the passing lane: an insider's account of life in a Japanese auto factory 924
Japan in the Victorian mind: a study of stereotyped images of a nation 1850-80 251
Japan in transition: from Tokugawa to Meiji 212
Japan Inc.: an introduction to Japanese economics (the comic book) 1480
Japan information resources in the United States, 1985 1565
Japan Journal 1510
Japan Labor Bulletin 1511
Japan Missionary Bulletin 1506
Japan 1990: an international comparison 824

683

Japan: official standard names approved by the United States Board on Geographic Names 57
Japan: past and present 122
Japan: patterns of continuity 17
Japan: photographs, 1854-1905 1278
Japan Pictorial 1512
Japan prepares for total war: the search for economic security, 1919-1941 679
Japan Quarterly 1513
Japan reader. Volume 1: Imperial Japan, 1800-1945 119
Japan reader. Volume 2: Postwar Japan, 1945 to the present 119
Japan re-armed 766
Japan Review of International Affairs 1514
Japan Society Newsletter 1515
Japan Society 1907-1982: 75 years of partnership across the Pacific 1515
Japan Society of London Bulletin 1516
Japan Society Review 1516
Japan solo: the independent traveller's passport to singular adventure 83
Japan Statistical Yearbook 825
Japan studies in Canada: 1987 1559
Japan subdued: the atomic bomb and the end of the war in the Pacific 254
Japan: the dilemmas of success 21
Japan: the Dutch experience 167
Japan: the fragile superpower 15
Japan, the hungry guest: Japanese business ethics vs. those of the U.S. 844
Japan: the shaping of daimyo culture, 1185-1868 1218
Japan: the story of a nation 122
Japan, the United States and a changing Southeast Asia 741
Japan: the years of trial, 1919-52 222
Japan through children's literature: an annotated bibliography 1596
Japan Times 1549
Japan today 5
Japan today! A Westerner's guide to the people, language and culture of Japan 1573
Japan: tradition and transformation 123
Japan unescorted 100
Japan Update 1517
Japan versus Europe: a history of misunderstanding 755
Japan vs. the West: implications for management 934

Japanalia: a concise cyclopaedia 1551
Japanese [Reischauer] 23
Japanese: a cultural portrait 20
Japanese: a major exploration of modern Japan 30
Japanese agriculture under siege: the political economy of agricultural policies 832
Japanese aircraft of the Pacific War 689
Japanese Americans: the evolution of a subculture 394
Japanese and Sukarno's Indonesia: Tokyo-Jakarta relations, 1951-1966 727
Japanese and the Japanese: words in culture 411
Japanese and the Jews 4
Japanese and U.S. inflation: a comparative analysis 859
Japanese antique dolls 1363
Japanese antiques: with a guide to shops 1215
Japanese army in north China, 1937-1941: the problems of political and economic control 702
Japanese art 1220
Japanese art of stone appreciation: suiseki and its use with bonsai 1362
Japanese art signatures: a handbook and practical guide 1571
Japanese automobile industry: model and challenge for the future? 870
Japanese automobile industry: technology and management at Nissan and Toyota 871
Japanese bamboo baskets 1366
Japanese blue collar: the changing tradition 918
Japanese bookbinding: instructions from a master craftsman 1479
Japanese brushes 1366
Japanese Buddhism 475
Japanese business language: an essential dictionary 422
Japanese business law and the legal system 776
Japanese castles 1306
Japanese character dictionary (with compound lookup via any kanji) = Kan-Ei jukugo ribāsu jiten 421
Japanese chronology 35
Japanese cloisonné: history, technique, and appreciation 1361
Japanese colleges and universities 1989: a

guide to institutions of higher education in Japan 1550
Japanese colonial empire, 1895-1945 223
Japanese communist movement, 1920-1966 635
Japanese Communist Party, 1922-1945 192
Japanese company 838
Japanese competition: phase 2 870
Japanese cooking 1434
Japanese cooking: a simple art 1438
Japanese costume and textile arts 1351
Japanese costume and the makers of its elegant tradition 1349
Japanese court poetry 1164
Japanese crafts 1369
Japanese crane: bird of happiness 58
Japanese criminal procedure 772
Japanese culture 37
Japanese culture and behavior: selected readings 591
Japanese dance 1388
Japanese death poems: written by Zen monks and haiku poets on the verge of death 1138
Japanese design through textile patterns 1344
Japanese Diet and the U.S. Congress 626
Japanese direct manufacturing investment in the United States 951
Japanese discovery of Europe: Honda Toshiaki and other discoverers 1720-1798 173
Japanese discovery of Europe, 1720-1830 173
Japanese drama and culture in the 1960s: the return of the gods 1171
Japanese economic development: a short introduction 818
Japanese economic growth: trend acceleration in the twentieth century 807
Japanese Economic Studies 1518
Japanese economy 791
Japanese education 35
Japanese education: a bibliography of materials in the English language 1610
Japanese education today: a report from the U.S. study of education in Japan 970
Japanese educational challenge: a commitment to children 978
Japanese electronics: a worm's-eye view

of its evolution 988
Japanese electronics technology: enterprise and innovation 985
Japanese emperor through history 35
Japanese enlightenment: a study of the writings of Fukuzawa Yukichi 194
Japanese etiquette & ethics in business 840
Japanese factory: aspects of its social organization 917
Japanese fan paintings from Western collections 1233
Japanese film: art and industry 1414
Japanese film directors 1415
Japanese finance:a guide to banking in Japan 861
Japanese Finance and Industry: Quarterly Survey 1519
Japanese financial system 864
Japanese flower arrangement: classical and modern 1466
Japanese flowering cherry trees of Washington, D.C.: a living symbol of friendship 663
Japanese folk festivals illustrated 501
Japanese folk literature: a core collection and reference guide 1577
Japanese folk plays: the Ink-smeared lady and other kyogen 1402
Japanese folk tales: a revised selection 1188
Japanese for busy people 436
Japanese for busy people II: intermediate level 436
Japanese for travellers 416
Japanese foreign policy and domestic politics: the peace agreement with the Soviet Union 728
Japanese foreign policy 1869-1942: Kasumigaseki to Miyakezaka 654
Japanese garden 1332
Japanese garden: an approach to nature 1332
Japanese gardens: design and meaning 1327
Japanese gardens revisited 1339
Japanese generative grammar 434
Japanese ghosts & demons: art of the supernatural 1189
Japanese grammar 433
Japanese history & culture from ancient to modern times: seven basic bibliographies 1583

Japanese house: a tradition for contemporary architecture 1300
Japanese ikat weaving: the techniques of kasuri 1354
Japanese imperial institution in the Tokugawa period 188
Japanese imperialism, 1894-1945 644
Japanese in action: an unorthodox approach to the spoken language and the people who speak it 454
Japanese in Hawaii: an annotated bibliography of Japanese Americans 1598
Japanese in Hawaii: 1868-1967: a bibliography of the first hundred years 1598
Japanese industrial policy 879
Japanese industrial policy: a descriptive account of postwar developments with case studies of selected industries 879
Japanese industrial system 878
Japanese industrialization and its social consequences 812
Japanese ink painting: Shubun to Sesshu 1253
Japanese ink paintings: from American collections – the Muromachi period; an exhibition in honor of Shūjirō Shimada 1248
Japanese inn 184
Japanese inn, ryokan: a gateway to traditional Japan 96
Japanese international negotiating style 645
Japanese investment in Southeast Asia 727
Japanese islands: a physical and social geography 46
Japanese Journal of Religious Studies 1520
Japanese journalists and their world 1484
Japanese kana workbook 449
Japanese knives 1366
Japanese lacquer art: modern masterpieces 1370
Japanese language [Kindaichi] 405
Japanese language [Miller] 407
Japanese language and culture for business and travel 439
Japanese language in contemporary Japan: some sociolinguistic observations 408
Japanese language patterns: a structural approach 435
Japanese legal system: introductory cases and materials 784
Japanese linked poetry: an account with translations of renga and haikai sequences 1165
Japanese literature: an introduction for Western readers 1002
Japanese literature in Chinese. Volume 1: Poetry & prose in Chinese by Japanese writers of the early period 1010
Japanese literature in Chinese. Volume 2: Poetry & prose in Chinese by Japanese writers of the later period 1010
Japanese literature in European languages: a bibliography 1588
Japanese Literature Today 1521
Japanese management: cultural and environmental considerations 927
Japanese management development system: generalists and specialists in Japanese companies abroad 949
Japanese manners and customs in the Meiji era 1188
Japanese manners and ethics in business 840
Japanese manufacturing techniques: nine hidden lessons in simplicity 936
Japanese marketing system: adaptations and innovations 839
Japanese Marxist: a portrait of Kawakami Hajime, 1879-1946 318
Japanese mind: essentials of Japanese philosophy and culture 522
Japanese mind: the goliath explained 8
Japanese money market 854
Japanese movie: an illustrated history 1426
Japanese music: an annotated bibliography 1611
Japanese music and musical instruments 1383
Japanese mythology 1186
Japanese names: a comprehensive index by characters and readings 423
Japanese national government publications in the Library of Congress: a bibliography 1602
Japanese navy in World War II: an anthology of articles by former officers of the Imperial Japanese Navy and Air Defence Force 688
Japanese navy in World War II: in the

words of former Japanese naval officers 688
Japanese, Nazis & Jews: the Jewish refugee community of Shanghai, 1938-1945 4
Japanese New Religion: Risshō Kōsei-kai in a mountain hamlet 507
Japanese novel of the Meiji period and the ideal of individualism 1129
Japanese oligarchy and the Russo-Japanese War 672
Japanese on trial: Allied war crimes operations in the East, 1945-1951 265
Japanese overseas: can they go home again? 572
Japanese painted porcelain: modern masterpieces in overglaze enamel 1285
Japanese painting in the literati style 1255
Japanese papermaking: traditions, tools, and techniques 1358
Japanese participation in British industry 944
Japanese party system: from one-party rule to coalition government 634
Japanese patterns of behavior 592
Japanese periodicals and newspapers in Western languages: an international union list 1601
Japanese Philately 1522
Japanese pilgrimage 73
Japanese poetic diaries 1149
Japanese police system today: an American perspective 570
Japanese policy and East Asian security 769
Japanese political culture: change and continuity 610
Japanese politics-an inside view: readings from Japan 611
Japanese porcelain 1283
Japanese: portrait of a nation 30
Japanese portrait sculpture 1292
Japanese pottery 1283
Japanese prefectures and policymaking 639
Japanese Press 1483
Japanese print: a historical guide 1271
Japanese print: its evolution and essence 1272
Japanese prints from the early masters to the modern 1270
Japanese private economic diplomacy: an analysis of business-government

linkages 887
Japanese proverbs and sayings 1183
Japanese radicals revisited: student protest in postwar Japan 969
Japanese rainmaking and other folk practices 500
Japanese religion:a cultural perspective 463
Japanese religion in the modern century 467
Japanese religion: unity and diversity 460
Japanese Religions 1523
Japanese rural society 531
Japanese school: lessons for industrial America 966
Japanese sculpture of the Tempyo period: masterpieces of the eighth century 1296
Japanese securities regulation 781
Japanese short stories 1045
Japanese social structure: its evolution in the modern century 532
Japanese Socialist Party and neutralism: a study of a political party and its foreign policy 637
Japanese society [Ishida] 537
Japanese society [Nakane] 539
Japanese society today 533
Japanese society: tradition, self, and the social order 544
Japanese spoons and ladles 1366
Japanese stencil dyeing: paste-resist techniques 1350
Japanese studies in Europe 1559
Japanese studies in Southeast Asia 1559
Japanese studies in the United Kingdom 1559
Japanese studies in the United States. Part 1: History and present condition 1559
Japanese studies in the United States. Part 2: Directory of Japan specialists and Japanese studies institutions in the United States and Canada 1559
Japanese style 1319
Japanese-style management: an insider's analysis 922
Japanese sword 1373
Japanese sword-fittings and associated metalwork: the Bauer Collection 1373
Japanese swordsmanship: technique and practice 1452
Japanese tales 1029
Japanese tattoo 1372
Japanese teapots 1366

Japanese technology: getting the best for
the least 990
Japanese: the spoken language 440
Japanese: the spoken language in
Japanese life 409
Japanese theatre 1394
Japanese thread: a life in the U.S.
Foreign Service 354
Japanese through American eyes 731
Japanese thrust into Siberia, 1918 684
Japanese today: change and continuity 23
Japanese touch for your garden 1337
Japanese touch for your home 1326
Japanese trade policy formulation 896
Japanese urbanism: industry and politics
in Kariya, 1872-1972 547
Japanese way of politics 632
Japanese women: constraint and
fulfillment 579
Japanese women's language 413
Japanese woodblock prints in miniature:
the genre of surimono 1263
Japanese woodworking tools: their
tradition, spirit and use 1343
Japanese words and their uses 420
Japanese workers and the struggle for
power, 1945-1947 275
Japanese working man: what choice?
what reward? 923
Japan's American interlude 273
Japan's civil service system: its structure,
personnel, and politics 613
Japan's Commission on the Constitution:
the final report 789
Japan's decision for war: records of the
1941 policy conferences 693
Japan's decision to surrender 683
Japan's decisive century, 1867-1967 324
Japan's economic aid: policy-making and
politics 746
Japan's economic challenge: a
bibliographic sourcebook 1590
Japan's economic security 885
Japan's economic security: resources as a
factor in foreign policy 885
Japan's economic strategy in Brazil:
challenge for the United States 898
Japan's economy: a bibliography of its
past and present 1614
Japan's economy: coping with change in
the international environment 903
Japan's emergence as a modern state:
political and economic problems of the

Meiji period 226
Japan's emerging multinationals: an
international comparison of policies
and practices 947
Japan's financial markets: conflict and
consensus in policymaking 857
Japan's first modern novel: 'Ukigumo' of
Futabatei Shimei 1124
Japan's first student radicals 244
Japan's foreign policy, 1868-1941: a
research guide 1599
Japan's foreign relations: a global search
for economic security 743
Japan's high schools 975
Japan's high technology industries:
lessons and limitations of industrial
policy 881
Japan's industrial economy: recent trends
and changing aspects 35
Japan's invisible race: caste in culture and
personality 373
Japan's longest day 703
Japan's managerial system: tradition and
innovation 943
Japan's market: the distribution system 839
Japan's militant teachers: a history of the
left-wing teachers' movement 967
Japan's modern century: from Perry to
1970 112
Japan's modern myth: the language and
beyond 408
Japan's modern myths: ideology in the
late Meiji period 203
Japan's multinational enterprises 952
Japan's new Buddhism: an objective
account of Soka Gakkai 512
Japan's new middle class: the salary man
and his family in a Tokyo suburb 564
Japan's new world role 732
Japan's Pacific mandate 227
Japan's parliament: an introduction 607
Japan's political revolution under
MacArthur: a participant's account 281
Japan's political system 627
Japan's postwar defense policy, 1947-
1968 770
Japan's postwar economy: an insider's
view of its history and its future 815
Japan's postwar peace settlements 283
Japan's public policy companies 612
Japan's quest for autonomy: national
security and foreign policy, 1930-1938
685

Japan's quest for comprehensive security: defence-diplomacy-dependence 762
Japan's reluctant multinationals: Japanese management at home and abroad 941
Japan's renaissance: the politics of the Muromachi bakufu 137
Japan's response to crisis and change in the world economy 909
Japan's role in Soviet economic growth: transfer of technology since 1965 900
Japan's technological challenge to the West, 1950-1974: motivation and accomplishment 993
JEI Report 1524
Jinnō Shōtōki 144
Journal of Asian Studies 1525
Journal of Japanese Studies 1526
Journal of Japanese Trade & Industry 1527
Journal of Northeast Asian Studies 1528
Journal of the Association of Teachers of Japanese 1529
Journal of the Japanese and International Economies 1530
JTECH panel reports 984

K
Kabuki 1400
Kabuki costume 1352
Kabuki encyclopedia: an English-language adaptation of 'Kabuki jiten' 1564
Kabuki: five classic plays 1396
Kabuki guide 1401
Kabuki handbook: a guide to understanding and appreciation, with summaries of favorite plays, explanatory notes, and illustrations 1401
Kabuki: the popular theater 1400
Kabuki theatre 1398
Kafu the scribbler: the life and writings of Nagai Kafū, 1879-1959 345
Kagayakeru yami 1062
Kagerō nikki 1013
Kagi 1100
Kaigai Nihon kenkyū kikan yōran 1554
Kaiseki: Zen tastes in Japanese cooking 1437
'*Kaisha': the Japanese corporation* 836
Kaisha, the Japanese corporation: the new competitors in world business 836

Kakiemon [Famous ceramics of Japan] 1281
Kamakura bakufu: a study in documents 148
Kamen no kokuhaku 1073
Kan-Ei jukugo ribāsu jiten 421
Kanashiki gangu 1140
Kanazawa: a seventeenth-century Japanese castle town 174
Kanban: shop signs of Japan 1368
'*Kani kōsen*' 1068
Kanji and kana: a handbook and dictionary of the Japanese writing system 438
Kanō Eitoku 1252
Kappa 1044
Kappa; a novel 1044
Karate training: the samurai legacy and modern practice 1448
Karate-dō kyōhan: the master text 1446
Karate-dō: my way of life 1446
Karate's history and tradition 1448
Karatsu [Famous ceramics of Japan] 1281
Karatsu ware: a tradition of diversity 1279
Karma of words: Buddhism and the literary arts in medieval Japan 1007
Katsura: a princely retreat 1305
Katsura: tradition and creation in Japanese architecture 1305
Keizai Tōkei Nenpō 819
Kempei tai: a history of the Japanese secret service 648
Kenji Mizoguchi: a guide to references and resources 1578
Kenkenroku: a diplomatic record of the Sino-Japanese War, 1894-95 668
Kenkyusha's new English-Japanese dictionary 417
Kenkyusha's new Japanese-English dictionary 418
Kenkyusha's new little English-Japanese dictionary = Shin ritoru Ei-Wa jiten 417
Kenkyusha's new little Japanese-English dictionary = Shin ritoru Wa-Ei jiten 418
Kenreimon'in Ukyō no Daibu shū 1142
Kenzo Tange, 1946-1969: architecture and urban design 1313
Key 1100
Key to Japan's economic strength: human

power 942
Kikkoman: company, clan, and
community 201
Kikuchi diary: chronicle from an
American concentration camp. The
Tanforan journals of Charles Kikuchi
393
Kikyō 1092
Kindai shūka 1135
Kinjiki 1075
Kinkakuji 1080
Kinoshita Yūji 1144
Kinship and economic organization in
rural Japan 561
Kinshū makura 59
Kiseto and Setoguro [Famous ceramics of
Japan] 1281
Kōda Rohan 1069
Kodansha encyclopedia of Japan 1556
Kodomo no tame ni: for the sake of the
children; the Japanese American
experience in Hawaii 397
Kōgun: the Japanese army in the Pacific
War 692
Kojiki 152
Kojinteki na taiken 1089
Kokin wakashū: the first imperial
anthology of Japanese poetry; with
Tosa nikki and Shinsen waka 1153
Kokinshū: a collection of poems ancient
and modern 1153
Kokoro 1086
Konjaku monogatari 1032
Konjaku monogatari-shū 1037
Konoe Fumimaro: a political biography
340
Korea and Japan in world politics 719
Korean minority in Japan 377
Koreans in Japan: ethnic conflict and
accommodation 376
Kōshoku gonin onna 1015
Kōshoku ichidai otoko 1014
Kosode: 16th-19th century textiles from
the Nomura Collection 1353
Kōtoku Shūsui: portrait of a Japanese
radical 337
Ko-uta: 'little songs' of the geisha world
576
Kūkai: major works, translated, with an
account of his life and a study of his
thought 482
Kumiuta and danmono traditions of
Japanese koto music 1378

Kura: design and tradition of the
Japanese storehouse 1311
Kuril Islands: Russo-Japanese frontier in
the Pacific 286
Kuroi ame 1058
Kuroshio: its physical aspects 47
Kuroshio: physical aspects of the Japan
Current 47
Kurozumikyō and the New Religions of
Japan 508
Kurusu: the price of progress in a
Japanese village, 1951-1975 556
Kutani ware 1284
Kyōgen 1402
Kyoto: a contemplative guide 89
Kyoto: seven paths to the heart of the city
77

L

La vie quotidienne au Japon à l'époque
des samouraï 1185-1603 136
Labor market in Japan: selected readings
930
Labor relations in Japan today 921
Lady who loved insects 1011
L'amiral Togo: samouraï de la mer 320
Land markets and land policy in a
metropolitan area: a case study of
Tokyo 42
Land reform in Japan 268
Landforms of Japan 51
Landscapes and portraits: appreciations
of Japanese culture 1003
Last writings: nothingness and the
religious worldview 524
Late chrysanthemum: twenty-one stories
from the Japanese 1051
Lateral view: essays on contemporary
Japan 26
Law and social change in postwar Japan
785
Law and society in contemporary Japan:
American perspectives 777
Law and trade issues of the Japanese
economy: American and Japanese
perspectives 783
Law in Japan: an Annual 1531
Law in Japan: the legal order in a
changing society 786
Lay Buddhism in contemporary Japan:
Reiyūkai Kyōdan 509
Learn Japanese: new college text 457
Learning to be Japanese: selected

readings on Japanese society and education 961
Lectures on developing economies: Japan's experience and its relevance 806
Legal reform in occupied Japan: a participant looks back 277
Legend in Japanese art: a description of historical episodes, legendary characters, folk-lore, myths, religious symbolism, illustrated in the arts of old Japan 1560
Legend of Semimaru: blind musician of Japan 1176
Legends of Tōno 1188
Lessons from history: the Tokushi yoron 298
Let's learn hiragana 442
Let's learn katakana 442
Letters from Sachiko: a Japanese woman's view of life in the land of the economic miracle 563
Liberalism in modern Japan: Ishibashi Tanzan and his teachers, 1905-1960 336
Libraries in Japan 1474
Lieutenant Lookeast, and other stories 1059
Life and death of Yukio Mishima 335
Life of an amorous man 1014
Life of an amorous woman, and other writings 1015
Limits of foreign policy: the West, the League, and the Far Eastern crisis of 1931-1933 711
Listening to Japan: a Japanese anthology 2
Literary life in Tokyo, 1885-1915: Tayama Katai's memoirs ('Thirty years in Tokyo') 1105
Live machines: hired foreigners and Meiji Japan 197
Living crafts of Okinawa 1222
Local government in Japan 641
Lonely furrow: farming in the United States, Japan and India 834
Long engagements: maturity in modern Japan 541
Look Japan 1532
Lost innocence: folk craft potters of Onta, Japan 553
"'Love'" and other stories of Yokomitsu Riichi 1108

Love match and arranged marriage: a Tokyo-Detroit comparison 558
Low city, high city: Tokyo from Edo to the earthquake 236
Lure of Japan's railways 954

M

MacArthur: his rendezvous with history 356
MacArthur, 1941-1951 356
Made in Japan: Akio Morita and Sony 332
Made in Japan: the methods, motivation, and culture of the Japanese, and their influence on U.S. business and all Americans 12
Major plays of Chikamatsu 1170
Makiguchi, the value creator, revolutionary Japanese educator and founder of Soka Gakkai 319
Making of a modern Japanese architecture: 1868 to the present 1320
Making of James Clavell's Shogun 1418
Making of modern Japan 121
Makioka sisters 1101
Makura no sōshi 1025
Management and worker: the Japanese solution 917
Management challenge: Japanese views 939
Management Japan 1533
Managing an alliance: the politics of U.S.-Japanese relations 721
Managing defense: Japan's dilemma 764
Managing diplomacy: the United States and Japan 729
Man'en gannen no futtōbōro 1090
Manga! manga! the world of Japanese comic books 1480
Manner of giving: strategic aid and Japanese foreign policy 757
Manpower policy in Japan 821
'Man'yōshū': a translation of Japan's premier anthology of classical poetry 1147
Manzanar 391
Marriage in changing Japan: community and society 560
Masaoka Shiki 1161
Mask and sword: two plays for the contemporary Japanese theater 1182
Masks 1052
Master of 'go' 1064

Masters' book of bonsai 1328
Masters' book of ikebana: background
and principles of Japanese flower
arrangement 1465
Masters of calligraphy, 8th-19th century
1249
Masters of the Japanese print 1267
Matsuo Bashō 1167
Measure and construction of the Japanese
house 1300
Medieval Japan [Cambridge history of
Japan] 115
Medieval Japan: essays in institutional
history 141
Meeting with Japan 70
Meiji 1868: revolution and
counter-revolution in Japan 191
Meiji ishin: restoration and revolution
191
Meiji Restoration 191
Meiji Western painting 1235
Meijin 1064
Meiroku zasshi: journal of the Japanese
enlightment 196
Memories of silk and straw: a self-
portrait of small-town Japan 234
Michio Ito: the dancer and his dances 322
Midaregami 1160
Migration in metropolitan Japan: social
change and political behavior 557
Mikado's empire 114
Military government in the Ryukyu
Islands, 1945-1950 285
Minamata 959
Minamata disease: methylmercury
poisoning in Minamata and Niigata,
Japan 959
Mind of the strategist: the art of Japanese
business 842
Minka: traditional houses of rural Japan
1312
Minobe Tatsukichi: interpreter of
constitutionalism in Japan 220
Miracle at Midway 706
Miracle by design: the real reasons
behind Japan's economic success 797
Mirror for the moon: a selection of
poems 1155
Mirror in the shrine: American
encounters with Meiji Japan 361
Mirror, sword and jewel: a study of
Japanese characteristics 593
Mirror, sword and jewel: the geometry of

Japanese life 593
Mishima: a biography 335
Mishima: a vision of the void 1131
Misunderstanding: Europe vs. Japan 755
Misunderstood miracle: industrial
development and political change in
Japan 872
Mitford's Japan: the memoirs and
recollections, 1866-1906, of Algernon
Bertram Mitford, the first Lord
Redesdale 357
MITI and the Japanese miracle: the
growth of industrial policy, 1925-1975
272
Mitsubishi and the N.Y.K., 1870-1914:
business strategy in the Japanese
shipping industry 250
Mitsui: three centuries of Japanese
business 231
Mizoguchi 1422
Mock Joya's things Japanese 1561
Modern bujutsu and budo 1444
Modern China and Japan: a brief history
126
Modern currents in Japanese art 1238
Modern history of Japan 111
Modern Japan: a historical survey 118
Modern Japan and Shinto nationalism: a
study of present-day trends in Japanese
religions 517
Modern Japan through its weddings:
gender, person, and society in ritual
portrayal 560
Modern Japanese drama: an anthology
1179
Modern Japanese fiction and its
traditions: an introduction 1008
Modern Japanese haiku: an anthology
1159
Modern Japanese literature in translation:
a bibliography 1588
Modern Japanese military system 761
Modern Japanese organization and
decision-making 39
Modern Japanese poetry 1145
Modern Japanese poets and the nature of
literature 1168
Modern Japanese print: an appreciation
1270
Modern Japanese prints: an art reborn
1274
Modern Japanese prose poem: an
anthology of six poets 1141

Modern Japanese stories: an anthology 1083

Modern Japanese writers and the nature of literature 1128

Modern reader's Japanese-English character dictionary 421

Modernization and the Japanese factory 929

Modernizers: overseas students, foreign employees, and Meiji Japan 197

Moetsukita chizu 1042

Monetary policy in Japan 821

Money and banking in contemporary Japan: the theoretical setting and its application 865

Money, finance, and macroeconomic performance in Japan 866

Monkey's straw raincoat and other poetry of the Bashō school 1150

Monumenta Nipponica: Studies in Japanese Culture 1534

More foot-loose in Tokyo: the curious traveler's guide to Shitamachi and Narita 91

Mori Arinori: a reconsideration 304

Mori Ōgai 1121

Mori Ōgai and the modernization of Japanese culture 1110

Morita psychotherapy 601

Morning glory: a history of the Imperial Japanese Navy 210

Mother of dreams and other short stories: portrayals of women in modern Japanese fiction 1106

Motoori Norinaga, 1730-1801 309

Mountain storm, pine breeze: folk song in Japan 1381

Multinationalism, Japanese style: the political economy of outward dependency 946

Multiple meanings: the written word in Japan – past, present, and future 1231

Murasaki Shikibu: her diary and poetic memoirs; a translation and study 1023

Murasaki Shikibu shū 1023

Murasaki Shikibu: The tale of Genji 1035

Musashi 1109

Music of a thousand autumns: the Tōgaku style of Japanese court music 1379

Musical structure of nō 1387

Mutual images: essays in American-Japanese relations 651

My life between Japan and America 360

Myth of Japanese uniqueness 587

N

Nabeshima [Famous ceramics of Japan] 1281

Nagasaki 1945: the first full-length eyewitness account of the atomic bomb attack on Nagasaki 258

Nagauta: the heart of kabuki music 1384

Nakahara: family farming and population in a Japanese village, 1717-1830 182

Namahage: a festival in the northeast of Japan 501

Namban art of Japan 1243

Nan'yō: the rise and fall of the Japanese in Micronesia, 1885-1945 227

Naomi 1102

Nara Buddhist art: Todai-ji 1290

Narrative of the expedition of an American squadron to the China Seas and Japan under the command of Commodore M. C. Perry, United States Navy 673

Narrative picture scrolls 1245

Narrow road to the deep north and other travel sketches 1149

National faith of Japan: a study in modern Shinto 515

National Museum: Tokyo 1473

National parks of Japan 48

Nationalism and the right wing in Japan: a study of post-war trends 276

Native sources of Japanese industrialization, 1750-1920 183

Natsume Soseki 1133

Neighborhood Tokyo 549

Neighbors across the Pacific: Canadian-Japanese relations 1870-1982 655

Netsuke: a bibliography 1288

Netsuke handbook 1288

New directions in Japanese architecture 1298

New fashion Japan 1348

New frontiers in American-East Asian relations: essays presented to Dorothy Borg 646

New generation in Meiji Japan: problems of cultural identity, 1885-1895 230

New geography of Japan 35

New Japanalia: past and present 1551

New Japanese architecture 1324

New Japanese photography 1277
New official guide: Japan 82
New Religions of Japan 513
New Religions of Japan: a bibliography
of Western-language materials 1584
New Zealand and Japan 1900-1941 665
Nihon eiga shisōshi 1428
Nihon kenkyū no tame no sankōtosho
1589
Nihon Tōkei Nenkan 825
Nineteenth century [Cambridge history of
Japan] 115
Ningen shikkaku 1049
Ninjutsu: the art of invisibility; Japan's
feudal-age espionage methods 1445
Nippon: a Charted Survey of Japan 826
Nippon Times 1549
Nippon-tō: art swords of Japan: the
Walter A. Compton Collection 1373
Nisei daughter 399
Nisei: the quiet Americans 390
No longer human 1049
Nō plays of Japan 1181
No surrender: my thirty-year war 341
Nō: the classical theatre of Japan 1405
Nobi 1091
Nobility of failure: tragic heroes in the
history of Japan 293
Noguchi and his patrons 343
Noh: the classical theater 1408
Noh theater: principles and perspectives
1406
Nomonhan: Japan against Russia, 1939
684
Normalization of Japanese-Soviet
relations, 1945-1970 728
Northeast Asia in prehistory 103
Nuclear energy and nuclear proliferation:
Japanese and American views 848

O

Occupation diplomacy: Britain, the
United States and Japan, 1945-1952
266
Ochikubo monogatari, or the tale of the
Lady Ochikubo: a tenth century
Japanese novel 1033
Ōkagami, the great mirror: Fujiwara
Michinaga (966-1027) and his times. A
study and translation 1017
Okage sama de: the Japanese in Hawai'i,
1885-1985 389
Okinawa, 1945: gateway to Japan 713

Okinawa problem: a chapter in Japan-
U.S. relations 285
Okinawa: the history of an island people
284
Okinawa: the last battle 713
Okinawa war 713
Okinawan religion: belief, ritual, and
social structure 466
Okubo Toshimichi: the Bismarck of
Japan 306
Ōkuma Shigenobu: statesman of Meiji
Japan 308
Old age in Japan: an annotated
bibliography of Western-language
materials 1595
Old friends, new enemies: the Royal
Navy and the Imperial Japanese Navy;
strategic illusions 1936-1941 698
Old Kyoto: a guide to traditional shops,
restaurants, and inns 78
Old maps in Japan 55
On the art of the nō drama: the major
treatises of Zeami 1413
On understanding Japanese religion 464
Once upon a time: visions of old Japan
1278
101 favorite songs taught in Japanese
schools 1386
101 letters of Hideyoshi: the private
correspondence of Toyotomi
Hideyoshi 299
One hundred famous views of Edo 1256
One hundred frogs: from renga to haiku
to English 1166
One hundred views of Mt. Fuji 1256
One robe, one bowl: the Zen poems of
Ryōkan 1154
One-straw revolution: an introduction to
natural farming 830
Ōnin War: history of its origins and
background with a selective translation
of 'The chronicle of Ōnin' 160
Onna-men 1052
Onnazaka 1053
Opening doors: contemporary Japan 36
Oraga haru 1146
Organization of the government of Japan
605
Organizational change in Japanese
factories 929
Organized workers and socialist politics
in interwar Japan 215
Organizing business: trade associations in

America and Japan 899
Oribe [Famous ceramics of Japan] 1281
Oriental Economist 1542
Orientations: the Monthly Magazine for
 Collectors and Connoisseurs of
 Oriental Art 1535
Origins of the modern Japanese state:
 selected writings of E. H. Norman 226
Origins of the Russo-Japanese War 671
Origins of the Second World War in Asia
 and the Pacific 694
Oritaku shiba no ki 298
Other Japan: postwar realities 34
Other Nuremberg: the untold story of the
 Tokyo war crime trials 265
Outline of a theory of civilization 194
Overseas Japanese studies institutions =
 Kaigai Nihon kenkyū kikan yōran
 1554
Ox against the storm; a biography of
 Tanaka Shozo: Japan's conservationist
 pioneer 312
Oxford-Duden pictorial English-Japanese
 dictionary 424
Ozu and the poetics of cinema 1416
Ozu: his life and films 1427

P
Pacific Affairs 1536
Pacific alliance: United States foreign
 economic policy and Japanese trade
 recovery, 1947-1955 264
Pacific estrangement: Japanese and
 American expansion, 1897-1911 662
Pacific rivals: a Japanese view of
 Japanese-American relations 643
Pacific War remembered: an oral history
 collection 699
Pacifism in Japan: the Christian and
 socialist tradition 288
Pagoda, skull and samurai: three stories
 1069
Painting in the Yamato style 1236
Palace and politics in prewar Japan 246
Papers relating to the foreign relations of
 the United States; Japan: 1931-1941
 690
Pariah persistence in changing Japan: a
 case study 374
Paris in Japan: the Japanese encounter
 with European painting 1251
Parties out of power in Japan, 1931-1941
 193

Partners in prosperity: strategic industries
 for the United States and Japan 873
Party in power: the Japanese Liberal-
 Democrats and policy-making 633
Party politics in Japan 629
Party rivalry and political change in
 Taishō Japan 198
Passport's Japan almanac 1553
Patent and know-how licensing in Japan
 and the United States 774
Patterns of Japanese economic
 development: a quantitative appraisal
 808
Patterns of Japanese policymaking:
 experiences from higher education 974
Peace conspiracy: Wang Ching-wei and the
 China War, 1937-1941 702
Pearl Harbor as history:
 Japanese-American relations,
 1931-1941 682
Pearl Harbor: the verdict of history 705
Pearl Harbor: warning and decision 705
Peasant protest in Japan, 1590-1884 161
Peasant protests and uprisings in
 Tokugawa Japan 161
Peasants, rebels, and outcastes: the
 underside of modern Japan 205
Penguin book of Japanese verse 1134
Personal matter 1089
Personality in Japanese history 289
Perspectives on Japan: a guide for
 teachers 9
PHP Intersect: Where Japan Meets Asia
 and the World 1537
Pictorial encyclopedia of Japanese
 culture: the soul and heritage of Japan
 1568
Pictorial encyclopedia of modern Japan
 1568
Pillow book of Sei Shōnagon 1025
Place called Hiroshima 256
Play of mirrors: eight major poets of
 modern Japan 1151
Pleasures of Japanese literature 1004
Poetic memoirs of Lady Daibu 1142
Poetry of postwar Japan 1143
Police and community in Japan 565
Policy and politics in Japan: creative
 conservatism 619
Policy and trade issues of the Japanese
 economy: American and Japanese
 perspectives 816
Policymaking in contemporary Japan 620

Political character of the Japanese press 1485
Political culture of Japan 621
Political development of modern Japan 239
Political dynamics of Japan 615
Political economy of Japan. Volume 1: The domestic transformation 817
Political economy of Japan. Volume 2: The changing international context 817
Political economy of Japan. Volume 3: Cultural and social dynamics 817
Political history of Japanese capitalism 117
Political leadership in contemporary Japan 636
Political opposition and local politics in Japan 642
Political women in Japan: the search for a place in political life 580
Politics and culture in wartime Japan 237
Politics and government in Japan 617
Politics in Japan 622
Politics in the Tokugawa bakufu, 1600-1843 185
Politics of Canadian-Japanese economic relations, 1952-1983 734
Politics of Japan's energy strategy: resources – diplomacy – security 849
Politics of labor legislation in Japan: national-international interaction 609
Politics of regional policy in Japan: localities incorporated? 640
Politics of the Meiji press: the life of Fukuchi Gen'ichirō 305
Pools of water, pillars of fire: the literature of Ibuse Masuji 1058
Population of Japan 371
Postwar industrial policy in Japan: an annotated bibliography 1581
Postwar Japanese economy: its development and structure 805
Postwar politics in Japan, 1945-1955 274
Postwar rearmament of Japanese maritime forces, 1945-71 759
Power and culture: the Japanese-American war, 1941-1945 695
Practical guide for teachers of elementary Japanese 455
Practical guide to Japanese signs. 1st part: Especially for newcomers 88
Practical guide to Japanese signs. 2nd part: Making life easier 88

Practical Japanese cooking: easy and elegant 1438
Prehistoric Japanese arts: Jōmon pottery 107
Prehistory of Japan 101
Price of affluence: dilemmas of contemporary Japan 567
Primer of Sōtō Zen: a translation of Dōgen's Shōbōgenzō Zuimonki 472
Primitive ukiyo-e from the James A. Michener Collection in the Honolulu Academy of Arts 1268
Princeton companion to classical Japanese literature 1566
Private academies of Tokugawa Japan 180
Proceedings of the British Association for Japanese Studies 1538
Programmed course on respect language in modern Japanese 450
Protest in Tokyo: the Security Treaty crisis of 1960 744
Protohistoric Yamato: archaeology of the first Japanese state 102
Psychological world of Natsume Sōseki 1112
Public administration in Japan 625
Public and private self in Japan and the United States: communicative styles of two cultures 584
Public finance in Japan 863
Public policy and private education in Japan 968
Puppet theatre of Japan 1411
Pure Land Buddhist painting 1244

Q

Quiet pilgrimage 362
Quiet therapies: Japanese pathways to personal growth 602
Quilt, and other stories by Tayama Katai 1105

R

Rabbits, crabs, etc.: stories by Japanese women 1048
Race to Pearl Harbor: the failure of the Second London Naval Conference and the onset of World War II 704
Radical nationalist in Japan: Kita Ikki, 1883-1937 348
Rashomon and other stories 1045
Read Japanese today 456

Reader of handwritten Japanese 451
Reader's guide to Japanese literature 1009
Reading Japanese 441
Rebellion and democracy in Meiji Japan:
  a study of commoners in the popular
  rights movement 195
Recent Japanese philosophical thought,
  1862-1962: a survey 527
Reckoning 874
Record of things heard from the Treasury
  of the Eye of the True Teaching: the
  Shōbōgenzō-zuimonki, talks of Zen
  master Dōgen, as recorded by Zen
  master Ejō 472
Red flag in Japan: international
  communism in action, 1919-1951 192
Reference grammar of Japanese 432
Reflections of reality in Japanese art 1205
Reflections on the way to the gallows:
  rebel women in prewar Japan 290
Religion and nothingness 525
Religion and society in modern Japan:
  continuity and change 468
Religion in Japanese history 465
Religion in the Japanese experience:
  sources and interpretations 461
Religions of Japan: many traditions
  within one sacred way 462
Reluctant admiral: Yamamoto and the
  Imperial Navy 317
Remaking Japan: the American
  occupation as New Deal 267
Report from Tokyo: a message to the
  American people 690
Requiem for battleship Yamato 716
Return to the Philippines 715
Return to Tsugaru: travels of a purple
  tramp 1116
Revolt in Japan: the young officers and
  the February 26, 1936 Incident 238
Revolutionary origins of modern Japan
  171
Rhetoric of confession: 'shishōsetsu' in
  early twentieth-century Japanese fiction
  1113
Riddle of MacArthur: Japan, Korea and
  the Far East 356
Rikishi: the men of sumo 1455
Rise of Japanese baseball power 1456
Rise of labor in Japan: the Yūaikai, 1912-
  1919 215
Rising sun 715
Rising sun: the decline and fall of the

Japanese empire, 1936-1945 712
River mist, and other stories 1070
Riverside counselor's stories: vernacular
  fiction of late Heian Japan 1011
Road to Komatsubara: a classical reading
  of the renga hyakuin 1165
Road to Tokyo 715
Roads to Sata: a 2000-mile walk through
  Japan 67
Roberts' guide to Japanese museums of
  art and archaeology 1475
Rodrigues the interpreter: an early Jesuit
  in Japan and China 352
Rōmaji diary 1140
Rōmaji diary and Sad toys 1140
Rōmaji nikki 1140
Romanized English-Japanese, Japanese-
  English dictionary 426
Roof in Japanese Buddhist architecture
  1322
Roof tile of Tempyō 1061
Roots of Japanese architecture: a
  photographic quest 1302
Ruined map 1042
Runaway horses 1077
Rural society in Japan 534
Rush hour of the gods: a study of new
  religious movements in Japan 510
Russia against Japan, 1904-05: a new
  look at the Russo-Japanese War 678
Russian push toward Japan:
  Russo-Japanese relations, 1697-1875
  664
Russia's Japan expedition of 1852 to 1855
  664
Ryōkan, Zen monk-poet of Japan 1154
Ryukyu: a bibliographical guide to
  Okinawan studies 1591
Ryukyu: an annotated bibliography 1591
Ryukyu Islands: a bibliography 1591

                    S
Sad toys 1140
Sadaharu Oh: a Zen way of baseball 338
Saga of Dazai Osamu: a critical study
  with translations 1116
Saiki kōi and other stories 1081
Sailor who fell from grace with the sea
  1076
'Saké': a drinker's guide 1431
Sakhalin: a history 287
Samurai 1054
Samurai and silk: a Japanese and

American heritage 297
Samurai film 1420
Samurai films of Akira Kurosawa 1420
Samurai sword: a handbook 1375
Sanshirō 1087
Sanshirō; a novel 1087
Sarashina nikki 1026
Sarumino 1150
Sasameyuki 1101
Say it in Japanese 416
Scholar painters of Japan: the Nanga
    school 1255
Scholars' guide to Washington, D.C. for
    East Asian studies (China, Japan,
    Korea, and Mongolia) 1562
Schooldays in imperial Japan: a study in
    the culture of a student elite 232
Science and culture in traditional Japan,
    A.D. 600-1854 157
Science and society in modern Japan:
    selected historical sources 992
Science & Technology in Japan 1539
Science and technology in Japan
    [Anderson] 980
Sculpture of the Kamakura period 1293
Sea of fertility: a cycle of four novels
    1077
Search for a new order: intellectuals and
    fascism in prewar Japan 199
Search for authenticity in modern
    Japanese literature 1130
Second to none: American companies in
    Japan 889
Secret history 1102
Secret history of the lord of Musashi, and
    Arrowroot 1102
Secret teachings in the art of Japanese
    gardens: design principles, aesthetic
    values 1338
Securities market in Japan 1988 858
Self-made man in Meiji Japanese
    thought: from samurai to salary man
    214
Senbazuru 1067
Sengoku and Edo [Cambridge history of
    Japan] 115
Sentimental imperialists: the American
    experience in East Asia 657
Setting sun 1050
Seven Japanese tales 1103
Shadows of the rising sun: a critical view
    of the 'Japanese miracle' 31
Shank's mare; being a translation of the

Tokaido volumes of Hizakurige,
    Japan's great comic novel of travel and
    ribaldry 1016
Shayō 1050
Sheathing the sword: the demilitarisation
    of Japan 271
Shibori: the inventive art of Japanese
    shaped resist dyeing: tradition,
    techniques, innovation 1355
Shiga hero 1125
Shigaraki, potters' valley 1280
Shikitei Sanba and the comic tradition in
    Edo fiction 1038
Shimoda story 676
Shinano! The sinking of Japan's secret
    supership 716
Shingū: a Japanese fishing community
    552
Shinichi Suzuki: the man and his
    philosophy 326
Shino and Oribe ceramics 1282
Shino [Famous ceramics of Japan] 1281
Shinohata: a portrait of a Japanese
    village 550
Shinran's gospel of pure grace 471
Shinto art: Ise and Izumo shrines 1325
Shinto arts: nature, gods, and man in
    Japan 1199
Shinto: at the fountain-head of Japan 516
Shintō bibliography in Western
    languages: bibliography on Shinto and
    religious sects, intellectual schools and
    movements influenced by Shintōism
    1606
Shinto: Japan's spiritual roots 519
Shinto: the kami way 518
Shinto: the way of Japan 520
Shinzō Hachiman imagery and its
    development 1289
Shiosai 1078
Shōbōgenzō: Zen essays 473
Shogi, Japan's game of strategy 1459
Shōgun 1418
Shogun Age Exhibition: from the
    Tokugawa Art Museum, Japan 1219
Shogunal politics: Arai Hakuseki and the
    premises of Tokugawa rule 177
Shoji Hamada: a potter's way and work
    331
Short economic history of modern Japan
    110
Short economic history of modern Japan,
    1867-1937 110

Shōwa: an inside history of Hirohito's Japan 294

Shōwa anthology: modern Japanese short stories. Volume 1: 1929-1961 1056

Shōwa anthology: modern Japanese short stories. Volume 2: 1961-1984 1056

Shrine Shinto after World War II 515

Shūkyō to wa nani ka 525

Shunga: the art of love in Japan 1259

Silence 1055

Silent cry 1090

Silent victory: the U.S. submarine war against Japan 681

Silk road and the Shoso-in 1194

Six hidden views of Japanese music 1385

Six lives, six deaths: portraits from modern Japan 292

Smart bargaining: doing business with the Japanese 893

Snow country 1065

Social basis for prewar Japanese militarism: the army and the rural community 243

Social change and the city in Japan: from earliest times through the industrial revolution 546

Social change and the individual: Japan before and after defeat in World War II 595

Social democratic movement in prewar Japan 247

Social protest and popular culture in eighteenth-century Japan 161

Socialist parties in postwar Japan 630

Socialization for achievement: essays on the cultural psychology of the Japanese 588

Society and education in Japan 973

Soga monogatari 1012

Sogoi shosha: the vanguard of the Japanese economy 914

Sōka Gakkai, builders of the third civilization: American and Japanese members 512

Sōka Gakkai, Japan's militant Buddhists 512

Sōkagakkai and mass society 514

Some Japanese portraits 291

Some prefer nettles 1104

Something like an autobiography 329

Song of the brush: Japanese paintings from the Sansō Collection 1246

Songs of gods, songs of humans: the epic tradition of the Ainu 380

Sony vision 877

Sound of the mountain 1066

Sound of the one hand: 281 Zen koans with answers 477

Sound of waves 1078

Sources of Japanese history 120

Sources of Japanese tradition 33

Southern barbarians: the first Europeans in Japan 132

Soviet policy towards Japan: an analysis of trends in the 1970s and 1980s 747

Soviet seizure of the Kuriles 285

Soviet Union and postwar Japan: escalating challenge and response 752

Space and illusion in the Japanese garden 1333

Space and spirit in modern Japan 1304

Space in Japanese architecture 1308

Speaking of Japan 1540

Speeches of Fukuzawa: a translation and critical study 194

Spirit of aikidō 1451

Spring snow 1077

State and diplomacy in early modern Japan: Asia in the development of the Tokugawa bakufu 677

State and economic enterprise in Japan: essays in the political economy of growth 239

State and labor in modern Japan 202

State and the mass media in Japan, 1918-1945 221

Statistical Handbook of Japan 827

Statistical Year Book of the Empire of Japan 825

Stepping stones to go: a game of strategy 1458

Stories by contemporary Japanese women writers 1071

Strange neutrality: Soviet-Japanese relations during the Second World War, 1941-1945 684

Strategy and structure of Japanese enterprises 926

Strategy of Japanese business 837

Structure of the Japanese language 429

Studies in Japanese folklore 503

Studies in Japanese literature and language: a bibliography of English materials 1615

Studies in kabuki: its acting, music, and historical context 1397

Studies in the institutional history of early modern Japan 168

Studies of Japan in Western languages of special interest to geographers 1592

Study of good 524

Study of the Ise-monogatari: with the text according to the Den-Teika-hippon and an annotated translation 1148

Suburban Tokyo: a comparative study in politics and social change 628

Sugawara and the secrets of calligraphy 1174

Sugawara denju tenarai kagami 1174

Sugawara no Michizane and the early Heian court 300

Summaries of Selected Japanese Magazines 1547

Sumo: from rite to sport 1453

Sun and steel 1079

Suna no onna 1043

Surimono: privately published Japanese prints in the Spencer Museum of Art 1263

Sushi made easy 1436

Suye mura: a Japanese village 551

Suzuki Harunobu: a selection of his color prints and illustrated books 1261

T

Tade kuu mushi 1104

Taiheiki: a chronicle of medieval Japan 1018

Taiyō to tetsu 1079

Takashima: a Japanese fishing community 554

Taking Japan seriously: a Confucian perspective on leading economic issues 795

Takuboku: poems to eat 1140

Tale of eleventh-century Japan: 'Hamamatsu Chūnagon monogatari' 1027

Tale of flowering fortunes: annals of Japanese aristocratic life in the Heian period 1021

Tale of Genji 1024

Tale of the Hamamatsu Middle Counselor 1027

Tale of the Heike 1019

Tale of the Soga Brothers 1012

Tales of Ise 1148

Tales of Ise: lyrical episodes from tenth-century Japan 1148

Tales of moonlight and rain: Japanese gothic tales 1031

Tales of the spring rain: Harusame monogatari 1030

Tales of times now past: sixty-two stories from a medieval Japanese collection 1032

Tales of Yamato: a tenth-century poem-tale 1028

Tall mountains and flowing waters: the arts of Uragami Gyokudō 1230

Tamba pottery: the timeless art of a Japanese village 1286

Tanaka Giichi and Japan's China policy 333

Tangled hair: selected tanka from 'Midaregami' 1160

Tanrokubon: rare books of seventeenth-century Japan 1481

Tansu: traditional Japanese cabinetry 1341

Tarawa: the story of a battle 707

Target Tokyo: the story of the Sorge spy ring 228

Taste of Japan: food fact and fable; what the people eat; customs and etiquette 1433

Tea ceremony 1472

Tea ceremony utensils 1468

Tea in Japan: essays on the history of 'chanoyu' 1467

Teachers and politics in Japan 977

Teachings essential for rebirth: a study of Genshin's 'Ōjōyōshū' 470

Technology and agricultural development in pre-war Japan 200

Technology and Development 1541

Technology policy and economic performance: lessons from Japan 983

Technopolis strategy: Japan, high technology, and the control of the twenty-first century 996

Teikoku's complete atlas of Japan 53

Temple of dawn 1077

Temple of the golden pavilion 1080

Temples of Nara and their art 1316

Tempyō no iroka 1061

Ten thousand leaves: a translation of the 'Man'yōshū', Japan's premier anthology of classical poetry 1147

Ten years in Japan: a contemporary record drawn from the diaries and private and official papers of Joseph C.

Grew, United States ambassador to Japan, 1932-1942 690
Tennin gosui 1077
Tense and aspect in modern colloquial Japanese 410
Tetsugaku no konpon mondai 524
Textile designs of Japan. Volume 1: Free-style designs 1347
Textile designs of Japan. Volume 2: Geometric designs 1347
Textile designs of Japan. Volume 3: Okinawan, Ainu, and foreign designs 1347
Textile wrangle: conflict in Japanese-American relations, 1969-1971 722
Theatres of Japan 1393
Theatrical world of Osaka prints: a collection of eighteenth and nineteenth century Japanese woodblock prints in the Philadelphia Museum of Art 1264
Theodore Roosevelt and Japan 659
Theory Z: how American business can meet the Japanese challenge 932
They call me Moses Masaoka: an American saga 395
They came to Japan: an anthology of European reports on Japan, 1543-1640 133
Thirty seconds over Tokyo 696
Thirty-six views of Mount Fuji by Hokusai 1265
This is kendo: the art of Japanese fencing 1449
This island of Japan: João Rodrigues' account of 16th-century Japan 153
This kind of woman: ten stories by Japanese women writers, 1960-1976 1098
This land . . . this beauty: Japan's natural splendor 44
Thorn in the chrysanthemum: suicide and economic success in modern Japan 568
Thought and behaviour in modern Japanese politics 618
Thought control in prewar Japan 221
Thousand cranes 1067
Thousand cranes: treasures of Japanese art 1217
Threat of Japanese multinationals: how the West can respond 945
Three decades in Shiwa: economic development and social change in a

Japanese farming community 555
Three pillars of Zen: teaching, practice, and enlightenment 478
Through harsh winters: the life of a Japanese immigrant woman; as told to Akemi Kikumura 400
Through Japanese eyes. Volume 1: The past: the road from isolation 18
Through Japanese eyes. Volume 2: The present: coping with affluence 18
Thunder gods: the kamikaze pilots tell their story 700
Titans of the seas: the development and operations of Japanese and American carrier task forces during World War II 680
To the distant observer: form and meaning in the Japanese cinema 1417
Together with the Ainu: a vanishing people 375
Tojo and the coming of the war 321
Tōkaidōchū Hizakurige 1016
Tokoname [Famous ceramics of Japan] 1281
Tokugawa Collection: nō robes and masks 1412
Tokugawa ideology: early constructs, 1570-1680 178
Tokugawa Ieyasu: shogun 314
Tokugawa religion: the cultural roots of modern Japan 459
Tokugawa religion: the values of pre-industrial Japan 459
Tokutomi Sohō, 1863-1957: a journalist for modern Japan 311
Tokyo: a bilingual atlas 56
Tokyo: a world financial centre 862
Tokyo and Washington: dilemmas of a mature alliance 750
Tokyo Business Today: a Monthly Magazine of Japan's Business and Finance 1542
Tokyo city guide 75
Tokyo Journal 1510
Tokyo now and then: an explorer's guide 99
Tokyo Rose: orphan of the Pacific 387
Tokyo: the city at the end of the world 22
Told round a brushwood fire: the autobiography of Arai Hakuseki 298
Tonkō 1061
Tōno monogatari 1188
Toshokan: libraries in Japanese society 1476

Totto-chan: the little girl at the window 330

Tough words for American industry 875

Toward a modern Japanese theatre: Kishida Kunio 1178

Towazugatari 310

Toyota: a history of the first 50 years 347

Toyota: fifty years in motion; an autobiography 347

Trade friction and economic policy: problems and prospects for Japan and the United States 907

Trade war: greed, power, and industrial policy on opposite sides of the Pacific 908

Trading places: how we allowed Japan to take the lead 904

Tradition and modernization in Japanese culture 239

Traditional domestic architecture of Japan 1303

Traditional folksongs of Japan: with piano accompaniment 1381

Traditional Japanese furniture 1342

Traditional Japanese houses 1303

Traditional music of Japan 1382

Traditional theater of Japan 1403

Traditions of Japanese art: selections from the Kimiko and John Powers Collection 1214

Training of the Zen Buddhist monk 491

Transactions of the Asiatic Society of Japan 1543

Transforming the past: tradition and kinship among Japanese Americans 403

Translations from early Japanese literature 1011

Travelers' Japanese 446

Travels in Japan 69

Treasures among men: the fudai daimyo in Tokugawa Japan 163

Treaty of Portsmouth: an adventure in American diplomacy 672

Treelike: the poetry of Kinoshita Yūji 1144

Triad power: the coming shape of global competition 902

Trilateralism in Asia: problems and prospects in U.S.-Japan-ASEAN relations 741

Troubled encounter: the United States and Japan 653

Tsugaru 1116

Tsujigahana: the flower of Japanese textile art 1346

Tsuki ni hoeru 1136

Tsurezuregusa 1034

Tsūshō hakusho 828

Tsutsumi Chūnagon monogatari 1011

Tun-huang 1061

Twelve doors to Japan 16

Twentieth century [Cambridge history of Japan] 115

Twenty plays of the nō theater 1175

Two hungry giants: the United States and Japan in the quest for oil and ores 913

Two Japanese novelists: Sōseki and Tōson 1117

Typhoon of steel: the battle for Okinawa 713

U

Ueda Akinari 315

Ugetsu monogatari: tales of moonlight and rain. A complete English version of the eighteenth-century Japanese collection of tales of the supernatural 1031

Uji shūi monogatari 1022

Ukifune: love in 'The tale of Genji' 1039

Unbeaten tracks in Japan: an account of travels on horseback in the interior, including visits to the aborigines of Yezo and the shrines of Nikkô and Isé 66

Under Japanese management: the experience of British workers 950

Understanding industrial relations in modern Japan 925

Understanding Japan 35

Understanding Japanese society 535

Uneasy partnership: competition and conflict in U.S.-Japanese trade relations 890

United States and Japan: a troubled partnership 753

United States and the Far Eastern crisis of 1933-1938: from the Manchurian Incident through the initial stage of the undeclared Sino-Japanese War 702

United States in East Asia: a historical bibliography 1575

United States-Japan economic problem 886

Unknown craftsman: a Japanese insight

into beauty 1228
Unspoken way. 'Haragei': silence in Japanese business and society 406
Unsui: a diary of Zen monastic life 486
Urban housewives: at home and in the community 577
Urban Japan: its foundations and growth 43
U.S./Japan foreign trade: an annotated bibliography of socioeconomic perspectives 1600
U.S.-Japan science and technology exchange: patterns of interdependence 998
U.S.-Japan strategic reciprocity: a neo-internationalist view 767
U.S.-Japanese agricultural trade relations 888
U.S.-Japanese energy relations: cooperation and competition 847
U.S.-Japanese security relations: a historical perspective 768
Utage no ato 1072
Utamaro: colour prints and paintings 1262
Utsukushisa to kanashimi to 1063

V

Valley of darkness: the Japanese people and World War Two 207
Venture Japan: the Journal of Global Opportunity 1544
Victorians in Japan: in and around the treaty ports 68
Victor's justice: the Tokyo war crimes trial 265
View by the sea 1107
Village Japan 548
Visions of virtue in Tokugawa Japan: the Kaitokudō Merchant Academy of Osaka 176
Voices and hands of bunraku 1391
Voices from the Japanese cinema 1423

W

Wagahai wa neko de aru 1085
Waiting years 1053
Wanderers and settlers in the Far East: a century of Jewish life in China and Japan 4
War criminal: the life and death of Hirota Koki 346
War under the Pacific 715

War without mercy: race and power in the Pacific War 686
Warbler's song in the dusk: the life and work of Ōtomo Yakamochi (718-785) 301
Warlords, artists, and commoners: Japan in the sixteenth century 135
Warrior government in early medieval Japan: a study of the Kamakura bakufu, shugo, and jitō 149
Warships of the Imperial Japanese Navy, 1869-1945 1572
Washi: the world of Japanese paper 1365
Water: a view from Japan 3
Waves at Genji's door: Japan through its cinema 1424
Way of tea 1467
Way of the samurai 156
Way of the samurai: Yukio Mishima on Hagakure in modern life 529
Way of Zen 494
Western Europe and Japan between the super powers 739
Western medical pioneers in feudal Japan 596
Western world and Japan: a study in the interaction of European and Asiatic cultures 674
What is Japanese architecture? 1314
Wheel Extended 1545
When the twain meet: the rise of Western medicine in Japan 597
White Paper on International Trade 828
White Papers of Japan: Annual Abstract of Official Reports and Statistics of the Japanese Government 829
Who's who in Japan 1574
Who's who in Japanese government, 1988/89 366
Who's who in modern Japanese prints 364
Why has Japan 'succeeded'? Western technology and the Japanese ethos 804
Widows of Hiroshima: the life stories of nineteen peasant wives 259
Wild geese 1082
Will Japan rearm? a study in attitudes 354
Windows for the crown prince 362
Windows on the Japanese past: studies in archaeology and prehistory 109
With respect to the Japanese: a guide for Americans 586
Within the barbed wire fence: a Japanese

man's account of his internment in Canada 383
Woman in the dunes 1043
Womansword: what Japanese words say about women 413
Women against war 583
Women in changing Japan 578
Women in Japan: discrimination, resistance and reform 575
Women of Suye mura 582
Words in motion: modern Japanese calligraphy 1231
Work and lifecourse in Japan 542
Work, mobility, and participation: a comparative study of American and Japanese industry 919
Workers and employers in Japan: the Japanese employment relations system 931
World destroyed: the atomic bomb and the grand alliance 261
World of Japanese ceramics 1287
World of origami 1364
World of sex: perspectives on Japan and the West. Volume 1: Sexual equality 536
World of sex: perspectives on Japan and the West. Volume 2: Sex and marriage 536
World of sex: perspectives on Japan and the West. Volume 3: Responsible parenthood 536
World of sex: perspectives on Japan and the West. Volume 4: Sex in ethics and law 536
World of the Japanese garden: from Chinese origins to modern landscape art 1335
World of the Meiji print: impressions of a new civilization 1269
World of the shining prince: court life in ancient Japan 150
World War II (Series) 715
World War II at sea: a bibliography of sources in English. Volume II: The Pacific theater 1609
World within walls: Japanese literature of the pre-modern era, 1600-1867 1005
Writers and society in modern Japan 1120

Y

Yakuza: the explosive account of Japan's criminal underworld 569

Yama no oto 1066
Yamagata Aritomo in the rise of modern Japan, 1838-1922 303
Yamato monogatari 1028
Yanagita Kunio guide to the Japanese folk tale 1188
Year of my life: a translation of Issa's 'Oraga haru' 1146
Years of infamy: the untold story of America's concentration camps 386
Years of MacArthur. Volume 3: Triumph and disaster, 1945-1964 356
Years of sorrow, years of shame: the story of the Japanese Canadians in World War II 383
Yen! Japan's new financial empire and its threat to America 853
Yō no bi: the beauty of Japanese folk art 1213
Yoakemae 1094
Yokomitsu Riichi: modernist 1114
Yoshida memoirs: the story of Japan in crisis 282
Yoshino kuzu 1102
Yoshitsune: a fifteenth-century Japanese chronicle 1020
You gotta have wa 1456
Young Japan: Yokohama and Yedo. A narrative of the settlement and the city from the signing of the treaties in 1858, to the close of the year 1879. With a glance at the progress of Japan during a period of twenty-one years 162
Yukiguni 1065

Z

Zeami's style: the Noh plays of Zeami Motokiyo 1172
Zen action/Zen person 480
Zen and Japanese culture 492
Zen and the fine arts 1195
Zen and Western thought 469
Zen at Daitoku-ji 1190
Zen Buddhism: a bibliography of books and articles in English, 1892-1975 1612
Zen Buddhism: a history 474
Zen Buddhism and its influence on Japanese culture 492
Zen culture 1196
Zen: dawn in the West 479
Zen forest: sayings of the masters 488
Zen guide: where to meditate in Japan 97

Zen life [Kuzunishi] 486
Zen life [Satō] 486
Zen life: D. T. Suzuki remembered 316
Zen master Hakuin: selected writings 476
Zen mind, beginner's mind 493
Zen no kenkyū 524

*Zen painting & calligraphy: an exhibition
 of works of art* [etc.] 1232
Zen poems of Ryōkan 1154
Zen poems of the five mountains 1152
Zen training: methods and philosophy
 487

Index of Subjects

The index is based primarily on key terms, concepts, and names mentioned in the titles and annotations of individual books.

A

Abby Aldrich Rockefeller Collection (Providence, Rhode Island)
  ukiyo-e prints 1257
Abe Akira
  short stories 1057
Abe Isoo
  as a pacifist 288
Abe Kōbō
  novels 1041-1043, 1127
  plays 1057, 1179
  search for authenticity in literature 1130
  short stories 1051, 1106, 1126
Abe Masahiro
  biography 289
  leadership 146
Abortion 536
  as a traditional practice 370
  Tokugawa period 169, 172
Academic achievement patterns 965
Academic freedom
  permissibility of limiting 788
Accent in the Japanese language 412
Accidents
  among Japanese Americans 385
  automobile factory 924
  motor-vehicle (legal aspects) 786
Accordion books 1479
Accounting practices
  corporate 852
Achievement
  cognitive 964
  educational 965-966, 971
  family influence on school 594
  mathematics 594
  motivation 588
  orientation (correlated with suicide rates) 568
Actors
  depicted in woodblock prints 1264, 1271
  interaction with theatrical audiences (history) 1410
  kabuki theatre 165, 1264, 1271, 1291, 1352, 1394, 1398, 1400-1401, 1410, 1564
  movie 1414
  noh theatre 1405-1406, 1408, 1410
  photographs 1278
  sarugaku noh and *dengaku noh* 1409-1410
Acupuncture
  clinical practice 598
Adams, Will 133
Addresses *see* Directories
Adjectives 411
  grammar 427, 429-433
Administration
  administrative counselling 625
  administrative inspection 625
  administrative law 777, 1582
  administrative practices (500-1700 AD) 138
  administrative practices (Kamakura period) 148
  agricultural 835
  educational 960
  judicial review of administrative actions 786-787
  maps of administrative divisions 53
  public 613, 625
  securities 858
  universities 963
Administrative guidance (*gyōsei shidō*) 625, 783
  concerning foreign enterprises 779
  doctrinal adaptation in the courts 777
  during the 1973-74 oil crisis 777
  pro-cartel policies and 816
Administrative reform
  Liberal Democratic Party's response to changing conditions in 619
  role in Japan's emergence as a 'headquarters country' 856
Admirals *see* Navy admirals
Adolescents *see* Youth
Adoption 536
Adult socialisation 595
Adultery
  plays about 1170

Advanced polymers
  research and development 984
Adverbs
  grammar 427, 430-433
Adversary method
  rejected for settling disputes 797
  used in criminal trials 780
Advertising
  business 788, 844
  consumer 841, 891
  ethics 844
  freedom 771
  newspaper 1483
  photographs of advertisements 1276
  see also Shop signs (kanban)
Advisers (Western) see 'Employed
  foreigners' (oyatoi gaikokujin)
Advisory bodies
  Shōwa Kenkyūkai 199
Aerospace
  industry 912
  research institutes and programmes
  980
Aesthetics 153, 1003-1004
  Ainu 380
  architecture 1198, 1300
  artistic accomplishments 1211
  bamboo 1357
  bonsai 1328
  Buddhist 1228
  bunraku theatre 1393
  buyō (dance) 1390
  calligraphy 1249
  cloisonné 1361
  clothing accessories 1198
  court poetry 1164
  cuisine 1196, 1435, 1437
  design motifs 1204
  esoteric Buddhist art 1216
  flower containers 1198
  foundation of Japanese 150
  gagaku 1377
  gardens 1332, 1335, 1338
  Hamada Shōji's views 331
  kabuki theatre 1393-1394
  kitchen utensils 1198
  kites 1198
  Kokinshū 1153
  Mori Ōgai's use of German aesthetic
  theory 1110
  music 1378
  musical instruments 1198
  noh theatre 1393
  Okakura Kakuzō's views 1470
  principles regarding forms in the
  Japanese universe 1202
  renga poetry 1166
  ritual objects 1198
  Shintō 516, 1289
  suiseki (stones) 1362
  swords 1373
  Tanizaki Junichirō's views 1225
  tea ceremony 135, 1467-1472
  toys 1198
  traditional craftsmanship 1198, 1228
  values 530
  wabi (aesthetic principle) 1467
  washi (handmade paper) 1365
  woodblock prints 1271-1272
  Yanagi Sōetsu's views 1228
  Yoshida Kenkō's views 1034
  Zen Buddhist 1195-1196
Affective expressions
  handbook 425
Affluence
  among farmers (1960s-1970s) 534
  problems 15, 18, 30, 34, 567
Afghanistan
  Japanese response to the Soviet
  invasion 758
Africa
  relations with Japan 743
After the banquet (Mishima Yukio)
  translation 1072
Agano ware (ceramics) 1281
Age groups 593
Ageing
  Japan's ageing society 820
  old age (bibliography) 1595
  process 327, 541, 579
  words pertaining to 413
  see also Elderly
Agrarian structure
  post-1945 40, 532
Agrarianist thought 206
Agricultural Basic Law
  enactment and consequences 835
  failure of structural policies under 832
Agriculture 46, 50, 791, 801, 888
  1870s-1980 803
  agricultural development 200, 223,
  242, 806, 834-835
  agricultural households (maps) 54
  agricultural policy 206, 623, 821, 832,
  835, 888
  agricultural practices 136, 548, 830

agricultural productivity 200, 831, 834
agricultural products (maps) 53-54
agricultural protection 832
'agricultural revolution' (16th century)
    139
annual statistics 824-827, 829
bibliographies 1592, 1594
Canadian-Japanese trade 895
changes (post-1945) 34, 805
contribution to economic growth
    (1868-1941) 218
co-operation among farmers 181, 200,
    268, 551, 555, 835
co-operatives 268, 550, 555, 723, 835
decline (post-1945) 556, 835
Dōsojin as a deity of 502
during the Allied occupation of Japan
    (1945-52) 273-274, 282
farming (comparison of Japan, the
    USA, and India) 834
government report (annual) 829
historical development 187, 831
impact of economic growth
    (post-1945) 534
land reform (Meiji period) 835
land reform (late 1940s) 267-268, 282,
    790, 835
laws 1582
long-term statistical data 808
mechanisation 555, 573
natural farming 830
periodicals 1488, 1502
photographs 835
political economy of agricultural
    policies 832
prehistoric 101
present conditions and trends (annual
    survey) 823
research institutes and programmes
    980
statistics (1870s-1970s) 835
structure (1970s) 835
Tokugawa period 181-182
US-Japan trade relations 888
women 578
see also Community studies, and
    Farmers
Aichi Prefecture
Kariya 547
Nagoya 70, 100, 350, 1412
Aikidō (martial art) 1444
history 1444, 1450-1451
introductory study 1450

philosophy 1451
photographs 1450-1451
Shintō dimensions 519
Ainu
burial practices 378
community life 372, 379
customs and religion 66, 372, 375,
    378-380
demography 379
education 961
experiences working with 359, 375
family life 375, 379
fishing 375
folk art 375
folklore 375, 380
history 372, 379
horticulture 375
kinship system 379
photographs 375
poetry 1006
social change among 961
social organisation 378-379
stories and legends 372
tattooing 375
textile designs (photographs) 1347
Air force
World War II 688-689
Air pollution *see* Pollution
Aircraft
flown by kamikaze pilots 700
industry 763, 911
military (descriptions) 680, 689
Aircraft carriers
encyclopaedic information about 1572
Shinano 716
task forces (World War II) 680, 687
Airports
Narita Airport 606
Akatsuki no tera (Mishima Yukio)
literary analysis 1131
translation 1077
Akazome Emon
Eiga monogatari 1021
Akihito (Crown Prince, now Emperor)
life during the 1940s 362
Akimoto Matsuyo
plays 1171
Akita Prefecture
Namahage festival 501
traveller's account 66
see also Tōhoku region
Akutagawa Ryūnosuke
as a member of the *bundan* 1120

Akutagawa Ryūnosuke *continued*
 biography 289
 concept of literature 1128
 haiku poetry 1159
 Kappa 1044
 life and writings 1132
 search for authenticity in literature
  1130
 short stories 1045, 1083, 1126
Alcock, Rutherford
 experiences and observations 349
Alcoves (*tokonoma*)
 element of interior design 1326
Aleutian Islands (Alaska)
 military occupation (World War II)
  687-688
Allen, George Cyril
 reminiscences 350
Allied occupation of Japan (1945-52)
 222, 249, 269, 271, 282
 activities of Nikkyōso (Japan Teachers
  Union) 967, 977
 American involvement 278, 657
 as a part of American East Asian
  diplomacy 279
 Australian involvement 266
 Australian trade with Japan 745
 bibliographies 1583, 1599, 1613-1614
 British involvement 266, 701
 Canadian involvement 655
 Christianity 495-497
 constitutional reform 266, 271,
  273-274, 280-282
 decline and reemergence of
  nationalism 276
 demilitarisation 271, 759
 democratisation 267, 273-274, 280,
  617
 economic changes 805
 economic reconstruction 264, 799
 educational reforms 273, 282, 651,
  960-961, 975
 emperor (new role and image) 273,
  334
 evolution of defence policy 770
 evolution of local government 641
 evolution of socialist parties 630
 experiences of Herbert Passin 359
 financial history 851
 high-ranking occupation personnel
  (list) 1613
 impact on American images of Japan
  731
 impact on city life 549
 impact on MITI 272
 impact on public policy companies 612
 impact on radio broadcasting 1486
 impact on rural society 268, 531, 548
 impact on Shintō 515, 517
 imperial family 362
 institutional reforms affecting
  economic development 818
 Japanese and American views 646
 land reform 267-268, 282, 790, 835
 legal and judicial reforms 277, 780
 MacArthur, Douglas 273, 278,
  281-282, 356
 Matsukawa case 780
 naval disarmament and rearmament
  759
 overview 273
 photographs 278
 political events 274
 portrayed in films 1424
 Ryūkyū Islands 285, 1591
 San Francisco Peace Treaty 266, 274,
  282-283, 285, 745
 Soviet policies and practices 752
 war crimes trials 265-266, 271, 321,
  346, 595
 women 581, 583
 Yoshida Shigeru 324
 zaibatsu dissolution 267, 270, 274
 see also Constitution
'Almanac prints' 1576
Almanacs 1553
Alternative energies
 market 850
 research and development 847, 849
Aluminium-refining industry
 industrial policy and 876, 879
Amae see Dependence (*amae*)
Amakudari (employment practice) 612
Amakusa Shirō
 life and times 293
Amaterasu Ōmikami (sun goddess) 516,
 519
 myths about 1186
Ambassadors
 Grew, Joseph C. 690
 private businessmen as roving 887
 Reischauer, Edwin O. 360
 Yoshida Shigeru 324
Ambiguity
 element of management style 933
Americans in Japan 162, 278

Barrett, Timothy 1358
baseball players 1456
business companies 889, 902
Cohen, Theodore 267
Dalby, Liza Crihfield 576
Emmerson, John K. 354
Gayn, Mark 269
Grew, Joseph C. 690
Griffis, William Elliot 114, 190, 197, 358, 361
Harris, Townsend 676
Hearn, Lafcadio 190, 361
Janes, Leroy Lansing 358
MacArthur, Douglas 278, 281-282, 356
Morse, Edward S. 361
Murray, David 197
Okimoto, Daniel I. 398
Oppler, Alfred C. 277
Passin, Herbert 359
Perry, Matthew C. 673
physicians (Meiji period) 597
Richie, Donald 71
Statler, Oliver 73
Vining, Elizabeth Gray 362
Whitney, Clara A. N. 363
Williams, Justin, Sr. 281
see also Allied occupation of Japan, (1945-52), and Westerners in Japan
Ami group of painters 1239
Amitābha Buddha
depicted in Buddhist painting 1244
Amulets
used to exorcise the spirits 506
Ananaikyō (New Religion) 513
see also New Religions
Anarchists
Kanno Suga 290
Kōtoku Shūsui 288, 337
Ancestor worship 485, 505
Reiyūkai practice 509
Ancestors
honoured in Buddhist observances 500
moral authority 505
Anchiku region (Nagano Prefecture)
leisure time among its residents 1460
And then (Natsume Sōseki)
psychoanalytical study 1112
synopses and analyses 1112, 1117
Andō Hiroshige
life and works 1256
ukiyo-e print series of Edo
(reproductions) 1256

ukiyo-e print series of the Tōkaidō
highway (reproductions) 1265
ukiyo-e prints of birds and flowers
1257
'Anecdotal literature' see Setsuwa
bungaku ('tale literature')
Anecdotes about the samurai 529
Anglo-Japanese alliance (1902-23) 666, 669-670
Anglo-Japanese commercial treaty
(1857-58) 658
Anglo-Japanese Convention (1854-55)
658
Animals
depicted in art (dictionary) 1567
depicted in netsuke 1291
depicted in sculpture 108
encyclopaedic and almanac-type
information about 1560-1561
folk tales about 1185-1187
Katsushika Hokusai's sketches
(reproductions) 1258
sumi-e techniques for painting 1254
see also Fauna
Annual celebrations
depicted in classical literature 1566
Annual events
encyclopaedic and almanac-type
information about 1551, 1557, 1561, 1568
Annual surveys see Yearbooks and
annual surveys
Ansei commercial treaties (1858) 658, 675
Anthologies (of readings, etc.)
contemporary society and political
economy 809
culture and behaviour 591
drama 1000, 1179
folk legends 1184
folk tales 1185, 1187-1188
jisei ('death poems') 1138
Kyōto School of Philosophy (essays)
521
labour market 930
life, past and present 1-2, 18
literature 1000
modern history and culture 119
naval action in World War II 688
noh plays 1175, 1181
poetry 1000, 1134, 1138, 1145, 1151, 1156-1157, 1159
poetry and prose in Chinese 1010

Anthologies (of readings, etc.) *continued*
  political and economic institutions 623
  religious life and practice 461
  short stories 1051, 1056-1057, 1071,
    1083, 1088, 1098, 1106
  society and education 961
  sources of Japanese tradition 33
  varieties of writing styles 404
Anthropomorphic imagery
  genesis 1289
Anti-Christian tracts 166
Anti-Comintern Pact (1936) 346, 708
Anti-Japanese legislation in the United
  States 384, 392, 402, 660
Anti-monopoly law
  bibliography 1582
  licensing agreements under 773-774
Anti-monopoly policy
  relaxation and modification 846
Antiques
  dolls 1215, 1363
  furniture 1340
  guidebook 1215
  shops (directories) 1215, 1340
Antitrust 774, 776
  environment 899
  industrial policy and 783
  zaibatsu dissolution 267, 270, 274
Anti-war activism
  during the Vietnam War 727
Anya kōro (Shiga Naoya)
  translation 1093
Anzai Fuyue
  poetry 1141
Aoki Shigeru
  painting 1235
Aomori Prefecture
  Tsugaru Peninsula 1116
  see also Tōhoku region
Aoneko (Hagiwara Sakutarō)
  translation 1136
Aoyama San'u
  calligraphy 1231
Apartments
  housewives in suburban Tokyo and
    577
Applied research
  evaluation 987
Apprenticeship 39
Arab-Israeli War (1973)
  Japanese diplomatic response to 758
Arai Hakuseki
  autobiography 298

  role in Tokugawa politics 177
  Tokugawa period Confucian
    historiography and 526
Arai Ryōichirō
  biography 297
Arakawa Hiroshi
  baseball coach to Oh Sadaharu 338
Arakawa Ward (Tokyo)
  family patterns and juvenile
    delinquency 571
Arbitration
  Kamakura period 148
  used in settling contractual disputes
    779
  used in settling environmental disputes
    775
Archaeology 1217
  excavations 101, 143
  haniwa 106, 108
  holdings of the Tokyo National
    Museum 1473
  museums (guidebook) 1475
  Nara Basin sites 102
  photographs 103-108, 143, 284, 1214,
    1217, 1473
  preservation of sites 109
  Ryūkyū Islands 284
Archery
  equipment (Kofun period) 105
  kyūjutsu (martial art) 1443
  Shintō dimensions 519
  Zen Buddhist dimensions 1196
Architects
  Ashihara Yoshinobu 1298
  biographical dictionaries 369, 1567
  Isozaki Arata 1298-1299, 1320
  Kikutake Kiyonari 1298
  Kurokawa Noriaki 1298
  Maekawa Kunio 1298
  Maki Fumihiko 1298
  Sakakura Junzō 1298
  Shinohara Kazuo 1320
  Tange Kenzō 1298, 1313
  Wright, Frank Lloyd 1320
  Yokoyama Kimio 1298
Architecture 1220
  16th century 153
  1950s-1960s 1324
  1960s-1980s 1297, 1321
  aesthetic qualities (photographs) 1198
  bibliographies 1212, 1314
  castles 1306-1307, 1314, 1317
  dictionary 1567

encyclopaedic and almanac-type
  information about 1552, 1556, 1568
evolution (1868-1968) 1209
floor plans 1297, 1299-1300, 1321,
  1324
guidebook 81
historical relationship with furnishings
  1342
history 1211-1212, 1314, 1320, 1322
Hōryūji temple 1208
Ise Shrine 1323, 1325
Japonization of world 1321
joinery and joints 1318
Katsura Detached Palace 1305, 1315
Katsushika Hokusai's sketches
  (reproductions) 1258
kura ('storehouses') 1311
minka (traditional-style houses) 1301,
  1303, 1312
'New Japan Style' (postwar) 1298
neighbourhoods of Kyōto 77
periodicals 1505
philosophical concepts 1302
principles 1297, 1300
Pure Land (Jōdo) Buddhist temples
  1192
regional styles and variations 1301,
  1303, 1311-1312
roofs 1302, 1322
ryōkan (inns) 96
Shintō shrines 518, 1323, 1325
shoin-style 140, 1307
space 1300, 1302, 1304-1305, 1308,
  1323, 1326
sukiya style 1309-1310
surroundings for the tea ceremony
  1467, 1471-1472
temples 131, 143, 1192, 1206, 1208,
  1212, 1316, 1322
Tōdaiji temple 1206
Tokyo 22
Tōshōgu Shrine (Nikkō) 1315
traditional houses 1300
Western influence 1297, 1319-1320
Zen Buddhist dimensions 1196
see also Photographs (architecture)
Archives
architecture (post-1945) 81
Japan-related sources in the USA
  (guidebook) 1562
Japan-related sources in Washington,
  DC (guidebook) 1562
Arishima Takeo

Aru onna 1046
Arita ware (ceramics) see Imari ware
  (ceramics), Kakiemon ware
  (ceramics), and Nabeshima ware
  (ceramics)
Ariwara no Narihira
poetry 1148
Ariyoshi Sawako
novel 1047
short stories 1106
Armed forces
air force (World War II) 688-689
armament programmes 704
kamikaze pilots 293, 686, 688, 691,
  700, 715
rearmament 271, 354, 754, 759
Self-Defence Forces 282, 754, 759
see also Army, History (military),
  Military, Military leaders, Navy,
  Sino-Japanese War of 1894-95,
  Sino-Japanese War of 1937-45,
  Warships, Weapons, World War I,
  and World War II (Pacific Theatre)
Armour
depicted in exhibition catalogues 1218,
  1227
illustrations 1566
samurai 156, 1218
used in the kabuki theatre 1352
yoroi kumi-uchi (martial art) 1443
Arms
control measures (post-1945) 762
exports 763
production (1980s) 763
see also Weapons
Army
abortive coup d'état (26 February
  1936) 209, 238, 245, 342, 348
activities in North China (1937-41)
  702
aircraft (guidebook) 689
developed with European assistance
  229
foreign policy-making role (1930s)
  654, 682
general staff 229, 654
growth of factions 245
High Command (World War II) 692
images of war with the USA 651
intervention in politics (1930s) 209,
  679
Kwantung Army 209, 342, 684-685,
  692, 702

Army *continued*
  military-civilian rift over Japan's
    China policy (1920s) 661
  mobilisation of rural support 243
  modernised by Yamagata Aritomo 303
  moral education and socialisation
    processes 595, 961
  participation in the 1941 policy
    conferences 693
  soldiers in the Philippines 341, 1091
  strengthened by Hirota Kōki 346
Army generals
  Honjō Shigeru 209
  Ishiwara Kanji 342
  MacArthur, Douglas 278, 281-282,
    356
  Nogi Maresuke 292
Army officers
  life-course of former 542
Arrowroot (Tanizaki Junichirō)
  translation 1102
Art
  book illustrations (history) 1477
  collection of Kimiko and John Powers
    (exhibition catalogue) 1214
  depiction of history 155
  depiction of water 3
  depiction of wildlife 58, 63
  dictionary 1567
  encyclopaedic and almanac-type
    information about 1552, 1556,
    1567-1568
  evolution (1868-1968) 1209
  geisha as 'curators of tradition and art'
    576
  introductory works and survey
    histories 32, 37, 1197, 1205, 1211,
    1220, 1223, 1226
  modern currents 1238
  periodicals 1489, 1496, 1535, 1543
  'reflections on art and society' (essays)
    1200
  Shintō arts (exhibition catalogue) 1199
  Western influence 1209, 1235, 1238,
    1243
  see also Artists, Bambooware,
    Bronzes, Buddhist art, Calligraphy,
    Ceramics, Cloisonné, Drawings,
    Exhibition catalogues, Fans, Folk
    art, Furniture, Ink painting
    (*suibokuga*), Ink painting (*sumi-e*),
    Inrō, Interior decoration,
    Lacquerware and lacquerwork,
    Masks, Metalwork, Murals,
    Museums, Netsuke, Painting,
    Photographs (art), Pottery, Rituals
    (ritual objects), Screens, Scrolls,
    Sculpture, Swords (sword guards),
    Textiles, Ukiyo-e paintings,
    Ukiyo-e prints, Woodblock prints,
    and Woodblock prints
    (reproductions)
Art collecting
  cloisonné 1361
  dolls 1363
  inrō 1360
  netsuke 1288, 1360
  periodicals 1489, 1535
  suiseki (stones) 1362
  swords 1375
  woodblock prints 1271-1272, 1576
Art collections
  Abby Aldrich Rockefeller Collection
    (ukiyo-e prints) 1257
  Bauer Collection (sword-fittings) 1373
  James A. Michener Collection
    (ukiyo-e prints) 1268
  Kimiko and John Powers Collection
    1214
  Nomura Collection (*kosode* textiles)
    1353
  Sansō Collection (paintings) 1246
  Walter A. Compton Collection (art
    swords) 1373
  see also Museums
Art galleries
  marketing of art 1376
Artificial intelligence
  research and development 982
  status, research, and focus 994
  traditional writing system and 997
Artisans *see* Craftsmen and craftswomen
Artists
  biographical dictionaries 364, 368-369,
    1567
  comic books produced by 1480
  patronage (1955-80) 1376
  signatures (handbook) 1571
  social position 1200
  techniques and styles (post-1945) 1203
Arts
  interrelationship with religion 463
  legends illustrated in 1560
  overview 6
  social context and organisation
    (1955-80) 1376

Aru onna (Arishima Takeo)
  translation 1046
Asahi Shimbun (newspaper)
  articles and editorials (translations and synopses) 1546-1547
  articles on US-Japanese relations 643
  news reporting 1484
  political character 1485
Asai Chū
  painting 1235
Asakura Setsu
  film-making activities 1423
ASEAN *see* Association of Southeast Asian Nations (ASEAN)
Ashihara Yoshinobu
  architectural work 1298
Ashikaga Takauji
  biographical sketch 295
  political activities 159
Ashikaga Yoshimitsu
  biographical sketch 295
  social change and patronage under 140
Ashio Copper Mine
  pollution caused by 312, 957
Asian Americans *see* Japanese Americans
Asian Development Bank
  Japanese involvement 756
Asiatic Society of Japan
  activities (news) 1543
  history 1543
Aspect 434
  in colloquial Japanese 410
Assassinations
  conspiracy against the Meiji Emperor 337, 1122
  political 245, 290
  practiced by the *ninja* 1445
  see also February 26, 1936 Incident
Association for Asian Studies activities (news) 1525
Association of Southeast Asian Nations (ASEAN)
  linkages among Japan, the USA, and 741
  relations with Japan 743, 810, 897
Associations
  professional 980
  trade 899
Astrology
  historical development 151, 157
Astronomy
  historical development 151, 157, 187

Tokugawa period 167
Asukadera (temple)
  architecture 1322
Asukata Ichio
  dilemmas of socialist leadership 636
Ataka (*sōgō shōsha*)
  evolution, role, and organisation 914
Atlases
  cultural 113
  nationwide 53-54
  Tokyo and environs 56, 75
Atomic bomb
  continuing legacy 34
  development 260-263
  see also Hiroshima, and Nagasaki
Atomic bomb literature 1058, 1088, 1173
Atomic energy
  government report (annual) 829
  policy (development) 846
  US-Japanese co-operation 847
  see also Nuclear energy
Atsumori (ballad-drama)
  translation 1169
Atsumori (Zeami Motokiyo)
  translation 1181
Attitudes
  affected by socio-economic trends (1945-1960s) 595
  Americans towards Japan (1940s-1980s) 731
  Bank of Japan 856
  blue-collar workers 918
  burakumin 373-374
  consumer 841, 891
  farmers 834
  police 570
  political 549, 621
  popular 537
  towards authority 373
  towards business negotiations 911
  towards death 598, 600
  towards environmental pollution 312, 957-959
  towards financial liberalisation 856
  towards health 600
  towards illness 588, 598, 600
  towards international problems 581
  towards law 782
  towards nature 1332
  towards Okinawa 285
  towards rearmament 354
  towards research and development 922
  towards the elderly 540

Attitudes *continued*
  towards the human body 598, 600
  towards work and leisure 1460
  women 581
Attu *see* Aleutian Islands (Alaska)
Audiences
  interaction with actors (history) 1410
  kabuki theatre 1398, 1400, 1410
  movie 1414, 1421
  noh theatre 1410
Audits
  independent corporate 852
  state audit system 625
Australia
  hostile attitudes towards Japan (1910s)
    666
  implications of Japanese economic
    growth for 814
  imports of coal from 885
  involvement in the Allied occupation
    of Japan (1945-52) 266
  involvement in World War II 711
  Japanese studies 1554, 1559
  migration to 751
  pressure on Japan to eliminate trade
    restrictions 833
  trade and commerce with Japan 723,
    745, 751
  see also Foreign relations with
    Australia
Authenticity
  concern in literature for 1130
Authority
  ancestors 505
  burakumin attitudes towards 373
  exercised before 1700 AD 138
  factories 920
  family 564
  individuals and 614
  industry 838
  public prosecutors 777
  village 531
Autobiographical novels
  analysis of *shishōsetsu* ('I-novels')
    1113
  Ie (Shimazaki Tōson) 1096
  Rōmaji nikki (Ishikawa Takuboku)
    1140
  Tsugaru (Dazai Osamu) 1116
  writings of Shiga Naoya 1125
Autobiographical poetry
  Takamura Kōtarō 1158
Autobiographies and memoirs

Akizuki Tatsuichirō 258
Alcock, Rutherford 349
Allen, George Cyril 350
Arai Hakuseki 298
Baelz, Erwin von 351
Barrett, Timothy 1358
Cohen, Theodore 267
Emmerson, John K. 354
Fraser, Mary Crawford 355
Fujiwara Michitsuna no haha 1013
Fukuoka Masanobu 830
Fukuzawa Yukichi 302
Funakoshi Gichin 1446
Gayn, Mark 269
Griffis, William Elliot 114
Guillain, Robert 691
Honjō Shigeru 209
Houston, Jeanne Wakatsuki 391
Inoue Yasushi 327
Ishimoto Shizue 328
Kamata Satoshi 924
Katō Shizue 328
Kido Kōin 307
Kikuchi, Charles 393
Kotsuji, Abraham 4
Kurosawa Akira 329
Kuroyanagi Tetsuko 330
Lady Daibu 1142
Lady Nijō 310
Lawson, Ted W. 696
Masaoka, Mike 395
Masatoshi 1291
Mishima Yukio 1079
Mitford, Algernon Bertram 357
Morita Akio 332
Mutsu Munemitsu 668
Nagai Takashi 258
Nagatsuka Ryūji 700
Nakano, Takeo Uyo 383
naval officers (World War II) 688
Oh Sadaharu 338
Ōhira Masayoshi 339
Okimoto, Daniel I. 398
Onoda Hiroo 341
Oppler, Alfred C. 277
Passin, Herbert 359
Reischauer, Edwin O. 360
Reischauer, Haru Matsukata 297
Shigemitsu Mamoru 708
Smith, Richard Gordon 72
Sone, Monica 399
Sueno Akira 845
Sugimoto, Etsu Inagaki 313

716

Suzuki, Daisetz Teitaro 316
Tanaka Michiko 400
Tayama Katai 1105
Toyoda Eiji 347
Vining, Elizabeth Gray 362
Wakatsuki, Jeanne 391
Whitney, Clara A. N. 363
widows of Hiroshima atomic bomb
    victims 259
Williams, Justin, Sr. 281
women activists (prewar) 290
women in World War II 583
Yoshida Mitsuru 716
Yoshida Shigeru 282
see also Diaries
Automation 8
flexible 986
role of invention and innovation in 985
Automobile industry 45, 883
blue-collar workers 918-919, 924
collaboration between Japanese and
    Western companies 912
collective bargaining 948
comprehensive examination 870
co-operation among Japanese and US
    companies 911
Honda Motor Company 344, 882
industrial policy and 876, 879
introduction of robotics 986
Mazda Motor Corporation 809
multinationalisation 948
Nissan Motor Company 871, 874, 942
penetration of the US market 874
quality control circles 919
targeted as a 'strategic industry' 873
technology 344, 347
technology and management at Nissan
    and Toyota 871
Toyota Motor Corporation 347, 547,
    871, 912, 919, 924, 926, 934-936
working conditions (assembly line) 924
Automobiles
congestion caused by 957
legal treatment of accidents 786
limitations on exports 892
Autumn wind (Natsume Sōseki)
synopsis and analysis 1117
Avant-garde theatre 26
Aviation
research institutes and programmes
    980
Ayukawa Nobuo
poetry 1143

Azaleas
growth and cultivation 59
Azuchi Castle 1306, 1317
wall paintings 135

B
Baelz, Erwin von
diary 351
medical activities 351, 597
Bajutsu (martial art) 1443
Bakufu (shogunate)
evolution of the term 146
historic role 146
Kamakura period 141, 146-149, 154,
    160
Muromachi period 137, 140-141, 146,
    160
Tokugawa period 139, 146, 163, 177,
    185-186, 289, 298, 349
Balance of payments 823
annual statistics 819, 824
current-account surpluses 798, 800,
    860, 884
during the 1970s 851
efforts towards a positive 815
Sterling payments agreements 745
trends (1980s) 820
Ballad-drama see Kōwaka
    (ballad-drama)
Bamboo
cultural, aesthetic, and technical
    aspects 1357
depicted in textile patterns 1344
growth and cultivation 64, 1357
photographs 64, 1357
sumi-e techniques for painting 1247,
    1257
used in gardens 1337, 1357
Bambooware
folk art 1193, 1213
Okinawan 1222
photographs 1193, 1213, 1222, 1357,
    1366
Banditry
13th century 147
Banking 217, 823, 861
annual statistics 819, 825-827
bibliography 1614
element of the industrial system 878
law 781, 783, 1582
managerial approaches (Japanese
    subsidiaries in Europe) 949
system 805, 811, 851, 861-862, 865

Banks
  architecture (post-1945) 81, 1299
  Asian Development Bank 756
  Bank of Japan 856, 861-862, 864, 866
  Bank of Yokohama 942
  commercial 864
  co-operation with corporations 836
  ethnographic study 543
  finance and 901
  foreign (in Japan) 861-862
  foreign business 851, 861
  impact of the government 868
  impact on international capital flows
    909
  long-term credit 862, 864
  personnel practices 809, 942
  regional 862
  rural 806
  services 901
Baoshan steel complex (Shanghai,
    China)
  Sino-Japanese construction 735
Bar talk 454
Bargaining style of businessmen 893
Baseball 338, 1456
Baseball players
  Oh Sadaharu 338
Bashō *see* Matsuo Bashō
Bashō school
  poetry 1137, 1150
Baskets and basketry
  folk art 1193, 1213
  Okinawan 1222
  photographs 1193, 1213, 1222, 1366
Bassui-*zenji* (Rinzai Zen master)
  teachings 478
Bath (*furo*)
  element of interior design 1326
  encyclopaedic and almanac-type
    information about 1552-1553, 1556
  overview (illustrated) 1457
Bathing 1457
  at *ryōkan* (inns) 96, 1457
  use of water (photo-essay) 3
  Victorian British writings about 68
  see also Hot springs (*onsen*)
Battlefield epithets
  racist stereotypes 686
Battleships *see* Warships
Battō-jutsu (martial art) 1444
Bauer Collection
  sword-fittings and associated
    metalwork 1373

Bauxite
  quest for dependable supplies 913
Bears 63
Beato, Felix
  photographs 1278
Beauty
  Hamada Shōji's views 331
  Yanagi Sōetsu's conception 1228
  see also Aesthetics
Beauty and sadness (Kawabata
    Yasunari)
  translation 1063
Beef
  increased US exports to Japan 892
  politics, production, marketing, and
    trade 833
Before the dawn (Shimazaki Tōson)
  synopsis and analysis 1117
  translation 1094
Behaviour 585
  abnormal forms 589
  blue-collar workers 918
  business world 894, 901, 916
  cultural context 439, 591
  entrepreneurial 816
  group 539
  negotiating 645, 893
  patterns 31, 592, 618, 622
  political 557, 628
  proper conduct of love affairs (Heian
    period) 1039
  protagonists of Natsume Sōseki's
    novels 1112
  relationship to juvenile delinquency
    571
  samurai 529
  social 916
  symbolic aspects 535
Beheiren anti-war movement (1965-74)
  727
Bells
  at the Tōdaiji temple 1206
  prehistoric 104
Belongingness
  as a factor influencing behaviour 592
Benten Kōzō (Kawatake Mokuami)
  translation 1407
Betrothal
  in an agricultural village 560
Betsuyaku Minoru
  plays 1173, 1179
Biblical studies
  post-1945 497

Bibliographies 1513, 1580, 1589,
    1607-1608
  agriculture 1592, 1594
  Allied occupation of Japan (1945-52)
    1583, 1599, 1613-1614
  architecture 1212, 1314
  art 1212
  artists 369
  banking 1614
  bunraku theatre 1588, 1603
  children's books 1596
  Christianity in Japan 497, 1587
  climate 1592
  Constitution 1582, 1613
  corporate world 1590
  doctoral dissertations 1607
  economic development (1868-1941)
    218, 1614
  economic development (post-1945)
    1581, 1590, 1592, 1594, 1614
  economic planning 1594, 1600, 1614
  education 1610
  employment 1590, 1614
  environment 1592
  essays 1588
  finance 1581, 1594, 1600, 1614
  folk literature 1577
  foreign policy (1868-1941) 1599
  foreign relations (history) 1583, 1599
  foreign relations with Southeast Asia
    727
  foreign relations with the United
    States 1575, 1600
  geography 1592
  government publications 1593, 1602
  haiku poetry 1162, 1588, 1605
  Hirohito (emperor) 334
  history 118, 126, 367, 1555, 1575,
    1583, 1592, 1614
  industry 1581, 1590, 1592, 1594, 1600,
    1614
  Japan (area studies) 1513, 1580, 1589,
    1607-1608
  Japanese Americans 1487, 1579, 1598,
    1607
  kabuki theatre 1588, 1603, 1615
  Kurosawa Akira (film director) 1425,
    1585
  Kuroshio Current 47
  kyōgen 1603
  labour 1594
  labour-management relations 1581,
    1590, 1614

  language and linguistics 1529, 1615
  law 778, 1582
  literature 1529, 1597, 1615
  literature in translation 1521, 1588,
    1597
  management 1581, 1590, 1594, 1614
  Mizoguchi Kenji (film director) 1578
  music 1383, 1611
  netsuke 1288
  New Religions 1584
  newspapers published in Japan 1601
  noh plays 1409, 1588, 1603, 1615
  novels 1588, 1597, 1615
  Okinawa 1591
  old age 1595
  periodicals published in Japan 1601
  plays 1588, 1603, 1615
  poetry 1156, 1588, 1605, 1615
  population and demography 371,
    1592, 1594
  productivity 1581, 1590, 1600
  reference works 1589
  religion 460, 1584, 1606, 1612
  Ryūkyū Islands 1591
  Shintō 1606
  short stories 1588, 1597
  social history of modern Japanese
    science 992
  Sōka Gakkai 1584
  swords 1375
  technology 1581, 1594
  trade and commerce 727, 1575, 1581,
    1590, 1594, 1600, 1614
  women 1590, 1595
  woodblock prints 1271, 1576
  World War II (Pacific Theatre) 1583,
    1591, 1609, 1614
  writings of D. T. Suzuki 316
  Zen Buddhism 1612
  see also Discographies, and
    Filmographies
Bill discount market 854
Biographical dictionaries 1574
  architects 369, 1567
  artists 364, 368-369, 1567
  businessmen 1574
  calligraphers 369
  Diet members 366
  government officials 366, 1574
  historical figures 367, 1555
  Japanese Americans 1563
  kabuki actors and playwrights 1564
  lacquer artists 368-369, 1567

Biographical dictionaries *continued*
  novelists 365
  metalwork artists 369
  painters 368-369, 1567
  photographers 364
  poets 365
  potters 368-369, 1567
  print-makers 364, 368-369, 1567
  sculptors 368-369
  swordsmiths 369
  writers 365
Biographical sketches
  Abe Isoo 288
  Andō Hiroshige 1256
  architects 1321
  artists (post-1945) 1203
  business leaders 823
  ceramic artists (20th century) 1285
  Chikamatsu Monzaemon 295
  Communist leaders 192
  eminent historical figures 295
  Fujiwara no Michinaga 295
  gozan bungaku poets 1152
  high-ranking army officers 692
  Higuchi Ichiyō 291
  Hōjō Masako 295
  Hosokawa Yūsai 291
  Ihara Saikaku 295
  Ikkyū Sōjun 291, 1003, 1139
  Isozaki Arata 1299
  Jien 130
  Kagawa Toyohiko 288
  Kanagaki Robun 291
  Kanō Eitoku 1252
  Kanō Mitsunobu 1252
  Kanō Shōei 1252
  Kanō Sōshū 1252
  Katsushika Hokusai 1260
  Kawabata Yasunari 295
  Kawakami Hajime 292
  Kinoshita Naoe 288
  Kitagawa Utamaro 1262
  Kitamura Tōkoku 288
  Kōtoku Shūsui 288
  Kūkai 295, 482
  Kurosawa Akira 1585
  lacquerwork artists 1370
  Masamune Hakuchō 292
  Masaoka Shiki 291
  Matsuo Bashō 295
  Mishima Yukio 292
  Mizoguchi Kenji 1578
  Mori Ōgai 292

Murasaki Shikibu 295, 1604
  Nakae Chōmin 292
  Nogi Maresuke 292
  Nomura Shōjirō 1353
  Ōkubo Toshimichi 289, 295
  Ozu Yasujirō 1415-1416
  painters (Meiji and Taishō periods) 1251
  poets 1141, 1143, 1145, 1151-1153, 1156-1157, 1159
  print-makers (post-1945) 364
  Rai Sanyō 295
  Sakamoto Ryōma 295
  Sei Shōnagon 295
  Sen no Rikyū 295
  Shikitei Sanba 1038
  Shinran 295
  Tabata Shinobu 288
  Takeda Shingen 295
  Tamenaga Shunsui 291
  Tanuma Okitsugu 295
  Uchimura Kanzō 288
  Ueda Akinari 1030-1031
  Yanaihara Tadao 288
  Zeami Motokiyo 291
Biographies
  Abe Masahiro 289
  Akutagawa Ryūnosuke 289, 1132
  Amakusa Shirō 293
  Arai Hakuseki 177
  Arai Ryōichirō 297
  Dazai Osamu 1116, 1119
  Fujiwara ministers of state 1017
  Fujiwara no Michinaga 1017, 1021
  Fukuchi Gen'ichirō 305
  Fukuda Tsuneari 239
  Futabatei Shimei 1124
  Griffis, William Elliot 358, 361
  Hamada Shōji 331
  Hara Kei 224, 296
  Hashimoto Sanai 289
  Hearn, Lafcadio 361
  Hirohito (emperor) 334
  Hirota Kōki 346
  Honda Sōichirō 344
  Honda Toshiaki 173
  Ikeda Mitsumasa 289
  Inukai Tsuyoshi 296
  Ishibashi Tanzan 336, 650
  Ishiwara Kanji 342
  Itō Hirobumi 296
  Ito Michio 322
  Itō Miyoji 289

Janes, Leroy Lansing 358
Kawakami Hajime 318
Kawakami Tōgai 239
Kawamata Katsuji 874
Kayahara Kazan 289
Kido Kōin 289
Kinoshita Yūji 1144
Kishida Kunio 1178
Kita Ikki 348
Kobayashi Hideo 239
Kōda Rohan 1069
Konoe Atsumaro 650
Konoe Fumimaro 340
Kōtoku Shūsui 337
Kusaka Genzui 171
Kusunoki Masashige 293
MacArthur, Douglas 356
Makiguchi Tsunesaburō 319
Masaoka Shiki 239, 1161
Masuda Tetsuo 874
Matsudaira Sadanobu 177
Matsukata Masayoshi 297
Matsuo Bashō 1167
middle-aged residents of Ōsaka and
    Kōbe 541
Minamoto no Yoshitsune 293, 1020
Minobe Tatsukichi 220
Mishima Yukio 335
Mizoguchi Kenji 1422
Mori Arinori 304
Mori Ōgai 1110, 1121
Morse, Edward S. 361
Motoori Norinaga 309
Mutsu Munemitsu 289
Nagai Kafū 345
Nagai Ryūtarō 289
Naitō Konan 650
Natsume Sōseki 239, 1133
Nishida Kitarō 239
Noguchi Hideyo 343
Norman, E. H. 226
Ōkubo Toshimichi 289, 306
Ōkuma Shigenobu 296, 308
Ōkura Nagatsune 289
Ōshio Heihachirō 289, 293
Ōtomo no Yakamochi 301
Ozaki Hotsumi 228
Ozu Yasujirō 1427
pacifists (19th-20th centuries) 288
political leaders (19th-20th centuries)
    296
Rodrigues, João 352
Saigō Takamori 293

Saionji Kinmochi 296, 323
Saitō Mokichi 325
Shimazaki Tōson 239
Shimazu Nariakira 289
Sugawara no Michizane 293, 300
Suzuki Shinichi 326
Takasugi Shinsaku 171
Tanaka Giichi 333
Tanaka Shōzō 312
Tōgō Heihachirō 320
Toguri, Iva 387
Tōjō Hideki 321
Tokugawa Ieyasu 314
Tokugawa Nariaki 289
Tokugawa Tsunayoshi 289
Tokutomi Sohō 311
Toyotomi Hideyoshi 299
tragic heroes in history (4th-20th
    centuries) 293
Ts'ao Ju-lin 650
Ueda Akinari 315
Ugaki Kazushige 650
Uragami Gyokudō 1230
Utsunomiya Haruko 573
Willis, William 353
Yamagata Aritomo 303
Yamamoto Isoroku 317
Yoshida Shigeru 324
Yoshida Shōin 171
Zeami Motokiyo 1172
see also Autobiographies and
    memoirs, Biographical dictionaries,
    and Biographical sketches
Biology
    historical development 187
    language textbook for reading
        materials in 437
Biotechnology
    industry 881
    research and development 984
    research institutes and programmes 980
    US-Japan scientific relationship 998
Bird, Isabella 66, 190
'Bird and flower' (*kachō*) painting
    tradition 1257
'Bird and flower' (*kachō*) prints by
    Katsushika Hokusai 1260
Birds
    cranes 58, 63
    crows (photographs) 1275
    depicted in netsuke 1291
    depicted in ukiyo-e prints by Andō
        Hiroshige 1257

Birds *continued*
  design motif of family crests and
    textile patterns 1191, 1344
  encyclopaedic and almanac-type
    information about 1551, 1556, 1561
  folk tales about 1185
  guidebooks 65
  origami figures 1364, 1367
  sumi-e techniques for painting 1247,
    1254
Birth
  birth control 328, 370-371
  maternity leave 575
  taboos and rituals 500
  see also Infanticide
Biruma no tategoto (Takeyama Michio)
  translation 1097
Biwa (lute) 1383
  music 1382
Bizen *han*
  history 138, 168
  Ikeda Mitsumasa (daimyō) 289
Bizen Province
  history 138
Bizen ware (ceramics) 1283, 1286
Black rain (Ibuse Masuji)
  literary analysis 1127
  quest for identity in 1115
  translation 1058
Blue cat (Hagiwara Sakutarō)
  translation 1136
Bodhidharma 483
Bohai Sea (China)
  Sino-Japanese petroleum
    development projects 735
Bokutō kitan (Nagai Kafū)
  translation 345
Bon celebrations 500
Bond markets 809, 823, 854, 857-858,
    862
Bonds
  government 863
Bonin Islands (Ogasawara Shotō)
  Perry expedition's visit 673
Bonkei (miniature landscapes)
  instruction manual 1330
Bonsai
  Chinese 1336
  combined with *suiseki* (stones) 1362
  history 1328
  instruction manuals 1328, 1336
  photographs 1328, 1330, 1336, 1362
  used in *bonkei* 1330

Bookbinding and book repair
  instructional manual 1479
Books
  comic books 1480
  depicting the USA as Japan's enemy
    651
  frontispiece prints in Meiji period
    novels 1269
  historical development and structure
    1479
  illustrations 1260-1261, 1477-1478
  see also Illustrated books, and Printing
Books (woodblock-printed) 1477-1478,
    1481
  holdings of the Chester Beatty Library
    1263
  produced by Suzuki Harunobu 1261
  theme of the supernatural in 1189
  Tokugawa period (exhibition
    catalogue) 1227
Botan kuroku (Masaoka Shiki)
  translation 1149
Botany
  introduced as a science 596
Botchan (Natsume Sōseki)
  literary analyses 1112, 1117, 1127
  psychoanalytical study 1112
  translation 1084
Bowls
  at the Tōdaiji temple 1206
  Kutani ware (photographs) 1284
  painted porcelain 1285
  tea ceremony 1228, 1467-1469,
    1471-1472
  see also Ceramics
Bowring, John
  British policy towards Japan (1850s)
    658
Box man (Abe Kōbō)
  translation 1041
Boxes
  holding tea ceremony utensils 1468
  owned by the Tokugawa shōguns
    (exhibition catalogue) 1219
  painted porcelain 1285
  see also Inrō (compartmentalised
    containers)
Boys' Festival (Tango no sekku) 501
Brand preferences 841
Bravery
  as a samurai value 529
Brazil
  images of Japan and the Japanese 898

investment in 898
place in Japan's foreign economic
strategy 898
relations with Japan 743, 897
Bribery
business 844
Bridges
across Tokyo Bay 640
British Columbia (Canada)
Japanese Canadians 382-383, 385
Japanese immigration 655
British Commonwealth Occupation
Force in Japan (1940s) 266
Britten, Benjamin
noh theatre's influence on his music
1393
Broadcast Law
text (excerpts) 1486
Broadcasting
development (1920s-1970s) 1482, 1486
radio 221, 387, 703, 1482, 1486
satellite 955
stations (directory) 1483
structure and activities 1482
television 1482, 1486
Brocades
at the Shōsōin 1194
Broken commandment (Shimazaki
Tōson)
literary analyses 1002, 1117, 1129
translation 1095
Broker-dealers
regulation 781
Bronzes
at the Tokyo National Museum 1473
colossal sculpture of Buddha 1290
depicting creatures of nature 1221
implements 104-106
Brooklyn Museum (Brooklyn, New
York)
ukiyo-e prints 1256
Brooms
craftsmanship 1369
Brushes
craftsmanship 1369
photographs 1357, 1366, 1369
Buddha
Amitābha Buddha 1244
colossal bronze sculpture 1290
Buddhism 464-465, 468, 485, 1217
ancestor worship 485, 505
Bon celebration 500
brief introductions 462-463

Buddhist writers (intellectual and
religious assumptions) 1007
co-existence with Christianity 498
history 484
idea of beauty 1228
influence on Chikamatsu
Monzaemon's plays 1399
influence on Shintō 1289
influence on Tokugawa period values
459
introduction into Japan 458, 484
introductory survey 460, 475
medieval literature and 1007
music 1380, 1382-1383
myths and stories derived from 1186
Nara period 458
nationalism and 517
notion of 'pure existence' 524
paradigm change 464
periodicals 1499, 1520, 1523, 1534
prints on Buddhist themes 1576
readings about 33, 461
relationship with portrait sculpture
1292
relationship with Shintō 519
relationship with the state (16th
century) 145
religious organisations (19th century)
212
scrolls illustrating sutras 1245
shōmyō (Buddhist chanting) 1382
stories about preachers 1017
supernatural beings in 499
survey of doctrines 475
terminology (dictionary) 415
see also Jōdo Buddhism, Nichiren
Buddhism, Religious leaders,
Religious practices, Religious texts,
Shin Buddhism, Shingon Buddhism,
Temples, Tendai Buddhism, and
Zen Buddhism
Buddhist art 1195
architecture (temples) 1192, 1208,
1212, 1316, 1322
at the Byōdōin temple 1192
at the Chūsonji temple 1192
at the Daitokuji temple 1190
at the Hōryūji temple 1208
at the Shōsōin 1194
at the Tōdaiji temple 1206, 1290
calligraphy 1232, 1249
esoteric Buddhism 1216, 1237
holdings of the Powers Collection 1214

Buddhist art *continued*
 Pure Land (Jōdo) Buddhist painting
  1244
 sculpture 1290, 1292-1293, 1295-1296,
  1316
 Zen Buddhist painting 1232, 1246
 Zen-influenced ink painting 1196,
  1239
 see also Photographs (Buddhist art)
Buddhist literature
 Konjaku monogatari 1029, 1032, 1037
 medieval 1007
 Uji shūi monogatari 1022, 1029
Buddhists
 novels about 1080, 1097
 tales about 1017, 1022, 1028-1029,
  1032
Budgets
 budgetary policy 909
 budgetary system 625
 defence 764
 foreign aid 746
 general account 863
 government 39, 608, 626
Budō ('martial ways')
 introductory studies 1442, 1444
Bugaku (dance) 1403
 audiences 1410
 influence on *kōwaka* 1169
 masks 1294
Bugyōnin system 140
Bujutsu ('martial arts')
 introductory studies 1443-1444
Bundan ('literary establishment')
 emergence, development, and decline
  1120
Bungei Shunjū (magazine)
 articles (translations and summaries)
  1547
Bunjinga (literati painting)
 art in the Powers Collection 1214
Bunraku theatre
 behind-the-scenes world 1391
 bibliographies 1588, 1603
 depicted in literature 1104
 history 1392-1393, 1411
 musical accompaniment and structure
  1382, 1395, 1399, 1611
 performance conventions and
  techniques 1391-1393, 1399
 photographs 1391-1392, 1404
 plays (literary analyses) 1002, 1170,
  1180

plays (synopses) 1411
plays (translations) 1170, 1174, 1176,
 1180
puppets 1174, 1391-1392, 1404, 1411
surveys 1392, 1403-1404, 1411
transformation of bunraku plays into
 kabuki plays 1174, 1395
Burakumin (minority group)
 1868-1945 205
Buraku Liberation League 777
delinquency among 588
depicted in *Hakai* (novel) 1095
discrimination against 205, 373-374,
 381, 1095
education 374
efforts to improve status 373, 381, 777
history 373-374, 381
kinship and marriage 374
living in the USA 373
periodicals 381
police treatment 565
psychology 373, 381
religion 374
social persistence 373
struggles against discrimination
 (post-1945) 785
Tokugawa period 165
Burden-sharing (US-Japan)
 defence 764, 767
Bureaucracy 20, 623, 723
 bureaucratism 612
 civil service system 613
 decision-making 620
 determination and administration of
  foreign aid 746
 directing firms toward high-profit
  markets 872
 functional and dysfunctional aspects
  39
 government's economic 612
 imperial palace 246
 in-fighting 856
 influence on US-Japanese relations
  (post-1945) 721
 limiting its staffing 625
 MITI 272
 Muromachi period 137, 140
 place of foreign service officers 729
 reform (post-1945) 274, 280
 relationship with big business 846
 relationship with organised labour and
  party governments 202
 relationship with private industry 791

role in economic administration 884
role in the supply of energy 850
Seiyūkai influence 224
Tokugawa period 163, 174, 177, 183, 185
Bureaucratic politics
effect on US-Japanese relations (1952-80) 750
Bureaucrats
decision-making style among 896, 906
involvement in politics 241, 809
profile of typical 613
role in defence policy decision-making 764
Burial practices
Ainu 378
Asuka and Nara periods 143
prehistoric 105-106, 109
Burma
peace settlement with Japan 283
World War II 697, 715
World War II (fiction) 1097
see also Southeast Asia
Bushidō (ethical code of the samurai)
classic exposition 529
Bushūkō no hiwa (Tanizaki Junichirō)
translation 1102
Business 15
advertising 788, 844
annual statistics 825-827
big business 39, 846, 883, 938
business-government relationship (post-1945) 623-624, 797, 801, 816, 846, 849, 852, 856, 878, 880, 887, 899, 951
commercial broadcasting 1482, 1486
compendium of information sources 1570
concern for company integrity 797
contracts 844
decision-making 894
democratisation 270
development (1600-1980) 208
directory 1574
encyclopaedic and almanac-type information about 1556
ethics 844
firms in transition 817
Fukuzawa Yukichi's views 302
industry (1950s-1970s) and 883
law 776
Liberal Democratic Party's relations with 633, 638

negotiations 776, 844, 893-894, 911, 916
newspaper reporting about 1546-1549
organisation (overview) 23, 843
periodicals 1494-1495, 1501, 1524, 1527, 1540, 1542
policy-making 801
present conditions and current trends (annual survey) 823
response to labour radicalism 275
shop signs (*kanban*) 1213, 1215, 1368
strategy 842, 901, 935
terms (dictionary) 422
ways of doing business in Japan (practical information) 776, 839-840, 843, 861, 889, 891, 893-894, 901, 904, 911, 916, 928
yakuza influence 569
see also Companies, Corporations, Enterprises, History (business), Industrial policy, Management, and Trade and commerce
Business community
defence policy and 761
involvement in Sino-Japanese relations 748
Business firms
group-centred, vertically-oriented nature 539
Business groups
big business and 883
Business Japanese (language)
dictionary 422
textbooks 436, 439, 447
Business management 840, 842, 845, 901, 935, 941
Business philosophy
corporations 894
Honda Sōichirō 344
Nissan and Ford (automobile manufacturers) 874
Sueno Akira 845
Business practices
guidebooks 891, 901, 916
influence on consumer buying habits 841
overview for businessmen 843
Business strategy
guide to (*Gorin no sho*) 1447
Business world 891
concepts, customs, practices, and values 422
dominated by Japan, the USA, and Europe 902

Business world *continued*
  guidebook 894
  hierarchical nature 840
Businessmen
  Arai Ryōichirō 297
  biographical dictionary 1574
  characteristics 891
  directory 1574
  Honda Sōichirō 344, 882
  interviews 1494-1495, 1527
  involved in private economic
    diplomacy 887
  Kawamata Katsuji 874
  language textbooks designed for 436,
    439, 447, 453
  Morita Akio 332, 877
  patronage of the arts (1955-80) 1376
  role in peace negotiations with the
    USSR (1950s) 728
  Sueno Akira 845
  Toyoda Eiji 347
Buson *see* Taniguchi (Yosa) Buson
Buyō (dance)
  introductory study 1390
By after the equinox (Natsume Soseki)
  psychoanalytical study 1112
Byōbu (folding screens) *see* Screens
Byōdōin (temple)
  architecture 1322
  Pure Land Buddhist art 1192

C

C. Itoh (*sōgō shōsha*)
  evolution, role, and organisation
    914-915
Cabinet 617, 625
  Cabinet Law (text) 605
  Liberal Democratic Party and the
    formation of a new 638
  members (names and dates of office)
    1555
  participation in the 1941 policy
    conferences 693
  power to dissolve the Diet 790
Cabinetry *see* Furniture
Calendrical astronomy
  historical development 151, 157
California
  anti-Japanese prejudice 659
  Issei population 385, 388, 400
  Nisei population 385, 388, 398
  see also Japanese Americans

Call money market
  1950s-1960s 851
Calligraphers
  Aoyama San'u 1231
  biographical dictionary 369
  Kuwata Sasafune 1231
  Miyamoto Chikukei 1231
  techniques and styles (post-1945) 1203
  Uragami Gyokudō 1230
  Yanagida Taiun 1231
Calligraphy 19, 1214, 1220
  at the Shōsōin 1194
  at the Tōdaiji temple 1206
  at the Tokyo National Museum 1473
  depicted in exhibition catalogues 1218,
    1227, 1229, 1231, 1249
  historical development 1249
  impact on American abstract
    expressionism 1231
  overview 1242
  produced in Kyōto (16th-17th
    centuries) 1249
  Rimpa school of art 1240
  role in society 1231
  Uragami Gyokudō 1230
  used in the tea ceremony 1469
  utensils (exhibition catalogue) 1219
  writing brushes (photographs) 1357,
    1366, 1369
  Zen Buddhist 1196,1232
  see also Photographs (calligraphy)
Campaigns *see* Election campaigns
Canada
  expansion of *yakuza* (gangster)
    operations into 569
  hostile attitudes towards Japan (1910s)
    666
  impact of imports from Japan on
    Canadian manufacturers 895
  involvement in the Allied occupation
    of Japan (1945-52) 266
  Japanese investment 734, 895
  Japanese migration 382, 655
  Japanese studies 1525, 1554, 1559
  trade and commerce with Japan 655,
    734, 895
  see also Foreign relations with
    Canada, and Japanese Canadians
Canadians in Japan
  Norman, E. H. 226
Canon, Inc.
  investment decision-making process 951
  personnel practices 942

strategic management practices 926
Capital
  concentration of 883
  contributions to economic growth
    (1868-1941) 218
  control of 552
  corporate capital structure 884
  cost of 884
  foreign capital in the Japanese
    economy 779
  liberalisation 779, 856
  markets 851, 856
  stock (statistical data) 808
Capital formation 811
  1868-1940 233
  1868-1970s 803, 855
  1953-73 792
  bibliography 1594
  colonial Korea and Taiwan 223
  long-term statistical data 808
  private (20th century) 793, 807
Capitalism
  nationalism (prewar) and 219
  history (1860s-1970s) 117
  manipulation of Zen Buddhism 34
  mode of production (post-1973) 545
Career patterns
  bureaucrats 613, 857
  foreign service officers 729
  higher civil servants 613
  journalists 1484
Career women 574
Careers 535
  in-company career development
    activities 919
  labour mobility and 542
  relationship to education 962
Caroline Islands see Micronesia
Carpentry
  historical evolution 1318
  Okinawan 1222ʳ
  see also Furniture
Cartels
  business and industry (post-1945) 270
  changes in government policy towards
    909
  oil cartel criminal cases 777
Cartography 52, 55
Cartoons
  images of Japan in American 731
  Meiji period 1269
  racist stereotypes in World War II 686
Carvers

bugaku masks 1294
Carvings
  stone 143, 502
  see also Netsuke (miniature carvings),
    and Sculpture
Case marking
  grammar 429
Cash management 861
Castaways
  on the Kamchatka Peninsula
    (Tokugawa period) 664
Castle towns
  1840s-1880s 212
  daimyō rule 168
  growth (mid-1800s-1970s) 40
  Kanazawa 174
Castles 133
  architectural history 1306-1307, 1314,
    1317
  Azuchi 135, 1306, 1317
  Edo 185, 1307, 1317
  Fushimi 1317
  Himeji 1306
  Kyōto 92
  Nijō 89, 1307, 1317
  Ōsaka 146, 1307, 1317
  photographs 156, 158, 1306, 1317
  tourist sites 90
Catalogues (art)
  artworks at the Seattle Art Museum
    1217
  netsuke by Masatoshi 1291
  primitive ukiyo-e in the Michener
    Collection 1268
  surimono in the Chester Beatty
    Library 1263
  surimono in the Spencer Museum 1263
  see also Exhibition catalogues
Cats
  novel about 1085
Cattle
  raising and supply 833
Causativisation 434
Censorship
  1868-1945 221, 1122
  centring on the play Chūshingura 1395
  colonial Korea 223
  opposition to 336, 1122
Centralisation
  post-1945 (misconceptions) 640
Ceramics 1220
  Agano ware 1281
  Asuka and Nara periods 143

Ceramics *continued*
  at the Seattle Art Museum 1217
  at the Shōsōin 1194
  at the Tokyo National Museum 1473
  Bizen ware 1283, 1286
  depicted in exhibition catalogues 1218, 1227, 1229
  design motifs and techniques 1204
  dictionary 1567
  Echizen ware 1283, 1286
  folk art 19, 542, 553, 1193, 1210, 1213, 1281
  Hagi ware 1281, 1283
  historical function and beauty 1435
  history 1211
  Iga ware 1283
  Imari ware 1281
  influence on lacquerwork and design 1374
  Kakiemon ware 1281
  Karatsu ware 1279, 1281, 1283
  Kiseto ware 1281
  Kutani ware 1284
  Meiji period 1229
  Nabeshima ware 1281
  Oribe ware 1281, 1283
  prehistoric production 101
  Rimpa school of art 1240
  Ryūkyū Islands 1201, 1222
  Satsuma ware 1283
  Seto ware 1283, 1286
  Setoguro ware 1281
  Shigaraki ware 1280, 1283, 1286
  Shino ware 1281, 1283
  Takatori ware 1281
  Tamba ware 1283, 1286
  Tokoname ware 1281, 1283, 1286
  world of 1287
  Zen Buddhist dimensions 1196
  see also Photographs (ceramics and pottery), and Pottery
Ceremonies (Buddhist)
  dictionary 415
Certain woman (Arishima Takeo)
  translation 1046
Certificates of deposit
  markets 854, 857
Chanoyu see Tea ceremony (*chanoyu*)
Character, National *see* National character
Characters *see* Chinese characters (*kanji*)
Charms (religious) 460-461
Chauvinism
  male 591
Chemical industry 217
Chemistry
  historical development 187
  language textbook for reading materials in 437
Cherry trees
  Washington, DC 663
Chester Beatty Library (Dublin, Ireland)
  holdings of *surimono* (woodblock prints) 1263
Chests *see Tansu* (wooden chests)
Chiba Prefecture
  Narita 91
  Narita Airport 606
  Noda 201
  policy-making 639
  Tateyama City 559
  Tone River area 109
  see also Kantō region
Chichibu, Prince
  ties with the Young Officers' Movement 238
Chichibu Incident (1884) 195
Chikamatsu Monzaemon 1005
  biographical sketch 295
  conventions in his plays 1399
  plays 1002, 1170, 1176, 1392, 1396, 1407
Chikamatsu Shūkō
  literary analysis 1113
Child-rearing 15, 559, 594
  among the Ainu 375
  behavioural patterns 591
  lower-class Tokyo families 571
  middle-class Tokyo families 564
  relationship to juvenile delinquency 571
  relationship to personality and behaviour 585
Children
  American views (World War II) of the Japanese as 686
  at Tomoe Gakuen (elementary school) 330
  child development 594
  commitment to educating 978
  conceptions of the child 594
  during World War II 207
  lives and behaviour of urban 564
  parental attitudes towards 571
  pre-school 559
  social readjustment following their

stay overseas 572
socialisation 535, 559
survivors of the atomic bombing of
Hiroshima 259
Children's books
portraying Japan and the Japanese
(bibliography) 1596
China
Chinese origins of ink painting
(*suibokuga*) 1239
Chinese sources for Nanga painting
1255
Chinese sources of Japanese gardens
1327, 1335
compared with Japan 10
depicted in Japanese literature 1027,
1032, 1061
depicted in Japanese textbooks 647
diplomacy of resistance against Japan
(1910s-1920s) 647
Doihara Kenji and the North China
Autonomy Movement 647
functions in Tokugawa period thought
650
images of Japan and the Japanese
649-650
impact of the Opium War (1840-42)
on Anglo-Japanese relations 658
imperialist expansion (Meiji period) in
250
influence on early Japanese culture
101, 151, 157, 1296
influence on early Japanese poetry
301, 1006, 1153, 1163
influence on Japanese art 179
influence on Japanese language 407
influence on Japanese textiles 1347
introduction of printing techniques
from 1477
Japanese aid (1910s) to 650, 666
Japanese espionage in 648
Japanese expansion (1897-1911) in
662
Japanese images of 647, 649-650
Japanese intervention in Shantung
(World War I) 647
Kwantung Leased Territory 223
modernisation (compared with Japan)
818
music imported from 1379
Okinawa as its tributary state 284
origins and development of Zen
Buddhism 474

press coverage of 1484
relations between the Japanese and
Chinese communist parties 635
Shanghai (World War II) 4
Tokugawa policy vis-à-vis the
Manchu assumption of power 677
transmission of esoteric Buddhism to
Japan via 1237
Ts'ao Ju-lin's role in shaping
Sino-Japanese perceptions 650
'Twenty-One Demands' (1915) 652,
666
see also Foreign relations with China,
Manchuria, Manchurian Incident,
(1931), Russo-Japanese War
(1904-5), Sino-Japanese War of
1894-95, and Sino-Japanese War of
1937-45
China (People's Republic of China)
as a source of raw materials and fuels
885
Baoshan steel complex project 735
Bohai Sea petroleum development
project 735
Japanese economic assistance 735-736
Senkaku Islands (Tiao-Yü-T'ai)
dispute 730
trade and commerce with Japan 738,
885
see also Foreign relations with China
(People's Republic of China)
China (Republic of China)
economic development (compared
with Japan) 806
relations with Japan 283, 647, 738, 743
China-Japan Peace and Friendship
Treaty (1978) 730
Chinese art in Japan
holdings of the Shōsōin 1194
Mu Chi's paintings at the Daitokuji
temple 1190
museum collections 1473, 1475
Zen Buddhist painting 1232
Chinese characters (*kanji*)
adapted to the Japanese spoken
language 404
dictionaries 421, 423, 437-438, 448,
1571
history and arrangement 438
introduction into Japan 404
textbooks focused on learning 438,
441, 448, 452, 456
Chinese Communist Party

Chinese Communist Party *continued*
 anti-Japanese movement in
  Manchuria and 647
 relations with the Japan Communist
  Party 635
Chinese in Japan
 Meiji period 650
 Tokugawa period traders 179
Chinese language
 Japanese literary works written in 488,
  1000, 1005, 1010, 1138-1139, 1152,
  1154
Chinese studies in Japan
 Tokugawa period 180
Chinmoku (Endō Shūsaku)
 translation 1055
Chinsō portraits 1232
Chishima Rettō *see* Kurile Islands
Chōka poetry
 literary format of Ōtomo no
  Yakamochi 301
 translations 1147, 1154, 1156
Chōshū *han*
 involvement in the Meiji Restoration
  168, 171
 origins of Yamagata Aritomo 303
'Christian century' in Japan 129,
  132-133, 166
Christianity in Japan 468, 498
 1500s-1600s 129, 133, 166, 293, 352,
  458, 465, 495
 1500s-1600s (novels) 1054-1055
 after World War II 497
 art 1243
 bibliography 1587
 brief introductions 462-463
 brief readings 461
 co-existence with Buddhism and
  Shintō 498
 encounter with Zen Buddhism 474
 history (1549-1960s) 495
 history (1859-1959) 496
 introductory survey 460
 Meiji period converts 235, 358
 missions (1870s) 66
 music 1383
 periodicals 1506, 1523
 Shintō nationalism and 517
Christians
 as pacifists 288
 involvement in social reform
  movements 235, 240
 persecution (1600s) 129, 133, 166, 179

resistance to centralised rule 614
Chronologies
 agricultural developments 831, 835
 archaeology of the Ryūkyū Islands 284
 books illustrated by Katsushika
  Hokusai 1260
 broadcasting (radio and television)
  1486
 bunraku theatre 1392
 classical literature 1566
 communist movement 635
 current economic events 823
 current events 1513
 events concerning libraries and
  librarianship 1476
 events concerning women 581
 historical 35, 122, 1569
 Imperial Japanese Navy 210
 Japan Communist Party 192, 635
 Jōmon pottery 107
 noh theatre 1408
 period of the *Ōkagami* (850-1025 AD)
  1017
Chrysanthemum Festival (Kiku no
  sekku) 501
Chrysanthemum textile patterns 1344
Chūō Kōron (magazine)
 articles (translations and summaries)
  1547
Churches 90, 179
 architecture (1940s-1960s) 1313
Chūshingura (Takeda Izumo et al.)
 historical background 1180, 1395
 kabuki and bunraku versions
  compared 1395
 Katsushika Hokusai's ukiyo-e prints
  based on 1260
 literary analyses 1180, 1395
 musical accompaniment 1395
 translations 1180, 1395
Chūsonji (temple)
 architecture 1322
 Pure Land (Jōdo) Buddhist art 1192
Chuzan (Ryūkyūan kingdom)
 history (15th-16th centuries) 284
Cinema 19, 37
 censorship (1918-45) 221
 depiction of women 26
 form and meaning in 1417
 history 1414, 1417, 1426
 images of Japan in American movies
  731
 influence of foreign films 1428

influence of traditional drama 1393
   'New Wave' cinema (introductory
     study) 1419
   overview 1424
   see also Film directors, Filmographies,
     and Films
Cinematographers
   Narushima Tōichirō 1423
Cinematography *see* Film-making
Cities and towns 50
   16th century 133
   burakumin ghettos 373, 381
   castle towns 40, 168, 174, 212
   city assembly members (life-course)
     542
   city halls (architecture) 81
   gazetteer 57
   historical growth and evolution 43,
     139, 546
   libraries 1476
   maps 53, 55
   megalopolis along the Pacific coast 46
   planning and administration 143
   political choice and policy change in
     642
   political opposition and big city
     elections 642
   solid waste (garbage) management
     programmes 956
   technopolises 996
   tourist guides (nationwide) 79, 82-83,
     94, 100
   see also Local government, Local
     politics, and the names of individual
     cities and towns
Citizens' movements
   environmental protests and 642, 958
   'Minamata disease' and 959
   political socialisation through 642
   viewed in historical perspective 616
Citizenship 9
Citrus fruit
   increased US exports to Japan 892
Civil Code 277, 280
Civil disputes
   techniques for resolving 778
Civil engineering projects
   Japanese involvement in Soviet 900
Civil law and procedure
   bibliography 1582
Civil liabilities 781
Civil religion
   secularisation 802

Civil service system 625
   examinations (1868-1945) 613
   labour relations 937
   structure, personnel, and politics 613
Civil wars
   Gempei War (1180-85) 154, 293, 1019
   Jōkyū War (1221) 148
   Meiji Restoration 162, 191, 226, 249,
     353, 357
   Ōnin War (1467-77) 160
   Satsuma Rebellion (1877) 293, 306
   Tengu Insurrection (1864) 175
   'Warring States' (Sengoku) period
     115, 124, 135, 139, 145, 299
Civilian-military relations
   post-1945 761
Class consciousness
   proverbs about 1183
Class divisions
   post-1945 society 545
Class struggle
   post-1945 616
Clauses
   grammar 427, 429
'Clean Government Party' *see* Kōmeitō
   ('Clean Government Party')
Cleverness
   folk tales about 1185, 1187
Climate 40-41, 50
   annual statistics 825-827
   bibliography 1592
   maps 53-54
Cliques
   political (1920s-1930s) 247
Cloisonné
   illustrated survey 1361
   Meiji period (exhibition catalogue)
     1229
Cloth
   production of *tsutsugaki* 1345
   tsujigahana 1346
   use of water for manufacturing
     (photo-essay) 3
Clothing
   Ainu 66
   design (photographs) 1224
   during the 1870s 66, 363
   encyclopaedic and almanac-type
     information about 1553, 1556-1557,
     1561
   fashion world of the 1970s-1980s 1348
   illustrations 1566
   industry 794

Clothing *continued*
  medieval 133, 136, 153
  owned by the Tokugawa shōguns
    (exhibition catalogue) 1219
  photographs 1219, 1345, 1351-1353,
    1356
  Tokugawa period 165, 1219
  worn by geisha 576
  see also Costumes, Kimono, and
    Kosode
Clothing accessories
  aesthetic qualities (photographs) 1198
  used in the kabuki theatre 1352
  worn with kimono 1356
Clouds
  design motif of textile patterns 1344
Coal
  imports from Australia 885
  Japanese development of Soviet
    resources 900
  market for 850
  miners 205, 328
  mining 38
  policy influenced by the Tokyo
    Electric Power Company 849
  US-Japanese co-operation in 847
Coca-Cola (company)
  business operations in Japan 889, 928
Cocks, Richard 132
Cognitive achievement
  among school children 964
Cohen, Theodore
  involvement in the Allied occupation
    of Japan (1945-52) 267
Coins
  economic use 143
Cold War
  impact on Australia and Japan 723
  influence on the postwar peace
    settlement 283
  origins in Asia 279
Collaboration (political)
  during the Sino-Japanese War of
    1937-45 702
Collections *see* Art collections
Collective bargaining
  1940s-1960s 931
  growth 267, 937
  innovations 948
Colleges *see* Universities
Colonial empire of Japan 223, 227
  disposition (post-1945) 282, 285-287
Colonialism

Japanese attitudes towards 223
  nature of Japanese 249
Colours
  component of kabuki theatrical
    costumes 1352
  expressed in Japanese 454
  used in costume (historical overview)
    1349
  used in *kosode* fabrics 1353
Combat swimming *see Suiei-jutsu*
  (martial art)
Combs
  craftsmanship 1369
Comic strip books *see Manga* (comic
  strip books)
Comic tradition
  element of *renga* poetry 140
Commerce *see* Trade and commerce
Commercial colleges
  Shōhō Kōshūjo (Hitotsubashi
    University) 304
Commercial law 786
  bibliography 1582
Commission on the Constitution
  activities 787, 789
  documents 787
  final report 789
Committee system
  Diet (parliament) 607
Communication 20, 46
  among students 406
  area of managerial activity 941
  basic facts and figures (annual
    handbook) 14
  business 891, 894
  cross-cultural 586
  equipment (research and
    development) 981
  haragei in interpersonal 406
  implicit 933
  interpersonal 406, 584
  law (bibliography) 1582
  methods 923
  modes and styles 439, 726
  new electronic media 955
  nonverbal 20, 406, 443
  postal 248
  radio broadcasting 221, 387, 703,
    1482, 1486
  roles of *omote* and *ura* in 590
  satellite broadcasting 955
  technology (promotion and diffusion)
    983

US-Japan scientific relationship in 998
see also Newspapers, and
   Telecommunications
Communism
   Japan as a bulwark against its
      expansion 271, 279
Communists
   alleged sabotage of a train at
      Matsukawa (1949) 780
   see also Japan Communist Party, and
      Marxism
Community
   affairs (housewives' involvement) 577
   associations 548, 551
   health and medicine 603
   life (Ainu) 372, 379
   life (Korean ghetto in Kawasaki,
      Kanagawa Prefecture) 376
   organisation 551, 554, 576
   readings about 1
Community studies
   Fuchū (Tokyo Prefecture) 565, 628
   Gunma Prefecture mountain farming
      hamlet 507
   Higashiuwa County (Ehime
      Prefecture) 573
   Kariya (Aichi Prefecture) 547
   Kurashiki (Okayama Prefecture) 565
   Kurotsuchi (Fukuoka Prefecture) 560
   Kurusu (Kagawa Prefecture) 556
   Kyōto (world of the geisha) 576
   Musashino (Tokyo Prefecture) 628
   Niiike (Okayama Prefecture) 548
   Noda (Chiba Prefecture) 201
   Sarayama (Ōita Prefecture) 553
   Shingū (Fukuoka Prefecture) 552
   Shin-machi (pseudonymous
      burakamin community) 374
   Shinohata (Tochigi Prefecture) 550
   Shiwa (Iwate Prefecture) 555
   Suye mura (Kumamoto Prefecture)
      551, 582
   Takashima (Okayama Prefecture) 554
   Tokyo 549, 557-558, 564-565,
      570-571, 577, 628
   Tsuchiura (Ibaraki Prefecture) 234
Companies 38
   adaptive patterns 935
   American companies in Japan 889,
      928
   career development activities for
      employees 919
   case study 838

company housing 543, 577
company unions 616, 797, 921, 940
directory 1574
employee loyalty 38, 543
engaged in artificial
   intelligence-related activities 994
handbook of leading 822
information networks 955
intra-firm wage differentials 930
job mobility patterns 919
Kokusai Denshin Denwa Company
   953
management 838, 941
Nippon Yūsen Kaisha (N.Y.K.) 250
Nomura Security Company 853
organisation 838, 894, 917
personnel practices 917
quality control circles 919
research and development strategies
   983
Tokyo Electric Power Company 849
see also Corporations, Enterprises,
   Management, Multinational
   corporations, *Sōgō shōsha* (general
   trading companies), and *Zaibatsu*
   (financial and industrial combines)
Comparative studies 10
   agriculture and agricultural policy
      (Japan, USA) 888
   approaches to research and
      development (Japan, USA) 881
   automobile manufacturers (Nissan,
      Ford) 874
   blue-collar workers (Japan, USA) 919
   business policy-making (Japan, USA)
      801
   calligraphy (Chinese, Japanese) 1242
   changing industrial relations (Japan,
      West Germany) 940
   choice of marriage partners (Japan,
      USA) 558
   Diet and US Congress 626
   economic development (Japan,
      Europe) 233
   economic development (Japan,
      developing countries) 806
   educational systems (Japan, USA) 965
   elderly (Japan, West) 540
   energy markets 850
   ethical basis of business practices
      (Japan, USA) 844
   factory life (Japan, China) 10
   family patterns and delinquency

Comparative studies *continued*
formation 571
farming (Japan, USA, India) 834
financial development (Japan, India, USA) 855
financial innovation, deregulation, and reform (Japan, USA) 860
industrial policy (Japan, USA) 884
industrial relations system 931
inflation (Japan, USA) 859
interpersonal communication (Japan, USA) 584
introduction of the oxygen steelmaking process (Japan, USA) 989
landholding patterns (Japan, England) 10
literary depiction of love and death (Japan, USA) 10
management (Japan, Great Britain) 941
management (Japan, USA) 927, 933
management of diplomacy (Japan, USA) 729
managerial behaviour (Japanese in Germany and Great Britain) 949
multinational corporations (Japan, Great Britain, USA) 947
multinational corporations (Japan, USA) 942
music of *Shakkyō* (noh and kabuki versions) 1385
nation-building (Japan, China) 10
navies (Japan, Great Britain) 698
patent and know-how licensing (Japan, USA) 774
patterns of adult socialisation 595
patterns of responding to the West (Japan, Korea) 10
patterns of social organisation (Japan, Great Britain) 920
police operations (Fuchū, Kurashiki) 565
political and economic institutions (Japan, China) 623
politics and social change (two Tokyo suburbs) 628
private and public school systems 968
quest for oil and ores (Japan, USA) 913
racist thought during World War II (American, English, Japanese) 686
science and technology (Japan, USA) 984, 998

semiconductor industry (Japan, USA) 880
social change (Ōsaka, Takashima) 562
trade associations (Japan, USA) 899
urban housewives 577
Compassion
as a samurai value 529
Compensation
non-monetary 845
paid to former landlords 633, 790
pollution-related health injuries 775, 777
wartime loss of overseas assets 620
Competition
among car-makers 610, 869-870, 874
among corporations 902, 939
business 883, 943
for leadership in the world's computer industry 982
for supremacy in information technology (Japan, USA) 981
industrial 883, 945
Japan's increasing economic competitiveness 813
law to prevent unfair 773, 786
over energy (Japan, USA) 847
over semiconductors (Japan, USA) 880
quest for oil and ores (Japan, USA) 913
science and technology (Japan, USA) 984, 996, 998
Competitive advantage pursued manufacturing 836
Complementation 434
Compton Collection
art swords 1373
Computers
artificial intelligence 982
computer industry 813, 873, 876, 911-912, 982
computer-guided machinery (development and adoption) 872
computer science (research and development) 984
incompatibility with the traditional writing system 997
research and development 981
role of invention and innovation in 985
terms (dictionary) 437
US-Japan scientific relationship 998
Concentration camps (Japanese American) *see* Japanese Americans

(relocation during World War II)
Conciliation
historical use (1740s-1964) 778
used in settling environmental disputes
775
Condominiums
housewives in Tokyo and 577
Confessions made under duress
inadmissibility 788, 790
Confessions of a mask (Mishima Yukio)
literary analyses 1127, 1131
translation 1073
Conflict
element of modern history
(1850s-1920s) 175
element of post-1945 policy-making
processes 619
labour 241, 538, 921
management 538, 721-722, 892, 921
over financial policy-making 857
over liberalisation 856
resolution 937
sources, expression, and management
538
see also Disputes, and Protest
movements and uprisings
Conformity
social and cultural 610
Confrontation
among Diet members 607
avoidance 522
Confucianism
adversely affected by the Meiji
Restoration 235
brief introduction 462
component of Tokugawa period
ideology and politics 177-178
during the Tokugawa period 458-459,
465, 526
institutions and thought (1868-1945)
528
introductory survey 460
readings 33, 461
rejected by Fukuzawa Yukichi 194
Zen Buddhism and 492
Congress (US)
compared with the Diet 626
Conjunctions
grammar 427, 430-433
Connoisseurship
ceramics and pottery 553, 1282
swords 1373
ukiyo-e prints 1256

woodblock prints 1576
Consensus
element of post-1945 policy-making
processes 619
importance in business relations 922
manipulative bases 616
resolving problems through 797
Conservation and environmental
protection
Chiba, Saga, and Saitama prefectures
639
energy conservation 849
environmental regulation 801
flora and vegetation 61
growth and impact of environmental
protest 642
Liberal Democratic Party's response
to changing conditions in 619
natural farming 830
practices (post-1945) 63
research institutes and programmes
980
Tanaka Shōzō (pioneer
environmentalist) 312
Conservative parties
1945-1955 274, 280, 324
loss of voter support in suburban
Tokyo 628
role of organised business in their
merger (1950s) 846
Consonants 412
Constitution 723, 784
Article 9 (renunciation of war) 784,
790
bibliographies 1582, 1613
Commission on the Constitution
(activities and report) 787, 789
constitutional revision 633, 789
constitutionality of the Self-Defence
Forces 761
Diet and 626, 629
guarantee of human rights 784
history (1947-67) 787
implementation 277
judicial interpretation 777
problems 624
procedural law 778
provisions affecting Shintō 515
provisions for local autonomy 641
reform (Allied occupation of Japan)
266, 271, 273-274, 280-282
Supreme Court's constitutional
decisions 788, 790

Constitution *continued*
  Tabata Shinobu (constitutional
    defender) 288
  text 112, 605, 617, 627, 784, 787
  see also Meiji Constitution
Constitutional development of Japan
    189, 305, 786
Constitutional monarchy
  Saionji Kinmochi's commitment 323
Constitutionalism
  Minobe Tatsukichi's interpretation 220
Construction
  annual statistics 825, 827
  private and government investment
    (1868-1940) 233
Consumer credit
  1950s-1960s 851
Consumer electronics
  role of invention and innovation in 985
Consumers
  business orientation towards 928
  buying habits (influences) 841
  consumer markets 841, 843, 891
  consumerism 815
  cultural idiosyncracies 841
  images of foreign products 891
  quality consciousness 889
Consumption (domestic) 823
  contribution to economic growth
    (1868-1941) 218
  long-term statistical data 808
  origins of the post-1945 mass
    consumption society 267
Continuity
  patterns (photo-essay) 17
Contraceptive methods 370
Contracts
  between Japanese and foreign
    enterprises 779
  business 844
  contract law 777
Conversion (ideological) 595
Conversion (religious)
  to Christianity 235, 358
  to Judaism 4
  to Nichiren Shōshū 319
Cookbooks
  general 1429-1430, 1434, 1438-1439
  shōjin ryōri (vegetarian cooking) 1440
  sushi 1432, 1436, 1438
Co-operation
  among farmers 181, 200, 268, 551
  among large firms in research and

    development 881
  among local governments 640
  between American and Japanese
    companies 911
  between business and government
    624, 797, 846, 849, 871, 881
  European-Japanese 910
  in energy (USA and Japan) 847
  in the business world 836, 883, 916,
    939
  promotion of Brazilian-Japanese 898
  scientific and technological 980
  Soviet-Japanese energy 847
Co-operatives
  agricultural 268, 550, 555, 723, 835
  fisheries 13
  silkworm-raisers 550
Copper
  Ashio Copper Mine 312, 957
  quest for dependable ore supplies 913
Copyright Law 773
  bibliography 1582
Coral Sea
  battle (1942) 680, 687
Corporations 8, 31
  bibliography 1590
  Canon 926, 942, 951
  competition and co-operation among
    939
  co-operation with banks and
    stockholders 836
  decision-making 926
  directory 1574
  disclosure system 858
  English-language instruction in 979
  financial behaviour 852, 862
  financing 922
  Fuji Xerox 935
  Fujitsu 912
  global competition among Japanese,
    American, and European 902
  Hitachi 920, 926, 951, 987
  Honda Motor 344, 882
  hostile corporate takeovers 868
  inner workings and behaviour 836
  Japanese National Railways 542, 612,
    625
  Kikkoman 201, 802
  life-course of employees 542
  lives and values of employees 564
  Mazda Motors 809
  Matsushita Electric 926, 933
  Mitsubishi Electric 987

NEC (Nippon Electric Company) 951, 987
Nippon Steel 942
Nippon Telegraph and Telephone 612, 625, 892, 953, 955
Nissan Motor 871, 874, 942
organisational structure 926, 929
patronage of the arts (1955-80) 1376
philosophy 894
public 605, 612, 625, 1558, 1593, 1602
Sharp 987
Sony 332, 877, 942, 951
strategies 895, 926, 951
tax burdens 884
tax incentives 884, 927
Toray Industries 987
Toshiba 951
Toyota Motor 347, 547, 871, 912, 924, 926, 934-936
Western corporations in Japan (operations) 902
see also Companies, Management, and Multinational corporations
Corruption
business 844
political 567
Cosmology 151
Costume
Ainu 66
historical evolution 1349, 1351
worn by practitioners of *iaidō* 1452
worn by the *ninja* 1445
Costume makers
bunraku theatre 1391
Costumes
at the Shōsōin 1194
depicted in ukiyo-e paintings 1250
gagaku 1377
kabuki theatre 1351-1352, 1400-1401, 1407, 1564
kyōgen 1351
noh theatre 1181, 1351, 1405-1406, 1408, 1412
Cotton
cotton spinning industry 806
textiles (*tsutsugaki*) 1345
trade (Tokugawa period) 170
Counselling
administrative counselling 625
Countryside
photographs 3, 11, 25, 28-29, 44, 1275-1276, 1278
see also Rural areas

Courage
depicted in the *Soga monogatari* 1012
Court, Imperial *see* Imperial court
Courtesans
depicted in ukiyo-e prints 1259, 1261-1262, 1268
'Courtly romances' *see Tsukuri monogatari* ('courtly romances')
Courts 617, 776, 782
cases affecting women 575
criminal proceedings 772
procedures 774, 784
reorganisation (1940s) 277
role in combatting environmental pollution 775
social role 785
Tokugawa period 778
Courtship
traditional and modern concepts 558
Courtyard gardens 1333
Craft tradition
influence on modern interior decoration 1319
Crafts 90
encyclopaedic and almanac-type information about 1552-1553, 1556-1557, 1561
evolution (1868-1968) 1209
folk-crafts (*mingei*) movement 331, 553, 1228
introduction (illustrated) 1369
Kyōto 77-78, 92
photographic survey 1198
Ryūkyū Islands 1201
Tōhoku region 74
traditional 153, 1369
Craftsmanship 1228
furniture-making 1341-1343
glass-making 1359
netsuke carving 1291
traditional (photo-essay) 1198
Craftsmen and craftswomen
biographical dictionary 369
bunraku theatre 1391
craftswomen in central Honshū 579
Hamada Shōji 331
'living national treasures' 13, 1222
Masatoshi (netsuke carver) 1291
Okinawan 1222
paper-makers (*washi*) 1365
photographs 13, 331, 1222, 1391
potters 331, 553, 1287
signatures (handbook) 1571

Craftsmen and craftswomen *continued*
    Tempyō period 1296
    textile designers 1349
    Tokugawa period 165
    villagers of Sarayama, Ōita Prefecture
        553
    villagers of Tsuchiura, Ibaraki
        Prefecture 234
Cranes (birds) 58, 63
    design motif of textile patterns 1344
'Crazy cloud anthology' (Ikkyū Sōjun)
    study and translation 1139
Credit
    consumer 851
    government programmes 863
    long-term credit banks 862, 864
    ways of securing 861
Creditor nation
    Japan's emergence as the world's
        largest 867
Crests *see* Family (crests)
Crime 588
    annual statistics 829
    basic facts and figures (annual
        handbook) 14
    control 38, 565-566, 616
    female 566
    government report (annual) 829
    investigation 565, 570
    low and declining rate 566
    oil cartel criminal cases 777
    stories about 1060
    treatment and rehabilitation of
        criminals 566
    see also Gangsters
Criminal Code 277
Criminal justice
    administration 772, 786, 788
    criminal law and procedure 772, 786,
        1582
    introduction of Anglo-American
        adversary proceedings 780
    system (historical evolution) 566
    war crimes trials (1946-48) 265-266,
        271, 321, 346, 595
Cross-cultural communication 586
Cross-cultural negotiations 893
Cross-cultural understanding 361, 776
Cuisine
    aesthetics (Zen Buddhist dimensions)
        1196, 1435, 1437
    of Kyōto 77-78
    of *ryōkan* (inns) 96

    see also Food, and Restaurants
Cults (religious) 460-461
Cultural relations
    Australian-Japanese 751
    European-Japanese 674
    foreign policies (1868-1941) in the
        cultural sphere (research guide)
        1599
    Sino-Japanese 650
    US-Japanese (bibliography) 1575
Culture 7, 9, 16-17, 31, 37, 531, 843, 916
    American infatuation with Japanese
        731
    basic facts and figures (annual
        handbook) 14
    behavioural manifestations 591
    cultural values 615
    daimyō 1218
    Daruma's interrelatedness with life
        and 483
    differences between American and
        Japanese 894
    documentary films (critical guide) 1586
    guidebook 1552
    Heian period 150
    language (cultural context) 411
    long-term evolution 101
    mass 533, 621
    material culture (mid-19th century)
        212
    Mori Ōgai and the modernisation of
        1110
    newspaper articles about 1546, 1549
    periodicals 1534, 1543
    place of Buddhism 485
    popular (and Tokugawa social protest)
        161
    popular (post-1945) 26
    readings about 33
    role of death and related poetry in
        1138
    student (1880s-1940s) 232
    women-related aspects 413
    Zen Buddhism and 489, 492, 1195
    see also History (cultural)
Currency reform (18th century) 298
Curriculum
    comparative studies 965
    pervasive egalitarianism 964
    reform 961
    role in educational achievement 971
    'units' about Japan 36
Customs

Ainu 66, 372, 375, 378
brief articles about 1551
business 422
depicted in contemporary photographs 1276, 1278
encyclopaedic and almanac-type information about 1553, 1556-1557, 1560-1561, 1568, 1573
household 114
Inland Sea area 71
Meiji period 1188
periodicals 1490
recorded by the Perry expedition (1853-54) 673
Tokugawa period 1014

D

Daibu, Lady
poetic memoirs 1142
Daigoji (temple)
architecture 1322
Daily life 1
at the Daitokuji temple 1190
at Manzanar internment camp 391
blue-collar workers 918
comparison of Ōsaka and Takashima, Okayama Prefecture 562
craftsmanship in 1198
during World War II 207
encyclopaedic and almanac-type information about 1552, 1568
farm women 573, 582
impact of the Allied occupation of Japan (1945-52) on 269
impact of the atomic bombings (1945) on 253
in castles (Tokugawa period) 1307
in a Tokyo neighbourhood 549
in the treaty ports 68
in Tsuchiura, Ibaraki Prefecture 234
in village communities 548, 550-551, 554, 582
Kamakura, Muromachi, and Momoyama periods 136
kamikaze pilots 700
pervasiveness of religion in 460-461
photographs 28, 1277
policemen 565
pre-school children 559
sumo wrestlers 1455
tales about 1022
Tokugawa period 165
use of bamboo in 1357

Zen monasteries 486
Daimyō
artistic and cultural contributions (exhibition catalogue) 1218
biographical studies 289
control over the samurai and the peasants (1500-1650) 139
fudai 163, 185
Go-Hōjō 139
Hosokawa Yūsai 291
house laws 139
Ikeda Mitsumasa 289
Matsudaira Sadanobu 177
regulation of trade 139
relationship with Toyotomi Hideyoshi 146, 299
role in Tokugawa political affairs 185
rule (Tokugawa period) 168
Shimazu Nariakira 289
Takeda Shingen 295
Tokugawa Nariaki 289
village communities and 140
Daisenin (temple)
garden 1327
Daitokuji (temple)
garden 1331-1332
history 1190
suibokuga painters associated with 1239
Zen-influenced art and daily life at 1190
Dance
aesthetics 1390
buyō 1390
historical evolution 1388, 1390
kabuki 1388, 1564
medieval 136
patronage (1955-80) 1376
Dancers
Ito Michio 322
Dances
as precursors to the theatrical arts 1393
bugaku 1169, 1294, 1403, 1410
choreographed by Michio Ito 322
depicted in Heian period handscrolls 1380
dramatising Kamaitachi's demonic imagery 1275
gagaku 1169, 1377, 1403
gigaku 1403
Gorō Tokimune (kabuki dance piece) 1384

Dances *continued*
  influence on *kōwaka* 1169
  noh (dances and movements) 1389,
    1405-1406, 1408
  performed by geisha 576
  photographs 322, 1275, 1377,
    1389-1390, 1408
  Shintō 518
Danchi see Public housing (*danchi*)
Danger
  idiomatic words and expressions 414
Danmono tradition of koto music 1378
Dark night's passing (Shiga Naoya)
  translation 1093
Daruma
  representation in art and popular
    culture 483
Data-processing
  incompatible with the traditional script
    997
  terms (dictionary) 437
  undertaken within the government 625
Dates
  guide to reading 1571
Day nurseries
  day-to-day life of children 559
Dazai Osamu 1003
  as a member of the *bundan* 1120
  concept of literature 1128
  life and writings 1116, 1119
  novels 1049-1050, 1116, 1118, 1127
  short stories 1051, 1083, 1106, 1116,
    1126
Death
  Ainu customs 378
  as an aspect of medieval life 136
  attitudes towards 292, 588, 600
  burial practices 105-106, 109, 143, 378
  constitutionality of the death penalty
    790
  'death poems' (*jisei*) 1138
  depicted in novels 10
  funerals 66, 485, 1556, 1561
  Shintō concepts 518
  taboos and rituals 500
  see also Ancestor worship, and
    Mortality
Debts
  code regulating repayments 585
Decay of the angel (Mishima Yukio)
  literary analysis 1131
  translation 1077
Deceit

proverbs about 1183
Decision-making
  allocation of foreign aid 746
  among bureaucrats 613, 896, 906
  business 894, 926
  concerning science 980
  curriculum unit about 36
  defence policy (post-1945) 754,
    763-764
  educational 962
  foreign policy 682
  impact of value-systems 618
  investment 951
  involving the imperial court (1930s)
    246
  leading to surrender to the Allies
    (1945) 683, 703
  leading to the San Francisco peace
    settlement (1951) 283
  leading to war with the USA (1941)
    321
  Liberal Democratic Party 638
  Manchurian Incident (1931) 702
  organisations 39
  political 620, 720
  process 23, 923, 941, 943
  role of organised business in political
    and economic 846
  related to new ocean policies 796
Decorations
  inrō 1360
  kites 1461
  see also Design, and Interior
    decoration
'Decorative' school of Tokugawa art *see*
  Rimpa school of art
Defamation
  media 771
Defence 624
  annual statistics 824, 829
  basic facts and figures (annual
    handbook) 14
  expenditures (statistics) 761
  government report (annual) 829
  newspaper articles (translations and
    synopses) 1547
  policies 27, 623, 718, 741, 751, 762,
    768-770
  policy-making process 613, 754, 764
  research institutes and programmes
    980
  role of the Diet 626
  see also Security (national),

Self-Defence Forces, United
States-Japan Security Treaty
(1951), and United States-Japan
Security Treaty of 1960
Deficit spending
government (1970s) 800
Deities 505
Ainu 375, 378, 380
Amaterasu Ōmikami 516, 519, 1186
as healers of illness 600
closeness with man and nature
460-461
depicted in art (dictionary) 1567
depicted in netsuke 1291
Dōsojin 502
encyclopaedic and almanac-type
information about 1551, 1556,
1560-1561
folk conceptions 530
Hachiman 1289
imperial family members 1163
kami 499, 503, 516, 518-520
myths and stories about 1186
pantheon of Buddhist 485
Shintō (depicted in paintings) 1199
Susanoo no Mikoto 516
village (Takashima, Okayama
Prefecture) 554
Yashiki-gami 503
Delinquency *see* Juvenile delinquency
Demilitarisation
post-1945 271, 759
Democracy
1960s-1970s 2, 27
1970s-1980s 616
championed by Ōkuma Shigenobu 296
consequences of the popular rights
movement for 195
future prospects 617
Taishō period 241, 249
views (1860) of American 667
Democratic Socialist Party 634
Democratisation
during the Allied occupation of Japan
(1945-52) 267, 273-274, 280, 617
effect on corporate management 802
post-1945 process 532
Demography 46, 371
Ainu 379
demographic transition in the
industrialisation process 812
mid-19th century 212
Tokugawa period 169, 172, 182

Demons
demonic imagery of Kamaitachi
(photographs) 1275
theme in art and culture (exhibition
catalogue) 1189
Demonstrative words
grammar 427
Dengaku noh (performing art) 1403,
1409
audiences 1410
Dependence (*amae*)
analysis of the concept 589
as a factor in crime control 566
as a factor influencing behaviour 592
as an element of human relationships
809
psychology 20
relationship to the dyadic concepts of
omote/ura and *tatemae/honne* 590
Deregulation
financial 860, 884
telecommunications transmission
953
see also Liberalisation
Deshima (Nagasaki)
Western physicians at 596
Design
Design Law 773
development of cloisonné 1361
elements 1191
encyclopaedic and almanac-type
information about 1552
historical evolution and aesthetic
conception 1204
industrial 773
interior 1326
motifs 1191, 1204, 1207
motifs (of textiles) 1344-1345, 1347,
1349, 1351, 1353
patterns (in lacquerwork) 1370
photographs 1224
Desserts
recipes 1429-1430, 1438
Destiny
folk tales about 1185
Detroit, Michigan
blue-collar workers (compared with
Yokohama) 919
ways of choosing marriage partners
(compared with Tokyo) 558
Developing countries
Japanese economic exploitation
567

Development *see* Agriculture
(agricultural development),
Economic development, Industrial
development, Political
development, and Research and
development
Development aid *see* Foreign aid
Deviant behaviour 588
among Japanese Americans 394
see also Crime, Gangsters, Juvenile
delinquency, and Suicide
Dialects 407, 454
Diaries
Baelz, Erwin von 351
bibliography 1597
Fujiwara Michitsuna no haha 1013
Gayn, Mark 269
Grew, Joseph C. 690
Hachiya Michihiko 259
Harris, Townsend 676
Honjō Shigeru 209
Izumi Shikibu 1149
Kamata Satoshi 924
Ki no Tsurayuki 1149
Kido Kōin 307
Kikuchi, Charles 393
Kobayashi Issa 1146
literary genre of poetic 1149
Masaoka Shiki 1149
Matsuo Bashō 1007, 1149
Murasaki Shikibu 1023
Perry, Matthew C. 673
Richie, Donald 71
Smith, Richard Gordon 72
Sugawara Takasue no musume 1026
Whitney, Clara A. N. 363
Diary of a mad old man (Tanizaki
Junichirō)
quest for identity in 1115
translation 1099
Diary of Izumi Shikibu
translation 1149
Dictionaries
affective expressions 425
art 1567
artistic names 423
Asian American history 1563
Buddhist terms 415
business terms 422
Chinese characters (*kanji*) 421, 423,
437-438, 448, 1571
classical literature 1566
computer and data-processing terms 437

English-Japanese 417, 424, 426
era names (*nengō*) 423
expressions pertaining to women 413
historical names 423
history (1853-1980) 1555
idiomatic words and expressions 414
Japanese-English 413-415, 418-423,
425-426
literary names 423
loanwords 419
personal names 415, 423
pictorial 424
place names 57, 423
proper usage 420, 425
romanised 426
signs in Japanese 88
surnames 423
ukiyo-e prints 1266
unique terms 453
see also Biographical dictionaries
Diet (food)
medieval period 136
Diet (parliament) 23, 617, 624, 782
Cabinet's power to dissolve 790
compared with the US Congress 626
conflict management in 538
development of parliamentary
government (1868-1900) 189
elections 631, 788
introductory study 607
members (biographical dictionary and
directory 366)
nature and role 626
operations and internal governance
629
organisation 607
origins and history 607
party politics 198, 224, 607, 629-630,
636
ratification of ILO Convention no.87
609
reactions to Prime Minister Tōjō's
wartime regime 237
restructuring (1945-52) 280-281
role in foreign policy-making 682, 748
role in peace negotiations with the
USSR (1950s) 728
Tanaka Shōzō as a Diet member 312
US-Japan Security Treaty crisis (1960)
744
see also National Diet Library
Diplomacy
basic facts and figures (annual

handbook) 14
Canadian-Japanese economic
    (1960s-1970s) 895
European-Japanese economic
    (1959-81) 906
Korean repatriation 377
management 729
negotiating style 645, 748
negotiations for the 1951 peace
    settlement 283
oil 849, 885
private economic 887
role of foreign aid policy 757
Sino-Japanese economic
    (1970s-1980s) 735
Diplomats
Alcock, Rutherford 349
biographical dictionary 367
comparison of Japan and the USA 729
Emmerson, John K. 354
Harris, Townsend 676
Hirota Kōki 346
Mitford, Algernon Bertram 357
Mori Arinori 304
Norman, E. H. 226
role in peace negotiations with the
    USSR (1950s) 728
round-table discussion on Japan-US
    relations (1980s) 733
Satow, Ernest 190, 675
Shigemitsu Mamoru 708
see also Ambassadors
Directories
antique shops 1215, 1340
broadcasting stations 1483
colleges and universities 1550
companies 822
Diet (parliament) members 366
government bodies 366, 605, 1574
government officials 366, 1574
information sources 1558, 1565
Japanese studies (outside Japan) 1554,
    1559, 1565, 1615
libraries 1474, 1558
museums of art and archaeology 1475
newspaper industry 1483
organisations engaged in artifical
    intelligence activities 994
prominent postwar figures 1574
published in Japan (union list) 1601
restaurants 84
ryōkan (inns) 96
scientific research establishments 980

Zen Buddhist temples 97
Disarmament
as part of post-1945 national security
    762
breakdown of naval negotiations
    (1930s) 704
Disasters
public and private responses 777
Disclosure system
corporations 858
for securities 781
Discographies 1383
bibliography 1611
folk songs 1381
Discrimination
against Japanese Americans 384, 389,
    392, 402
against Japanese Canadians 382-383
against Koreans in Japan 376-377
against the burakumin 205, 373-374,
    381, 785
against women 575, 785
as an issue in the 'New Wave' cinema
    1419
Diseases see Illness
Disinvestment policies 801
Disobedience
patterns 614
Disputes
business 779, 797
labour 921, 930-931
methods of resolving 778-779, 786,
    797, 921, 931
see also Conflict
Dissertations
bibliographies 1607
Distribution system 838, 891
government publications 1593
marketing imported Canadian
    products 895
structure 801
wholesale and retail 839
Divorce 536, 574
legal obstacles 777
Doctors
Akizuki Tatsuichirō 258
Baelz, Erwin von 351, 597
Hachiya Michihiko 255
involvement in politics 604
Kaempfer, Engelbert 596
life-course 542
Meiji period 597
Mohnike, Otto 597

Doctors *continued*
  Nagai Takashi 258
  Pompe van Meerdervoort, J. L. C.
    596
  profession of biomedical 600
  Siebold, Philipp Franz von 596
  survivors of the atomic bombing of
    Hiroshima (1945) 255, 259
  Ten Rhijne, Willem 596
  Thunberg, Carl Pieter 596
  Tokugawa period 165, 596
  Willis, William 353, 597
Doctor's wife (Ariyoshi Sawako)
  translation 1047
Documents
  at the Shōsōin 1194
  belonging to the family of Iriki-in
    (12th-14th centuries) 148
  education (1615-1947) 973
  historical sources 120
  Kamakura period 148
  peace settlements (1950s) 283
  records of the 1941 policy conferences
    693
  Sino-Japanese relations (1949-80) 730
  Soviet-Japanese treaties and
    agreements 752
  US-Japanese relations, (1931-41) 690
Dōgen
  life and thought 474, 481
  Shōbōgenzō 473
  Shōbōgenzō-zuimonki 472
  teachings 480
Doihara Kenji
  role in the North China Autonomy
    Movement 647
Dolls
  as antiques 1215, 1363
  introductory study (illustrated) 1363
Domestic violence 591
Doolittle air raid (1942) 696, 699
Dormitory life
  companies 543
  university preparatory academies
    (1880s-1940s) 232
Dōsojin (deity) 502
Dōzoku (corporate group of people) 561
Drainage
  effect of improvements in 831
Drama
  history 999
  history (1868-1940s) 1001
  influence on cinema 1393

introductory studies 1002, 1004
  kōwaka 1169
  realism and unreality in 1003
  television home 538
  theatre and culture in the 1960s 1171
  Tokugawa period 1005
  see also Bugaku, Bunraku theatre,
    Gigaku, Kabuki, *Kyōgen*, Noh,
    Shingeki, Theatre
Dramatists *see* Playwrights
Drawings
  aircraft (World War II) 689
  bunraku theatre 1392
  Katsushika Hokusai 1258, 1260
  made during the Perry expedition
    (1853-54) 673
Dreams
  in *Hamamatsu Chūnagon monogatari*
    1027
  in *Sarashina nikki* 1026
Dress *see* Clothing
Drifting clouds (Futabatei Shimei)
  ideal of individualism in 1129
  study and translation 1124
Drinks and drinking
  among farmers 573
  encyclopaedic and almanac-type
    information about 1551-1553,
    1556-1557, 1561
  overview 1433
  recipes for beverages 1429, 1434, 1438
  saké 929, 1431, 1433, 1436, 1438
  tea 1433, 1438
  see also Tea ceremony (*chanoyu*)
Drugs
  use 566, 570
  yakuza (gangster) involvement in 569
Drums
  played in kabuki ensembles 1384-1385
  played in noh ensembles 1385, 1387
Dual structure of the economy 805, 883
  labour demand and supply 803, 807
  national policy for eliminating 815
  wage structure 812
Dulles, John Foster 283
Dutch in Japan at Nagasaki (Tokugawa
  period) 167, 173, 179
  Pompe van Meerdervoort, J. L. C.
    596
  Ten Rhijne, Willem 596
'Dutch learning' (*Rangaku*) 167, 173,
  180
Dyes and dyeing 1349, 1351

ikat weaving (*kasuri*) 1354
kimono 1356
stencil dyeing (*katazome*) 1350
stencils for dyeing fabrics 1344
tsujigahana 1346
tsutsugaki fabrics 1345
use of dyes in *kosode* fabrics 1353

E

Earth sciences
   research institutes and programmes
      980
Earthquakes 22, 236
   research institutes and programmes
      980
Eastern Solomons
   battle (1942) 680
Ebina Danjō 358
   writings and activities 235
Echizen ware (ceramics) 1283, 1286
Economic assistance *see* Foreign aid
Economic change
   economy's responsiveness to 925
   village communities 550, 555-556
Economic co-operation *see*
      Co-operation, Co-operatives, and
      Foreign aid
Economic development 16, 533
   1868-1941 (survey) 218
   1868-1973 (overview) 818
   1870s-1980 (quantitative study) 803
   Asian Development Bank and Japan
      756
   bibliographies 218, 1581, 1590, 1592,
      1594, 1614
   British involvement in Meiji 660
   comparison of Japan and Asian
      countries 806
   comparison of Japan and Europe 233
   Japan International Cooperation
      Agency 746
   labour market and 938
   long-term patterns 808
   offshore petroleum resources 735, 796
   prospects by the year 2000 AD 954
   role of trade unions 780
   social consequences 555-556
   sustained by 'strategic industries' 873
   Tokugawa period 169, 182
Economic growth
   1868-1941 225

post-1945 5, 350, 791-793, 799-800,
   813, 883
agriculture 831
automobile manufacturing 871
determinants 793, 797, 799, 804, 807,
   810-811, 814-815, 875
impact of foreign trade 807
impact on foreign relations 743
machine tools industry 872
mechanism and policies 805
MITI's role (post-1945) 272
negative aspects 567
organisers (post-1945) 208
overview for businessmen 843
pollution accompanying 775
role of education 966
role of financial policies 863
role of industrial strategy 934
role of social and cultural factors 811
sectoral growth patterns and
   intersectoral relations 807
shift from export-led to demand-led
   growth 798
social consequences 532-534, 564, 567
technopolises as engines for future 96
Economic history *see* History (economic)
Economic missions
   use of private businessmen 887
Economic planning 810, 939
   bibliographies 1594, 1600, 1614
Economic policies 910
   adjustment (post-1973) 794, 816, 859,
      903
   advocated by Arai Hakuseki 177
   advocated by the socialist parties 630
   annual surveys 821
   decision-making process 856
   determinants 882
   developed by MITI 272, 748, 785
   entrepreneurial behaviour and 816
   institutional framework for foreign 906
   Liberal Democratic Party's response
      to changing 619
   prewar foreign (research guide) 1599
   responsible for post-1945 economic
      growth 799, 811, 814-815
Economic prosperity *see* Affluence
Economists
   Yanaihara Tadao 288
Economy 7, 9, 32, 791
   adoption of economies of scale
      (1953-71) 793
   annual statistics 819-829

Economy *continued*
  annual surveys 820-821, 823
  basic facts and figures (annual
    handbooks) 14
  character and structure 6
  depicted in comic books 1480
  development and structure (1945-80)
    805
  dual structure 803, 805, 807, 812, 815,
    883
  economic welfare 817
  encyclopaedic and almanac-type
    information about 1556, 1568
  government report (annual) 820, 829
  impact of labour disputes 841, 930
  impact of the robotics industry 995
  internationalisation 798, 802
  Japan as a model for the West 795
  Japan's central role in East Asia's
    economic expansion 724
  Japan's emergence as a global
    economic power (post-1945) 5, 726,
    740, 755, 805, 904
  macroeconomic interdependence of
    Japan and the USA 903
  Muromachi period 137
  newspaper reporting about 1546-1549
  overview 21, 23, 30
  periodicals 1488, 1491, 1493, 1498,
    1500-1501, 1517-1518, 1524, 1526,
    1530, 1536, 1540, 1542
  political decision-making and 620
  structural adjustment (1970s) 794
  survey (1953-73) 792
  technology policy and economic
    performance 983
  Tokugawa period 169-170
Ecumenicity
  post-1945 497
Edo *see* Tokyo
Edo Castle 185, 1307, 1317
Edo school of painting 1239
Education 6, 16, 35, 38, 723, 960
  access to good high schools 639
  achievements 966, 971
  adaptive qualities 976
  administration 960
  American perceptions 965
  among Tokyo residents 549
  among the *burakumin* 374
  annual statistics 825-827
  as an agent of social change 379
  at Tomoe Gakuen 330

  at university preparatory academies
    (1880s-1940s) 232
  basic facts and figures (annual
    handbook) 14
  bibliographies 1610
  Christian involvement (post-1945) 497
  colonial Korea and Taiwan 223
  contribution to industrialisation 216
  Crown Prince Akihito (1940s) 362
  development (1930s-1950s) 973
  during the Allied occupation of Japan
    (1945-52) 271, 273, 282, 651,
    960-961, 975
  during the Meiji period 194, 197, 205,
    217, 239, 304, 343, 351, 353, 358
  during the Taishō period 217, 350
  during the Tokugawa period 164, 168,
    176, 180, 973
  during World War II 207
  educational aspects of
    Australian-Japanese relations 751
  employment system and 923
  finance 960, 968
  freedom of expression and 771
  government resolution of problems
    affecting 620
  health 603
  high standards 971
  higher civil servants 613
  history of 594, 960
  influence on job mobility 919
  influence on student radicalism 969
  kindergartens 559, 960, 970
  Korean minority in Japan 376
  labour markets and 962
  legal 776, 786
  Liberal Democratic Party's response
    to changing conditions in higher 619
  librarianship 1474, 1476
  management recruitment and 878
  medical 343, 353, 596-598
  moral 9, 595
  music teaching 326, 1385-1386
  naval officers and sailors 698
  newspaper articles 1546, 1549
  policy 623
  post-1945 537, 651, 964
  private schools 968
  promotion of egalitarianism 964
  readings about 961
  reform 619, 970, 972
  reform (Allied occupation of Japan)
    273, 282, 651, 960-961, 975

reform (comparison of Japan and the
  USA) 965
rural 573
schools that teach *kanpō* (Chinese
  herbal medicine) 598
science 980
selection of schools 962
shortcomings and problems 966
social, economic, and political
  importance 976
system 8, 212, 239, 535, 970-971
system (comparison of private and
  public) 968
vocational 217
widespread commitment to
  precollegiate 978
women 240, 578
see also Elementary education, High
  schools, Higher Education,
  Instructional materials, Schools,
  Textbooks, Training, and
  Universities
'Education mamas'
women as 574
Educators
Abe Isoo 288
changing role of professors (1970s) 963
Fukuzawa Yukichi 302
Griffis, William Elliot 114, 190, 197,
  358, 361
Janes, Leroy Lansing 358
Kawakami Hajime 241, 318
Kobayashi Sosaku 330
Makiguchi Tsunesaburō 319
Minobe Tatsukichi 220
Mori Arinori 304, 972
Murray, David 197
productivity of schools 963
support for World War II among 237
Suzuki Shinichi 326
Yanaihara Tadao 288
Ehime Prefecture
farm life 573
natural farming near Matsuyama Bay
  830
see also Inland Sea area, and Shikoku
Eiga monogatari
translation and study 1021
Ejima Kiseki
life and writings 1036
Elderly
bibliography 1595
during World War II 207

health care 599, 603, 1595
literary works about 1053, 1060, 1066,
  1099, 1172, 1595
status and social integration 540
women 574, 1595
see also Ageing
Election campaigns 632
freedom of expression during 771
Satō Bunsei in Ōita Prefecture 631
Elections 23, 627
annual statistics 825
July 6, 1986 election 629
long-term trends 628, 642
novel about 1072
Nikkyōso's influence 977
parliamentary 624, 631, 638, 788
political opposition and big city 642
Electoral behaviour *see* Voting
  behaviour
Electoral system 27, 629, 631, 634
impact on political parties 634
influence on Diet proceedings 607
Electric power 812, 850
Tokyo Electric Power Company 849
Electrical appliance factory
organisational structure 929
Electrical equipment industry 217
Electronic media
socio-economic role 955
Electronics
research and development 984
research institutes and programmes 980
Sony Corporation 332, 877
Electronics industry 813, 985
collaboration between Japanese and
  Western firms 912
evolution (post-1945) 988
industrial policy and 879
managerial approaches (Japanese
  subsidiaries in Europe) 949
overseas market strategies 948
Elementary education
child development and 594
comparison of Japan and the USA 965
equality among schoolchildren 964
history and current issues 960
overview (1980s) 970
school years of Kuroyanagi Tetsuko
  330
Elementary Particle Theory Group 992
Elgin, Lord
negotiation of the Anglo-Japanese
  commercial treaty 658

Elites
  business 208, 219
  industrial 219
  intellectual 232
  see also Leadership
Emaki see Handscrolls
Embroidery
  textile 1346, 1351
Emigration see Migration
Emigration companies (imingaisha) 396
Emmerson, John K.
  autobiography 354
Emotions
  attitudes towards one's 585
  emotional interdependence 530
  kamikaze pilots 700
  vocabulary for 405
Empathy
  factor influencing behaviour 592
'Emperor-organ theory' 209, 220
'Emperor system' (tennōsei) 203, 617
Emperors 35, 188
  16th century 133
  Akihito 362
  biographical dictionary 367
  Go-Daigo 159, 1018
  Go-Fukakusa 310
  Go-Sanjō 142
  Go-Shirakawa 142
  Hirohito 23, 209, 237, 273, 280, 334,
    362, 693
  history (Heian period) 1017
  legal status (post-1945) 782
  position in Shintō 515-516, 520
  Shirakawa 142
  Tenmu Tennō 295
  Toba 142
  see also Imperial court, and Imperial
    institution
'Employed foreigners' (oyatoi
    gaikokujin)
  Meiji period 197, 229, 351, 353, 358
Employment
  annual statistics 824
  bibliographies 1590, 1614
  changing occupational structure
    (19th-20th centuries) 812
  corporate practices 836
  during World War II 207
  education and 962, 970
  increase in labour employment
    (1953-71) 793
  lifetime employment 204, 332, 542,

  795, 809, 869, 917, 919, 923, 938
  occupational trends among Japanese
    Americans 349
  opportunities 535
  patterns (women) 542, 574
  social readjustment problems of
    overseas employees 572
  structure 532
  system 23, 917, 920, 923
  unemployment (early 1970s) 930
'Emptiness'
  tenet of Buddhism 469, 477, 487, 493,
    525
Enamelling technology
  historical evolution 1361
Enchi Fumiko
  novels 1052-1053
  short stories 1048, 1071, 1098, 1106
Encyclopaedias
  culture and history 1568
  Imperial Japanese Navy 1572
  kabuki theatre 1564
  Kodansha encyclopaedia of Japan 1556
  legends illustrated in art 1560
  modern Japan 1568
  things Japanese 1551-1553, 1561
Endō Shūsaku
  novels 1008, 1054-1055
Energy 45
  alternative sources 847, 849-850
  annual statistics 824-827, 829
  basic facts and figures (annual
    handbook) 14
  coal 847, 849-850, 885, 900
  dependence on overseas supplies 762,
    903
  diversification of supplies 885
  electric power 812, 849-850
  imported from Siberia 747
  involvement of government
    corporations 612
  laws relating to (bibliography) 1582
  liquefied natural gas 847, 849, 885
  markets 801, 850
  natural gas 900
  nuclear power 34, 796, 829, 846-849,
    885
  policies 27, 623, 801, 849, 884
  research institutes and programmes
    980
  resources 46
  Soviet-Japanese energy co-operation
    847

US-Japanese energy relations 847
see also Petroleum
Enfranchisement of women 267
Engineering
historical development 187
Engineering industry
managerial approaches (Japanese
subsidiaries in Europe) 949
Engineers
Honda Sōichirō 344, 882
England *see* Great Britain
English language
contrasted with Japanese 429
teaching 362
teaching (guidebook) 979
words and terms adopted in the
Japanese language 419
English men and women in Japan 68,
132, 162
Adams, Will 133
Alcock, Rutherford 349
Allen, George Cyril 350
Batchelor, John 372
Bird, Isabella 66, 190
Black, John R. 162
Booth, Alan 68
British Commonwealth
Occupation Force in Japan 266
depicted in *Shōgun* 1418
Fraser, Mary Crawford 355
Mitford, Algernon Bertram 357
physicians (Meiji period) 597
Satow, Ernest 190, 675
Smith, Richard Gordon 72
Willis, William 353, 597
see also Westerners in Japan
Enlightenment (*satori*) 487-490, 493
accounts 478-479
Ennen noh (performing art) 1403
Enola Gay (aeroplane)
atomic bombing mission (1945) 260,
262
Enpukuji monastery
Zen Buddhist life and routines 486
Enterprise unions *see* Companies
(company unions)
Enterprises
corporate groupings 231, 935
foreign enterprises in Japan 779
government report (annual) 829
Japanese enterprise as a community
920
packaging 845

public 937
Small and Medium-Sized Enterprises
Organization Law 611
small-scale family 817
Entertainers
female 574
geisha 234, 576
Entertainment
dinner 591
during World War II 207
in Tokyo (1867-1923) 236
industries controlled by *yakuza*
(gangsters) 569
Meiji period 355, 363
newspaper articles about 1546, 1549
see also Games, Leisure activities,
Recreational activities, and Sports
Entrance examinations (university) 971,
975-976, 978
Entrepreneurial mentality
business elite (prewar) 943
economic policy and 816
urban lower class 588
Entrepreneurs
Fujisawa Takeo 882
Honda Sōichirō 344, 882
Meiji period 208
Morita Akio 332, 877
Entsuji (temple)
garden 1327
Environment
annual statistics 829
bibliography 1592
environmental law and policy 775
environmental protest 642, 958
government report (annual) 829
politics 642
solid waste (garbage) management
956
see also Conservation and
environmental protection, and
Pollution
Environmentalists
Tanaka Shōzō 312
Epidemics
Tokugawa period 172
Epic songs (Ainu) 380
Equality
educational 38, 964
Japan's search for equality with the
West 654
problems 611
unequal pay for women 575

Equipment
electrical equipment industry 217
investment (1868-1940) in 233
Erotic literature *see* Pornography
Eroticism
photographs 1277
Esoteric Buddhism *see* Shingon
Buddhism
Espionage
overseas 648
practiced by the *ninja* 1445
Sorge spy ring 228
Essayists
biographical dictionary 365
Kitamura Tōkoku 288, 1129
Uchimura Kanzō 288
Essays
architecture (Tange Kenzō) 1313
bibliography of translations 1588
gardens in Kyōto 1334
'In praise of shadows' (Tanizaki
Junichirō) 1225
Kitamura Tōkoku 1129
nature of poetry (Fujiwara Teika)
1135
postwar cinema (Tadao Satō) 1428
Shōsetsu shinzui (Tsubouchi Shōyō)
1123
Taiyō to tetsu (Mishima Yukio) 1079
tea ceremony (Okakura Kakuzō) 1470
see also Haibun, and *Zuihitsu*
('random essays')
Essays in idleness (Yoshida Kenkō)
aesthetics 1004
translation 1034
Eta *see* Burakumin
Ethics
business 844
ethical values 530
samurai 529, 1452
Shintō 516, 520
views of Fukuzawa Yukichi 194
see also Morality, and Work ethic
Etiquette
business 840, 901, 916, 928
food 1432-1433
kendō 1449
saké-drinking 1431
tea ceremony 1467, 1471-1472
Europe
economic and trade frictions with
Japan 720, 755, 910
economic development (compared
with Japan) 233

foreign relations with Japan 720, 732,
743, 755, 906, 910
images of Japan and the Japanese 216,
755
impact of Japanese exports on
manufacturers in 910
influence on Japanese art 179
influence on Japanese astronomy 151
Japanese direct investment (Western
Europe) 909-910
Japanese images 755
Japanese studies 1554, 1559
Japanese visitors 302, 307, 328, 334
Tokugawa period views 173
trade and commerce with Japan 720,
906, 910
see also the names of individual
European countries
Evil
folk tales about 1184-1185, 1187
Examinations
higher civil servants 613
university entrance 971, 975-976, 978
Exchange rates *see* Foreign exchange
rates
Exhibition catalogues
artistic depiction of natural creatures
1221
Buddhist art from the Tōdaiji temple
1206
Buddhist sculpture (AD 600-1300) 1295
calligraphy (8th-19th centuries) 1249
collection of John and Kimiko Powers
1214
daimyō culture (1185-1868) 1218
design (traditional and modern) 1224
development of colour printing 1261
fan paintings 1233
folk art 1193, 1213
French influence on Japanese painting
1251
handicrafts from the Ryūkyū Islands
1201
ink paintings (Muromachi period)
1248
kosode in the Nomura Collection 1353
lacquerwork 1370
Meiji period art 1229
modern calligraphy 1231
Nanga school of painting 1255
painted porcelain (20th century) 1285
paintings from the Sansō Collection
1246

photography 1275, 1277
realism in art 1205
Shintō arts 1199
shop signs (*kanban*) 1368
supernatural in art and culture 1189
Suzuki Harunobu's ukiyo-e prints
    1261
tea ceremony utensils 1469
theatrical world of Ōsaka prints 1264
Tokugawa Collection of artworks 1219
Tokugawa Collection of noh robes and
    masks 1412
Tokugawa period art 1227
traditional packaging 1371
tsutsugaki fabrics 1345
ukiyo-e paintings (Freer Gallery of
    Art) 1250
woodblock prints 1576
Zen-inspired painting and calligraphy
    1232
see also Catalogues (art)
Exiles
    Sugawara no Michizane 300
Existence
    Buddhist notion of 'pure existence'
    524
Exorcism of evil spirits 378
Exorcists 499
Expenditures (government)
    long-term statistical data 808
Exports
    armaments 763
    automobiles 344, 874, 892
    contribution to economic growth
        (1868-1941) 218
    government encouragement 815
    government policies (post-1945) 814
    impact of labour policies on 909
    impact on Canadian manufacturers
        895
    impact on European manufacturing
        industries 910
    industrial technology 900, 993
    machinery 900
    protection of world export markets
        801
    semiconductors 880
    silk 297
    steel 892
    television sets 783
    textiles 721-722
    see also Sōgō shōsa (general trading
        companies), and Trade and

commerce (foreign)
Expressions
    affective 425
    use of terse 405
Extracurricular activities
    among high school students 975

F

Factions and factionalism
    army 245
    influence on politics in the Diet 607
    Japan Socialist Party 637
    Liberal Democratic Party 629,
        633-634, 638
    socialist parties 630, 634
Factory
    automation 985-986
    economic and social structure 920
    organisational change 929
    social organisation 917
    women workers 578
    workers' concept of social justice 183,
        578
    working conditions 10, 204-205, 918,
        924, 937
Fairs and expositions
    participation in American 651
Fairy tales
    bibliography 1577
Family
    altered social relationships in 556
    as an element of post-1945 society 537
    business (involvement of women)
        578-579
    change depicted in films 1424, 1428
    counselling 570
    crests 1204, 1207, 1352
    crests (handbook) 1191
    enterprises 817
    history 560
    importance for bank employees 543
    institutions (form and function) 530
    juvenile delinquency and 571
    law 786
    members (terminology) 430
    members (women) 574, 579
    readings about 1
    relationships (views of Fukuzawa
        Yukichi) 194
    religious character 460-461
    role in caring for the sick 600
    role in education 574, 594, 962, 970
    role in political socialisation 969

Family *continued*
  socialisation 10, 533
  solidarity 564
  structure of the rural 531
  system 136, 535, 549, 564, 723
  vocabulary for 405
  see also Ie system
Family (Shimazaki Tōson)
  synopsis and analysis 1117
  translation 1096
Family life 8, 20
  Ainu 375, 379
  attitudes towards 18
  comparison of Ōsaka and Takashima,
    Okayama Prefecture 562
  depicted in novels 1047, 1050, 1053,
    1066, 1090, 1092, 1096, 1100-1101
  early medieval 154
  in the new electronic media age 955
  of farmers 534, 573
  of Japanese Americans 388, 392, 394
  of the elderly 540
  of Tokyo residents 549, 563-564
  privatisation of 594
Family planning 169, 172, 182-183, 370
Fans 155
  as antiques 1215
  craftsmanship 1369
  design motif of textile patterns 1344
  fan paintings 1233, 1240
  made of bamboo (photographs) 1357
  used in the kabuki theatre 1352, 1388
Farmers
  activities of Nōkyō (nationwide
    farmers' group) 723
  attitudes, beliefs, and behaviour 834
  Fukuoka Masanobu 830
  impact of post-1945 economic growth
    534, 550, 555-556
  involvement in national politics 531,
    534
  leisure time activities among 1460
  living conditions (1868-1945) 205
  mentality 531, 548, 550
  Ōkura Nagatsune 289
  opposition to Narita Airport 606
  receipt of government subsidies 620
  support for the socialist parties 630
  tenant 175, 181, 205, 241-242, 268,
    1068
  Tokugawa period 165
  transformed into supporters of the
    army 243

  Utsunomiya Haruko 573
  way of life 548, 550, 573
Farmhouses
  minka 1301, 1303, 1312
Farming *see* Agriculture
Farming communities *see* Hamlets, and
  Villages
Fascism
  ideology and dynamism 618
  intellectuals of the 1930s 199
Fashion
  language of 26
  world of (illustrated guide) 1348
Fauna
  attitudes towards wild life 63
  geological periods 49
  national parks 48
  Tokyo area 91
Feast of all souls (*shinurapa*) 378
February 26, 1936 Incident 209, 238,
  245, 685, 690, 708
  Ishiwara Kanji's role 342
  Kita Ikki's association 348
Feminine sensibility
  Heian period literature 1003
Feminism 574
  Meiji period beginnings 240
Fencing *see* Kendō (martial art)
Fenellosa, Ernest
  writings about Japan 216
Ferns 62
Fertility invocations
  festivals based on 501
Festivals
  16th century 133, 153
  as precursors of the theatrical arts
    1393, 1403, 1410
  Autumn Festival of thanksgiving 519
  dolls 1363
  encyclopaedic and almanac-type
    information about 1551, 1556-1557,
    1561, 1568
  folk festivals (*matsuri*) 460-462,
    500-501
  kite-flying 1461
  Namahage festival 501
  Nii-name-sai 520
  of Kyōto 77, 92
  of the Tōhoku region 74
  photographs 77, 92, 501, 1461
  relationship with marriage 560
  Shintō 516, 518-520
  Shinurapa 378

tales about 1017, 1022
tourist guides 80
Feudal lords *see* Daimyō
Feudalism 134, 154
  abolition of Tokugawa 307
  development and character 148
'Fifth generation' of computers
  research and development 982, 997
Fifty-three Stages of the Tōkaidō (Andō
  Hiroshige)
  print series (reproductions) 1265
Filial piety
  as a samurai value 529
  law and 790
  literary depiction 1012
Filial relations
  among Japanese Americans 403
Film companies
  government control (1918-45) 221
Film directors 1414
  Gosha Hideo 1420
  Hani Susumu 1423
  Hidari Sachiko 1423
  Ichikawa Kon 1415, 1421, 1423
  Imai Tadashi 1423
  Imamura Shōhei 1415, 1419
  Inagaki Hiroshi 1420
  Ishida Tamizo 1417
  Itō Daisuke 1423
  Kinoshita Keisuke 1415, 1421
  Kobayashi Masaki 1415, 1423
  Kurosawa Akira 329, 1415, 1417,
    1420-1421, 1423-1425, 1585
  Mizoguchi Kenji 1415, 1417,
    1421-1422, 1424, 1428, 1578
  Naruse Mikio 1415, 1417, 1424, 1428
  Okamoto Kihachi 1420
  Ōshima Nagisa 1415, 1417, 1419,
    1421, 1423-1424
  Ozu Yasujirō 1415-1417, 1421, 1424,
    1427-1428
  Shimizu Hiroshi 1417
  Shindō Kaneto 1423
  Shinoda Masahiro 1415, 1419-1421,
    1423-1424
  Suzuki Seijun 1419
  Terayama Shūji 1423
  Teshigahara Hiroshi 1421, 1423
  Yamanaka Sadao 1417
  Yoshida Yoshishige 1419
Film distributors
  Kawakita Kashiko 1423
Film scripts

Ikiru (translation) 1057
Tōkyō monogatari (translation) 1057
  used by Ozu Yasujirō 1427
Film-making 1416, 1421, 1423, 1425,
  1427-1428
  modes of representation 1417
  production of *Shōgun* 1418
Filmographies
  documentary and theatrical films 1586
  Ichikawa Kon 1415
  Imamura Shōhei 1415
  Kinoshita Keisuke 1415
  Kobayashi Masaki 1415
  Kurosawa Akira 1415, 1425, 1585
  Mizoguchi Kenji 1415, 1578
  Naruse Mikio 1415
  Ōshima Nagisa 1415
  Ozu Yasujirō 1415, 1427
  Shinoda Masahiro 1415
Films
  as a resource for teachers 9
  critical essays about major 1421
  depiction of robots 995
  developments during the 1960s 1428
  encyclopaedic and almanac-type
    information about 1552, 1556
  racist stereotypes in wartime 686
  samurai films of Kurosawa Akira 1420
  see also Cinema
Finance 110
  banks and 901
  basic facts and figures (annual
    handbook) 14
  bibliographies 1581, 1600, 1614
  corporate 822, 836, 852, 862, 880, 922
  debt financing 852
  deregulation 800
  educational 960, 963
  equity financing 852
  financial reporting 852
  history (1945-71) 851
  impact of regulatory policy-making 857
  international 811, 851
  intersectoral resource flows and 806
  Japanese inroads into the US financial
    services sector 853
  liberalisation 779, 820-821, 856, 860,
    884
  local government 641
  management 861-862
  merging and non-merging firms 935
  newspaper reporting about 1546,
    1548-1549

Finance *continued*
    periodicals 1495, 1500, 1519, 1542,
        1544
    political parties 632-634, 638
    procedures of the Diet 626
    public policy companies 612
    strategy for financing energy imports
        849
    structure and development
        (1868-1977) 855
    Tokyo as a world centre 861-862
    see also Foreign investment, Money,
        and Public finance
Finance Ministry *see* Ministry of Finance
Financial institutions 801, 853, 864, 866
    1868-1977 855
    bibliography 1594
    influence on the semiconductor
        industry 880
    internationalisation 948
    personnel practices 942
    see also Banks, and Securities
        (securities companies)
Financial markets
    1980s 860, 862
    annual statistics 824
    internationalisation of Japan's 909
Financial system 939
    forces of change (1970s) 903
    overview (1980s) 868
    post-1945 791, 813, 864
    structure and monetary instruments
        865
Fire-bombing of Japanese cities
    (1944-45) 583, 691, 715
Fires on the plain (Ōoka Shōhei)
    literary analysis 1127
    quest for identity in 1115
    translation 1091
First Japanese embassy to the USA
    (1860) 667
Fiscal policies
    1950s-1960s 811, 851
    1970s-1980s 801
    comparisons of Japan and the USA
        801, 884, 886
    contribution to economic growth 799
    external safeguard of domestic 909
    management (1970s) 859
    of Arai Hakuseki 177, 298
    of Matsukata Masayoshi 297
Fish
    depicted in netsuke 1291

design motif of textile patterns 1344
    encyclopaedic and almanac-type
        information about 1556, 1561
    guidebook 60
    recipes 1429-1430, 1434, 1438-1439
    sumi-e techniques for painting 1254
    sushi 1369, 1432-1433, 1436,
        1438-1439
Fisheries
    annual statistics 825, 827, 829
    government report (annual) 829
    periodicals 1502
    policy 796
Fishermen
    folk culture 503
    literary works about 1068, 1078
    Tsuchiura, Ibaraki Prefecture 234
    women in central Japan 579
Fishing 46
    Ainu 375
    co-operatives 13
    fish markets 552, 1432
    industry's role in peace negotiations
        with the USSR (1950s) 728
    Japan in global ocean politics 717
    North Pacific Fisheries Convention
        734
    rights off the Siberian coasts 752
    socio-economic organisation 552
Fishing communities
    central Japan 579
    Shingū, Fukuoka Prefecture 552
    Takashima, Okayama Prefecture 554
Flexner, Simon
    patron of Noguchi Hideyo 343
'Floating world' culture *see* Society
    (cultural world of Tokugawa), and
    Ukiyo-e prints
Floor mats *see* Tatami (floor mats)
Flora 61-62
    bamboo 64, 1357
    described by Carl Pieter Thunberg 596
    design motif of family crests and
        textiles 1191, 1344
    folk tales about plants 1185
    geological periods 49
    national parks 48
    origami figures 1364, 1367
    photographs 17, 44, 64, 1357
    Tokyo area 91
Flower-arrangement *see* Ikebana (flower
    arrangement)
Flower containers

aesthetic qualities (photographs) 1198
used in ikebana 1462, 1465
used in the tea ceremony 1467-1469,
    1471-1472
Flowers
    azaleas 59
    design motif of textile patterns 1344
    encyclopaedic and almanac-type
        information about 1551, 1557,
        1560-1561
    Katsushika Hokusai's sketches
        (reproductions) 1258
    sumi-e techniques for painting 1254
    ukiyo-e prints by Andō Hiroshige
        1257
    used in the tea ceremony 1470
    see also Flora
Flutes
    bamboo (photographs) 1357
    flute-playing (Shintō dimensions) 519
    hayashi ensemble 1384
    noh 1387
    shakuhachi 1369, 1382-1383
Folk art 1226
    Ainu 375
    exhibition catalogues 1193, 1213
    introductory study 1210
    Okinawan 1222, 1228
    pottery 19, 553
    representations of Daruma 483
Folk beliefs
    in the supernatural 1189
Folk festivals *see* Festivals
Folk legends
    anthology 1184
Folk religion 460-462, 499-505, 530
Folk songs 1381-1383
    annotated collection 1381
    discography 1381
    history 1380-1381
    rice-planting (16th century) 135
Folk tales 1, 1186, 1189
    anthologies 1185, 1187-1188
    bibliography 1577
    scrolls illustrating 1245
    Yanagita Kunio guide to 1188
Folk-crafts (*mingei*) movement 331, 553,
    1228
Folklore 1186
    Ainu 375, 380
    bibliography 1577
    concerned with Daruma 483
    encyclopaedic and almanac-type

information about 1560-1561
folklorists 503
Inland Sea area 71
periodicals 1490
research opportunities 503
Food 19, 86
    16th century 133, 153
    arrangement on serving dishes 1432,
        1435, 1437-1438, 1440
    buying (guidebook) 85
    cookbooks 1429-1430, 1434,
        1438-1440
    during prehistoric times 101, 106, 109
    during World War II 207
    encyclopaedic and almanac-type
        information about 1551-1553,
        1556-1557, 1561
    Festival of New Food (*Nii-name-sai*)
        520
    fruit production 40
    guidebooks 87, 90
    imports 762, 832-833, 885, 892
    Meiji period 363
    overview 1433
    Tokugawa period 165
    Victorian British writings about 68
    see also Agriculture, Beef, Cuisine,
        Drinks and drinking, Fish,
        Restaurants, and Sushi
Forbidden colors (Mishima Yukio)
    translation 1075
Ford Motor Company
    compared with Nissan 874
Foreign aid 742
    annual statistics 824, 829
    decision-making process 746
    economic assistance to China 735-736
    government report (annual) 829
    Japan and the Asian Development
        Bank 756
    loans to Korea (1980s) 737
    Overseas Economic Cooperation Fund
        612
    periodicals 1502, 1541
    policy 757
    programmes 746, 946
Foreign economic policy 898, 910
Foreign exchange
    annual statistics 819, 824
    controls 783
    laws 857, 909
    management 861
    markets 862, 864, 909

Foreign exchange rates
  before and after the G5 agreement
    (1980s) 907
  during the 1970s 866
  policy 816, 909
  revaluation of the yen 851, 860, 892
  revaluation of the yen (economic
    impact) 805, 820, 853, 886, 946
Foreign investment 27, 791, 823, 867,
    905, 952
  annual statistics 824
  in Brazil 898
  in Canada 734, 895
  in Great Britain 944
  in Southeast Asia 727, 952
  in the Netherlands 948
  in the USA 801, 951
  in West Germany 948
  in Western Europe 909-910
  law (bibliography) 1582
  private economic diplomacy and 887
  undertaken by multinational
    corporations 912, 951
Foreign investment in Japan 791, 905
  American 801
  Canadian 895
  corporate acquisitions 837
Foreign ministers
  Hirota Kōki 346
  Mutsu Munemitsu 668
  personalities and actions (1869-1942)
    654
  Shidehara Kijurō 333
  Shigemitsu Mamoru 708
Foreign Ministry see Ministry of Foreign
  Affairs
Foreign policy 623-624, 748
  1868-1941 (research guide) 1599
  1869-1942 654
  1930s 249, 682, 685, 694, 708
  constitutional structure and
    components (Meiji period) 672
  general background 724, 748
  government report (annual) 829
  impact of the Manchurian Incident 702
  interaction with domestic politics
    (post-1945) 718, 754, 817
  interrelationship with security policy
    762
  Japan Socialist Party 637
  political development,
    decision-making, and 720
  resources as a factor in 885

role of foreign aid 757
role of the Diet 626
socialist parties 630
Soviet-Japanese peace agreement and
  728
trends (1970s) 718
Foreign Press Centre
  activities 1483
Foreign relations 6, 23, 30, 617, 739
  1334-1573 (Muromachi period) 140
  1853-1952 (bibliographical guide) 1599
  1858-1879 162
  1862-1868 186
  1868-1912 (Meiji period) 351
  1894-1943 656
  post-1945 5-6
  bibliographies 1583, 1599
  Fukuzawa Yukichi's views 194
  impact of post-1945 economic growth
    743
  influence on foreign aid policy 746
  Japan and the Asian Development
    Bank 756
  Japan's emerging role (1980s) in
    international affairs 724-725, 732,
    740
  Japan's involvement in global ocean
    politics 717
  Japan's role in regional security
    arrangements 760
  newspaper articles about 1546-1547,
    1549
  periodicals 1491, 1493, 1514, 1524,
    1536, 1540
Foreign relations with Africa 743
Foreign relations with ASEAN
  (Association of Southeast Asian
    Nations) 741, 743, 810, 897
Foreign relations with Australia
  1960s-1970s 751
  post-1945 723, 743
  trade and commerce 723, 745, 751,
    833, 885
  see also World War II (Pacific
    Theatre)
Foreign relations with Brazil 743, 897
Foreign relations with Burma
  peace settlement (World War II) 283
Foreign relations with Canada
  1870-1982 655
  post-1952 734, 743
  impact of the Law of the Sea 895
  trade and commerce 655, 734, 895

Foreign relations with China
  17th century 677
  1868-1941 (research guide) 1599
  1894-1972 652
  1911-1915 666
  1915-1970s 647
  1920s 324, 333, 661
  1930s 209, 346
  political and cultural relationship
    (1850-1945) 650
  see also Sino-Japanese War of
    1894-95, and Sino-Japanese War of
    1937-45
Foreign relations with China (People's
  Republic of China)
  1945-76 738
  1949-72 736
  1950s-1980s 724, 730
  1960s 633, 742
  1970s-1980s 735, 743, 762
  1980s 725, 732, 754
  China-Japan Peace and Friendship
    Treaty (1978) 730
  influence of the US-Japan security
    alliance 765
  normalisation of relations 339, 620,
    647, 652, 730, 736, 738, 748-749
  peace settlement (World War II) 283
  Soviet perceptions 747
  trade and commerce 738, 885
Foreign relations with China (Republic
  of China) 738, 743
  terminating the state of war (1952)
    283, 647
Foreign relations with Europe 720
Foreign relations with Europe
  (European Community) 732, 743
  755, 906, 910
Foreign relations with France
  early 1940s 711
  massacre of French sailors at Sakai
    (1868) 675
  Triple Intervention (1895) 668
Foreign relations with Germany
  1868-1941 (research guide) 1599
  1930s 228, 245, 346, 708
  concerning Jews in Shanghai 4
  Triple Intervention (1895) 668
Foreign relations with Great Britain
  1858-79 162
  1858-83 660
  1860s 186, 349, 353, 675
  1868-1941 (research guide) 1599

  1894-1907 669
  1894-1943 656
  1908-23 670
  1911-15 666
  1919-52 701
  1930s 209, 323-324, 697-698, 704, 708,
    711
  1937-41 697
  opening of Japan (1834-58) 658
  peace settlement (World War II) 283
  trade and commerce 349, 658, 660
  see also Allied occupation of Japan
    (1945-52), and World War II
    (Pacific Theatre)
Foreign relations with India 742
  peace settlement (World War II) 283
Foreign relations with Indonesia
  1951-66 727
  peace settlement (World War II) 283
  US-Japan-ASEAN relations 741, 891
Foreign relations with Iran 758
Foreign relations with Israel
  post-1973 Middle East diplomacy 758
Foreign relations with Italy
  1930s 245, 346, 708
Foreign relations with Korea
  17th century 677
  Hideyoshi's invasion (1590s) 299
Foreign relations with Korea (North
  Korea)
  1950s-1960s 377
  peace settlement (World War II) 283
Foreign relations with Korea (Republic
  of Korea) 719, 737
  1950s-1960s 377, 742
  1970s 743
  1980s 725
  offshore petroleum development
    negotiations 796
  peace settlement (World War II) 283,
    737
  trade and commerce 719
Foreign relations with Latin America
  743
Foreign relations with Malaysia
  US-Japan-ASEAN relations 741, 897
Foreign relations with NATO
  common security interests 765
Foreign relations with New Zealand 743
  1900-1941 665
Foreign relations with Oceania 743
Foreign relations with the Philippines
  US-Japan-ASEAN relations 741

Foreign relations with Russia/USSR
1697-1875 664
1868-1941 (research guide) 1599
1945-78 752
1970s 743
1970s-1980s 747
1980s 725, 732, 766
dispute over the 'Northern Territories'
(southern Kuriles) 285-286, 752
influence of the US-Japan security
alliance 765
Japanese thrust into Siberia (1918) 684
Kurile Islands as a focus 285-286
Manchurian crisis (1930s) 684
neutrality during World War II 684
Nomonhan Incident (1939) 684
normalisation of relations (1945-70)
728
patterns and prospects (post-1945)
720, 724
peace agreement (1956) 283, 728
response to the Soviet invasion of
Afghanistan 758
Sakhalin as a focus 287
trade and commerce 747, 752, 885,
900
Triple Intervention (1895) 668
see also Russo-Japanese War (1904-5)
Foreign relations with Singapore
US-Japan-ASEAN relations 741, 897
Foreign relations with Southeast Asia
bibliography 727
Japan in postwar Asia 742, 749, 757,
762
Foreign relations with Taiwan see
Foreign relations with China
(Republic of China)
Foreign relations with Thailand
peace settlement (World War II) 283
US-Japan-ASEAN relations 741, 897
Foreign relations with the Middle East
743, 758, 885
Foreign relations with the Philippines
peace settlement (World War II) 283
US-Japan-ASEAN relations 741, 897
Foreign relations with the Ryūkyū
Islands 284, 677
Foreign relations with the Third World
810
foreign aid as a political tool 757
Foreign relations with the United States
8, 12, 15, 649
1850s-1970s 643, 651, 657

1860s 186, 667
1868-1912 (Meiji period) 197
1868-1941 (research guide) 1599
1890-1941 653
1897-1911 662
1921-31 661
1931-41 209, 323, 340, 354, 679, 682,
690, 693, 704, 708, 711
1940s-1950s 264, 279, 283, 324
1940s-1980s 271, 725
1960s 354, 360
1965-75 (Vietnam War period) 727
1970s 339, 718, 743, 749, 897
1980s 726, 733, 741, 753, 766, 873
bibliographies 1575, 1600
bilateral alliance relationship
(1952-80) 750
cherry trees of Washington, DC 663
conflict over textile exports 721-722
consequences of Japan's technological
progress 988
diverging Middle East policies 758
economic and security dimensions
(1980s) 724
economic relations (post-1950s) 27,
801
energy relations (1980s) 847
Far Eastern crisis of 1933-38 702
historiographical essays 646
history (bibliography) 1575
impact of the internationalisation of
the yen 860
influence of politics and bureaucratic
processes 721
Japan Socialist Party's attitude 637
Okinawa as a focus 285
Perry expedition (1853-54) 673
portrayed in films 1428
prospects for stability (1980s) 817
response to the Iran hostage crisis 758
role of Japan's foreign aid policy 757
role of organised business 846
security ties (post-1951) 754, 765,
767-769
Security Treaty crisis of 1960 744, 754,
1485
Soviet perceptions 747
Townsend Harris at Shimoda
(1856-58) 676
under Theodore Roosevelt 659
see also Allied occupation of Japan
(1945-52), Pearl Harbor (1941
attack on), Trade and commerce

with the United States, United States Japan Security Treaty (1951), United States-Japan Security Treaty of 1960, and World War II (Pacific Theatre)
Foreign relations with Vietnam
  peace settlement (World War II) 283
Foreign service officers
  comparison of Japan and the USA 729
Foreign trade *see* Trade and commerce (foreign)
Foreign trade law bibliography 1582
Foreign trade control law
  reform 909
Foreign words in Japanese *see* Loanwords
Forest processing industries
  Japanese involvement in Soviet 900
Forestry
  annual statistics 825, 827
  maps 54
  periodicals 1502
Forests
  bamboo 64
  photographs 44
  vegetation 61
Formosa *see* Taiwan
Forms
  in the Japanese universe (aesthetic principles) 1202
Fortification technology
  castles 1306
'Forty-seven *rōnin*'
  subject of the play *Chūshingura* 1180, 1395
Fossils 49
France
  images of Japan and the Japanese 216, 755
  influence on Japanese painting (1890-1930) 1251
  relations with Japan 668, 675, 711
  see also Europe, and Frenchmen in Japan
Fraser, Mary Crawford
  reminiscences 355
Free trade
  Meiji period views 196
Freedom
  academic 788
  evolution (1860s-1980s) 771
  of advertising 771
  of assembly 771, 790

of association 771
of expression 771, 787, 790
of information 771
of the individual 336
Freer Gallery of Art
  (Washington, DC) exhibition catalogues 1250
Free-style textile designs photographs 1347
Frenchmen in Japan
  as military advisers 229
  Guillain, Robert 691
Friendships
  comparison of Ōsaka and Takashima, Okayama Prefecture 562
Frog
  subject of a poem by Matsuo Bashō 1166
Frois, Luis 132-133
Fruit
  citrus (imports) 892
  production 40
Fuchū (Tokyo Prefecture)
  police operations 565
  politics and social change 628
Fudai daimyō 163, 185
Fuji (Mount) *see* Mount Fuji
Fuji Xerox (company)
  quality control at 935
Fujimoto Kizan 1003
Fujisawa Takeo 882
Fujishima Takeji
  painting 1235
Fujitsu (company)
  joint venture with Amdahl 912
Fujiwara family
  as rivals of Sugawara no Michizane 300
  tales about 1017, 1021
Fujiwara Kaneie
  depicted in *Kagerō nikki* 1013
Fujiwara Michitsuna no haha
  diary 1013
Fujiwara no Michinaga
  biographical sketch 295
  tale about (*Eiga monogatari*) 1021
  tale about (*Ōkagami*) 1017
Fujiwara no Shunzei
  Korai fūteishō 1007
Fujiwara Seika
  writings 178
Fujiwara Teika
  Kindai shūka 1135

Fujiwara Teika *continued*
　life and writings 1135
Fukuchi Gen'ichirō
　biography 305
Fukuda Hideko
　as an advocate of people's rights 290
Fukuda Takeo
　political leadership 636
Fukuda Tsuneari
　biographical essay 239
Fukuda Yoshiyuki
　plays 1171
Fukui *han*
　tradition and change in 197
　William Elliot Griffis as a teacher in
　　358
Fukuoka 69
　work with refugees in 359
Fukuoka Masanobu
　natural farming methods 830
Fukuoka Prefecture
　Kurotsuchi 559-560
　Mitsui coal mines 328
　Shingū 552
　see also Kyūshū
Fukushima Incident (1882) 195
Fukushima Prefecture
　sabotage at Matsukawa 780
　see also Tōhoku region
Fukuzawa Ichirō
　artistic techniques and styles 1203
Fukuzawa Yukichi
　autobiography 302
　writings 194
Funa-dansu ('sea chests') 1341
Funakoshi Gichin
　memoirs 1446
Funasaka Yoshisuke
　woodblock print techniques 1273
Funerals
　Buddhist 485
　ceremonies 66
　encyclopaedic and almanac-type
　　information about 1556, 1561
Furniture
　as antiques 1215, 1340
　at the Shōsōin 1194
　design (photographs) 1224
　folk art 1193, 1213
　historical development 1341-1342
　illustrated survey 1342
　joints 1318, 1341-1342
　restoration (instruction manual) 1340

woodworking tools 1343
　see also Tansu (wooden chests)
Furo see Bath (*furo*)
Furoshiki (carrying cloths)
　craftsmanship 1369
Fushimi Castle 1317
Futabatei Shimei
　search for authenticity in literature
　　1130
　novels 1118, 1124, 1129
Fūten rōjin no nikki (Tanizaki Junichirō)
　quest for identity in 1115
　translation 1099
Futon (Tayama Katai)
　ideal of individualism in 1129

G
Gagaku (imperial court orchestra music)
　1382-1383, 1403
　influence on *kōwaka* ballad-drama
　　1169
　introductory study (illustrated) 1377
　masks 1215, 1377
　revival (post-1945) 1377, 1380
　Tōgaku style of music 1379
Gaimushō *see* Ministry of Foreign
　Affairs
Gairaigo (loanwords) 407, 454
　dictionary 419
Gambling 569
Games
　children's 66
　'go' 1064, 1458
　pachinko (pinball game) 26
　played by geisha 576
　shōgi 1459
Gan (Mori Ōgai)
　literary analysis 1127
　translation 1082
Gandhi, Mahatma
　changing Japanese images of 610
Gangsters 569
　gangsterism 566
　organisation 588
　police ways of handling 565
　resident in Tsuchiura, Ibaraki
　　Prefecture 234
　tattoos 1372
　yakuza 565, 569
Ganjin (abbot) 1296
Gappo ga Tsuji (Suga Sensuke and
　Wakatake Fuemi)
　translation 1394

760

Garbage
recycling and special handling
programmes 956
Gardens 1220, 1302
19th century (photographs) 1278
as a setting for the tea ceremony 1467,
1471-1472
courtyard 1333
creating Japanese-style (guidebook)
1337
Daitokuji temple 1190
design and meaning 1327
design motifs and techniques 1204
encyclopaedic and almanac-type
information about 1556, 1568
history 1211, 1329, 1332
influence of Zen Buddhism 492, 1226
Katsura Detached Palace 1305
landscape gardening 37, 369, 1196,
1327, 1338
of Kyōto 89, 98, 1327, 1331-1335
of Tokyo 91
principles of visual and spatial design
1327, 1331, 1333, 1335, 1338-1339
stone (dry-landscape) 1196, 1327,
1329, 1332, 1335, 1339
tourist guides 98, 1331
use of bamboo 1337, 1357
use of space 1327, 1329, 1333
use of water 3, 1331
see also Photographs (gardens)
Gas
Japanese development of Soviet
resources 900
liquefied natural 847, 849, 885
Gate (Natsume Sōseki)
psychoanalytical study 1112
synopses and analyses 1112, 1117
Gayn, Mark
diary 269
Gazetteers 57
Gedatsukai (New Religion) see New
Religions
Geisha
resident in Kyōto (ethnographic study)
576
resident in Tsuchiura, Ibaraki
Prefecture 234
songs sung by 576
talk 454
Gempei War (1180-85) 154, 293
depicted in the Heike monogatari 1019
kōwaka ballad-dramas about 1169

Lady Daibu's poetic reactions to 1142
Genealogies
artists 369
history 367
kabuki acting families 1564
General-interest periodicals 1497, 1503,
1507, 1510, 1512-1513, 1515-1516,
1532, 1537, 1545
General trading companies see Sōgō
shōsha (general trading companies)
Generals see Army generals
Genji clan see Minamoto family
Genji monogatari (Murasaki Shikibu) see
Tale of Genji
Genji monogatari ekotoba
illustrated translation 1241
Genrō ('elder statesmen')
Russo-Japanese War (1904-5) and 672
Saionji Kinmochi 296
Yamagata Aritomo 303
Genroku era (1688-1703) 1036
Tokugawa Tsunayoshi (shōgun) 289
Gensaki (bond repurchase) market 854
Genshin (priest)
Ōjōyōshū 470
Gentlemen's Agreement of 1907-8 384,
659
Genyōsha (ultranationalistic society)
connections with Hirota Kōki 346
Geography 32, 35, 40, 43, 46, 50
bibliography 1592
encyclopaedic and almanac-type
information about 1556
historical development 187
industrial 45
Niiike, Okayama Prefecture
(geographical setting) 548
overview 7, 9, 16, 23
Geology 49
historical development 187
Ijiri Shōji and the Chindanken 992
maps 49, 53-54
Geometric textile designs
compendium of photographs 1347
Germans in Japan
Baelz, Erwin von 351, 597
Kaempfer, Engelbert 596
Kleinsorge, Wilhelm 255
Meckel, Jakob 229
Mohnike, Otto 597
physicians (Meiji period) 597
Siebold, Philipp Franz von 596
Sorge, Richard 228

Germans in Japan *continued*
  Stillfried, Raimund von 1278
Germany
  cultural influence on Mori Ōgai 1110
  see also Foreign relations with
    Germany
Germany (Federal Republic)
  changing industrial relations
    (compared with Japan) 940
  Japanese branch operations 949
  Japanese direct investment and
    subsidiaries 948
  see also Europe
Gerontology *see* Ageing, and Elderly
Gesaku fiction 1005
  Kanagaki Robun 291
  Shikitei Sanba 1038
Gestures 26
Ghosts
  folk tales about 1185, 1189
  Katsushika Hokusai's sketches
    (reproductions) 1258
  stories about 1031-1032, 1069
  theme in art and culture (exhibition
    catalogue) 1189
  see also Demons, Spirits, and
    Supernatural beings
Gidō Shūshin
  poetry 1152
Gifu Prefecture
  agriculture and demography
    (Tokugawa period) 182
  Hida District 1301
  kilns (Shino and Oribe ware) 1282
  Takayama 100
Gigaku (masked dance drama) 1403
  audiences 1403
  masks 1296
Gikeiki
  translation 1020
Ginkakuji (temple)
  garden 1327, 1335
Ginza (Tokyo)
  'Gucci on the Ginza' 841
Gion Festival 500
Giri (social obligations) 522, 782
Girls' Festival (Hinamatsuri) 501
Glass
  illustrated history 1359
  Okinawan 1222
  recycling 956
Glazes 1279-1282, 1284, 1286-1287
Glossaries
  antiques 1215

archaeology 109
bonsai 1336
business 840
finance 863
'go' (game) 1458
haiku poetry 1162
history 1569
kabuki theatre 1396
literature 365, 1566
music 1383
names found in the *Kojiki* 152
names of corporate bodies and laws
  863
paper-making (*washi*) 1365
sumo 1454
swords 1373, 1375
theatrical forms 1399
'Go' (game)
  introductions and manuals 1458
  novel about 1064
Go-Daigo (Emperor) 144, 159, 1018
Go-Fukakusa (Emperor)
  concubine of 310
Go-Hōjō (daimyō)
  political history 139
Go-Sanjō (Emperor) 142
Go-Shirakawa (Emperor) 142
Gods and goddesses *see* Deities, and
  Kami (divinities)
Gogo no eikō (Mishima Yukio)
  translation 1076
Golovnin, Vasilii Mikhailovich
  role in Russo-Japanese relations 664
Gondo Seikyō 206
Gosha Hideo
  films 1420
Gosho (*sōgō shōsha*)
  evolution, role, and organisation 914
Gossamer years (Fujiwara Michitsuna no
  haha)
  translation 1013
Gotō Seikichirō
  work as a paper-maker 1365
Government 535
  assistance to and relations with
    scientific institutes 157
  assistance to firms relocating overseas
    946
  attempts to influence news reporting
    1484
  basic facts and figures (annual
    handbook) 14
  bonds 863

business-government relationship
(post-1945) 623-624, 797, 801, 816,
846, 849, 852, 856, 878, 880, 887,
899, 951
central (1840s-1880s) 212
central-local government relations
625, 639, 641-642
construction of Narita Airport 606
economic functions 791
economic policies (1953-73) 792
employees (lives and values) 564
expenditures and revenues (statistical
data) 808
funding for applied research 987
impact on securities companies,
banks, and the stock exchange 868
interaction with trade associations 899
introductory textbook 617
local power (500-1700 AD) and 138
manipulation of the legal environment
785
newspaper articles about 1546-1549
organisation 605
participation in economic affairs
(post-1945) 805
patronage of the arts (1955-80) 1376
performance in allocating funds and
resources 627
periodicals 1488, 1526
policy conflict and resolution within
538
pressured by the Japan Medical
Association 604
regulation of industrial production
(1930s-1940s) 872
relations with Shintō 515, 517-518
role in promoting economic
co-operation with Brazil 898
role in the business law system 776
role in the financial intermediation of
saving and investment 859
structure and process 624
subsidies to private schools 968
system of censorship (1868-1945) 221,
1122
see also Bakufu (shogunate),
Bureaucracy, Cabinet, Diet
(parliament), Imperial institution,
Industrial policy, Local government,
Officials (government), Public
administration, and The State
Government officials see Officials
(government)

Government publications
bibliography 1593
holdings of the Library of Congress
(bibliography) 1602
guidebook 1593
Government reports
annual abstract 829
Economic survey of Japan (annual)
820
White Paper on International Trade
(annual) 828
Gozan ('five mountains') system of Zen
Buddhist temples 131, 140
Gozan bungaku poetry
study and translations 1152
Grain consumption
mid-19th century 212
Grammar 407, 427-434
methods of teaching 455
Grappling in armour *see Yoroi
kumi-uchi* (martial art)
Grass on the wayside (Natsume Sōseki)
synopsis and analysis 1117
Grasses
Katsushika Hokusai's sketches
(reproductions) 1258
Great Britain
comparison of Japan and England 10
growth of Japanese subsidiary
companies 948
images of Japan and the Japanese 68,
216, 251, 266, 686, 755
involvement in the Allied occupation
of Japan (1945-52) 266
involvement in World War II 686,
697-698, 701, 711
Japanese art in British collections 1261
Japanese images of the British 686,
701
Japanese investment 944
Japanese managerial methods 941,
947, 949-950
Japanese participation in industry 944
Japanese studies 1508-1509, 1538,
1554, 1559
managerial methods (compared with
Japan) 941
patterns of social organisation
(compared with Japan) 920
policy towards Japan 658, 660, 666,
669-670, 697
trade and commerce with Japan (19th
century) 349, 658, 660

Great Britain *continued*
trade rivalry with Japan 758
transfer of Japanese managerial styles
and technologies 944
see also Anglo-Japanese [etc.],
English men and women in Japan,
Europe, Foreign relations with
Great Britain, and Westerners in
Japan
Greater East Asia Co-Prosperity Sphere
as a pattern of imperialism 644
Hawaii's expected role 710
Greater Japan National Defence
Women's Association 243
Greater Japan Youth Association 243
Grew, Joseph C.
diaries (1932-42) 690
Griffis, William Elliot 190
biographies 358, 361
experiences and observations
(1870-74) 114, 197, 358
Group-centred orientation of the
Japanese 15, 19, 31, 39, 532, 539,
990
baseball players 1456
bank employees 543
blue-collar workers 918
burakumin 373
company work groups 39
influence on business ideology
(1868-1941) 219
reinforced by corporate philosophy
and values 928
relationship between individual psyche
and 590
villagers (communal solidarity) 268,
553
Guadalcanal
military campaign (1942-43) 687-688,
699, 715, 1609
Guandong Army *see* Kwantung Army
Guandong Leased Territory *see*
Kwantung Leased Territory
Guidebooks
aikidō (martial art) 1450
aircraft (World War II) 689
antique furniture 1340
antiques 1215
architecture 81
artificial intelligence-related activities
994
artists' signatures 1571
behaviour and values 586

birds 65
business law system 776
business negotiations 893
business practices and procedures 891,
901, 916
business world 894
classical literature 1566
colleges and universities 1550
culture 1552
drama 1603
family crests 1191
folk tales 1188
food arrangement 1435
food buying 85
gardening 1337
haiku poetry 1162
hot springs (*onsen*) 80, 1457
ikebana (flower arrangement)
1462-1466
interior design incorporated into
American homes 1326
Japan and the Japanese 1573
Japan-related archival and manuscript
sources in the USA 1562
Japan-related resources in
Washington, DC 1562
Japanese expressions for travellers 416
kabuki theatre 1401
kaiseki cuisine 1437
Kamakura 76
karate (martial art) 1446, 1448
kimono 1356
Kyōto 89, 92
libraries 1474
literature in translation 1009
masterpieces of prose 1597
museums of art and archaeology 1475
Nara 93
netsuke 1288
poetry 1605
samurai ethics 529
samurai swords 1375
signs 88
strategy (*Gorin no sho*) 1447
Tale of Genji 1035, 1604
tansu (wooden chests) 1340
Tokyo 56, 95, 99
world of saké 1431
world of sushi 1432
see also Tourist guides
Guides for teachers *see* Teaching guides
Gukanshō (Jien) 130
Gunki monogatari see 'War tales' (*gunki*

monogatari)
Gunma Prefecture
  mountain farming hamlet 507
  see also Kantō region
Gyōsei shidō see Administrative
  guidance (*gyōsei shidō*)
Gyōsho (calligraphic script) 1242

H

Habeus corpus 790
Habomai Islands
  Japanese-Soviet dispute over 285-286
Hachiman (deity)
  wooden statues 1289
Hachiman cycle 516
Hachiya Michihiko
  diary 259
Hagi (Yamaguchi Prefecture) 69
Hagi ware (ceramics) 1281, 1283
Hagiwara Sakutarō
  ideas about poetry 1168
  poetry 1136
Hagoromo (Zeami Motokiyo)
  translation 1181
Haibun
  Oraga haru (Kobayashi Issa) 1146
  survey 1162
  translations 1156
Haikai poetry 1003, 1005, 1150, 1165
  translations 1150, 1165
Haiku poetry
  anthology 1159
  bibliographies 1162, 1588, 1605
  composed by Western poets 1162,
    1166
  curriculum unit about 36
  handbook 1162
  history 1162
  introductory studies 1137, 1159, 1166
  jisei ('death poems') 1138
  Masaoka Shiki 1161
  Matsuo Bashō 1002, 1137, 1167
  Oku no hosomichi (Matsuo Bashō)
    1007, 1149
  Oraga haru (Kobayashi Issa) 1146
  Shintō's contributions 519
  translations 1156-1157, 1159
  Zen Buddhist dimensions 492, 1196
Hakai (Shimazaki Tōson)
  literary analyses 1002, 1117, 1129
  translation 1095
Hako otoko (Abe Kōbō)
  translation 1041

Hakodate (Hokkaidō)
  life in (19th century) 68
  traveller's account 66
Haku rakuten (Zeami Motokiyo)
  translation 1181
Hakuin Ekaku
  epistolatory treatises 476
  teachings 480
  Zen mysticism 474
Halberds
  used in the martial arts 1443-1444
Hamada Shōji
  biography 331
  pottery 331
Hamamatsu (Shizuoka Prefecture)
  kite-flying festivals 1461
Hamamatsu Chūnagon monogatari
  translation 1027
Hamlets
  power structure 531
  religious practices 507
  Sarayama, Ōita Prefecture 553
  Shinohata, Tochigi Prefecture 550
  social structure 507, 531, 534, 553
  Takashima, Okayama Prefecture 554
  see also Villages
Hanaoka Seishū no tsuma (Ariyoshi
  Sawako)
  translation 1047
Handbooks *see* Guidebooks, and
  Instruction manuals
Handicapped employees 923
Handicrafts *see* Crafts
Handscrolls
  at the Tōdaiji temple 1206
  depicting creatures of nature 1221
  depicting music and dance 1380
  introduction to narrative picture
    scrolls 1245
  owned by the Tokugawa shōguns
    (exhibition catalogue) 1219
  painted in the *yamato-e* style 1236
  Tale of Genji picture scroll 1200
Handwriting
  language textbook 451
  styles 451
Hanging scrolls (kakemono)
  as antiques 1215
  at the Tōdaiji temple 1206
  depicting creatures of nature 1221
Hani Susumu
  films and film-making activities 1423
Haniwa (prehistoric clay figures) 106, 108

Hara Kei
  political leadership 198, 224, 296
Hara Tamiki
  short stories 1088
Haragei ('belly play') 406
Harbours
  gazetteer 57
Harmony
  importance in interpersonal relations
    522, 586, 592-593
  importance in the business world 840,
    922, 933-934
Harp of Burma (Takeyama Michio)
  translation 1097
Harris, Townsend
  as first US consul to Japan (1856-58)
    676
Haru (Shimazaki Tōson)
  synopsis and analysis 1117
Haru no yuki (Mishima Yukio)
  literary analysis 1131
  translation 1077
Harunobu *see* Suzuki Harunobu
Harusame monogatari (Ueda Akinari)
  translation 1030
Harvard University
  East Asian studies 360
Hashimoto Sanai
  biography 289
Hatano Seiichi
  philosophy 527
Hawaii
  Honolulu Academy of Arts (primitive
    ukiyo-e) 1268
  invasion and occupation plans (World
    War II) 710
  Japanese Americans (bibliography)
    1598
  Japanese Americans (history of
    immigration and settlement) 385,
    389, 396-397, 402
  Japanese Americans (Issei) 392
  Japanese Americans (relationship with
    Japan and the USA) 710
  see also Japanese Americans, and
    Pearl Harbor (1941 attack on)
Hayashi Fumiko
  short stories 1051, 1071, 1083, 1088,
    1126
Hayashi Razan
  writings 178
Headgear
  used in the kabuki theatre 1352

Healing-cults
  spirit possession 592
Health 34
  among the elderly 540, 1595
  annual statistics 825-827
  attitudes towards 598
  benefits of hot springs 80
  care 207, 599-600, 603
  compensation for pollution-related
    injuries 775, 777
  cultural and social dimensions 599-600
  education 603
  impact of urbanisation 603
  insurance 604
  relationship to natural farming 830
Hearn, Lafcadio
  experience living in Japan 190, 361
  writings 216
Heavy machinery industry 217
Hebiichigo (Hakuin Ekaku) 476
Heike clan *see* Taira family
Heike monogatari literary analyses 1008,
    1019
  translation 1019
Heisei Emperor *see* Akihito (emperor)
Hekiganshū (Engo Kokkin)
  mondo from 492
Heraldic design and practice
  history and social significance 1191
Herbal medicine 598
Heroes
  Ainu 380
  folk legends about 1184, 1186
  tragic heroes in history 293
  see also Warriors and heroes
Hibakusha (atomic bomb victims)
    252-253, 255-259
  depicted in novels 1058
Hibiya riot (1905) 175, 672
Hida District (Gifu Prefecture)
  minka 1301
Hidari Sachiko
  film-making activities 1423
Hideyoshi *see* Toyotomi Hideyoshi
Hierarchy
  as a factor influencing behaviour 592
  business world 840
  job 923
  of authority and function in factories
    920
  patterns 539
  ranking system of sumo wrestlers
    1453-1454

social 535, 539, 585, 809
Higan sugi made (Natsume Sōseki)
  psychoanalytical study 1112
  synopsis and analysis 1112
High schools
  access to good education in 639
  American images 965
  bibliography 1610
  career options of students 962
  description and analysis 975
  education (post-1952) 960
  educational choices of students 962
  English-language instruction 979
  Kōbe 975
  Kōtō Shōgyō Gakkō (Nagoya) 350
  Kyōto 964
  libraries 1474, 1476
  overview (1980s) 970
  university preparatory academies
    (1880s-1940s) 232
High technology *see* Technology
Higher education
  American images 965
  bibliography 1610
  changes (1970s) 963
  chaotic state (late 1960s) 972
  Christian involvement 497
  comparison of the private and public
    sectors 968
  comprehensive guidebook 1550
  conservative reforms 619, 961
  government policy towards 619-620,
    974
  post-1952 960
  see also Universities
Highways *see* Roads
Higuchi Ichiyō
  biographical sketch 291
  biography 1111
  short stories 1111, 1126
Hikari goke (Takeda Taijun)
  quest for identity in 1115
Himeji (Hyōgo Prefecture)
  tourist guide 100
Himeji Castle 1306
Hinamatsuri (Girls' Festival) 501
Hino Sōjō
  haiku poetry 1159
Hirabayashi Taiko
  short stories 1071
Hiragana see Kana syllabaries
Hirata Atsutane
  pursuit of Western learning 173

Hiratsuka Un'ichi
  woodblock prints 1274
Hirohito (Emperor) 23
  advised by Saionji Kinmochi 323
  biography 334
  during the 1930s 209
  during the Allied occupation of Japan
    (1945-52) 273, 280, 362
  ratification of key foreign-policy
    decisions (1941) 693
  reactions to Prime Minister Tōjō's
    wartime regime 237
  role in Japan's decision to surrender
    (1945) 703
Hiroshige *see* Andō Hiroshige
Hiroshima
  atomic bombing (1945) 255, 260,
    262-263, 691, 715
  atomic bombing (depicted in literary
    works) 731, 1058, 1088, 1173
  atomic bombing (human victims)
    252-253, 255-257, 259, 583
  'Hiroshima maidens' 252
  Peace Centre (architectural project)
    1313
Hiroshima Prefecture
  Kinoshita Yūji as a local poet 1144
  Miyajima 19
  see also Inland Sea area
Hirota Kōki
  biography 346
Hishikawa Moroyasu
  ukiyo-e paintings 1250
Historians
  Rai Sanyō 295, 1010
Historical fiction 184, 1012, 1017-1021,
    1047, 1054-1055, 1061, 1068-1069,
    1081, 1094, 1102, 1109
Historical tables 421
'Historical tales' (*rekishi monogatari*)
  Eiga monogatari 1021
  Ōkagami 1017
Historiography 144, 249
  colonialism (19th-20th centuries) 223
  Eiga monogatari's contributions to
    1021
  Kamakura period 130, 147
  Kemmu Restoration (1333-36) 159
  pre-13th century 130
  Tokugawa Confucianism 526
  US-Japanese relations 646
  US-Japanese relations during the
    1930s 682

Historiography *continued*
  writings of E. H. Norman 226
History 6, 13, 16, 21, 29, 32, 82, 86
  Origins of Japan–7th century 152
  Origins of Japan–8th century 115
  Origins of Japan–12th century 1569
  Origins of Japan–13th century 130
  Origins of Japan–14th century 144
  Origins of Japan–19th century 114,
    125, 151
  Origins of Japan–20th century 113,
    115-116, 120, 122-123, 155, 284,
    286-287, 293, 1359, 1380
  3rd-19th centuries 1212, 1223
  3rd-20th centuries 23, 1211
  4th-20th centuries 1374
  6th-8th centuries 143
  6th-16th centuries 484, 1164
  6th-17th centuries 138
  6th-19th centuries 134, 523, 1477
  6th-20th centuries 295, 1006
  7th-19th centuries 128, 157, 546
  8th century 301
  8th-12th centuries (Heian period) 115
  8th-19th centuries 92
  8th-20th centuries 999
  9th century 300
  9th-11th centuries 1017
  9th-16th centuries 141
  9th-17th centuries 298
  10th-11th centuries 150, 1021
  11th-12th centuries 142
  12th century 154, 1019
  12th-13th centuries 148-149
  12th-14th centuries (Kamakura
    period) 147
  12th-15th centuries 131, 160
  12th-16th centuries 115, 136
  12th-19th centuries 146, 156, 158,
    1218
  13th century 310
  14th century 159, 1018
  14th-16th centuries (Muromachi
    period) 137, 140
  16th century 135, 145, 153, 299
  16th-17th centuries 129, 132-133, 139,
    166, 178, 352
  16th-19th centuries 115, 161, 179
  16th-20th centuries 121, 184, 495, 648
  17th century 174, 314, 677
  17th-18th centuries 298
  17th-19th centuries 664, 674, 1005,
    1271

  17th-19th centuries (Tokugawa
    period) 124, 163, 165, 167-169, 172,
    180-181, 185, 188, 596, 1227
  17th-20th centuries 18-19, 187, 201,
    208, 231, 289
  18th century 161, 177, 309, 315
  18th-19th centuries 164, 170, 173, 176,
    182
  18th-20th centuries 183, 211
  19th century 115
  19th-20th centuries 110-112, 117-119,
    127, 650
  1830s-1850s 658
  1830s-1870s 306
  1830s-1890s 302
  1830s-1920s 303, 308
  1840s-1860s 191
  1840s-1870s 213
  1840s-1880s 212, 304
  1840s-1910s 312
  1840s-1930s 320, 323
  1840s-1940s 1276
  1850s 673
  1850s-1860s 171, 175, 190, 349
  1850s-1870s 162, 251
  1850s-1880s 660
  1850s-1900s 216
  1850s-1950s 204
  1850s-1970s 643, 651, 1555
  1860s 186, 357, 667, 675
  1860s-1870s 307, 353
  1860s-1880s 229
  1860s-1890s 189-190, 226, 305
  1868-1912 (Meiji period) 197, 235,
    240, 248, 250, 361
  1860s-1920s 157, 236, 297
  1860s-1940s 200, 202, 205-206,
    217-219, 221, 225, 233, 239, 246,
    311, 528, 613, 654, 1001
  1860s-1950s 249, 288, 496
  1860s-1960s 324, 1209
  1860s-1970s 818, 855, 1320
  1870s 196, 358
  1870s-1880s 195, 363
  1870s-1910s 351
  1870s-1940s 242, 247, 318-319, 346,
    517, 641, 1572
  1870s-1970s 547, 581, 835
  1870s-1980s 655
  1880s-1890s 230, 355
  1880s-1930s 348
  1880s-1940s 227, 232, 317, 321
  1890s 669

1890s-1910s 203, 357, 662
1890s-1920s 175
1890s-1940s 210, 223, 340, 644, 653,
  656
1890s-1960s 648
1890s-1970s 652, 1426
1890s-1980s 1414
20th century 115
1900-1909 659, 671-672, 678
1900s-1910s 224, 663
1900s-1940s 665
1900s-1930s 243, 290, 328
1900s-1950s 324, 334, 336
1910s 215, 666
1912-1926 (Taishō period) 198, 241
1910s-1940s 221, 234, 329
1910s-1950s 222, 701
1910s-1960s 360, 967
1910s-1970s 647
1920s 244, 350, 661
1920s-1930s 333, 758
1920s-1940s 192, 215, 342, 679
1920s-1970s 272, 628, 1486
1920s-1980s 294
1930s 193, 199, 209, 220, 238,
  684-685, 701-702, 704
1930s-1940s 207, 228, 245, 330, 682,
  690, 694, 697-698, 702, 708-712
1930s-1960s 354
1930s-1980s 347, 871-872
1940-1945 237, 254-255, 258, 260-263,
  285, 680-681, 683, 686-688,
  691-693, 695-696, 699-700, 703,
  705-707, 709, 711, 713-716
1945-1950 265, 267-270, 275, 279,
  285, 359, 362
1940s-1950s 264, 266, 273-274,
  276-278, 280-283, 356
1940s-1960s 759
1940s-1970s 851
1940s-1980s 271, 799
agricultural 835
architectural 1211-1212, 1314, 1320,
  1322
art 1205, 1211-1212, 1220, 1223, 1271,
  1576
bibliographies 118, 126, 367, 1555,
  1575, 1583, 1592, 1614
biographical dictionary 367
bonsai 1328, 1336
business 201, 208, 219, 231, 250, 347
constitutional 220
cultural 37, 113, 125, 237, 239, 1534

depicted by Japanese artists 155
detailed chronology (ca. 40 BC-AD
  1167) 1569
dictionary 1555, 1563
diplomatic 279, 354, 645, 654,
  658-660, 664, 666, 668-673,
  676-677, 690, 697, 1599
documentary films (critical guide) 1586
documentary sources 120
economic 110, 119, 139, 169-170,
  181-182, 218, 225, 233, 270, 297,
  758, 799, 1614
education 164, 180, 217, 244
encyclopaedic and almanac-type
  information about 1551, 1553, 1556,
  1560-1561, 1568
financial 851, 855
furniture 1341-1342
gardens 1329, 1332
ikebana 1462-1466
institutional 116, 138, 141, 148, 168,
  170, 250, 272, 484, 682
intellectual 178, 199, 203, 206, 211,
  999
Japanese American (dictionary) 1563
labour 202, 204, 215, 217, 275
legal 277, 384
literary 999, 1001, 1005-1006, 1162,
  1566
maps 53
medical 172, 343, 353
military 210, 229, 238, 303, 317,
  320-321, 342, 678, 680-681, 684,
  696, 698-700, 702-703, 705-707,
  709, 711, 713-716, 1572, 1609
Mori Ōgai's attitude towards 1110
oral histories 234, 383, 400-401, 403,
  583, 699
periodicals 1493, 1504, 1526, 1534,
  1543
philosophy 523, 527-528
photographic record (1840-1945) 1276
photographic record (1854-1905) 1276
political 117, 124, 130, 137-142,
  145-149, 154, 159-160, 163, 177,
  185-186, 188-189, 191-193, 195,
  198, 202, 224, 237, 245-247, 281,
  306-308, 323, 333, 336, 340, 346,
  628
postal 1522
readings about 33, 119
religious 145, 458, 465, 474-475, 484,
  495-496, 511, 516-517, 520

History *continued*
role of comics in 1480
scientific 151, 157, 187, 992
social 119, 124, 157, 161, 173,
183-184, 205, 207, 214, 230,
234-236
sports 1453, 1456
tea ceremony 1467, 1469, 1472
theatrical 1175, 1181, 1392-1394,
1396-1398, 1400, 1402-1405,
1408-1411
Tōdaiji temple in 1206
urban 174, 179, 236, 546
women's 240, 290, 313, 581
see also Allied occupation of Japan
(1945-52)
History textbook controversy (1980s)
613
Hitachi (company)
evaluation of applied research 987
factory (economic and social
structure) 920
investment decision-making process
951
strategic management practices 926
Hitomaro *see* Kakinomoto no Hitomaro
Hitotsubashi University
establishment 304
Hizō hōyaku (Kūkai)
translation 482
Hōjō family
political ascendancy 147
Hōjō Masako
biographical sketch 295
Hōjō military government *see Bakufu*
(shogunate): Kamakura period
Hōjōki (Kamo no Chōmei) 1007
Hokkaidō
Ainu 66, 359, 372, 375, 378-380
cranes (birds) 58
crows 1275
discovery and mapping 52
geography 50
Hakodate 66, 68
national parks 48
police operations 570
Sapporo 100
tenant farmers 1068
travellers' accounts 66-67
Hokku poetry
survey 1166
Hokuriku region
geography 50

Hokusai *see* Katsushika Hokusai
Holidays
encyclopaedic and almanac-type
information about 1551, 1553,
1556-1557, 1561, 1568
Home Affairs Ministry *see* Ministry of
Home Affairs
Home life
pre-school children 559
Home Ministry
under Ōkubo Toshimichi 306
under Yamagata Aritomo 303
Homecoming (Osaragi Jirō)
quest for identity in 1115
translation 1092
Homma (Mishima Yukio)
literary analysis 1131
translation 1077
Hon'ami Kōetsu
artworks and artistic environment
1240
artworks in the Powers Collection
1214
Honda Motor Company 344
history 882
Honda Sōichirō 882
biography 344
Honda Toshiaki
career and writings 173
Honjō Shigeru
diaries 209
Honolulu Academy of Arts (Honolulu,
Hawaii) Michener Collection of
primitive ukiyo-e prints 1268
Honorific language (*keigo*)
grammar 407, 427, 430-434, 443
textbooks 443, 450
Honour
literary depiction 1012
sense of 15, 585
Horsemanship *see Bajutsu* (martial art)
Horse-racing
Shintō dimensions 519
Horticulture
Ainu 375
Hōryūji (temple)
architecture 1322
early Buddhist art 1208
Hosokawa Shin
fashion-design work 1348
Hosokawa Yūsai
biographical sketch 291
Hospitals

during the 1870s 66
founding of Western-style 596
Hot springs (*onsen*)
use of water (photo-essay) 3
gazetteer 57
guides 80, 1457
overview 1457
Hotels
architecture (1958-84) 1321, 1324
Imperial Hotel (Tokyo) 1320
see also Ryōkan (inns), Tourist guides
Hotta Kiyomi
plays 1173
House (Shimazaki Tōson)
synopsis and analysis 1117
translation 1096
House laws
daimyō 139
House of the sleeping beauties (Kawabata Yasunari)
quest for identity in 1115
Households
composition 549
customs 114
deity (Yashiki-gami) 503
finances (annual statistics) 825, 827
in village communities 548, 551-552, 554, 560
savings behaviour 783
social organisation 561
Houses
architecture (post-1945) 1299, 1309, 1313, 1321, 1324
depicted as sculptures 108
encyclopaedic and almanac-type information about 1556, 1561, 1568
house-building ceremonies 560
rural types 40
Housewives
folk culture 503
life-style, role, and community involvement 577
political involvement 580
shopping behaviour 841
Housing
annual statistics 825
basic facts and figures (annual handbook) 14
effect on housewives' behaviour 577
land used for 42
medieval 133, 136
Meiji period 363
private and government investment

(1868-1940) 233
projects (architecture) 1313
public housing (*danchi*) 577, 639
Tokugawa period 165
Howling at the moon (Hagiwara Sakutarō)
translation 1136
Human biology
vocabulary 405
Human body
attitudes towards 598, 600
Human fertility
Dōsojin (deity) 502
festivals 501
Human nature
attitudes towards 530
Human rights 616
consciousness 611
constitutional guarantee 784
Humour
kyōgen 1402
Hundred stanzas related to 'person' by Sōgi alone
translations 1165
Husband-wife relationships 375, 536, 549-550, 558, 564
among the Ainu 375
among Tokyo residents 549
among villagers (Shinohata, Tochigi Prefecture) 550
conversational disclosure in 584
depicted in literary diaries 1013
depicted in novels 1046-1047, 1053, 1066, 1072, 1093, 1100, 1104
depicted in short stories 1031, 1098, 1106
Hydrology
bibliography 1592
Hygiene
everyday practices and beliefs 600
introduction of methods of public 597
medieval 136
Tokugawa period 172
Hyōgo Prefecture
cotton trade (Tokugawa period) 170
Himeji 100
Himeji Castle 1306
Kōbe 68, 72, 100, 975
Tachikui (Tamba ware) 1286

I

I am a cat (Natsume Sōseki)
  synopses and analyses 1112, 1117
  translation 1084
I-Thou relationship in Zen Buddhism
  Nishitani Keiji's views 521
Iaidō (martial art)
  introductory studies 1441, 1452
Iai-jitsu see Iaidō
Ibaraki Prefecture
  Mito Castle 1317
  Tsuchiura 234
  Tsukuba 980
  see also Kantō region, and Mito *han*
IBM (International Business Machines)
  Corporation
  business operations in Japan 889, 928
  challenged by the Japanese 982
Ibuse Masuji
  literary analysis 1058
  novels 1008, 1058, 1127
  short stories 1056, 1059, 1088, 1126
Ichikawa Kon
  film-making activities 1415, 1423
  films 1421, 1423
Ichinotani futaba gunki (Namiki Sōsuke
  et al.)
  translation 1396
Iconography
  Buddhist sculpture 1295
  Daruma 483
  esoteric Buddhism 1237
  ink painting (*suibokuga*) 1239
  shinzō 1289
  Tale of Genji 1039, 1241
  tattoos 1372
Ideals of beauty
  Tanizaki Junichirō's views 1225
Idemitsu Art Museum (Tokyo)
  holdings of Karatsu ware 1279
Identity
  female (dictionary of expressions) 413
  foundations of Japanese 535
  Koreans in Japan 376
  Nisei's personal search for 398
  problems of cultural (Meiji period)
    230
  problems of overseas employees 572
  quest for (literary depiction) 1115
  relationship to the Japanese language
    408
  sense of Japanese 30-31, 36, 211
  social self-identity 588

  see also National character, and
    Nihonjinron
Ideology
  business leaders 219, 943
  Christian-Japanese conflict of 166
  ideological conversion (*tenkō*) 595
  influence on news reporting 1484
  internationalisation as an 802
  labour unions 918
  Meiji period 20, 203, 206
  Nikkyōso (Japan Teachers Union)
    967, 977
  propagated through the schools 973
  regional bank 543
  relationship with publishing,
    education, and freedom of
    expression 771
  social classes 545
  social democratic 247
  Tengu Insurrection 175
  Tokugawa period 178, 526
  Young Officers' Movement 238
Idiomatic expressions
  collection 1183
  dictionary 414
  grammar 427
Ie (Shimazaki Tōson) synopsis and
    analysis 1117
  translation 1096
Ie system 531, 549
  central role in society 532
  disintegration 532, 555
Iga ware (ceramics) 1283
Ihara Saikaku 1005
  biographical sketch 295
  literary career 1015
  novels 1004
  short stories 1014-1015, 1036
Iijima Kōichi
  poetry 1151
Ijiri Shōji 992
Ikat weaving (*kasuri*)
  instruction manual 1351
Ike no Taiga
  fan-shaped paintings 1233
Ikebana (flower arrangement)
  illustrated guidebooks 1462-1466
  Shintō's contributions 519
  Zen Buddhist dimensions 1196
Ikeda Daisaku 512
Ikeda Mitsumasa
  biography 289
Ikeno Taiga

painting 1255
Ikenobō School of ikebana 1464-1466
Ikiru (film script)
  translation 1057
Ikki (Muromachi period military
  organisations) 141
Ikkyū Sōjun
  biographical sketches 291, 1003, 1139
  poetry 1139
Illness
  attitudes towards 588, 598, 600
  caused by environmental pollution 34,
    312, 567, 957, 959
  caused by industrialisation and
    urbanisation 603
  caused by malevolent spirits 506
  cultural and social dimensions 599-600
  'itai-itai' disease 957
  'Minamata disease' 34, 567, 957, 959
  Tokugawa period diseases 172
Illustrated books
  Meiji period (exhibition catalogue)
    1229
  Rimpa school of art 1240
  Suzuki Harunobu 1261
Illustrated handscrolls (*emaki*) *see*
  Handscrolls
Illustrations
  contained in *tanrokubon* 1481
  printed book (history) 1477-1478
  printed book (Katsushika Hokusai)
    1260, 1478
Images held by the Japanese (of)
  Britain and the British 686, 701
  British and Japanese navies 698
  China and the Chinese 647, 649-650
  defence system 761
  diplomats 729
  Europe 755
  foreign products 891
  nihonjinron 4, 587
  robots 995
  self-image 566
  USA and Americans 649, 651, 667,
    686, 721, 727, 753
  women (self-images) 580
  yazuka 569
Images of Japan and the Japanese
  American 216, 361, 643, 649, 651, 686,
    690, 721, 731, 753, 945, 965
  Brazilian 898
  British (19th century) 68, 216, 251,
    755

British (1940s) 266, 686, 698
  Chinese 649-650
  European 755
  French 216, 755
  Soviet 747
Imai Tadashi
  films and film-making activities 1423
Imari ware (ceramics) 1281
Imamura Shōhei
  film-making activities 1415, 1419
Immigration *see* Migration
Imperial court
  1868-1945 246
  bugaku (court dance) 1169, 1294,
    1403, 1410
  depicted by Lady Nijō 310
  gagaku (court music) 1377, 1382-1383,
    1403
  Heian period 141-142, 150, 300, 1021
  Heian period (literary depictions)
    1011, 1013, 1021, 1023-1026,
    1028-1029
  Kamakura period 147, 149, 310
  Kamakura period (literary depiction)
    1018
  poetry 1153, 1164
  relations with Toyotomi Hideyoshi 299
  Sugawara no Michizane and 300
  Tōgaku style of court music 1379
  Togukawa period 165
  see also Tsukuri monogatari ('courtly
    romances')
Imperial family
  deified in Hitomaro's poetry 1163
  depicted in Meiji period prints 1269
Imperial Hotel (Tokyo) 1320
Imperial household
  Baelz's services as physician 351
Imperial institution 30, 159
  concept of imperial prerogative 246
  origins and early history 144, 152, 516
  palace politics (structure and style) 246
  position in the governing process 246
  retained after World War II 266, 280
  role and image after World War II 273
  Tokugawa period 188
  see also Palaces
Imperial Japanese Army *see* Army
Imperial Japanese Navy *see* Navy
Imperial Military Reserve Association
  243
Imperialism
  1897-1911 662

Imperialism *continued*
  British reactions 656
  impact of Western 186
  in China (1920s) 661
  Japanese perspectives 223, 342
  Meiji period 249
  origins and nature (1894-1945) 644
  overseas expansion of State Shintō 517
  overseas propagation of Confucianism 528
  role of the secret service 648
  search for economic self-sufficiency 679, 685
  US reactions 657
Impermanence of life
  as a psychological concept 593
Imports
  agricultural 832-833, 885, 892
  beef 833, 892
  Canadian goods 734
  coal 885
  manufactured goods 816
  petroleum 794, 847, 849, 885, 913
  raw materials 885, 913
  relationship with the domestic marketing system 909
  technology 869, 871, 989, 993
  see also Sōgō shōsha (general trading companies), and Trade and commerce (foreign)
Impressionist school of painting in Japan 1235, 1238
In no cho (ex-sovereign's administrative office) 142
Inagaki Hiroshi
  films 1420
Incense
  boxes 331, 1221, 1370
  burners 1215, 1219, 1285
  craftsmanship 1369
  containers 1469
Income
  among the elderly 540, 1595
  distribution 792, 843
  from capital (taxation) 884
  in a village community (Niiike, Okayama Prefecture) 548
  Income Tax Law 788
  National Income-Doubling Plan (1960s) 815
  taxation 786
India
  economic development (compared
    with Japan) 806
  farming (compared with Japan and the USA) 834
  financial development (compared with Japan) 855
  hostile attitudes towards Japan (1910s) 666
  Japanese images of Mahatma Gandhi 610
  relations with Japan 283, 742
Indian Ocean
  naval raids (World War II) 680, 687
Individual
  authority and 614
  literary depiction 1129
  social change and 595
  status and role 522
Individual psyche
  relationship to group-oriented behaviour 590
Individualism
  belief in 203, 214
  family law and 786
  influence on the Meiji period novel 1129
  suppression of individuality 567
Indonesia
  relations with Japan 283, 727, 741, 891
  see also New Guinea, and Southeast Asia
Industrial areas
  formation 40
  maps 53-54
Industrial designs
  Japanese-Western collaboration in 912
  protection 773
Industrial development 43, 45
  British involvement (Meiji period) 660
  human resources in 216
  Mitsui's involvement 231
  political change and 872
  theory 873
Industrial economy
  relationship to imperialism (1894-1945) 644
  trends and changing aspects 35
Industrial groups
  influence on the economy 869
  relations with the Liberal Democratic Party 638
Industrial machinery industry 879
Industrial management 878, 928, 936

bibliography 1600
corporate strategies 895
industrial collaboration with foreign
    firms 911-912
industrial reforms 27
see also Management
Industrial organisation and structure
    811, 820, 869
1970s-1980s 813, 816-817
bibliographies 1581, 1600, 1614
Industrial policy 623, 821, 837, 869, 901,
    909-910, 939
1950s-1970s 883
1950s-1980s 876, 904
antitrust and 783
applicability in the West 795
bibliographies 1581, 1590, 1614
case studies 876, 879, 881
comparison of Japan and the USA 884
costs 809
declining industries 884
deregulation of the
    telecommunications market 953
detailed analysis 876, 879
encouraging co-operation among rival
    companies 881
future prospects 817
high technology industries 881, 905
high-profit markets 872
industrial machinery industry 879
influence on overseas business
    strategies 951
integrated-circuit industry 884
location of industry 45
MITI 272, 814, 879
origins and evolution 813, 908, 981
overview 823, 907
semiconductor industry 880
structural adjustment in the economy
    (1970-80) and 794
targeting strategic industries 873, 876,
    880, 945
Industrial pollution
caused by the Ashio Copper Mine
    312, 957
government responses 620
industry's compliance with
    environmental policies 775
'Minamata disease' 34, 567, 957, 959
policy of controlling 785
'red tides' of the Inland Sea 957
Yokkaichi 'asthma' 957
Industrial property law

bibliography 1582
Industrial relations 939
bibliography 1600
conflict and resolution 538, 937
during the 1970s 937
electrical engineering factories 920
function of law in 937
strike at the Noda Soy Sauce
    Company 241
system 204, 791, 921, 925, 931, 940
violence 921
see also Labour-management relations
Industrialisation
1870s-1980 803
post-1945 264, 532
health problems resulting from 603
political consequences 547
role of the sōgō shōsha 914
social 547, 812
Industry 45-46, 50, 82, 110, 791, 869
aerospace 912
aircraft 689, 763, 911
aluminium-refining 876, 879
annual statistics 819, 824
annual survey 823
automobile 45, 344, 347, 547, 809,
    870-871, 873-874, 876, 879,
    882-883, 912, 918-919, 924, 926,
    934-936, 942
automotive chemicals 911
basic facts and figures (annual
    handbook) 14
bibliographies 1592, 1594, 1600, 1614
biotechnology 881
business and (1950s-1970s) 883
chemical 217, 911
clothing 794
computer 813, 873, 876, 911-912, 982
cotton spinning 806
declining public ownership 777
directory 1574
electrical engineering 920
electrical equipment 217, 929
electronics 332, 813, 879, 912,
    948-949, 985, 988
encyclopaedic and almanac-type
    information about 1556, 1568
heavy 204
heavy machinery 217
high technology 881, 905, 996
industrial machinery 879
information industry 879, 881
integrated-circuit 884

Industry *continued*
  iron and steel 45, 899
  laws relating to (bibliography) 1582
  long-term statistical data 808
  machine tools 38, 872, 899
  maps 53-54
  metal-processing 762
  military armaments and munitions 229
  newspaper 1483, 1485
  newspaper reporting about 1546,
    1548-1549
  periodicals 1494, 1500, 1517, 1519,
    1527, 1542, 1545
  petrochemical 813
  pharmaceuticals 911
  present conditions and current trends
    (annual survey) 823
  research institutes and programmes
    980
  robotics 899, 986, 995
  saké brewing 929
  semiconductor 873, 880, 904, 907, 945
  shifts in industrial structure (1970s)
    794
  shipbuilding 38, 45, 217, 763, 796,
    812-813, 876, 879, 929
  space and missile 763
  steel 217, 876, 879, 942, 945, 989
  synthetic fibre 945
  technological change and
    rationalisation (1970s) 940
  telecommunications 217, 813
  television 945, 947
  textile 217, 794, 876
  trade associations 899, 1565
  zaibatsu dissolution 270
  see also Labour-management
    relations, Manufacturing, and
    Quality control (circles)
Infanticide
  Tokugawa period 169, 172, 182
Inflation
  comparison of Japan and the USA 859
  control (1970s) 794
  debate (1970s) over 866
  land prices 42
Information
  centres (directory) 1558
  exchange (in business) 899
  freedom 771
  industry 38, 879, 881
  Japan as an information-oriented
    society 8

networks (created by private
    companies) 955
  scientific and technological 991
  sources (business and commerce) 1570
  sources (directories) 1558, 1562, 1565
  technology 981, 983
  see also Computers (computer
    industry)
Ink painting (*suibokuga*) 140
  artworks in the Sansō Collection 1246
  exhibition catalogue 1248
  illustrated surveys 1239, 1253
  Rimpa school of art 1240
  Zen Buddhist dimensions 1196
Ink painting (*sumi-e*)
  introduction and manual 1247, 1254
Inland Sea area
  customs 71
  environmental pollution 957
  folklore 71
  geography 50
  minka 1301
  national park 48
  travellers' accounts 71-73
Innovation 983
  automobile industry 344, 871, 882
  collective bargaining 948
  electronics technology 877, 985
  management (comparison of Japan
    and the USA) 998
  semiconductor industry 880
  steel industry 989
  technological 344, 836, 871, 875, 877,
    880, 882, 989, 993, 996
Inns *see Ryōkan* (inns)
Inoki Masamichi
  report on national security 760
Inoue Kowashi 961
Inoue Mitsuharu
  short stories 1088
Inoue Yasushi
  autobiography 327
  essay on the Katsura Detached Palace
    garden 1334
  novels 1061
  poetry 1141
  short stories 1060, 1106
Inrō (compartmentalised containers)
  depicting creatures of nature 1221
  guide to legends and historical
    episodes embodied in 1560
  handbook 1360
  photographs 1189, 1221, 1360

theme of the supernatural in 1189
Inscriptions on swords 1375
Insects
  depicted in netsuke 1291
  design motifs of family crests and
    textile patterns 1191, 1344
  encyclopaedic and almanac-type
    information about 1551
Insei system of government 141-142
Insider trading
  in securities 781, 868
Institutional history *see* History
    (institutional)
Instruction
  classroom (high schools) 975
Instruction manuals
  bonkei 1330
  bookbinding 1479
  cultivation of bonsai 1328, 1336
  'go' (game) 1458
  ikat weaving (*kasuri*) 1354
  ikebana (flower arrangement)
    1462-1466
  martial arts 1446, 1448-1450, 1452
  origami 1364, 1367
  producing *washi* (handmade paper)
    1358
  restoring antique furniture 1340
  shōgi (game) 1459
  stencil dyeing (*katazome*) 1350
  sumi-e painting 1247, 1254
  tea ceremony 1471-1472
  see also Guidebooks
Instructional materials
  about haiku 1162
  about Japan 9, 18, 21, 36
  educational films (critical guide) 1586
  Focus on Asian Studies (periodical)
    1503
  for teaching Japanese 455
Instruments *see* Musical instruments
Insults 454
  avenging 585
Insurance 823, 862
  companies 851
  health 604
  laws (bibliography) 1582
  life 862
Integrated-circuit industry 884
Intellectual history *see* History
    (intellectual)
Intellectual property law 773
  role in US-Japanese licensing

transactions 783
Intellectuals
  biographical dictionary 367
  during the 1930s 199, 228
  Hashimoto Sanai 289
  Kawakami Hajime 318
  Meiji period 194, 196, 214, 230, 302,
    304, 404, 999
  Meirokusha 196, 304
  Mori Ōgai 1110
  Motoori Norinaga 309
  political and cultural socialisation 232
  role in decision-making 39
  role in formulating fascist ideas and
    programmes 199
  Sugawara no Michizane 293, 300
  Taishō period 175, 241
  Tokugawa period 165, 167, 173, 178,
    309
  see also Religious leaders
Inter-cultural activities
  participation of women 581
Interest articulation
  political 622
Interest groups 617, 627
  impact on political behaviour 628
  inability to influence industrial
    policy-making 880
  influence on foreign policy-making
    (1930s) 682
  involvement in the legislative process
    611
  Japan Medical Association 604
  Japan Teachers Union (Nikkyōso)
    967, 977
  nationwide farmers' group (Nōkyō)
    723
  repatriated Japanese 620
  role in peace negotiations with the
    USSR (1950s) 728
  role in political decision-making 620
Interest rates
  annual statistics 824
  decontrol (1970s) 866
  money markets 854
Interior decoration
  castles 1307
  elements of interior design 1326
  houses and apartments (post-1945)
    1319
  Pure Land Buddhist temple 1192
Interjections
  grammar 430

Intermarket groups
role 869
International Christian University library
holdings of English-language books
about Japan (bibliography) 1589
International House of Japan library
(Tokyo)
holdings of English-language books
about Japan (bibliography) 1589
International Labour Organisation
Convention no.87
politics of ratification 609
International Military Tribunal for the
Far East *see* Tokyo war crimes trial
(1946-48)
International relations *see* Foreign
relations
International trade *see* Trade and
commerce (foreign)
International Trade and Industry,
Ministry of *see* Ministry of
International Trade and Industry
(MITI)
Internationalisation 572
automobile industry 870
challenge for Japan 802
consumer markets 841
domestic controversies over 798
economy (1980s) 798, 820
financial institutions 948
financial markets 909
higher education 963
MITI's espousal 272
securities market 858
yen 860-861
Interpersonal communication
haragei in 406
comparison of Japan and the USA 584
Interpersonal relations 1, 20, 23
among geisha 576
among the women of Suye mura,
Kumamoto Prefecture 582
concern for harmonious 522, 544, 586,
592-593
concern for the quality of 795
conflict in 538
dependence in 589, 809
group-centred, vertically-oriented
nature 539
impact on individual behaviour and
development 541
importance in business 916
importance in industrial relations 921

in rural communities 588
modern politics 618
roles of *omote* and *ura* in 590
see also Husband-wife relationships,
Kinship, and Social relations
Interrogative words
grammar 430-433
Interviews
businessmen 1494-1495, 1527
fashion designers 1348
film directors 1423
Hamada Shōji 331
important personalities 1539
Into a black sun (Kaikō Takeshi)
translation 1062
Inukai Tsuyoshi
biography 296
Invasion of privacy 771
Inventory management system
Nissan Motor Company 871
Toyota Motor Corporation 871, 934,
936
Investment 800, 817, 884, 886
basic facts and figures (annual
handbook) 14
behaviour (comparison of Japan and
the USA) 859
climate (1980s) 868
contribution to economic growth
(1868-1941) 218
cycles 814
in agricultural improvements 831
in company facilities 822
in construction, housing, and
equipment 233
petroleum investment strategies 847
trusts 781, 858
see also Foreign investment, and
Foreign investment in Japan
Iran-Iraq War (1980s)
Japanese diplomatic response to 758
Ireland
surimono in the Chester Beatty
Library (Dublin) 1263
Iriki
documents of 148
Iron and steel industry 45
trade associations 899
Iron ore
quest for dependable supplies 913
Iron workers
folk culture 503
Irregularity

beauty of 1228
Irrigation
  improvements and technological
    innovations 200, 555, 831
  use of water (photo-essay) 3
Irwin, Robert Walker
  role in Japanese migration to Hawaii
    385
Ise (Mie Prefecture) 70
Ise monogatari
  literary analyses 1004, 1008, 1148
  translations 1148
Ise national park 48
Ise Shrine
  architecture 1323, 1325
  mythological background and history
    1323
  photographs 1323, 1325
  status (post-1945) 515
  traveller's account 66
Ishibashi Tanzan
  biography 336, 650
Ishida Baigan
  Shingaku movement 459
Ishida Tamizo
  film-making activities 1417
Ishikawa Prefecture
  electoral behaviour 611
  Kanazawa 100, 174
  kilns (Kutani ware) 1284
  see also Kaga *han*
Ishikawa Prefecture Art Museum
  holdings of Kutani ware 1284
Ishikawa Takuboku
  ideas about poetry 1168
  opposition to literary censorship 1122
Ishikawa Toyonobu
  primitive ukiyo-e prints 1268
Ishimoto Shizue
  biography 328
Ishiwara Kanji
  careeer and thought 342
Islands
  gazetteer 57
Isozaki Arata
  architectural work 1298-1299, 1320
Israel
  relations with Japan 758
Issa *see* Kobayashi Issa
Issei 390, 392, 403
  Arai Ryōichirō 297
  as founders of Japanese American
    trade 385

in California 385, 388, 392
in Hawaii 385, 392, 396-397
in Seattle, Washington 403
Sugimoto, Etsu Inagaki 313
Tanaka Michiko 400
'Itai-itai' disease 957
Italians in Japan
  Beato, Felix 1278
  Maraini, Fosco 70
  Valignano, Alessandro 133
Italy
  relations with Japan 245, 346, 708
  see also Europe
Itō Daisuke
  films and film-making activities 1423
Itō Hirobumi
  biography 296
  diplomatic involvement in the
    Sino-Japanese War of 1894-95 668
Ito Michio
  career and dances 322
Itō Miyoji
  biography 289
Itōh (*sōgō shōsha*)
  evolution, role, and organisation
    914-915
Ittōen (New Religion) 513
  see also New Religions
Iwai (*sōgō shōsha*)
  evolution, role, and organisation
    914-915
Iwakura mission (1871-73) 239, 307
Iwata Hiroshi
  poetry 1143
Iwate Prefecture
  Chūsonji temple 1192, 1322
  legends of Tōno 1188
  Shiwa 555
  see also Tōhoku region
Iwo Jima
  battle (1945) 699, 714-715, 1609
Izumi Shikibu nikki
  translation 1149
Izumo Shrine
  architecture 1325
Izutsu (Zeami Motokiyo)
  translation 1172

J
James A. Michener Collection
  (Honolulu Academy of Arts)
  holdings of primitive ukiyo-e prints
    1268

Janes, Leroy Lansing
  biography 358
Japan Broadcasting Corporation
  organisation and activities 1482, 1486
Japan Communist Party 634
  development (1922-45) 192
  doctrine, political strategy, and
    electoral record 635
  involvement of Koreans (1920s-1930s)
    377
  leadership and membership 635
  opposition to a revised US-Japan
    Security Treaty 744
  political role (post-1945) 635
  relations with the student movement
    (1920s) 244
  ties with Moscow 635, 752
'Japan Current' (Kuroshio)
  physical aspects 47
Japan Defence Agency
  annual review of defence policy 764
Japan External Trade Organisation
  (JETRO) 612
Japan Foundation (Tokyo) 612
  library holdings of English-language
    books about Japan (bibliography)
    1589
Japan General Federation of Labor
  (Nihon Rōdō Sōdōmei)
  activities (1920s-1930s) 215
Japan International Cooperation Agency
  746
Japan Iron and Steel Federation
  role in co-ordinating economic and
    political activity 899
Japan-Labor clique 247
Japan Library Association
  organisation and activities 1474
Japan Machine Tool Builders
  Association
  role in co-ordinating economic and
    political activity 899
Japan Medical Association
  pressure group politics 604
Japan Newspaper Publishers and Editors
  Association 1483
Japan Socialist Party 634
  as a perpetual opposition party 632
  Asukata Ichio and the dilemmas of
    leadership 636
  factions and factionalism 637
  links with China (1960s-1970s) 736
  political and ideological history 637

see also Socialist parties
Japan Society of London
  activities 1516
Japan Society of New York
  activities 1515
  history 1515
Japan Teachers Union (Nikkyōso)
  origins, development, and activities
    967, 977
Japan Times 1549
  collections of brief articles from 1551,
    1561
Japanalia 1551-1553, 1561
Japanese Alps
  minka 1301
Japanese American Citizens League
  origins and activities 390, 395
Japanese Americans 385
  acculturation 394, 397, 403
  achievement, culture, and personality
    588
  as domestic workers in San Francisco
    388
  autobiographies and memoirs 297,
    313, 391, 393, 395, 398-400
  bibliographies 1487, 1579, 1598, 1607
  biographies 387
  compensation for wartime internment
    395
  doctoral dissertations about
    (bibliography) 1607
  encyclopaedic and almanac-type
    information about 1563
  history (dictionary) 1563
  history (survey) 402
  images of Japan 651
  immigration and settlement 385,
    388-389, 396, 402
  in Hawaii 385, 389, 392, 396-397, 402,
    710
  kinship change among 403
  legislation affecting 384
  periodicals 1487
  photographs 389, 391
  racial discrimination experienced by
    384, 389, 392, 400, 402
  relocation during World War II
    384-386, 390-391, 393, 395, 398-402
  see also Issei, and Nisei
Japanese Canadians
  immigration and settlement 382
  racism experienced by 382, 385
  relocation during World War II

382-383, 655
Japanese Evacuation Claims Act (1948) 384
Japanese Exclusion Act (1924) 384, 392
Japanese language *see* Language
Japanese National Railways 612, 625
life-course of employees 542
Japanese studies
archival and manuscript sources in the USA (guidebook) 1562
directories 1554, 1559, 1565, 1615
doctoral dissertations (bibliography) 1607
in Australia 1554, 1559
in Canada 1525, 1554, 1559
in Europe 1554, 1559
in Great Britain 1508-1509, 1538, 1554, 1559
in Southeast Asia 1554, 1559
in the United States 359-360, 1509, 1525, 1554, 1559, 1562, 1565
newsletters 1509, 1525, 1543
periodicals (multidisciplinary) 1504, 1508-1509, 1525-1526, 1528, 1534, 1536, 1538, 1543
precollegiate (in the USA) 9, 18
resources in Washington, DC (guidebook) 1562
Jesuit Mission Press
influence on printing 1477
Jesuit missionaries (1500s-1600s) 129, 132-133, 153, 166, 352
Jews
anti-Semitism (World War II) 237
compared with the Japanese 4
life in Japan (history) 4
life in Japanese-occupied Shanghai (1941-45) 4
Jidai-geki genre (movies) 1414
Jien (priest)
life and writings 130
Jikigyō Miroku 526
Jinnō Shōtōki (Kitabatake Chikafusa)
translation 144
Jinrikisha
Victorian British writings about 68
Jippensha Ikku
Tōkaidōchū Hizakurige 1016
Jisei ('poetry composed on the verge of death') 1138
jitō (estate stewards) 149
Jiun Sonja 526
Jiyū minken undō ('movement for

freedom and popular rights') 195
leadership of Tanaka Shōzō 312
Job satisfaction
expatriate managers in multinational corporations 948
industrial employees 948
Jōdo Buddhism 475
absorption of elements of esoteric Buddhist painting 1237
artworks at the Byōdōin and Chūsonji temples 1192
doctrines 471
during the Kamakura and Muromachi periods 458, 465, 484
historical evolution 470, 1244
nenbutsu 470, 504
painting (survey) 1244
Shinran's cardinal ideas 471
terminology (dictionary) 415
Jōdo Shin Buddhism *see* Shin Buddhism
Johnson and Johnson (company)
business operations in Japan 889
Joinery and joints 1318
joints employed by *tansu* craftsmen 1341
Joint economic committees
utilisation of private businessmen 887
Joint ventures 916
financial management 861
negotiations for establishing 911
special problems 891
Jōkyū War (1221) 148
Jōmon period
art 104
culture (Tone River area) 109
excavated sites 101
human evolution and cultural development 103
pottery 104, 107, 1283
Jōruri (dramatic narrative chanting) 1005
development (bunraku theatre) 1392
handbook of classical literature 1566
influence of folk songs 135
structural units of plays 1399
Josetsu
ink painting 1239, 1253
Journalism
historical development 305, 999
impact on pre-1945 autobiographical fiction 1113
Journalists
Fukuchi Gen'ichirō 305
Gayn, Mark 269

Journalists *continued*
  Guillain, Robert 691
  Ishibashi Tanzan 336
  Kamata Satoshi 924
  Kayahara Kazan 289
  Kinoshita Naoe 288
  professional and political attitudes
    1485
  Ryū Shintarō 199
  Tokutomi Sohō 311
  world of 1484
Judiciary 782
  judicial appeals 772
  judicial interpretation of the
    constitution 777
  judicial review 784, 786-787
  Kamakura period 148
  Matsukawa case (1949-70) 780
  treatment of Koreans in Japan 376
Jūdō (martial art) 1444
Jugōya (Chrysanthemum Festival) 501
Juku (private schools)
  overview (1980s) 970
'Just-in-time' production
  at the Toyota Motor Corporation
    934-935
  corporate practices 836
  see also Inventory management system
Justice
  administration 780, 1582
  annual statistics 825
  social (concept among factory
    workers) 183
  see also Criminal justice
Juvenile delinquency 566, 588
  family and personality factors causing
    571
  influence on behaviour 592
  police ways of handling 565

K
Kabasan Incident (1884) 195
Kabuki 1004
  19th century 1005
  acting forms 1397, 1407
  actors 1264, 1394, 1398, 1400-1401,
    1564
  actors depicted in netsuke 1291
  audiences 1410
  bibliographies 1588, 1603, 1615
  comprehensive overview 1398
  costumes 1351-1352, 1400-1401, 1407,
    1564

  dance 1388, 1564
  depicted in Ōsaka prints 1264
  depicted in primitive ukiyo-e prints
    1268
  encyclopaedia 1564
  guidebooks 1401
  handbook of classical literature 1566
  history 1352, 1393, 1396-1398, 1400
  influenced by folk songs 135
  introductory studies 1394, 1400, 1403
  major types 1394, 1401
  make-up 1401, 1407, 1564
  musical accompaniment 1382-1385,
    1396-1398, 1401, 1407, 1564, 1611
  nagauta 1384-1385
  performance conventions and
    techniques 1174, 1393, 1396-1398,
    1400-1401, 1407
  photographs 1351-1352, 1395, 1398,
    1400-1401, 1407
  plays (literary analyses) 1170, 1180,
    1398
  plays (synopses) 1394, 1400, 1407,
    1564
  plays (translations) 1170, 1174,
    1395-1396
  playwriting system 1396
  relationship to the world of public
    entertainment 1397
  stage 1394, 1398, 1400, 1564
  transformation of bunraku plays into
    kabuki plays 1174, 1395
  versions of the play *Chūshingura* 1180
  Western influences 1398
Kachō ('bird and flower') painting
  tradition 1257
Kachō prints of Katsushika Hokusai
  1260
Kaempfer, Engelbert
  as a cultural intermediary 596
Kaga *han*
  tradition and change in 197
Kagawa Prefecture
  Kurusu 556
  Sanuki 69
  see also Inland Sea area, Sanuki
    Province, and Shikoku
Kagawa Toyohiko
  as a pacifist 288
Kagayakeru yami (Kaikō Takeshi)
  translation 1062
Kagerō nikki (Fujiwara Michitsuna no
  haha)
  translation 1013

Kagi (Tanizaki Junichirō)
  literary analysis 1127
  translation 1100
Kagoshima (Kagoshima Prefecture)
  Allied bombardment (1863) 353, 675
  tourist guide 100
  William Willis' medical activities
    (1870s) 353
Kagoshima Prefecture
  documents of Iriki 148
  Satsuma Rebellion (1877) 293, 306
  see also Kyūshū, and Satsuma *han*
Kagura 1403
Kaifusō
  translation (excerpts) 1010
Kaigetsudō Ando
  ukiyo-e paintings 1267
Kaikei
  Kamakura period sculpture 1293
Kaikō Takeshi
  Kagayakeru yami 1062
Kaiseki (cuisine)
  association with the tea ceremony
    1437, 1471-1472
  guidebook 1437
  utensils for the *kaiseki* meal 1468
Kaisho (calligraphic script) 1242
Kaitokudō Merchant Academy
  as a centre of scholarly learning 176
Kakemono *see* Hanging scrolls
  (kakemono)
Kakiemon ware (ceramics) 1281
Kakinomoto no Hitomaro
  poetry 1163-1164
Kakugyō Tōbutsu 526
Kamaitachi (demon)
  demonic imagery depicted in
    photographs 1275
Kamakura (Kanagawa Prefecture) 19,
  68-69
  antique shops and dealers (directory)
    1215
  guidebook 76
  temples 76, 131, 463
Kamakura *bakufu see Bakufu*
  (shogunate): Kamakura peiod
Kamakura school of painting 1239
Kamata Satoshi
  diary 924
Kamchatka Peninsula (Siberia)
  Tokugawa period castaways 664
Kamen no kokuhaku (Mishima Yukio)
  literary analyses 1127, 1131

translation 1073
Kami (divinities)
  shamanistic techniques for dealing
    with 499
  Shintō 499, 516, 518-520
  Yashiki-gami 503
  see also Deities
Kamikaze pilots 691, 715
  as tragic heroes 293
  comprehensive accounts 700
  during the Okinawa campaign 688
  tradition of sacrifice 686
Kamo no Chōmei
  Hōjōki 1007
Kampō see Kanpō (Chinese herbal
  medicine)
Kamui ('gods') 378
Kana syllabaries 438
  historical evolution 404, 1242
  language textbooks 441-442, 449
Kana zōshi (popular literary books) 1005
Kanagaki Robun
  biographical sketch 291
Kanagawa
  Treaty (1854) 667, 673
Kanagawa Prefecture
  Bank of Yokohama 942
  Kamakura 19, 68-69, 76, 131, 463,
    1215
  Kawasaki 376
  labour relations (1853-1955) 204
  Odawara Castle 1317
  Yokohama 56, 68, 162, 353, 919
  see also Kantō region
Kanai Mieko
  poetry 1057
  short stories 1048
Kanamajiribun (writing system)
  historical development 404
Kan'ami
  noh plays 1175, 1181
Kanashiki gangu (Ishikawa Takuboku)
  translation 1140
Kanazawa (Ishikawa Prefecture)
  A. B. Mitford's visit 357
  history (17th century) 174
  tourist guide 100
Kanban see Shop signs (*kanban*)
Kanban system *see* Inventory
  management system
Kaneko Fumiko 290
Kaneko Mitsuharu
  poetry 1057

Kaneko Tōta
  haiku poetry 1159
Kanemi Rice Oil poisoning case 957
Kanji see Chinese characters (*kanji*)
Kanno Suga 240, 290
Kannon (bodhisattva)
  depicted in paintings 1244
Kanō Eitoku
  life and painting 1252
  wall paintings 135, 1252
Kanō Mitsunobu
  life and painting 1252
Kanō school of painting 1239, 1252
  influence on styles of book illustration
    1477
Kanō Shōei
  life and painting 1252
Kanō Sōshū
  life and painting 1252
Kanpō (Chinese herbal medicine)
  598, 600, 603
Kansei reforms (1787-93) 177
Kantō region
  geography 50
  geomorphic surfaces 51
  minka (traditional-style houses) 1301
  Muromachi period *bakufu* rule 146
Kappa (Akutagawa Ryūnosuke)
  translation 1044
Kappa (supernatural creatures)
  stories about 1044, 1188
Kara Jūrō
  plays 1171
Karafuto (southern Sakhalin)
  Japanese colonial rule 223
Karate (martial art) 1444
  history 1448
  introductory manual 1446
  Karate-dō kyōhan (text) 1446
  memoirs of Funakoshi Gichin 1446
  training 1446, 1448
Karatsu ware (ceramics) 1281, 1283
  history and stylistic analysis 1279
Kariya (Aichi Prefecture)
  industry and politics 547
Karuizawa (Nagano Prefecture)
  as a summer resort 362
Kasai Zenzō
  literary analysis 1113
Kashiwabara (Nagano Prefecture)
  depicted in Kobayashi Issa's poetic
    diary 1146
Kasuri (ikat weaving)

instruction manual 1351
Katagami (stencils for dyeing fabrics)
  1344
Katakana see Kana syllabaries
Katazome see Stencil dyeing (*katazome*)
Katō Hajime
  painted porcelains 1285
Katō Kanji 206, 210
Katō Kōmei
  political leadership 198
Katō Shizue
  biography 328
Katō Tomosaburō 210
Katsukawa Shunshō
  ukiyo-e paintings 1250
Katsura Detached Palace
  cultural and architectural history 1305,
    1315
  gardens 1332, 1334-1335
  photographs 1305, 1315
Katsushika Hokusai
  book illustrations 1478
  books and albums of woodblock prints
    1478
  drawings 1258, 1260
  erotic prints (*shunga*) 1259, 1478
  life and works (introductory study)
    1260
  ukiyo-e paintings 1250, 1260
  ukiyo-e print series of Mount Fuji
    (reproductions) 1256, 1265
  ukiyo-e prints 184, 1260
Kawabata Yasunari
  biographical sketch 295
  concept of literature 1128
  novels 1008, 1063-1067, 1118, 1127
  search for authenticity in literature
    1130
  short stories 1051, 1057, 1083, 1106,
    1126
  vignette 24
Kawakami Hajime
  biographical sketch 292
  biography 318
  life and thought 241
Kawakami Tōgai
  biographical essay 239
  painting 1235
Kawakita Kashiko
  film-distributing activities 1423
Kawakubo Rei
  fashion-design work 1348
Kawamata Katsuji

mini-biography 874
Kawaradera (temple)
architecture 1322
Kawasaki (Kanagawa Prefecture)
Korean ghetto 376
Kawatake Mokuami
kabuki plays 1394, 1407
Kayahara Kazan
biography 289
Kegon sect of Buddhism
absorption of esoteric Buddhist
painting elements 1237
Keibō-sōhō (martial art) 1444
Keidanren Defence Production
Committee 761
Keigo see Honorific language (*keigo*)
Keijo Shūrin
poetry 1152
Keijo-jutsu (martial art) 1444
Keio University
establishment 302
Keiretsu (business groups)
growth (post-1945) 270
system of oligopoly trading 886
Kemmu Restoration (1333-36) 144, 159
depicted in the *Taiheiki* 1018
Kempeitai (military police)
history 648
Kendō (martial art) 1444
introductory study 1449
kata ('forms') 1441
Kenjutsu ('use of the sword') 1443
Kenkō *see* Yoshida Kenkō
Kenreimon'in Ukyō no Daibu shū
translation 1142
Kenseikai (political party)
political rivalry with the Seiyūkai 198
Kenshō ('seeing one's true nature') 487
Key (Tanizaki Junichirō)
literary analysis 1127
translation 1100
Ki no Tsurayuki
Kokinshū 1004, 1153
Shinsen wakashū 1153
Tosa nikki 1149
Kido Kōichi 246
Kido Kōin
biography 289
diary 307
Kido Takayoshi *see* Kido Kōin
Kijima Hajime
poetry 1143
Kikkoman Corporation

corporate management 802
history (1660s-1970s) 201
Kiku no sekku (Chrysanthemum
Festival) 501
Kikuchi, Charles
'Tanforan journals' (diary) 393
Kikuchi Takeo
fashion-design work 1348
Kikutake Kiyonari
architectural work 1298
Kikyō (Osaragi Jirō)
quest for identity in 1115
translation 1092
Kilns 1279-1280, 1282-1284, 1286-1287
Kimiko and John Powers Collection
art (exhibition catalogue) 1214
Kimono
as antiques 1215
at the Seattle Art Museum 1217
guidebook 1356
historical background 1351
photographs 1217, 1356
textile patterns 1344
see also Kosode
Kinai region
cotton trade (Tokugawa period)
170
Kindai shūka (Fujiwara Teika)
translation 1135
Kindergartens
day-to-day life of children 559
education (post-1952) 960
overview (1980s) 970
Kinjiki (Mishima Yukio)
translation 1075
Kinkakuji (temple)
garden 1327, 1335
novel about 1080
Kinkakuji (Mishima Yukio)
literary analysis 1131
quest for identity in 1115
translation 1080
Kinki region
geography 50
Kinnō ('imperial loyalism') 188
Kinoshita Keisuke
film-making activities 1415
films 1421
Kinoshita Naoe
as a pacifist 288
Kinoshita Yūji
biography 1144
poetry 1144

Kinship
among Japanese Americans 403
among the *burakumin* 374
associations (in Niiike, Okayama
Prefecture) 548
form and function 530
patrilineal groups 531
relations 535
relationships (rural society) 561
relationships (Tokyo ward) 549
system (Ainu) 379
Kipling, Rudyard
writings about Japan 216
Kisei Reigen
poetry 1152
Kiseto ware (ceramics) 1281
Kishi Nobusuke
Security Treaty crisis (1960) 744
Kishi school of art
influence on styles of book illustration
1477
Kishida Kunio
life and writings 1178
plays 1178
Kishida Ryūsei
paintings 1251
Kishida Toshiko 240
Kiska *see* Aleutian Islands (Alaska)
Kiso District (Nagano Prefecture)
novel about 1094
Kita Ikki
life and ideas 348
Kitabatake Chikafusa
Jinnō Shōtōki 144
Kitagawa Utamaro
erotic prints (*shunga*) 1259
prints and paintings 1262
Kitamura Tōkoku
as a pacifist 288
individualism in his essays 1129
search for authenticity in literature
1130
Kitaōji Rosanjin
painted porcelains 1285
Kitchens
furnishings 1342
utensils (aesthetic qualities) 1198
Kites 1461
aesthetic qualities (photographs) 1198
kite-making 1461
Knives
craftsmanship 1369
photographs 1366, 1369

Know-how
legal protection 773-774
taxation of know-how licensing 774
Kōan (catechetic questions) 490, 494
sermons and commentaries on 473
'Sound of the One Hand' 476-477
Kōan zaza 478
Kobayashi Hideo
biographical essay 239
Kobayashi Issa
haiku poetry 1137, 1146
Oraga haru 1146
Kobayashi Masaki
film-making activities 1415, 1423
films 1423
Kobayashi Sakae
influence on Noguchi Hideyo 343
Kobayashi Sosaku
educational methods 330
Kobayashi Takiji
novellas 1068
Kōbe (Hyōgo Prefecture)
high schools 975
life in (Meiji period) 68, 72
tourist guide 100
Kōbō Daishi *see* Kūkai
Kōchi Prefecture *see* Tosa *han*
Kōda Rohan
literary analysis 1069
short stories 1069
Kōenkai (mass membership
organisation)
used in election campaigning 631
Kōetsu *see* Hon'ami Kōetsu
Kōfu (Natsume Sōseki)
psychoanalytical study 1112
synopsis and analysis 1112
Kōfukuji (temple)
architecture and sculpture 1316
Kofun (Tumulus) period (AD 250-552)
art 104-105
excavated sites 101
human evolution and cultural
development 103
pottery 104
Kohōan (temple)
garden 1327
Koide Narashige
paintings 1251
Koiso Cabinet (1944-45)
activities 237
Kojiki
creation myths recorded in 502
Motoori Norinaga's study of 309

translation 152
Kojima Nobuo
    short stories 1057
Kōjin (Natsume Sōseki)
    psychoanalytical study 1112
    synopses and analyses 1112, 1117
Kojinteki na taiken (Ōe Kenzaburō)
    literary analysis 1127
    quest for identity in 1115
    translation 1089
Kokedera ('Moss Temple') see Saihōji
    (temple)
Kōkei
    Kamakura period sculpture 1293
Kokinshū
    Chinese influences 1153
    literary analysis 1153
    poetry 1004
    translations 1153
Kokinwakashū see Kokinshū
Kokoro (Natsume Sōseki)
    literary analysis 1127
    psychoanalytical study 1112
    synopses and analyses 1112, 1117
    translation 1086
Kokugaku ('national learning') 180
    promoted by Motoori Norinaga 309
Kokusai Bunka Kaikan see International
    House of Japan library (Tokyo)
Kokusai Denshin Denwa Company
    deregulation of telecommunications
    transmission 953
Kokusaika see Internationalisation
Kokutai ('national polity') 203
Kōmeitō ('Clean Government Party')
    514, 634
Komparu Zenchiku
    noh plays 1175, 1181
Konjaku monogatari
    literary analyses 1032, 1037
    relationship with Uji shūi monogatari
    1022
    translations 1029, 1032
Konkōkyō (New Religion) 510, 513
    see also New Religions
Kōno Taeko
    short stories 1048, 1071, 1098
Kōno Yōhei 636
Konoe Atsumaro
    intellectual biography 650
Konoe Fumimaro
    advised by the Shōwa Kenkyūkai 199
    biography 340

role in launching the Sino-Japanese
    War (1937) 685
Konoe Memorial
    Yoshida Shigeru and 324
Konparu Zenchiku noh plays 1175, 1181
Korai fūteishō (Fujiwara no Shunzei)
    1007
Korea
    accounts of World War II refugees
    from 583
    early cultural influence 101
    influence on early Japanese poetry
    1163
    invaded by Toyotomi Hideyoshi 299
    Japanese colonial rule (1910-45) 223
    Japanese imperialist expansion
    (1897-1911) 662
    Japanese museum collections of
    Korean art 1473, 1475
    Japanese response to the Tonghak
    Rebellion (1894-95) 668
    migration of Koreans to and from
    Japan 376-377
    movable type introduced from 1477
    relations with Japan 299, 677
    response to the West (comparison
    with Japan) 10
Korea (North Korea)
    relations with Japan 283, 377
    relations with Japan's Korean minority
    376
    right of Koreans in Japan to visit 788
Korea (Republic of Korea)
    economic development (compared
    with Japan) 806
    relations with Japan's Korean minority
    376
    trade and commerce with Japan 719
    see also Foreign relations with Korea
    (Republic of Korea)
Korean War (1950-53)
    economic impact on automobile
    manufacturing companies 871
Koreans in Japan 376-377, 565, 788
Kōrin see Ogata Kōrin
Kōrin school of art see Rimpa school of
    art
Kōshoku gonin onna (Ihara Saikaku)
    translation 1015
Kōshoku ichidai onna (Ihara Saikaku)
    translations (excerpts) 1015, 1036
Kōshoku ichidai otoko (Ihara Saikaku)
    translation 1014

Kosode (clothing)
  evolution (illustrated survey) 1351
  exhibition catalogue (Nomura
    Collection) 1353
Koto (zither) 1383
  music 1378, 1382-1383
  music (*kumiuta* and *danmono*
    compositions) 1378
Kōtoku Shūsui
  as a pacifist 288
  biography 337
  reactions to his trial 1122
Kotsuji, Abraham
  autobiography 4
Kōwaka (ballad-drama) 1169
Kōwakamai
  handbook of classical literature 1566
Kozaki Hiromichi 358
  writings and activities 235
Kūkai
  biographical sketches 295, 482
  Buddhist writings 458, 482
  pilgrimages in his honour 73
Kumagai Morikazu
  artistic techniques and styles 1203
Kumamoto Castle 1317
Kumamoto Prefecture
  Kumamoto School for Western
    Learning (Kumamoto Yōgakko) 358
  'Minamata disease' 34, 567, 957, 959
  Suye mura 551, 582
  see also Kyūshū
Kume Kunitake 211
Kumiuta tradition of koto music 1378
Kunikida Doppo
  literary analysis 1070
  short stories 1070, 1126
Kuniyoshi see Utagawa Kuniyoshi
Kura ('storehouses')
  architectural design and tradition 1311
Kurahashi Yumiko
  short stories 1098
Kurashiki (Okayama Prefecture)
  police operations 565
  Takashima as a suburb 554
  tourist guide 100
Kurile Islands
  19th-century claims to 664
  comprehensive history 286
  discovery and mapping 52
  Soviet military occupation 285
  territorial dispute over 752
Kuroda Kio

  poetry 1141
Kuroda Seiki
  painting 1235
Kuroi ame (Ibuse Masuji)
  literary analysis 1127
  quest for identity in 1115
  translation 1058
Kurokawa Noriaki
  architectural work 1298
Kurosawa Akira
  autobiography 329
  bibliographies 1425, 1585
  film-making activities 1415, 1417,
    1423, 1425
  filmographies 1415, 1425, 1585
  films 1421, 1423-1425, 1428
  Ikiru (translation) 1057
  samurai films 1420
Kuroshio ('Japan Current')
  physical aspects 47
Kurotsuchi (Fukuoka Prefecture)
  child-rearing 559
  marriage practices 560
Kuroyanagi Tetsuko
  autobiography 330
Kurozumikyō (New Religion) 513
  ethnographic study 508
  see also New Religions
Kurusu (Kagawa Prefecture)
  community study (1951-75) 556
Kuruwa bunshō (Chikamatsu
    Monzaemon)
  translation 1396
Kusakabe Kinbei
  photographs 1278
Kusamakura (Natsume Sōseki)
  synopsis and analysis 1117
Kusaka Genzui
  political biography 171
Kusemai music and songs 1409
Kusunoki Masashige
  life and times 293, 1018
Kutani ware (ceramics)
  illustrated study 1284
Kuwata Sasafune
  calligraphy 1231
Kwantung Army
  activities in Manchuria 209
  defeated by Soviet armed forces 684,
    692
  Ishiwara Kanji's involvement 342
  Manchurian Incident (1931) 245, 342,
    685, 702

Kwantung Leased Territory
 Japanese colonial rule (1905-45) 223
Kyōgen (form of comic drama) 26, 1007
 bibliography 1603
 costumes 1351
 handbook of classical literature 1566
 performance conventions and
  techniques 1402
 photographs 1405
 survey 1402-1403, 1405
 synopses 1402
 translations 1181, 1402
Kyōka poets
 Hokusai's illustrations to 1260
Kyōkai
 Nihon ryōiki 1007
Kyōto
 ageing among its residents 541
 antique shops and dealers (directory)
  1215
 as a literary centre 1005
 Daigoji temple 1322
 Daitokuji temple 1190
 Enpukuji Monastery 486
 Fushimi Castle 1317
 gardens 89, 98, 1327, 1331-1335
 geisha 576
 Gion Festival 500
 growth and development 546
 history (794-1868) 92
 history of printing 1477
 imperial court 141, 147, 188
 Katsura Detached Palace 1305, 1315,
  1332, 1334-1335
 medical beliefs and practices among its
  residents 598
 minka 1301
 Muromachi period 140
 Muromachi period *bakufu* rule 146
 Nijō Castle 89, 1307, 1317
 Ōnin War 160
 photographs 25, 77-78, 89, 92, 1026
 population distribution and movement
  40
 primary and secondary school life 964
 Shigaraki ware 1280
 temples 77, 89, 92, 131, 463
 Tōji temple 1289
 tourist guides 77-78, 89, 92, 98, 100
 travellers' accounts 66, 68-70
Kyōto Imperial University
 Kawakami Hajime at 318
Kyōto Prefecture

Byōdōin temple 1192, 1322
 leftist government 642
 Ōhara 100
 Uji 69, 100, 1192
Kyōto School of Philosophy
 anthology of essays 521
Kyōunshu (Ikkyū Sōjun)
 study and translation 1139
Kyūjutsu (archery) 1443
Kyūshū
 geography 50
 minka 1301
 Muromachi period *bakufu* rule 146
 ornamented tombs 105
 traveller's account 67

L

Labels
 price and packaging 85, 88
 annual statistics 819, 825-827, 829
Labour
 automobile industry 870
 basic facts and figures (annual
  handbook) 14
 bibliography 1594
 blue-collar workers 870, 918-920,
  923-925
 contribution to economic growth
  (1868-1941) 218
 during the Allied occupation of Japan
  (1945-52) 267, 273-275, 282
 education of skilled 217, 925, 942
 force 181, 808, 930
 government report (annual) 829
 increase in labour employment
  (1953-71) 793
 industrial (pre-1945) 202
 law 538, 1582
 legislation 609
 manpower policy 821, 895
 manpower strategy of business 836
 market 803, 811, 895, 930, 938, 940,
  962-963
 mobility 542, 919, 930
 movement 202, 215, 244, 275, 282, 938
 organisations (Japanese American)
  392
 organisations (Yūaikai) 215
 organisers (Tanno Setsu) 290
 overview for businessmen 843
 periodicals 1500, 1511
 policy 909
 political party preference 611

Labour *continued*
political role of organised 215
problems (robot-related) 995
sectoral reallocation (1953-71) 793
support for the socialist parties 630
supply 792, 803, 806-807
unit labour costs in manufacturing 859
white-collar workers 13, 564, 574, 579, 870, 1460
see also Employment, History (labour), Paternalism, Personnel, Productivity, Recruitment, Wages, and Working conditions
Labour-Farmer faction 247
Labour leaders
alleged sabotage of a train at Matsukawa (1949) 780
Kagawa Toyohiko 288
Masuda Tetsuo 874
Suzuki Bunji 215
women 580
Labour-management relations 894, 921, 937, 941
bibliographies 1581, 1590, 1614
collective bargaining 267, 931, 937
consultation 940
consumer behaviour and 841
heavy industry 204, 547
historical evolution 204, 208
human resource development and 817
labour relations law 786
large companies 917
Liberal Democratic Party's response to changing conditions in 619
medium-sized manufacturing enterprise 838
Nissan Motor Company 871, 874
Toyota Motor Corporation 547, 871, 924
Westernisation 929
see also Industrial relations, and Management
Labour unions 723, 811, 891, 895, 923, 938, 940
administration 937
autonomy and ideology 918
company unions 616, 797, 921, 940
decision-making 39
during the 1920s-1930s 215
farmers 268
finances 937
legal right to organise 921
legislation (pre-1945) 202

links with politics 937
membership 920
Nikkyōso (Japan Teachers Union) 967, 977
organisation 920
practices 921
regional bank 543
response to microelectronisation 940
role in post-1945 economic development 780
under the Allied occupation of Japan (1945-52) 267
union take-overs 921
Lacquer artists
biographical dictionaries 368-369, 1567
signatures 1360, 1571
Lacquerware and lacquerwork
as antiques 1215
at the Seattle Art Museum 1217
at the Tokyo National Museum 1473
depicted in exhibition catalogues 1218-1219, 1227, 1229, 1370
design motifs and techniques 1204
dictionary 1567
folk art 1193, 1213
historical function and beauty 1435
history 1211, 1370, 1374
lacquer finishes for *tansu* (wooden chests) 1341-1342
netsuke 1288, 1291
Okinawan 1201, 1222
Rimpa school of art 1240
see also Photographs (lacquerwork and lacquerware)
Ladles
photographs 1366
Lady Daibu
poetic memoirs 1142
Lady Nijō
autobiographical narrative 310
Lakes
gazetteer 57
species of fish 60
Land
allotment 143
basic facts and figures (annual handbook) 14
classification (maps) 54
landholding patterns 10
markets and policy (Tokyo metropolitan area) 42
reform (Allied occupation of Japan)

267-268, 282, 790, 835
reform (Meiji period) 835
shōen (landed estates) 140-141, 149
surveys (Hideyoshi) 299
system (Tokugawa period) 181
taxation 42, 138, 183, 212
tenure (pre-1700) 138
use 548, 1592
Landforms 40, 51
bibliography 1592
Landlord-tenant relations
1870-1940 242
Tokugawa period 181
Landlords
government compensation to former
633, 790
Landscape gardening 37 1327
designers (biographical dictionary) 369
'secret teachings' 1338
Zen Buddhist dimensions 1196
Landscapes
19th century (photographs) 1278
depicted in *bonkei* 1330
depicted in *yamato-e* painting 1236
design motif of textile patterns 1344
Edo depicted in woodblock prints
1256
Katsushika Hokusai's prints 1260
Katsushika Hokusai's sketches
(reproductions) 1258
Mount Fuji depicted in woodblock
prints 1256, 1260, 1265, 1478
sumi-e techniques for painting 1254
Tōkaidō highway depicted in
woodblock prints 1265
see also Gardens
Language 8, 23, 916
1500s-1600s 132-133, 153
adjectives 411, 427, 429-433
as an expression of culture 16, 31
aspect 410, 434
bar talk 454
bibliographies 1529, 1615
business Japanese 422, 436, 439, 447
comparatives 411
comparison of Japanese and
Indo-European languages 411
courses for foreign students
(guidebook) 1550
daily usage 409
dialects 407, 454
encyclopaedic and almanac-type
information about 1552-1553,

1556-1557
grammar 407, 427-434, 455
guide for teachers of Japanese 455
history 404, 407
honorific language (*keigo*) 407, 427,
430-434, 443, 450, 454
kana syllabaries 404, 438, 441-442,
449, 1242
learning process 359, 594
loanwords 407, 419, 454
meaning and definition of words 411
myths 408
nature of 405
negation 432, 434
newspaper Japanese 445
nonverbal communication 406, 443,
535, 584
overviews 407, 454
patterns 435
periodicals 1529, 1543
personal pronouns 411, 427
phonology 405, 407, 412
phrase books 416, 446, 453
politeness in Japanese 443
pronunciation 405, 454-455
proper usage of basic words and
phrases 420
proverbs and idiomatic sayings 1183
reform 196, 404, 997
relationship to patterns of behaviour
411
sentence structure 405
slang 454
sociolinguistic observations 408
syntax 407
technical Japanese 437
tense 410
textbooks 85, 88, 419-420, 425,
427-428, 431, 435-457
varieties of ordinary speech 405
verbs 410, 412, 427, 429-433
women's 413
word order 427, 429
words and terms pertaining to women
413
see also Calligraphy, Chinese
characters (*kanji*), Dictionaries,
Glossaries, and Writing system
Language teaching
guide to teaching English 979
guide to teaching Japanese 455
teaching reading skills to scientists and
engineers 991

Lanterns
  as antiques 1215
  at the Tōdaiji temple 1206
  chōchin ('paper lanterns') 1326
  craftsmanship 1369
  folk art 1213
  used in gardens 1337, 1339
Latin America
  relations with Japan 743
Laughter
  idiomatic words and expressions 414
Laundry
  procedures for cleaning kimono 1356
Law 20
  administrative 777, 1582
  arbitration 148, 775, 779
  banking 781, 783, 1582
  bibliography 1582
  business 776
  commercial 786, 1582
  concept and role (Tokugawa period)
    778
  contract 777
  court cases affecting women 575
  criminal 772, 786, 1582
  education for lawyers 776, 786
  environmental 775
  environmental lawsuits 958
  ethics of legal action 844
  family 786
  function in industrial relations 937
  impact on US-Japanese economic
    relations 783
  intellectual property 773, 783
  introductory studies 16, 32, 782
  Japanese Americans (legal history)
    384
  Kamakura period 147-148
  labour 538, 921, 1582
  labour relations 786
  legal framework of public
    administration 625
  legal problems of foreign enterprises
    in Japan 779
  legal profession 776, 782, 784, 786
  legal status of the Korean minority in
    Japan 376-377
  legal system 535, 771, 776, 782, 901
  legal system (introductory cases and
    materials) 784
  legal system (role of the police) 570
  newspaper publishing 1484
  overview for businessmen 843

  patent 774
  periodicals 1531
  post-1867 development 784, 786
  reforms (Allied occupation of Japan)
    277, 780
  relating to libraries 1474, 1476
  role in society 784-785
  social change (post-1945) and 785
  Tokugawa period 168, 778
  see also Legislation
Law of the Sea
  impact on Japanese-Canadian
    relations 895
  United Nations Conference 717
Law on Foreign Securities Firms
  text 781
Laws
  Agricultural Basic Law 832, 835
  alien land laws (USA) 384
  Antimonopoly Law 773-774
  Banking Law 781
  Broadcast Law (excerpts) 1486
  broadcasting 1482
  Cabinet Law 605
  censorship 221
  Civil Code 277, 280
  Copyright Law 773
  Criminal Code 277
  criminal compensation law 772
  Design Law 773
  Election Law 631
  foreign exchange law 857, 909
  foreign trade control law 909
  governing the management of solid
    wastes (garbage) 956
  Income Tax Law 788
  Japanese Exclusion Act of 1924 384
  Land Reform Law 268
  law for compensating
    pollution-related health damage 777
  Law of the Sea 717, 895
  Law on Foreign Securities Firms 781
  law to prevent unfair competition 773,
    786
  Library Law of 1950 1474, 1476
  National Diet Library Law (1955
    revision) 1476
  National Government Organisation
    Law 606
  Peace Preservation Law 221
  police laws 788
  Procedural Code 277
  Securities and Exchange Law 781

Securities Investment Trust Law 781
Small and Medium-Sized Enterprises
    Organization Law 611
Trademark Law 773
Utility Model Law 773
see also Constitution, Meiji
    Constitution
Lawyers 776, 782, 784, 786
Laxman, Adam Erikovich
    role in Russo-Japanese relations 664
LDP *see* Liberal Democratic Party
Leadership
    at Nissan and Ford 874
    business 208, 219, 943
    fishing crews 552
    government 627
    Japan Communist Party 635
    mayoral 636
    naval (World War II) 687-688
    Nikkyōso (Japan Teachers Union) 967
    political 30, 185, 296, 379, 611, 623,
        634, 636
    role of *de facto* leaders 922
    styles 726, 750
    see also Labour leaders, Military
        leaders, Political leaders, and
        Religious leaders
League of Nations
    involvement in the Manchurian crisis
        (1931-33) 711
    Japanese mandate over Micronesia
        227
    Japan's withdrawal from membership
        685
Learned societies 980
    Asiatic Society of Japan 1543
    Association for Asian Studies 1525
    Japan Societies in the USA (directory)
        1565
    Japan Society of London 1516
    Japan Society of New York 1515
    Meirokusha 196, 304
Learning
    proverbs about 1183
Leasing
    1950s-1960s 851
Leftists
    opposition to Narita Airport 606
Legends 1186
    about Daruma 483
    about *ninjutsu* and the *ninja* 1445
    about the Japanese crane 58
    about the 'other world' 499

Ainu 372
associated with Semimaru of Ausaka
    1176
bibliography 1577
encyclopaedic and almanac-type
    information about 1560-1561
folk 1184
of Kamakura 76
of the Tōhoku region 74
of Tōno, Iwate Prefecture 1188
scrolls illustrating 1245
see also Folk tales, Folklore, and
    Myths
Legislation
    censorship (1868-1945) 221
    environmental protection 775
    judicial review of 787
    labour union 202
    legislative process 611, 626
    legislative statutes (post-1945) 782
    Nikkyōso's influence 977
Legislature *see* Diet (parliament)
Legitimacy, Political *see* Political
    legitimacy
Leisure activities 8, 26
    among residents of Ōsaka and
        Takashima, Okayama Prefecture
        (comparison) 562
    among residents of Tokyo 549
    among the elderly (bibliography)
        1595
    among villagers (Shinohata, Tochigi
        Prefecture) 550
    basic facts and figures (annual
        handbook) 14
    see also Entertainment, and
        Recreational activities
Letters
    correspondence of Toyotomi
        Hideyoshi 299
    describing family life 563
    letter-writing 451
Lew Chew *see* Ryūkyū Islands
Leyte Gulf
    battle (1944) 210, 680, 687-688, 699,
        715, 1609
Liberal Democratic Party 624
    dominance and organisation
        (post-1954) 632
    election campaign of Satō Bunsei 631
    factions and factionalism 629, 633, 638
    interaction with government ministries
        and financial institutions 857

Liberal Democratic Party *continued*
  intergenerational conflict among
    members 636
  involved in budget-making 608
  involvement of ex-bureaucrats 809
  links with China (1960s-1970s) 736
  loss of voter support in Tokyo 628
  membership 633
  organisation, internal structure, and
    operation 638
  origins 274
  policy-making (1950s-1960s) 633, 638
  relations with business and industrial
    interests 638
  responses to postwar change 619
  role in peace negotiations with the
    USSR (1950s) 728
  selection of a party president 638
  support for a revised US-Japan
    Security Treaty (1960) 744
Liberalisation
  capital 779
  economic process (1980-84) 856
  finance 820-821, 856, 860, 884
  foreign trade 896, 906
  money markets 856, 861
  telecommunications transmission 953
Liberalism in Japan
  Ishibashi Tanzan 336
  readings about 33
  resistance to centralised rule 614
Librarians 1474
Librarianship
  comprehensive survey 1476
  education 1474, 1476
Libraries
  architecture (1960-80) 1299
  college and university (guidebook)
    1550
  comprehensive survey 1476
  Diet Library holdings (bibliography)
    1589
  directories 1474, 1558
  holdings of English-language books
    about Japan in Tokyo area libraries
    (bibliographies) 1589
  Library Law (1950) 1474, 1476
  union list of periodicals and
    newspapers 1601
Library of Congress (Washington, DC)
  holdings of calligraphy 1231
  holdings of national government
    publications 1602

Librettos
  kōwaka (ballad-drama) 1169
Licensing
  agreements 773-774
  of public gatherings 790
  role of intellectual property law in 783
  taxation of know-how 774
Life after death
  Ainu views 375
Life insurance 862
Life sciences
  research institutes and programmes
    980
Life-course
  women (case studies) 579
  workers (case studies) 542
Life-cycle 535
  families in Ōsaka and Takashima,
    Okayama Prefecture 562
  villagers in Niiike, Okayama
    Prefecture 548
Life-styles
  prehistoric Japanese 103
  production workers 918
  relationship to language 411
  urban housewives 577
  village residents (Shinohata, Tochigi
    Prefecture) 550
Light and darkness (Natsume Sōseki)
  psychological study 1112
Linguistics
  bibliographies 1529, 1615
  see also Language
Linked verse *see Haikai* poetry, and
    Renga poetry
Liquefied natural gas 885
  policy influenced by the Tokyo
    Electric Power Company 849
  US-Japanese co-operation involving
    847
Literacy 164
Literary activities and groups
  bundan 1120
  Shinkankakuha 1114
  student (1880s-1940s) 232
  Tokyo (late Meiji period) 1105
Literary criticism
  critics (biographical dictionary) 365
  history 999
  history (1868-1940s) 1001
  Kobayashi Hideo 239
Literati
  calligraphy 1249

painting 1255
Literature
  bibliographies of translations 1521,
    1588, 1597
  bibliography 1615
  biographical dictionary 365
  Buddhist (medieval) 1007
  censorship 221, 1122
  Chinese influence 301, 1006, 1153,
    1163
  chronologies 1566
  depicted in *yamato-e* painting 1236
  depiction of wildlife 58, 63
  encyclopaedic and almanac-type
    information about 1552, 1556, 1564,
    1566
  guidebooks 1009, 1566, 1597
  history 999, 1001, 1005-1006, 1162,
    1566
  ideal of individualism in 1129
  introductory studies 16, 32, 1002, 1004
  Korean influence 1163
  'Japanese Literature in Translation'
    (symposium proceedings) 1231
  nature of (modern novelists' concepts)
    1128
  Okinawan 1006
  periodicals 1493, 1496, 1504, 1521,
    1526, 1534, 1543
  portrayal of old people (bibliography)
    1595
  proletarian literary movement (1920s)
    241
  Russian influence 1124
  scrolls illustrating medieval 1245
  search for authenticity in 1130
  social context (modern) 1120
  Western influence 1002, 1006,
    1113-1114, 1123, 1129, 1133, 1141
  see also Drama, Essays, Folk tales,
    Novels, Poetry, Short stories,
    Translations, and Writers
Litigation 785-786
Little master (Natsume Sōseki)
  literary analyses 1112, 1117, 1127
  psychoanalytical study 1112
  translation 1084
Livelihood
  basic facts and figures (annual
    handbook) 14
Livestock industry
  economics 833
Living arrangements

changes in 556
of foreign businessmen 891
of the elderly 540
'Living national treasures'
  photo-essay 13
Living standards
  1870s-1980 803
  impact of land reform 268
  revolution in rural 556
  Tokugawa period 169
Loanwords 407, 454
  dictionary 419
Lobbying (political) 30
  big business 30, 39
  Japan Medical Association 604
Local government 617
  1860-90 212
  1945-1950s 280, 531
  citizen participation 641
  city assembly members 542
  comprehensive introduction 641
  economic functions 791
  finance 625, 641, 863
  history (1871-1952) 641
  local autonomy 616, 640-641, 790
  Niiike, Okayama Prefecture 548
  offices (directory) 1574
  participation in regional
    policy-making 640
  relations with the national government
    625, 639, 641-642, 863
  Tokugawa period 168
  Tokyo Metropolitan Government 625
  Tokyo suburbs 628
Local politics
  impact of citizens' movements 958
  leadership and power structure 611
  lobbying activities of organised labour
    609
Local power
  Bizen Province (pre-1700) 138
  structure (Muromachi period) 140
London (England)
  compared with Tokyo 10
London Naval Arms Limitation talks 209
London Naval Treaty (1930)
  military discontent with 685
Los Angeles, California
  assimilation of Nisei residents 385
  images of Japan among Japanese
    American residents 651
Loti, Pierre
  writings about Japan 216

Lotus Sutra
venerated by the Reiyūkai 509
Love
affairs (in novels) 10, 1024, 1046,
1052, 1063, 1065, 1067, 1076, 1078,
1082, 1086, 1099, 1102, 1109, 1124
affairs (in plays) 1170
affairs (in poetry) 1142
affairs (governing principles) 1039
as a factor in choosing marriage
partners 558
as an aspect of medieval life 136
depicted in *shunga* (erotic prints) 1259
idiomatic words and expressions 414
in marriage 591
in *The tale of Genji* 1039
language of 454
poetry about 1148, 1153, 1155, 1160
proverbs about 1183
stories about 1011, 1014-1015, 1021,
1027-1028
see also Dependence (*amae*)
Loyalty
company 845
Japanese Americans 386-387, 397, 401
managers of multinational
corporations 942
plays about 1180, 1395
Toyota Motor Corporation employees
924
value among businessmen 840
value among policemen 565
value among samurai 529
Luminous moss (Takeda Taijun)
quest for identity in 1115
Lute *see Biwa* (lute), and Shamisen
(lute)

M

MacArthur, Douglas
biography 356
character and role 278, 281-282
McDonald's Corporation
business operations in Japan 889
Machine tools industry 38
evolution (1930s-1980s) 872
trade associations 899
Machine translation
future prospects 991
Macroeconomic policy
changes in (1980s) 860
Maeda family
as the daimyō of Kanazawa 174

Maekawa Commission Report (1986)
798
Maekawa Kunio
architectural work 1298
Maekawa Senpan
woodblock prints 1274
Magazines
Bungei Shunjū 1547
Chūō Kōron 1547
government control (pre-1945) 221
Tōyō Keizai Shinpō 336
translations and summaries of articles
1547
see also Periodicals
Magic
employed in a New Religion 506
Mainichi Shimbun (newspaper)
articles and editorials (translations and
synopses) 1547
news reporting 1484
political character 1485
Tōkyō Nichi Nichi Shimbun as its
forerunner 305
Maitreya (Miroku)
depicted in paintings 1244
Make-up (facial)
as an aspect of medieval life 136
kabuki theatre 1352, 1401, 1407, 1564
Maki Fumihiko
architectural work 1298
Makiguchi Tsunesaburō
biography 319
Makioka sisters (Tanizaki Junichirō)
literary analyses 1002, 1127
translation 1101
Makura no sōshi (Sei Shōnagon)
translation 1025
Malaysia
relations with Japan 741, 897
see also Southeast Asia
Male chauvinism 591
Man
closeness with the gods and nature
460-461
Shintō concepts 518
Management 811, 837, 939
attitudes (of Sueno Akira) 845
baseball teams 1456
bibliographies 1581, 1590, 1594, 1614
business 840, 842, 845, 901, 935, 941
cash 861
concern for production schedules 924
conflict 538, 721-722, 892, 921

contributions of middle-level
  managers 922
corporate practices 838, 844, 926, 929,
  932
diplomacy 729
efficiency 837
environment 927
expatriate managers 948
financial 861-862
fishing crews 552
high technology 802
Honda Motor Company 882
impact of internationalisation on
  corporate 802
impact of Japanese culture 939
industrial 878, 928, 936
industrial (bibliography) 1600
influence of Japanese values 927
'insider's analysis' 922
Kikkoman Corporation 802
managerial councils (1940s) 280
multinational corporations 802, 877,
  926, 941, 944-945, 947-952
new-product development 926
newspaper industry 1483
Nissan Motor Company 871, 874
ocean resources 796
people-centred orientation of 797,
  922, 928
periodicals 1500, 1518, 1533
personnel 922-923, 926, 931, 933, 943,
  947-948
policies and practices (comparison of
  Japan and Great Britain) 941
politics of economic 817
practices 934, 941, 943
production-line 936
sociocultural aspects 927
solid waste programmes 956
strategies 822, 878, 882, 926, 940
styles 20, 332, 586, 874, 932-933
sumo wrestlers 1453
technique of simplification 936
'Theory Z' 932
Toyota Motor Corporation 871, 926,
  934, 936
transferability of Japanese techniques
  to the West 922, 927, 932-934, 936
values of managers 948
see also Labour-management relations
Management and Coordination Agency
  613
Manchuria

accounts of World War II refugees
  from 583
anti-Japanese movements (1930s) 647
establishment of Manchoukuo (1932)
  702
Ishiwara Kanji's activities (1930s) 342
Japanese expansion (1897-1911) 662
Kwantung Army 209, 342, 684, 692
Kwantung Leased Territory 223
promotion of Sino-Japanese
  co-prosperity in 661
Soviet-Japanese warfare (1939) in 684
Soviet Union and crises (1924-35) in
  684
stamps of Manchoukuo 1522
US-Japanese economic rivalry over 659
see also Russo-Japanese War (1904-5)
Manchurian Incident (1931) 245, 342,
  685, 702, 708
League of Nations' involvement 711
Mandalas
artistic world of 1192
esoteric Buddhist (Mikkyō) 1216, 1237
Pure Land (Jōdo) Buddhist 1244
Man'en gannen no futtōbōro (Ōe
  Kenzaburō)
translation 1090
Manga (comic strip books)
depicting robots 995
widespread popularity 26
world of 1480
Manga (Katsushika Hokusai) 1258,
  1260, 1478
Manganese nodules
policy for mining 796
Manpower see Labour
Manuals see Instruction manuals
Manufacturing 875
affected by the introduction of electric
  power 812
annual statistics 819, 825-827
flexible manufacturing strategies 872
flexible manufacturing systems 986
manufacturer-supplier relations
  (automobile industry) 870
movements of wage rates, labour
  costs, and prices in 859
see also Industry
Manuscripts
Japan-related resources in the USA
  (guidebook) 1562
Japan-related resources in
  Washington, DC (guidebook) 1562

Manyōshū
  Kakinomoto no Hitomaro's poetry
    1163
  Ōtomo Yakamochi as compiler 301
  poetry 301, 1004
  translation 1147
Manzanar (World War II Japanese
    American internment camp)
  autobiographical account of internees
    391
  photographs of daily life 391
Maps 14
  administrative divisions 53
  agricultural households 54
  agricultural products 53-54
  ancient Japan 1569
  antique maps 52, 55
  archaeological sites 101-102, 107, 109
  bird habitats 65
  cities and towns 53-54, 79, 82-83
  climate 41, 53-54
  flora and vegetation 61
  forestry 54
  gardens 1327, 1331
  geography 40, 50
  geology 49, 53-54
  Hiroshima 253
  history 53, 113, 124, 138, 314, 546
  hot springs (*onsen*) 80
  industrial and mining areas 53-54
  industrial geography 45
  international trade by ports 54
  Kanazawa (castle town) 174
  Kuroshio ('Japan Current') 47
  Kyōto 77-78, 89, 92
  land classification 54
  landforms 51
  locations of important libraries 1474
  Micronesia 227
  Nagasaki 179, 253
  Nara 93, 102
  national parks 48, 53-54
  nationwide tourism 82-83, 86, 100
  Niiike, Okayama Prefecture 548
  occupational patterns 54
  Okinawa (1945 battle) 713
  'Old Yamato' (Nara Basin) 102
  physical features 53
  population 53-54, 371
  Russo-Japanese relations (1697-1875)
    664
  soils 53
  Tōhoku region 74

  Tokyo 56, 75, 84, 86-87, 91, 99, 1256
  topography 54
  transportation routes 53-54, 56
  urban development 546
  villages 548
  World War II 681, 687, 692, 699, 713,
    715
Marianas *see* Micronesia
Marine science and technology
  research institutes and programmes
    980
Maritime Self-Defence Force
  role and development (1945-71) 759
Marketing 878, 939
  art through museums and galleries
    1376
  beef 833
  Canadian products in Japan 895
  competition for photovoltaic markets
    overseas 847
  foreign access to Japanese markets 905
  influences on consumer buying habits
    841
  Japanese-Western collaboration 912
  market research 901
  overview for businessmen 843
  practices 891, 901
  product-market strategy of major
    companies 926
  relationship between imports and the
    domestic marketing system 909
  strategy of multinational corporations
    945, 948
  system (1960s) 839
Marriage 536, 558, 574
  among Japanese Americans 403
  among the *burakumin* 374
  among residents of Tokyo 549, 558
  arranged marriages 558, 560
  as an aspect of medieval life 136
  associated taboos and rituals 500
  customs 1
  encyclopaedic and almanac-type
    information about 1556, 1561
  evolution of its form and function 530
  expressions pertaining to married life
    413
  folk tales about 1185
  love in 591
  mechanics of matchmaking 560
  memoirs about 1013
  patterns 379
  policies of the daimyō 163

role in forming ties between households 561
trends 371
weddings 66, 413, 560
Marshall Islands *see* Micronesia
Martial arts
aikidō 519, 1444, 1450-1451
bujutsu (classical and modern) 1443-1444
encyclopaedic and almanac-type information about 1553, 1556-1557, 1573
iaidō 1441, 1452
internationalisation 1444, 1448, 1451
jūdō 1444
karate 1444, 1446, 1448
kendō 1441, 1444, 1449
ninjutsu 1445
Martial ways (*budō*)
introductory studies 1442, 1444
Marubeni (*sōgō shōsha*)
evolution, role, and organisation 914-915
personnel practices 942
Maruyama school of art
influence on styles of book illustration 1477
Marxism
1926-45 527
ideology of students (1950s-1960s) 969
introduced into Japan 318
Kawakami Hajime 241, 292, 318
resistance to centralised rule 614
Masamune Hakuchō
biographical sketch 292
Masaoka, Mike
life and achievements 395
Masaoka Shiki
biographical sketch 291
biography 239
Botan kuroku 1149
haiku poetry 1137, 1159
ideas about poetry 1168
life and writings 1161
Masculine speech 454
Mashiko (Tochigi Prefecture)
Hamada Shōji's life in 331
Masks
as antiques 1215
at the Seattle Art Museum 1217
at the Shōsōin 1194
at the Tōdaiji temple 1206
bugaku dance 1294

depicted in netsuke 1291
gagaku 1215, 1377
gigaku dance drama 1296
kyōgen 1402
noh theatre 1215, 1219, 1405-1406, 1408, 1412
origami figures 1364, 1367
owned by the Tokugawa shōguns (exhibition catalogue) 1219
see also Photographs (masks)
Masks (Enchi Fumiko)
translation 1052
'Mass age' 537
Mass culture 533
mass political attitudes 621
Mass media 15
basic facts and figures (annual handbook) 14
freedom of expression 771
media defamation 771
political dynamics and 615
women employees 578
see also Broadcasting, Journalism, Magazines, Newspapers, and Publishing
Mass society 533
development of a 532
Sōka Gakkai and 514
Massage
clinical practice 598
Master of 'go' (Kawabata Yasunari)
literary analysis 1127
translation 1064
Masuda Tetsuo
biography 874
Masuho Zankō
as a populariser of Shintō 526
Maternity leave 575
Mathematics
achievement 594
historical development 157, 187
Matsudaira Sadanobu
political biography 177
Matsukata Haru *see* Reischauer, Haru Matsukata
Matsukata Masayoshi
biography 297
Matsukawa (Fukushima Prefecture)
sabotage of a train (1949) at 780
Matsumoto (Nagano Prefecture)
leisure time among residents 1460
Matsumoto Akira
woodblock print techniques 1273

Matsumoto Seichō
  short stories 1106
Matsumoto Shigeharu 211
Matsunaga Yasuzaemon 636
Matsuo Bashō 1005
  biographical sketch 295
  haikai poetry 1165
  haiku poetry 1002, 1137, 1167
  life and writings 1167
  Oku no hosomichi 1007, 1149
  renga poetry 1166
  Sarumino 1150
  see also Bashō school
Matsuri see Festivals
Matsushita Electric Company
  personnel policies 933
  strategic management practices 926
Matsuyama Bay (Ehime Prefecture)
  natural farming on land near 830
Max Factor & Company
  business operations in Japan 889
Mazda Motor Corporation
  recovery from near bankruptcy 809
Meat dishes
  recipes 1429-1430, 1434, 1438-1439
Mechanisation
  agricultural 555, 573
Mechatronics 995
  research and development 984
  US-Japan scientific relationship in 998
Meckel, Jakob
  as adviser to the army 229
Mediation 785
  used in settling environmental disputes
    775
Medical sociology
  review and future prospects 603
Medicine 596-604
  acupuncture 598
  at the Shōsōin 1194
  British influence (Meiji period) 660
  during medieval times 136
  encyclopaedic and almanac-type
    information about 1552-1553, 1561
  historical development 157, 187,
    596-597
  kanpō (Chinese herbal medicine) 598,
    600, 603
  medical care 540, 599, 826
  medical clinics (architecture) 1299
  medical education 343, 353, 596-598
  medical effects of the 1945 atomic
    bombings 253, 255-257

medical practices (mid-1800s) 353
moxibustion 598
Noguchi Hideyo 343
psychotherapy 592, 601-602
reconstructive surgery of 1945
  bombing victims 252
reliance on medications 603
research institutes and programmes
  980
Tokugawa period 167, 596
Western medicine in Japan 596-598,
  600
see also Doctors
Meditation 480, 489
  at a Zen monastery 486, 491
  central to Dōgen's thought 481
  seiza ('quiet-sitting therapy') 602
  zazen (sitting meditation) 478, 487,
    494
Megalopolis
  along the Pacific coast 46
Meian (Natsume Sōseki)
  psychoanalytical study 1112
Meiji Constitution 189
  bibliography 1582
  foreign policy and 672
  interpreted by Minobe Tatsukichi 220
  Itō Hirobumi as its 'father' 296
  text 112, 784
Meiji Restoration (1868) 162, 191, 226,
  249, 675
  as a 'revolt from below' 171
  medical care during 353
  Sakamoto Ryōma 295
  Western observations 353, 357
Meijin (Kawabata Yasunari)
  literary analysis 1127
  translation 1064
Meiroku zasshi (magazine) 196
Meirokusha ('Meiji 6 Society')
  involvement of Mori Arinori 304
Meisho Edo Hyakkei (Andō Hiroshige)
  print series (reproductions) 1256
Membership
  Japan Communist Party 635
  Kurozumikyō 508
  Liberal Democratic Party 633
  Reiyūkai 509
  Risshō Kōseikai 507
  Sōka Gakkai 511-512, 514
  Sūkyō Mahikari 506
Memorial tablets 505
Menopause 599

Menstrual taboos 503
Mental illness
among Japanese Americans 394
Merchant shipping
World War II losses to US submarines
681
Merchants
Tokugawa period 165, 170, 176, 208,
231
Mercury poisoning
'Minamata disease' 34, 567, 957, 959
Meritocracy
emphasis on 795
Metal-processing industries
economic importance 762
Metals
recycling 956
Metalwork
associated with sword-fittings 1373
at the Shōsōin 1194
at the Tokyo National Museum 1473
craftsmen (biographical dictionary)
369
craftsmen (handbook of signatures)
1571
design motifs and techniques 1204
folk art 1193, 1210, 1213
furniture 1341-1342
influence on lacquerwork and design
1374
Kofun (Tumulus) period 105
Meiji period (exhibition catalogue)
1229
see also Photographs (metalwork)
Metaphysics
Shintō 516
Methylmercury poisoning 'Minamata
disease' 34, 567, 957, 959
Mibu kyōgen (pantomime theatre)
handbook of classical literature 1566
Michener Collection (Honolulu
Academy of Arts)
holdings of primitive ukiyo-e prints
1268
Michikusa (Natsume Sōseki)
psychoanalytical study 1112
synopses and analyses 1112, 1117
Microbiologists
Noguchi Hideyo 343
Micro-electronics
research and development 984
Micro-electronisation
trade union responses 940

Micronesia
Japanese colonial rule 223, 227
Japanese enterpreneurs 227, 385
relations with Japan (post-1945) 743
Midaregami (Yosano Akiko)
translation 1160
Middle class
housewives 577
in Tokyo 549, 563-564, 577
life of salaried workers 13, 564
Meiji period origins 214
structure and composition (1970s) 545
support for the socialist parties 630
Middle East
Anglo-Japanese trade rivalry
(1920s-1930s) 758
heavy reliance on oil from 885
relations with Japan 743, 758, 885
Midway
battle (1942) 210, 680, 687-688, 710,
715
battle (comprehensive account) 706
battle (bibliography) 1609
Mie Prefecture
Ise 48, 66, 70, 1323, 1325
Yokkaichi 'asthma' 957
Migration
internal 40, 371, 557
Koreans to and from Japan 376-377
overseas (1920-55) 371
to Australia 751
to Canada 382, 655
to Hawaii 385, 389, 396-397, 662
to Micronesia 227
to the United States 384, 392,
396-397, 402, 659, 662
Miki Kiyoshi 199
Mikkyō (esoteric Buddhism) see Shingon
Buddhism
Militarism
during the 1930s 193, 222, 238, 321,
323, 340, 690
public fear of resurgent 764
social basis for pre-1945 243
Military
assistance (1860s-1880s) 229
conscription (1868-1945) 205
demilitarisation (Allied occupation of
Japan) 271, 759
equipment (medieval) 136
foreign policies (1868-1941) in the
military sphere (research guide)
1599

Military *continued*
  fortifications (7th-8th centuries) 143
  nationalist trends (1945-57) in 276
  organisation (Muromachi period) 137
  organisations (1840s-1880s) 212
  periodicals 1488, 1491
  prehistoric development of military
    power 101
  rearmament (post-1945) 271, 354,
    754, 759, 766
  system (Tokugawa period) 185
  tradition 761
  US military bases in Japan
    (constitutionality) 790
  see also Air force, Army, Castles,
    Defence, History (military), Navy,
    Self-Defence Forces, Weapons,
    and the names of individual wars
Military leaders
  biographical dictionary 367
  prosecution (war crimes trials)
    265-266, 271, 321, 346, 595
  Oda Nobunaga 135, 139, 145
  Toyotomi Hideyoshi 146, 299
  Yamagata Aritomo 303
  see also Army generals, Navy
    admirals, and Warriors and heroes
'Military tales' *see* 'War tales' (*gunki
  monogatari*)
'Minamata disease' 567, 957, 959
  impact 34
  photographs 959
Minamoto family
  depicted in the *Heike monogatari* 1019
  rivalry with the Taira family 149, 154
  stories about 1017
Minamoto no Yoshitsune
  life and times 293
Minamoto Sanetomo
  play about 1182
Minase sangin hyakuin
  translation 1165
Miner (Natsume Sōseki)
  psychological study 1112
  synopsis and analysis 1112
Mineral waters *see* Hot springs (*onsen*)
Minerals
  manganese nodules 796
  ocean mineral rights 717
  significance of imported 762
  survey of resources 50
Mingei (folk-crafts) movement 331, 553,
  1228

Miniature carvings *see* Netsuke
  (miniature carvings)
Miniature landscapes (*bonkei*)
  instruction manual (illustrated) 1330
Miniature trees *see* Bonsai
Mining 217
  annual statistics 825
  areas (maps) 53-54
  coal 38
  coal miners 205, 328
  copper (Ashio Copper Mine) 312, 957
Ministries (government)
  concerned with foreign enterprises in
    Japan 779
  control of public corporations 612
  inter-ministerial conflict 856-857
  major scientific programmes 980
  organisation 605
  publications 1593, 1602
Ministry of Education
  relationship with Nikkyōso (Japan
    Teachers Union) 967, 977
Ministry of Finance 862
  career and retirement patterns of
    officials 857
  organisation 605
  policy-making (institutional nature)
    856
  role in foreign policy decision-making
    (1930s) 682
  role in regulating banks 861
  role in the budget-making process 608
Ministry of Foreign Affairs
  evolving role (1869-1942) 654
  organisation and administration 605,
    729
  policy-making (Tyumen oil
    development project) 748
  role in foreign policy decision-making
    (1930s) 682
  role in peace negotiations with the
    USSR (1950s) 728
Ministry of Home Affairs 202
  inability to amalgamate prefectures
    640
  organisation 605
  see also Home Ministry
Ministry of International Trade and
    Industry (MITI)
  decision-making (case study) 39
  evaluation of applied research at 987
  formulation of industrial policy 814,
    879

formulation of trade policy 896
history (1925-75) 272
implementation of economic policy 785
international economic policy 748
organisation 605
promotion of high technology 880, 996
Minka (traditional-style houses)
comprehensive study 1312
photo-essays 1301, 1303
Mino ware (ceramics) *see* Oribe ware (ceramics), and Shino ware (ceramics)
Minobe Affair (1935) 220
Minobe Tatsukichi
'emperor-organ theory' 209, 220
Minorities see Ainu, *Burakumin*, and Koreans in Japan
Minseitō (political party)
efforts to enact labour union legislation 202
Minyūsha ('Society of the People's Friends') 230
Miracles
tales about 1022
Mirrors
at the Shōsōin 1194
at the Tōdaiji temple 1206
bronze 104-105
maps on the backs of 55
Mishima (Shizuoka Prefecture)
citizens' movements and environmental politics 642
Mishima Yukio 1003
biographical sketch 292
biography 335
concept of literature 1128
essay on the Sentō Imperial Palace garden 1334
life and work (interpretive essay) 1131
novels 1072-1073, 1075-1078, 1080, 1118, 1127
plays 1074, 1177, 1179
search for authenticity in literature 1130
short stories 1057, 1074, 1083, 1126
writings on bushidō 529
Missile industry 763
Missionaries
Christian (19th-20th centuries) 495-497, 1587
depicted in *Nanban* art 132, 1243
Jesuit (16th-17th centuries) 129,

132-133, 153, 166, 352, 495, 498, 1587
Mitford, Algernon Bertram
memoirs 357
MITI *see* Ministry of International Trade and Industry (MITI)
Mito Castle 1317
Mito *han*
Tokugawa Nariaki (daimyō) 289
Mitsubishi (company)
aircraft manufactured during World War II 689
origins and growth (1870-1914) 250
see also Zaibatsu
Mitsubishi Electric Corporation
evaluation of applied research by 987
Mitsubishi enterprise group
inter-firm relations 935
Mitsubishi Shōji (*sōgō shōsha*)
evolution, role, and organisation 914-915
Mitsui
competition with Mitsubishi 250
history (1673-1960s) 231
see also Zaibatsu
Mitsui Bussan (*sōgō shōsha*)
evolution, role, and organisation 914-915
personnel practices 942
Mitsui coal mines (Fukuoka Prefecture) 328
Miyagawa Chōshun
ukiyo-e paintings 1250, 1267
Miyagi Prefecture
nuclear power generating plant at Onagawa 796
Sendai 100
see also Tōhoku region
Miyajima (Hiroshima Prefecture) 19
Miyake Issey
fashion-design work 1348
Miyamoto Chikukei
calligraphy 1231
Miyamoto Musashi
Book of five rings (*Gorin no sho*) 1447
novel about 1109
Miyamoto Yuriko
short stories 1071
Miyashita Tokio
woodblock print techniques 1273
Miyazawa Kenji
ideas about poetry 1168

Miyoshi Tatsuji
  poetry 1141, 1145
Mizoguchi Kenji
  bibliography 1578
  biography 1422
  film-making activities 1415, 1417, 1428
  filmographies 1415, 1578
  films 1421, 1424
Mobility *see* Labour (mobility)
Modality 434
Model
  exemplary features of the educational
    system 966, 971
  Japan as a model for the West 795,
    797
  Japanese automobile industry as a 870
  Japanese industry as an example for
    Americans 875
  relevance of Japanese corporate
    practices for the West 836
  relevance of Japan's development
    experience for the Third World 806,
    810, 818, 831
  transferability of Japanese
    management techniques to the West
    922, 927, 932-934, 936
Modernisation 7, 190, 530
  as an historiographical concept 249
  changing atitudes towards 239
  depicted in Meiji period prints 1269
  depicted in photographs (1840-1945)
    1276
  drama 1178
  human costs 205
  impact (overview for businessmen)
    843
  impact upon cultural identity 230
  impact upon culture 239
  impact upon the peasantry 205, 242,
    550
  literature 1110, 1123
  managerial practices 943
  Meiji period 190, 196-197, 206, 214,
    226, 230, 239, 248, 303-307, 358,
    1110, 1269, 1276
  military 229, 303
  role of education in 973
  role of Mori Ōgai in 1110
  Tokugawa period origins 164, 168,
    180-181, 183, 218, 459, 818
  Tokutomi Sohō's views 311
  see also Industrial development
Modernism (literary movement)

Yokomitsu Riichi 1114
Moetsukita chizu (Abe Kōbō)
  translation 1042
Mohnike, Otto
  medical activities 597
Mon see Family (crests)
Mon (Natsume Sōseki)
  psychoanalytical study 1112
  synopses and analyses 1112, 1117
Monasteries
  Enpukuji Monastery 486
  Rinzai Zen (14th-15th centuries) 131
  role in Kamakura period society 147
  see also Temples
Monastic life
  depicted in Mishima Yukio's novel
    1080
  jisei poetry by Zen monks 1138
  reflected in *gozan bungaku* poetry
    1152
  Zen Buddhism 131, 472, 486, 491
Monetary policies 811, 821
  1950s-1960s 851
  1950s-1970s 791, 799, 815, 865
  1970s 866
  Bank of Japan 864-865
  bibliography 1594
  development and structure
    (post-1945) 805
  external safeguards of 909
  management (1970s) 859
Money
  annual statistics 819
  Fukuzawa Yukichi's views 302
  emerging global role of Japanese 817,
    867
  markets 854, 856, 861-862, 864
  money-making (stories about) 1015
  see also Capital, Capital formation,
    Finance, Foreign exchange, Foreign
    investment, and Foreign investment
    in Japan
Mongolia
  Soviet-Japanese warfare (1939) in 684
Mongols
  wars against invading 141
Monkeys 63
  American wartime views of the
    Japanese as apes 686
Monkey's straw raincoat (Matsuo Bashō)
  translation 1150
Monks *see* Monastic life, and Religious
  leaders

Monopolies
  administrative guidance and pro-cartel
    policies 816
  Antimonopoly Law 773-774
  control of monopoly power 786
  relaxation of anti-monopoly policy
    846
Monsoons
  winter 41
Monsters
  folk legends about 1184
Morality
  among Tokyo residents 549
  business world 840, 844
  moral education 9, 595
  pollution viewed in moral terms 775
  protected by government literary
    censorship 1122
  shared values and 591
  see also Ethics
Moras 412
Mori Arinori
  career and personality 304
  educational policies 972
Mori Ōgai
  biographical sketch 292
  biographies 1110, 1121
  'historical literature' 1081
  life and writings 1121
  literary, intellectual, and cultural
    contributions 1110
  novels 1082, 1118, 1127
  opposition to literary censorship 1122
  short stories 1081, 1083, 1126
Morita Akio
  autobiography 332
  history of Sony, Inc. 877
Morita psychotherapy 601
  shinkeishitsu and 592
Morozumi Osamu
  woodblock print techniques 1273
Morse, Edward S.
  experience living in Japan 361
Mortality
  during the Tokugawa period 172
  trends (1920-55) 371
Moss
  used in gardens 1334, 1337, 1339
Mothers
  as motivating source for children 978
  'education mamas' 574
  expressions pertaining to motherhood
    413

Motivation
  achievement motivation 588
  among blue-collar employees 918, 925
  among schoolchildren 971, 978
  among workers 923, 939
Motoda Eifu
  efforts to revive Confucianism 528
Motoori Norinaga
  biography 309
Motorcycles
  produced by the Honda Motor
    Company 344
Mount Fuji
  as a volcano 51
  depicted in ukiyo-e prints by Andō
    Hiroshige 1256, 1260, 1478
  depicted in ukiyo-e prints by
    Katsushika Hokusai 1265
  Fuji-Hakone-Izu national park 48
  travellers' accounts 68
Mountains 51
  gazetteer 57
  maps 53-54
  photographs 44
  religious importance 504
  sumi-e techniques for painting 1247,
    1254
  vegetation 61
Mouth organ (sho) 1379
Movements
  folk-crafts (mingei) 331, 553, 1228
  labour 202, 215, 244, 275, 282
  Popular Rights Movement (Jiyū
    minken undō) 195, 312
  proletarian literary movement (1920s)
    241
  Shingaku movement 459
  social reform 235, 240, 290
  student 2, 175, 244, 276, 565, 588, 595,
    961, 963, 969
  teachers' 967, 977
  women's 581
  see also Protest movements and
    uprisings
Movies see Cinema, Film directors, and
  Films
Moxibustion
  clinical practice 598
Mu Gai Ryū (iaidō style)
  basic styles 1441
Mukden
  battle (1905) 678
Mukyōkai ('Non-Church Christianity') 497

Multinational corporations 39, 836, 902
  competitive threat of Japanese 945
  evolution 946, 952
  expatriate managers 948
  in Canadian-Japanese relations 895
  in Great Britain 941, 944, 947-950
  in West Germany 948-949
  investment 912
  investment decision-making processes
    951
  Japanese policy toward foreign 905
  Kikkoman 201
  management 802, 926, 941-942, 947
  problems and successes (assessment)
    946
  Sony 877
  work-related values of employees 802
  see also Sōgō shōsha (general trading
    companies)
Munakata Shikō
  artistic techniques and styles 1203
  woodblock prints 1274
Murals 155
  Hōryūji temple 1208
  Kanō Eitoku 135, 1252
Murano Shirō
  poetry 1145
Murasaki Shikibu 150
  biographical sketch 295
  diary and poetic memoirs 1023
  see also Tale of Genji
Murasaki Shikibu shū
  translation 1023
Murder
  plays about 1170
Murōji (temple)
  architecture 1322
  photographs 1277
Muromachi bakufu see Bakufu
  (shogunate): Muromachi
Murray, David
  contributions to educational
    modernisation 197
Musashi (Yoshikawa Eiji)
  translation 1109
Musashino (Tokyo Prefecture)
  politics and social change 628
Museums
  architecture (post-1945) 81, 1299,
    1309, 1321, 1324
  Freer Gallery of Art (Japanese art)
    1250
  Freer Gallery of Art (ukiyo-e

  painting) 1250
  guidebook and directory 1475
  holdings of Japanese art (list) 368
  Honolulu Academy of Arts (primitive
    ukiyo-e) 1268
  Idemitsu Art Museum (Karatsu ware)
    1279
  Ishikawa Prefecture Art Museum
    (Kutani ware) 1284
  marketing of art through 1376
  periodicals 1489, 1535
  Philadelphia Museum of Art (Ōsaka
    prints) 1264
  Seattle Art Museum (premodern
    artworks) 1217
  Spencer Museum of Art (surimono)
    1263
  Tokugawa Art Museum (artworks)
    1219
  Tokugawa Art Museum (noh robes
    and masks) 1412
  Tokyo National Museum (overview)
    1473
  see also Art collections
Music 19
  accompaniment to the bunraku
    theatre 1382, 1395, 1399, 1404
  accompaniment to the kabuki theatre
    1382-1385, 1396-1398, 1401, 1407,
    1564
  bibliographies 1383, 1611
  biwa music 1382
  comprehensive history 1380
  discographies 1381, 1383
  during the Azuchi-Momoyama period
    135
  encyclopaedic and almanac-type
    information about 1552, 1556
  folk songs 135, 1380-1383
  gagaku (imperial court orchestra
    music) 1169, 1377, 1382-1383, 1403
  general principles 1385
  influenced by Japan's modernisation
    239
  koto music 1378, 1382
  kōwaka (ballad-drama) 1169
  kusemai music and songs 1409
  medieval 136
  musical transcriptions 1378-1379, 1384
  musical notation 1382-1383, 1387
  noh music 1181, 1382-1383, 1385,
    1387, 1389, 1405, 1408-1409
  patronage (1955-80) 1376

performances 1377, 1379, 1385
shakuhachi music 1382
Shintō 518, 1380, 1383
shōmyō (Buddhist chanting) 1382
songs 135, 380, 576, 1378, 1386
survey history 1383
survey of traditional genres 1382
teaching 326, 1385-1386
Tōgaku style of court music 1379
Western 1380, 1386
Musical compositions
Goro *Tokimune* (*nagauta*
composition) 1384
kumiuta and *danmono* (koto music)
1378
Tōgaku 1379
Tsuru-kame (*nagauta* composition)
1384
written by Uragami Gyokudō 1230
Musical instruments
aesthetic qualities (photographs) 1198
at the Shōsōin 1194
biwa 1382-1383
design (photographs) 1224
development (16th century) 135
drums 1385, 1387
drums and flutes of the *hayashi*
ensemble 1384
flutes 519, 1357
gagaku 1377
general survey 1383
history 1380
ko tsuzumi drums 1385
koto 1378, 1382-1383
mouth organ (*sho*) 1379
noh flute 1387
Okinawan 1201, 1222
owned by the Tokugawa shōguns
(exhibition catalogue) 1219
shakuhachi 1369, 1382-1383
shamisen 576, 1382-1385, 1399, 1404,
1411
Tōgaku ensemble 1379
used in the bunraku theatre 1382,
1399, 1404
used in the kabuki theatre 1382-1385,
1397
used in the noh theatre 1382-1383,
1385, 1387, 1405
see also Photographs (musical
instruments)
Musicians
bunraku theatre 1391

Semimaru of Ausaka 1176
Uragami Gyokudō 1230
Mutsu Munemitsu
as foreign minister 654, 668
biography 289
Myōshinji (temple)
garden 1332
Mythological characters
Katsushika Hokusai's sketches
(reproductions) 1258
Myths 1186
about Japan's divine origins 114, 130,
144, 152, 502, 516, 520
about the 'other world' 499
about the Ryūkyūs Islands' ancient
past 284
bibliography 1577
encyclopaedic and almanac-type
information about 1560-1561, 1568
folk festivals 501
periodicals 1490
Shintō mythology 458, 516, 520

N

Nabeshima ware (ceramics) 1281
Nagai Kafū
concept of literature 1128
life and writings 345
opposition to literary censorship 1122
short stories 345, 1126
Nagai Ryūtarō
biography 289
Nagano Prefecture
Anchiku region 1460
Karuizawa 362
Kashiwabara 1146
Kiso District 1094
Matsumoto 1460
Shinano 69
Nagasaki
atomic bombing 253, 258, 1275, 1277
atomic bombing depicted in literary
works 1088, 1173
Dutch physicians at 596
history (1500s-1800s) 179
life in (19th century) 68
prints and paintings 179
tourist guide 100
traveller's account 69
Nagauta (lyric form of shamisen music)
introductory study 1384
performance interpretations 1385
Naginata-dō (martial art) 1444

Nagoya (Aichi Prefecture) 70
  during the 1920s 350
  Tokugawa Art Museum 1219, 1412
  tourist guide 100
Naikan ('introspection therapy') 592, 602
Naitō Konan
  intellectual biography 650
Nakae Chōmin
  biographical sketch 292
  Confucianism and 526
Nakagami Kenji
  short stories 1056
Nakamura Hōchū
  fan-shaped paintings 1233
Nakano, Takeo Uyo
  account of internment (World War II)
    383
Nakarai Tōsui
  relationship with Higuchi Ichiyō 1111
Namahage (festival)
  anthropological account 501
Names see Dictionaries, and Signatures
Nanban art 132
  survey 1243
Nanga school of art
  influence on styles of book illustration
    1477
  painting 1255
  paintings in the Sansō Collection 1246
  Uragami Gyokudō 1230
  see also Bunjinga (literati painting)
Nan'yo see Micronesia
Naomi (Tanizaki Junichirō)
  translation 1102
Naozamurai (Kawatake Mokuami)
  translation 1407
Nara
  guidebook 93
  history 93
  history of printing in 1477
  Hōryūji temple 1208, 1322
  Kōfukuji temple 1316
  major religious sites 463
  minka (traditional-style houses) 1301
  pictorial survey 25
  Shōsōin 1194
  temples (architecture and sculpture)
    1316
  Tōdaiji temple 147, 1194, 1206,
    1289-1290, 1316
  Tōshōdaiji temple 1322
  tourist guide 100
  travellers' accounts 69-70

Nara Basin
  archaeology 102
Nara Prefecture
  Asukadera temple 1322
  Kawaradera temple 1322
  minka (traditional-style houses) 1301
  Murōji temple 1277, 1322
  Yakushiji temple 1289-1290, 1316,
    1322
  Yoshino region 1102
Narcissism 588
Narita (Chiba Prefecture)
  guidebook 91
  movement against airport construction
    at 606
Narrators
  bunraku theatre 1391-1392, 1404,
    1411
Narrow road to the far north (Matsuo
  Bashō) see Oku no hosomichi
Narrow road through the provinces
  (Matsuo Bashō) see Oku no
  hosomichi
Narukami Fudō Kitayama zakura
  (Tsuuchi Hanjurō et al.)
  translation 1396
Naruse Mikio
  film-making activities 1415, 1417, 1428
  films 1424
Narushima Tōichirō
  film-making activities 1423
National accounts
  annual statistics 819
National character 1-2, 4, 7-8, 15, 20,
    23, 31
  Buddhism's pervasive presence 485
  debate over (Meiji period) 230
  nihonjinron 4, 587
  proverbs illustrating 1183
  World War II studies 585, 686
National Defence Programme Outline
    764
National Diet Library 1474, 1476
  holdings of English-language books
    about Japan (bibliography) 1589
  National Diet Library Law (1955)
    1476
National income
  annual statistics 824
  National Income-Doubling Plan
    (1960s) 815
'National learning' (kokugaku) 180
  promoted by Motoori Norinaga 309

National parks 48
  maps 48, 53-54
  tourist guide 79
National Personnel Authority 613
National security *see* Security (national)
Nationalism
  agrarian (1890s-1930s) 206, 243
  capitalism (1868-1941) and 219
  during the 1930s 245, 348, 618
  Meiji period 20, 363, 517
  readings about 33
  right-wing (1945-57) 276
  State Shintō's formative role 517
  see also Ultranationalism
Natsume Sōseki
  biographical essay 239
  Chinese-language poetry 1010
  concept of literature 1128
  haiku poetry 1159
  life and writings 1117, 1133
  novels 1008, 1084-1087, 1118, 1127
  opposition to literary censorship 1122
  political thought 241
  psychological world 1112
  search for authenticity in literature
    1130
  short stories 1126
Natural gas *see* Liquefied natural gas
Natural resources
  bibliography 1594
Naturalism (literary movement)
  government censorship 1122
  impact on autobiographical fiction
    1113
Nature
  artistic depictions of natural creatures
    1221
  attitudes towards 63, 530, 1332
  belief in its beauty and power 516
  close bonds with man 593
  closeness with man and the gods
    460-461
  encyclopaedic and almanac-type
    information about 1556, 1561
  gozan bungaku poetry about 1152
  influence of Zen on the love of 492
  natural farming 830
  photographs 3, 17, 44, 48
  prints about (bibliography) 1576
  use in haiku poetry 1162
  vocabulary for 405
Navy
  aircraft (guidebook) 689

  during the Russo-Japanese War
    (1904-5) 210, 320, 678
  during the Sino-Japanese War of
    1894-95 210, 320
  during World War II 210, 317,
    680-681, 687-688, 705-706
  during World War II (bibliography)
    1609
  encyclopaedic and almanac-type
    information about 1572
  expansion programme (1930s) 704
  history (1870s-1945) 1572
  history (1895-1945) 210
  history (1945-71) 759
  images of war with the USA 651
  kamikaze pilots 293, 686, 688, 691,
    700, 715
  London Naval Arms Limitation talks
    (1930s) 209, 704
  London Naval Treaty (1930) 685
  mutual images of the British and
    Japanese navies (1936-41) 698
  participation in the 1941 policy
    conferences 693
  planning for the conquest of Hawaii
    710
  role in foreign policy-making (1930s)
    679, 682, 698
Navy admirals
  Katō Kanji 206, 210
  Katō Tomosaburō 210
  Tōgō Heihachirō 210, 320, 678
  Yamamoto Isoroku 210, 317, 699,
    705-706, 710
NEC (Nippon Electric Company)
  evaluation of applied research by 987
  investment decision-making 951
Negation
  grammar 432, 434
Negotiations
  business 776, 844, 893-894, 911, 916
  diplomatic 283, 645
  labour 267, 931
  trade 721-722, 892, 895-896, 904
Neighbours
  in a Tokyo ward 549
  neighbourhood associations 641
Nemureru bijo (Kawabata Yasunari)
  quest for identity in 1115
Nenbutsu (Buddhist invocation) 504
  theory and practice 470
Neo-Confucianism *see* Confucianism

Netherlands
  Dutch traders at Nagasaki 167, 173,
    179, 596
  involvement in World War II 711
  Japanese direct investment 948
  see also Europe
Netsuke (miniature carvings)
  as antiques 1215
  bibliography 1288
  carving (craftsmanship) 1291
  depicting creatures of nature 1221
  guide to legendary characters
    embodied in 1560
  handbooks 1288
  introductory study 1288
  photographs 1189, 1221, 1227, 1288,
    1291, 1360, 1489, 1535
  signatures of netsuke carvers
    (handbook) 1571
  theme of the supernatural in 1189
  Tokugawa period (exhibition
    catalogue) 1227
Neuroses
  shinkeishitsu 592
  treatment 592, 601-602
Neurotic savages
  American wartime views of the
    Japanese as 686
Neutralism
  Japan Socialist Party's avowed policy
    637
New Guinea
  Japanese capture (1942) 687
New Left youth movement
  drama of the 1960s and 1171
New Liberal Club (political party) 634,
    636
New life (Shimazaki Tōson)
  ideal of individualism in 1129
  synopsis and analysis 1117
New materials
  US-Japan scientific relationship in 998
New Religions 465, 468, 485, 506-514
  bibliography 1584
  introductions 462-463
  living goddesses 499
  readings about 461
  shamanistic tendencies 504
'New Theatre' movement *see Shingeki*
    ('new theatre')
New Tokyo International Airport at
    Narita
  opposition to its construction 606

'New Wave' cinema
  motifs and cultural concerns 1419
New Year's celebrations and customs
    153, 500-501
New Zealand
  involvement in World War II 711
  relations with Japan 665, 743
Newsletters
  Asian Studies Newsletter 1525
  Asiatic Society of Japan. *Bulletin* 1543
  Japan Foundation Newsletter 1509
  Japan Society Newsletter 1515
  Japan Society Review 1516
News agencies
  directory 1483
Newspaper Japanese
  textbook 445
Newspapers
  Asahi Evening News 1546
  Asahi Shimbun 643, 1484-1485,
    1546-1547
  British influence (1860s-1880s) on 660
  characteristics and readership 1484
  competition and conformity among 39
  directory 1483
  government control and censorship
    (pre-1945) 221
  influence on foreign policy-making
    (1931-41) 682
  influence on Soviet-Japanese relations
    (1950s-1970s) 728, 752
  Japan Economic Journal 1548
  Japan Times 1549, 1551, 1561
  Mainichi Shimbun 1484-1485, 1547
  Meiji period 212, 248, 305, 660
  newspaper industry 1483, 1485
  newspaper reporting 1483-1484
  Nihon Keizai Shimbun 1547-1548
  political character 1485
  Sankei Shimbun 1484, 1547
  Tōkyō Nichi Nichi Shimbun 305
  Tōkyō Shimbun 1547
  translations and synopses of articles
    and editorials 1547
  union list of library holdings 1601
  vilification of Iva Toguri as 'Tokyo
    Rose' 387
  Yomiuri Shimbun 1484-1485, 1547
  see also Journalists, and Mass media
NHK (Nippon Hōsō Kaisha)
  organisation and activities 1482, 1486
Nichimen (*sōgō shōsha*)
  evolution, role, and organisation 914

Nichiren
  biographical sketch 295
  Risshō Ankokuron 511
Nichiren Buddhism 475
  during the Kamakura and Muromachi
    periods 458, 465, 484
  healing priests 499
  see also Reiyūkai, Risshō Kōseikai,
    and Sōka Gakkai
Nichiren Shōshū
  Makiguchi Tsunesaburō's conversion
    to 319
  Nichiren Shōshū of America 511
Nightclubs
  bar hostesses 578
  bar talk 454
  controlled by the *yakuza* 569
Nihon eitaigura (Ihara Saikaku)
  translation (excerpts) 1015
Nihon Keizai Shimbun (newspaper)
  articles and editorials (translations and
    synopses) 1547
  weekly English-language edition 1548
Nihon Kyōshokuin Kumiai *see* Nikkyōso
    (Japan Teachers Union)
Nihon Rōdō Sōdōmei (Japan General
    Federation of Labour)
  activities (1920s-1930s) 215
Nihon ryōiki (Kyōkai) 1007
  translation (excerpts) 1010
Nihonga (Japanese-style painting) 1238
Nihongi
  creation myths recorded in 502
Nihonjinron 4, 587
Nii-name-sai (Festival of New Food)
    520
Niigata (Niigata Prefecture)
  life in (19th century) 68
  methylmercury poisoning in 959
  traveller's account 66
Niigata Prefecture
  kite-flying festival at Shirone 1461
  Sado (island) 69
Niiike (Okayama Prefecture)
  community study (1950s) 548
Niijima Jō
  writings and activities 235
Nijō, Lady
  autobiographical narrative 310
Nijō Castle (Kyōto) 89, 1307, 1317
Nikkō (Tochigi Prefecture)
  national park 48
  Tōshōgu Shrine 1315

  traveller's account 66
Nikkyōso (Japan Teachers Union)
  origins, development, and activities
    967, 977
Nimitz, Chester
  role in the battle of Midway (1942)
    706
Ningen shikkaku (Dazai Osamu)
  literary analysis 1127
  translation 1049
Ninja ('secret agents') 1445
Ninjutsu (martial art)
  introductory study 1445
Nippon Electric Company *see* NEC
    (Nippon Electric Company)
Nippon Hōsō Kaisha (NHK)
  organisation and activities 1482, 1486
Nippon Kisha Club
  activities 1483
Nippon Steel Corporation
  personnel practices 942
Nippon Telegraph and Telephone Public
    Corporation 612, 625
  controversial procurements 892
  deregulation of telecommunications
    transmission 953
  plans for new electronic media
    infrastructure 955
Nippon Yūsen Kaisha (N.Y.K.)
  history (Meiji period) 250
Nisei 390, 403
  assimilation into American life 385
  contributions to American war efforts
    390, 395
  Kikuchi, Charles 393
  Masaoka, Mike 395
  Okimoto, Daniel I. 398
  Sone, Monica 399
  Toguri, Iva 387
  Wakatsuki, Jeanne 391
  see also Japanese Americans, and
    Japanese Canadians
Nishida Kitarō
  biographical essay 239
  philosophy 524, 527
Nishikawa Sukenobu
  ukiyo-e paintings 1250
Nishimura Shigeki
  efforts to revive Confucianism 528
Nishimura Shigenaga
  primitive ukiyo-e prints 1268
Nissan Motor Company
  history, management, and leadership 874

Nissan Motor Company *continued*
  personnel practices 942
  quality control 871
  technology and management 871
Nisshō (*sōgō shōsha*)
  evolution, role, and organisation
    914-915
Nitobe Inazō
  value system 385
Nō *see* Noh
No longer human (Dazai Osamu)
  literary analysis 1127
  translation 1049
No requiem (Moriya Tadashi)
  quest for identity in 1115
Nobi (Ōoka Shōhei)
  literary analysis 1127
  quest for identity in 1115
  translation 1091
Nobunaga *see* Oda Nobunaga
Noda (Chiba Prefecture)
  history (17th-20th centuries) 201
Noda Shōyu Corporation
  history 201, 241
Noda Tetsuya
  woodblock print techniques 1273
Nogami Yaeko
  short stories 1071
Nogi Maresuke
  biographical sketch 292
Noguchi Hideyo
  biography 343
Nōgyō Kyōdō Kumiai *see* Nōkyō
  (agricultural co-operative
  association)
Noh 26, 1002
  actors 1405-1406, 1408
  audiences 1410
  costumes 1181, 1351, 1405-1406, 1408,
    1412
  dances and movements 1389,
    1405-1406, 1408
  evolution (1300-1450) 1409
  handbook of classical literature 1566
  history 1175, 1181, 1393, 1403,
    1408-1410
  influence on *kōwaka* ballad-drama
    1169
  influence on Western culture 1393
  introductory surveys 1405, 1408
  masks 1215, 1219, 1405-1406, 1408,
    1412
  music 1181, 1382-1383, 1385, 1387,
    1389, 1405, 1408-1409, 1611
  performance conventions and
    techniques 1172, 1175, 1393, 1406,
    1408, 1413
  photographs 1219, 1405-1406, 1408,
    1412
  principles (explanation and analysis)
    1406
  robes 1219, 1412
  schools of 1405
  works related to the noh theatre 1218
  Zeami Motokiyo's treatises 1413
  Zen Buddhist dimensions 1196
Noh plays
  bibliographies 1409, 1588, 1603, 1615
  literary analyses 1172, 1181, 1405
  performance analyses 1406
  rhythmic organisation 1387
  synopses 492, 1181
  Zeami Motokiyo 1004, 1007, 1172
Noh plays in translation
  anthologies 1175, 1181
  Ausaka madman (Zeami Motokiyo)
    1176
  Dōjōji (Mishima Yukio) 1074
  Izutsu (Zeami Motokiyo) 1172
  modern noh plays of Mishima Yukio
    1177
  Nonomiya (Zeami Motokiyo) 1406
  Semimaru (Zeami Motokiyo) 1176
  Shunkan (Zeami Motokiyo) 1406
  Tadanori (Zeami Motokiyo) 1172
  Takasago (Zeami Motokiyo) 1172
  Teika (Zeami Motokiyo) 1156
Nōkyō (agricultural co-operative
  association)
  activities 723
Nomonhan Incident (1939) 684
Nomura Collection
  kosode textiles 1353
Nomura Securities Company
  financial success 853
  personnel practices 942
Nomura Shōjirō
  life and work 1353
'Non-Church Christianity' (Mukyōkai)
  497
Non-duality
  as a Zen Buddhist concept 493
Nonomiya (Zeami Motokiyo)
  translation and performance analysis
    1406
Nonverbal communication 406, 443, 535, 584

Noren ('shop-curtains')
  produced out of *tsutsugaki* fabrics 1345
Norman, Egerton Herbert
  biography 226
  scholarship about 19th-century
    history 226
North Atlantic Treaty Organization
  (NATO)
  common security interests with Japan
    765
North China Autonomy Movement
  role and involvement of Doihara
    Kenji 647
North Pacific Fisheries Convention 734
Northern Expedition (China, 1927)
  Japanese reaction 661
'Northern Territories' problem 285-286,
  752
Nouns
  grammar 427, 429-433
Novelists
  Abe Kōbō 1130
  Akutagawa Ryūnosuke 1128, 1130,
    1132
  biographical dictionary 365
  Chikamatsu Shūko 1113
  Dazai Osamu 1003, 1116, 1119, 1128
  Futabatei Shimei 1124, 1129-1130
  Higuchi Ichiyō 291
  Inoue Yasushi 327
  Kasai Zenzō 1113
  Kawabata Yasunari 295, 1128, 1130
  Kinoshita Naoe 288
  Kitamura Tōkoku 1130
  Masamune Hakuchō 292
  Mishima Yukio 1003, 1128, 1130
  Mori Ōgai 292, 1121
  Nagai Kafū 345, 1128
  Natsume Sōseki 1112, 1117, 1128,
    1130, 1133
  Ōe Kenzaburō 1130
  Shiga Naoya 1113, 1128, 1130
  Shimazaki Tōson 239, 1117, 1129-1130
  Tanizaki Junichirō 1003, 1128, 1130
  Tayama Katai 1129
  Tsubouchi Shōyō 1123, 1130
  Yamashiro Tomoe 290
  Yokomitsu Riichi 1114
  see also Writers
Novels 1118
  background, structural principles, and
    development 1008
  bibliographies of translations 1588, 1597

censorship of modern 1122
central themes compared with real life
  541
history (1868-1940s) 1001
images of Japan in American 731
influence of individualism on Meiji
  period 1129
introductory studies 1002, 1004
pedagògically oriented essays about
  1127
Tokugawa period 1005
see also Autobiographical novels,
  Translations (novels), and the
  section 'Literature: Modern Fiction
  and Prose: Translations'
Nowaki (Natsume Sōseki)
  synopsis and analysis 1117
Nuclear energy 849, 885
  Canadian efforts to sell Japan a
    CANDU reactor 734
  dependence on the USA for supplies
    of nuclear fuel 848
  government report (annual) 829
  Japanese and American views 848
  nuclear power plants 34, 796
Nuclear proliferation
  Japan Socialist Party's attitudes
    towards nuclear weapons 637
  Japanese and American views 848
  non-proliferation treaty 754
Numbers
  counting system 427, 430-432
Nuns
  Lady Nijō as a wandering Buddhist
    nun 310
Nurseries
  children at day 559
N.Y.K. (Nippon Yūsen Kaisha)
  history (Meiji period) 250

O

Ōba Minako
  short stories 1071, 1098
Obedience
  patterns (vis-à-vis political authority)
    614
Obi (sash) 1356
Obligations
  importance of reciprocal 15, 585
Obscenity
  freedom of expression and 771, 790
Oceans
  involvement in global ocean politics 717

Oceans *continued*
  Kuroshio ('Japan Current') 47
  'law of the sea' 717, 895
  modern ocean policy 796
Ochikubo monogatari
  translation 1033
Oda Katsuzō
  short stories 1088
Oda Nobunaga
  historical role 135
  policies 139, 145
Odawara Castle 1317
Odoriko (Nagai Kafū)
  translation (excerpts) 345
Ōe Kenzaburō
  novels 1089-1090, 1127
  search for authenticity in literature
    1130
  short stories 1057, 1126
Office buildings
  architecture (post-1945) 81, 1299,
    1313, 1321, 1324
'Office ladies' 574, 578
Official regulations
  promotion of freedom and 771
Officials (government)
  directories 366, 1574
  employed in public and private
    corporations 612
  ethics of elected and non-elected 844
Ōgai *see* Mori Ōgai
Ogasawara Islands *see* Bonin Islands
  (Ogasawara Shotō)
Ogata Kenzan
  artworks and artistic environment
    1240
Ogata Kōrin
  artworks and artistic environment
    1240
  fan-shaped paintings 1233
  screen paintings 1234
Ogawa Isshin
  photographs 1278
Ogiwara Seisensui
  ideas about poetry 1168
Ogyū Sorai
  writings 526
Oh Sadaharu
  autobiography 338
Ōhara (Kyōto Prefecture)
  tourist guide 100
Ohara School of ikebana 1464-1465
Ohba Minako

  short stories 1071, 1098
Ōhira Masayoshi
  life and personal views 339
Oil *see* Petroleum
Oil cartel criminal cases 777
Oil crisis of 1973-74 749, 805
  administrative guidance during 777
  economic prospects following 811
  economic response to 794, 816, 859,
    903, 940
  Japan's new Middle East diplomacy
    758
Ōita Prefecture
  election campaigning (1966-67) 631
  Sarayama 553
  see also Kyūshū
Ōjōyōshū (Genshin)
  background and teachings 470
Okada Kōtama
  founder of Sūkyō Mahikari 506
Ōkagami
  translation and study 1017
Okakura Tenshin
  promotion of *nihonga* 1238
Okamoto Kanoko
  short stories 1048
Okamoto Kihachi
  films 1420
Okayama Prefecture
  Kurashiki 100, 565
  Niiike 548
  Takashima 554, 562
  see also Bizen *han*, Bizen Province,
    and Inland Sea area
Okimoto, Daniel I.
  personal search for identity 398
Okinawa
  attitudes towards (1950s-1960s) 285
  battle (1945) 688, 713, 715-716, 1609
  bibliographies 1591
  comprehensive history 284
  folk art 1222, 1228
  indigenous religion 466
  literature 1006
  military occupation (1945-72) 280, 285
  minka (traditional-style houses) 1303
  reversion to Japanese sovereignty
    (1972) 721, 727, 754
  studies of (bibliography) 1591
  textiles 1201, 1222, 1347
  see also Ryūkyū Islands
Okinoshima (Shiga Prefecture)
  folk activities and ceremonies 500

Okitsu (Shizuoka Prefecture)
  local history 184
Oku no hosomichi (Matsuo Bashō) 1007
  literary analysis 1167
  translations 1149
Ōkubo dayori (Nagai Kafū)
  translation (excerpts) 345
Ōkubo Toshimichi
  biographical sketches 289, 295
  biography 306
Ōkuma Shigenobu
  biography 296, 308
  political leadership 296
Okumura Masanobu
  primitive ukiyo-e prints 1268
Ōkura Nagatsune
  biography 289
Old age see Elderly
Omote/ura
  dyadic concept of 590
Ōmoto (New Religion) 513
  see also New Religions
Onagawa (Miyagi Prefecture)
  nuclear power generating plant 796
Onchi Kōshirō
  woodblock prints 1274
One hundred famous views of Edo
    (Andō Hiroshige)
  print series (reproductions) 1256
One hundred stanzas by three poets at
    Minase see Minase sangin hyakuin
One hundred views of Mount Fuji
    (Katsushika Hokusai)
  print series 1256, 1260, 1478
  reproductions 1256
Ōnin War (1467-77) 160
Onna-men (Enchi Fumiko)
  translation 1052
Onnazaka (Enchi Fumiko)
  translation 1053
Onoda Hiroo
  autobiography 341
Onomatopoeic words 430
Onsen see Hot springs (onsen)
Onta pottery
  production, marketing, and aesthetics
    553
Ōoka Makoto
  poetry 1151
Ōoka Shōhei
  Nobi 1091, 1127
  short stories 1106
Opium War (China, 1840-42)

impact on Anglo-Japanese relations
    658
Oppenheimer, J. Robert
  role in creating the atomic bomb 263
Oppler, Alfred C.
  role in legal and judicial reforms 277
Opposition
  politics of 624, 642
  to censorship 336, 1122
  to the construction of Narita Airport
    606
Oraga haru (Kobayashi Issa)
  translation 1146
Oral histories 234, 383, 400-401, 403,
    583, 699
Oral literature
  Ainu 372, 380
Orategama (Hakuin Ekaku) 476
Orchids
  design motif of textile patterns 1344
Organic mercury poisoning
  'Minamata disease' 34, 567, 957, 959
Oribe ware (ceramics) 1281, 1283
  illustrated survey 1282
Origami (art of paper folding)
  instruction manuals 1364, 1367
  overview 1364
  photographs 1364, 1367
Ōsaka
  ageing among its inhabitants 541
  as a literary centre (Tokugawa period)
    1005
  bunraku theatre 1391-1392
  cotton trade (Tokugawa period) 170
  family life among its inhabitants 562
  growth and development 546
  Kaitokudō Merchant Academy 176
  life in (19th century) 68
  Ōsaka prints 1264
  population distribution and movement
    40
  tourist guide 100
Ōsaka Bunraku Troupe
  behind-the-scenes world of 1391
Ōsaka Castle 1307, 1317
  administrative role 146
Ōsaka Prefecture
  minka (traditional-style houses) 1301
  Sakai 135, 140, 675
Osaragi Jirō
  essay on the Shūgakuin Detached
    Palace garden 1334
  Kikyō 1092

Ōshima Nagisa
film-making activities 1415, 1417,
1419, 1423
films 1421, 1423-1424
Ōshio Heihachirō
biographies 289, 293
Ōta Yōko
short stories 1088
'Other world'
conceptions of 499, 504
Ōtomo no Yakamochi
life and poetry 301
Ōuchi (daimyō)
political history 139
Outcastes *see* Burakumin
Outlaws
Tokugawa period 165
Overseas Economic Cooperation Fund
612
Overseas trade *see* Trade and commerce
(foreign)
Overtime work
obligatory 924
Oyabun-kobun (patron-client)
relationships 142, 539, 593
Oyatoi gaikokujin ('employed
foreigners')
Meiji period 197, 229, 351, 353, 358
Ozaki Hōsai
haiku poetry 1159
Ozaki Hotsumi
role in the Sorge spy ring 228
Ozaki Shirō
short stories 1051
Ozaki Yukio
flowering cherry trees of Washington,
DC 663
Ozu Yasujirō
film-making activities 1415-1417,
1427-1428
filmographies 1415, 1427
films 1416, 1421, 1424, 1427
Tōkyō monogatari (translation) 1057

P

Pachinko (pinball game) 26
Pacific Ocean
Japan in global ocean politics 717
Japan's modern ocean policy 796
Kuroshio ('Japan Current') 47
'law of the sea' 717, 895
species of fish 60
see also Micronesia, and World War II

(Pacific Theatre)
Pacifism
Christian and socialist traditions 288
Packaging
enterprises (Shōwa Bōeki) 845
historical evolution 1371
photographs 1371
Painted porcelain
exhibition catalogue 1285
Painters
Asai Chū 1235
biographical dictionaries 368-369,
1567
Ikeno Taiga 1255
Josetsu 1239, 1253
Kaigetsudō Ando 1267
Kanō Eitoku 1252
Kanō Mitsunobu 1252
Kanō Shōei 1252
Kanō Sōshū 1252
Katsushika Hokusai 1260
Kawakami Tōgai 239
Kishida Ryūsei 1251
Kitagawa Utamaro 1262
Koide Narashige 1251
Kuroda Seiki 1235
Miyagawa Chōshun 1250, 1267
Sesshū 1239, 1253
Shūbun 1239, 1253
Takahashi Yūichi 239
Taniguchi (Yosa) Buson 1255
Uragami Gyokudō 1230
Yorozu Tetsugorō 1251
Painting 1220
American responses to Western-style
Japanese 1251
'bird and flower' (*kachō-ga*) genre
1257
dictionary 1567
encyclopaedic and almanac-type
information about 1552, 1556
evolution (1868-1968) 1209
French influence on 1251
hand-painted *tsujigahana* fabrics 1346
history 1211-1212
instruction manuals 1241, 1247, 1255
Meiji period Western-style 1235, 1251
modern 1203, 1238
patronage (1955-80) 1376
scenes from *The tale of Genji* 1241
Shintō contributions 519
shorthand convention 1226
signatures of artists (handbook) 1571

style of the Sōtatsu school 1200
yamato-e style 1236
see also Ink painting (*suibokuga*), Ink
    painting (*sumi-e*), Painters,
    Photographs (painting), Screens,
    and Scrolls
Paintings
    at the Daitokuji temple 1190
    at the Freer Gallery of Art 1250
    at the Seattle Art Museum 1217
    at the Shōsōin 1194
    at the Tōdaiji temple 1206
    at the Tokyo National Museum 1473
    depicting Daruma 483
    depicting Shintō deities 1199
    depicting the bunraku theatre 1392
    design motifs and techniques 1204
    esoteric Buddhist 1216, 1237
    fan 1233, 1240
    folk art 1193, 1213
    from the Powers Collection
        (exhibition catalogue) 1214
    from the Sansō Collection (exhibition
        catalogue) 1246
    guide to legends and historical
        episodes embodied in 1560
    Meiji period (exhibition catalogue)
        1229
    murals 135, 155, 1208, 1240, 1252
    Nagasaki paintings 179
    owned by the Tokugawa shōguns
        (exhibition catalogue) 1219
    product of daimyō culture (exhibition
        catalogue) 1218
    Pure Land (Jōdo) Buddhist 1192, 1244
    theme of the supernatural in 1189
    Tokugawa period (exhibition
        catalogue) 1227
    ukiyo-e 1212, 1250, 1260, 1262, 1267
    used in the tea ceremony 1469, 1472
    Zen Buddhist 1190, 1232
Palaces
    architecture (historical survey) 1314
    Asuka and Nara periods 143
    Katsura Detached Palace 1305, 1315,
        1332, 1334-1335
    Sentō Imperial Palace (garden) 1334
    Shūgakuin Detached Palace (garden)
        1334-1335
Palanquins 1219
Palestine Liberation Organisation
    relations with Japan 758
Pamphlets

right to distribute politically
    inflammatory 788
Paper
    lanterns (*chōchin*) 1369
    recycling 956
    stencils for dyeing fabrics (*katagami*)
        1344
    umbrellas (*karakasa*) 1369
    see also Washi (handmade paper)
Paper folding *see* Origami
Pariahs *see Burakumin*
Paris (France)
    influence on Japanese painting
        (1890-1930) 1251
Parks, National *see* National parks
Parliament *see* Diet (parliament)
Particles
    grammar 427, 429-433
Parties *see* Political parties
Passin, Herbert
    memoirs (1944-47) 359
Passivisation 434
Patent system 773-774
Paternalism 39, 204
    among blue-collar workers 918
    in large companies 917, 929
    prewar business elite 943
Patience
    proverbs about 1183
Patriotism
    Tokugawa period concepts 188
Patron-client (*oyabun-kobun*)
    relationships 142, 539, 593
Patronage
    of *sarugaku* and *dengaku* noh 1409
    of *shinzō* 1289
    of the noh theatre 1410
    of the performing and visual arts
        (1955-80) 1376
    under Ashikaga Yoshimitsu 140
PCB poisoning
    Kanemi Rice Oil poisoning case 957
Peace
    anti-war activism during the Vietnam
        War 727
    consciousness and national security
        611
    efforts (1940s) to redirect the Japanese
        towards 595
    traditional concept 610
Peace Preservation Law 221
    violated by Kawakami Hajime
        318

817

Peace settlement with Japan (1951) 266,
274, 282-283, 647, 745
Soviet-Japanese peace agreement
(1956) 283, 728
Pearl Harbor (1941 attack on)
bibliography 1609
Japanese American reactions 393
Japanese civilian reactions 691
planning and execution 680, 687-688,
693, 699, 705, 711, 715
US-Japan negotiations preceding 645,
690
Yamamoto Isoroku and 317
see also Foreign relations with the
United States (1931-41)
Peasants
controlled by the daimyō (16th
century) 139
folk legends about rich 1184
lives and thoughts (1868-1945) 205
uprisings 161, 175, 195, 213
women in Hiroshima (1945) 259
see also Farmers
Pedagogy
pervasiveness of egalitarianism in 964
Peer groups
influence on student radicalism 969
Peeresses' School
education of Ishimoto Shizue 328
Peninsulas
gazetteer 57
Pension funds 862
People's rights see Human rights, and
Rights
Performances
bunraku theatre 1391-1393
kabuki theatre 1393, 1400
kōwaka ballad-drama 1169
noh theatre 1172, 1393
performance texts of plays 1174,
1395-1396, 1407
Periodicals
agriculture 1488, 1502
architecture 1505
art 1489, 1496, 1535, 1543
art history 1489, 1534
Buddhism 1499, 1520, 1523, 1534
burakumin 381
business 1494-1495, 1501, 1524, 1527,
1540, 1542
Christianity in Japan 1506, 1523
culture 1534, 1543
customs 1490

doctoral dissertations (bibliographical
journal) 1607
economy 1488, 1491, 1493, 1498,
1500-1501, 1517-1518, 1524, 1526,
1530, 1536, 1540, 1542
finance 1495, 1500, 1519, 1542, 1544
fisheries 1502
folklore 1490
foreign aid 1502, 1541
foreign relations 1491, 1493, 1514,
1524, 1536, 1540
forestry 1502
general-interest 1497, 1503, 1507,
1510, 1512-1513, 1515-1516, 1532,
1537, 1545
government 1488, 1526
guides to government periodicals
1593, 1602
history 1493, 1504, 1526, 1534, 1543
industry 1494, 1500, 1517, 1519, 1527,
1542, 1545
Japanese Americans 1487
Japanese studies (multidisciplinary)
1504, 1508-1509, 1525-1526, 1528,
1534, 1536, 1538, 1543
labour 1500, 1511
language and linguistics 1529, 1543
law 1531
literature 1493, 1496, 1504, 1521,
1526, 1534, 1543
management 1500, 1518, 1533
military 1488, 1491
museums 1489, 1535
myths 1490
philately 1522
philosophy 1496, 1504, 1543
politics 1491, 1493, 1498, 1501, 1524,
1536, 1542
religion 1499, 1504, 1506, 1520, 1523,
1526, 1534, 1543
science 1539
society 1488, 1491, 1493, 1498, 1517,
1526, 1536
speeches 1540
tea ceremony 1496
technology 1494-1495, 1500, 1539,
1541, 1544-1545
theatre 1492
trade and commerce (foreign)
1500-1501, 1524, 1540, 1544
translating and summarizing magazine
articles 1507, 1547
union list of periodicals published in

Japan 1601
women 1488, 1493
see also Magazines
Permanent employment *see* Employment
(lifetime employment)
Perry, Matthew C.
expedition to Japan (1852-54) 673
Personal connections
political dynamics and 615
Personal matter (Ōe Kenzaburō)
literary analysis 1127
quest for identity in 1115
translation 1089
Personal pronouns 411
grammar 427
Personality 585
among Japanese Americans 588
as a factor in history 289
development 594-595
psychology 16
relationship to juvenile delinquency
571
Personnel
Asian Development Bank 756
management 922-923, 926, 931, 933,
943
management (multinational
corporations) 947-948, 950
naval (1950s-1970s) 759
practices (large companies) 917, 942
practices discriminatory to women 785
sōgō shōsha (general trading
companies) 914-915
systems 729
Petrochemical industry 813
Petroleum
development projects (with China)
735
development projects (with the
USSR) 748, 900
investment strategies 847
market 850
offshore development negotiations
(with Korea) 796
oil diplomacy 849, 885
politics of US exports to Japan 847
problems of depending on foreign 849
quest for dependable supplies 913, 952
response to increased prices (1970s)
794, 816, 859, 903, 940
see also Oil crisis of 1973-74
Phallicism
in folk religion 502

Pharmaceuticals industry
co-operation among US and Japanese
companies 911
Pharmacy
herbal medicine 598
Philadelphia Museum of Art
(Philadelphia, Pennsylvania)
Ōsaka prints 1264
Philately
periodicals 1522
stamps of Japan (1871-1979) 1522
Philippines
accounts of World War II refugees
from 583
autobiography of a World War II
soldier (Onoda Hiroo) in 341
Battle of Leyte Gulf (1944) 210, 680,
687-688, 699, 715, 1609
economic development (compared
with Japan) 806
relations with Japan (post-1945) 741
World War II 341, 680, 687, 715
World War II (fiction) 1091
see also Southeast Asia
Philosophers
Fukuzawa Yukichi 194
Kyōto School of philosophy 521
Miki Kiyoshi 199
Nishida Kitarō 239, 524
Nishitani Keiji 525
Suzuki, Daisetz Teitaro 316, 489-492
Tanaka Ōdō 336
Philosophy 16, 469, 521-529
aikidō (martial art) 1451
corporate 894
history 999
iaidō (martial art) 1441
ikebana (flower arrangement)
1464-1465
periodicals 1496, 1504, 1543
readings about 33
treatises (translations) 524-525, 1447
underlying the tea ceremony 1470
Phonemes 405
phonemicisation 412
Phonology
historical 407
introductory study 412
Photographers
biographical dictionary 369
Beato, Felix 1278
Fukase Masahisa 1275
Hosoe Eikoe 1275

Photographers *continued*
  Kusakabe Kinbei 1278
  Moriyama Daidō 1275
  Ogawa Isshin 1278
  Stillfried, Raimund von 1278
  Tōmatsu Shōmei 1275
Photographs
  agriculture 835
  aikidō (martial art) 1450-1451
  Ainu 375
  aircraft (World War II) 689
  Allied occupation of Japan (1945-52)
    278
  animals 63
  archaeology 103-108, 143, 284, 1214,
    1217, 1473
  architecture (modern) 22, 81,
    1297-1299, 1304, 1309, 1313,
    1319-1321, 1324, 1326, 1505
  architecture (traditional) 81, 113,
    1212, 1300-1303, 1305, 1307,
    1310-1312, 1315-1318, 1322-1323,
    1325
  arms and armour 108, 156, 158
  art 155, 1197, 1209, 1211-1212, 1214,
    1217-1220, 1223, 1473, 1489
  art (pre-7th century) 104-105
  art (16th century) 132
  art (1950s-1960s) 1203
  artistic depictions of natural creatures
    1221
  arts and crafts 19, 25, 77-78, 92, 1210,
    1369
  bamboo 64, 1357
  bambooware 1193, 1213, 1222, 1357,
    1366
  baskets 1193, 1213, 1222, 1366
  baths and bathing 3, 1326, 1457
  birds 58, 63, 65, 1275
  bonkei (miniature landscapes) 1330
  bonsai 1328, 1330, 1336, 1362
  bookbinding 1479
  brushes 1357, 1366, 1369
  Buddhism in Japan 485-486
  Buddhist art 1190, 1192, 1194-1195,
    1206, 1208, 1214, 1216, 1232, 1237,
    1244, 1246, 1249, 1290, 1292-1293,
    1295-1296, 1316, 1322
  Buddhist sculptures 1290, 1292-1293,
    1295-1296
  bugaku masks 1294
  bunraku theatre 1391-1392, 1404
  calligraphy 1194, 1206, 1214, 1218,

  1220, 1227, 1229-1232, 1240, 1242,
    1249, 1469, 1473, 1535
  castles 156, 158, 1306, 1317
  ceramics and pottery 104-108, 331,
    1193-1194, 1201, 1210-1211, 1213,
    1217-1218, 1220, 1222, 1224, 1227,
    1229, 1240, 1279-1287, 1435, 1437,
    1473, 1489, 1535
  Christianity in Japan 498
  cloisonné 1229, 1361
  clothing 1219, 1345, 1351-1353, 1356
  countryside 3, 11, 25, 28-29, 44,
    1275-1276, 1278
  craftsmen and craftswomen 13, 331,
    1222, 1391
  culture 1568
  culture (guidebook) 1552
  daily life (general) 11, 13, 28
  Daitokuji temple 1190, 1331-1332
  dances 322, 1275, 1377, 1389-1390,
    1408
  Daruma (reproductions) 483
  design (traditional and modern) 1224
  design motifs 1204, 1207
  Diet (parliament) members 366
  dolls 1363
  Dōsojin (deity) 502
  fan paintings 1233
  festivals 77, 92, 501, 1461
  film directors 1423, 1426
  fisheries co-operative 13
  flora 61, 64, 663
  folding screens 1234
  folk art 483, 1193, 1210, 1213, 1222,
    1281
  food and drink 1430-1440
  furniture 1193, 1213, 1219, 1224,
    1341-1342
  gagaku 1377
  gardens 3, 89, 92, 1190, 1211, 1278,
    1305, 1327, 1329, 1331-1335, 1337,
    1339, 1467, 1472
  glass 1359
  Hamada Shōji 331
  handicrafts from the Ryūkyū Islands
    1201
  haniwa figures 108
  Hiroshima (atomic bombing) 256, 715
  history of Japan 113, 1276, 1278, 1568
  Hōryūji temple 1208, 1322
  hot springs (*onsen*) 3, 1457
  ikat weaving (*kasuri*) 1354
  ikebana (flower arrangement)

1462-1466
illustrated handscrolls (*emaki*) 1245
illustrating Matsuo Bashō's *Oku no
hosomichi* 1149
illustrating forms within the Japanese
universe 1202
ink painting (*suibokuga*) 1239-1240,
1246-1248, 1253
Inland Sea area 71-72
inrō (compartmentalised containers)
1189, 1221, 1360
interior decoration 1319
Ise Shrine 1323, 1325
Iwo Jima (1945 battle) 714-715
Japan and the Japanese in general 11,
17, 19, 25, 28-29, 50, 70, 94, 1497,
1512, 1545, 1556
Japanese Americans 389, 391
Japanese bath (*furo*) 1457
Japanese Canadians 383
kabuki theatre 1351-1352, 1395, 1398,
1400-1401, 1407
karate (martial art) 1446, 1448
kendō (martial art) 1449
kimono 1217, 1356
kites 1461
knives 1366, 1369
kyōgen 1405
Kyōto 25, 77-78, 89, 92, 1026
lacquerwork and lacquerware 1193,
1201, 1204, 1211, 1213, 1215,
1217-1219, 1222, 1227, 1229, 1240,
1370, 1374, 1435, 1473, 1489, 1535
landscapes 3, 44, 48, 64
'living national treasures' 1222
masks 1194, 1206, 1217, 1219, 1291,
1294, 1296, 1377, 1402, 1405, 1408,
1412
Meiji period art 1229, 1235, 1269
Meiji period feminists 240
metalwork 1193-1194, 1210, 1213,
1229, 1373, 1473, 1535
'Minamata disease' 959
modern Japan (pictorial
encyclopaedia) 1568
monastic Zen life 486
musical instruments 1194, 1198, 1201,
1219, 1222, 1224, 1357, 1369, 1377,
1382-1383, 1400, 1404-1405
Nagasaki (atomic bombing) 1275, 1277
Nanban art 132, 1243
Nara 25, 93, 1316
national parks 48

nature 3, 17, 44, 48
netsuke 1189, 1221, 1227, 1288, 1291,
1360, 1489, 1535
New Religions 513
noh theatre 1219, 1405-1406, 1408,
1412
Okinawa (1945 battle) 713
Okinawan folk art and craftsmen 1222
origami 1364, 1367
Ōsaka prints 1264
painting 113, 483, 1205, 1209,
1211-1214, 1218, 1220, 1227,
1229-1230, 1232-1241, 1243-1248,
1250-1255, 1260, 1489, 1535
paper-making 1358, 1365
patterns of continuity 17
people 11, 28, 95, 1277
periodicals containing 1489,
1496-1497, 1505, 1512, 1535, 1537,
1545
production of the movie *Shōgun* 1418
railways 954
Russo-Japanese War (1904-5) 678
ryōkan (inns) 96
samurai culture 156, 158, 1218
sculpture 93, 108, 502, 1192, 1189,
1197, 1199, 1205-1206, 1208-1209,
1211, 1213-1214, 1216-1218, 1220,
1227, 1229, 1289-1290, 1292-1293,
1295-1296, 1316, 1489, 1535
seasons of the year 44
shibori textiles 1355
Shintō 519
Shintō arts 1199, 1289
shop signs (*kanban*) 1213, 1215, 1368
Shōsōin 1194
shunga (erotic prints) 1259
spoons and ladles 1366
stencil dyeing (*katazome*) 1350
still photographs of various films 158,
1414-1416, 1423-1427
suiseki stones 1362
sumo wrestlers 1278, 1455
supernatural in art 1189
surimono woodblock prints 1263
Suzuki, Daisetz Teitaro 316
swords and sword guards 1211, 1219,
1221, 1227, 1373, 1375
swordsmanship (*iaidō*) 1452
tansu chests 1213, 1219, 1341-1342
tattoos 1372
tea ceremony 1467, 1471-1472,
1496

Photographs continued
   tea ceremony utensils 1218-1219,
      1279-1280, 1282, 1357, 1467-1469,
      1471-1472
   tea kettles 1366, 1468-1469
   temples 77, 92, 1026, 1190, 1192,
      1208, 1216, 1277, 1290, 1316, 1322
   textiles and textile design 1345-1347,
      1349, 1351, 1353-1355
   Tokyo 22, 25, 28, 95, 236, 1256, 1275
   traditional packaging 1371
   ukiyo-e paintings 1250, 1262, 1267
   ukiyo-e prints 1256-1257, 1259-1262,
      1264-1268, 1478
   US-Japanese relations (1860s) 667
   vegetation 61
   warships (1870s-1945) 1572
   water 3, 17
   woodblock prints 1270-1274, 1344
   woodworking tools 1343
   world of fashion 1348
   world of saké 1431
   world of sushi 1432
   World War II 713-715, 1276
   yamato-e painting 1236
   Zen Buddhist practices 486
Photography
   historical development (1840-1945)
      1276
   survey of contemporary 1277
Photovoltaics
   competition for the world market in
      847
Phrase books 416, 446, 453
Physical anthropology
   prehistoric Japanese 109
Physicians see Doctors
Physics
   historical development 187
   language textbook for reading
      materials in 437
Physiography
   national parks 48
Picture scrolls (emaki) see Handscrolls
Pilgrimage routes
   Buddhist 73, 97
'Pillar prints' (hashira-e)
   bibliography 1576
Pillow book (Sei Shōnagon)
   translation 1025
Pillow of grass (Natsume Sōseki)
   synopsis and analysis 1117
PL Kyōdan (New Religion) 468, 510,

      513
   see also New Religions
Place names
   catalogue 1571
Plains
   as a landform 51
Planning
   corporate 836, 926
   economic 810, 939
   economic (bibliography) 1594
   industrial 878
   strategic (business) 842
Plants see Flora
Plateaus
   gazetteer 57
Plays see Bunraku theatre, Drama,
      Kabuki, Kyōgen, Noh plays,
      Shingeki ('new theatre'), Theatre,
      and Translations (plays)
Playwrights
   biographical dictionary 365
   Chikamatsu Monzaemon 295, 1170
   Fukuda Tsuneari 239
   kabuki theatre (encyclopaedia) 1564
   Kishida Kunio 1178
   Shimamura Hōgetsu 336
   Yamazaki Masakazu 1182
   Zeami Motokiyo 291, 1172, 1182,
      1406, 1408-1409, 1413
Plot summaries (synopses)
   bunraku plays 1411
   Dazai Osamu's works 1119
   films 1415, 1421-1422, 1425, 1578,
      1585-1586
   folk tales 1577
   kabuki plays 1394, 1400, 1407, 1564
   Kishida Kunio's plays 1178
   kōwaka ballad-dramas 1169
   kyōgen 1402
   masterpieces of prose 1597
   medieval literary works 1481
   modern novels 1001, 1009, 1112, 1117,
      1521
   noh plays 492, 1181
   Tale of Genji 1035, 1604
   'Poem-tales' (uta monogatari)
   Ise monogatari 1004, 1008, 1148
   Yamato monogatari 1028
Poetry
   accompanying ukiyo-e prints 1257
   Ainu 1006
   anthologies 1000, 1134, 1138, 1145,
      1151, 1156-1157, 1159

bibliographies 1156, 1588, 1605, 1615
Chinese-style poetry of Uragami
    Gyokudō 1230
chōka 301, 1147, 1154, 1156
contained in surimono prints 1263
court poetry 1164
court style in classical 1153
folk-song 1381
gozan bungaku 1152
haibun 1146, 1156, 1162
haikai 1003, 1005, 1150, 1165
Heian period 1028
historical use 1004
history 999, 1006, 1162, 1164-1166,
    1168
hokku 1166
introductory studies 1002, 1004, 1134,
    1143, 1156, 1162, 1164, 1166
jisei ('death poems') 1138
Kojiki 152
Manyōshū 301, 1147
modern 1001, 1003, 1141, 1143, 1145,
    1151, 1157, 1159, 1168
poetic diaries 1149
poetics 1566
renga 135, 140, 1156, 1162, 1165-1166
ritual origins 1163
role in The tale of Genji 1039
waka 1005, 1148, 1153, 1155, 1245
written in Chinese 488, 1000, 1005,
    1010, 1138-1139, 1152, 1154
see also Haiku poetry, Tanka poetry,
    and Translations (poetry)
Poets and poetesses
    biographical dictionary 365
    Fujiwara Teika 1135
    Hagiwara Sakutarō 1136, 1168
    Hosokawa Yūsai 291
    Ikkyū Sōjun 291, 1003, 1139
    Ishikawa Takuboku 1122, 1140, 1168
    Kakinomoto no Hitomaro 1163
    Ki no Tsurayuki 1153
    Kinoshita Yūji 1144
    Kitamura Tōkoku 288
    Kobayashi Issa 1137, 1146
    Masaoka Shiki 239, 291, 1137, 1161,
        1168
    Matsuo Bashō 295, 1137, 1149, 1167
    Miyazawa Kenji 1168
    Murasaki Shikibu 1023
    Ogiwara Seisensui 1168
    Ōtomo no Yakamochi 301
    Rai Sanyō 295
    Ryōkan 1010, 1154
    Saigyō 1007, 1155
    Saitō Mokichi 325
    Satomura Jōha 135
    Shōhaku 1165
    Sōchō 1165
    Sōgi 1165
    Sugawara no Michizane 300
    Takahashi Shinkichi 1168
    Takamura Kōtarō 1158, 1168
    Taniguchi (Yosa) Buson 1137
    Uragami Gyokudō 1230
    Yosano Akiko 1160, 1168
Police
    confrontations at Narita Airport 606
    crime control 566
    laws 788
    operations (Kurashiki, Okayama
        Prefecture) 565
    operations (Hokkaidō) 570
    operations (Tokyo) 565, 570
    reform 282
    system (pre-1945) 223, 248
Police stick
    used in keijo-jutsu (martial art) 1444
Policy
    agricultural 206, 623, 821, 832, 835,
        888
    atomic energy 846
    automobile industry and public 870
    budgetary 909
    defence 27, 613, 623, 718, 741, 751,
        754, 761-762, 768-770
    disinvestment 801
    education 623
    energy 27, 623, 801, 849, 884
    environmental 775
    export 814
    fiscal 799, 801, 811, 851, 859, 884, 886,
        909
    fisheries 796
    food 833
    foreign aid 757
    foreign economic 898, 910
    foreign exchange rate 909
    foreign trade 623, 817, 896-897, 907
    human resource 895
    industrial pollution control 785
    international economic 748
    labour 609, 821, 909
    macroeconomic 860
    monetary 791, 799, 811, 815, 821, 851,
        859, 864-866, 909

Policy *continued*
  nuclear 754
  public 870
  science 980
  security 720, 761-762, 768
  social welfare 623
  technology 983
  wage 940
  see also Economic policies, Foreign
    policy, and Industrial policy
Policy-making
  at the prefectural level 611, 639-640
  business 801
  characterised by consensus and
    conflict 619
  educational 974, 977
  financial 857
  government (post-1945) 611, 620, 622,
    809
  in the civil service system 613
  in the Liberal Democratic Party 633,
    638
  in the Ministry of Finance 856
  in the Ministry of Foreign Affairs 747
  in the yen bond market 857
  in US-Japanese economic relations
    721-722, 892
  labour policy 609
  leading up to the Russo-Japanese War
    (1904-5) 671
  national defence 613
  overview of the published literature
    about 620
  records of the 1941 policy conferences
    693
Polite speech 454
Politeness
  in Japanese culture 443
  language textbook 443
Political crisis of 1881
  downfall of Ōkuma Shigenobu 308
Political development
  19th-20th centuries 239
  decision-making, foreign policy, and
    720
Political economy
  changing international context 817
  cultural and social dynamics 817
  domestic transformation 817
  of agricultural policies 832
  of energy 850
  of European-Japanese relations 906
Political leaders

Abe Isoo 288
Abe Masahiro 146, 289
Arai Hakuseki 177, 298, 526
Asukata Ichio 636
biographical dictionary 367
Fujiwara no Michinaga 295, 1017,
  1021
Inukai Tsuyoshi 296
Kido Kōin 289, 307
Konoe Atsumaro 650
Meiji period oligarchs 189, 672
Mori Arinori 304, 972
Mutsu Munemitsu 289, 654, 668
Ōkubo Toshimichi 289, 295, 306
Saigo Takamori 293
Saionji Kinmochi 296, 323
socialist party leaders 630
Tanaka Shōzō 312
Tanuma Okitsugu 295
Toyotomi Hideyoshi 299
Ugaki Kazushige 650
World War II (thought and behaviour)
  618
see also Daimyō, Foreign ministers,
  Prime Ministers, and Shōguns
Political legitimacy 139, 142
  sought by the Tokugawa shogunate
    178, 677
  sought by Toyotomi Hideyoshi 299
  theory 138, 246
Political parties 23, 27, 617, 622-623, 627
  conservative parties (1945-55) 274,
    280, 846
  Democratic Socialist Party 634
  factions and factionalism 607,
    629-630, 633-634, 637-638
  historical development (1874-1981)
    1555
  Japan Socialist Party 632, 634,
    636-637, 736
  Kenseikai 198
  Kōmeitō 514, 634
  loss of power and influence (1931-41)
    193
  Meiji period 189, 224
  Minseitō 202
  New Liberal Club 634, 636
  operating manner in the Diet
    (1960s-1970s) 607
  party politics (1905-15) 224
  party politics (1910s-1920s) 198
  party politics (1945-55) 274, 281
  party politics (1970s-1980s) 629

party preference of labourers 611
party system (introductory studies)
    629, 634
noncommunist proletarian parties
    (prewar) 247
reformist parties (1945-52) 280
Rikken Kaishintō 308
role in foreign policy-making (1930s)
    682
Seiyūkai 198, 224
shifts in voter support 628
socialist parties 628, 630
Taishō period 198
see also Japan Communist Party, and
    Liberal Democratic Party
Political reforms
    Allied occupation of Japan (1945-52)
        266, 273 280-281, 622
Political scientists
    Rōyama Masamichi 199
Politics
    1950s-1980s 632
    1960s-1970s 27, 622
    among Koreans in Japan 376-377
    budget-making 608
    centralisation of political authority
        (1868-71) 307
    dynamics of contemporary 615, 620
    environmental protest and citizen 958
    impact of internationalisation 802
    impact on foreign policy (post-1952)
        817
    influence of the agrarian sector 832
    influence of the yakuza (gangsters)
        569
    influence on post-1952 US-Japanese
        relations 721, 754
    introductory textbooks 617, 623-624,
        627
    involvement of big business 39, 846
    involvement of Christians 497
    involvement of labour unions 937
    involvement of sōgō shōsha (general
        trading companies) 914
    involvement of teachers 967, 975, 977
    involvement of women 578, 580-581
    newspaper articles about 1546-1547,
        1549
    of alternative energy research and
        development 849
    of defence policy (1970s-1980s) 762,
        764
    of economic management 817
    of energy strategy 849
    of Soviet-Japanese trade 747
    of the foreign aid budgetary process
        746
    of trade liberalisation 732
    of US crude oil exports to Japan 847
    overview 5-7, 16, 21, 23, 30, 32, 38,
        535, 843
    periodicals 1491, 1493, 1498, 1501,
        1524, 1536, 1542
    political behaviour 557, 628
    political change 547, 628, 632, 872
    political character of the press 1485
    political consequences of
        industrialisation 547
    political corruption 567
    political culture 610, 621, 627
    political offences 566
    political opposition in local politics 642
    political power 547, 618, 632
    political recruitment 622, 628, 634
    political rights of women 267, 580
    political socialisation 580, 642
    political structure (rural villages) 534
    political theories of Kitabatake
        Chikafusa 159
    political thought (of Natsume Sōseki
        and Yoshino Sakuzō) 241
    politicisation of strategic aid policy 757
    role of the China question
        (1950s-1970s) in domestic 736, 738
    role of the Diet in post-1945 politics
        607
    Soviet comprehension of Japanese 747
    see also Elections, History (political),
        Interest groups, Political
        development, Political leaders,
        Political legitimacy, and Political
        parties
Pollution
    air 41, 957
    anti-pollution movements 785,
        957-959
    compensation for pollution-related
        health injuries 775, 777, 959
    environmental 45-46, 533, 567, 801,
        826, 957-959
    environmental (photographs) 959,
        1277
    industrial 34, 312, 567, 620, 957-959
    ritual 466, 530
    see also Conservation and
        environmental protection

Pompe van Meerdervoort, J. L. C.
  as an instructor of Western medicine
    596
Popular Rights Movement (*Jiyū minken
    undō*)
  grassroots level study 195
  leadership of Tanaka Shōzō 312
Population 50, 371
  1870s-1980 803
  annual statistics 824, 825-827
  basic facts and figures (annual
    handbook) 14
  bibliographies 371, 1592, 1594
  change in Kurusu, Kagawa Prefecture
    (1951-75) 556
  distribution and movement 40
  growth and economic development
    810
  long-term statistical data 808
  maps 53-54
  see also Demography
Porcelain
  as antiques 1215
  depicting creatures of nature 1221
  painted (exhibition catalogue) 1285
  Tokugawa period 1283
Pornography
  erotic comic books 1480
  in movies 26
  shunga (erotic prints) of the
    Tokugawa period 1259, 1478
  yakuza (gangster) involvement 569
Port Arthur (Manchuria)
  naval blockade and battle (1904) 210,
    320, 678
Portraiture
  Buddhist portrait sculpture 1292-1293
  product of daimyō culture (exhibition
    catalogue) 1218
  Zen Buddhist 1232
Ports *see* Treaty ports
Portsmouth Peace Conference (1905)
    672, 678
  Hibiya riot as a reaction to 175, 672
  mediation of Theodore Roosevelt 659
Portuguese in Japan
  Frois, Luis 132-133
  Rodrigues, João 132, 153, 352
Postal savings system
  inter-ministerial conflict over 857
Postal system
  history 1522
  Meiji period 248

Posters
  regulation of poster displays 788
  used in labour unrest 921
Postindustrial society 7, 38, 812
Potters
  biographical dictionaries 368-369,
    1567
  folk craft potters of Sarayama, Ōita
    Prefecture 553
  Hamada Shōji 331
  Katō Hajime 1285
  Kitaōji Rosanjin 1285
  overview 1285, 1287
  signatures (handbook) 1571
  Tomimoto Kenkichi 1285
Pottery
  associated with Japanese cuisine 1430,
    1435, 1437
  design (photographs) 1224
  pre-6th century AD 104-109
  folk art 19, 542, 553, 1193, 1210, 1213,
    1281
  Hamada Shōji 331
  historical evolution 1283, 1287
  Jōmon period 104, 107
  life-course of pottery-making
    households 542
  Okinawan 1222
  Ontayaki 553
  problems in dating and attributing
    1283
  Yamashiro 1283
  see also Ceramics, Flower containers,
    and Photographs (ceramics and
    pottery)
Poverty
  perceptions and realities 812
  rural (1868-1945) 205, 234
Powers (Kimiko and John Powers)
    Collection
  art (exhibition catalogue) 1214
Prefectures
  establishment (1870s) of the system of
    212
  private school education in 968
  unsuccessful schemes to amalgamate
    640
  see also Local government, and the
    names of individual prefectures
Prejudice
  as an issue in the 'New Wave' cinema
    1419
  see also Discrimination, and Racism

Pressure groups *see* Interest groups
Prices 823
  1868-1970s 803, 855
  annual statistics 819, 824-827
  during World War II 207, 237
  long-term statistical data 808
  stabilisation 859, 866
Priests
  folk legends about 1184
  healing priests (Buddhist) 499
  photographs 1278
  Shintō 503, 516, 518
  survivors of the atomic bombing of
    Hiroshima 255
  see also Religious leaders
Prime Ministers
  biographical dictionary 367
  Hara Kei 198, 296
  Hirota Kōki 346
  Inukai Tsuyoshi 296
  Ishibashi Tanzan 336
  Itō Hirobumi 296, 668
  Katō Kōmei 198
  Kishi Nobusuke 744
  Konoe Fumimaro 340
  Matsuka Masayoshi 297
  Ōhira Masayoshi 339
  Ōkuma Shigenobu 296, 308
  Saionji Kinmochi 296
  Satō Eisaku 727
  Tanaka Giichi 333
  Tanaka Kakuei 620, 636, 647, 652
  Tōjō Hideki 237, 321
  Yamagata Aritomo 303
  Yoshida Shigeru 282-283, 324
Primitive ukiyo-e prints
  holdings of the Michener Collection
    1268
Prince of Wales (British battleship)
  sunk by the Japanese (1941) 698
Printing
  1500s-1600s 132
  development of colour 1261
  history 1477
  textile printing techniques 1351
Print-makers
  Andō Hiroshige 1256-1257
  bibliographies 1576
  biographical dictionaries 364, 368-369,
    1567
  Funasaka Yoshisuke 1273
  Katsushika Hokusai 1256, 1258, 1260,
    1478

Kitagawa Utamaro 1262
  lives and careers (bibliography) 1576
  Matsumoto Akira 1273
  Miyashita Tokio 1273
  Morozumi Osamu 1273
  Noda Tetsuya 1273
  post-1945 print-makers 364, 1270,
    1273-1274
  signatures (handbook) 1571
  survey 1267, 1271
  Suzuki Harunobu 1261
  ukiyo-e 1266-1267, 1270
  Yoshida Hodaka 1273
Print-making
  bibliography 1576
  comparison of activities in Ōsaka and
    Edo 1264
  dictionary 1567
  patronage (1955-80) 1376
  techniques and styles (post-1945) 1203
Prints *see Surimono* (woodblock prints),
  Ukiyo-e prints, and Woodblock
  prints
Prisoners-of-war
  Soviet indoctrination (1940s-1950s)
    752
Privacy
  among students 584
  invasion of 771
Private international law
  bibliography 1582
Private language-schools
  English-language instruction 979
Privy Council
  Yamagata Aritomo as president 303
Procuratorial system 780
Product liability rules 783
Production
  ceramics and pottery 107, 553,
    1279-1280, 1282, 1284, 1286-1287
  glass 1359
  structures 801
  systems 934-936, 983
  washi (handmade paper) 1358, 1365
  workers' control (1946) over 275
  see also Techniques
Productivity 908, 939
  agricultural 200, 831, 834
  among schools 963
  annual statistics 824
  automobile industry 871
  bibliography 1581, 1590, 1600
  effect of reducing working hours 930

Productivity *continued*
  factor inputs and aggregate 807
  high labour 945
  manufacturing industries 895
  principles of human 875
  role in industrial development 875
  structuring company operations to
    maximise 928
  trends (comparison of Japan and the
    USA) 859
Proletarian literary movement (1920s)
  241
Promotions
  among bank employees 543
  among foreign service officers 729
  as a managerial activity 941
  senority-based (determinants) 938
Pronouns
  grammar 430-433
Pronunciation 405, 454
  methods of teaching 455
Propaganda
  government (1968-1945) 221
  photographs of 1276
  World War II 387, 686
  'yellow peril' 384
Property rights
  constitutional protection 787
Props *see* Stage Properties
Prose
  written in Chinese 1000, 1005, 1010,
    1153-1154
Prose poetry (*sanbunshi*)
  study and translation 1141
Prosecutors
  discretionary authority 777
Prosperity *see* Affluence
Prostitution 205, 536
  campaign to abolish 240
  courtesans depicted in ukiyo-e prints
    1259, 1261-1262, 1268
  during the Allied occupation of Japan
    (1945-52) 583
  Victorian British writings about 68
  yakuza (gangster) involvement 569
Protectionism
  Japanese views of US 897
Protest movements and uprisings
  against constructing Narita Airport
    606
  anti-pollution movements 785,
    957-959
  Beheiren anti-war movement 727

  citizen protest 614, 616
  environmental protest 642, 958-959
  February 26, 1936 Incident 209, 238,
    245, 342, 348, 685, 690, 708
  Hibiya riot (1905) 175, 672
  peasant (17th-19th centuries) 161,
    175, 195, 213
  Satsuma Rebellion (1877) 293, 306
  Security Treaty crisis (1960) 744, 754,
    969, 1485
  Shimabara Rebellion (1637-38) 129,
    293
  Tempō Uprising (1837) 289, 293
  see also Movements
Protestantism *see* Christianity in Japan
Proverbs
  collection 1183
Proxy regulation 781
Psychology 584-595
  burakumin 373, 381
  businessmen 894
  Dazai Osamu 1116
  haragei as a principle of 406
  human effects of the 1945 atomic
    bombings 253, 256-259
  kendō (martial art) 1449
  leading writers and public figures 292
  personality 16
  politically active women 580
  protagonists of Natsume Sōseki's
    novels 1112
  tattooing 1372
  ultra-nationalism (1930s-1940s) 618
  World War II soldiers 341
Psychotherapy
  models 599
  Morita psychotherapy 592, 601
  types 592, 602
Public administration 613
  structure and operations 625
Public corporations 612, 625
  information sources (directory) 1558
  organisation 605
  publications 1593, 1602
Public employees
  rights 609, 771, 788
  see also Bureaucracy
Public finance 817, 823
  1870s-1980 803
  annual statistics 819, 824-827
  overview 863
  public spending on social facilities 533
Public gatherings

licensing 790
Public housing (*danchi*)
  housewives in suburban Tokyo and 577
  provided by local governments 639
Public international law
  bibliography 1582
Public opinion
  foreign affairs (1964-73) and 748
  research and surveys 359, 621, 753
  support of foreign aid programmes 757
  towards the USSR 728, 752
Public prosecutors
  discretionary authority 777
Public relations 891
Publishing
  censorship (1868-1945) 221
  freedom of expression 771
  government imprints 1593
Pumps
  electric irrigation 200
Punctuation 430, 438
Puppet plays *see* Bunraku theatre
Puppets
  dolls used as 1363
  makers of 1391
  puppeteers (bunraku theatre) 1391-1392
  used in the bunraku theatre 1174, 1391-1392, 1404, 1411
Pure Land Buddhism *see* Jōdo Buddhism
Purges
  World War II militarists 271, 282
Purification
  religious significance 460-461
Putiatin, Evfimii Vasil'evich
  role in Russo-Japanese relations 664

Q

Quality
  consciousness among consumers 889, 990
  emphasis on 38, 922
Quality control 908, 923, 936
  at Fuji Xerox 935
  bibliography 1590
  circles 919, 934, 990
  Morita Akio's views 332
  pursuit of 797, 928, 996
  systems at the Nissan and Toyota motor companies 871
Quality of life
  curriculum unit about 36

in factories 937
Quaternary period
  chronology (Kantō region) 51
  geological research 49
  tephra and its implications for 40
Questions
  grammatical formation 427

R

R & D *see* Research and development
Race
  Japanese comments (1860) on 667
Racism
  during World War II 686
  experienced by Japanese Americans 384, 389, 392, 398, 400, 402
  experienced by Japanese Canadians 382, 385
  in Japanese culture 373, 376
  see also Discrimination
Radicals
  Kwantung Army officers 702
  Red Army activist 580
  student 244, 565, 969
Radio broadcasting
  censorship (1920s-1945) 221
  development (1920s-1970s) 1482, 1486
  surrender to the Allied Powers (1945) 703
  'Tokyo Rose' (World War II) 387
Raguna ko no kita (Moriya Tadashi)
  quest for identity in 1115
Rai Sanyō
  biographical sketch 295
  writings 1010
Railways
  alleged sabotage at Matsukawa, Fukushima Prefecture (1949) 780
  development (Japanese) in the Yangtze River valley 666
  history 954
  industry 217
  Japanese National Railways 542, 612, 625
  maps 53-54, 56, 82
  photo-essay 954
  research institutes and programmes 980
  signs 88
  train schedules 83
  Yamanote railway line (Tokyo) 91
Rain 41
  design motif of textile patterns 1344

829

Rain *continued*
  rainmaking ceremonies 500
  rainy season (*baiu*) 41
Rangaku ('Dutch learning') 167, 173,
  180
'Rashomon' (Akutagawa Ryūnosuke)
  translation 1045
Rationalisation
  technological changes (in industry)
  and 940
Raw materials
  quest for dependable supplies 913, 952
Reading
  process of learning to read 594
Readings *see* Anthologies (of readings,
  etc.)
Realism
  in art (exhibition catalogue) 1205
  used in Tsubouchi Shōyō's novels 1123
Reality
  Kyōto School's conception 521
  perception of 36
Rearmament
  post-1945 271, 354, 754, 759, 766
Rebellions *see* Protest movements and
  uprisings
Recipes *see* Cookbooks
Reciprocity
  as an element of social relationships
  585
  as an influence on behaviour 592
Recreational activities 31
  among bank employees 543
  among residents of the Anchiku
  region, Nagano Prefecture 1460
  during the Tokugawa period 165, 174
  encyclopaedic and almanac-type
  information about 1552, 1556-1557,
  1561
  kite-flying 1461
  see also Entertainment, Games,
  Leisure activities, and Sports
Recruitment
  bank employees 543
  company workers 838, 917, 928, 941
  diplomats and foreign service officers
  729
  electrical engineering industry workers
  920
  employees 891, 923
  fishermen 552
  higher civil servants 613
  journalists 1484

managers 878, 948
methods 928
policemen 565
political 622, 628, 634
scientists (Meiji period) 157
Self-Defence Forces 759, 761
Recycling
  solid wastes (garbage) 956
Red Army activist
  case history 580
Reference works *see* Bibliographies,
  Biographical dictionaries,
  Chronologies, Dictionaries,
  Encyclopaedias, Gazetteers,
  Glossaries, Guidebooks, and
  Instruction manuals
Reflexivisation 434
Reforms
  administrative 619, 856
  constitutional (1940s) 266, 271,
  273-274, 280-282
  economic (1940s) 267, 270, 273-274
  educational (1940s) 273, 282, 651,
  960-961, 975
  educational (1950s-1980s) 619, 965,
  970, 972
  egalitarian 964
  employment 575
  financial 860
  industrial 27
  initiated by Arai Hakuseki 298
  Kansei (1787-93) 177
  land (1940s) 267-268, 282, 790, 835
  language 196, 404, 997
  legal (1940s) 277, 780
  political (1940s) 266, 273, 280-281,
  356
  social (1940s) 267, 269, 273
  Tokugawa (1860s) 186
Refugees
  World War II 4, 359, 583
Regulation
  banking (1980s) 861
  broker-dealers 781
  development of financial markets 857
  environmental 801
  exchange markets 781
  licensing agreements 773-774
  machine tools industry 872
  ownership of industry 777
  posters on telephone poles 788
  securities 781
  stock exchange 868

see also Deregulation
Reischauer, Edwin O.
  autobiography 360
Reischauer, Haru Matsukata 297, 360
Reiyūkai (New Religion) 513
  ethnographic study 509
  see also New Religions
Rekishi monogatari ('historical tales')
  Eiga monogatari 1021
  Ōkagami 1017
Relativisation 434
Religion 9, 16, 32, 37, 460-465
  Ainu beliefs and rites 375, 378-380
  among the burakumin 374
  annual statistics 825
  architecture of post-1945 religious
    buildings 1313, 1321, 1324
  attitudes towards 18
  bibliographies 460, 1584
  conceptual worlds of 463
  contribution to modernisation 459
  encyclopaedic and almanac-type
    information about 1552, 1556,
    1560-1561, 1568
  impact of internationalisation 802
  influence on business ethics 844
  influence on contemporary politics 615
  introductory survey 460
  national and international dimensions
    802
  Okinawan 466
  periodicals 1499, 1504, 1506, 1520,
    1523, 1526, 1534, 1543
  prehistoric background 464
  readings about 1, 33, 461
  religious beliefs of villagers 548, 551,
    554
  religious life since the Meiji
    Restoration 467-468
  religious toleration (influence by the
    British) 660
  roots of religious symbolism 1323
  secularisation of civil 802
  see also Buddhism, Christianity in
    Japan, Deities, Folk religion,
    History (religious), Monastic life,
    New Religions, Rituals, Shintō,
    Shrines, Taoism, and Temples
Religious leaders
  Abe Masao 469
  Bassui-zenji 478
  biographical dictionary 367
  depicted in portrait sculpture 1292

Dōgen 472-474, 480-481
Ebina Danjō 235
Ganjin 1296
Genshin 470
Hakuin Ekaku 474, 476, 480
Ikkyū Sōjun 1139
Jien 130
Kōbō Daishi (Kūkai) 295, 482
Kōzaki Hiromichi 235
Kūkai 295, 458, 482
Nichiren 295
Niijima Jō 235
Rennyo 140
Ryōkan 1010, 1154
Saichō 295, 458
Saigyō 1007, 1155
Shinran 295, 471
Suzuki, Daisetz Teitaro 316
Uchimura Kanzō 288
Uemura Masahisa 235
Yasutani-rōshi 478
Yoshida Kenkō 1034
Religious practices
  decline (post-1945) 556
  in a pseudonymous mountain hamlet 507
  in Ōsaka and Takashima, Okayama
    Prefecture compared 562
  in Suye mura, Kumamoto Prefecture
    551
  in Tokyo 549
  medieval 136
  prehistoric 106
Religious texts
  dictionary of Buddhist 415
  English translations 472-473, 476-478,
    482, 488, 1499
  Ōjōyōshū of Genshin 470
  Shōbōgenzō of Dōgen 473
  Shōbōgenzō-zuimonki of Dōgen 472
  'Sound of the One Hand' (kōan) 477
Reliquaries
  at the Tōdaiji temple 1206
Renga poetry
  comic tradition in 140
  composed by Western poets 1166
  evolution and literary analysis 1165
  Satomura Jōha 135
  survey 1162, 1166
  translations 1156, 1165-1166
Rennyo
  Shinshū religious revival and 140
Reparations
  payments to Southeast Asia 742, 846

Repatriation
government compensation to World
War II repatriates 620
of Koreans in Japan 376-377
of Soviet-indoctrinated
prisoners-of-war 752
Repulse (British battle-cruiser)
sunk by the Japanese (1941) 698
Research
formation of a modern tradition of
scientific 157
Research and development 763, 837
alternative sources of energy 847, 849
artificial intelligence 982, 994, 997
at the Honda Motor Company 882
attitudes towards 922
computer industry 982
contrasting Japanese and American
approaches 881
corporate programmes 836
electronics industry 984-985, 988
evaluation methods and techniques
987
government-industry projects
(description) 980
information technology 981
involvement of trade associations 899
manufacturing industry 986
relationship to Japanese-style
management 990
robotics 995
science and technology 980, 983-984,
993, 996
technopolises as the focal point for 996
Research institutes
as sources of information (directory)
1558
overseas Japanese studies (directories)
1554, 1559, 1565
scientific (Meiji period) 157
scientific and technological 980
university (guidebook) 1550
Resignations
company workers 838
Resource allocation
aggregate demand and 807
'Respect language' *see* Honorific
language (*keigo*)
Restaurants
architecture (1960s) 1309
Buddhist 97
entertainment provided by geisha at
576

in Kyōto 78
in Tokyo 84, 87, 91
McDonald's 889
saké drinking places (guide) 1431
Retirement 540
bibliography 1595
discriminatory policies 575
emperors 142
fixed-age retirement system 930
higher civil servants 612-613
patterns in the Ministry of Finance 857
practice of *amakudari* 612
Revenge
novel about 1063
plays about 1180, 1395
tales about 1012, 1031, 1033
Revenues (government)
long-term statistical data 808
Tokugawa *bakufu* sources 185
Rewards
system of 917, 923, 931
Rezanov, Nikolai Petrovich
role in Russo-Japanese relations 664
Rice
brewing saké from fermented 1431
cultivation 200, 548
folk culture of rice farmers 503
government subsidies 620
Rice and rice dishes
recipes for 1429-1430, 1434,
1438-1440
see also Food
Richardson affair (1862) 675
Right-wing
in politics (1930s) 238, 245
in politics (1945-57) 276
Rights
Fukuda Hideko as an advocate of
people's 290
human rights 611, 616, 784
'movement for freedom and popular
rights' (Jiyū minken undō) 195, 312
of labour unions to organise 921
of participation in election politics 788
of public employees 609, 771, 788
of women 280, 328, 580, 777
of workers 771
property 787
related to environmental pollution 775
'right of silence' in law 787
see also Constitution, and Freedom
Rikken Kaishintō (political party) 308
Rikyū *see* Sen no Rikyū

Rimpa school of art
  influence on styles of book illustration
    1477
  survey 1240
Rinzai sect of Zen Buddhism
  Bassui-*zenji* (teachings) 478
  Daitokuji temple 1190
  during the Kamakura period 474, 484
  gozan bungaku poetry 1152
  gozan system of temples 131, 140
  Hakuin Ekaku 474, 476, 480
  kōan (catechetic questions) 477-478
  kōan zaza 478
  monasteries 131, 486
Riots
  Hibiya riot (1905) 175, 672
Risshō Ankokuron (Nichiren) 511
Risshō Kōseikai (New Religion) 468,
    510, 513
  ethnographic case-study 507
  see also New Religions
Rituals 460-463, 535, 593
  Ainu 375, 378
  ancestor worship 485, 505, 509
  associated with birth, marriage, and
    death 500
  associated with rice culture 503
  diplomatic (Tokugawa period) 677
  family 549
  initiation rites for young men 503
  New Religions 506, 509
  origins of poetry in 1163
  ritual objects 1193-1194, 1198, 1206,
    1214
  ritual pollution 466, 530
  ritual purity 516, 520, 530
  shamanistic 499
  Shintō 516, 518, 520
  sumo tournaments 1453-1455
  traditional festivals 501
  wedding rites 560
  wine drinking 153
  water rituals in religious practices 3
Rivers
  contamination of Tokyo's waterways
    957
  gazetteer 57
  photographs 44
  species of fish 60
Riverside Counselor's Stories
  translation 1011
Roads
  Dōsojin as their guardian spirit 502

encyclopaedic and almanac-type
    information about 1551
  novel about life along the Kiso Road
    1094
  see also Tōkaidō highway
Robes
  noh theatre (Tokugawa period) 1412
Robotics 986, 995
  industry 38, 995
  industry trade association 899
  role of invention and innovation in 985
Rockefeller (Abby Aldrich Rockefeller)
    Collection (Providence, Rhode
    Island)
  ukiyo-e prints 1257
Rockefeller Institute for Medical
    Research (New York)
  Noguchi Hideyo's work at 343
Rocks
  geological study 49
  sumi-e techniques for painting 1247
  used in gardens 1337
  see also Stones
Rodrigues, João 132, 153
  biography 352
Roesler, Hermann
  role in drafting the Meiji Constitution
    189
Role behaviour 588
Role orientations
  journalists 1484
Role strain
  among women 580
Rōmaji nikki (Ishikawa Takuboku)
  translation 1140
Roman Catholicism *see* Christianity in
    Japan
Romanisation
  romanised dictionaries 426
  system 438
Rōnin (masterless samurai)
  'Forty-seven *rōnin*' (subject of the
    play *Chūshingura*) 1180, 1395
Roof tile of Tempyō (Inoue Yasushi)
  translation 1061
Roofs 1302, 1322
  minka (traditional-style houses) 1312
  roof tiles (Okinawan) 1222
Roosevelt, Theodore
  role in the Portsmouth Peace
    Conference (1905) 672
  US-Japanese relations (1901-9) and
    659

Rōyama Masamichi 199
Ruined map (Abe Kōbō)
   translation 1042
Runaway horses (Mishima Yukio)
   literary analysis 1131
   translation 1077
Rural areas
   banks (19th century) 806
   comparison of rural and urban life 562
   concern over death and illness in 588
   economy (1840s-1880s) 212
   education 573
   group-centred, vertical orientation of
      society 539
   life in the Inland Sea area 71
   life in Tsuchiura, Ibaraki Prefecture
      234
   neighbourhood associations 641
   photographs of rural life 3, 11, 28-29,
      1275-1276, 1278
   production of *tsutsugaki* fabrics 1345
   society of Shimoda (1850s) 676
   socio-economic change (1940s-1970s)
      34, 531, 534, 835
   structural forms and cultural patterns
      of society 531
   see also Hamlets, and Villages
Russia
   expansion towards Japan (1697-1875)
      664
   Japanese espionage in 648
   Japanese response to Russian
      imperialism in China 669
   perceived threat to Japan 173
   see also Foreign relations with
      Russia/USSR, and Union of Soviet
      Socialist Republics (USSR)
Russian Orthodox Church *see*
   Christianity in Japan
Russians in Japan
   Golovnin, Vasilii Mikhailovich 664
   Putiatin, Evfimii Vasil'evich 664
   Rezanov, Nikolai Petrovich 664
Russo-Japanese War (1904-5)
   analytical narrative 678
   as an historical turning point 249
   Hibiya riot 175, 672
   Japanese reactions 72, 175, 672
   Kōtoku Shūsui's opposition 337
   naval operations and battles 210, 320
   oligarchic control of foreign policy 672
   origins 671
   photographs 678

Portsmouth Peace Conference 659,
   672
Ryōanji (temple)
   garden 1327, 1332, 1335
Ryōkan
   poetry 1154
   prose 1010
Ryōkan (inns) 90
   bathing in 1457
   depicted in literature 184
   illustrated overview 96
   Kyōto 78
   Victorian British writings about 68
Ryū Shintarō 199
Ryūkyū Islands
   bibliographies 1591
   flora 62
   handicrafts 1201
   history 284, 1201
   Iriomote Island (national park) 48
   Perry expedition's visit (1853-54) 673
   postage stamps 1522
   relations with Japan 284, 677
   textile designs (photographs) 1347
   textiles 1201, 1222
   US military government (1945-72) 285
   see also Okinawa

S

Sado Island (Niigata Prefecture) 69
Safety practices 923
Saga Plain (Saga Prefecture)
   agricultural development
      (1880s-1930s) 200
Saga Prefecture
   kilns (Karatsu ware) 1279
   policy-making 639
   Saga Plain 200
   see also Kyūshū
Saichō
   biographical sketch 295
   Buddhist writings 458
Saigō Takamori
   life and times 293
Saigyō
   poetry 1007
   Sankashū 1155
Saihōji (temple)
   garden 1327, 1331
Saikaku *see* Ihara Saikaku
Sailor who fell from grace with the sea
   (Mishima Yukio)
   translation 1076

Saionji Kinmochi
  biography 296, 323
  political leadership 296
Saipan
  battle (1944) 699, 715, 1609
Saitama Prefecture
  Chichibu Incident (1884) 195
  policy-making 639
  see also Kantō region
Saitō Kiyoshi
  woodblock prints 1274
Saitō Mokichi
  life and poetry 325
Sakai (port city)
  historical evolution (Muromachi
    period) 140
  massacre of French sailors (1868) 675
  urban autonomy (16th century) 135
Sakakura Junzō
  architectural work 1298
Sakamoto Ryōma
  biographical sketch 295
Saké 1433, 1436, 1438
  brewery 929
  guidebook 1431
Sakhalin
  19th-century claims to 664
  accounts of World War II refugees
    from 583
  history 287
  under Japanese colonial rule
    (1905-45) 223
Sakura-ga-ike-miya (shrine) 520
Sakura Hime Azuma bunshō (Tsuruya
    Namboku IV et al.)
  translation 1396
Sakuteiki (Tachibana no Toshitsuna)
    1338
'Salary men' see White-collar workers
Salvation
  Buddhist concepts 470-471
  Shinran's doctrines of 471
  Shintō concepts 518
Samurai 139, 214
  1840s-1880s 212, 226
  converts to Christianity (Meiji period) 235
  daughters 313
  depicted in the Azuma kagami 154
  depicted in the novel Musashi 1109
  depicted in the Soga monogatari 1012
  education 164, 1452
  effect of the Meiji Restoration on 235, 307
  ethics (guidebook) 529

  ethos and traditions 1448
  everyday life (1185-1603) 136
  everyday life (1600-1868) 165
  'Forty-seven rōnin' 1180, 1395
  historical development of the samurai
    class 1443
  history (1180s-1220s) 149
  history (12th-19th centuries) 156, 158
  influenced by Zen Buddhism 492
  samurai films 1420
Samurai (Endō Shūsaku)
  translation 1054
Samurai swords see Swords
San Francisco Bay area (California)
  Japanese American women 388
San Francisco Peace Treaty (1951) 266,
    274, 282-283, 285, 745
San Francisco school crisis (1906)
  Japanese Americans and 384, 659
Sanbōin (temple)
  garden 1327
Sanbunshi ('prose poems')
  study and translation 1141
Sanetomo (Yamazaki Masakazu)
  translation 1182
Sangō shiki (Kūkai)
  translation 482
Sankashū (Saigyō)
  translation 1155
Sankei Shimbun (newspaper)
  articles and editorials (translations and
    synopses) 1547
  news reporting 1484
Sanrizuka farmers
  opposed to constructing Narita
    Airport 606
Sanshirō (Natsume Sōseki)
  psychoanalytical study 1112
  synopses and analyses 1112, 1117
  translation and study 1087
Sansō Collection
  paintings (exhibition catalogue) 1246
Santa Cruz
  battle (1942) 680
Sad toys (Ishikawa Takuboku)
  translation 1140
Saddles
  owned by the Tokugawa shōguns
    (exhibition catalogue) 1219
Sanuki (Kagawa Prefecture) 69
Sanuki Province
  Sugawara no Michizane's
    governorship 300

Sanya district (Tokyo)
    labourers 34
Sapporo (Hokkaidō)
    tourist guide 100
Sarashina nikki (Sugawara Takasue no
    musume)
    translation 1026
Sarayama (Ōita Prefecture)
    folk craft potters 553
Sarcophagi
    Kofun (Tumulus) period 105
Sarugaku noh (performing art) 1403,
    1409
    audiences 1410
Sarumino (Matsuo Bashō)
    translation 1150
Sasameyuki (Tanizaki Junichirō)
    literary analyses 1002, 1127
    translation 1101
Sata Ineko
    short stories 1071, 1088
Satellite broadcasting 955
Satō Bunsei
    election campaign (1966-67) 631
Satō Eisaku
    support for the USA during the
        Vietnam War 727
Satoh Makoto
    plays (translations) 1171, 1173
Satomura Jōha
    poetic career 135
Satori (enlightenment) 487-490, 493
    accounts 478-479
Satow, Ernest
    activities and travels 190, 675
Satsuma *han*
    Allied bombardment of Kagoshima
        (1863) 353, 675
    historical case-study 168
    Mori Arinori's early years in 304
    Okinawa as its vassal state 284
    Shimazu Nariakira (daimyō) 289
Satsuma Rebellion (1877) 293, 306
Satsuma ware (ceramics) 1283
Savings 817
    1868-1977 855
    behaviour 20, 783, 859
    high level of household 816
    investment and savings rates 884, 886
    Japan-US savings-rate gap 809
    postal savings 857
    private savings (economic role) 814
    savings-investment imbalance (1970s) 800

Sayings
    collection of 1183
Scandals
    business 844
Scholarships
    government and university 1550
Schools
    architecture (1960s-1980s) 1299, 1324
    collection of school songs 1386
    David Murray's contributions to
        school administration 197
    life (1880s-1940s) 232
    moral education and socialisation 595
    organisation (Tokugawa period) 164
    schoolchildren 594, 964, 971
Science
    annual statistics 825, 827, 829
    assessment of scientific advances 984
    astronomy 151, 157, 167, 187
    basic facts and figures (annual
        handbook) 14
    bibliography 992
    biology 187, 437
    botany 596
    British influence (Meiji period) 660
    chemistry 187, 437
    education 980
    formation of a scientific research
        tradition 157
    geology 49, 53-54, 187, 992
    government report (annual) 829
    history 157, 187, 992
    medieval 136
    Nagasaki's transmission of Western
        179
    periodicals 1539
    physics 187, 437
    policies (government) 980
    research institutes and programmes
        (overview) 980
    training Americans to read Japanese
        scientific materials 991
    US-Japan relations in science and
        technology 897, 998
    US-Japanese scientific contacts (Meiji
        period) 197
Science and Technology Agency
    evaluation of applied research by 987
Scientific Japanese
    language textbook 437
Scientists
    Morse, Edward S. 361
    Noguchi Hideyo 343

recruitment, training, and socialisation
(Meiji period) 157
Scoundrels
stories about 1016
Screens 155
as an artistic medium 1234
as antiques 1215
at the Seattle Art Museum 1217
at the Tōdaiji temple 1206
decorated with fan-shaped paintings
(exhibition catalogue) 1233
depicting creatures of nature 1221
historical overview 1234
lacquered 1370
maps on 55
owned by the Tokugawa shōguns
(exhibition catalogue) 1219
painted by the Kanō school of painting
1252
painted by the Rimpa school of art
1240
painted in the *yamato-e* style 1236
six masterpieces (detailed study) 1234
theme of the supernatural in 1189
Scrolls 155
hanging scrolls (kakemono) 1206,
1215, 1221
illustrated handscrolls (*emaki*) 1200,
1206, 1219, 1221, 1236, 1245, 1380
painted by the Rimpa school of art
1240
Sculptors
biographical dictionaries 368-369
Kaikei 1293
Kōkei 1293
techniques and styles (post-1945) 1203
Unkei 1293
Sculpture 155, 1214, 1220
at temples in Nara 1316
at the Freer Gallery of Art 1250
at the Hōryūji temple 1208
at the Shōsōin 1194
at the Tōdaiji temple 1206, 1290
at the Tokyo National Museum 1473
at the Yakushiji temple 1290
depicted in exhibition catalogues 1218,
1227, 1229
Dōsojin 502
esoteric Buddhist (Mikkyō) 1216
evolution of Buddhist (AD 600-1300)
1295
evolution of modern (1868-1968)
1209, 1238

folk art 1193, 1213
haniwa 106, 108
history 1211-1212
Kamakura period 1293
patronage (1955-80) 1376
portrait (Buddhist) 1292-1293
Pure Land (Jōdo) Buddhist 1192
representations of Daruma 483
Shintō 1199, 1289
style of Buddhist 1200, 1292-1293, 1295
Tempyō period 1296
theme of the supernatural in 1189
see also Photographs (sculpture)
Sea of Japan
fishing industry 552
species of fish 60
Tsushima Current 47
Seal-engraving (*tenkoku*)
craftsmanship 1369
Seals
of Uragami Gyokudō (reproductions)
1230
on prints (bibliography) 1576
Seasons
bamboo during the four seasons 64
cuisine associated with 1431, 1435,
1437, 1440
designs of the four seasons 1224
flower arrangements attuned to 1462
painting on themes involving 1236
poetry about 1152-1153, 1155, 1162
seasonal guide to bonsai cultivation
1336
Seattle Art Museum (Seattle,
Washington)
premodern art treasures 1217
Seattle, Washington
Japanese Americans 399, 403
Secondary education *see* High schools
Secret history of the lord of Musashi
(Tanizaki Junichirō)
translation 1102
Secret service
history 648
'Secret teachings'
about garden design 1338
about the Noh theatre 1413
about Zen Buddhism 477
Secrets
idiomatic words and expressions
pertaining to secrecy 414
legal protection of trade 773-774
role in personal relations 590

Securities
  co-operation between corporations
    and stockholders 836
  credit 858
  international transactions 781
  investment advisers 858
  market 811, 858, 864, 868
  Nomura Securities Company 853, 942
  regulation 781, 1582
  Securities and Exchange Law 781
  securities companies 851, 853, 858,
    862, 864, 868, 909, 942
  Securities Investment Trust Law 781
  shareholder-management relations
    (legal aspects) 786
  see also Stock exchanges
Security
  blue-collar workers' search for
    economic 918
  maintenance of public 565
Security (national) 6, 354, 732, 738-739,
  761
  common interests of Japan, the USA,
    and NATO 765
  concept of comprehensive 760
  consciousness of peace and 611
  East Asian regional security 732, 738,
    742, 762, 765, 769
  energy-related strategy 849
  foreign aid policy and 757
  foreign policy (post-1960) and 748
  interrelationship of economic and
    military 903
  Japan's search for economic 679, 685,
    749, 885
  Japan's self-defence requirements 765
  policy 720, 748, 761-762, 768
  potential Soviet military threat 747,
    752, 766-767
  security debate within Japan 768-769
  US-Japan mutual security ties
    724-725, 750, 753-754, 765-769, 897
  see also Defence, Self-Defence
    Forces, United States-Japan
    Security Treaty (1951), and United
    States-Japan Security Treaty of
    1960
Security Treaty crisis (1960) 744, 754,
  969, 1485
Sei Shōnagon
  biographical sketch 295
  Pillow book 1025
Seichō-no-Ie (New Religion) 468, 510, 513

see also New Religions
Seikyōsha ('Society for Political
  Education') 230
Seiyūkai (political party)
  growth and activities (1905-15) 224
  political rivalry with the Kenseikai 198
Seiza ('quiet-sitting therapy') 602
Sekai Kyūseikyō (New Religion)
  overview 513
  see also New Religions
Seken munesanyo (Ihara Saikoku)
  translation (excerpts) 1015
Seken musuko katagi (Ejima Kiseki)
  translation (excerpts) 1036
Seken musume katagi (Ejima Kiseki)
  translation (excerpts) 1036
Sekine Hiroshi
  poetry 1057
Sekino Junichirō
  woodblock prints 1274
Sekirankai ('Red Wave Society') 290
Self-awareness
  roles of *omote* and *ura* in 590
Self-Defence Forces 754, 762
  constitutionality 761
  establishment 282
  Maritime Self-Defence Force 759
  origins and nature 761, 766
  reliance on domestically produced
    goods 763
  role in defence policy (1950s-1960s)
    770
Self-discipline
  traditional concern for 544, 585
Self-government
  village 531
Self-help (Samuel Smiles)
  impact on Meiji period values 214
Selfhood
  as a factor influencing behaviour 592
Self-made man
  concept (Meiji period) 214
Self-sacrifice
  literary depiction 1012
Self-sufficiency
  quest for economic (1920s-1930s) 679,
    685
Semiconductors
  role of invention and innovation in 985
  semiconductor industry 873, 880, 904,
    907, 945
Semimaru of Ausaka
  as a legendary figure 1176

literary works associated with 1176
Sen no Rikyū 1467
  biographical sketch 295
  calligraphy 1249
  tea master 295, 1460, 1470, 1472
Senbazuru (Kawabata Yasunari)
  translation 1067
Sendai (Miyagi Prefecture)
  tourist guide 100
Seniority
  promotion based on 938
  wages based on 208, 930, 940
Senkaku Islands
  Sino-Japanese dispute (1960s-1970s)
    730
Senryū (comic poetry)
  survey 1162
  translations 1156
Senryū Namiki
  Chūshingura 1180, 1395
Sentence structure 405
Sentimentality
  as a factor in US policy towards Japan
    657
Sentō Imperial Palace
  garden 1334
Senzui narabi ni yagyō no zu (Zōen)
  translation 1338
Separation of church and state
  Meiji period views 196
Servants
  agricultural 181
Service industries
  women employees 578
Service sector
  annual statistics 824
  long-term statistical data 808
Sesshū
  ink painting 1239, 1253
Set designers
  Asakura Setsu 1423
Seto ware (ceramics) 1283, 1286
Setoguro ware (ceramics) 1281
Setouchi Harumi
  short stories 1098
Setsuwa bungaku ('tale literature')
  evolution 1022
  Konjaku monogatari 1029, 1032, 1037
  Uji shūi monogatari 1022, 1029
Setting sun (Dazai Osamu)
  literary analysis 1127
  translation 1050
Settlement archaeology

Nara Basin 102
Settlement patterns
  Ainu 379
Sewage system
  inadequacies 957
Sex 31, 536
  among farmers 573
  depicted in *shunga* (erotic prints) 1259
  expressions pertaining to sexuality 413
  sex roles 31, 536
  sexism in society 31
  sexual morality 536
  sexuality 536, 599
  see also Pornography
Shadan ('isolation therapy') 602
Shakkei ('borrowed scenery')
  concept of garden design 1333
Shakuhachi (flute) 1383
  craftsmanship 1369
  music 1382-1383
Shamans and shamanism 499, 504
Shame
  proverbs about 1183
  sense of 585
Shamisen (lute) 1383
  as an accompaniment to songs of
    geisha 576
  music 1382-1385
  used in the bunraku theatre 1391,
    1399, 1404, 1411
  used in the kabuki theatre 1384, 1397
Shanghai (China)
  interaction of Japanese and Jews
    (World War II) 4
  Sino-Japanese economic collaboration
    735
Shantung (China)
  occupied by Japan (World War I) 647
Sharp Corporation
  evaluation of applied research by 987
Shashin gafu (Katsushika Hokusai)
  book illustrations 1260
Shayō (Dazai Osamu)
  literary analysis 1127
  translation 1050
Shibata Zenshin
  fan-shaped paintings 1233
Shibori (shaped resist-dyed textiles)
  illustrated study 1355
Shibunkai (society)
  activities 528
Shidehara Kijurō
  China policy (1924-27) 333

Shiga Naoya
  Anya korō 1093
  as a member of the *bundan* 1120
  concept of literature 1128
  literary analyses 1113, 1125
  search for authenticity in literature
    1130
  short stories 1051, 1126
Shiga Prefecture
  Azuchi Castle 135, 1306, 1317
  Okinoshima 500
  Shigaraki Valley 1280
Shigaraki ware (ceramics) 1283, 1286
  stylistic development 1280
Shigemitsu Mamoru
  'struggle for peace' (1931-45) 708
Shijō school of art
  influence on styles of book illustration
    1477
Shijuku (private academies) 180
Shikan-taza 478
Shikitei Sanba
  life and writings 1038
  Ukiyoburo 1038
Shikoku
  geography 50
  minka (traditional-style houses) 1301
  occupied by the British
    Commonwealth Occupation Force
    in Japan 266
  pilgrimages in honour of Kōbō Daishi
    73
  see also Ehime Prefecture, Kagawa
    Prefecture, and Tosa *han*
Shikotan Island
  Japanese-Soviet dispute over 285-286
Shimabara Rebellion (1637-38) 129, 293
Shimaki Kensaku
  short stories 1051
Shimamura Hōgetsu
  liberal thought and activities 336
Shimane Prefecture
  Izumo Shrine 1325
Shimazaki Tōson
  biography 239
  life and writings 1117
  novels 1094, 1129
  search for authenticity in literature
    1130
Shimazu Nariakira
  biography 289
Shimizu Hiroshi
  film-making activities 1417

Shimoda (town)
  during the 1850s 676
  Townsend Harris' sojourn (1856-58)
    676
Shimonoseki (town)
  Allied naval operations (1864) against
    675
  Treaty of Shimonoseki (1895) 645, 668
Shin Buddhism 521
  Shinshū religious revival 140
Shinagawa Takumi
  woodblock prints 1274
Shinano (Nagano Prefecture) 69
Shinano (super-battleship)
  sunk by Americans (1944) 716
Shindō Kaneto
  films and film-making activities 1423
Shingaku movement 459
Shingeki ('new theatre') 1001, 1179
  bibliographies 1588, 1603
  examined through Kishida Kunio's
    career 1178
  interview with Yamazaki Masakazu
    about 1182
  survey 1393
Shingon Buddhism 475, 484-485
  artworks 1216
  growth (Heian period) 458
  healing priests 499
  painting 1237
  terminology (dictionary) 415
Shingū (Fukuoka Prefecture)
  ethnographic study 552
Shinjinkai ('New Man Society')
  as a student movement (1920s) 244
Shinkankakuha (modernist literary
    group)
  Yokomitsu Riichi as a member 1114
Shinkeishitsu (neuroses)
  treatment through Morita therapy 592
Shino ware (ceramics) 1281, 1283
  illustrated survey 1282
Shinoda Masahiro
  film-making activities 1415, 1419, 1423
  films 1420-1421, 1423-1424
Shinoda Morio
  artistic techniques and styles 1203
Shinohara Kazuo
  architectural work 1320
Shinohata (Tochigi Prefecture)
  community study 550
Shinran
  biographical sketch 295

cardinal ideas 471
Shinsei (Shimazaki Tōson)
  ideal of individualism in 1129
  synopsis and analysis 1117
Shinsen wakashū (Ki no Tsurayuki)
  translation 1153
Shinshū religious revival (15th century)
  140
Shintō 458, 464-465, 468, 515-520
  aesthetic attitudes 1289
  architecture 518, 1323, 1325
  art 1199
  as the state religion 515
  bibliography 1606
  co-existence with Christianity 498
  cultural contributions 519
  deities assimilated into Buddhist
    iconography 1237
  devotional practices pertaining to
    shinzō 1289
  early ritual sites 143
  early role in Japanese life 458
  encyclopaedic study 516
  festivals 516, 518-520
  history 516-517, 520
  introductory survey 460
  Ise Shrine 66, 515, 1323, 1325
  kagura 1403
  kami 499, 516, 518-520
  Kurozumikyō 508, 513
  music 518, 1380, 1383
  mythology 458, 516, 1186
  overseas expansion of State Shintō 517
  overviews 462-463
  popularised by Masuho Zankō 526
  practised in a mountain farming
    hamlet 507
  priests 503, 516, 518
  readings about 33, 461
  relationship to bathing 1457
  relationship to sumo wrestling 1453
  role in the development of nationalism
    517
  shinzō statues of deities 1289
  Shrine Shintō (post-1945) 515
  State Shintō (1868-1945) 517
  Tokugawa period revival 309, 458
  see also Shrines
Shinzō (statues of Shintō deities)
  stylistic and iconographic evolution
    1289
Shiosai (Mishima Yukio)
  translation 1078

Shipbuilding industry 38, 45, 217, 763,
  812
  competitive decline 813
  fundamental changes 796
  industrial policy and 876, 879
  shipyards 929
Shipping industry
  Meiji period 212, 250
Ships *see* Warships
Shiraishi Kazuko
  poetry 1143, 1151
Shirakawa (Emperor) 142
Shirone (Niigata Prefecture)
  kite-flying festivals 1461
Shisendō (temple)
  garden 1327
Shishōsetsu ('I-novels') 1113
Shiwa (Iwate Prefecture)
  community study 555
Shiwa Agricultural Cooperative 555
Shizuoka Prefecture
  Hamamatsu 1461
  Minaguchi-ya inn at Okitsu 184
  Mishima 642
  Sakura-ga-ike-miya (shrine) 520
  Shimoda 676
Shōbōgenzō (Dōgen)
  translation 473
Shōbōgenzō-zuimonki (Dōgen)
  translation 472
Shōdenji (temple)
  garden 1327
Shōen ('landed estates')
  Heian period development 141
  jitō (estate stewards) 149
Shōgi (game)
  introduction to 1460
Shōgun (film)
  production of 1418
Shōgun (John Clavell)
  American image of the Japanese in
    731
Shogunate *see Bakufu* (shogunate)
Shōguns
  artworks owned by the Tokugawa
    shōguns (exhibition catalogue) 1219
  Ashikaga Takauji 159, 295
  Ashikaga Yoshimitsu 140, 295
  biographical dictionary 367
  Minamoto Sanetomo 1182
  Tokugawa Ienobu 177, 298
  Tokugawa Ietsugu 177, 298
  Tokugawa Ieyasu 139, 314, 1315

Shōguns *continued*
Tokugawa Tsunayoshi 289
Shōhaku
renga poetry 1165
Shoin style of architecture 140, 1307
Shōji (translucent paper screens) 1326
Shōji jissō gi (Kūkai)
translation 482
Shōjin ryōri (vegetarian cooking)
cookbook 1440
Shōkokuji (temple)
suibokuga painters associated with
1239
Shōmyō (Buddhist chanting) 1382
Shōnai Plain (Yamagata Prefecture)
protest movements (1840-75) 213
Shop signs (*kanban*)
as antiques 1215
folk art 1213
photographs 1213, 1215, 1368
Shopkeepers
of Tsuchiura, Ibaraki Prefecture 234
Shōraku Miyoshi
Chūshingura 1180, 1395
Short stories
background, structural principles, and
development 1008
collection of essays about 1126
history (1868-1940s) 1001
see also Translations (short stories)
Shōsōin
collection of art objects at 1194
Shōtoku Taishi 93, 523
Shōwa Bōeki (packaging enterprise)
case history 845
Shōwa Emperor *see* Hirohito (emperor)
Shōwa Research Association (Shōwa
Kenkyūkai) 199
Shrines 90
architecture (historical survey) 1314
folk legends about 1184
Ise Shrine 66, 515, 1323, 1325
Kofun (Tumulus) period 106
of Kamakura (guidebook) 76
of Kyōto 77, 92
of Nara 93
Sakura-ga-ike-miya 520
Shintō 66, 515-516, 518-520, 1323,
1325
Shintō art treasures 1199
Tōshōgu Shrine 1315
Yasukuni Shrine 515
Shūbun

ink painting 1239, 1253
Shūgakuin Detached Palace
garden 1334-1335
Shūgen noh (performing art) 1403
Shugendō (religious order)
yamabushi 499
Shugo (provincial constables) 149, 160
Shunga (erotic prints and paintings)
illustrated study 1259
prints of Katsushika Hokusai 1478
Shunkan (Zeami Motokiyo)
noh, kabuki, and bunraku theatrical
versions compared 1393
performance analysis and translation
1406
Shyness
among Japanese 19
Siberia
as a source of raw materials and fuels
885
Japanese involvement in its
development 747-748, 752, 900
Japanese military thrust (1918) into
684
Soviet-Japanese energy co-operation
in 847
Siblinghood
among Japanese Americans 403
Sickles and chains
used in the martial arts 1443
Siebold, Philipp Franz von
as a cultural intermediary 596
Signatures
handbook for depicting artists 1571
lacquer artists 1360
netsuke carvers 1288
table of facsimiles of artists 1264
Signs 26, 88
guidebook 88
shop signs (*kanban*) 1213, 1215, 1368
Silent cry (Ōe Kenzaburō)
translation 1090
Silk
exports to the USA 297
Silkworm-raisers
Shinohata, Tochigi Prefecture 550
Simplification
as a managerial technique 936
Singapore
relations with Japan 741, 897
Single-mindedness
as a samurai value 529
Sino-Japanese War of 1894-95 652

842

activities of Tōgō Heihachirō 320
Chinese attitudes towards Japan 650
depicted in Meiji period prints 1269
impact on culture and literature 1003
memoirs of Mutsu Munemitsu 668
naval battle at Yalu Bay 210
negotiations for the Treaty of
Shimonoseki 645, 668
Sino-Japanese War of 1937-45 647, 652,
679, 690, 695, 702, 708, 712, 715
British involvement 694, 697, 711, 715
Chinese collaboration 650, 702
Ishiwara Kanji's role 342
Japanese army in North China
(1937-41) 702
Japanese atrocities 650
Konoe Fumimaro's role 685
occupation of Shanghai 4
outbreak 245
Tientsin crisis 697
US involvement 649, 702, 711, 715
Wang Ching-wei 702
see also World War II (Pacific
Theatre)
Sino-Soviet conflict (1960s-1970s)
influence on Sino-Japanese relations
730
reactions of the Japan Communist
Party 635
Slang 454
Sliding doors
as an element of interior design 1326
Slogans
racist stereotypes in World War II 686
Small and Medium-Sized Enterprises
Organization Law 611
Smallpox
Tokugawa period 172
vaccination (introduced by Otto
Mohnike) 597
Smith, Richard Gordon
diaries 72
Smog (photochemical) 957
Smuggling
yakuza (gangster) involvement 569
Snow country (Kawabata Yasunari)
literary analysis 1127
translation 1065
Sōchō
renga poetry 1165
Social change
20th-century 239, 531-534, 537, 544,
546, 588

among Japanese Americans 400
among migrants 557
among the Ainu 379
among the burakumin 374
cities and 546
impact on folk crafts 553
in rural society (1930s) 551
in rural society (post-1945) 531, 550,
553-556, 562, 573
in suburban Tokyo 628
individuals and 595
law and 785
marriage practices 560
police adjustment to 565
resulting from egalitarianism in
education 964
violence as an instrument 777
Social classes
structure and composition 545
Social control
among Japanese Americans 394
Social Democratic clique 247
Social democratic movement
1920s-1930s 247
Social development
backwardness of Japan's 533
prospects by the year 2000 AD
954
Social history see History (social)
Social integration
elderly 540
migrants to Tokyo 557
Social law
bibliography 1582
Social obligations (giri)
concern for fulfilling 522, 782
Social order
traditional concern for 544
Social organisation 23, 38
Ainu 378-379
factory workers 917, 920
influence of feelings of amae
589
local corporate groups 561
Rinzai Zen monasteries 131
rural households 561
villages 548, 551, 553, 561, 573
Social policy
1868-1930s 202
Social reformers
Ishimoto Shizue 328
Kagawa Toyohiko 288
Tanno Setsu 290

Social reforms
  Allied occupation of Japan (1945-52)
    267, 269, 273
  movements (1900-40) 290
  movements (Meiji period) 235, 240,
    290
Social relations 2, 9, 532, 561, 585
  16th century 133
  among bank employees 543
  among high school students 975
  among the residents of Shinohata,
    Tochigi Prefecture 550
  see also Husband-wife relationships,
    and Interpersonal relations
Social responsibility
  sense of 30
Social security 931
  annual statistics 825-827
  bibliography 1594
Social status
  hierarchy as a mechanism for assigning
    585
Social stratification
  changes in the system of 530
Social structure 9, 31, 533, 537, 627, 723
  Japanese American community 394
  regional bank 543
  rural 534
  Tokugawa period 459
Social values 916
  in primary human relations 588
Social welfare
  policy 623
  political response to changing
    conditions in 619
Social work
  Christian involvement (post-1945) 497
Socialisation 533, 588, 595
  adults 595
  as a factor influencing behaviour 592
  burakumin 373
  children 535, 559
  intellectual elite (1880s-1940s) 232
  policemen 565
  political 580, 642, 969
  readings about 961
  scientists (Meiji period) 157
  students 595, 969
Socialism
  1898-1921 192
  readings about 33
Socialist parties
  1945-55 274

1945-1960s (comprehensive study) 630
increased voter support in suburban
  Tokyo 628
opposition to a revised US-Japan
  Security Treaty 744
see also Japan Socialist Party
Socialist politics
  1920s-1940 215
Socialists
  as pacifists 288
  Kōtoku Shūsui 337
  Sekirankai (1920s) 290
Societies (learned) see Learned societies
Society 32, 544, 593, 904
  basic contradictions in post-1945 537
  Buddhism's role in modern 485
  cultural world of Tokugawa 1005,
    1014-1015, 1036, 1038, 1259
  depicted in Dazai Osamu's novels
    1116
  emergence of a 'controlled' 567
  impact of the Vietnam War 727
  impact of World War II 207
  influence of the company 838
  interaction with politics 622
  interrelationship with religion 463
  introductory studies 535, 537
  mass society 514, 532-533
  Meiji period 305, 313, 351, 355, 363
  newspaper articles about 1546, 1549
  overviews 6, 21, 23, 29-30, 843
  periodicals 1488, 1491, 1493, 1498,
    1517, 1526, 1536
  pervaded by tension and conflict 538
  reintegration of overseas employees
    into 572
  relationship with the individual 549
  rural 531, 534, 548, 550-556
  social consequences of
    industrialisation 812
  social contributions of women 574
  social effects of the 1945 atomic
    bombings 252-253, 256-257
  social perception of the person 480
  social place and function of geisha 576
  social position of the artist 1200
  social role of law and lawyers 784
  social role of marriage 560
  social role of women 580-581
  structural principles guiding 539
  vocabulary for 405
Sōdōmei see Nihon Rōdō Sōdōmei
  (Japan General Federation of

844

Labour)
Software (computer)
    research and development 981
    role of invention and innovation in 985
Sōfū School of ikebana 1464
Soga monogatari
    translation 1012
Soga school of painting 1253
Sōgetsu School of ikebana 1462,
    1464-1466
Sōgi
    renga poetry 1165
Sōgi dokugin nanibito hyakuin
    translations 1165
Sōgō shōsha (general trading companies)
    activities in Brazil 898
    assistance to firms relocating overseas
        946
    evolution, role, and organisation
        914-915
    financial role (1950s-1960s) 851
    life-course of their employees 542
    management 922, 949
    multinational character 952
    origins and growth 812
    personnel practices 942
    role in expanding foreign trade 806
Sōhyō (General Council of Trade
        Unions of Japan)
    opposition to a revised US-Japan
        Security Treaty 744
Soils 50
    maps 53
Sōka Gakkai (New Religion) 468, 510,
    513
    bibliography 1584
    doctrine and teachings 511-512, 514
    history 319, 511-512
    involvement in politics 511-512, 514,
        634
    Makiguchi Tsunesaburō 319
    publications 511
Sokushin jōbutsu gi (Kūkai)
    translation 482
Solomons Seas
    battles (1942) 680, 687
Some prefer nettles (Tanizaki Junichirō)
    translation 1104
Sone, Monica
    autobiography 399
Songs
    Ainu epic 380
    European-style school 1386

    folk 135, 1380-1383
    gagaku 1377
    geisha 576
    koto music 1378
    kusemai 1409
    nagauta 1384-1385
    noh theatre 1387
    racist stereotypes in World War II 686
Sono Ayako
    short stories 1048
Sony Corporation
    history 332, 877
    investment decision-making process
        951
    personnel practices 942
Sorekara (Natsume Sōseki)
    psychoanalytical study 1112
    synopses and analyses 1112, 1117
Sorge, Richard 228
Sorge spy ring 228
Sōseki see Natsume Sōseki
Sōsho (calligraphic script) 1242
Sōtatsu see Tawaraya Sōtatsu
Sōtatsu school of art
    style 1200
Sōtō sect of Zen Buddhism
    Dōgen and his teachings 472-474,
        480-481
    Kamakura and Muromachi periods
        484
    practices 493
    practised in a mountain farming
        hamlet 507
    Ryōkan 1010, 1154
    shikan-taza 478
    teachings of Yasutani-roshi 478
Sotoba Komachi (Kan'ami)
    translation 1181
Sound of the mountain (Kawabata
        Yasunari)
    literary analysis 1127
    translation 1066
Sound of waves (Mishima Yukio)
    translation 1078
Sound systems
    of Japanese 405
Soups
    recipes 1429-1430, 1434, 1438-1440
Southeast Asia
    evolution of Japan's economic role
        and position in 264, 727, 817
    expansion of yakuza (gangster)
        operations into 569

Southeast Asia *continued*
  Japanese espionage 648
  Japanese investment 727, 952
  Japanese studies 1554, 1559
  relations with Japan (post-1945) 727,
    741-743, 749, 757, 762, 810, 897
  reparations agreements with 846
  trade and commerce with Japan
    (bibliography) 727
  see also Burma, Indonesia,
    Philippines, Thailand, Vietnam, and
    World War II (Pacific Theatre)
Soy sauce
  production and sale 201
Space
  attitudes and use of 1304
  city-dwellers' ways of using 1304, 1319
  evolving treatment of exterior and
    interior 1308
  in architecture 1300, 1302, 1304-1305,
    1308, 1323, 1326
  in gardens 1327, 1329, 1333
  Isozaki Arata's concept 1320
  Shinohara Kazuo's concept 1320
  spatial layout of *ryōkan* (inns) 96
  spatial layout of the Ise Shrine 1323
Space and missile industry 763
Spears
  used in the martial arts 1443
Speech
  government controls (1868-1945) 221
Speeches 1
  Fukuzawa Yukichi (collection of
    speeches) 194
  periodical containing 1540
  policy speech of Ōhira Masayoshi 339
Spencer, Herbert
  adoption of his educational ideas 972
Spencer Museum (Lawrence, Kansas)
  holdings of *surimono* woodblock
    prints 1263
Spirits 505
  exorcism of 506
  folk legends about 1184
  spirit possession in a healing-cult 592
  spiritual healing in Reiyūkai 509
  spiritual relationship between
    craftsmen and their tools 1343
  see also Demons, Ghosts, and
    Supernatural beings
Spoons
  photographs 1366
Sports 90

baseball 338, 1456
basic facts and figures (annual
  handbook) 14
centres (architecture) 1313, 1321, 1324
during World War II 207
encyclopaedic and almanac-type
  information about 1552, 1556, 1561
newspaper articles about 1546, 1549
sports comics 1480
sumo wrestling 519, 1278, 1453-1455
women in 578
see also Martial arts
Spring (Shimazaki Tōson)
  synopsis and analysis 1117
Spring snow (Mishima Yukio)
  literary analysis 1131
  translation 1077
St. Petersburg
  Treaty (1875) 664
Stage properties
  bunraku theatre 1391, 1411
  kabuki theatre 1398, 1400, 1407, 1564
  kyōgen 1402
  noh theatre 1175, 1181, 1405-1406,
    1408
Stamps (postage) *see* Philately
Star Festival (Tanabata) 501
The State 38
  intervention in the market-place 880
  labour and 202
  mass media and 221
  readings about 1
  religion and 460-461, 464, 517
  role in economic development
    (1868-1941) 218, 239
  separation of church and 196
  supply of energy and 850
Statistics 14
  capital formation (1868-1941) 233
  demographic 371
  economic growth (1868-1941) 225
  economic growth (1870s-1980) 803,
    808
  economy (1868-1970s) 110
  economy (annual survey) 820
  financial development (1868-1977) 855
  statistical yearbooks 819, 824-827
Statues
  at the Seattle Art Museum 1217
  at the Tōdaiji temple 1290
  depicting lay people 1292
  depicting religious personages 1292
  depicting the Shintō deity Hachiman
    1289

see also Sculpture
Steel
  industry 45, 217, 876, 879, 945, 989
  industry trade associations 899
  limitations on Japanese exports 892
  political economy of US-Japanese
    trade in 816
Stencil dyeing (katazome)
  illustrated study 1350
Stencil patterns (reproductions) 1344
Stencils
  depicting creatures of nature 1221
  katagami (used in stencil dyeing) 1344
Stereotypes held by the Japanese see
    Images held by the Japanese, and
    Images of Japan and the Japanese
Sterling payments agreements
  Australian-Japanese trade 745
Stirling, James
  negotiation of the Anglo-Japanese
    Convention (1854-55) 658
Stillfried, Raimund von
  photographs 1278
Stock exchanges 809, 851, 858, 862
  current news 1501
  handbook of companies listed on 822
  weekly transactions 1548
  see also Securities
Stone carvings 143, 502
Stone gardens
  Zen Buddhist dimensions 1196
Stone lanterns
  as antiques 1215
  used in gardens 1337, 1339
Stonemasonry
  Okinawan 1222
Stones
  suiseki 1362
  used in gardens 1331, 1334, 1337, 1339
Stoneware
  see Ceramics
Storehouses see Kura ('storehouses')
Stories, Short see Short stories
'Strategic industries'
  for the USA and Japan 873
Strategy
  British and Japanese navies (1936-41)
    698
  business and corporate 39, 842, 895,
    901, 915, 926, 935, 951
  during World War II 687-688, 692,
    701, 705-706, 709-712
  economic 718, 898

energy (politics of) 849
'go' as a game of 1458
guide to (Gorin no sho) 1447
industrial 934
management 822, 878, 882, 926, 940,
    945
multinational corporations 945, 948
overseas markets 939
shōgi as a game of 1459
strategic aid policy 757
strategic planning (concepts and
    fundamentals) 842
strategic thinking (1980s) 767
Stratigraphy
  geological periods 49
Strikes (labour)
  as an element of labour relations 921
  at the Noda Soy Sauce Company 241
  public employees' right to strike 609
Student movements 961, 963
  1945-57 276
  police ways of handling 565
  Shinjinkai (1920s) 244
  socialisation patterns 595, 969
  violence in 588
Students
  at university preparatory academies
    (1880s-1940s) 232
  bibliography 1610
  conflict among 538
  expansion of enrollments 974
  female 574
  novels about 1082, 1086-1087
  overseas (Meiji period) 197
  patterns of communication among 584
  political socialisation among 969
  rioting at universities (1960s) 972
  student protest (meaning to society) 2
  survivors of the atomic bombing of
    Hiroshima 259
Study abroad
  guidebook to studying in Japan 1550
Stupidity
  folk tales about 1187
Style
  historical and social determinants 1200
  realism in (art) 1205
Submarines
  encyclopaedic information about 1572
  World War II (Pacific Theatre) 681,
    688, 715-716
Subsidies
  price of rice 620

Sue mura *see* Suye mura (Kumamoto Prefecture)
Sugawara denju tenarai kagami (Takeda Izumo II et al.)
  literary anaysis 1174
  translations 1174, 1407
Sugawara no Michizane
  biographies 293, 300
  play about 1174
  poems and prose 300, 1010
Sugawara Takasue no musume
  Hamamatsu Chūnagon monogatari 1027
  life and times 1026-1027
  Sarashina nikki 1026
Sugita Genpaku 211
Suibokuga see Ink painting (*suibokuga*)
Suicide 566
  aetiology 588
  among Japanese Americans 394
  among women 568, 578
  among writers 568
  among young males 568
  as a factor influencing behaviour 592
  for the sake of one's honour 585
  Mishima Yukio's act of ritual 335, 1131
  patterns 568, 578
  plays about 1170
Suiei-jutsu (martial art) 1443
Suiseki (stones)
  illustrated study 1362
Sukeroku Yukari no Edo zakura (Tsuuchi Jihei II and Tsuuchi Hanemon)
  translations 1394, 1396
Sukiya style of architecture 1309-1310
Sūkyō Mahikari (New Religion)
  ethnographic account and sociological analysis 506
  see also New Religions
Sumidagawa (Kanze Motomasa)
  musical techniques involved in 1385
Sumi-e painting
  introduction and manual 1247, 1254
Sumitomo Shōji (*sōgō shōsha*)
  evolution, role, and organisation 914-915
Sumo (wrestling)
  introductory studies 1453-1454
  role of Shintō 519, 1453-1454
  wrestlers (*rikishi*) 1278, 1453-1455
Sun and steel (Mishima Yukio)

translation 1079
Sun Goddess *see* Amaterasu Ōmikami (sun goddess)
Suna no onna (Abe Kōbō)
  literary analysis 1127
  quest for identity in 1115
  translation 1043
Suō (province)
  imperial authority (Kamakura period) 147
Supernatural beings
  depicted in netsuke 1291
  encyclopaedic and almanac-type information about 1551
  kappa 1044, 1188
  myths, novels, and stories about 1044, 1186-1188
  shamanistic communication with 499
  see also Demons, Ghosts, and Spirits
Supernatural world
  folk beliefs in 1189
  in art and culture (exhibition catalogue) 1189
  Okinawan concepts 466
  tales about 1031
Superstitions 66, 114
  proverbs about 1183
Supreme Court
  noteworthy constitutional decisions 788, 790
Surgery
  development of Western (19th century) 353, 597
Surimono (woodblock prints)
  at the Chester Beatty Library, Dublin 1263
  at the Spencer Museum (catalogue) 1263
  introductory study 1263
  Katsushika Hokusai as a designer of 1260
Susanoo no Mikoto 516
Sushi 1433
  craftsmanship 1369
  guidebook 1432
  recipes for 1436, 1438-1439
  see also Food
Suye mura (Kumamoto Prefecture)
  community study 551
  women of 582
Suzuki Bunji
  leadership of the Yūaikai 215
Suzuki, Daisetz Teitaro

life and significance 316
philosophical writings 489-492, 521
reminiscences 316
Suzuki Cabinet (1945)
   activities 237
Suzuki Harunobu
   erotic prints (*shunga*) 1259
   ukiyo-e prints (exhibition catalogue)
      1261
Suzuki Heizaburō
   mayoral leadership 636
Suzuki Seijun
   film-making activities 1419
Suzuki Shinichi
   life and philosophy 326
Suzuki Shōsan 526
   writings 178
Suzuki violin teaching method 326
Swedes in Japan
   Thunberg, Carl Pieter 596
Swimming
   suiei-jutsu (martial art) 1443
Swords 1452
   basic characteristics 1441
   bibliography 1375
   depicted in exhibition catalogues 1219,
      1227, 1373
   glossaries of technical terms 1373,
      1375
   handbook 1375
   history 1211, 1373, 1375
   photographs 1211, 1219, 1227, 1373,
      1375
   sword guards (*tsuba*) 1215, 1221, 1227,
      1373, 1560
   used in the kabuki theatre 1352
Swordsmanship
   Gorin no sho (*Book of five rings*) 1447
   battō-jutsu (martial art) 1444
   iaidō (martial art) 1441, 1452
   kenjutsu (martial art) 1443
   Zen Buddhist dimensions 489, 492,
      1196
Swordsmen
   Miyamoto Musashi 1109, 1447
Swordsmiths
   biographical dictionary 369
   signatures (handbook) 1571
Syllabaries *see* Kana syllabaries
Syllables 405, 412
Symbolism
   encyclopaedic and almanac-type
      information about 1560

of classical literature 1566
of family crests 1191
of major films 1421
of traditional festivals 501
of weddings 560
Shintō 516, 1323
Symbols
   in the Japanese language 26
   on prints (bibliography) 1576
Syncretism
   in religious life 461
Synopses (literary) *see* Plot summaries
   (synopses)
Syntax 407
Synthetic fibre industry
   competition (Japanese, American, and
      European) 945
Syphilis
   Noguchi Hideyo's research on 343
Szilard, Leo
   role in creating the atomic bomb 263

T

Tabata Shinobu
   as a pacifist 288
Taboos
   associated with births, marriages, and
      deaths 500
   fishermen 503
   menstrual 503
   Okinawan religious 466
Tachibana Kōzaburō 206
Tachibana no Toshitsuna
   Sakuteiki 1338
Tachikui (Hyōgo Prefecture)
   Tamba ware 1286
Tada Chimako
   poetry 1151
Tadanori (Zeami Motokiyo)
   translation 1172
Tade kuu mushi (Tanizaki Junichirō)
   translation 1104
Taiheiki
   translation and study 1018
Taira family
   depicted in the *Heike monogatari* 1019
   rivalry with the Minamoto family 149,
      154
Taishō political crisis (1912-13) 224
Taiwan
   air battle (1944) off 688
   economic development (compared
      with Japan) 806

Taiwan *continued*
  Japanese colonial rule (1895-1945) 223
  see also China (Republic of China),
    and Foreign relations with China
    (Republic of China)
Taiyō to tetsu (Mishima Yukio)
  translation 1079
Takahashi Shinkichi
  ideas about poetry 1168
Takahashi Takako
  short stories 1071, 1098
Takahashi Yūichi
  painting 239, 1235
Takamura Kōtarō
  ideas about poetry 1168
  poetry 1158
Takasago (Zeami Motokiyo)
  translation 1172
Takashima (Okayama Prefecture)
  community studies 554
  extended family households 562
Takasugi Shinsaku
  political biography 171
Takatori ware (ceramics) 1281
Takayama (Gifu Prefecture)
  tourist guide 100
Takeda Izumo II
  Chūshingura 1180, 1395
  Sugawara denju tenarai kagami 1174,
    1407
Takeda Shingen
  biographical sketch 295
Takeda Taijun
  short stories 1057
Takemitsu Tōru
  vignette 24
Takenishi Hiroko
  short stories 1088
Taketori monogatari 1004
Takeyama Michio
  Biruma no tategoto 1097
Tale of flowering fortunes translation and
  study 1021
Tale of Genji (Murasaki Shikibu)
  iconography 1039, 1241
  introductory guides 1035, 1604
  literary analyses 1035, 1039-1040
  Motoori Norinaga's pioneering study
    309
  parallels with *Hamamatsu Chūnagon
    monogatari* 1027
  picture scroll 1200
  poetics 1040

  studies 150, 1002, 1008
  translations 1024
  'Ukifune' (literary analysis) 1039
Tale of Ise
  literary analyses 1004, 1008, 1148
  translation 1148
Tale of the Bamboo Cutter 1004
*Tale of the Hamamatsu Middle
  Counselor*
  translation 1027
Tale of the Heike
  literary analyses 1008, 1019
  translation 1019
Tale of the Lady Ochikubo
  translation 1033
Tale of the Soga Brothers
  translation 1012
Tales of moonlight and rain (Ueda
  Akinari)
  literary analysis 315
  translations 1031
Tales of the spring rain (Ueda Akinari)
  translation 1030
Tales of Yamato
  literary analysis and translation 1028
Tales *see* Folk tales
Tamba ware (ceramics) 1283
  illustrated study 1286
Tamenaga Shunsui
  biographical sketch 291
Tamura Ryūichi
  poetry 1057, 1141, 1143, 1151
Tanabata (Star Festival) 501
Tanabe Hajime
  philosophy 527
Tanaka Chikao
  plays 1173
Tanaka Giichi
  China policy (1927-29) 333
Tanaka Kakuei
  normalisation of relations with China
    620, 647, 652
  political leadership 636
Tanaka Memorial (1927)
  wrongly attributed to Tanaka Giichi
    333
Tanaka Michiko
  life as an immigrant in the USA 400
Tanaka Ōdō
  liberal thought and activities 336
Tanaka Shōzō
  biography 312
Tanforan Race Track (California)

World War II Japanese American
  internees 393
Tange Kenzō
  architectural work 1298, 1313
Tango no sekku (Boys' Festival) 501
Taniguchi (Yosa) Buson
  poetry 1137, 1165
  painting 1255
Tanikawa Shuntarō
  poetry 1141, 1143, 1151
Tanizaki Junichirō 1003
  concept of literature 1128
  essay on aesthetics 1225
  novels 1008, 1099-1104, 1127
  search for authenticity in literature
    1130
  short stories 1057, 1083, 1126
Tanka poetry
  Masaoka Shiki 1161
  survey 1162
  Saitō Mokichi 325
  translations 1013, 1135, 1140, 1142,
    1147, 1154, 1156-1157, 1160-1161
Tanno Setsu 290
Tanrokubon (illustrated
  woodblock-printed books) 1481
Tansu (wooden chests)
  as antiques 1215, 1340
  folk art 1210, 1213
  guide to evaluating and restoring 1340
  history 1341
  owned by the Tokugawa shōguns
    (exhibition catalogue) 1219
  photographs 1213, 1219, 1341-1342
Tantric paintings 1237
Tanuma Okitsugu
  biographical sketch 295
Taoism
  influence on the tea ceremony 1470
  introductory survey 460
  readings about 461
Tarawa Atoll
  battle (1943) 707, 715, 1609
Tatami (straw floor mats)
  as an element of interior design 1326
  craftsmanship 1369
Tatemae/honne
  analysis of the dyadic concept of 590
Tateyama City (Chiba Prefecture)
  child-rearing 559
Tattoos
  Ainu 375
  illustrated study 1372

Tawaraya Sōtatsu
  artworks and artistic environment
    1214, 1240
  screen paintings 1234
Taxation
  annual statistics 824
  corporate 884, 927
  foreign investors 862
  income 786, 788, 884
  land 42, 138, 183, 212
  patent and know-how licensing 774
  reform 823
  securities 858
  system 811, 863
  tax law 788, 1582
Tayama Katai
  Futon 1129
  short stories 1105
Tea 1433, 1438
  see also Drinks and drinking
Tea ceremony (chanoyu) 37, 77, 153,
    1200
  at the Daitokuji temple 1190
  comprehensive examination 1467
  encyclopaedic and almanac-type
    information about 1552-1553, 1556
  history 135, 1467, 1469, 1472
  influence of Shino and Oribe ceramics
    1282
  influence of Shintō 519
  influence of Zen Buddhism 492, 1196,
    1226
  introductory studies 1471-1472
  kaiseki cuisine 1437, 1471-1472
  Okakura Kakuzō's essays 1470
  philosophy 1470
  photographs 1467, 1471-1472, 1496
Tea ceremony utensils 1467, 1471-1472
  depicted in exhibition catalogues
    1218-1219, 1469
  illustrated introduction 1468
  Karatsu ware 1279
  Kizaemon tea-bowl 1228
  made of bamboo (photographs) 1357
  Oribe ware 1282
  periodical 1496
  Shigaraki ware 1280
  Shino ware 1282
  see also Photographs (tea ceremony
    utensils)
Tea kettles 1467-1469, 1471-1472
  as antiques 1215
  photographs 1366, 1468-1469

Tea masters 1470, 1472
  calligraphy 1249
  Sen no Rikyū 295, 1249, 1467
Teachers 970-971
  involvement in teachers' unions 967,
    975, 977
  novels about 1084-1085, 1095
  status, power, and preparation 960
  training, role, and practices 978
  women 574
Teaching guides 9, 36
  elementary Japanese 455
  English in Japan 979
  haiku poetry for Westerners 1162
  principles of the noh theatre (Zeami
    Motokiyo) 1413
  Tale of Genji 1604
  see also Instructional materials
Teahouses
  architecture (historical survey) 1314
  built in the *sukiya* style 1309-1310
  entertainment by geisha 576
  within garden landscapes 1334
Technical education
  promoted by the government 974
Technical Japanese
  textbook 437
Technical know-how
  protection of unpatented 773
Techniques
  architectural 1318
  artistic 1203-1204, 1569
  bonsai cultivation 1328, 1336
  bugaku mask carving 1294
  ceramics 107, 331, 1279-1280, 1282,
    1286-1287
  cloisonné production 1361
  creating *bonkei* (miniature landscapes)
    1330
  English-language teaching 979
  film-making 1414, 1421-1423, 1425
  furniture-making 1340-1342
  gagaku 1377
  gardening 1337, 1339
  glass-making 1359
  haniwa production 108
  inrō production 1360
  Jōmon pottery production 107
  lacquerwork 1370, 1374
  manufacturing 936
  martial arts 1441-1446, 1448-1452
  musical 1378-1379, 1384-1385
  netsuke carving 1291

newspaper production 1483
  origami 1364, 1367
  paper-making 1358, 1365
  photography 1278
  print-making 1256, 1266, 1270, 1273,
    1576
  sculpture 1293, 1295-1296
  stencil dyeing (*katazome*) 1350
  sumo wrestling 1453-1455
  tattooing 1372
  textile production 1345-1346, 1351,
    1353-1355
Technological change
  bibliographies 1581, 1594
  impact upon art 1200
  industrial rationalisation and 940
  nature and impact (1940s-1970s) 555
Technology
  agricultural 181, 200
  annual statistics 825, 829
  automobile 344, 347, 870-871, 924
  bibliography 1581
  communication 983
  contribution to post-1945 economic
    growth 332, 793, 811, 982, 993, 996
  corporate drive for technological
    leadership 836
  electronics 985, 988
  exchange agreements 763
  fishing 552
  'getting the best for the least' 990
  government report (annual) 829
  government support of high tech
    industries 814, 880-881, 905
  historical development (pre-1945)
    181, 187, 200, 218, 660
  imports 779, 807, 869, 993
  inadequate for preventing pollution
    957
  industrial 806, 869, 871-872, 875,
    877-879, 986
  information 981, 983
  Japan's growing technological
    pre-eminence 795, 817, 897,
    904-905, 983-984
  military 759, 763
  nuclear 848-849
  overview of research institutes and
    programmes 980
  periodicals 1494-1495, 1500, 1539,
    1541, 1544-1545
  prehistoric 109
  robotic 985-986, 995

steelmaking 989
technological innovation 344, 836,
  871, 875, 877, 880, 882, 983, 989
training Americans to read Japanese
  technological materials 991
transfer of industrial technology
  abroad 900, 944, 993
US-Japan relations in science and
  technology 897, 998
Western technology and the Japanese
  ethos 804
see also Research and development
Technopolises (hi-tech towns)
development strategy 996
Telecommunications
deregulation 953
industry 217, 813, 953
Nippon Telegraph and Telephone
  Public Corporation 612, 625, 892,
  953, 955
research and development 984
role of invention and innovation in 985
Television 1414
alleged dumping of TV sets 783
as a part of popular culture 26
broadcasting 1482, 1486
home drama 538
images of Japan on American 731
industry 945, 947
role in health education 603
Shōgun (TV mini-series) 1418
Teller, Edward
role in creating the atomic bomb 263
Temple of dawn (Mishima Yukio)
literary analysis 1131
translation 1077
Temple of the golden pavilion (Mishima
  Yukio)
literary analysis 1131
quest for identity in 1115
translation 1080
Temples 90, 114
architecture 143, 1314, 1322
Asukadera 1322
Byōdōin 1192, 1322
Chūsonji 1192, 1322
Daigoji 1322
Daitokuji 1190, 1239, 1331-1332
encyclopaedic and almanac-type
  information about 1556, 1560-1561,
  1568
Enpukuji 486
Entsuji 1327

esoteric Buddhist (Mikkyō) 1216
folk legends about 1184
Ginkakuji 1327, 1335
guidebooks 76, 97
Hōryūji 1208, 1322
Kawaradera 1322
Kinkakuji 1080, 1327, 1335
Kōfukuji 1316
loss of economic and political power
  (16th century) 145
Murōji 1277, 1322
Myōshinji 1332
of Kamakura 76, 131, 463
of Kyōto 77, 89, 92, 131, 463
of Nara 93, 1316
of the Tōhoku region 66
Ryōanji 1327, 1332, 1335
Saihōji 1327, 1331
Shōdenji 1327
Shōkokuji 1239
Tōdaiji 147, 1194, 1206, 1289-1290,
  1316
Tōji 1289
Tōshōdaiji 1322
Yakushiji 1289-1290, 1316, 1322
see also Photographs (temples)
Tempō Uprising (1837)
led by Ōshio Heihachirō 289, 293
Tempyō no iroka (Inoue Yasushi)
translation 1061
Ten Rhijne, Willem
as a cultural intermediary 596
Tenant farmers 205
landlord-tenant relations 181, 242
novella about 1068
origins of tenant unrest 241
tenant unions (1920s) 175
tenancy system 268
Tendai Buddhism 475, 484-485
healing priests 499
Ōjōyōshū of Genshin 470
terminology (dictionary) 415
Tengu Insurrection (1864) 175
Tenkō (ideological conversion) 595
Tenmu Tennō
biographical sketch 295
Tennin gosui (Mishima Yukio)
literary analysis 1131
translation 1077
Tenrikyō (New Religion) 513
see also New Religions
Tense 434
in colloquial Japanese 410

Tensho (calligraphic script) 1242
Tenshō-Kōtai-Jingūkyō (New Religion)
513
see also New Religions
Tephra 40
Terakoya schools 164
Terayama Shūji
films and film-making activities 1423
Terms (linguistic) *see* Glossaries
Teshigahara Hiroshi
film-making activities 1423
films 1421, 1423
Texas Instruments, Inc.
business operations in Japan 889
Textbooks
controversies over their contents 613,
961
government not obliged to provide
free 788
high school 975
portrayal of China 647
portrayal of World War II 737
Textiles 1220
at the Shōsōin 1194
at the Tokyo National Museum 1473
biographical dictionary of artists 369
depicted in exhibition catalogues 1218,
1227
design motifs 1204, 1344-1345, 1347
dispute over exports to the USA
721-722
factory workers 205, 240, 595
folk art 1193, 1210, 1213
history 1211
industry 45, 217, 794, 876
influence on lacquerwork and design
1374
kosode fabrics 1351, 1353
Okinawan 1201, 1222, 1347
photographs 1345-1347, 1349, 1351
shibori 1355
stencil dyeing (*katazome*) 1350
tsujigahana 1346
tsutsugaki fabrics 1345
Yūsoku textile patterns 1207
see also Clothing, Costume,
Costumes, Dyes and dyeing
Thailand
economic development (compared
with Japan) 806
modernisation (compared with Japan)
818
relations with Japan 283, 741, 897

see also Southeast Asia
Theatre 37
architecture (historical survey) 1314
history 1403
introductory study 1393
prints on theatrical themes
(bibliography) 1576
see also Bunraku theatre, Kabuki,
Kyōgen, Noh, Performances, and
Shingeki ('new theatre')
Theory Z (management theory) 932
Therapy *see* Psychotherapy
Thin snow (Tanizaki Junichirō)
literary analyses 1002, 1127
translation 1101
Thirty-six Views of Mount Fuji
(Katsushika Hokusai)
print series (reproductions) 1265
Thought
cultural assumptions of Japanese
modes of 439
thought control (1920s-1940s) 221
Thousand cranes (Kawabata Yasunari)
translation 1067
Thrift
proverbs about 1183
Thunberg, Carl Pieter
as a cultural intermediary 596
Tiao-Yü-T'ai *see* Senkaku Islands
Tientsin crisis (1939) 697
Tiles (roof) 1222
Time
attitude towards 530
Tinian
battle (1944) 699
Toba (Emperor) 142
Tobacco
encyclopaedic and almanac-type
information about 1551, 1561
Tochigi Prefecture
Ashio Copper Mine 312, 957
Mashiko 331
Nikkō 48, 66, 1315
Shinohata 550
Yanaka 312
see also Kantō region
Toda Jōsei 512
Tōdaiji (temple)
architecture and sculpture 1289-1290,
1316
Buddhist art treasures (exhibition
catalogue) 1206
fiscal fortunes (Kamakura period) 147

Shōsōin 1194
Tōdaiji school of sculpture 1290
Tofu 1433, 1438-1439
 see also Food
Tōgaku style of court music
 comprehensive study 1379
Tōgō Heihachirō 210, 678
 biography 320
Toguri, Iva
 biography 387
Tōhoku region
 crafts 74
 geography 50
 minka (traditional-style houses) 1301,
 1303
 tourist guide 74
 traveller's account 66
Tōji (temple)
 statue of Hachiman 1289
Tōjō Cabinet (1941-44)
 establishment and activities 237
Tōjō Hideki
 biography 321
 during World War II 237
Tōkai region
 geography 50
Tōkaidō highway
 brief articles about 1551
 depicted in literary works 184, 1016
 depicted in ukiyo-e prints 1265
 travellers' accounts (Meiji period) 68,
 114
Tōkaidōchū Hizakurige (Jippensha
 Ikku)
 translation 1016
Tokonoma (alcoves)
 element of interior design 1326
Tokoname ware (ceramics) 1281, 1283,
 1286
Tokugawa Art Museum
 collection of art 1219
 collection of noh robes and masks
 1412
Tokugawa bakufu see Bakufu
 (shogunate): Tokugawa
'Tokugawa house'
 structure and organisation 185
 support of the noh theatre 1412
Tokugawa Ienobu
 advised by Arai Hakuseki 177, 298
Tokugawa Ietsugu
 advised by Arai Hakuseki 177, 298
Tokugawa Ieyasu

biography 314
buried at the Tōshōgu Shrine (Nikkō)
 1315
political legitimacy 139
Tokugawa Nariaki
 biography 289
Tokugawa Tsunayoshi
 biography 289
Tokushi yoron (Arai Hakuseki)
 translation 298
Tokutomi Sohō
 life and thought 311
Tokyo 22, 26, 70
 antique shops and dealers (directories)
 1215, 1340
 architecture of Tange Kenzō 1313
 as a literary centre (Tokugawa period)
 1005
 as a world financial centre 853,
 861-862
 atlas 56, 75
 compared with London 10
 cultural activities (monthly guide)
 1510
 depicted in literature 345, 1038, 1087,
 1116, 1140
 depicted in woodblock prints 236,
 1256, 1262, 1265
 die-casting factory employees 918
 Doolittle air raid (1942) 696, 699
 Edo Castle 185, 1307, 1317
 Edo during the Tokugawa period 165
 family life 549, 563-564
 family patterns and juvenile
 delinquency 571
 family planning 370
 fashion world 1348
 fire-bombing (World War II) 691
 'garbage war' 957
 growth and development 546
 Hibiya riot (1905) 175, 672
 history (1850s-1880s) 162, 212
 history (1867-1923) 236
 hospital and medical school (1860s)
 353
 hospital practice of Morita
 psychotherapy 601
 housewives 577
 Imperial Hotel 1320
 land markets and policy 42
 libraries (directory) 1474
 library holdings (English-language
 books about Japan) 1589

Tokyo *continued*
life during the early 1890s 355
literary life (Meiji period) 1105
major religious sites 463
mayoral leadership 636
metropolitan government 625
migration and migrants 557
neighbourhood life 549
photographs 22, 25, 28, 95, 236, 1256, 1275
police operations 565, 570
politics and social change 628
population distribution and movement 40
print-making in Edo and Ōsaka (comparison) 1264
restaurants 84, 87
Sanya flophouse district 34
Tokyo Stock Exchange 858, 1548
Tomoe Gakuen (elementary school) 330
tourist guides and guidebooks 56, 75, 86, 91, 99-100
travellers' accounts (1860s-1870s) 66, 68, 114
Tsukiji fish market 1432
ways of choosing marriage partners 558
William Elliot Griffis' teaching experiences 358
Yasukuni Shrine 515
see also Kantō region
Tokyo Bay
bridge construction 640
Tokyo Electric Power Company
role in shaping coal and LNG policies 849
Tōkyō monogatari (film script)
translation 1057
Tokyo National Museum
illustrated introduction 1473
Tōkyō Nichi Nichi Shimbun (newspaper)
history (Meiji period) 305
Tokyo Prefecture
Fuchū 565, 628
Musashino 628
see also Kantō region
'Tokyo Rose' 387
Tōkyō Shimbun (newspaper)
articles and editorials (translations and synopses) 1547
Tokyo University
novel about student life 244

organisation and decision-making 39
student movement (1920s) 244
Tokyo war crimes trial (1946-48) 271
accounts of the proceedings 265
British involvement 266
Hirota Kōki 346
redirecting the Japanese towards peace 595
Tōjō Hideki 321
Toleration (religious)
influence of the British 660
Toleration of deviant behaviour
as a factor in crime control 566
Tomb sculpture *see* Haniwa
Tombs
Kofun (Tumulus) period 105-106, 109
Tomimoto Kenkichi
painted porcelains 1285
Tomioka Taeko
poetry 1143
short stories 1071, 1098
Tomodachi (Abe Kōbō)
translation 1057
Tone River area (Chiba Prefecture)
Jōmon culture 109
Tonkō (Inoue Yasushi)
translation 1061
Tōno (Iwate Prefecture)
village legends 1188
Tools
bookbinding 1479
creating *bonkei* (miniature landscapes) 1330
cultivating bonsai 1328
furniture-restoring 1340
machine tools industry 38, 872, 899
netsuke-carving 1291
paper-making 1358
pottery production 1287
stencil dyeing (*katazome*) 1350
woodworking 1343
Topography
maps 54
Toray Industries
evaluation of applied research by 987
Torii Kiyomasu I
primitive ukiyo-e prints 1268
Torii Kiyomasu II
primitive ukiyo-e prints 1268
Tosa *han*
historical case studies 168
Tosa nikki (Ki no Tsurayuki)
translations 1149, 1153

Tosa school of art
  influence on styles of book illustration
    1477
Tōsan region
  geography 50
Toshiba Corporation
  investment decision-making 951
Tōshōdaiji (temple)
  architecture 1322
Tōshōgu Shrine (Nikkō)
  architectural history 1315
Tōson see Shimazaki Tōson
Tourist guides 69, 90, 1573
  antiques 1215
  architecture 81
  birds 65
  gardens 98, 1331
  hot springs (onsen) 80, 1457
  kabuki theatre 1401
  Kamakura 76
  Kyōto 77-78, 89, 92, 98, 100
  museums of art and archaeology 1475
  nationwide ('all-Japan') 79, 82-83, 86,
    94, 100
  one-day excursions 86, 91, 94
  phrase books 416, 446, 453
  restaurants 78, 84, 87, 97
  Tōhoku region 74
  Tokyo 56, 75, 86, 91, 99-100
  world of saké 1431
  Zen Buddhist meditation 97
  see also Guidebooks
Tourists
  language textbooks designed for 436,
    439, 446, 453
Town halls
  architecture (post-1945) 1299, 1313,
    1324
Town planning
  architecture (1950s-1960s) 1324
Tōyō Keizai Shinpō (magazine)
  Ishibashi Tanzan's editorship 336
Tōyō Menka (sōgō shōsha)
  evolution, role, and organisation 914
Toyoda Eiji
  autobiography 347
Toyota Motor Corporation
  assembly line working conditions 924
  employee career development
    activities 919
  history 347, 547, 871
  inventory management system 934,
    936

joint venture with General Motors 912
  labour-management relations 547,
    871, 924
  production system 934-935
  quality control 871, 919
  strategic management practices 926
  technology and management 871
Toyotomi Hideyoshi
  biography 299
  efforts to attain legitimacy 135
  policies 139
  relationship with the daimyō 146
  secret service under 648
Toys
  aesthetic qualities (photographs) 1198
  depicted in netsuke 1291
  design (photographs) 1224
  Okinawan 1222
  robots 995
Trade and commerce 50
  accelerated growth (1550-1650) 139
  annual statistics 819, 825-827
  basic facts and figures (annual
    handbook) 14
  bibliographies 1594, 1600, 1614
  cotton (Tokugawa period) 170
  historical development 43
  long-term statistical data 808
  medieval 136, 140
  regulated by the daimyō 139
  role of the Diet (parliament) 626
  urban 40
  see also Marketing
Trade and commerce (foreign) 6, 14,
    806, 823
  1870s-1980 803, 818
  annual statistics 819, 824-828
  Arai Ryōichirō's developmental role
    297
  bibliographies 1581, 1590, 1594, 1614
  'coming shape of global competition'
    902
  foreign trade control law (reform) 909
  government reports (annual) 828-829
  impact of the Vietnam War 727
  impact on economic growth
    (1900s-1960s) 807
  involvement of trade associations 899
  Meiji period 218, 250, 297
  MITI's role 39, 272
  newspaper reporting about 1546-1549
  periodicals 1500-1501, 1524, 1540,
    1544

Trade and commerce (foreign) *continued*
private economic diplomacy 887
recovery and growth (post-1945) 264,
791-792, 805, 811, 814
Tokugawa period 167, 177, 179, 298,
349, 677
trade associations (comparison of
Japan and the USA) 899
trade barriers and restrictions 745,
832, 886, 890, 905
trade competitiveness 843
trade conflict 844, 867
trade conflict (over food imports)
832-833
trade conflict (with Europe) 720, 755
trade conflict (with the USA) 721-722,
725, 733, 740, 750, 753, 783, 798,
875, 886, 890, 892, 903, 907
trade liberalisation (politics) 732
trade policy 623, 817, 896-897, 907
see also Business (ways of doing
business in Japan: practical
information), Exports, Imports, and
Sōgō shōsha (general trading
companies)
Trade and commerce with Australia 723,
745, 751, 833, 885
Trade and commerce with Brazil 898
Trade and commerce with Canada 655,
734, 895
Trade and commerce with China
(People's Republic of China) 738,
885
Trade and commerce with Europe
post-1945 trade 720, 906
trade imbalance and its perceptions
910
Trade and commerce with Great Britain
19th century 349, 658, 660
Trade and commerce with Korea
(Republic of Korea) 719
Trade and commerce with Southeast
Asia
bibliography 727
Trade and commerce with the Middle
East 758, 885
Trade and commerce with the United
States 297, 332, 718, 897
1970s 816
1980s 724, 732-733, 767, 837, 886, 904
agricultural imports 888
American companies in Japan 889,
894

automobile exports 344, 874, 892
beef imports 833
bibliographies 1575, 1581, 1590, 1600,
1614
dynamics of US-Japanese business
negotiations 911
evolution (1960s-1980s) 890
history (bibliography) 1575
industrial policy and trade competition
908
legal aspects 783
problematic areas 905
problems in trade negotiations
(case-studies) 896
trade imbalance (1980s) 837, 875, 884,
886
see also Trade and commerce (foreign:
trade conflict)
Trade and commerce with the USSR
747, 752, 885, 900
Trade secrets
legal protection 773-774
Trade unions *see* Labour unions
Trademark Law 773
Trading companies *see Sōgō shōsha*
(general trading companies)
Tradition
composing poetry on the verge of
death 1138
encyclopaedic and almanac-type
information about 1551-1553,
1556-1557, 1561, 1568
folk traditions in art 1193
formation of a scientific research 157
geisha as 'curators of tradition and art'
576
sources of 33
Training
bank employees 543, 809
bunraku artists and craftsmen 1391
electrical engineering industry workers
920
employees 923, 928
foreign service officers 729
geisha 576
kamikaze pilots 700
karate 1446, 1448
manual workers 925
martial arts 1443-1446
multinational corporation employees
941-942
netsuke carvers 1291
ninja ('secret agents') 1445

noh actors 1405, 1408, 1413
policemen 565
scientists (Meiji period) 157
Self-Defence Forces 759, 761
sumo wrestlers 1453-1455
sushi chefs 1432
teachers 960, 978
Trains *see* Railways
Translation
  machine 955, 991
  problems and experience of translating
    literature 1003
  techniques of translating poetry 1166
Translations
  anti-Christian tracts 166
  appearing in periodicals 1492,
    1499-1500, 1505, 1507, 1513, 1518,
    1521, 1531, 1534, 1541
  autobiographies 18, 298, 302, 310,
    327, 330, 339, 341, 347
  bibliographies listing 1521, 1588, 1597
  biographies 317, 340, 346
  botanical guide to azaleas 59
  case-histories of companies 845, 882
  Commission on the Constitution's
    report 789
  Constitutions (texts) 112, 189, 605,
    617, 625, 784, 787
  diaries 18, 209, 307, 924, 1000, 1013,
    1023, 1149, 1153
  epic songs (Ainu) 380
  essays 2, 290, 1025, 1034, 1079, 1428
  film scripts 1057
  folk tales 1, 1185, 1187-1188
  gesaku fiction 1038
  government economic reports 820
  guides to bonsai 1328, 1336
  historical documents 18, 148
  histories of Japan 130, 144, 152-154,
    160
  histories of literature 999, 1006
  kōwaka ballad-dramas 1169
  laws (texts) 605, 764, 781
  letters and correspondence 299, 451
  magazine articles 18, 1547
  Meiroku zasshi 196
  memoirs 1, 234, 282, 290, 583, 668,
    688, 691, 700, 708, 1023, 1026
  Mori Ōgai's literary translations into
    Japanese 1110
  National Defence Programme Outline
    (1985) 764
  newspaper articles and editorials 1, 18,

    1546-1547
  novels 1, 18, 345, 1016, 1041-1044,
    1046-1047, 1049-1050, 1052-1055,
    1058, 1061-1068, 1072-1073,
    1075-1078, 1080, 1082, 1084-1087,
    1089-1097, 1099-1104, 1107, 1109,
    1116, 1124, 1140
  painting manual 1241
  periodical articles on economic topics
    1500
  philosophical writings 521, 524-525,
    529
  plays 1000, 1492
  plays (bunraku) 1170, 1174, 1176,
    1180
  plays (*dengaku noh*) 1409
  plays (kabuki) 1170, 1174, 1394, 1396,
    1407
  plays (*kyōgen*) 1402
  plays (modern) 1057, 1171, 1173,
    1177-1179, 1182
  plays (noh) 1172, 1175-1177, 1406
  poetry 18, 1000, 1134, 1156
  poetry (Chinese-language) 488, 1000,
    1010, 1138-1139, 1152, 1154
  poetry (classical) 152, 300-301, 1013,
    1023, 1028, 1135, 1137-1138, 1142,
    1146-1150, 1152-1155, 1163-1167
  poetry (collections of multiple
    authorship) 1134, 1137-1138, 1141,
    1143, 1145, 1151-1153, 1156-1157,
    1159
  poetry (modern) 2, 325, 1057, 1136,
    1140-1141, 1143-1145, 1151,
    1157-1161
  prose written in Chinese 1010,
    1153-1154
  proverbs and sayings 1183
  readings about culture 1, 2, 18, 33
  readings about history 18, 33, 119-120
  readings about politics 611
  readings about religion and philosophy
    33
  readings (high school-level) 18
  readings (undergraduate-level) 1, 33
  records of the 1941 policy conferences
    693
  religious texts 472-473, 476-479, 482,
    488, 1499
  report on national security (official
    summary) 760
  Requiem for battleship Yamato
    (prose-poem) 716

Translations *continued*
  short stories 1-2, 345, 1000, 1011,
    1014-1015, 1036, 1045, 1048, 1051,
    1056-1057, 1059-1060, 1069-1071,
    1074, 1081, 1083, 1088, 1098, 1103,
    1105-1108, 1111, 1116, 1125, 1513,
    1521
  songs (texts) 1378, 1381, 1386
  speeches 1, 194, 339
  studies of architecture 1302-1303,
    1306-1310, 1312, 1314-1316, 1318,
    1322, 1324-1326, 1505
  studies of art 104, 1192, 1194-1195,
    1199-1202, 1207-1208, 1210-1211,
    1216, 1222
  studies of economic growth 225, 799,
    803, 805, 815
  studies of finance and banking 865-866
  studies of gardens and gardening 1329,
    1332-1334, 1338-1339
  studies of *haniwa* 108
  studies of Hiroshima and Nagasaki
    (atomic bombing) 253, 258-259, 583
  studies of international relations 668,
    708
  studies of labour relations 924-925
  studies of lacquerwork 1370, 1374
  studies of language 405, 409, 411
  studies of law 772, 778, 1531
  studies of music 1377, 1387
  studies of painting 1235-1240,
    1243-1245, 1252-1255
  studies of politics 615, 618
  studies of pottery and ceramics
    1281-1282, 1284-1285
  studies of psychology 589-590
  studies of sculpture 1290, 1292-1294
  studies of society 531-534, 546, 567
  studies of technology 988, 990, 1541
  studies of textiles 1346, 1351
  studies of the economy 1518
  studies of the theatre 1392, 1400,
    1402, 1408
  studies of World War II (Pacific
    Theatre) 688, 693, 700, 708, 716
  study of calligraphy 1242
  study of furniture 1342
  study of industrial policy 876
  study of modern political leadership
    296
  study of national identity 4
  study of old maps 55
  study of religion 467
  study of swords 1373
  study of woodblock prints 1272
  study of Zen monastic practices 486
  Supreme Court decisions 788, 790
  tales 1012, 1017-1022, 1024,
    1027-1033
  treatises on the art of noh drama
    (Zeami Motokiyo) 1413
  works about ikebana (flower
    arrangement) 1463-1464
  works about origami 1364
  works about the martial arts 1446,
    1451
  works about the tea ceremony
    1468-1469, 1471
  writings of Fukuzawa Yukichi 194
  writings of Honda Toshiaki 173
Transportation 50
  annual statistics 825-827, 829
  basic facts and figures (annual
    handbook) 14
  companies 949
  government report (annual) 829
  Japanese National Railways 542, 612,
    625
  jinrikisha 68
  law (bibliography) 1582
  maps of routes 53-54, 56, 82
  ocean shipping 88, 250
  railways 666, 780, 954
  signs 88
  train schedules 83
Travel
  encyclopaedic and almanac-type
    information about 1552-1553, 1557
  poetry about 1153
  stories about 1014, 1016
Travel information *see* Guidebooks, and
  Tourist guides
Travellers' accounts 66-73, 114, 133,
  153, 269, 349, 667, 673
Treaties
  Ansei commercial treaties (1858) 658,
    675
  China-Japan Peace and Friendship
    Treaty (1978) 730
  Harris Treaty (1858) 676
  London Naval Treaty (1930) 685
  San Francisco Peace Treaty (1951)
    266, 274, 282-283, 285, 745
  Treaty of Kanagawa (1854) 667, 673
  Treaty of Portsmouth (1905) 659, 672,
    678

Treaty of Shimonoseki (1895) 645, 668
Treaty of St. Petersburg (1875) 664
US-Japan Security Treaty (1951)
    282-283, 324, 770, 1613
US-Japan Security Treaty (1960) 112,
    627, 721, 744, 761, 766, 770, 846
Treaty ports
    British pressure for opening 660
    life 68, 162, 190, 353
Trees
    bonsai 1328, 1330, 1336, 1362
    depicted as art objects (photographs)
    17
    design motif of family crests and
        textile patterns 1191, 1344
    encyclopaedic and almanac-type
        information about 1551, 1557, 1561
    folk tales about 1185
    flowering cherry trees of Washington,
        DC 663
    Katsushika Hokusai's sketches
        (reproductions) 1258
    sumi-e techniques for painting 1254
Trials 772
    Kōtoku Shūsui (1910-11) 337, 1122
    Matsukawa case (1949-70) 780
    settlement by conciliation in civil 778
    war crimes trials (1946-48) 265-266,
        271, 321, 346, 595
'Triple Intervention' of France,
    Germany, and Russia (1895) 668
Trudeau, Pierre Elliot
    Canadian-Japanese relations under
    655
Tsuba (sword guards) see Swords (sword
    guards)
Tsubouchi Shōyō
    friendship with Futabei Shimei 1124
    realism in his fiction 1123
    search for authenticity in literature
    1130
Tsuchigumo (Kawatake Mokuami)
    translation 1394
Tsuchiura (Ibaraki Prefecture)
    daily life (1900s-1930s) 234
Tsugaru (Dazai Osamu)
    translations 1116
Tsugaru Peninsula (Aomori Prefecture)
    depicted in Dazai Osamu's novel 1116
Tsujigahana (textiles)
    illustrated study 1346
Tsuki ni hoeru (Hagiwara Sakutarō)
    translation 1136

Tsukiji fish market (Tokyo)
    operations 1432
Tsukioka Yoshitoshi
    artworks (supernatural theme) 1189
Tsukuba (Ibaraki Prefecture)
    development as a 'science city' 980
Tsukuri monogatari ('courtly romances')
    Hamamatsu Chūnagon monogatari
    1027
    Ochikubo monogatari 1033
    Taketori monogatari 1004
    Tsutsumi Chūnagon monogatari 1011
    see also Tale of Genji
Tsumura Setsuko
    short stories 1098
Tsurezuregusa (Yoshida Kenkō)
    aesthetics 1004
    translation 1034
Tsushima
    naval battle (1905) 210, 320, 678
Tsushima Current 47
Tsushima Yūko
    short stories 1098
Tsutsugaki (textiles)
    illustrated study 1345
Tsutsumi Chūnagon monogatori
    translation 1011
Tumuli see Tombs
Tun-huang (Inoue Yasushi)
    translation 1061
Turtles 63
'Twenty-One Demands' on China (1915)
    652, 666
Typhoons 3, 41
Tyumen oil development project
    (Siberia)
    Japanese involvement 748

U

Uchimura Kanzō
    as a pacifist 288
Ude kurabe (Nagai Kafū)
    translation (excerpts) 345
Ueda Akinari 1005
    Harusame monogatari 1030
    life and writings 315, 1030-1031
    Ugetsu monogatari 1031
Uemura Masahisa
    writings and activities 235
Ueshiba Morihei
    biographical sketch 1450
Ugaki Kazushige
    intellectual biography 650

Ugetsu monogatari (Ueda Akinari)
  literary analysis 315
  translations 1031
Uji (Kyōto Prefecture) 69
  Byōdōin temple 1192, 1322
  tourist guide 100
Uji shūi monogatari
  literary analysis 1022
  translations 1022, 1029
Ukigumo (Futabatei Shimei)
  ideal of individualism in 1129
  study and translation 1124
Ukiyoburo (Shikitei Sanba)
  translation (excerpts) 1038
Ukiyo-e paintings
  exhibition catalogue 1250
  history 1212, 1267
  Kitagawa Utamaro 1262
Ukiyo-e prints 19, 1036, 1270
  Andō Hiroshige 1256-1257, 1265
  bibliographies 1271, 1576
  history 1212, 1266-1267, 1271-1272
  influence on tattoos 1372
  Katsushika Hokusai 1256, 1260, 1265
  Kitagawa Utamaro 1262
  Ōsaka prints 1264
  primitive (Michener Collection) 1268
  shunga (erotic prints) 1259, 1478
  Suzuki Harunobu 1261
  Yokohama prints 1269, 1576
  see also Woodblock prints, and
    Woodblock prints (reproductions)
Ukiyo-e school of art
  influence on styles of book illustration
    1477
Ukiyo-zōshi (popular fiction of the
  1680s-1770s) 1036
Ultranationalism
  Confucianism propagated by
    ultranationalists 528
  Mishima Yukio's ultranationalistic
    orientation 292, 335
  theory and psychology (1930s-1940s)
    618
  Tokutomi Sohō's support 311
  ultranationalistic associations 245, 346
Umbrellas
  craftsmanship 1369
'Umikibe no kōkei' (Yasuoka Shōtarō)
  translation 1107
Union of Soviet Socialist Republics
  espionage undertaken for (Sorge spy
    ring) 228

ideological views of Japan 747
Kurile Islands (under Soviet
  occupation since 1945) 285-286, 752
Nomonhan Incident (1939) 684
Siberia and Japan 747-748, 752, 847
ties with the Japan Communist Party
  635, 752
trade with Japan 747, 752, 885, 900
see also Foreign relations with
  Russia/USSR
Unions *see* Labour unions
Uniqueness
  myth of Japanese 587
United Kingdom *see* Great Britain
United Nations
  Japan's changing role 732
  Japan's voting behaviour 611
United Nations Conference on the Law
  of the Sea
  Japan's participation 717
United States
  agriculture and agricultural policy
    (compared with Japan) 888
  Aleutian Islands (Japanese military
    occupation during World War II)
    687-688
  American companies in Japan 889,
    928
  anti-Japanese legislation
    (1900s-1920s) 384, 392, 402, 659
  blue-collar workers (compared with
    Japan) 919
  burakumin in 373
  business policy-making (compared
    with Japan) 801
  competition with Japan for supremacy
    in information technology 981
  Congress and the Diet (comparative
    study) 626
  co-operation and conflict over energy
    with Japan 847
  courtship and marriage (compared
    with Japan) 558
  dynamics of US-Japanese business
    negotiations 911
  economic and trade frictions with
    Japan 721-722, 725, 733, 750, 753,
    833, 847
  education (compared with Japan) 965
  expansion of *yakuza* (gangster)
    operations into 569
  farming (compared with Japan) 834
  financial development (compared with

862

Japan) 855
flowering cherry trees of Washington,
DC 663
government organisations concerned
with Japan 1562, 1565, 1570
images of Japan and the Japanese 216,
361, 643, 649, 651, 686, 690, 721,
731, 753, 965
industrial policy (compared with
Japan) 884
inflation (compared with Japan) 859
interpersonal communication
(compared with Japan) 584
Ito Michio (artistic career in the USA)
322
Japan-related archival and manuscript
sources (guidebook) 1562
Japan-related information resources
(directory) 1565
Japan-related resources in
Washington, DC (guidebook) 1562
Japan-US savings-rate gap 809
Japanese art in American collections
1213-1214, 1217, 1221, 1231, 1233,
1248-1250, 1256-1257, 1263-1264,
1268
Japanese business communities 12
Japanese cultural and economic
influence 12
Japanese espionage 648
Japanese images of Americans 649,
651, 667, 686, 721, 753
Japanese investment 801, 951
Japanese managers of multinational
corporations in 942
Japanese migration 384-385, 389, 392,
396-397, 402, 659, 662
Japanese participation in American
fairs 651
Japanese studies 359-360, 1509, 1525,
1554, 1559, 1562, 1565
Japanese travellers' views 651, 667
Japanese visitors 302, 307, 328, 337,
651, 667
loss of economic and technological
pre-eminence to Japan 813, 853,
904
macroeconomic interdependence with
Japan 903
military bases in Japan (constitutional
status) 790
military occupation and return of
Okinawa 280, 285, 721, 727, 754

Noguchi Hideyo (medical career in the
USA) 343
patent and know-how licensing
(compared with Japan) 774
Perry expedition to Japan (1853-1854)
673
policy towards Japan (1890-1941) 653
policy towards Japan (1930s) 354
policy towards Japan (1945-52) 264,
267-268, 270, 279-281, 354
policy towards Japan (1960s) 354
pressure on Japan to rearm 764, 766
relevance of Japan's high-tech
industrial policy for 881
responses to Western-style Japanese
painting 1251
science and technology (compared
with Japan) 984
semiconductor industry (compared
with Japan) 880
steelmaking (compared with Japan)
989
'strategic industries' for Japan and 873
Sugimoto, Etsu Inagaki (adulthood in
the USA) 313
Theodore Roosevelt's mediation in
the Portsmouth Peace Conference
659
US-Japan mutual security ties 750
visit by the first Japanese embassy
(1860s) 667
see also Allied occupation of Japan
(1945-52), Americans in Japan,
Foreign relations with the United
States, Japanese Americans, Pearl
Harbor (1941 attack on), Trade and
commerce with the United States,
and World War II (Pacific Theatre)
United States-Japan Exchange of
Technology Agreement (1983)
text 763
United States-Japan Security Treaty
(1951) 282-283, 324, 1613
influence on Japan's defence policy
770
United States-Japan Security Treaty of
1960 766
attainment of military security under
846
crisis surrounding its revision 744, 754,
969, 1485
influence on Japan's defence policy 770
text 112, 627, 721, 761

Universities
  architecture (1950s-1960s) 1324
  changing styles of university life 961
  comprehensive guidebook 1550
  English-language instruction 979
  foreign universities with Japanese
    studies programmes (directories)
    1554, 1559, 1565
  historical development (1870s-1960s)
    972
  Hitotsubashi University 304
  intellectuals and 972
  International Christian University
    (bibliography of library holdings)
    1589
  Keio University 302
  Kyōto Imperial University 318
  libraries 1474, 1476, 1589
  organisation and administration 963
  Tokyo University 39, 244
  see also Higher education
University preparatory academies 232
Unkei
  Kamakura period sculpture 1293
Unkoku school of painting 1253
Uno Chiyo
  short stories 1048, 1071
Uragami Gyokudō
  fan-shaped paintings 1233
  life and artistic accomplishments 1230
Uranium
  imports from Canada 734
Urban development 533
  architectural approaches 1320
Urban history see History (urban)
Urban life
  compared with rural life 562
Urban society
  group centred, vertical orientation 539
Urbanisation
  20th century 40, 371, 532, 811
  Kanazawa (1583-1700) 174
  Kariya, Aichi Prefecture 547
  resulting health problems 603
  Takashima, Okayama Prefecture 554
  Tokyo 628
USSR see Union of Soviet Socialist
  Republics
Uta monogatari ('poem-tales')
  Ise monogatari 1004, 1008, 1148
  Yamato monogatari 1028
Utagawa Kuniyoshi
  artworks (supernatural theme) 1189

erotic prints (shunga) 1259
Utago no ato (Mishima Yukio)
  translation 1072
Utamaro see Kitagawa Utamaro
Utility Model Law 773
Utsukushisa to kanashimi to (Kawabata
  Yasunari)
  translation 1063

V
Valignano, Alessandro 133
Values
  business-related 208, 422, 543, 802,
    840, 868
  effect on interpersonal
    communications and relationships
    586
  human values in Zen Buddhism 489
  impact of internationalisation on
    personal 802
  influence of Zen Buddhism on samurai
    492
  management-related 927, 948
  middle-class 563-564
  modern 194, 537, 592
  morality and shared 591
  of baseball players 1456
  of Japanese Americans 394
  of Nitobe Inazō 385
  social 588, 916, 1200
  traditional 20, 194, 219, 459, 544-545,
    550
Van Reed, Eugene
  role in Japanese immigration to
    Hawaii 385
Vegetarian cooking 1440
Vegetation 50, 61
  during prehistoric times 109
Verbs
  grammar 427, 429-433
  morphology 412
  semantic characteristics 410
Verse record of my peonies (Masaoka
  Shiki)
  translation 1149
Vertical relationships in society see
  Hierarchy
Vietnam
  relations with Japan 283
  Vietnam War (1965-75) 727, 1062,
    1484
  see also Southeast Asia
Villages 50

administration (Tokugawa period) 168
daimyō power and (Muromachi
  period) 140
economy (Tokugawa period) 181-182
folk ceremonies in Okinoshima, Shiga
  Prefecture 500
gazetteer 57
Higashiuwa County, Ehime Prefecture
  573
historical formation 40
impact of land reform (1940s) 268
Kurotsuchi, Fukuoka Prefecture 560
Kurusu, Kagawa Prefecture 556
legends of Tōno, Iwate Prefecture
  1188
local self-government 531
Niiike, Okayama Prefecture 548
Noda, Chiba Prefecture 201
organisation 530, 551, 555, 561
political and authority structures 531,
  534
population (Tokugawa period) 182
role behaviour of village women 588
Shiwa, Iwate Prefecture 555
social basis for militarism in 243
society (Tokugawa period) 181
Suye mura, Kumamoto Prefecture
  551, 582
Tachikui, Hyōgo Prefecture 1286
village life (pre-1945) 205, 243, 551,
  582
Yanaka, Tochigi Prefecture 312
see also Hamlets, and Rural areas
Vining, Elizabeth Gray
as tutor to Crown Prince Akihito 362
Violence
as an instrument of social change 777
domestic 591
in industrial relations 921
in student movements 588
Vocational training
historical evolution 217
Volcanoes 51, 66
gazetteer 57
vegetation 61
Voluntary organisations
political activities 628
Volunteerism
political (among women) 580
von Baelz, Erwin
diary 351
medical activities 351, 597
von Siebold, Philipp Franz

as a cultural intermediary 596
von Stillfried, Raimund
photographs 1278
Voting behaviour 621, 632
impact of citizens' movements 958
Ishikawa Prefecture 611
Japan in the United Nations 611
party preference of labour and 611
suburban Tokyo 628
Vowels 412
Vulgarity
idiomatic words and expressions 414

W
Wabi (aesthetic principle) 1467
Wagahai wa neko de aru (Natsume
  Sōseki)
synopses and analyses 1112, 1117
translation 1084
Wages 811, 859
among blue-collar employees 918, 920
annual statistics 819, 824-827
banks 543
determination of wages 930
discrimination against women 785
during World War II 207
evolution of the dualistic wage
  structure 812
intra-firm differentials 930
long-term statistical data 808
policy 940
responsiveness to labour market
  conditions 938
seniority-based 208, 930, 940
Waiting years (Enchi Fumiko)
translation 1053
Waka poetry
Kokinshū 1153
scrolls illustrating 1245
Tokugawa period 1005
translations 1148, 1153, 1155
Wakan konkōbun (writing style) 404
Walter A. Compton Collection
art swords 1373
Wang Ching-wei
collaboration with Japan during World
  War II 702
War and warfare
against the invading Mongols (13th
  century) 141
ballad-drama about 1169
Ishiwara Kanji's perceptions 342
maritime 3

War and warfare *continued*
  medieval 136
  renounced in the constitution 784
  see also Civil wars, Russo-Japanese
    War (1904-5), Sino-Japanese War
    of 1894-95, Sino-Japanese War of
    1937-45, Vietnam (Vietnam War),
    World War I, and World War II
    (Pacific Theatre)
War brides
  Japanese Americans 388
War crimes trials (1946-48) 265-266,
  271, 321, 346, 595
'War tales' (*gunki monogatari*)
  Heike monogatari 1019
  scrolls illustrating medieval 1245
  Soga monogatari 1012
  Taiheiki 1018
Warehouses *see Kura* ('storehouses')
Warriors and heroes
  ballad-drama about 1169
  plays about 1172, 1175
  stories about 1019-1020, 1032, 1069,
    1102, 1109
  see also Samurai
Warships
  aircraft carriers 680
  encyclopaedic information about 1572
  photographs 1572
  Shinano (super-battleship) 716
  submarines (World War II) 681,
    715-716, 1572
  Yamato (super-battleship) 687, 688,
    716
Washi (handmade paper) 1273, 1479
  historical evolution 1365
  instruction manual 1358
  introductory studies (illustrated) 1358,
    1365
Washington, DC
  flowering cherry trees 663
  Japan-related resources (guidebook)
    1562
Water
  photo-essays 3
  depicted as art objects (photographs)
    17
  design motif of textile patterns 1344
  resources 40
  used in gardens 3, 1331
  water rituals (photo-essay) 3
  see also Hot springs (*onsen*)
Watsuji Tetsurō
  philosophy 527
Wayfarer (Natsume Sōseki)
  psychoanalytical study 1112
  synopses and analyses 1112, 1117
Wayō (calligraphic script) 1242, 1249
Weapons
  16th century 133
  ancient ceremonial 104
  at the Shōsōin 1194
  development and production (1980s)
    763
  illustrations 1566
  naval (1950s-1960s) 759
  nuclear 848
  products of daimyō culture (exhibition
    catalogue) 1218
  used by the *ninja* 1445
  used by the samurai 156
  see also Armour, Martial arts, and
    Swords
Weather 40-41
  gozan bungaku poetry about 1152
Weaving 1351
  Ainu 375
  ikat weaving (*kasuri*) 1354
  industry (history) 1353
  kimono 1356
  tsutsugaki cloth 1345
  see also Textiles
Weber, Max
  scholarly interpretations of 610
Weddings *see* Marriage
Weights and measures 85, 421
Welfare 38
  basic facts and figures (annual
    handbook) 14
  benefits 923
  economic 817
  social 619, 623
Western civilisation
  inquiry into its nature (Fukuzawa
    Yukichi) 194
'Western learning' (*Rangaku*)
  Tokugawa period 167, 173, 180
Western-style painting (*yōga*)
  evolution (Meiji period) 1235
Westerners in Japan
  as 'employed foreigners' (Meiji
    period) 197, 229, 351, 353, 358
  as missionaries after World War II 497
  Canadians 226
  depicted in Meiji period prints 1269
  depicted in *Nanban* art 132, 1243

Dutch 167, 173, 179, 596
Frenchmen 229, 691
Italians 70, 133, 1278
Jesuit missionaries (1500s-1600s) 129,
    132-133, 153, 166, 352
Jews 4
Meiji period 190
Portuguese 132-133, 153, 352
Russians 664
Swedes 596
see also Americans in Japan, English
    men and women in Japan, and
    Germans in Japan
Westernisation
depicted in Meiji period prints 1269
impact on a village community 554
Meiji period 196, 302, 304, 306, 674,
    1094
of Tokyo 236
Wetlands
vegetation 61
Whales 63
White-collar workers
in Tokyo 564
leisure-time activities among 1460
photo-essay 13
women as 574, 579
'White papers' (periodic government
    reports)
annual abstract 829
concerned with international trade 820
concerned with the economy 820
see also Government publications
Whitney, Clara A. N.
life in Japan (1875-84) 363
Widows 259, 583
Wig masters
bunraku theatre 1391
Wigs
used in the kabuki theatre 1352
Wild geese (Mori Ōgai)
literary analysis 1127
translation 1082
Williams, Justin, Sr.
role in the Allied occupation of Japan
    (1945-52) 281
Willis, William
biography 353
medical activities 353, 597
Wind 41
Wives see Husband-wife relationships,
    and Women
Woman in the dunes (Abe Kōbō)

literary analysis 1127
quest for identity in 1115
translation 1043
Women 616
1865-1945 205
advocates of equality for 336
ageing 327
Ainu 375
Akazome Emon 1021
as artists 579
as atomic bombing victims 252, 255,
    259
as radical activists 290
autobiographies and memoirs 259,
    290, 297, 310, 313, 328, 330, 355,
    362-363, 391, 399-400, 583, 1013,
    1142
bibliographies 1590, 1595
biographies and biographical sketches
    291, 295, 387, 573, 1604
changing employment patterns 542
clothing (kimono and kosode) 1215,
    1217, 1344, 1351, 1353, 1356
company wives 845
contemporary attitudes towards 18
costumes of female impersonators in
    kabuki 1352
depicted in shunga (erotic prints) 1259
depicted in the cinema 26, 1419, 1422,
    1424, 1428
depicted in ukiyo-e prints 1259,
    1261-1262, 1268
discrimination against 575, 785
during the 1870s 114
during the 1980s 574
during World War II 207, 583
educational and career opportunities
    536
enfranchisement 267
female crime 566
female workers in a sōgō shōsha
    (general trading company) 542
feminine ideal of the wife/mother 578
feminine sensibility in literature 1003
Fujiwara Michitsuna no haha 1013
Fukuda Hideko 290
geisha 234, 576
health, illness, and medical care of 599
Heian period 150, 1003, 1011, 1013,
    1021, 1023-1026, 1028, 1035, 1039
Higuchi Ichiyō 291, 1111
history (1870s-1970s) 581
Hōjō Masako 295

Women *continued*
  housewives in suburban Tokyo 577
  impact of World War II 595
  in a fishing and tourist-oriented city
    579
  in industry 937
  in political life 580
  in the employment system 923
  in the New Religions 508-509
  in various occupational roles 578
  Ishimoto Shizue 328
  Japanese American 313, 388, 399-400
  Japanese views (1860) of American
    667
  Kaneko Fumiko 290
  Kanno Suga 240, 290
  Katō Shizue 328
  Lady Daibu 1142
  Lady Nijō 310
  major women's organisations (listing)
    581
  Meiji period feminists 240
  Meiji period views 196
  menopause 599
  menstrual taboos 503
  Murasaki Shikibu 150, 295, 1023-1024
  novels about 1043, 1046-1047,
    1052-1053, 1058, 1099-1101
  novels written by 1047, 1052-1053
  of Suye mura, Kumamoto Prefecture
    582
  of Tsuchiura, Ibaraki Prefecture 234
  plays about 1172, 1175
  poetry about 1158
  prostitution 68, 205, 240, 536, 569, 583
  rights of 280, 328, 580, 777
  roles and role behaviour 8-9, 508-509,
    578-579, 588, 595, 1047, 1071
  rural 205, 548, 550-551, 554, 556, 573,
    582, 588
  Sei Shōnagon 295, 1025
  sexism in society 31
  shopping behaviour of housewives 841
  short stories by 1048, 1071, 1098, 1111
  short stories concerning 1098, 1106
  smokers 603
  Sone, Monica 399
  stories and tales about 1011, 1015,
    1019, 1033, 1186-1187, 1189
  Sugawara Takasue no musume
    1026-1027
  Sugimoto, Etsu Inagaki 313
  suicide among 568, 578

  Tanaka Michiko 400
  Tanno Setsu 290
  Toguri, Iva 387
  views of Fukuzawa Yukichi 194
  Westerners in Japan 66, 190, 355,
    362-363
  woman's view of life in the 1980s 563
  women's speech 413, 454
  words and terms pertaining to 413
  Yamashiro Tomoe 290
  Yosano Akiko 1160, 1168
  see also Family, Family life, Family
    planning, Husband-wife
    relationships, and Marriage
Women's Reform Society 240
Wood
  carpentry 1222, 1318, 1341-1343
  Okinawan woodwork 1222
  types used in furniture-making
    1341-1342
  wooden combs (*kushi*) 1369
  woodworking tools 1343
  see also Sculpture, and *Tansu* (wooden
    chests)
Woodblock prints 1220
  20th century 364, 1270, 1273-1274
  as antiques 1215
  bibliographies 1271, 1576
  depicting the supernatural 1189
  design motifs and techniques in 1204
  facsimile signatures on 1571
  folk art 483, 1193, 1210
  guide to legends and historical
    episodes embodied in 1560
  history 1209, 1211, 1271-1272
  Katsushika Hokusai's books and
    albums 1478
  Meiji period 1269
  representations of Daruma 483
  see also Print-makers, Print-making,
    Surimono (woodblock prints), and
    Ukiyo-e prints
Woodblock prints (reproductions) 184
  'bird and flower' (*kachō*) prints (Andō
    Hiroshige) 1257
  depicting azaleas 59
  depicting Edo/Tokyo 236, 1256, 1265
  depicting gardens 1327
  depicting history 155
  depicting Kyōto 92
  depicting Nagasaki 179
  depicting Nara 93
  depicting samurai society and culture 158

depicting the 'floating world' (*ukiyo*) 1036
Fifty-three Stages of the Tōkaidō (Andō Hiroshige) 1265
illustrating textile patterns (Tokugawa period) 1344
Kitagawa Utamaro's prints 1262
Meiji period (exhibition catalogue) 1229
One Hundred Famous Views of Edo (Andō Hiroshige) 1256
One Hundred Views of Mount Fuji (Katsushika Hokusai) 1256
Ōsaka prints 1264
post-1945 364, 1270
primitive ukiyo-e 1268
shunga (erotic prints) 1259
surimono 1263
Suzuki Harunobu's prints 1261
Thirty-six Views of Mount Fuji (Katsushika Hokusai) 1265
Tokugawa period (exhibition catalogue) 1227
ukiyo-e (multiple artists) 1267, 1272
Words 405
loanwords 419
meaning and definition 411
pertaining to women 413
proper usage 420
word order (grammar) 427, 429
see also Dictionaries
Work ethic 20, 30, 36, 38, 214, 797, 844
among Japanese and Americans (comparison) 919
Working conditions
blue-collar workers 918-920, 937
major social classes (1970s) 545
women 575, 785
Toyota automobile assembly line 924
working hours 924, 930, 945
World-views
influenced by feelings of dependence (*amae*) 589
of Shigemitsu Mamoru 708
of the women of Suye mura, Kumamoto Prefecture 582
World War I (1914-18)
Anglo-Japanese alliance and its benefits 666, 670
impact on the scientific community 157
military occupation of Micronesia 227
military occupation of Shantung, China 647

military thrust into Siberia (1918) 684
negotiations over Japan's entry into 666
World War II (Pacific Theatre) 222, 657
aircraft 680, 689
aircraft carrier task forces 680, 687
Allied policies, strategies, and military operations 711
American reminiscences (oral history collection) 699
Anglo-Japanese naval battle (1941) 698
Army High Command (actions) 692
bibliographies 1583, 1591, 1609, 1614
British involvement 686, 697-698, 701, 711
Burma Road crisis 697, 715
Canadian involvement 655
comprehensive history 709, 712, 715
controversy over its portrayal in textbooks 737
depicted in novels 1091-1092, 1097
Doolittle air raid (1942) 696, 699
Emperor Hirohito's role 237, 334, 693, 703
fire-bombing of Japanese cities 583, 691, 715
government compensation to repatriated Japanese 620
impact on American images of Japan 731
impact on culture and literature 1003
impact on Japanese Americans in Hawaii 389, 392, 705, 710
impact on Koreans in Japan 376-377
impact on MITI 272
impact on society 207, 691, 715
impact on women 583, 595
interplay between culture and international relations 695
Iwo Jima (battle) 699, 714-715
Japanese and British strategies 701
Japanese-Jewish relations 4
Japan's decision for war (1941) 321, 693
Japan's decision to surrender (1945) 683, 703
kamikaze pilots 293, 686, 688, 691, 700, 715
life during 70, 207, 715
machine tools industry 872
Micronesia 227
Midway (battle) 210, 680, 687-688, 706, 715

World War II *continued*
naval battles 210, 687-688, 698-700, 706, 715
Nisei participation 390, 395
Okinawa (battle) 688, 713, 715-716
Onoda Hiroo's personal account 341
origins 694, 697
peace settlements 266, 274, 282-283, 647, 728, 745
photographs 713-715, 1276
planning for the conquest of Hawaii 710
political and cultural developments 237
portrayed in films 1424, 1428
prisoners-of-war 752
processes of army socialisation 961
propaganda 387, 686, 1276
racist stereotypes 686
radio broadcasting 221, 387, 703, 1486
records of the 1941 policy conferences 693
relocation of Japanese Americans 384-386, 390-391, 393, 395, 398-402
relocation of Japanese Canadians 382-383, 655
reparations (1950s) to Southeast Asia 742, 846
San Francisco Peace Treaty (1951) 266, 274, 282-283, 285, 745
Shigemitsu Mamoru's personal interpretation 708
sinking of the *Yamato* 687-688, 716
Soviet-Japanese neutrality 684
Soviet seizure of Sakhalin 287
Soviet seizure of the Kurile Islands 285-286
submarine warfare 681, 688, 715-716, 1572
Tarawa (battle) 707, 715
termination (1945) 254, 261-263, 647, 683, 703, 708, 715
thought and behaviour of wartime leaders 618, 693, 703, 708, 712
'Tokyo Rose' 387
US Army Intensive Japanese Language School 359
war crimes trials 265-266, 271, 321, 346, 595
warships (encyclopaedic information) 1572
wartime objectives of Japan and the USA 695

wartime planning for postwar Japan 266, 280, 360, 701, 745
Yamamoto Isoroku 210, 317, 699, 705-706, 710
see also Atomic bomb, Foreign relations with the United States, Hiroshima (atomic bombing), Nagasaki (atomic bombing), Pearl Harbor (1941 attack on), and Sino-Japanese War of 1937-45
Wrappings *see* Packaging
Wrestling *see* Sumo (wrestling)
Writers
Akutagawa Ryūnosuke 289
biographical dictionaries 365, 1566
Ejima Kiseki 1036
Higuchi Ichiyō 1111
Ihara Saikaku 295, 1015, 1036
Kanagaki Robun 291
members of the *bundan* 1120
Mishima Yukio 292, 335
Murasaki Shikibu 295, 1023, 1035
Natsume Sōseki 239
Sei Shōnagon 295
Shimazaki Tōson 239
Sugawara Takasue no musume 1027
suicide among 568
support for World War II among 237
Tamenaga Shunsui 291
Ueda Akinari 315, 1030
Yoshida Kenkō 1034
see also Novelists, Playwrights, and Poets and poetesses
Writing-boxes and cases
as antiques 1215
depicting creatures of nature 1221
Writing script *see* Calligraphy
Writing styles 404
Writing system
history 407
incompatibility with data-processing technology 997
methods of teaching 455
resistance to script reform 997
see also Chinese characters (*kanji*), *Kana* syllabaries, *Kanamajiribun*, and *Wakan konkōbun*

X

Xavier, Francis
missionary activities 129

Y

Yabukōji (Hakuin Ekaku) 476
Yajima Kajiko 240
Yakushiji (temple)
    architecture 1316, 1322
    sculpture 1289-1290, 1316
Yakuza (gangsters)
    history and activities 569
    police ways of handling 565
    see also Gangsters
Yalu Bay
    battle (1894) 210
Yama no oto (Kawabata Yasunari)
    literary analysis 1127
    translation 1066
Yamabushi (religious ascetics)
    of Shugendō 499
Yamagata Aritomo
    biography 303
Yamagata Prefecture
    Shōnai Plain 213
    see also Tōhoku region
Yamaguchi Prefecture
    Hagi 69
    Shimonoseki 675
    see also Chōshū *han*
Yamaguchi Takeo
    artistic techniques and styles 1203
Yamamoto Isoroku 210
    attack on Pearl Harbor (1941) 210,
        317, 705
    biography 317
    death in World War II 699
    defeated at Midway (1942) 706
    planning for the conquest of Hawaii
        710
Yamamoto Kanae
    woodblock prints 1274
Yamamoto Kansai
    fashion-design work 1348
Yamamoto Michiko
    short stories 1098
Yamamoto Yohji
    fashion-design work 1348
Yamanaka Sadao
    film-making activities 1417
Yamanashi Prefecture
    agricultural development and tenancy
        disputes 242
Yamanote railway line (Tokyo) 91
Yamashiro pottery 1283
Yamashiro Tomoe 290
Yamato

    archaeology of 'old Yamato' 102
Yamato (super-battleship)
    sinking (1945) 687-688, 716
Yamato-e ('Japanese-style') painting
    evolution and nature 1236
Yamato monogatari
    literary analysis and translation 1028
Yamato Takeru
    life and times 293
Yama-uba (noh play)
    synopsis 492
Yamazaki Ansai
    philosophical writings 178
Yamazaki Masakazu
    plays 1179, 1182
Yanagi Sōetsu (Muneyoshi)
    biographical sketch 1228
Yanagida Taiun
    calligraphy 1231
Yanaihara Tadao
    as a pacifist 288
Yanaka (Tochigi Prefecture)
    physical destruction (1906-7) 312
Yangtze River Valley (China)
    Japanese interest in its railway
        development (1913-14) 666
Yashiki-gami (deity) 503
Yashiro Seiichi
    plays 1179
Yasukuni Shrine
    status (post-1945) 515
Yasuoka Shōtarō
    short stories 1057, 1107
Yasutani-*rōshi* (Sōtō Zen master)
    teachings 478
Yayoi period
    art 104
    excavated sites 101
    human evolution and cultural
        development 103
    pottery 104, 109
Yeats, William Butler
    noh theatre's influence on his drama
        1393
Yearbooks and annual surveys 819-829
    union list of Japanese publications in
        Western languages 1601
Yedo see Tokyo
Yen
    prospects for becoming the world's
        key currency 853
    internationalisation 860-861
    yen bond market 857

Yen *continued*
 yen call money market 854
 see also Foreign Exchange, and
  Money
Yezo *see* Hokkaidō
Yoakemae (Shimazaki Tōson)
 synopsis and analysis 1117
 translation 1094
Yokkaichi (Mie Prefecture)
 municipal air pollution (Yokkaichi
  'asthma') 957
Yokohama
 Bank of Yokohama (personnel
  practices) 942
 blue-collar workers (compared with
  Detroit, Michigan) 919
 history (1858-79) 162
 life during the 1860s 353
 life in (19th century) 68
 maps 56
 'Yokohama prints' (*Yokohama-e*) 1269,
  1576
Yokoi Tokio 358
Yokomitsu Riichi
 life and writings 1108
 literary analysis 1114
 short stories 1108
Yokoyama Kimio
 architectural work 1298
Yomiuri Shimbun (newspaper)
 articles and editorials (translations and
  synopses) 1547
 news reporting 1484
 political character 1485
Yoroi kumi-uchi (martial art) 1443
Yorozu Tetsugorō
 paintings 1251
Yosa Buson *see* Taniguchi (Yosa) Buson
Yosano Akiko
 ideas about poetry 1168
 poetry 1160
Yoshida Hodaka
 woodblock print techniques 1273
Yoshida Kenkō
 Tsurezuregusa 1034
Yoshida Shigeru
 political leadership during the Allied
  occupation of Japan (1945-52)
  282-283, 324
 biography 324
Yoshida Shōin
 life and ideas 188
 political biography 171

Yoshida Yoshishige
 film-making activities 1419
Yoshikawa Eiji
 Musashi 1109
Yoshimasu Gōzō
 poetry 1143, 1151
Yoshino kuzu (Tanizaki Junichirō)
 translation 1102
Yoshino region (Nara Prefecture)
 depicted in Tanizaki Junichirō's
  novella 1102
Yoshino Sakuzō
 political thought 241
Yoshioka Minoru
 poetry 1057, 1141, 1151
Yoshishige no Yasutane
 'Record of the pond pavilion' 1010
Yoshitoshi *see* Tsukioka Yoshitoshi
Yoshitsune *see* Minamoto no Yoshitsune
Young Officers' Movement
 role in the February 26, 1936 Incident
  238
Youth
 folk culture 503
 juvenile delinquency 565-566
 'New Wave' cinema's concern with
  1419
 nationalist trends in youth groups
  (1950s) 276
 personality development 594
 patterns of suicide among 568
 police relations with 570
 training centres (1900s-1930s) 243
Yūaikai ('Friendly Society')
 institutional history 215
Yūkar epics
 representative epic songs
  (translations) 380
Yukiguni (Kawabata Yasunari)
 literary analysis 1127
 translation 1065
Yūsoku textile patterns 1207

Z

Zaibatsu (financial and industrial
  combines)
 assistance to the Young Officers'
  Movement 238
 dissolution (1940s) 267, 270, 274
 Mitsui (history) 231
 oligopolisation of the economy
  (1911-30) 241
Zattaisho (calligraphic script) 1242

Zazen (sitting meditation) 478, 487, 494
Zeami (Yamazaki Masakazu)
    translation 1182
Zeami Motokiyo
    biographical sketch 291
    noh plays 1004, 1007, 1156, 1172,
        1175-1176, 1181, 1406, 1408-1409
    play about 1182
    treatises on the art of noh drama 1413
Zekkai Chūshin
    poetry 1152
Zen Buddhism 469, 475, 479, 602
    art related to 1190, 1195-1196, 1214,
        1232
    begging for alms (practice) 1154
    bibliography 1612
    compared with Western thought 469
    cuisine associated with 1437, 1440
    Daruma 483
    'death poems' (*jisei*) by Zen monks
        1138
    Dōgen (monk) 472-474, 480-481
    drawings and photographs of Zen life
        486, 491
    encounter with Christianity
        (Tokugawa period) 474
    gozan bungaku poetry 1152
    gozan system of temples 131, 140
    Hakuin Ekaku (monk) 474, 476, 480
    history 458, 465, 474, 484, 494, 1196
    I-Thou relationship in 521
    Ikkyū Sōjun (monk) 291, 1003, 1139
    influence on a baseball player (Oh
        Sadaharu) 338
    influence on art and daily life at the
        Daitokuji temple 1190
    influence on art 1195, 1239
    influence on culture 474, 489, 492,
        494, 1195-1196
    influence on gardens 1226, 1329
    influence on kendō 1449
    influence on the tea ceremony 1226,
        1470
    introduced to the West 316, 479
    introductory works 478, 489-490,
        493-494
    kōan 473, 476-478, 490, 494

    manipulated by capitalism 34
    monasteries and monastic life 131,
        147, 472, 486, 491
    moral and social responsibility in 479
    paintings by Zen monks in the Sansō
        Collection 1246
    philosophical basis 469
    poetry (translations) 488, 1138-1139,
        1152, 1154
    practices 472-474, 477-480, 486-487,
        491, 493-494, 507
    Ryōkan (monk) 1010, 1154
    Shōbōgenzō of Dōgen 473
    Shōbōgenzō-zuimonki of Dōgen 472
    stories about early Zen masters 491
    Suzuki, Daisetz Teitaro 316
    terminology (dictionary) 415
    zazen (sitting meditation) 478, 487,
        494
    Zen action and Zen person (concepts)
        480
    Zen gardens 1327, 1331-1332, 1335
    Zen masters, temples, and
        programmes (guidebook) 97
    Zen training 487, 491
    see also Temples
Zenchiku *see* Komparu Zenchiku
Zengakuren (All-Federation of Student
    Self-Governing Associations)
    opposition to a revised US-Japan
        Security Treaty 744
Zenrin kushū
    translation 488
Zodiac
    encyclopaedic and almanac-type
        information about 1551
Zoen (priest)
    Senzui narabi ni yagyō no zu
        (translation) 1338
Zokugaku instrumental music 1380
Zoologists
    Morse, Edward S. 361
Zoology
    mythical 114
Zuihitsu ('random essays')
    Pillow book of Sei Shōnagon 1025
    Tsurezuregusa of Yoshida Kenkō 1034

Maps of Japan

These maps show the prefectural boundaries, the more important cities, and certain other features.

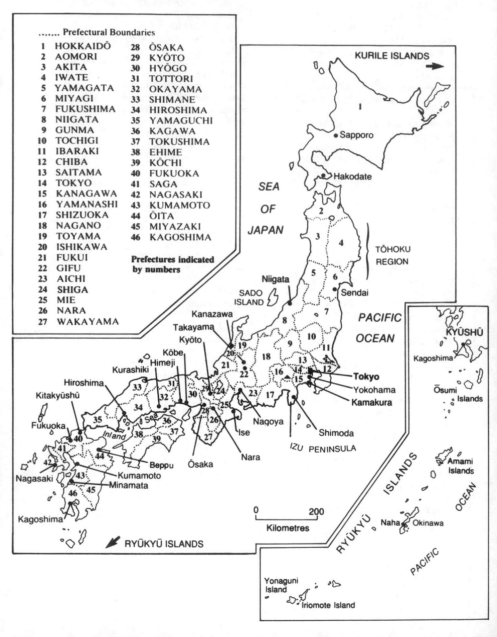

...... Prefectural Boundaries

1	HOKKAIDŌ	28	ŌSAKA
2	AOMORI	29	KYŌTO
3	AKITA	30	HYŌGO
4	IWATE	31	TOTTORI
5	YAMAGATA	32	OKAYAMA
6	MIYAGI	33	SHIMANE
7	FUKUSHIMA	34	HIROSHIMA
8	NIIGATA	35	YAMAGUCHI
9	GUNMA	36	KAGAWA
10	TOCHIGI	37	TOKUSHIMA
11	IBARAKI	38	EHIME
12	CHIBA	39	KŌCHI
13	SAITAMA	40	FUKUOKA
14	TOKYO	41	SAGA
15	KANAGAWA	42	NAGASAKI
16	YAMANASHI	43	KUMAMOTO
17	SHIZUOKA	44	ŌITA
18	NAGANO	45	MIYAZAKI
19	TOYAMA	46	KAGOSHIMA
20	ISHIKAWA		
21	FUKUI	**Prefectures indicated**	
22	GIFU	**by numbers**	
23	AICHI		
24	SHIGA		
25	MIE		
26	NARA		
27	WAKAYAMA		

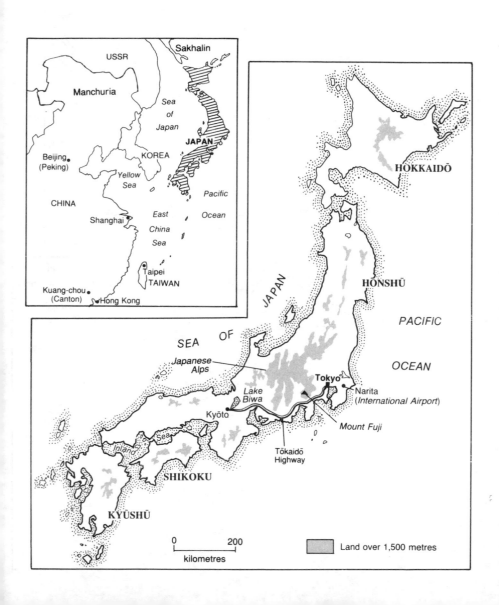

USSR

Sakhalin

Manchuria

Sea
of
Japan

JAPAN

Beijing
(Peking)

KOREA

Yellow
Sea

CHINA

Shanghai

East
China
Sea

Pacific

Ocean

Kuang-chou
(Canton)

Taipei
TAIWAN

Hong Kong

HOKKAIDŌ

HONSHŪ

PACIFIC

OCEAN

SEA   OF

JAPAN

Japanese
Alps

Lake
Biwa

Kyōto

Tokyo

Narita
(*International Airport*)

Mount Fuji

*Tōkaidō
Highway*

Inland   Sea

SHIKOKU

KYŪSHŪ

0   200

kilometres

Land over 1,500 metres